The Concise Companion to Language Assessment

The Concise Companion to Language Assessment

Edited by

Antony John Kunnan

WILEY Blackwell

Copyright © 2025 by John Wiley & Sons, Inc. All rights reserved, including rights for text and data mining and training of artificial technologies or similar technologies.

Published by John Wiley & Sons, Inc., Hoboken, New Jersey.
Published simultaneously in Canada.

No part of this publication may be reproduced, stored in a retrieval system, or transmitted in any form or by any means, electronic, mechanical, photocopying, recording, scanning, or otherwise, except as permitted under Section 107 or 108 of the 1976 United States Copyright Act, without either the prior written permission of the Publisher, or authorization through payment of the appropriate per-copy fee to the Copyright Clearance Center, Inc., 222 Rosewood Drive, Danvers, MA 01923, (978) 750-8400, fax (978) 750-4470, or on the web at www.copyright.com. Requests to the Publisher for permission should be addressed to the Permissions Department, John Wiley & Sons, Inc., 111 River Street, Hoboken, NJ 07030, (201) 748-6011, fax (201) 748-6008, or online at http://www.wiley.com/go/permission.

Trademarks: Wiley and the Wiley logo are trademarks or registered trademarks of John Wiley & Sons, Inc. and/or its affiliates in the United States and other countries and may not be used without written permission. All other trademarks are the property of their respective owners. John Wiley & Sons, Inc. is not associated with any product or vendor mentioned in this book.

Limit of Liability/Disclaimer of Warranty: While the publisher and author have used their best efforts in preparing this book, they make no representations or warranties with respect to the accuracy or completeness of the contents of this book and specifically disclaim any implied warranties of merchantability or fitness for a particular purpose. No warranty may be created or extended by sales representatives or written sales materials. The advice and strategies contained herein may not be suitable for your situation. You should consult with a professional where appropriate. Further, readers should be aware that websites listed in this work may have changed or disappeared between when this work was written and when it is read. Neither the publisher nor authors shall be liable for any loss of profit or any other commercial damages, including but not limited to special, incidental, consequential, or other damages.

For general information on our other products and services or for technical support, please contact our Customer Care Department within the United States at (800) 762-2974, outside the United States at (317) 572-3993 or fax (317) 572-4002.

Wiley also publishes its books in a variety of electronic formats. Some content that appears in print may not be available in electronic formats. For more information about Wiley products, visit our web site at www.wiley.com.

Library of Congress Cataloging-in-Publication Data
Names: Kunnan, Antony John, editor.
Title: The concise companion to language assessment / edited by Antony John
    Kunnan, USA.
Description: Hoboken, New Jersey : Wiley-Blackwell, 2025. | Includes index.
Identifiers: LCCN 2023054316 (print) | LCCN 2023054317 (ebook) | ISBN
    9781394179596 (paperback) | ISBN 9781394179602 (adobe pdf) | ISBN
    9781394179619 (epub)
Subjects: LCSH: Language and languages–Ability testing. | Language and
    languages–Examinations. | LCGFT: Essays.
Classification: LCC P53.4 .C586 2024 (print) | LCC P53.4 (ebook) | DDC
    418.0076–dc23/eng/20231206
LC record available at https://lccn.loc.gov/2023054316
LC ebook record available at https://lccn.loc.gov/2023054317

Cover Design: Wiley
Cover Image: © TrishaMcmillan/Getty Images

Set in 10/12pt STIXTwoText by Straive, Pondicherry, India

SKY10082430_082024

This volume is dedicated to all those who inspired me to write and edit:

Lyle F, Bachman, Alister Cumming, Jim Purpura, Nick Saville, and Suchitra Sadanandan

CONTENTS

About the Editor	xi
List of Contributors	xiii
Acknowledgments	xix
Introduction	xxi

THEME 1 Fundamental Considerations

1 How to Conceptualize and Implement a Language Assessment 3
Lyle F. Bachman and Barbara Damböck

2 Learning-Oriented Language Assessment 22
James Enos Purpura

3 Assessing Integrated Skills 42
Alister Cumming

4 Dynamic Assessment in the Classroom 55
Matthew E. Poehner

5 Designing Evaluations for Validation of Language Assessments 67
Carol A. Chapelle, Erik Voss, and Haeun Kim

6 Fairness and Justice in Language Assessment 80
Antony John Kunnan

7 Statistics and Software for Test Revisions 93
Yo In'nami and Rie Koizumi

8 Language Assessment and Artificial Intelligence 112
Erik Voss

THEME 2 Assessing Language Skills and Resources

9 Assessing Listening 129
Elvis Wagner

10 Assessing Speaking 143
Barry O'Sullivan

11 Assessing Reading 154
William Grabe and Xiangying Jiang

12 Assessing Writing 168
Cecilia Guanfang Zhao

vii

viii Contents

13 Assessing the Linguistic Resources of Meaningful
Communication 181
James Enos Purpura and Saerhim Oh

14 Assessing Vocabulary 205
John Read

15 Assessing Pronunciation 216
Talia Isaacs

16 Assessing Interactional Competence and Pragmatics 230
Carsten Roever

THEME 3 Assessment Development and Evaluation

17 Assessing English as a Lingua Franca 245
Jennifer Jenkins and Constant Leung

18 Scenario-Based Language Assessment 255
Heidi Liu Banerjee

19 Adapting or Developing Source Materials for Listening and
Reading Tests 270
Anthony Green

20 Automated Writing Assessment and Feedback 285
Sara T. Cushing and Sha Liu

THEME 4 Assessment Contexts

21 Classroom-Based Assessment Issues for Language Teacher
Education 303
Constant Leung

22 Assessment of Young Language Learners 312
Mikyung Kim Wolf

23 Monitoring Progress in the Classroom 326
Matthew E. Poehner and Rama Mathew

24 Diagnostic Assessment Feedback in the 21st-Century
Technology-Rich Classroom 339
Eunice Eunhee Jang, Maryam Wagner, Liam Hannah, and Hyunah Kim

25 Evolution and Future Trends in Tests of English for University
Admissions 355
Xiaoming Xi, Brent Bridgeman, and Cathy Wendler

26 Assessing Health and Other Professionals 371
Lynda Taylor and John Pill

Contents ix

27 Acoustic and Temporal Analysis for Assessing Speaking 383
Okim Kang and Lucy Pickering

THEME 5 Assessment for Immigration and Citizenship

28 Language Testing for Residence and Citizenship in Europe: Justifications, Consequences, and Debates 401
Cecilie Hamnes Carlsen

29 Language Assessment for Immigration in Australia: Test-Policy-Discourse Entanglements and Their Ethical Implications 417
Kellie Frost

30 U.S. Immigration, Citizenship, and the Naturalization Test: Policies and practices 432
Antony John Kunnan

THEME 6 Qualitative Research Methods

31 Introspective Methods 453
Miyuki Sasaki and Yuhang Hu

32 Test-Taking Strategies 473
Yuyang Cai

33 Consequences, Impact, and Washback 496
Liying Cheng

34 Language Testing in the Dock 509
Glenn Fulcher

THEME 7 Quantitative Research Methods

35 Historical Overview of Classical Theory: Reliability 527
James Dean Brown

36 Classical Test Theory – Reliability 541
Yasuyo Sawaki

37 Norm-Referenced and Criterion-Referenced Score Interpretations in Language Assessment 555
Ikkyu Choi

38 Practical Uses of EFA and SEM for Language Assessment Researchers 570
Gary J. Ockey

39 Item Response Theory in Language Assessment 588
Shangchao Min and Lianzhen He

x   Contents

40 Many-Facet Rasch Analysis for Evaluating Second Language
Tests   602
Khaled Barkaoui

41 Psychometric Considerations for a Computerized
Adaptive Language Test   619
Steven W. Nydick, J.R. Lockwood, and Mancy Liao

THEME 8   The Role of Technology

42 Computer-Assisted Language Testing   637
Ruslan Suvorov, Yasin Karatay, and Volker Hegelheimer

43 Computer-Adaptive Language Testing: Focus on Language
Issues   649
Ramsey Cardwell, Ben Naismith, and Micheline Chalhoub-Deville

44 Automated Writing Evaluation   661
Jill Burstein and Yigal Attali

45 Detecting Plagiarism and Cheating   671
Ardeshir Geranpayeh

Index   681

ABOUT THE EDITOR

Antony John Kunnan is a language assessment specialist who is currently a Senior Research Fellow at Carnegie Mellon University. His research interests are fairness of tests and testing practice, assessment literacy, research methods and statistics, ethics and standards, and language assessment policy. After completing his Ph.D. at UCLA, he held academic positions in Ann Arbor, Los Angeles, Taichung, Hong Kong, Singapore, and Macau.

He has conducted more than 130 seminars, workshops, and plenary and invited talks in over 40 countries and completed close to 100 publications as author and editor of books and author of journal articles and book chapters. He was also Founding Editor of *Issues in Applied Linguistics* at UCLA (1989–1991), Founding Editor of *Language Assessment Quarterly* (2003–13; 2020–2023), and the Chief Editor of *Journal of Asia TEFL* (2017–2024). In terms of international service, he was past President of the International Language Testing Association (ILTA) and Founding President of the Asian Association for Language Assessment (AALA). In 2024, he was awarded the Cambridge-ILTA Distinguished Achievement Award for Language Assessment.

This volume is partly based on the Antony John Kunnan's four-volume edited collection titled *The Companion to Language Assessment* (Wiley, 2014).

LIST OF CONTRIBUTORS

Yigal Attali
Duolingo, Inc.
Pittsburgh, PA
USA

Lyle F. Bachman
Emeritus, Department of Applied
Linguistics
The University of California
Los Angeles, CA
USA

Heidi Liu Banerjee
PSI Service LLC
Olathe, KS
USA

Khaled Barkaoui
Faculty of Education
York University
Toronto, ON
Canada

Brent Bridgeman
Educational Testing Service
NJ, USA

James Dean Brown
Kailua, HI
USA

Jill Burstein
Duolingo, Inc.
Pittsburgh, PA
USA

Yuyang Cai
Center for Language Education and
Assessment Research (CLEAR) & School
of Languages
Shanghai University of International
Business and Economics
Shanghai
China

Ramsey Cardwell
Duolingo, Inc
Pittsburgh, PA
USA

Cecilie Hamnes Carlsen
Department of Language, Literature
Mathematics and Interpreting, Western
Norway University of Applied Sciences
Bergen
Norway

Micheline Chalhoub-Deville
Educational Research Methodology
University of North Carolina
Greensboro, NC
USA

Carol A. Chapelle
Department of English, Applied Linguistics
& Technology Program
Iowa State University
Ames, IA
USA

Liying Cheng
School of Education
City University of Macau
Macau

Ikkyu Choi
Research, Educational Testing Service
Princeton, NJ
USA

Alister Cumming
Department of Curriculum, Teaching and
Learning, University of Toronto
Toronto, Ontario
Canada

xiv List of Contributors

Sara T. Cushing
Department of Applied Linguistics & ESL
Georgia State University
Atlanta, GA
USA

Barbara Damböck
Emerita, English Department
Teacher Training Academy
(Akademie für Lehrerfortbildung
und Personalführung)
Dillingen
Germany

Kellie Frost
School of Languages and Linguistics
Faculty of Arts
University of Melbourne
Parkville, VIC
Australia

Glenn Fulcher
School of Education
University of Leicester
Leicester
UK

Ardeshir Geranpayeh
Cambridge Computational Psychometrics
Ltd
Cambridge
UK

William Grabe
Emeritus Regents Professor of Applied
Linguistics
Northern Arizona University
Flagstaff, AZ
USA

Anthony Green
Centre for Research in English Language
Learning and Assessment
University of Bedfordshire
UK

Liam Hannah
Department of Applied Psychology and
Human Development
Ontario Institute for Studies in Education
University of Toronto
Toronto, ON
Canada

Lianzhen He
Institute of Applied Linguistics
Zhejiang University
Hangzhou
China

Volker Hegelheimer
Department of English
Iowa State University
Ames, IA
USA

Yuhang Hu
Department of English
Northern Arizona University
Flagstaff, AZ
USA

Yo In'nami
Division of English Language Education
Faculty of Science and Engineering
Chuo University
Tokyo
Japan

Talia Isaacs
UCL Centre for Applied Linguistics, IOE,
UCL's Faculty of Education and Society
University College London
London
UK

Eunice Eunhee Jang
Department of Applied Psychology and
Human Development
Ontario Institute for Studies in Education
University of Toronto
Toronto, ON
Canada

Jennifer Jenkins
Department of Modern Languages and
Linguistics
University of Southampton
Southampton
UK

Xiangying Jiang
Duolingo, Lead Learning Scientist
Pittsburgh, PA
USA

List of Contributors xv

Okim Kang
Applied Linguistics, Department of English
Northern Arizona University
Flagstaff, AZ
USA

Yasin Karatay
English Research
Cambridge University Press & Assessment
Cambridge
UK

Haeun Kim
Department of English, Applied Linguistics
& Technology Program
Iowa State University
Ames, IA
USA

Hyunah Kim
Department of Applied Psychology and
Human Development
Ontario Institute for Studies in Education
University of Toronto
Toronto, ON
Canada

Rie Koizumi
Institute of Humanities and Social Sciences
University of Tsukuba, Subprogram in
English Language Education
Tsukuba, Ibaraki
Japan

Antony John Kunnan
San Gabriel, CA
USA

Mancy Liao
Duolingo
Pittsburgh, PA
USA

Constant Leung
School of Education, Communication
and Society
King's College London
London
UK

Sha Liu
British Council
London
UK

J.R. Lockwood
Duolingo
Pittsburgh, PA
USA

Rama Mathew
Faculty of Education, Delhi University
Delhi
India

Shangchao Min
Institute of Applied Linguistics, Zhejiang
University
Hangzhou
China

Ben Naismith
Duolingo, Inc
Pittsburgh, PA
USA

Steven W. Nydick
Duolingo
Pittsburgh, PA
USA

Gary J. Ockey
Applied Linguistics and Technology
Iowa State University
Ames, IA
USA

Saerhim Oh
Educational Testing Service
Princeton, NJ
USA

Barry O'Sullivan
British Council English Language Research
The British Council
London
UK

xvi List of Contributors

Lucy Pickering
Department of Literature and Languages
Texas A&M University-Commerce
Commerce, TX
USA

John Pill
Department of Linguistics and English
Language
Lancaster University
Lancaster
UK

Matthew E. Poehner
Departments of Curriculum and Instruction
and Applied Linguistics
The Pennsylvania State University
State College, PA
USA

James Enos Purpura
Department of Arts and Humanities,
Applied Linguistics and TESOL Program
Teachers College
Columbia University
New York, NY
USA

Lynda Taylor
Centre for Research in English Language
Learning and Assessment
University of Bedfordshire
Luton
UK

John Read
Emeritus Professor of Applied Language
Studies, School of Cultures, Languages and
Linguistics
University of Auckland
Auckland
New Zealand

Carsten Roever
School of Languages and Linguistics
The University of Melbourne
Parkville, VIC
Australia

Miyuki Sasaki
Faculty of Education and Integrated
Arts and Science, Waseda University
Tokyo
Japan

Yasuyo Sawaki
Faculty of Education and Integrated
Arts and Sciences
Waseda University
Tokyo
Japan

Ruslan Suvorov
Faculty of Education
University of Western Ontario
London, ON
Canada

Erik Voss
Department of Arts & Humanities,
Applied Linguistics & TESOL Program
Teachers College
Columbia University
New York, NY
USA

Elvis Wagner
Department of Teaching and Learning
Temple University
Philadelphia, PA
USA

Maryam Wagner
Institute of Health Sciences Education
Faculty of Medicine and Health Sciences
McGill University
Montreal, QC
Canada

Cathy Wendler
Educational Testing Service
Midlothian, VA
USA

Mikyung Kim Wolf
Educational Testing Service
Princeton, NJ
USA

Xiaoming Xi
Hong Kong Examinations and Assessment
Authority
Hong Kong
China

Cecilia Guanfang Zhao
Department of English, Faculty of
Arts and Humanities
University of Macau
Taipa, Macau
China

ACKNOWLEDGMENTS

I thank all the authors who agreed to write the 45 chapters and then faced an avalanche of email reminders, requests to review other chapters, comments for revisions, and final proofs. My thanks are also due to many scholars who commented on the proposal and other aspects of the volume: Lyle Bachman, J. D. Brown, Alister Cumming, and Gary Ockey. All deficiencies, of course, are mine.

I also thank Coral Yiwei Qin, my editorial assistant, who assisted me ably in many phases of this project.

Finally, I thank Rachel Greenberg for persuading me to undertake this project. And the Wiley staff, including the staff in Chennai, for completing the production process extremely well.

INTRODUCTION

If we were to outline the history of language assessment, depending on how wide we draw this circle, we could include the Chinese imperial civil service examinations as the earliest recorded public assessments. These assessments had language elements such as poetry writing, calligraphy, and knowledge of classic Chinese texts. Many scholars believe that the examinations were established in A.D. 605 during the Sui Dynasty, expanded during the Song Dynasty, and finally discontinued in 1905 before the fall of the Qing Dynasty. The almost 1300 years of examinations, despite some interruptions, is the longest use of an examination system, which lasted until a little more than 100 years ago.

In Europe, scholars have documented that, Matteo Ricci, a Jesuit missionary, took ideas of the Chinese examinations in the late 16th century to Europe. France soon started using examinations in Catholic schools, but it was under Napoleon, in 1808, that the Baccalauréat was introduced. The examination has many subject areas, such as French, philosophy, and science. It is still in use and is used to admit students into college as well as qualify them for certain government positions. This examination started just a little more than 200 years ago.

In the United States and the United Kingdom, the year 1913 was important. In the United States, the first committee appointed by the Association of Modern Language Teachers of the Middle States of Maryland for the assessment of French, German, and Spanish was formed. In the United Kingdom, the Certificate of Proficiency in English, the first examination in English as a foreign language, was established by the University of Cambridge Local Examinations Syndicate (now Cambridge University Press and Assessment). A quick review of the components of the 1913 examination started over 100 years ago shows they are not very dissimilar to the ones used today. These components included translation from English into French or German, translation from French or German into English, questions on English grammar, English essay writing, English literature, English phonetics, dictation and reading aloud, and conversation.

More recently, three important events took place in the United States in 1961. First, a conference sponsored by the Center for Applied Linguistics in Washington, DC, adopted a plan to assess the English ability of foreign students entering US colleges and universities. This later became known as the Test of English as a Foreign Language (TOEFL, now known as the Internet-based TOEFL or iBT). Second, Robert Lado's *Language Testing: The Construction and Use of Foreign Language Tests*, the first full-length textbook on language assessment, was published by Longman. As the title indicates, it was primarily focused on the development and construction of tests. Finally, John Carroll's significant paper titled "Fundamental Considerations in Testing for English Language Proficiency of Foreign Students" was published. He promoted the idea of integrative testing (of skills and components) with a focus on what has come to be known as communicative ability. Many scholars, therefore, consider 1961 as the start of the modern era of language assessment. This occurred a little more than 60 years ago!

The Concise Companion to Language Assessment with 45 chapters continues the tradition of discussing the language assessment's past, present, as well as future possibilities. It also discusses critical approaches, methods, and issues in assessment conceptualization, development, research, and policy. All chapters are accessible to interested readers with some background in language education and assessment. A few technical chapters may need more

xxii Introduction

background as they deal with psychometrics and technology. On the other hand, a few chapters bring outside knowledge and relate it to language assessment in an interdisciplinary fashion.

How to Use the Collection?

This book is presented in eight themes. Theme 1 (Chapters 1–8), Fundamental Considerations, has chapters that offer a sound basis for assessment development and research. The theme has chapters on conceptualizing an assessment, learning-oriented assessment, assessing integrated skills and dynamic assessment, and evaluation and fairness, and statistics and AI's role of language assessment. These chapters can be used for graduate students who need the fundamentals before they dip into more detailed and complex chapters.

Themes 2 and 3 (Chapters 9–20) are devoted to assessment of different skills (listening, speaking, reading, writing, linguistic resources, vocabulary, pronunciation, and intercultural competence), and assessment development and evaluation (scenario-based and English as lingua franca, developing materials, and automated writing and speaking). This set of chapters are useful in developing assessments and scoring guidelines as well as considerations for an innovative concept in scenario-based assessment and automated scoring of performances.

Themes 4 and 5 (Chapters 21–30) are related to different assessment contexts (classroom, young language learners, diagnostic feedback, tests for university admission, health professionals, and immigration and citizenship). As considerations for assessments may vary for different contexts (classrooms, universities, employment, and immigration and citizenship), these chapters provide insights and discussions.

Themes 6 and 7 (Chapters 31–41) offer chapters on qualitative and quantitative research methods. Qualitative research methods discussed include introspective methods; test-taker strategies; consequences, impact, and washback; and legal matters. Quantitative research methods discussed include classical reliability, norm-referenced and criterion-referenced score interpretations, exploratory factor analysis and structural equation modeling, item response theory, many-faceted Rasch analysis, and psychometric considerations for computer-adaptive testing. All chapters that would be required research for planning and conducting research.

Theme 8 (Chapters 42–45) has chapters that underscore the importance of the role of technology in operationalizing assessments in a computer-adaptive format and its related topics of automated writing evaluation and detecting plagiarism and cheating. These chapters are essential reading if technology is part of assessment development and operations.

In summary, the ideal way to use this collection would be to read the chapters from Theme 1 first, to ensure a solid background given the range of ideas in the chapters and then to read the chapters from the other themes based on desired expertise. If the desired expertise is assessment development or research, then Themes 2 and 3 would be necessary reading. Assessment contexts are critical readings from Themes 4 and 5. For researchers embarking on qualitative and/or quantitative research, chapters from Themes 6 and 7 are absolutely necessary. The role of technology today cannot be understated; therefore, the chapters in Theme 8 would be particularly useful. In addition, the suggested readings and discussion questions at the end of chapters should help enhance the understanding of the chapters.

July 2024
San Gabriel, California

THEME 1

Fundamental Considerations

CHAPTER 1

How to Conceptualize and Implement a Language Assessment

Lyle F. Bachman and Barbara Damböck

Introduction

Language assessments have been pervasive in human societies for centuries. They have played a vital role in shaping the nature of societies, while at the same time reflecting the values of those societies. Although language assessments have taken many different forms, have been implemented with many different kinds of test takers, and have been used for many different purposes, they can all be conceptualized in essentially the same way. In this chapter, we first provide a brief historical overview of language assessments over the centuries and present what we believe to be the central conceptualization that informs all language assessments, both in their design and development and in their use. We then describe an approach to language assessment that is based on the work of Bachman and Palmer (2010) and Bachman and Damböck (2018) and that we believe instantiates the central conceptualization of language assessment. We describe the process of using language assessments to help us make decisions that will have beneficial consequences. Next, we discuss fairness and accountability in assessment and the process of assessment justification. We then discuss the process of designing and developing language assessments, using an example of a language assessment to illustrate this.

Brief Historical Overview of Language Assessments

The oldest and longest continuously implemented language assessment on record is the Chinese Imperial Civil Service Examination,[1] which was initiated during the Sui dynasty (581–618) and lasted over a thousand years, until it was abolished in 1905, toward the end of the Qing dynasty (1644–1911) (Weerdt, 2022).[2] The initial purpose of the examination was to

---

[1] For more complete discussions of the history of language testing, see, e.g., Barnwell (1996) and Spolsky (1995).
[2] At about the same time, similar examinations were initiated in Japan and Korea.

The Concise Companion to Language Assessment, First Edition. Edited by Antony John Kunnan.
© 2025 John Wiley & Sons, Inc. Published 2025 by John Wiley & Sons, Inc.

4 Chapter 1 How to Conceptualize and Implement a Language Assessment

select exceptionally talented young men to serve as senior bureaucrats by merit, rather than by birth. As the examination evolved over the years, it became a tool for selecting government officials who were loyal to the emperor, thus countering the influence of the military and the aristocracy on the imperial government.

The content of the examinations was based on the classic texts of Confucianism, i.e., *The Analects* and *Mencius*. However, they assessed not only a young man's knowledge of Confucian philosophy but also his writing and calligraphy, formal essay writing techniques, mathematics, law, government, poetry, and clear and coherent speaking (Cartwright, 2019). In the later years of the examinations, beginning during the Ming dynasty (1368–1644) and continuing into the Ching dynasty, the focus became more and more on language, especially the candidates' mastery of the "eight-legged" essay, an elaborate structure of formal writing which candidates were expected to follow strictly (Elman, 2009). Candidates' written answers were double marked, once by an associate examiner and once by a senior examiner, using a system of symbols indicating the quality of the answer. Only when both examiners agreed on the mark was the pass/fail decision made (O'Sullivan & Cheng, 2022).

In the earliest European universities, which were established during the 11th through 15th centuries, there were no formal "examinations." Students were assessed through the lectures they gave and through a series of "disputations," in which a student engaged in a formal debate with another student or a master. In these disputations, the student was assessed according to how well he demonstrated his ability to plausibly and convincingly argue a particular position according to Aristotle's syllogistic rules of argumentation. These disputations were conducted in Latin and covered the content of the university's curriculum, which included the writings of Aristotle and Euclid, as well as the Trivium (grammar, rhetoric, and logic), the Quadrivium (arithmetic, geometry, music, and astronomy), and the three philosophies (natural, moral, and metaphysical). Once students passed all of their disputations, they were considered to be "masters" and could take on students of their own (Rashdall, 1975).

It was not until the 18th century that formal written examinations were introduced in Europe. The first of these, the German *Abitur*, was introduced in Prussia in 1788 and later established in the other German states. Prior to this, each university in Germany had its own entrance examination, and the government wanted to standardize this to assure that all students accepted to German universities had the same qualifications. Although the Abitur served initially as a university entrance qualification, over time it also came to be used as a school-leaving examination. The written examination assessed both old languages, e.g., Latin and Greek; new languages, e.g., French; and the mother tongue, German. It also assessed knowledge of the sciences, especially history (Bölling, 2010). In 1808, the French Baccalauréat was established by Napoleon Bonaparte as a way to provide the opportunity for anyone with talent or intelligence to pass its rigorous exams. The original Baccalauréat assessed test takers' knowledge in the areas of science, literature, law, medicine, and theology (Villinger, 2018). Both the Abitur and the Baccalauréat continue to be administered up to the present day.

The late 18th century saw the rapid emergence of secondary school-leaving examinations in the United Kingdom. These were administrated largely by agencies within universities, e.g., the Royal Society of Arts Examinations Board (est. 1856), the University of Oxford Delegacy of Local Examinations (est. 1857), and the University of Cambridge Local Examinations Syndicate (est. 1858). All of these examinations aimed at the general goal of improving society. The purpose of the Cambridge examinations, for example, was to "raise standards in education by administering exams for people who were not members of the University and inspecting schools" (Cambridge Assessment International Education, 2023b). Similarly, the Oxford examinations were intended to "confer a great benefit on that large class of persons who cannot afford, or do not require, a University education for their children, by undertaking to examine boys, about the time of their leaving school" (Cambridge University Libraries, 2023). These examinations covered a wide range of academic subjects,

Brief Historical Overview of Language Assessments **5**

including, e.g., drawing, English language, English literature, French, geography, German, Greek, history, Latin, law, mathematics, religious knowledge, and zoology (Cambridge Assessment International Education, 2023a).

Standardized tests began to appear in the United States in the mid-18th century. It is important to note that "standardized" at that time meant simply that "the tests were published, that directions were given for administration, that the exam could be answered in consistent and easily graded ways, and that there would be instructions on the interpretation of results" (U.S. Congress Office of Technology Assessment, 1992, p. 108). The first such test was a written examination initiated in the Boston Public School system in 1845 to replace oral examinations, which were seen as subjective and were expensive to administer. This written examination was intended to be used for two purposes: (i) classify schoolchildren according to how much they had learned and (ii) monitor the effectiveness of the school system (U.S. Congress Office of Technology Assessment, 1992). In 1865, the first preliminary Regents Examinations were administered to eighth-grade students in the state of New York; the High School Regents Examinations were administered for the first time in 1878. These examinations were intended to inform the distribution of state funding to encourage academic education. Although only 5 subjects, algebra, American history, elementary Latin, natural philosophy, and physical geography, were assessed in the first, by 1879 the list was expanded to 41 subjects, including rhetoric and English composition, Greek, French, and German (New York State Education Department, n.d.).

Testing for university and college admissions began in the United States in 1901 with the administration of the College Entrance Examination Board's first examinations. These "College Boards" consisted of essay examinations in English, French, German, Latin, Greek, history, mathematics, chemistry, and physics (Lawrence et al., 2003). Over the years, these subjects were greatly expanded to include literature, reading, and writing and became a part of the family of Scholastic Aptitude Tests (SATs), first as SAT Achievement Tests, and eventually as the SAT II (Atkinson & Geiser, 2009; Lawrence et al., 2003).

Probably the most influential assessment of speaking ability in the United States, in terms of its prestige and range of use, is the Oral Proficiency Interview (OPI), which is used both within numerous U.S. government agencies and by colleges, universities, and high schools as a measure of speaking ability. This assessment had its origins in the Foreign Service Oral Proficiency Interview that was developed in the 1950s.[3] By 1956, this had been officially adopted by the U.S. Department of State for new employees and became mandatory for all Foreign Service Officers in 1957. Subsequently, it was adopted by a number of other U.S. government agencies and was renamed as the Interagency Language Roundtable (ILR) oral interview. In the early 1960s, the OPI was adopted by the U.S. Peace Corps to assess the language proficiency of Peace Corps Volunteers around the world (Lowe Jr., 1988). Inspired by the success of this project, in 1982 Educational Testing Service and the American Council on the Teaching of Foreign Languages collaborated to modify the OPI scale to better suit the population of foreign language learners in U.S. high schools, colleges, and universities (Clark & Clifford, 1988; Liskin-Gasparro, 2003).

From the 1960s to the present, there has been a proliferation of large-scale, high-stakes assessments of English as a foreign language, such as the *Test of English as a Foreign Language* (TOEFL) first administered in 1964 and the *International English Language Testing System* (IELTS) first administered in 1989. These tests include multiple-choice questions that are machine-scored for listening and reading. For writing, test takers produce samples of writing that are scored by trained human raters for the IELTS, and by a combination of human and AI-based scoring for the TOEFL. For speaking, test takers produce samples of spoken language that are scored by trained human raters. The content of the tests is generally based on

---

[3] According to Lowe, the OPI's "ultimate antecedents are shrouded in mystery" (Lowe Jr., 1983).

6   Chapter 1 How to Conceptualize and Implement a Language Assessment

the content of academic studies in colleges and universities. Both of these tests are intended for essentially the same purposes: to help college admissions officers determine (i) if an applicant is sufficiently proficient in English to successfully complete an academic degree program and (ii) whether an applicant might benefit from ESL instruction at the college or university.

Although all of these assessments over the years have covered different domains, e.g., Confucian philosophy and ethics, natural, moral, and metaphysical philosophy, geography, mathematics, science, and history, many of them explicitly assessed languages, e.g., Latin, Greek, French, German, and English, as well as various aspects of language, e.g., grammar and rhetoric. Furthermore, in many of the examinations, even those that were focused on other topics, e.g., Confucian philosophy in the Chinese Civil Service Examination, test takers' answers have been evaluated at least in part according to the quality of the language they have used in the examination. For these reasons, virtually all of these assessments can be considered to be assessments of language.

Central Conceptualization of Language Assessment

Language assessments over the years and up to the present time have been used for a wide variety of purposes, have been administered to a wide range of individuals, in a variety of institutional settings, and have been implemented using a diversity of assessment tasks and procedures. Despite these differences in intended use, intended test takers, and assessment formats and tasks, all of these language assessments can be conceptualized in the same way, as follows:

> Language assessment is the process of collecting information about individuals and using this information to make decisions that will lead to beneficial consequences. The process of language assessment is socioculturally embedded, reflects the values of the culture, and helps realize these.

Using Language Assessments

The primary purpose of a language assessment is to collect information about individuals' language ability. The reason we collect this information is so that we can use this to help us make decisions that we believe will lead to beneficial consequences for the intended stakeholders. We define stakeholders as "people, language programs or courses, or institutions that may be affected by or benefit from the use of the assessment" (Bachman & Damböck, 2018, p. 13). Stakeholders may include some or all of the following:

- Individuals, e.g., the test developer/user, test takers, teachers, school administrators, parents, guardians, caretakers, college/university admissions officers, employers, and government officials.
- Institutions or organizations, e.g., schools, colleges/universities, government agencies, and businesses that the test developer/user wants to be affected by the use of the assessment.

Using a language assessment thus involves linking test takers' assessment performance to the consequences we want to help bring about. When we use a language assessment, we do the following:

1. collect samples of test takers' language performance;
2. arrive at an assessment record (a description or score);

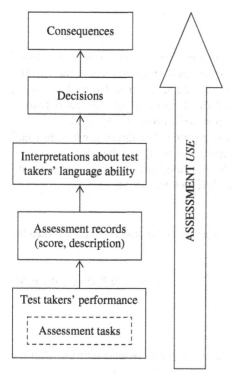

FIGURE 1.1 Links between assessment performance and intended consequences. *Source:* Adapted from Bachman and Damböck (2018), figure 2.3, p. 20.

3. interpret these assessment records as indicators of test takers' language ability;
4. make decisions based on these interpretations; and
5. hence lead to beneficial consequences for stakeholders.

The links in assessment use are illustrated in Figure 1.1.

Fairness and Accountability in Assessment

Fairness as an overarching quality of an assessment has been discussed extensively in the language assessment literature (Bachman, 2005; Davies, 2010; see, e.g., Elder, 1997; Kane, 2010; the articles in Kunnan, 2000; Xi, 2010). The most extensive discussion of fairness is Kunnan (2018), who approaches this from the perspective of what he calls an "ethics-based approach to assessment evaluation." Drawing on Toulmin's approach to practical argumentation (Toulmin, 2003), he operationalizes this approach as a "fairness and justice argument."

We define fairness as "a quality of assessment use. Fairness depends on how well each link from test takers' performance on assessment tasks, to assessment records, to interpretations, to decisions, to consequences can be supported or justified to stakeholders" (Bachman & Damböck, 2018, p. 28).

Many of the decisions we make on the basis of assessments are high stakes, potentially affecting the lives of many people and institutions. That is, they have major, life-affecting consequences for stakeholders. If we want stakeholders to believe in or trust the way our assessments are used, then these assessments need to be fair. In order to convince stakeholders that our assessments are fair, we must be accountable to them. Accountability means "being able to *demonstrate* to stakeholders that the intended uses of our assessments are justified" (Bachman & Palmer, 2010, p. 92). The process that we will utilize to do this is assessment justification.

8 Chapter 1 How to Conceptualize and Implement a Language Assessment

Assessment Justification

There are several approaches to accountability in assessment. One approach, which is based on the measurement quality of validity, is to follow a list of qualities or standards, such as the *Code of Ethics* (International Language Testing Association, 2000) and *Guidelines for Practice* (International Language Testing Association, 2005) of the International Language Testing Association. Another approach is called an "argument-based approach" to validation (e.g., Kane, 2006). Bachman and Palmer (2010) have used this approach to develop what they call "assessment justification." They define assessment justification as "the process that test developers will follow to investigate the extent to which the intended uses of an assessment are justified" (p. 95). Assessment justification includes two interrelated activities.

The test developer/user

1. articulates an Assessment Use Argument (AUA) that supports the links between the intended consequences and test takers' performance, and
2. provides backing (evidence) to support the AUA.

(Bachman & Palmer, 2010, p. 95)

Assessment Use Argument (AUA)

An AUA includes a series of claims that correspond to the links in assessment use that we discussed above.

> *Claims* are statements that the test developer and/or user makes that specify the intended uses of the assessment, what it aims to assess, and how it intends to do this.
>
> (Bachman & Damböck, 2018, p. 30)

The AUA for a given assessment will include four claims, about the following:

1. the intended consequences of using the assessment;
2. the intended decisions to be made;
3. the intended interpretations; and
4. the intended assessment records (scores and descriptions).

We provide examples of these claims for an example assessment below.

Backing

Backing consists of the evidence that we need to provide to support the claims in the AUA. Backing can be collected from a variety of different sources. Two kinds of backing can be provided to support the claims in an AUA:

1. *Backing from procedures*: This comprises essentially the documentation of the procedures that were followed in the development of the assessment, procedures that are followed in creating assessment tasks, administering and scoring these, procedures for making decisions, and for reporting the assessment results to test users.
2. *Backing that is collected specifically for the purpose of supporting warrants in the AUA*: This includes the collection of documentation such as laws, rules, and regulations, as well as the collection and analyses of specific empirical data, using a range of qualitative and quantitative approaches, as appropriate to the particular claim.

We provide examples of backing for an example assessment below.

Developing Language Assessments

In this section, we discuss three parts of our approach to developing language assessments: (i) using an AUA to guide the development of an assessment, (ii) developing assessment task templates, and (iii) creating multiple assessment tasks. All of these procedures will be illustrated with an example of a specific classroom-based language assessment (adapted from Bachman & Damböck, 2018).

Using an AUA to Guide Assessment Development

An AUA provides the rationale and basis for designing and developing a language assessment. Each claim in an AUA has two parts: an outcome (consequence, decision, interpretation, and assessment record) and one or more qualities that are claimed for the outcome. The outcomes and qualities of the claims in an AUA are illustrated in Figure 1.2.

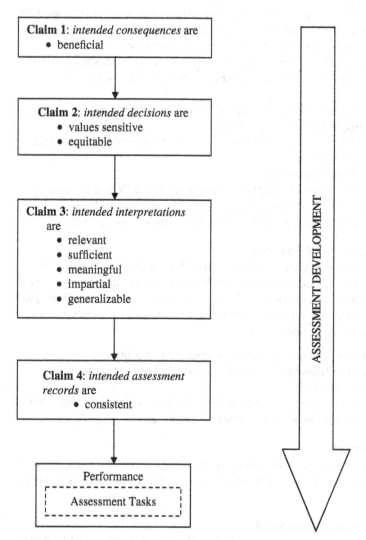

FIGURE 1.2 Claims, outcomes, and qualities in an Assessment Use Argument. *Source:* Adapted from Bachman and Damböck (2018), Figure 3.1, p. 31.

10   Chapter 1 How to Conceptualize and Implement a Language Assessment

Qualities of the Claims in an AUA

We define the qualities of claims in an AUA as follows (Bachman & Damböck, 2018, pp. 41–76):

1. Quality of consequences: **beneficence**: the degree to which the consequences of using an assessment and of the decisions made promote good and are not detrimental to stakeholders.
2. Qualities of decisions: values-sensitivity and equitability
   - **Values-sensitivity**: the degree to which the use of an assessment and the decisions that are made take into consideration existing educational and societal values and follow relevant laws, rules, and regulations.
   - **Equitability**: the degree to which different test takers who are at equivalent levels on the ability to be assessed have an equivalent chance of being classified into the same group.
3. Qualities of interpretations: relevance, sufficiency, meaningfulness, generalizability, and impartiality.
   - **Relevance**: the degree to which the intended interpretations provide the information the test user needs to make the intended decisions.
   - **Sufficiency**: the degree to which the intended interpretations provide *enough* information for the test user to make the intended decisions.
   - **Meaningfulness**: the extent to which the intended interpretation
     1. provides stakeholders with information about the ability to be assessed and
     2. conveys this information in terms that stakeholders can understand and relate to.
   - **Generalizability**: the degree to which the intended interpretations apply or extend to the test takers' target language use (TLU) domains.
     A TLU *domain* is a specific context outside the assessment itself in which test takers need to perform language use tasks.
4. Quality of assessment records: consistency
   - **Consistency**: the extent to which takers' performance on different assessments (e.g., different administrations, different tasks, and different scorers/raters) of the same area of language ability yields essentially the same assessment records.

An AUA as an Operationalization of Fairness

As indicated in our definition above, fairness is a function of how well the individual links from test takers' performance to intended decisions are justified. More specifically, it is a function of the extent to which the qualities associated with the claims are justified. The qualities of the claims in the AUA for a given assessment thus provide a mechanism for operationalizing the concept of fairness. Specifically,

1. if the assessment records are not consistent, the assessment is not fair;
2. if the interpretations are not meaningful, impartial, generalizable, relevant, and sufficient, the assessment is not fair;
3. if the decisions are not values-sensitive and equitable, the assessment is not fair; and
4. if the consequences are not beneficial, the assessment is not fair.

Example Language Assessment

We begin the development of a language assessment by articulating a series of claims that will guide us as we develop the assessment. An overview of the example assessment is given in Table 1.1.

AUA for the Example Language Assessment

The claims in the AUA for the example assessment, along with potential sources of backing, are discussed below.

Developing Language Assessments 11

> **TABLE 1.1**
>
> ### Overview of the example assessment
>
> | | |
> |---|---|
> | Setting | An ESL/EFL classroom in a college, university, or an adult education program |
> | Test takers | Students |
> | Age group | Adults |
> | Level of ability | Advanced |
> | Language | ESL/EFL |
> | Ability to be assessed | Four aspects of a student's writing ability – task achievement, grammar, vocabulary, and cohesion |
> | Assessment task | Writing a letter of application |
> | Intended uses | Make medium-stakes summative decisions about which students pass to the next level of instruction (This assessment is one of several assessments that will be given throughout the year for this intended use) |

Claim 1: Intended Consequences. The consequences of using the classroom writing assessment will be beneficial to stakeholders as indicated in Table 1.2.

Consequences are **beneficial** when they promote good and are not detrimental to stakeholders.

Some possible backing for the beneficence of the intended consequences of using the example assessment is shown in Table 1.3.

Claim 2: Intended Decisions. The medium-stakes summative decisions are made by the teacher at the end of the instructional term and will affect the stakeholders, as shown in Table 1.4. The decisions take into consideration the educational values of the university or adult education program and the societal values of the community and follow the rules and regulations of the university or adult education program. They are equitable for the stakeholders.

Decisions are **values-sensitive** when they take into consideration existing educational and societal values and follow relevant laws, rules, and regulations.

> **TABLE 1.2**
>
> ### Intended consequences and intended stakeholders in example assessment
>
> | Intended consequences | Intended stakeholders |
> |---|---|
> | 1. Students who have mastered the learning objectives of the entire term will benefit by receiving appropriate instruction at the next level of instruction | Students ESL/EFL teachers in the next level |
> | 2. Students who have not mastered the learning objectives of the entire term will benefit by receiving appropriate instruction at the same level of instruction | Students ESL/EFL teachers in the current level |

12   Chapter 1 How to Conceptualize and Implement a Language Assessment

> **TABLE 1.3**
>
> ### Intended consequences and possible backing in example assessment
>
> | Intended consequences | Possible backing |
> | --- | --- |
> | 1. Students who have mastered the learning objectives of the entire term will benefit by receiving appropriate instruction at the next level of instruction | The teacher talks with ESL/EFL teachers in the *next* grade level about how well students who moved on to the next course/grade are performing in writing |
> | 2. Students who have not mastered the learning objectives of the entire term will benefit by receiving appropriate instruction at the same level of instruction | The teacher talks with ESL/EFL teachers in the *same* grade level about how well students who did not move on to the next course/grade are performing in writing |

> **TABLE 1.4**
>
> ### Intended decisions in the example assessment
>
> | Decision(s) to be made | Individual(s) who will make the decision(s) | When the decision(s) will be made | Stakeholders who will (or might be) affected by the decision(s) |
> | --- | --- | --- | --- |
> | Decide which students pass to the next level in their language class (scores from this assessment will count as part of students' total grade for the term) | Teacher | At the end of the term | Students

Teachers

(Future teachers)

Administrators in the university or adult education program |

Some possible backing for the values sensitivity of the intended decisions:

- The teacher meets with students, fellow teachers, and school administrators to discuss the relevant values that need to be considered in the decisions to be made, and provides documentation that these are being considered in the decisions that are made.
- The teacher reviews school rules and regulations regarding the use of assessments for decisions about which test takers will pass to the next level.

Decisions are **equitable** when different test takers who are at the same levels on the ability to be assessed are classified into the same groups. Equitability is a concern with summative decisions, which will be made to classify test takers into different groups, such as classes at different levels of ability, progress/not progress, pass/not pass, and certify/not certify. Thus, if test takers with the same test scores are classified differently, the decision is not equitable. Likewise, if test takers with different test scores are classified the same, the decision is not equitable. In order to use test scores to classify test takers, we will need to specify a *cut score*, which is a test score, grade, or mark that will be used to classify test takers into different groups.

Some possible backing for the equitability of the intended decisions:

The teacher documents procedures for

- setting standards and cut scores based on all of the assessments given during the course of the school year,
- monitoring how these are implemented in practice, and
- informing test takers and other stakeholders about these.

Claim 3: Intended interpretations. The interpretations about four aspects of test takers' writing ability – task achievement, grammar, vocabulary, and cohesion – based on this single assessment are relevant to the medium-stakes summative decisions to be made, but are *not* sufficient for these decisions. This is because these decisions will be made on the basis of this assessment *and* other assessments that will be given during the course of instruction. The interpretations are meaningful with respect to the content of the course and of the current lesson, generalizable to the current language class, and are impartial to all test takers.

Interpretations are **relevant** when they provide the information the decision-maker needs. That is, interpretations are relevant when they actually help decision-makers make the intended decisions.

Some possible backing for the relevance of the interpretations in the example assessment:

- During the development of the assessment:
  The teacher meets with ESL/EFL teachers in the current and next level about the interpretations of writing ability that will be relevant for making the intended decisions.
- *After the use* of the assessment:
  The teacher conducts a follow-up meeting with these ESL/EFL teachers on how useful the interpretations actually were in making these decisions.

In this example assessment, the interpretations are *not* **sufficient** since they provide only partial information for the decision-maker to make the intended decisions.

Some possible backing for the sufficiency of the interpretations in the example assessment:

- The teacher provides descriptions of the additional assessments that will be used to make the pass/fail decisions.
- The teacher provides descriptions of and how these and the present assessment will be weighted in making these decisions.

Interpretations are **meaningful** when they provide stakeholders with information about the ability to be assessed and convey this information in terms that they can understand and relate to.

Some possible backing for the meaningfulness of the interpretations in the example assessment:

- The teacher provides documentation of relevant course materials, with specific assessment tasks that are aligned with these.
- The teacher collects feedback from students and other relevant stakeholders about their understanding of the areas of writing ability to be assessed.

Interpretations are **generalizable** when they apply or extend to the test takers' target use domain(s).

Some possible backing for the generalizability of the interpretations in the example assessment:

- The teacher provides an analysis of the characteristics of the instructional tasks in the language classroom.
- The teacher compares these characteristics with those of the assessment tasks.
- The teacher collects feedback from students and fellow teachers about the degree of correspondence between the instructional tasks and the assessment tasks.

Interpretations are **impartial** when the format and content of the assessment tasks and all aspects of the administration of the assessment are free from bias that may favor or disfavor some test takers.

Some possible backing for the impartiality of the interpretations in the example assessment:

- The teacher carefully reviews all of the assessment tasks for possible sources of bias.
- The teacher collects feedback from students and fellow teachers about assessment tasks they felt were possibly biased.

14   Chapter 1 How to Conceptualize and Implement a Language Assessment

Claim 4: Assessment Records. The scores from the writing assessment are consistent across different times and days of administration, and across different administrations to different groups of test takers. Test takers' performances are scored consistently by the teacher, according to an analytic rating scale with four components: task achievement, grammar, vocabulary, and cohesion.

Assessment records are **consistent** when test takers' performance on different assessments (e.g., different administrations, different tasks, and different scorers/raters) of the same construct yields essentially the same assessment records.

To help assure the consistency of our assessment records, the teacher needs to do two things:

- identify the specific possible sources of inconsistency in the example assessment and
- provide a description of the procedures followed to minimize the effects of these sources of inconsistency on the assessment records.

These are shown in Table 1.5 for the example assessment.

TABLE **1.5**

Possible sources of inconsistency and procedures to minimize the effects of the sources of inconsistency

Possible sources of inconsistency	Procedures used to minimize the effects of the sources of inconsistency

1. Inconsistencies in the way the assessment is administered
  a. at different times
  b. to different groups of students
  c. by different teachers
	1. Clearly specify the procedures for administering the assessment. Then make sure that the assessment is always administered in the same way at different times, with different groups of students, and by different teachers

2. Inconsistencies across different assessment tasks
  a. Inconsistencies in the information in the prompts that students need to process and respond to across different assessment tasks of the same task type
    i. in the length of the input
    ii. in the language (e.g., grammar, vocabulary, and organization) of the task input
    iii. in the topical content of the input
	2. Prepare specifications or an assessment task template for each assessment task type. Make sure that all tasks that are developed follow this template

3. Inconsistencies in how students' written responses are scored
  a. For ratings of the written responses:
    i. Inconsistencies in the ratings of the same rater
      1. at different times
      2. for different tasks
      3. for different students
    ii. Inconsistencies in the ratings of different raters
	3. Clearly specify the scoring method for each assessment task type. Make sure that the scoring method is followed consistently
	  • Develop a clear and understandable rating rubric
	  • If there will be multiple raters, train raters in the use of these scoring rubrics
	  • Periodically monitor ratings for consistency (e.g., estimates of intra- and interrater reliability)

Developing Assessment Task Templates

We need to base our assessments on the claims in our AUA. This assures that the qualities of our claims are realized in the assessments we develop. Claims 3 and 4 provide specific information that is relevant to developing assessment tasks. Claim 3 defines the area(s) of language ability to be assessed, which is related to the quality of meaningfulness. It also identifies the TLU domain, which is related to the quality of generalizability. These parts of Claim 3 will determine the kinds of assessment tasks we develop. Claim 4 identifies possible sources of inconsistency, which pertains to the quality of consistency. The kinds of assessment tasks we use, plus the concern for consistency, determine the administrative procedures we follow and the scoring method we specify.

The key link between these claims and the assessment tasks we develop is an **assessment task template**, which provides the basis for developing multiple assessment tasks with similar characteristics. To develop an assessment task template, we will first select a "target language use" (TLU task that engages the ability we want to assess). A TLU task is a language use task that the test takers may need to perform in one or more of their TLU domains. This will help assure that the assessment task is related to the content of the course (meaningfulness) and will apply or extend to the TLU tasks in the language classroom (generalizability). We will then describe the characteristics of that task. Next, we will need to modify the teaching task to make it usable for the purpose of assessment. This is because it is seldom possible to use a teaching task as is for assessment. For one thing, students have already performed the teaching task in class, so using this as an assessment task will not provide us with the information we need to generalize about students' ability beyond the classroom. Another reason is that the teaching task might be too long to be practical as an assessment task. Finally, we will specify a method for scoring or describing the students' performance on the assessment task. The result of this process is an assessment task template. This process is illustrated in Figure 1.3.

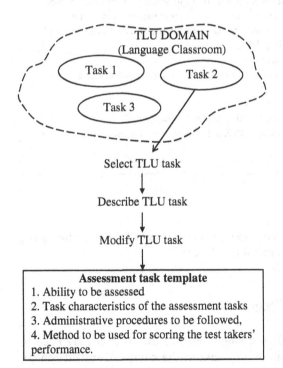

FIGURE 1.3 Process for creating assessment task templates. *Source:* Bachman and Damböck (2018), Figure 8.1, p. 89.

16   Chapter 1 How to Conceptualize and Implement a Language Assessment

---

TABLE 1.6

Assessment task template for the example assessment

Assessment Task: Writing a formal letter of application for a job	
Areas of language ability to be assessed: Task achievement – following the format of a formal letter of job application, using appropriate range of grammar, vocabulary, and cohesion	
Task Characteristics (TCs)	
Setting	Physical circumstances: the teacher in front of the classroom; students are seated individually Equipment/materials: pen/pencil and paper (or computer) Participants: teacher and all students (adults; advanced) Time of the task: during the regular class period; task requires one class period to complete

Input	Form:
	    Aural: teacher's spoken description of the task
	    Visual: writing prompt
	Language: English;
	    Teacher: aural: short spoken description and explanation; simple grammar and vocabulary
	    Length: aural: short utterances; visual: long
	Topical content: letter of application for a summer job as a sales assistant

Expected response	Form:
	    Visual: written text
	Language: English; written text, grammar, and vocabulary appropriate to the writing task; well organized, with cohesion; genre: formal letter of application
	    Length: 250–300 words
	Topical content: application for a summer job as a sales assistant

Administrative procedures	The teacher reads the test takers' letters of application and arrives at scores according to the "Rating Scale." The teacher enters these scores in the "Recording Form" and then adds up the scores to arrive at a Total Score and enters this in the "Recording Form."

Scoring method for the assessment task	Type of assessment record: score
	Aspects of ability: writing: task achievement, grammar, vocabulary, and cohesion
	Scoring method:
	    Criteria: See "Rating Scale" below.
	        For each aspect: 1–4, according to the "Rating Scale"
	        Score reported: Total score = Task achievement + Grammar + Vocabulary + Cohesion

The assessment task template for the example assessment is shown in Table 1.6. The Rating Scale for scoring students' responses is shown in Table 1.7.

Creating Multiple Assessment Tasks

A language assessment may include more than a single task, or the teacher may need to develop several different tests of the same ability throughout the course of instruction. In either case, the teacher will need to create multiple assessment tasks. An assessment task template provides the basis for developing multiple assessment tasks with similar

Developing Language Assessments · 17

TABLE 1.7

Rating Scale for scoring students' responses to the example assessment task

Points	Task achievement	Grammar	Vocabulary	Cohesion
4	• Includes *all* content points • Meets *all* job application letter requirements	• *Wide* range of grammar structures with *very few* inaccuracies	• *Wide* range of vocabulary with *very few* inaccuracies	• *Wide* range of cohesive devices with *very few* inaccuracies
3	• Includes *most* content points • Meets *most* job application letter requirements	• *Good* range of grammar structures with *occasional* inaccuracies	• *Good* range of vocabulary with *occasional* inaccuracies	• *Good* range of cohesive devices with *occasional* inaccuracies
2	• Includes *some* content points • Meets *some* job application letter requirements	• *Limited* range of grammar structures with *frequent* inaccuracies	• *Limited* range of vocabulary with *frequent* inaccuracies	• *Limited* range of cohesive devices with *frequent* inaccuracies
1	• Includes *few* content points • Meets *few* job application letter requirements	• *Very limited* range of grammar structures with *very frequent* inaccuracies	• *Very limited* range of vocabulary *with very frequent* inaccuracies	• *Very limited* range of cohesive devices with *very frequent* inaccuracies

characteristics. To create multiple assessment tasks to assess the same area of language ability from a single assessment task template, the teacher will do the following:

1. Create one task, a "model task" following the specifications in the assessment task template.
2. Create additional tasks by:
   - keeping the definition of the ability to be assessed the same;
   - keeping the attributes of the students (e.g., age and ability level) the same; and
   - changing one or more of the other task characteristics of the template (e.g., type of letter and type of writing activity).

The process for creating multiple assessment tasks from an assessment task template is illustrated in Figure 1.4.

Example "Model" assessment task

The assessment takes place during one class period. The teacher explains the assessment task and the scoring procedure, including the Rating Scale, at the beginning of the class period. The assessment is administered to the class as a group, with students working individually. They write a job application letter about a job they have seen advertised in the newspaper.

Teacher's description of the task

"Here's the prompt for your writing test." (The teacher gives students the writing prompt.) "Read it through and let me know if you have any questions." (Teacher allows time for students to read the prompt.) "Are there any questions?" (The teacher answers any clarification questions the students may have.) "You'll have 45 minutes to complete your letter. You may begin now."

18   Chapter 1   How to Conceptualize and Implement a Language Assessment

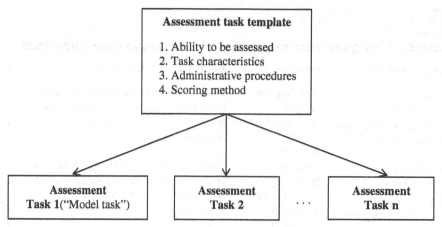

FIGURE 1.4 Creating multiple assessment tasks from a single assessment task template. *Source:* Adapted from Bachman and Dambӧck (2018), Figure 9.1, p. 112.

Writing prompt for "Model" assessment task

Imagine that you have read a description of a job in the newspaper. You want to apply for this job and so you write a letter of application (**250–300 words**) to the human resources department of the company. Use the same structure for your letter that we have been using in class. Include all the necessary information. Your letter will be scored according to the rating scale we discussed in class.

The job description for the model assessment task is given in Table 1.8.

TABLE 1.8

Job description for the model assessment task

Summer job: sales assistant

If you are a motivated and outgoing person who is looking for a great summer job that offers flexible hours and good income, join our team at "The Market Place"! Working hours are Monday through Friday from 9.00 a.m. to 5 p.m. You will receive interesting benefits such as discounts on merchandise.

Your duties will be to assist the sales manager in the following: ©

- Answer customers' queries about merchandise needs
- Offer recommendations based on customers' needs and interests
- Restock inventory
- Being responsible for processing cash and card payments
- Dealing with customer refunds
- Responsible for dealing with customer complaints

Please apply in writing to the Human Resources Department at:

The Market Place

132 Main Street

St Louis, MI, 63105

Writing Prompt for Assessment Task 2

Imagine that you have read a description of a job (different from the job in the "Model" assessment task) in the newspaper. You want to apply for this job and so you write a letter of application (**250–300 words**) to the human resources department of the company. Use the same structure for your letter that we have been using in class. Include all the necessary information. Your letter will be scored according to the rating scale we discussed in class.

Summary and Conclusion

Language assessments have been used for centuries for a variety of purposes, with many different types of test takers, and using a wide variety of assessment tasks. They have reflected the values of the societies in which they were used and have also played an important role in shaping these societies. Despite the wide variations in their intended uses, in the individuals who took them, and in the assessment methods that were used, all of these assessments can be conceptualized as procedures for gathering information about individuals for the purposes of making decisions that were intended to have beneficial outcomes for the societies in which they were embedded.

It cannot be assumed, however, that these intended benefits will accrue simply on the basis of the assessment developer's position of authority, good reputation, or assertions. Rather, the test developer must be held accountable for the claimed benefits of using the assessment. Accountability means being able to convince stakeholders that the intended uses of the assessment are justified.

Using an assessment involves making a series of inferences from a test taker's performance to an interpretation, to a decision, and to the intended consequences. In order to justify these inferential links in the use of an assessment to stakeholders, the test developer can employ the process of assessment justification. This provides a basis for being accountable to stakeholders. Assessment justification includes two processes:

1. articulating an AUA and
2. collecting backing to support the AUA.

An AUA consists of a series of four claims, each corresponding to an inferential link between assessment performance and assessment use. Each claim also includes the articulation of one or more qualities that contribute to the overall fairness of the assessment. An AUA thus provides an explicit rationale and conceptual framework for justifying the intended use of the assessment. Backing provides the evidence we need to support the claims in the AUA.

An AUA can also guide the development and use of language assessments. In developing a language assessment, we begin by articulating a series of claims about:

1. the intended consequences of using the assessment,
2. the intended decisions to be made,
3. the areas of language ability to be assessed, and
4. the kinds of assessment records (e.g., scores, marks, and descriptions) we intend to use to characterize test takers' performances.

Following the assessment development process, what we have described will enable test developers to develop and use language assessments that assess the intended areas of language to be assessed and provide information that is useful for making decisions that lead to consequences that can be justified to stakeholders.

Discussion Questions

1. Think of a language assessment you have either taken or administered. For this assessment, describe the following:
   - the intended consequences of the assessment
   - the intended stakeholders
   - the intended decisions
   - the intended interpretations – the aspects or components of language ability to be assessed.
2. Reread the description of the Chinese Imperial Civil Service Examination on p. ## above. Discuss the ways in which this assessment might or might not have had:
   1. consequences that were beneficial to stakeholders
   2. decisions that were values-sensitive and equitable
   3. interpretations that were relevant, sufficient, meaningful, and generalizable
   4. marks that were consistent.

References

Atkinson, R. C., & Geiser, S. (2009). Reflections on a century of college admissions tests. *Educational Researcher*, *38*(9), 665–676.

Bachman, L. F. (2005). Building and supporting a case for test use. *Language Assessment Quarterly*, *2*(1), 1–34.

Bachman, L. F., & Damböck, B. E. (2018). *Language assessment for classroom teachers*. Oxford University Press.

Bachman, L. F., & Palmer, A. S. (2010). *Language assessment in practice: Developing language assessments and justifying their use in the real world*. Oxford University Press.

Barnwell, D. P. (1996). *A history of foreign language testing in the United States: From its beginnings to the present*. Bilingual Press.

Bölling, R. (2010). *Kleine geschichte des Abiturs*. Ferdinand Schöningh.

Cambridge Assessment International Education. (2023a). *How have school examinations changed over the past 150 years?* Retrieved 08/21/2023 from https://www.cambridgeassessment.org.uk/news/how-have-school-exams-changed-over-the-past-150-years/.

Cambridge Assessment International Education. (2023b). *Our history*. Retrieved 08/21/2023 from https://www.cambridgeinternational.org/about-us/our-history/.

Cambridge University Libraries. (2023). *University of Oxford delegacy of local examinations (UODLE) (1857–1000)*. Retrieved 08/21/2023 from https://archivesearch.lib.cam.ac.uk/agents/corporate_entities/2574.

Cartwright, M. (2019). *The civil service examinations of imperial China*. World History Encyclopedia. Retrieved 08/13/2023 from https://www.worldhistory.org/article/1335/the-civil-service-examinations-of-imperial-china/.

Clark, J. L. D., & Clifford, R. T. (1988). The FSI/ILR/ACTFL proficiency scales and testing techniques: development, current status and needed research. *Studies in Second Language Acquisition*, *10*(2), 129–147.

Davies, A. (2010). Test fairness: a response. *Language Testing*, *27*(2), 171–176.

Elder, C. (1997). What does test bias have to do with fairness? *Language Testing*, *14*(3), 261–277.

Elman, B. A. (2009). Eight-legged essay. In L. Cheng (Ed.), *Berkshire encyclopedia of China* (pp. 695–989). Berkshire Publishing Group.

International Language Testing Association. (2000). *ILTA code of ethics*. https://cdn.ymaws.com/www.iltaonline.com/resource/resmgr/docs/ILTA_2018_CodeOfEthics_Engli.pdf.

International Language Testing Association. (2005). *Guidelines for practice*. International Language Testing Association. Retrieved 5/24/08 from https://cdn.ymaws.com/www.iltaonline.com/resource/resmgr/docs/guidelines_for_practice/2020_revised/ilta_guidelines_for_practice.pdf.

Kane, M. T. (2006). Validation. In R. L. Brennan (Ed.), *Educational measurement* (4th ed.). American Council on Education and Praeger Publishers.

Kane, M. T. (2010). Validity and fairness. *Language Testing, 27*(2), 177–182.

Kunnan, A. J. (Ed.). (2000). *Fairness and validation in language assessment: selected papers from the 19th Language Testing Research Colloquium*. Orlando: Cambridge University Press.

Kunnan, A. J. (2018). *Evaluating language assessments*. Routledge.

Lawrence, I. M., Rigol, G. W., Essen, T. V., & Jackson, C. A. (2003). *A historical perspective on the content of the SAT*. ETS Research Report Series, 2003(1), i–19.

Liskin-Gasparro, J. E. (2003). The ACTFL proficiency guidelines and the Orfal proficiency interview: a brief history and analysis of their survival. *Foreign Language Annals, 36*(4), 483–490.

Lowe, P. Jr. (1983). The ILR oral interview: origins, applications, pitfalls, and implications. *Die Unterrichtspraxis/ Teaching German, 16*(2), 230–244.

Lowe, P. Jr. (1988). The unassimilated history. In P. Jr. Lowe & C. W. Stansfield (Eds.), *Second language proficiency: Current issues* (pp. 11–51). Prentice-Hall Regents.

New York State Education Department. (n.d.). *History of New York state assessments*. Retrieved 08/21/2023 from https://www.nysed.gov/state-assessment/history-new-york-state-assessments.

O'Sullivan, B., & Cheng, L. (2022). Lessons from the Chinese imperial examination system. *Language Testing in Asia, 12*(1), 52. https://doi.org/10.1186/s40468-022-00201-5.

Rashdall, H. (1975). Chapter 1: foundings. In A. B. Cobban (Ed.), *The medieval universities: Their development and organization* (pp. 1–41). Methuen.

Spolsky, B. (1995). *Measured words*. Oxford University Press.

Toulmin, S. E. (2003). *The uses of argument* (updated ed.). Cambridge University Press.

U.S. Congress Office of Technology Assessment. (1992). Chapter 4 – Lessons from the past: a history of educational testing in the United States. In *Testing in American schools: Asking the right questions*. U.S. Government Printing Office.

Villinger, M. (2018). Bildungsreform in Frankreich: Schul- und Hochschulbereich. *Aktuelle Frankreich-Analysen, 33*.

Weerdt, H. D. (2022). The Chinese civil examinations. *Inference: International Review of Science, 7*(3).

Xi, X. (2010). How do we go about investigating fairness? *Language Testing, 27*(2), 147–170.

Suggested Readings

Bachman, L. F., & Damböck, B. E. (2018). *Language assessment for classroom teachers*. Oxford University Press.

Bachman, L. F., & Palmer, A. S. (2010). *Language assessment in practice: Developing language assessments and justifying their use in the real world*. Oxford University Press.

CHAPTER 2

Learning-Oriented Language Assessment

James Enos Purpura

Introduction

Communication involves the ability to draw on a range of social, mental, and dispositional resources in order to understand, express, negotiate, and co-construct variegated meanings through goal-oriented activities across a range of contexts (Purpura, 2016a). As second or foreign language (SFL) speakers, we communicate in social–interpersonal contexts to build and maintain relationships; in social–transactional contexts to navigate daily operations; in academic or instructional contexts to build knowledge, develop skills, and share understandings; and in professional or occupational contexts to build and share expertise. In all these domains of human endeavor, learning is essential for getting things done, and opportunities for SFL learning are ubiquitous. More technically, in all these encounters, we draw on what we know, in conjunction with contextual catalysts and other mediational supports, to build understandings so that we can ultimately use this contextualized knowledge to think productively and perform tasks in specific contexts. In short, the successful communication of ideas (i.e., instruction), the processing and retention of these ideas (i.e., learning), and the evaluation of communicative success (or infelicities) through performance are essential components of human activity, whether they transpire in one's native language or in a SFL or whether that they occur in formally structured learning environments or in informal learning contexts such as negotiating the purchase of a new phone in a foreign country.

Given that learning, instruction, and assessment are implicated in almost *all* domains of real-world language use, it stands to reason that these components, implicitly or explicitly, would be implicated in assessments that claim to generalize to real-world language use, or for that matter, in pedagogical contexts that claim to prepare students to handle real-world competencies. The idea that assessment might have a critical role in promoting SFL learning processes and informing instructional practices, or that SFL teaching, learning, and assessment success could be severely impacted by other factors (e.g., affect) in the assessment context has led to a relatively new approach to assessment, referred to as *learning-oriented language assessment* (LOLA) (Purpura, 2004; Turner & Purpura, 2016).

Given that a learning-oriented approach to SFL assessment involves much more than principled approaches to the instrument design and use, this chapter begins with a

---

The Concise Companion to Language Assessment, First Edition. Edited by Antony John Kunnan.
© 2025 John Wiley & Sons, Inc. Published 2025 by John Wiley & Sons, Inc.

broadened definition of SFL assessment and reflections on what might count as an SFL assessment in educational and other language use contexts. It then provides a definition of LOLA. This is followed by a discussion of the research in mainstream and language education that not only inspired theoretical reflections about LOLA but also motivated the need for this new approach. Following this, three Learning-Oriented Assessment (LOA) frameworks will be discussed along with how these frameworks have been used in LOLA research and practice.

A Broadened Conceptualization of Second or Foreign Language Assessment

Assessments, Assessment Events, and LOLA Events

Technically speaking, language assessment at its core can be defined as a process for collecting SFL performance information from an individual under certain elicitation or observational conditions for a specific purpose, so that the ensuing data can be used to make claims (also inferences or interpretations) about the individual's targeted attributes (e.g., SFL ability) or some other feature of interest (e.g., the characteristics of SFL production). In SFL assessment, we are specifically interested in evidence related to what language learners know, what skills they have, and their ability to use language resources, along with other resources (e.g., topical knowledge) to communicate effectively across a range of SFL use domains (Purpura & Oh, 2024). The inferences about test takers should be grounded in theoretical models (of proficiency, for example), standards, frameworks, or accumulated knowledge from experience or principled practice. These inferences are then used to produce records of performance quality in the form of scores and score reports, verbal descriptions of performance quality, or simply mental or written notes. In many instances of assessment (e.g., standardized tests), the assessment event stops here – test takers are given a score and possibly a generic description of what the score means, and they are left on their own to figure out how to improve. This is a classic example of *summative assessment* (SA) or *assessment OF learning* (AofL). Beyond the assessment protocol, the scores are then typically used to make decisions related to placement in a SFL program, certification of proficiency, or advancement to the next lesson – all decisions intended to provide beneficence to stakeholders (Kunnan, 2018).

A slightly different example of SA in SFL classrooms is an end-of-unit exam. The inferences from these assessments are primarily used to provide a summative evaluation (i.e., a grade) related to an examinee's knowledge, skills, or abilities (KSAs). However, information from the SA can just as well be and often is used for *formative* purposes. In this case, the assessment event extends beyond the interpretation of performance to decisions that may lead to further actions by teachers, learners, or technology. An *assessment event* in this instance can be defined as a situationally bound sequence of actions (or episodes) for the purpose of observing or eliciting language behavior so that the performance data can (i) be interpreted and judged according to some evaluative criteria and (ii) serve as the basis for further activities taken to close the learning gap.

To illustrate, in one assessment event, teachers may decide to use inferences about learning outcomes to move on to the next lesson, or despite noticing errors, may decide to ignore them, and still move on. In other events, teachers may decide to use inferences about the learners' strengths and weaknesses to assist these learners in narrowing knowledge gaps. In such cases, they might engage in interactions that involve repair practices (Wong & Waring, 2021), where

24 Chapter 2 Learning-Oriented Language Assessment

instructional assistance in the form of corrective feedback is provided. Alternatively, they may engage in collaborative scaffolding or assisted performance practices where instructional guidance serves to help learners consolidate understandings through various socio-cognitive supports. Or teachers might just decide to reteach the lesson. These are classic examples of *FA* or *assessment FOR learning* (AforL), where assessment information complements teaching and learning.

In many instances of FA, the assessment event ends with the provision of instructional assistance via some form of feedback. In these cases, however, teachers have no evidence regarding the *efficacy* of the assistance as a catalyst for further processing or as a vehicle for producing concrete learning outcomes. *Instruction* in this context refers generically to the provision of topical information that an interlocutor needs to process – e.g., feedback from an informed other or further reading; *processing* pertains to the social and mental activities used to understand input and remember it, so that when needed, the new information can be automatically and flexibly retrieved for use; and *learning* is defined as the end state of processing represented by a conceptual reorganization of information manifested by a qualitative shift in knowledge representation, skill, or situated use. In fact, the *only* way for teachers to be sure that further processing or learning has transpired is to provide learners with a second opportunity to display their new understandings. This is referred to as *follow-through*. By providing follow-through opportunities, teachers are, explicitly or implicitly, getting validation evidence in support of a validity argument and an efficacy argument. The validity argument seeks evidence for two claims, namely the claim that the performance-based inferences about the writing ability are accurate (e.g., wrong logical connector) and the claim that the implementation of instructional assistance (e.g., providing corrective feedback) was appropriate. The second argument, which is critical to LOA, is the efficacy argument, which seeks evidence to support the claim that the performance-based inferences and enacted choices about instructional assistance effectively advanced learning processes and or achieved learning outcomes (e.g., the logical connector was used correctly on subsequent occasions).

Thus, the basic structure of an assessment event and an expanded assessment event meant to be learning oriented would involve the following sequence of actions:

An assessment event
elicitation/observation > performance data > inferences > decision for *no further action* > [performance record] > presumed beneficence.

A learning-oriented assessment event
elicitation/observation > performance data > inferences > [performance report] > decision to *provide assistance* > implementation of assistance > opportunity to display learning development > inference about development > performance report > presumed beneficence

To summarize, an LOA event is broader than a simple assessment event as a learning-oriented event utilizes information from the assessment event to conceptualize follow-through for the purpose of furthering learning processes, or with any luck, achieving concrete learning outcomes.

In some assessment contexts, though, the distinctions between summative and formative assessment are much more fluid and complex. This occurs when the goal of assessment is not just for learners to display previously acquired competencies (AofL), but also for them to develop new competencies (AforL) through task completion during the assessment process. In other words, the act of responding to the task demands of assessment serves as an educational experience in its own right (Bennett, 2010b). This is referred to as *assessment AS learning* (AasL) (Earl, 2003).

The Synergies of Assessment, Instruction, and Learning

Assessments Independent from Instruction and Learning

When most people think of "language assessment," they mostly imagine formal, standardized tests designed to elicit SFL performance indicators that can be used to make decisions for placement into a program of study or certification regarding a criterion level of SFL proficiency for university entry, employment, or citizenship. Traditionally, the only instructional assistance to examinees embedded in these protocols is an occasional graphic or reminders about the process (e.g., check your grammar). In other words, instruction and learning within these protocols are not engineered into the design. Rather, the main goal of these tests is to generate fair, reliable, and valid scores that the public can trust for their intended sociocultural, political or institutional purpose. These assessments are considered *external* to the classroom, as they have no formative mandate beyond the assessment event, and their only links to the classroom, in some cases, involve the frameworks they both use to define proficiency (e.g., the CEFR).

When people think of "assessments" *internal* to the classroom, again formal tests, exams or quizzes, happening after instruction, come to mind. Their goal is again to provide meaningful performance records, however, with the intention of making inferences about SFL mastery related to decisions about progress, promotion, diagnosis, or readiness. In many cases, these classroom tests mirror the design of standardized tests, notwithstanding their mandate being very different.

Assessments Embedded in Instruction and Learning

Given the stakes associated with SAs and their use as accountability measures, the focus in CBA, understandably, has long been centered on principled approaches to the construction and use of assessments OF learning. However, as many educators (Turner, 2012) have noted, the paradigm has shifted with discussions turning to understanding the potential of assessment as catalysts for furthering learning processes when embedded in SFL instruction. This is seen in SFL classrooms when teachers use ready-made activities (e.g., tasks from textbooks, teacher-generated activities, or quizzes) for assessment and instructional purposes. The tasks have a wide range of purposes and design specifications. For example, they can be simple independent tasks involving a reading passage followed by comprehension questions; they can be integrated tasks requiring learners to use information from the passage to write an extended response; or they can be complex activities where the information for a reading serves as one source of information to be used alongside others in a careful sequence of sub-tasks as part of a problem-solving scenario. These tasks can be done alone or in groups, but there is always the expectation that learners will receive some form of feedback on their work – e.g., static feedback in the form of a list of answers or words circled on an essay.

In learner-centered classrooms, teachers regularly assign these activities to be carried out in pairs or groups. While completing the activities, learners have the opportunity to observe and evaluate each other's contributions and then to spontaneously provide peer guidance. These naturally occurring episodes can be conceptualized as assessments-on-the-fly, referred to as *spontaneous assessments*. The rationale for conceptualizing these interactions as "assessments" is that performance data are either elicited or observed. The data generate inferences about performance quality. These inferences then translate into decisions, which may involve further actions – providing feedback. In these assessment episodes, the feedback, assisted performance, or scaffolded assistance provided to learners by informed others (teachers, peers)

26   Chapter 2 Learning-Oriented Language Assessment

can be conceptualized as a form of "instruction," often revolving around issues with language, topic, or process. The intended effect of this instruction is to further learning processes and outcomes, thereby providing a clear example of the synergies created by assessment, instruction, and learning. Finally, spontaneous assessments obviously do not produce performance records other than a mental note.

Assessment, Instruction, and Learning Embedded in Naturalistic Conversation

Beyond the classroom, spontaneous assessment episodes are very frequent in naturalistic conversations, for example, when a person needs to clarify meaning by providing an SFL speaker with linguistic assistance. Spontaneous assessments embedded in instruction or naturalistic talk are clear instances of LOLAs mediated through social interaction. The interactional structure of these assessments and their role in promoting learning processes are a relatively new area of inquiry in CBA research.

Instruction and Learning Embedded in Assessment

More recently, several researchers have successfully created assessments that do a better job of mirroring situated SFL use in the real world, where instruction, learning, and assessment are integral components of the design. In these assessments, *instruction and learning are embedded within the assessment*, thereby engineering the protocol to support performance claims similar to those one would encounter in real-world communication. These LOLAs are often made possible by the affordances of technology. Such assessments are represented by a relatively new assessment technique called *scenario-based language assessment* (SBLAs) (Banerjee, 2019, 2024; Beltrán, 2024; Purpura & Banerjee, 2021, 2022; Seong, 2023). These assessments are built around a problem-solving narrative that requires examinees to work collaboratively with simulated online characters to build understandings, consolidate understandings, and work together to solve the problem and share their findings. In this context, teaching, learning, and assessment occur naturally. In the end, SBAs intentionally give examinees the opportunity not only to *display* acquired competencies but also to *develop* them as a result of the assessment experience. To summarize, this broadened conceptualization of SFL assessment is needed if we hope to understand the pervasive role that assessment plays in educational contexts and beyond.

What Is Learning-Oriented Language Assessment?

Turner (2012) defined Classroom-Based Assessment generally as:

> a repertoire of methods and the reflective procedures that teachers and students use for evidence to gauge student learning on an ongoing basis. In this way teaching is adjusted to meet student needs. In addition, CBA is a contextually bound and socially constructed activity involving different stakeholders in learning. (p. 66)

Within the context of CBA, then, several independent approaches to the study of how planned or spontaneous assessments can support learning and learning outcomes have been proposed. Among them are alternative assessment, authentic assessment, formative assessment, AfL, diagnostic assessment, dynamic assessment, and more recently, LOA. While all share a learning orientation, each approach differs with respect to context and focus – e.g., alternative versus standardized assessments; diagnosis and remediation of learning problems; or the moment-by-moment dynamics of mediation. Each also differs in terms of theoretical underpinnings, procedures for implementation, utility, and approaches to research.

With respect to LOLA, there is no one, coherent definition of what constitutes a learning-oriented approach, as Saville (2021) has pointed out. In my view, though, a learning-oriented assessment (LOA) approach to SFL assessment can be characterized by (i) the critical role that assessment information can play in promoting learning processes, practices, and outcomes in educational and other language use contexts and (ii) the role that instruction and learning can play in promoting quality performance and development in classroom and standardized assessment contexts. Importantly though, an LOA approach can also be characterized by a re-envisioning of the kinds of information we can get from SFL assessments so that a wider range of information can be used to support learning and instruction. Such a reconceptualization would begin with an acknowledgment that all assessments are situated and should be described within the various and interacting systems of a localized sociocultural context (e.g., academic, socio-interpersonal) (Brookhart, 2003).

Thus, within the ecology of an SFL assessment, it is essential, from an LOA perspective, not only to view assessments as indicators of learning or performance but also to consider factors in the system that potentially moderate performance and learning (e.g., cognitive demand of the tasks, technological characteristics of delivery). It is also important to understand how these subsystems interact across different agents (e.g., teachers, learners, curriculum, technology). The proposal then is that educators need to explicitly consider these subsystems in the design, collection, and interpretation of assessment evidence, in the decisions that result from the interpretations, and importantly, in determining the effectiveness of these decisions for their intended purpose. As a result, LOA can be defined as a framework for helping to conceptualize the different factors that come into play in assessment events so that these factors can be explicitly considered (i) in the design and development of planned assessments, (ii) in spontaneous assessments mediated through talk-in-interaction, and (iii) in the interpretation of claims related to the assessment event (Turner & Purpura, 2016). A principled approach to LOA would then require that these subsystems be grounded in research, theory, and informed practice.

What Research Has Motivated a Learning-Oriented Approach to SFL Assessment

In order to understand LOLA as an emerging strand of SFL assessment, we need to situate it in its historical framework.

The Foundations of LOLA

While SFL teachers might not have always had formal training in assessment principles and practices, they have always known intuitively that a well-designed test could give them the information they need to do their job – i.e., to give fair grades and help learners close learning gaps with targeted feedback. SFL testers, on the other hand, have mostly been concerned with principled approaches to the design and development of fair, reliable, and valid tests so the performance information could be used to make inferences about learners' KSAs for decision-making. This interest has resulted in dozens of books designed to provide professional guidance on the principles and practices of SFL test design, development, administration, and scoring with a handful of books focusing also on the analysis of test scores and the validation of assessment claims. Implicit in all these books is the belief that if teachers are able to develop technically sound tests, then the use of the test information for teaching and learning would come naturally.

28   Chapter 2 Learning-Oriented Language Assessment

Doubting this assumption, several researchers in the late 1990s published books (e.g., Brown, 1998) designed specifically for classroom teachers, in an attempt to bridge the gap between assessment principles and instructional practices. Rather than focus on technicalities, these books offered teachers practical strategies, with lots of examples, for planning and carrying out assessments (not just tests) in SFL classrooms. They also emphasized the value of linking assessment information to classroom practices. In terms of LOLA, it is important to recognize that both types of guidebooks have been indispensable resources for understanding how to conceptualize, create, use, and evaluate assessments within a learning-oriented framework.

While this body of work emphasized how well-designed assessments could support instruction, only a handful of researchers attempted to ground assessment practice to a theory of SFL testing, a theory of learning and cognition, and insights from SFL pedagogy. An early exception to this was Lado (1961), who argued that test design and interpretation should be informed by how SFLs are learned in classrooms, which at the time meant behaviorism and findings from contrastive analysis. Others (e.g., Bachman, 1990; Bachman & Palmer, 2010) highlighted the importance of relating test design to the underlying cognitive processes engaged in test performance through task completion. Still others (e.g., Bachman & Cohen, 1998; Canale & Swain, 1980) underscored the interfaces between second language acquisition and language testing research. Missing in this work, however, were recommendations for how assessment information could directly support instruction and learning. Skehan (1998), drawing on a theory of cognition and language learning, a model of language proficiency, and task-based language teaching (TBLT), was the first, in my opinion, to unpack the synergies among teaching, learning, and assessment. While his cognitive approach to language learning was mostly agnostic to the social dimension of learning or the sociocultural context in which teaching, learning, and assessment transpire, this body of work was important for a learning-oriented approach to SFL assessment as it underscored how tasks designed in terms of cognitive resources and demands served as important moderators of learning and performance. Hence, it underscored the role of the cognitive dimension in teaching, learning, and assessment.

Probably the most influential stimulus to the systematic study of CBA in general, and LOA in specific, came from research on policy school reform initiatives in the United States and the United Kingdom in the 1990s. These initiatives, at least in the United States, sought to address growing concerns about (i) the quality of public education and its effect on global competitiveness, (ii) the usefulness of assessment information measured by standardized multiple-choice tests, and (iii) the need for accountability systems to track progress through assessment. This focus on assessment as the cornerstone of educational reform, however, coincided with disenchantment with traditional forms of assessment and their lack of congruence with learning and instruction (Linn et al., 1991). Educators were thus looking not just for alternative forms of assessment, but rather for a paradigm shift, where "good assessment is an integral part of good instruction" (Herman et al., 1992, p. 5). Resonating with the goals of LOA today, 10 issues were proposed to characterize this shift (Pace Marshall, 1992):

1. Assessments must be congruent with significant instructional goals.
2. Assessment must involve the examination of the processes as well as the products of learning.
3. Performance-based activities do not constitute assessment per se.
4. Cognitive learning theory and its constructivist approach to knowledge acquisition support the need to integrate assessment methodologies with instructional outcomes and curriculum content.
5. An integrated and active view of student learning requires the assessment of holistic and complex performance.
6. Assessment design is dependent on assessment purpose; grading and monitoring student progress are distinct from diagnosis and improvement.

7. The key to effective assessment is the match between the task and the intended student outcome.
8. The criteria used to evaluate student performance are critical; in the absence of criteria, assessment remains an isolated and episodic activity.
9. Quality assurance provides substantive data for making informed decisions about student learning.
10. Assessment systems that provide the most comprehensive feedback on student growth include multiple measures taken over time. (pp. v–vi)

Similarly in the United Kingdom, in the context of a school reform initiative in the late 1980s, the government convened a task force that became known as the Assessment Reform Group (ARG) (2002) to examine the relationship between the public reporting of student performance following government-mandated curricula and assessments, and assessments in classrooms that tracked student progress relevant to teaching and learning. The ARG concluded, among other findings, that summative forms of assessment used to evaluate school performance should be decoupled from formative forms of assessment, in that assessment "should provide a basis for decisions about pupils further learning needs: they should be formative" (Lewkowicz & Leung, 2022). The ARG's argument for FA or AfL resulted in a landmark study on FA by Black and Wiliam (1998). This study reviewed 681 publications using FA methods of various sorts, locations, and educational levels to examine reported effects on disciplinary learning (math, science, not SFL). The findings suggested that FA activities, undertaken by teachers and students, with the goal of modifying teaching and promoting learning, led to significant learning gains – a finding that got the attention of educators and policymakers alike.

While this study was later criticized (Bennett, 2010a), it successfully highlighted the need for assessment literacy in terms of teachers' choice of assessment tasks, the role of classroom discourse (i.e., questioning) in promoting learning, the importance of feedback and the use of grades, and student involvement in the assessment process (self and peer assessment). More importantly, it provided the impetus for AfL research in many mainstream educational contexts around the world. Beyond this, the ARG received government endorsement to publish a poster outlining 10 principles related to AfL. This poster highlighted the multifaceted complexity of AfL, and contributed to heightened teacher understanding of its goals.

Assessment for learning. . .

1. Should be part of effective planning of teaching and learning.
2. Should focus on how students learn.
3. Should be recognized as central to classroom practice.
4. Should be regarded as a key professional skill for teachers.
5. Should be sensitive and constructive because any assessment has an emotional impact.
6. Should take account of the importance of learner motivation.
7. Should promote commitment to learning goals and a shared understanding of the criteria by which they are assessed.
8. Should ensure that learners receive constructive guidance about how to improve.
9. Should develop the learner's capacity for self-assessment so that they can become reflective and self-managing.
10. Should recognize the full range of achievements of all learners.

A second landmark study that provided a strong motivation for LOLA research was commissioned in the United States in 1998 by the National Research Council (NRC) through its Board of Testing and Assessment (BOTA), and tasked with trying to understand how the confluence of advances in testing and measurement sciences, cognition and learning sciences, and technology could help reshape educational assessment and assessment policy. The committee's work resulted in a seminal book entitled *Knowing what students know: The science and design of educational assessment* edited by Pellegrino et al. (2001) – a sort of companion

30 Chapter 2 Learning-Oriented Language Assessment

book to *How people learn: Brain, mind, experience, and school* edited by Bransford et al. (2000). This impressive work is based on the premise that cognition (a mental representation of both disciplinary knowledge and the development of that knowledge) should be at the core of assessment, curriculum, and instruction, none of which happens in a vacuum. Assessment, as one of three core elements, depends, therefore, on cognition (aligned with a model of proficiency and a theory of learning), observation (i.e., beliefs about how best situations and tasks elicit targeted KSAs), and interpretation (i.e., the process of reasoning about KSAs based on statistical methods and tools, or in classroom contexts, intuition or qualitative data).

The highly influential studies by Black and Wiliam and Pellegrino et al. also inspired many SFL assessment researchers (e.g., Davison & Leung, 2009) to examine the role of FA in SFL classrooms. This research is summarized in Turner (2012), Fox et al. (2022), and Lewkowicz and Leung (2022). Many of the themes emerging from this work laid the groundwork for the study of LOLA. For example, one important line of inquiry involved the *instructional dimension* of FA. Several studies examined issues related to teacher assessment literacy, specifically how teachers conceptualized assessments and used them for formative purposes.

Another line of inquiry focused on the moderators of test performance. Some studies looked at the *socio-cognitive dimension* of FA, addressing learners and learning processes in the context of diagnostic assessment while others examined the effects of self and peer assessment on self-regulation, autonomy, motivation, and learner outcomes (e.g., Patri, 2002). Still other studies were concerned with cognition and the processes involved in making use of feedback or processing related to test performance (e.g., Pellegrino et al., 1999). Several papers focused on the *affective dimension* of FA by examining the social or emotional dispositions of learners in relation to learning and performance (e.g., Broadfoot, 2005; Poehner & Ableeva, 2011). Several researchers addressed the *contextual dimension* of FA by examining institutional policy issues related to the incongruences and resulting problems associated with standardized assessments in classroom contexts or issues related to accountability measures. Others examined the affordances and pitfalls of FA and recommendations for a systemwide approach to FA practice. Finally, several researchers investigated the *social–interactional dimension* of FA by looking at the interface among assessment, instruction, and learning through the lens of talk-in-interaction (Hamp-Lyons & Tavares, 2011).

While the impressive body of research in SFL CBA provided many important insights on critical factors, it remains unclear how the different dimensions worked together within a coherent system conceptual framework – a system that accounts for multiple agents as they use assessments or naturalistic talk to elicit or observe performance data (*elicitation dimension*) indexing what participants know or what learning gaps exist (*proficiency dimension*); a system in which the learning gaps can be narrowed through targeted interventions (e.g., feedback) by informed others (*instructional dimension*), sometimes mediated through cooperative discourse (*social–interactional dimension*) and sometimes delivered though technology (*technological dimension*); a system in which the participants can process the information and maybe learn something new (*socio-cognitive dimension*), provided they are mentally, emotionally and behaviorally engaged coupled with the right attitudes (*affective dimension*); and finally, a system that is organized around competencies and activities that have value in the real world (*contextual dimension*). LOLA is an attempt to provide such a conceptual framework highlighting not only the individual dimensions but also their synergies.

Frameworks for Learning-Oriented Language Assessment

In order to delineate how assessment could be systematically linked to learning and instruction, three LOA framworks have been proposed.

Carless (2007, 2015)

In the context of a project in Hong Kong to help mainstream teachers implement assessment practices related to learning, Carless (2007) proposed a model of LOA in which systemwide certification exams and classroom learning could be directly linked. His model was based on three interconnected components: assessment tasks as learning tasks, participant involvement and engagement, and the central role of feedback as feedforward (i.e., follow through) related to the following three principles.

> **Principle 1:** Assessment tasks should be designed to stimulate sound learning practices amongst students.
> **Principle 2:** Assessment should involve students actively in engaging with criteria, quality, their own and/or peers' performance.
> **Principle 3:** Feedback should be timely and forward-looking so as to support current and future student learning. (p. 22)

Jones and Saville (2016) and Saville (2021)

Sharing the concern that the micro-level of teaching, learning, and assessment should have a direct link to the macro-level social context in which they are situated (i.e., the contextual dimension), Jones and Saville (2016) proposed the LOA cycle as a systematic framework for situated LOA. The framework proposes on the macro-level that learning objectives for an LOA-related syllabus be based on performance descriptors linked to the CEFR. In this system, learning in the LOA syllabus is monitored with summative assessments again associated with the CEFR. On the micro-level, teachers use LOA tasks and activities to monitor performance through a range of methods, and if needed, provide feedback, which aims to close learning gaps. In this way, learning from the micro and macro can be formally evaluated and certified through an external exam rooted to the CEFR, thereby completing the cycle. This framework provides a clear link for micro- and macro-level performance to be interpreted and used by all agents in the system – students, teachers, schools, and policymakers.

In a more recent description of this model, Saville (2021) characterized the framework as an ecosystem in which several subsystems interact to promote the teaching, learning, and assessment of real-world competencies. The system is organized around internal classroom evaluations and large-scale external exams (e.g., the Cambridge suite of exams), both linked to an external reference of scale descriptors, presumably the CEFR. Jones and Saville's comprehensive framework can be credited for highlighting the importance of using a common reference of SFL proficiency, based on functional descriptors, to link elements of LOA internal to the classroom to those in the wider social context.

One caveat with this framework is the need to link the system directly to a formal set of external standards like the CEFR. Not all language teaching or testing programs are, or even should be, linked to an external framework like the CEFR. This is not the venue for this debate; however, adoption of the CEFR comes with assumptions that may not be appropriate in all localized settings, for example, in scenario-based assessment programs, where situated SFL proficiency is linked to the habits of mind related to real-world integrated content and language competencies rather than to a decontextualized set of functional descriptors, which form the basis of the can-do statements in the CEFR. Another caveat is that the use of one "official" de facto model of L2 proficiency by stakeholders institutionalizes (i.e., fossilizes) the model of SFL proficiency upon which the exam construct is based, and the nature of constructs should naturally evolve as we learn more about proficiency.

Purpura (2004, 2014)

Purpura introduced the term *learning-oriented assessment* in 2004 in an attempt to demonstrate how well-constructed assessments, firmly rooted to language assessment theory, could be used in classroom teaching (specifically related to theme-base instruction), in the service of promoting learning processes and outcomes (associated with a model of information processing). This proposal was in reaction to calls from mainstream and language testing researchers to decouple conventional testing practices, typified by discrete-point, multiple choice test tests similar to those in standardized exams, from classroom assessment practices that attempted to use "authentic" or "alternative" tasks that better reflected the types of competencies educators valued and wished to promote. It was also influenced by calls to better align assessment with classroom goals, curricula, instruction, and learning processes.

Purpura initially conceptualized LOA in the context of testing "grammar." In this conceptualization, "grammar" referred broadly to the linguistic resources of meaningful communication, where the goal of classroom assessment could be to target some grammatical form like the use of the past tense to recount personal narratives or some pragmatic meaning like the ability to use context, topic, and language to convey politeness or humor in a language use event. Learning was conceptualized in terms of information processing. In the excerpt below, Purpura (2004) describes the approach, foreshadowing the need to have a comprehensive framework that addresses not only the elicitation of proficiency indicators but also critical moderators of learning, namely the role of learner dispositions:

> Unlike the other approaches, LOA of grammar draws on both a theory of grammar testing [. . .] and a theory of second language learning (i.e., grammar processing [. . .]). It is concerned not only with issues of grammar testing and measurement, but also with issues of instructed learning. For this reason, LOA of grammar aims to provide information about the grammar that students know, understand, or can use in certain contexts, and the implications that this information might have for grammar processing. Finally, moving beyond grammar performance per se, LOA can also provide teachers with information about what students feel or believe about learning grammar and about themselves as learners of grammar – other aspects of the instructional variable. (p. 216)

Purpura further explained that teachers need to strategically embed assessments into instruction at pivotal moments in the learning process, so that learning outcomes can be confirmed and gaps filled through follow-on activities. He explains:

> LOA is designed to be an integral part of instruction, occurring formally or informally at any stage of the learning process. Learning-oriented assessment data can also be collected at one point in time or over a period of time. Unlike large-scale assessments, LOA is fundamentally iterative and recursive in that feedback from one assessment is intended to provide information for subsequent learning and assessment, until a criterion level of mastery has been achieved. (pp. 216–217)

To operationalize LOA, learning was conceptualized in terms of information processing, drawing on VanPatten's (1996) model of grammar processing. This model is based on three components. To illustrate, when learners are presented with new information or "input," they need to use strategies to map the form of the input onto its meaning (*1. Input processing*). The end result is "intake." After intake, learners then consolidate their understandings through different types of practice, until they have (theoretically) developed skill – or the ability to retrieve this information flexibly in real time. In other words, they accommodate the new information in long-term memory by restructuring their mental representation of the acquired knowledge (*2. System development*). Finally, when learners are presented with tasks to perform, they will need to access knowledge automatically in meaningful communication, a form of output (*3. Output processing*).

Purpura (2004) argued that teachers needed to use different types of assessments to target each stage in the learning process if they wanted to promote learning processes. One assessment opportunity would be to *assess for readiness* or background knowledge before the lesson. Another opportunity could be to *assess for intake* after input processing (e.g., comprehension checks). Another would be to *assess to help consolidate understandings* or *promote system development* by providing different types of practice activities. A final opportunity would be first to ask learners to perform tasks that made them actively use strategies while communicating ideas, and then, to *assess for output* quality. Feedback on the quality could be given, and a second opportunity to demonstrate output could be provided. Finally, Purpura (2004) provided several examples of tasks that could be used to measure these processes. Figure 2.1 shows a graphic description of how assessment can be strategically embedded in instructed learning processes.

Purpura (2004) summarized the LOA approach as follows:

> In sum, a learning-oriented approach to [language] assessment raises critical issues for classroom teachers when it comes to decisions for constructing assessments designed to fulfill a learning mandate. One set of decisions relates to test construction, especially as this pertains to test design and issues of purpose, construct definition, task selection, and method of scoring. Another set of issues relates to the role that assessment can play in promoting learning in general and grammar processing in particular. Teachers must grapple with issues related to *what* exactly should be assessed *when* in the learning process, what kinds of assessments should be presented at different learning junctures, how assessment results should be presented to learners to promote further development, and how learners can collaborate with their teachers and peers in their own learning and assessment. (p. 217)

Purpura significantly updated this model in 2014, and it was used by Seong (2023) to examine the cognitive resources underlying integrated academic speaking performance. Seong's assessment of speaking ability and strategy use was implemented in the context of a scenario-based language assessment revolving around a journalism competency. This important study provides compelling evidence of the role of cognitive competence in the display and development of topical understandings in journalism; it also shows the intricate relationships between strategy use and L2 speaking performance when topical learning is involved.

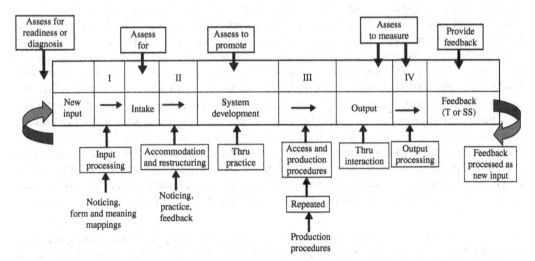

FIGURE 2.1 Assessment embedded in the learning process. *Source:* Adapted from VanPatten (1996, p. 154).

Turner and Purpura (2016), Purpura and Turner (2018) and Purpura (2021, 2022)

By 2014, CBA had attracted the interest of researchers both in mainstream education and in SFL assessment, witnessed by a virtual explosion of articles and books. CBA researchers in SFL assessment were mostly concerned with issues related to teacher assessment processes, and the development of teacher assessment competencies in classroom contexts with much less attention paid to learners, learning processes, and the role that assessment plays when embedded in instruction and mediated through interaction. And scant attention was paid to how the construct of SFL proficiency might need to expand when situating assessment in classroom learning contexts. Similarly, researchers in mainstream education were mostly concerned with issues of assessment literacy and how classroom assessment practices could increase learning gains. Much less work was devoted to learners and learning processes. And even less appeared with respect to how the construct of content knowledge might need to be broadened, when learners might know the content, but not have the linguistic resources to show it. To bring these two worlds together, Purpura and his students organized the first three-day Roundtable on LOA in language classrooms and large-scale assessment contexts.[1] Turner and Purpura opened the Roundtable with a theoretical paper entitled, "A learning-oriented approach to understanding the complexities of CBA." This paper served as the basis for Turner and Purpura (2016) and for its later expansion and refinements (Purpura & Turner, 2018; Purpura, 2021, 2022).

Purpura's (2022) framework is conceptualized in terms of eight interrelated dimensions. With respect to planned assessments, for example, the first three dimensions specify the context of the learning or assessment activity, the elicitation of performance by means of tasks (i.e., the task architecture), and the intended targets of learning or performance measured by these tasks (e.g., SFL proficiency constructs). The responses to the tasks produce data that can be judged according to several criteria: meaningfulness, accuracy, and appropriateness. Thus, the responses serve as *performance indicators*. The performance indicators allow teachers or testers to identify learning successes and gaps. Furthermore, in all language use, instruction, or assessment events, there are factors, aside from the task elicitation characteristics and proficiency, that can moderate performance (e.g., anxiety). Besides context, elicitation and proficiency, the LOA framework specifies five other factors that can potentially moderate learning or performance: *instructional, socio-cognitive, affective, social-interactional, and technological factors*. These are referred to as *performance moderators*. Another consideration in that framework is that each of the eight dimensions can be viewed independently, but in actuality, the dimensions are highly *interrelated* and often overlap. This captures the complexity of the phenomenon, and in fact, understanding what each dimension refers to, and how they interact can provide a nuanced understanding of the whole, which can ultimately be used to inform learning-oriented pedagogy. Finally, these dimensions can be viewed from the lens of different *agents* in language use context. For example, "instruction" can be conceptualized from the perspective of learners, teachers, peers, the curriculum (textbook), the test (a reading passage, embedded feedback) or even technology. Understanding how the different dimensions interact across the agents may lead to deeper understanding of the whole.

While many approaches can be used to organize curriculum or assessment, the LOA framework forces educators to think about the complexity from the design stage. In other words, the framework can be used to organize SFL use, pedagogy, and assessment around the specification of independent *or inter-related* tasks and activities (*elicitation dimension*), which serve to elicit SFL performance indicators (*proficiency dimension*) situated within, and often constrained by a particular sociocultural or institutional context (*contextual dimension*).

---

[1]Teachers College Columbia University Roundtable in Second Language Studies, Teachers College Columbia University. http://www.tc.columbia.edu/tccrisls/. The videos and author responses to questions are still available on the website.

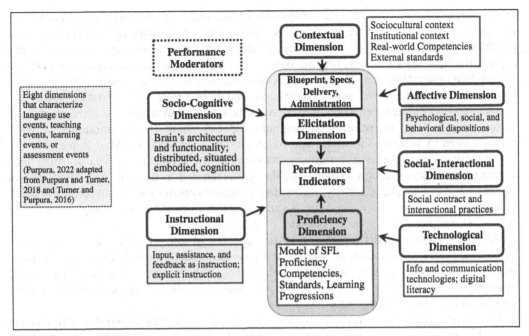

FIGURE 2.2 The LOA framework (Purpura, 2021).

The framework also forces educators to acknowledge and account for performance moderators within the language use, teaching, or testing event. These relate to the instructional role of topical input and assistance (*instructional dimension*) and the processing of input or assistance (*socio-cognitive dimension*). Importantly, the framework accounts for the role of affect in task engagement (*affective dimension*). And when communication is mediated through social interaction, it forces us to consider social factors (gender) and the interactional practices associated with situated language use (*social–interactional dimension*). Importantly, the framework, post-pandemic, forces us to consider the role of technology in language use, teaching, and assessment. Finally, the framework makes us consider the synergies among these dimensions. The framework is presented in Figure 2.2.

Contextual dimension: This dimension characterizes the sociocultural, socio-political, or institutional context in which the language use event is situated. It also characterizes competencies learners need to display in real-world language use domains and the types of tasks and settings they need to display these competencies in. The competencies and the resources needed to perform these competencies should drive instruction, learning, and assessment. Ultimately, test performance should generalize to these competencies.

Proficiency dimension: This dimension characterizes the targets of learning and performance. They can be linked to a set of competencies (e.g., ability to give a presentation), to a model of proficiency (SFL knowledge, science knowledge), or a set of performance standards. The proficiency dimension is usually the object of instruction, learning, and assessment. This dimension serves as an indicator of performance.

Elicitation dimension: This dimension characterizes the tasks or sequence of tasks used the elicit evidence of the performance related to the targeted construct. In the case of tests, to ensure consistency, this dimension should be based on a principled approach to test design, development, administration, delivery, and scoring of the performance. In the case of spontaneous assessments, this dimension relates to effective questioning. The elicitation dimension can be a moderator of performance.

Instructional dimension: This dimension characterizes the kinds of information learners are presented with and what they need to process. Information or input (e.g., a passage to read, interpersonal or transactional information in talk) can serve an instructional purpose as it aims to help learners build mental models of the content. Assistance in the form of glosses, graphics, scaffolded input, other accommodations, feedback and other repair practices, and explicit teaching are all seen as instructional as they help learners build mental models and consolidate understandings. The instructional dimension is obviously related to the socio-cognitive dimension and vice versa. This dimension can be a moderator of performance.

Socio-cognitive dimension: This dimension is characterized in terms of the architecture of socio-cognition (e.g., attention span, memory capacity, mental representation), or what learners need to be able to focus on and remember. It is also characterized in terms of the functionality of cognition (e.g., processes, strategies, ability to reason), or what learners need to process or reason through. It can be further characterized in terms of an activity system (including people, artifacts, activity, and settings) situated within socially and culturally structured space and time, where cognition is situated and distributed across components of the system. This dimension can be a moderator of performance.

Affective dimension: This dimension is characterized in terms of learners' psychological perceptions and dispositions (e.g., triggering high engagement, interest), their social perceptions and dispositions (e.g., triggering helpfulness, appreciation), and their behavioral dispositions (e.g., triggering level of effort or persistence) in relation language use tasks, all of which can moderate performance.

Social–interactional dimension: This dimension is important in mediated interaction and is characterized by the social contract among interlocutors and the interactional practices (e.g., turn-taking) this contract engages (e.g., deference). Participants in interaction come with individual and group identities, which impact the social and cultural norms, assumptions, preferences, and expectations that become relevant in language use events. This dimension can be a moderator of performance.

Technological dimension: This dimension is important when technology is used in teaching, learning, assessment, or everyday language use. It is characterized in terms of learners' digital literacy and computer literacy skills. As many of us saw during the pandemic, this dimension can be a moderator of performance.

In sum, when we communicate naturally in any of the language use domains, we are, consciously or unconsciously, engaging many of these dimensions. The same is true when we teach and take tests.

Current Research

Current research on LOA falls into three categories: theoretical papers on some aspects of LOLA, practice-based papers on the use of LOLA in different instructional settings, and papers related to the use of LOLA in test development or validation. Of particular note is Gebril's edited volume (Gebril, 2021a) in which several theoretical and practical topics of LOLA were addressed. Saville (2021) provided an excellent overview of the concepts and issues related to LOLA, followed by a discussion of the major LOA frameworks. Of particular note in the paper is the review of how LOLA has been conceptualized and implemented in different regions of the world. In this volume Banerjee (2021) then discussed different approaches to researching LOA in classroom contexts. She surveyed 17 studies in which she addressed data collection and analytic methods along with evidence presented for and of learning according to Turner and Purpura's (2018) LOA dimensions. She found that the studies fell into three categories: observation data with conversation analysis methods, interview data with content analysis methods, and narrative inquiries with narrative analysis. Finally, she found that all of the studies in the sample provided evidence related to two or more dimensions, with the elicitation dimension being addressed most. Lam's (2021) paper in this volume addressed the topic of feedback as learning-oriented practice. He first discussed the role of feedback in LOA. Later he discussed six practical principles of feedback practices. He discussed how feedback should be specific, forward-looking, at the appropriate level, related to success criteria, behavior-oriented, and conducive to self-regulated learning. Of particular note in this study were the transcript data to illustrate the provision and uptake of feedback as a component of interactional competence.

Gebril's book also presented several papers on how LOLA has been implemented in instructional settings. Gebril (2021b) reported on a national assessment reform initiative in Egypt, where he discussed the affordances and intriguing challenges of using LOA in such an exam-based instructional setting as Egypt; Amer (2021) reported on a case study of using LOA in Egyptian schools, and Khan and Hassan (2021) explored insights from different stakeholders after implementing LOA in a School in Malaysia.

Chong and Reinders (2023) edited volume addressed the topic of innovation in LOA. Their book documents what are considered to be innovative practices in using LOA. These papers covered topics such as digital literacy. the use of padlets, virtual reality, gamification, hybrid feedback, e-portfolios, and technology-mediated tasks. Then, using Turner and Purpura (2016) LOA dimensions, Chong and Reinders synthesized the practices in these papers and derived the following 10 practical principles for implementing LOA.

1. Language teachers need a renewed understanding of what "language assessment" entails, especially its close relationship with teaching and learning.
2. Language assessment tasks need to be designed to represent language use in authentic communicative situations.
3. Opportunities should be provided to learners to be more proactive in the feedback process.
4. The potential of gamification in language assessment can be explored to maximize learner engagement and sustain learner motivation.
5. Through assessment tasks, learners need to be orientated toward focused, purposeful, and deep self-reflection.
6. A community of practice approach can be adopted by making learners' work visible and accessible.
7. Language teachers need to develop and exercise their autonomy in developing appropriate assessment or feedback strategies.
8. The learning aspect of summative assessment can be maximized when it is designed, implemented, and followed up appropriately.
9. Language teachers can explore the opportunity to personalize learners' assessment experience.
10. Language assessment can be used to promote language learner autonomy.

In recent years, several researchers have reported using LOLA in the design and validation of scenario-based language assessments. Much of this research has, unsurprisingly, been associated with the Scenario-Based Language Assessment Research Lab at Teachers College, Columbia University, where LOLA has been used to develop an online battery of SFL assessments. In these SBAs, test takers are presented with scenarios in which they need to work collaboratively with imaginary team members to solve the scenario goal. In order to do this, however, they need to build understandings by reading and listening and then consolidate these understandings through instruction in the form of corrective feedback, peer assistance, and targeted lessons. They then need to use the acquired information to write summaries and ultimately give a presentation on behalf of the team. To develop this complex assessment, all eight dimensions are implicated in the scenario narrative and in the specifications. Similarly, validation involves quantitative and qualitative evidence from all dimensions to support the assessment claims. These assessments were developed for B1-level SBAs in English, Italian, Arabic, Korean, and Farsi. A2 and B2 level English exams will be piloted soon. Over the years,

38   Chapter 2 Learning-Oriented Language Assessment

there have been numerous conference presentations on this project around the world. Purpura (2022), in a Duolinguo Webinar, reported on the use of the LOA framework to reimagine how CBAs could be reimagined by means of scenarios.

Other researchers have also used the LOLA framework as a basis for designing and validating SBLAs. Banerjee (2019) used it to investigate the construct of topical knowledge in an SBA designed to simulate real-life second language use. Joo et al. (2023) used it to design a Korean SBA of writing ability. Peri (2023) used it to design and validate a B1 test of Italian. Seong (2023) used it to design and validate an SBA used to examine the cognitive dimension underlying academic speaking ability related to journalism competencies. And Beltrán (2024) used the framework to design and validate an SBA in which Mexican learners were exposed to different types of assistance as they prepared to deliver an evidence-based spoken presentation with the goal of persuading the audience of their position. In sum, the LOLA framework is a highly useful heuristic for test design and validation of SBAs, where all dimensions are so explicitly implicated.

Conclusions

LOLA grew out of the desire to better align assessment with instruction and learning and to use assessment tasks that better reflected the characteristics of the target language use domain to which assessment inferences were meant to generalize. The research on FA served as a catalyst for change. However, once researchers began to look at the multifaceted nature of CBA, it became eminently evident that this complex endeavor needed greater articulation. The LOA frameworks attempt to solve this problem. Since then, numerous researchers and practitioners have used Purpura and Turner's framework to get answers to theoretical and practical questions alike. It is an emerging strand in SFL assessment, and it will be interesting to see what LOLA has to offer in the years to come.

Discussion Questions

1. Take any assessment task in one of your courses. Using Purpura (2021) framework, what needs to be considered when using this as a test task? Describe each dimension.

2. What are the affordances and drawbacks of using Purpura's (2021) LOLA Framework when designing test tasks? What information can you get about students from using this framework?

References

Amer, A. (2021). Implementing learning-oriented assessment in Egyptian schools: a case study. In A. Gebril (Ed.), *LOA: Putting theory into practice* (pp. 123–139). Routledge.

Assessment Reform Group. (2002). *Assessment for learning: 10 principles*. University of Cambridge.

Bachman, L. F. (1990). *Fundamental considerations of language testing*. Oxford University Press.

Bachman, L. F., & Cohen, A. S. (Eds.). (1998). *Interfaces between second language acquisition and language testing research*. Cambridge University Press.

Bachman, L. F., & Palmer, A. S. (2010). *Language assessment in practice*. Oxford University Press.

Banerjee, H. L. (2019). Investigating the construct of topical knowledge in second language assessment: a scenario-based assessment approach. *Language Assessment Quarterly, 16*(2), 133–160. https://doi.org/10.1080/15434303.2019.1628237.

Banerjee, H. L. (2021). Approaches to researching learning-oriented assessment in second and foreign language classrooms. In A. Gebril (Ed.), *Learning-oriented language assessment: Putting theory into practice* (pp. 49–68). Routledge.

References   **39**

Banerjee, H. L. (2024). Scenario-based assessment. In A. J. Kunnan (Ed.), *Companion to language assessment*. John Wiley & Sons.

Beltrán, J. L. (2024). *Examining the role of assistance in a scenario-based test of L2 argumentative speaking ability: A learning-oriented approach to the assessment of complex competencies* [Unpublished doctoral dissertation]. Teachers College, Columbia University.

Bennett, R. (2010a). *Formative assessment: a critical review.* Presentation at the University of Washington, College of Education, Seattle, November 4.

Bennett, R. E. (2010b). Cognitively based assessment of, for, and as learning (CBAL): a preliminary theory of action for summative and formative assessment. *Measurement, 8*, 70–91. https://doi.org/10.1080/15366367.2010.508686.

Black, P., & Wiliam, D. (1998). Assessment and classroom learning. *Assessment in Education: Principles, Policy & Practice, 5*(1), 7–74.

Bransford, J. D., Brown, A. L., & Cocking, R. R. (2000). *How people learn: Brain, mind, experience, and school.* National Academy Press.

Broadfoot, P. (2005). Dark alleys and blind bends: testing the language of learning. *Language Testing, 22*(2), 123–141.

Brookhart, S. M. (2003). Developing measurement theory for classroom assessment purposes and uses. *Educational Measurement: Issues and Practices, 22*(4), 5–12.

Brown, J. D. (1998). *Testing in language programs.* Prentice Hall Regents.

Canale, M., & Swain, M. (1980). Theoretical bases of communicative approaches to second language teaching and testing. *Applied Linguistics, 1*, 1–47.

Carless, D. (2007). Learning-oriented assessment: conceptual bases and practical implications. *Innovations in Education and Teaching International, 44*(1), 57–66.

Carless, D. (2015). Exploring learning-oriented assessment processes. *Higher Education, 69*, 963–976. https://doi.org/10.1007/s10734-014-9816-z.

Chong, S. W., & Reinders, H. (2023). Introduction: learning-oriented language assessment – insights for evidence based-practices. In W. Chong & H. Reinders (Eds.), *Innovation in learning-oriented language assessment* (pp. 1–12). Springer. https://doi.org/10.1007/978-3-031-18950-0_1.

Davison, C., & Leung, C. (2009). Current issues in English language teacher- based assessment. *TESOL Quarterly, 43*(3), 393–415.

Earl, L. M. (2003). *Assessment as learning: Using classroom assessment to maximize student learning.* Sage.

Fox, J., Abdulhamid, N., & Turner, C. E. (2022). Classroom based assessment. In G. Fulcher & L. Harding (Eds.), *The Routledge handbook of language testing* (2nd ed., pp. 119–135). Routledge.

Gebril, A. (Ed.). (2021a). *Learning-oriented language assessment: Putting theory into practice.* Routledge.

Gebril, A. (2021b). Nationwide assessment reform in Egypt: challenges and potentials of learning-oriented assessment in an examinations-based instructional setting. In A. Gebril (Ed.), *LOA: Putting theory into practice* (pp. 109–122). Routledge.

Hamp-Lyons, L., & Tavares, N. (2011). Interactive assessment – a dialogic and collaborative approach to assessing learners' oral language. In D. Tsagari & I. Csépes (Eds.), *Classroom-based language assessment* (pp. 29–46). Peter Lang.

Herman, J. L., Aschbacher, P. R., & Winters, L. (1992). *A practical guide to alternative assessment.* The Regents of the University of California.

Jones, N., & Saville, N. (2016). *Learning-oriented assessment; A systematic approach.* Cambridge University Press.

Joo, S. H., Seong, Y., Suh, J., Jung, J. Y., & Purpura, J. E. (2023). Assessing writing through a scenario-based Korean proficiency test. *Assessing Writing, 58*. https://doi.org/10.1016/j.asw.2023.100766

Khan, A., & Hassan, N. (2021). Implementing learning-oriented assessment in Malaysia: insights from key stakeholders. In A. Gebril (Ed.), *LOA: Putting theory into practice* (pp. 140–161). Routledge.

Kunnan, A. J. (2018). *Evaluating language assessments.* Routledge.

Lado, R. (1961). *Language testing.* Longman.

Lam, D. M. K. (2021). Feedback as a learning-oriented assessment practice: principles, opportunities, and challenges. In A. Gebril (Ed.), *LOA: Putting theory into practice* (pp. 85–106). Routledge.

40   **Chapter 2** Learning-Oriented Language Assessment

Lewkowicz, J., & Leung, C. (2022). Classroom-based assessment. *Language Teaching, 54*(1), 47–57. https://doi.org/10.1017/S0261444820000506.

Linn, R. L., Baker, E. L., & Dunbar, S. B. (1991). Complex, performance-based assessment: expectations and validation criteria. *Educational Researcher, 20*(8), 15–21.

Pace Marshall, S. (1992). Forward. In J. L. Herman, P. R. Aschbacher & L. Winter (Eds.), *A practical guide to alternative assessment* (pp. v–vi). The Regents of the University of California.

Patri, M. (2002). The influence of peer feedback on self-and peer-assessment of oral skills. *Language Testing, 19*(2), 109–132.

Pellegrino, J. W., Baxter, G. P., & Glaser, R. (1999). Addressing the "two disciplines" problem: linking theories of cognition and learning with assessment and instructional practice. In A. Iran-Nejad & D. Pearson (Eds.), *Review of research in education* (Vol. 24, pp. 307–353).

Pellegrino, J. W., Chudowsky, N., & Glaser, R. (2001). *Knowing what students know: The science and design of educational assessment*. National Academy Press.

Peri, G. (2023). *Topical knowledge in L2 Italian speaking performances*. A Scenario-Based Language Assessment for L2 Italian. PhD Dissertation University for Foreigners of Siena, Siena, Italy.

Poehner, M. E., & Ableeva, R. (2011). Dynamic assessment and learner engagement in the activity of development. In D. Tsagari & I. Csépes (Eds.), *Classroom-based language assessment* (pp. 15–28). Peter Lang.

Purpura, J. E. (2004). *Assessing grammar*. Cambridge University Press.

Purpura, J. E. (2014). Cognition and language assessment. In A. J. Kunnan (Ed.), *The companion to language assessment*. John Wiley & Sons, Inc. https://doi.org/10.1002/9781118411360.wbcla150.

Purpura, J. E. (2016). Assessing meaning. In E. Shohamy & L. Or (Eds.), *Encyclopedia of language and education, Vol. 7. Language testing and assessment*. Springer.

Purpura, J. E. (2021). A rationale for using a scenario-based assessment to measure competency-based, situated second and foreign language proficiency. In M. Masperi, C. Cervini & Y. Bardière (Eds.), *Évaluation des acquisitions langagières: Du formatif au certificatif. MediAzioni* (Vol. 32, pp. A54–A96). http://www.mediazioni.sitlec.unibo.it. ISSN 1974-4382.

Purpura, J. E. (2022). *Using an LOA framework to reimagine classroom assessments by means of scenarios (Duolinguo Webinar Series)*. Duolinguo Inc.

Purpura, J. E., & Banerjee, H. L. (2021). *Rethinking second language proficiency assessment using a scenario-based assessment approach*. LTRC: Tunis, Tunisia.

Purpura, J. E. & Banerjee, H. L. (2022). *(Invited AAAL/ILTA Joint Colloquium). Exploring the cross-linguistic insights of using scenario-based assessment across four typologically different languages. AAAL Conference, Pittsburgh, PA*.

Purpura, J. E., & Oh, S. (2024). Assessing the linguistic resources of meaningful communication. In A. J. Kunnan (Ed.), *Companion to Language Assessment* (pp. 100–124). John Wiley & Sons.

Purpura, J. E., & Turner, C. E. (2018). *A learning-oriented assessment approach in classroom contexts: an expanded conceptualization of performance*. Invited pre-conference workshop at the 40th Language Testing Research Colloquium (LTRC 2018), International Language Testing Association, Auckland, New Zealand.

Saville, N. (2021). Learning-oriented assessment: basic concepts and frameworks in using assessments to support learning. In A. Gebril (Ed.), *Learning-oriented language assessment: Putting theory into practice* (pp. 13–33). Routledge.

Seong, Y., (2023). *Using a scenario-based assessment approach to examine the cognitive dimension of second language academic speaking ability through the assessment of an integrated academic speaking competency [Unpublished doctoral dissertation]. Teachers College, Columbia University*.

Skehan, P. (1998). *A cognitive approach to language learning*. Oxford University Press.

Turner, C. E. (2012). Classroom assessment. In G. Fulcher & F. Davidson (Eds.), *The Routledge handbook of language testing* (pp. 65–78). Routledge, Taylor and Francis Group.

Turner, C. E., & Purpura, J. E. (2016). Learning-oriented assessment in second and foreign language classrooms. In D. Tsagari & J. Baneerjee (Eds.), *Handbook of second language assessment* (pp. 255–272). De Gruyter, Inc.

VanPatten, B. (1996). *Input processing and grammar instruction in second language acquisition*. McGraw Hill.

Wong, J., & Waring, H. Z. (2021). *Conversation analysis and second language pedagogy*. Routledge.

Suggested Readings

Carless, D. (2007). Learning-oriented assessment: conceptual bases and practical implications. *Innovations in Education and Teaching International, 44*(1), 57–66.

Gebril, A. (Ed.). (2021a). *Learning-oriented language assessment: Putting theory into practice*. Routledge.

CHAPTER 3

Assessing Integrated Skills

Alister Cumming

Introduction

It is rare to write extended texts without reference to some source reading or to some audio or visual material – or to both – just as it is unusual to speak a language without interacting with some other speakers and engaging in ideas. In academic and many workplace contexts, the fundamental purpose of extended writing or speaking is usually to display one's knowledge appropriately with reference to the relevant source information – be that, in academic settings, from course assignments or lectures, required readings, or textbooks or, in workplace settings, from relevant policies, communications, data, or authorities.

Language tests have taken a while to address this fundamental dimension of literate human communication and, particularly, to establish how to evaluate it systematically, through writing and speaking tasks that integrate language production with the interpretation of source content from reading and listening material. Conventionally, language tests have assessed – in separate test components and with separate scores – individuals' abilities to speak, listen to, read, or write a language or their knowledge of its grammar or vocabulary. All these elements of language are, of course, interrelated to some extent, but tests have typically sought to separate them as objects of measurement rather than to address them as fundamentally integrated wholes. Over the last decades, however, an increasing number of language tests, particularly for academic or vocational purposes, have been designed to require examinees to demonstrate their writing and/or speaking abilities not as isolated or separate skills but rather as the ability to write or speak appropriately, in an integrated manner, about source content, ideas, and texts. The guiding rationale for these initiatives in language test design is that the abilities to write or speak coherently about relevant ideas, to handle source documents appropriately, and to display knowledge in relevant ways are primary abilities required for successful performance in universities, colleges, and high schools, as well as in many workplaces. This chapter describes the development of concepts about assessing integrated language skills over recent decades; the current state of understanding, practices, and research in this field; and the particular challenges and future directions faced in the assessment of integrated language skills.

The Concise Companion to Language Assessment, First Edition. Edited by Antony John Kunnan.
© 2025 John Wiley & Sons, Inc. Published 2025 by John Wiley & Sons, Inc.

Previous Views

The impetus to assess language abilities in an integrated rather than separate or componential manner arose from a variety of concerns. Most generally, from the 1970s onward educators argued that assessments of language proficiency needed to focus on students' abilities to communicate purposefully in a language rather than merely to demonstrate knowledge of its grammar, vocabulary, or single skills – which had become the primary, conventional basis for designing language tests (since, e.g., Lado, 1961). Concerted research attempts were made to develop assessments that expanded the range of competencies evaluated in language tests to those considered to be fundamental to communicating in a second or foreign language (e.g., Bachman, 1990; Davies, 2008; Harley et al., 1990; Hawkey, 2004). These efforts retained, however, the conventional distinction – articulated influentially through Carroll (1975) and subsequently instantiated in most educational curricula around the world – that language abilities can be distinguished, and hence comprehensively assessed, as four separate "skills," namely those of reading, writing, listening, and speaking.

The autonomy and categorical separation of these so-called four skills have been challenged for a number of reasons. First, the word "skill" is too broad a term to apply to modes of communication such as writing, speaking, listening, and reading, as is shown by theories and by empirical evidence about skill learning in domains of human activity other than languages (e.g., Anderson, 1995). Koda (2007), for instance, reviewed the substantial theories and research about reading that have accumulated in order to show that (just) reading in a second language requires the development and integration of a large number of distinct but interrelated componential subskills. That is, reading is not a single skill, but rather comprises many interrelated subskills, and the same can certainly be said of other modes of communication such as writing, speaking, and listening. Abilities to produce or interpret languages inherently involve many interdependent rather than separate skills and modes of interaction: In ordinary interactions, for example, people are compelled to talk about what they have read or listened to, and extended texts are usually written about things people have read, heard, or done. Moreover, the particular skills that are called upon for the specific tasks of reading, writing, listening, or speaking vary greatly according to such situational factors as the context, purpose, and age and status of participants.

In academic contexts in particular, educators criticized the types of tasks that conventionally appeared in tests of second language writing (i) for lacking authenticity with respect to the abilities that are really required for academic performance (see Lewkowicz, 2000; Morrow, 1977) and (ii), as a consequence, for negatively affecting teaching and learning by reducing them to the practice of simple, rhetorically formulaic types of writing in preparation for such tests (see Raimes, 1990). These criticisms, which are directed at the tendency for tests to under-represent the construct of writing for academic purposes, are even more predominant and worrying now, as formal testing has assumed greater importance and impact in educational policies (see Hillocks Jr., 2002). Parallel concerns about lack of authenticity appeared in criticisms of oral interviews as a conventional means of assessing speaking abilities (e.g., van Lier, 1989). As Peirce (1992) observed, high-stakes language tests tended to establish certain genres of communication that were unique to test formats, because they facilitated objective measurement; but these genres required in tests were scarcely representative of how people really use language to interact in their ordinary lives.

Performance assessments were designed to address and counter these kinds of concerns: Examinees perform tasks that represent realistically the complex types of communication and the knowledge demands imposed by university or workplace activities – for instance, extended writing and speaking with reference to source information. Morrow (1977) articulated an influential conceptualization of communication assessment on the basis of ideas emerging at the University of Reading and from the Council of Europe's notional–functional

44   **Chapter 3** Assessing Integrated Skills

syllabi and leading to innovative, integrated language tests for the Royal Society of Arts (Hawkey, 2004). Davies (2008) documented how the English Language Testing System attempted in the 1980s to integrate academic language skills in a systematic way as well as to distinguish between macro- and microlevels of skills. Wesche (1987) documented a notable example following from these ideas in the Ontario Test of English as a Second Language (ESL), a post-admissions university test that involved examinees writing and speaking critically about lengthy source texts they had to read and interpret as they would for an assignment in a university course.

Current Views

Assessments of integrated language skills follow interactionist conceptualizations of assessment; evaluating examinees' "capability to use language in a specified space of contexts, and demonstrating that capability jointly requires knowledge of substance, practices, conventions, and modes of interaction in those contexts" (Mislevy & Yin, 2009, p. 263; cf. Chalhoub-Deville, 2003; Cumming et al., 2021; Knoch & Chapelle, 2017). The interactionist view of assessment differs from traditional views, which conceive of language ability as a fixed set of traits (such as grammar or vocabulary) that people have – or have not – acquired, irrespective of situational contexts. Instead of evaluating or scoring acquired traits, interactionist-oriented assessments make claims about examinees' abilities to perform specific types of complex tasks, which represent crucial activities, skills, and strategies in a target domain of language use. This interactionist orientation puts integrated skills assessment in sync with recent trends, in education, work, and multimedia communications, to promote multiliteracies rather than traditional assessments that conceive of reading, writing, listening, speaking, or visual representations as autonomous skills (Cope & Kalantazis, 2000). From a psychological perspective, too, integrated skills assessments take an orientation toward literate task performance, which realizes constructivist principles of knowledge integration and synthesis, as articulated in the theories of Kintsch (1998) or Bereiter (2002).

For example, integrated skills assessments may involve writing or speaking tasks that require examinees to interpret source information on a particular topic and then to write or speak about the information for a specified purpose. Examinees' writing or speaking is then later rated holistically or analytically on scales that specify criteria for gradations of greater or lesser effective performance. The integrated writing tasks on the Test of English as a Foreign Language, Internet-Based Test (TOEFL iBT) exemplify this kind of task and (as described below) have been widely researched; see samples at Educational Testing Service (2005). These tasks emulate the kinds of behaviors expected of students writing exams on a particular academic topic, under timed conditions, at university. Justification for assessing these behaviors in language tests for admissions to programs of higher education follows from a considerable amount of research showing that students' writing for courses at universities or colleges mostly involves their displaying knowledge – gained from source readings, lectures, and discussions – in ways that are "responsible" to the relevant content and in appropriate genres and academic conventions (see Byrnes, 2008; Cumming et al., 2016, 2018; Knoch & Sitajalabhorn, 2013; Leki, 2007; Leki & Carson, 1997; Llosa & Malone, 2019; Rosenfeld et al., 2001; Sternglass, 1997). In brief, university students require abilities to integrate reading, listening, and writing in order to be able to perform competently in and learn from academic courses, so these language abilities need to be assessed in order for assessments to be able to fulfill the purpose of establishing individuals' preparedness for university studies.

Akin to the integrated writing and speaking tasks on the TOEFL iBT, integrated skills assessments feature internationally in various other established English tests for university admissions. In Canada, the Carleton Academic English Language (CAEL) Assessment (Carleton University, n.d.) features refined and elaborated versions of the task types established initially in the Ontario Test of ESL (see Wesche, 1987), requiring examinees to read a lengthy text on a certain topic, hear segments of a lecture or other discussion about it, and then write and speak about the information from the source materials. In New Zealand, the Diagnostic English Language Needs Assessment (DELNA) (University of Auckland, n.d.) asks doctoral students to read several short excerpts from varied sources about a topic and then to write an essay in answer to a specific question about the topic by referring to the statements read.

A cline can be distinguished between weak and strong versions of integrated skills assessments. A weaker version appeared, for example, in the writing component of the Cambridge First Certificate in English, now called B2 First, which requires examinees to read a letter or email of about 160 words and then to compose a reply to it of 120–150 words (see Cambridge English Language Assessment, 2024). Expectations for both reading and writing performances are pitched within the intended ability level of the examinees, at Common European Framework of Reference for Languages (CEFR) B or pre-academic, intermediate proficiency, and only writing performance is scored. A middle-range version of skills integration appears in the TOEFL iBT (described above), which requires all test takers, regardless of English proficiency levels, to integrate and synthesize material from relatively lengthy reading and listening source materials to answer specific academic-type questions in both written and oral production. A strong version of skills integration appears in task-based assessments, which may involve the integration of information and language production across a range of media and task conditions, as these have been determined (e.g., from needs analyses) to represent authentic communication tasks in target domains (see Colpin & Gysen, 2006; Deane, 2011; Hawkey, 2004; Norris, 2002).

Current Research

Cumming's (2013) review of recent research on integrated writing assessments for academic purposes highlights five of their widely acknowledged benefits. Integrated skills assessments (i) provide realistic, challenging literacy activities; (ii) engage examinees in writing that is responsible for specific ideas and content; (iii) counter test method or practice effects associated with conventional item types on writing tests; (iv) evaluate language abilities in accordance with construction–integration or multiliteracies models of literacy; and (v) offer diagnostic value for instruction or self-assessment. Six approaches to research have been taken in the studies leading up to these claims.

One approach has been to document and analyze the processes or strategies that examinees use during integrated skills assessment tasks that involve writing (see Cheong et al., 2019; Cumming et al., 1989; Delgado-Osorio et al., 2023; Esmaeili, 2002; Fraser, 2002; Pan & Lu, 2023; Plakans, 2008; Plakans & Gebril, 2012; Shin & Ewert, 2014; Yang & Plakans, 2012; Ye & Ren, 2023). Fewer studies have analyzed examinees' performances on integrated speaking tasks: See Huang and Hung (2018), Huang et al. (2018), Swain et al. (2009), and Zhang et al. (2021). These studies have shown that integrated skills tasks elicit from examinees a broad variety of relevant interpretive, analytic, self-monitoring, and composing strategies, seemingly (i) surpassing the range and depth of strategies observed in less complex writing or speaking tasks, on assessments that do not require reference to the source material; (ii) approximating the cognitive demands of writing or speaking for academic purposes in the ordinary situations of studying and learning in university or in college courses; and (iii) being welcomed by participating students as more authentic, interactive, and challenging than conventional writing tasks tend to be on language tests. However, this line of inquiry, like the other approaches described below, has been primarily descriptive, confined to performance on limited sets of integrated tasks and populations, and it has produced a range of individual differences among participating students, so that any

46 **Chapter 3** Assessing Integrated Skills

assertions about the value of, and specific outcomes from, integrated skills assessment tasks – for example, by comparison with other types of complex writing or speaking tasks – remain to be verified.

A second approach to research has been to analyze the discourse features of written or spoken texts produced under conditions that involve summarizing or interpreting source reading or listening material. Many of these studies have compared a range of text features that appear in compositions written for assessment purposes (i) with reference to source documents and (ii) written under similar conditions, but without reference to source material. Studies by Chan and May (2022), Chan and Yamashita (2022), Cumming et al. (2005, 2006), Guo et al. (2013), Knoch (2009), Kyle (2020), Ohta et al. (2018), Plakans (2009), Plakans and Gebril (2017), Plakans et al. (2019), Uludag et al. (2019), and Yu (2009) have showed that the written compositions that university-level learners of English produce in integrated skills tasks tend to display more complex lexical, syntactic, rhetorical, and pragmatic features (in contrast to comparable compositions written for tasks that do not require source information or in contrast to less proficient learners). Related results for integrated speaking assessments in comparison with other types of speaking tasks were reported by Frost et al. (2021) and Kyle et al. (2016). Frost et al. (2012) analyzed the content dimensions of the spoken discourse produced in listening–speaking tasks in Oxford English tests, establishing that the quantity and quality of the content conveyed by examinees from source materials corresponded to their speaking proficiency scores. These studies have also revealed numerous points of variability in integrated skills tasks – points related to such factors as the length, the topic, or other qualities of the source texts, the levels of language proficiency, the individual writers' skills at synthesizing or citing source material, their comprehension of source texts, or their interpretation of task instructions.

A related, third approach to research has evaluated the apparent authenticity of integrated assessment tasks in comparison with real academic tasks in university courses. Studies addressing issues of generalizability of test tasks to relevant real-world contexts have been conducted on integrated writing by Riazi (2016) and Llosa and Malone (2019), finding mainly similarities between writing in the test and real-world contexts, and on integrated speaking tasks by Brooks and Swain (2014) and by Brown and Ducasse (2019), observing similarities but also certain differences between the contexts compared.

A fourth approach to research has been to investigate instructors' or raters' perceptions of integrated skills assessment tasks. Findings from research by Brown et al. (2005), Cumming et al. (2004), Knoch (2009), and Wall and Horak (2008) indicate that experienced instructors or raters are positively impressed by innovative assessment tasks for writing and speaking, which require students or examinees to integrate source materials from reading or listening sources, because these integrated tasks seem to be more authentic representations of abilities required for academic performance, are intellectually more complex and challenging, and produce opportunities for language learning.

A fifth approach probes deeper into the processes of rating used during integrated writing tasks to provide evidence for the construct validity of such assessment tasks (see Gebril & Plakans, 2014; Knoch & Chapelle, 2017). Chan and May (2022) took up Chan et al.'s (2015) and Knoch and Sitajalabhorn's (2013) recommendations that integrated writing tasks deserve unique criteria for rating. Their research produced evidence for new rating criteria from expert raters' judgments that included "relevance of ideas, paraphrasing skills, accuracy of source information, academic style, language control, coherence and cohesion, and task fulfilment" (p. 1).

The sixth approach to research has considered integrated skills assessments for their diagnostic value, either (i) for purposes of assisting instructors to identify needs for students to learn or improve their abilities or (ii) for purposes of learners' own self-assessments and self-guided learning. The contexts, issues, and assessments investigated in these studies vary greatly, constraining any general conclusions other than to affirm that the researchers assert the particular value of integrated skills assessments for diagnostic purposes in diverse educational settings. The DELNA (Knoch, 2009), described above, is aimed specifically at eliciting diagnostic information relevant to the teaching and learning of writing among university students. Sawaki et al. (2013) showed the TOEFL iBT integrated writing tasks to be potentially useful for profiling differences among English language learners with varied needs for instruction according to their proficiency levels and writing abilities. Chapelle et al.'s (2015) account of the Intelligent Academic Discourse Evaluator exemplified an innovative approach to helping graduate students evaluate discourse features of research articles they were writing for their academic disciplines. Artemeva and Fox (2010) demonstrated how university students of engineering and their instructors can benefit alike from analyzing their existing knowledge of the genre and their intended aims for writing improvement in relation to integrated skills tasks and assessments.

Challenges

Integrated skills tasks do, nonetheless, pose several challenges when used for assessment purposes. Cumming (2013), in describing the benefits of integrated skills assessments, also observed the following five constraints, which are also documented in most of the publications cited above. Integrated skills assessments confound the measurement of writing or speaking abilities with the measurement of abilities to comprehend source materials; they muddle assessment and diagnostic information together; they involve genres that are ill-defined, and hence difficult to score; they require threshold levels of abilities for competent performance, producing results for examinees that may not compare neatly across different ability levels; and they elicit texts in which the language from source materials is hard to distinguish from the examinees' own language production.

The major constraint on complex integrated tasks arises from their involving, together, both comprehension (i.e., of source information from reading and/or listening) and production (of either writing or speaking), so they require a threshold level of language proficiency for examinees to perform on them competently. In order to write or speak about source information, examinees have to be able to understand it – at least partially, and perhaps even fully in terms of a source text's verbatim, propositional, and situational representations (to use Kintsch's terms for the construction of comprehension, see Kintsch, 1998). Comprehension and production are inextricably linked in integrated skills tasks, and so they are impossible to separate for assessment purposes. Technically, psychometricians call this a problem of task dependencies. The practical consequence, however, is that examinees who cannot comprehend source materials are not able to write or speak about them effectively. For this reason, most of the research cited above has concluded that integrated skills assessments tend to produce meaningful results only for learners who have attained an intermediate or advanced proficiency in a second language. Cumming (2013), Knoch and Sitajalabhorn (2013), and Sawaki et al. (2013) have suggested that this requirement of integrated skills tasks makes them especially suitable for university admissions tests, because the threshold level of comprehension they require appears to be what actually demarcates the language abilities of students who are prepared to begin academic studies in a second language from those of students who are not. But, also for this reason, as Charge and Taylor (1997) explained, at least one major English test, the International English Language Testing System (IELTS), decided to exclude integrated skills tasks so as to be able to provide score reports that are meaningful and comparable across a full range of language proficiency and that do distinguish consistently between language comprehension and production abilities.

A further implication from the inherent combination of language comprehension and production in integrated tasks is that interpreting their results can be tricky for diagnostic

48   Chapter 3 Assessing Integrated Skills

purposes. What, on the basis of results from an integrated skills assessment, are the specific abilities that students should be taught or should focus on in self-study? Comprehension? Writing? Speaking? Or all combined? And, if the latter, how can one separate or isolate appropriately teachable elements? A response could reasonably be that in general people learn to write or speak from reading or listening, particularly for academic or professional purposes. However, other perspectives on this complex issue have emerged from research. Knoch (2009) provided evidence that, for advanced writers, in academic contexts it may be only complex integrated skills tasks that can produce the kinds of relevant information needed in order to reveal the abilities that such learners truly need to acquire or have already mastered. Likewise, Sawaki et al. (2013) demonstrated that there are certain indicators of language proficiency (i.e., comprehension of source material, productive vocabulary, and sentence conventions) that emerge from the TOEFL iBT's integrated tasks and are especially robust and sensitive in demarcating between students who need further English study or are prepared to engage in literate academic tasks in higher education. Powers (2010) too has offered a spirited defense of language assessments that assess a broad range of language abilities comprehensively, recognizing that language abilities are at once integrated as well as distinct.

Another challenge for integrated skills assessment is that there are no fixed – or even conventional – genres for tasks such as summarization, précis, synthesis, or responses on academic-type exams. On the contrary, such text forms, either written or spoken, are highly variable according to context, purpose, and intended audience. This constraint has long been recognized in research on writing in first language education; it involves not just expectations for written text forms but also the cognitive and other self-control strategies adopted by examinees or students in performing integrated skills tasks (see Hidi & Anderson, 1986). Yu (2009, 2013) has shown how this variability in expectations for integrated skills tasks has profound implications for the quality of the information about people's abilities that arises from their performance on such tasks. The obvious implications for test designers and for educators preparing students for assessments are to specify precisely the expectations for performance on integrated skills tasks, to ensure that examinees are oriented to and familiar with these expectations, and to pilot assessment tasks carefully, so as to determine if the tasks produced any unintended, irrelevant sources of variance.

A final, related challenge for integrated skills assessment concerns the state of knowledge about how people learn to write from sources. Systematic scholarly inquiry into this matter has only emerged over the past two decades, and a broad range of novel findings and conceptualizations have developed from it, shifting perspectives from naive, alarmist concerns over plagiarism to a substantial appreciation of the complex challenges and contextual variability associated with learning how to cite information appropriately from source texts while displaying one's own knowledge in written texts, particularly in a second language and unfamiliar discourse domains (see Cumming et al., 2016; Flowerdew & Li, 2007; Harwood & Petric, 2012; Shi, 2004, 2010). For examinees performing integrated skills tasks as well as for raters of the written compositions or spoken texts that arise from them, demarcations are difficult to discern between what are – or are not – appropriate citation practices, learning strategies, expressions of individual viewpoints, and practiced formulaic routines. Considerably more research on this matter is needed to inform both the preparation of instructions for integrated skills assessments and the guidelines for scoring them.

Future Directions

Among the many possible directions for the future development of integrated language skills assessment, the most fundamental is to refine the constructs and purposes that define language tests for academic and professional purposes (see Knoch & Chapelle, 2017). Integrated skills assessment presupposes an interactionist theory of human communication in which knowledge is constructed through the interpretation and expression of relevant ideas through multiple media. These abilities are fundamental to being able to use language effectively for extensive writing and speaking in academic and professional contexts, so they need to be the guiding principles in language assessments made for these purposes. For assessments in other types of contexts, conventional models of language as four separate skills or as componential knowledge may suffice – for example, in courses where accumulating knowledge about the vocabulary of grammar may be a goal of education, or for limited purposes such as reading abilities or sojourning travel. However, considerable work needs to be done to understand and define the constructs that are essential to performing integrated writing and speaking tasks for academic or professional purposes. Moreover, these abilities are highly complex, and so they require extensive, interactive assessments, as Deane (2011) has shown in pioneering studies of multiliteracies assessments for adolescents writing in English as a mother tongue.

Most research and test developments involving integrated skills assessments have, to date, focused on contexts related to English for academic purposes with populations of international or migrant students. But examples of inquiry and assessment practices have also appeared in relation to other languages, taught and studied to advanced levels of proficiency (e.g., German at a U.S. university: Byrnes et al., 2010, or Dutch for occupational purposes internationally: Certificaat Nederlands als Vreemde Taal, 2012), or in English competency tests for secondary school completion (Part 3 of New York State's *Regents Examination*: New York State Education Department, 2012 – but curiously not in these schools' tests of various foreign languages). These and many other assessment contexts and purposes need to be developed and analyzed further to determine if the benefits and challenges described above are obtained as they do in tests of English for university admission. Innovative uses of new technologies also hold promise, not only for providing modes of assessment delivery that capitalize on and evaluate the increasing uses of new multimedia for communications but also for overcoming certain challenges that have beset integrated skills tests in the past – particularly for managing test materials, for disentangling the focus and components of assessment, and for monitoring the processes of test takers responding to tasks in ways that may reveal how they integrate language and content appropriately to achieve communicative goals.

At the practical level of designing language assessments, an important future direction is to specify clearly the purpose, context, audience, and evaluation criteria of tasks that involve integrated skills. To whom, where, how, and why exactly is an examinee expected to write or speak? As Yu (2013) has demonstrated, a summary can involve many different forms, genres, or purposes, so expectations for writing summary-type tasks vary greatly in the instructions given on major English-language tests, ranging from (i) a single sentence about a reading passage in the Pearson Test of English (Academic), to (ii) summaries that involve interpreting pictorial or schematic information rather than extended source texts in the IELTS, and to (iii) complex, open-ended writing and speaking tasks, judged on multiple criteria, in the TOEFL iBT. Likewise, for integrated speaking tasks, this range and ambiguity in expectations may be a reason why studies such as Xi et al. (2008) have found distinct variation in interpretations, both in raters' scoring and in examinees' performances, on these kinds of tasks, posing a difficult challenge for modeling these performance criteria precisely through automated scoring by computer programs.

A final direction for future research and development is to establish if and how integrated skills assessments really do produce a positive impact on teaching and learning. Wall and Horak (2008) have shown that the introduction of the integrated writing and speaking tasks on the TOEFL iBT had a distinct, positive washback effect on the teaching practices and classroom activities of a small sample of teachers in Central and Eastern Europe. Much of this impact appears to have occurred through changes in the textbooks that adopted integrated tasks and in their uses in classrooms to prepare students for the new version of the test. More studies of this kind need to be conducted on a broader basis and in a variety of contexts in relation to major language tests, particularly to establish exactly how integrated language tasks can promote effective teaching, learning, and instructional materials, and further to demonstrate how these processes can be most productively acted upon in educational practices. Such research, however, may be dependent (as suggested above) on further refinements in the construct definitions of integrated skills assessment so as to know precisely what abilities they involve and consequently how they can be taught, studied, learned, and assessed.

Discussion Questions

1. Do you agree that "the threshold level of comprehension" in a second language required for integrated skills tasks is "what actually demarcates the language abilities of students who are prepared to begin academic studies in a second language from those of students who are not"? Why or why not?

2. What can designers of assessments do to minimize the confounding effects of examinees' second-language comprehension (of source reading or listening materials) on their production (through writing or speaking) in integrated skills tasks?

References

Anderson, J. R. (1995). *Learning and memory*. John Wiley.

Artemeva, N., & Fox, J. (2010). Awareness vs. production: probing students' antecedent genre knowledge. *Journal of Written and Business Communication*, *24*, 476–515. https://doi.org/10.1177/1050651910371302.

Bachman, L. (1990). *Fundamental considerations in language testing*. Oxford University Press.

Bereiter, C. (2002). *Education and mind in the knowledge age*. Lawrence Erlbaum. https://doi.org/10.4324/9781410612182.

Brooks, L., & Swain, M. (2014). Contextualizing performances: comparing performances during TOEFL iBT™ and real-life academic speaking activities. *Language Assessment Quarterly*, *11*, 353–373. https://doi.org/10.1080/15434303.2014.947532.

Brown, A., & Ducasse, A. (2019). An equal challenge? Comparing TOEFL iBT™ speaking tasks with academic speaking tasks. *Language Assessment Quarterly*, *16*, 253–270. https://doi.org/10.1080/15434303.2019.1628240.

Byrnes, H. (2008). Assessing content and language. In E. Shohamy & N. H. Hornberger (Eds.), *Encyclopedia of language and education. Volume 7: Language testing and assessment* (2nd ed., pp. 37–52). Springer. https://doi.org/10.1007/978-0-387-30424-3_166.

Byrnes, H., Maxim, H., & Norris, J. (2010). Realizing advanced foreign language writing development in collegiate education curricular design, pedagogy, assessment. *Modern Language Journal*, *94*(Supplement), 1. https://doi.org/10.1111/j.1540-4781.2010.01136.x.

Cambridge English Language Assessment. (2024). *B2 First*. Retrieved April 3, 2024 from https://www.cambridgeenglish.org/exams-and-tests/first/.

Carroll, J. B. (1975). *The teaching of French as a foreign language in eight countries*. John Wiley and Sons.

Chalhoub-Deville, M. (2003). Second language interaction: current perspectives and future trends. *Language Testing*, *20*, 369–383. https://doi.org/10.1191/0265532203lt264oa.

Chan, S., & May, L. (2022). Towards more valid scoring criteria for integrated reading–writing and listening–writing summary tasks. *Language Testing*, *40*(2), 410–439. https://doi.org/10.1177/02655322221135025.

Chan, S., & Yamashita, J. (2022). Integrated writing and its correlates: a meta-analysis. *Assessing Writing*, *54*. https://doi.org/10.1016/j.asw.2022.100662.

Chan, S. H. C., Inoue, C., & Taylor, L. (2015). Developing rubrics to assess the reading-into-writing skills: a case study. *Assessing Writing*, *26*, 20–37. https://doi.org/10.1016/j.asw.2015.07.004.

References

Chapelle, C., Cotos, E., & Lee, J. (2015). Validity arguments for diagnostic assessment using automated writing evaluation. *Language Testing, 32*, 385–405. https://doi.org/10.1177/0265532214565386.

Charge, N., & Taylor, L. (1997). Recent developments in IELTS. *ELT Journal, 51*, 374–380.

Cheong, C. M., Zhu, X., Li, G. Y., & Wen, H. (2019). Effects of intertextual processing on L2 integrated writing. *Journal of Second Language Writing, 44*, 63–75. https://doi.org/10.1016/j.jslw.2019.03.004.

Colpin, M., & Gysen, S. (2006). Developing and introducing task-based language tests. In K. van den Branden (Ed.), *Task-based language education* (pp. 151–174). Cambridge University Press.

Cope, B., & Kalantzis, M. (Eds.). (2000). *Multiliteracies: Literacy learning and the design of social futures.* Routledge.

Cumming, A. (2013). Assessing integrated writing tasks for academic purposes: promises and perils. *Language Assessment Quarterly, 10*, 1–8. https://doi.org/10.1080/15434303.2011.622016.

Cumming, A., Rebuffot, J., & Ledwell, M. (1989). Reading and summarizing challenging texts in first and second languages. *Reading and Writing: An Interdisciplinary Journal, 2*, 201–219. https://doi.org/10.1007/BF00377643.

Cumming, A., Grant, L., Mulcahy-Ernt, P., & Powers, D. (2004). A teacher-verification study of speaking and writing prototype tasks for a new TOEFL. *Language Testing, 21*, 159–197. (See also TOEFL Monograph Report 26 at http://www.ets.org/research/policy_research_reports/rm-04-05_toefl-ms-26).

Cumming, A., Kantor, R., Baba, K., Erdosy, U., Eouanzoui, K., & James, M. (2005). Differences in written discourse in independent and integrated prototype tasks for next generation TOEFL. *Assessing Writing, 10*, 5–43. https://doi.org/10.1016/j.asw.2005.02.001.

Cumming, A., Lai, C., & Cho, H. (2016). Students' writing from sources for academic purposes: a synthesis of recent research. *Journal of English for Academic Purposes, 23*, 47–58. https://doi.org/10.1016/j.jeap.2016.06.002.

Cumming, A., Yang, L., Qiu, C., Zhang, L., Ji, X., Wang, J., Wang, Y., Zhan, J., Zhang, F., Xu, C., Cao, R., Yu, L., Chu, M., Liu, M., Cao, M., & Lai, C. (2018). Students' practices and abilities for writing from sources in English at universities in China. *Journal of Second Language Writing, 39*, 1–15. https://doi.org/10.1016/j.jslw.2017.11.001.

Cumming, A., Cho, Y., Burstein, J., Everson, P., & Powers, D. (2021). Assessing academic writing. In X. Xi & J. Norris (Eds.), *Assessing academic English for higher education admissions* (pp. 107–151). Routledge. https://doi.org/10.4324/9781351142403.

Davies, A. (2008). *Assessing academic English: Testing English proficiency 1950–2005, the IELTS solution.* Cambridge University Press.

Delgado-Osorio, X., Koval, V., Hartig, J., & Harsch, C. (2023). Strategic processing of source text in reading-into-writing tasks: a comparison between summary and argumentative tasks. *Journal of English for Academic Purposes, 62*. https://doi.org/10.1016/j.jeap.2023.101227.

Esmaeili, H. (2002). Integrated reading and writing tasks and ESL students' reading and writing performance in an English language test. *The Canadian Modern Language Review, 58*, 599–622. https://doi.org/10.3138/cmlr.58.4.599.

Flowerdew, J., & Li, Y. (2007). Language re-use among Chinese apprentice scientists writing for publication. *Applied Linguistics, 28*, 440–465. https://doi.org/10.1093/applin/amm031.

Frost, K., Elder, C., & Wigglesworth, G. (2012). Investigating the validity of an integrated listening–speaking task: a discourse-based analysis of test takers' oral performances. *Language Testing, 29*, 345–369. https://doi.org/10.1177/0265532211424479.

Frost, K., Wigglesworth, G., & Clothier, J. (2021). Relationships between comprehension, strategic behaviours and content-related aspects of test performances in integrated speaking tasks. *Language Assessment Quarterly, 18*, 133–153. https://doi.org/10.1080/15434303.2020.1835918.

Gebril, A., & Plakans, L. (2014). Assembling validity evidence for assessing academic writing: rater reactions to integrated tasks. *Assessing Writing, 21*, 56–73. https://doi.org/10.1016/j.asw.2014.03.002.

Guo, L., Crossley, S. A., & McNamara, D. S. (2013). Predicting human judgments of essay quality in both integrated and independent second language writing samples: a comparison study. *Assessing Writing, 3*, 218–238. https://doi.org/10.1016/j.asw.2013.05.002.

Harley, B., Allen, P., Cummins, J., & Swain, M. (Eds.). (1990). *The development of second language proficiency.* Cambridge University Press.

Harwood, N., & Petric, B. (2012). Performance in the citing behavior of two student writers. *Written Communication, 29*, 55–103. https://doi.org/10.1177/0741088311424133.

52 **Chapter 3** Assessing Integrated Skills

Hawkey, R. (2004). *A modular approach to testing English language skills: The development of the certificates in english language skills (CELS) examination.* Cambridge University Press.

Hidi, S., & Anderson, V. (1986). Producing written summaries: task demands, cognitive operations, and implications for instruction. *Review of Educational Research, 56,* 473–493. https://doi.org/10.3102/00346543056004473.

Hillocks, G. Jr. (2002). *The testing trap: How state assessments of writing control learning.* Teachers College Press.

Huang, H. T. D., & Hung, S. T. A. (2018). Investigating the strategic behaviours in integrated speaking assessment. *System, 78,* 201–212. https://doi.org/10.1016/j.system.2018.09.007.

Huang, H.-T. D., Hung, S.-T. A., & Plakans, L. (2018). Topical knowledge in L2 speaking assessment: comparing independent and integrated speaking test tasks. *Language Testing, 35,* 27–49. https://doi.org/10.1177/0265532216677106.

Kintsch, W. (1998). *Comprehension: A paradigm for cognition.* Cambridge University Press.

Knoch, U. (2009). *Diagnostic writing assessment: The development and validation of a rating scale. Dissertation. University of Melbourne, Melbourne.* https://doi.org/10.3726/978-3-653-00929-3.

Knoch, U., & Chapelle, C. (2017). Validation of rating processes within an argument-based framework. *Language Testing, 35,* 477–499. https://doi.org/10.1177/0265532217710049.

Knoch, U., & Sitajalabhorn, W. (2013). A closer look at integrated writing tasks: towards a more focused definition for assessment purposes. *Assessing Writing, 18,* 300–308. https://doi.org/10.1016/j.asw.2013.09.003.

Koda, K. (2007). Reading and language learning: crosslinguistic constraints on second language reading development. *Language Learning, 57*(Supplement 1), 1–44. https://doi.org/10.1111/j.1467-9922.2007.00411.x.

Kyle, K. (2020). The relationship between features of source text use and integrated writing quality. *Assessing Writing, 45.* https://doi.org/10.1016/j.asw.2020.100467.

Kyle, K., Crossley, S. A., & McNamara, D. S. (2016). Construct validity in TOEFL iBT speaking tasks: insights from natural language processing. *Language Testing, 33,* 319–340. https://doi.org/10.1177/0265532215587391.

Lado, R. (1961). *Language testing: The construction and use of foreign language tests.* Longman.

Leki, I. (2007). *Undergraduates in a second language: Challenges and complexities of academic literacy development.* Erlbaum. https://doi.org/10.4324/9781315084442.

Leki, I., & Carson, J. (1997). "Completely different worlds": EAP and the writing experiences of ESL students in university courses. *TESOL Quarterly, 31,* 39–69. https://doi.org/10.2307/3587974.

Lewkowicz, J. A. (2000). Authenticity in language testing: some outstanding questions. *Language Testing, 17,* 43–64. https://doi.org/10.1177/026553220001700102.

Llosa, L., & Malone, M. E. (2019). Comparability of students' writing performance on TOEFL iBT and in required university writing courses. *Language Testing, 36,* 235–263. https://doi.org/10.1177/0265532218763456.

Mislevy, R., & Yin, C. (2009). If language is a complex adaptive system, what is language assessment? *Language Learning, 59*(S1), 249–267. https://doi.org/10.1111/j.1467-9922.2009.00543.x.

Morrow, K. (1977). *Techniques of evaluation for a notional syllabus.* Royal Society of Arts.

Norris, J. (2002). Interpretations, intended uses and designs in task-based language assessment. *Language Testing, 19,* 337–346. https://doi.org/10.1191/0265532202lt234ed.

Ohta, R., Plakans, L. M., & Gebril, A. (2018). Integrated writing scores based on holistic and multi-trait scales: a generalizability analysis. *Assessing Writing, 38,* 21–36. https://doi.org/10.1016/j.asw.2018.08.001.

Pan, R., & Lu, X. (2023). The design and cognitive validity verification of reading-to-write tasks in L2 Chinese writing assessment. *Assessing Writing, 56,* 100699. https://doi.org/10.1016/j.asw.2023.100699.

Peirce, B. (1992). Demystifying the TOEFL reading test. *TESOL Quarterly, 26,* 665–689. https://doi.org/10.2307/3586868.

Plakans, L. (2008). Comparing composing processes in writing-only and reading-to-write test tasks. *Assessing Writing, 13,* 111–129. https://doi.org/10.1016/j.asw.2008.07.001.

Plakans, L. (2009). Discourse synthesis in integrated second language writing assessment. *Language Testing, 26,* 561–587. https://doi.org/10.1177/0265532209340192.

Plakans, L., & Gebril, A. (2012). A close investigation into source use in integrated second language writing tasks. *Assessing Writing, 17,* 18–34. https://doi.org/10.1016/j.asw.2011.09.002.

Plakans, L., & Gebril, A. (2017). Exploring the relationship of organization and connection with scores in integrated writing assessment. *Assessing Writing, 31*, 98–112. https://doi.org/10.1016/j.asw.2016.08.005.

Plakans, L., Gebril, A., & Bilki, Z. (2019). Shaping a score: complexity, accuracy, and fluency in integrated writing performances. *Language Testing, 36*, 161–179. https://doi.org/10.1177/0265532216669537.

Raimes, A. (1990). The TOEFL test of written English: causes for concern. *TESOL Quarterly, 24*, 427–442. https://doi.org/10.2307/3587228.

Riazi, M. (2016). Comparing writing performance in TOEFL-iBT and academic assignments: an exploration of textual features. *Language Assessment Quarterly, 28*, 15–27. https://doi.org/10.1016/j.asw.2016.02.001.

Rosenfeld, M., Leung, S., & Oltman, P. (2001). *The reading, writing, speaking, and listening tasks important for academic success at the undergraduate and graduate levels (TOEFL Monograph Report 21)*. Educational Testing Service.

Sawaki, Y., Quinlin, T., & Lee, Y. (2013). Understanding learner strengths and weaknesses: assessing performance on an integrated writing task. *Language Assessment Quarterly, 10*, 73–95. https://doi.org/10.1080/15434303.2011.633305.

Shi, L. (2004). Textual borrowing in second-language writing. *Written Communication, 21*, 171–200. https://doi.org/10.1177/0741088303262846.

Shi, L. (2010). Textual appropriation and citing behaviors of university undergraduates. *Applied Linguistics, 31*, 1–24. https://doi.org/10.1093/applin/amn045.

Shin, S.-Y., & Ewert, D. (2014). What accounts for integrated reading-to-write task scores? *Language Testing, 32*, 259–281. https://doi.org/10.1177/0265532214560257.

Sternglass, M. (1997). *Time to know them: A longitudinal study of writing and learning at the college level*. Erlbaum.

Uludag, P., Lindberg, R., McDonough, K., & Payant, C. (2019). Exploring L2 writers' source-text use in an integrated writing assessment. *Journal of Second Language Writing, 46*, 1–7. https://doi.org/10.1016/j.jslw.2019.100670.

van Lier, L. (1989). Reeling, writhing, drawling, stretching, and fainting in coils: oral interviews as conversation. *TESOL Quarterly, 23*, 489–508. https://doi.org/10.2307/3586922.

Wesche, M. (1987). Second language performance testing: The Ontario Test of ESL as an example. *Language Testing, 4*, 28–47. https://doi.org/10.1177/026553228700400103.

Xi, X., Higgins, D., Zechner, K., & Williamson, D. (2008). *Automated scoring of spontaneous speech using SpeechRater V 1.0 (ETS Research Report 08-62). Educational Testing Service.*

Yang, H., & Plakans, L. (2012). Second language writers' strategy use and performance on an integrated reading-listening-writing task. *TESOL Quarterly, 46*, 80–103. https://doi.org/10.1002/tesq.6.

Ye, W., & Ren, W. (2023). Toward a better understanding of skill integration in integrated writing: a structural equation modeling study of EFL secondary learners' test performance. *Reading and Writing*, 1–24. https://doi.org/10.1007/s11145-023-10419-1.

Yu, G. (2009). The shifting sands in the effects of source text summarizability on summary writing. *Assessing Writing, 14*, 116–137. https://doi.org/10.1016/j.asw.2009.04.002.

Yu, G. (2013). The use of summarization tasks: some conceptual and lexical analyses. *Language Assessment Quarterly, 10*, 96–109. https://doi.org/10.1080/15434303.2012.750659.

Zhang, W., Zhang, L. J., & Wilson, A. (2021). Supporting learner success: revisiting strategic competence through developing an inventory for computer-assisted speaking assessment. *Frontiers in Psychology, 12*. https://doi.org/10.3389/fpsyg.2021.689581.

On-line Resources

Brown, A., Iwashita, N., & McNamara, T. (2005). *An examination of rater orientations and test-taker performance on English-for-Academic-Purposes speaking tasks (TOEFL Monograph Report 29). Princeton, NJ: Educational Testing Service.* Retrieved December 7, 2012 from https://www.ets.org/Media/Research/pdf/RR-05-05.pdf.

Carleton University. (n.d.). *Carleton academic English language (CAEL) assessment practice test. Topic: Rainforest. Ottawa: Carleton University.* Retrieved May 14, 2012 from http://www.cael.ca/taker/Rainforest.shtml.

Certificaat Nederlands als Vreemde Taal. (2012). *Centre for Language and Education, Catholic University of Leuven.* Retrieved July 26, 2012 from http://www.cnavt.org/main.asp.

54 **Chapter 3** Assessing Integrated Skills

Cumming, A., Kantor, R., Baba, K., Eouanzoui, K., Erdosy, U., & James, M. (2006). *Analysis of discourse features and verification of scoring levels for independent and integrated prototype tasks for the new TOEFL. (TOEFL Monograph Report 30). Princeton, NJ: Educational Testing Service.* Retrieved December 7, 2012 from http://www.ets.org/Media/Research/pdf/RR-05-13.pdf.

Deane, P. (2011). *Writing assessment and cognition.* Princeton, NJ: Educational Testing Service. Retrieved May 14, 2012 from http://www.ets.org/Media/Research/pdf/RR-11-14.pdf.

Educational Testing Service. (2005). *TOEFL iBT writing sample responses.* Princeton, NJ: Educational Testing Service. Retrieved May 14, 2012 from http://www.ets.org/Media/Tests/TOEFL/pdf/ibt_writing_sample_responses.pdf.

Fraser, W. (2002). *The role of reflection in the Canadian Academic English Language (CAEL) Assessment.* Ottawa, Canada: Carleton University. Retrieved May 14, 2012 from http://www.cael.ca/pdf/wendypaper.pdf.

Powers, D. E. (2010). *The case for a comprehensive, four-skills assessment of English language proficiency.* (TOEIC Compendium Report 12). Educational Testing Service. Retrieved May 14, 2012 from http://www.ets.org/Media/Research/pdf/TC-10-12.pdf.

Swain, M., Huang, L., Barkaoui, K., Brooks, L., & Lapkin, S. (2009). *The speaking section of the TOEFL iBT (SSTiBT): Test-takers' reported strategic behaviors* (TOEFL iBT Research Report 10). Princeton, NJ: Educational Testing Service. Retrieved May 14, 2012 from http://www.ets.org/Media/Research/pdf/RR-09-30.pdf.

University of Auckland. (n.d.). *Diagnostic English Language Needs Assessment (DELNA): Handbook for candidates at the University of Auckland.* Auckland, New Zealand: University of Auckland. Retrieved May 14, 2012 from http://www.delna.auckland.ac.nz/webdav/site/delna/shared/delna/documents/delna-handbook.pdf.

Wall, D., & Horak, T. (2008). *The impact of changes in the TOEFL examination on teaching and learning in central and eastern Europe: Phase 2, coping with change* (TOEFL-iBT Research Report 5). Educational Testing Service. Retrieved May 14, 2012 from http://www.ets.org/Media/Research/pdf/RR-08-37.pdf.

Suggested Readings

Chapelle, C., Enright, M., & Jamieson, J. (Eds.). (2008). *Building a validity argument for the Test of English as a Foreign Language (TOEFL).* Routledge.

Shaw, S., & Weir, C. (2007). *Examining writing: Research and practice in assessing second language writing.* Cambridge University Press.

Xi, X., & Norris, J. (Eds.). (2021). *Assessing academic English for higher education admissions.* Routledge. https://doi.org/10.4324/9781351142403.

Yu, G. (Ed.). (2013). Use of integrated writing tasks in language assessment. *Special issue of Language Assessment Quarterly,* 10. https://doi.org/10.1080/15434303.2013.766744.

CHAPTER 4

Dynamic Assessment in the Classroom

Matthew E. Poehner

Introduction

Since first introduced to the field of second language (L2) studies in the early 2000s (Antón, 2003; Kozulin & Garb, 2002; Lantolf & Poehner, 2004), dynamic assessment (henceforth, DA) has gained considerable attention from assessment researchers, teachers, and those interested in processes of L2 development. In a representative, but not exhaustive, timeline of L2 DA publications, Poehner and Wang (2021) include 74 scholarly articles and book chapters reporting uses of DA with learners of different languages, at varying levels of proficiency, and in a range of instructional contexts. DA offers a systematic framework for relating assessment practices to teaching and learning. Indeed, its central tenet is that fully diagnosing learner abilities requires taking account of their responsiveness when support, or mediation, is offered to help them address difficulties. This process reveals abilities that are still forming and are therefore most amenable to instructional intervention (Lantolf & Poehner, 2014). Equally important, providing mediation during the assessment procedure is a means of integrating teaching into the assessment itself (Poehner, 2008).

To be sure, this conceptualization of assessment diverges from psychometrically oriented approaches to standardized testing. This may explain why L2 DA has frequently been associated with formative assessment (e.g., Rea-Dickins & Poehner, 2011) and learning-oriented assessment (e.g., Baker & Germain, 2020). These comparisons are not without merit as there is a shared commitment to situating assessment within educational (i.e., teaching and learning) activity more broadly. However, in this chapter, I argue that the distinguishing characteristic of DA is the theoretical orientation to development that guides the organization and goals of DA procedures and interpretations of outcomes. For this reason, while DA may overlap with other formulations of assessment that support teaching and learning, this does not exhaust its relevance to the L2 field. As I will attempt to show, classroom-based DA demonstrates theoretical principles that may be recontextualized in the service of more formal assessments. To help the reader appreciate this argument, the following section offers additional remarks on the origins of DA in Vygotskian Sociocultural Theory (SCT) and its subsequent elaboration in psychology and general education.

The Concise Companion to Language Assessment, First Edition. Edited by Antony John Kunnan.
© 2025 John Wiley & Sons, Inc. Published 2025 by John Wiley & Sons, Inc.

Previous Views or Conceptualization

Central to SCT is the understanding that humans do not relate to the world in a direct manner like other animals, but rather we are *mediated* by artifacts available to us in our culture as well as through our interactions with others (Vygotsky, 2012). Following Vygotsky (1978), mediation may be understood as the affordances with which we act, that render our activity possible, and that also result from our activity. Just as humans act on and shape our environment in a manner mediated by *physical* tools (hammers, saws, bulldozers, etc.), our psychological functioning is similarly mediated by *symbolic* tools, such as counting systems, charts, models, and, most importantly, language. Symbolic tools, like their physical counterparts, are created by humans and become features of our cultural heritage. Through interaction with others, we are brought into relation with these tools, using them for our own purposes while simultaneously coming to think and act through them in new ways. Developmentally, Vygotsky (1978) explained this process as beginning in dialog with others, on what he termed the *intermental plane*; subsequently, abilities re-emerge on the *intramental* plane as individuals rely increasingly on internalized forms of mediation to regulate their thinking and actions, that is, to *self-regulate*.

Following what he referred to as the *genetic method* of research, Vygotsky (2012) observed the psychological functioning of children at different ages (as well as children with various special needs). His interest was not simply in child development but rather to understand the human mind by studying the processes of its formation, that is, by tracing development as it occurred. An important element of this work involved what he described as *developmental experiments* in which children were first asked to carry out tasks independently and then were offered mediation in the form of either resource or, in many cases, interaction with an adult (i.e., a mediator). This research led him to empirically establish not only those psychological functions that had already fully developed and could therefore be understood according to learner-independent performance but also abilities that were still in the process of forming, or *ripening*, and that could be observed through their responsiveness to mediation. The former he termed the *zone of a person's actual development* and the latter the *zone of proximal development (ZPD)*. In short, Vygotsky's (2012) genetic method led to an understanding of the mind and its formation as a process of becoming ourselves (i.e., individuals) through the social world.

Lantolf and Poehner (2014) explain that Vygotsky's approach to science may best be described as a form of praxis, a departure from the dominant view that theory building and constructing models of the world may be conducted independently from the people and contexts they concern, with "applications" to be worked out only after researchers have arrived at confidence in their knowledge. Instead, praxis regards theory/research as providing an appropriate orientation to practical activity in the world, which in turn serves as a testing ground for the revision, acceptance, or rejection of theory. Thus, Vygotsky's psychological research was always in dialogue with his efforts to address problems of practice, particularly in education. The importance of the ZPD for education that Vygotsky (2011) saw was that by specifying emerging abilities, it was possible to orient instruction to optimally intervene in and guide learner development. At the same time, doing so required a "diagnosis of development" that revealed not merely the products of past development (the zone of actual development) but also the ZPD. As Vygotsky (2011, p. 203) put it, "what is indicative of the child's intellectual development is not only what he [sic] can do himself, but probably more so what he can do with the help of others," that is, through cooperation on the intermental plane.

A crucial finding in his empirical work tracing school performance among children entering school with different performances on standard measures of intelligence concerns the relation between the zone of actual development and the ZPD. Vygotsky (2011) reported children with very similar levels of independent performance can respond very differently while interacting with a mediator, indicating different ZPDs. Some learners with poor initial performance, for example, were found to show substantial improvement, while among the learners with initial high performance, not all made gains when mediation was available. Decades later, in his use of the Learning Potential Measurement approach to DA with under-performing racial minority children in the United States, Budoff (1968) reported similar findings. Importantly, Budoff leveraged these findings to argue for different placement decisions into special education programs for children with low scores on cognitive measures but who proved responsive to mediation. In short, the ZPD varies independent of the learner actual level of development such that the one cannot be used to predict the other.

Budoff (1968) was among the first outside of Russia to apply Vygotsky's approach to diagnosing development. This followed Luria's (1961) introduction of the ZPD and its relevance to assessments, which he described as "dynamic," to psychologists and educators in the West. Beginning in the 1970s, a wide range of procedures devised by researchers around the world working with a variety of populations came to be known collectively as *dynamic assessment* (Haywood & Lidz, 2007; Sternberg & Grigorenko, 2002). Procedurally, they are united by the integration of mediation (e.g., leading questions, prompts, hints, models, or feedback) into the procedure; theoretically, they share the view that diagnosing abilities requires both learner-independent performance of assessment tasks and their responsiveness to mediation that is offered when they encounter problems. The amount, or explicitness, of mediation provided and whether it leads learners to overcome difficulties during the procedure are interpreted as indicating the ZPD (Poehner, 2008).

Beyond these principles for conducting DA and interpreting results, a good deal of variation exists among approaches. In their review of prevailing models of DA, Lantolf and Poehner (2004) propose that they may be grouped according to whether they approach mediation as prescribed treatment, designed in advance of interaction and administered to learners in a standardized manner, or if mediation is negotiated through interaction, unfolding through mediator–learner dialoguing. The former orientation to DA, which Lantolf and Poehner term *interventionist*, typically organizes mediation as scripted prompts or hints that are arranged from least explicit to most explicit, often culminating in presenting the solution and explaining the principles involved. Prompts are offered one at a time until either the learner responds correctly or the final prompt is reached. An advantage of this approach is that the number of prompts a learner required for particular tasks can simply be recorded and the results of the procedure easily reported. The open-ended orientation to DA, which Lantolf and Poehner describe as *interactionist*, conceives of mediation as a process that involves mediator probing of learner understanding, and leading questions and feedback as learners work through difficulties. Although the procedure is open-ended, the mediator nonetheless follows principles to organize the interaction, as will be explained in detail in the next section.

The decision to follow either an interventionist or interactionist approach should be informed by the purpose behind employing DA. For example, if assessment results serve to inform teachers and learners of progress and areas in need of additional work, an interactionist approach may be preferred. If the context demands comparisons among learners for purposes of ranking or selection, an interventionist approach would be advantageous. It is worth noting that this distinction may be similar to the formative–summative divide, but this is not an exact parallel. Specifically, it needs to be remembered that both interactionist and interventionist DA involve mediation, a form of teaching, and that this process of probing learner abilities may also promote those same abilities, as they stretch beyond their actual level of independent performance.

An additional way of categorizing DA concerns whether the procedure occurs during a single session or is spread across multiple steps. Haywood and Lidz (2007) explain that DA is most frequently conceived as a three-stage process mirroring the classic pretest – intervention – posttest experimental design. This organization, which Sternberg and Grigorenko (2002)

58   Chapter 4 Dynamic Assessment in the Classroom

dubbed the *sandwich* format of DA, begins with a traditional assessment – without mediator–learner interaction – to establish a baseline of learner performance. A brief intervention then reviews learner performance, probes their understanding of relevant principles, and may introduce models. Finally, the same or a parallel version of the original test is administered, again without interaction between mediator and learner. The two sets of scores that are produced for each learner are then compared to ascertain the degree of change, and observations are noted of particular dimensions of task performance where changes occurred. This results in a profile of the learner's ZPD. Sternberg and Grigorenko (2002) contrast this format with the *cake* format, in which the entire DA occurs in a single administration. As learners complete assessment tasks or items, mediation is presented whenever a response is incorrect. ZPD profiling highlights tasks a learner completed independently, those for which mediation was required, and the quality of mediation and learner responsiveness.

Regardless of the DA approach or format followed, the literature outside the L2 field is replete with reports of nuanced insights into learner abilities and challenges and how these may be overcome through enrichment programs. Such work has been conducted with learners with special needs, immigrants, learners from diverse cultural backgrounds, minority children, and others who struggle to succeed in mainstream schooling.

Current Views or Conceptualization

In the L2 field, DA research has often been conducted in classroom contexts, through partnerships with teachers, and following the existing language curriculum and has tended to favor qualitative analyses of interactionist approaches (Poehner & Lantolf, to appear). There are numerous exceptions to this trend, many of which are included in Poehner and Wang's (2021) timeline, and again, the selection of DA approach very much depends upon context and goals. The reason for the preponderance of interactionist, classroom-focused studies likely reflects the commitment to praxis in SCT research. As explained, Vygotsky held that research needed to be engaged in addressing problems of practice, and it is through such work that theory continues to be elaborated and refined.

L2 SCT research began to pursue a praxis orientation in earnest in the early 2000s. Lantolf and Thorne (2006) identify two recent (at that time) doctoral dissertations that opened lines for L2 praxis: Negueruela (2003) and Poehner (2005). Following Vygotsky's (2012) view that schooling creates the possibility for introducing abstract conceptual knowledge as a special form of symbolic mediation, Negueruela (2003) proposed organizing L2 curricula around linguistic concepts rather than grammar rules. Just as the value of conceptual knowledge for Vygotsky is that it provides systematic resources beyond direct experience for perceiving, reasoning, and planning actions, Negueruela argued that linguistic concepts permit an understanding of how language features may be drawn upon to convey nuanced meanings, an advantage over selecting the "correct" rule to follow in a given communicative situation. According to Lantolf and Thorne (2006), concept-based language instruction understands concepts such as tense, mood, aspect, and voice among others, as features of human languages that may be realized in different ways from one language to another but that provide resources from which learners may consciously select. Concept-based language instruction has generated a considerable number of studies working in different languages and with a range of linguistic concepts (for an overview, see Lantolf et al., 2021). As will be discussed below, the integration of a conceptual orientation to the language curriculum and DA to organize interactions and to monitor learner development offers a powerful framework for L2 education.

Poehner's (2005) dissertation was the most in-depth study of L2 DA at the time, and it brought into focus three essential and interrelated features of ZPD activity: quality of mediation; forms of learner responsiveness, or *reciprocity*; and the *transcendence*, or transfer, of abilities to new problems and contexts. With regard to mediation, the general principle in much DA work has been to begin with very implicit support and to become more explicit only when required by learners. The reason is that as a diagnosis, DA aims to determine the minimum level of support learners require to identify problems in their language performance and make corrections. An overt correction would "fix" the immediate error, but it would not provide insight into how close learners are to appropriate independent use of the language. Several studies now report inventories of mediating behaviors arranged from implicit, such as pausing, inviting the learner to reflect on their performance, asking if there is anything they might wish to revise, etc., to explicit, such as offering an example of a principle or pattern or providing a metalinguistic explanation (e.g., Davin et al., 2017; Zhang, 2023). In addition to differentiating learners according to the mediation they require to complete challenging tasks, the development of individuals over time may also be tracked not only as a shift from unsuccessful to successful independent performance but also through changes in the mediation they require (see Yu, 2023).

In DA research with young children, Van der Aalsvoort and Lidz (2002) highlighted various learner behaviors in DA that include but are not limited to, correctly completing tasks. Referring to these behaviors as reciprocity, the authors argued that including these in profiles of learner engagement in DA can further inform diagnoses of development. Examples of reciprocity they described include self-regulating of attention and impulses (including avoidance of guessing), reaction to challenge (including managing feelings of frustration and a desire to give up), and using the mediator as a resource (i.e., eliciting suggestions and clarifications and talking through possibilities together). In DA studies with L2 learners, among the forms of learner reciprocity that have been described are repeating after the mediator, requesting additional support, rejecting mediating, and seeking confirmation or approval from the mediator (Ableeva, 2010; Poehner, 2005).

Finally, transcendence emerged from Feuerstein's work with learners with special needs (e.g., Feuerstein et al., 2015). Feuerstein's Mediated Learning Experience program employs DA to diagnose learner underlying difficulties and then designs individualized instructional plans, which he refers to as *enrichment*, to promote abilities identified during DA. Given that his goal is not to train learners using very specific problem types, subsequent assessments involve a range of tasks requiring learners to use their emerging abilities in the face of new challenges, that is, to transcend the contexts and tasks they originally encountered. The related notion of *transfer*, associated with the Graduated Prompting Approach to DA (Brown & Ferrara, 1985), formalizes this idea through a series of post-mediation or post-intervention assessments that introduce tasks of increasing complexity, which they term *near, far,* and *very far transfer assessments*. In L2 DA, this may take several forms. For instance, it could involve pushing learners to extend their understanding of one feature of language, such as perfect and imperfect verbal aspect, to a related feature, such as the pluperfect (Poehner, 2008). In Ableeva's (2010) implementation of DA in the context of listening comprehension, transfer involved introducing increasingly sophisticated aural texts, while in Yu's (2023) study of DA and integrated academic reading–writing assessment, transfer occurred as additional reading texts were included in the tasks and as those readings addressed more complex topics. One may similarly consider transfer assessments that require learners to use different communicative modalities from those employed in the initial DA or in instructional enrichment (e.g., moving from writing to speaking tasks).

Current Research

A recent study by Yu (2023) provides an example of the direction much L2 DA research has taken with regard to integrating assessment procedures with subsequent instructional programming, tracking learner progress over time, and comparing the experiences of learners receiving instruction aligned with their ZPD to those receiving general instruction.

An important contribution of this work is that it counters the perception that DA is simply "good teaching" rather than an assessment framework that includes a teaching element and that can orient future instruction. In addition, the work examines the SCT premise that teaching focused on the ZPD (i.e., abilities that are emerging) will be particularly effective at promoting development. Yu's (2023) study employed DA with international students in an academic English writing program at a US university. A three-stage, one-to-one DA was implemented as follows: (i) students first prepared a draft of an argumentative essay on an assigned topic and then carefully reviewed it to identify any potential questions or revisions; (ii) each student read and discussed the essay with a mediator, who offered leading questions, prompts, and feedback in order to gain insights into their thinking and to determine their responsiveness to this support; and (iii) students individually revised their essays, endeavoring to take account of the mediation they had received. A particularly innovative feature of Yu's study was that an analytic rubric developed by Weigle (2004) was employed by double-blind raters to score the drafts students produced prior to and following their interaction with the mediator (i.e., at stages one and three of the DA). Given that the rubric follows a 10-point scale for content, organization, language accuracy, and language range and complexity, it was possible to ascertain learner responsiveness to mediation according to areas of improvement between stages one and three. These particular areas were interpreted as within the ZPD of individual learners. Moreover, the study followed a pre- and post-test design and used a control group to allow for comparisons. Thirteen students were divided into an enrichment (six students) and a non-enrichment (seven students) group. While the former met with the mediator for five weekly sessions in which instruction was focused on the identified ZPD areas of writing, the non-enrichment group received standard writing instruction and feedback according to a set curriculum. At the end of the five weeks, a parallel version of the initial three-stage DA was administered to both groups. According to Yu (2023), both groups evidenced improvement in certain areas of their writing (again, according to blind ratings following the analytic rubric). However, gains were greater among the enrichment group participants, and in some cases those learners made a dramatic improvement, supporting the theoretical arguments in favor of orienting instruction to the ZPD.

A similar multi-step DA procedure and research design featuring a control group was implemented on a much larger scale by Levi (2017). Her project integrated DA with the English language oral proficiency component of the national matriculation exam in Israel. An additional interesting feature of Levi's work is that her 73 Israeli secondary school learners were divided into three groups, a control group that received only standard administrations of the oral language proficiency test and two treatment groups: one that participated in individualized DA and another in which students were organized into small clusters of four to five for a group DA session. The idea behind group DA, as explained by Poehner (2009), is that tasks are set that are beyond the actual abilities (i.e., independent performance) of any individual but that are within the ZPD of each learner. In this way, mediation may be directed toward the group or individuals within the group and should be of relevance to the development of all. In Levi's project, all learners were administered the oral assessment in its standard form as a pre-test. Learners in the group DA treatment were then shown a video recording of the performance of one member of the group and worked together to discuss and evaluate the performance relative to the Ministry of Education's criteria for "communicative ability" and "accuracy." Their work was further supported by the provision of resources, including a guide for focusing their attention on particular aspects of the recorded performance as well as a rubric. In addition, a teacher–mediator was present to provide dialogic support. This 20–25-minute session was followed by a re-administration of the oral assessment. Students in the individualized DA treatment engaged in a similar session but without peers while those in the control group simply had a break before the post-test. Results showed significant improvement on the post-test for both the DA treatment groups while the control group's scores actually declined slightly. Levi (2017) interpreted these results as evidence of the effectiveness of a short-term DA mediation session in promoting learners' "ripening" abilities. She further noted that the results are promising with regard to moving DA from one-to-one to group-based formats.

More recently, Wang and Zhang (2023) conducted an exploratory case study targeting oral communication in the context of the ACTFL (American Council on the Teaching of Foreign Languages) Oral Proficiency Interview, or OPI. Using the ACTFL proficiency scale as their reference, the authors sought to determine how far learners might stretch their abilities beyond what was observed in a regular administration of the OPI (i.e., learner-independent performance). As Wang and Zhang explain, the context of the study is a Chinese language program at a U.S. university where students take the OPI at various points in their course of study. As such, their case study is an early stage of a larger project integrating DA into the OPI framework to yield diagnoses of each learner's ZPD that can orient subsequent instruction, thereby aiming to promote individuals' emerging abilities. In their case study, a standard OPI placed the learner at an intermediate level on the ACTFL proficiency scale. A series of three DA sessions then explored the kinds of support learners required as communicative functions at the advanced proficiency level were introduced (e.g., narration, description, handling complicated role-play scenarios). This allowed an investigation of which of the advanced-level communicative functions were within a learner's ZPD and how much future instruction might be required to develop those abilities. In addition, analysis of the DA interactions led to the identification of mediational moves as well as learner-reciprocating behaviors that characterized the sessions. Wang and Zhang explain that these inventories may be used to guide future dynamic administrations of the OPI.

Finally, another area that has seen considerable interest is computerized DA. Technology has long been recognized as opening possibilities for administering DA procedures, with mediation provided by a computer program rather than a person (e.g., Guthke & Beckmann, 2000). An early example of DA with L2 learners was reported by Poehner and Lantolf (2013), in which learner listening and reading comprehension were evaluated. Computerized tests presented learners with listening or reading texts followed by multiple-choice comprehension questions. If learners answered the question correctly, the test continued to the next item. However, if an incorrect response was selected, a mediating prompt was provided, and the learner was invited to attempt the question again. This process continued until there were no options left to choose. At the end of the test, two sets of scores were produced, one indicating whether the learner answered questions correctly on the first attempt and another score weighted to indicate the number of attempts and mediating prompts received. Since that project, a number of other approaches to computerized DA have been developed (see Leontjev, 2016). An advantage of these procedures is that they yield scores or sets of scores that allow for comparisons among learners, and the assessments themselves can be simultaneously administered to large numbers of learners. Moreover, newer approaches to computerized DA are finding creative ways to render mediation better aligned to learner needs. For instance, a recent study by Randall and Urbanski (2023) focused on learner knowledge of L2 Spanish grammar generates greater nuance in the system's capacity to address difficulties underlying learner performance. The authors explain that their computerized system presents learners with two kinds of tasks: ones for which they must either construct a response by selecting components and placing them in order or multiple-choice questions. In both cases, the response that learners select opens up different menus of mediating prompts such that a learner who chooses a present tense form rather than a past tense form initiates a different sequence of mediation from a learner who selects a third-person verbal form instead of a first-person form. Following Randall and Urbanski, both learners failed to answer the question correctly but for different reasons, and so the mediation they are offered should reflect this. To be sure, limitations remain in this system, but it offers an important advance over earlier work, and, as will be discussed, emerging technologies hold promise for even greater individualization of computerized DA procedures.

Challenges

While it has certainly been beneficial to the elaboration of DA in L2 contexts that much of the research to date has been conducted through also brings to light certain challenges. These include the language curriculum followed in any given context, as this has shaped how development is construed and the aims of DA, and teacher preparedness to conceive of assessment and instruction as processes of promoting learner L2 development. These challenges are interrelated, and so, too, maybe how they can be addressed moving forward.

To begin, it remains the case that traditional approaches to language teaching predominate around the world (e.g., Lightbown & Spada, 2021). So-called grammar-translation models of L2 education approach language as lists of "equivalent" lexical items to be memorized and sets of morpho-syntactic rules to be mechanically practiced. Introducing DA into such a context raises the question of what the procedure may seek to reveal about learners. As explained, DA follows Vygotsky's (2012) reasoning concerning teaching–learning activity as promoting the development of new abilities. Successful application of grammar rules may indeed be a developmental process, entailing reflection, memory, judgment, etc. However, it is unclear to what extent such processes involve new understandings of language or knowledge of how language resources may be intentionally employed to construct and convey meanings. This is precisely the goal of the other approach to Vygotskian praxis mentioned earlier, concept-based language instruction. Thus, one possibility for development-oriented L2 education is to simultaneously shift the existing curriculum to one focused on linguistic concepts and introduce DA for the purpose of understanding learners' initial awareness and subsequent development of conceptual knowledge. Such a two-pronged approach – altering the "content" of the language classroom as well as forms of interaction – can of course be very ambitious. Nonetheless, by integrating symbolic mediation (in the form of conceptual knowledge of language) with dialogic mediation (as occurs during DA interactions), these two forms of praxis together offer a compelling form of development-oriented L2 education (for an example of this work, see Infante, 2018; Levi, 2017).

It is worth pointing out that much concept-based language instruction research to date has favored situations in which the classroom teacher has sophisticated knowledge of language. This cannot always be assumed, and indeed this returns us to the second challenge mentioned, that of teacher preparation to engage in development-oriented activity. According to Poehner and Lantolf (to appear), such engagement requires three forms of expertise: a theoretical understanding of development; conceptual knowledge of language; and knowledge of language teaching, or pedagogical content knowledge. First, without a theory of development to guide decision-making, it is difficult to imagine how teachers can systematically create the conditions necessary for ZPD activity or how they would respond in appropriate ways to learner needs. Expertise is necessary to make thoughtful choices regarding the focus of assessment and intervention, the forms of mediation that will be made available, how interactions will be approached, and the ways in which development may manifest. Swain et al. (2015) offer an accessible introduction to SCT directed specifically to teachers that employs narratives of language teacher and learner experiences to illustrate concepts and principles of the theory.

With regard to the second and third forms of teacher knowledge (language and pedagogy), two approaches have been discussed in the literature in recent years, the Barcelona Formative Model, or BFM (Esteve, 2018), and Praxis-Oriented Pedagogy, or PROP (Johnson et al., 2023). Detailed discussion of these approaches to language teacher preparation is beyond the scope of this chapter (for a recent overview, see Poehner & Lantolf, to appear). Briefly, BFM aims to guide teachers to a systematic and conceptual understanding of language, communication, and grammar and the implications of such understanding for L2 instruction. Text genre is taken as the basic unit of communication, and specific linguistic concepts (rather than grammar rules) are analyzed with regard to how forms available in a language are arranged to create textual meaning. Teachers are led through a process of identifying their current assumptions about language and language education, and they collaborative analyze teaching activities and materials to identify the extent to which they are likely to promote learner development of abilities to engage in authentic communication through the L2. They then work to engage with linguistic concepts to re-orient practices to better support learners. PROP, in contrast, maintains an emphasis on pedagogical concepts or principles intended to help teachers shift from instructor-focused transmission approaches to language education to what Johnson and colleagues refer to as *teaching as dialogic mediation*. This view stresses teaching as a collaborative undertaking with learners, one that requires monitoring of and responsiveness to learner backgrounds, interests, and needs while organizing the classroom environment and instructional interactions.

Future Directions

While DA has been employed in a wide variety of L2 instructional contexts and has focused on a range of language abilities, there are a number of important emerging possibilities for further investigation. I limit my remarks here to three: extensions of DA to new cultural situations; consideration of uses of artificial intelligence (AI) technologies within DA procedures; and uses of DA linked to concerns of social justice. With regard to cultural contexts, while DA in the psychology and general education research literature has been documented in North America and Europe, relatively little work has been reported in other countries (notable exceptions including Israel and, of course, Russia, the site of Vygotsky's original studies). Similarly, L2 DA research to date has been heavily dominated by Western researchers. If we take seriously Vygotsky's commitment to praxis, then both testing DA as a framework and elaborating it requires us to expand our research to new situations and populations. Some of this work is currently underway. For example, a recent special issue of the journal *Language Assessment Quarterly* was devoted to L2 DA research in China. The papers contained in the special issue report original studies by researchers in China investigating topics ranging from listening comprehension assessment among middle school learners of English to the development of translation revision competence among university students and new methods for calculating scores to capture the outcomes of DA procedures. Such research is crucial for the continued development of DA as a framework to address the needs of all L2 learners.

As explained earlier in this chapter, there is a growing body of research concerned with computerized DA. Emerging forms of AI raise new questions concerning whether human mediators might effectively be replaced by technology. While I will not address this issue here, I will suggest that AI may offer new resources to teachers and learners for both DA and enrichment. An ongoing project (Huhta et al., 2023) investigates precisely this idea. Drawing on both diagnostic language assessment and DA, Huhta and colleagues are collaborating with secondary school teachers and learners as they prepare for the English language portion of the Finnish national matriculation exam. A dynamic administration of the exam provides an initial diagnosis of the learner emerging language abilities relative to the underlying constructs. An AI system then is used to analyze online texts that can be used to practice reading comprehension, automatically generating sets of questions and mediating prompts that target particular language dimensions identified for individual learners. The project is still in its early stages, but the use of AI to support mediational opportunities within DA shows promise.

Finally, the increased emphasis on social justice in L2 education offers new opportunities for applications of DA. There is in fact an extensive history of such work in the general education and psychology literature (e.g., Budoff's Learning Potential Measurement with low-performing minority students, Feuerstein's Mediated Learning Experience research with learners with special needs). More recently, Feuerstein et al. (2019) report a project to support Ethiopian immigrant students applying to Israeli universities. The authors explain that these

64 **Chapter 4** Dynamic Assessment in the Classroom

students are from "culturally different" backgrounds, often lacking many of the resources that characterize the educational experiences of students matriculating through the Israeli school system. Consequently, students of Ethiopian background tend to perform poorly on the standardized tests of academic achievement required for university admission. The use of DA to provide insights into the students' abilities, along with a course focused on academic metacognition, has been shown to alter educational trajectories. According to Feuerstein, a longitudinal study across several universities over a six-year period found participants enrolling in highly competitive programs of study at higher rates than the national average and dropping out of university at lower rates. The DA screening exam has now become commonplace for applicants to Israeli universities. It is not difficult to imagine similar procedures being implemented with various at-risk or low-performing learners in order to better understand the sources of academic difficulty, abilities that have begun to develop but are not yet fully formed, and how enrichment programs may be designed to help such learners realize academic success.

Discussion Questions

1. This chapter explained that Dynamic Assessment is informed by a specific theory of mind and development, namely Vygotskian Sociocultural Theory. As such, DA research and practice are framed by notions of mediation, internalization, and Zone of Proximal Development that together offer a way of thinking about L2 development, what forms of evidence of development might be sought, how such evidence can be analyzed, and so on. How does this differ from other forms of L2 assessment, including approaches to formal testing as well as those intended to support teaching and learning?

2. At the level of practice, a defining characteristic of DA is the inclusion of mediation in the assessment procedure in order to probe learner difficulties and emerging abilities according to their responsiveness. This chapter discussed different approaches to mediation, including one-to-one DA procedures, mediation aimed at groups of learners, and procedures in which mediation is delivered via a computer program. What advantages or challenges do you see to each of these? What other approaches to mediating learners during DA can you imagine?

References

Ableeva, R. (2010). *Dynamic assessment of listening comprehension in second language learning (Unpublished doctoral dissertation)*. University Park, PA: The Pennsylvania State University.

Antón, M. (2003). *Dynamic assessment of advanced foreign language learners. Paper presented at the annual meeting of the American Association of Applied Linguistics. Washington, DC.*

Baker, B., & Germain, J. (2020). Narrative inquiry as praxis: examining formative assessment practices in a nature-based Indigenous language classroom. In M. E. Poehner & O. Inbar-Lourie (Eds.), *Toward a reconceptualization of second language classroom assessment. Praxis and researcher–teacher partnership* (pp. 107–127). Springer.

Brown, A. L., & Ferrara, R. A. (1985). Diagnosing zones of proximal development. In J. V. Wertsch (Ed.), *Culture, communication, and cognition: Vygotskian perspectives* (pp. 273–305). Cambridge University Press.

Budoff, M. (1968). Learning potential as a supplementary testing procedure. In J. Hellmuth (Ed.), *Learning disorders* (Vol. *3*, pp. 295–343). Special Child.

Davin, K. J., Herazo, J. D., & Sagre, A. (2017). Learning to mediate: teacher appropriation of dynamic assessment. *Language Teaching Research, 21,* 632–651.

Esteve, O. (2018). Concept-based instruction in teacher education programs in Spain as illustrated by the SCOBA-mediated Barcelona formative model. Helping teachers to become transformative practitioners. In J. P. Lantolf, M. E. Poehner, with M. Swain, eds., *The Routledge handbook of sociocultural theory and second language development*. Routledge, pp. 487–504.

References

Feuerstein, R., Feuerstein, R., & Falik, L. H. (2015). *Beyond smarter: Mediated learning and the brain's capacity for change*. Teachers College Press.

Feuerstein, R., Tzuriel, D., Cohen, S., Cagan, A., Yosef, L., Devisheim, H., Falik, L., & Goldenberg, R. (2019). Integration of Israeli students of Ethiopian origin in Israeli universities. *Journal of Cognitive Education and Psychology, 18*(1), 18–34.

Guthke, J., & Beckmann, J. F. (2000). The learning test concept and its applications in practice. In C. S. Lidz & J. G. Elliott (Eds.), *Dynamic assessment: Prevailing models and applications* (pp. 17–69). Elsevier.

Haywood, H. C., & Lidz, C. S. (2007). *Dynamic assessment in practice. Clinical and educational applications*. Cambridge University Press.

Huhta, A., Poehner, M. E., & Leontjev, D. (2023). *Integrating dynamic and diagnostic assessment. A new approach to supporting L2 development. Paper presented at the Annual Meeting of the International Language Testing Association. New York.*

Infante, P. (2018). Mediated development: promoting learner internalization of L2 concepts through cognitive-process focused activities. In J. P. Lantolf, M. E. Poehner, with M. Swain, eds., *The Routledge handbook of sociocultural theory and second language development*. Routledge, pp. 229–246.

Johnson, K. E., Verity, D. P., & Childs, S. S. (2023). *Praxis-oriented pedagogy for novice L2 teachers. Developing teacher reasoning*. Routledge.

Kozulin, A., & Garb, E. (2002). Dynamic assessment of EFL text comprehension. *School Psychology International, 23*(1), 112–127.

Lantolf, J. P., & Poehner, M. E. (2004). Dynamic assessment: bringing the past into the future. *Journal of Applied Linguistics, 1*(1), 49–74.

Lantolf, J. P., & Poehner, M. E. (2014). *Sociocultural Theory and the pedagogical imperative in L2 education. Vygotskian praxis and the research/practice divide*. Routledge.

Lantolf, J. P., & Thorne, S. L. (2006). *Sociocultural theory and the genesis of second language development*. Oxford University Press.

Lantolf, J. P., Xi, J., & Minakova, L. (2021). Research timeline for sociocultural theory: concept-based language instruction (C-BLI). *Language Teaching, 54*(3), 327–342.

Leontjev, D. (2016). *I can do it: The impact of computerised adaptive corrective feedback on L2 English learners (Unpublished doctoral dissertation). Jyväskylä, Finland: The University of Jyväskylä.*

Levi, T. (2017). Developing L2 oral language proficiency using concept-based dynamic assessment within a large-scale testing context. *Language and Sociocultural Theory, 4*(1), 77–100.

Lightbown, P. M., & Spada, N. (2021). *How languages are learned* (5th ed.). Oxford University Press.

Luria, A. (1961). Study of the abnormal child. *American Journal of Orthopsychiatry: A Journal of Human Behavior, 31*, 1–16.

Negueruela, E. (2003). *A sociocultural approach to the teaching and learning of second languages: Systemic–theoretical instruction and L2 development (Unpublished Ph.D. dissertation). University Park, PA: The Pennsylvania State University.*

Poehner, M. E. (2005). *Dynamic assessment of oral proficiency among advanced L2 learners of French. Unpublished doctoral dissertation. The Pennsylvania State University, University Park, PA.*

Poehner, M. E. (2008). *Dynamic assessment: A Vygotskian approach to understanding and promoting second language development*. Springer Publishing.

Poehner, M. E. (2009). Group dynamic assessment: mediation for the L2 classroom. *TESOL Quarterly, 43*(3), 471–491.

Poehner, M. E., & Lantolf, J. P. (2013). Bringing the ZPD into the equation: capturing L2 development during computerized dynamic assessment. *Language Teaching Research, 17*(3), 323–342.

Poehner, M. E., & Lantolf, J. P. (to appear). *Sociocultural theory and L2 developmental education*. Cambridge University Press.

Poehner, M. E., & Wang, Z. (2021). Dynamic assessment and second language development. *Language Teaching, 54*, 472–490.

Randall, T. S., & Urbanski, K. (2023). Development of a computerized dynamic assessment program for second language grammar instruction and assessment. *Language and Sociocultural Theory, 10*(1), 50–81.

Rea-Dickins, P., & Poehner, M. E. (2011). Addressing issues of access and fairness in education through dynamic assessment. *Assessment in Education: Principles, Policy and Practice, 18*(2), 95–97.

Sternberg, R. J., & Grigorenko, E. L. (2002). *Dynamic testing. The nature and measurement of learning potential.* Cambridge University Press.

Swain, M., Kinnear, P., & Steinman, L. (2015). *Sociocultural theory in second language education. An introduction through narratives* (2nd ed.). Multilingual Matters.

Van der Aalsvoort, G. M., & Lidz, C. S. (2002). Reciprocity in dynamic assessment in classrooms: taking contextual influences on individual learning into account. In G. M. Van der Aalsvoort, W. C. M. Resing & A. J. J. M. Ruijssenaars (Eds.), *Learning potential assessment and cognitive training, 7* (pp. 111–144). Elsevier.

Vygotsky, L. S. (1978). *Mind in society. The development of higher psychological processes.* Harvard University Press.

Vygotsky, L. S. (2011). The dynamics of the schoolchild's mental development in relation to teaching and learning. *Journal of Cognitive Education and Psychology, 10*, 198–211.

Vygotsky, L. S. (2012). *Thought and language.* MIT Press.

Wang, Z., & Zhang, J. (2023). Mediation and learner reciprocity: applying dynamic assessment to the oral proficiency interview framework. *Language and Sociocultural Theory, 10*(1), 82–105.

Weigle, S. C. (2004). Integrating reading and writing in a competency test for non-native speakers of English. *Assessing Writing, 9*(1), 27–55. https://doi.org/10.1016/j.asw.2004.01.002.

Yu, L. (2023). *Dynamic assessment of academic writing among L2 learners of English* (Unpublished doctoral dissertation). University Park, PA: The Pennsylvania State University.

Zhang, Y. (2023). Promoting young EFL learners' listening potential: a model of mediation in the framework of dynamic assessment. *The Modern Language Journal, 107*(S1), 113–136.

Suggested Readings

Levi, T. (2017). Developing L2 oral language proficiency using concept-based dynamic assessment within a large-scale testing context. *Language and Sociocultural Theory, 4*(1), 77–100.

Poehner, M. E., & Yu, L. (2022). Dynamic assessment of L2 writing: exploring the potential of rubrics as mediation in diagnosing learner emerging abilities. *TESOL Quarterly, 56*(4), 1191–1217. https://doi.org/10.1002/tesq.3098.

Randall, T. S., & Urbanski, K. (2023). Development of a computerized dynamic assessment program for second language grammar instruction and assessment. *Language and Sociocultural Theory, 10*(1), 50–81.

Zhang, Y., & Xi, J. (2023). Fostering self-regulated young writers: dynamic assessment of metacognitive competence in secondary school EFL class. *Language Assessment Quarterly, 20*(1), 88–107. https://doi.org/10.1080/15434303. 2022.2103702.

CHAPTER 5

Designing Evaluations for Validation of Language Assessments

Carol A. Chapelle, Erik Voss, and Haeun Kim

Introduction

Language test scores are used to make important decisions about people in many different contexts, and consequently, the tests that evaluate language users' abilities need to be evaluated themselves. Evaluation processes are needed to give test users confidence that the test scores are valid for their intended purposes. Evaluation of assessments and tests is a special case of evaluation of materials in language education, but "validation" is distinguished from other forms of evaluation that are not necessarily focused on test scores and other summaries of students' performance. Validation is defined as the justification of the interpretations and uses of testing outcomes. In this sense, validation at first appears to be a one-sided evaluation if the aim is solely to produce justifications, but the idea is that in the process of attempting to justify something, one confronts both sides of an argument. Despite the intended aim of justification, validation is supposed to entail inquiry into the meaning of test scores, their use, and their consequences. Therefore, practices testing professionals use for validation are critically important to their work.

Language test developers and researchers work in many different contexts to conduct validation research for a variety of tests and assessments using many different approaches. The terms "tests" and "assessments" are both used in this chapter to refer to the systematic procedures for gathering samples of performance to make inferences about test takers' language knowledge, competence, or performance in other contexts. This chapter provides an overview of validation from a scholarly perspective by examining the approaches to validation appearing in the published research in the two major language testing research journals in the field, *Language Testing* and *Language Assessment Quarterly*. With the aim of compiling an empirically based chronological description of validation, we conducted searches of the titles and abstracts of published articles in these two journals at two points in time: 2012 and 2023. Each of the searches was conducted using the search terms "validity," "validation," "validating," "evaluation," "usefulness," and "argument." The terms were chosen to find studies focusing on validation research from any of the variety of perspectives in use since the journal *Language Testing* appeared in 1984 through 2011 for the first search and from 2012 through 2022 for the second search. For each search, the results were compiled in an Excel document and some of

---

The Concise Companion to Language Assessment, First Edition. Edited by Antony John Kunnan.
© 2025 John Wiley & Sons, Inc. Published 2025 by John Wiley & Sons, Inc.

68 Chapter 5 Designing Evaluations for Validation of Language Assessments

the initial results were omitted because the paper did not report an empirical study, or the keyword was used in a manner that did not refer to the validation of test interpretations and uses.

We classified each article from each of the searches under one of four approaches to validation that had appeared in language testing by 2012: (i) one question and three validities, (ii) evidence gathering, (iii) test usefulness, and (iv) argument-based (Chapelle, 2012). These approaches are defined with examples below. In addition, we had a category for studies in which the approach to validation was not explicitly expressed, and we kept an open category for the discovery of additional approaches not captured by the four indicated above. The following sections describe the overall results from each of the two time periods and highlight examples of indicators for approaches to validity that were identified in the research articles. Overall, the more recent sample contained a smaller proportion of articles with no identifiable approach to validation than the earlier sample, but there remained a considerable number of empirical studies in which the conceptual framework for the validation research was not evident or open to question.

Validation in Language Assessment Journals 1984–2011

The first search contained a list of 123 titles published from 1984 through 2011. Table 5.1 shows a tabulation of these results divided into five-year periods and categorized by the approach to validation that each study was judged to use. Overall, the number of empirical validation studies published in language testing journals in the final period, 2006–2011, increased sharply. This is in part due to the launch of *Language Assessment Quarterly* in 2003, but the effect is that the field has more professional validation research open to review and discussion. With the increase in number came an increase in the variety of explicitly identified approaches taken in validation research, especially over the most recent period, 2006 through 2011.

One Question and Three Validities

The question that this category refers to is the following: "Does the test measure what it claims to measure? If it does, it is valid" (Lado, 1961, p. 321). This means of conceptualizing validity and introducing validity research seemed to resonate with testing researchers for some time. It appeared, for example, in Henning's textbook: "A test is said to be valid to the extent that it

---

TABLE **5.1**

Validation approach results from the first search of validation studies (1984–2011) in *Language Testing* and *Language Assessment Quarterly*

Time period	No. of articles	Not explicit % (*n*)	One question % (*n*)	Gathering evidence % (*n*)	Test use-fulness % (*n*)	Argument-based % (*n*)
1984–1990	20	70.00 (14)	30.00 (6)	0.00 (0)	0.00 (0)	0.00 (0)
1991–1995	18	61.11 (11)	11.11 (2)	27.78 (5)	0.00 (0)	0.00 (0)
1996–2000	18	88.89 (16)	0.00 (0)	11.11 (2)	0.00 (0)	0.00 (0)
2001–2005	22	77.27 (17)	0.00 (0)	13.64 (3)	9.09 (2)	0.00 (0)
2006–2011	45	66.67 (30)	0.00 (0)	13.33 (6)	8.89 (4)	11.11 (5)
Total (*n*)	123	71.54 (88)	6.50 (8)	13.01 (16)	4.88 (6)	4.07 (5)

measures what it is supposed to measure" (Henning, 1987, p. 89). Books such as Lado's and Henning's in the United States described procedures associated with demonstrating three "types of validity." Content validity referred to expert opinion systematically gathered indicating the test items or tasks were appropriate for assessing specific aspects of the construct to be measured. Concurrent and criterion-related validity was investigated through the use of correlations between the test and other tests intended to measure the relevant construct. Construct validity referred to other quantitative evidence such as factor analysis showing that the data obtained from examinees conformed to theorized expectations when analyzed statistically.

In 1984–1990 when the results came from the only journal at that time, *Language Testing*, many papers reflected the "one question" approach to validity. A paper by Hudson and Lynch (1984), for example, introduced their approach to validity by stating, "Validity is usually defined as the extent to which a test is actually measuring what it claims to be measuring" (p. 182). They described their study as an initial investigation of content validity and construct validity.

Despite the persistence of the one question, three validities approach among nonspecialists today, measurement specialist Sireci (2009) pointed out that it is an artifact from the past: "to claim that validity refers simply to demonstrating that a 'test measures what it purports to measure' or that it is an inherent property of a test is to ignore at least 70 years of research on validity theory and test validation as well as the consensus Technical Recommendations and Standards that have existed since 1954" (p. 28). Sireci was referring to the fact that contemporary sources refer to validity as one overarching concern with the aim of using a variety of content-related, correlational, and other statistical and qualitative evidence in support of test interpretation and use. Sources that capture this professional consensus include the *Standards for Educational and Psychological Measurement, 7th edition*, published jointly by the American Psychological Association, the American Educational Research Association, and the National Council on Measurement in Education (AERA et al., 2014). Another such source is an edited collection, *Educational measurement, 4th edition* (Brennen, 2006). According to these authoritative sources, the problem for evaluating any particular test interpretation and use would more aptly be characterized as a problem of gathering the appropriate evidence.

Evidence Gathering

In the period 1991–1995, some papers in *Language Testing* began to refer to Messick's (1989) presentation of evidence gathering in support of construct validity, and from 1996 to 2000, studies continued to adopt an evidence-gathering approach and dropped the terminology "content validity and criterion-related validity." Messick (1989) defined validity as "an overall evaluative judgment of the degree to which evidence and theoretical rationales support the adequacy and appropriateness of interpretations and actions based on test scores" (p. 13). This perspective was presented in Bachman's (1990) seminal book. According to these sources in the 1980s and 1990s, validation research should consist of gathering evidence about the meaning and consequences of test scores. A study in *Language Testing* by Shohamy and Inbar (1991) explicitly framed their research as gathering evidence through hypothesis testing concerning the type of text and questions in a listening comprehension test rather than from the perspective of types of validity.

During the period 2001–2005, when the first issues of *Language Assessment Quarterly* were published (in 2004), authors continued to adopt an evidence-gathering approach. For example, Snellings et al. (2004) applied Messick's (1989) framework to their validation of measures of written lexical retrieval, referring to it as a unified validity framework and citing both Bachman (1990) and the 1999 version of the Standards. They explain that the framework states ". . . different kinds of validity evidence are not alternatives but supplement each other in assessing the unifying concept of construct validity" (p. 178). They define construct validity as involving "an integration of any evidence on what the interpretation or meaning of the test scores is for a particular purpose. In other words, what does this evidence tell us about the meaning of the score" (p. 178).

Another important strand from Messick's perspective is what Davies and Elder (2005) in language assessment called the social turn in the conception of validity. This turn included critical forms of inquiry as part of the validation process with the aim of uncovering the values and social consequences underlying test interpretation and use. This presentation of validity as an evidence-based judgment – including judgments about the consequences of testing – continues to be important for validation researchers despite expressed frustrations about research gathering evidence about score meaning and consequences. Davies and Elder (2005) expressed the frustration of many who attempt to conduct validation research within this frame of reference: "If the notion of test validity and the process of test validation . . . are to be regarded as credible rather than dismissed as the arcane practices of a self-serving élite, they need to be simplified or at least rendered more transparent to test users" (p. 810).

Test Usefulness

In language assessment, Bachman and Palmer (1996) responded to the need for a more transparent framing of the goals and processes of validation, and this framing began to appear in the journals in the early 2000s. It is consistent with the perspective of validation that advocates gathering evidence that can be used in an overall evaluation of test use, but it is easy to spot as distinct because of the reliance on a single source (Bachman & Palmer, 1996) and the term, "test usefulness." Test usefulness can be thought of as a shorthand way of expressing "validity of test score interpretation and use." The types of analysis Bachman and Palmer cite for investigation of test usefulness are construct validity, reliability, authenticity and interactiveness, impact, and practicality. In language testing research, this perspective and the practices that they suggested were used in materials aimed at practitioners (e.g., Stoynoff & Chapelle, 2005). The journal articles show that this framework gained some traction in language testing research, as well: A course-based assessment was evaluated by Spence-Brown (2001) using authenticity and interactiveness, which are components of Bachman and Palmer's (1996) test usefulness framework. Chapelle et al.'s (2003) evaluation of a web-based ESL proficiency test was conducted by outlining for each of the qualities of test usefulness the evidence suggesting positive results and limitations or evidence yet to be gathered. Use of such a framework illustrates how the problems of endless evidence gathering can be addressed in a practical setting, where parameters of time and money have to be considered. Many more such cases exist than those that appear in the journals.

Argument-Based Approach

Within the period of 2006–2011, another praxis-oriented approach to validation appeared – an argument-based approach to validation. The principal characteristics of an argument-based approach are (i) the interpretive argument that the test developer specifies to identify the various components of meaning that the test score is intended to have and its uses, (ii) the claims and inferences that are used as the basic building blocks in an interpretative argument, and (iii) the use of the interpretive argument as a frame for gathering validity evidence. Within this time frame, these tenets of validity argument were presented in a number of papers by Kane (2006), most notably in his chapter in the 4th edition of *Educational measurement*, but also in the influential work of Mislevy (e.g., Mislevy et al., 2003; Mislevy & Chengbin, 2009). In language testing, the approach was also evident in Bachman (2005), Bachman and Palmer (2010), and Chapelle et al. (2008). Several studies in the journals also use an argument-based approach.

Articles in journals show the many possible arguments that can be constructed from the basic idea of inferences and claims. In a high-stakes test, Enright and Quinlan (2010) presented an argument-based approach to contextualize their research that collects evidence in the evaluation of human and e-rater scoring of a writing task. The authors develop their argument for the TOEFL iBT writing task using the following four inferences: evaluation, generalization, extrapolation, and utilization. Support for each inference comes from their empirical studies of the relationship between human raters and e-rater scoring, reliability estimates for combinations of human and computer scoring, correlational studies with other measures and other non-test criteria, and evidence that will be collected regarding the consequences of using automatic essay scoring. In another test intended for high-stakes use, Bernstein et al. (2010) presented an argument-based approach for their validation of a test of speaking ability, which used automatic scoring of spoken language. While the authors do not use the same terminology for inferences in the interpretive argument, they gather evidence related to (i) the accuracy of the test score (evaluation), (ii) evidence of test score consistency (generalization), (iii) the relationship between the automated test and score on other communicative tests (explanation), and (iv) with the target domain (extrapolation). In addition, the authors present counterclaims and support for a potential rebuttal to the argument.

Other articles within the final five-year period of the first search describe validation procedures for low-stakes testing. For example, Pardo-Ballester (2010) applied Bachman's (2005) Assessment Use Argument approach to a Spanish listening test to support the score interpretation and use for placement of students into university Spanish classes. The claims about the test score meaning included three of Bachman and Palmer's (1996) qualities of usefulness: reliability, construct validity, and authenticity. Another example of an argument-based approach in a low-stakes test is a test of productive grammatical ability (Chapelle et al., 2010). The validity argument outlined in the paper provided support for five inferences: *evaluation, generalization, explanation, extrapolation, and utilization.* Finally, a study by Koizumi et al. (2011) provided an example of a validity argument for a low-stakes diagnostic test of grammar for Japanese learners of English. The evidence from the research supported three inferences in a validity argument: statistical characteristics of test items were appropriate for making intended decisions (evaluation), reliability was high (generalization), and test scores were consistent with the difficulty of certain grammatical features (noun phrase groups) (explanation).

These studies do not include all of the steps in the examples shown above from domain definition through utilization; they include the claims and inferences that are important for the score meaning of a particular test. Alternatively, the formulation of the argument and the evidence presented may be due, in part, to the length restriction of the publication. Another reason may be that authors chose to write about the inferences that needed the most attention rather than all of the evidence that pertained to the complete argument. "Validity evidence is most effective when it addresses the weakest parts of the interpretive argument" (Kane, 1992, p. 530). Some authors, therefore, may focus on these more challenging links such as those made on the basis of automated scoring. In fact, the formulation of an interpretive argument may help test developers and researchers to better deal with the challenges in validation.

Summary 1984–2011

The empirically based chronological description of validation compiled from the research journals found examples of all four approaches. From 1996 on, the "one question three validities" approach seemed to be left as a thing of the past. Once evidence-gathering and usefulness approaches were introduced, they continued to be used through 2011, even as argument-based approaches appear. In 2011, the research published in the two primary journals in the field did not suggest that there was only one conceptual framework used for validation. As shown in Table 5.1, the papers that explicitly present an approach to validation

72 Chapter 5 Designing Evaluations for Validation of Language Assessments

are split among an evidence-gathering approach to validation (13.33%), a usefulness framework (8.89%), and an argument-based approach (11.11%). The second analysis investigated how these trends evolved through the following 11 years.

Validation in Language Assessment Journals 2012–2022

The second search of the titles and abstracts of published articles in *Language Testing* and *Language Assessment Quarterly* included articles from 2012 through 2022. The same search terms and process of evaluation were used to classify the articles into six categories: the four validation approaches identified in the first time period, one category for articles not explicitly indicating an approach, and one category for other approaches appearing in the articles. Relative to previous decades, the results of the second search found an increased tendency for research to explicitly present the basis for the validation research they reported, as shown in Table 5.2. In contrast to the 88 (72%) articles in which researchers gave no explicit indication of a validation approach until 2011, the second search found only 15 (23%) of articles that did not indicate a validation framework. One example of an empirical study that does not explicitly introduce the approach or framework guiding the study is the article "Does test preparation work? Implications for score validity" (Xie, 2013). This study investigated the effects of students' varying test preparation strategies on their test scores. It introduced the study with discussion of potential effects of test preparation on "score validity," "construct validity," and "test washback," and it claims implications of the study for "extrapolation validity." Despite the use of the term "validity" throughout the article, our analysis did not find an approach to validation outlined or implied.

The other notable trend revealed in the results of the second search was the approaches and frameworks presented by researchers. One was that argument-based was up from 5 (4%) of articles in the first search results to 22 (34%) in the second search. A third trend was that the socio-cognitive framework for validation (Weir, 2005), which had not been identified in the first search, appeared in the second search results, so this is included in Table 5.2. Finally, an additional category (other) was added to hold two studies using approaches that did not fit into any of the named categories.

One Question and Three Validities

The one question (Does the test measure what it claims to measure?) three validities (content, validity, criterion-related validity, and construct validity) category is used to code the studies in which the researcher uses these (or other terms) to indicate a type of validity as an inherent property of a test. The number of articles identified as adopting this perspective was the same in the first and second searches, but because the overall number of articles in the first search was larger, the percentage was smaller (6.50%) in the first than in the second search (12.31%). Within the second search, the earlier and later year groups contain the same number of articles coded as "one question, three validities," as well, indicating that this perspective from the 1960s remains with the field.

Evidence Gathering

Articles identified as "evidence gathering" increased somewhat from the first to second searches, from 13% to almost 17%. Evidence gathering can provide a means for researchers to present a research methodology with reference to a specific validation goal. An example of an

TABLE 5.2

Validation approach results from the second search of validation studies (2012–2022) in *Language Testing* and *Language Assessment Quarterly*

Time period	No. of articles	Not explicit % (*n*)	One question % (*n*)	Gathering evidence % (*n*)	Test useful-ness % (*n*)	Argument-based % (*n*)	Socio-cognitive % (*n*)	Other % (*n*)
2012–2016	25	32.00 (8)	16.00 (4)	12.00 (3)	4.00 (1)	28.00 (7)	8.00 (2)	0.00 (0)
2017–2022	40	17.50 (7)	10.00 (4)	20.00 (8)	0.00 (0)	37.50 (15)	10.00 (4)	5.00 (2)
Total (*n*)	65	23.08 (15)	12.31 (8)	16.92 (11)	1.52 (1)	33.85 (22)	9.23 (6)	3.08 (2)

Note. The "socio-cognitive" framework for validation (Weir, 2005) and "other" categories were added to accommodate approaches to validation referred to by authors in the second search that did not appear in the first search. The "other" category consists of a study using a validation framework for standard setting, and one citing several approaches that we were unable to categorize within one of the identified categories.

74 Chapter 5 Designing Evaluations for Validation of Language Assessments

article that clearly presents the rationale for their evidence-gathering research is "Development and validation of extract the base: An English Derivational Morphology Test for third through fifth grade monolingual students and Spanish-speaking English language learners" (Goodwin et al., 2012). The authors begin with the one question: "Test validity refers to a test's accuracy in terms of measuring what it is intended to measure" (p. 275). Rather than going on to refer to various types of validity, however, the authors establish the conceptual basis for their research by adding an appropriate definition of validity: "More specifically, Messick (1989) defined test validity as an evaluative judgment of the adequacy and appropriateness of inferences based on test performance" (p. 275). Messick's definition added the technical specificity the authors need to explain their research: "In our context, we needed theoretical rationales and empirical evidence to support the hypothesis that the Extract the Base Test measures a participant's 'conscious awareness of the morphemic structure of words and their ability to reflect on and manipulate that structure' (Carlisle, 1995, p. 194)" (p. 275). The rest of the paragraph explained the basis for the theoretical rationales and methodology for obtaining the empirical evidence, and it ends with the statement of the scope of the research findings from this study and leaves it to "future research to take into account rival or alterative interpretations of the test results" (p. 275). This example demonstrates the clarity of purpose that can be obtained in the presentation of validation research when authors use evidence gathering as an approach to validation. This clarity might be expected to mark a popular path for researchers wanting to describe the rationale for their research without elaborating a framework, but the percentage increase in articles using evidence gathering in the second search was negligible.

Test Usefulness

Test usefulness, a framework that appeared to be increasing in frequency at the end of the first search period, was identified in only one article in the second search period. The article, "Scratching where they itch: Evaluation of feedback on a Diagnostic English grammar test for Taiwanese university students," provides an example of how the test usefulness framework served as a basis for the study (Yin et al., 2012). The authors introduced the framework as follows:

> Therefore, any evaluation of such a test's usefulness must include an examination of the feedback provided. In fact, in Bachman and Palmer's (1996) list of possible questions for evaluating a language test's usefulness, one item under the aspect of impact upon test takers is, 'How relevant, complete, and meaningful is the feedback that is provided to test takers? (p. 146).' The article reports a study that sought to answer this question for a diagnostic grammar test for Taiwanese university students. (pp. 78–79)

The authors then used the test usefulness framework's specification of "impact" to guide their development of research questions as they explain:

> Bachman and Palmer (1996) recommend that test makers examine (a) the extent to which and (b) the ways in which feedback is "relevant, complete and meaningful" to test takers (p. 146). For this study, these questions were reformulated into two primary research questions: RQ1: How useful do test takers perceive the Grammar Test feedback to be? RQ2: In what ways do the test takers perceive the feedback to be useful or not? (p. 82)

By connecting the research questions in the study to the usefulness framework, the authors state from the beginning the scope of their study relative to the larger issue of validity.

Argument-Based Approach

The percentage increase in articles identified as using an argument-based approach from 4% in the first search to almost 34% in the second search was accompanied by an increase in the variety of ways that this framework was used in the research. The use of argument-based validity was flagged by authors who indicated that they had created or were investigating a validity argument. One example was in the article, "Can the test support student learning? Validating the use of a second language pronunciation diagnostic" (Isbell, 2021). The author wrote that he "developed a validity argument for the [Korean Pronunciation Diagnostic] spanning the interpretation and use of scores" (p. 335). His validation research is framed by current research on diagnostic assessment, validation, and the intersection of these two areas. Specifically, as background for the validity argument, he cited Chapelle et al. (2008), Kane (2013), Kunnan (2018), and Chapelle et al. (2015), each one a source that uses the same basic concepts for developing validity arguments.

The author continued by describing what his argument contains by using the validity argument terminology of inferences, warrants, and assumptions: "This argument comprises a series of inferences that ultimately connect the design of the test to impact on learning" (p. 335). He used the terminology of the cited sources to introduce the form of the validity argument: "Each inference is explicated in detail by one or more warrants (propositions) which advance the argument, and for each warrant to hold, one or more assumptions must be met" (p. 335). He did not present the entire validity argument in this article, but instead delimited the scope of this investigation relative to the complete validity argument:

> In this article, however, I limit my focus to the test score use portion of the argument, which includes two inferences: utilization and impact . . . The utilization inference pertains to how test users are able to interpret and apply diagnostic information, and the potential for that information to raise or correct awareness of strengths/weaknesses. The impact inference relates directly to the (potential) beneficial consequences of applying diagnostic feedback to learning activity. (p. 335)

A second example focuses on two different inferences in their validity argument, but similarly begins the paper with an unmistakable introduction of the validity approach they are using. The article, "Fitting MD analysis in an argument-based validity framework for writing assessment: Explanation and generalization inferences for the ECPE" (Yan & Staples, 2020) cited Kane (2013) and Chapelle et al. (2008). It then named six inferences that can be made in validity arguments before explaining how the research questions for the study were developed to address the assumptions underlying the two inferences, explanation and generalization, that they investigate through their linguistic analysis of the responses on a writing test. By proposing the "warrants, assumptions and evidence for inferential steps pertaining to investigations of performance characteristics in language assessments" (p. 189), the authors illustrated how quantitative corpus linguistic methods are used to investigate certain assumptions underlying the inferences and uses of the test scores.

A third example developed an evaluation of a testing policy using the principles of fairness, including "the subprinciples of opportunity to learn, meaningfulness, absence of bias, and access," and justice that "covers subprinciples of beneficial consequences and positive values" (Saito et al., 2022, p. 427). The article "Evaluating fairness and justice of external English language test score interpretation and use for Japanese university admission" (Saito et al., 2022) showed how the principles and subprinciples (proposed by Kunnan, 2018) offered a basis in ethics that can be developed into the specific claims and warrants, required to motivate research questions and the interpretation of the results as providing evidence or failing to do so. For example, based on the opportunity to learn sub-principle, the authors stated "An assessment ought to provide adequate opportunity for test-takers to acquire the

76   Chapter 5 Designing Evaluations for Validation of Language Assessments

knowledge, abilities, or skills to be assessed on the external tests" (p. 433). The claim relative to the test being evaluated is "The opportunity to learn the vocabulary knowledge assessed in the external tests is available in classrooms in Japan" (p. 433). This claim would be supported if "test agency surveys and literature reviews indicate some of their test suites are within the suggested vocabulary range, and test-taking techniques and glossary aid this gap in vocabulary knowledge" (p. 433).

These are just 3 of the 22 examples illustrating how authors of articles included in the second search all worked from a common intent to make explicit the validity framework they were using as well as the specific claims and inferences that their validation research was addressing. The clarity of purpose in each of these cases has the benefit of delineating how far the results of the validation extend and therefore what remains in question.

Summary 2012–2022

The increased clarity of validation approaches in the second search results is consistent with a growing interest in research methods and epistemology in applied linguistics throughout the 11-year period covered in the second search. In fact, validation research, which can span a range of theoretical and empirical questions, reflects a microcosm of applied linguistics issues, including defining constructs, generating and investigating hypotheses about language performance, and extrapolating research results to the real world of language users and technologies. Validation frameworks that extend beyond the question of whether the test measures what it claims to measure create the potential for increasing understanding of the dimensions of validation in language testing and the research methods appropriate for investigating each dimension. Over half of the articles found in the second search supported this goal of increased transparency and therefore provide examples for the next generation of language testers.

Conclusion

This chapter began with a definition of validation as the justification of the interpretations and uses of testing outcomes, but then found that the paths that language testing researchers take to conduct validation research are varied. The searches of the two major research journals in language testing at two periods of time revealed that with time the approaches to validation have become increasingly clearly stated in the articles indicating that authors recognize the need to state the basis of their research design in terms of the rationale it is intended to support. Nevertheless, not all researchers make an explicit reference to an approach to validity that we were able to identify. Moreover, even within the approaches that were identified in the articles in the second search, several ($n = 20$) required discussion between the two of us who reviewed the articles, and only one ($n = 1$) required adjudication by the third. In short, readers seeking examples of validation in language testing cannot assume published articles always provide a clear link between validation – justification of the interpretations and uses of testing outcomes – the rationales for study designs, and research results. Many do, however, and these tend to rely on a framework for validation that indexes authoritative sources and examples where readers can gain a fuller understanding of the fit of the article into the overall justification of the interpretations and uses of testing outcomes.

Language assessments are used by many different people and for a range of different purposes in language education and research. Therefore, there is a need to better understand and conceptualize how principles and methods in validation research can best be used to investigate the quality of assessments for their respective purposes. Norris (2008) pointed out that in view of the variety of reasons for conducting validation research, appropriate variations in validation practices need to be formulated. "Accountability, knowledge generation, development, improvement, learning, advocacy, and other rationales each may be posited as the primary driving force behind a validity evaluation" (p. 73). Each of these purposes is likely to be served by a distinct set of data collection procedures during validation. Moreover, each purpose will affect the manner of dissemination of results.

The historical perspective outlined in this chapter relied on an analysis of published work on validation, but this is only a selective subset of all of the validation work conducted over this time period. It reveals a fraction of validation research carried out by testing programs that publish tests; language programs that develop, use, and revise tests; and researchers including doctoral students who write research reports and dissertations. A systematic review of this larger pool of validation studies from a research methodological perspective is beginning to appear (e.g., Dursun & Li, 2021). Such reviews can promote a level of transparency that invites new researchers into a community whose technical language and concepts are up to the task of evaluating language tests in the many ways required for justification of the interpretations and uses of testing outcomes.

Discussion Questions

1. How do researchers select an approach to validity for their research? Consider one or more of the validation studies cited in this chapter, and explain why you think the chosen validation approach was selected.

2. What role does technology play in evaluation of language assessments? Give an example of how you would use one of the approaches to validation to take advantage of technology for validation research.

References

AERA, APA, & NCME. (2014). *Standards for educational and psychological testing* (7th ed.). American Educational Research Association.

Bachman, L. F. (1990). *Fundamental considerations in language testing*. Oxford University Press.

Bachman, L. F. (2005). Building and supporting a case for test use. *Language Assessment Quarterly, 2*(1), 1–34.

Bachman, L. F., & Palmer, A. S. (1996). *Language testing in practice*. Oxford University Press.

Bachman, L. F., & Palmer, A. S. (2010). *Language assessment in practice*. Oxford University Press.

Bernstein, J., Van Moere, A., & Cheng, J. (2010). Validating automated speaking tests. *Language Testing, 27*(3), 355–377.

Brennan, R. L. (Ed.). (2006). *Educational measurement* ((4th ed.). ed.). Greenwood Publishing.

Chapelle, C. A. (2012). Conceptions of validity. In G. Fulcher & F. Davidson (Eds.), *The Routledge handbook of language testing* (pp. 19–30). Routledge.

Chapelle, C. A., Jamieson, J., & Hegelheimer, V. (2003). Validation of a web-based ESL test. *Language Testing, 20*(4), 409–439.

Chapelle, C. A., Enright, M. K., & Jamieson, J. (Eds.). (2008). *Building a validity argument for the Test of English as a Foreign Language*. Routledge.

Chapelle, C. A., Chung, Y.-R., Hegelheimer, V., Pendar, N., & Xu, J. (2010). Towards a computer-delivered test of productive grammatical ability. *Language Testing, 27*(4), 443–469.

Chapelle, C. A., Cotos, E., & Lee, J. (2015). Validity arguments for diagnostic assessment using automated writing evaluation. *Language Testing, 32*(3), 385–405.

Davies, A., & Elder, C. (2005). Validity and validation in language testing. In E. Hinkel (Ed.), *Handbook of research in second language teaching and learning* (pp. 795–813). Lawrence Erlbaum Associates.

78 **Chapter 5** Designing Evaluations for Validation of Language Assessments

Dursun, A., & Li, Z. (2021). A systematic review of argument-based validation studies in the field of language testing. In C. A. Chapelle & E. Voss (Eds.), *Validity argument in language testing: Case studies of validation research.* Cambridge University Press.

Enright, M. K., & Quinlan, T. (2010). Complementing human judgment of essays written by English language learners with e-rater scoring. *Language Testing, 27*(3), 317–334.

Goodwin, A. P., Huggins, A. C., Carlo, M., Malabonga, V., Kenyon, D., Louguit, M., & August, D. (2012). Development and validation of extract the base: an English derivational morphology test for third through fifth grade monolingual students and Spanish-speaking English language learners. *Language Testing, 29*(2), 265–289. https://doi.org/10.1177/0265532211419827.

Henning, G. (1987). *A guide to language testing: Development, evaluation, research.* Newbury House.

Hudson, T., & Lynch, B. (1984). A criterion-referenced measurement approach to ESL achievement testing. *Language Testing, 1*(2), 171–201.

Isbell, D. R. (2021). Can the test support student learning? Validating the use of a second language pronunciation diagnostic. *Language Assessment Quarterly, 18*(4), 331–356. https://doi.org/10.1080/15434303.2021.1874382.

Kane, M. T. (1992). An argument-based approach to validity. *Psychological Bulletin, 112*, 527–535.

Kane, M. T. (2006). Validation. In R. Brennen (Ed.), *Educational measurement* (4th ed., pp. 17–64). Greenwood Publishing.

Kane, M. T. (2013). Validating the interpretations and uses of test scores. *Journal of Educational Measurement, 50*(1), 1–73.

Koizumi, R., Saka, H., Ido, T., Ota, H., Hayama, M., Sato, M., & Nemoto, A. (2011). Development and validation of a diagnostic grammar test for Japanese learners of English. *Language Assessment Quarterly, 8*(1), 53–72.

Kunnan, J. A. (2018). *Evaluating language assessments.* Routledge.

Lado, R. (1961). *Language testing.* Longman.

Messick, S. (1989). Validity. In R. L. Linn (Ed.), *Educational measurement* (3rd ed., pp. 13–103). Macmillan Publishing Co.

Mislevy, R. J., & Chengbin, Y. (2009). If language is a complex adaptive system, what is language assessment? *Language Learning, 59*(Supplement 1), 249–267.

Mislevy, R. J., Steinberg, L. S., & Almond, R. G. (2003). On the structure of educational assessments. *Measurement: Interdisciplinary Research and Perspectives, 1*, 3–62.

Norris, J. (2008). *Validity evaluation in language assessment.* Peter Lang.

Pardo-Ballester, C. (2010). The validity argument of a web-based Spanish listening exam: test usefulness evaluation. *Language Assessment Quarterly, 7*(2), 137–159.

Saito, H., Sawaki, Y., & Kasahara, K. (2022). Evaluating fairness and justice of external English language test score interpretation and use for Japanese university admission. *Language Assessment Quarterly, 19*(4), 422–448. https://doi.org/10.1080/15434303.2022.2083965.

Shohamy, E., & Inbar, O. (1991). Validation of listening comprehension tests: the effect of text and question type. *Language Testing, 8*(1), 23–40.

Sireci, S. G. (2009). Packing and unpacking sources of validity evidence: history repeats itself again. In R. Lissitz (Ed.), *The concept of validity: Revisions, new directions and applications* (pp. 19–37). Information Age Publishing Inc.

Snellings, P., van Gelderen, A., & de Glopper, K. (2004). Validating a test of second language written lexical retrieval: a new measure of fluency in written language production. *Language Testing, 21*(2), 174–201.

Spence-Brown, R. (2001). The eye of the beholder: authenticity in an embedded assessment task. *Language Testing, 18*(4), 463–481.

Stoynoff, S., & Chapelle, C. A. (2005). *ESOL tests and testing: A resource for testers and administrators.* TESOL.

Weir, C. (2005). *Language testing and validation.* Palgrave Macmillan.

Xie, Q. (2013). Does test preparation work? Implications for score validity. *Language Assessment Quarterly, 10*(2), 196–218. https://doi.org/10.1080/15434303.2012.721423.

Yan, X., & Staples, S. (2020). Fitting MD analysis in an argument-based validity framework for writing assessment: Explanation and generalization inferences for the ECPE. *Language Testing, 37*(2), 189–214. https://doi.org/10.1177/0265532219876226.

Yin, M., Sims, J., & Cothran, D. (2012). Scratching where they itch: evaluation of feedback on a diagnostic English grammar test for Taiwanese university students. *Language Assessment Quarterly*, *9*(1), 78–104. https://doi.org/10.1080/15434303.2010.516043.

Suggested Readings

Chalhoub-Deville, M., & O'Sullivan, B. (2020). *Validity: Theoretical development and integrated arguments*. Equinox.

Chapelle, C. A. (2021). *Argument-based validation in testing and assessment*. SAGE Publications.

Chapelle, C. A., & Voss, E. (Eds.). (2021). *Validity argument in language testing: Case studies of validation research*. Cambridge University Press.

Fox, J., & Artemeva, N. (2022). *Reconsidering context in language assessment: Transdisciplinary perspectives, social theories, and validity*. Routledge.

CHAPTER 6

Fairness and Justice in Language Assessment

Antony John Kunnan

Introduction

The concept of *fairness*, as related to assessment and assessment practice, has been debated regularly since the late 1980s by researchers and practitioners. In the field of educational assessment, the concept of fairness was first introduced in employment-related testing of the General Aptitude Test Battery (see Hartigan & Wigdor, 1989). In language assessment, the term was first discussed at the Language Testing Research Colloquium in Finland when Kunnan (1997) presented a case for a fairness research agenda. Fairness also soon made its way into the influential *Standards for Educational and Psychological Testing* (APA (American Psychological Association) et al., 1999) with a section titled "Fairness in Testing" and subsections on fairness in testing and test use, the rights and responsibilities of test takers, testing individuals of diverse linguistic backgrounds, and testing individuals with disabilities. Codes of ethics and practice based on this pioneering work have now been established by many assessment agencies such as the International Language Testing Association, Educational Testing Service, Princeton, University of Cambridge, and the Association of Language Testers of Europe, among others. Since 2000, there have been frequent publications on fairness as a concept (see Kunnan, 2000, 2004, 2008; Walters, 2012), situated ethics (Kunnan & Davidson, 2004), how to investigate fairness (Kunnan, 2010; Xi, 2010), differential item functioning as a method for detecting biased items (Ferne & Rupp, 2007), accommodations for test takers with disabilities (see Chapter 67, Accommodations in the Assessment of English Language Learners), the intersection of fairness and justice (McNamara & Ryan, 2011), and legal matters related to fairness.

Disagreements, however, have regularly surfaced in these debates. The first is to do with the interpretation of the term. Depending on the researcher's perspective, fairness has meant "absence of bias," "equal opportunity," "equitable treatment," "similar outcomes in terms of scores," and so on. Additionally, the scope of the term has been contested (see Kane, 2010; Xi, 2010): Does fairness include validity or does validity include fairness? Or are they two separate entities? This has led many researchers to set aside the concept of fair assessments as inferior to validation efforts. Davies (2010) even asked whether it was worth paying attention to. Finally, no foundational principles that drive the concept have been articulated; as a result, critics have argued that fairness studies are incoherent (e.g., Bachman, 2005). As a result, fairness is often invoked with ad hoc and post hoc investigations after assessments are written and launched but it is not part of the assessment design, development, administration, and

---

The Concise Companion to Language Assessment, First Edition. Edited by Antony John Kunnan.
© 2025 John Wiley & Sons, Inc. Published 2025 by John Wiley & Sons, Inc.

standard-setting processes. A good example is the class of DIF/bias studies that examine test performance, often with no a priori hypotheses.[1]

The term *justice*, on the other hand, is rarely mentioned in the assessment literature, although the idea of justice has been discussed in writings from Plato to recent work by John Rawls and Amartya Sen. Once again, the term is difficult to define. A few interpretations include "distributive justice," which refers to institutions providing benefits that are distributed to a society in a just manner, "retributive or corrective justice," which refers to whether punishments are just, and "compensatory justice," which refers to fair compensation for injuries. In language assessment, Kunnan has tied the two concepts of fairness and justice together (Kunnan, 2004, 2008) and McNamara and Ryan (2011) have wrestled with the two concepts to offer separation and clarity to the concepts.

This chapter attempts to provide principled bases for fairness and justice as applied to the institution of assessment. It does this by applying the *idea of fairness as relating to persons – how assessments ought to be fair to test takers –* and the *idea of justice as relating to institutions – how institutions ought to be just to test takers.*

Preliminaries

Despite the disagreements regarding the concept of fairness, the very concept of the public examination (or assessment) includes notions of fairness and justice. This can be seen as the main goal of such examinations, which is to bring about a level playing field in awarding benefits through a process that assesses desired abilities; not to award benefits based on privilege and patronage. This was the main goal of the civil service selection process in China centuries ago, and in France, Germany, the United Kingdom, and colonial India in the late 18th and early 19th centuries. In more recent times, related concepts of equality, equal protection, and equal representation have become part of public discourse in most parts of the world, although such discussions have not always resulted in the active promotion of fairness, equality, and civil rights. Thus, in many countries, fairness in schooling and employment has been advanced through fair assessments and just institutions.

The more practical aspects of fairness are noticeable. For example, anonymizing examination responses by removing test takers' personal information so that test takers cannot be identified; the use of topics in test materials that are familiar to test takers; investigations regarding biases toward test takers from different language, gender, age, and ethnic backgrounds and biases of raters and ratings; checks regarding whether test takers have had the opportunity to acquire the knowledge or skills prior to the assessment, and the use of appropriate accommodations for test takers with disabilities. Therefore, in many contexts, the practical aspects of fairness are not new. With this background, a few preliminary questions can be articulated:

1. Does every test taker have the right to a fair assessment? Is this rule inviolable? Are rights of test takers to a fair assessment universal or only applicable in states that provide equal rights?
2. Is it adequate that most test takers are assessed fairly while a few are not? Would it be appropriate to use a cost–benefit analysis to evaluate whether assessments should be improved or not? And, if harm is done to test takers, does such harm need to be compensated?

---

[1] Most assessment agencies have a publicly declared they have a sensitivity review phase in which all items are subject to careful review.

82 Chapter 6 Fairness and Justice in Language Assessment

3. Would the rights of test takers to a fair assessment be supported in authoritarian states that do not provide for equal rights? Would institutions in such states feel less compelled to provide a fair assessment?
4. Should an assessment be beneficial to the society in which it is used?
5. Should assessment developers and users be required to offer public justification or reasoning?

This chapter continues with hypothetical vignettes and real-world examples and reflections on these scenarios. These vignettes exclude concrete realistic details so that we can focus on a limited number of issues. Arguments from normative ethics regarding fairness and justice are then discussed in order to provide appropriate background for the proposed principle of fairness and principle of justice. This chapter concludes with how these principles can be used to advance fairness and justice in language assessment.

Vignette 1: Pretesting of Assessment Tasks

Imagine a new staff member has joined a large professional language assessment organization (university or commercial) that develops assessments for high-stakes contexts. After she had worked at the organization for three months, she began to be concerned about many of the agency's practices. She took note of them: First, they did not pretest or trial their test tasks; instead, they used the non-pretested tasks in a real administration and did not delete the scores from those tasks when they computed the scores for the test takers. In other words, the test takers received scores that included tasks that were not pretested. The staff member approached her supervisor who was head of assessment development. He was at first disinterested in the staff member's concern but later admitted that pretesting tasks would cost too much money for the organization, and, if they conducted a pretest, the assessment would also cost the test taker much more.

The main questions here are: Did the staff member do the right thing in bringing to the attention of her supervisor the lack of pretesting? Is pretesting of tasks for high-stakes assessments a requirement? Is the head of assessment development's lack of understanding of the situation acceptable? Are his reasons for not conducting any pretesting justified? Would people of any persuasion (teachers, test takers, business leaders, etc.) be able to defend such a practice? Is there a violation of an accepted code of ethics and practice? Would this be an example of an unfair assessment?

Vignette 2: Checks for Biased Assessment Items/Tasks

Continuing with Vignette 1 ... The staff member also found that the organization did not conduct any review or investigation to examine whether the assessment was fair to all test takers in terms of content, dialect, test delivery, or test performance. She brought this matter up with her supervisor too. The supervisor said that, while these are important matters, the organization did not have staff with expertise to conduct such investigations. He also reminded her that, once again, these investigations would cost the organization a lot of money and the final result would be that the assessment would cost the test taker more.

Once again, the main questions here are: Did the staff member do the right thing by bringing to the attention of her supervisor the lack of any investigations regarding fairness? Are such investigations required in an assessment that is a high-stakes assessment? Are the supervisor's reasons for not conducting these investigations defensible? Is there a violation of an accepted code of ethics and practice? Would this be an example of an unfair assessment?

Arguments from Philosophy

One way to understand the concept of fairness and justice is to step back from its current theory and practice in assessment and to examine how the concept is used in normative ethics (an important branch of philosophy). In this field, there have been numerous attempts at debating the concept of moral reasoning from normative ethical theories. Ethical dilemmas that we face include right and wrong, fair and unfair, equality and inequality, just and unjust, and individual rights and common good. The main theoretical perspectives and proponents in philosophy are utilitarianism (Bentham, Mill) and social contract/deontology (Kant, Rawls, Sen).[2]

Utilitarianism

The dominant Western philosophical doctrine for many centuries until Rawls's work appeared was that of *utilitarianism* advanced by Bentham and Mill.[3] Its thinking is that the highest principle of morality is to maximize utility and to balance pleasure over pain. It promotes the notion of the greatest happiness of the greatest number of people. As a result, the utility principle trumps individual rights. Related to this, the most important aspect of utilitarianism is *consequentialist* thinking in which outcomes of an event are used as tools to evaluate an institution. Thus, implementing utilitarianism in the assessment context would mean that decisions about an assessment would be made solely on the basis of utility and consequences.

Rawls's *Justice as Fairness*

Rawls' (1971, 2001) theory and arguments of justice and fairness have been the basis for wide discussions in moral philosophy/reasoning from the 1970s onwards. His main focus is on inequalities in citizens' life prospects. In formulating a theory and principle of fairness and justice, he argues that *fairness is prior to justice* but foundational and central to justice and that *fairness relates to persons* and *justice relates to choice over institutions*. In this chapter, these two terms will be used accordingly. To quote from Sen's (2009) summary of Rawls's work:

> In the Rawlsian theory of "justice as fairness", *the idea of fairness relates to persons* (*how to be fair between them*) whereas the Rawlsian principles of *justice apply to the choice of institutions* (*how to identify "just institutions"*). The former leads to the latter in Rawls's analysis. (p. 72, emphasis added)

The case for justice as fairness that Rawls makes is a moral philosophy for a "well-ordered society" that has a "fair system of social cooperation" and has "citizens who are free and equal persons." Rawls's intention here is that, for his theory to work, society has to be well ordered – in other words, democratic – with a representative government and, as Sen puts it, with a "government by discussion" and not just with elections and balloting. Further, Rawls argues that members of such a society should accept the concept of justice and be free and equal to have the moral capacity to do this.

Rawls presents a procedural plan for how a just institution can provide social arrangements that promote justice. He introduces three inter-related concepts: the hypothetical thought experiment, which he called "the original position and the veil of ignorance," "public justification," and "reflective equilibrium." In Rawls's original position and veil of ignorance,

---

[2] Other perspectives include virtue ethics, cosmopolitanism, communitarianism, and postmodernism.
[3] This does not include traditional and theological ethics such as the divine command theory or the natural law theory.

84 Chapter 6 Fairness and Justice in Language Assessment

members of a society are not allowed to know their social position in society, any of their backgrounds (race, ethnicity, or gender), or their endowments (capabilities, talents). Therefore, as members do not know anything about themselves, they will not be able to gamble to become beneficiaries of any benefits. This setup, Rawls argues, would give members a way to derive principles of justice without any biases or prejudices as they know any decisions they make could affect them as well.

The principles of justice Rawls posits that would emerge from such a procedure would have unanimous agreement, although he amended this later (Rawls, 2001, p. 32) to accommodate the idea of "overlapping consensus," as he recognized the limits of agreement on justice in pluralistic democracies where conflicting religious, philosophical, and moral doctrines may make unanimity unlikely. Finally, for justice as fairness to work, Rawls contends, public justification is a necessary part of the process. He argues that it is necessary to justify political judgments to fellow citizens so that public consensus can be reached. He also suggests the use of the methodology of "reflective equilibrium" to help in the public justification process. In this methodology, initial ideas, beliefs, or theories are subjected to reason, reflection, and revision until the ideas, beliefs, or theories reach a state of equilibrium in public justification.[4]

Rawls offers two principles of justice as way of guidance in the design of just institutions. The *first principle of justice* states: Each person has the same indefeasible claim to a fully adequate scheme of equal basic rights and liberties, which scheme is compatible with the same scheme for all (2001, p. 42).

This principle includes five sets of basic liberties: liberty of conscience and freedom of thought, freedom of association, equal political liberties, the rights and liberties that protect the rights and liberties of the person, and rights and liberties covered by the law.

The *second principle of justice* has two parts: The first part, the *equal opportunity principle*, is familiar as examinations in general provide fair equality of opportunity. The institution of examination by assessing abilities opens up opportunities that would otherwise be available only in terms of heredity, nobility, and social position by birth. The second part, *the difference principle*, refers to economic opportunities in which the least advantaged members of society are better off when primary goods are unequally distributed (between least advantaged and more advantaged members) than when primary goods are equally distributed between the two groups.

In summary, in Rawls's theory of justice as fairness, the focus is on developing ideal just institutions by identifying what just institutions would look like. This, Rawls proposes, can be achieved in a well-ordered society with free and equal citizens interested in social cooperation to bring about justice as fairness. By using the original position and the veil of ignorance, principles of justice can be publicly justified by the process of reflective equilibrium.[5] When this is done, principles of justice would emerge as guidance to build a just institution.

Sen's *Idea of Justice*

Sen advances Rawls's thinking significantly with some major ideas. First, he contends that Rawls's theory of justice as fairness is primarily aimed at the ideal of establishing just institutions (which Sen terms "transcendental institutionalism") and that it does not have any

---

[4] Rawls's reflective equilibrium is remarkably similar to Habermas's idea of discourse ethics in which principles are not mirrors of truth but something that emerges from fair argumentation by members in a society.
[5] Rawls is a secular theorist and his theory is in this tradition. There are traditional virtues from religion-based ethics that might overlap with the major secular theories. These could include virtues of consciousness, benevolence, and self-restraint (from Buddhist ethics), humanity and goodness, rightness and duty, consideration and reciprocity, loyalty and commitment (Chinese ethics), neighborly love, natural morality (Judeo-Christian ethics), social and individual duties (classic Hindu ethics), and charity, kindness, and prayer (Islamic ethics).

mechanism to evaluate human transgressions that bring about unjust societies through public reasoning.[6] Sen (2009) contends that Rawls's approach is *arrangement-focused* (justice conceptualized in terms of organizational arrangements like institutions, regulations, behavioral rules, and the active presence of these would indicate that justice is being done). This is in contrast to Sen's view of justice as *realization-focused* understanding of justice (examining what emerges in society, the kind of lives people can lead, given the institutions and rules, but also actual behavior that would inescapably affect human lives).

Second, Sen (2009) invokes Adam Smith's thought experiment of the "impartial spectator." This device, Sen argues, could be used "when judging one's own conduct, 'to examine it as we imagine an impartial spectator would examine it'" (p. 124). Sen argues that this approach of the impartial spectator has a major advantage over Rawls's original position with a veil of ignorance in arriving at principles of justice. Although both approaches attempt to remove the vested interests and goals of individuals, spectators or disinterested people from other societies can participate in deliberations in Smith's approach, whereas outsiders are restricted in the Rawlsian approach. Sen argues that Smith's open impartiality – including the voice of the people who do not belong to the focal group – is superior to Rawls's closed impartiality – restricting the voice of the people to focal group members – as it provides the opportunity for cross-societal and cross-border deliberations.

In a related point, the non-parochial, global perspective view is a central part of Sen's thesis. He is concerned about the parochial nature of nations when it comes to the service of justice for two reasons: First, what happens in a particular country in terms of how its institutions operate can have huge consequences on the rest of the world, and, second, each country or society may have parochial practices that need to come under examination and scrutiny from others with distant judgments who are impartial spectators.[7] Further, the global reach of justice is necessary in a world where globalization is taking place in other areas: trade, commerce, business, travel, technology, and so on.[8] Similarly, Sen also criticizes the view of Asian government leaders from Singapore, Malaysia, and China regarding "(East) Asian values." Their leaders argue that the denial of political and personal freedoms and suppression of media freedoms in exchange for economic growth are part of "Asian values," different from those of the West. This is defective reasoning, Sen argues, as Asian countries have a tradition of democratic values and principles as well.[9] Recall Martin Luther King's warning: "Injustice anywhere is a threat to justice everywhere."[10]

---

[6] This idea is similar to the thinking of Schopenhauer, although Sen does not mention him.

[7] Although Sen does not put it this way, we can assume he advocates, in Cohen and Sabel's words, "equal concern, equal respect, and equal opportunity regardless of any background conditions" (2006, p. 148). Sen cites many examples of this parochial nature: the common practice of the murder of newborn infants in ancient Greece despite the presence of Aristotle and Plato in their midst; more recently, stoning of adulterous women in Taliban Afghanistan, selective abortion of female fetuses in China, Korea, and parts of India, female genital mutilation in parts of Africa, capital punishment in China and the United States and restrictions of personal and media freedoms in North Korea and China.

[8] Nagel (2005) argued against global justice: that outside the state, there is no justice, and therefore as there is no global state, there can be no global justice. But does this mean that a state does not have any humanitarian obligations to its citizens even if the obligations do not lead to egalitarian justice?

[9] Sen (1999) illustrated this through a variety of examples that show the use of democratic ways from the past in Asian states. Examples include democratic Buddhist councils in the 1st and 2nd century AD; Japanese Prince Shotoku's "Constitution of 17 Articles" in the 7th century AD; Emperor Ashoka of India in the 3rd century BCE; and the Moghul Emperor Akbar in the 16th century. It is also not true that all Western or European states are liberal democracies with media freedoms and all Asian states are authoritarian. There are counterexamples too: the early to mid-20th century saw authoritarian regimes in Germany, Italy, Spain, and apartheid South Africa. In contrast, in the mid- to late-20th century, there have been Asian democracies with full media freedoms in India, Japan, South Korea, and Taiwan.

[10] But Sen, like Rawls, for different reasons shied away from a full cosmopolitan approach to justice which holds moral universalism as paramount to moral value.

86 Chapter 6 Fairness and Justice in Language Assessment

Third, Sen argues that public reasoning is a critical component in advancing justice. His requirements are similar to those of Rawls: in this case, a well-ordered society – in other words, a democratic state (in the sense of "government by discussion" with political and personal freedoms) – with free and equal persons (who are capable of challenging injustice) that would be able to safeguard principles of fairness through public justification and reasoning. Such states would have in place transparent mechanisms for the fair selection and use of assessments, public reasoning of the assessment in use (in public forums), and regulations and laws that have adequate provisions for appeals and redress. An authoritarian regime, on the other hand, with few or no political and personal freedoms, will be less compelled to need or allow public justification and reasoning of principles of fairness. The lack of such reasoning along with inadequate accompanying regulations and laws for appeals and redress would make it difficult for such institutions to be just.

In summary, Sen argues that the focus of justice must be on the advancement of the cause of justice through the methodology of public reasoning. His methodology for doing this is through the distant judgment of the impartial spectator in his open partiality mode with outsiders and the world examining and scrutinizing the practices of just institutions. He also indicates the need for a global reach of justice.

Applying Fairness and Justice

General Issues

Drawing on insights from Rawls and Sen on fairness and justice, we can now consider how their ideas and arguments can be applied to language assessment. First, individual rights and inequalities in test takers' life prospects have to be the central focus of the application. The main idea is that assessments ought to be fair and assessment institutions ought to be just to all test takers. Second, Rawls's idea of public justification and Sen's public reasoning have to be part of this application.

Two Principles of Fairness and Justice

Based on Rawls and Sen, two general principles and subprinciples of fairness and justice are proposed[11]:

> **Principle 1** – *the principle of fairness*: An assessment *ought* to be fair to all test takers, that is, there is a presumption of treating every test taker with equal respect.
> **Subprinciple 1**: An assessment *ought* to provide adequate opportunity to acquire the knowledge, abilities, or skills to be assessed for all test takers.
> **Subprinciple 2**: An assessment *ought* to be consistent and meaningful in terms of its test score interpretation for all test takers.
> **Subprinciple 3**: An assessment *ought* to be free of bias against all test takers, in particular by avoiding the assessment of construct-irrelevant matters.
> **Subprinciple 4**: An assessment *ought* to use appropriate access, administration, and standard-setting procedures so that decision making is equitable for all test takers.
> **Principle 2** – *the principle of justice*: An assessment institution *ought* to be just and bring about benefits in society and advance justice through public reasoning.
> **Subprinciple 1**: An assessment institution *ought* to bring benefits to society by making a positive social impact.
> **Subprinciple 2**: An assessment institution *ought* to advance justice through public reasoning of their assessment.

---

[11] Previous versions of the principles were presented in Kunnan (2000, 2004). This revision is more extensive.

A few remarks regarding the principles are necessary here. To begin with, the first principle, the principle of fairness, is prior to the second, the principle of justice, because if the first principle is not satisfied, then the second principle cannot be satisfied. In other words, if the presumption that treating every test taker with equal respect in an assessment is not satisfied, then the assessment will not succeed in being beneficial to society and bring justice to society. In terms of the relationship between the general principles and the subprinciples, the respective subprinciples provide the framings for the two general principles, and therefore, the subprinciples have to be individually satisfied in order for the general principle to be satisfied.

Second, the principles and subprinciples are written as obligations (obligatory actions signaled with the use of *ought*) and not as categorical or unconditional imperatives, but the assumption is that there will be universal application. As argued earlier, justice should be nonparochial and impartial beyond one's society as everyone should be treated in the same manner. This is particularly true of current globalized assessment institutions that operate in numerous countries. It does not seem defensible to propose otherwise, despite the objection of being imperialist as to how there could be different approaches to fairness and justice.

The Principle of Fairness: Grounds and Objections

It is necessary to explicitly make a general case for this principle by articulating the grounds and rejecting some common objections. First, the principle states that an assessment ought to be fair to all test takers, which includes a presumption of treating every test taker with equal respect. This emphasis on the test taker rather than an assessment or its scores should be sufficient to reject the argument that validity of an assessment (or valid score interpretations or validity arguments) guarantees that all test takers will be treated with equal respect. The focus of validity concerns has been either on the assessment itself or at most on various aspects of assessment practice; the focus has never been on the individual test taker.

Second, the subprinciples provide guidance for detailed investigations of assessments so that a number of grounds for the compliance or noncompliance with the principle can be arrived at. Researchers could conduct investigations relevant to the subprinciples to build arguments regarding the general principle of fairness. The subprinciples focus on the test takers' opportunity to learn, the meaningfulness of the assessment to the test taker, and whether the assessment is free of bias and standard setting has been conducted in an equitable manner. These matters are relevant to the individual test taker and affect the test taker positively or adversely depending on the qualities of the assessment. Thus, they are essential components of the general first principle.

The Principle of Justice: Grounds and Objections

As mentioned earlier, this principle follows the first principle but it is a necessary component. First, the principle states that an assessment ought to bring about benefits to society and that such institutions promote just institutions. The overall benefit to society should be the primary motivation to build any assessment in society; that is, if the motivation to build an assessment is not to resolve some difficulties and bring about benefits to society, one could conclude that there may not be a need for the assessment. This is particularly the case if an assessment is likely to cause adverse effects on test takers and society.

Second, the institution of assessment is not any different from institutions like banks or universities. But assessment institutions have a higher responsibility in society than the Department for Beautiful Gardens as assessment institutions are responsible for awarding benefits to test takers that can alter their life prospects. If such institutions bring benefits and just institutions, then the principle of justice is satisfied.

Finally, while it is possible that assessment institutions may have different ways of defending their assessments, it is essential that there is public reasoning of assessments. This can be offered through public forums such as conferences or research reports available to the public.

88   Chapter 6 Fairness and Justice in Language Assessment

Challenges from Vignettes

Let us now consider vignettes from different assessment contexts that illustrate some real-world challenges. These challenges need to be resolved by assessment developers, administrators, score users such as administrators, teachers, and test takers, and decision makers. Some of the vignettes are related to the principle of fairness while others are related to the principle of justice.

Vignette 3: Defective Tasks

Imagine there were two forms of a paper and pencil assessment – Forms A and B. The forms belonged to a high-stakes university admissions assessment. It was known previously through pretesting that there were a few defective tasks in the 2 forms: 10 tasks in Form A and 5 tasks in Form B out of a total of 100 tasks in each. But the administrator went ahead and used both forms as a cost–benefit analysis conducted earlier showed that only 10% of the test takers who took Form A and 5% of the test takers who took Form B were misclassified as failed due to the defective tasks. She felt these figures were within the usual margin of error. The administrator also wrote in her report that the cost of replacing the defective tasks (designing and writing new tasks, pretesting them, assembling them into the forms, and printing the new assessments) would be much higher than that of errors in classification, although she did not assign a monetary value to the misclassified test takers' lost opportunities due to the errors.

If we consider the different philosophical persuasions, each may take a view that supports or criticizes the actions of the administrator. The utilitarian could take the view that the cost–benefit analysis provided the basis for the administrator's decision, and that such decisions have to be made in order to run a profitable business. The utilitarian could also concede though that the administrator should have preferred Form B to Form A as it had utility. The contractarian could argue that the administrator did not act morally as she did not uphold the rights of all test takers to a fair assessment by holding defective assessments. These arguments could lead us to some important questions: What should the administrator have done? Which of these perspectives appeals to us? What is the right thing to do?

Vignette 4: Compensation for Misclassification

Continuing with Vignette 3 and expanding it ... Imagine further that the administrator was convinced of her error and agreed to pay compensation to the test takers who were misclassified as failed. She offered a free retake of the assessment at a later date (as per the contract issued by the agency) but the results would be available only after the completion of the university admissions cycle. The test takers were not satisfied with the remedy offered: Some test takers wanted more compensation, while others planned to file a lawsuit in court against the assessment agency.

This action raises additional questions regarding the right thing to do. The utilitarian could claim that the consequences of the assessment were mostly successful as most test takers were assessed appropriately, thus satisfying the principle of maximizing utility and the maxim of "greatest good for the greatest number of people." Further, as the assessment did not provide sufficient utility for these test takers who were erroneously misclassified, they were offered compensation as per the contract. The contractarian could argue that the administrator did not carry out her duty and therefore should be tried for dereliction or breach of duty, as she did not uphold the rights of all test takers to a fair assessment. The argument could then be made that the administrator and her agency should face a tort, product liability, or a similar lawsuit that would be available in a just institution. These are simplified arguments from different perspectives, but they nevertheless indicate how difficult it is to do the right thing. Both the vignettes above pose problems for the principle of fairness and in particular subprinciples 3 and 4 and the principle of justice and in particular subprinciple 2.

Vignette 5: Selecting an Assessment

Now imagine a school teacher – or a group of teachers – were authorized by the school principal to choose an assessment for a grade 8 reading class in English. The teachers had to choose from three assessments that were commercially available: Test A was developed by a well-established company known for its quality products, the test was traditional and was broadly suitable in terms of content, it was normed for the national population, and it cost $500 for a class of 40. Test B was developed by a small local company, it was highly suitable in terms of content, it was normed for the local population and checked for fairness, it was proven to offer accurate results and useful diagnostic information, and it cost $800 for a class set of 40. Test C was an innovative test developed by teachers from another local school, it had not been analyzed yet but was available for free for the class.

The main question is: On what grounds should the teachers choose from these assessments? Should the decision be based on cost? If the decision were to be made on this ground, the choice would be Test C even though the assessment had not been analyzed; the argument could be that the assessment was not high stakes in grade 8. Another consideration would be consequences and fairness – whether the assessment would have consequences that were beneficial to the students and the community. If the decision were to be made on this ground, the choice would be Test B. This would appeal to the consequentialist doctrine. Yet another consideration would be the quality of the organization developing the assessment. If this was the ground, then it would be Test A. You will see that the choice is not straightforward and the teachers have to weigh several factors such as quality, cost, and so on in order to make their choice.

Vignette 6: What Was the Quality of the Assessment?

Imagine a high-stakes high school exit examination that is conducted by the ministry of education in a country. The examination had been in use for many years, and students worked hard during the months prior to the examination. After the examination, some students got together and exchanged thoughts on the examination. They concluded that some of the questions were tasks and topics that were new to them. When the results were announced, it turned out these students had received low grades. Apart from feeling upset, the students could do nothing else (there was no review or appeal process in place) but their parents went to the ministry and complained that something was wrong with the examination. The ministry officials said that there could not be anything wrong as their examinations were written by expert senior teachers who had been doing this for decades. When pressed to show that the examination was an appropriate assessment procedure, the ministry officials defended their examination by saying there were no prior complaints and therefore no analysis of the examination was conducted as it was not necessary.

The main question here is whether the ministry had the motivation and expertise to provide the best possible examination. There were numerous problems with the examination from an equal rights perspective (a Rawlsian concern): Did some of the students not have the opportunity to learn all the material? Did their school or teacher perhaps not cover all the topics? In which case, did the assessment have utility (a utilitarian concern)? Did the ministry's regulations not have any provision for review or appeals? Further, were there no analyses of the examination tasks conducted although they were written by experts? Were there no research studies that examined the quality of the assessments and the test performance?

90   Chapter 6 Fairness and Justice in Language Assessment

Was the examination providing a beneficial service to the community? Did the ministry owe the student community public justification (Rawlsian requisites)? Finally, was the ministry acting responsibly? In general, Rawlsian theorists would in particular be up in arms with the ministry's lack of provision for basic rights to the students and its dereliction of duty to the students and community.

Vignette 7: Public Reasoning of the Assessment

Continuing with Vignette 7 and expanding it ... Imagine that the parents of the students who received low grades protested against the ministry's approach and demanded that they provide a public justification of the assessment. The ministry replied with a firm NO as it had never responded to such a request before and did not consider it necessary to do so.

Once again, the test takers were denied basic freedoms such as the basic right to be treated with respect and dignity and to have fair assessments and assessment practice. They could also argue that public reasoning (in public forums) would be the only way to ensure that the assessment is fair and the institution is just. Both these vignettes pose problems in terms of the principle of fairness and all its subprinciples. Vignette 7 in particular poses a problem for the principle of justice and its subprinciple 2.

Vignette 8: The Role of Differential Pricing

Imagine you received a questionnaire from a well-known assessment developer and publisher who is planning on introducing differential pricing to test takers for different services. Which of these would you find acceptable? The proposal is higher test-taker fees for new services. Thus, there would be two levels of pricing: regular pricing for regular assessment and premium pricing for additional services. Here are the additional services for premium pricing: Better assessments with higher reliability and thorough validation and fairness studies, individual diagnostic feedback instead of generic feedback, better raters who are experienced and not severe in their ratings, faster turn-around time for results, front row seating for the listening section (where audio speakers are in front of the test room), fast-track line for speaking tests/interviews, better test room facilities (air-conditioning, heating, plus seats), relaxed time conditions (more and frequent breaks), assistance from spell and grammar checks for the writing test, upgraded technology (computers, monitors, keyboard and mouse, color photos, and video), accommodations for test takers with disabilities, no experimental section included in the assessment, repeat assessment within a few days, re-evaluation of assessment performance by two human raters, and return of responses to tasks to test taker (selected and constructed responses on items/tasks).

The main questions are: For which of these services would we consider differential pricing appropriate? On what grounds would we accept or not accept differential pricing? Is the market forcing us to change our ethical behavior? Is there an obligation on the part of the assessment developer to offer some of these services without differential pricing? Would the differential pricing for some of these services violate the principles of fairness and justice?

Advancing Fairness and Justice

The earlier section considered how Rawls's and Sen's ideas can be applied to language assessments in order to design and establish just institutions by examining hypothetical vignettes. But it is also important to simultaneously explore how institutions can advance the principles of fairness and justice and remove existing unfairness and injustice in current society. Any example of unjust practice should motivate skeptics about the need for action should such practices be identified. For example, recalling the discriminatory practice behind the dictation test given to immigrants in Australia in the 1900s during the country's White Australia policy (see McNamara & Ryan, 2011). If such a policy were to be in place now, we could ask on what moral principles such an assessment could be defended.

Conclusion

This chapter provides a principled foundational basis for fairness and justice in language assessment by drawing on work from Rawls and Sen. Applying arguments from Rawls and Sen to language assessment has provided the background that led to the principles of fairness and justice as instruments being used to evaluate assessments and assessment institutions. The methodology of how principles of fairness and justice may be derived by assessment agencies remains a concern. Rawls and Sen offer ways in which this can be done through the original position/veil of ignorance and the impartial spectator. These or other methods should help put in place mechanisms that enable the development of fair assessments and just institutions.

As Sen argued, it is not sufficient to use principles to design and establish just institutions: Efforts should be made to remove manifest injustice that exists in the world today. He argued that a nonparochial global justice view would be best suited to establish and review unjust institutions. This is critical with globalized assessment institutions. These institutions need to be evaluated by enforcing categorical imperatives with obligations and *ought-to* principles, particularly general principles. This chapter also put forth the idea that there should be public reasoning of assessments. This would mean that whether an assessment is fair or not and whether an institution is just or not should be a matter of public discourse for which public reasoning is necessary. This is a critical part of justifying fair assessments and just institutions.

Finally, the main point of this chapter is not to debate whether the putative principles of fairness and justice (proposed in this chapter) are appropriate or workable for all contexts but to find principles that can guide us to the right action when we encounter examples of unfair assessments and unjust institutions. We hope therefore the answers to the preliminary questions that were raised at the beginning of this chapter can now be answered by focusing on the right thing to do in setting up fair assessments and just institutions and the right thing to do to remove any unfairness and injustice.

Discussion Questions

1. Which aspects of fairness or unfairness have you experienced yourself or in your teaching or professional career?
2. How can you find ways to advance justice in your institutional setting?

References

APA (American Psychological Association), AERA (American Educational Research Association), & NCME (National Council for Measurement in Education). (1999). *Standards for educational and psychological testing*. Author.

Bachman, L. F. (2005). Building and supporting a case for test use. *Language Assessment Quarterly*, 2(1), 1–30.

Davies, A. (2010). Test fairness: a response. *Language Testing*, 27, 171–176.

Ferne, T., & Rupp, A. (2007). A synthesis of 15 years of research on DIF in language testing: methodological advances, challenges, and recommendation. *Language Assessment Quarterly, 4*(2), 113–148.

Hartigan, J., & Wigdor, A. (1989). *Fairness in employment testing.* National Academy Press.

Kane, M. (2010). Validity and fairness. *Language Testing, 27,* 177–182.

Kunnan, A. J. (1997). Connecting validation and fairness in language testing. In A. Huhta, V. Kohonen, L. Kurki-Suonio & S. Luoma (Eds.), *Current developments and alternatives in language assessment* (pp. 85–105). University of Jyväskylä.

Kunnan, A. J. (2000). Fairness and justice for all. In A. J. Kunnan (Ed.), *Fairness and validation in language assessment* (pp. 1–14). Cambridge University Press.

Kunnan, A. J. (2004). Test fairness. In M. Milanovic & C. Weir (Eds.), *European language testing in a global context* (pp. 27–48). Cambridge University Press.

Kunnan, A. J. (2008). Towards a model of test evaluation: using the test fairness and wider context frameworks. In L. Taylor & C. Weir (Eds.), *Multilingualism and assessment: Achieving transparency, assuring quality, sustaining diversity: Papers from the ALTE Conference in Berlin, Germany* (pp. 229–251). Cambridge University Press.

Kunnan, A. J. (2010). Fairness matters and Toulmin's argument structures. *Language Testing, 27,* 183–189.

Kunnan, A. J., & Davidson, F. (2004). Situated ethics in language assessment. In D. Douglas (Ed.), *English language tests and testing practice* (pp. 115–132). NAFSA.

McNamara, T., & Ryan, K. (2011). Fairness versus justice in language testing: the place of English literacy in the Australian Citizenship Test. *Language Assessment Quarterly, 8,* 161–178.

Nagel, T. (2005). The problem of global justice. *Philosophy & Public Affairs, 33,* 113–147.

Rawls, J. (1971). *A theory of justice.* Harvard University Press.

Rawls, J. (2001). In E. Kelly (Ed.), *Justice as fairness: A restatement.* Harvard University Press.

Sen, A. (1999). *Development as freedom.* Random House.

Sen, A. (2009). *The idea of justice.* Penguin Books.

Walters, F. S. (2012). Fairness. In G. Fulcher & F. Davidson (Eds.), *The Routledge handbook of language testing* (pp. 469–494). Routledge.

Xi, X. (2010). How do we go about investigating test fairness? *Language Testing, 27,* 147–170.

Suggested Readings

Freeman, S. (2007). *Rawls.* Routledge.

Rawls, J. (1999). *The law of peoples.* Harvard University Press.

Sandel, M. (2009). *Justice: What's the right thing to do?* Penguin.

Smith, A. (1759/2009). *The theory of moral sentiments.* Penguin Books.

CHAPTER 7

Statistics and Software for Test Revisions

Yo In'nami and Rie Koizumi

Introduction

Statistical analysis plays an important role in language assessment because quantified information available from tests/tasks/questionnaires helps test developers and users to provide a clear and defensible interpretation of test scores. Therefore, it is not surprising that language testers have taken advantage of statistical analysis to examine the quality of test items (e.g., Kunnan et al., 2022), pre–post changes of variables of interest (e.g., Elder et al., 2005), and variables related to test performance (e.g., Ockey, 2011), to name just a few. Although statistical analysis itself is a topic of interest in psychometrics, language testers must embed it in the validity argument of test interpretation and use, specifically in relation to the bridges of inferences, such as evaluation, generalization, explanation, and utilization (Bachman & Palmer, 2010; Chapelle & Voss, 2021; see Chapelle & Lee, 2021, for reviews of approaches to validation). This chapter mainly focuses on the stages that provide evidence related to the evaluation and generalization inferences – key stages from which the remaining inferences can evolve and in which tests are revised iteratively. To achieve this goal, this chapter is divided into a theoretical overview followed by examples.

Evaluation, Generalization, and Test Revision

Evaluation concerns the appropriateness of the processes through which an examinee's performance is converted into test scores (Chapelle et al., 2008; Kunnan & Carr, 2013). Generalization concerns the consistency of test scores across raters, test items or tasks, test occasions, test forms, or others that may produce variability in test scores (Chapelle et al., 2008). Test performance should be appropriately quantified and scored so that the resulting scores are representative of the examinee's performance. This process is simpler for multiple-choice tests, which can be scored dichotomously (as right or wrong), either by machine or by hand, according to a set of answer keys and/or a list of acceptable answers. The situation becomes more complex for performance testing of speaking and writing skills. These skills are scored polytomously (for example, on a scale of 0–2) by raters according to rating scales describing a typical response or ability for each level. Compared to machine scoring, use of human raters can bring in irrelevant factors that may affect score judgments, undermining the score-based validity (Knoch et al., 2021).

The Concise Companion to Language Assessment, First Edition. Edited by Antony John Kunnan.
© 2025 John Wiley & Sons, Inc. Published 2025 by John Wiley & Sons, Inc.

94 **Chapter 7** Statistics and Software for Test Revisions

When researching the evaluation and generalization inferences, language testers should understand the distributions of examinee scores; evaluate the statistical characteristics of items, tasks, and tests; and analyze the rating scales and raters. The analysis of rating scales and raters is a more advanced topic but is addressed as it is essential for performance assessment. The following sections examine each of these issues in turn and are intended to serve as an introduction to relevant chapters in the volume.

Understanding the Distributions of Examinee Scores

Quantifying score distributions is important as it helps us understand what scores are typically observed and how much variability there is in the scores. The distributions of examinee scores can be examined using measures of central tendency, which describe the location of most scores in the distribution. Measures of central tendency include the mean, median, and mode. The mean is the average and is the most used of the three measures. The mean is calculated by summing all responses and dividing the number by the number of responses. The median is the middle value of an ordered list. It is calculated by first arranging all values from smallest to largest, and then identifying the middle value. If the list contains an even number of items, then the median is the average of the middle two. The mode is the most frequently observed number in a sample or population. For example, when the responses of 10 students in a 5-scale questionnaire item are 1, 1, 2, 2, 2, 3, 3, 4, 5, and 5, the mean is 2.8 ([1+1+2+2+2+3+3+4+5+5]/10). The median is 2.5 ([2+3]/2) and the mode is 2, as the number 2 appears most frequently. The median and mode are particularly useful for small samples and/or non-normally distributed data. In such cases, the mean can be influenced by extreme scores and so is less likely to represent the distribution of data well.

In addition to the above measures of central tendency, it is useful to study measures of dispersion, which show the degree of variation in the distribution of scores. They allow one to understand the data distribution from a different perspective. Further, because many statistical methods are based on score variability, it is important to report and interpret measures of dispersion. One of the most widely used measures is the standard deviation, a measure of the degree to which test scores deviate from the mean, expressed in terms of the original metric unit. This is obtained by first calculating the variance: Calculate the difference between each individual score and the mean, square the results, sum them, and divide the answer by the sample size minus 1. The standard deviation is defined to be the square root of the variance. The formula is shown in equation 7.1, where X represents individual scores, M is the mean, and N is the sample size. The Greek letter sigma Σ is a summation sign and indicates the sum of the values $(X - M)^2$. Note that the denominator $N - 1$ is used to estimate the standard deviation in the population based on the sample that is currently analyzed (in case of equation 7.1). This standard deviation is termed a *sample* standard deviation, or an *estimated population* standard deviation. In contrast, the denominator N is used to calculate the standard deviation in the sample that is currently analyzed, by considering this sample is the reflection of the population the researchers are investigating (termed a *population* standard deviation). Although there are two types of standard deviation, equation 7.1 is typically employed.

$$\text{Standard deviation} = \sqrt{\frac{\Sigma(X - M)^2}{N - 1}} \tag{7.1}$$

Another useful distribution measure is the skewness of the data, which shows the degree to which the distribution is asymmetrical relative to a normal distribution. A distribution with few low test scores and many high test scores is negatively skewed (with a long tail on the left side and most of the values on the right side of the distribution), whereas a distribution with many low test scores and few high test scores is positively skewed (with a longer tail on the right side and most of the values on the left side of the distribution). The shape of the distribution is further described by its kurtosis, which can be interpreted as measuring how peaked the distribution is relative to a normal distribution. Peaked distributions result from many examinees achieving similar scores. A distribution with a flat-topped curve has negative kurtosis and is called a platykurtic distribution. In contrast, a distribution with a high peak has positive kurtosis and is called a leptokurtic distribution. A distribution somewhere between these two has zero kurtosis and is called a mesokurtic distribution. The details of calculating skewness and kurtosis indices are out of the scope of this chapter. Readers are referred to Glass and Hopkins (1996).

An example of a distribution with zero skewness and kurtosis is the normal distribution. When data conform to a normal distribution, the mean, median, and mode have the same value. Data normality holds significance because many inferential statistical techniques rely on the assumption of normality in the data. Consequently, when dealing with datasets that deviate severely from normality, the results may be questionable. In such cases, addressing non-normality through data transformation or opting for statistical methods less sensitive to non-normality might be necessary.

One way to judge whether the distribution is normal is to conduct statistical significance tests for skewness and kurtosis (e.g., Tabachnick & Fidell, 2019). The statistical significance of the skewness is examined using z-values (equation 7.2), which show the degree to which the distributions are skewed in terms of the units of standard error of skewness, s_s, defined in equation 7.3 (N is the sample size).

$$z = \frac{\text{skewness}}{s_s} \tag{7.2}$$

$$S_s = \sqrt{\frac{6}{N}} \tag{7.3}$$

The statistical significance of kurtosis is again examined using z-values (equation 7.4), but this time showing the degree to which the distributions are peaked compared with the units of standard error of kurtosis, s_k. See equation 7.5 for the definition of s_k (N is again the sample size).

$$z = \frac{\text{kurtosis}}{s_k} \tag{7.4}$$

$$S_k = \sqrt{\frac{24}{N}} \tag{7.5}$$

If the z-values exceed 2.58 ($p < 0.01$) or 3.29 ($p < 0.001$), the data are considered to be non-normally distributed. However, as stressed by Tabachnick and Fidell (2019), the standard errors of skewness and kurtosis shrink in large sample sizes, which can produce statistically significant skewness and kurtosis values, even though the distribution looks normal. Thus, with large samples, making substantive decisions based on the visual inspection of the data, using histograms or box plots, for example (see the Reporting Practice and Examples section), is preferred.

Evaluating the Statistical Characteristics of Items, Tasks, and Tests

Along with the score distribution of examinee scores, we should also be concerned with the statistical properties of items, tasks, and tests. This is important, particularly in pilot testing, because such analysis (called item analysis) shows whether items, tasks, and tests are functioning as expected. Some items may be too easy or too difficult, or some distractors (i.e., any incorrect options in a multiple-choice item) may not be working properly, for example, because they are so irrelevant to the text that they were little chosen by examinees. Thus, item analysis contributes to revising and improving test items so that the test facilitates valid and fair score-based decision-making.

Item analysis can be conducted in terms of item facility, item discrimination, and distractor analysis. First, item facility (or item difficulty) shows the proportion of examinees who responded to an item correctly. It ranges from 0.00 to 1.00, with a high value suggesting that the item was easy for the test-taker sample. In norm-referenced tests (NRTs), we compare an examinee's performance against that of other examinees. Here, item facility should be around 0.50 to maximally differentiate examinees (e.g., Bachman, 2004; Brown & Hudson, 2002), with values between 0.30 and 0.70 generally considered permissible. In criterion-referenced tests (CRTs), we want to know whether an examinee has reached a certain level of skill/ ability, as judged by a predetermined criterion (e.g., mastery/non-mastery). However, there are no guidelines on the standard of item facility. This is because, in CRTs such as achievement tests, everyone should ideally master the skills taught in the course, so it is not uncommon or undesirable for item facility values to be close to 1.00. Items with high facility values show that examinees have generally mastered a particular skill, whereas items with low facility values show that examinees generally need more time to master such a skill. Another reason is that CRTs also include professional certification/licensing (e.g., the Occupational English Test) and general proficiency tests. In these contexts, it is arguably not at all expected for all examinees to do well on the test.

Second, item discrimination is a measure of how well an item distinguishes between groups of examinees with different proficiency levels. For NRTs, one measure is the item discrimination index. This is calculated by subtracting the item facility for the lower group from that of the higher group. Upper and lower groups can be defined as either the upper 50% and lower 50% of the examinee group, based on the total test score, or as the upper and lower 27% or 33% of the examinee group. For example, if everyone in the higher group answered an item correctly (item facility is 1.00) and everyone in the lower group answered it incorrectly (item facility is 0.00), the item discrimination has a perfect value of 1.00 (1.00 − 0.00). Values over 0.40 are generally considered adequate (Carr, 2011). For CRTs, Brown and Hudson (2002) explain two statistics. First, the difference index is calculated by subtracting the item facility for the non-mastery group from that of the mastery group. This is similar to the item discrimination index for NRTs, the difference being that we focus here on the mastery/ non-mastery groups rather than higher/lower groups. The mastery and non-mastery groups are defined on the basis of some independent criterion. Alternatively, in a pre–post, repeated-measures design, students take a pretest, receive instruction, and then take a posttest. Here, we obtain the difference index by subtracting the item facility of the students before instruction (the non-mastery group) from that after instruction (the mastery group). However, it is not always possible to calculate the difference index, because it requires that two different groups, identified by experts, complete a test or that the same group completes the test on two different occasions. Another useful method for CRTs is the B index, which is the difference between examinees who passed and those who failed a test. The mastery and non-mastery groups are defined on the basis of their test performance. This requires determining the cut-off score for passing or failing the test before analyzing the data. In general, values over 0.40 are considered adequate for CRTs.

Another measure of item discrimination is based on the correlation between the item (a dichotomous variable) and the total score (of all the items or of the remaining items except for the item in focus; either is a continuous variable). One example for NRTs is the point-biserial correlation, a type of Pearson correlation ranging from –1.00 to +1.00. Another is the biserial correlation, which assumes underlying continuity for a dichotomous variable, in contrast with the point-biserial correlation that does not. The biserial correlation generally shows higher values than the point-biserial and can lie outside the range –1.00 to 1.00. Positive values on either correlation show that high-scoring examinees on the entire test performed better on a given item than low-scoring examinees, whereas negative values show the opposite. Values over 0.30 are considered adequate for both correlations. For CRTs, item discrimination is based on the correlation between the item and mastery/non-mastery. Another measure of item discrimination is ϕ (phi), which is considered adequate when the value is over 0.30. Item discrimination indices for NRTs may not work well for CRTs, because CRTs do not often have sufficient variance in test scores.

Analysis on distractors can provide further information on item quality that may not be revealed through item facility and discrimination. For example, when inadequate item facility or low item discrimination is observed, a distractor analysis may indicate that distractors perform poorly because they are evidently incorrect and thus not selected by examinees or that distractors are overly attractive that even high-proficiency test takers may select them. A comprehensive explanation of distractor analysis is beyond the scope of this chapter, and interested readers can refer to Carr (2011) for details. Note that this section has described classical test theory, which contrasts with item response theory (described in another chapter in this volume). For details on the relationships between classical test theory values and item response theory parameters, see de Ayala (2022).

Analyzing Rating Scales and Raters

Rating scales refer to a set of level descriptions on behavior against which an examinee's ability is judged (e.g., McNamara et al., 2019). Well-known examples include the speaking rating scale of the Internet-based Test of English as a Foreign Language® (TOEFL iBT), which judges performance on a five-point scale in terms of delivery, language use, and topic development (Educational Testing Service, 2022). In human-scored tests of speaking or writing, or even in tests of listening or reading in an open-ended format, some kinds of rating scales are used. Thus, unless scoring is dichotomous, as in conventional multiple-choice tests, rating scales play an essential role in assessment.

There are a few issues surrounding rating scales and raters. First, rating scales, both holistic and analytic, must be developed carefully to eliminate ambiguity and ensure consistent scoring. Consistent scoring is important as it indicates the performance was less likely to be influenced by unintended variables. A well-constructed scale articulates the construct being measured, signaling to the raters what aspects they should focus on in performance and to the examinees what skill or behavior they are expected to demonstrate and how the skill or behavior is evaluated.

Second, raters must be trained to familiarize themselves with the assessment tasks and rating criteria. Newly hired raters are presented with previously scored exemplar performances and are required to rate a different set of performances at a predetermined level of consistency (i.e., reliability). Rater consistency or rater variability can be checked using *inter*-rater reliability and *intra*-rater reliability. Inter-rater reliability is the degree of rating consistency between different raters on the same set of examinee responses, while intra-rater reliability concerns a single rater on the same set of examinee responses on different occasions. These two concepts of reliability are calculated using correlations between different raters or correlations of a single rater between different occasions. However, correlations are not sensitive to differences in the mean between ratings, and even a perfect correlation of 1 can be achieved with zero

98 Chapter 7 Statistics and Software for Test Revisions

agreement (Council of Europe, 2009). This underlines the importance of reporting agreement percentages (exact and adjacent). Further, for a scale with a small number of categories, exact agreement could occur by chance alone. Kappa statistics corrects for this and should also be reported (Cook, 2005).

A broader tool that can be employed for analyzing rater variability is generalizability (G) theory. G theory is a flexible, statistical framework for systematically investigating the reliability of instruments under specific conditions by considering multiple sources of error (Shavelson & Webb, 1991). These sources of error are called facets (i.e., variables) in G theory and also in many-facet Rasch measurement as will be discussed below. G theory allows us to investigate, in a single analysis, the relative and interactive effects of various factors such as examinees (persons), raters, items/tasks, and occasions on reliability (e.g., Kunnan, 1992; Sawaki & Xi, 2019). For example, it is possible to estimate what percentage of the variance of test scores is due to factors associated with rater or rater-by-task interaction. This analysis is referred to as a G study. The G study is a variance components analysis that is used to calculate the G- and D-coefficients. Further, we can determine optimum measurement designs by systematically simulating how a change in factors would affect reliability. For example, would four raters rating once be more reliable than two raters rating twice? This type of question can be answered in the optimization phase, called a decision (D) study.

Additionally, valuable information on rating scales and raters can be gained by using many-facet Rasch measurement (McNamara et al., 2019). It is particularly well suited to analyzing rater-based performance assessments. Many-facet Rasch measurement can model the characteristics of rating scales, raters, and other aspects of performance assessment settings (e.g., task and interviewer) and consider those (and interactive) effects on estimates of examinee ability and task difficulty. The results include rater severity/leniency, rater consistency, interaction between rater and item (called rater-by-item bias), and the difficulty level of each task. Such information is useful in rater training and item/task revision (e.g., McNamara et al., 2019). It should be noted that, although G theory indicates various sources of error separately, it does not help us correct such errors in the calibration of ratings (Eckes, 2015). For example, even if we know some raters are too harsh, we cannot take that into consideration in rating calibration using G theory. However, this is possible in many-facet Rasch measurement, which presents examinees' ability and task difficulty estimates that are statistically adjusted if raters are found to be consistently severe or lenient, although this is only possible if rater behavior is consistent and does not fluctuate considerably (see Eckes, 2015; McNamara et al., 2019, for further comparisons of G theory and many-facet Rasch measurement). Finally, it is worth noting that both G theory and many-facet Rasch measurement can be used for both NRT and CRT analyses.

Software for Test Revision

Many computer programs, such as R, SAS, and SPSS, can deal with the statistics described in this chapter and can compute the distributions of examinee scores (mean, median, mode, standard deviation, skewness, and kurtosis), item characteristics (item facility and item discrimination), and rater consistency (inter-rater and intra-rater reliability). For guidance on using R and SPSS, see Larson-Hall (2016), and for SAS, see Field and Miles (2010). If rater consistency is not a primary concern, ITEMAN – software tailored for item analysis – will suffice and may be preferable as it is easy to use and has been written particularly for the purpose of item analysis. Its output is particularly informative, giving a detailed figure and table of statistics for each item. It also allows users to specify criteria for an acceptable range for item facility, item mean, and point-biserial and biserial values. For example, one can specify that all point-biserial correlations be between 0.30 and 1.00, and any items outside this range (e.g., items with negative point-biserials) are flagged and presented in a list. Particularly useful for item analysis and revision are quantile plots, which graphically show the behavior of each item. Plots are created by dividing the examinees into subgroups (the number of which we can decide) based on the total test score and by examining the proportion of examinees in each subgroup that selected each option. Quantile plots are a newly added feature to ITEMAN version 4. For video tutorials on how to use ITEMAN, see ASCpsychometrics (2011a, b).

However, ITEMAN, SAS, and SPSS are all commercial programs, and statistics for CRTs are usually not available. Using spreadsheet editing software such as Microsoft Excel is another possibility. Although this is a general-purpose software, Excel is widely available and provides a range of basic statistics in a friendly graphic user interface. To the best of our knowledge, the most useful resource for Excel currently available for language testers is Carr (2011), which comes with Excel worksheets for hands-on practice and three hours of video tutorials that demonstrate the procedures used in the worksheets. The worksheets and tutorials cover the issues of item analysis comprehensively, ranging from creating a class grade book in Excel, calculating descriptive statistics and correlations, constructing a histogram and a frequency polygon, performing item analysis for NRTs and CRTs, to calculating reliability (e.g., Cronbach's alpha) and standard error of measurement. Step-by-step procedures for completing the worksheets are also offered in the book. However, Carr cautions that Excel would be adequate and useful for item analysis for low-stakes tests, but that specialized software is recommended for high-stakes tests.

Further, although R, SAS, and SPSS can be used for G theory analysis, GENOVA, mGENOVA, urGENOVA (Brennan, 2001), and EduG (Cardinet et al., 2010) offer a variety of analytical options and are fast and efficient, as they are written specifically with G theory analyses in mind. GENOVA and EduG are used for univariate analysis, and mGENOVA and urGENOVA for multivariate analysis. A multivariate analysis is appropriate when a test includes multiple sections or subtests, and one can investigate the reliability of each section or the whole test (see Kim, 2022 for details).

For many-facet Rasch measurement, FACETS has often been used among language testers. It is designed to construct measures from rater-mediated ratings and complex data. FACETS can manage heterogeneous tests, such as those consisting of a mixture of dichotomous responses and rater-mediated polytomous ratings, with a complete rating design, in which all raters rate all examinees. FACETS can also analyze data with a partial rating design, in which some rate a group of examinees and others rate a partially overlapping different group of examinees. ConQuest, RUMM, PARSCALE, LPCM-WIN, and eRm all offer many-facet Rasch measurement analysis. These programs differ in their parameter estimation methods, although this may make little difference in practice. For details and further comparison of programs, see Eckes (2015), Sick (2009), and Aryadoust et al. (2021).

Reporting Practice and Examples

In this section, we describe the reporting practice and examples with the research community as the target audience in forms of academic articles. While researchers analyze data in test development using methods from many perspectives, they may focus on reporting the results most relevant to their research purposes or contexts, making less relevant ones available as supplementary materials. Furthermore, even with the same results, they can be conveyed more effectively using adequate types of tables and figures.

Distribution of Examinee Scores

Box plots provide a good way to report statistics showing the distributions of examinee scores. Larson-Hall and Herrington (2010) strongly recommend box plots (box-and-whisker plots)

Chapter 7 Statistics and Software for Test Revisions

over bar graphs. Although bar graphs are the most basic graph and have been conventionally used, they are far less informative than box plots because they only convey central tendency, whereas box plots also show the distributions of groups, including the degree of dispersion and outliers in the data. Figure 7.1 shows an example of a bar graph and a box plot for four groups of examinees ($n = 140$ each) taking the Test of English for International Communication (TOEIC). In Figure 7.1b, the bold horizontal line in each box represents the median value. The length from the bottom to the top of the box shows the range between the first quartile

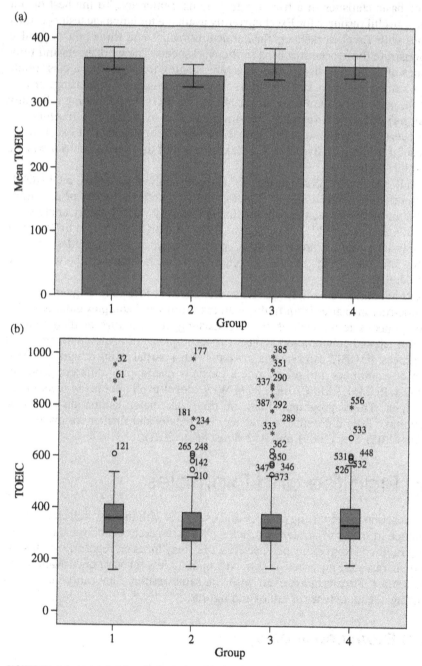

FIGURE 7.1 A bar graph (a) and a box plot (b) visualizing the same data. *Note.* Error bars in the bar graph represent 95% confidence intervals for means.

(the 25th percentile) and the third quartile (the 75th percentile), which encompasses the middle 50% of the score distribution. This is also called the interquartile range (IQR). There are two *whiskers* above and below the box: The bottom bar of the whisker shows either the minimum value or the median minus 1.5 × IQR, whichever is greater; the top bar of the whisker shows either the maximum value or the median plus 1.5 × IQR, whichever is lesser. Values outside the whiskers are outliers. For example, group 1 had a median of approximately 360, first- and third-quartile scores of 300 and 400, and a minimum value of 180 (as seen by the bottom bar of the whisker). A score of 510, calculated as 360 + 1.5 × [400 − 300], constitutes the highest non-outlier score (see the top bar). In actual data interpretation, one needs to refer to descriptive statistics to know the exact values of boxes and bars. While the means and the 95% confidence intervals in the bar graph in Figure 7.1a seem to be essentially the same across the groups, the box plot in Figure 7.1b shows in addition that the range of scores was equally wide (based on the upper and lower bars) and that groups 2–4 had more outliers than did group 1. These results suggest that, even if confidence intervals are reported along with means in a bar graph, the score distributions are better depicted in a box plot. However, box plots do not show mean scores. Therefore, since means are widely used, not only in primary studies but also in secondary studies (such as meta-analysis), the mean and other descriptive statistics (e.g., standard deviation, skewness, and kurtosis) should be reported along with box plots. The SPSS syntax for the bar graphs and box plots described here is included in Appendices 7.A and 7.B.

Item Analysis

To report statistics showing item characteristics, a quantile plot for each item is recommended. For example, Figure 7.2a shows a three-option, multiple-choice grammar item with five ability groups in an NRT (1 being low, 5 being high, and $n = 10$ per group). A good item has an upward trend in the line for the correct answer, with a downward trend for the incorrect answers. For item 5 (see below), the line for the correct answer (option 1) was generally upward, whereas the lines for the two distractors (2 and 3) were generally downward across the five ability groups. This shows that examinees with higher ability were more likely to answer this item correctly. In fact, approximately 70% of the lowest-ability examinees chose the correct answer, whereas almost all of the highest-ability examinees chose the correct answer. These results show that the item discriminated well between examinees. Table 7.1 shows that the point-biserial discrimination value was 0.370. As it exceeded 0.300, it is

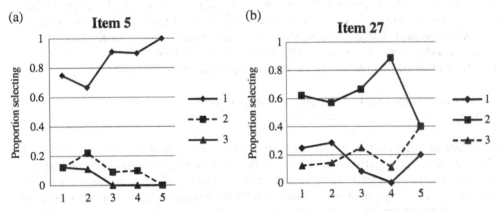

FIGURE 7.2 Quantile plots for well functioning (a) and poorly functioning (b) items. *Note.* Correct answers = Option 1 for item 5; Option 2 for item 27. The *x*-axis represents five ability groups, with 1 indicating the lowest ability and 5 indicating the highest ability.

102 Chapter 7 Statistics and Software for Test Revisions

TABLE 7.1

Item statistics for well- and poorly functioning items

Option	N	Prop.	r_{pbis}	r_{bis}	Mean	SD	
Good item (Item 5)							
1	41	0.820	0.370	0.541	38.780	9.532	**KEY**
2	5	0.100	−0.184	−0.315	30.400	9.607	
3	2	0.040	−0.181	−0.412	27.000	2.828	
Omit	2	0.040	−0.138	−0.313	23.000	22.627	
Poor item (Item 27)							
1	7	0.140	−0.143	−0.224	33.000	13.166	
2	29	0.580	0.101	0.127	37.517	8.971	**KEY**
3	10	0.200	0.144	0.206	40.600	9.524	
Omit	4	0.080	−0.134	−0.245	29.250	16.661	

Note. Prop. = item facility. r_{pbis} = point-biserial correlation. r_{bis} = biserial correlation.

considered acceptable. The facility value was 0.820 (i.e., 82% of the examinees answered correctly). Although the value is higher than the generally recommended threshold of 0.70, a combination of high item discrimination and slightly high item facility is deemed less problematic (Carr, 2011). Note that the point-biserials for the distractors were negative (−0.184 and −0.181 for distractors 2 and 3, respectively). This is desirable because it shows that those who got the item wrong were likely to have a lower total score than those who got the item right.

> Item 5: What are you (   ) about?
> 1. talking*   2. saying   3. telling

Figure 7.2b shows an example of response patterns for an item that did not function well in the examinee sample. For item 27 (see below), although the slope for the correct answer (2) went up overall as proficiency increased from groups 1 to 4, group 5 performed substantially worse than group 4. More problematic was that distractor 3 was selected as often as the correct answer in group 5. There was clearly something wrong with the options, and a closer scrutiny of the content of the item is warranted. Item 27 tests the knowledge of the grammar pattern "not + comparative + than." Although the intended correct answer was option 2, option 3 is also grammatical and sensical, and group 5 examinees seemed to be confused. The item relies not only on grammatical ability but also on value judgment and clearly needs revision. Table 7.1 shows that the facility value was 0.580 and the point-biserial value was 0.101. The point-biserial was far below 0.300, and therefore unacceptable. Note that the point-biserial value for distractor 3 was positive (0.144), which (weakly) suggests that those who scored incorrectly by choosing distractor 3 were likely to have a higher total score.

> Item 27: Good sleep is not (   ) important than good food.
> 1. better   2. less*   3. more

Two issues are particularly crucial in item analysis. First, having too many items with high/low facility and negative/low discrimination values is problematic, particularly for NRTs, since such items cannot separate proficient from less proficient examinees. However, this does not necessarily mean these items should be discarded. They may be statistically flawed, but still represent the construct being assessed well. Including such items could make the test look more trustworthy, and prompt examinees to be more motivated and better prepared to complete the test. It is more sensible to keep the items if the item statistics are not conspicuously unfavorable or to revise them rather than to delete them. Second, item statistics tend to fluctuate particularly with small sample sizes. It would be advisable to pilot items to a reasonably large number of examinees to investigate whether they function as intended. Stakeholders may be interested to know how they were revised and how effective the revision was, so it is better to provide pre- and post-revision statistics for the items in question when it is possible to do so.

Analysis of Rating Scales and Raters

To report statistics showing characteristics of rating scales and raters in performance assessment, it is useful to report outputs from GENOVA and FACETS (see In'nami & Koizumi, 2022 for the data, syntax, and output files from FACETS version 3.85.0 and GENOVA version 3.1). Among GENOVA outputs, it is advisable to report G study estimates of variance components and D study results. Table 7.2 shows analysis of variance (ANOVA) estimates of variance components for a two-facet crossed design, with tasks and raters included as facets. The data are the speaking scores of 145 respondents for four tasks rated by two raters, with no missing values. The design was fully crossed, meaning all respondents completed all tasks, which were rated by all raters using a holistic rating scale of 1–5. The tasks and raters were both modeled as random facets (i.e., they were considered to be randomly sampled from a universe of conditions; Sawaki & Xi, 2019).

Of great interest is the percentage of variance components, which shows the relative contribution of the sources of variation in this speaking test. Half the variation was attributable to persons (52.642%), indicating that examinee scores were spread well. The non-negligible variance components of the interactions between persons and tasks (19.667%) and between persons and raters (10.372%) suggest that the relative standing of examinees differed somewhat across tasks and across raters. For example, regarding the person-by-rater interaction, rater 1 may have judged that examinee 1 was more proficient than examinee 2 and that examinee 2 was more proficient than examinee 3. In contrast, rater 2 may have judged that examinee 3 was the most proficient, followed by examinee 2 and then examinee 1. Approximately 16% of the variation was due to residual effects, indicating that a somewhat small proportion of the variance was due to the three-way interaction between persons, tasks, and raters, and measurement error that was not captured in this analysis.

TABLE 7.2

G study ANOVA estimates of variance components for a two-facet crossed design for the speaking test ($p \times t \times r$)

Source of variation	Sum of squares	Degree of freedom	Estimated mean square	Estimated variance component	Percentage of variance component
Persons (p)	763.232	144	5.300	0.538	52.642
Task (t)	2.217	3	0.739	0.000	0.000
Rater (r)	3.986	1	3.986	0.005	0.489
pt	246.532	432	0.570	0.201	19.667
pr	85.263	144	0.592	0.106	10.372
tr	1.889	3	0.629	0.003	0.294
ptr, e (residual)	72.860	432	0.168	0.169	16.536
Total				1.022	100.000

TABLE 7.3
D study for the speaking test ($p \times T \times R$)

	1 task	2 tasks	3 tasks	4 tasks
1 rater	0.530 (0.526)	0.649 (0.644)	0.701 (0.695)	0.730 (0.725)
2 raters	0.614 (0.611)	0.733 (0.730)	0.784 (0.780)	0.812 (0.808)
3 raters	0.647 (0.645)	0.766 (0.764)	0.816 (0.813)	0.843 (0.841)
4 raters	0.666 (0.664)	0.784 (0.782)	0.833 (0.831)	0.860 (0.858)

Note. Values outside parentheses are generalizability coefficients for norm-referenced tests. Values in parentheses are phi coefficients for criterion-referenced tests.

D study results in Table 7.3 show two types of reliability indices: generalizability coefficients used for NRT, and phi (ϕ) coefficients used for CRT. They are both predicted values, changing as a function of the number of tasks and raters. If the current speaking test is used for placement (i.e., NRT), the test is considered reliable in general, with a generalizability coefficient for four tasks with two raters of 0.812. However, the relatively large person-by-task and the person-by-rater interactions compromise the generalizability of test performance. If the test needs to be shorter, we can still expect a similar level of reliability with three tasks and three raters (0.816). These changes are often effectively reported as a graph like Figure 7.3. The GENOVA control card for this analysis is included in Appendix 7.C.

FACETS generates numerous, useful outputs, with certain ones being particularly beneficial to test revision (see In'nami & Koizumi, 2022). First, it is advisable to report a facets map, as presented in Figure 7.4. Results are based on the same data used in the G and D studies above. The map shows the relative abilities of examinees (column 2), the relative severity of raters (column 3), and the relative difficulty of tasks (column 4). Column 1 shows

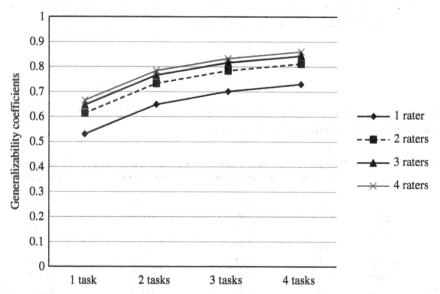

FIGURE 7.3 Generalizability coefficients for the speaking test ($p \times T \times R$). *Note.* The values presented are generalizability coefficients for norm-referenced tests, as shown in Table 7.3. Phi coefficients for criterion-referenced tests can likewise be displayed using a comparable format.

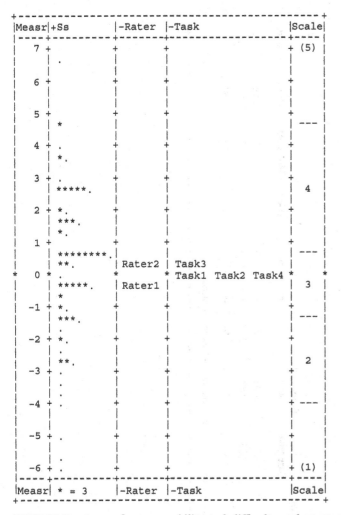

FIGURE 7.4 Facets map for person ability, task difficulty, and rater severity/leniency.

a ruler of a logit scale, and column 5 shows the ranges of each level of the rating scale. The examinees were relatively normally distributed; the raters rated similarly in terms of severity, as they clustered around zero; and the tasks were of similar difficulty. If tasks of various difficulty are needed relative to the distribution of examinee ability for NRTs, new tasks should be added to the current test. Alternatively, new tasks can replace some of the present tasks.

A second instructive statistic to report from FACETS is the bias analysis, which examines systematic patterns of interaction between variables of interest (e.g., Kondo-Brown, 2002). For example, the aforementioned G study person-by-rater interaction from GENOVA can be further analyzed through bias analysis in FACETS. Three significant interactions were found, as shown in Table 7.4. Column 4 shows the average difference between the observed (column 1) and expected (column 2) scores. On average, this student (number 59 [column 10]; ability measure of −0.93 [column 11]) was being rated 1.17 score-points higher by rater 1 than expected ([16 − 11.3]/4). This corresponded to a change in rater severity of 3.35 logits, with the standard error being 1.05 logits. The t-value was 3.20, $df = 3$, $p = 0.049$. These results indicate that rater 1 was significantly and much less severe (more lenient) in rating student 59 at the 0.05 level (two-tailed) than s/he normally is. In contrast, rater 2 was more severe for the same student, assigning scores (−1.17 score-points) lower than expected. Rater 1 was also more severe for

Bias analysis: person-by-rater interaction

Observed score	Expected score	Observed count	Observed-expected average	Bias size[a]	Standard error	t	df	p	Student	Measure	Rater	Measure
16	11.3	4	1.17	3.35	1.05	3.20	3	0.049	59	−0.93	Rater1	−0.17
6	10.7	4	−1.17	−2.86	0.88	−3.23	3	0.048	59	−0.93	Rater2	0.17
14	17.2	4	−0.79	−2.99	0.83	−3.62	3	0.036	68	3.65	Rater1	−0.17

[a]Positive bias size shows less severity (more leniency) of raters, whereas negative bias size shows more severity (less leniency) of raters.

student 68, giving lower scores (−0.79 score-points) than expected. To summarize, significant bias of rater behavior was found for only 3 of the 290 cases (145 examinees rated by 2 raters), and the degree of bias was relatively small with similarly severe and consistent ratings of the raters (rater severity measures for raters 1 and 2 = −0.17, 0.17; see rater consistency or fit below). This suggests that the person-by-rater interaction, which was non-negligible in the G study, was adjusted in many-facet Rasch analysis when examinees' abilities were estimated. If many cases of rater-related bias are found, problematic rater behavior should be examined by inspecting the actual examinee performance and ratings, and/or interviewing raters to identify factors causing the discrepancies, such as rater fatigue or failure to understand the rating criteria. Information on the sources of rater divergence can be incorporated into rater training. Further, pre–post training data can be examined through a pre- and post-facets map, similar to Figure 7.4, and bias analyses (e.g., Elder et al., 2005).

FACETS also produces statistics for evaluating the fit of each examinee, rater, and task with the Rasch model, although these statistics are not shown in Table 7.4. A model fit shows whether the data patterns of examinees, raters, and tasks are similar to the ones expected from the Rasch model. The model and data are deemed consistent when the infit and outfit mean square fit statistics fall within the range of 0.4–1.2 for judged ratings, and 0.8–1.2 for high-stakes multiple-choice questions (Wright & Linacre, 1994). Depending on the type and stakes of a test, different ranges might be acceptable (see Wright & Linacre, 1994). For raters 1 and 2 above, the infit mean squares were, respectively, 0.90 and 1.09, and the outfit mean squares were 0.88 and 1.10. These results indicate that both raters' ratings fit the model.

Other relevant outputs are the category statistics (Table 7.5) and probability curve (Figure 7.5) of the rating scale. Bond et al. (2021) summarize four types of the properties of appropriate rating scales: First, difficulty estimates in reaching a certain band level (category) should increase steadily as levels get higher, with at least 10 ratings at each level. Results in columns 2 and 3 in Table 7.5 indicate that difficulty estimates gradually increased from levels 1 to 5 (−3.29 to 3.56), with more than 10 rating at each level (e.g., $n = 62$ for level 5). Second, thresholds or step calibrations are difficulty estimates for selecting one level over another (e.g., −3.73 from levels 1 to 2 in column 4). The degree of distances between thresholds between adjacent levels should be at least 1.4 logits, but less than 5.0 logits. Results suggest all distances satisfied this criterion (2.05–3.92). Third, a probability curve shows the probability of examinees obtaining a rating at a certain level of a rating scale (e.g., examinees with an ability of −2.0 logits have an approximately 50% chance of obtaining level 2). Each level should have its own distinctive peak, as seen in Figure 7.5. Further, the intersection of level probabilities equals the threshold estimate in Table 7.5. For example, the intersection of levels 1 and 2 in Figure 7.5 is −3.73, as also observed in Table 7.5. Fourth, level fit statistics, as seen in column 5 in Table 7.5, have an average of 1.0. If the value is more than 2.0, ratings are considered

---

TABLE 7.5

Category statistics for the rating scale

Level	Number of observations and percentage	Average measure for all examinees who selected the level	Rasch–Andrich thresholds measure (distance), standard error	Outfit mean square
1	63 (6%)	−3.29		1.2
2	203 (18%)	−1.82	−3.73, 0.17	1.0
3	369 (32%)	0.05	−1.43 (2.30), 0.10	0.9
4	447 (39%)	1.64	0.62 (2.05), 0.08	1.0
5	62 (5%)	3.56	4.54 (3.92), 0.15	1.0

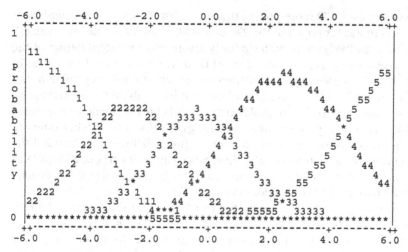

FIGURE 7.5 Probability curve for the rating scale.

to depart from rating patterns predicted from the Rasch model and thus problematic. Results show that all the ratings for each level fit the model well. Therefore, we can conclude that this rating scale functioned well and requires no revision. However, if results do not satisfy these criteria, test developers should consider collapsing adjacent levels and/or rewording descriptors in the levels. They should then analyze rescored or newly collected data.

Finally, regardless of the statistics used, reporting commands/scripts/syntax whenever possible and appropriate is highly recommended. Although readers peruse the method section of a journal article to try to understand how the analysis was conducted, method sections often do not include all information that should be reported. This may be due to word limits or authors not being familiar with data reporting practices. In these cases, reporting commands/scripts/syntax (with annotated comments) makes data analysis more transparent, so readers can see exactly how the data were analyzed. For example, for G theory analysis, GENOVA requires specifying whether variables are considered random or fixed. For variables to be considered random, they must be considered to be randomly drawn from the universe (population) of examinees, raters, or tasks and exchangeable with any other samples of variables in the population. If such exchangeability is not assured, variables are considered fixed. Since the random/fixed specification affects results and, more importantly, any generalizations we make, this should be clearly reported with the syntax. Reporting syntax helps readers become familiar with different analyses and helps them apply these methods to their own data. Syntax and data should ideally be made available in Instrument for Research Into Second Language Learning and Teaching (IRIS) and Open Science Framework (OSF; see In'nami & Koizumi, 2022 for an example) to facilitate open science and ensure transparency (In'nami et al., 2022).

Challenges and Future Directions

To further promote the use of statistics addressed in this chapter in actual data analyses among language testers, an important challenge is to ensure that statistical analyses are reported so that readers can understand how items/tests/tasks have been revised based on those analyses, and how this has improved the validity argument for a particular instrument. In their seminal book on building a validity argument for the TOEFL, Chapelle et al. (2008) report unique and important studies that contributed to the revision of one of the world's most widely taken high-stakes tests. For example, Chapelle (2008) reviews studies investigating various aspects of the TOEFL and synthesizes them into one validity argument for TOEFL score interpretation and use. Chapelle organizes studies according to (i) the appropriateness of scoring rubrics (e.g., whether scoring rubrics for writing should be holistic or analytic; how various factors are addressed, such as copying verbatim material from the reading text in an integrated writing task), (ii) task administration conditions (e.g., whether note-taking is allowed for a listening task), and (iii) the psychometric quality of tests (e.g., whether tasks have the appropriate difficulties and discriminations). An iterative process of revision through these three phases led to an improvement in the validity of interpretation and use of TOEFL scores. Therefore, a revision of the items/tests/tasks in relation to the inferences that language testers intend to draw from tests would make the whole process of test development and validation more valuable and meaningful. Statistics discussed in this chapter will put language testers in a better position to revise items/tests/tasks and, eventually, to hone arguments for interpretation and use based on the test scores.

Discussion Questions

1. Analyze your data using FACETS. Is the rating scale functioning as intended? For instance, as demonstrated in the probability curve for the rating scale in Figure 7.5 of this chapter, are all levels of the scale performing effectively? If any level is not functioning as expected, would you retain the scale as is? Would you consider collapsing adjacent levels and/or rephrasing descriptors within the levels?

2. As with many-facet Rasch measurement, you can include various facets (i.e., variables) into G theory analyses, depending on the purpose(s) of your study. Researchers have frequently included persons, tasks, and raters. What other facets would you consider including in your analysis?

Appendix A: SPSS Syntax for Bar Graphs

```
DATASET ACTIVATE DataSet1.
GRAPH
  /BAR(SIMPLE)=MEAN(TOEIC) BY group
  /INTERVAL CI(95.0).
```

Appendix B: SPSS Syntax for Box Plots

```
GET
FILE='G:\Research\Descriptive_stat.sav'.
DATASET NAME DataSet1 WINDOW=FRONT.
EXAMINE VARIABLES=TOEIC BY group
  /PLOT=BOXPLOT
  /STATISTICS=NONE
  /NOTOTAL.
```

Appendix C: GENOVA Control Card

(*Note.* See In'nami & Koizumi, 2022 for the data, syntax, and output files from FACETS version 3.85.0 and GENOVA version 3.1)

```
GSTUDY      P X T X R DESIGN -- RANDOM MODEL
OPTIONS     RECORDS 2
```

Chapter 7 Statistics and Software for Test Revisions

```
EFFECT        * P 145 0
EFFECT        + T  4  0
EFFECT        + R  2  0
FORMAT        (8F2.0)
PROCESS
3 3 4 3 3 4 3 4
(snipped)
2 3 2 3 2 3 2 3
COMMENT
COMMENT       FIRST SET OF D STUDY CONTROL CARDS
DSTUDY        #1 -- P X T X R DESIGN -- T, R RANDOM
DEFFECT       $ P
DEFFECT       T 1 1 1 1 2 2 2 2 3 3 3 3 4 4 4 4
DEFFECT       R 1 2 3 4 1 2 3 4 1 2 3 4 1 2 3 4
ENDDSTUDY
FINISH
```

References

Aryadoust, V., Ng, L. Y., & Sayama, H. (2021). A comprehensive review of Rasch measurement in language assessment: recommendations and guidelines for research. *Language Testing*, *38*(1), 6–40. https://doi.org/10.1177/0265532220927487.

ASCpsychometrics. (2011a). *Running classical test theory analysis with Iteman 4*. Retrieved April 4, 2024 from http://www.youtube.com/watch?v=dAAxpJTa-mc&feature=plcp.

ASCpsychometrics. (2011b). *Interpreting classical test theory analysis – Iteman 4 output*. Retrieved April 4, 2024 from http://www.youtube.com/watch?v=IWoMY4OJQrs.

de Ayala, R. J. (2022). *The theory and practice of item response theory* (2nd ed.). Guilford.

Bachman, L. F. (2004). *Statistical analyses for language assessment*. Cambridge University Press.

Bachman, L., & Palmer, A. (2010). *Language assessment in practice*. Oxford University Press.

Bond, T. G., Yan, Z., & Heene, M. (2021). *Applying the Rasch model: Fundamental measurement in the human sciences* (4th ed.). Routledge.

Brennan, R. L. (2001). *Generalizability theory*. Springer-Verlag.

Brown, J. D., & Hudson, T. (2002). *Criterion-referenced language testing*. Cambridge University Press.

Cardinet, J., Johnson, S., & Pini, G. (2010). *Applying generalizability theory using EduG*. Routledge.

Carr, N. T. (2011). *Designing and analyzing language tests*. Oxford University Press.

Chapelle, C. A. (2008). The TOEFL validity argument. In C. A. Chapelle, M. K. Enright & J. M. Jamieson (Eds.), *Building a validity argument for the test of English as a Foreign language* (pp. 319–352). Routledge.

Chapelle, C. A., & Lee, H.-W. (2021). Understanding argument-based validity in language testing. In C. A. Chapelle & E. Voss (Eds.), *Validity argument in language testing: Case studies of validation research* (pp. 19–44). Cambridge University Press.

Chapelle, C. A., & Voss, E. (Eds.). (2021). *Validity argument in language testing: Case studies of validation research*. Cambridge University Press.

Chapelle, C. A., Enright, M. K., & Jamieson, J. M. (Eds.). (2008). *Building a validity argument for the test of English as a foreign language*. Routledge.

Cook, R. J. (2005). Kappa. In P. Armitage & T. Colton (Eds.), *The encyclopedia of biostatistics* (pp. 2166–2168). John Wiley & Sons.

Council of Europe. (2009). *Relating language examinations to the common European framework of reference for languages: Learning, teaching, assessment (CEFR): A manual*. Language Policy Division. https://www.coe.int/en/web/common-european-framework-reference-languages/relating-examinations-to-the-cefr.

Eckes, T. (2015). *Introduction to many-facet Rasch measurement: Analyzing and evaluating rater-mediated assessments* (2nd rev. and updated ed.). Peter Lang.

Educational Testing Service. (2022). *TOEFL iBT® independent speaking rubrics.* Retrieved April 4, 2024 from https://www.ets.org/pdfs/toefl/toefl-ibt-speaking-rubrics.pdf.

Elder, C., Knoch, U., Barkhuizen, G., & von Randow, J. (2005). Individual feedback to enhance rater training: does it work? *Language Assessment Quarterly, 2*(3), 175–196. https://doi.org/10.1207/s15434311laq0203_1.

Field, A., & Miles, J. (2010). *Discovering statistics using SAS.* Sage.

Glass, G. E., & Hopkins, K. D. (1996). *Statistical methods in education and psychology* (3rd ed.). Allyn and Bacon.

In'nami, Y., & Koizumi, R. (2022). *Data, syntax, and output files for GENOVA and FACETS from "Statistics and software for test revisions.".* OSF Database, Center for Open Science. https://osf.io/af6tu.

In'nami, Y., Mizumoto, A., Plonsky, L., & Koizumi, R. (2022). Promoting computationally reproducible research in applied linguistics: recommended practices and considerations. *Research Methods in Applied Linguistics, 1*(3), 100030. https://doi.org/10.1016/j.rmal.2022.100030.

Kim, S. Y. (2022). Using generalizability theory software suite: GENOVA, urGENOVA, and mGENOVA. *Measurement: Interdisciplinary Research and Perspectives, 20*(3), 181–194. https://doi.org/10.1080/15366367.2022.2025569.

Knoch, U., Fairbairn, J., & Jin, Y. (2021). *Scoring second language spoken and written performance: Issues, options and directions.* Equinox.

Kondo-Brown, K. (2002). A FACETS analysis of rater bias in measuring Japanese second language writing performance. *Language Testing, 19*(1), 3–31. https://doi.org/10.1191/0265532202lt218oa.

Kunnan, A. J. (1992). An investigation of a criterion-referenced test using G-theory, and factor and cluster analysis. *Language Testing, 9*(1), 30–49.

Kunnan, A. J., & Carr, N. T. (2013). Statistical analysis of test results. In C. Chapelle (Ed.), *The encyclopedia of applied linguistics* (pp. 5396–5403). Wiley-Blackwell.

Kunnan, A. J., Qin, C. Y., & Zhao, C. G. (2022). Developing a scenario-based English language assessment in an Asian university. *Language Assessment Quarterly, 19*(4), 368–393. https://doi.org/10.1080/15434303.2022.2073886.

Larson-Hall, J. (2016). *A guide to doing statistics in second language research using SPSS and R* (2nd ed.). Routledge.

Larson-Hall, J., & Herrington, R. (2010). Improving data analysis in second language acquisition by utilizing modern developments in applied statistics. *Applied Linguistics, 31*(3), 368–390. https://doi.org/10.1093/applin/amp038.

McNamara, T., Knoch, T., & Fan, J. (2019). *Fairness, justice, and language assessment.* Oxford University Press.

Ockey, G. J. (2011). Assertiveness and self-consciousness as explanatory variables of L2 oral ability: a latent variable approach. *Language Learning, 61*(3), 968–989. https://doi.org/10.1111/j.1467-9922.2010.00625.x.

Sawaki, Y., & Xi, X. (2019). Univariate generalizability theory in language assessment. In V. Aryadoust & M. Raquel (Eds.), *Quantitative data analysis for language assessment (Vol. I: Fundamental techniques)* (pp. 30–53). Routledge.

Shavelson, R. J., & Webb, N. M. (1991). *Generalizability theory: A primer.* Sage.

Sick, J. (2009). Rasch analysis software programs. *Shiken: JALT Testing & Evaluation SIG Newsletter, 13*(3), 13–16. https://hosted.jalt.org/test/sic_4.htm.

Tabachnick, B. G., & Fidell, L. S. (2019). *Using multivariate statistics* (7th ed.). Pearson.

Wright, B. D., & Linacre, J. M. (1994). Reasonable mean-square fit values. *Rasch Measurement Transactions, 8*(3), 370. https://www.rasch.org/rmt/rmt83b.htm.

Suggested Readings

Larson-Hall, J. (2015). *A guide to doing statistics in second language research using SPSS and R* (2nd ed.). Routledge. https://doi.org/10.4324/9781315775661.

Plonsky, L. (Ed.). (2015). *Advancing quantitative methods in second language research.* Routledge.

Vispoel, W. P., Lee, H., Hong, H., & Chen, T. (2023). Applying multivariate generalizability theory to psychological assessments. *Psychological Methods.* Advance online publication. https://doi.org/10.1037/met0000606.

Wind, S. A. (2023). *Exploring rating scale functioning for survey research.* Sage.

CHAPTER 8

Language Assessment and Artificial Intelligence

Erik Voss

Introduction

Artificial intelligence (AI) is gaining interest as it plays an increasingly important role in language assessment. Although the term AI is becoming a prominent area of interest today, AI research has been around since the mid-1900s focusing on applications of machine learning, natural language processing (NLP), and AI that have been the underlying techniques for applications in language assessment. For example, Ellis Page developed a computer rater to "analyze" students' essays more than 50 years ago (Page, 1966). The title of the publication about this project was "The Imminence of . . . Grading Essays by Computer" foreshadowing the unstoppable progress of technology's role in language assessment. His vision was most likely positive, however, despite the negative connotation associated with the term "imminence." The advancements in technology have made it possible for a computer to carry on a simple conversation as a tutor or language coach and provide feedback not only on linguistic features such as vocabulary use and rate of speech but also on nonlinguistic gestures such as head nods and facial expressions (Hoque, 2013). Because of the linguistic and biometric data that are collected, the complex algorithms that process the data are capable of performing tasks in language assessment that typically require human intelligence. Although most readers will understand this as a general concept, the definition of AI has not been agreed upon. The next section will explain two subfields in AI that have made it possible for computers to "learn" and simulate tasks that were previously only possible by humans.

What Is Artificial Intelligence?

Although the notion of AI has been around since the 1950s, a precise definition is difficult to present. Nonetheless, it is essential to agree on a working definition of AI to guide research and evaluation. Most definitions are broad, such as "Artificial intelligence [. . .] can deal with new problems, once it has learnt the general principle" (Dodigovic, 2005, p. 2). However, since the main goal for implementation of AI in language assessment is to replicate tasks that have traditionally been done by a human, a working definition would include reference to the replication of human intelligence as implemented through computer systems (Wang, 2019).

The Concise Companion to Language Assessment, First Edition. Edited by Antony John Kunnan.
© 2025 John Wiley & Sons, Inc. Published 2025 by John Wiley & Sons, Inc.

Wang (2019) defined intelligence as "the capacity of an information-processing system to adapt to its environment while operating with insufficient knowledge and resources" (p. 17), which would resemble human cognition. Because the reality of insufficient knowledge and resources has been an immense challenge for AI researchers, working definitions of AI have defaulted to the comparison of whether a task is completed as well as a human could complete the task.

For instance, the most famous measure of AI is the imitation experiment proposed by Turing (1950), which tests whether a computer can imitate an adult human mind. The basic premise is that if a computer replaces a human, will another human know? In language assessment, research has sought to imitate the adult human mind in tasks such as scoring, test development, and proctoring. The automation of these tasks falls under the term AI; however, the underlying computational technique that has made these applications possible is a subarea of AI called machine learning.

The field of machine learning (ML) was pioneered in the 1950s by Arthur Samuel (McCarthy & Feigenbaum, 1990) exploring the potential for computers to learn without explicitly being programmed. A subfield of ML that has led to advances in AI applications in language assessment is called deep learning. Deep learning architecture was designed to replicate neurons in the human brain in a dense neural network that identifies patterns and can embed syntactic and semantic information into numerical vectors that are easier for computers to process (Goldberg, 2022). ML and deep learning are frequently mentioned in conjunction with or as a substitute for AI. Figure 8.1 shows the relationship among AI, machine learning, and deep learning.

In Figure 8.1, AI is the umbrella term referring to the development of computer systems that can perform tasks requiring human-like intelligence, such as learning, problem-solving, and decision-making. ML is a subfield of AI that focuses on training computer systems to learn from data and improve their performance without being explicitly programmed. Finally, deep learning is a subfield of ML that uses neural networks with multiple layers to understand and analyze complex patterns in data, similar to how the human brain processes information. Although NLP techniques are an important component for developing AI language applications, the next section will present a survey of how three terms – AI, machine learning, and deep learning – have been used in language assessment publications to identify the study as AI research.

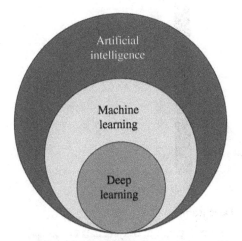

FIGURE 8.1 The relationship among AI, machine learning, and deep learning.

Artificial Intelligence Research in Language Assessment

Although research in AI has been around since the 1950s, AI applications and research in language assessment have arrived much later. AI research in language assessment can be found in many places; however, in order to explore the degree to which research is published in language assessment journals, this chapter presents the findings from a survey of articles referring to the use of AI in the two leading journals in language assessment, *Language Assessment Quarterly* and *Language Testing*. In order to explore how AI is positioned in these two journals, I conducted a survey of articles that reference AI using "artificial intelligence," "machine learning," and "deep learning" as search terms based on the relationship in Figure 8.1. There are, of course, articles that reference intelligent machines, automated scoring, and NLP. However, the three terms were selected as general terms that are used when discussing AI applications as explained in the previous section. Test reviews, book reviews, and article commentaries were not included in the results. Figure 8.2 shows the number of articles that include these terms in the two journals identified by five-year time periods except the period before 2010 and the period that begins in 2020, which spans only three years.

Artificial Intelligence

At a glance, it is clear that the term "artificial intelligence" has been referenced in articles in each time period. However, the use of the term differs through the publication dates. The earliest references to AI in the 80s and 90s discuss AI as a model for future applications supported by a theory in modern cognitive psychology called information processing (Grotjahn, 1986) and language understanding systems for a listening test (Yi'an, 1998), both related to theories in the field of AI. In the periods between 2010 and 2014, the term AI was used to describe NLP as a means or engineering features for scoring writing and speech performance (Chapelle & Chung, 2010) with a focus on automated speech recognition (ASR) (Van Moere, 2012) and automated essay scoring (AES) (Park, 2014). During the period from 2015 to 2019, research referencing AI focused on the assessment of speaking through research

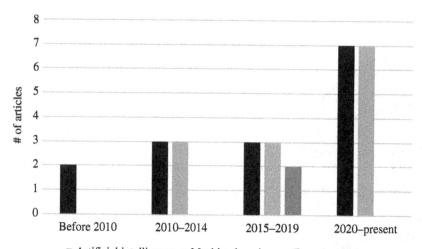

FIGURE 8.2 Number of articles that include one or more of the search terms in the journals *Language Testing* and *Language Assessment Quarterly*.

on scoring features for speaking proficiency (Kang & Johnson, 2018), ASR (Litman et al., 2018), and although the article does not focus on AI, the authors highlight the progress that needs to be made to improve interactional competence with at-home AI devices (Plough et al., 2018). During the period from 2020 through May of 2023, less than a five-year period, the number of published articles referring to AI more than doubled. Research during this period has diversified following agendas to explore AES (Latifi & Gierl, 2021) and features of fluency in automated speaking assessment (Tavakoli et al., 2023). The familiar topics of ASR of L2 speech (Hannah et al., 2022) and assessing conversation through spoken dialogue systems (Youn, 2023) including conversational agents to assess language in content areas (Grapin, 2023) continue as relevant research in language assessment. Research on the validation of AI systems for language assessment was emerging during this period as test developers explore the construct definition with new technologies (Aryadoust, 2023; Isaacs et al., 2023).

Machine Learning

The term "machine learning" first appeared in the journals during the 2010–2014 period. The research at this time explored the linguistic features that were relevant to the construct of speaking and writing (Chapelle et al., 2010; Chodorow et al., 2010; Granfeldt & Ågren, 2014). The identification of characteristics of grammatical ability including article and preposition usage held potential for scoring, feedback, and diagnostic testing. The next period from 2015 to 2019 shared results from commercial feedback systems (Hoang & Kunnan, 2016) and ML approaches discussed related to AES and ASR. During the current period beginning in 2020, articles started to reference ML approaches at more than twice the rate as the previous two periods in the first three years of this five-year time period. These approaches refer to typical research themes of AES systems (Latifi & Gierl, 2021; Shin & Gierl, 2020) and speaking assessment (Grapin, 2023; Hannah et al., 2022; Khabbazbashi & Galaczi, 2020) as additional research topics emerged. For instance, Choi and Deane (2021) used a ML approach to develop a tool to explore the potential of keystroke logs as features of writing performance. In an eye behavior study of an online assessment, Burton (2023) suggested that ML could be used to include nonverbal behavior as features in a speaking assessment. This is a topic that is being explored in affective computing and AI-based proctoring.

Deep Learning

The subfield of ML known as "deep learning" has shown promise in research in many fields including language assessment. Due to newer architecture using this approach, language modeling has made great progress. ChatGPT is an example of a foundation model with a transformer-based deep learning architecture that was trained as a conversational agent using a technique called reinforcement learning from human feedback (RLHF) (Heaven, 2023). The only period with any published work in language assessment with reference to deep learning in these two journals is during the period between 2015 and 2019. These articles both mention deep learning in reference to ASR (Litman et al., 2018; Xu, 2018).

Since 2015, articles began referencing more than one term. For example, the term ML was often found in the same article mentioning AI. In fact, articles describing a deep learning application would always include AI demonstrating the relationship between the terms in the field of AI. There are already twice as many articles referencing these terms during the first half of 2023 than the prior two periods, and there are two and a half years to go in this time period. If this trend continues, it demonstrates a substantial growth in research and applications of AI in language assessment.

According to the analysis of the two journals, published research of AI in language assessment has undergone significant changes over time. The early references in the 80s and

90s focused on AI as a theoretical model and language understanding systems. In the following years, the term AI was used to describe NLP and feature engineering for scoring writing and speech performance. As we progressed into the 2010s, research expanded to include speaking proficiency assessment and conversational agents. More recently, from 2020 to 2023, there has been a notable increase in research articles mentioning AI, with a particular emphasis on automated essay scoring, fluency in automated speaking assessment, ASR of L2 speech, and assessing conversation through spoken dialogue systems. ML began to be discussed in publications, with a focus on NLP, feedback systems, and feature identification for writing and speaking assessment. Deep learning, another subfield of machine learning, has shown promise in language assessment research, particularly in the area of ASR. This increasing trend in research and terminology reflects the expanding applications of AI in language assessment and signifies the ongoing growth of the field.

The next section will outline applications and challenges of AI use in language assessment.

Applications and Challenges

Current applications of AI technologies for language assessment are part of research agenda to explore assessment of writing, speaking, and sign language as well as automatic item generation (AIG) and assessment security.

AI in Writing Assessment

The assessment of L2 learner writing has experienced significant progress through the use of AI techniques and algorithms. This automated scoring process involves evaluating the quality of essays, written compositions, or short constructed responses produced by learners of a second language. Ellis Page's "Project Essay Grade" (PEG) system, developed in the 1960s (Page, 1966), was among the first AES systems. PEG identified features in a text and calculated a score using standard multiple regression. Early AES systems employed feature engineering and traditional ML techniques such as regression analysis, random forest, and support vector machines to analyze text and make scoring judgments. These approaches proved effective in learning patterns from large datasets. However, this approach faced challenges in capturing the semantic and contextual aspects of writing.

Building on the research since PEG, commercial testing companies have implemented high-stakes essay scoring systems for essays written by second-language learners such as e-rater® Scoring Engine by ETS (Attali & Burstein, 2006) and Pearson's Intelligent Essay Assessor (Foltz et al., 2013). These examples utilize automated scoring for extended responses in high-stakes tests to contribute to a measure of language proficiency. In addition, low-stakes applications for more specific purposes have also been developed such as feedback on rhetorical move analysis in academic research writing (Cotos, 2016).

In recent years, neural network-based models, particularly those utilizing deep learning architectures, have gained prominence in AES and automated writing evaluation (AWE) that provide feedback to the test taker. These models are developed based on the learning process of neurons in the brain, enabling them to understand complex patterns and relationships within text. Deep learning algorithms have shown promise in evaluating the overall quality, coherence, grammar, and style of written compositions (Alikaniotis et al., 2016; Taghipour & Ng, 2016). State-of-the-art research incorporates neural networks and transformers, which are trained on large language models (LLMs) or foundation models. These LLMs, exemplified by models like ChatGPT (OpenAI, 2023), have sparked research on using AI language models for automated scoring. Since this is a new area of research, and the models are in their infancy, the successful application of LLMs for scoring varies. Although some research has shown success, Mizumoto and Eguchi (2023) found that adding engineered features improved the accuracy of performance over using just the LLM. While LLMs can offer valuable feedback and evaluation, current models should not be the sole basis for assessing language proficiency. Human evaluation and feedback are essential for considering broader aspects of communication, cultural nuances, and context-specific requirements. Integrating automated scoring systems with human evaluation can provide a comprehensive and balanced assessment of second-language learners' essays.

Despite recent advancements, challenges persist in the development of automated writing scoring systems. One challenge involves ensuring fairness and mitigating potential bias in scoring. Efforts are underway to address bias and ensure that automated systems provide fair evaluations across different demographics and writing styles (Loukina et al., 2019). By addressing challenges, such as fairness, bias, and creativity, the field of automated writing scoring can continue to advance and provide valuable assessment tools for second-language learners.

AI in Speaking Assessment

Recent advances in ASR have improved the assessment of spoken language skills. The objective of AI-based speech assessment systems is to process responses, identify errors, and generate pronunciation and fluency scores that align closely with human ratings (Van Moere, 2012). These systems employ a combination of signal processing and ML techniques to convert spoken language into written transcript, extract relevant acoustic features from the sound files, and identify linguistic features in the written text. While the evaluation of ASR systems is typically based on word error rate (WER), by measuring the rate of errors in transcribing spoken language into written text, recent studies have highlighted the impact of task type and linguistic background on their performance of oral language proficiency (Hannah et al., 2022). Considerations for relevant features that represent the construct of speaking ability are crucial for the development of effective assessment of speaking abilities, particularly in multilingual and plurilingual contexts involving code switching and translanguaging.

To further improve ASR systems for L2 speech, one approach involves training ML algorithms on larger datasets of learner language (Loukina et al., 2018). Expanding the training data can lead to improved accuracy and generalization, enabling ASR systems to effectively evaluate a broader range of spoken language expressions. However, the collection of language samples for the development of suitable datasets remains a significant challenge in this domain.

Challenges also persist in collecting appropriate datasets and improving the authenticity and naturalness of computer interlocutors in spoken dialogue assessments. An emerging area of research focuses on replacing humans with computers as interlocutors in spoken dialogue assessments. Ockey and Chukharev-Hudilainen (2021) conducted a study comparing the discourse elicited between language learners and a human interlocutor versus a computer as an interlocutor. Surprisingly, the findings indicated that language elicited with a computer interlocutor was more dependable for assessing interactional competence than when language elicited with a human interlocutor. On the other hand, language elicited with human partners was found to be more natural. Therefore, efforts are needed to enhance the authenticity and naturalness of conversational agents.

These developments have prompted the investigation into the use of avatars as interlocutors in spoken interaction assessments. The use of avatars in speaking assessment serves as an active research area, aiming to simulate human interlocutors in language assessments. Many of these systems, known as tutoring systems, perform dual functions of assessment and tutoring. For instance, My Automated Conversation coacH (MACH) (Hoque, 2013) is a tutoring system that employs a 3D human avatar on a computer screen, simulating a job interview scenario while collecting diagnostic data. It records various features, including facial expressions, speech, and prosody, such as voice pitch, volume, and language use. A feedback dashboard provides valuable insights for students to improve their performance. While these spoken dialogue systems demonstrate significant potential, a debate persists regarding the extent to which computers should exhibit emotions, act, and speak as humans.

Monologic and semi-direct speaking assessment has been the standard for high-stakes language assessment powered by SpeechRater[SM] by ETS (Chen et al., 2018), Versant scoring system for Versant language tests (Pearson, 2022) and the Custom Automated Speech Engine (CASE) for Linguaskill (Xu et al., 2020). The research on interactive conversation tasks such as in Interactional Competence Elicitor (ICE) (Ockey & Chukharev-Hudilainen, 2021) is an innovative direction to expand the construct of speaking ability. For progress to be made in this area, however, advances are needed not only in the automated systems for language assessment but also in the systems that are used in real-world settings (e.g., smart home devices, digital assistants, and customer phone support systems).

Research in AI-powered speech recognition technology for assessing spoken language faces several notable challenges including the collection of appropriate datasets representative of diverse linguistic backgrounds, the quest for authenticity and naturalness in computer interlocutors, and the debate about the extent to which computers should exhibit emotions and human-like behavior. Overcoming these challenges requires continued research, innovation, and interdisciplinary collaboration.

AI in Sign Language Assessment

An area of research related to automated speaking assessment is the potential application of signed language recognition technology in assessing second-language (L2) signed language proficiency (Liu et al., 2022; Ritchings et al., 2012). This application relies on a trained model using computer vision to identify hand gestures and facial expressions. A notable example of this application is the utilization of signed language recognition for a vocabulary test in Swiss German Sign Language (Ebling et al., 2021). The system captures hand and facial gestures using computer vision for discrete signs and provides feedback on how to improve based on a comparison with a reference sign. While this research has primarily focused on isolated signs and manual features, the availability of datasets like the Scalable Multimodal Sign Language Technology for Sign Language Learning and Assessment (SMILE) Dataset (Ebling et al., 2018) is expected to attract more attention from computational linguists and computer vision researchers working with AI technology. The next logical step in this field is to transition toward assessment that incorporates continuous features, which necessitates a larger amount of annotated data. To address the challenge of annotating continuous sequences, one potential approach is the utilization of generative adversarial networks for image synthesis, as they have demonstrated promising results in generating poses that have not been previously seen. However, all research endeavors within this domain require a more comprehensive and explicit modeling of sign language linguistics, including the examination of sign syntax, grammar, and linguistic constructs.

Sign language recognition using AI technology has been employed to develop a system for sign language tutoring using wearable devices. For instance, Ritchings et al. (2012) designed a system for training Arabic sign language utilizing a cost-effective data glove worn by the trainee and real-time processing of sign movements. By employing pattern matching techniques, the system evaluates trainees' replication of recorded sign movements that are produced by an animated 3D model of a hand and arm. Evaluations conducted with teachers and trainees demonstrate a high level of accuracy in replicating signs, highlighting the system's efficacy as an alternative and preferred method for sign language tutoring when compared to traditional human-based approaches. Such tutoring systems hold promise for standardized assessment of sign language proficiency. The assessment could also involve integrating avatar-based signed language production systems that simulate humans with both hand and facial movements as interlocutors during signed conversations.

These research efforts underscore the potential of AI technology in the domains of sign language recognition, tutoring, and assessment. Despite challenges related to data availability, modality-specific considerations, and the necessity for further technological advancements, the application of AI technology in sign language assessment exhibits promising prospects in supporting effective teaching and assessment methods in sign language education.

AI in Automated Item Generation (AIG)

Automated item generation (AIG) can take different forms such as using NLP techniques to extract multiple-choice questions from an existing passage (ACT Inc, 2021). However, the development of LLMs, also known as foundation models, in the field of AI has led to advancements in AIG for developing both the passage and corresponding questions for language assessments. For instance, AIG can involve using a foundation model to automatically generate reading passages and associated questions by prompting the model with specific criteria to produce items that are appropriate for the proficiency level and purpose of the assessment. This approach has been utilized for various task types such as multiple choice, gap fill, sentence completion, and development of reading comprehension assessments. For example, in a study conducted by Attali et al. (2022), GPT-3 (OpenAI, 2020) was employed to develop reading comprehension items for the Duolingo English Test operational test and piloted on the practice test. By providing the language model with an example target text and example questions, the model was prompted to generate similar texts and questions about the new texts. In November of 2022, ChatGPT was released to the public allowing a large audience to experiment with similar tasks. Brunfaut (2022) notes that although AI systems can produce items and passages comparable to those created by human item writers, the need for human review remains, indicating the continued requirement for a significant amount of human capital and human reviewers that represent the intended population of test takers. The degree to which humans remain "in the loop" remains a challenge in order to balance the time-affordance of automating a process while retaining human monitoring and evaluation of the product.

The use of LLMs for developing language assessments presents a range of challenges that need to be addressed. These challenges include the potential for bias and fairness issues, the limited contextual understanding of LLMs, the overreliance on surface-level features, the lack of dynamic assessment capabilities, ethical considerations (e.g., addressing bias, promoting fairness, and striving for equity, ensuring privacy, security, and transparency), and the continued necessity for human involvement and expertise. Overcoming these challenges requires a balanced approach that combines the capabilities of LLMs with human oversight and validation. By carefully addressing these challenges, language assessment developers can harness the potential of LLMs while ensuring the fairness, validity, and comprehensiveness of language assessments in measuring diverse dimensions of language proficiency.

Addressing these challenges requires a balanced approach that combines the strengths of LLMs with human expertise. The collaboration between AI systems and human assessors is essential to overcome limitations, ensure fairness, incorporate contextual understanding, and design comprehensive language assessments that accurately measure various dimensions of language proficiency.

AI in Assessment Security

The advancement of AI technology has led to the application of AI-based technologies to ensure security utilizing computer vision and biometrics during remote language assessment administrations. These systems employ techniques like facial recognition, keystroke analysis,

120   Chapter 8 Language Assessment and Artificial Intelligence

and behavior analysis to monitor test takers and detect potential cheating behaviors (Purpura et al., 2021; Voss, 2023). During the pandemic, issues of test security and proctoring considerations were extremely relevant for all high- and low-stakes language assessments. Duolingo English Test, TOEFL iBT Special Home Edition, and Versant were a few of the language tests that utilized proprietary or third-party AI technology for proctoring and test security (Isbell & Kremmel, 2020). The AI technology is trained to identify suspicious behavior (e.g., plagiarism, unknown voices, and suspicious eye gaze) and flag the event for human review. One of the primary challenges with remote proctoring, however, lies in the state of current technology. Despite the potential benefits, the system's flags for suspicious activities may produce false positives, incorrectly flagging test takers for cheating when no such attempt was made. This limitation calls for further refinement and enhancement of the AI-based systems to improve accuracy and reduce false alarms.

Another challenge pertains to the concerns surrounding privacy and user consent. Test takers may experience anxiety or reluctance when asked to comply with certain security measures, such as scanning their identification documents, undergoing biometric facial scanning, or accepting audio and video recording in the privacy of their homes. Ensuring clear communication, obtaining informed consent, and addressing privacy concerns are essential to maintain trust and alleviate any apprehensions among test takers (American Educational Research Association et al., 2014).

Moreover, providing technical assistance to test takers with low language proficiency poses a significant challenge (Purpura et al., 2021). Both language testing and proctoring companies generally do not have the capability to offer high-quality, real-time technical support in the all languages of the test taker population, placing an undue burden on test takers to troubleshoot technical issues in English as a second language. This language barrier can hinder effective communication and may disproportionately affect test takers who require additional assistance. While the use of AI in remote proctoring systems enhances assessment security and its applications are promising, challenges remain. Improving violation detection, addressing privacy concerns, obtaining consent, ensuring clear communication, and providing multilingual technical support are vital for advancing remote proctoring and establishing secure assessment practices.

This section has highlighted the application and challenges with existing AI technologies in language assessment. The next section will present future directions in the development and use of AI-based language assessments.

Future Directions

Future directions in the use of AI for developing and administering language assessments involve several key areas of focus. These areas include the utilization of LLMs for assessment development and scoring, validating language assessments by reevaluating the construct in writing assessment, exploring affective computing, and considering technology literacy, ethics, and policy to better understand the role of AI in language education and assessment.

The emergence of LLMs, such as GPT-3 and its successors, has generated great interest for language assessment development and scoring. Test item generation is an area where AI could play a significant role. With the help of AI algorithms, it may be possible to automatically generate diverse and contextually relevant test items that assess various language skills. However, while AI can automate various aspects of language assessment, it is crucial to incorporate human expertise through the "human in the loop" approach. This involves using AI as a tool to support human judgment rather than replacing it entirely. One of the challenges in using AI for language assessments is addressing "hallucinations". Language models can sometimes generate plausible yet incorrect responses called hallucinations. Developers must explore techniques to identify and mitigate such issues, ensuring the reliability and accuracy of the assessments. Further research is needed into how experts can supervise and guide AI systems, ensuring the assessments are fair, reliable, and valid.

Language assessment validation research is once again challenged to include new construct definitions with the introduction of AI technologies. One consideration is the extent to which technology is relevant to the interpretation and uses of test scores (Chapelle, 2021; Voss, 2022). Frameworks such as argument-based validation (Chung, 2017; Fan & Yan, 2020; Williamson et al., 2012; Xu et al., 2020) can help guide validation research of AI-driven language assessments to support their use in appropriate contexts.

Expanding the construct being assessed is an area of future direction. Language assessments often focus on linguistic knowledge and skills, but there is a growing recognition of the importance of assessing other competencies, such as intercultural communicative competence, critical thinking, and digital literacy. AI can support the development of assessments that encompass a broader range of competencies, providing a more authentic assessment of learners' communicative abilities and their ability to navigate real-life language situations. One suggestion is to develop a language use profile rather than a proficiency score (Aryadoust, 2023). Software is already able to record all interactions a test taker has throughout the day in any language. An AI application could analyze the collected data at any time for any time period to provide not only personalized language assessment reports but also appropriate feedback and tutorials that support language learning (Voss, 2021).

Affective computing (Picard, 2000) is an emerging field that focuses on understanding and incorporating emotions in assessment processes. Affective computing research is already on the agenda for intelligent tutoring systems (Hoque, 2013). Soon AI will be able to analyze linguistic cues and nonverbal signals to assess learners' affective states, providing insights into their engagement, motivation, and emotional responses, and can be applied to analysis during language assessment tasks. Integrating affective computing into language assessments can expand the construct being assessed and yield a more comprehensive understanding of learners' language abilities. With the assistance of computer vision, affective computing approaches are integrated into tutoring systems that, enhanced with AI, can provide personalized and adaptive instruction, catering to learners' specific needs and optimizing their language learning experiences. By analyzing learners' performance, AI systems can identify areas of weakness, offer targeted feedback, and provide tailored learning materials (Hoque, 2013). This approach can enhance the effectiveness of language education and assessment, promoting individual growth and development.

Wearable AI as assistive technology will emerge as humans learn how to best utilize data analysis with new technology (Williamson et al., 2020). There is also potential for integration with the social aspects of language assessment. For example, instead of developing avatars and speech recognition system as the sole "rater" or a second rater, technology can assist a human rater in real time to be more efficient and produce more reliable ratings with augmented reality. Diagnostic information about a student or test taker can be displayed through smart glasses, also known as AR glasses, that can collect data through microphones and cameras, process the data, and present information to the wearer on an external screen or a screen embedded in the lens of the glasses (Kumar et al., 2018; Spitzer & Ebner, 2016). More specifically, when a rater administers an interview with a candidate, the rater could be able to see information about the candidate such as their name, the rubric or rating, and dynamic automated assessment presenting feedback on the test taker's linguistic performance (e.g., rate of speech and lexical profile score). With the assistive feedback, a rater is able to attend to interacting with the test taker, rating social aspects of the interaction, and potentially remain more consistent with the aid of the AI feedback.

Supportive AI through wearable AI is an example of how technology can help humans do more than what humans can do alone (Brynjolfsson, 2022; Hoque, 2013). Consider the image in Figure 8.3 recreated from Brynjolfsson (2022). The white circle is the domain of what humans are capable of doing alone. The black circle inside the white circle is the domain of what

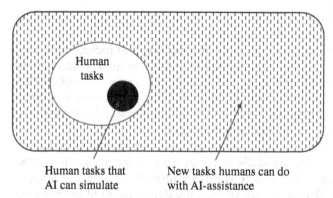

FIGURE 8.3 The domains of human tasks, AI tasks, and AI-assisted human tasks. *Source:* Adapted from Brynjolfsson (2022).

computers are capable of doing that can simulate human performance. The first assumption is that we want the black circle to fill the white circle so that artificial general intelligence is capable of doing all tasks that humans do. However, the box around the circle indicates the domain of tasks that humans can do with the help of AI technology. Brynjolfsson (2022) claims that "opportunities for augmenting humans are far greater than opportunities to automate existing tasks" (p. 279). As technology assists humans, the potential expands exponentially.

Finally, considering technology literacy, ethics, and policy is paramount when incorporating AI into language education and assessment. There is a need to promote digital literacy among learners and educators, ensuring they have the necessary skills to interact with AI systems ethically and responsibly. Additionally, policymakers should establish guidelines and regulations to ensure the ethical use of AI in language assessment, addressing issues of bias, privacy, and fairness.

Understanding the risks and benefits associated with AI in language education and assessment is essential. While AI offers promising opportunities, it is crucial to be aware of potential risks, such as overreliance on automated systems, lack of human interaction, and potential biases in algorithmic decision-making. By critically evaluating the benefits and risks, stakeholders can make informed decisions about the implementation and use of AI in language assessment to enhance the validity, efficiency, and inclusivity.

Discussion Questions

1. To what extent and in what ways will AI-based language assessment change the construct to be measured?
2. To what extent and how can AI-based language assessment support instruction and learning?

References

ACT Inc. (2021). *Automatic item generation for passage-based assessment.* U.S. Patent No. 10,332,416.

Alikaniotis, D., Yannakoudakis, H., & Rei, M. (2016). Automatic text scoring using neural networks. *Proceedings of the 54th annual meeting of the association for computational linguistics,* pp. 715–725. Berlin, Germany, August 7–12, 2016.

American Educational Research Association, American Psychological Association, & National Council on Measurement in Education. (2014). *Standards for educational and psychological testing.* American Psychological Association.

Aryadoust, V. (2023). The vexing problem of validity and the future of second language assessment. *Language Testing*, *40*(1), 8–14.

Attali, Y., & Burstein, J. (2006). Automated essay scoring with e-rater® V.2. *The Journal of Technology, Learning, and Assessment*, *4*(3), 1–30.

Attali, Y., Runge, A., LaFlair, G. T., Yancey, K., Goodwin, S., Park, Y., & von Davier, A. A. (2022). The interactive reading task: transformer-based automatic item generation. *Frontiers in Artificial Intelligence*, *5*, 903077. https://doi.org/10.3389/frai.2022.903077.

Brunfaut, T. (2022). Future challenges and opportunities in language testing and assessment: basic questions and principles at the forefront. *Language Testing*, *40*(1), 15–23. https://doi.org/10.1177/02655322221127896.

Brynjolfsson, E. (2022). The turing trap: the promise & peril of human-like artificial intelligence. *Daedalus*, *151*(2), 272–287.

Burton, J. D. (2023). Gazing into cognition: eye behavior in online L2 speaking tests. *Language Assessment Quarterly*, *20*(2), 190–214. https://doi.org/10.1080/15434303.2022.2143680.

Chapelle, C. A. (2021). *Argument-based validation in testing and assessment*. Sage.

Chapelle, C. A., & Chung, Y. R. (2010). The promise of NLP and speech processing technologies in language assessment. *Language Testing*, *27*(3), 301–315. https://doi.org/10.1177/0265532210364405.

Chapelle, C. A., Chung, Y. R., Hegelheimer, V., Pendar, N., & Xu, J. (2010). Towards a computer-delivered test of productive grammatical ability. *Language Testing*, *27*(4), 443–469.

Chen, L., Zechner, K., Yoon, S. Y., Evanini, K., Wang, X., Loukina, A., Tao, J., Davis, L., Lee, C. M., Ma, M., Mundkowsky, R., Lu, C., Leong, C. W., & Gyawali, B. (2018). *Automated scoring of nonnative speech using the SpeechRater*[SM] *v. 5.0 engine*. Research Report, ETS RR-18-10.

Chodorow, M., Gamon, M., & Tetreault, J. (2010). The utility of article and preposition error correction systems for English language learners: feedback and assessment. *Language Testing*, *27*(3), 419–436.

Choi, I., & Deane, P. (2021). Evaluating writing process features in an adult EFL writing assessment context: A keystroke logging study. *Language Assessment Quarterly*, *18*(2), 107–132.

Chung, Y. R. (2017). Validation of technology-assisted language tests. In C. A. Chapelle & S. Sauro (Eds.), *The handbook of technology and second language teaching and learning* (pp. 332–346). Wiley.

Cotos, E. (2016). Computer-assisted research writing in the disciplines. In S. A. Crossley & D. S. McNamara (Eds.), *Adaptive educational technologies for literacy instruction* (pp. 225–242). Routledge. https://doi.org/10.4324/9781315647500-15.

Dodigovic, M. (2005). *Artificial intelligence in second language learning: Raising error awareness*. Multilingual Matters.

Ebling, S., Camgöz, N. C., Braem, P. B., Tissi, K., Sidler-Miserez, S., Stoll, S., Hadfield, S., Haug, T., Bowden, R., Tornay, S., Razavi, M., & Magimai-Doss, M. (2018). *SMILE Swiss German sign language dataset*. In *Proceedings of the 11th international conference on language resources and evaluation (LREC) 2018*. The European Language Resources Association (ELRA). https://aclanthology.org/L18-1666.pdf.

Ebling, S., Camgöz, N. C., & Bowden, R. (2021). New technologies in second language signed assessment. In T. Haug, W. Mann & U. Knoch (Eds.), *The handbook of language assessment across modalities*. New York: Oxford Academic. https://doi.org/10.1093/oso/9780190885052.003.0036, accessed 8 April 2024.

Fan, J., & Yan, X. (2020). Assessing speaking proficiency: a narrative review of speaking assessment research within the argument-based validation framework. *Frontiers in Psychology*, *11*, 330.

Foltz, P. W., Streeter, L. A., Lochbaum, K. E., & Landauer, T. K. (2013). Implementation and applications of the intelligent essay assessor. In M. D. Shermis & J. Burstein (Eds.), *Handbook of automated essay* (pp. 68–88). Routledge.

Goldberg, Y. (2022). *Neural network methods for natural language processing*. Springer Nature.

Granfeldt, J., & Ågren, M. (2014). SLA developmental stages and teachers' assessment of written French: exploring Direkt Profil as a diagnostic assessment tool. *Language Testing*, *31*(3), 285–305.

Grapin, S. E. (2023). Assessment of English learners and their peers in the content areas: expanding what "counts" as evidence of content learning. *Language Assessment Quarterly*, *20*(2), 215–234. https://doi.org/10.1080/15434303.2022.2147072.

Grotjahn, R. (1986). Test validation and cognitive psychology: some methodological considerations. *Language Testing*, *3*(2), 159–185. https://doi.org/10.1177/026553228600300205.

124 Chapter 8 Language Assessment and Artificial Intelligence

Hannah, L., Kim, H., & Jang, E. E. (2022). Investigating the effects of task type and linguistic background on accuracy in automated speech recognition systems: implications for use in language assessment of young learners. *Language Assessment Quarterly, 19*(3), 289–313. https://doi.org/10.1080/15434303.2022.2038172.

Heaven, W. D. (2023, March 3). The inside story of how ChatGPT was built from the people who made it: Exclusive conversations that take us behind the scenes of a cultural phenomenon. *MIT Technology Review.* https://www.technologyreview.com/2023/03/03/1069311/inside-story-oral-history-how-chatgpt-built-openai/.

Hoang, G. T. L., & Kunnan, A. J. (2016). Automated essay evaluation for English language learners: a case study of MY Access. *Language Assessment Quarterly, 13*(4), 359–376. https://doi.org/10.1080/15434303.2016.123012.

Hoque, M. E. (2013). *Computers to help with conversations: Affective framework to enhance human nonverbal skills (Doctoral dissertation).* ProQuest Dissertations and Theses database. ProQuest No. 1647765699.

Isaacs, T., Hu, R., Trenkic, D., & Varga, J. (2023). Examining the predictive validity of the Duolingo English Test: evidence from a major UK university. *Language Testing,* 1–23. https://doi.org/10.1177/02655322231158550.

Isbell, D. R., & Kremmel, B. (2020). Test review: current options in at-home language proficiency tests for making high-stakes decisions. *Language Testing, 37*(4), 600–619.

Kang, O., & Johnson, D. (2018). The roles of suprasegmental features in predicting English oral proficiency with an automated system. *Language Assessment Quarterly, 15*(2), 150–168. https://doi.org/10.1080/15434303.2018.1451531.

Khabbazbashi, N., & Galaczi, E. D. (2020). A comparison of holistic, analytic, and part marking models in speaking assessment. *Language Testing, 37*(3), 333–360. https://doi-org.ezproxy.cul.columbia.edu/10.1177/0265532219898635.

Kumar, N. M., Krishna, P. R., Kumar, P., Pagadala, P. K., & Kumar, N. M. S. (2018). *Use of smart glasses in education: a study.* In *Proceedings of the second international conference on I-SMAC (IoT in Social, Mobile, Analytics and Cloud),* pp. 56–59.

Latifi, S., & Gierl, M. (2021). Automated scoring of junior and senior high essays using Coh-Metrix features: implications for large-scale language testing. *Language Testing, 38*(1), 62–85.

Litman, D., Strik, H., & Lim, G. S. (2018). Speech technologies and the assessment of second language speaking: approaches, challenges, and opportunities. *Language Assessment Quarterly, 15*(3), 294–309. https://doi.org/10.1080/15434303.2018.1472265.

Liu, A., Pang, L., & Qi, X. (2022). MEN: mutual enhancement networks for sign language recognition and education. *IEEE Transactions on Neural Networks and Learning Systems,* 1–15.

Loukina, A., Davis, L., & Xi, X. (2018). Automated assessment of pronunciation in spontaneous speech. In O. Kang & A. Ginther (Eds.), *Assessment in second language pronunciation* (pp. 153–171). Routledge.

Loukina, A., Madnani, N., & Zechner, K. (2019). The many dimensions of algorithmic fairness in educational applications. In *Proceedings of the fourteenth workshop on innovative use of NLP for building educational applications* (pp. 1–10). Association for Computational Linguistics.

McCarthy, J., & Feigenbaum, E. (1990). In memoriam Arthur Samuel: pioneer in machine learning. *AI Magazine, 11*(3).

Mizumoto, A., & Eguchi, M. (2023). Exploring the potential of using an AI language model for automated essay scoring. *Research Methods in Applied Linguistics, 2*(2), 1–13.

Ockey, G. J., & Chukharev-Hudilainen, E. (2021). Human versus computer partner in the paired oral discussion test. *Applied Linguistics, 42*(5), 924–944.

OpenAI. (2020). *Language models are few-shot learners (GPT-3).* arXiv:2005.14165 [cs.CL].

OpenAI. (2023). *ChatGPT (Mar 14 version) [Large language model].* https://chat.openai.com/chat.

Page, B. E. (1966). The imminence of … grading essays by computer. *The Phi Delta Kappan, 47*(5), 238–243.

Park, K. (2014). Corpora and language assessment: the state of the art. *Language Assessment Quarterly, 11*(1), 27–44. https://doi.org/10.1080/15434303.2013.872647.

Pearson (2022). *Versant™ English test: test description and validation summary.* https://www.pearson.com/content/dam/one-dot-com/one-dot-com/english/SupportingDocs/Versant/ValidationSummary/Versant-English-Test-Description-Validation-Report.pdf.

Picard, R. (2000). *Affective computing.* The MIT Press.

Plough, I., Banerjee, J., & Iwashita, J. (2018). Interactional competence: genie out of the bottle. *Language Testing, 35*(3), 427–445.

Purpura, J. E., Davoodifard, M., & Voss, E. (2021). Conversion to remote proctoring of the community English language program online placement exam at Teachers College, Columbia University. *Language Assessment Quarterly*, *18*(1), 42–50. https://doi.org/10.1080/15434303.2020.1867145.

Ritchings, T., Khadragi, A., & Saeb, M. (2012). An intelligent computer-based system for sign language tutoring. *Assistive Technology*, *24*(4), 299–308. https://doi.org/10.1080/10400435.2012.680662.

Shin, J., & Gierl, M. (2020). More efficient processes for creating automated essay scoring frameworks: a demonstration of two algorithms. *Language Testing*, *38*(2), 247–272.

Spitzer, M., & Ebner, M. (2016). Use cases and architecture of an information system to integrate smart glasses in educational environments. In *Proceedings of EdMedia 2016 – world conference on educational media and technology* (pp. 57–64). Vancouver, BC, Canada: Association for the Advancement of Computing in Education (AACE). https://www.learntechlib.org/primary/p/172932/.

Taghipour, K., & Ng, H. T. (2016). A neural approach to automated essay scoring. In J. Su, K. Duh, & X. Carreras (Eds.), *Proceedings of the 2016 conference on empirical methods in natural language processing* (pp. 1882–1891). https://aclanthology.org/volumes/D16-1/.

Tavakoli, P., Kendon, G., Mazhurnaya, S., & Ziomek, A. (2023). Assessment of fluency in the test of English for educational purposes. *Language Testing*, *40*(3), 1–23.

Turing, A. M. (1950). Computing machinery and intelligence. *Mind*, *59*(236), 433–460. http://www.jstor.org/stable/2251299.

Van Moere, A. (2012). A psycholinguistic approach to oral language assessment. *Language Testing*, *29*(3), 325–344. https://doi.org/10.1177/0265532211424478.

Voss, E. (2021). The role of technology in learning-oriented assessment. In A. Gebril (Ed.), *Learning-oriented language assessment: Putting theory into practice*. Routledge.

Voss, E. (2022). Argument-based validation in the time of the COVID-19 pandemic. In K. Sadeghi (Ed.), *Language assessment at the time of the COVID-19 pandemic: Technological affordances and challenges*. Routledge.

Voss, E. (2023). Proctoring remote language assessments. In K. Sadeghi & D. Douglas (Eds.), *Fundamental considerations in technology mediated language assessment*. Routledge.

Wang, P. (2019). On defining artificial intelligence. *Journal of Artificial General Intelligence*, *10*(2), 1–37. https://doi.org/10.2478/jagi-2019-0002.

Williamson, D. M., Xi, X., & Breyer, F. J. (2012). A framework for evaluation and use of automated scoring. *Educational Measurement: Issues and Practice*, *31*(1), 2–13.

Williamson, B., Bayne, S., & Shay, S. (2020). The datafication of teaching in higher education: critical issues and perspectives. *Teaching In Higher Education*, *25*(4), 351–365.

Xu, J. (2018). Measuring "spoken collocational competence" in communicative speaking assessment. *Language Assessment Quarterly*, *15*(3), 255–272.

Xu, J., Brenchley, M., Jones, E., Pinnington, A., Benjamin, T., Knill, K., Seal-Coon, G., Robinson, M., & Geranpayeh, A. (2020). *Linguaskill: building a validity argument for the speaking test*. Cambridge Assessment English. https://doi.org/10.13140/RG.2.2.18138.98242.

Yi'an, W. (1998). What do tests of listening comprehension test?: a retrospection study of EFL test-takers performing a multiple-choice task. *Language Testing*, *15*(1), 21–44.

Youn, S. J. (2023). Test design and validity evidence of interactive speaking assessment in the era of emerging technologies. *Language Testing*, *40*(1), 54–60.

Suggested Readings

Chapelle, C. A., & Douglas, D. (2006). *Assessing language through computer technology*. Cambridge University Press.

Wang, N., Rebolledo-Mendez, G., Dimitrova, V., Matsuda, N. & Santos, O. C. (Eds.). (2023). *Artificial intelligence in education: posters and late breaking results, workshops and tutorials, industry and innovation tracks, practitioners, doctoral consortium and blue sky. Proceedings from 24th international conference, AIED 2023*.

Yan, D., Rupp, A. A., & Folz, P. W. (2020). *Handbook of automated scoring: Theory in practice*. Routledge.

Zechner, K., & Evanini, K. (Eds.). (2019). *Automated speaking assessment: Using language technologies to score spontaneous speech*. Routledge.

THEME 2

Assessing Language Skills and Resources

CHAPTER 9

Assessing Listening

Elvis Wagner

Introduction

The ability to listen is recognized as an integral component of communicative language ability, as well as language learning. Children learn their first language almost exclusively through listening and responding to spoken input. It is estimated that 50% or more of a person's time in communicative situations is spent listening. Similarly, L2 researchers (e.g., Rost, 2016) have stressed the importance of listening in language acquisition because so much of the input needed for language acquisition is provided orally. Nevertheless, assessing a person's L2 listening ability presents unique challenges to teachers and test developers, and perhaps because of these challenges, the assessment of listening has historically been somewhat neglected and even overlooked in the language assessment literature. This chapter provides a brief overview of L2 listening assessment and the necessity of assessing this component of interactional competence. It will also present some of the unique challenges that the assessment of listening ability presents for test developers, and will provide theoretical justification for how to address these particular challenges.

It is now widely accepted that individual language learners have varying levels of ability in the different language skills and that a divisible model of language ability with a general factor plus distinct traits is the most plausible model (Bachman & Palmer, 1996). As a result, it is recognized by language assessment researchers that listening ability, being a distinct trait, should be assessed. Nevertheless, because of the unique and challenging aspects of assessing listening ability, test developers might be tempted to avoid including a listening section. After all, many of the components of listening are similar to the other modalities, especially reading. However, there are also many characteristics that are unique to listening. Listening ability is obviously a subset of general language ability, and any assessment of listening ability will also be an assessment of general language ability (Rost, 2016). The reverse is not necessarily true, however, in that an assessment of general language ability might not assess listening ability specifically. Buck (2001) argued that because the testing of listening is technically more complicated than testing the other language modalities (i.e., it requires audio or video equipment to create the texts and then to play these texts for test takers), it might not actually be worth the trouble unless the test developer was "particularly interested in the knowledge, skills and abilities that are unique to listening" (p. 32). Similarly, Rost (2016) argued that if the goal is to test listening ability, it is necessary to focus on those characteristics that are unique to listening.

Each skill or modality presents challenges for test developers, but assessing a person's listening ability presents unique challenges. Perhaps the most obvious difficulty is that

The Concise Companion to Language Assessment, First Edition. Edited by Antony John Kunnan.
© 2025 John Wiley & Sons, Inc. Published 2025 by John Wiley & Sons, Inc.

130 Chapter 9 Assessing Listening

listening (like reading) is an internal process. While speaking and writing involves some sort of output that can be observed and measured, listening goes on inside a person's head. Thus, a test developer must create some sort of task that the listener must respond to in some way, and based on this response output, the test developer is able to make inferences about the individual's listening ability. In addition, reading and listening assessments require selecting or creating the written or spoken input to present to test takers. For reading tests, it is relatively simple to present the written input to test takers, either on paper (for a paper and pencil test) or on a computer monitor for a computer-based test. But the presentation of spoken texts to listening test takers proves more problematic. How should the spoken texts be presented the listeners? Should the text be spoken by a test interlocutor, or should it be recorded and played using technology? How long should the text be? How fast should the texts be spoken? What sort of language characteristics should the spoken texts include? One way to address these sorts of questions is to utilize Bachman and Palmer's (1996) framework of task characteristics when selecting, creating, and developing spoken texts for listening assessment, and this notion of the "characteristics of the input" will be investigated in more depth below.

Identifying the Target Language Use Domain and Construct Validity

For this section, two separate yet complementary notions fundamental to language assessment will be reviewed and applied to the assessment of listening. The first notion is that of defining the target language use domain, as described by Bachman and Palmer (1996). The second is the two major threats to construct validity, as described by Messick (1989, 1996).

To determine appropriate texts and response formats for a particular listening assessment, it is vital that the test developer identifies the purpose and the situational context for the assessment (Buck, 2001). In other words, how is the construct of listening ability defined, and what aspects of listening ability should be tested? It is very rare for the goal to be to assess an individual's overall listening proficiency. Instead, the test developer usually has some sort of listening context in which the test takers' ability is to be assessed. Bachman and Palmer (1996) define the target language use (TLU) domain as the "situation or context in which the test-taker will be using the language outside of the test itself" (p. 18). In other words, what type of listening ability should be assessed? For example, if the goal of the test is to assess a learner's ability to comprehend an academic lecture (an academic TLU domain), then it is necessary to identify the distinguishing characteristics of academic lecture texts and include those characteristics in the assessment task. The test developer needs to first identify those distinguishing language characteristics of the TLU domain and then make the test task characteristics similar to and representative of the TLU domain. The characteristics of the listening test tasks are always going to affect test scores to some extent, and thus, it is necessary to control them as much as possible so that the tests will be appropriate for their intended use. Bachman and Palmer (1996) created a framework of language task characteristics that allows test developers to understand how the test task characteristics can be varied to tailor tests for different purposes. Their framework of task characteristics has five sections: characteristics of the setting, characteristics of the test rubrics, characteristics of the input, characteristics of the expected response, and relationship between input and response (pp. 49–50).

Utilizing this framework should serve to minimize threats to construct validity. For listening assessment, particularly relevant are the third and fourth components of the framework ("characteristics of the input" and "characteristics of the expected response"). To relate it back to the academic lecture example, the first step would be to identify the characteristics of academic lecture spoken texts. For "characteristics of the input," things to consider would be the "format" of the input, including the channel of the input (an academic lecture obviously involves oral input, but also includes visual input because the listeners can see the speaker, her gestures and body language, as well as things like PowerPoint slides and other types of visuals) as well as the length of the lecture, and the speech rate of academic lecturers. Also important are characteristics of the language of input, including the way academic lectures are typically organized textually, the grammatical and vocabulary characteristics of typical academic lectures, as well as pragmatic and topical characteristics of academic lectures. The test developer also needs to consider how the listening test taker is expected to respond to the input. Again, using an academic lecture TLU domain, what is the listener in an academic lecture expected to do with the input? How is she expected to respond to the input? For an academic lecture, the listener might be expected to remember the information so that she can create some sort of future response, which might include answering questions for a future test (and these test questions might include selected response, limited production, and/or extended production items). The listener might be expected to discuss the information with classmates and write a paper in which she can demonstrate that she has understood the information presented in the lecture.

Identifying the distinguishing language characteristics of the TLU domain and then making the test task characteristics similar to and representative of the TLU domain should serve to minimize threats to the construct validity of the test and should allow the test developer to make more valid inferences about the test takers' listening ability beyond the testing context. L2 listening tests that have tasks that are not representative of the TLU domain present threats to construct validity in two ways: unrepresentative tasks introduce sources of invalidity and also lead to construct underrepresentation (Messick, 1989, 1996). An example of an unrepresentative listening task would be the use of a speaking text that involves two friends discussing their vacations on a listening test meant to assess academic lecture listening ability. Because this speaking text is not representative of the textual characteristics of academic lectures, using such a text would introduce sources of invalidity (construct irrelevant variance). The test might provide information about a listener's ability to understand conversational language, but not the TLU domain of interest (i.e., academic lectures). Similarly, a speaking text that includes characteristics of the TLU domain, but is not an adequate representation of that domain, would represent a threat to construct validity. For example, using an oral text taken from a real academic lecture for a listening test, but having that text be only 30 seconds long might be a source of construct underrepresentation. A 30-second academic lecture is very different from a 30-minute academic lecture. Longer texts require the speaker to utilize textual organizational characteristics (such as discourse markers and other cohesive devices) that would not be appropriate or necessary for a 30-second utterance. Thus, test developers have to be cognizant of the importance of not only using speaking texts that are similar to those of the TLU domain; they must also make sure that the characteristics are representative of the characteristics of the TLU domain.

With criterion-referenced listening testing, the criteria to be assessed will dictate the characteristics of the test task. For a classroom teacher, the assessment context is necessarily closely aligned with the curricular goals of the class, and not all listening test tasks must necessarily be listening comprehension tasks. For example, for some learners, the learning goals might include promoting learners' ability to discriminate different sounds in the target language, or the ability to segment incoming speech into words. If the curricular goals and the teaching focus on this type of decoding (Field, 2008), then the test tasks should as well. There are of course many times when it might not be advisable to use texts spoken at a normal speaking rate, or that contain the characteristics of unplanned spoken discourse.

Current Research and Challenges for L2 Listening Assessment

Current research in second language listening suggests a number of issues that are particularly relevant for L2 listening assessment pertaining to specific language characteristics of possible TLU domains and will be discussed here.

Assessing a Learner's Interactive Speaking and Listening Ability

Traditionally, language assessment has often involved separating the different skills to assess them. There are many justifications for doing this. First, there is often a diagnostic component to assessment, where the test developers want to examine what specific aspects of language a person might be weaker in than in other areas, and use this information for placement purposes, and to design and personalize instruction according to that test taker's needs. Another reason for separating the skills in language assessment involves validity and reliability issues. For example, an integrated skills assessment task might include reading a written text and then writing some sort of response to that text. The writing sample that is produced by the test takers is then scored. The difficulty for test developers here, however, is how to interpret the score from this writing sample. If a test taker performs poorly on the writing sample, is it because she has weaker writing skills? Or perhaps it is because she has weaker reading skills and was not able to understand the text she was required to read. The test taker's inability to respond appropriately in writing to the prompt might not have been because she lacked the writing ability to do so, but because her weaker reading ability made it impossible for her to demonstrate her writing ability.

This phenomenon presents difficulties for language test developers. However, in most real-life listening domains, listeners must listen to and process oral information, and then immediately do something with that information. The obvious example would be a communicative situation where a person is using language to interact with another person. Here, the person is both listener and speaker. The person must listen to the oral text provided by the speaker, and simultaneously formulate an appropriate response, and then speak that response at the correct time. This is cognitively demanding of many language learners, which is exactly the point. Working memory capacity has emerged as an area of intense research in second language learning, with the theory being that individuals with more working memory capacity are better able to learn and use a second language (Juffs & Harrington, 2011; Mackey et al., 2010), because of the intense cognitive processing demands found in interactive language contexts. Again, test developers need to identify and incorporate the characteristics of the TLU domain into the test tasks, and thus, creating integrated test tasks that mimic the intensive cognitive processing demands of real-life oral interaction should result in more valid inferences about a test taker's interactional competence outside of the testing situation.

Being able to interact in a conversation is obviously a language use domain of interest for language learners and language teachers. Yet, it presents difficulties for assessment, due mainly to reliability issues. For a classroom assessment, where reliability concerns are of less importance, it is certainly feasible to create an interactive speaking/listening test task that can assess this ability. But for a larger-scale exam, in which reliability is of great importance, this type of task is problematic. Standardized tests, by definition, involve the same testing conditions for every test taker. The same (or equivalent) prompts are given to all test takers, who are all exposed to the same or equivalent input. With an interactive task, involving two or more speakers, standardization is not possible, presenting real reliability challenges for test developers. This is an example where the tension between validity and reliability is apparent. In an attempt to maximize the validity of the inferences made from the results of the test, a test developer might identify some of the distinguishing characteristics of a conversational domain

Current Research and Challenges for L2 Listening Assessment **133**

and then include some of these characteristics in the assessment task. In so doing, however, reliability might suffer. Similarly, with advances in technology, test developers are increasingly relying on computers to administer and interactive speaking and listening test tasks, in which the computer acts as an interlocutor and the test taker listens to and responds to the computer-prompted spoken input (e.g., Ockey & Chukharev-Hudilainen, 2021; Ockey & Wagner, 2018).

Some standardized tests of English proficiency provide examples of how different components of a conversational TLU domain can be assessed. The Test of English as a Foreign Language internet-based test (TOEFL iBT) would seem to focus more on the reliability of the scoring of the speaking and listening components of the test, with less of a focus on including many of the characteristics of interactive conversational language use on the assessment. While some of the listening and speaking tasks are integrated, in that the listener must first listen to a spoken text, and then speak a response based on the oral input, there is no interlocutor for the test taker to interact with. The test taker listens to a recorded response from a computer, then has time to formulate a response, and then speaks that response into a microphone, where it is later scored by trained raters. For the International English Language Testing System (IELTS), there is a human interlocutor that administers the speaking task, and the interlocutor asks (prescribed) questions that the test taker must respond to. Here, there are more of the characteristics of interactive conversational language, but still the domain coverage is fairly narrow, in that the interlocutor seeks to provide standardized input to the test taker, rather than an authentic conversation in which the language is unscripted. For the *Cambridge English: Advanced* test, the speaking section of the test is also face-to-face with two test takers and two assessors. The test takers converse with each other in completing a collaborative task. Then, they speak with the interlocutor about the task they just completed.

Integrating speaking and listening tasks to maximize coverage of an interactive conversational language use domain remains challenging in assessment, but it is a necessary and advisable goal. Douglas (1997) argues that "... because listening and speaking are theoretically and practically very difficult to separate" (p. 25), the two skills should be integrated in assessment. Similarly, other skills can also be integrated with listening tasks on assessments. For example, many tests (e.g., TOEFL iBT, with an academic listening TLU domain) involve tasks that require the test taker to listen to a spoken text, and then incorporate this information into some sort of written response.

Including Linguistics Features Characteristic of Unplanned Spoken Discourse in the Spoken Texts Used in L2 Listening Assessment

Again, returning to the need to identify and incorporate the characteristics of the TLU domain into the test tasks, an important consideration for test developers is the linguistic characteristics of unplanned spoken discourse. Written texts and spoken texts are often very different because of these features found in unplanned spoken discourse. These can include things like hesitations, filled and unfilled pauses, false starts, and the phonological characteristics of connected speech (i.e., assimilation, vowel reduction, epenthesis, linking, and elision) (Celce-Murcia et al., 1994). In addition, spoken language can be seen as having a different set of rules than written language. Spoken language often has run-on sentences, grammatical "mistakes," shorter idea units, and ellipses. Spoken language usually involves shared knowledge between two speakers and is often deictic in nature (the here and now, when a speaker says "I" or "that" or "now," or points to an object) (Brown, 1995). Finally, because of the nature of most speaking events (with obvious exceptions), planning what is going to be said is usually done in real-time. This results in texts that are less logically and systematically organized. Most spoken texts are "first draft," unedited, and messy, as compared to written texts, in which the writer can plan, organize, and revise the written text.

134 **Chapter 9** Assessing Listening

These linguistics characteristics of unplanned spoken discourse often present difficulties for L2 listeners. Many or even most L2 listeners are often not even aware of the differences between written and spoken texts. Tannen (1982) described how spoken texts can be arranged on a continuum of orality – some texts will be more oral than others. It is necessary for test developers to identify the TLU domain and the characteristics of spoken texts in that domain. Texts that are written, rehearsed, and then read aloud will be on one end of the continuum (literate), while extemporaneous conversations will be on the other end (oral). According to the theory that individual differences in working memory capacity influence learner performance, the processing of unplanned speech might require more of a listener's cognitive resources than speech that is planned and rehearsed. Because more attentional resources have to be devoted to segmenting and decoding the oral input, the listeners have fewer resources to devote to other parts of the comprehension process. The difficulty L2 listeners face in comprehending unplanned spoken texts is probably exacerbated in part by the nature of the spoken input that many language learners (especially foreign language learners) receive. Audio-texts that are created for language textbooks and classrooms usually involve a scripted text that is written and revised, and then read aloud, often by professional actors trained to speak clearly and comprehensibly. Some TLU domains might involve spoken texts on the literate end of the spoken text continuum (e.g., the ability to listen to television or radio), but it would seem more likely that the TLU domains most teachers and test developers would be interested in would include spoken texts on the "oral" end of the continuum. To not include these types of spoken texts on tests of L2 listening ability would be an example of construct underrepresentation (Messick, 1989, 1996; Ockey & Wagner, 2018).

The most obvious way to include these natural characteristics of unplanned spoken discourse is to use authentic spoken texts, in which speakers are recorded in a real-life communicative language situation, rather than to use scripted and polished written texts that are read aloud. However, in reality, it is difficult to use unscripted texts. As assessment researchers have described (e.g., Buck, 2001; Carr, 2011), it is often difficult to create comprehension questions using authentic, unplanned spoken texts. Usually, test developers will create a text to be used on a listening test and simultaneously write comprehension items based on the text. Doing so is efficient, in that the test developer can make sure that there is enough testable information in a text of a given length of time. Authentic texts usually do not have the same amount of testable information in the same duration of time. For high-stakes exams, created by high-profile companies or organizations, there is also the issue of "face validity," in that spoken texts with pauses, false starts, grammar mistakes, and "poor pronunciation" might appear unprofessional. A review of the spoken texts used in the listening section of some of the high-stakes English proficiency tests (i.e., the IELTS, TOEFL, and the Duolingo English Test) suggests that virtually all of the texts are indeed scripted, written, and read aloud, and tend to fall on the "literate" end of the orality continuum. For classroom tests, the goal is to assess what is taught in the curriculum. If the curriculum includes communicative language ability, and being able to listen to and comprehend spontaneous spoken discourse, then it is essential that the assessment includes those linguistic phenomena found in spoken discourse.

Types and varieties of the spoken language to use as input

Another consideration for test developers includes the types and varieties of spoken texts to include. Spoken language tends to have much more variety than written language, and phenomena like dialects, accents and regional variations, and colloquial language and slang are much more likely to be found in spoken texts than written texts. The dilemma for test developers is if and how this variation should be integrated into listening tests. For classroom tests tied to a specific curriculum, this issue is less problematic, because the curriculum and goals of the class dictate the criteria to be assessed. If the goal of the class is to teach listeners to be able to comprehend the standard variety of a language, then the standard variety should be used on the listening assessment. But for other assessments in which the construct definition is less easily defined, this issue of language variety can be problematic. For example, the

TOEFL iBT purports to assess a test taker's ability to use North American English or academic English in a higher education context. Thus, North American-accented English is used in the listening test task. However, very few, if any, of the listening texts use speakers that are non-native speakers of English, even though a substantial proportion of higher education instructors in North America are non-native speakers of English (and thus, this variety of English is part of the TLU domain). The IELTS (Academic) also purports to assess a test taker's ability to use academic English in a higher education context, but it is used by North American, British, Australian, and institutions of higher learning in other areas. Because of this, the IELTS uses speakers with American, Canadian, British, Australian, and New Zealand-accented English. Similarly, the Cambridge ESOL exams use regional varieties of British English in their spoken texts. Finally, another point to consider is that in many language use contexts, the variety of English that listeners might usually encounter is that in which none of the speakers are native speakers of the language, and English is being used as a lingua franca.

While this issue of the particular variety of a language to use on a listening test has begun to receive research attention (e.g., Taylor, 2008), many of the major proficiency tests in English have been reluctant to use texts with speakers that have regional or non-native accents, or who speak nonstandard varieties of English. This might be due to resistance of the use of nonstandard varieties of English by the test stakeholders, including the test developers, test users, and the test takers themselves. Again, the TLU domain should dictate the language variety and dialect that should be used as the input for listening tests, yet social and political considerations often override these dictates, which can be a threat to the validity of the test results (Ockey & Wagner, 2018).

Using the visual channel to include the nonverbal components of spoken texts

Traditionally, tests of L2 listening ability have focused on the oral information in a spoken text (Wagner, 2010) and have neglected to include the visual, nonverbal components of spoken language. Numerous second language acquisition researchers have described how the visual components of a spoken text can assist listeners in comprehending that text, including the physical appearance of the speaker, the physical background setting, gestures, body language, lip movements, facial expressions, and many others (e.g., Baltova, 1994; Gruba, 1997; Wagner, 2008, 2010, 2013). Second language listening teachers have incorporated audio-visual texts into their classrooms in the last few decades, and with the proliferation of technology into everyday life, it seems likely that the use of audio-visual input for L2 learners will only continue to expand.

For a few limited domains such as listening to the radio, or participating in a telephone conversation, the listener is not able to see the speaker, and thus, it would be inappropriate to include the visual channel in assessing a listener's ability in this particular domain, because doing so would serve to introduce construct irrelevant variance into the measurement. However, for the vast majority of TLU domains, the listener is able to see the speaker and is able to utilize the information provided by the physical setting, the speaker's appearance, gestures, and body language. Again, the listening test developer must incorporate the characteristics of the TLU domain into the test tasks, and if the TLU domain includes these nonverbal components, then the test task should as well. A number of researchers (Cross, 2011; Ockey, 2007; Sueyoshi & Hardison, 2005; Wagner, 2008) have found that L2 listeners vary in their ability to interpret and utilize the nonverbal information provided by the speaker. Because this varying ability to interpret the nonverbal information can be seen as part of the construct, to not include the visual channel on L2 listening tests is an example of construct underrepresentation (Ockey & Wagner, 2018; Wagner, 2008). However, large testing organizations have resisted using the visual channel in delivering input to L2 listening test takers. Currently, the PTE and IELTS exams have listening sections that use audio-only input. The TOEFL uses audio-visual input, but the visual input is limited to a series of still pictures and graphics, rather than video. Although the theoretical justification for the use of both the oral and visual channels for the input for listening tests is strong, practicality constraints have often overridden these theoretical arguments.

Item types and response formats

The previous discussion has focused on the type of input that the test takers listen to during listening tests. Listening, like reading, presents challenges to test developers because it is an internal process, and since the test taker cannot see inside the brain of the test takers, the test developer is forced to make inferences about test takers' ability based on their response to the input. This section will focus on the types of response formats that can be used with L2 listening tests, and will explore related issues including how many times to present the oral text, providing some sort of context for test takers before the listening text is played, and the issue of question preview.

Unfortunately, looking to the TLU domain for the most appropriate type of item response format to use on a test of listening is less clear cut than the type of input to provide. For a writing and speaking test, the output of the test takers can be modeled on the type of output learners are expected to produce in that TLU domain. Even with reading, the TLU domain provides more clues to the most appropriate type of item response format to utilize. Readers (especially in academic settings) are usually expected to read a text and respond to it in some ways, perhaps in writing, or perhaps by answering a series of questions about the text that they have read. In an academic listening domain, the learner is usually expected to listen to a text (e.g., a lecture). However, how the listener is expected to respond to the input is less clear. The inherent artificiality of a testing situation becomes apparent in choosing or creating a response format for a listening test, so the test developer has to try and make the best informed and theoretically plausible decisions possible.

Perhaps the most common response format in listening tests is a set of usually discrete point comprehension questions. The listener must read (or listen to) the question and then choose the most appropriate answer or answers (selected response such as a multiple-choice item), or write (or speak) the answer (constructed response). Because these types of items are relatively easy to create and can be reliably scored, they are commonly used in listening tests, and some examples are provided below.

Types of selected-response items that are sometimes used in listening tests include filling out a timetable, itinerary, calendar, or chart based on the spoken input. An example (http://www.ets.org/Media/Tests/TOEFL/pdf/TOEFL_Tips.pdf, p. 17) from the TOEFL iBT is provided here:

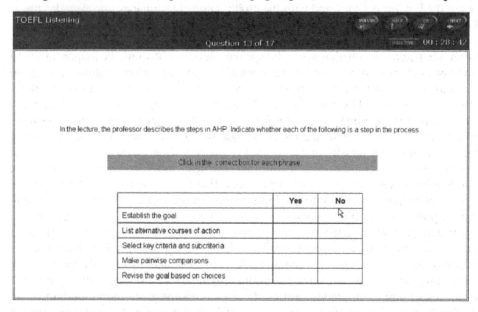

These types of response format presuppose that the learner is proficient enough to be able to read the items and prompts. With lower-ability test takers, some listening tests require the test taker to respond orally, or with some sort of nonverbal physical response to the input.

Alternatively, test takers might have to repeat a phrase or sentence that they have heard, or to summarize an oral text, as shown in the example from the PTE (http://pearsonpte.com/PTEAcademic/Tutorial/Documents/PTEA_Tutorial.pdf, p. 12):

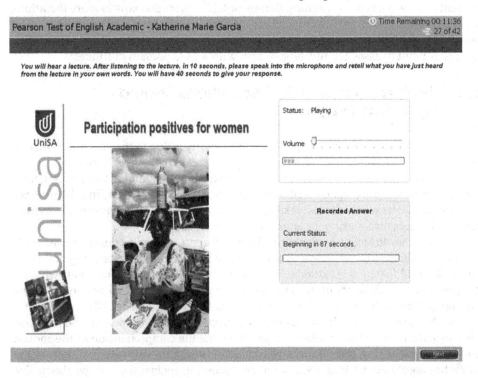

The oral summary response described above is an example of more integrative test tasks. Other integrative tasks include things like dictation, or listening cloze tasks, as shown here, also from the PTE (http://pearsonpte.com/PTEAcademic/Tutorial/Documents/PTEA_Tutorial.pdf, p. 25):

138 Chapter 9 Assessing Listening

While the desire to move beyond discrete point testing in listening is understandable, the more integrative tasks shown here are also problematic in their own ways. Dictation as a listening test task can be criticized because the word-for-word listening required in dictation is not representative of the type of listening that most L2 listeners do. How to score dictations also presents reliability concerns. Listening cloze tests necessarily involve a written text, and these types of tasks can be seen as more of a reading assessment than a test of listening ability, and again, it is difficult to associate this type of task with a TLU domain of interest.

How the Listening Texts and Test Questions Should Be Presented to Test Takers

One of the unique challenges in assessing L2 listening ability is due to the ethereal nature of spoken texts. With written input, test takers can repeatedly refer to the input as needed (within the time constraints of the test). The nature of spoken texts, however, makes this less or nearly impossible, and thus, test developers need to make difficult decisions regarding the number of times the text should be played for test takers, and how to present the test questions (written versus orally, or both; before, during, or after the spoken text).

To some extent, the difficulty in deciding the most appropriate (according to the TLU domain) testing procedures comes down to the artificial nature of testing listening ability. In virtually all real-world listening situations, the listener has some sort of idea what an imminent speech event will be about. Knowledge of the situation, the physical context of the setting, the appearance of the speaker, the co-text, and real-world knowledge all provide useful information to the listener and help her anticipate aspects of what the speaker will say, thus allowing her to activate the relevant schemata and facilitate the comprehension of the spoken text. However, many listening tasks (both teaching and testing) are very different, in that the listener often has absolutely no idea about what an upcoming spoken text will be about. The tester (or teacher) pushes the play button, and the listeners hear a text that could be on virtually any subject. The listener is then forced to do intensive and cognitively demanding bottom-up processing, listening for each individual word, in the attempt to discern what the topic of the text is. Once the listener is able to do this, she can then simultaneously perform bottom-up and top-down (interactive) processing, similar to most real-world listening situations.

This manner of presenting a listening text to the test takers, without providing any background context to the text, presents threats to validity, in that this is usually not representative of the TLU domain of interest. A relatively simple thing testers can do to make the test task demands more authentic is to provide some sort of introduction or summary of the listening text before it is played for the test takers. That is, by introducing and providing information about what the upcoming text will be about, the test developer can better mimic real-world listening situations, and result in assessing the desired TLU domain.

Regarding the number of times that a text should be played, a superficial analysis of the TLU domain would suggest that in most instances, listeners do not get repeated chances to listen to spoken input, and thus, playing the text one time would usually be the most appropriate. However, it could also be argued that in many dialogic communication settings, listeners often have the ability to ask the speaker to repeat herself. In most listening test settings, it seems that the text is usually played one time, sometimes it is played two times, and very rarely is it played three times. Not surprisingly, research (Sakai, 2009) has shown that the more times a text is played, the higher the test takers score on the test.

A related issue is when (and in what manner) to present the test questions to the test takers. Buck (1991) argued that by allowing the test takers to preview the test questions before the text is played, the listeners are provided with contextual information that allows them to know what to listen for and will serve as positive motivation. Some studies have found that question preview led to increased test scores, while others have found no effect on performance.

Similarly, Yanagawa and Green (2008) investigated how full multiple-choice question preview, preview of the multiple-choice answer options only, and preview of the multiple-choice stems only affected test performance, and found that the answer-only preview condition scored significantly lower than the other two conditions.

As can be seen, the research on these different issues is ambiguous and certainly incomplete and illustrates the difficulties developers of listening assessment face. While there is no single right answer to these issues, one thing that testers can do is to try and make the test tasks as authentic as possible by making the characteristics of test task as similar as possible to the language tasks in the TLU domain.

Test Impact and Washback

A test's impact on stakeholders is an important (yet often overlooked) consideration for test developers. Tests obviously have many important functions and are a necessary part of most educational systems. But large-scale, high-stakes language tests can have profound impact on course curricula, national curricula, and even whole societies. It is thus important to consider test washback in relation to some of the issues unique to the testing of listening as described above. It seems obvious that teachers and testers should be interested in L2 learners developing the ability to listen to and comprehend authentic spoken discourse, which usually includes things like connected speech, reduction, phonological modifications, vernacular language, language variation, and nonverbal communication. The need to assess a learner's ability to speak and understand conversational language in an interactive speaking and listening communicative language use setting would also seem to be obvious. Yet, most large-scale, high-stakes tests of listening focus on a very narrow aspect of the construct, using spoken texts that include almost none of these natural characteristics, but instead use texts that are planned, prepared, practiced, polished, and then read aloud and artificially enunciated. These texts are usually recorded, then played back using the audio channel only, with listening and speaking ability being assessed separately, rather than as a part of interactive speaking/listening ability. This can have a direct (and negative) impact on how listening is taught to language learners. If the goal of the learners is to pass the test, then it is understandable that learners are not interested in learning how to listen to and comprehend authentic spoken discourse. It is also understandable that teachers and curriculum designers would decide against focusing instruction on these aspects of listening. Similarly, if the high-stakes tests that drive curriculum design do not include the nonverbal components of spoken language in the listening process, then the curriculum (often driven by those high-stakes tests) will not include them either. In addition, it is important that high-stakes tests include the varieties of language that learners would encounter in the target language use (TLU) domain, rather than just the standard variety of the language. "Consequential validity" involves the idea that a validity of a test should be gauged at least in part on the extent to which it has a positive influence on teaching (Messick, 1989). Thus, creating L2 listening tests that include these components of unplanned spoken discourse could have a positive impact on how second language listening is taught, and the test's potential impact on test takers and educational systems should be part of the test development and validation process (Chalhoub-Deville & O'Sullivan, 2020).

Future Directions and Conclusion

There has been a decided movement in assessment in recent years toward more integrated tasks that are a better measure of test takers' interactional competence. For L2 listening testing, this is evidenced by tasks in which the listening text is presented, and then, test takers have to respond by speaking or even writing about the text. In addition, there has been a

140 Chapter 9 Assessing Listening

strong movement toward the use of group oral testing, in which two, three, or even four test takers are tested simultaneously, and the test takers have to interact appropriately, listening to the discourse from one participant, and responding orally (e.g., Ockey, 2014). This type of testing is necessary, in that it seeks to truly assess test takers interactive speaking and listening ability. However, it also presents a number of reliability and validity concerns, and while it has been the subject of a large amount of recent research (e.g., Galaczi, 2008, 2014), most of this research seems to have been focused on the speaking component, and less on the listening. One of the obvious concerns is how the test taker's listening ability is assessed in group oral testing, since the rater can only guess as to how well the participant comprehended the spoken input based on her spoken response. While this seems a fruitful direction for assessment, much more research is needed on this type of test task.

Another obvious future direction of testing listening includes the increased use of technology to allow test developers to address at least some of the threats to the construct validity of current testing formats, by allowing testers to more fully include important components of the TLU domain in tests. Increased use of computers to deliver the input to test takers would allow for the inclusion of the visual channel, thus reducing the amount of construct underrepresentation found in many tests of listening. Similarly, innovations in assessing interactive speaking and listening ability seem possible, going beyond the current two-turn design found in many tests where the first turn is a spoken text delivered (usually only in oral form), and the second turn requires the test taker to respond in some way. Rather, a more innovative design might involve multiple turns, allowing for a more authentic assessment of interactive speaking and listening ability. Another area in which technology has made great progress is in the analysis of large corpora, especially spoken corpora. Using the results of these analyses, future test developers can create texts for listening assessments that include the characteristics of unplanned spoken discourse, thus resulting in the assessment of a much broader construct of L2 listening ability than is usually assessed currently. Even for the assessment of low-ability listeners, in which it might not be appropriate to use texts spoken at a normal rate of speech, technology can be used to slow down the speech rate electronically, or by inserting pauses at the appropriate speech boundaries.

However, technology in itself is certainly no panacea. Lynch (2009) questions how useful technology is for teaching and testing L2 listening ability, and the increased use of technology also presents issues that need to be much more thoroughly researched. Vanderplank (2010) argues that various facets of the use of technology related to L2 listening are only beginning to be researched. While there has been some research into how the use of the visual channel affects test taker performance, and how test takers interact with a video listening test (e.g., Batty, 2015; Suvorov, 2015; Wagner, 2008, 2010, 2013), much more research is needed on how the use of different types of technology affects L2 listening test taker performance.

Discussion Questions

1. The idea of interactional competence has been the dominant theme in second language acquisition for decades. How can test developers create tests that truly assess learners' listening ability as a part of interactional competence? Why is this so hard to do?

2. Tests are, by their very nature, inauthentic. What are the advantages and disadvantages to creating "authentic" listening tests? What makes an L2 listening test authentic?

References

Bachman, L., & Palmer, A. (1996). *Language testing in practice*. Oxford University Press.

Baltova, I. (1994). The impact of video on comprehension skills of core French students. *Canadian Modern Language Review, 50*(3), 507–531. https://doi.org/10.3138/cmlr.50.3.507.

References   141

Batty, A. (2015). A comparison of video- and audio-mediated listening tests with many-facet Rasch modelling and differential distractor functioning. *Language Testing, 32*(1), 3–20. https://doi.org/10.1177/0265532214531254.

Brown, G. (1995). *Speakers, listeners, and communication.* Cambridge University Press. https://doi.org/10.1017/CBO9780511620942.

Buck, G. (1991). The test of listening comprehension: an introspective study. *Language Testing, 8*(1), 67–91. https://doi.org/10.1177/026553229100800105.

Buck, G. (2001). *Assessing listening.* Cambridge University Press. https://doi.org/10.1017/CBO9780511732959.

Carr, N. (2011). *Designing and analyzing language tests (Oxford handbooks for language teachers).* Oxford University Press.

Celce-Murcia, M., Brinton, D., & Goodwin, J. (1994). *Teaching pronunciation: A reference for teachers of English to speakers of other languages.* Cambridge University Press.

Chalhoub-Deville, M., & O'Sullivan, B. (2020). *Validity: Theoretical developments and integrated arguments.* Equinox.

Cross, J. (2011). Comprehending news videotexts: the influence of the visual content. *Language Learning & Technology, 15*(2), 44–68.

Douglas, D. (1997). *Testing speaking ability in academic contexts: Theoretical considerations* (TOEFL Monograph Series, Number 8). Educational Testing Service.

Field, J. (2008). *Listening in the language classroom.* Cambridge University Press. https://doi.org/10.1017/CBO9780511575945.

Galaczi, E. (2008). Peer-peer interaction in a speaking test: the case of the *First Certificate in English* examination. *Language Assessment Quarterly, 5*(2), 89–119. https://doi.org/10.1080/15434300801934702.

Galaczi, E. (2014). Interactional competence across proficiency levels: How do learners manage interaction in paired tests? *Applied Linguistics, 35*(5), 553–574. https://doi.org/10.1093/applin/amt017.

Gruba, P. (1997). The role of video media in listening assessment. *System, 25*(3), 335–345. https://doi.org/10.1016/S0346-251X(97)00026-2.

Juffs, A., & Harrington, M. (2011). State-of-the-art article: Aspects of working memory in L2 learning. *Language Teaching, 44*(2), 137–166. https://doi.org/10.1017/S0261444810000509.

Lynch, T. (2009). *Teaching second language listening.* Oxford University Press.

Mackey, A., Adams, R., Stafford, C., & Winke, P. (2010). Exploring the relationship between modified output and working memory capacity. *Language Learning, 60*(3), 501–533. https://doi.org/10.1111/j.1467-9922.2010.00565.x.

Messick, S. (1989). Validity. In R. Linn (Ed.), *Educational measurement* (3rd ed., pp. 13–103). American Council on Education and Macmillan.

Messick, S. (1996). Validity and washback in language testing. *Language Testing, 13*(3), 242–256. https://doi.org/10.1177/026553229601300302.

Ockey, G. (2007). Construct implication of including still image or video in computer-based listening tests. *Language Testing, 24*(4), 517–537. https://doi.org/10.1177/0265532207080771.

Ockey, G. (2014). The potential of the L2 group oral to elicit discourse with a mutual contingency pattern and afford equal speaking rights in an ESP context. *English for Specific Purposes, 35*, 17–29. https://doi.org/10.1016/j.esp.2013.11.003.

Ockey, G. J., & Chukharev-Hudilainen, E. (2021). Human versus computer partner in the paired oral discussion test. *Applied Linguistics, 42*(5), 924–944. https://doi.org/10.1093/applin/amaa067.

Ockey, G. J., & Wagner, E. (2018). *Assessing L2 listening: Moving towards authenticity.* John Benjamins. https://doi.org/10.1075/lllt.50.

Rost, M. (2016). *Teaching and researching listening* (3rd ed.). Routledge. https://doi.org/10.4324/9781315732862.

Sakai, H. (2009). Effect of repetition of exposure and proficiency level in L2 listening tests. *TESOL Quarterly, 43*(2), 360–371. https://doi.org/10.1002/j.1545-7249.2009.tb00179.x.

Sueyoshi, A., & Hardison, D. (2005). The role of gestures and facial cues in second language listening comprehension. *Language Learning, 55*(4), 661–699. https://doi.org/10.1111/j.0023-8333.2005.00320.x.

Suvorov, R. (2015). The use of eye tracking in research on video-based second language (L2) listening assessment: A comparison of context videos and content videos. *Language Testing, 32*(4), 464–483. https://doi.org/10.1177/0265532214562099.

142 **Chapter 9** Assessing Listening

Tannen, D. (1982). The oral/literate continuum in discourse. In D. Tannen (Ed.), *Spoken and written language: Exploring orality and literacy* (pp. 1–33). Ablex.

Taylor, L. (2008). Language varieties and their implications for testing and assessment. In L. Taylor & C. Weir (Eds.), *Multilingualism and assessment: Achieving transparency, assuring quality, sustaining diversity.* Cambridge University Press.

Vanderplank, R. (2010). De´ja`vu? A decade of research on language laboratories, television and video in language learning. *Language Teaching, 43,* 1–37. https://doi.org/10.1017/S0261444809990267.

Wagner, E. (2008). Video listening tests: what are they measuring? *Language Assessment Quarterly, 5*(3), 218–243. https://doi.org/10.1080/15434300802213015.

Wagner, E. (2010). The effect of the use of video texts on ESL listening test-taker performance. *Language Testing, 27*(4), 493–513. https://doi.org/10.1177/0265532209355668.

Wagner, E. (2013). An investigation of how the channel of input and access to test questions affect L2 listening performance. *Language Assessment Quarterly, 10*(2), 178–195. https://doi.org/10.1080/15434303.2013.769552.

Yanagawa, K., & Green, A. (2008). To show or not to show: The effects of item stems and answer options on performance on a multiple-choice listening comprehension test. *System, 36*(1), 107–122. https://doi.org/10.1016/j.system.2007.12.003.

Suggested Readings

Field, J. (2013). Cognitive validity. In A. Geranpayeh & L. Taylor (Eds.), *Examining listening: Research and practice in assessing second language listening* (Studies in Language Testing, Vol. 35, pp. 77–151). UCLES/Cambridge University Press.

Gilmore, A. (2007). Authentic materials and authenticity in foreign language learning. *Language Teaching, 40,* 97–118. https://doi.org/10.1017/S0261444807004144.

Goh, C., & Vandergrift, L. (2022). *Teaching and learning second language listening: Metacognition in action* (2nd ed.). Routledge. https://doi.org/10.4324/9780429287749.

Wagner, E. (2022). Assessing listening. In G. Fulcher & L. Harding (Eds.), *Routledge handbook of language testing* (2nd ed., pp. 223–235). Routledge. https://doi.org/10.4324/9781003220756-18.

CHAPTER 10

Assessing Speaking

Barry O'Sullivan

Introduction

Since the publication of the first version of this chapter a decade ago (O'Sullivan, 2013), the testing of speaking has undergone some significant changes. Some of these changes have come about through updated thinking around test development and validation, others through research. Also, the COVID pandemic led to the normalization of the changes in test delivery brought about through technological advances, while the emergence of large language models in late 2022 threatens to take us in previously unexplored directions.

Concerns about construct definition (what exactly we are assessing), the predictability of task response (task description), the effect of test-taker characteristics on performance, the effect of on performance of characteristics associated with the interlocutor (the person with whom the candidate is interacting), and the appropriateness of the scoring system (the reliability and validity of the rating process) remain with us. In this chapter, I will focus on these issues while also taking into consideration emerging technologies.

As with the original chapter, I will first turn to the underlying model of test development and validation that underpins this version. While the basic model remains the same, it too has changed over the past decade, with updates from O'Sullivan (2021) and most notably from Chalhoub-Deville and O'Sullivan (2020). Most of the discussion will be related to large-scale speaking assessments although applications can be made to classroom assessments. The discussion will also be related to assessments with an examiner in person, raters who rate the assessments later as well as automated scoring of speaking.

Defining Speaking

In the 1970s, the field of psycholinguistics was most obviously associated with studies that focused on understanding and processing spoken language. The most important model of the psychological process of language production to emerge from early work in the area was that of Levelt (1999). This model (or blueprint as Levelt called it) shows how the speech process is organized from the constraints on conversational appropriateness to articulation and self-monitoring. Levelt saw the speaker as an information processor, proposing a blueprint in which message generation, grammatical encoding, phonological encoding, and articulation are seen as relatively autonomous processors (encoding here refers to the process by which the message is prepared for delivery). While Levelt's model stops largely at the point of

The Concise Companion to Language Assessment, First Edition. Edited by Antony John Kunnan.
© 2025 John Wiley & Sons, Inc. Published 2025 by John Wiley & Sons, Inc.

144 **Chapter 10** Assessing Speaking

utterance, he goes on to describe at length the three essential aspects of conversation in which the speaker plays the part of both a participant and interlocutor. Levelt saw conversation as being highly contextualized and purposeful, having a spatiotemporal setting. In addition, the basic mechanisms of speech processing are conceptualized in his model in an uncomplicated way: speech is produced by first conceptualizing the message, then formulating its language representation (encoding) and finally articulating it. In terms of reception, speech is hypothesized as being perceived initially by an acoustic-phonetic processor, it is then linguistically encoded in the speech comprehension system (the parser), and it is finally interpreted by the conceptualizer.

Levelt's model continues to underpin much research on speaking (see, e.g., Field, 2011). However, O'Sullivan (2000a) argued that the essentially cognitive model of spoken language was not sufficient in explaining how communication actually works. Instead, he argued that we should also take into account the social aspect of human communication, demonstrating that speaking test performance is significantly impacted by an individual's affective reaction to their perception of their interlocutor (in terms of variables such as gender, age, relative language level, and extraversion). His suggestion that we take a broader socio-cognitive approach to speaking (op. cit., p. 277) informed thinking on a new approach to test development and validation (O'Sullivan & Weir, 2020), which was detailed in Weir's (2005) seminal work. Since O'Sullivan (2013) outlines this approach in some detail, I will instead focus here on how the approach has been updated in the intervening years.

In their book on validity, Chalhoub-Deville and O'Sullivan (2020) argued that the argument-based approach to test validation proposed by Kane (for example: 2013) is, in practice, overly dependent on a test's underlying measurement model. Chalhoub-Deville and O'Sullivan proposed a more nuanced approach with specific arguments focusing on four areas, theory of change, communication with stakeholders, test development, and delivery and measurement approach. Their *Integrated Arguments* concept reflects this thinking by a further updating of the Weir approach first proposed by O'Sullivan (2016) in which the test is situated in a specific context of development and use.

The version of the socio-cognitive model presented here (Figure 10.1) represents a significant change to that of O'Sullivan (2013). The central core of the model presented here (test taker, test system, scoring system, and performance) as well, the underlying philosophy (focusing on the social and cognitive aspects of language use), and the validation approach (building the argument around the development and delivery process) all remain true to Weir (2005). However, it is important to make explicit several elements:

- *Theories of change and action.* This refers to the intended consequences and to the clarification of how these will be achieved. In other words, it is expected that the developer will be clear and transparent in their description of what the test is meant to measure and how they intend to ensure that this happens.
- *Communication.* Up to now, validation has always been one-way traffic. The developer produces a validation argument and presents it as a completed (and complex) text. It is argued that for any educational innovation to be successful, it must be understood and accepted by key stakeholder groups. For this to happen, they must be involved in decisions around the development and publication of any validation argument, which should reflect their expectations and be presented using appropriate channels and language.
- *Test development.* While this chapter takes the Weir (2005) approach to test development as its basis, other models (e.g., Mislevy et al., 2003) can be used. The important thing is that the developer specifies a development model and demonstrates how their processes reflect that model.
- *Language development.* While Weir (2005) includes direct reference to the need to clearly specify the language targeted by a test, it ought to be placed within a broader model of language development such as the Common European Framework of Reference for

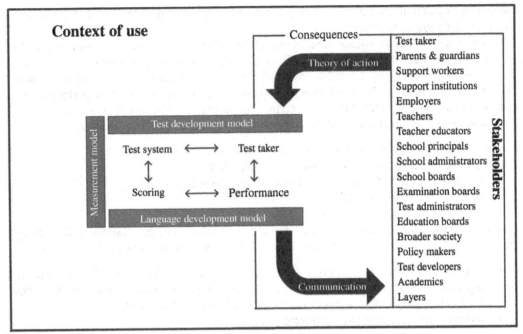

FIGURE 10.1 Reconsidering Weir's socio-cognitive framework. *Source:* Based on Chalhoub-Deville and O'Sullivan (2020) and O'Sullivan (2021).

Languages (CEFR) or other language benchmarks (e.g., the Canadian Language Benchmarks).

- *Measurement model.* This refers to the psychometric qualities of the test with regard to its use in a particular context and with a particular population. It is a vital element of the test validation argument, but I strongly believe that is must be seen as just one of several elements.

The important matter of consequences is also highlighted in the updated approach. Here, it is argued that intended consequences must be addressed in any validation argument. We see this as being achieved through more qualitative approaches focusing on key stakeholder groups. A quantitative approach can often offer that something is happening but not what that something is or what it means to the people who are affected. By taking a qualitative approach to the exploration of test consequence, it is open to identify unintended consequences during the development phase.

What follows in this chapter should be seen as a reflection of the validation model shown in Figure 10.1 supporting the contention of O'Sullivan and Weir (2011) that validation lies at the heart of test development.

Test Design

Speaking tests, like other direct tests of language performance, are designed to allow the test developer to make a claim or set of claims about an individual test taker's ability to use language under specific conditions. The nature of the claim is inextricably linked to both the ability model (i.e., the model or definition of the ability being assessed) upon which the test will be based and the test-taking population. This is because the test developer must consider a whole series of variables (or characteristics) that are associated with the intended population to ensure that the resulting test is appropriate for use with that population. These have been

146   Chapter 10 Assessing Speaking

categorized by O'Sullivan (2000a) as physical, psychological, and experiential characteristics and are briefly discussed later.

The test task is then developed to reflect the ability model and the intended population while the rating scale is devised to reflect the ability model in terms of both the criteria to be included and the level or amount of the ability expected of a successful test taker. When it comes to the administration phase of the development process, the test taker produces a performance in response to the task, which is then assessed by a human rater or the scoring is automated.

It is likely that the test taker will be affected by several factors. These include:

- the interlocutor, where this person is another candidate (O'Sullivan, 2002),
- affective reactions to the examiner (O'Sullivan, 2000b),
- examiner behavior (Brown & Lumley, 1997; Plough & Bogart, 2008),
- the task topic (Lumley & O'Sullivan, 2005),
- the task format (Berry, 2007), and
- knowledge of the scoring (or rating) criteria – it is also likely that the candidate will be affected by their knowledge (or lack of knowledge) of how their performance is to be assessed.

Of course, the factors will apply differently depending on the mode of administration involving human interview, computer avatar, or monologic response. Therefore, the above factors will affect the human rating or the automated scoring differently.

In addition, several factors affect human raters:

- *The test taker*. The implication of research that focused on the affective reactions of test takers to examiners (O'Sullivan, 2000a) is that the examiner may also react to the candidate in a positive or negative way (see Carey et al., 2011).
- *The task*. There is ample anecdotal evidence of examiners selecting a narrow range of tasks where they are offered a choice, and this suggests that there may be some bias toward or against particular tasks, which could be translated into significant effects on scores awarded.
- *The rating scale*. See McNamara (1996) who reported on the unexpected reaction of raters to a scale, which did not conform to their expectations (they simply inserted their criterion).
- Rater background (L1 v L2; novice v. expert) and rater training.

Once the final score or grade has been awarded, it is necessary to establish evidence of the value of the score in terms of the claim or claims upon which the test is based.

In speaking assessments, this typically includes evidence from sources such as performance on other tasks (e.g., performed in class), teacher estimates of each test taker's ability, or post-test longitudinal data of test taker spoken performance. An example of this is in a test of language for immigration where the developer/user will gather data through tracking studies of test takers' success in using spoken language in the target country, though the limitation of tracking studies (only successful test takers are typically tracked) must be acknowledged. It is also possible to look to test taker performances to establish evidence that the language predicted by the test developer when the task was designed emerges in the test event (see O'Sullivan et al., 2002) or to compare test taker language with descriptions of ability level in established standards such as the Common European Framework of Reference (CEFR) published by the Council of Europe (2001) and its Companion Volume (CoE, 2020).

Issues in Assessing Speaking

In this section of the paper, the focus will be on current issues of significance in testing speaking and present these in terms of the model of validation (Figure 10.1).

Issues in Assessing Speaking   **147**

Focusing on Test-Specific Issues

The test taker

Here, we consider the test taker from several perspectives, understanding that we should consider the test taker as the central player in our test, and of course in our learning system.

- *Physical characteristics.* There is some evidence that factors such as test taker age (e.g., O'Sullivan, 2000a) and gender (e.g., Moe et al., 2023) can have a significant impact on test performance. The situation with the provision of special accommodations for test takers with physical (and other) disabilities appears to have changed dramatically in the last decade.
- *Psychological characteristics.* Both Berry (2007) and Ockey (2009) demonstrated that personality can have a significant impact on speaking test performance in live test events. In addition, O'Sullivan (2000a) also demonstrated that a test taker's perception of their interlocutor (e.g., as being outgoing and fluent) can also influence performance. Other psychological characteristics have been explored in the broader language learning domain include motivation (e.g., Dörnyei, 2010) and anxiety (e.g., Bailey et al., 1999; Horwitz, 2001), though only the latter has received systematic attention in assessment.
- *Experiential characteristics.* This can refer to education (both formal and informal) and background knowledge (general and test-specific). There is evidence that test performance will be positively affected by education (i.e., exposure to the language in formal and informal settings) (Spurling & Illyin, 1985). In terms of task topic, there appears to be mixed evidence with studies such as Jennings et al. (1999) and Lumley and O'Sullivan (2005) reporting some evidence that choice of topic is unlikely to impact on performance, while Moe et al. (2023) found the opposite. Kunnan (1995) found that of the four variables associated with subject background (formal instruction and informal exposure to English either in the subject's own country or in an English-speaking country), only one proved to have a substantial effect on test performance, and this was formal instruction in an English-speaking country.
- *Cognitive aspects.* Apart from Field (2011), little significant research has been undertaken into this area, though Shaw and Weir (2007) and Khalifa and Weir (2009) have investigated the cognitive perspective of writing and reading, respectively.

The test system

The test system includes those aspects of the test that relate to the performance parameters, the linguistic demands, and the administration conditions through which the test is delivered.

- *Performance parameters.* The most often researched aspect of task performance has been that of planning time (Yuan & Ellis, 2003) and it is now well accepted that the appropriate inclusion of planning time is likely to result in significantly improved performance on speaking test tasks. Other parameters that might benefit from more extensive research include the way in which knowledge of how the performance will be assessed (i.e., knowing the rating criteria) will affect subsequent test performance; how the amount of language output expected or the degree of support offered will impact the performance (see Weir et al., 2004). Mode of delivery has been researched over the years, with mixed results where comparisons were made between traditional face-to-face tests with recorded semi-structured oral proficiency interviews (SOPIs). In an early study, Stansfield and Kenyon (1992) concluded that "both tests are highly comparable as measures of the same construct – oral language proficiency" (p. 363). However, later studies by Shohamy (1994), Wigglesworth and O'Loughlin (1993, 1995) all report that the different formats result in different kinds of language – thus reflect different underlying constructs. More recent research by Nakatsuhara et al. (2017b) suggests that comparisons between live tests of

148 Chapter 10 Assessing Speaking

speaking across two delivery modes (face-to-face and computer-mediated) show no significant differences in linguistic performance or in terms of scores achieved.

- *Linguistic demands.* Bygate (1999) argued that it was not possible to predict the language used in task performance at the macro level as learners were always able to find ways of responding to tasks that were not predicted by the developers. The linguistic demands of task input have long been recognized as impacting on subsequent performance, and it is common practice to ensure that the input language is set at a level below that of the target level. With the recent rise in awareness of the need to move toward a more inclusive multilingual approach to testing (see, e.g., De Backer & Van Avermaet, 2017; Gorter and Cenoz, 2017), it seems reasonable to present test rubrics/instructions either in a bilingual format or even in the test taker's primary language. This latter suggestion has become more feasible with the rise of digital testing and the increasingly powerful translation abilities supported by ChatGPT and other major large language models (LLMs). As we move into the realm of machine-based assessment and testing, we also need to consider important issues such as test takers' affective reaction to interacting with increasing human-like agents.

- *Non-linguistic input.* In the 2014 version of this chapter, I argued that we should explore the impact on task performance under test conditions of a range of input-related variables, including language and/or visual stimuli. While this has been explored for listening by Ginther (2002) and Wagner (2010), we have yet to see the topic explored for testing speaking.

- *Test administration.* For a clear and comprehensive description of one approach to the area of administration of a speaking test, see Taylor (2011). This impressive piece offers the reader a broad overview of the main issues and also an insight into how one major examination board addresses them. In light of the increased move toward digital tests since the COVID pandemic, it seems clear that further research is needed into administrative areas such as remote invigilation. While mixed findings around privacy issues have been reported (e.g., see Selwyn et al., 2023; Jaap et al., 2021 who report opposing results), the impact of remote invigilation on speaking test performance, which is based on human–machine communication remains unexplored.

- *Test format and delivery.* While technology-driven scenario-based language tests have been around for some time (see Holland et al., 2013), over the past decade we have seen growing interest in the approach, principally through the work of Purpura (2021). In this approach, the candidate is expected to display a broad range of mental, social, linguistic, affective resources (Purpura, 2021) while participating in a scripted interaction. Ockey and Chukharev-Hudilainen (2021) take this a step further with their use of a spoken dialogue system (SDS), which sees the human test taker interacting with a machine specifically trained to target and assess interactional competence. When combined with the potential that lies behind the new large language models (LLMs), this approach seems likely to offer interesting new avenues of research and development for the testing of spoken language. This approach has been taken at the British Council in the UK, where a series of practice tasks were launched into their English Online learning system in April 2024.

The scoring system

The scoring system includes everything that is done to transform a test performance into a test score that is meaningful and useful. Limitations of space mean that only some key aspects of this very complex system can be addressed in this paper.

- *Theoretical fit.* The most obvious aspect of this is the fit between the underlying ability model and the rating scale. We have already seen that there are some serious issues related to the way in which grammar and fluency are defined in typical scale descriptors. Whether the scales are holistic (where there is a single global score), analytic (where the overall score comprises of a number of scores awarded on a set of pre-determined criteria), or boundary recognition (essentially a series of yes/no distinctions based on a series of task-specific questions or statements, see Upshur & Turner, 1999), it is vital that a clearly defined link can be made between the content, the format of the scale and the ability model. Without this, any resulting score is clearly meaningless in relation to the claims the developer wishes to make.

Theoretical fit also refers to the selection and training of the raters. The developer must maintain the integrity of the scoring system by ensuring that the raters are appropriately qualified and trained. A typical issue here is that of bias. While Lumley and McNamara (1995) conclude "that judge differences survive training" (p. 69), it is important that training is offered, though it should probably focus on things like intra-rater consistency (i.e., within the individual – is the person him/herself consistent?) and critical boundary internalization (internalizing important decision points such as the pass/fail boundary – does the rater automatically recognize a passing or failing performance?). It is also important that training should focus on acquainting raters not just with the scale and the tasks, but with the rationale that lies behind these.

Where the rater is also the interlocutor, it is also very important to ensure that participants are trained for their role as interlocutor (and not just in the management of the event, e.g., score recording and timekeeping). This training would also benefit from a focus on affect – highlighting how this can impact on their rating. The contribution of raters with different behavior patterns to the co-construction of the live test event (and test taker proficiency), explored by Brown (2003), highlights the importance of this aspect of training.

It is important to point to the work of Carter and McCarthy (for example 2006). These studies suggest that the traditional descriptors of grammar used in rating scales, which are typically focused on accuracy and range, are unlikely to result in meaningful measures due to the often-significant differences between spoken and written grammar. It may be that more formal, monologic, or individual long-turn/presentation tasks are more likely to reflect the expectations of a written grammar, while more interactive tasks may require descriptors, which are more systematically based on grammars of spoken discourse. A second area for concern is that of fluency. McCarthy (2010) argues convincingly that fluency should be regarded in a different way for monologic discourse (the traditional view) and interactive discourse, where he has shown it to be co-constructed by the participants. This again suggests that current practice, in which descriptions of fluency are based on the monologic model, is again likely to result in misleading claims and as such needs revision.

- *Accuracy of decisions.* The scoring of spoken performance has been described by Leclercq and Edmonds (2014, p. 5) as "a moving target." Nevertheless, the accuracy of the decisions made by the rater (or the machine for that matter) is one of the central elements of the scoring system. It is clear from writing assessment research that training is a key contributor to accuracy and consistency (see Weigle, 2000), though as pointed out by Lumley and McNamara (1995), training is unlikely to eradicate all differences between raters (see also Kim, 2015). However, little empirical work has been reported for the impact of training on raters of speaking tests (though see Elder et al., 2005) and we can assume that the impact of training in both areas will be similar.

Multifaceted Rasch analysis has been used to explore rater error (see Myford & Wolfe, 2003, 2004) and other aspects of the rating process (e.g., Lumley & O'Sullivan, 2005; Ockey, 2009) and offers a valuable tool to take rater harshness or leniency into account when calculating test scores (Lumley & McNamara, 1995). The broader use of probability-based (or alternative) statistical procedures to estimate ability level is clearly an area worth further exploration as is the use of technology (e.g., voice recognition and artificial intelligence) to refine automated scoring engines. It is also important to investigate how technology can support human rating by looking at a more collaborative model of rating in which each plays a distinctive role.

150 Chapter 10 Assessing Speaking

A final comment here on the rater is that much has been made over the years of differences between native and non-native speakers (or L1 and L2) raters. But recent studies seem to demonstrate that there are no significant differences in the consistency of raters from the two groups, though they may well be assessing different aspects of test taker language (see Zhang & Elder, 2011). Gallardo del Puerto et al. (2014) reported that trained non-native judges are very similar to native judges in their assessment of accent. This is clearly an area that needs further exploration, though it is not always an easy matter to make a definitive distinction between a native and non-native speaker as it is not a matter of dichotomy but of degree.

- *Value of decisions.* While this aspect of validation can include the collection of evidence from sources such as other tests or from teachers, peers, or self-assessments, it is critical to focus on the concept of establishing evidence of the value, or meaning, of test scores in contexts outside of the testing arena. The most referenced documents these days are the CEFR and its *Companion Volume* (Council of Europe, 2020). In terms of speaking, the CEFR offers perhaps the most valuable descriptors (certainly in comparison with the other skills). In addition two manuals have been published which are designed to help developers of tests, assessments, curricula, classroom materials, teacher education, as well as professional development materials and programs to align their work to the CEFR (Council of Europe, 2009; ALTE et al., 2022). As valuable as these resources are, it should be noted that the resources needed to generate a fully convincing alignment argument are significant and are likely to be available only to large organisation.

- *The increased use of AI technology.* In recent years, the autoscoring of test performance has become more prominent. High-stakes test providers are increasingly turning to AI technology to develop scoring solutions, which either support (e.g., as a second marker) or replace human judgment (except in cases where the technology is unable to award a score for some reason, e.g., sound quality). With the introduction of ChatGPT in late 2022, the situation has begun to change rapidly, with accessibility to the technology becoming more widespread. The costs associated with developing automated scoring systems have fallen dramatically though little or no critical questioning of how this has impacted on test content or scoring has taken place to date. Critical outstanding issues remain including construct representation and underrepresentation (for example, read-aloud and listen-and-repeat items do not measure speaking ability), scoring model transparency in automated scoring systems, security of the proctoring systems, and bias. To date, this latter issue has been dealt with only once in the language testing literature (O'Sullivan et al., 2023), and in this context only a very low stakes placement test was examined. Clearly, when it comes to bias, developers who rely on technology-based scoring solutions should be held to account.

Conclusion

This chapter outlined a view of testing speaking that is based on the socio-cognitive model of test development and validation. Despite the growing use of speaking tests worldwide, the area remains quite under-researched. This may well be because most speaking tests are essentially local in nature, meaning that there is a distinct likelihood that factors such as familiarity with the language and culture of the population play a greater part in the test (from its inception through to administration) than is the case with other skills.

The introduction of ChatGPT and other large language models (LLMs) in late 2022 has added interest and innovation to an already burgeoning area of interest to researchers and test developers. Many governments and institutions are beginning to see the potential of these technologies to help them introduce accessible and affordable tuition, learner-oriented language assessment (LOLA), and even high-stakes testing of speaking. While there are undoubted benefits to this, there should be caution due to ongoing concerns with these large learning models.

Discussion Questions

1. What are the most important factors to consider in designing speaking assessments?
2. What are the likely issues that are critical to automated speaking assessments?

References

ALTE, British Council, EALTS, & UKALTA. (2022). *Aligning language education with the CEFR: A handbook.* Retrieved 04/10/2024: https://www.britishcouncil.org/sites/default/files/cefr_alignment_handbook_layout.pdf.

Bailey, P., Daley, C., & Onwuegbuzie, A. (1999). Foreign language anxiety and learning style. *Foreign Language Annals, 32,* 64–72. https://doi.org/10.1111/j.1944-9720.1999.tb02376.x.

Berry, V. (2007). *Personality differences and oral test performance.* Frankfurt: Peter Lang.

Brown, A. (2003). Interviewer variation and the co-construction of speaking proficiency. *Language Testing, 20,* 1–25.

Brown, A., & Lumley, T. (1997). Interviewer variability in specific-purpose language performance tests. In A. Huhta, V. Kohonen, L. Kurki-Suonio & S. Luoma (Eds.), *Current developments and alternatives in language assessment* (pp. 137–150). Jyväskylä: University of Jyväskylä and University of Tampere.

Bygate, M. (1999). Quality of language and purpose of task: patterns of learners' language on two oral communication tasks. *Language Teaching Research, 3,* 185–214.

Carey, M. D., Mannell, R. H., & Dunn, P. K. (2011). Does a rater's familiarity with a candidate's pronunciation affect the rating in oral proficiency interviews? *Language Testing, 28,* 201–219.

Carter, R. A., & McCarthy, M. J. (2006). *Cambridge grammar of English.* Cambridge: Cambridge University Press.

Chalhoub-Deville, M., & O'Sullivan, B. (2020). *Validity: Theoretical development and integrated arguments* (British Council Monograph Series 3). Sheffield: Equinox Publishing.

Council of Europe. (2001). *The common European framework of reference for languages: Learning, teaching, assessment.* Cambridge: Cambridge University Press. Also available at: http://www.culture2.coe.int/portfolio/documents_intro/common_framework.html.

Council of Europe. (2009). *Relating language examinations to the common European framework of reference for languages: Learning, teaching, assessment (CEFR): A manual.* Strasburg: Language Policy Division. Available at: http://www.coe.int/T/DG4/Linguistic/Manuel1_EN.asp.

Council of Europe (2020). *Common European framework of reference for languages: learning, teaching, assessment: Companion volume.* Available at: https://rm.coe.int/common-european-framework-of-reference-for-languages-learning-teaching/16809ea0d4

De Backer, F., & Van Avermaet, P. (2017). Schools as laboratories for exploring multilingual assessment policies and practices. *Language and Education, 31*(3), 217–230. https://doi.org/10.1080/09500782.2016.1261892.

Dörnyei, Z. (2010). Researching motivation: from integrativeness to the ideal L2 self. In S. Hunston & D. Oakey (Eds.), *Introducing applied linguistics: Concepts and skills* (pp. 74–83). London: Routledge.

Elder, C., Knoch, U., Barkhuizen, G., & von Randow, J. (2005). Individual feedback to enhance rater training: does it work? *Language Assessment Quarterly, 2,* 175–196.

Field, J. (2011). Cognitive validity. In L. Taylor (Ed.), *Examining speaking* (pp. 65–111). Cambridge: Cambridge University Press.

Gallardo del Puerto, F., García Lecumberri, M. L., & Gómez Lacabex, E. (2014). The assessment of foreign accent and its communicative effects by naïve native judges vs. experienced non-native judges. *International Journal of Applied Linguistics, 25*(2), 202–224. https://doi.org/10.1111/ijal.12063.

Ginther, A. (2002). Context and content visuals and performance on listening comprehension stimuli. *Language Testing, 19,* 133–167.

Gorter, D., & Cenoz, J. (2017). Language education policy and multilingual assessment. *Language and Education, 31*(3), 231–248. https://doi.org/10.1080/09500782.2016.1261892.

Holland, V. M., Kaplan, J. D., & Sabol, M. A. (2013). Preliminary tests of language learning in a speech-interactive graphics microworld. *CALICO Journal, 16*(3), 339–359. https://doi.org/10.1558/cj.v16i3.339-359.

152 **Chapter 10** Assessing Speaking

Horwitz, E. K. (2001). Language anxiety and achievement. *Annual Review of Applied Linguistics, 21,* 112–126.

Jaap, A., Dewar, A., Duncan, C., Fairhurst, K., Hope, D., & Kluth, D. (2021). Effect of remote online exam delivery on student experience and performance in applied knowledge tests. *BMC Medical Education, 21*(86), 1–7. https://doi.org/10.1186/s12909-021-02521-1.

Jennings, M., Fox, J., Graves, B., & Shohamy, E. (1999). The test-takers' choice: an investigation of the effect of topic on language-test performance. *Language Testing, 16,* 426–456.

Kane, M. (2013). Validating the interpretations and uses of test scores. *Journal of Educational Measurement, 50*(1), 1–73. https://doi.org/10.1111/jedm.12000.

Khalifa, H., & Weir, C. J. (2009). *Examining reading: Research and practice in assessing second language reading.* Cambridge: Cambridge University Press.

Kim, H. J. (2015). A qualitative analysis of rater behavior on an L2 speaking assessment. *Language Assessment Quarterly, 12*(3), 239–261. https://doi.org/10.1080/15434303.2015.1049353.

Kunnan, A. J. (1995). *Test taker characteristics and test performance: A structural modelling approach.* Cambridge: Cambridge University Press.

Leclercq, P., & Edmonds, A. (2014). How to assess L2 proficiency? An overview of proficiency assessment research. In P. Leclercq, A. Edmonds & H. Hilton (Eds.), *Measuring L2 proficiency: Perspectives from SLA* (pp. 3–23). Bristol: Multilingual Matters.

Levelt, W. J. M. (1999). Producing spoken language: a blueprint of a speaker. In C. M. Brown & P. Hagoort (Eds.), *The Neurocognition of Language.* Oxford: Oxford University Press.

Lumley, T., & McNamara, T. F. (1995). Rater characteristics and rater bias: Implications for training. *Language Testing, 12,* 54–71. https://doi.org/10.1177/026553229501200104.

Lumley, T., & O'Sullivan, B. (2005). The effect of test-taker gender, audience and topic on task performance in tape-mediated assessment of speaking. *Language Testing, 22,* 415–437.

McCarthy, M. J. (2010). Spoken fluency revisited. *English Profile Journal, 1,* 1–15.

McNamara, T. F. (1996). *Measuring second language performance.* London: Longman.

Mislevy, R. J., Almond, R., & Lukas, J. (2003). *A brief introduction to evidence-centered design.* Princeton, NJ. ETS Research Report No. RR-03-16. https://doi.org/10.1002/j.2333-8504.2003.tb01908.x.

Myford, C. M., & Wolfe, E. W. (2003). Detecting and measuring rater effects using many-facet Rasch measurement: Part II. *Journal of Applied Measurement, 5*(2), 189–227. PMID: 15064538.

Myford, C. M., & Wolfe, E. W. (2004). Detecting and measuring rater effects using many-facet Rasch measurement: Part I. *Journal of Applied Measurement, 4*(4), 386–422. PMID: 14523257.

Moe, E., Helness Lahlum, H. & Verhelst, N. (2023). *Exploring gender differences in the results of a language test. Paper presented at the EALTA conference,* Helsinki, June 2023.

Nakatsuhara, F., Inoue, C., Berry, V. and Galaczi, E. (2017b). *Exploring performance across two delivery modes for the IELTS Speaking Test: Face-to-face and videoconferencing delivery (Phase 2).* IELTS Partnership Research Papers 3/2017. British Council, Cambridge English Language Assessment and IDP: IELTS Australia. Available online at: https://www.ielts.org/-/media/research-reports/ieltsresearch-partner-paper-3.ashx.

O'Loughlin, K. (1995). Lexical density in candidate output on direct and semi-direct versions of an oral proficiency test. *Language Testing, 12,* 217–237.

O'Sullivan, B. (2013). Assessing speaking. In A. J. Kunnan (Ed.), *Wiley companion to language assessment.* Oxford: Wiley.

O'Sullivan, B. (2016). Validity: What is it and who is it for? In Yiu-nam Leung (ed.). *Epoch Making in English Teaching and Learning: Evolution, Innovation, and Revolution,* (pp. 157–175). Taipei: Crane Publishing Company Ltd.

O'Sullivan, B. (2000a). *Towards a model of performance in oral language tests.* PhD dissertation, University of Reading, UK (submitted).

O'Sullivan, B. (2000b). Exploring gender and oral proficiency interview performance. *System, 28*(3), 373–386. https://doi.org/10.1016/S0346-251X(00)00018-X.

O'Sullivan, B. (2002). Learner acquaintanceship and oral proficiency test pair-task performance. *Language Testing, 19*(3), 277–295. https://doi.org/10.1191/0265532202lt205oa.

O'Sullivan, B. (2021). *Can tests be fair and valid? Plenary paper at the 1st ALTE digital symposium,* April 30.

O'Sullivan, B., & Weir, C. J. (2011). Language testing and validation. In B. O'Sullivan (Ed.), *Language testing: Theory & practice*. Oxford: Palgrave.

O'Sullivan, B. & Weir, C. J. (2020). Research issues in testing speaking. In L. Taylor & N. Saville (Eds.), *Papers in honour of Professor Cyril J. Weir*, (pp.23–53). Cambridge: Cambridge University Press.

O'Sullivan, B., Weir, C. J., & Saville, N. (2002). Using observation checklists to validate speaking-test tasks. *Language Testing, 19*, 33–56.

O'Sullivan, B., Breakspear, T., & Bayliss, W. (2023). Validating an AI-driven scoring system: the model card approach. In K. Sadeghi & D. Douglas (Eds.), *Fundamental considerations in technology mediated language assessment* (pp. 115–134). New York: Routledge. https://doi.org/10.4324/9781003292395-10.

Ockey, G. J. (2009). The effects of group members' personalities on a test taker's L2 group oral discussion test scores. *Language Testing, 26*, 161–186.

Ockey, G., & Chukharev-Hudilainen, E. (2021). Human versus computer partner in the paired oral discussion test. *Applied Linguistics, 42*(5), 924–944. https://doi.org/10.1093/applin/amaa067.

Plough, I. C., & Bogart, P. S. H. (2008). Perceptions of examiner behavior modulate power relations in oral performance testing. *Language Assessment Quarterly, 5*, 195–217.

Purpura, J. E. (2021). A rationale for using a scenario-based assessment to measure competency-based, situated second and foreign language proficiency. *MediAzioni, 32*, A54–A96. Retrieved from: https://mediazioni.sitlec.unibo.it/images/stories/PDF_folder/document-pdf/32-2021/3-purpura%20def.pdf.

Shaw, S., & Weir, C. J. (2007). *Examining writing in a second language*. Cambridge: Cambridge University Press.

Selwyn, N., O'Neill, C., Smith, G., Andrejevic, M., & Gu, X. (2023). A necessary evil? The rise of online exam proctoring in Australian universities. *Media International Australia, 186*(1), 149–164. https://doi.org/10.1177/1329878X211005862.

Shohamy, E. (1994). The validity of direct versus semi-direct oral tests. *Language Testing, 11*, 99–123.

Spurling, S., & Ilyin, D. (1985). The impact of learner variables on language test performance. *TESOL Quarterly, 19*, 283–301. https://doi.org/10.2307/3586830.

Stansfield, C. W., & Kenyon, D. M. (1992). Research on the comparability of the oral proficiency interview and the simulated oral proficiency interview. *System, 20*(3), 347–364. https://doi.org/10.1016/0346-251X(92)90045-5.

Taylor, L. (Ed.). (2011). *Examining speaking*. Cambridge: Cambridge University Press.

Upshur, J. A., & Turner, C. E. (1999). Systematic effects in the rating of second language speaking ability: test method and learner discourse. *Language Testing, 16*, 82–111.

Wagner, E. (2010). The effect of the use of video texts on ESL listening test-taker performance. *Language Testing, 27*(4), 493–513.

Weigle, S. C. (2000). *Assessing writing*. Cambridge: Cambridge University. Press.

Weir, C. J. (2005). *Language testing and validation: An evidence-based approach*. Oxford: Palgrave.

Weir, C. J., O'Sullivan, B., & Horai, T. (2004). Exploring difficulty in speaking tasks: an intra-task perspective. *IELTS Research Reports, 6*, 1–42.

Wigglesworth, G., & O'Loughlin, K. (1993). An investigation into the comparability of direct and semi-direct versions of an oral interaction test in English. *Melbourne Papers in Language Testing, 2*, 56–67.

Yuan, F., & Ellis, R. (2003). The effects of pre-task planning and on-line planning on fluency, complexity and accuracy in L2 monologic oral production. *Applied Linguistics, 24*, 1–27.

Zhang, Y., & Elder, C. (2011). Judgments of oral proficiency by non-native and native English speaking teacher raters: competing or complementary constructs? *Language Testing, 28*, 31–50.

Suggested Readings

Luoma, S. (2004). *Assessing speaking*. Oxford: Oxford University Press.

O'Sullivan, B. (2012). Assessing speaking. In C. Coombe, P. Davidson, B. O'Sullivan & S. Stoynoff (Eds.), *Cambridge guide to second language assessment*. Cambridge: Cambridge University Press.

Weir, C. (2005). *Language testing and validation: An evidence-based approach*. Oxford: Palgrave. Sections 7.3, 8.3 and 9.3.

CHAPTER 11

Assessing Reading

William Grabe and Xiangying Jiang

Introduction

In this review, we discuss the construct of reading comprehension abilities in relation to reading assessment, examine prior and current conceptualizations of reading abilities in assessment contexts, and describe why and how reading abilities are assessed. From a historical perspective, the "construct of reading" is a concept that has followed far behind the formal assessment of reading abilities (leaving aside for the moment the issue of classroom assessment of reading abilities). In fact, the construct of reading comprehension abilities, as well as all the relevant component subskills, knowledge bases, and cognitive processes (hereafter "component skills"), had not been well thought out and convincingly described in assessment contexts until the 1990s. It is interesting to note, in light of this point, a quote by Clapham (1996) on efforts to develop the IELTS reading modules:

We had asked applied linguists for advice on current theories of language proficiency on which we might base the IELTS test battery. However, the applied linguists' responses were varied, contradictory and inconclusive, and provided little evidence for a construct for EAP tests on which we could base the test. (p. 76)

Similar limitations can be noted for the TOEFL of the 1980s (Taylor & Angelis, 2008) and the earlier versions of the Cambridge ESOL suite of tests (see Hawkey, 2009; Khalifa & Weir, 2009; Weir & Milanovich, 2003). Parallel limitations with classroom-based assessments in second language contexts were evident until fairly recently with the relatively narrow range of reading assessment options typically used (often being limited to multiple-choice items, true/false items, matching items, and brief open-ended response items). Fortunately, this situation has changed remarkably in the past 15 years, and very useful construct research (and construct statements for assessment purposes) is now available to help conceptualize reading assessment.

The transition from reliability to validity as the driving force behind standardized reading assessment development in the past 20 years has focused on efforts to reconceptualize reading assessment practices (Chapelle, 2021; Schmidgall & Xi, 2020). Most importantly, this reconceptualization reflects a more empirically supported reading construct, one that has also led to a wider interpretation of reading purposes generally (Grabe & Yamashita, 2022; Yamashita, 2022) and in reading assessment contexts more specifically, e.g., reading to learn, and expeditious reading (Chapelle et al., 2008; Khalifa & Weir, 2009; Weir & Chan, 2019; Weir et al., 2012). Reading assessment itself involves a range of purposes that reflect multiple

The Concise Companion to Language Assessment, First Edition. Edited by Antony John Kunnan.
© 2025 John Wiley & Sons, Inc. Published 2025 by John Wiley & Sons, Inc.

assessment contexts: standardized proficiency assessment, classroom-based formative and achievement testing, placement and diagnostic testing, assessment for reading research purposes (Grabe & Yamashita, 2022), and assessment-for-learning purposes (Wiliam, 2016, 2018). The first two of these contexts take up the large part of this review.

In the process of discussing these purposes for reading assessment, questions related to how reading assessments should be carried out are also addressed. The changing discussions of the reading construct, the redesign of standardized assessments for second language learners, and the need to assess aspects of the reading construct have led to a wide range of assessment task types.

Previous Conceptualizations

Reading comprehension ability has a more intriguing history than is commonly recognized, and it is a history that has profoundly affected how it is assessed. Before the 20th century, most people did not read large amounts of material silently for comprehension. For the much smaller percentage of test takers in academic settings, assessment emphases were placed on literature, culture, and interpretation involving more subjectively measured items. The 20th century, in its turn, combined a growing need for many more people capable of reading large amounts of text information for comprehension with many more uses of this information in academic and work contexts. In the United States, as an example, while functional literacy has been estimated at 90% at the turn of the 20th century, this may have been defined simply as completing one or two years of schooling. In the 1930s, functional literacy in the United States was placed at 88%, being defined as a third-grade completion rate (Stedman & Kaestle, 1991). The pressure to educate a much larger percentage of the population in informational literacy skills, and silent reading comprehension skills in particular, was driven, in part, by the need for more literate soldiers in WWs I and II, more literate industrial workers, and increasingly higher demands placed on student performance in educational settings (Pearson & Goodin, 2010).

Within academic settings, the rise of objective testing practices from a rapidly developing field of educational psychology and psychological measurement spurred large-scale comprehension assessment. However, for the US context, it was only in 1970 that comprehension assessments provided a reliable national picture of English first language (L1) reading abilities, and their patterns of variation, through the NAEP (National Assessment of Educational Progress) testing program and public reports. If broad-based reading comprehension skills assessment has been a relatively recent development, so also has been the development of reading assessment measures that reflect an empirically derived construct of reading abilities.

During the period from the 1920s to the 1960s, objective assessment practices built on psychometric principles were powerful shaping forces for reading assessment in US contexts. In line with these pressures for more objective measurement, L2 contexts were not completely ignored. The first objectively measured foreign language reading test was developed in 1919 (Spolsky, 1995). In the United Kingdom, in contrast, there was a strong counter-balancing emphasis on expert validity. In the first half of the 20th century, this traditional validity emphasis sometimes not only led to more interesting reading assessment tasks (e.g., summarizing, paraphrasing, text interpretation) but also sometimes led to relatively weaker assessment reliability (Weir & Milanovich, 2003).

By the 1960s and 1970s, the pressure to deliver objective test items led to the development of the TOEFL as a multiple-choice test and led to changes in assessment practices with the Cambridge ESOL suite as well as the precursor of the IELTS (i.e., ELTS and the earlier EPTB, the English Proficiency Test Battery) (Clapham, 1996; Weir & Milanovich, 2003). At the same time, the constraints of using multiple-choice and matching items also limited which aspects of reading abilities could be reliably measured. Starting in the 1970s, the pressures of

156 Chapter 11 Assessing Reading

communicative competence and communicative language teaching led to strong claims for the appropriateness of integrative reading assessments (primarily cloze testing). However, from 1980 onwards, the overwhelming output of cognitive research on reading abilities led to a much broader interpretation of reading abilities, one that was built from several component subskills and knowledge bases. From 1990 onwards, research on reading comprehension has been characterized by the roles of various component subskills on reading performance, and on reading for different purposes (reading-to-learn, reading for general comprehension, expeditious reading, etc.). This expansion of reading research also led to more recent conceptualizations of the reading construct as the driving force behind current standardized reading assessment practices.

Current Conceptualizations of Reading and Reading Assessment

In considering current views on reading assessment, we focus primarily on standardized assessment and classroom-based assessment practices. These are the two most widespread uses of reading assessment, and the two purposes that have the greatest impact on test takers. In both cases, the construct of reading abilities is a central issue. The construct of reading has been described recently in a number of ways, mostly with considerable overlap (see Alderson et al., 2015; Grabe & Yamashita, 2022; Khalifa & Weir, 2009). Based on what can now be classified as thousands of empirical research studies on reading comprehension abilities, the consensus that has emerged is that reading comprehension comprises several component language skills, knowledge resources, and general cognitive abilities. The use of these component abilities in combinations varies by proficiency, overall reading purpose, and specific task.

Research in both L1 and L2 contexts has highlighted those factors that strongly impact reading abilities and account for individual differences in reading comprehension performance:

1. Efficient word recognition processes (phonological, orthographic, morphological, and semantic processing)
2. A large recognition vocabulary (vocabulary knowledge)
3. Efficient grammatical parsing skills (grammar knowledge under time constraints)
4. The ability to formulate the main ideas of a text (formulate and combine appropriate semantic propositions)
5. The ability to engage in a range of strategic processes while reading more challenging texts (including goal setting, academic inferencing, and monitoring)
6. The ability to recognize discourse structuring and genre patterns, and use this knowledge to support comprehension
7. The ability to use background knowledge appropriately
8. The ability to interpret text meaning critically in line with reading purposes
9. The efficient use of working memory abilities
10. The efficient use of reading fluency skills
11. Extensive amounts of exposure to L2 print (massive experience with L2 reading)
12. The ability to engage in reading, to expend effort, to persist in reading without distraction, and achieve some level of success with reading (reading motivation)

These factors, in various combinations, explain reading abilities for groups of readers reading for different purposes and at different reading proficiency levels. Given this array of possible factors influencing (and explaining) reading comprehension abilities, the major problems facing current L2 assessment development are (i) how to explain these abilities to wider audiences, (ii) how best to measure these component skills within constrained assessment contexts, and (iii) how to develop assessment tasks that reflect these component skills and reading comprehension abilities more generally (Grabe & Stoller, 2018, 2020; Grabe & Yamashita, 2022).

Standardized Reading Assessment

Major standardized reading assessment programs consider the construct of reading in multiple ways. It is possible to describe the reading construct in terms of purposes for reading, representative reading tasks, or cognitive processes that support comprehension. To elaborate, a number of purposes for engaging in reading can be identified, a number of representative reading tasks can be identified, and a set of cognitive processes and knowledge bases can be considered constitutive of reading comprehension abilities. Of the three alternative descriptive possibilities, reading purpose provides the most transparent explanation to a more general public as well as to test takers, text users, and other stakeholders. Most people can grasp intuitively the idea of reading-to-learn, reading for general comprehension, reading-to-evaluate, expeditious reading, etc. Moreover, these purposes incorporate several key reading tasks and major component skills (many of which vary in importance depending on the specific purpose), thus providing a useful overarching framework for the "construct of reading" (see Chapelle et al., 2008; Clapham, 1996; Grabe & Yamashita, 2022; Khalifa & Weir, 2009). This depiction of reading abilities, developed in the past two decades, has also led to a reconsideration of how to assess reading abilities within well-recognized assessment constraints. It has also led to several innovations in test tasks in standardized assessments. This trend is exemplified by new revisions to the Cambridge ESOL suite of exams, the IELTS, and the iBT TOEFL.

The Cambridge ESOL suite of exams (KET, PET, FCE, CAE, CPE) has undergone important changes in its conceptualization of reading assessment (see Khalifa & Weir, 2009; Weir et al., 2013). As part of the process, the FCE, CAE, and CPE have introduced reading assessment tests and tasks that require greater recognition of the discourse structure of texts, recognition of main ideas, careful reading abilities, facility in reading multiple text genres, and a larger amount of reading itself. Reading assessment tasks now include complex matching tasks of various types, multiple-choice items, short response items, and summary writing (once again).

IELTS (The International English Language Testing System) similarly expanded its coverage of the purposes for reading to include reading for specific information, reading for main ideas, reading to evaluate, and reading to identify a topic or theme. Recent versions of the IELTS include an academic version and a general training version (see Read, 2022 review). The IELTS academic version increased the amount of reading required, and it includes short response items of multiple types, matching of various types, several complex readings with diagrams and figures, and innovative fill-in summary tasks (see Weir & Chan, 2019; Weir & O'Sullivan, 2017).

The iBT TOEFL has similarly revised its reading section based on the framework of reader purpose. Four reading purposes were initially considered in the design of iBT TOEFL reading assessment: reading to find information, reading for basic comprehension, reading to learn, and reading to integrate (Chapelle et al., 2008; Schedl et al., 2022), although reading to integrate was not pursued after the pilot study. iBT TOEFL uses three general item types to evaluate readers' academic reading proficiency: basic comprehension items, inferencing items, and reading-to-learn items. Reading-to-learn has been defined as "developing an organized understanding of how the main ideas, supporting information, and factual details of the text form a coherent whole" (Chapelle et al., 2008), for which two new tasks, prose summary and schematic table, were included. In addition, the iBT TOEFL uses longer, more complex texts than the ones used in the earlier traditional TOEFL.

In all three of these standardized test systems, revisions drew upon well-articulated and empirically supported constructs of reading abilities as they apply to academic contexts. In all three cases, greater attention has been given to longer reading passages, to discourse organization, and to an expanded concept of reading-to-learn or reading-to-evaluate. At the same time, a number of component reading abilities are obviously absent, reflecting the limitations of international standardized reading assessment imposed by cost, time, reliability demands, equating challenges, and fairness across many country settings. (Standardized English L1 reading assessment practices are far more complex.) These limited operationalizations of L2 reading abilities are noted by Alderson (2000), Grabe and Yamashita (2022), Khalifa and Weir (2009), and Schedl et al. (2022).

Among the abilities that the new iBT TOEFL did not pursue are word recognition efficiency, reading to scan for information, summarizing, and reading to integrate information from multiple texts. Khalifa and Weir (2009) note that the Cambridge Suite did not pursue reading to scan, reading to skim, or reading rate (fluency). All three come under the umbrella term "expeditious reading," and for their analysis, this gap represents a limitation in the way the reading construct has been operationalized in the Cambridge Suite (and in IELTS). IELTS revisions had considered including short response items and summary writing. In recent versions, it has settled for a more limited but still innovative cloze summary task.

Two other general standardized assessments are becoming more widely used: the Pearson Test of English-Academic (PTE) and the Duolingo English Test (DET). Both of these tests have carried out successful benchmarking with the CEFR framework and reasonable concurrent validity studies with more established L2 standardized assessments (TOEFL-iBT, IELTS). The PTE-Academic is carefully reviewed in Wang et al. (2012) and Zheng and DeJong (2011). The DET is far more innovative and does not conform with more traditional standardized measures, nor with more standardized assessment tasks, but it makes interesting validity arguments based on psychometric results and research assessment approaches (LaFlair & Settles, 2020) (see also discussion of these innovations in Grabe & Yamashita, 2022).

Returning to the list of component skills noted earlier, the current standardized reading assessment has yet to measure a full range of component abilities of reading comprehension (and may not be able to do so in the near future). Nonetheless, an assessment of reading abilities should reflect, as far as possible, the abilities a skilled reader engages in when reading for academic purposes (leaving aside adult basic literacy assessments and early child reading assessments). The following is a list of the component abilities of reading comprehension that are not yet widely incorporated into L2 standardized reading assessment (from Grabe & Yamashita, 2022, p. 465):

1. Passage reading fluency and reading rate
2. Automaticity and rapid word recognition
3. Search processes
4. Morphological knowledge
5. Text–structure awareness and discourse organization
6. Spelling knowledge
7. Strategic-processing abilities
8. Summarization abilities
9. Synthesis skills
10. Complex evaluation and critical reading

How select aspects of these abilities find their way into standardized L2 reading assessment practices is currently being explored, but these abilities remain as important challenges for the future.

Although researchers working with standardized reading tests have made a serious effort to capture crucial aspects of the component abilities of reading comprehension (e.g., Chapelle et al., 2008; Hawkey, 2009; Khalifa & Weir, 2009), construct validity still represents a major challenge for L2 reading assessment because the number and the types of assessment tasks are strictly constrained in the context of standardized testing. If the construct is underrepresented by the test, it is difficult to claim that reading comprehension abilities are being fully measured (see Chapelle, 2021). This difficulty also suggests that efforts to develop an explanation of the reading construct *from* L2 reading tests face the challenge of construct underrepresentation in the very tests being used to develop the construct (a fairly common problem until recently). Perhaps with greater uses of computer technology in testing, the control over time for individual items or sections can be better managed, and innovative item types can be incorporated without disrupting assessment procedures. In addition, as suggested by Shiotsu (2010), test taker performance information recorded by computers not only may assist decision-making but might also be used for diagnostic purposes. One of the most obvious potential applications of the computer is to more easily incorporate skimming, reading to search, reading fluency, and reading rate measures. Such an extension in the future would be welcome.

Classroom-Based Reading Assessment

Moving from standardized assessments, the second major use of L2 reading assessments takes place in classroom contexts. In certain respects, classroom-based assessment provides a complement to standardized assessment in that aspects of the reading construct not accounted for by the latter can easily be included in the former. In many classroom-based assessment contexts, teachers observe, note, and chart students' reading rates, reading fluency, summarizing skills, use of reading information in multistep tasks, critical evaluation skills, and motivation and persistence to read.

Reading assessment in these contexts is primarily used to measure student learning (and presumably to improve student learning). This type of assessment usually involves the measurement of skills and knowledge gained over a period of time based on course content and specific skills practiced. Typically, classroom teachers or teacher groups are responsible for developing the tests and deciding how the scores should be interpreted and what steps to take as a result of the assessment outcomes (Jamieson, 2011). Classroom learning can be assessed at multiple points in any semester and some commonly used classroom assessments include unit achievement tests, quizzes of various types, and midterm and final exams. In addition to the use of tests, informal and alternative assessment options are also useful for the effective assessment of student learning, using, for example, student observations, self-reporting measures, and portfolios. A key issue for informal reading assessment is the need for multiple assessment formats (and multiple assessment points) to evaluate a wide range of student performances for any decisions about student abilities or student progress. The many small assessments across many tasks help overcome the subjectivity of informal assessment and strengthen the effectiveness and fairness of informal assessments (Grabe & Yamashita, 2022).

Classroom-based assessment makes use of the array of test-task types found in standardized assessments (e.g., cloze, gap-filling formats [rational cloze formats], text segment ordering, text gaps, multiple choice questions, short-answer responses, summary writing, matching items, T/F/not stated questions, editing, information transfer, skimming, scanning). Much more importantly, for the validity of classroom assessment, though less commonly recognized, is the day-to-day informal assessments and feedback that teachers regularly provide to students. Grabe and Yamashita (2022) identify 6 categories of classroom-based assessment practices and note 25 specific informal assessment activities that can be, and often are, carried out by teachers. These informal activities include (i) having students read aloud in class and evaluating their reading, (ii) keeping a record of student responses to questions in class after a reading, (iii) observing how much time

160 Chapter 11 Assessing Reading

students spend on task during free reading or sustained silent reading (SSR), (iv) observing students reading with an audio tape or listening to an audio-taped reading, (v) having students list words they want to know after reading and why, (vi) having students write simple book reports and recommending books to others, (vii) keeping charts of student reading rate growth, (viii) having students read aloud for the teacher/tester and making notes, or using a checklist, or noting miscues on the text, (ix) noting students' uses of texts in a multistep project and discussing these uses, and (x) creating student portfolios of reading activities or progress indicators.

Among these informal assessment activities, it is worth pointing out that oral reading fluency assessment (reading aloud) has attracted much research interest in L1 contexts. Oral reading fluency has been found to serve as a strong predictor of general comprehension (Fuchs et al., 2001; Shinn et al., 1992; Valencia et al., 2010). Even with a one-minute oral reading measure, teachers can look into multiple indicators of oral reading fluency (e.g., rate, accuracy, prosody, and comprehension) and obtain a fine-grained understanding of students' reading ability, particularly if multiple aspects of student reading performances are assessed (Kuhn et al., 2010; Valencia et al., 2010). However, research on fluency assessment has not been carried out in L2 reading contexts. Reading aloud tasks as an L2 reading assessment tool have certain challenges (conflating reading fluency with oral language fluency), but for informal assessment settings, it may be worth exploring the validity of oral reading fluency assessment in the L2 context.

Another aspect of classroom-based assessment that is gaining recognition is the concept of assessment *for* learning (Black & Wiliam, 2009; Wiliam, 2011). This approach draws on explicit classroom tests, informal assessment practices, and opportunities for feedback from students to teachers that indicate a need for assistance or support. The critical goal of this assessment approach is to provide immediate feedback on tasks and to teach students to engage in more effective learning instead of evaluating their performance. An important element of assessment for learning is the follow-up feedback and interaction between the teacher and the students. Through this feedback, teachers respond with ongoing remediation and fine-tuning of instruction when they observe non-understanding or weak student performances. Grabe and Yamashita (2022) note 17 ideas and techniques for assessment for learning.

The key is not to provide answers but to enhance learning, work through misunderstandings that are apparent from student performance, develop effective learning strategies, and encourage student self-awareness and motivation to improve. Although these ideas and techniques apply to any learning and assessment context, they are ideally suited to reading tasks and reading comprehension development. The real goal of assessment for learning is not to provide effective teacher feedback but to get students to act on teacher feedback in ways that improve student learning.

Diagnostic Assessment and Research-Driven Assessment

For the sake of completeness, two further types of reading assessment involve diagnostic assessment and researcher-driven assessment practices. In the case of diagnostic assessment, the goal is to provide a more detailed profile of specific strengths and weaknesses rather than an overall proficiency measure of reading ability. Recent research on diagnostic assessment for L2 reading is outlined in Alderson et al. (2015). Researcher-based assessment practices are not well-documented in any single overview (because they are so varied and used in such varied contexts), but such assessment practices are essential for any research study of individual differences among learners that do not replicate a real-world language use context (e.g., speed of word recognition, spelling quizzes, response time recognition measures). A key commonality among the many varieties of researcher-driven assessment practices is that they are not constrained to target language use (TLU) domains as one tenet of good assessment practices (cf. Bachman & Palmer, 1996). (For a simple taxonomy and commentary on research-driven assessment practices, see Grabe & Yamashita, 2022.)

Key L2 Reading Assessment Research

In addition to the volume-length publications on assessment development and validation with three large-scale standardized L2 tests (e.g., Chapelle et al., 2008; Clapham, 1996; Hawkey, 2009; Khalifa & Weir, 2009; Weir & Milanovich, 2003) reviewed above, this section will focus on key journal publications related to reading assessment. We searched through the two most important assessment journals, *Language Testing* and *Language Assessment Quarterly*, for their publications in the past 20 years. These reading assessment articles focused mainly on the topics of background knowledge, test tasks, discourse structure knowledge, and reading strategies.

We note here seven studies relevant to conceptualizations of the L2 reading construct and ways to assess reading ability. The first two studies explore the relationship between background knowledge and reading comprehension in the school context. The subsequent four studies look at discourse structure awareness, summary writing as a reading task, text types, and the role of metacognitive and cognitive strategies in reading assessment. The final study examines the role of memory in reading assessment as a possible source of bias. Overall, it is important to note that research articles on L2 reading assessment are relatively uncommon in comparison with research on speaking and writing assessment (and performance scoring issues).

It is well known that background knowledge facilitates reading comprehension, but relatively little is known about whether lack of background knowledge impedes comprehension and how much knowledge is needed to prevent comprehension from being compromised. O'Reilly et al. (2019) explored the knowledge threshold hypothesis with the goal of identifying a point below which reading comprehension is limited and not predicted by background knowledge, and above which reading comprehension is facilitated by background knowledge. They tested 3534 high school students with a reading comprehension test and a background-knowledge test. The results of the study showed that the relation between reading comprehension and background knowledge was affected by a knowledge threshold. Below the threshold, background knowledge did not predict comprehension while above the threshold, it was positively related to comprehension, thus supporting the knowledge threshold hypothesis. The finding suggests that readers might need a minimum amount of background knowledge to comprehend a text about a certain topic.

Min et al. (2022) explored the interplay between content knowledge and reading ability in a large-scale EAP reading assessment in a K-12 context, and how the relation was moderated by grade levels and proficiency levels. The data used in the study were item-level responses to a total of 360 reading items targeting 5 grade clusters (1, 2–3, 4–5, 6–8, and 9–12) in the WIDA ACCESS for ELLs (Online 2.0) test administered in 40 states in the school year 2018–2019. Students' overall proficiency levels were coded as low, intermediate, and high based on their listening scores in the test. The results showed that content-specific factors played a significant role only in the performance of Grade 1 students but not the other grade clusters and contributed to the performance of low-ability-level students across all grade clusters. In this study, with younger L2 learners, as grade level and proficiency level increase, the importance of content knowledge decreases. Interestingly, the participants of this study and in O'Reilly et al. (2019) were either high school students or a range of mostly lower-grade L2 students. In contrast, the majority of the studies in the literature have focused instead on tertiary-level language learners; these latter studies have tended to support the facilitative effect of background knowledge in reading comprehension. The varying results for what is considered a major component of reading comprehension ability deserve much more attention in reading assessment research.

Kobayashi (2002) examined the impact of discourse organization awareness on reading performance. Specifically, she investigated whether text organization (association, description,

162 Chapter 11 Assessing Reading

causation, and problem-solution) and response format (cloze, open-ended questions, and summary writing) have a systematic influence on test results of learners at different proficiency levels (high, middle, and low). She found that text organization did not lead to strong performance differences for test formats that measured less integrative comprehension such as cloze tests or for learners of limited L2 proficiency. On the contrary, stronger performance differences due to organizational differences in texts were observed for testing formats that measure more integrative forms of comprehension tasks (open-ended questions and summary writing), especially for learners with higher levels of L2 proficiency. The more proficient students benefited from texts with a clear structure for summary writing and open-ended questions. She suggested that "it is essential to know in advance what type of text organization is involved in passages used for reading comprehension tests, especially in summary writing with learners of higher language proficiency" (p. 210). The study confirms previous findings that different test formats seem to measure different aspects of reading comprehension and that text organization can influence reading comprehension based on more complex reading tasks.

Yu (2008) also contributed to issues in discourse processing by exploring the use of summaries for reading assessment with 157 Chinese university students in an undergraduate EFL program. The study looked at the relationships between summarizing an L2 text in the L2 versus in the L1, as well as relationships among both summaries (L1 and L2) and an L2 reading measure, an L2 writing measure, and a translation measure. Findings showed that test takers wrote longer summaries in the L1 (Chinese) but were judged to have written better summaries in their L2 (English). Perhaps more importantly, summary writing in Chinese and English only correlated with L2 reading measures at 0.30 and 0.26 (r^2 of 0.09 and 0.07, respectively, for only the stronger of the two summary quality measures). These weak correlations suggest that summary writing measures something quite different than the TOEFL reading and writing measures used. Yu found no relationships between summary writing quality and the TOEFL writing or translation measures. In a questionnaire and follow-up interviews, test takers also felt that summary writing was a better indicator of their comprehension abilities than their writing abilities. While this is only one study in one context, it raises interesting questions about the role of summarizing in reading assessment, which needs to be examined further.

Green et al. (2010) focused on the role of texts, and especially disciplinary text types, for testing purposes. They examine the authenticity of reading texts used in IELTS by comparing IELTS Academic Reading texts with the texts that first-year undergraduates most needed to read and understand once enrolled at their universities. The textual features examined in the study included vocabulary and grammar, cohesion and rhetorical organization, genre and rhetorical task, subject and cultural knowledge, and text abstractness. The authors found that the IELTS texts have many of the features of the kinds of text encountered by first-year undergraduates and there are few fundamental differences between them. The findings support arguments made by Clapham (1996) that nonspecialist texts of the kind employed in IELTS can serve as a reasonable substitute for testing purposes.

Zhang et al. (2014) investigated the relationship between the use of metacognitive and cognitive strategies and the relationship between the use of such strategies and reading performance. Metacognitive strategies in this study include planning, evaluating, and monitoring and cognitive strategies consist of initial reading, identifying important information, inference making, and integrating. A total of 593 Chinese college students responded to a 38-item metacognitive and cognitive strategy questionnaire and took the CET-4 Reading subtest. The researchers took a multi-sample SEM approach to their analyses. The results suggested that metacognitive and cognitive strategies were not clearly distinguishable in the test context. Test takers used multiple strategies simultaneously in a unitary manner and the two types of strategies functioned in synergy to maximize their reading test performance.

The CET-4 reading subtest had two underlying factors: lexico-grammatical ability and text comprehension. Test takers' strategy use affected their lexico-grammatical ability significantly but played a minor role in text comprehension.

Finally, Chang (2006) examined whether and how the requirement of memory biases our understanding of readers' comprehension. The study compared L2 readers' performance on an immediate recall protocol (a task requiring memory) and on a translation task (a task without the requirement of memory). The study revealed that the translation task yielded significantly more evidence of comprehension than did the immediate recall task, which indicates that the requirement of memory in the recall task may hinder test takers' abilities to demonstrate fully their comprehension of the reading passage. The results also showed that the significant difference found in learners' performance between the immediate recall and the translation task spanned the effect of topics and proficiency levels. This study provides evidence that immediate free recall tasks might have limited validity as a comprehension measure due to its memory-related complication. Certainly, more research is needed on the role and relevance of memory processes as part of reading comprehension abilities.

Challenges

A number of important challenges face reading assessment practices. One of the most important challenges for reading assessment stems from the complexity of the construct of reading ability itself. Reading comprehension is a multi-component construct that involves many skills and subskills (at least the 14 listed above). The question remains how such an array of component abilities can best be captured within the operational constraints of standardized testing, what new assessment tasks might be developed, and what component abilities might best be assessed indirectly (Grabe & Yamashita, 2022). In standardized assessment contexts, practices that might expand the reading-assessment construct are constrained by concerns of validity, reliability, time, cost, usability, and consequence, which limit the types of reading-assessment tasks that can be used. In classroom-based contexts, effective reading assessments are often constrained by relatively minimal awareness among teachers that a range of reading abilities, reflecting the reading construct, need to be assessed.

A second challenge is the need to reconcile the connection between reading in a testing context and reading in non-testing contexts. Whether or not a text or task has similar linguistic and textual features in a testing context with texts in non-test uses (that is, TLU, Bachman & Palmer, 1996) does not address what test takers actually do when encountering these texts in a high-stakes testing situation. When students read a text as part of standardized assessment, they know that they are reading for an assessment purpose. So, for example, although the characteristics of the academic reading texts used in IELTS were said to share most of the textual characteristics of first-year undergraduate textbook materials (Green et al., 2010), the context for standardized assessment may preclude any strong assumption of a match to authentic reading in the "real world" (see also Cohen & Upton, 2007; Rupp et al., 2006). One outcome is that it is probably not reasonable to demand that the reading done in reading assessments exactly replicates the "real world" reading experiences. However, the use of realistic texts, tasks, and contexts should be expected because it supports positive washback for reading instruction; that is to say, texts being used in testing and language instruction should be realistic approximations for what test takers will need to read in subsequent academic settings.

A third challenge is how to assess reading strategies, or "the strategic reader" (Grabe & Yamashita, 2022). Rupp et al. (2006) found that the strategies readers use in assessment contexts were different from the ones they use in real reading contexts and even the construct of reading comprehension is assessment-specific and determined by the test design and text

164   Chapter 11 Assessing Reading

format. On the other hand, Cohen and Upton (2007) found that although the participants approached the reading test as a test taking task, the successful completion of the test requires both local and general understanding of the texts, which reflects academic reading-like abilities. This debate leaves open a key question: If readers use strategies in non-testing contexts differently from how they are used in testing contexts, how should we view the validity of reading assessments (assuming strategy use is a part of the reading construct)? Clearly, more research is needed on the use of, and assessment of, reading strategies in testing contexts.

A fourth challenge is the possible need to develop a notion of the reading construct that varies with growing proficiency in reading. In many L2 reading assessment situations, this issue is minimized (except for the Cambridge ESOL suite of language assessments). Because English L2 assessment contexts are so often focused on EAP contexts, there is relatively little discussion of how reading assessments should reflect a low-proficiency interpretation of the L2 reading construct (whether for children, or beginning L2 learners, or for basic adult literacy populations). It is clear that different proficiency levels require distinct types of reading assessments, especially when considering research in L1 reading contexts (Adlof et al., 2011; Grabe & Yamashita, 2022). In L2 contexts, Kobayashi (2002) found that text organization and response format have an impact on the performance of readers at different proficiency levels. The implication of this finding is that different texts, tasks, and task types are appropriate at different proficiency levels. In light of this finding, how should reading assessment tasks and task types change with growing L2 proficiency? Can systematic statements be made in this regard? Should proficiency variability be reflected at the level of the L2 reading construct, and if so, how?

Future Directions

In some respects, the challenges to L2 reading assessment and future directions for reading assessment are two sides of the same coin. In closing this chapter, we suggest five future directions as a set of issues that L2 reading assessment research and practice should give more attention to. These directions do not necessarily reflect current conflicts in research findings or immediate challenges to the validity of reading assessment, but they do need to be considered carefully and acted upon in the future.

First, different L2 reading tests likely measure students differently. This is not news to reading assessment researchers, but this needs to be explored more explicitly and systematically in L2 reading contexts. Standardized assessment programs may not want to know how their reading tests compare with other reading tests, so this is work that might not be carried out by testing corporations. At the same time, such work can be expensive and quite demanding on test takers. Nonetheless, with applied linguists regularly using one or another standardized test for research purposes, it is important to know how reading measures vary. One research study in L1 contexts (Keenan et al., 2008) has demonstrated that widely used L1 reading measures give different sets of results for the same group of test takers. Work of this type would be very useful for researchers studying many aspects of language learning.

Second, the reading construct is most likely underrepresented by all well-known standardized reading assessment systems. A longer-term goal of reading assessment research should be to try to expand reading measures to more accurately reflect the L2 reading construct. Perhaps, this work can be most usefully carried out as part of recent efforts to develop diagnostic assessment measures for L2 reading because much more detailed information could be collected in this way. Such work would, in turn, improve research on the L2 reading construct itself. At issue is the extent to which we can (and should) measure reading passage fluency, main idea summarizing skills, information synthesis from multiple text sources, strategic reading abilities, morphological knowledge, and possibly other abilities.

Third, L2 readers are not a homogeneous group and they bring different background knowledge when reading L2 texts. They vary in many ways such as cultural experiences, topic interest, print environment, knowledge of genre and text structures, and disciplinary knowledge. In order to control for unnecessary confounding factors related to these differences in prior knowledge, more attention should be paid to issues of individual variation, especially in classroom-based assessments, so no test takers are advantaged or disadvantaged due to these differences.

Fourth, computers and new media are likely to alter how reading tests and reading tasks evolve. Although we believe that students reading for academic purposes are not going to magically bypass the need to read print materials and books for at least the near future, we need to recognize that the ability to read online texts is becoming an important part of the general construct of reading ability. As a result, more attention needs to be paid to issues of reading assessment tied to reading of online texts, especially when research has indicated a low correlation between students who are effective print readers versus students who are effective online readers (Coiro, 2021; Grabe & Yamashita, 2022). At the same time, reading assessment research will need to examine the uses of computer-based assessments and assessments involving new media. A major issue is how to carry out research that is fair, rigorous, and relatively free of enthusiastic endorsements or the selling of the "new" simply because it is novel.

Finally, teachers need to be trained more effectively to understand appropriate assessment practices. A large number of teachers still have negative attitudes to the value of assessment measures for student evaluation, student placement, and student learning. In many cases, L2 training programs do not require an assessment course, or the course is taught in a way that seems to turn off future teachers. As a consequence, teachers allow themselves to be powerless to influence assessment practices and outcomes. In such settings, teachers, in effect, cheat themselves by being excluded from the assessment process, and they are not good advocates for their students. Perhaps most importantly, teachers lose a powerful tool to support student learning and to motivate students more effectively (Grabe & Yamashita, 2022). The problem of teachers being poorly trained in assessment practices is a growing area of attention in L1 contexts; it should also be a more urgent topic of discussion in L2 teacher training contexts.

Discussion Questions

1. Suppose you are developing a reading comprehension test. Describe your testing context to include testing purpose, testing type, and characteristics of test takers. How do you conceptualize the construct of reading comprehension? What abilities will you test and what abilities will you leave out. Explain why.

2. In classroom-based reading assessment, teachers use assessment for different purposes. Explain how reading assessment **of** learning differs from reading assessment **for** learning.

References

Adlof, S., Perfetti, C., & Catts, H. (2011). Developmental changes in reading comprehension: implications for assessment and instruction. In S. Samuels & A. Farstrup (Eds.), *What research has to say about reading instruction* ((4th ed.) ed., pp. 186–214). International Reading Association.

Alderson, J. (2000). *Assessing reading.* Cambridge University Press.

Alderson, J. C., Haapakangas, E.-L., Huhta, A., Nieminen, L., & Ullakonoja, R. (2015). *The diagnosis of reading in a second and foreign language.* Routledge.

Bachman, L. F., & Palmer, A. S. (1996). *Language testing in practice: Designing and developing useful language tests.* Oxford University Press.

Black, P., & Wiliam, D. (2009). Developing the theory of formative assessment. *Educational Assessment, Evaluation, and Accountability, 21,* 5–31.

166   Chapter 11 Assessing Reading

Chang, Y.-F. (2006). On the use of the immediate recall task as a measure of second language reading comprehension. *Language Testing, 23*(4), 520–543.

Chapelle, C. A. (2021). *Argument-based validation of testing and assessment.* Sage.

Chapelle, C. A., Enright, M. K., Jamieson, J. M., & . (2008). *Building a validity argument for the Test of English as a Foreign Language.* Routledge.

Clapham, C. (1996). *The development of IELTS: A study in the effect of background knowledge on reading comprehension.* Cambridge University Press.

Cohen, A. D., & Upton, T. A. (2007). 'I want to go back to the text': response strategies on the reading subtest of the new TOEFL®. *Language Testing, 24*(2), 209–250. https://doi.org/10.1177/0265532207076364.

Coiro, J. (2021). Toward a multifaceted heuristic of digital reading to inform assessment, research, practice, and policy. *Reading Research Quarterly, 56*(1), 9–31.

Fuchs, L., Fuchs, D., Hosp, M., & Jenkins, J. (2001). Oral reading fluency as an indicator or reading competence: a theoretical, empirical, and historical analysis. *Scientific Studies of Reading, 5,* 239–256.

Grabe, W., & Stoller, F. (2018). How reading comprehension works (Chapter 2). In J. Newton, D. Ferris, C. Goh, W. Grabe, F. Stoller & L. Vandergrift (Eds.), *Teaching English to second language learners: Reading, writing, listening, and speaking* (pp. 9–27). Routledge.

Grabe, W., & Stoller, F. (2020). Teaching reading: foundations and practices. In C. Chapelle (Ed.), *The concise encyclopedia of applied linguistics* (pp. 1063–1071). Wiley Blackwell.

Grabe, W., & Yamashita, J. (2022). *Reading in a second language: Moving from theory to practice* (2nd ed.). Cambridge University Press.

Green, A., Unaldi, A., & Weir, C. (2010). Empiricism versus connoisseurship: establishing the appropriacy of texts in tests of academic reading. *Language Testing, 27*(2), 191–211.

Hawkey, R. (2009). *Examining FCE and CAE: Key issues and recurring themes in developing the first certificate in English and certificate in advanced English exams.* Cambridge University Press.

Jamieson, J. (2011). Assessment of classroom language learning. In E. Hinkel (Ed.), *Handbook of research in second language teaching and learning* (Vol. *II*, pp. 768–785). Routledge.

Keenan, J., Betjemann, R., & Olson, R. (2008). Reading comprehension tests vary in the skills they assess: differential dependence on decoding and oral comprehension. *Scientific Studies of Reading, 12*(3), 281–300.

Khalifa, H., & Weir, C. J. (2009). *Examining reading.* Cambridge University Press.

Kobayashi, M. (2002). Method effects on reading comprehension test performance: text organization and response format. *Language Testing, 19*(2), 193–220.

Kuhn, M. R., Schwanenflugel, P. J., & Meisinger, E. B. (2010). Aligning theory and assessment of reading fluency: automaticity, prosody, and definitions of fluency. *Reading Research Quarterly, 45*(2), 230–251.

LaFlair, G.T., & Settles, B. (2020). *Duolingo English Test: Technical manual.* Duolingo. Retrieved May 30, 2021 from https://duolingo-papers.s3.amazonaws.com/other/det-technical-manual-current.pdf.

Min, S., Bishop, K., & Cook, H. G. (2022). Reading is a multidimensional construct at child-L2-English-literacy onset, but comprises fewer dimensions over time: evidence from multidimensional IRT analysis. *Language Testing, 39*(2), 265–288. https://doi.org/10.1177/02655322211045296.

O'Reilly, T., Wang, Z., & Sabatini, J. (2019). How much knowledge is too little? When a lack of knowledge becomes a barrier to comprehension. *Psychological Science, 30*(9), 1344–1351.

Pearson, P. D., & Goodin, S. (2010). Silent reading pedagogy: a historical perspective. In E. Hiebert & D. R. Reutzel (Eds.), *Revisiting silent reading* (pp. 3–23). Reading Association.

Read, J. (2022). Test review: the International English Language Testing System (IELTS). *Language Testing, 39*(4), 679–694.

Rupp, A. A., Ferne, T., & Choi, H. (2006). How assessing reading comprehension with multiple-choice questions shapes the construct: a cognitive processing perspective. *Language Testing, 23*(4), 441–474. https://doi.org/10.1191/0265532206lt337oa.

Schedl, M., O'Reilly, T., Grabe, W., & Schoonen, R. (2022). Assessing academic reading. In X. Xi & J. M. Norris (Eds.), *Assessing academic English for higher education admissions* (pp. 22–60). Routledge.

Schmidgall, J., & Xi, X. (2020). Validation of language assessment. In C. Chapelle (Ed.), *The concise encyclopedia of applied linguistics* ((2nd ed.) ed., pp. 1123–1135). Wiley Blackwell.

Shinn, M. R., Knutson, N., Good, R. H., Tilly, W. D., & Collins, V. L. (1992). Curriculum-based measurement of oral reading fluency: a confirmatory analysis of its relation to reading. *School Psychology Review, 21*, 459–479.

Shiotsu, T. (2010). *Components of L2 reading: Linguistic and processing factors in the reading test performances of Japanese EFL learners.* Cambridge University Press.

Spolsky, B. (1995). *Measured words.* Oxford University Press.

Stedman, L., & Kaestle, C. (1991). Literacy and reading performance in the United States from 1880 to the present. In C. Kaestle, H. Damon-Moore, L. C. Stedman, K. Tinsley & W. W. Jr. Trollinger (Eds.), *Literacy in the United States* (pp. 75–128). Yale University Press.

Taylor, C., & Angelis, P. (2008). The evolution of the TOEFL. In C. Chapelle, M. Enright & J. Jamieson (Eds.), *Building a validity argument for the Test of English as a Foreign Language* (pp. 27–54). Routledge.

Valencia, S. W., Smith, A. T., Reece, A. M., Li, M., Wixson, K. K., & Newman, H. (2010). Oral reading fluency assessment: issues of construct, criterion, and consequential validity. *Reading Research Quarterly, 45*(3), 270–291.

Wang, H., Choi, I., Schmidgall, J., & Bachman, L. F. (2012). Review of Pearson test of English academic: building an assessment use argument. *Language Testing, 29*(4), 603–619.

Weir, C. J., & Chan, S. (2019). *Research and practice in assessing academic reading: The case of IELTS.* Cambridge University Press.

Weir, C., Hawkey, R., Green, A., & Devi, S. (2012). The cognitive processes underlying the academic reading construct as measured by IELTS. In L. Taylor & C. J. Weir (Eds.), *Studies in Language Testing 34, IELTS collected papers 2: Research in reading and listening assessment* (pp. 212–269). New York: Cambridge University Press.

Weir, C. J., & Milanovich, X. M. (Eds.). (2003). *Continuity and innovation: Revising the Cambridge Proficiency in English examination 1913–2002.* Cambridge University Press.

Weir, C. J., & O'Sullivan, B. (2017). *Assessing English on the global stage: The British Council and English language testing, 1941–2016.* Equinox Publishing.

Weir, C. J., Vidaković, I., & Galaczi, E. D. (2013). *Measured constructs: A history of Cambridge English Language Examinations 1913-2012.* Cambridge University Press.

Wiliam, D. (2011). What is assessment for learning. *Studies in Educational Evaluation, 37*, 3–14.

Wiliam, D. (2016). The secret of effective feedback. *Educational Leadership, 73*(7), 10–15.

Wiliam, D. (2018). *Embedded formative assessment* ((2nd ed.) ed.). Solution Tree Press.

Yamashita, J. (2022). L2 reading comprehension: theory and research. In E. H. Jeon & Y. In'nami (Eds.), *Understanding L2 proficiency: Theoretical and meta-analytic investigation* (pp. 5–28). John Benjamin.

Yu, G. (2008). Reading to summarize in English and Chinese: a tale of two languages. *Language Testing, 25*(4), 521–551.

Zhang, L., Goh, C. C. M., & Kunnan, A. J. (2014). Analysis of test takers' metacognitive and cognitive strategy use and EFL reading test performance: a multi-sample SEM approach. *Language Assessment Quarterly, 11*(1), 76–102. https://doi.org/10.1080/15434303.2013.853770.

Zheng Y., & De Jong, J. H. A. L. (2011). *Establishing construct and concurrent validity of Pearson Test of English Academic [Research note].* Retrieved www.pearsonpte.com/research/Documents/PTEAcademicValidityPaper.pdf.

Suggested Readings

Coiro, J. (2021). Toward a multifaceted heuristic of digital reading to inform assessment, research, practice, and policy. *Reading Research Quarterly, 56*(1), 9–31.

Geva, E., Xi, Y., Massey-Garrison, A., & Mak, J. Y. (2019). Assessing reading in second language learners: development, validity, and educational considerations. In D. A. Kilpatrick, R. M. Joshi & R. K. Wagner (Eds.), *Reading development and difficulties: Bridging the gap between research and practice* (pp. 117–155). Springer.

Schedl, M., O'Reilly, T., Grabe, W., & Schoonen, R. (2022). Assessing academic reading. In X. Xi & J. M. Norris (Eds.), *Assessing academic English for higher education admissions* (pp. 22–60). Routledge.

Yamashita, J. (2022). L2 reading comprehension: theory and research. In E. H. Jeon & Y. In'nami (Eds.), *Understanding L2 proficiency: Theoretical and meta-analytic investigation* (pp. 5–28). John Benjamin.

CHAPTER 12

Assessing Writing

Cecilia Guanfang Zhao

Introduction

Writing and writing competence have been conceptualized differently over time from different perspectives. As a result, different approaches to writing assessment have emerged in various contexts. This chapter surveys such theoretical conceptions and existing writing assessment practices that inform the subsequent discussions of major challenges as well as future directions for writing assessment research and practice. A synthesis of the current scholarship on writing assessment is also offered to highlight recurring and emerging themes, such as the validation of writing assessment in large-scale high-stakes contexts, the development of alternative writing assessment approaches in low-stakes classroom-based settings, and the application of AI and technology in writing assessment research and practice. Major challenges are then identified, based on which future directions are highlighted, including the need for the field to reconceptualize and define the construct of writing in situ; to incorporate digital, multimodal, and multilingual elements into writing assessments; and to further exploit AI and technology for more effective automated scoring and evaluation of writing and more innovative design of the next generation of writing assessment.

The Construct of Writing

Writing was once conceptualized largely as mechanical and linguistic accuracy. As such, the assessment of writing also focused almost exclusively on the evaluation of mechanical and grammatical accuracy in a written product, be it a direct composition or an indirect standardized test. Interested readers may refer to Crusan (2014) and Cumming (2009) for a quick overview of the early histories of writing assessment that moved from prescientific to psychometric-structuralist approaches in both the U.S. context and an international context. Later in the 1960s and 1970s, writing started to be conceptualized as a set of linear processes that involve prewriting, writing, and rewriting (see Britton et al., 1975; Rohman, 1965). This process-centered view of writing continued to evolve in the ensuing decades, resulting in a more sophisticated conception of writing as a hierarchical mental process. Flower and Hayes's (1981) cognitive process model is probably the most influential, highlighting the complexity of various cognitive mental activities (e.g., goal setting, idea generation, organization, translating,

The Concise Companion to Language Assessment, First Edition. Edited by Antony John Kunnan.
© 2025 John Wiley & Sons, Inc. Published 2025 by John Wiley & Sons, Inc.

reviewing, and monitoring) and their interactions with individual writers' long-term and short-term memory, as well as their affective and motivational states.

This focus on individual writers and their cognitive activities in the composing process was soon challenged by scholars in the 1980s and 1990s from a sociocultural perspective. They argue that while writing is a cognitive process, it is also highly social and that a primary focus on the writer and their cognition is ineffective in preparing student writers, particularly second language (L2) writers, for academic writing tasks in authentic educational settings. They further point out that writing processes are often based on and influenced by interactions between the writer and their audience, as well as other contextual factors and materials in a specific writing situation. As a response to this sociocultural turn, researchers and practitioners proposed various genre-based conceptions and models of writing, including the systemic functional linguistics (SFL) approach (e.g., Halliday, 1985; Schleppegrell, 2004) and the English for specific purposes (ESP) conceptions (e.g., Swales, 1990) that see writing as a process of how writers choose lexico-grammatical features as their meaning-making resources in specific contexts (see Bawarshi & Reiff, 2010; Hyland, 2003). Overall, therefore, researchers believe that genres are both social and cognitive (Johns, 2008), and that analyses of "context, complex writing processes, and intertexuality" are all critical (Johns, 2011, p. 64).

In addition to such models of writing in general, conceptions of *academic literacy/literacies* also exist (cf. Bloome et al., 2018), covering similar perspectives of writing in academic contexts as a cognitive process (academic literacy, Scardamalia & Bereiter, 1991) and social practice (academic literacies; see Lea & Street, 2006). Snow and Uccelli (2009), for example, highlight three levels of challenges associated with the development of academic literacies, including the ability to organize discourse following conventions, the ability to represent an often abstract and complicated message, and ultimately the ability to represent the self and the audience in and through writing. Yu and Zhao (2021) further highlight the role of information literacy in the discussion of academic literacy practices in an information age. They point out that the process of academic writing in this particular context entails both an information process and a composing process, whereas the social dimension of writing covers rhetorical, disciplinary, and information contexts that together afford and constrain information and writing practices.

Writing Assessment Practices

As theoretical conceptions of the construct of writing and writing competence have evolved over the years, writing assessment practices, too, have undergone some major changes. The initial focus on linguistic and mechanical accuracy in the early days and a goal to achieve standardized objective testing once led to indirect discrete-point assessment of writing, particularly in the United States (see Crusan, 2014). The shift of focus from the accuracy of written products to the composing process in writing theories gradually gave rise to direct, performance-based writing assessments, although arguably such assessment formats had been around since the early 20th century (e.g., Shaw & Weir, 2007). The most prevalent type of direct writing assessment, especially on large-scale high-stakes language tests, is perhaps the timed, prompt-based impromptu essay writing. Test takers are often given a general statement that presents a particular perspective regarding a specific topic; they are then required to take a stance and explain why they agree or disagree with the given statement within a specified time limit (often 20–30 minutes). The use of such decontextualized generic essay tasks, however, fails to see writing as a social activity and interaction situated in a particular context; nor does it test writing as a cognitive process, when the evaluation is still exclusively product-based with the use of an often-holistic rubric. Such an assessment approach, therefore, significantly underrepresents the construct of writing ability and reduces the level of

170 Chapter 12 Assessing Writing

authenticity in its task design, which in turn calls into question the usefulness and validity of such writing assessment (e.g., Moore & Morton, 2005).

Perhaps as a response, some large-scale language tests started to tackle this issue at the turn of the century by adding an integrated writing task to supplement the prompt-based impromptu essay task (e.g., TOEFL iBT®). Oftentimes, such integrated tasks involve the provision of input in various modes (aural and/or visual); test takers need to process such input before writing in response to the task. It is a commendable effort, as this new form of integrated reading, listening, and writing assessment reflects more faithfully the type of writing activities and scenarios in actual language use domains, particularly for educational purposes, hence making integrated writing assessment more authentic. A closer look at such tasks, however, reveals that these source-based integrated writing tasks are also limited in that they only require test takers to summarize the main points presented in the two sources, rather than to use these sources to support their own ideas and arguments. Other forms of writing assessment also exist, including more contextualized and practical writing tasks such as letter/memo writing and report or proposal of events/activities to a specified audience. Although they are not as prevalent as independent essay writing tasks or integrated summary writing tasks on large-scale high-stakes language tests, some believe that such alternative tasks help broaden the construct by capturing the social and cognitive aspects of writing (e.g., Shaw & Weir, 2007). Others, however, point out that despite such genre and task variations, the evaluation of writing ability is still overwhelmingly product-based, thus falling short of truly reflecting recent theoretical conceptions of the construct of writing as a cognitive process and social practice. Zhao (2022), for example, points out that aspects of writing ability such as cognitive processes and metacognitive strategy use are less likely to be readily observable in a written product, hence unlikely to be captured by any rubric that defines text quality, be it holistic or analytic. Perhaps as Hamp-Lyons and Kroll (1997) openly acknowledged 25 years ago, socio-cognitive models of writing are simply "unhelpful" and even "problematic for the design of academic writing assessment" (p. 7). In other words, they accepted the "fact" that writing assessment on these high-stakes tests with summative purposes can only be product-based, despite the well-established process-oriented practices endorsed and implemented by many writing teachers in the classroom setting.

Indeed, a quick survey of formative classroom-based writing assessment practices shows much more diverse forms of assessment that go beyond the evaluation of text quality or linguistic accuracy alone. Writing teachers often adopt learning-oriented and diagnostic assessments that involve self-assessment, peer-assessment, portfolio assessment, or other forms of dynamic assessment practices. Many of such alternative writing assessment forms do attend to the long-neglected writing processes by collecting multiple drafts over a longer period of time, rather than a single essay produced within a very limited time frame. They also align more closely with the socio-constructivist view of writing and interactionist approach to assessment by incorporating teacher and peer support and feedback into the assessment practices (e.g., Hamp-Lyons & Condon, 2000). Lee (2017), for example, provides a comprehensive examination of classroom-based writing assessment and feedback practices in a wide range of school contexts across ESL and EFL settings at both primary and secondary levels with students of varying backgrounds. Through concrete examples and case studies of formative and learning-oriented writing assessment practices in such school contexts, Lee (2017) highlights the importance of aligning classroom assessment with teaching and learning objectives and offers practical guidelines for writing teachers to support young learners with tailor-made assessment tasks and effective feedback. Of course, new innovations in writing assessment design, in both classroom-based assessment settings and large-scale testing contexts, are still needed to keep abreast with the developments in theoretical conceptions of writing in an increasingly digital and information age, with new technological affordances and breakthroughs that affect how people communicate in writing.

Current Research

Going beyond a concise overview of the theoretical conceptions of the construct of writing in the literature and its operationalizations in actual testing practices, this section examines the current writing assessment research to highlight recurring and emerging themes in recent scholarship. While research into the reliability and validity of writing assessment of various types continues to dominate much of the scholarship on writing assessment, new themes also gradually surface in response to recent changes in educational and assessment settings, advances in natural language processing (NLP) and artificial intelligence (AI) technologies, and the field's evolving conceptions of the construct of writing.

Validation of Writing Assessment

Validation research in writing assessment follows theories of test validation in general (e.g., Chapelle, 2008; Xi, 2008). Argument-based validation frameworks outline various inferences that need to be supported by theoretical rationales and empirical evidence. Such inferences include *domain representation* that links test content to that in the target language use (TLU) domain; *evaluation* that links test performances to observed scores; *generalization* that examines the consistency of observed scores across similar measurement contexts; *explanation* that connects the interpretation of performance to the underlining construct; *extrapolation* that links the observed performance on the test to that on other measures or performance in the TLU domain; and *utilization* that examines how scores are used to make appropriate decisions and produce desirable outcomes. A survey of the existing writing assessment literature shows a clear focus on the examination of the *evaluation, generalization, explanation*, and *extrapolation* inferences, although other links are also investigated.

A large proportion of such validation research, for example, has focused on issues of consistency in the ratings provided by raters using a rubric. Holistic rubrics are often adopted in large-scale testing contexts for scoring efficiency, although analytic or primary trait rubrics may be preferred in classroom assessment settings for their diagnostic and pedagogical value. Overall, evidence of reliability could come from analysis of an individual rater's consistency in their evaluative judgments over time (intra-rater reliability), or from analysis of the degree of consistency in multiple raters' ratings (inter-rater reliability). Empirical research has therefore primarily focused on raters themselves, rating processes, and rating scales, examining their impact on the consistency and meaningfulness of the scores observed. Studies on raters include those that explore the impact of rater background and experience (e.g., Barkaoui, 2011a; Johnson & Lim, 2009; Zhao & Wu, 2022), rater bias and types (e.g., Eckes, 2008; Schaefer, 2008), and rater training (e.g., Knoch et al., 2007; Weigle, 1994, 1998) on writing performance evaluation. Studies on the rating processes mainly examine raters' decision-making in the rating process, often using qualitative methods such as think-aloud and rater interview (e.g., Barkaoui, 2011b; Cumming et al., 2002), while studies on rating scales focus primarily on the development of rubrics or their interactions with raters in the rating process (e.g., Knoch, 2011; Lumley, 2002).

Additionally, validity evidence often also comes from studies that compare task types and test performances across testing contexts and authentic TLU domains (e.g., Llosa et al., 2020; Llosa & Malone, 2019), as well as studies that examine the impact of various factors on writing performances. Such factors include writer characteristics and abilities (e.g., demographic background, proficiency level, strategy use, motivation level, working memory capacity, and source use), task conditions (e.g., time allotment, task complexity, and input characteristics), as well as other contextual variables, cognitive factors, and consequential

172 Chapter 12 Assessing Writing

aspects (cf. Shaw & Weir, 2007). Other research also investigates various features of the text produced during the assessment to examine the construct of writing in relation to the evaluative criteria. These features include, among others, lexical, syntactic, and cohesive features (e.g., Kim & Crossley, 2018), discourse and argumentation structure (e.g., Bax et al., 2019; Chuang & Yan, 2022), as well as voice and identity features (e.g., Yoon & Tabari, 2023; Zhao, 2017; Zhao & Llosa, 2008).

Alternative Approaches to Writing Assessment

In addition to the focus on reliability and validity issues in writing assessment, current research also documents and discusses the development or implementations of various alternative writing assessment approaches and forms, often in relation to different assessment purposes and contexts. Researchers, for example, have explored various forms of diagnostic or dynamic writing assessment with new designs, new scoring methods, and even new perspectives such as using think-aloud protocols as an assessment instrument (e.g., Beck et al., 2015; Knoch, 2009; Llosa et al., 2011; Wang & Xie, 2022). Others focused on the implementation of such alternative writing assessments that are often learning-oriented and process-based, including assessment for learning in writing classrooms (e.g., Lee & Coniam, 2013; Mak & Lee, 2014), peer- and self-assessment practices (e.g., Chung et al., 2021), and portfolio assessment (e.g., Lam, 2018).

Other than research on the aforementioned alternative writing assessment approaches and practices, a large volume of scholarship has examined integrated writing assessment practices. Cumming (2013) highlights the high authenticity, interactiveness, and the inclusion of multiliteracies with the use of integrated writing tasks. Research on this front, therefore, has focused on exploring the composing processes and writing strategies employed in such an assessment setting (e.g., Plakans et al., 2019), examining discourse features of texts produced in response to such integrated writing tasks (e.g., Cumming et al., 2005; Gebril & Plakans, 2016), and documenting stakeholder perceptions about integrated writing assessment (e.g., Knoch, 2009).

While integrated writing assessment has gained much recognition from both researchers and practitioners, novel assessment designs, often tech-enhanced, continue to be proposed and implemented. Educational Testing Service (ETS®), for example, announced in 2023 that "a more concise and modern writing task" (ETS, 2023) called "Writing for an Academic Discussion" would replace the long-standing "Independent Writing" task on TOEFL iBT®. This new writing assessment task simulates the online discussion tasks often assigned by professors in their courses via learning management systems. Test takers need to read the question posted by a professor and several responses from other students before they are prompted to post their own response that would contribute meaningfully to the academic discussion. Such a task appears to be more authentic and interactive than the integrated summary writing task; it also better represents the construct of academic writing as contextualized meaning-making and interaction. The online discussion context, in addition, highlights the affordances of digital and multimodal composing and their applications in future assessment practices.

AI and Technology in Writing Assessment

Another emerging theme in the current writing assessment scholarship is the increasingly extensive applications of AI and technology in various aspects of writing assessment practice and research. The most notable and widely discussed applications of AI in writing assessment are perhaps automated essay scoring (AES) and automated writing evaluation (AWE). In large-scale high-stakes testing settings, human scoring of written responses is often expensive and time-consuming. In addition, consistency in human ratings is, as discussed above, subject to the influence of various factors, presenting additional threats to reliability. As a response, NLP-based AES systems emerged in an attempt to provide more consistent, time-efficient, and cost-effective evaluations of written responses.

Since the debut of the first AES system, Project Essay Grade (PEG), in as early as the 1960s (see Page, 2003), many automated scoring systems have been developed. Shermis and Hamner's (2013) comparison of nine AES systems, together with other studies (see Shermis & Burstein, 2003, 2013), shows that the performance of these systems is largely comparable to that of human raters in terms of score consistency and accuracy. On the other hand, writing researchers tend to voice concerns regarding the use of such systems (Ericsson & Haswell, 2006), arguing that they may seriously underrepresent or misrepresent the construct of writing and even bring about a dehumanizing effect on writers and their writing practices (e.g., Conference on College Composition and Communication, 2004). Indeed, research reveals that some test takers may game the system by transcribing irrelevant texts they have memorized to secure a higher score from the machine rater in high-stakes testing contexts (e.g., Powers et al., 2002).

In classroom-based assessment settings, AWE systems (e.g., Criterion® by ETS; WriteToLearn® by Pearson; My Access!® by Vantage Learning) that provide automated feedback on essays for formative purposes also become popular among teachers and learners. Research on automated feedback provided by such AWE systems often focuses on feedback accuracy, coverage, usefulness, and user perceptions and attitudes. Results seem to indicate that current AWE systems tend to provide satisfactory feedback more at the linguistic level than at the content or discourse level and that AWE feedback can also be rather generic, redundant, and vague (e.g., Lavolette et al., 2015; Wilson & Roscoe, 2020; Zhang & Hyland, 2018). Researchers, therefore, advise the integration of automated feedback and teacher feedback to maximize the effectiveness of feedback giving (e.g., Fu et al., 2022; Warschauer & Ware, 2006). Little research, however, exists to further detail optimal means of human and machine feedback integration that could bring about a positive impact on learning.

Other than a primary focus on automated essay scoring and feedback giving, research on the application of AI and technology also examines the impact of such tech-enhanced writing assessment on writing performance and on validity interpretations (e.g., Jin & Yan, 2017; Tate et al., 2019). Additionally, there are also discussions and debates on whether language-editing tools, such as spelling and grammar check should be made available on computerized writing assessment and whether such tools would influence writing performance and score interpretations (e.g., East, 2007; Oh, 2022; Shin et al., 2021). Recent research on writing assessment has also benefited from the use of such technologies as eye-tracking, keystroke, and input logging that enable researchers to further probe into the writing processes rather than the written products alone (e.g., Anson & Schwegler, 2012; Choi & Deane, 2021; de Smet et al., 2018). As AI and computer technologies become increasingly more sophisticated, more complex and innovative applications of such new technologies are likely to emerge and influence writing assessment practice and research in the near future.

Challenges

New developments in writing assessment theory and practice also bring about new challenges. Defining the construct of writing is one of such challenges. When writing is assessed using impromptu essay tasks, for example, writing ability is often evaluated as text quality, using either holistic or analytic rubrics that define or describe what "good" writing is. The challenge or controversy, however, lies in the fact that writing, and assessment of writing, is often highly contextualized (see Cumming, 2001). In other words, different people in

174 **Chapter 12** Assessing Writing

different contexts may have very different views about what good writing is. It thus becomes unreasonable, or even unethical, to impose one set of standards on all, especially in large-scale high-stakes tests that affect an international test-taker population.

When writing is assessed using integrated tasks that more faithfully reflect authentic writing activities, especially those in an academic context, the issue of confounding the construct of writing ability with that of other abilities, such as listening or reading abilities, arises as a common concern among researchers and test developers. Many believe that integrated writing assessment presents the issue of task dependencies (see Cumming, 2014), when it requires test takers to first process and comprehend various sources of input before they write in response to such input. Researchers therefore argue that integrated writing assessment is meaningful only when used in the Higher Education context with test takers who have hopefully attained a threshold level of intermediate or advanced language proficiency (see Cumming, 2013; Sawaki et al., 2013). Even in such assessment contexts, however, integrated writing performance could be difficult to score and interpret. Raters, for example, would find it difficult to distinguish test takers' language from the language used in the source materials. Instructors, or test users, may also find it challenging to interpret the scores on such integrated writing performance, especially for diagnostic and instructional purposes.

In addition to the challenges associated with defining the construct of writing in various assessment contexts, the enduring predicament of relying on a product-based approach as the only viable method for assessing writing in large-scale testing contexts persists without a clear resolution. It appears that writing assessment practices have not kept pace with the widely accepted conception that writing "is text, is composing, and is social construction" (Cumming, 1998, p. 61). Almost all the writing tasks, independent or integrated, aim to elicit a text of a particular genre for rubric-based evaluation. The composing process, which is critical in composition theories, is, however, largely ignored in such assessment practices. Many believe that the large-scale testing setting makes it inherently impossible to assess the composing process due to time and resource constraints. Zhao (2022), however, challenges this view and argues that with the recent technological advances, writing assessment practices could and should be better aligned with writing theories. Thus, a major challenge facing the writing assessment community is to reinstate the socio-cognitive aspects of writing and assess not only the product but also the processes and the social functions of writing as situated in a particular sociocultural and communicative context.

Future Directions

While many researchers may be concerned with construct validity issues in integrated writing assessment practices, it should be noted that such concerns are not always warranted. In fact, no meaningful or useful assessment design should start with a general definition of a particular concept or skill; instead, all assessment considerations should start with a clearly articulated purpose of the test intended for a particular group of test takers situated in a particular context. We should not assume that "writing ability" is a generic, static, and always already defined construct agreed upon by all across all assessment situations. This conception of writing ability itself goes against the situated, contextualized, dynamic, and sociocultural view of writing that many advocate in the literature. Instead, the construct of a given writing assessment can and should only be defined and operationalized in relation to all such contextualized assessment elements as test purpose, test taker population, and test context.

In the case of the TOEFL iBT integrated writing assessment, for example, the construct of the writing section is not a generic "writing ability" anymore; rather, it is the type of writing ability required of international students seeking admission into US Higher Education institutions for academic purposes. In this case, integrated writing tasks that involve the processing of input presented in multiple modes, and the synthesis of such input in writing following academic conventions, are of critical importance and highly relevant to the test purpose and to the meaningful interpretation of results for such purposes. Integrated writing tasks such as these therefore should not be viewed as a threat to construct validity, because the construct in this particular assessment context is never simply the basic language skill of writing; instead, it is specified as "source-based academic writing" operationalized as a summary writing task. Similarly, writing assessment for kindergarteners in an EFL context, for instructional and diagnostic purposes, is unlikely to involve timed impromptu essay tasks or integrated writing tasks, as young learners in an EFL kindergarten context are often only just starting to learn the alphabet and the spelling of a few high-frequency vocabulary items. The construct of writing ability for these learners is, therefore, more likely to be handwriting ability in terms of tracing and copying upper- or lower-case letters or simple words and sentences, based on a specific curriculum. In other words, the construct of writing is not static and independent of test purposes, contexts, and test-taker characteristics. In fact, if writing is always a situated and contextualized social act, the assessment of writing should also be situated and contextualized, and so should be the construct. Future writing assessment design and research into the construct validity of writing assessments should, therefore, be conceptualized and discussed in situ, rather than being confined to and constrained by the concept of writing only as a language skill.

Another direction for future writing assessment design and research is to respond to the increasingly more digital and information-based writing environment and behaviors. Powerful and sophisticated technological innovations are likely to enable future test developers to reinstate the long-neglected composing process and strategic competence in the evaluation of writing ability, highlighting also the concept of multiliteracy, when information literacy, digital literacy, and academic literacy function together in this writing process. In the context of Higher Education, writing to learn and to construct new knowledge often entails the access, evaluation, and use of various sources in an argument-building process. Computerized testing platforms in the future can thus be used to not only supply source materials but also provide a potential pool of such sources of varying degrees of relevancy and credibility using an embedded task-specific database. Computer technology could then help monitor the writers' access, evaluation, and eventually also actual use of such sources in their written product. In the meantime, pre-writing items could be designed to assess specific aspects of the cognitive and metacognitive competences, including task interpretation, audience awareness, goal setting, planning, information processing, and plans of source use. Likewise, post-writing questions and items could be used to further capture writers' self-assessment of their performance, to reveal their regulations of affective states and strategy use with varying degrees of success, and to elicit revision plans if given more time and resources. Such composing process data, when interpreted together with analysis of the written product, could help to provide more precise and meaningful interpretations of one's writing ability as situated in that particular context. With enhanced technology, the written product could also be analyzed using keystroke and input logging data to further examine and compare the reported composing process with the observed composing process. This new assessment approach thus offers the potential to materialize what Hamp-Lyons (2001) envisioned two decades ago as the next generation of writing assessment, one that is "both humanistic and technological, drawing on advances in computer applications and an understanding of writing assessment as a complex of processes" (p. 117).

In addition to the efforts into innovative writing assessment design and development, automated scoring and evaluation will certainly continue to be refined and applied in various writing assessment contexts. The challenge identified earlier by many regarding the difficulty for raters to distinguish test takers' own language from the language of the source text in integrated writing assessment, for example, can be easily addressed using similarity detection

176 **Chapter 12** Assessing Writing

technology when machine scoring is employed. Certainly, automated scoring is still limited in its current capacity to evaluate the more sophisticated aspects of written communication. To date, therefore, AES systems have been used mainly to supplement, rather than replace, human scoring. Attali (2013) proposed three means of integrating AES and human scoring, i.e., the contributory, the confirmatory, and the division-of-labor approaches. The contributory approach reports the average of human and AES scores as the final score. The confirmatory approach uses the ASE scores only to confirm the tenability of human scores or flag potentially problematic human scores. The division-of-labor approach, as indicated by its name, means that human raters and AES systems evaluate separate dimensions of writing. While AES systems can assess mechanical and linguistic accuracy reliably and efficiently, human raters can focus on the evaluation of content and communicative effect. Although these blended scoring approaches have been proposed for a decade, little research exists to have compared the effectiveness of these approaches or provided evidence on the optimal means of blended scoring that could enhance validity and assessment usefulness. Similarly, little is known about how automated feedback and teacher feedback could be best integrated to benefit both classroom teachers and language learners. Future research, therefore, could further examine the various means of integrating automated and human evaluation across various assessment contexts. As generative AI technology becomes more sophisticated, new breakthroughs in automated scoring and human–machine interaction will likely emerge to further inform and shape up future writing assessment practices, which in turn would call for more future research.

Moreover, as assessments are now designed for use with an increasingly diverse test taker population in multilingual and multicultural communities, writing assessment also needs to be sensitive to the linguistic and cultural backgrounds of test takers. This involves exploring alternative assessment formats and considering issues of fairness and equity in writing assessment design, development, and implementation. Researchers have even started to consider and call for the incorporation of translanguaging into multilingual assessment practices (e.g., Baker & Hope, 2019; Schissel et al., 2019), although a series of serious questions (see Chalhoub-Deville, 2019) need to be addressed before multilingual and translanguaging assessment can be meaningfully implemented. Further complicating issues of writing assessment is the current digital age and the prevalence of digital multimodal composing practices in this age. Writing assessment in the future may, therefore, seek to incorporate the assessment of new literacies such as digital writing, multimodal writing, and online collaborative writing. Much research is needed, however, before we could satisfactorily define the construct of multimodal composing and assess various multimodal genres across different contexts (e.g., Cheung, 2023).

Overall, the field of writing assessment has evolved significantly in the past few decades and will continue to evolve as new technologies and social practices emerge. At the core, however, is the ongoing need for assessment tools and approaches that are fair and responsive to the changing needs of writers, communities, and assessment contexts. As such, innovative writing assessment design and practices, and research into the reliability, validity, and fairness of such practices, will continue to be important areas of inquiry in the years to come.

Discussion Questions

1. Reflect on your local assessment context, and discuss how writing could be best assessed with different groups of learners for different purposes in that particular context.

2. What might be the optimal means of integrating automated and human scoring and feedback that may maximize scoring and feedback efficiency and effectiveness?

References

Anson, C. M., & Schwegler, R. A. (2012). Tracking the mind's eye: a new technology for researching twenty-first-century writing and reading processes. *College Composition and Communication*, 151–171. https://www.jstor.org/stable/23264924.

Attali, Y. (2013). Validity and reliability of automated essay scoring. In M. D. Shermis & J. Burstein (Eds.), *Handbook of automated essay evaluation* (pp. 181–198). Routledge.

Baker, B., & Hope, A. (2019). Incorporating translanguaging in language assessment: the case of a test for university professors. *Language Assessment Quarterly*, *16*(4–5), 408–425. https://doi.org/10.1080/15434303.2019.1671392.

Barkaoui, K. (2011a). Effects of marking method and rater experience on ESL essay scores. *Assessment in Education: Principles, Policy & Practice*, *18*(3), 277–291. https://doi.org/10.1080/0969594X.2010.526585.

Barkaoui, K. (2011b). Think-aloud protocols in research on essay rating: an empirical study of their veridicality and reactivity. *Language Testing*, *28*(1), 51–75. https://doi.org/10.1177/0265532210376379.

Bawarshi, A. S., & Reiff, M. J. (2010). *Genre: An introduction to history, theory, research, and pedagogy*. Parlor Press.

Bax, S., Nakatsuhara, F., & Waller, D. (2019). Researching L2 writers' use of metadiscourse markers at intermediate and advanced levels. *System*, *83*, 79–95. https://doi.org/10.1016/j.system.2019.02.010.

Beck, S. W., Llosa, L., Black, K., & Trzeszkowski-Giese, A. (2015). Beyond the rubric: think-alouds as a diagnostic assessment tool for high school writing teachers. *Journal of Adolescent and Adult Literacy*, *58*(8), 668–679. https://doi.org/10.1002/jaal.423.

Bloome, D., Carvalho, G. T., & Rue, S. (2018). Researching academic literacies. In A. Phakiti, P. D. Costa, P. Plonsky & S. Starfield (Eds.), *The Palgrave handbook of applied linguistics research methodology* (pp. 887–902). Palgrave Macmillan.

Britton, J., Burgess, T., Martin, N., McLeod, A., & Rosen, H. (1975). *The development of writing abilities (11–18)*. Macmillan.

Chalhoub-Deville, M. B. (2019). Multilingual testing constructs: theoretical foundations. *Language Assessment Quarterly*, *16*(4–5), 472–480. https://doi.org/10.1080/15434303.2019.1671391.

Chapelle, C. (2008). The TOEFL validity argument. In C. Chapelle, M. Enright & J. Jamieson (Eds.), *Building a validity argument for the test of English as a foreign language* (pp. 319–352). Routledge.

Cheung, A. (2023). Developing and evaluating a set of process and product-oriented classroom assessment rubrics for assessing digital multimodal collaborative writing in L2 classes. *Assessing Writing*, *56*, 100723. https://doi.org/10.1016/j.asw.2023.100723.

Choi, I., & Deane, P. (2021). Evaluating writing process features in an adult EFL writing assessment context: a keystroke logging study. *Language Assessment Quarterly*, *18*(2), 107–132. https://doi.org/10.1080/15434303.2020.1804913.

Chuang, P. L., & Yan, X. (2022). An investigation of the relationship between argument structure and essay quality in assessed writing. *Journal of Second Language Writing*, *56*, 100892. https://doi.org/10.1016/j.jslw.2022.100892.

Chung, H. Q., Chen, V., & Olson, C. B. (2021). The impact of self-assessment, planning and goal setting, and reflection before and after revision on student self-efficacy and writing performance. *Reading and Writing*, *34*, 1885–1913. https://doi.org/10.1007/s11145-021-10186-x.

Conference on College Composition and Communication. (2004). *Position statement on teaching, learning, and assessing writing in digital environments*. https://dtext.org/f14/505/readings/ncte-CCCC-digital-environments.pdf.

Crusan, D. (2014). Assessing writing. In A. J. Kunnan (Ed.), *The companion to language assessment* (pp. 201–215). Wiley Blackwell. https://doi.org/10.1002/9781118411360.wbcla067.

Cumming, A. (1998). Theoretical perspectives on writing. *Annual Review of Applied Linguistics*, *18*, 61–78. https://doi.org/10.1017/S0267190500003482.

Cumming, A. (2001). Learning to write in a second language: two decades of research. *International Journal of English Studies*, *1*(2), 1–23. https://revistas.um.es/ijes/article/view/48331.

Cumming, A. (2009). Assessing academic writing in foreign and second languages. *Language Teaching*, *42*(3), 329–366. https://doi.org/10.1017/S0261444808005430.

Cumming, A. (2013). Assessing integrated writing tasks for academic purposes: promises and perils. *Language Assessment Quarterly*, *10*(1), 1–8. https://doi.org/10.1080/15434303.2011.622016.

178 Chapter 12 Assessing Writing

Cumming, A. (2014). Assessing integrated skills. In A. J. Kunnan (Ed.), *The companion to language assessment* (pp. 216–229). Wiley Blackwell. https://doi.org/10.1002/9781118411360.wbcla131.

Cumming, A., Kantor, R., & Powers, D. E. (2002). Decision making while rating ESL/EFL writing tasks: a descriptive framework. *Modern Language Journal, 86*, 67–96. https://doi.org/10.1111/1540-4781.00137.

Cumming, A., Kantor, R., Baba, K., Erdosy, U., Eouanzoui, K., & James, M. (2005). Differences in written discourse in independent and integrated prototypes for next generation TOEFL. *Assessing Writing, 10*, 5–43. https://doi.org/10.1016/j.asw.2005.02.001.

East, M. (2007). Bilingual dictionaries in tests of L2 writing proficiency: do they make a difference? *Language Testing, 24*(3), 331–353. https://doi.org/10.1177/0265532207077203.

Eckes, T. (2008). Rater types in writing performance assessments: a classification approach to rater variability. *Language Testing, 25*, 155–185. https://doi.org/10.1177/0265532207086780.

Educational Testing Service. (2023). *Practice tests.* https://www.ets.org/toefl/test-takers/ibt/prepare/practice-tests.html.

Ericsson, P. F., & Haswell, R. H. (Eds.). (2006). *Machine scoring of student essays: Truth and consequences.* Utah State University Press.

Flower, L., & Hayes, J. R. (1981). A cognitive process theory of writing. *College Composition and Communication, 32*(4), 365–387. https://doi.org/10.2307/356600.

Fu, Q. K., Zou, D., Xie, H., & Cheng, G. (2022). A review of AWE feedback: types, learning outcomes, and implications. *Computer Assisted Language Learning*, 1–43. https://doi.org/10.1080/09588221.2022.2033787.

Gebril, A., & Plakans, L. (2016). Source-based tasks in academic writing assessment: lexical diversity, textual borrowing and proficiency. *Journal of English for Academic Purposes, 24*, 78–88. https://doi.org/10.1016/j.jeap.2016.10.001.

Halliday, M. A. K. (1985). *Introduction to functional grammar.* Arnold.

Hamp-Lyons, L. (2001). Fourth generation writing. In T. Silva & P. K. Matsuda (Eds.), *On second language writing* (pp. 117–129). Lawrence Erlbaum Associates, Inc.

Hamp-Lyons, L., & Condon, W. (2000). *Assessing the portfolio: Principles for practice, theory, and research.* Hampton Press.

Hamp-Lyons, L., & Kroll, B. (1997). *TOEFL 2000 writing: Composition, community and assessment (TOEFL Monograph Series Report No. 5).* Educational Testing Service.

Hyland, K. (2003). Genre-based pedagogies: a social response to process. *Journal of Second Language Writing, 12*(1), 17–29. https://doi.org/10.1016/S1060-3743(02)00124-8.

Jin, Y., & Yan, M. (2017). Computer literacy and the construct validity of a high-stakes computer-based writing assessment. *Language Assessment Quarterly, 14*(2), 101–119. https://doi.org/10.1080/15434303.2016.1261293.

Johns, A. M. (2008). Genre awareness for the novice academic student: an ongoing quest. *Language Teaching, 41*(2), 237–252. https://doi.org/10.1017/S0261444807004892.

Johns, A. M. (2011). The future of genre in L2 writing: fundamental, but contested, instructional decisions. *Journal of Second Language Writing, 20*(1), 56–68. https://doi.org/10.1016/j.jslw.2010.12.003.

Johnson, J. S., & Lim, G. S. (2009). The influence of rater language background on writing performance assessment. *Language Testing, 26*, 485–505. https://doi.org/10.1177/0265532209340186.

Kim, M., & Crossley, S. A. (2018). Modeling second language writing quality: a structural equation investigation of lexical, syntactic, and cohesive features in source-based and independent writing. *Assessing Writing, 37*, 39–56. https://doi.org/10.1016/j.asw.2018.03.002.

Knoch, U. (2009). Diagnostic assessment of writing: a comparison of two rating scales. *Language Testing, 26*(2), 275–304. https://doi.org/10.1177/0265532208101008.

Knoch, U. (2011). Rating scales for diagnostic assessment of writing: what should they look like and where should the criteria come from? *Assessing Writing, 16*(2), 81–96. https://doi.org/10.1016/j.asw.2011.02.003.

Knoch, U., Read, J., & von Randow, J. (2007). Re-training raters online: how does it compare with face-to-face training? *Assessing Writing, 12*, 26–43. https://doi.org/10.1016/j.asw.2007.04.001.

Lam, R. (2018). *Portfolio assessment for the teaching and learning of writing.* Springer Briefs in Education.

Lavolette, E., Polio, C., & Kahng, J. (2015). The accuracy of computer-assisted feedback and students' responses to it. *Language, Learning & Technology, 19*(2), 50–68.

Lea, M. R., & Street, B. V. (2006). The "academic literacies" model: theory and applications. *Theory into Practice, 45*(4), 368–377. https://doi.org/10.1207/s15430421tip4504_11.

Lee, I. (2017). *Classroom writing assessment and feedback in L2 school contexts*. Springer Singapore. https://doi.org/10.1007/978-981-10-3924-9.

Lee, I., & Coniam, D. (2013). Introducing assessment for learning for EFL writing in an assessment of learning examination-driven system in Hong Kong. *Journal of Second Language Writing, 22*(1), 34–50. https://doi.org/10.1016/j.jslw.2012.11.003.

Llosa, L., & Malone, M. E. (2019). Comparability of students' writing performance on TOEFL iBT and in required university writing courses. *Language Testing, 36*(2), 235–263. https://doi.org/10.1177/0265532218763456.

Llosa, L., Beck, S. W., & Zhao, C. G. (2011). An investigation of academic writing in secondary schools to inform the development of diagnostic classroom assessments. *Assessing Writing, 16*, 256–273. https://doi.org/10.1016/j.asw.2011.07.001.

Llosa, L., Grapin, S. E., Friginal, E., Cushing, S. T., & Malone, M. E. (2020). Linguistic dimensions of TOEFL iBT essays compared with successful student disciplinary writing in the university. *TESOL Quarterly, 54*(1), 251–265. https://doi.org/10.1002/tesq.553.

Lumley, T. (2002). Assessment criteria in a large-scale writing test: what do they really mean to the raters? *Language Testing, 19*(3), 246–276. https://doi.org/10.1191/0265532202lt230oa.

Mak, P., & Lee, I. (2014). Implementing assessment for learning in L2 writing: an activity theory perspective. *System, 47*, 73–87. https://doi.org/10.1016/j.system.2014.09.018.

Moore, T., & Morton, J. (2005). Dimensions of difference: a comparison of university writing and IELTS writing. *Journal of English for Academic Purposes, 4*(1), 43–66. https://doi.org/10.1016/j.jeap.2004.02.001.

Oh, S. (2022). The use of spelling and reference tools in second language writing: their impact on students' writing performance and process. *Journal of Second Language Writing, 57*, 100916. https://doi.org/10.1016/j.jslw.2022.100916.

Page, E. B. (2003). Project essay grade: PEG. In M. D. Shermis & J. C. Burstein (Eds.), *Automated essay scoring: A cross-disciplinary perspective* (pp. 43–54). Routledge.

Plakans, L., Liao, J. T., & Wang, F. (2019). "I should summarize this whole paragraph": shared processes of reading and writing in iterative integrated assessment tasks. *Assessing Writing, 40*, 14–26. https://doi.org/10.1016/j.asw.2019.03.003.

Powers, D. E., Burstein, J. C., Chodorow, M., Fowles, M. E., & Kukich, K. (2002). Stumping e-rater: challenging the validity of automated essay scoring. *Computers in Human Behavior, 18*(2), 103–134. https://doi.org/10.1016/S0747-5632(01)00052-8.

Rohman, D. G. (1965). Pre-writing the stage of discovery in the writing process. *College Composition and Communication, 16*(2), 106–112. https://doi.org/10.2307/354885.

Sawaki, Y., Quinlan, T., & Lee, Y. W. (2013). Understanding learner strengths and weaknesses: assessing performance on an integrated writing task. *Language Assessment Quarterly, 10*(1), 73–95. https://doi.org/10.1080/15434303.2011.633305.

Scardamalia, M., & Bereiter, C. (1991). Literate expertise. In K. A. Ericsson & J. Smith (Eds.), *Toward a general theory of expertise: Prospects and limits* (pp. 172–194). Cambridge University Press.

Schaefer, E. (2008). Rater bias patterns in an EFL writing assessment. *Language Testing, 25*, 465–493. https://doi.org/10.1177/0265532208094273.

Schissel, J. L., Leung, C., & Chalhoub-Deville, M. (2019). The construct of multilingualism in language testing. *Language Assessment Quarterly, 16*(4–5), 373–378. https://doi.org/10.1080/15434303.2019.1680679.

Schleppegrell, M. J. (2004). *The language of schooling: A functional linguistics perspective*. Lawrence Erlbaum Associates Publishers.

Shaw, S., & Weir, C. J. (2007). *Examining writing: Research and practice in assessing second language writing, Studies in Language Testing, 26*. UCLES/Cambridge University Press.

Shermis, M. D., & Burstein, J. C. (Eds.). (2003). *Automated essay scoring: A cross-disciplinary perspective*. Routledge.

Shermis, M. D., & Burstein, J. C. (Eds.). (2013). *Handbook of automated essay evaluation: Current applications and new directions*. Routledge.

Shermis, M. D., & Hamner, B. (2013). Contrasting state-of-the-art automated scoring of essays. In M. D. Shermis & J. Burstein (Eds.), *Handbook of automated essay evaluation: Current applications and new directions* (pp. 313–346). Routledge.

Shin, D., Kwon, S. K., & Lee, Y. (2021). The effect of using online language-support resources on L2 writing performance. *Language Testing in Asia*, *11*(1), 1–23. https://doi.org/10.1186/s40468-021-00119-4.

de Smet, M. J., Leijten, M., & Van Waes, L. (2018). Exploring the process of reading during writing using eye tracking and keystroke logging. *Written Communication*, *35*(4), 411–447. https://doi.org/10.1177/0741088318788070.

Snow, C. E., & Uccelli, P. (2009). The challenge of academic language. In D. R. Olson & N. Torrance (Eds.), *The Cambridge handbook of literacy* (pp. 112–133). Cambridge University Press.

Swales, J. (1990). *Genre analysis: English in academic and research settings.* Cambridge University Press.

Tate, T. P., Warschauer, M., & Kim, Y. S. G. (2019). Learning to compose digitally: the effect of prior computer use and keyboard activity on NAEP writing. *Reading and Writing*, *32*, 2059–2082. https://doi.org/10.1007/s11145-019-09940-z.

Wang, Y., & Xie, Q. (2022). Diagnosing EFL undergraduates' discourse competence in academic writing. *Assessing Writing*, *53*, 100641. https://doi.org/10.1016/j.asw.2022.100641.

Warschauer, M., & Ware, P. (2006). Automated writing evaluation: defining the classroom research agenda. *Language Teaching Research*, *10*(2), 157–180. https://doi.org/10.1191/1362168806lr190oa.

Weigle, S. C. (1994). Effects of training on raters of ESL compositions. *Language Testing*, *11*(2), 197–223. https://doi.org/10.1177/026553229401100206.

Weigle, S. C. (1998). Using FACETS to model rater training effects. *Language Testing*, *15*(2), 263–287. https://doi.org/10.1177/026553229801500205.

Wilson, J., & Roscoe, R. D. (2020). Automated writing evaluation and feedback: multiple metrics of efficacy. *Journal of Educational Computing Research*, *58*(1), 87–125. https://doi.org/10.1177/0735633119830764.

Xi, X. (2008). Methods of test validation. In E. Shohamy & N. H. Hornberger (Eds.), *Encyclopedia of language and education. Vol. 7: Language testing and assessment* (2nd ed., pp. 177–196). Springer.

Yoon, H. J., & Tabari, M. A. (2023). Authorial voice in source-based and opinion-based argumentative writing: patterns of voice across task types and proficiency levels. *Journal of English for Academic Purposes*, *62*, 101228. https://doi.org/10.1016/j.jeap.2023.101228.

Yu, C., & Zhao, C. G. (2021). Continuing the dialogue between writing experts and academic librarians: a conceptual model of information-based academic writing in higher education. *The Journal of Academic Librarianship*, *47*, 102454. https://doi.org/10.1016/j.acalib.2021.102454.

Zhang, Z. V., & Hyland, K. (2018). Student engagement with teacher and automated feedback on L2 writing. *Assessing Writing*, *36*, 90–102. https://doi.org/10.1016/j.asw.2018.02.004.

Zhao, C. G. (2017). Voice in timed L2 argumentative essay writing. *Assessing writing*, *31*, 73–83. https://doi.org/10.1016/j.asw.2016.08.004.

Zhao, C. G. (2022). Theory-based approach to academic writing assessment in higher education: a conceptual framework for assessment design and development. In L. Hamp-Lyons & Y. Jin (Eds.), *Assessing the English language writing of Chinese learners of English* (pp. 137–154). Cham: Springer. https://doi.org/10.1007/978-3-030-92762-2_9.

Zhao, C. G., & Llosa, L. (2008). Voice in high-stakes L1 academic writing assessment: implications for L2 writing instruction. *Assessing Writing*, *13*(3), 153–170. https://doi.org/10.1016/j.asw.2008.10.003.

Zhao, C. G., & Wu, J. (2022). Perceptions of authorial voice: why discrepancies exist. *Assessing Writing*, *53*, 100632. https://doi.org/10.1016/j.asw.2022.100632.

Suggested Readings

Cumming, A., Cho, Y., Burstein, J., Everson, P., Kantor, R., & Powers, D. (2021). Assessing academic writing. In X. Xi & J. Norris (Eds.), *Assessing academic English for higher education admissions* (pp. 107–151). Routledge. https://doi.org/10.4324/9781351142403.

Poehner, M. E., & Yu, L. (2022). Dynamic assessment of L2 writing: exploring the potential of rubrics as mediation in diagnosing learner emerging abilities. *TESOL Journal*, *56*, 1191–1217. https://doi.org/10.1002/tesq.3098.

Weigle, S. C. (2002). *Assessing writing.* Cambridge University Press.

CHAPTER 13

Assessing the Linguistic Resources of Meaningful Communication

James Enos Purpura and Saerhim Oh

Introduction

Written and spoken communication, by definition, involves the ability to draw on contextual, topical, linguistic, socio-cognitive, and other mental and dispositional resources to express, understand, or negotiate propositional meanings (e.g., ideas, opinions, and beliefs) along with the contextualized extensions of those meanings (e.g., stance and politeness) across a range of language use contexts (Purpura, 2004, 2016). We use these resources to build and maintain relationships (i.e., social–interpersonal domain of language use), navigate service encounters and other institutional transactions (socio-transactional domain), develop topical or disciplinary understandings to present or write reports (academic or professional domains), or to persuade others in oral pitches or editorials (social-persuasive domain). In all these domains of language use, the one area requiring special attention for second or foreign language (SFL) users is the ability to use linguistic resources to communicate in grammatically precise, semantically meaningful, and pragmatically appropriate ways. *SFL proficiency*, therefore, can be defined as an individual's mental capacity to use linguistic and other resources in communication, while *situated SFL proficiency* refers to the ability to use linguistic resources in conjunction with other resources to communicate meanings interactively in a sociocultural context.

While acknowledging that linguistic resources (i.e., phonology, syntax, semantics, discourse, and pragmatics) are critical to the expression, comprehension, and negotiation of meaning, the role these resources play can be somewhat complex. Before going further, we should acknowledge that having linguistic resources without topical resources is like having language knowledge with nothing to say. And, having topical understandings without linguistic resources is like having something to say with no means of expressing it. As a result, communication at its most basic level involves the integration of propositional or topical meanings with linguistic forms (Purpura, 2004), often referred to as semantico-grammatical (S-G) resources, lexico-grammatical (L-G) resources, or integrated content and language resources. In other words, "*how* something is said is part of *what* is said" (Hymes, 1972, p. 59).

Based in part on Purpura (2014), with permission.

The Concise Companion to Language Assessment, First Edition. Edited by Antony John Kunnan.
© 2025 John Wiley & Sons, Inc. Published 2025 by John Wiley & Sons, Inc.

Unsurprisingly, however, the ability to express grammatically accurate and semantically meaningful utterances does not guarantee the resulting propositions will be understood as situationally intended, if the pragmatic conditions of the communicative event are not accounted for (Bachman & Palmer, 1996; Purpura, 2004). Thus, having the ability to generate well-formed and semantically meaningful utterances, without having pragmatic ability, is like having the ability to say things without realizing we're making no sense in a given situation or saying something socially, culturally, or emotionally inappropriate or unsuitable (Gumperz, 1972). In other words, the ability to express or understand a humorous or sarcastic remark in a given context involves more than well-formed and propositionally meaningful utterances; it also involves the ability to see how literal meanings expressed in propositions can be extended or contextualized in any given local situation. Thus, communicative effectiveness requires "situated" SFL proficiency, or the ability to use linguistic resources, along with other resources, to understand, express, or negotiate propositions in meaningful and contextually appropriate ways within the social structure of a given communicative event.

This chapter considers why it is important to study the linguistic resources of communication for assessment purposes. It then addresses how these resources have been conceptualized in the literature, operationalized in tests, and researched. It also looks at some current work in this area.

Why Examine the Linguistic Resources of Communication?

Language testers have always been interested in measuring the linguistic resources of communication (Purpura, 2004; Purpura & Dakin, 2020). This interest derives from the fundamental role that S-G knowledge plays in the ability to generate well-formed utterances and texts at different levels of proficiency. It also stems from the fact that S-G knowledge is a consistently strong predictor of SFL proficiency. Moreover, in classroom settings, SFL teachers need to teach the linguistic foundations of the language, and assessment, in whatever form, allows them to monitor the development of these resources for the purpose of closing learning gaps. SFL learners also need this information to focus their learning efforts. In sum, the assessment of linguistic resources is important because it is an integral part of how we teach, learn, and use an SFL – something that teachers have always known.

As a result, language testing researchers have long pursued questions related to the role of S-G resources in the ability to communicate effectively. And unsurprisingly, this research has demonstrated that S-G knowledge is an essential indicator of communicative success, dispelling myths that SFL education should focus only on meaning with no or little attention to the resources of meaning making. This finding, however, does not mean that the ability to convey propositional meanings is a weak predictor of communicative success; it's just that the ability to use linguistic forms precisely generally appears stronger. The critical takeaway from this research, though, is that communication involves the integration of linguistic resources with topical resources relevant to a localized speech community, and teaching, learning, and assessment practices should acknowledge this in construct definition. To support these claims, let us consider the following research.

As early as 1998, Purpura used structural equation modeling (SEM) to show that S-G resources had an extremely strong effect on how well candidates sitting for the Cambridge *First Certificate Exam* (currently named *B2 First*) (Cambridge University Press, 2023) were able to achieve high reading comprehension scores – an effect that seemed to conflate the two constructs. However, when modeled separately across high- and low-ability candidates, the effects were more moderate, and more in line with expectations of the perceived need to access S-G resources to understand the meanings encoded in different types of written texts (Purpura, 1998).

Similar results were found by Ameriks (2009), who, again using SEM, examined the contribution of L-G knowledge to reading ability across two forms of the University of Michigan *Examination for the Certificate of Proficiency in English (ECPE)* (English Language Institute, 2006). In two test forms, the ability to use L-G resources had a moderately strong effect on the ability to perform well on the reading test.

In the context of speaking assessment, Grabowski (2013) used multivariate generalizability (M-G) theory to investigate the relative contribution of S-G and pragmatic knowledge to total score variance of a speaking test. Examinees had to accomplish task goals through the accurate and meaningful use of S-G resources on the one hand and the contextually appropriate conveyance of sociolinguistic, sociocultural, and psychological meanings on the other, as outlined in Purpura (2004). The results showed that S-G resources contributed systematically more to total speaking score variance than did the ability to convey pragmatic meanings, although their contributions cannot be discounted. Thus, Grabowski clearly showed that the ability to perform well on contextually bound oral role-play tasks depended not only on the ability to produce well-formed and propositionally meaningful utterances but also on the ability to appropriately communicate stance and tone (psychological meanings), sensitivity toward both the interlocutors' social identity (sociolinguistic meanings), and toward the cultural norms, assumptions, preferences, and expectations inherent in the role-play contexts (sociocultural meanings).

Probably, the most comprehensive study to date on the relationship between S-G resources and the ability to read and listen in a SFL was done by Liao (2009), who in the context of the *General English Proficiency Test* (GEPT), developed by the Language Training and Testing Center in Taiwan, examined the degree to which S-G resources contributed to the candidates' ability to perform well on reading and listening comprehension tests. Liao, also drawing on Purpura (2004), defined S-G resources in terms of knowledge of grammatical forms and semantic meanings. Then, drawing on Purpura (1998), she characterized listening and reading comprehension as the ability to understand both (i) literal meanings explicitly stated in oral or written texts (coded as "endophoric literal reference") and (ii) implied pragmatic meanings implicitly inferred from cues within or beyond the text (coded as "endophoric/exophoric implied reference"). Using M-G theory, Liao found that the semantic meaning items in the GEPT contributed more than the grammatical form items to total S-G score variance. She also observed that the reading items measuring literal meanings explicitly stated in the text (i.e., endophoric literal meanings) contributed more to total reading score variance than items measuring implied pragmatic meanings in the text.

Following this, Liao examined these relationships using SEM, finding first that the association between knowledge of integrated grammatical forms and semantic meanings was very high. She also observed that the relationship between the ability to understand literal explicit meanings and pragmatic-implicit meanings in the context of both reading and listening comprehension was very high. More interestingly though, in investigating the simultaneous effects of S-G knowledge on reading and listening comprehension, she found that the use of S-G resources had a very strong effect on the ability to understand written texts but had a lesser effect on the ability to comprehend spoken texts. Liao concluded by examining the extent to which knowledge of grammatical forms and semantic meanings, measured separately, impacted reading and listening comprehension, finding that knowledge of semantic meaning was a slightly stronger predictor of reading and listening comprehension than was knowledge of grammatical forms. Taken together, these studies show that the ability to use a SFL depends on the ability to integrate linguistic with topical resources to achieve communicative goals.

Besides these theoretical questions, language testers have studied the linguistic resources of communication in an attempt to characterize linguistic features associated with different levels of proficiency when operationalized as performance level descriptors such as those in

184 Chapter 13 Assessing the Linguistic Resources of Meaningful Communication

the *Common European Framework of Reference* (CEFR) (Council of Europe, 2020). Specifically, these studies have explored links between linguistic characteristics and examinee response patterns at different proficiency levels, the goal being to inform the design of level-appropriate curricula, teaching materials, and assessments.

To investigate these links, researchers have pursued many lines of inquiry. Hawkins and Filipovic (2012), using data from the University of Cambridge exams and textual data from Cambridge curricular materials, characterized the distinguishing linguistic features of proficiency from the A2 to C2 level. This work led to the *University of Cambridge English Profile*, an online tool for understanding what features of English grammar and vocabulary are suitable for instruction or assessment at different CEFR levels. Taking a different approach, Hulstijn et al. (2012) related grammatical production features, defined in terms of syntactic complexity (e.g., mean sentence length, length of clause or T-units, and clauses per T-units or sentence), to the CEFR writing ability levels. Finally, Milton and Alexiou (2008, 2009), among others, linked production features for lexical complexity (e.g., word properties, level of frequency, and multi-word expressions) to CEFR writing levels.

While descriptive work in this area continues, the prospects of providing descriptions of the linguistic resources linked to proficiency levels that can be generalized beyond any one assessment or educational context, while intuitively appealing, seem somewhat aspirational. This is because the performance level descriptors in the CEFR, or other standards frameworks, are framed as *functional* or *can-do* statements, where performance is characterized in terms of speech acts describing what functions learners can perform at the different levels, rather than in terms of what specific linguistic features learners need to have mastered to implement the functions in task completion (trait descriptors), a theoretical conundrum first discussed by Upshur (1979).

Finally, interest in assessing the linguistic resources of communication has grown considerably over the years, given the role these resources play in developing speech and writing recognition and processing technologies on the one hand and automated scoring and feedback systems on the other (Xi, 2010). An example of this is illustrated in Zechner and Evanini (2020), who, in their state-of-the-art, authoritative synthesis of work on automated scoring of speaking over the last 20 years at the Educational Testing Service (ETS), discussed the measurement of several speech features (e.g., vocabulary, grammar, fluency, pronunciation, content, and discourse coherence) associated with "the ability to speak about everyday familiar topics, to summarize, synthesize and integrate written and audio materials; and to present the information orally in a comprehensible, coherent, and appropriate manner" (Zechner, 2020, p. 99).

In sum, SFL educators continue to be interested in measuring the fundamental linguistic resources of an examinee's communicative ability. And while most current language assessments are generally designed to measure these resources in tandem with other resources (e.g., topical knowledge) in performance tests, this by no means precludes the need to measure independent aspects of these resources in certain assessment contexts. No matter how we choose to measure the linguistic resources of communication, however, we can only do so if we have a deep understanding of what these resources are, how they are related to a comprehensive model of SFL proficiency, and how they can be elicited and measured. The following section discusses different conceptualizations of these resources along with ideas on how to measure them.

Unpacking the Linguistic Resources of Communication

When most SFL educators refer to the "linguistic resources of communication," they often think only of "grammar" conceptualized in terms of structural linguistics, where "grammar" is defined as a set of structural rules, patterns, norms, or conventions that govern the generation of well-formed and meaningful utterances within some specific domain of language use. This conceptualization defines the linguistic resources of communication only in terms of "grammatical knowledge," limited to phonology, morphology, syntax, and semantics – a definition that would likely be rejected by most SFL educators today as being too limited. Currently, SFL educators would argue that communication also involves resources such as discourse and pragmatics, especially in context-rich instances of SFL use. Thus, they would argue for a broader depiction of SFL proficiency and the resources that define it.

Given that conceptualizations of the linguistic resources of communication in applied linguistics have evolved over the years, language testers have proposed and refined several models of SFL knowledge, each generally building upon and expanding former models. In the next section, we describe some of the more consequential conceptualizations.

Evolving Conceptualizations of SFL Knowledge

Prominent Frameworks of Language Knowledge

Lado (1961) was one of the first language testers to propose a model of SFL proficiency in which the linguistic resources of communication were specified. His model was operationalized in terms of a skills-and-elements approach to assessment, where individual elements (e.g., lexis and syntax) were seen as the principal building blocks of SFL proficiency. This view led to a discrete-point approach to assessment, where discrete linguistic elements (e.g., 20 multiple-choice [MC] grammar items) are presented to learners and scored dichotomously for accuracy (e.g., 1 for a right answer and 0 for wrong). The scores from the correct responses are then aggregated to produce an overall proficiency estimate, often reported as a percent correct. While Lado's model was visionary for the time, operationalizing proficiency as discrete morphosyntactic, cohesive, and lexical elements constituted a highly restricted view of "proficiency." Nonetheless, Lado's approach to assessment remains useful for measuring isolated forms, when this is the assessment goal.

Another highly influential conceptualization of language knowledge was proposed by Canale and Swain (1980) and further refined by Canale (1983) in their model of communicative competence. Moving beyond linguistic elements associated with language skills, they operationalized the construct of *communicative competence* in terms of grammatical, sociolinguistic, and discourse competence, and their interaction during language use with *strategic competence*, or the mental ability to notice and adjust for communication failures. Canale and Swain's model significantly broadened our understanding of the individual components of communicative competence and shifted notions of proficiency from grammatical forms to functional meanings expressed in social interaction. It also highlighted how contextualized utterances carried sociolinguistic meanings. It also underscored the role of discourse meanings in communication. While this model transformed our conceptualization of communication, it unfortunately failed to address how topical understandings impact one's ability to communicate.

Building on prior work, Bachman (1990) and later Bachman and Palmer (1996, 2010) proposed a model of SFL proficiency, referred to as *communicative language ability or communicative language use*, in which linguistic resources again played a critical role. They defined language use as an interaction between the individual characteristics of the language user and the context of language use. The user characteristics were further specified as the interaction among an individual's language ability, topical knowledge, and affective schemata. Language knowledge was further defined in terms of organizational knowledge (involving grammatical and textual knowledge) and pragmatic knowledge (comprising functional and sociolinguistic knowledge). The context of language use is defined in terms of task characteristics. Bachman

Other Refinements to the SFL Proficiency Construct

and Palmer's model of language knowledge has been used as a heuristic for guiding test development in numerous L2 testing contexts, including the *Test of English as a Foreign Language* (TOEFL), *the Cambridge suite of exams*, and the *Canadian language benchmarks*.

Other Refinements to the SFL Proficiency Construct

Building on Bachman and Palmer, many others have offered important refinements to how SFL proficiency is defined. Most notably, Chapelle (1998) proposed an interactionist approach in which she highlighted the importance of context in shaping a learner's ability to communicate in a SFL. Chalhoub-Deville (2003) described how proficiency is located not only within an individual but also across interlocutors as they engage interactively in the co-construction of ideas. And Douglas (2000) argued that in language for specific purposes (LSP) contexts, an examinee's specific purpose background knowledge is, together with L2 knowledge and strategic competence, a critical component of specific purpose language ability (SPLA), thereby highlighting the role that topical knowledge plays in domain-specific communication.

Purpura's (2016) Conceptualization of Language Knowledge Within a Meaning-Oriented Approach to Situated SFL Proficiency

A more recent development in the evolution of SFL proficiency models, and one we will use to discuss the assessment of the linguistic resources of communication, is the meaning-oriented model (MOM) of situated SFL proficiency, proposed by Purpura (2016). Inspired by language assessment theory, research in the sciences of thinking and learning, and years of experience teaching and testing SFLs, this slightly different conceptualization of SFL proficiency prioritizes meaning and meaning conveyance as it assumes that meaning making and exchange are the quintessential goals of communication, and language knowledge is one of many resources needed for communicative success. The MOM also acknowledges "the risks associated with meaning-related conversational breakdowns or flat-out miscommunications, due not only to S-G deficiencies but also, and more insidiously, to pragmatic infelicities, which can easily lead to mutual misjudgment of intentions and abilities, miscommunication, and even cultural stereotyping (Gumperz, 1999), which could ultimately support linguistic manipulation (i.e., fake news), discrimination, and social inequity" (Purpura, 2016, p. 18).

In this context, *situated SFL proficiency* is conceptualized as "a network of resources that enable users to effectively express, understand, dynamically co-construct, negotiate, and repair variegated meanings in a wide range of language use contexts" (Purpura, 2016, p. 18). And the ability to communicate meanings in some domain of L2 use depends conjointly on the conditions of the language use situation, language resources, topical resources, socio-cognitive resources, and the dispositional resources of task engagement. This model is schematized in Figure 13.1.

The MOM assumes that an individual's situated SFL proficiency is triggered by the need to communicate in some goal-oriented, language use situation, where one objective might be to socialize with friends (socio-interpersonal), another to resolve a billing problem (socio-transactional), another to give a presentation in class (academic) or at a conference (professional), and another to convince someone of an opinion (socio-persuasive). Each situation requires a coherent sequence of related tasks, and each task needs to be specified for different conditions in an assessment context. Figure 13.1 identifies several situational and task characteristics that need to be considered for domain-related tasks.

To communicate in these situations, individuals first need something to say – topical resources. For example, in socio-interpersonal contexts, individuals might need to access

SITUATIONAL CONSIDERATIONS

- **Purpose:** Assess ability to...
- **Domain of generalization:** Social-interpersonal, social-transactional, academic, professional, combination
- **Link to standards:** CEFR, ACTFL...

TASK CONSIDERATIONS (related to the input & expected response)

- **Task setting:** location
- **Event within setting:** discursive practice

- **Participatory roles:** symmetry
- **Topical requirements:** domain-general; domain specific
- **Task goal(s)/functions:** to...
- **Subtask goal(s)/functions:** to...
- **Semantico-grammatical requirements:** forms, meanings
- **Sociolinguistic requirements:** register, identity considerations
- **Sociocultural requirements:** inter/cross-cultural expectations

- **Psychological requirements:** stance, affect
- **Rhetorical requirements:** coherence, structuring expectations,
- **Interactional requirements:** turn-taking, preference, structuring expectations
- **Socio-cognitive considerations:** cognitive load expectations, processability-rate of recall, processing, fluid reasoning
- **Literary/religious considerations:** references
- **Dispositional considerations:** level of engagement, effort, interest

Socio-cognitive (individually/group)
- Architecture: attention span memory capacity,
- Functionality: strategic processing, reasoning

Dispositional (perceptions & dispositions)
- Psychological (engagement, confidence)
- Behavioral (effort, grit, initiative)
- Social (trust, cooperation,)

Adapted from Purpura (2014, 2018)

[Central diagram: Situated SFL proficiency — Consideration of domain-related features, Socio-cognitive & dispositional resources, Topical resources, Language resources]

Explicit semantic memory
- Access to ideas, facts, concepts, principles, rules, scripts, frames, & habits of mind for solving problems
- Access to networks organized in categories, classifications, hierarchies, associations, & schemas

Adapted from Baddeley, Eysenck, & Anderson (2009)

Explicit episodic memory
- Access to episodes, states, situations, or events experienced in real life or vicariously

Autobiographical memory
- Access to facts about ourselves & past (also involves semantic & episodic memory)

Implicit memory
- Access to scripts & algorithms based on proceduralized performance

Visuo-spatial memory
- Access to mental images, objects, or locations

Semantico-grammatical (S-G) knowledge
- Knowledge of forms & associated semantic meanings
- Propositional Knowledge (topical information)

Pragmatic knowledge
- Functional Knowledge (intended or functional meanings)
- Implicational Knowledge (contextualized meanings)

Adapted from Purpura (2004) and Purpura & Dakin (2020).

FIGURE 13.1 Meaning-oriented model of situated SFL proficiency. *Source:* Purpura (2016) / Springer Nature.

188 Chapter 13 Assessing the Linguistic Resources of Meaningful Communication

information from autobiographical or episodic memory to exchange personal information, while in academic or professional contexts, they would need to tap into explicit semantic memory or implicit memory to communicate facts or opinions.

In certain situations, examinees can tap into domain-general topical knowledge (i.e., information available to all individuals such as going grocery shopping) in order to respond to questions. In other situations, however, examinees need to access domain-specific topical knowledge. In these cases, examinees need specialized information available to select individuals within a content area, such as disciplinary information about photosynthesis (i.e., LSP background knowledge proposed by Douglas, 2000). Testers need to pay attention to the assumed topical resources that examinees need to have access to when creating test tasks. We also need to remember that even native speakers lack topical resources in certain language use domains (e.g., aerodynamics).

To perform these goal-related tasks, individuals also have to tap into the mental resources that govern cognitive functionality. These socio-cognitive resources determine what is noticed and attended to in social situations, and they influence how new information is understood, stored, represented in memory, revised, accessed, and used to reason and solve problems. Language testers need to give careful thought to the kinds of socio-cognitive resources needed to complete tasks, keeping in mind the level of focus, cognitive load, and processability.

The need to complete a task naturally engages an individual's perceptions of the task request and their dispositions toward completing it. Different tasks arouse diverse psychological dispositions (e.g., mental engagement, anxiety), behavioral dispositions (e.g., effort, defeat), and social dispositions (e.g., cooperation, superiority). Testers should obviously attempt to engineer tasks that promote positive affective responses from individuals, all the while keeping track of occasions in which examinees respond negatively to the task demands and the potential effects on performance.

Last but not least, communication involves linguistic resources (i.e., language knowledge) without which the conveyance of literal and implied meanings would be impossible. Language knowledge as specified in the MOM involves two highly related sets of resources: S-G knowledge and pragmatic knowledge. Given that each set of resources can be assessed independently or in tandem depending on the assessment goal, we next explain this conceptualization of language knowledge and use it to examine how the linguistic resources of meaningful communication can be defined, elicited, and measured in SFL assessments.

Conceptualizing and Measuring Linguistic Resources Within the MOM

Knowledge of Language Forms as a Resource for Communication

Many SFL educators continue to think of the resources of communication as grammatical knowledge defined in terms of discrete grammatical forms often categorized as morphosyntactic structures with little explicit acknowledgment of their relationship to meaning (Purpura, 2004). This conceptualization of language knowledge has a long history and is the mainstay of many traditional grammar tests today.

In a form-based approach to grammar assessment, the selection of forms to be measured is often based on a principled list of morphosyntactic structures. For example, in deciding on grammatical forms to be measured on the *Oxford Online Placement Test*, Purpura and colleagues compiled a list of structures drawn from Celce-Murcia and Larsen-Freeman's (1999) pedagogical grammar, as seen in Figure 13.2. Once organized, this list became a critical resource for item selection and development.

Nouns and noun phrases:
- predeterminers, determiners, post-determiners
- nouns (countability, affixation, compounding)

Verbs, verb phrases, tense and aspect:
- tense–present, past; aspect–progressive
- subject–verb agreement

Modals and phrasal modals (*be able to*):
- forms–present, past, future, perfective, progressive
- obligation–*should, supposed to*

Phrasal verbs:
- form–two-word, three-word
- separability

Prepositions and prepositional phrases:
- co-occurrence with verb, adjective or noun–*rely on, fond of*
- spatial or temporal relationships–*at the store, at 5*

Adjectives and adjectival phrases:
- formation (*-ous, -ive*)
- adjective order–*the lovely, little, plastic Cher doll*

Logical connectors:
- relationships of time, space, reason, and purpose
- subordinating and coordinating conjunctions

Relative clauses:
- forms–animate, inanimate, zero, place
- subject noun phrase, (in)direct object noun phrase, genitive noun phrase

Nonreferential *It* and *There*:
- time, distance, environment–*it's noisy in here*
- existence–*there is/are*

Pronouns and reference (cohesion):
- personal, demonstrative, reciprocal
- relative, indefinite, interrogative

Questions and responses:
- yes/no, *wh-*, negative, uninverted
- tags

Conditionals:
- forms–present, past, future
- factual, counterfactual

Passive voice:
- form–present, past, future, perfective
- other passives–*get something done*

Complements and complementation:
- verb + noun phrase + (preposition) noun phrase
- infinitive or gerund complements–*want (him) to; believe him to; get used to + gerund*

Comparisons:
- comparatives and superlatives
- equatives–*as/so big as*

Adverbials and adverbial phrases:
- forms–adverb phrase, clause, prepositional phrase
- placement–sentence initial, medial, and final

Reported speech:
- backshifting
- indirect imperatives or questions

Focus and emphasis:
- emphasis–emphatic *do*
- marked word order–*him I see*

FIGURE 13.2 List of morphosyntactic forms (Purpura, 2014).

Similarly, the list of phonological forms in Figure 13.3, based on Ellis and Barkhuizen (2005) and Bonk and Oh (2019), could inform item selection for a pronunciation test.

Since a form-based approach can involve hundreds of forms, Purpura (2004, 2016) proposed a model of grammatical knowledge that organized the forms according to the (sub)sentential or discourse level of occurrence. The (sub)sentential-level forms include graphological/ phonological, lexical, and morphosyntactic forms, and the discourse-level forms comprise cohesive, information management, and interactional forms. These six categories can be used to track content representativeness. In the MOM of SFL proficiency (Figure 13.4), knowledge of grammatical forms is one component of S-G knowledge.

In Figure 13.4, knowledge of grammatical forms is assessed by means of selected-response (SR), limited-production (LP), or extended-production (EP) tasks. SR tasks are commonly used when the aim is to isolate and measure knowledge of individual grammatical forms. For example, Figure 13.4 presents a morphosyntactic form (tense-aspect), where the forms vary in the response options, but the meaning of the verb "spend" is held constant, thereby measuring knowledge of form. It also presents a lexical form item where the prepositional options for

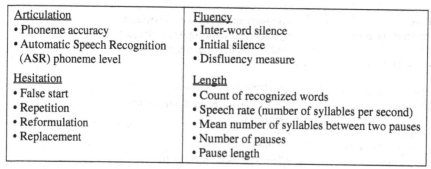

FIGURE 13.3 List of phonological forms.

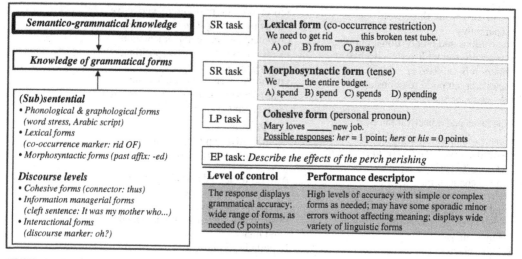

FIGURE 13.4 Model of knowledge of grammatical forms. *Source:* Purpura (2016) / Springer Nature.

lexical phrase vary, but the preposition "of" in *get rid of* is not meaning bearing; thus, the item measures form and not meaning. SR items are typically scored dichotomously (1 for accurate; 0 for wrong).

Figure 13.4 presents another way of assessing knowledge of forms – by means of LP tasks, a method designed to assess relatively discrete units of S-G knowledge. LP tasks present test input in the form of an item that requires examinees to *produce* a limited amount of language. LP tasks provide fine-grained, developmental information on grammatical knowledge – a major advantage over SR tasks. The cohesive form item in Figure 13.4 asks examinees to fill in the blank with a limited amount of language. The response encodes both form and meaning. For example, the response, *his*, indicates the correct form, but the wrong meaning (biological sex), whereas the response *hers* indicates the right meaning, but the wrong form. In these cases, responses can be scored dichotomously right/wrong, or we can give partial credit, 0.5 for the correct form and 0.5 for the correct meaning.

Finally, many L2 testers believe the assessment of grammatical resources is best accomplished through *performance tasks*, where examinees are presented with input in the form of a prompt and required to produce extended amounts of spoken or written text. Performance tasks are EP tasks that are best designed when they reflect the tasks learners might encounter in the language use domain. Because of the amount of data produced by these tasks, assessment may involve multiple areas of L2 knowledge depending on the assessment goal, or the response can be assessed only by means of a rubric targeting knowledge of S-G resources. In the EP task in Figure 13.4, examinees have to speculate about what would happen to an ecosystem if one species perished. Their performance is then evaluated on how accurate, elaborated, and organized their responses are. For a more elaborated discussion of this topic, see Purpura (2004) and Purpura & Dakin (2020).

Knowledge of Semantic Meaning as a Resource for Communication

As almost all grammatical forms (in English) are associated with at least one semantic meaning. Another resource of communication is knowing the literal semantic meaning(s) of the forms. For example, the plural -s affix added to a count noun conveys plurality – the semantic meaning. The fact that a form simultaneously encodes a meaning dimension can present learning challenges in cases where the SFL uses different grammatical forms from those in the L1. For example, to convey plurality, Italian uses the "i" affix as in *ragazzi (boys)* or "e" as in *ragazze (girls)*. As a result, English native speakers learning Italian often encounter no problem conceptualizing the notion of plurality, but face challenges getting the two plural forms correct.

Another example of the semantic dimension is seen when a patient calls his doctor for advice, and the doctor replies: "I *work* with a patient now" (literal meaning, my current job is to do this work). This response reflects a knowledge gap in the link between the morphosyntactic form *work* and its associated meaning (habitual time), and in this context, such an error may result in a misunderstanding. However, if the doctor had responded: "I *working* with a patient now" or "I'*m working* with a patient now," the meaning in both cases, despite the form error, would be: "I am currently occupied – and therefore, unavailable to talk." The intended meaning of the proposition would have been conveyed. If we were to assess these three responses, the interpretation of the knowledge base would be different, and the scoring decisions would vary, again underscoring the importance of the meaning dimension. In sum, given the learning challenges and ambiguities associated with these two dimensions, testers need to stop treating "grammar" as a monolithic whole, but rather should think of grammatical content in terms of forms and meanings.

The semantic meanings associated with the forms occur on the (sub)sentential and discourse levels with respect to phonology or graphology, lexis, morphosyntax, cohesion, information management, and interaction. In certain contexts, it is necessary to assess *just* the semantic meaning. This is often the case in classroom contexts when teachers question if students have processed a new grammatical concept or have consolidated their understanding of a new concept (e.g., assess the lexical meaning of a new vocabulary or the cohesive meaning of logical connectors). To accommodate this possibility, the S-G knowledge component of the MOM was expanded to include the knowledge of semantic meanings component, as seen in Figure 13.5.

Figure 13.5 provides examples of how semantic meanings can be elicited and measured separately, if needed. In the two SR items, the meanings vary, but the forms are held constant; scoring is dichotomous. However, in the LP items, a short response encodes both form and meaning, allowing each to be scored separately (e.g., 1 for accuracy and 1 for meaningfulness). Or the response can be treated as a whole, constituting a form-meaning mapping with one point being assigned for a completely correct response and zero for flawed responses. In the EP item, the precision, effectiveness, or the efficiency of the form-meaning mappings can be rated holistically for different levels of semantic control based on a rubric. In this conceptualization, having knowledge of forms and meanings constitutes a fundamental resource for being able to create or understand utterances, and it is sometimes important to test these building blocks alone.

In developing a comprehensive grammar test designed to stream candidates into multi-level scenario-based language assessments (SBLA), the *SBLA lab at Teachers College, Columbia*

Chapter 13 Assessing the Linguistic Resources of Meaningful Communication

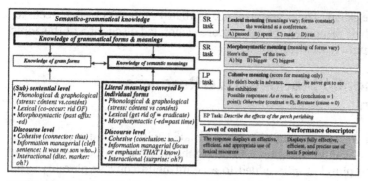

FIGURE 13.5 Model of knowledge of semantic meanings. *Source:* Purpura (2016) / Springer Nature.

TABLE 13.1

Taxonomy of SBA screening test

	CEFR levels (# of items)				
	A2	B1	B2	C1	Totals
Grammatical forms					
Lexical	1	1	1	0	3
Morphosyntactic	4	7	5	0	16
Cohesive	0	1	1	1	3
Info management	1	1	0	0	2
	6	10	7	1	24
Semantic meanings					
Lexical	3	3	2	1	9
Morphosyntactic	0	3	0	0	3
Cohesive	2	0	1	1	4
Info management	0	0	2	0	2
	5	6	5	2	18
CEFR totals	11	16	12	3	42

Source: Beltrán et al. (2023).

University, used this model of grammatical knowledge to create a taxonomy of test content at different levels of proficiency (Beltrán et al., 2023). The list of forms and meanings was drawn from English as a second language textbooks and from Celce-Murcia and Larsen-Freeman (1999). The taxonomy served to balance the content across different aspects of grammatical knowledge at different proficiency levels, so that forms from all the categories could be represented in the test content. This taxonomy appears in Table 13.1.

Knowledge of Propositional Meaning as a Resource for Communication

While it is possible and sometimes necessary to test the resources of communication at this smaller grain size, the heart and soul of communication, in our opinion, relate to how forms and meanings conspire to create well-formed utterances that communicate *literal propositional meanings* – i.e., information units about people, events, beliefs, and other ideational content. This is referred to as the propositional or topical meaning of an utterance or text.

All utterances encode propositional meaning, since without propositional content there would be nothing to say. And in order to generate utterances, examinees need *propositional* or *topical knowledge*.

As seen in Figures 13.6, propositional knowledge is considered an integral part of S-G knowledge, even though the source of that knowledge might be in long-term memory (Seong, 2023).[1] Thus, to accommodate this complexity, the model of S-G knowledge was again extended to include a separate propositional dimension as part of the language knowledge construct, since the proposition is the product of the form-meaning mappings.

The propositional content of utterances or texts is critical because it provides the information base of communication. As seen in Figure 13.6, propositional meaning can be measured at the sentence level through the synonymous-sentence technique. More commonly, however, propositional meaning questions are used on reading or listening comprehension tests to measure the examinees' ability to comprehend explicitly stated information in the text (e.g., *What is the main takeaway from the text? What is the first stage of change according to the article?*).

Propositional knowledge is always elicited in written or spoken tasks. For example, the prompt in Figure 13.6 provides examinees with a graphic about an ecosystem and then asks them to explain the phenomenon. The elicited response is then assessed for topical or content control based on a performance level descriptor on a scoring rubric (e.g., scored for the quality of content, relevance of response to the task, and development of the topical information).

In fact, all SFL use can be judged for propositional accuracy, relevance, and elaboration; however, scoring expectations in assessments should vary based on whether or not examinees come to the assessment event only with background knowledge, whether they have access via the assessment protocol to the needed informational input, or whether they had access to the information through prior instruction. For example, in traditional writing tasks where examinees are given no informational support, examinees will have to draw exclusively on background knowledge to generate responses. Such is the case with the following prompt:

Write a paragraph about someone you admire. Who is this person and what did the person do? What are their special characteristics and how are they similar or different from others?

(Purpura et al., 2001, Unit 4 Achievement Test)

In these cases, testers make assumptions about what background knowledge examinees likely have access to, a judgment that may introduce topical bias into the assessment for those not having the opportunity to gain that knowledge.

In integrated content and language (ICL) assessments or in SBLAs, however, examinees are first asked to build understandings about a topic by listening or reading. They are then asked to use this information as a basis for their written or spoken response. In these cases, it is possible to create *content-responsible rubrics*, where topical information in the expected response can be specified from the input in the listening or reading and later judged for accuracy, relevance, and elaboration. In this context, all candidates have equal access to the information base.

---

[1] The location of topical knowledge in the mind has been a matter of much debate. Interestingly, though, Seong (2023) provided compelling theoretical and statistical evidence, showing that topical knowledge is both within and external to the language knowledge construct, as suggested by Douglas (2000) in LSP contexts and by Purpura (2004, 2016) in all contexts.

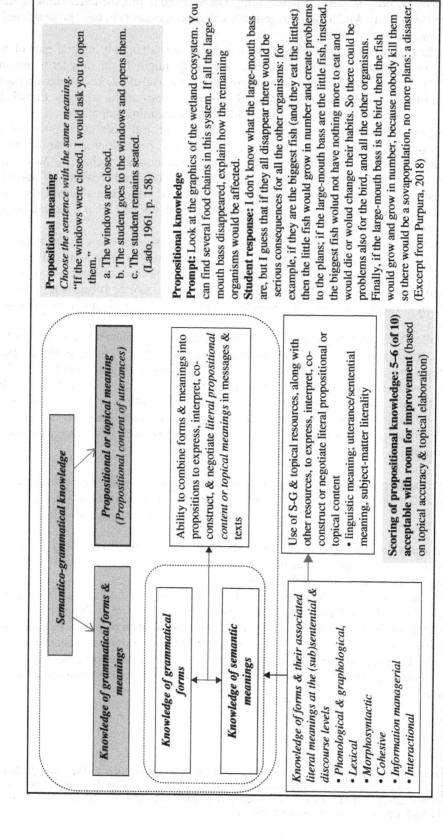

FIGURE 13.6 Model of semantico-grammatical knowledge. *Source:* Purpura (2016) / Springer Nature.

Conceptualizing and Measuring Linguistic Resources Within the MOM

The MOM model highlights the interface between language forms and their meanings on the one hand and the ability to generate propositional content on the other. As a result, this model would be a useful heuristic in educational contexts with an ICL approach to instruction and assessment (e.g., LSP, CLIL, and English medium instruction).

Functional Knowledge as a Resource for Communication

In many assessment contexts, examinees have to express and understand propositions with very little reference to context beyond what is stated in a sentence or two (i.e., the linguistic meaning) (see the propositional item in Figure 13.6). Without context encoding a speaker's intentionality, these utterances are open to interpretation and may introduce error into an assessment.

In other assessment contexts, or in real-life language use, however, SFL users have full access to the situational conditions of the language use event. In these contexts, the situational parameters help interlocutors understand not only what is being said literally (i.e., the propositional content) but also what is being implied. For example, the statement, *"it's hot in here,"* in one situation might refer literally to a description of the room temperature and, in another, a request to turn on the AC. Thus, the intended meaning of the utterance depends on the context in which it was implicated.

In communication, the comprehension and expression of meanings not derivable from the literal meanings of words arranged in syntax but interpretable *only* from an understanding of the context are called *pragmatic meanings* (Purpura, 2004). And the ability to use the situational context to understand or express implied pragmatic meanings encoded in propositions is called *pragmatic knowledge*. Having pragmatic knowledge is another core linguistic resource of communication since much of what is actually said is interpreted through a contextual frame.

One important component of pragmatic knowledge is *functional knowledge*. When a SFL user expresses a proposition in context, this proposition has a social purpose or *function*, encoding the contextualized intentionality of the speaker. In the example above, we do not know if the speaker intends to describe the room temperature (the literal meaning) or request a change in temperature (an implied meaning); more context is necessary to interpret intentionality. Functional knowledge gives SFL users the capacity to use context to express, interpret, co-construct, or negotiate one's intentionality vis-à-vis another interlocutor by performing direct (e.g., *open the window*) or indirect speech acts (e.g., *some air might be good*). Since the ability to use functional knowledge to achieve socially situated goals is another critical linguistic resource of communication, the MOM was extended to accommodate this component, as seen in Figure 13.7.

Functional knowledge is often conceptualized in language tests as language functions, operationalized as "can-do" statements, that appear in frameworks such as the *CEFR*, or in skill level performance descriptors similar to those in the *ILR*, the *ACTFL*, or the *Canadian Benchmarks*.

Given the importance of determining if examinees can understand more than *what* is being said, but *why* it is being said, and *what* the interlocutor is attempting to achieve, functional knowledge questions are common on reading and listening tests. Two such questions, as seen in Figure 13.7, might be as follows: *What was the underlying purpose of ...?* or *What was the goal of ...?*

Functional knowledge is also elicited when examinees are asked to write or speak in relation to a prompt. The completion of the task allows examinees to demonstrate their functional ability. To illustrate, the results section of a chemistry lab report is minimally organized around three language functions: state the action (*was dipped*), state the observed result (*turned the paper red*), and make a conclusion (*the solution was, therefore, an acid*). If one or

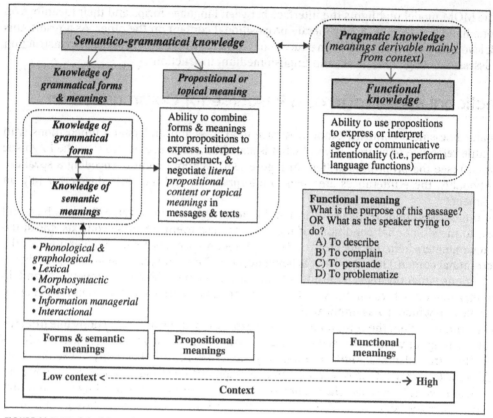

FIGURE 13.7 Model of functional knowledge. *Source:* Purpura (2016) / Springer Nature.

more of these functions were missing, the examinee would have demonstrated a gap in functional knowledge. If the conclusion drawn was incorrect, however, this does not demonstrate lack of functional knowledge, but a gap in propositional knowledge. And if the passive form was ill-formed (e.g., *was add), this would not demonstrate lack of functional or propositional knowledge, but a gap in knowledge of grammatical form.

Implicational Knowledge as a Resource for Communication

In context-rich situations of language use, grammatical, propositional and functional knowledge are always implicated in language production. Besides this, however, many other nuanced meanings can be *simultaneously* implicated based on the shared presuppositions, experiences, and associations of the interlocutors relevant to the situation. Thus, the second component of pragmatic knowledge is *implicational knowledge*, as seen in Figure 13.8. It refers to the ability to understand or express other layers of implied meaning encoded in the context of the situation.

To illustrate, consider the sentence *I'm Italian*. If there were no context other than this sentence (as in many grammar tests), then the *literal semantic meaning* would be the default meaning (statement of nationality), as it is based on the meanings of the words arranged in syntax. If, however, this sentence occurred with a little more context – an interlocutor who asked about nationality – then, as seen in the extract below, the response *I'm Italian* would encode both a statement about nationality (propositional content) and the speaker's intent *to inform* or *provide information* [about nationality] – the implied functional meaning.

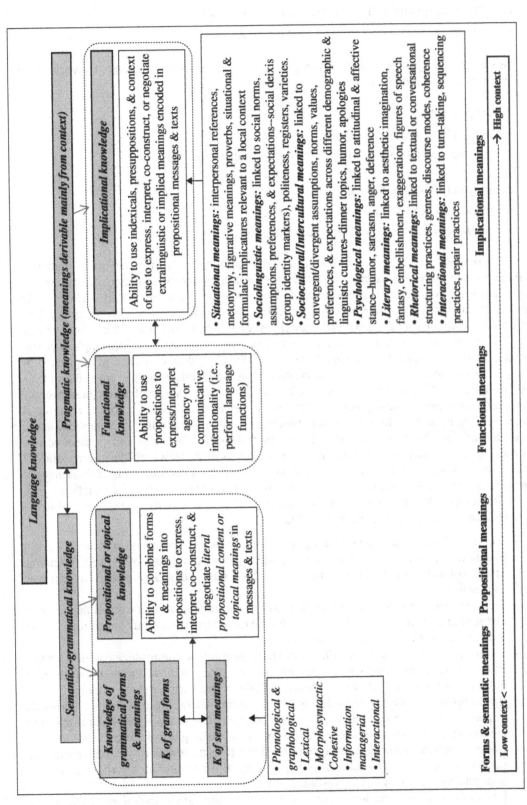

FIGURE 13.8 Meaning-oriented model of language knowledge. *Source:* Adapted from Purpura (2016) / Springer Nature.

Chapter 13 Assessing the Linguistic Resources of Meaningful Communication

A: What's your nationality? [request for information]

B: *I'm Italian.* [provide information]

However, with a just little more context, the same sentence could be used to convey a range of other contextualized meanings:

A: Do you like red wine?

B: [smile] *I'm Italian.*

[= Come on! Of course, I like red wine! All Italians like red wind.]

A: Do you lie about bad pizza?

B: [condescending look] *I'm Italian.*

[= Oh please! Italians will tell you if the pizza sucks!]

In these cases, the response *I'm Italian* encodes more than an expression of nationality. It *simultaneously* conveys a *sociocultural/intercultural* association between Italian identity and the shared presupposition that Italians generally like red wine or are not usually inclined to lie about substandard pizza. Such an utterance could also convey *sociolinguistic meanings* (e.g., informality between friends) and *psychological meanings* (e.g., playfulness). Thus, the utterance *I'm Italian* uses the same grammatical resources to convey literal semantic meaning in a proposition (i.e., nationality), intended meaning (i.e., to inform), and other meanings implicated by the context and solely derivable from the context. Thus, pragmatic meanings are different from but intrinsically linked to both a learner's S-G resources and the contextual characteristics of the communicative event. Consequently, having implicational knowledge is a critical resource of communication, as this allows us to communicate situational implicatures, metaphors, social and cultural identity; social and cultural appropriateness – formality and politeness; and affective stance – emotionality, humor, sarcasm, and so forth. However, the complexities of pragmatic inference relevant to extralinguistic context and the sheer range of meanings that can be encoded in an utterance can pose challenges to SFL users depending on the situation.

A definition of the pragmatic meanings that could be operationalized in scoring rubrics is provided below (adapted from Purpura, 2016, pp. 20–21).

- *Situational meanings*: understanding how to communicate meanings specific to a given situation; e.g., assessment of appropriate and/or conventional use of indirect functions, interpersonal or situational references, metaphors, figures of speech, and local formulaic expressions.
- *Sociolinguistic meanings*: understanding how to communicate with a given person (and identity) in a given social context; e.g., assessment of appropriate and conventional use of social deixis, politeness, registers, formality, etc.
- *Sociocultural/intercultural meanings*: understanding how to communicate within a given culture or across cultures; e.g., assessment of appropriate and conventional use of topic, humor, gratitude, and criticism; avoidance of taboos; etc. within a given situation.
- *Psychological meanings*: understanding how to communicate attitudes, feelings, and other dispositions; e.g., assessment of appropriate or conventional use of humor or sarcasm or the conveyance of anger, deference, affection, etc. within a given situation.
- *Literary/religious meanings*: understanding how to communicate symbolic meanings; e.g., assessment of appropriate, creative, or original use of literary or religious conventions and references within a given situation.
- *Rhetorical meanings*: understanding how to communicate a logical or conventional sequence of actions; e.g., assessment of appropriate and conventional use of organizational patterns or genres.

- *Interactional meanings*: understanding how to communicate meanings such as collaborative talk through interactional practices; e.g., assessment of appropriate and conventional practices associated with conversational norms, assumptions, and expectations (e.g., turn-taking, repair).

For a more detailed description of the implicational meanings, see Purpura (2004, 2016).

In sum, the MOM of situated SFL proficiency has been a useful organizing heuristic for conceptualizing the full range of resources that underlie communication. It is particularly useful, however, for assessments that prioritize the ability to use linguistic resources to understand and express meanings. That said, the framework can be used selectively to measure individual resources or a range of resources depending on the purpose of the assessment.

To illustrate, the MOM can be used to define the ability to use a range of resources to communicate meanings through one of the language modalities. For example, speaking or writing ability can be aligned with a comprehensive model of SFL proficiency by means of propositional, S-G, and pragmatic resources. Knowledge of these resources can then be operationalized through different language components (e.g., topical, language, rhetorical, sociolinguistic, and psychological control) and then measured for certain criteria (e.g., accuracy, development, and appropriateness), as shown in Figures 13.9 and 13.10.

The MOM has also been a useful framework for conceptualizing language assessment research. Liao (2009) used an earlier version to examine the relationships between S-G knowledge and reading and listening ability. Grabowski (2013) used it to investigate examinees' ability to use implicational meanings in the context of a reciprocal role-play speaking task. Kim (2009) used it to examine the effects of context and task type on different components of speaking ability. Oh (2022) used it to examine test takers' use of linguistic tools in L2 academic writing assessment. Purpura and Cumming (2023) used it to analyze the construct underlying the upper-level French and Chinese DLPT5s at the Defense Language Institute in Monterey. In the context of SBLAs, Banerjee (2019) used it to examine the construct of topical knowledge in an SFL nutrition test, Seong (2023) to explore the role of the socio-cognitive

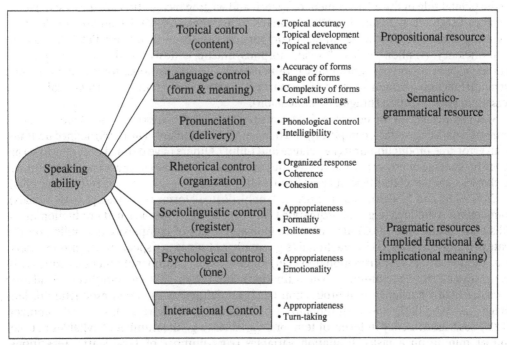

FIGURE 13.9 Defining of speaking ability through the MOM of language knowledge. *Source:* Adapted from Purpura (2016) / Springer Nature.

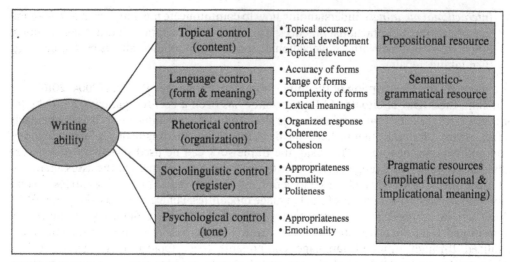

FIGURE 13.10 Defining writing ability through the MOM of language knowledge. *Source:* Purpura (2016) / Springer Nature.

dimension of an integrated academic speaking task involving journalism, Beltrán (2023) to investigate the role of assistance in an SBA of argumentative speaking ability in Mexico, Joo et al. (2023) to examine writing performance in an SBA of Korean writing ability, and Beltrán et al. (2023) to investigate the use of linguistic resources to stream candidates into proficiency-level appropriate SBAs of situated SFL proficiency.

Future Directions

The importance of linguistic resources of communication has expanded over the years, driven by the pivotal role in the advancement of speech and writing recognition and processing technologies (Zechner & Evanini, 2020). In many cases, measures of L2 production features revolving around the following language components have been used to predict differences in L2 proficiency: (i) phonological, lexical, morphosyntactic, cohesive, and interactional forms and associated meanings (grammatical dimension); (ii) propositions, topics, or idea units (semantic meaning dimension); and (iii) markers of stance, coherence, and rhetorical or conversational organization (pragmatic dimension).

SLA researchers, on the other hand, have mainly examined the resources of L2 production in terms of linguistic accuracy, complexity, and fluency. Wolfe-Quintero et al. (1998) defined *accuracy* as an error-free production unit (i.e., clause and t-unit). Others have defined accuracy in terms of the percentage of errors per 100 words, the percentage of error-free clauses per total number of clauses, and the percentage of error-free t-units per total number of t-units (Skehan, 1998).

Complexity can be defined as the use of "sophisticated" forms (e.g., past passive modals), complex constructions (e.g., subordination), and various other late-learned production units. Ellis and Barkhuizen (2005) identified the following types of complexity depending on the feature being analyzed: (i) interactional (e.g., number of turns per speaker), (ii) propositional (e.g., the density of the information unit), (iii) functional (e.g., number of functions expressed), (iv) grammatical (e.g., amount of subordination), and (v) lexical (e.g., number of academic words). Finally, *fluency* in oral production has been defined as the rapid production of language (Skehan, 1998) and operationalized by numerous measures. Ellis and Barkhuizen (2005) described fluency in terms of temporal variables (e.g., the number of syllables per second or minute on a task), hesitation variables (e.g., number of false starts, repetitions, reformulations, replacements, or other disfluencies), and the quantity of production (e.g., the response time or the number of syllables in a response).

Drawing from prior research, the use of accuracy, complexity, and fluency indicators have proven to be strong predictors of L2 speaking and writing quality and have been employed to characterize and examine various aspects related to L2 speaking and writing proficiency. To illustrate, in a review of measures of linguistic accuracy in L2 writing research, Polio and Shea (2014) revealed that some of the reasons for measuring grammatical accuracy in L2 writing research have been to investigate the difference between individual and collaborative writing, learners' writing performance over time, and the effects of planning and feedback.

However, learners' performance can vary depending on the attributes of the tasks and the interaction between the task characteristics and the learners' background (Ortega, 2003; Révész, 2009). As a result, the measures of accuracy, complexity, and fluency derived from performance across different tasks may also exhibit differences. For instance, Gan (2012) compared measures of grammatical complexity in performance on a monologic and interactive task uncovering greater indications of complexity in the results of the monologue task.

Additionally, these indicators of accuracy, complexity, and fluency exhibit a multidimensional and dynamic nature. Yan et al. (2021) underscored the multidimensionality of speech fluency and advocated for the incorporation of both macro features (e.g., speech rate and number of silent pauses) and micro features (e.g., subordinate clause per C-unit) when measuring fluency. Similarly, Norris and Ortega (2009) stress the importance of employing multiple measures of complexity, as these measures may tap into distinct facets of language proficiency.

Therefore, it is evident that the selection of measures of accuracy, complexity, and fluency as key features representing learners' language knowledge should be approached with caution, and researchers should exercise prudence when utilizing these features to gauge learners' language knowledge.

When scoring L2 oral and written performance, automated scoring systems have increasingly been used to systematically extract relevant production features (or cluster of features), such as the linguistic resources related to speed, pause, intonation, lexical diversity, syntactic complexity, and content and discourse coherence (see Zechner & Evanini, 2020 for a review of production features used in automated speech evaluation technology). These extracted linguistic resources are then funneled into a scoring model, wherein the relevant production features are combined to generate scores. A few examples of products built upon these automated scoring technologies include e-rater® and SpeechRater® developed by ETS, Intelligent Essay Assessor™ (IEA) and Versant™ Technology offered by Pearson, and amiSCORE from Analytic Measures Inc.

The advancement of AI in recent years has notably expanded the array of tools available to testers, enabling them to characterize L2 production within different assessment contexts. Simultaneously, the evolution of automated scoring technologies shows potential in enhancing resources and expanding the effectiveness of language learning and assessment. However, there persists a lack of clarity of how automated systems actually operationalize the constructs being measured, and it remains unclear whether automated scores fully measure the language ability of interest. It is also unclear how production features in this work might align with a comprehensive model of situated SFL proficiency. Perhaps in the future with greater collaboration, the questions regarding the resources of meaningful communication will be answered.

Discussion Questions

1. What are your main takeaways from this chapter in terms of how to conceptualize and measure the linguistic resources of communication?

2. What are some advantages and disadvantages of using SR, LP, and EP tasks to assess knowledge of grammatical forms, semantic meanings, propositional meanings, functional meanings, and implicational meanings?

3. What are the benefits and drawbacks of using automated scoring technologies to provide feedback on learners' linguistic resources of meaningful communication?

References

Ameriks, Y. (2009). *Investigating validity across two test forms of the examination of proficiency in English (ECPE): A multi-group structural equation modeling approach [Unpublished doctoral dissertation].* Teachers College, Columbia University.

Bachman, L. F. (1990). *Fundamental considerations of language testing.* Oxford University Press.

Bachman, L. F., & Palmer, A. S. (1996). *Language testing in practice.* Oxford University Press.

Bachman, L. F., & Palmer, A. S. (2010). *Language assessment in practice.* Oxford University Press.

Banerjee, H. L. (2019). Investigating the construct of topical knowledge in second language assessment: a scenario-based assessment approach. *Language Assessment Quarterly, 16*(2), 133–160.

Beltrán, J. L. (2023). *Examining the role of assistance in a scenario-based test of L2 argumentative speaking ability: A learning-oriented approach to the assessment of complex competencies [Unpublished doctoral dissertation].* Teachers College, Columbia University.

Beltrán, J. L., Joo, S. H., Eskin, D., Ralston, M., Vafaee, P., & Purpura, J. E. (2023). *Examining the use of a test of linguistic resources to stream candidates into proficiency-level appropriate scenario-based assessments of situated second & foreign language proficiency. Paper presented at 2023 language testing research colloquium,* New York, NY.

Bonk, W., & Oh, S. (2019). *What aspects of speech contribute to the perceived intelligibility of L2 speakers? Paper presented at 2019 language testing research colloquium,* Atlanta, GA.

Cambridge University Press, & Assessment. (2023). *B2 first: Handbook for teachers for exams.* Cambridge University Press & Assessment.

Canale, M. (1983). On some dimensions of language proficiency. In J. Oller (Ed.), *Issues in language testing research* (pp. 333–342). Newbury House.

Canale, M., & Swain, M. (1980). Theoretical bases of communicative approaches to second language teaching and testing. *Applied Linguistics, 1,* 1–47.

Celce-Murcia, M., & Larsen-Freeman, D. (1999). *The grammar book: An ESL/EFL teacher's course* (2nd ed.). Heinle.

Chalhoub-Deville, M. (2003). Second language interaction: current perspectives and future trends. *Language Testing, 20*(4), 369–383.

Chapelle, C. A. (1998). Construct definition and validity inquiry in SLA research. In L. F. Bachman & A. D. Cohen (Eds.), *Interfaces between second language acquisition and language testing research* (pp. 32–70). Cambridge University Press.

Council of Europe. (2020). *Common European Framework of Reference for Languages: Learning, teaching, assessment – Companion volume.* Council of Europe Publishing.

Douglas, D. (2000). *Assessing languages for specific purposes: Theory and practice.* Cambridge University Press.

Ellis, R., & Barkhuizen, G. (2005). *Analysing learner language.* Oxford University Press.

English Language Institute. (2006). *Michigan certificate examinations general information bulletin 2005–2006.* English Language Institute, The University of Michigan.

Gan, Z. (2012). Complexity measures, task types, and analytic evaluations of speaking proficiency in a school-based assessment context. *Language Assessment Quarterly, 9,* 133–151.

Grabowski, K. (2013). Investigating the construct validity of a role-play test designed to measure grammatical and pragmatic knowledge at multiple proficiency levels. In S. J. Ross & G. Kasper (Eds.), *Assessing second language pragmatics.* Palgrave Macmillan.

Gumperz, J. J. (1972). Introduction. In J. J. Gumperz & D. Hymes (Eds.), *Directions in sociolinguistics: The ethnography of communication* (pp. 1–25). Holt, Rinehart and Winston, Inc.

Gumperz, J. J. (1999). On interactional sociolinguistic methods. In S. Sarangi & C. Roberts (Eds.), *Talk, work, and institutional order* (pp. 453–471). Mouton de Gruyter.

Hawkins, J. A., & Filipovic, L. (2012). *Criterial features in L2 English: Specifying the reference levels of the common European framework* (English Profile Series, Vol. 1). Cambridge University Press.

Hulstijn, J. H., Schoonen, R., de Jong, N. H., Steinel, M. P., & Florijn, A. (2012). Linguistic competences of learners of Dutch as a second language at the B1 and B2 levels of speaking proficiency of the common European framework of reference for languages (CEFR). *Language Testing, 29*(2), 203–221.

Hymes, D. (1972). Models of interaction of language and social life. In J. J. Gumperz & D. Hymes (Eds.), *Directions in sociolinguistics: The ethnography of communication* (pp. 35–71). Holt, Rinehart and Winston, Inc.

Joo, S. H., Seong, Y., Suh, J., Jung, J. Y., & Purpura, J. E. (2023). Assessing writing through a scenario-based Korean proficiency test. *Assessing Writing, 58*, 100766.

Kim, H. J. (2009). *Investigating the effects of context and task type on second language speaking ability [Unpublished doctoral dissertation]*. Teachers College, Columbia University.

Lado, R. (1961). *Language testing*. Longman.

Liao, Y.-F. A. (2009). *Construct validation study of the GEPT reading and listening sections: Re-examining the models of L2 reading and listening abilities and their relations to lexico-grammatical knowledge [Unpublished doctoral dissertation]*. Teachers College, Columbia University.

Milton, J., & Alexiou, T. (2008). Vocabulary size in Greek as a foreign language and the common European framework of reference for languages. *Journal of Applied Linguistics, 24*, 35–52.

Milton, J., & Alexiou, T. (2009). Vocabulary size and the common European framework of reference for languages. In *Vocabulary studies in first and second language acquisition: The interface between theory and application* (pp. 194–211). Palgrave Macmillan UK.

Norris, J. M., & Ortega, L. (2009). Towards an organic approach to investigating CAF in instructed SLA: the case of complexity. *Applied Linguistics, 30*(4), 555–578.

Oh, S. (2022). The use of spelling and reference tools in second language writing: their impact on students' writing performance and process. *Journal of Second Language Writing, 57*, 100916.

Ortega, L. (2003). Syntactic complexity measures and their relationship to L2 proficiency: a research synthesis of college level L2 writing. *Applied Linguistics, 4*, 492–518.

Polio, C., & Shea, M. C. (2014). An investigation into current measures of linguistic accuracy in second language writing research. *Journal of Second Language Writing, 26*, 10–27.

Purpura, J. E. (1998). Investigating the effects of strategy use and second language test performance with high- and low-ability test takers: a structural equation modeling approach. *Language Testing, 15*(3), 333–379.

Purpura, J. E. (2004). *Assessing grammar*. Cambridge, England: Cambridge University Press.

Purpura, J. E. (2014). Assessing grammar. In A. J. Kunnan (Ed.), *The companion to language assessment*. Oxford: Wiley.

Purpura, J. E. (2016). Assessing meaning. In E. Shohamy & L. Or (Eds.), *Encyclopedia of language and education, Vol. 7. Language testing and assessment*. Springer International Publishing.

Purpura, J. E. (2018). *Learning-oriented language assessment: a framework for considering the nexus of instruction, learning, and assessment in classroom contexts. Roundtable on teaching assessment to L2 teachers. Language testing research colloquium*, Auckland, New Zealand.

Purpura, J. E., Bino, A., Gallagher, J., Ingram, M., Kim, H.-J., Kim, H.-J., Kim, J.-W., & Tsai, C. (2001). *Achievement tests for on target 1*. Pearson Publishers.

Purpura, J. E., & Cumming, A. (2023). *Using a meaning-oriented model of second and foreign language proficiency to examine the higher-level French and Chinese DLPT5 exams*. Monterey, CA: Defense Language Institute's Foreign Language Center.

Purpura, J. E., & Dakin, J. W. (2020). Assessment of the linguistic resources of communication. In C. Chapelle (Ed.), *The concise Encyclopedia of applied linguistics: Assessment and evaluation* (pp. 1–10). Wiley.

Révész, A. (2009). Task complexity, focus on form, and second language development. *Studies in Second Language Acquisition, 31*, 437–470.

Seong, Y., (2023). *Using a scenario-based assessment approach to examine the cognitive dimension of second language academic speaking ability through the assessment of an integrated academic speaking competency [Unpublished doctoral dissertation]*. Teachers College, Columbia University.

Skehan, P. (1998). *A cognitive approach to language learning*. Oxford University Press.

Upshur, J. A. (1979). Functional proficiency theory and a research role for language tests. *Concepts in Language Testing: Some Recent Studies*, 75–100.

Wolfe-Quintero, K., Inagaki, S., & Kim, H.-Y. (1998). *Second language development in writing: Measures of fluency, accuracy and complexity (Technical report 17). University of Hawai'i Press*.

Xi, X. (2010). Automated scoring and feedback systems. *Language Testing, 27*(3), 291–300.

Yan, X., Kim, H. R., & Kim, J. Y. (2021). Dimensionality of speech fluency: examining the relationships among complexity, accuracy, and fluency (CAF) features of speaking performance on the Aptis test. *Language Testing, 38*(4), 485–510.

Zechner, K. (2020). Speech features: introduction to Part III. In K. Zechner & K. Evanini (Eds.), *Automated speaking assessment: Using language technologies to score spontaneous speech* (pp. 99–100). Routledge.

Zechner, K., & Evanini, K. (Eds.). (2020). *Automated speaking assessment: Using language technologies to score spontaneous speech.* Routledge.

Suggested Readings

Ellis, R., & Barkhuizen, G. (2005). *Analyzing learner language.* Oxford University Press.

Grabowski, K. (2013). Investigating the construct validity of a role-play test designed to measure grammatical and pragmatic knowledge at multiple proficiency levels. In S. J. Ross & G. Kasper (Eds.), *Assessing second language pragmatics.* Palgrave Macmillan.

Purpura, J. E. (2004). *Assessing grammar.* Cambridge University Press.

Purpura, J. E. (2016). Assessing meaning. In E. Shohamy & L. Or (Eds.), *Encyclopedia of Language and Education, Vol. 7. Language testing and assessment.* Springer International Publishing.

Zechner, K., & Evanini, K. (Eds.). (2020). *Automated speaking assessment: Using language technologies to score spontaneous speech.* Routledge.

CHAPTER 14

Assessing Vocabulary

John Read

Introduction

Vocabulary assessment as a distinct area of interest within language testing and assessment dates back to the 1980s. Of course, tests of vocabulary knowledge were created and used for educational purposes well before then, but it is difficult to locate more than a few published articles on the design and validation of vocabulary tests for second language learners in earlier decades of the 20th century. In the United Kingdom, vocabulary assessment did not receive much attention from the major examining boards. In the best-documented case, the Cambridge proficiency exams were originally based on subjectively marked essay writing, translation, and the appreciation of literature. It was not until the mid-1970s that these exams included multiple-choice vocabulary items in their reading papers (Weir et al., 2013). On the other hand, partly in reaction to the elitist form of foreign language education represented by the Cambridge exams, Harold Palmer emerged in the 1920s as a major figure in English Language Teaching, advocating a functional method that gave priority to the careful selection and grading of course material. This meant a focus on useful, high-frequency vocabulary as the basis for both communication in the classroom and the provision of simplified reading materials. Another key figure was Michael West, who is best remembered as the author of the *General Service List of English Words* (GSL) (West, 1953), composed of around 2000 of the most frequent and useful word families, including figures for the relative frequency of different meanings and uses of the words. The GSL remained as the definitive statement of high-frequency vocabulary in English for L2 learners until the early 21st century. Although the work of these scholars did not involve vocabulary testing as such, the principles of frequency of occurrence and usefulness of words are fundamental to the design of the vocabulary assessments to be discussed in this chapter.

Vocabulary tests had a more prominent role in the United States than in Britain. Beginning in the 1920s, American educational assessment came to be dominated by psychometric principles, with the multiple-choice format being generally accepted as the most reliable and practical basis for measurement. The testing of word knowledge lent itself well to this form of assessment, as is clear from Lado's (1961) pioneering work on language testing. Vocabulary items were a key component of the Test of English as a Foreign Language (TOEFL) from its launch in 1965 at least until the 1990s (Read, 2000). The testing of vocabulary in a relatively decontextualized manner came under increasing criticism in the 1980s from those who advocated more integrative and communicative test formats, especially for

The Concise Companion to Language Assessment, First Edition. Edited by Antony John Kunnan.
© 2025 John Wiley & Sons, Inc. Published 2025 by John Wiley & Sons, Inc.

206 Chapter 14 Assessing Vocabulary

assessing language proficiency. It is worth noting that Bachman and Palmer's (1996) influential model of communicative language ability assigned vocabulary a very subsidiary role as a component of organizational competence. Similarly, Purpura (this volume) sees the testing of vocabulary knowledge as an integral component of grammar assessment. Thus, there is a real sense that vocabulary testing went outside the mainstream of language assessment until it has come back in the past two decades.

Some Key Concepts

The construct that vocabulary tests set out to assess has never been fully articulated. Henriksen (1999) proposed that there were three dimensions involved in the development of second language vocabulary knowledge: partial to precise knowledge of word meaning; depth of knowledge; and receptive to productive use ability. However, the most influential statement of what constitutes vocabulary knowledge is Nation's often-quoted table of what it means to know a word (see Table 14.1). This can be seen as essentially a static statement about declarative knowledge of words, which does not presume to specify the relative significance of the different aspects of knowledge and how they develop. Table 14.1 embodies two distinctions that have long been the focus of attention in vocabulary testing – one implicit and the other explicit. The implicit distinction is between breadth and depth of knowledge, and the explicit one is receptive versus productive knowledge. These also figure prominently in Henriksen's (1999) three dimensions, as cited above. Let us look at each of these in turn.

TABLE 14.1

What is involved in knowing a word?

Form	spoken	R	What does the word sound like?
		P	How is the word pronounced?
	written	R	What does the word look like?
		P	How is the word written and spelled?
	word parts	R	What parts are recognizable in this word?
		P	What word parts are needed to express the meaning?
Meaning	form and meaning	R	What meaning does this word form signal?
		P	What word form can be used to express this meaning?
	concepts and referents	R	What is included in the concept?
		P	What items can the concept refer to?
	associations	R	What other words could we use instead of this one?
Use	grammatical functions	R	In what patterns does the word occur?
		P	In what patterns must we use this word?
	collocations	R	What words or types of words occur with this one?
		P	What words or types of words must we use with this one?
	constraints on use (register, frequency, . . .)	R	Where, when, and how often would we expect to meet this word?
		P	Where, when, and how often can we use this word?

Notes: In column 3, R = receptive knowledge, P = productive knowledge.
Source: Nation (2022, p. 54) / Cambridge University Press.

Breadth and Depth of Knowledge

Anderson and Freebody (1981) are credited with distinguishing *breadth* as being "the number of words for which the person knows at least some of the significant aspects of meaning," from *depth*, where a person's understanding of a word "conveys to him or her all of the distinctions that would be understood by an ordinary adult under normal circumstances" (pp. 92–93). The focus here is on a limited versus richer understanding of word meaning. Other authors have made the distinction in different terms (Read, 2004), but it remains a somewhat ill-defined concept.

In practice, breadth of knowledge normally involves being able to make the form – meaning link: knowing the meaning of an L2 word, given its written form, or vice versa: knowing the written form of an L2 word, giving its meaning. This link has typically been assessed by means of test formats such as multiple-choice items or multiple matching of words and definitions. Such formats are favored for tests of vocabulary size because the simplicity of the task allows for a large sample of words to be assessed within a single test, to provide more reliable estimates of the learners' vocabulary size.

Looking back at Nation's table, it can be seen that the form and meaning link is just one aspect of vocabulary knowledge. Thus, we can understand *depth* as encompassing in principle all of the other aspects of word knowledge. A number of researchers (e.g., González-Fernández & Schmitt, 2019; Read & Dang, 2022) have administered multiple tests of aspects such as knowledge of word parts, multiple meanings, collocations, and associations for a set of target words in order to investigate depth of knowledge in this sense. Other projects have operationalized depth of knowledge primarily in terms of one particular aspect: Wesche and Paribakht's (1996) Vocabulary Knowledge Scale was designed to elicit learners' self-assessment of how well they know the meaning of particular target words; Sasao and Webb's (2017) Word Part Levels Test assesses knowledge of the form, meaning, and use of affixes in English; and several authors have devised tests of collocational knowledge (Gyllstad, 2020).

One type of test that has come to be most widely linked with assessing depth of knowledge is the word associates format (Read, 1993, 1998). As the name indicates, it mostly draws on word associations, along with collocations, as in this example:

team			
alternative	chalk	ear	<u>group</u>
orbit	<u>scientists</u>	<u>sport</u>	<u>together</u>
(The intended answers are underlined.)			

The format was originally conceived as an efficient means of assessing some aspects of vocabulary depth, so that a reasonably large sample of target words could be covered in a similar manner to a vocabulary size test. Although Read's two tests have the highest profile, there have been numerous other initiatives to devise word associates tests and explore the potential of the format in a variety of educational contexts (for a review, see Zhang & Koda, 2017).

Word association is one component of Nation's table of word knowledge, as shown above. However, it is also the basis for a distinctly different approach to defining the construct of depth, which draws on the psycholinguistic concept of the mental lexicon (Fitzpatrick & Thwaites, 2020), envisaged as a complex and dynamic network of connections among the words that a language user has some knowledge of. This is in fact how Henriksen (1999) defined her second dimension of vocabulary development, which she labeled as depth of knowledge. It has also inspired a considerable body of research by Meara (2009) and his associates, who developed several measures that elicit associations from learners in order to explore what they reveal about the changing states of the learners' lexical knowledge. These measures are interesting, small-scale tools for use by researchers rather than tests that have been developed for pedagogical purposes.

208 Chapter 14 Assessing Vocabulary

Thus, although breadth is a relatively straightforward concept, depth is more varied in the way that it is conceived and measured. From a teaching perspective, it is probably most useful to think of it as encouraging learners to go beyond the form–meaning link to acquire the various other aspects of word knowledge specified in Nation's table. One question that arises, though, is to what extent learners' word knowledge naturally deepens as the size of their vocabulary and their general proficiency in the language expand over time. In a comprehensive review of research on the breadth–depth distinction, Schmitt (2014) found that few definite conclusions could be drawn, because of the diverging ways in which depth was defined, the interrelated nature of the components of vocabulary knowledge, and the generally poor quality of tests intended to measure depth.

Receptive and Productive Knowledge

The receptive and productive distinction is incorporated as an additional component in Nation's (2022) table of word knowledge above and is the third of Henriksen's (1999) three dimensions of vocabulary development. It reflects two familiar observations: that the number of words we can recognize and understand is somewhat larger than the number that we use in speech or writing, and it seems that we need to know more about a word in order to use it ourselves. When it comes to assessment, though, the two terms have been used rather loosely, as Read (2000) pointed out. In particular, "receptive" knowledge has typically been assessed by means of selected-response test formats such as multiple choice or multiple word–definition matching, whereas tests of "productive" knowledge have used constructed-response formats such as gap-filling or cloze-type tasks. Another strategy, which arguably provides the most direct comparison, is to set twin translation tasks, whereby giving the meaning of an L2 word in L1 is "receptive," whereas giving the L2 word in response to an L1 meaning is "productive" (Webb, 2008). It is better to use the terms "recognition" and "recall" when these types of test format are involved, to avoid any implication that performance on such test items gives direct evidence of the test takers' ability either to comprehend words when they occur in spoken or written texts or to use words in their own speaking or writing. These abilities are better assessed through embedding vocabulary assessment in more communicative tasks.

Measuring Vocabulary Size

One of the enduring issues in vocabulary assessment is how to estimate the vocabulary size of various groups of language users: adult L1 users, children of varying ages, and, more recently, learners at various stages of L2 development. As Nation and Coxhead (2021) show in their comprehensive account of work on the vocabulary size of L1 users, most previous studies dating back to the early 20th century suffered from methodological flaws, particularly related to obtaining an adequate sample of words to be tested and in defining what is meant by a "word." These errors have been largely corrected in contemporary work. Estimates of the vocabulary size of comparable L1 users represent useful benchmarks for determining the adequacy of learners' vocabulary knowledge at various stages of their L2 acquisition. Vocabulary size tests have practical value for placement and diagnostic purposes, in planning vocabulary teaching in the classroom, and as research tools.

The Vocabulary Levels Test (VLT)

Two tests that are broadly seen as measuring vocabulary size have had an outsize influence on second language vocabulary assessment since the 1980s. We begin with the Vocabulary Levels Test (VLT), a modest instrument originally designed for classroom use and published in 1983 by Paul Nation in a magazine for teachers. It consisted of five sections sampling four word-frequency levels (2000, 3000, 5000, and 10,000) and a selection of academic vocabulary.

This reflected its origins in a preuniversity EAP program at the author's university in New Zealand. It used a simple word-definition matching format, with 18 test items at each level. Intended as a diagnostic tool, it was accompanied by a table to guide teachers in planning vocabulary learning activities according to which level(s) of the test their learners had mastered (Nation, 1990, p. 263).

The test gained wider currency when it was included as an appendix in Nation's (1990) pioneering book on L2 vocabulary teaching and learning and started to be used for other purposes, such as for placement in language teaching programs and as a kind of standard measure of vocabulary knowledge in research studies on vocabulary learning. In the early 1990s, Norbert Schmitt wrote a larger pool of test items that became the basis for two forms of a revised version of the test. The number of items for each section of the test was increased from 18 to 30, in the interests of reliability. To conduct a validation study, Schmitt et al. (2001) assembled a large convenience sample of 801 English learners from about 30 different countries. The majority were preparing for or engaging in English-medium study at the university level, but more than a third were studying General English. Thus, the test was validated more as a generic measure of vocabulary knowledge than one that was tailored for a clearly defined purpose or learner population. The researchers undertook numerous analyses of the test scores, including reliability, item analysis, implicational scaling of the four frequency levels, factor analysis of the five sections, equivalence of the two test forms, and retrospective verbal reports from a small subsample of the test takers. Collectively, the results produced ample evidence for the quality of the test in the terms under which it was evaluated, and the study set a new benchmark for the validation of vocabulary tests.

A more recent development is the "updated" VLT (Webb et al., 2017). It draws on Nation's (2020) BNC/COCA word frequency data, but more significantly it covers a continuous sequence of word frequencies from the first 1000 to the fifth 1000 (K1–K5) levels and excludes the previous academic vocabulary section. The authors argue that this gives a more coherent coverage of the English vocabulary that most learners will know or need to know. Validation of the test was undertaken within Messick's framework, drawing primarily on a series of Rasch analyses of test data obtained from a similarly diverse worldwide learner population as that used by Schmitt et al. (2001). As with the earlier study, Webb et al. (2017) discuss the uses of the test only in broad terms, focusing particularly on what cut score represents mastery of each frequency level.

The VLT has often been described as a measure of vocabulary size. This represents a misunderstanding of its original purpose and its suitability to estimate how many words are known overall in any meaningful way. It was restricted in its frequency range and its discontinuous coverage of the levels. In fact, Nation (2016) defines levels tests as a separate category of instruments that assess a limited range of high-frequency vocabulary for pedagogical purposes, whereas size tests are designed to make a more comprehensive estimate of vocabulary knowledge in research studies. The updated VLT is now a good example of a levels test in this redefined sense.

Other measures of size

An early initiative to measure vocabulary size was the set of tests developed by Goulden et al. (1990). The tests each consisted of a list of 50 words ordered by frequency, and the task was simply to self-assess whether the test taker knew a meaning of each word or not, with a provision to check words on the margin of being known or unknown. The reliance on a relatively pure form of self-assessment restricted the pedagogical utility of the tests, and they were used largely for research purposes to estimate the vocabulary size of native speakers and advanced learners.

Self-assessment is an essential element of another size measure, the Yes/No format, introduced in the L2 assessment literature by Meara and Buxton (1987). Again, test takers were

210 **Chapter 14** Assessing Vocabulary

presented with a list of words to respond to from a wide range of frequency levels, but a key feature was the inclusion of a certain proportion of pseudo-words. This provided a basis for adjusting the scores of test takers who were assumed to be overstating their vocabulary knowledge if they responded "Yes" to pseudo-words. The simplicity of the task was belied by the complexity involved in finding a scoring procedure that would accurately fit the range of response behaviors of the test takers in different educational contexts (Huibregtse et al., 2002). Versions of the Yes/No format have been used as placement measures in language schools. Meara's current version, which is available on his website (www.lognostics.co.uk), estimates vocabulary size up to the 10,000 word level.

On a much larger scale, Brysbaert et al. (2021) used the Yes/No format in their crowdsourcing research to determine which English words are actually known by L2 learners around the world. Their numbers were huge – 17 million participants responding to 61,000 words, presented in individual tests of 70 words and 30 pseudo-words – and this allowed them to generate a word list ranked in terms of degree and speed of recognition by this large body of learners. The ranking of words was noticeably at variance with that found in conventional word frequency lists derived from computer corpora. This certainly has implications for the design of vocabulary size tests in the future, although it should be noted that Brysbaert et al. (2021) did not set out to estimate the vocabulary size of individual learners.

The Vocabulary Size Test (VST)

However, for now the most prominent measure of size is another creation by Paul Nation, the Vocabulary Size Test (VST). Developed in the 2000s, it made a similarly low-key entry into circulation as the VLT did before it. It was made freely available on Nation's website, but for the first few years the only published account of it was a short article in a teachers' journal in Japan in 2007. There was no validation study available until Beglar (2010). Even now, the most comprehensive description of the test is found in an unpublished paper on Nation's website (Nation, 2012). Nevertheless, the test has been very influential in the last 15 years. On the one hand, it has blossomed into a family of tests, and on the other, it has produced directly and indirectly a large amount of research and debate on issues related to the design and use of such tests.

The VST grew out of Nation's long-standing interest in measuring vocabulary size and drew on his ongoing work to compile an authoritative word frequency list based initially on the British National Corpus (BNC), with later input from the Corpus of Contemporary American English (COCA) (Nation, 2016). At the time the VST was developed, the word list comprised fourteen 1000-word-family sublists. Thus, 10 words were sampled from each sublist as the target words for a 140-item test consisting of four-option multiple-choice items, with the target word presented in a short non-defining sentence in the stem:

ERRATIC: He was erratic.
a. without fault
b. very bad
c. very polite
d. unsteady

The raw score out of 140 was intended to be multiplied by 100 to give an estimate of the test taker's vocabulary size, within the limits of the overall 14,000 word frequency list. Beglar's (2010) study was based on Rasch analysis conducted within Messick's framework for test validation, with a total of 197 participants, including Japanese university students with varying levels of English proficiency and a small group of L1 users. The results showed the test had excellent measurement characteristics in terms of reliability, unidimensionality, and measurement invariance, and a shorter 70-item version exhibited similar qualities.

Since the original test, a 100-item version has been developed, sampling from an expanded 20,000 word-family list, with just 5 words from each frequency level. With its larger coverage of English vocabulary, this version is intended for use primarily with L1 users at secondary school level and above to investigate, for example, the comparative vocabulary size of students from mainstream and disadvantaged backgrounds (Nation & Coxhead, 2021).

For L2 learners, there are also bilingual versions of the original VST for at least nine languages, where the multiple-choice options are written in the learners' L1 rather than in English. The bilingual versions have been consistently shown to yield higher scores for specific learner groups, with the assumption that definitions in L1 reduce the potentially confounding factor of ability to comprehend definitions in English, especially for lower-level learners (Nguyen & Nation, 2011). With regard to the Russian bilingual version, Elgort (2013) raised the issue of the role of cognates in test performance. She found that 34% of the English target words in the test were Russian cognates, a significantly higher proportion than in Russian vocabulary generally, and there was evidence that this had boosted the test takers' scores. This is a broader issue in target word selection, especially if the concept of cognates is extended to include loanwords from English. It is a particular concern in designing tests for Japanese learners, whose everyday L1 vocabulary includes a substantial proportion of English loanwords. In tests tailored for particular L1 populations, it is possible to take account of this variable in test development, but it is a potentially uncontrolled factor in monolingual versions of tests administered to learners from diverse language backgrounds.

However, it should be emphasized that the full VST, whether it be the 14K or the 20K version, is suitable primarily for advanced learners. For those at lower levels of proficiency, a levels test such as the updated VLT (Webb et al., 2017) will be more appropriate for most purposes. Rather than estimating total vocabulary size, a levels test is designed to assess mastery of the specific word-frequency levels included in the test.

Current Issues

There are other issues that apply to the VST but that have become matters for more general debate among vocabulary researchers. One is the appropriate unit of analysis for vocabulary. The VLT and the VST are both based on word lists that are organized into **word families**, consisting of a stem or headword, together with its inflected forms and regular, frequent derivatives of the word, according to criteria originally formulated by Bauer and Nation (1993). For example, the *preserve* family includes the inflections *preserves*, *preserved*, and *preserving* as well as the derived forms *preserver(s)*, *preservative(s)*, and *preservation*. The argument is that if learners know the core meaning of *preserve* – to keep something alive, safe, or in good condition – it is not difficult for them to understand the other members of the family with some basic knowledge of English morphology, especially if the words are supported by contextual clues in a written text.

This assumption is being increasingly questioned by those who advocate the **lemma** as a more appropriate unit of analysis. A lemma is a stem word that represents just its inflected forms. In the example above, *preserve* is a lemma that covers *preserves*, *preserved*, and *preserving*; the three derived forms are separate lemmas. Several research studies have shown that learners, particularly at lower levels of proficiency, often cannot make the semantic connection between derived forms and the headword within a word family (McLean, 2018; Sasao & Webb, 2017). Classification by lemma helps to distinguish words according to their part of speech (e.g., *pick* as a noun and a verb) and to separate derived forms with distinct meanings from the stem word. It also takes account of the fact that a derived form can be more frequent than the stem form (e.g., *organization* and *organize*). Nation (2016) argues that the choice of unit should reflect the proficiency level of the learners and the purpose of the assessment. A unit like the lemma is more appropriate in assessing vocabulary knowledge for productive use.

A second issue is the choice of item format for vocabulary size tests. The conventional approach has been to use selected-response formats such as Yes/No, multiple-choice, and

212 Chapter 14 Assessing Vocabulary

multiple matching of words and definitions, which all offer the opportunity to guess from the responses provided. Each format can be designed to reduce the chances of successful blind guessing; however, numerous recent studies have shown that guessing and test-taking strategies can boost test takers' scores substantially – and differentially (Gyllstad et al., 2015; Stewart, 2014). This is of particular concern in a test like the VST where the raw score is multiplied by 100 (or 200 in the case of the 20 K version) to give an estimate of vocabulary size.

Selected-response test items assess vocabulary knowledge at the recognition level. However, some authors (e.g., Stoeckel et al., 2021) consider that meaning recall is more appropriate, which means the use of constructed-response test items requiring the test takers to supply the meanings of a set of target words either in L1 or L2. The case for meaning recall is supported by studies that show the superior performance of such tests in correlating with reading comprehension ability (Zhang & Zhang, 2020). There are practical constraints in using these tests that need to be weighed up against the convenience and objective scoring of selected-response test items. Meaning recall involves more time-consuming and less reliable scoring because of the range of possible answers that test takers may produce. It is more feasible when the test takers share a common L1 and when a bank of accepted responses can be built, either as a manual answer key or as automated scoring in a computer-based test. As researchers continue to investigate measures of meaning recall, it is very likely that meaning recognition tests will have an ongoing place in classroom assessments.

Future Directions

As has been shown so far, vocabulary assessment has always had a close relationship to the development of reading comprehension ability. Conversely, too little attention has been paid to the aural vocabulary required for listening. A small amount of research confirms that a vocabulary test with spoken input correlates better with a listening comprehension measure than a conventional written vocabulary test does (Matthews, 2018; Milton et al., 2010). However, few tests of listening vocabulary are available. Milton et al. (2010) adopted the Yes/No format in their test AuralLex, whereas Matthews (2018) used a partial dictation task, in which the test takers write the target word in a sentence as it is read aloud. There is also the Listening Vocabulary Levels Test (LVLT) created by McLean et al. (2015), which has a similar structure to the updated VLT (Webb et al., 2017). The items have a VST-type bilingual format, with the stem sentence and the target word spoken in English and the response options written in Japanese. These represent three models of listening vocabulary tests, but much more work is needed to explore further how knowledge of words in spoken form contributes to the listening comprehension ability of learners at different proficiency levels and to produce operational tests for particular assessment purposes.

Selected-response vocabulary items have lent themselves well to computer-based testing from an early stage in its development. Computer administration allows for a more controlled presentation of the input material and for the recording of reaction times to individual test items. Speed of access to the mental lexicon underlies fluent performance of both receptive and productive tasks, and reaction times are a basic tool in more psycholinguistic investigations of vocabulary ability (Gottfroid, 2020). To date, there have been only a few applications of this approach in educational contexts, notably by Harrington (2018) and his colleagues with their Timed Yes/No (TYN) tests combining accuracy and speed of response as predictors of achievement. The recording of reaction times was also a component of the data-gathering by Brysbaert et al. (2021) in their crowdsourcing project to rank English words according to their familiarity and usefulness to learners on a worldwide scale. A more targeted application of computer technology would be the use of item response theory to establish difficulty estimates for large numbers of vocabulary test items, which could then be used in computer-adaptive tests for learners with different L1s and levels of proficiency (Stoeckel et al., 2021).

More generally, an obvious future direction for large-scale language testing is the use of artificial intelligence (AI) and other automated technologies to substantially reduce costs and time in the development and administration of tests. Vocabulary test formats are particularly suited to the application of such tools. Settles et al. (2020) describe how machine learning and natural language processing were used to produce automated estimates of the difficulties of both real words and pseudo-words for the Yes/No vocabulary sections of the Duolingo English Test, thus obviating the need for costly pilot testing of test items. In another context, Luo et al. (2022) have explored how effectively AI could generate distractors for multiple-choice items to test vocabulary in Chinese, as compared to items written by human experts. In a validation study, the two types of item functioned somewhat differently, but the results showed the promise of automated item generation techniques.

In a recent critique of vocabulary assessment, Schmitt et al. (2020) point out weaknesses in the design and validation of some vocabulary tests that have been widely disseminated, and they call for the implementation of higher professional standards in the development of such tests in the future. This would include a clearer specification and justification of the purposes for which the assessments can be used and with which populations of learners. It represents a move away from the generic approach that has tended to dominate the field until now. Although well-constructed vocabulary tests are quite robust, there is still a need to obtain evidence that they will work effectively for their intended purpose in specific educational settings, regardless of whether they are developed in the conventional manner or by automated procedures.

Discussion Questions

1. To what extent do the different aspects of vocabulary knowledge identified by Nation (Table 14.1) need to be explicitly taught or assessed? Does such knowledge naturally grow as one's proficiency in a second language develops?

2. Discuss the advantages and disadvantages of using selected-response and constructed-response test items to assess vocabulary knowledge.

References

Anderson, R. C., & Freebody, P. (1981). Vocabulary knowledge. In J. T. Guthrie (Ed.), *Comprehension and teaching: Research reviews* (pp. 77–177). International Reading Association.

Bachman, L. F., & Palmer, A. S. (1996). *Language testing in practice*. Oxford University Press.

Bauer, L., & Nation, P. (1993). Word families. *International Journal of Lexicography, 6*(4), 253–279. https://doi.org/10.1093/ijl/6.4.253.

Beglar, D. (2010). A Rasch-based validation of the Vocabulary Size Test. *Language Testing, 27*(1), 101–118. https://doi.org/10.1177/0265532209340194.

Brysbaert, M., Keuleers, E., & Mandera, P. (2021). Which words do English non-native speakers know? New supranational levels based on yes/no decision. *Second Language Research, 37*(2), 207–231. https://doi.org/10.1177/0267658320934526.

Elgort, I. (2013). Effects of L1 definitions and cognate status of test items on the Vocabulary Size Test. *Language Testing, 30*(2), 253–272. https://doi.org/10.1177/0265532212459028.

Fitzpatrick, T., & Thwaites, P. (2020). Word association research and the L2 lexicon. *Language Teaching, 53*(3), 237–274. https://doi.org/10.1017/s0261444820000105.

214 Chapter 14 Assessing Vocabulary

González-Fernández, B., & Schmitt, N. (2019). Word knowledge: exploring the relationships and order of acquisition of vocabulary knowledge components. *Applied Linguistics, 41*(4), 481–505. https://doi.org/10.1093/applin/amy057.

Gottfroid, A. (2020). Sensitive measures of vocabulary knowledge and processing: expanding Nation's framework. In S. Webb (Ed.), *The Routledge handbook of vocabulary studies* (pp. 433–453). Routledge. https://doi.org/10.4324/9780429291586-28.

Goulden, R., Nation, P., & Read, J. (1990). How large can a receptive vocabulary be? *Applied Linguistics, 11*(4), 341–363. https://doi.org/10.1093/applin/11.4.341.

Gyllstad, H. (2020). Measuring knowledge of multiword items. In S. Webb (Ed.), *The Routledge handbook of vocabulary studies* (pp. 387–405). Routledge. https://doi.org/10.4324/9780429291586-28.

Gyllstad, H., Valkaite, L., & Schmitt, N. (2015). Assessing vocabulary size through multiple-choice formats: issues with guessing and sampling rates. *ITL International Journal of Applied Linguistics, 166*(2), 276–303. https://doi.org/10.1075/itl.166.2.04gyl.

Harrington, M. (2018). *Lexical facility: Size, recognition speed and consistency as dimensions of second language vocabulary knowledge.* Palgrave Macmillan. https://doi.org/10.1057/978-1-137-37262-8.

Henriksen, B. (1999). Three dimensions of vocabulary development. *Studies in Second Language Acquisition, 21*(2), 303–317. https://doi.org/10.1017/S0272263199002089.

Huibregtse, I., Admiraal, W., & Meara, P. (2002). Scores on a yes/no vocabulary test: correction for guessing and response style. *Language Testing, 19*(3), 227–245. https://doi.org/10.1191/0265532202lt229oa.

Lado, R. (1961). *Language testing.* Longmans Green.

Luo, Y., Wei, W., & Zheng, Y. (2022). Artificial intelligence-generated and human expert-designed vocabulary tests: a comparative study. *SAGE Open*, 1–12. https://doi.org/10.1177/21582440221082130.

Matthews, J. (2018). Vocabulary for listening: emerging evidence for high and mid-frequency vocabulary knowledge. *System, 72*, 23–36. https://doi.org/10.1016/j.system.2017.10.005.

McLean, S. (2018). Evidence for the adoption of the flemma as an appropriate word counting unit. *Applied Linguistics, 39*(6), 823–845. https://doi.org/10.1093/applin/amw050.

McLean, S., Kramer, B., & Beglar, D. (2015). The creation and validation of a listening vocabulary levels test. *Language Teaching Research, 19*(6), 741–760. https://doi.org/10.1177/1362168814567889.

Meara, P. (2009). *Connected words: Word associations and second language vocabulary acquisition.* John Benjamins. https://doi.org/10.1075/lllt.24.

Meara, P., & Buxton, B. (1987). An alternative to multiple choice vocabulary tests. *Language Testing, 4*(2), 142–151. https://doi.org/10.1177/026553228700400202.

Milton, J., Wade, J., & Hopkins, N. (2010). Aural word recognition and oral competence in a foreign language. In R. Chacón-Beltrán, C. Abello-Contesse, M. Torreblanca-López & M. D. López-Jiménez (Eds.), *Further insights into nonnative vocabulary teaching and learning* (pp. 83–97). Multilingual Matters. https://doi.org/10.21832/9781847692900-007.

Nation, I. S. P. (1990). *Teaching and learning vocabulary.* Newbury House.

Nation, P. (2012). *The Vocabulary Size Test* (Unpublished paper). https://www.wgtn.ac.nz/lals/resources/paul-nations-resources/vocabulary-tests/the-vocabulary-size-test/Vocabulary-Size-Test-information-and-specifications.pdf.

Nation, I. S. P. (2016). *Making and using word lists for language learning and teaching.* John Benjamins. https://doi.org/10.1075/z.208.

Nation, I. S. P. (2020). *The BNC/COCA word family lists* (Unpublished paper). https://www.wgtn.ac.nz/lals/resources/paul-nations-resources/vocabulary-lists.

Nation, I. S. P. (2022). *Learning vocabulary in another language* (3rd ed.). Cambridge University Press. https://doi.org/10.1017/9781009093873.

Nation, I. S. P., & Coxhead, A. (2021). *Measuring native-speaker vocabulary size.* John Benjamins. https://doi.org/10.1075/z.233.

Nguyen, L. T. C., & Nation, P. (2011). A bilingual vocabulary size test of English for Vietnamese learners. *RELC Journal, 42*(1), 86–99. https://doi.org/10.1177/0033688210390264.

Read, J. (1993). The development of a new measure of L2 vocabulary knowledge. *Language Testing, 10*(3), 355–371. https://doi.org/10.1177/026553229301000308.

Read, J. (1998). Validating a test to measure depth of vocabulary knowledge. In A. J. Kunnan (Ed.), *Validation in language assessment* (pp. 41–60). Routledge. https://doi.org/10.4324/9780203053768.

Read, J. (2000). *Assessing vocabulary*. Cambridge University Press. https://doi.org/10.1017/CBO9780511732942.

Read, J. (2004). Plumbing the depths: how should the construct of vocabulary knowledge be defined? In P. Bogaards & B. Laufer (Eds.), *Vocabulary in a second language: Selection, acquisition and testing* (pp. 209–227). John Benjamins. https://doi.org/10.1075/lllt.10.

Read, J., & Dang, T. Y. N. (2022). Measuring depth of academic vocabulary knowledge. *Language Teaching Research.* Online First. https://doi.org/10.1177/13621688221105913.

Sasao, Y., & Webb, S. (2017). The Word Part Levels Test. *Language Teaching Research*, *21*(1), 12–30. https://doi.org/10.1177/1362168815586083.

Schmitt, N. (2014). Size and depth of vocabulary knowledge: what the research shows. *Language Learning*, *64*(4), 913–951. https://doi.org/10.1111/lang.12077.

Schmitt, N., Nation, P., & Kremmel, B. (2020). Moving the field of vocabulary assessment forward: the need for more rigorous test development and validation. *Language Teaching*, *53*(1), 109–120. https://doi.org/10.1017/S0261444819000326.

Schmitt, N., Schmitt, D., & Clapham, C. (2001). Developing and exploring the behaviour of two new versions of the Vocabulary Levels Test. *Language Testing*, *18*(1), 55–88. https://doi.org/10.1177/026553220101800103.

Settles, B., LaFlair, G. T., & Hagiwara, M. (2020). Machine learning-driven language assessment. *Transactions of the Association for Computational Linguistics*, *8*, 247–263. https://doi.org/10.1162/tacl_a_00310.

Stewart, J. (2014). Do multiple-choice options inflate estimates of vocabulary size on the VST? *Language Assessment Quarterly*, *11*(3), 271–282. https://doi.org/10.1080/15434303.2014.922977.

Stoeckel, T., McLean, S., & Nation, P. (2021). Limitations of size and levels tests of written receptive vocabulary knowledge. *Studies in Second Language Acquisition*, *43*(1), 181–203. https://doi.org/10.1017/S027226312000025X.

Webb, S. (2008). Receptive and productive vocabulary sizes of L2 learners. *Studies in Second Language Acquisition*, *30*(1), 79–95. https://doi.org/10.1017/S0272263108080042.

Webb, S., Sasao, Y., & Ballance, O. (2017). The updated Vocabulary Levels Test: developing and validating two new forms of the VLT. *ITL – International Journal of Applied Linguistics*, *168*(1), 34–70. https://doi.org/10.1075/itl.168.1.02web.

Weir, C. J., Vidakovic, I., & Galaczi, E. D. (2013). *Measured constructs: A history of Cambridge English examinations, 1913–2012.* Cambridge University Press.

Wesche, M. B., & Paribakht, T. S. (1996). Assessing second language vocabulary knowledge: depth vs. breadth. *Canadian Modern Language Review*, *53*(1), 13–39. https://doi.org/10.3138/cmlr.53.1.13.

West, M. (1953). *A general service list of English words.* Longmans Green.

Zhang, D., & Koda, K. (2017). Assessing L2 vocabulary depth with word associates format tests: issues, findings, and suggestions. *Asian-Pacific Journal of Second and Foreign Language Education*, *2*(1), 1–30. https://doi.org/10.1186/s40862-017-0024-0.

Zhang, S., & Zhang, X. (2020). The relationship between vocabulary knowledge and L2 reading/listening comprehension. *Language Teaching Research*, *26*(4), 696–725. https://doi.org/10.1177/1362168820913998.

Suggested Readings

Meara, P., & Miralpeix, I. (2017). *Tools for researching vocabulary.* Multilingual Matters. 10.21832/9781783096473.

Read, J. (2013). Research timeline: second language vocabulary assessment. *Language Teaching*, *46*(1), 41–52. https://doi.org/10.1017/S0261444812000377.

Schmitt, N. (2010). *Researching vocabulary: A vocabulary research manual.* Palgrave Macmillan. https://doi.org/10.1057/9780230293977.

Webb, S. (Ed.). (2020). *The Routledge handbook of vocabulary studies.* Routledge. https://doi.org/10.4324/9780429291586.

CHAPTER 15

Assessing Pronunciation

Talia Isaacs

Introduction

Accents are one of the most perceptually salient aspects of spoken language. Previous research has shown that linguistically untrained listeners are able to distinguish between native and non-native speakers under nonoptimal experimental conditions, including when the speech is played backward (Munro et al., 2010) or when it is in a language that listeners do not understand (Major, 2007). In fact, one of the earliest documented examples of language testing, the biblical Shibboleth test described in the *Book of Judges*, involved testing the identity of members of warring tribes based on whether they pronounced the word *shibboleth* "sheave of wheat" with a /ʃ/ or a /s/ sound at syllable onset, with fatal consequences if the "wrong" pronunciation betrayed their enemy status (Spolsky, 1995). In modern times, a less brutal but still high-stakes example is the use of so-called experts' analyses of speech to determine the legitimacy of asylum seekers' claims based on their *perceived* group identity (Fraser, 2009). Of course, such identity tests are far from foolproof, can lead to erroneous conclusions that could inform high-stakes decisions, and raise concerns about fairness. It is often unclear, for example, whether it is aspects of the speech signal that trigger unfavorable listener responses, or whether listener expectations that arise as a result of linguistic stereotyping lead listeners to assign qualities to the speech that are absent or distorted (Kang & Rubin, 2009).

Foreign accents tend to receive a disproportionate amount of attention precisely due to their perceptual salience. Despite the enduring reference to the native speaker as the "gold standard" of language knowledge (Levis, 2005), eradicating traces of a foreign accent is widely viewed by applied linguists as an unsuitable goal for L2 pronunciation instruction for several reasons. First, native-like attainment of phonology is an unrealistic goal for most adult L2 learners, not least possibly an undesirable goal for L2 speakers, since accent and identity are intertwined (Gatbonton & Trofimovich, 2008). Second, L2 speakers do not need to sound like native speakers to fully integrate into society or successfully carry out their academic or professional tasks (Derwing & Munro, 2009). Third, the global spread of English and its emergence as the international lingua franca renders conformity to native speaker norms inappropriate in many EFL settings (Jenkins, 2002). In fact, many native English speakers themselves do not speak prestige (standard) varieties of English (e.g., Received Pronunciation, General American English). For all of these reasons, having a native-like accent is an unsuitable benchmark for pronunciation assessment in the vast majority of language use contexts.

The emerging consensus among applied linguists is that what really counts in oral communication is not accent reduction or attaining a native-like standard but rather simply being

---

The Concise Companion to Language Assessment, First Edition. Edited by Antony John Kunnan.
© 2025 John Wiley & Sons, Inc. Published 2025 by John Wiley & Sons, Inc.

understandable to one's interlocutors and able to get the message across (Jenkins, 2002). In fact, over a decade of L2 pronunciation research has shown that having an L2 accent does not *necessarily* preclude L2 speech from being perfectly understandable, although it might. It is in cases when the presence of an L2 accent impedes listener understanding that explicit instruction is most needed to address learners' pronunciation difficulties (Derwing & Munro, 2009).

The theme of defining and operationalizing an appropriate assessment criterion for L2 pronunciation permeates this chapter. After providing reasons for the exclusion of pronunciation from L2 classrooms and its marginalization from mainstream L2 assessment research over the past several decades, the role of pronunciation in theoretical models of communicative competence and in L2 oral proficiency scales will be examined. Next, existing empirical evidence on the pronunciation features that should be taught and, by implication, tested will be considered, and research on individual differences in rater characteristics that could influence their judgments of L2 pronunciation will be discussed. This chapter will conclude with future directions in L2 pronunciation assessment research, with particular emphasis on technological innovations.

Previous Views or Conceptualization

In 1957, the English linguist J. R. Firth famously wrote, "you shall know a word by the company it keeps" (1957, p. 11). A quick perusal of the past several decades of L2 pronunciation research reveals that "pronunciation" has kept close company with the term "neglect" (e.g., Derwing & Munro, 2009). This disparaging association generally refers to the devaluation of pronunciation by some communicative proponents and its resulting de-emphasis in ESL classrooms. One reason for the exclusion of pronunciation from L2 communicative teaching is the belief that an overt focus on pronunciation is extraneous to helping learners achieve communicative competence (Celce-Murcia et al., 2010). To counter this view, Morley (1991) argued that "intelligible pronunciation is an essential component of communicative competence" and that "ignoring students' pronunciation needs is an abrogation of professional responsibility" (pp. 488–489), since poor pronunciation can be professionally and socially disadvantageous to L2 speakers. There is also evidence that adult L2 learners with "fossilized" pronunciation benefit from explicit pronunciation instruction (Derwing & Munro, 2009) and that a focus on pronunciation can be embedded in genuinely communicative activities (Trofimovich & Gatbonton, 2006).

Although the subject of L2 pronunciation *teaching* conjures up reference to neglect, there is at least a body of literature documenting this neglect. Not the same can be said about L2 pronunciation *assessment*, which, with the exception of literature on automated scoring, has been essentially dropped from the research agenda since the publication of Lado's seminal book, *Language Testing*, over six decades ago (Lado, 1961). In what remains the most comprehensive treatment of L2 pronunciation assessment to date, Lado devoted separate chapters to testing L2 learners' perception and production of individual sounds, stress, and intonation, offering concrete guidelines on item construction and test administration. Some of Lado's views on L2 pronunciation are timely, including challenges in defining a standard of intelligible (i.e., easily understandable) pronunciation. However, other ideas are clearly outdated. For example, operating under the premise that "language is a system of habits of communication" (p. 22), Lado held that where differences exist between sounds in the learner's first language (L1) and the target language, there will be problems, and these need to be systematically tested. However, predicting learner difficulties appears to be more nuanced than a simple inventory of differences between the L1 and L2 can account for. There is growing evidence, for example, that the accurate perception and production of L2 segments (i.e., vowel or consonant sounds) is mediated by learners' *perceptions* of how different a given sound is from

218 Chapter 15 Assessing Pronunciation

their existing L1 sound categories (Flege et al., 2003). In general, accurate perception/ production is more likely if the learner does not perceptually identify an L2 sound with any L1 sounds. This is because, if no difference is perceived, the learner will simply substitute the L1 sound for the L2 sound. In addition, contextual factors such as phonetic environment and lexical frequency also contribute to learner performance (Flege et al., 2003). Clearly, Lado's (1961) view that differences between L1 and L2 phoneme inventories should form the basis of L2 pronunciation tests oversimplifies the situation.

Due to advances in language testing and speech sciences research, there is a pressing need for an updated guide on L2 pronunciation assessment and item writing. As reported above, Lado's work is the only extensive treatment on the subject. Therefore, several decades later, this reference remains the starting point for any discussion on L2 pronunciation assessment and, thus, features prominently in this chapter.

Lado expressed concern about the subjective scoring of test takers' speech and proposed the use of more objective paper and pencil tests as an alternative to assessing test takers' L2 pronunciation production (e.g., using multiple choice). Such written tests have the advantage of facilitating the testing of large numbers of students without the added time or expense of recording and storing speech samples or double marking them. For example, the National Centre Test in Japan, a gatekeeping test used until recently for university admissions purposes, employed decontextualized written items of the sort that Lado proposed to test oral pronunciation skills (see http://school.js88.com/sd_article/dai/dai_center_data/pdf/2010Eng. pdf). The pronunciation component consisted of (i) *segmental items*, in which the test taker selects the word where the underlined sound is pronounced differently from the others (e.g., boot, goose, proof, wool; the vowel sound in "wool" /ʊ/ is different from the /u/ sound in the other choices) and (ii) *word stress items*, in which the test taker selects the word that follows the same primary stress pattern as the item in the prompt (e.g., fortunately → appreciate, elevator, manufacture, sympathetic; both "fortunately" and "elevator" have primary stress on the first syllable).

In an empirical study on retired National Centre Test items entitled "Written tests of pronunciation: Do they work?" conducted in a Japanese junior college, Buck (1989) found no evidence that they do. First, internal consistency coefficients (KR-20) for six pronunciation subtests were unacceptably low (range: −0.89 to 0.54) as were correlations between scores on the written items and on test takers' oral productions of those items (0.25 to 0.50). Correlations with read-aloud and extemporaneous speech task ratings were even lower (0.18 to 0.43). Several decades after the publication of Lado's (1961) book and Buck's (1989) article, there is still no empirical evidence that written pronunciation items constitute a reliable or valid measure of L2 pronunciation speaking ability. Thus, such written items should not be used as a proxy for oral pronunciation production in any assessment context.

Current Views or Conceptualization

Theoretical Conceptualization

The field of language testing has moved beyond Lado's (1961) focus on discrete-point testing and theoretical view of language as consisting of separate skills (speaking, reading, writing, listening) and components (e.g., vocabulary, grammar, pronunciation) toward expanded notions of communicative competence and communicative language ability. However, the assessment of L2 pronunciation has been left behind, with communicatively oriented theoretical frameworks not adequately accounting for the role of pronunciation. In Bachman's (1990) influential communicative language ability framework, for example, "phonology/graphology" appears to be a carryover from the skills-and-components models of the early 1960s

(Lado, 1961). However, the logic of pairing "phonology" with "graphology" (legibility of handwriting) is unclear. Notably, Bachman and Palmer's (1982) multitrait–multimethod study, which informed the development of Bachman's (1990) model, omitted the "phonology/graphology" variable from the analysis even though it was hypothesized to be an integral part of grammatical competence. This is because the authors claimed that phonology/graphology functions more as a channel than as a component, since pronunciation accuracy (and legibility) cannot be examined below a critical level at which communication breaks down. Bachman's reincorporation of phonology/graphology as a component in his 1990 model without explanation demonstrates the need for greater clarity on the role of pronunciation in communicative models.

In the L2 pronunciation literature, Levis (2005) characterized two "competing ideologies" or "contradictory principles" that have long governed research and pedagogical practice (p. 370). The first principle, the "*nativeness principle*," holds that the aim of pronunciation instruction should be to help L2 learners achieve native-like pronunciation by reducing L1 traces from their speech. The construct of "accentedness" in the L2 pronunciation literature, defined as listeners' *perceptions* of how different an L2 utterance sounds from the native-speaker norm (measured using rating scales), aligns with this principle. The second principle, the "*intelligibility principle*," holds that the goal of L2 pronunciation instruction should simply be to help L2 learners be understandable to their interlocutors – a view that most L2 researchers endorse and which is also "key to pronunciation assessment" (Levis, 2006, p. 252). However, the issue that Lado (1961) raised of "intelligible to whom" still resonates. To complicate matters, some scholars have depicted intelligibility as interactional between the speaker and the listener, whereas others have underscored that intelligibility is principally "hearer-based," or a property of the listener (Fayer & Krasinski, 1987, p. 313). Still others have criticized the burden that is implicitly placed on L2 speakers to achieve intelligibility, arguing that native speakers need to assume their share of the communicative responsibility (Lindemann, 2002).

Part of the problem is that intelligibility has been defined and measured in multifarious ways, which makes cross-study comparisons difficult (Isaacs, 2008). At least some of the confusion lies in the existence of broad and narrow definitions of the term. In its broad meaning, "intelligibility" refers to listeners' ability to understand L2 speech and is synonymous with "comprehensibility" (Levis, 2006). Reference to intelligibility as the appropriate goal of L2 pronunciation instruction and assessment conforms to this broad meaning. In its narrower sense, Derwing and Munro's (1997) conceptually clear definitional distinction between intelligibility and comprehensibility, which is increasingly pervasive in L2 pronunciation research, is useful to examine. Derwing and Munro define intelligibility as the amount of speech that listeners are able to understand (i.e., listeners' *actual* understanding). This construct is most often operationalized by computing the proportion of an L2 learner's utterance that the listener correctly orthographically transcribes. In contrast, comprehensibility, the more subjective measure, is defined as listeners' *perceptions* of how easily they understand L2 speech. This construct is operationalized by having raters record the degree to which they can understand L2 speech on a rating scale. Thus, comprehensibility, in its narrow definition, is instrumentally defined in that it necessitates a scale (i.e., a measurement apparatus) in the same way that measuring temperature necessitates a thermometer. That is, what distinguishes narrowly defined intelligibility from comprehensibility is not theory but, rather, the way these constructs have been operationalized. Hereafter, the term "comprehensibility" will therefore be used in its narrow sense whenever the notion of understandability is evoked in rating scales, with the exception of when the original wording from a given rating descriptor is retained. The term "intelligibility" will be used in both its broad and its narrow senses in the remainder of this chapter, and the sense in which it is being used will be specified. The role of pronunciation in general and comprehensibility and accentedness in particular in current L2 speaking scales is the subject of the next section.

220 Chapter 15 Assessing Pronunciation

The Role of Pronunciation in Rating Scales

Theory often informs rating scale development. Because the theoretical basis for L2 pronunciation in communicative frameworks is weak as is our understanding of major holistic constructs, it follows that there are numerous shortcomings in the way pronunciation has been modeled in existing rating scales. First, pronunciation is sometimes omitted as a rating criterion. For example, pronunciation was excluded from the Common European Framework of Reference benchmark levels due to the high misfit values (i.e., substantial unmodeled variance) obtained for the pronunciation descriptors (North, 2000). Other scales that do include pronunciation only incorporate this criterion haphazardly. For instance, in the recently retired version of the 10-level ACTFL oral Proficiency Guidelines (1 = novice low, 10 = superior), pronunciation is referred to in levels 1, 3, 4, and 5 of the scale but is omitted from level 2 (novice mid). It is unlikely that pronunciation does not contribute to L2 oral proficiency at this precise point of the scale (level 2) when it is relevant at both neighboring levels. The inconsistency of reference to pronunciation or its exclusion altogether implies that pronunciation is not an important component of L2 speaking proficiency, making it likely that "pronunciation will become a stealth factor in ratings and a source of unsystematic variation in the test" (Levis, 2006, p. 245).

Another limitation of proficiency scales is that their descriptors are often too vague to articulate a coherent construct. For example, the highest level of the TOEIC Speaking Proficiency Level Descriptors reads "their pronunciation and intonation and stress are at all times highly intelligible," and the level immediately below describes "minor difficulties with pronunciation, intonation, or hesitation when creating language" (Educational Testing Service, 2018). Similarly, the level 2 descriptor for the TOEFL iBT "Integrated Speaking Rubrics" (Educational Testing Service, 2009) states, "speech is clear at times, though it exhibits problems with pronunciation, intonation, or pacing and so may require significant listener effort" (p. 190).

Problems with intelligibility may obscure meaning in places (but not throughout). These descriptors only vaguely reference the error types that lead to listener difficulty. In addition, the use of the term "pronunciation" differs across the scales. In the IELTS scale, "pronunciation" could be interpreted as referring to both segmental (individual sounds) and suprasegmental phenomena (e.g., intonation, rhythm, word stress), although this is not specified. In contrast, in the TOEFL iBT, the juxtaposition of "pronunciation" with "intonation" suggests that "pronunciation" refers only to segmental features. Clarifying the meaning of "pronunciation" is necessary to convey what exactly is being measured and is crucial for score interpretation.

Scales that employ relativistic descriptors offer even less clarity about the focal construct. For example, Morley's (1991) Speech Intelligibility Index makes reference to "basically unintelligible," "largely unintelligible," "reasonably intelligible," "largely intelligible," and "fully intelligible" speech (p. 502). However, these semantic differences do little to guide raters on how the qualities manifested in test takers' performance samples align with the scale levels.

Finally, a major shortcoming in the way that pronunciation is modeled in current L2 oral proficiency scales is that some scales conflate the dimensions of comprehensibility and accentedness. For example, the highest level of the now retired Cambridge ESOL "Common Scale for Speaking" groups "easily understood" pronunciation with "native-like" control of "many features" (University of Cambridge ESOL Examinations, 2008, p. 70). Similarly, in a scale showing assessed traits for the automatically scored Pearson Test of English (PTE) Academic picture description task, the test provider characterizes the highest level of pronunciation performance as, "all vowels and consonants are produced in a manner that is easily understood by regular speakers of the language" (Pearson, 2023, p. 16). Although this part of the descriptor aligns with a comprehensibility construct, they also explicitly label this Pronunciation level as "Native-like" at the top of the descriptor. This practice contradicts a large volume of L2 pronunciation research showing that comprehensibility and accentedness, while related, are partially independent dimensions (Derwing & Munro, 2009). That is, L2 speakers with detectable L1 accents may be perfectly understandable to their listeners, whereas speech that is difficult to understand is almost always judged as being heavily accented. Clearly, there is a need for a greater understanding of the linguistic factors that underlie L2 comprehensibility ratings, particularly at high levels of ability, so that reference to accent or native-like speech can be left aside.

Current Research

Overview

Although the increased visibility and momentum of L2 pronunciation within the broader field of applied linguistics over the past few years is evidenced in pronunciation-specific journal special issues, invited symposia, special interest groups, and, most recently, in the establishment of the annual Pronunciation in Second Language Learning and Teaching conference, this momentum has yet to extend to L2 pronunciation assessment specifically. This notwithstanding, there are two areas in the L2 assessment literature in which discussions on pronunciation are noteworthy. One is in the North American literature on international teaching assistants (ITAs) in light of concerns about ITAs' spoken proficiency; the other is in the growing body of research on automated scoring for L2 speaking – a subject that is likely to continue to inspire debate as speech recognition technologies become increasingly sophisticated and implementable in a variety of assessment contexts. Both areas will be discussed in the remainder of this chapter. In particular, research aimed at gaining a deeper understanding of major holistic constructs in L2 pronunciation research will be emphasized.

Linguistic Influences on L2 Intelligibility and Comprehensibility

In an increasingly globalized world with greater human mobility, a growing number of students face the challenge of conducting academic tasks in their L2. This includes international graduate students who bear instructional responsibilities in higher education settings in a medium of instruction that is different from their L1, referred to here as ITAs. ITAs' pronunciation has been singled out as problematic by different university stakeholders, including undergraduate students, English for academic purposes experts, and ITAs themselves (Isaacs, 2008). However, "pronunciation" (or "accent") sometimes serves as a scapegoat for other linguistic or nonlinguistic barriers to communication that may be more difficult to identify (e.g., ITAs' acculturation issues or listeners' discriminatory attitudes toward accented speech; see Kang & Rubin, 2009). In cases where listener understanding is genuinely at stake, targeted training of the factors that are most consequential for achieving successful communication should be prioritized in ITA instruction and assessment while taking into account their teachability/learnability (e.g., for adult learners with "fossilized" pronunciation). Unless concrete, empirically substantiated guidelines on what matters most for intelligibility and comprehensibility are provided to teachers, there is a risk that pronunciation features that are perceptually salient (i.e., are noticeable or irritating) but that have little bearing on listener understanding will be targeted (e.g., English interdental fricatives) in lieu of features that have more communicative impact (Derwing & Munro, 2009).

Jenkins (2002) proposed a core set of pronunciation features that should be emphasized in instruction for a new, global variety of English – the "lingua franca core." Although her argument for a transnational standard of English that is an alternative to native-speaker varieties is compelling, her recommendations are based on a limited data set. Further, the inclusion criteria for speech samples in the English as a lingua franca corpus that Jenkins

222 Chapter 15 Assessing Pronunciation

and her colleagues frequently cite have not been clarified (e.g., Seidlhofer, 2010). Therefore, substantially more empirical evidence is needed before the lingua franca core can be generalized across instructional contexts or adopted as a standard for assessment.

A growing volume of empirical studies have examined which pronunciation features are most important for intelligibility and/or comprehensibility. Perhaps the most conclusive findings arise from controlled studies that have systematically isolated a particular pronunciation feature to examine its effect on intelligibility (narrowly defined; see above). Generally, different experimental conditions are created either through manipulating sound files using digital editing techniques (e.g., for syllable duration) or through having the same speaker record different renditions of an utterance (e.g., correct versus displaced primary stress placement). Taken together, the studies reveal that prosodic (i.e., suprasegmental) aspects of pronunciation related to stress and timing have a direct effect on intelligibility or comprehensibility (e.g., Hahn, 2004), although other features have yet to be methodically examined. This emerging evidence supports previously unsubstantiated claims about the negative effects of prosodic errors on communication.

As for segmental errors, the available evidence suggests that a nuanced approach to instruction and assessment is needed, since some segmental contrasts (e.g., /s/ versus /ʃ/ in English) appear to be more detrimental to intelligibility and comprehensibility than others (e.g., /θ/ versus /f/). This is dependent, in part, on the frequency of the contrast in distinguishing between lexical items (i.e., the so-called functional load principle; Munro & Derwing, 2006). It is likely that segmental errors are more problematic for learners from some L1 backgrounds than others and that the occurrence of segmental errors in conjunction with prosodic errors (e.g., word stress) can be particularly problematic (Zielinski, 2008). Overall, prosodic errors seem to be more crucial for listener understanding than segmental errors, although some segmental errors clearly lead to reduced intelligibility and comprehensibility and should be addressed (Munro & Derwing, 2006). In order to target the problem, it is important to first diagnose whether the learner's difficulty lies in perception, production, orthographic influence (particularly in languages with poor sound–symbol correspondence), or a combination of these factors. In addition to systematically testing the perception and production of target features at the individual sound, word, and/or sentential levels, in the case of speech production, a diagnostic passage (read-aloud task crafted to elicit particular segmental or prosodic features that may not occur in natural speech) could be used in conjunction with a prompt eliciting an extemporaneous L2 speech sample (see Celce-Murcia et al., 2010).

Beyond diagnosing learner problem areas for pedagogical reasons, gaining a deeper understanding of the linguistic factors that most influence listeners' L2 comprehensibility ratings is crucial for adequately operationalizing the construct in assessment instruments. In low-stakes research contexts, comprehensibility and accentedness are conventionally measured using nine-point numerical rating scales (1 = very difficult to understand, 9 = very easy to understand; 1 = very accented, 9 = not accented at all; e.g., Munro & Derwing, 2006). A minority of studies have instead used sliding scales (i.e., the rater places a cursor along a continuum to indicate his/her scoring decision) or Likert-type scales with a different number of scale levels. Such scales are appealing to L2 pronunciation researchers precisely due to their generic nature, since they can be used with L2 learners from virtually any L1 background and proficiency level. However, a caveat is that the raters receive no guidance on how to make level distinctions and, in the case of the conventionally used nine-point scales, are unlikely to converge on what the nine levels "mean" in terms of performance qualities, particularly between scalar extremes where no descriptors are provided (Isaacs & Thomson, 2013). While these scales have been shown to work well for rank-ordering speakers, the lack of clarity on what is being measured at each scale level limits the precision of the instruments and raises questions about the validity of the ratings (e.g., it is unclear whether comprehensibility refers to comprehensibility of the overall message or of each individual word).

In a study examining the linguistic factors that underlie listeners' L2 comprehensibility ratings for the purpose of deriving a preliminary L2 comprehensibility scale for formative assessment purposes, Isaacs and Trofimovich (2012) analyzed speech samples of 40 Francophone learners of English on a picture narrative task using 19 speech measures drawn from a wide range of linguistic domains, including segmental, suprasegmental, temporal, lexicogrammatical, and discourse level measures. The speech measures were analyzed using both auditory and instrumental techniques. For example, in terms of suprasegmentals, "pitch contour" at clause boundaries was measured using listeners' perceptions of pitch patterns at the end of intonation phrases (auditory), whereas "pitch range" was measured using the pitch tracker function in the Praat speech analysis software (instrumental). The analyzed measures were then correlated with 60 raters' mean L2 comprehensibility ratings using the nine-point numerical comprehensibility scale. By bringing together statistical indices and raters' accounts of influences on their judgments, it was possible to identify a subset of measures that best distinguished between three different levels of L2 comprehensibility. Overall, lexical richness and fluency measures differentiated between low-level learners, grammatical and discourse level measures differentiated between high-level learners, and word stress differentiated between learners at all levels. Such a formative assessment tool could help teachers integrate pronunciation with grammar and vocabulary teaching in communicative classrooms. However, follow-up validation studies are needed to refine the scale and clarify the range of tasks and settings that scale descriptors can be extrapolated to.

Isaacs and Trofimovich's (2012) study represents an initial step at "deconstructing" L2 comprehensibility by focusing on linguistic properties of speech. However, the scores that raters assign may also be influenced by individual differences in rater characteristics – factors that are external to the test takers' performance that is the object of the assessment. This topic is examined in the next section.

The Influence of Rater Characteristics on Their Judgments of L2 Pronunciation

A growing body of L2 speaking assessment research has examined the influence of rater background characteristics on rater processes and scoring outcomes. Research focusing on L2 pronunciation specifically is a subset of this literature. For example, Isaacs and Trofimovich (2010, 2011) examined the effects of three rater cognitive variables – phonological memory, attention control, and musical ability (aptitude) – on rater judgments of L2 comprehensibility, accentedness, and fluency. The rationale was that, if individual differences in rater cognitive abilities were found to influence raters' scoring, then this could pose a threat to the validity of their ratings. There were two major findings. First, no significant effects were detected for phonological memory and attention control, which is reassuring because it removes these variables as a possible source of rater bias. Second, musical raters were overall more severe in their judgments of L2 comprehensibility and accentedness than their less musical peers. Follow-up analyses revealed that musical raters' heightened sensitivity to melodic aspects of music and speech (i.e., pitch phenomena) likely accounted for these differences. Although these findings are intriguing from a research perspective, the statistical findings were relatively weak (e.g., yielded small effect sizes) and it is unclear how *practically* significant these findings are. Further evidence is needed before recommending, for example, that raters for high-stakes speaking tests need to be screened for musical ability or that a homogeneous group of raters should be sought on the basis of their musical training. Therefore, until future research suggests otherwise, language testers need not be overly concerned by these findings.

Recent L2 pronunciation research has begun to establish a link between individual differences in L2 *learners'* sociolinguistic variables, such as ethnic group affiliation and willingness to communicate, and their L2 pronunciation attainment (e.g., Gatbonton &

224 Chapter 15 Assessing Pronunciation

Trofimovich, 2008). Although not examined from an assessment angle, Lindemann (2002) observed that native speakers' perceptions of how well they understood their non-native interlocutors were mediated by their attitudes toward their partners' L1 (see also Kang & Rubin, 2009). Research on motivational and attitudinal factors in relation to pronunciation assessment bears further exploration.

Rater familiarity with a particular L2 accent is often not controlled for in L2 pronunciation research, and studies that have investigated this have produced inconsistent findings. Some studies have shown that greater rater familiarity is associated with a tendency toward higher scoring and better listener understanding, although other studies have found no facilitative effects (see Carey & Szocs, 2024, for a review and discussion of this and related constructs, particularly in the context of L2 listening assessment). At least some of the difficulties can be accounted for by the multifarious ways in which familiarity, which is sometimes framed as listener experience or expertise, is defined (e.g., in terms of the amount of exposure to a particular L2 accent, ESL/EFL teaching experience, or phonetic training) and the "novice," "inexperienced," or "lay" listener comparison group is defined (Isaacs & Thomson, 2013). Clearly, greater consensus on the meaning of these terms in the context of L2 pronunciation research would be desirable.

Because subjective measures of pronunciation are contingent upon both the message sender and the message receiver, the effect of rater background characteristics on the rating processes and the scores assigned is important to examine. One way of removing rater idiosyncrasies from the scoring process is through automated (i.e., machine) scoring. This subject is discussed in the next section.

Automated Scoring

Lado's (1961) concern about the reliability of subjective scoring of test takers' L2 pronunciation productions can now be addressed through an alternative that was unavailable during Lado's time – automated scoring. Because the machine scoring system (i.e., speech recognition algorithm) is trained on pooled ratings across a large cross section of human raters, it has the effect of averaging out individual rater idiosyncrasies in a way that operational ratings of L2 speech involving two or three human raters do not. Research on Pearson's fully automated Versant English Test (previously Phonepass) has revealed high correlations between machine-generated scores and human ratings (Bernstein et al., 2010) and has established criterion validity with traditional large-scale L2 speaking proficiency tests (e.g., TOEFL, IELTS). While this suggests that these tests are measuring a related construct, it is unlikely that the automated system is sensitive to the same properties of speech that human raters attend to when rating, which raises questions about the validity of the assessment. In fact, studies from the speech sciences literature have demonstrated that some aspects of listeners' auditory perceptions conflict with acoustic facts obtained using instrumental measures. For example, human listeners often perceive stressed syllables to be higher than they are revealed to be in spectral analysis (Crystal, 2008). Further, because pattern matching is involved in automated scoring, controlled tasks that generate highly predictable test taker output (e.g., utterance repetition, sentence unscrambling) are much easier for automatic scoring systems to deal with than spontaneous speech arising from more communicative tasks (Xi, 2010). However, the use of constrained tasks, which, at present, are necessary to replicate scores that human raters are likely to assign, has led to concerns about the narrowing of the construct of speaking ability. This said, fully automated tests may introduce new task types or update them to make them more communicative as technological capabilities improve (see e.g., Attali et al., 2022, for an reading example from the Duolingo English Test, although the same logic of evolving he test could conceivably apply to speaking when further improvements are possible). Finally, automated speaking tests may claim to measure intelligibility in the broad sense of the term.

However, much of the emphasis in the automated system is on pronunciation accuracy (e.g., of vowels and consonants). While automated feedback can inform the test user of the presence of mispronunciations, the type of mispronunciations, even if specified, will not likely all have the same impact on an interlocutor's ability to understand the utterance. Thus, the need to define the pronunciation features that most contribute to breakdowns in communication also applies to the automated scoring of speech.

Because human interlocutors involved in real-world communication are the ultimate arbiters of the qualities of speech that promote the successful exchange of information (and not machines), it is important not to lose sight of human raters as the gold standard to which automated assessments must conform. As speech recognition technologies continue to improve, automated scoring is becoming increasingly prominent in the language testing research literature and testing products. However, there will always be constraints on what automated systems are able to do.

Challenges

This chapter has brought to the fore key issues in L2 pronunciation assessment. Numerous challenges have emerged thus far. Among the most salient are the need to:

- unparse the role of pronunciation (i.e., "phonology/graphology") in theoretical models of communicative competence and communicative language ability;
- discontinue the use of pronunciation item types or assessment methods that do not meet high standards of reliability and validity (e.g., paper and pencil items purportedly testing pronunciation production) or that are methodologically unsound or of questionable fairness (e.g., speech analyses for asylum purposes by authorities who know little about language or linguistics), particularly when they are being used for high stakes purposes;
- clarify the role of pronunciation within the broader construct of L2 speaking ability;
- disambiguate terms in the L2 pronunciation research literature that are not used with consistency, such as intelligibility and comprehensibility or listener (rater) expertise, experience, and familiarity;
- recognize that intelligibility (broadly defined) is the appropriate goal of L2 pronunciation instruction and assessment in the vast majority of language use contexts but needs to be more clearly understood;
- prioritize empirical studies that isolate a particular segmental or suprasegmental feature to examine measurable effects of that feature on intelligibility or comprehensibility (narrowly defined), the findings of which can then be examined in conjunction with evidence from observational studies;
- develop a greater understanding of the linguistic factors that underlie listeners' perceptions of L2 comprehensibility for the purpose of operationalizing comprehensibility more clearly in rating scales, including without resorting to a native speaker standard;
- examine systematic sources of variance (e.g., psycholinguistic, sociolinguistic, or experience-related rater variables) that have the potential to influence ratings of L2 pronunciation but that may be extraneous to the construct being measured (i.e., are possible sources of rater bias);
- provide L2 teachers with more precise information on the error types that most contribute to communication breakdowns so that these can be targeted in L2 speaking and listening instruction and assessment;
- continue to investigate the relationship between human-mediated and machine-mediated assessments of L2 pronunciation, including the extent to which automated speech recognition can predict human scoring on more communicatively oriented tasks and the quality of the feedback delivered to test users.

226 Chapter 15 Assessing Pronunciation

While these areas, both individually and as a unit, constitute major challenges, there is one challenge that underpins all of these points and that is fundamental to propelling L2 pronunciation assessment into a post-Lado era. That is, the most significant challenge in the area of pronunciation assessment research today is to reinvigorate the conversation on L2 pronunciation in L2 assessment circles. To say that the area of L2 pronunciation assessment has been under-researched over the past several decades would be an understatement, as repercussions of the view that pronunciation is incidental to L2 learning and is unessential for communicative competence still resonate. Although, in the minds of some applied linguists, pronunciation hearkens back to tedious, mechanical drills, and decontextualized discrete-point items of the past, the potential for communicatively oriented items is evident in some currently available teaching materials (e.g., Grant, 2016) if it has not yet infiltrated pronunciation assessments.

There is evidence of some reversal of the marginalization of L2 pronunciation from discussions on L2 assessment. For example, at the time of writing, the most recent issue of the prominent journal *Language Testing*, features three full-length articles (out of 8 total) on pronunciation-related constructs for L2 speaking and listening (Isaacs & Yan, 2024; see e.g., Carey & Szocs, 2024).These studies reflect burgeoning research, for example, on accent familiarity effects and related constructs. Also this chapter cannot possibly be comprehensive, some fruitful areas for future research are discussed in the final section of this chapter.

Future Directions

As the debate on automated scoring in relation to L2 speaking has gained momentum with the launch of fully automated tests (e.g., PTE Academic), the topic of pronunciation has resurfaced in L2 assessment circles. However, this is only one area of research that merits attention. If we accept the argument that pronunciation (and, in particular, broadly defined intelligibility) needs to be assessed as part of the construct of L2 oral proficiency, then there is an urgent need to better define the constructs that we intend to measure for assessment purposes, including filtering out accentedness from L2 proficiency scales. While accentedness is of substantive interest to L2 pronunciation researchers due to its potential to influence listeners' attitudes toward L2 speech (Kang & Rubin, 2009), intelligibility (broadly defined) is by far the more important construct for L2 pronunciation pedagogy and assessment (see above). It follows that operationalizing comprehensibility in more explicit terms in rating scales without resorting to the native speaker standard should be the focus of L2 pronunciation scale development and use. Isaacs et al., (2018) described such an approach to L2 English comprehensibility scale development, triangulating evidence from Isaacs and Trofimovich (2012) with experienced teachers' ratings and suggestions for improving the scale. However, the resulting instrument, which is constrained for use with monologic tasks, has yet to be validated, and, therefore, its generalizability and applicability to other contexts is unclear. Notably, the Common European Framework of Reference for Languages (CEFR) updated its original Phonological control scale descriptors, which *implied* a native speaker standard (Harding, 2017), with substantial amendments that now much more robustly articulate pronunciation-relevant constructs in a new set of improved scales (Council of Europe, 2018). Drawing on Isaacs and Trofimovich's (2011) finding that musical raters, who are more attuned to certain aspects of the speech signal than their less musical counterparts, overall perceive comprehensibility and accentedness to be more independent dimensions, eliciting musicians' perceptions may be helpful in teasing these constructs apart.

One final substantive area not yet addressed in this chapter that needs to be flagged as a research priority relates to examining learners' L2 pronunciation performance on tasks that elicit a wider range of interactional patterns. Most of the pronunciation research cited above has involved native speakers' ratings of non-native speakers' performances on relatively inauthentic monologic tasks. Generally, this involves L2 learners (i.e., research participants) speaking into the microphone without the presence of an interlocutor, which does not foster genuine communication. To reflect the reality of English as a global language more closely, including the likelihood that L2 learners will need to interact not only with native speakers but also with non-native interlocutors (depending, of course, on the context), performance on more collaborative tasks that bear greater resemblance to the real-world tasks that learners will be expected to carry out would be desirable. From an L2 assessment perspective, paired speaking tasks generally involve dyadic interactions among non-native interlocutors, although pairing procedures can be somewhat haphazard. Future research could, for example, investigate the effects of same versus different L1 group pairings on factors such as communicative efficiency and the production of target-like pronunciation.

Discussion Questions

1. What is the difference between comprehensibility and intelligibility?
2. What assessment norms would you use in assessing pronunciation if you consider English as a lingua franca?
3. What are the opportunities and challenges for fully automated (machine administered and scored) speaking and pronunciation assessments?
4. What do you think has driven a renewed interest in pronunciation assessment in research circles?

References

Attali, Y., Runge, A., LaFlair, G. T., Yancey, K., Goodwin, S., Park, Y., & von Davier, A. A. (2022). The interactive reading task: Transformer-based automatic item generation. *Frontiers in Artificial Intelligence, 5,* 903077. https://doi.org/10.3389/frai.2022.903077.

Bachman, L. F. (1990). *Fundamental considerations in language testing.* Oxford University Press.

Bachman, L. F., & Palmer, A. S. (1982). The construct validation of some components communicative proficiency. *TESOL Quarterly, 16,* 449–465.

Bernstein, J., Van Moere, A., & Cheng, J. (2010). Validating automated speaking tests. *Language Testing, 27,* 355–377.

Buck, G. (1989). Written tests of pronunciation: do they work? *ELT Journal, 43,* 50–56.

Carey, M. D., & Szocs, S. (2024). Revisiting raters' accent familiarity in speaking tests: evidence that presentation mode interacts with accent familiarity to variably affect comprehensibility ratings. *Language Testing, 41*(2), 290–315. https://doi.org/10.1177/02655322231200808.

Celce-Murcia, M., Brinton, D. M., Goodwin, J. M., & Griner, B. (2010). *Teaching pronunciation: A course book and reference guide* (2nd ed.). Cambridge University Press.

Council of Europe. (2018). *Common European framework of reference for languages: learning, teaching, assessment. Companion volume with new descriptors.* Council of Europe.

Crystal, D. (2008). *A dictionary of linguistics and phonetics* (6th ed.). Wiley-Blackwell.

Derwing, T. M., & Munro, M. J. (1997). Accent, intelligibility, and comprehensibility: evidence from four L1s. *Studies in Second Language Acquisition, 19,* 1–16.

Derwing, T. M., & Munro, M. J. (2009). Putting accent in its place: rethinking obstacles to communication. *Language Teaching, 42,* 1–15.

Educational Testing Service. (2009). *The official guide to the TOEFL test* (3rd ed.). McGraw-Hill.

Educational Testing Service. (2018). *TOEIC Speaking Proficiency Level Descriptors.* https://www.ets.org/pdfs/toeic/toeic-speaking-writing-score-descriptors.pdf

Fayer, J. M., & Krasinski, E. (1987). Native and nonnative judgments of intelligibility and irritation. *Language Learning, 37,* 313–326.

Chapter 15 Assessing Pronunciation

Firth, J. R. (1957). *A synopsis of linguistic theory, 1930–1955*. Blackwell.

Flege, J. E., Schirru, C., & MacKay, I. R. A. (2003). Interaction between the native and second language phonetic subsystems. *Speech Communication, 40*, 467–491.

Fraser, H. (2009). The role of "educated native speakers" in providing language analysis for the determination of the origin of asylum seekers. *International Journal of Speech Language and the Law, 16*, 113–138.

Gatbonton, E., & Trofimovich, P. (2008). The ethnic group affiliation and L2 proficiency link: empirical evidence. *Language Awareness, 17*, 229–248.

Grant, L. (2016). *Well said: Pronunciation for clear communication* (4th ed.). Heinle ELT.

Hahn, L. D. (2004). Primary stress and intelligibility: research to motivate the teaching of suprasegmentals. *TESOL Quarterly, 38*, 201–233.

Isaacs, T. (2008). Towards defining a valid assessment criterion of pronunciation proficiency in non-native English speaking graduate students. *Canadian Modern Language Review, 64*, 555–580.

Isaacs, T., & Thomson, R. I. (2013). Rater experience, rating scale length, and judgments of L2 pronunciation: revisiting research conventions. *Language Assessment Quarterly, 10*(2), 135–159.

Isaacs, T., & Trofimovich, P. (2010). Falling on sensitive ears? The influence of musical ability on extreme raters' judgments of L2 pronunciation. *TESOL Quarterly, 44*, 375–386.

Isaacs, T., & Trofimovich, P. (2011). Phonological memory, attention control, and musical ability: effects of individual differences on rater judgments of second language speech. *Applied Psycholinguistics, 32*, 113–140.

Isaacs, T., & Trofimovich, P. (2012). "Deconstructing" comprehensibility: identifying the linguistic influences on listeners' L2 comprehensibility ratings. *Studies in Second Language Acquisition, 34*, 475–505.

Isaacs, T., & Yan, X. Eds. (2024). [Journal issue]. *Language Testing, 41*(2), 233–455.

Jenkins, J. (2002). A sociolinguistically based, empirically researched pronunciation syllabus for English as an international language. *Applied Linguistics, 23*, 83–103.

Kang, O., & Rubin, D. L. (2009). Reverse linguistic stereotyping: measuring the effect of listener expectations on speech evaluation. *Journal of Language and Social Psychology, 28*, 441–456.

Lado, R. (1961). *Language testing: The construction and use of foreign language tests*. Longman.

Levis, J. M. (2005). Changing contexts and shifting paradigms in pronunciation teaching. *TESOL Quarterly, 39*, 369–377.

Levis, J. M. (2006). Pronunciation and the assessment of spoken language. In R. Hughes (Ed.), *Spoken English, TESOL and applied linguistics: Challenges for theory and practice* (pp. 245–270). Palgrave Macmillan.

Lindemann, S. (2002). Listening with an attitude: a model of native-speaker comprehension of non-native speakers in the United States. *Language in Society, 31*, 419–441.

Major, R. C. (2007). Identifying a foreign accent in an unfamiliar language. *Studies in Second Language Acquisition, 29*, 539–556.

Morley, J. (1991). The pronunciation component of teaching English to speakers of other languages. *TESOL Quarterly, 25*, 481–520.

Munro, M. J., & Derwing, T. M. (2006). The functional load principle in ESL pronunciation instruction: an exploratory study. *System, 34*, 520–531.

Munro, M. J., Derwing, T. M., & Burgess, C. S. (2010). Detection of nonnative speaker status from content-masked speech. *Speech Communication, 52*, 626–637.

Seidlhofer, B. (2010). Giving VOICE to English as a lingua franca. In R. Facchinetti, D. Crystal & B. Seidlhofer (Eds.), *From international to local English – and back again* (pp. 147–163). Peter Lang.

Spolsky, B. (1995). *Measured words: The development of objective language testing*. Oxford University Press.

Trofimovich, P., & Gatbonton, E. (2006). Repetition and focus on form in processing L2 Spanish words: implications for pronunciation instruction. *Modern Language Journal, 90*, 519–535.

University of Cambridge ESOL Examinations. (2008). *Certificate of proficiency in English: Handbook for teachers*. UCLES.

Xi, X. (2010). Automated scoring and feedback systems: where are we and where are we heading? *Language Testing, 27*, 291–300.

Zielinski, B. W. (2008). The listener: no longer the silent partner in reduced intelligibility. *System, 36*, 69–84.

Suggested Readings

Derwing, T. M., Munro, M. J., & Thomson, R. I. (2022). *The Routledge handbook of second language acquisition and speaking*. Routledge. https://doi.org/10.4324/9781003022497.

Harding, L., & McNamara, T. (2018). Language assessment: the challenge of ELF. In J. Jenkins, W. Baker & M. J. Dewey (Eds.), *Routledge handbook of English as a lingua franca* (pp. 570–582). Routledge.

Isaacs, T., & Harding, L. (2017). Research timeline: pronunciation assessment. *Language Teaching, 50*(3), 347–366. https://doi.org/10.1017/S0261444817000118.

Isaacs, T. (2018). Fully automated speaking assessment: changes to proficiency testing and the role of pronunciation. In O. Kang, R. I. Thomson & J. Murphy (Eds.), *The Routledge handbook of English pronunciation* (pp. 570–584). Routledge.

Kang, O., & Ginther, A. (2018). *Assessment in second language pronunciation*. Routledge.

Moyer, A. (2013). *Foreign accent: The phenomenon of non-native speech*. Cambridge University Press. http://www.jstor.org/stable/10.21832/j.ctt1xp3wcc.

Saito, K., & Plonsky, L. (2019). Effects of second language pronunciation teaching revisited: a proposed measurement framework and meta-analysis. *Language Learning, 69*(3), 652–708. https://doi.org/10.1111/lang.12345.

CHAPTER 16

Assessing Interactional Competence and Pragmatics

Carsten Roever

Introduction

The assessment of second language (L2) learners' ability to use language for social purposes has seen burgeoning research interest but has so far had little impact on operational language assessment. The theoretical framework for research in this area has shifted from speech act pragmatics in the 1990s and 2000s to interactional competence (IC) from the early 2010s. This has had a notable impact on the test construct and test instruments used. This chapter will review existing research on the assessment of pragmatics and IC and outline some future research directions.

Pragmatics as a construct was developed in philosophy (Austin, 1962; Searle, 1969) but has resonated strongly in linguistics. In a commonly cited definition, Crystal (1997) conceptualizes pragmatics as "the study of language from the point of view of users, especially of the choices they make, the constraints they encounter in using language in social interaction and the effects their use of language has on other participants in the act of communication" (p. 301). Mey (2001) specified some subareas of pragmatics, including implicature, speech acts, deixis, and extended discourse.

To conceptualize language users' pragmatic knowledge and ability for use, Leech (1983) distinguished between sociopragmatics, the social rules of language use, and pragmalinguistics, the linguistic tools of such language use. Language users' sociopragmatic knowledge is their knowledge of social norms and conventions, social relationships, politeness and appropriateness levels, common ways of doing things, and mutual rights and obligations. A sociopragmatically competent language user understands the context factors of power, social distance, and imposition (Brown & Levinson, 1987) and knows what level of politeness is appropriate given different settings of context factors. Pragmalinguistics concerns linguistic tools, that is, a language user's linguistic knowledge that can be made available for pragmatic use. Pragmatically competent language users need both sociopragmatic and pragmalinguistic knowledge. They need to map the two systems onto each other, and they need to be able to activate their knowledge within the time constraints of a communicative situation.

The Concise Companion to Language Assessment, First Edition. Edited by Antony John Kunnan.
© 2025 John Wiley & Sons, Inc. Published 2025 by John Wiley & Sons, Inc.

> You are having dinner at a friend's house. As you are handing your friend the salt shaker you accidentally drop it. It breaks and spills salt all over the floor.
>
> *What would you say?*
>
> _____
>
> _____

FIGURE 16.1 DCT item.

Most work on L2 pragmatics has focused on speech acts, with the most commonly investigated acts being request, apology, and refusal (Taguchi & Roever, 2017). These speech acts have been commonly investigated by means of discourse completion tests (DCTs), which consist minimally of a situation description (the prompt), a stimulus question ("What would you say in this situation?"), and a gap for participants to write their response, as exemplified in Figure 16.1.

DCTs, however, are far from faithful emulations of actual conversation. They cannot emulate the sequential nature of conversation, responses are not constructed under the time pressure of an online communicative situation, and respondents have been shown to write what they think they might say in the given situation, which is not necessarily what they actually do say in reality (Golato, 2003). So the range of conclusions that can be drawn from performances and scores obtained through DCTs is limited to test takers' offline knowledge of semantic formulas for implementing speech acts and does not extend to their ability to perform them in real-world interaction.

Other aspects of pragmatics have also been researched in L2 pragmatics, most notably comprehension of implicature (Bouton, 1999) and routine formulae (Bardovi-Harlig, 2009).

IC as a concept originates from Kramsch's (1986) critique of the ACTFL proficiency guidelines as underemphasizing the social dimension of language. It has since been elaborated and uses conversation analysis (CA) as its framework, which originated in sociology and sees language as a tool for community members to carry out social actions and manage social life (see Hepburn & Potter, 2021, for a concise introduction). Pekarek Doehler (2021) defined IC as "the ability to deploy procedures for the management of social interaction (turn taking, opening or closing a conversation, disagreeing, initiating a storytelling, and so forth) in ways that are relevant, i.e., adapted, to the local circumstances of the interaction and to the specific others who participate therein. IC includes both the ability to understand the interactional context and the expected practices therein, and to deploy locally relevant conduct based on verbal and non-verbal resources" (p. 24).

While much of CA takes an agnostic position toward cognition and mental models (Te Molder & Potter, 2005) and would struggle with etic judgments of interactional performance, IC research recognizes development and qualitative differences in learners' interactional conduct. Still, many studies do not interpret developmental findings from the perspective of a cognitive model of learning and use.

Research on L2 IC has focused on the development of particular social actions, such as refusals (Wu & Roever, 2021), proposals (Youn, 2019), disagreements (Pekarek Doehler & Pochon-Berger, 2011), turn-taking (Cekaite, 2007), or complaints (Skogmyr Marian, 2021). IC research is typically based on recordings of extended conversation, which can be natural, unelicited discourse in keeping with CA (e.g., Skogmyr Marian, 2021) or role plays designed to elicit a specific feature of interest (e.g., Wu & Roever, 2021).

The research traditions of speech act pragmatics and IC have strongly influenced approaches to assessment.

232 Chapter 16 Assessing Interactional Competence and Pragmatics

Previous Conceptualization and Research

The first major test development project in the assessment of L2 pragmatics was Hudson et al.'s (1995) battery, which focused on request, apology, and refusal and was designed contrastively for L1 Japanese-speaking learners of American English. The test consisted of four measures and two self-assessment questionnaires:

- 24 written DCT items administered as a paper and pencil test;
- 24 multiple choice DCT items as a paper and pencil test;
- 24 oral DCT items administered in a language lab;
- 8 role-play situations, each containing a request, an apology, and a refusal; and
- 2 self-assessment questionnaires, asking participants to rate how well they would perform in some of the DCT situations, and how well they thought they performed in the immediately preceding role play.

Hudson et al. (1995) trained native speaker (NS) raters to evaluate learner production using a five-point scale from "very unsatisfactory" to "completely appropriate" on six criteria: ability to use the correct speech act; formulaic expressions; amount of speech used and information given; and degrees of formality, directness, and politeness. Hudson (2001) reported on a piloting of the battery, which showed that the test was somewhat easy for a sample of Japanese ESL students. Inter-rater reliabilities ranged from 0.75 to 0.86.

Hudson et al.'s test sparked a number of subsequent test development projects. Yoshitake (1997) used the original battery EFL learners in Japan, Yamashita (1996) adapted the test for Japanese as a second language (JSL), and Brown and Ahn (2011) report on an adaptation of the test for Korean as a foreign language (KFL), though without the multiple choice DCT and the self-assessment on the DCT situations. Analyses by Brown (2001, 2008) showed that most parts of the test were reliable except for the multiple choice DCT, which showed low reliabilities in Yamashita's JSL data than in Yoshitake's EFL data. Liu (2006) and Tada (2005) tackled the challenge of developing a reliable multiple-choice DCT, and both developed instruments with satisfactory reliability.

The first test battery that included multiple aspects of pragmatics was Roever's Web-based test of English pragmalinguistics (Roever, 2005). Roever assessed three areas: comprehension of implicature; recognition of routine formulas; and knowledge of speech act strategies for the speech acts of request, apology, and refusal.

The implicature section was based on Bouton's (1999) work and tested learners' ability to interpret general conversational implicature (e.g., "Do you know where the blender is?" "Try the kitchen cabinet") and formulaic implicature (e.g., "Is the Pope Catholic?"). The routines section assessed recognition of situational routine formulas ("Can I get you anything else?").

Both sections contained 12 items, and learners had 12 minutes to complete each section. The speech act section also consisted of 12 items, but learners were given 18 minutes to complete it. It included the speech acts of request, apology, and refusal and varied only the context factor of imposition, keeping power, and distance low. Roever ran the test with a total of 335 L2 learners of English in the United States, Australia, Japan, and Germany, and 13 NSs of American English as a comparison group and achieved good overall reliability.

In contrast to Hudson et al. (1995), who had designed their test specifically for Japanese learners of English, Roever's test was not contrastively designed, and Roever (2010) showed in a differential item functioning (DIF) analysis that neither test takers of Asian nor those of European language background had an advantage. Itomitsu (2009) developed a battery similar to Roever's for JFL.

Roever's and Itomitsu's tests can be seen as direct descendants of the battery developed by Hudson et al. (1995). Roever and Itomitsu extended the construct measured in the original battery to include other aspects of pragmatics while at the same time increasing practicality through the use of computer technology. However, their tests primarily elicited knowledge rather than online performance and did not allow conclusions to be drawn as to test takers' ability to produce routines, speech acts, implicatures, speech styles, or all of these under real-world conditions. Hudson et al.'s battery elicited more performance-based data through its role play but was otherwise limited to one aspect of pragmatic competence.

A later group of tests aimed to combine a speech act-based construct with more interactional elements. Roever et al. (2014) developed a test battery of ESL sociopragmatics, including metapragmatic judgment tasks of utterances contextualized in a scenario or a dialogue, as well as judgments of the success of entire dialogues, productive pragmatic error correction tasks, and productive multiturn DCT tasks. While they achieved good overall reliability of Cronbach's alpha of 0.81, test takers' scores predicted only 7.1% of their overall ease of communication, making extrapolation to real-world performance questionable.

Timpe (2013, see also Timpe & Choi, 2017) developed a battery that assessed comprehension of speech acts and idiomatic language use, metapragmatic judgment of routine formulae, and organization and appropriateness of oral production in role plays. Timpe's inclusion of idiomatic language was in line with her overall construct being interculturally rather than exclusively pragmatically oriented.

In a psycholinguistic "twist" on pragmatics testing, Ellis et al. (2023) designed a test battery to elicit implicit and explicit pragmatic knowledge. The battery included six tests, assessing judgment about social context variables, metapragmatic judgment and reasoning, comprehension of irony, monologic and dialogic recipient-designed talk, and processing of pragmatic meaning through an elicited conversation task. Roever et al. (2023) found a Cronbach alpha reliability of 0.78 for the battery, though without the social context variables test. Ellis et al.'s (2023) battery was designed for research purposes rather than assessment with real-world consequences but its instruments are potentially usable for other assessment purposes. However, their approach to pragmatics testing seems somewhat old-fashioned given that work on testing IC began a decade before their battery.

Two other test developments followed theoretical frameworks other than the speech acts approach. Grabowski (2009, 2013) based her test on Purpura's (2004) model of communicative language ability, investigated the relationship between pragmatics and grammar by having 102 ESL learners do four role plays, and rating their performance on two indicators of grammatical ability and three indicators of pragmatic ability. She found moderate to strong relationships between measures of pragmatic and grammatical ability, indicating that the constructs are related though distinct, as has been discussed in interlanguage pragmatics research (e.g., Kasper & Rose, 2002). Grabowski's test was billed as a "speaking test" rather than a test of L2 pragmatics, but the strong performance orientation of her role plays is an interesting innovation over the knowledge-oriented tests in the Hudson et al. (1995) tradition.

The battery by Walters (2007) was a precursor to current tests focusing on interactional abilities. Walter designed his battery from a conversation analytic perspective and included a listening test, role play, and DCT to assess how learners comprehend and produce compliment responses as well as upgraded or downgraded assessments following an interlocutor assessment. Walters administered his test to 42 ESL learners in a fairly narrow proficiency range, which may help explain the low reliabilities he obtained. However, his instrument was creative and innovative in that it assessed aspects of conversational ability, which none of the other tests did.

Current Conceptualization and Research

Just like research on second language pragmatics has undergone a paradigm shift from investigating pragmatic competence to focusing on IC, so has assessment. In a pioneering study with IC as the test construct, Youn (2013, 2015) developed a test of IC for ESL learners.

234 **Chapter 16** Assessing Interactional Competence and Pragmatics

One-hundred and two learners completed two role plays with a trained interlocutor and one pragmatic monologue, together with two monologues used as measures of general speaking proficiency. One role play was centered around requesting and the other around proposing (see also Youn, 2019) with the monologues eliciting constructive criticism. Youn then developed five rating criteria for the role plays bottom-up from the data by comparing representative performances of learners at three different proficiency levels:

- *Content delivery*: sequential organization of the core social action.
- *Language use*: effective use of language tools to achieve pragmatic meaning.
- *Sensitivity to the situation*: management of contingencies.
- *Engaging with interaction*: responses fitted to the previous turn and listener responses.
- *Turn organization*: smooth turn-taking.

Youn (2013, 2015) achieved separation reliability provided by Rasch measurement of 0.96, indicating that her test was able to clearly distinguish test taker performance levels.

Youn's study was groundbreaking for the assessment of IC as it demonstrated that IC features like sequential organization, turn management, and listener responses can be reliably assessed and interactions at different score levels differ systematically in identifiable features (see also Youn, 2020). One potential limitation of Youn's study was that she tied interactional features to proficiency levels in her bottom-up analysis, which potentially conflated IC and proficiency, and led to a very high correlation of 0.9 between the role-play scores and scores on the two monologues serving as proficiency measures. While IC and proficiency are conceptually related, they are not necessarily congruent, and conflating them calls into question the need for separate measurements of IC.

Ikeda (2017, 2021) designed and validated a test battery of IC consisting of three dialogues and three monologues in two task sets. Tasks delivered as dialogues in Set A were set as monologues in Set B and vice versa. All tasks involved requests, and dialogic tasks were designed to include a complication, e.g., when asking a classmate to partner up for a presentation, the classmate is already thinking about partnering with someone else and has a slightly different topic in mind. Ikeda recruited 67 university and pre-entry students at approximately B2 and C1 levels of the Common European Framework of Reference for Languages (Council of Europe, 2020). Similar to Youn, he developed rating criteria bottom-up from the data and arrived at six criteria:

- *Language use for mitigation*: control varied linguistic resources to mitigate imposition.
- *Facility with the language*: deliver contents smoothly and clearly with sound variation and repair when necessary.
- *Language use for intended meanings*: employ linguistic resources naturally to deliver intended meaning, minimizing the addressee's effort.
- *Social actions*: take adequate and appropriate actions tailored to the context to achieve a communicative goal.
- *Engagement in interaction*: engage in interaction naturally by responding with varied patterns of responses.
- *Turn organization*: smooth turn taking and projection of TRPs.

Ikeda (2017, 2021) achieved highly reliable test-taker separation and also reported high inter-rater reliability. He found that in most cases, dialogs were more difficult than the equivalent monologue tasks, and language-oriented rating criteria were more difficult than interactional criteria. In investigating the extrapolation inference following Kane (2006), Ikeda (2017) found that test takers assessed their task performance as similar to their real-world performance, did not feel that having the same interlocutor for all tasks impacted their performance, and were not affected by fatigue.

Ikeda's study further demonstrated the feasibility of IC testing, and his extrapolation findings support the meaningfulness of scores as being indicative of IC. Also similar to Youn, some of Ikeda's scoring criteria were quite strongly influenced by language proficiency, raising the question of the relationship between proficiency and IC.

A recent IC assessment study took a somewhat different approach, which also differentiated IC more clearly from proficiency. Dai (2022) developed IC tests for L2 Mandarin Chinese consisting of nine tasks: three monologic first-pair part tasks where test takers produce a voicemail based on a prompt, three monologic second-pair part tasks where test takers respond to a voicemail, and three dialogues with a trained interlocutor. Instead of developing rating criteria bottom-up using CA, Dai elicited indigenous criteria (Jacoby & McNamara, 1999) from domain experts, in his case, L1 Mandarin-speaking linguistic lay people with extensive experience working, living, and studying in China. Using a variation of the analytical judgment method (Plake & Hambleton, 2001), Dai had the raters sort performance into three groups (successful/average/unsuccessful) and comment on positive and negative features of the performance. From these comments, Dai abstracted five rating criteria:

- *Role enactment and orientation*: speaking in a way appropriate to one's social role and the relationship to the interlocutor, e.g., employee to manager.
- *Reasoning*: making sensible, logical points when laying out problems and suggesting solutions.
- *Morality*: showing desirable personal qualities and behaviors in line with social category membership, e.g., self-display as a diligent student.
- *Affiliative resources*: building rapport and maintaining a harmonious relationship with the interlocutor.
- *Disaffiliation management*: managing instances of disagreement and conflict.

Dai's test rendered a Cronbach alpha reliability of 0.864, and a Rasch analysis showed no significant severity difference between raters.

It is noticeable that Dai's criteria do not focus on sequential organization or specific linguistic resources deployed to achieve intersubjectivity but they view the quality of interaction from the perspective of social roles and the relevant attributes associated with them (see Dai & Davey, 2023, for a detailed explication). Dai's approach also avoided the issue of a confound between proficiency and IC, which affected both Youn's (2013) and Ikeda's (2017) study with proficiency only accounting for 17.5% of the variance in IC scores (Dai & Roever, 2023). Comparing the IC scores of native and non-native speakers, Roever and Dai (2021) showed that native speakers do not automatically have flawless IC. In fact, the lowest IC score in their sample was obtained by a native speaker.

Dai's study constitutes a significant step forward in IC testing. Unlike Youn's (2013) and Ikeda's (2017) tests that scored components of IC, Dai's criteria allow a more holistic perspective of IC in action by evaluating the outcome of test takers' deployment of interactional skills in terms of fulfillment of social roles and display of role-congruent behaviors, and his reliance on linguistic laypersons' indigenous judgments successfully sidestep the proficiency issue. A possible concern with this approach is its inherent perpetuation of prevalent social norms of expected behavior, which potentially disavows language users' agency to behave in ways that are non-conforming and non-mainstream.

In addition to the studies by Youn (2013), Ikeda (2017) and Dai (2022), which have developed complete IC test batteries, other studies have investigated IC with existing tests and developed rating criteria for assessment settings and classroom assessment. Pill (2016) reports on a project (see Elder, 2016 for an overview) that was a pre-cursor to Dai's (2022) work, though embedded in the theoretical framework of language for specific purposes (LSP) testing, rather than IC. Pill (2016) described the process of adding interactional scoring criteria to the speaking section of the Occupational English Test (OET), an LSP English test

236 Chapter 16 Assessing Interactional Competence and Pragmatics

for health professionals wishing to practice in Australia, New Zealand, and some other predominantly English-speaking environments. The OET speaking test consisted of a role-play between the test taker and a simulated patient, which was scored on linguistic criteria (Intelligibility, Fluency, Appropriateness of language, Resources of grammar and expression, and Overall communicative effectiveness). In light of stakeholders' concerns about the real-world interactional abilities of test takers, Pill (2016) used the analytical judgment method (Plake & Hambleton, 2001) to elicit domain experts' indigenous criteria of expected performance in the target professional roles of doctor, nurse, and physiotherapist. Based on their comments, he developed two new criteria: clinical engagement, which encompasses a supportive, non-judgmental, patient-centered attitude, and management of interaction, which assesses to what extent test takers effectively elicited and provided information in their consultations. O'Hagan et al. (2016) showed that the new criteria contributed to the measurement beyond the original criteria in a way that extended the construct.

Also working with an existing test, Galaczi (2014) identified rateable features in paired speaking tasks from Cambridge English tests. She compared test takers at levels B1–C2 of the CEFR, and described differences in topic management, turn taking, and listener responses, but did not develop a rating scale. This was done in later work by May et al. (2020, see also Nakatsuhara et al. 2018), who used verbal protocols from raters commenting on videotaped performances in paired speaking tests to develop a checklist with nine criteria of successful interactional performance: opening and continuing the interaction, being responsive, maintaining and developing the interaction, requiring support or providing it, using body language, using routine formulae, and talking confidently. Their checklist was formatively oriented, and they also developed an abbreviated version for classroom assessment.

Kley (2019) used data from classroom learner interactions to develop a rubric on topic management, encompassing topic initiation, responding to topic initiation, topic shifting, and expanding a topic. Barth-Weingarten and Freitag-Hild (2021, 2023) took a different approach, creating a rating rubric first and then applying it to classroom data from secondary school learners. They developed rubrics for turn taking (Barth-Weingarten & Freitag-Hild, 2021) and action accomplishment (Barth-Weingarten & Freitag-Hild, 2023).

Challenges

A vexed theoretical question for IC assessment is epistemology since testing of IC requires a combination of two mostly incompatible theoretical frameworks. IC is rooted in CA, whose orientation is emic, bottom-up, and descriptive. CA is not concerned with judgments of right or wrong, better or worse, whereas testing must make these etic judgments based on a clearly definable standard. Work on IC has gone some way toward accepting that there are qualitative differences in interactional performance but does not lend itself easily to scoring performances based on fixed criteria. It is difficult to find a balanced compromise position between these frameworks, and the etic perspective of assessment will likely have to take precedence. Still, deriving assessment standards from indigenous criteria (as Dai, 2022; Pill, 2016, did) at least grounds assessments in the members' knowledge of domain experts, be they medical professionals or community members with experience of mundane everyday life.

An important and under-explored research issue in IC and pragmatics testing is Extrapolation from a universe score based on the universe of items (as reliability and generalizability theory might support) to a target score across the domain of interest. In attempts to address this question, Ikeda (2017) investigated features of the test situation and Dai (2022) experimented with peer judgments but important questions remain, such as how representative are test scenarios of real-world interactional needs? And to what extent does test takers' orientation to the social situation of being in a role play affect performance and limit the generalizability of scores to real-world interaction?

The greatest practical challenge for testing L2 pragmatics and IC is ensuring practicality while providing sufficient construct coverage. An ideal test of L2 pragmatics or IC assesses learners' ability to use language in a variety of social settings and social roles and can be delivered to large groups simultaneously, rather than one-on-one as it is common for role plays. The obvious solution to this problem would be a computer-based test, possibly powered by artificial intelligence (AI), and some studies have started to investigate the affordances and drawbacks of test takers interacting with computers to assess IC. Ockey and Chukharev-Hudilainen (2021, see also Chukharev-Hudilainen & Ockey, 2021) used a computer-based system (though not AI based) to interact with test takers, and compared it with a traditional paired speaking test. They found that test takers obtained lower scores when interacting with a computer and that their score for IC was particularly affected. This raises the larger question of whether differences in interacting with a computer and a human are due to test takers' orientation to these different types of interlocutors, or if the computer-based system in Ockey and Chukharev-Hudilainen's studies needed to be improved to resemble a human more closely in its interaction. Even if it were possible to design a computer-based system that is indistinguishable from a human in its interactional style, it is unclear to what extent test takers' awareness that they are interacting with a machine rather than a human might affect their display of interactional abilities.

The practicality challenge is an important one to tackle as it is directly related to the lack of IC in major tests. While awareness of the importance of IC has increased dramatically over the last decade, it is primarily the resource-intensive nature of IC testing that is hindering its more large-scale adoption. In addition, it has also not been entirely clear that integrating dedicated IC tasks in test would add value to test scores in the form of previously uncaptured variance. Youn's (2013) and Ikeda's (2017) analyses seem to indicate a great deal of overlap between IC and proficiency, which might obviate the need for separate testing of IC. However, their rating criteria were quite sensitive to proficiency, and studies with criteria focusing on social role fulfillment like Pill (2016) and Dai (2022) showed much less impact of proficiency on scores. In addition, fine-grained analyses in recent studies by Roever and Ikeda (2022) and Roever (2023) showed that proficiency is not a good predictor of IC in a test taker population typical of tests like TOEFL iBT, IELTS, or PTE even when using Ikeda's criteria. Still the practical question remains: is the value gained from including expensive IC assessments large enough to justify their inclusion?

And what is the future of tests based on speech act pragmatics? The speech act paradigm can mostly be considered as outdated these days. There is little room for assessing learners' knowledge of the appropriateness of isolated speech acts, and it is highly questionable what conclusions about learners' real-world language use can be drawn from tests designed around isolated speech acts. There is scope for testing recognition of routine formulae, especially at lower proficiency levels where these formulae are an important component of learners' repertoires. However, IC exists at any proficiency level and can be assessed at any proficiency level (see also Roever, 2022) so it should be given priority over pragmatics.

Future Directions

Given the technical challenges of developing human-equivalent computer systems for interaction, an option that deserves research attention is to investigate the potential of recipient-designed talk from monologic tasks. All three IC test developments (Dai, 2022; Ikeda, 2017; Youn, 2013) included monologic tasks, and the correlation between the monologic tasks and the role plays was above $r = 0.85$ on all criteria in Ikeda's study. It appears that an appreciable amount of IC variance can be captured through recipient-designed monologues embedded in a social scenario but the exact relationship between overall IC and the part of it that is assessable through monologues still remains to be determined.

238 Chapter 16 Assessing Interactional Competence and Pragmatics

As outlined above, the use of AI as a conversation partner also requires much more investigation. Designing conversational AI tools that can simulate a variety of social roles in a variety of scenarios is useful for assessment and practice purposes, though the exact degree to which interaction even with a highly realistic AI allows conclusions as to test takers' ability to interact with people still requires more research. Work in the area of digital pragmatics has been ongoing (for example, Timpe-Laughlin et al., 2022) and will no doubt increase in the coming years as AI tools become more sophisticated.

Finally, written pragmatics and IC are as yet an underexplored but promising area for research. IC in writing could be explored through text chat (see Wang, 2023), which shares many features of spoken discourse though with some medium-specific characteristics, including the use of emojis to express emotion and a radically different turn taking system than in spoken language. Text chat has the additional practical advantage that it does not require computing-intensive automated speech recognition and lags in response times are unproblematic, which they are not in spoken dialog system. Email pragmatics has never been incorporated in a test, though this would be relatively easy to implement technologically and could even involve interactive email chains (Haider, 2019).

Undoubtedly the use of technology will increase in pragmatics and IC assessment to mitigate the practicality challenge but it is important not to lose sight of interaction's fundamental human function as the "primordial site of sociality" (Schegloff, 1987, p. 102). Any test must extrapolate to real-world, person-to-person communication.

Discussion Questions

1. What abilities are covered by the construct of Interactional Competence (IC) that are not covered by the construct of pragmatic competence?

2. Why might even role-play data not provide a completely accurate reflection of real-world ability for language use?

3. What is the fundamental difference between Dai's scoring rubric and the rubrics developed by Youn and Ikeda?

References

Austin, J. L. (1962). *How to do things with words*. Oxford University Press.

Bardovi-Harlig, K. (2009). Conventional expressions as a pragmalinguistic resource: recognition and production of conventional expressions in L2 pragmatics. *Language Learning*, *59*(4), 755–795. https://doi.org/10.1111/j.1467-9922.2009.00525.x.

Barth-Weingarten, D., & Freitag-Hild, B. (2021). Assessing interactional competence in secondary schools. In M. R. Salaberry & A. R. Burch (Eds.), *Assessing speaking in context* (pp. 237–262). Multilingual Matters.

Barth-Weingarten, D., & Freitag-Hild, B. (2023). Assessing interactional competence in secondary schools: action accomplishment in English as a foreign language. *Applied Pragmatics*, *5*(2), 240–272. https://doi.org/10.1075/ap.00016.bar.

Bouton, L. F. (1999). Developing non-native speaker skills in interpreting conversational implicatures in English: explicit teaching can ease the process. In E. Hinkel (Ed.), *Culture in second language teaching and learning* (pp. 47–70). Cambridge University Press.

Brown, J. D. (2001). Six types of pragmatics tests in two different contexts. In K. Rose & G. Kasper (Eds.), *Pragmatics in language teaching* (pp. 301–325). Cambridge University Press.

Brown, J. D. (2008). Raters, functions, item types and the dependability of L2 pragmatics tests. In E. Alcón Soler & A. Martínez-Flor (Eds.), *Investigating pragmatics in foreign language learning, teaching and testing* (pp. 224–248). Multilingual Matters.

Brown, J. D., & Ahn, R. C. (2011). Variables that affect the dependability of L2 pragmatics tests. *Journal of Pragmatics, 43*, 198–217. https://doi.org/10.1016/j.pragma.2010.07.026.

Brown, P., & Levinson, S. D. (1987). *Politeness: Some universals in language usage.* Cambridge University Press.

Cekaite, A. (2007). A child's development of interactional competence in a Swedish L2 classroom. *The Modern Language Journal, 91*(1), 45–62. https://doi.org/10.1111/j.1540-4781.2007.00509.x.

Chukharev-Hudilainen, E., & Ockey, G. J. (2021). *The development and evaluation of interactional competence elicitor for oral language assessments (TOEFL Research Report RR 92).* Educational Testing Service.

Council of Europe. (2020). *Common European framework of reference for languages: Learning, teaching, assessment. Companion volume with new descriptors.* Council of Europe. https://www.coe.int/en/web/common-european-framework-reference-languages.

Crystal, D. (1997). *A dictionary of linguistics and phonetics.* Blackwell.

Dai, D. W. (2022). *Design and validation of an L2-Chinese interactional competence test [Unpublished doctoral dissertation].* The University of Melbourne.

Dai, D. W., & Davey, M. (2023). On the promise of using membership categorization analysis to investigate interactional competence. *Applied Linguistics.* https://doi.org/10.1093/applin/amad049.

Dai, D., & Roever, C. (2023, June). *Is measuring interactional competence the same as measuring proficiency? An empirical study on L2-Chinese IC. Paper presented at the 2023 language testing research colloquium, New York City, NY.*

Elder, C. (2016). Exploring the limits of authenticity in LSP testing: the case of a specific-purpose language test for health professionals. *Language Testing, 33*(2), 147–152. https://doi.org/10.1177/0265532215607397.

Ellis, R., Roever, C., Shintani, N., & Zhu, Y. (Eds.). (2023). *Measuring second language pragmatic competence: A psycholinguistic perspective.* Multilingual Matters.

Galaczi, E. D. (2014). Interactional competence across proficiency levels: How do learners manage interaction in paired speaking tests? *Applied Linguistics, 35*(5), 553–574. https://doi.org/10.1093/applin/amt017.

Golato, A. (2003). Studying compliment responses: a comparison of DCTs and recordings of naturally occurring talk. *Applied Linguistics, 24*(1), 90–121. https://doi.org/10.1093/applin/24.1.90.

Grabowski, K. (2009). *Investigating the construct validity of a test designed to measure grammatical and pragmatic knowledge in the context of speaking [Unpublished doctoral dissertation]. Columbia University.*

Grabowski, K. (2013). Investigating the construct validity of a role-play test designed to measure grammatical and pragmatic knowledge at multiple proficiency levels. In S. Ross & G. Kasper (Eds.), *Assessing second language pragmatics* (pp. 149–171). Palgrave MacMillan. https://doi.org/10.1057/9781137003522_6.

Haider, I. (2019). Cyberpragmatics: assessing interlanguage pragmatics through interactive email communication. In S. Papageorgiou & K. M. Bailey (Eds.), *Global perspectives on language assessment* (pp. 152–166). Routledge.

Hepburn, A., & Potter, J. (2021). *Essentials of conversation analysis.* American Psychological Association.

Hudson, T. (2001). Indicators for cross-cultural pragmatic instruction: some quantitative tools. In K. Rose & G. Kasper (Eds.), *Pragmatics in language teaching* (pp. 283–300). Cambridge University Press.

Hudson, T., Detmer, E., & Brown, J. D. (1995). *Developing prototypic measures of cross-cultural pragmatics (Technical Report No. 7). University of Hawai'i, Second Language Teaching and Curriculum Center.*

Ikeda, N. (2017). *Measuring L2 oral pragmatic abilities for use in social contexts: Development and validation of an assessment instrument for L2 pragmatics performance in university settings. [Unpublished doctoral dissertation]. University of Melbourne.*

Ikeda, N. (2021). Assessing L2 learners' pragmatic ability in problem-solving situations at English-medium university. *Applied Pragmatics, 3*(1), 51–83. https://doi.org/10.1075/ap.19039.ike.

Itomitsu, M. (2009). *Developing a test of pragmatics of Japanese as a foreign language [Unpublished doctoral thesis]. Ohio State University.*

Jacoby, S., & McNamara, T. (1999). Locating competence. *English for Specific Purposes, 18*(3), 213–241. https://doi.org/10.1016/S0889-4906(97)00053-7.

Kane, M. T. (2006). Validation. In R. L. Brennan (Ed.), *Educational measurement* (4th ed., pp. 17–64). American Council on Education/Praeger Publishers.

Kasper, G., & Rose, K. R. (2002). *Pragmatics development in a second language.* Blackwell.

240 **Chapter 16** Assessing Interactional Competence and Pragmatics

Kley, K. (2019). What counts as evidence for interactional competence? Developing rating criteria for a German classroom-based paired speaking test. In R. Salaberry & R. Burch (Eds.), *Teaching and testing L2 interactional competence: Bridging theory and practice* (pp. 291–321). Multilingual Matters.

Kramsch, C. (1986). From language proficiency to interactional competence. *The Modern Language Journal, 70*(4), 366–372. https://doi.org/10.1111/j.1540-4781.1986.tb05291.x.

Leech, G. (1983). *Principles of pragmatics*. Longman.

Liu, J. (2006). *Measuring interlanguage pragmatic knowledge of EFL learners*. Peter Lang.

May, L., Nakatsuhara, F., Lam, D., & Galaczi, E. (2020). Developing tools for learning oriented assessment of interactional competence: bridging theory and practice. *Language Testing, 37*(2), 165–188. https://doi.org/10.1177/0265532219879044.

Mey, J. L. (2001). *Pragmatics: An introduction* (2nd ed.). Blackwell.

Nakatsuhara, F., May, L., Lam, D., & Galaczi, E. (2018). *Learning oriented feedback in the development and assessment of interactional competence (IELTS Research Notes, Issue 70). Cambridge Assessment.*

Ockey, G. J., & Chukharev-Hudilainen, E. (2021). Human versus computer partner in the paired oral discussion test. *Applied Linguistics, 42*(5), 924–944. https://doi.org/10.1093/applin/amaa067.

O'Hagan, S., Pill, J., & Zhang, Y. (2016). Extending the scope of speaking assessment criteria in a specific-purpose language test: operationalizing a health professional perspective. *Language Testing, 33*(2), 195–216. https://doi.org/10.1177/0265532215607920.

Pekarek Doehler, S. (2021). Toward a coherent understanding of L2 interactional competence: epistemologies of language learning and teaching. In S. Kunitz, N. Markee & O. Sert (Eds.), *Classroom-based conversation analytic research: Theoretical and applied perspectives on pedagogy* (pp. 19–33). Springer.

Pekarek Doehler, S., & Pochon-Berger, E. (2011). Developing 'methods' for interaction: a cross-sectional study of disagreement sequences in French L2. In J. K. Hall, J. Hellermann & S. Pekarek Doehler (Eds.), *L2 interactional competence and development* (pp. 206–243). Multilingual Matters. https://doi.org/10.21832/9781847694072-010.

Pill, J. (2016). Drawing on indigenous criteria for more authentic assessment in a specific-purpose language test: health professionals interacting with patients. *Language Testing, 33*(2), 175–193. https://doi.org/10.1177/0265532215607400.

Plake, B. S., & Hambleton, R. K. (2001). The analytic judgement method for setting standards on complex performance assessments. In G. J. Cizek (Ed.), *Setting performance standards: Concepts, methods, and perspectives* (pp. 283–312). Lawrence Erlbaum.

Purpura, J. (2004). *Assessing grammar*. Cambridge University Press.

Roever, C. (2005). *Testing ESL pragmatics*. Peter Lang.

Roever, C. (2010). Effects of native language in a test of ESL pragmatics: A DIF approach. In G. Kasper, H. thi Nguyen, D. R. Yoshimi & J. Yoshioka (Eds.), *Pragmatics & Language Learning* (Vol. 12, pp. 187–212). Honolulu, HI: National Foreign Language Resource Center.

Roever, C. (2022). *Teaching and testing second language pragmatics and interaction: A practical guide*. Routledge.

Roever, C. (2023). Testing and CA: the test makers' perspective – a discussion paper. *Applied Pragmatics, 5*(2), 289–296. https://doi.org/10.1075/ap.00019.roe.

Roever, C., & Dai, W. (2021). Interactional competence and language testing. In M. R. Salaberry & R. Burch (Eds.), *Assessing speaking* (pp. 23–49). Palgrave Macmillan.

Roever, C., & Ikeda, N. (2022). What scores from monologic speaking tests can(not) tell us about interactional competence. *Language Testing, 39*(1), 7–29. https://doi.org/10.1177/02655322211003332.

Roever, C., Fraser, C., & Elder, C. (2014). *Testing ESL sociopragmatics: development and validation of a web-based test battery*. Peter Lang.

Roever, C., Shintani, N., Zhu, Y., & Ellis, R. (2023). Proficiency effects on L2 pragmatics. In A. Martínez-Flor, J. Barón & A. Sánchez-Hernández (Eds.), *L2 pragmatics in action: Teachers, learners and the teaching–learning interaction process* (pp. 145–168). John Benjamins.

Schegloff, E. A. (1987). Analyzing single episodes of interaction: an exercise in conversation analysis. *Social Psychology Quarterly, 50*(2), 101–114. https://doi.org/10.2307/2786745.

Searle, J. R. (1969). *Speech acts*. Cambridge University Press.

Skogmyr Marian, K. (2021). Initiating a complaint: change over time in French L2 speakers' practices. *Research on Language and Social Interaction, 54*(2), 163–182. https://doi.org/10.1080/08351813.2021.1899709.

Tada, M. (2005). *Assessment of EFL pragmatic production and perception using video prompts* [Unpublished doctoral dissertation]. Temple University.

Taguchi, N., & Roever, C. (2017). *Second language pragmatics.* Oxford.

Te Molder, H., & Potter, J. (Eds.). (2005). *Conversation and cognition.* Cambridge University Press.

Timpe, V. (2013). *Assessing intercultural language learning.* Peter Lang. https://doi.org/10.3726/978-3-653-03884-2.

Timpe, V., & Choi, I. (2017). Exploring the validity of a second language intercultural pragmatics assessment tool. *Language Assessment Quarterly, 14*(1), 19–35. https://doi.org/10.1080/15434303.2016.1256406.

Timpe-Laughlin, V., Sydorenko, T., & Dombi, J. (2022). Human versus machine: investigating L2 learner output in face-to-face versus fully automated role-plays. *Computer Assisted Language Learning.* https://doi.org/10.1080/09588221.2022.2032184.

Walters, F. S. (2007). A conversation-analytic hermeneutic rating protocol to assess L2 oral pragmatic competence. *Language Testing, 24*(2), 155–183. https://doi.org/10.1177/0265532207076362.

Wang, X. (2023). *Second language interactional competence in mobile text chat: Developmental pathways and assessment* [Unpublished manuscript]. The University of Melbourne.

Wu, J., & Roever, C. (2021). Proficiency and preference organization in second language Mandarin Chinese refusals. *The Modern Language Journal, 105*(4), 897–918. https://doi.org/10.1111/modl.12736.

Yamashita, S. O. (1996). *Six measures of JSL pragmatics* (Technical Report No. 14). University of Hawai'i, Second Language Teaching and Curriculum Center.

Yoshitake, S. S. (1997). *Measuring interlanguage pragmatic competence of Japanese students of English as a foreign language: A multi-test framework evaluation* (Unpublished doctoral dissertation). Columbia Pacific University.

Youn, S. J. (2013). *Validating task-based assessment of L2 pragmatics in interaction using mixed methods* [Unpublished doctoral dissertation]. University of Hawai'i at Manoa.

Youn, S. J. (2015). Validity argument for assessing L2 pragmatics in interaction using mixed methods. *Language Testing, 32*(2), 199–225. https://doi.org/10.1177/0265532214557113.

Youn, S. J. (2019). Managing proposal sequences in role-play assessment: validity evidence of interactional competence across levels. *Language Testing, 37*(1), 76–106. https://doi.org/10.1177/0265532219860077.

Youn, S. J. (2020). Interactional features of L2 pragmatic interaction in role-play speaking assessment. *TESOL Quarterly, 54*(1), 201–233. https://doi.org/10.1002/tesq.542.

Suggested Readings

Betz, E., Malabarba, T., & Barth-Weingarten, D. (Eds) (2023). Describing and assessing interactional competence in a second language [Special issue]. *Applied Pragmatics, 5*(2).

Dai, D. W., & Davey, M. (2023). On the promise of using membership categorization analysis to investigate interactional competence. *Applied Linguistics.* https://doi.org/10.1093/applin/amad049.

Roever, C. (2022). *Teaching and testing second language pragmatics and interaction: a practical guide.* Routledge.

Salabarry, M. R., & Burch, R. (Eds.). (2021). *Assessing speaking.* Palgrave Macmillan.

Youn, S. J., & Burch, R. (2020). Where conversation analysis meets language assessment [Special issue]. *Papers in Language Testing and Assessment, 9*(1).

THEME 3

Assessment Development and Evaluation

CHAPTER 17

Assessing English as a Lingua Franca

Jennifer Jenkins and Constant Leung

Introduction: The Changing Global Role of English

During the past few decades, largely as a result of its position as the main language of globalization, English has undergone a major speaker-demographic transformation. Broadly speaking, up until the 1950s it was spoken primarily as a first/native language in the anglophone countries and as a nativized language in the postcolonial countries, as well as being learned as a foreign language (i.e., for communication between native and non-native speakers) in many other parts of the world. Nowadays, however, its most extensive use is as a lingua franca among speakers from different first languages, particularly, but not exclusively, non-native English speakers from countries with little or no connection to English-speaking colonial administrations.

A substantial body of empirical research into English as a lingua franca (henceforth ELF) conducted over the past 20 years or so has identified a number of linguistic features that differ from native English. More recent research has demonstrated that ELF is also characterized by extensive contingent variability, with speakers accommodating their language to an extent not found in other language use in order to make it appropriate to the diverse interlocutors engaged in the interaction in hand. ELF thus presents a twofold problem for English language teaching and assessment. First, the prolific global growth in ELF use, which is predicted to continue for several decades (see Coupland, 2010; Graddol, 2006), calls into question the prioritizing of standard native English grammatical and pragmatic norms in evaluating the competence of the majority of non-native learners. For, as Tomlinson (2010, p. 299) points out, these norms represent a kind of English that they "do not and never will speak." Second, ELF's inherent variability implies not only that language yardsticks need to be updated but also that new approaches to language modeling and norming in assessment, a key part of the international English teaching enterprise, are needed if we are to be able to judge whether ELF users' English is fit for purpose. In the discussion that follows, "assessment" will be used as a superordinate term, and the narrower term "testing" will be used where appropriate.

In the next section, we take a look at a high-stakes language curriculum and assessment framework, the Common European Framework of Reference for Languages (CEFR), and a sample of tests that are widely used around the world: Test of English as a Foreign Language (TOEFL), Test of English for International Communication (TOEIC), International English Language Testing System (IELTS), and the Pearson Test of English (PTE Academic) with

---

The Concise Companion to Language Assessment, First Edition. Edited by Antony John Kunnan.
© 2025 John Wiley & Sons, Inc. Published 2025 by John Wiley & Sons, Inc.

Chapter 17 Assessing English as a Lingua Franca

reference to language modeling. In the third section, we turn to ELF, report some of the key findings of empirical ELF research, and consider what these findings imply for conceptualizations of English. We go on in the fourth section to explore the implications of ELF for the testing of English and, in the final section, to consider the challenges involved in, and possible future directions for (research into), the assessment of English if it is to embrace ELF.

Popular Norms and Values Underpinning Curriculum and Assessment

We start with the CEFR (Council of Europe, 2001, 2020). Although, as its name suggests, the CEFR was originally devised for the teaching and assessment of second or foreign learners' proficiency in European languages, it has been widely adopted as a key reference point well beyond Europe; its presence can be found in parts of North and South America, Australia, and Asia (McNamara, 2011; Read, 2019). For instance, the suite of Cambridge ESOL examinations is aligned to the CEFR (https://www.cambridgeenglish.org/exams-and-tests/cefr/cefr-exams/?hc_location=ufi). The CEFR proficiency scales assess a range of language knowledge and skills against six levels, from A1 (the lowest), through A2, B1, B2, and C1, to C2 (the highest), according to the degree of linguistic complexity involved at each level. The descriptors for the six levels are not language specific, i.e., they are meant to be "universally" applicable. The wording of the descriptors for the highest level implies that ultimate achievement in the CEFR corresponds to linguacultural insider knowledge and skills in the focal language. For example, on the "C2 – Overall" scale, the candidate "can express him/herself spontaneously, very fluently and precisely, differentiating finer shades of meaning even in more complex situations" (Council of Europe, 2001, p. 24). In terms of the "qualitative aspects of spoken language use," at C2 the candidate's range includes "a good command of idiomatic expressions and colloquialisms" (p. 28). As regards listening with understanding, at the C2 level the candidate is expected to be able to "... follow specialised lectures and presentations employing a high degree of colloquialism, regional usage or unfamiliar terminology" (Council of Europe, 2020, p. 50).

While the CEFR is intended as a proficiency framework for languages in Europe including English, the tests we will now consider are specific to English. Given our focus for this discussion, a salient question here is the following: What kind of English underlies the internationally marketed proficiency tests? To promote the relevance and usefulness of their products, the test providers tend to present their tests as having wide currency in the target English-speaking environments. That said, it is interesting to note that a company representative described the modeling of English for the Pearson Test of English (PTE, Academic) thus:

> To create an international exam, we started by hiring item writers from the UK, the US and Australia ... Because we are not using a single standard model of English, we can grade all non-native students on a single scale. The first thing we look for is comprehensibility – are they understandable to the native speaker?
>
> (*EL Gazette*, September 2008, p. 10)

On this view, the "international" nature of the PTE presumably resides in the fact that it draws on a range of native English varieties (rather than only one native variety); by extension, it is concerned with non-native speakers' intelligibility to native speakers of all these varieties (rather than only with, say, native speakers of British English).

This pluralistic native speaker variety approach seems to reflect a good deal of the on-the-ground professional sensibility. A cursory glance at the English Language Teaching (ELT) discussions on the Internet would suggest that teachers and students are concerned with the variety of English they should be adopting. Emilie Pooler, speaking as the Director of Client

Management at Educational Testing Service (ETS), a U.S.-based company that offers both TOEFL and TOEIC, told the Hindu Education:

> The good news is that yes, you can, and as long as you speak (and write) in proper, correct English, you will be fine. Assessment experts will not penalize you if your accent is Australian, British, or Irish. If you have studied British English at school and this is the variety of English you are most comfortable with, there is absolutely nothing wrong with using British spelling and speaking with a British accent. (https://www.unimy.com/article/mba-preparation/toefl/blog-mba-preparation-toefl-british-american-english-advice)

Trina Duke, speaking as ETS assessment director, gave a talk on TOEIC with the title "Assessment of English as an International Language," at the 4th International ELF Conference in Hong Kong (May 2011). In her talk, she pointed out that TOEIC accepts non-native English-speaking raters provided that they first pass an English language test but added (when asked) that native speakers are not required to take any such test, only to demonstrate that they are "comfortable" with English. Evidently, TOEIC is "international" in the sense of being *used* (and marketed and administered) internationally, rather than in the sense of reflecting international *use* (the diverse ways in which English is used internationally).

The adherence to the putative "native speaker" norm appears to be a good deal more relaxed now, especially after the removal of all references to it in the CEFR Companion Volume (Council of Europe, 2020). Even so, it does raise its head occasionally. For instance, in the IELTS Speaking band descriptors under Grammatical Range and Accuracy at Band 9 (public version), it is stated that the candidate

- uses a full range of structures naturally and appropriately
- produces consistently accurate structures apart from 'slips' characteristic of native speaker speech.
(https://www.ielts.org/-/media/pdfs/speaking-band-descriptors.ashx)

Of course, the largely native speaker variety perspective adopted by the large international English-language-testing organizations represents just one view, albeit a very powerful one. Some test developers and researchers have explored other approaches. For instance, Brown and Lumley (1998, p. 94) developed a test of English proficiency for teachers of English in Indonesia in which "the native speaker was not set as the 'ideal'"; they consciously tried to incorporate appropriate local cultural content and English language usage (also see Hill, 1996 for a discussion on the case for using local non-English native speaker raters). There has also been research into shared first-language advantages in language testing; for example, Harding (2012) investigates whether test takers from a particular first-language background gain advantage when listening to English passages delivered in their own accents (e.g., Japanese test takers listening to Japanese-accented English passages). These are interesting early efforts designed to move beyond the confines of English native speakerdom in language testing. However, the use of ELF involves speakers from diverse linguacultural backgrounds. They are not necessarily oriented toward a particular variety of English (native or otherwise); they use ELF to communicate with one another, to get things done, and to socialize. Therefore the language assessment issues raised by ELF transcend questions of proficiency conceptualized in terms of a stable variety; they are concerned with what counts as effective and successful communication outcomes through the use of English that can include emergent and innovative forms of language and pragmatic meaning.

In the next section, we explore ELF research and its implications for the way we conceptualize the English language in its global contexts. We then return in the fourth section to the assessment of English, in order to consider the issues that ELF raises for the kinds of tests discussed above.

ELF Studies and Their Implications for Conceptualizations of English

The earliest empirical ELF research was that of Jenkins, who in the late 1980s began exploring the ways in which non-native English interlocutors from different first languages adjusted their pronunciation in order to render their speech more mutually intelligible.[1] She found accommodation at the phonological level to be a crucial aspect of ELF communication, while also identifying a "lingua franca core" of target features that contribute to mutual intelligibility, along with a larger "non-core" in which speakers can "safely" replace a target item with their preferred (often first language-influenced) variant (see Jenkins, 2000).

The next major development was Seidlhofer's (2001) call for corpus descriptions of ELF communication. Practicing what she preached, Seidlhofer set up the Vienna-Oxford International Corpus of English (VOICE, www.univie.ac.at/voice) in 2001. It now numbers over a million words, all meticulously transcribed, many with speech files, and is available online for free download. As a result of the wealth of new empirical evidence available in VOICE, Seidlhofer and her team were soon able to identify a number of lexico-grammatical ELF features that differ from native English use and are communicatively effective in ELF communication. These features include the use of count nouns where they are uncountable in native English (e.g., *informations*), zero marking of the third person present tense -*s*, and the use of an all-purpose tag question such as *isn't it?* or *no?* (Seidlhofer, 2004). Seidlhofer presented these features as a set of hypotheses rather than as definitive ELF features, but they have nevertheless proved remarkably durable, being repeatedly identified in subsequent empirical ELF studies (e.g., Dewey, 2007), and thus likely to indicate language change in progress among ELF users.

Soon after VOICE had been launched, Mauranen established the English as a Lingua Franca in Academic Settings (ELFA) corpus (www.helsinki.fi/englanti/elfa/elfacorpus) (see Mauranen, 2003) that focused, as its name suggests, on one particular – and highly prevalent – global context of ELF use, higher education.

Like the VOICE researchers, Mauranen and her ELFA team have since identified a number of lexico-grammatical features that differ from native English use. These include some of the features that have been identified in more general ELF corpus studies, as well as others that appear to be specific to academic settings. An example of the latter is the extending of an attention-catching function to the progressive involving its use where native speakers would typically use a stative verb, e.g., *are belonging* rather than *belong* (Ranta, 2006).

Another major branch of ELF research is pragmatics. Some of the pragmatics research focuses on miscommunication, particularly the preempting, negotiation, and resolution of nonunderstanding by means of various kinds of accommodation strategies. This research has tended to find that miscommunication is less frequent than in traditional English as a foreign language (EFL) communication and that when it occurs, it is dealt with discreetly in ways that do not interrupt the flow of conversation (Pitzl, 2005) by strategies such as repetition, clarification, and paraphrasing.

Studies of ELF pragmatics also focus on the ways in which speakers exploit their plurilingual resources, particularly by means of code switching. For example, Cogo (in Cogo & Dewey, 2006, p. 68) demonstrates how a French speaker uses the French

---

[1]Space constraints inevitably mean that our account of the vast amount of ELF research that has been conducted, particularly over the past decade, is somewhat truncated. A fuller account of the key studies and findings is available in a state-of-the-art article on developments in ELF research (Jenkins et al., 2011) and more recently in Jenkins et al. (2018).

expression *fleur bleue* for the English idiom *cheesy* in order to signal his cultural identity rather than to explain the meaning of *cheesy* to his German and Italian interlocutors. Other studies demonstrate how ELF speakers code switch into the languages of their interlocutors in order both to signal their plurilingual identity and to promote solidarity. These kinds of moving from one language to another enrich communication and have nothing to do with the lexical gaps that are so frequently cited in the traditional EFL literature as the prime motivation for code switching.

More recently, in line with the increasing availability of ELF data, there has been a growing realization that, despite the observed regularities in ELF forms, ELF communication is inherently more fluid, flexible, dynamic, and ad hoc than traditional language varieties used by putatively traditional speech communities. As a result, the focus of research has shifted from features to the underlying processes that motivate their use and, in turn, to the need for new conceptualizations of language and language practices. As Seidlhofer (2009, p. 238) points out, the terms "language variety" and "speech community" are "still used in the same way as they were long before the days of mass international travel, let alone electronic communication", and "at a time of pervasive and widespread global communication, the notion of community based purely on frequent face-to-face contact among people living in close proximity to each other clearly does not hold any more." Or, to put it another way, ELF "is a use- and context-driven phenomenon not primarily tied to any particular ethnic or racial group, nation, or geographic space" (Leung & Lewkowicz, 2006, p. 229). The heavy reliance on technology-mediated distal communication triggered by the COVID pandemic has amplified the need for further thinking. The (teaching and) testing of English therefore needs to reflect this reality if it is to be relevant to the ways in which the majority of non-native English learners will use the language in their future lives. Still more recently, ELF has undergone a further reconceptualization that foregrounds ELF's multilingual nature more than previously and focuses on the multilingualism of the vast majority of ELF users (see Jenkins, 2015). Let us now consider language assessment further in relation to ELF.

The Implications of ELF for Assessing English

The tests we described above (second section) all claim international status. This, we argue, relates to their international spread as well as to the use of test developers from a range of native English countries in the case of the PTE, and the use of non-native raters (provided they first pass a test) in the case of TOEIC. On the other hand, their interpretation of "internationalness" reflects a particular set of values and perspectives. For instance, the tests are all predicated on the notion of "foreign language," according to which the learner, and, therefore, the test candidate, is assumed to be learning the language in order to communicate with its native speakers, often for occupational or academic purposes. Consequently, the ultimate goal of learning is seen as a standard native variety of the target language. Any differences in forms from those that would be used by the notional native speaker of a standard variety of the language are thus regarded as learner errors in need of remediation.

Seidlhofer (2011, p. 18) sums up the characteristics of EFL as follows: Its linguacultural forms are "pre-existing, reaffirmed"; its objectives are "integration" and "membership in [a native speaker] ... community"; and the processes involved in its learning are "imitation" and "adoption." She contrasts these characteristics with those of an ELF perspective, whose linguacultural forms are "ad hoc" and "negotiated," whose objectives are "intelligibility" and "communication in [a non-native speaker] ... or mixed [non-native speaker–native speaker] ... community," and whose processes involve "accommodation" and "adaptation." From this perspective, differences from native English forms are not automatically errors. More importantly, those forms that according to traditional approaches are said to have fossilized may, by contrast, be considered evidence of English language change in progress.

250 **Chapter 17** Assessing English as a Lingua Franca

Indeed, Widdowson (2011) argues that from an ELF perspective "it is the [traditional] norms that are the fossils."

Despite claims to the contrary (e.g., Elder & Harding, 2008, argue that intercultural skills are already addressed in testing; Taylor, 2002, states that Cambridge ESOL "has been grappling with these issues for some time"), up to now, it is almost exclusively those scholars working with a critical perspective who have engaged with ELF (see, for example, Canagarajah, 2006; Leung, 2022a; Leung & Lewkowicz, 2006; Lowenberg, 2002; McNamara, 2009, 2011). Others seem to consider themselves to take a "liberal" approach in relation to ELF, but turn out, on closer inspection, to largely regard ELF as a surface-level phenomenon or to fall back on the established certainties in psychometrically oriented language testing that have been built up in the past 50 years or so (e.g., Elder & Davies, 2006; Elder & Harding, 2008; Taylor, 2006). This is implicit, for example, in Taylor's (2006) response to an article by Jenkins (2006a) on the implications of ELF for assessment. Instead of engaging with Jenkins's points about the changing global demographic of English and the contemporary importance of successful accommodation skills over narrow versions of "correctness," Taylor presents Cambridge ESOL's standard response and argues, for instance, that tests of standard native English fulfil test takers' and users' expectations and implies that an ELF approach patronizes learners and teachers (see Jenkins, 2006b). Others suggest that those scholars arguing for an ELF orientation to testing are politically motivated "bleeding hearts." In this respect, Canagarajah (2006, p. 241) argues that "debates in English-language testing should not be conducted with the condescending attitude that we scholars are just trying to be kind to those non-native speakers outside the inner circle."

Current assessment of English as a second language, then, continues to focus primarily on native English norms, while no substantial adjustments have been made to the basic assumptions of what English is in a wider world context. Decisions of momentous importance in people's lives are thus taken on the basis of their ability to pass tests such as IELTS and TOEIC that are grounded in kinds of English that are often insufficient and inadequate in relation to their situated language practices (Leung & Jenkins, 2020; Leung & Lewkowicz, 2012). Even when students are hoping to study in universities in native countries with English-speaking majorities, the communities they will circulate in are largely lingua franca groups made up of other students from a range of first-language backgrounds. These days, even many of their lecturers are non-native English speakers. Universities in countries such as Australia, Canada, New Zealand, the United Kingdom, and the United States that like to call themselves "international" need, therefore, to think more carefully about the linguistic implications of their proclaimed international status, including whether their *native* English-speaking staff and students would benefit from developing greater intercultural language skills for use on campus and beyond (see Jenkins, 2013).

While many of these issues have not been given sufficient attention in language assessment research, there are opportunities for interesting and informative enquiries. For instance, Kim's (2013) work on aviation communication points to the need for more attention. Her doctoral study investigated the attitudes within the Korean aviation industry to the English language-testing policy of the International Civil Aviation Organization (ICAO) (also see Kim, 2018; Kim & Elder, 2009). This study shows that a substantial amount of miscommunication between pilots and air traffic controllers is not the fault of the non-native English speaker but arises from the native English speakers' inability to accommodate to their ELF interlocutors, that the test is insufficiently oriented to the international (i.e., ELF) community for whom it is designed because of its privileging of native English norms, and that native English-speaking pilots need to be trained and tested in ELF communication. This study has much to offer others researching English language testing, and it is to be hoped that they will follow its example. (Also see Kim's, 2018, study on the communication issues involving a Russian pilot and a Korean air traffic controller.)

From an ELF standpoint, a fundamental problem with second language assessment is that the basis of its language modeling and norming has not kept in touch with contemporary developments in English. At a very broad theoretical level, the second language assessment community tends to regard the pedagogically rendered notion of communicative competence as the bedrock of their paradigm (e.g., Bachman, 1990; Canale & Swain, 1980). Established assessment frameworks such as the CEFR (Council of Europe, 2001) and tests such as IELTS and TOEFL all claim such affiliation. This concept, as first elaborated by Hymes some 50 years ago (Hymes, 1972), suggests that competence in language use is more than just having a knowledge of lexicogrammar and abstracted pragmatic conventions; it also involves the use of such knowledge with reference to social purposes in actual contexts of communication. According to this Hymesian view, communicative competence should be empirically derived – that is, what counts as effective communication should be based on observations of what people actually say and do. The Hymesian ethnographic impulse will continue to serve us well in future for as long as we pay close-up attention to the ways in which users of English in multiethnic and transcultural interactions make use of its lexico-grammatical (and other semiotic) resources to serve their pragmatic real-life purposes. In a world where this kind of lingua franca use of English is fast becoming the default scenario, language assessment has no alternative but to return to its empirical roots. The need for a major 're-think' has been made all the more urgent by the CEFR's recent efforts to expand the notion of language proficiency to take account of mediation and plurilingualism (see Leung, 2022b, 2023).

ELF: Challenges and Possible Future Directions for Teaching and Assessment

Apart from the less-than-productive impact that current English language teaching and testing paradigm has on candidates and their life chances, it also has a negative impact on the English language itself. As McNamara (2011, p. 1) points out, the testing status quo "makes us less able to respond to ... the fact that communication in the globalized workplace takes place using English as a lingua franca." The washback effect, then, is that testing promotes an outdated view of communication in English as relatively fixed and native-normative, whereas a major result of the globalization of English is that the language in its global contexts has become relatively fluid, flexible, contingent, and often non-native-influenced. Assessment is therefore not encouraging learners from exploiting the potential of the English language and their own resources as multilingual English speakers, and thus holding up English language change.

The challenge for English language education and assessment professionals, then, is to move away from a strong investment in abstracted native variety-referenced norms of language use, to take a broader account of the global sociolinguistic reality that is ELF, and to find effective ways of testing the receptive and productive skills relevant to that reality. While we understand the argument that the more fluid aspects of ELF do not lend themselves to fixed templates of rules and standards for teaching and assessment (see Ockey & Hirch, 2020), there are promising avenues to be explored. ELF researchers have for several years pointed out that language testing could, for example, refrain from penalizing the use of forms that are emerging as potential ELF variants, reward the successful use of accommodation strategies even where the result would be an error in native English, and penalize the use of forms that are not mutually intelligible in ELF, such as native English idioms (Jenkins, 2006a). But more than this: Now that there is clear evidence of the extent of ELF's fluidity and flexibility, test designers need to devise new approaches altogether to assessing English, so that, as we argued in our introduction, they can assess whether ELF users' English is fit for ELF use and the

252 Chapter 17 Assessing English as a Lingua Franca

extent to which contingent uses of ELF in context have facilitated communication. We believe that these are the directions for English-related language assessment research efforts.

Discussion Questions

1. Conventionally the assessment of vocabulary and grammar has been normed on regular patterns of usage sampled from English-medium communication data. How might ELF-oriented assessment deal with these aspects of language use, which are likely to involve elements of situated multilingualism and variable forms of use?

2. It is suggested that ELF-oriented assessment should be focused on communicative effectiveness in context. What kinds of assessment tasks or test items would allow us to tap into this dimension of language use?

References

Bachman, L. (1990). *Fundamental considerations in language testing*. Oxford University Press.

Brown, A., & Lumley, T. (1998). Linguistic and cultural norms in language testing: a case study. *Melbourne Papers in Language Testing, 7*(1), 80–96.

Canagarajah, A. S. (2006). Changing communicative needs, revised assessment objectives: testing English as an international language? *Language Assessment Quarterly, 3,* 229–242.

Canale, M., & Swain, M. (1980). Theoretical bases of communicative approaches to second language teaching and testing. *Applied Linguistics, 1*(1), 1–47.

Cogo, A., & Dewey, M. (2006). Efficiency in ELF communication: from pragmatic motives to lexicogrammatical innovation. *Nordic Journal of English Studies, 5,* 59–94.

Council of Europe. (2001). *Common European framework of reference for languages: Learning, teaching, assessment.* Cambridge University Press.

Council of Europe. (2020). *Common European framework of reference for languages: Learning, teaching, assessment – companion volume.* Council of Europe.

Coupland, N. (Ed.). (2010). *The handbook of language and globalization.* Wiley-Blackwell.

Dewey, M. (2007). *English as a lingua franca: An empirical study of innovation in lexis and grammar* (Unpublished doctoral dissertation). King's College London.

Elder, C., & Davies, A. (2006). Assessing English as a lingua franca. *Annual Review of Applied Linguistics, 26,* 282–301.

Elder, C., & Harding, L. (2008). Language testing and English as an international language. *Australian Review of Applied Linguistics, 31*(3), 1–34.

Graddol, D. (2006). *English next. Why global English may mean the end of "English as a foreign language".* British Council.

Harding, L. (2012). Accent, listening assessment and the potential for a shared-L1 advantage: a DIF perspective. *Language Testing, 29*(2), 163–180.

Hill, K. (1996). Who should be the judge? The use of non-native speakers as raters on a test of English as an international language. *Melbourne Papers in Language Testing, 5*(2), 29–50.

Hymes, D. (1972). On communicative competence. In J. B. Pride & J. Holmes (Eds.), *Sociolinguistics* (pp. 269–293). Penguin.

Jenkins, J. (2000). *The phonology of English as an international language.* Oxford University Press.

Jenkins, J. (2006a). The spread of English as an international language: a testing time for testers. *ELT Journal, 60*(1), 42–50.

Jenkins, J. (2006b). The times they are (very slowly) a-changin'. *ELT Journal, 60*(1), 61–62.

References   **253**

Jenkins, J. (2013). *English as a lingua franca in the international university.* Routledge.

Jenkins, J. (2015). Repositioning English and multilingualism in English as a lingua franca. *Englishes in Practice, 2*(3), 49–85.

Jenkins, J., Cogo, A., & Dewey, M. (2011). Review of developments in research into English as a lingua franca. *Language Teaching, 44*(3), 281–315.

Jenkins, J., Baker, W., & Dewey, M. (2018). *The Routledge handbook of English as a lingua franca.* Routledge.

Kim, H. (2013). Exploring the construct of radiotelephony communication: A critique of the ICAO English testing policy from the perspective of Korean aviation experts. *Papers in Language Testing and Assessment, 2*(2), 103–110.

Kim, H. (2018). What constitutes professional communication in aviation: is language proficiency enough for testing purposes? *Language Testing, 35*(3), 403–426. https://doi.org/10.1177/0265532218758127.

Kim, H., & Elder, C. (2009). Understanding aviation English as a lingua franca: perceptions of Korean aviation personnel. *Australian Review of Applied Linguistics, 32*(3), 1–17.

Leung, C. (2022a). Action-oriented plurilingual mediation: a search for fluid foundations. In N. Figueras & D. Little (Eds.), *Reflecting on the common European framework of reference for languages and its companion volume* (pp. 78–92). Multilingual Matters.

Leung, C. (2022b). Language proficiency: from description to prescription and back? *Educational Linguistics, 1*(1), 56–81.

Leung, C. (2023). English language proficiencies – recasting disciplinary and pedagogic sensibilities. *Critical Inquiry in Language Studies, 20*(4). https://www.tandfonline.com/doi/full/10.1080/15427587.2023.2292185.

Leung, C., & Jenkins, J. (2020). Mediating communication – ELF and flexible multilingualism perspectives on the common European framework of reference for languages. *Australian Review of Applied Linguistics, 3*(1), 26–41.

Leung, C., & Lewkowicz, J. (2006). Expanding horizons and unresolved conundrums: language testing and assessment. *TESOL Quarterly, 40*, 211–234.

Leung, C., & Lewkowicz, J. (2012). Language communication and communicative competence: a view from contemporary classrooms. *Language and Education, 26*(6), 1–17.

Lowenberg, P. (2002). Assessing English proficiency in the expanding circle. *World Englishes, 21*, 431–435.

Mauranen, A. (2003). The corpus of English as a lingua franca in academic settings. *TESOL Quarterly, 37*, 513–527.

McNamara, T. (2009). Principles of testing and assessment. In K. Knapp & B. Seidlhofer (Eds.), *Handbook of foreign language communication and learning* (pp. 607–627). Berlin, Germany: De Gruyter.

McNamara, T. (2011). Managing learning: authority and language assessment. *Language Teaching, 44*(4), 500–515.

Ockey, G. J., & Hirch, R. R. (2020). A step toward the assessment of English as a lingua franca. In G. J. Ockey & B. A. Green (Eds.), *Another generation of fundamental considerations in language assessment: A Festschrift in honor of Lyle F. Bachman* (pp. 9–28). Springer Singapore. https://doi.org/10.1007/978-981-15-8952-2_2.

Pitzl, M.-L. (2005). Non-understanding in English as a lingua franca: examples from a business context. *Vienna English Working Papers, 14*, 50–71.

Ranta, E. (2006). The "attractive" progressive – why use the *-ing* form in English as a lingua franca? *Nordic Journal of English Studies, 5*, 95–116.

Read, J. (2019). The influence of the common european framework of reference (CEFR) in the Asia-Pacific region. *Language Education and Acquisition Research Network Journal, 12*(1), 12–18.

Seidlhofer, B. (2001). Closing a conceptual gap: the case for a description of English as a lingua franca. *International Journal of Applied Linguistics, 11*, 133–158.

Seidlhofer, B. (2004). Research perspectives on teaching English as a lingua franca. *Annual Review of Applied Linguistics, 24*, 209–239.

Seidlhofer, B. (2009). Common ground and different realities: world Englishes and English as a lingua franca. *World Englishes, 28*, 236–245.

Seidlhofer, B. (2011). *Understanding English as a lingua franca.* Oxford University Press.

Taylor, L. (2002). *Assessing learners' English: But whose/which English(es)? Research notes 10.* University of Cambridge ESOL Examinations.

Taylor, L. (2006). The changing landscape of English: implications for language assessment. *ELT Journal*, *60*, 51–60.

Tomlinson, B. (2010). Which test of English and why? In A. Kirkpatrick (Ed.), *The Routledge handbook of world Englishes* (pp. 599–616). Routledge.

Widdowson, H. G. (2011 May). *Only connect. Plenary address given at the 4th international English as a lingua franca conference*, Hong Kong.

Suggested Readings

Gorter, D., & Cenoz, J. (2017). Language education policy and multilingual assessment. *Language and Education*, *31*(3), 231–248.

Mirhosseini, S.-A., & De Costa, P. (Eds.). (2019). *The sociopolitics of English language testing*. Bloomsbury Academic.

Schissel, J. L., Leung, C., & Chalhoub-Deville, M. (2019). The construct of multilingualism in language testing. *Language Assessment Quarterly*, *16*(4–5), 373–378.

Shohamy, E., Tannenbaum, M., & Gani, A. (2022). Bi/multilingual testing for bi/multilingual students: policy, equality, justice, and future challenges. *International Journal of Bilingual Education and Bilingualism*. https://doi.org/10.1080/13670050.2022.2062665.

CHAPTER 18

Scenario-Based Language Assessment

Heidi Liu Banerjee

Introduction

In recent years, the opportunities offered by rapid technological advances as well as an ongoing effort to broaden the measured constructs in language assessment have led to the creation of new approaches to assessing language learners' communicative competence that is more closely aligned with their real-life language use. One of these approaches is scenario-based language assessment (SBLA). As defined by Purpura (2019), a scenario is:

> a description of an internally consistent set of naturally-occurring, imagined scenes or events in which characters carry out actions and interact with each other until they bring the overarching scenario goal to conclusion. Given that scenarios are proxies for real-life situations, they are used to create a context in which engaged examinees use their mental and dispositional resources to perform a series of carefully sequenced tasks to achieve some intended goal. Scenarios are naturally flexible in that they can present straightforward scripts with few complications or surprising features, or they can be varied in complex ways that present storylines with surprising features such as novel insights, shifts in values or perspectives, feedback, and so forth. Similar to real life, just about anything can be modeled to create dynamic scenarios. (37:03)

Building on the conceptualization of *scenario* in an assessment context, Purpura and Banerjee (2021, 2022, see also Purpura, 2021) described SBLA as a digitally delivered assessment technique that utilizes scenarios to provide test takers with a purposeful, real-life-like situation in which they are expected to act as a fully contributing member to achieve an overarching goal (e.g., present a solution to a community problem and pitch an idea to a committee) with their imaginary team, until the scenario goal is fulfilled. As part of the scenario narrative, the scenario goal is contextualized using a coherent set of tasks that are carefully sequenced to model the habits of mind of those who would be capable of achieving the scenario goal effectively. Purpura and Banerjee further noted that, to achieve the scenario goal, test takers are required to display a range of linguistic, topical, socio-cognitive, and other dispositional resources within each task throughout the scenario narrative. In addition, test takers are generally expected to engage in several tasks in a collaborative manner with their imaginary team. Through simulated collaboration and social interaction with the imaginary team, test takers have an opportunity to develop topical knowledge, apply relevant strategies to solve

---

The Concise Companion to Language Assessment, First Edition. Edited by Antony John Kunnan.
© 2025 John Wiley & Sons, Inc. Published 2025 by John Wiley & Sons, Inc.

any challenge presented in the scenario, receive assistance or feedback within the assessment space, and support or be supported emotionally. Therefore, while the ultimate purpose of SBLA is to assess test takers' situated language proficiency, the entire scenario – including the narrative, the simulated interaction, and the overarching goal – is intended to be a worthwhile educational experience in its own right.

Broadening the Measured Constructs of Language Knowledge, Skills, and Abilities Using a Scenario-Based Language Assessment Approach

Considering that the components in SBLA carry the capabilities of allowing test takers to perform in a way that is aligned with their behaviors in a similar situation in real life, SBLA has gained increasing attention to assess broadened constructs of language knowledge, skills, and abilities (KSAs). In the K-12 context, some of the first applications of SBLA in language assessments include the Cognitive Based Assessment of, for, and as Learning (CBAL) initiative (Bennett, 2010; Bennett & Gitomer, 2009) and Global, Integrated Scenario-Based Assessment (GISA) under the Reading for Understanding initiative (RfU; O'Reilly & Sabatini, 2013; Sabatini & O'Reilly, 2013), where SBLA has been utilized to capture the complex performances of reading and writing skills required to succeed in the 21st century.

One of the targeted KSAs in CBAL that has benefited greatly from the use of SBLA is integrated reading and writing skills (Deane, 2011; Deane et al., 2012; O'Reilly et al., 2015; Sheehan & O'Reilly, 2012) given that the assessment design features allow for the simulation of the way students engage in and process academic tasks in real life, such as conducting research and critically reading and summarizing sources. To illustrate, O'Reilly et al. (2015) provided an SBLA example, *Dolphin Intelligence*, where the task sequence is modeled after the cognitive activities of building and sharing knowledge. In the scenario, test takers are expected to research the topic of dolphin intelligence with their simulated classmates and create a poster for the upcoming science fair. To achieve the scenario goal, test takers are first asked to evaluate and determine the relevance of a list of Web search entries (*activate background knowledge*); then, they are presented with an informational text based on which they demonstrate their reading comprehension, vocabulary knowledge, and summary writing ability (*understand the text*); next, test takers will use a graphic organizer to populate and organize the information they have received (*consolidate knowledge*); finally, they write a report on dolphin intelligence that is designed to be used in the poster (*convey knowledge*). Through this assessment example, O'Reilly et al. demonstrated not only how SBLA can be properly contextualized but also how the design process of an SBLA can be informed so that the assessment can yield meaningful and generalizable interpretations.

Along the same line of reasoning as CBAL, GISA was developed to address the need to measure a broadened scope of reading skills that resemble test takers' cognitive activities in real-life situations and how they would realistically engage in reading in these situations. In order for test takers' reading comprehension to be assessed in an authentic environment, SBLA is used to provide a purpose or goal for reading, establish coherence among reading sources, probe students' reading strengths and weaknesses, promote collaboration, simulate valid literacy contexts, and promote motivation and engagement (O'Reilly & Sabatini, 2013). In addition to utilizing a sequence of thematically related tasks as well as simulated assistance and interaction to assess test takers' reading skills, GISA operationalizes background knowledge, metacognitive or self-regulatory strategies, language-related strategies, and motivation or engagement as performance moderators to enhance the reading process (O'Reilly & Sabatini, 2013; Shore et al., 2017). Empirical evidence collected has been in support of the validity and usability of SBLA in GISA (O'Reilly et al., 2014; Sabatini et al., 2014), and researchers have demonstrated that SBLA is more capable of capturing the multifacetedness of reading KSAs than the traditional assessment systems (Sabatini et al., 2019).

Inspired by the potentials SBLA has demonstrated in the mainstream educational context, several researchers have applied SBLA in the second and/or foreign language (L2) assessment context to broaden the measured constructs of L2 KSAs. Banerjee (2019a, b) developed an SBLA, *Nutrition Ambassador*, to measure high-intermediate L2 learners' topical knowledge and their L2 KSAs as part of the broadened construct of L2 communicative competence. Following the key literacy practice of *building and sharing knowledge* identified in the CBAL initiatives (Deane et al., 2015), the *Nutrition Ambassador* SBLA simulated the cognitive process of how L2 learners work with others, listen to and read a variety of resources and identify relevant information, and synthesize or summarize the relevant information to share what they know in a socio-interpersonal target language use domain. Test takers' topical knowledge was measured by a set of items that were presented to test takers both at the beginning (i.e., to gauge and activate prior topical knowledge) and at the end (i.e., to measure topical learning) of the scenario. The study found that different aspects of topical knowledge appeared to have some effect on test takers' ability to achieve the scenario goal: The amount of topic-related factual information test takers already knew about appeared to facilitate their knowledge-building process, whereas the amount of topic-related lexical knowledge they already had seemed to influence their ability to share knowledge through writing. Furthermore, test takers' proficiency levels were shown to positively contribute to their ability to learn more about the topic as they progressed through the scenario. In other words, the more proficient an L2 learner is, the more likely they learn about the topic as they engage with resources for a communicative purpose and subsequently utilize it to fulfill the scenario goal.

In response to having a placement exam that represents better construct coverage and as a result can better place incoming undergraduate students into the appropriate English class levels than the existing exam at a university in Asia, Kunnan et al. (2022) developed multiple SBLA modules for a Test of Academic English (TAE) at the Common European Framework of Reference (CEFR) A2, B1, and B2 levels. Specifically, the research group developed three scenarios at the A2 level, two scenarios at the B1 level, and two scenarios at the B2 level. In each scenario module, test takers were asked to demonstrate a range of level-appropriate independent and integrated L2 KSAs. For instance, in one of the B2-level scenarios, test takers were presented with two tasks, both assessing integrated skills. In Task 1, test takers had to first read an article about a topic related to the scenario, followed by watching a video of students discussing the topic. Then, test takers were asked to summarize how the opinions in the two test inputs differed in an oral response. In Task 2, test takers were presented with the notes they took on both the reading passage and discussion video in Task 1, and they were required to write an essay to express their own opinions to fulfill the scenario goal. The design of the TAE reaffirms how SBLA can be used to measure both independent and integrated L2 KSAs using thematically related tasks in a coherent storyline. The TAE also highlights how an SBLA approach can address topics that are culturally relevant to the local contexts.

Examining the nature of strategic competence and its role as a broadened construct of L2 learners' speaking ability, Seong (2023) designed an SBLA, *SBEST*, in which a set of strategy tasks was used to measure the metacognitive and cognitive strategies L2 learners would typically engage in when preparing for an oral response to an academic discussion forum. In *SBEST*, where the culminating scenario goal is for test takers to present their opinions about journalism based on the videos they have watched, test takers were asked to plan how they would achieve the scenario goal, predict the content of the videos, take notes of the videos, use their notes to prepare an outline of their responses, monitor their speaking performance, and finally, reflect on their performance. The sequence of the strategy tasks mirrored the habits of mind of how L2 learners would process audiovisual resources to prepare for an academic discussion topic and produce the final oral responses. Seong's study offered valuable insights into the role strategic competence plays in L2 learners' academic speaking ability. It also demonstrated the capability of SBLA to capture and assess aspects of communicative competence, in this case, strategy use, that is typically not considered in traditional assessments.

At Teachers College, Columbia University in New York City, the Scenario-Based Language Assessment Lab[1] (hereafter the SBLA Lab, or the Lab) was founded in 2016 to comprehensively explore the potentials of SBLA in L2 assessment contexts. One of the main missions of the SBLA Lab is to design assessments with meaningfully contextualized tasks that reflect how L2 learners would realistically use their L2 KSAs as well as essential 21st-century skills, such as active learning, critical thinking, and complex problem-solving (World Economic Forum, 2020), to communicate successfully in modern society. The first SBLA module the Lab has developed simulated a classroom setting where learners needed to decide on the destination of their class trip. In the scenario, test takers were formed into groups with three simulated peers, learned about the two destinations their group was interested in through listening and reading tasks, summarized the pros and cons of each destination for their simulated teacher through writing tasks, and finally, pitched the final decision on their group's behalf to a simulated selection committee through a speaking task (Eskin et al., 2022; Purpura et al., 2021; Purpura & Banerjee, 2018). A key feature of this SBLA is that throughout the scenario, feedback and assistance from the simulated peers and teacher were embedded to moderate performance, create an authentic classroom-based collaboration environment, ease test takers' anxiety, and promote engagement. Results from several test administrations have shown that the SBLA functioned as intended and reliably elicited construct-relevant performances. Test takers also reported high levels of positive affective dispositions, such as enjoyment and engagement, during the scenario, and they valued the learning opportunities and authentic experience the SBLA provided.

Thus far, the SBLA approach to language assessments has shown great potentials and promising results in both the mainstream educational context, where the focus is on literacy skills essential for college and career readiness, and the L2 assessment context where the assessment purposes and target language use domains vary more widely. The studies described in this section have demonstrated that SBLA allows for a more comprehensive measurement of learners' real-life language use. Furthermore, SBLA is highly customizable and can be flexibly tailored to specific language use contexts, such as health care, business, or education, making it a more relevant and useful tool for language learners who have specific goals. As SBLA continues to gain popularity, it is likely that we will see more widespread adoption of this approach in language assessment.

Guiding the Design of Scenario-Based Language Assessment Using a Learning-Oriented Assessment Framework

With the increasing interest in and discussion of applying SBLA to L2 assessment contexts, the development of a theoretical framework is critical to systematically guide the development of SBLA. Purpura (2019; see also Purpura & Banerjee, 2018, 2021, 2022) argued that even though SBLA is a relatively "new" L2 assessment approach, its merits are well connected to the learning-oriented assessment (LOA) framework (Purpura, 2022, 2023; Purpura & Turner, 2014, 2018; Turner & Purpura, 2016) in that both SBLA and LOA consider assessment to be a multifaceted and dynamic activity that involves testing, teaching, and learning.

---

[1]To learn more about the SBLA Lab, visit https://tinyurl.com/TCSBLA.

Through the lens of eight interrelated, yet independent, dimensions, the LOA framework addresses the interactions between teaching, learning, and assessment that can be applied in both classroom-based and large-scale assessment contexts. Consolidating what learner-centered assessment should entail from various classroom-based assessment approaches (e.g., formative assessment, Black & Wiliam, 2004; diagnostic assessment, Alderson, 2005; and dynamic assessment, Lantolf & Poehner, 2011), the LOA framework "highlights learning goals, performance evaluation and feedback, and the role they play in developing individual learning progressions" (Turner & Purpura, 2016, p. 260). Each of the dimensions and its connection to SBLA are described below.

The first and the most fundamental dimension of the LOA framework is the contextual dimension. The contextual dimension concerns the real-life language use domains in which learners would realistically demonstrate their L2 KSAs, such as a socio-interpersonal domain where learners plan an event with friends, or an academic domain where learners collaborate with classmates on a school project (Purpura & Turner, 2018). The design of an SBLA begins with defining a scenario in which a communicative goal needs to be fulfilled (Purpura & Banerjee, 2021). The contextual dimension relates to the settings, scenarios, or themes chosen to guide the storyline of the SBLA. Ideally, these contextual factors should reflect what learners would encounter or be modeled after how learners would behave in real-life situations, so that the performance results can be generalizable across similar contexts.

The second dimension of the LOA framework is the proficiency dimension. With L2 assessment, the proficiency dimension is concerned with the targeted proficiency components in terms of what L2 KSAs learners are expected to demonstrate based on curriculum, instruction, or standards. The specifications of the proficiency dimension are used to inform what needs to be assessed, how the performance results should be interpreted, and what types of feedback and assistance should be provided (Turner & Purpura, 2016). In SBLA, learners-situated L2 proficiency is elicited through a series of thematically related tasks where the sequence of the tasks closely resembles the habits of mind (Purpura, 2021; Purpura & Banerjee, 2021). The situated proficiency components include foundational L2 KSAs, topical resources, and cognitive and metacognitive strategies that learners may need to display in the process of achieving the scenario goal. In other words, compared to the other approaches to L2 assessment, SBLA allows learners to demonstrate their situated L2 proficiency in a broader scope.

The third dimension, the elicitation dimension, relates to how evidence of learners' KSAs can be elicited to reflect their expected proficiency. In the LOA framework, the elicitation dimension is conceptualized to include both planned (e.g., tests and quizzes) and unplanned (e.g., talk-in-interaction) assessments, particularly when an assessment is internal to the classroom (Turner & Purpura, 2016). With respect to SBLA, the elicitation dimension focuses on the various planned methods test developers may employ to elicit the targeted KSAs in the scenario. Because SBLA is often deployed through computer-based platforms, the technological capabilities of the platforms have allowed for the utilization of a variety of item types (e.g., multiple choice, matching, graphic organizers, editing, and paragraph writing) to elicit both discrete and constructed responses.

The fourth dimension, the socio-cognitive dimension, is related to the cognitive (e.g., attention span and cognitive processing), socio-cognitive (e.g., collaborative effort), and strategic demands (e.g., planning and reasoning) of the assessment tasks and the extent to which these demands remain construct relevant within an assessment (Purpura & Turner, 2018). In SBLA, the tasks are thematically and logically sequenced to reflect the habits of mind. Such a design not only allows learners to explicitly apply strategies and KSAs as they would in real-life situations but also ensures broader representation of the targeted proficiency components (Bennett, 2010).

The fifth dimension of the LOA framework, the instructional dimension, concerns how teachers, peers, or learners themselves utilize the information from planned or unplanned assessment to provide assistance or feedback and to promote further processing and learning. Such an assessment component, while largely embraced by the assessment for learning proponents (e.g., Black, 1986; Wiliam, 2011), was rarely, if ever, operationalized in traditional language assessments. SBLA, however, considers the instructional dimension a vital component during the goal-achieving process. Through the implementation of simulated teachers, peers, or other characters, SBLA demonstrates how guided assistance and feedback can be embedded within an assessment to not only provide a language use context that is natural to learners but also allow learners' KSAs to be further probed with proper guidance.

The sixth dimension, the social–interactional dimension, relates to the interactions between teachers, peers, and learners that are embedded in instruction within an assessment. It also relates to how these interactions may promote or impede learning (Purpura & Turner, 2018). Because one of the main features of SBLA is the use of simulated characters to interact with test takers, the social–interactional dimension plays a central role in the effectiveness of the scenario narrative. In academic-oriented SBLA, interactions mostly occur in two forms: (i) between simulated teachers and test takers, where instructions are given and assistance is provided and (ii) between test takers and simulated peers, where knowledge is co-constructed and problems are solved collaboratively.

The seventh dimension of the LOA framework, the affective dimension, brings attention to how assessments tap into learners' socio-psychological dispositions, such as engagement, motivation, and anxiety. The affective dimension also highlights how these affective factors may promote or impede learning (Purpura & Turner, 2018). While research on the relationships between L2 learners' affective characteristics and their learning abounds, these characteristics have not been explicitly addressed within an assessment. In SBLA, the affective dimension is explicitly addressed with many of its design features. For instance, through the incorporation of authentic tasks and simulated characters, SBLA shows great potential in promoting test takers' engagement and motivation. At the same time, the interaction between simulated characters and test takers can potentially ease test takers' anxiety and allow them to demonstrate their KSAs in a construct-relevant manner.

Finally, the eighth dimension of the LOA framework, the technological dimension, highlights the indispensable role technologies play in L2 contexts. This newly added LOA dimension (Purpura, 2022, 2023) concerns both the extent to which technologies may enhance (or impede) L2 learning processes and how L2 teachers' and learners' own digital literacy and familiarity with technologies may affect the overall teaching, learning, or assessment experience. Given that one key feature of SBLA is it is being digitally delivered, the technological aspect of assessment is central to the design and development of SBLA. To illustrate, SBLA utilizes the technological capacities of the chosen assessment delivery platforms to present the storyline of the scenario, embed simulated characters for interactions, and implement feedback or assistance where necessary, all while recording test takers' L2 performance throughout the assessment process. Currently, except for large testing organizations (e.g., Educational Testing Service where CBAL and GISA were developed) that rely on their in-house assessment delivery platforms, locally developed SBLA modules (e.g., Banerjee, 2019a, b; Eskin et al., 2022; Kunnan et al., 2022; Purpura et al., 2021; Purpura & Banerjee, 2018; Seong, 2023) mainly utilized learning management systems, such as Moodle, or experience management software, such as Qualtrics, to deliver the assessments. Because neither learning management systems nor experience management software were developed specifically for language assessment purposes, many desired features of SBLA required customizations with technical expertise, which can be challenging and costly.

Through the lens of the LOA framework, the added value of SBLA compared to other approaches to language assessment can be highlighted. Specifically, the key differences between SBLA and trait-based or task-based language assessment approaches include the following: (i) SBLA allows for the implementation of guided assistance and feedback to scaffold test takers' performance as a part of the storyline (the instructional dimension); (ii) SBLA utilizes

An Example of Scenario-Based Language Assessment: *Nutrition Ambassador* **261**

simulated characters to collaborate with test takers to co-construct KSAs, actions, and dispositions (the social–interactional dimension); and (iii) the design features in SBLA explicitly seek to engage test takers' participation and ease their anxiety (the affective dimension). For trait-based or task-based language assessment approaches, the instructional and social–interactional aspects of the test design are not a part of the assessment considerations, and the affective aspect of the test design is not explicitly incorporated.

In L2 assessment contexts, several SBLAs have applied the LOA framework as a theoretical foundation to justify the use of the SBLA approach and guide the SBLA design process (e.g., Banerjee, 2019a, b; Davoodifard et al., 2022; Eskin et al., 2022; Joo et al., 2021, 2022; Machetti et al., 2022). With SBLAs' capabilities of measuring complex constructs, having a consistent design framework allows test developers to ensure the validity across tasks in an SBLA, and test users to make meaningful interpretations of the assessment results. In the following section, the SBLA developed by Banerjee (2019a, b), *Nutrition Ambassador*, is described to exemplify how the LOA framework can guide the development of an SBLA.

An Example of Scenario-Based Language Assessment: *Nutrition Ambassador*

The *Nutrition Ambassador* SBLA was designed as a high-intermediate placement exam module for the Community English Program at a major research university in the United States. All students enrolled in this program are adult ESL learners, and they represent a wide range of nationalities, professional backgrounds, English proficiency levels, and learning motivations. The assessment was developed in and delivered via Qualtrics with some customization using HTML and JavaScript.

One of the crucial features of SBLA is to have a coherent storyline embedded in the scenario so that test takers can perform in a way that is natural to their real-life behaviors (O'Reilly et al., 2015). Therefore, the first step of creating an SBLA is to define its context and the culminating scenario goal, addressing the contextual dimension of the LOA framework. In *Nutrition Ambassador*, test takers were set in a scene where they were to work with two neighbors for the town's "Nutrition Ambassador" event. With their neighbors, they would learn something about nutrition – food additives, specifically – and share what they learned with the town. Figure 18.1 shows how *Nutrition Ambassador* was contextualized for the test takers.

As part of the contextualization, the simulated characters with whom test takers will fulfill the scenario goal are then introduced. Throughout the scenario, the simulated characters interact constantly with test takers through chats. The simulated characters in SBLA serve several key purposes: (i) to provide test takers with instructions on the assessment tasks; (ii) to provide assistance or feedback to the test takers; (iii) to create a sense of collaboration; and (iv) to encourage engagement and ease anxiety, connecting to the social–interactional, instructional, and affective dimensions of the LOA framework. In *Nutrition Ambassador*, after learning about the context, test takers were introduced to Ms. Norman, the event organizer, and Jane and Paul, test takers' "neighbors" who would work on the tasks together. Figure 18.2 shows the initial interaction between the simulated characters and test takers. Due to technological constraints at the time of test development, all interactions were conducted through static images and text chats.

Following the introduction of the simulated characters, the sequence of the tasks within the scenario should be defined. For the results from SBLA to yield meaningful interpretations, it is critical for the sequence of the tasks to mirror the habits of mind, or the way test takers would naturally use the target language in a similar real-life situation, which is related to the socio-cognitive dimension of the LOA framework. In order to have a logical, coherent design of the test structure, the theoretical framework of *Nutrition Ambassador* followed the building

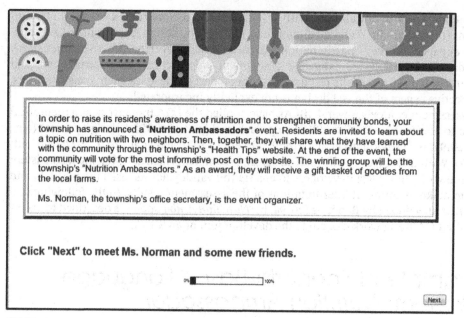

FIGURE 18.1 Context and scenario goal. *Source:* From Banerjee (2019a), p. 141. Copyright 2019 by Routledge / Taylor and Francis Group.

Ms. Norman: Hello there! I'm so happy to have you participate in this event. Learning about nutrition is important! Don't we all want to live a healthy life? I've paired you up with Jane and Paul. Come and meet them!

Jane: Hi! I don't think we've met before. I just moved here 6 months ago. I'm really looking forward to working with you and Paul to promote nutrition knowledge in the community!

Paul: Hi, nice to meet you! This is such a cool event. For me, it's not just about promoting nutrition knowledge in the community. I want to learn more about nutrition for my own health, too!

FIGURE 18.2 Initial interactions with the simulated characters. *Source:* From Banerjee © 2019a / Taylor and Francis.

and sharing knowledge key literacy practice described in O'Reilly et al. (2015). Figure 18.3 summarizes the assessment tasks in *Nutrition Ambassador* and their purpose in relation to building and sharing knowledge.

As the assessment tasks are where test takers' target KSAs are being measured within an SBLA, the constructs each task intends to measure must be carefully defined. The measured

An Example of Scenario-Based Language Assessment: *Nutrition Ambassador* 263

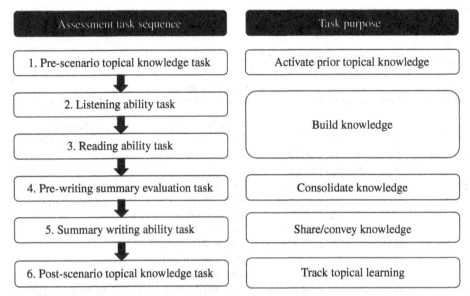

FIGURE 18.3 A summary of the assessment tasks in the *Nutrition Ambassador* SBLA.

constructs and elicitation methods of the assessment tasks address the proficiency and elicitation dimensions of the LOA framework. In *Nutrition Ambassador*, the pre-scenario topical knowledge task was used to determine the extent to which test takers already knew about the topic in the scenario (i.e., food additives), and the post-scenario topical knowledge task was used to track test takers' topical knowledge gains at the end of the scenario. The two topical knowledge tasks shared the same set of items. Each of the L2 assessment tasks elicits specific L2 KSAs that are appropriate for high-intermediate L2 learners with respect to the curriculum adopted in the Community English Program. Given that *Nutrition Ambassador* involved complex constructs, the evidence-centered design (ECD) framework (Almond et al., 2015; Mislevy et al., 2003) was used to ensure that the evidence gathered from each of the assessment tasks was systematic, logical, and coherent. Specifically, the conceptual assessment framework (CAF) within the ECD framework was used as the test specification blueprint in this SBLA, as shown in Table 18.1.

With the sequence and nature of the assessment tasks identified, the next step is to determine how instructions should be presented as part of the coherent storyline in SBLA, where instructions as well as feedback and assistance are commonly embedded in interactions with the simulated characters. In other words, test takers learn about what is expected of them, or what they need to do, through engaging in the chats with the simulated characters. As mentioned earlier, such a design feature is closely connected to the social–interactional, instructional, and affective dimensions of the LOA framework. In *Nutrition Ambassador*, Ms. Norman provided the general scenario instructions and assistance to guide the "event participants" (i.e., Paul, Jane, and test takers) through the scenario, whereas Paul and Jane provided test takers with specific instructions as a way to facilitate their collaboration. Figure 18.4 depicts the instruction of the culminating summary writing task, where all three simulated characters provided test takers with a part of the task instruction and assistance.

As illustrated through *Nutrition Ambassador*, the LOA framework is a useful theoretical framework for guiding the design process of assessments with complex constructs. To create a successful SBLA, how each of the eight LOA dimensions is manifested through the assessment design and components needs to be carefully documented, as each dimension, where appropriate, plays a unique role in contributing to an authentic experience for test takers in an SBLA. In other words, when designing an SBLA, it is important to carefully

264 Chapter 18 Scenario-Based Language Assessment

> ### TABLE 18.1
>
> ### The assessment blueprint using the CAF
>
> | Assessment task | Proficiency claims | Evidence to be collected | Item/Task type |
> | --- | --- | --- | --- |
> | 1. Pre-scenario topical knowledge task | Test takers have some relevant topical knowledge that may have an effect on their language performance | Test takers' responses to the topical knowledge items | Multiple choice and matching |
> | 2. Listening ability task | Test takers have the ability to understand the information conveyed in the video either implicitly or explicitly and to identify inaccurate information in peers' notes | Test takers' responses to the comprehension questions related to the "*What are food additives?*" video and their evaluation and correction of their peers' notes | True/false and error correction |
> | 3. Reading ability task | Test takers have the ability to identify main ideas and details and make inferences | Test takers' responses to the comprehension questions related to the "*What's really on your dinner plate?*" article | Multiple choice |
> | 4. Pre-writing summary evaluation ability task | Test takers have the ability to evaluate the quality of the model summaries written by their peers based on the summary guideline | Test takers' identification of whether their peers' summaries meet the criteria of a good summary, and if not, what quality is lacking | Multiple choice |
> | 5. Summary writing ability task | Test takers can write a coherent and accurate summary to convey the information they have obtained | Test takers' written summary | Constructed written response |
> | 6. Post-scenario topical knowledge task | Test takers will have gained topical knowledge related to the topic through the process of building and sharing knowledge | Test takers' responses to the same topical knowledge items as appeared at the beginning | Multiple choice and matching |
>
> *Source:* Adapted from Banerjee (2019a, p. 144). Copyright 2019 by Routledge.

consider each dimension throughout the entire design process, from defining the context to creating appropriate simulated characters, and from specifying the measured constructs to embedding construct-relevant and helpful assistance and feedback. However, it is equally important to note that the dimensions in the LOA framework simply serve as a guide for designing SBLA; it does not mean that all eight dimensions must be included in the design for an assessment tool to be considered SBLA. For example, in Kunnan et al. (2022) where multiple SBLA modules were developed, the authors explicitly explained that while the contextual, proficiency, and elicitation dimensions were addressed in all modules, the socio-cognitive, social–interactional, and affective dimensions were only included in some modules, and the instructional dimension was not considered for any module as it did not fit the purpose of the assessment. In all, through a systematic design

Paul: Great! Now, we need a paragraph to introduce the unsafe food additives. I think we can do that by summarizing Paragraphs 6-10 in the article Mike showed us.

Jane: I agree! Why don't you try and write a 1-paragraph summary to tell people about the unsafe food additives? Since we want to teach our neighbors about these unsafe food additives, I think the summary should include:

- What are the unsafe food additives?
- Where can we find these unsafe food additives?
- What can these unsafe food additives do to our health?

Ms. Norman: Sounds like a plan! Again, in your paragraph, please make sure:

- All of the information is correct.
- Only the important and necessary information is included.

FIGURE 18.4 Summary writing task instruction embedded in interactions. *Source:* From Banerjee © 2019 / Taylor and Francis.

process, SBLA can be used to effectively measure broadened constructs of language KSAs in a natural way that is reflective of real-life situations.

Challenges and Future Directions

SBLA has opened up possibilities for us to measure a broadened scope of L2 learners' real-life communicative competence, including how they may apply their language KSAs to demonstrate 21st-century skills. However, while the approach offers exciting opportunities to expand assessment practices, Purpura and Banerjee (2021) have identified some challenges to be considered when selecting SBLA as the assessment approach.

The first challenge relates to scenario selection. While a scenario provides rich contextualization for test takers, the sociocultural elements associated with the scenario could affect test takers' interaction with and engagement in the scenario, which subsequently could have an impact on their test performance. To ensure that the selected scenario is fair for the intended test takers, it is important to consider what is socioculturally relevant, appropriate, and meaningful to the test takers. At the SBLA Lab where one of the ongoing projects is to develop SBLA in multiple languages (specifically Korean, Persian, Italian, and Arabic), institutional collaborations were formed. Test developers of each foreign language SBLA all spoke the

Chapter 18 Scenario-Based Language Assessment

target language as first language or with native-like fluency, were highly familiar with the culture of the target language, and had had extensive experience teaching and assessing the language (Davoodifard et al., 2022; Joo et al., 2022; Machetti et al., 2022). By recruiting test developers who are closely connected to the sociocultural context of the target language, aspects of the sociocultural elements within a scenario that could play a role in test takers' situated L2 performance can be monitored. In Kunnan et al. (2022), the scenario selection was a collaborative effort between faculty and students to ensure that the scenarios were culturally relevant to the test takers. In addition, a fairness review was conducted to ensure that the content, topics, and tasks were appropriate and that the locations and characters that appeared in the scenario had adequate representation.

The second challenge relates to understanding the relationships between the complex constructs measured within a scenario. Purpura and Banerjee (2021) pointed out that, while SBLA allows for the flexibility to embed assistance within an assessment, we have yet to fully understand the role various types of performance moderators play in test takers' situated L2 performance and how performance as a result of assistance can be most properly scored. As an attempt to understand the relationships between complex constructs within an SBLA through a measurement model, Banerjee (2019b) constructed a Bayesian network to examine how L2 learners' ability to achieve the scenario goal was dependent on their topical knowledge and L2 KSAs. The results, while exploratory in nature, provided a glimpse of how the probabilistic graphical model can offer a holistic understanding of complex constructs in an SBLA. Nevertheless, the use of Bayesian networks to understand complex constructs has not gained much attention in L2 assessment.

The third, and likely the most fundamental, challenge relates to technology. As mentioned earlier, a key feature of SBLA is that it is digitally delivered; therefore, having an appropriate delivery platform is essential to building a successful SBLA. Thus far, most L2 SBLA modules that have been administered reported being built either on a learning management system with limitations or on an experience management platform with paid customizations that require programming expertise. For L2 test developers who do not have flexible access to a dedicated assessment delivery platform or on-demand technical support, there has not seemed to be a technological solution where all aspects of SBLA design features can be easily and efficiently supported.

Despite the challenges, SBLA has shown to be a promising approach to language assessment. As the application of SBLA in language assessment continues to grow, it is critical for test developers to carefully review the appropriateness of a scenario from various perspectives related to test takers' sociocultural, sociopolitical, and socioeconomic experiences in real life. Further research is also greatly needed to better understand the interrelationships between the complex constructs within an SBLA so that the components embedded in an SBLA can be finetuned to better represent test takers' real-life communication. Finally, finding an appropriate and reliable assessment delivery solution is needed in order to fully realize the potential of SBLA as an effective measure of complex constructs. As SBLA continues to be developed, it will be important to assess their validity, reliability, and fairness in order to ensure that they are an effective and equitable assessment tool for L2 learners.

Discussion Questions

1. In what ways might generative AI, such as GPT-4, be used to support the development of SBLA? What challenges might such an implementation encounter?

2. What psychometric approaches can be considered to comprehensively capture the complexity of L2 performance within an SBLA?

References

Alderson, C. (2005). *Diagnosing foreign language proficiency: The interface between learning and assessment.* Continuum.

Almond, R. G., Mislevy, R. J., Steinberg, L., Yan, D., & Williamson, D. (2015). *Bayesian networks in educational assessment.* Springer.

Banerjee, H. L. (2019a). Investigating the construct of topical knowledge in second language assessment: a scenario-based assessment approach. *Language Assessment Quarterly, 16*(2), 133–160. https://doi.org/10.1080/15434303.2019.1628237.

Banerjee, H. L. (2019b). *Investigating the construct of topical knowledge in a scenario-based assessment designed to simulate real-life second language use* [Doctoral dissertation, Teachers College, Columbia University]. Columbia University Academic Commons. https://doi.org/10.7916/d8-r7t4-pe76.

Bennett, R. E. (2010). Cognitively based assessment of, for, and as learning: a preliminary theory of action for summative and formative assessment. *Measurement: Interdisciplinary Research and Perspectives, 8*, 70–91. https://doi.org/10.1080/15366367.2010.508686.

Bennett, R. E., & Gitomer, D. H. (2009). Transforming K-12 assessment: integrating accountability testing, formative assessment and professional support. In C. Wyatt-Smith & J. Cumming (Eds.), *Assessment issues of the 21st century* (pp. 43–61). Springer.

Black, H. (1986). Assessment for learning. In D. L. Nuttall (Ed.), *Assessing educational achievement* (pp. 7–18). Falmer Press.

Black, P. J., & Wiliam, D. (2004). The formative purpose: assessment must first promote learning. In M. Wilson (Ed.), *Towards coherence between classroom assessment and accountability: 103rd yearbook of the National Society for the Study of Education* (Vol. Part II, pp. 20–50). University of Chicago Press.

Davoodifard, M., Akbari-Saneh, N., & Vafaee, P. (2022). *Examining Persian learners' situated language proficiency and topical learning through a scenario-based assessment. In J. E. Purpura & H. L. Banerjee (Chairs), Exploring the cross-linguistic insights of using scenario-based assessment across four typologically different languages [AAAL-ILTA joint colloquium]. American Association for Applied Linguistics Annual Conference, March 19–22, Pittsburgh, PA.*

Deane, P. (2011). *Writing assessment and cognition* (Research Report No. RR-11-14). Educational Testing Service. https://doi.org/10.1002/j.2333-8504.2011.tb02250.x.

Deane, P., Sabatini, J., & O'Reilly, T. (2012). *English language arts literacy framework.* Princeton, NJ: Educational Testing Service. Retrieved from https://www.ets.org/s/research/pdf/ela_literacy_framework.pdf.

Deane, P., Sabatini, J., Feng, G., Sparks, J., Song, Y., Fowles, M., O'Reilly, T., Jueds, K., Krovetz, R. and Foley, C. (2015), *Key practices in the English Language Arts (ELA): Linking learning theory, assessment, and instruction* (Research Report No. RR-15-17). Princeton, NJ: Educational Testing Service. https://doi.org/10.1002/ets2.12063.

Eskin, D., Beltrán, J., Joo, S. H., Puprura, J. E., & Banerjee, H. L. (2022). *Examining ESL learners' situated language proficiency and topical learning through a scenario-based assessment. In J. E. Purpura & H. L. Banerjee (Chairs), Exploring the cross-linguistic insights of using scenario-based assessment across four typologically different languages [AAAL-ILTA joint colloquium]. American Association for Applied Linguistics Annual Conference, March 19–22, Pittsburgh, PA.*

Joo, S. H., Seong, Y., Suh, J., Jung, J.-Y., & Purpura, J. E., (2021). *Developing a scenario-based Korean proficiency assessment using a learning-oriented approach* [Paper presentation], November 4–5. Seoul, South Korea.

Joo, S. H., Jung, J.-Y., Seong, Y., & Suh, J. (2022). *Examining Korean learners' situated language proficiency and topical learning through a scenario-based assessment. In J. E. Purpura & H. L. Banerjee (Chairs), Exploring the cross-linguistic insights of using scenario-based assessment across four typologically different languages [AAAL-ILTA joint colloquium]. American Association for Applied Linguistics Annual Conference, March 19–22, Pittsburgh, PA.*

Kunnan, A. J., Qin, C. Y., & Zhao, C. G. (2022). Developing a scenario-based English language assessment in an Asian university. *Language Assessment Quarterly, 19*(4), 368–393. https://doi.org/10.1080/15434303.2022.2073886.

Lantolf, J. P., & Poehner, M. E. (2011). Dynamic assessment in the classroom: Vygotskyan praxis for second language development. *Language Teaching Research, 15*(1), 11–33. https://doi.org/10.1177/1362168810383328.

Machetti, S., Peri, G., & Masillo, P. (2022). *Examining Italian learners' situated language proficiency and topical learning through a scenario-based assessment. In J. E. Purpura & H. L. Banerjee (Chairs), Exploring the cross-linguistic* insights of using scenario-based assessment across four typologically different languages [AAAL-ILTA Joint Colloquium]. American Association for Applied Linguistics Annual Conference, March 19–22, Pittsburgh, PA.

Mislevy, R. J., Steinberg, L. S., & Almond, R. G. (2003). On the structure of educational assessments. *Measurement: Interdisciplinary Research and Perspectives, 1*(1), 3–62. https://doi.org/10.1207/S15366359MEA0101_02.

O'Reilly, T., & Sabatini, J. (2013). *Reading for understanding: How performance moderators and scenarios impact assessment design* (Research Report No. RR-13-31). Educational Testing Service. http://doi.org/10.1002/j.2333-8504.2013.tb02338.x.

O'Reilly, T., Weeks, J., Sabatini, J., Halderman, L., & Steinberg, J. (2014). Designing reading comprehension assessments for reading interventions: how a theoretically motivated assessment can serve as an outcome measure. *Educational Psychology Review, 26,* 403–424. https://doi.org/10.1007/s10648-014-9269-z.

O'Reilly, T., Deane, P., & Sabatini, J. (2015). *Building and sharing knowledge key practice: What do you know, what don't you know, what did you learn?* (Research Report No. RR-15-24). Educational Testing Service. http://doi.org/10.1002/ets2.12074.

Purpura, J. E. (2019). *Questioning the currency of second and foreign language certification exams [Video].* A&H Distinguished Speaker Series. https://vimeo.com/367018433.

Purpura, J. E. (2021). A rationale for using a scenario-based assessment to measure competency-based, situated second and foreign language proficiency. In M. Masperi, C. Cervini & Y. Bardière (Eds.), *Évaluation des acquisitions langagières: Du formatif au certificatif. MediAzioni 32* (pp. A54–A96). http://www.mediazioni.sitlec.unibo.it.

Purpura, J. E., (2022). *Using a learning-oriented assessment framework to reimagine classroom assessments* [Video]. Duolingo English Test Assessment Research Webinar. https://www.youtube.com/watch?v=S5hO4sP5XxI.

Purpura, J. E., (2023). *The intriguing complexities of classroom-based assessment through the lens of a competency-based, learning-oriented, professional development initiative in Algeria [Alan Davis lecture]. The 44th Annual Language Testing Research Colloquium, June 5–9, New York, NY.*

Purpura, J. E. & Banerjee, H. L. (2018). *An introduction to scenario-based assessment: opportunities for construct expansion. In J. E. Purpura & H. L. Banerjee (Chairs), The affordances of scenario-based assessment for broadening measurement opportunities in second or foreign language assessment [Colloquium]. American Association for Applied Linguistics Annual Conference, March 24–27, Chicago, IL.*

Purpura, J. E., & Banerjee, H. L. (2021). *The affordances of scenario-based assessment for measuring 21st century language-driven competencies. In J. E. Purpura & H. L. Banerjee (Chairs), Rethinking second language proficiency assessment using a scenario-based approach: Opportunities and challenges [Symposium]. The 42nd annual Language Testing Research Colloquium, June 14–17, Tunis, Tunisia.*

Purpura, J. E., & Banerjee, H. L. (2022). *The affordance of using scenario-based assessment in cross-linguistic assessment context. In J. E. Purpura & H. L. Banerjee (Chairs), Exploring the cross-linguistic insights of using scenario-based assessment across four typologically different languages [AAAL-ILTA joint colloquium]. American Association for Applied Linguistics Annual Conference, March 19–22, Pittsburgh, PA.*

Purpura, J. E., & Turner, C. E. (2014). *A learning-oriented assessment approach to understanding the complexities of classroom-based language assessment [Paper presentation]. Roundtable on learning-oriented assessment in language classrooms and large-scale contexts, October 10–12. New York, NY: Teachers College, Columbia University.*

Purpura, J. E., & Turner, C. E. (2018). *A learning-oriented assessment approach in classroom contexts: an expanded conceptualization of performances [Workshop], July 2–6. The 40th annual language testing research colloquium, Auckland, New Zealand.*

Purpura, J. E., Banerjee, H. L., Beltrán, J., Robinson, B., & Vafaee, P. (2021). *Developing a scenario-based assessment for placement purposes: takeaway and challenges. In J. E. Purpura & H. L. Banerjee (Chairs), Rethinking second language proficiency assessment using a scenario-based approach: Opportunities and challenges [Symposium]. The 42nd Annual Language Testing Research Colloquium, June 14–17, Tunis, Tunisia.*

Sabatini, J., & O'Reilly, T. (2013). Rationale for a new generation of reading comprehension assessments. In B. Miller, L. Cutting & P. McCardle (Eds.), *Unraveling reading comprehension: Behavioral, neurobiological, and genetic components* (pp. 100–111). Brookes Publishing.

Sabatini, J., O'Reilly, T., Halderman, L., & Bruce, K. (2014). Integrating scenario-based and component reading skill measures to understand the reading behavior of struggling readers. *Learning Disabilities Research & Practice, 29*(1), 36–43. https://doi.org/10.1111/ldrp.12028.

Sabatini, J., O'Reilly, T., Weeks, J., & Wang, Z. (2019). Engineering a twenty-first century reading comprehension assessment system utilizing scenario-based assessment techniques. *International Journal of Testing, 20*(1), 1–23.

Seong, Y. (2023). *Using a scenario-based assessment approach to examine the cognitive dimension of second language academic speaking ability through the assessment of an integrated academic speaking competency [Unpublished doctoral dissertation]. Teachers College, Columbia University.*

Sheehan, K., & O'Reilly, T. (2012). The case for scenario-based assessments of reading competency. In J. Sabatini, T. O'Reilly & L. Albro (Eds.), *Reaching an understanding: Innovations in how we view reading assessment* (pp. 19–33). Rowman & Littlefield.

Shore, J. R., Wolf, M. K., O'Reilly, T., & Sabatini, J. P. (2017). Measuring 21st-centruy reading comprehension through scenario-based assessment. In M. K. Wolf & Y. G. Butler (Eds.), *English language proficiency assessment for young learners* (pp. 234–252). Routledge.

Turner, C. E., & Purpura, J. E. (2016). Learning-oriented assessment in second and foreign language classrooms. In D. Tsagari & J. Banerjee (Eds.), *Handbook of second language assessment* (pp. 255–273). De Gruyter.

Wiliam, B. (2011). What is assessment for learning? *Studies in Educational Evaluation, 37*, 3–14. https://doi.org/10.1016/j.stueduc.2011.03.001.

World Economic Forum (2020). *Top 10 skills of 2025* [Infographic]. https://www.weforum.org/reports/the-future-of-jobs-report-2020/in-full/infographics-e4e69e4de7.

Suggested Readings

Banerjee, H. L. (2019). Investigating the construct of topical knowledge in second language assessment: a scenario-based assessment approach. *Language Assessment Quarterly, 16*(2), 133–160. https://doi.org/10.1080/15434303.2019.1628237.

Kunnan, A. J., Qin, C. Y., & Zhao, C. G. (2022). Developing a scenario-based English language assessment in an Asian university. *Language Assessment Quarterly, 19*(4), 368–393. https://doi.org/10.1080/15434303.2022.2073886.

O'Reilly, T., & Sabatini, J. (2013). *Reading for understanding: How performance moderators and scenarios impact assessment design* (Research Report No. RR-13-31). Educational Testing Service. 10.1002/j.2333-8504.2013.tb02338.x.

Purpura, J. E. (2021). A rationale for using a scenario-based assessment to measure competency-based, situated second and foreign language proficiency. In M. Masperi, C. Cervini & Y. Bardière (Eds.), *Évaluation des acquisitions langagières: Du formatif au certificatif. MediAzioni 32* (pp. A54–A96).

Sabatini, J., O'Reilly, T., Weeks, J., & Wang, Z. (2020). Engineering a twenty-first century reading comprehension assessment system utilizing scenario-based assessment techniques. *International Journal of Testing, 20*(1), 1–23. https://doi.org/10.1080/15305058.2018.1551224.

CHAPTER 19

Adapting or Developing Source Materials for Listening and Reading Tests

Anthony Green

Introduction

Because it is an essential aspect of using a language, assessing language learners' abilities in receptive skills – their ability to understand spoken and written language – has always been an important element in language tests. A major challenge for language assessors is that, unlike the ability to speak or to write, the ability to comprehend what is read or heard cannot be observed directly. Instead, evidence of comprehension has to be indirect. The learner draws on his or her competence in the target language to read a text or listen to a recording and is given a task of some kind to perform to convey how well he or she has understood. The score given to this performance is taken to represent the learner's ability to understand not only the particular text on the test but also other similar texts.

Language test batteries have for many years included components assessing test takers' ability to follow reading and listening texts or "passages," but the kinds of tasks used and the kinds of texts they are based on have changed along with shifting fashions in test design. This chapter looks at how different approaches and purposes for assessment have shaped the ways in which texts for use in tests of reading and listening skills have been chosen and adapted.

Whatever the testing technique employed, producing a test of comprehension must also involve either locating or creating appropriate source material to use as input: The obvious choice for the assessor lies between creating material specifically for use in a test and selecting material created for some other purpose and using it, with or without adaptation, as a basis for test tasks. This chapter traces developments in the advice given to assessors on how this choice should be made and, in the practices, employed in actual language tests over the past century.

Early Uses of Input Texts

The source materials chosen for use in language tests inevitably reflect underlying conceptions of the nature and purpose of language learning. A century ago, the 1913 Cambridge Certificate of Proficiency in English (CPE), following earlier precedents in foreign language

The Concise Companion to Language Assessment, First Edition. Edited by Antony John Kunnan.
© 2025 John Wiley & Sons, Inc. Published 2025 by John Wiley & Sons, Inc.

education, included a variety of input texts used as a basis for dictation (as an indication of listening abilities), reading aloud, and translation of English into other languages (as indicators of reading comprehension) (Weir & Milanovic, 2003). The oral test of foreign languages developed in the United States by the New England Modern Language Association and used in college admissions (Barnwell, 1996) showed similar influences, supplementing the more widespread tests involving translation and the statement of grammatical rules with a 10-minute dictation, a written summary of an oral passage read by the examiner, and written answers to general classroom questions read by the examiner.

It is interesting to note that, although much has changed in the way we have thought about language tests since the beginning of the 20th century and such techniques have perhaps rather fallen out of favor, they have all remained in use in language tests throughout the period: Reading aloud, retelling spoken texts, and dictation all appear in the Pearson Test of English (PTE) Academic launched in 2010.

During the early years of the 20th century, the dominant liberal educational paradigm in the teaching of foreign languages in Europe favored extending the supposed benefits of high culture to all sectors of society. Key objectives of language learning included accessing the classics of literature and history in the target language and, following the model set by the teaching of classical languages, puzzling out the complex grammar of literary works. In the 1913 CPE, test takers were asked to translate extracts from texts by recognized literary figures, including Thomas Arnold and Thomas Carlyle, and to "correct or justify" sentences such as "Comparing Shakespeare with Æschylus, the former is by no means inferior to the latter" (Weir & Milanovic, 2003, appendix one). The reading of "set books" – literary works used as a basis for essays of critical appreciation – has continued in Cambridge tests as an option to the present day. As an example of this, in the 1984 Cambridge First Certificate in English (FCE), test takers were simply asked to "write on one of the following": Austen's *Sense and Sensibility*, Shaw's *Arms and the Man* (both of which had also featured in the original 1939 test), and Greene's *The Third Man*.

The liberal educational tradition, with its stress on literature, history, grammar, and translation, has continued to exert a strong influence on testing practices, although it was regularly and increasingly challenged by alternatives. In 1913, phonetics held a central place in British linguistics, being allied with the oral method, which prioritized the spoken language in the teaching of modern foreign languages. Dictation and reading aloud were both favored teaching tools in the oral method, and their place in the 1913 CPE and in the 1915 Maryland tests reflects this.

Language teaching and linguistic theory have retained their influence, but another recurrent theme is reflected in early revisions to the CPE. Alongside the liberal agenda of cultural enrichment, language learning has always embraced more utilitarian objectives. Learners themselves often wish to acquire a language not so much to access the cultural highlights as to facilitate travel, to access technical information, and to do business. During the 1930s, the University of Cambridge came under pressure from CPE test score users to address business uses of language, and a paper on "economic and commercial knowledge" was offered as an alternative to literature. This presages the later interest in target language use and performance or work sample approaches to testing in which future uses of the language become the basis for test design – in other words, the view that the reading and listening material used in tests should be taken from the real-world contexts in which learners would be expected to use the language.

Reading and Listening Comprehension

Short reading passages with accompanying questions were already firmly entrenched in tests of first language reading comprehension when Thorndike (1918) began to explore reading comprehension as a mental process. It was perhaps natural that such tasks should find their

272 Chapter 19 Adapting or Developing Source Materials

way into language tests, as indicators of how well learners could follow a written text. Barnwell (1996) described Handschin's *Silent Reading Test in French and Spanish* (which appeared in 1919 and consisted of a written paragraph accompanied by 10 comprehension questions) as the first standardized modern language test. Barnwell recorded that the ambitious and highly influential Modern Foreign Language Study in the United States in the 1920s viewed both reading and listening comprehension as core components of foreign language ability, but only produced tests of the former (paragraphs accompanied by "True/False" questions).

Early examples of listening tests tended to involve isolated words or questions spoken in the target language, with translation equivalents or appropriate responses presented as multiple-choice options. According to Barnwell (1996), it was not until 1954 that the first test named "Listening Comprehension" appeared in the United States. The College Board test of 1954 had clear work sample elements and involved a range of text types, from informal conversation to lectures and extracts from plays.

In Cambridge, although not elsewhere in the United Kingdom (see, for example, the language laboratory-based Association of Recognized English Language Schools [ARELS] Oral Examinations described by Hawkey, 2004), resistance to "objective type" multiple-choice tests meant that listening comprehension tests did not appear until much later. The first listening comprehension papers were introduced to CPE and FCE in 1975 (Weir & Milanovic, 2003). Input for the latter took the form of extracts from written (literary) sources read out by the examiner.

In the 1950s, while the eclectic stew of linguistic theory, educational practice, and pragmatic influences continued to simmer in Cambridge, a fourth element was bubbling to the surface in the United States. Here educational testing had, since the 1920s, been more heavily influenced by psychometric theory, which attempts to extend to the social sciences the kinds of precise and consistent measurement that can be achieved in the physical sciences in the measurement of distance, temperature, or time. For language testing, this would imply an emphasis on consistent, reliable results and componential theoretical models centered on the individual language learner. In what has become known as a discrete-point approach, Lado (1961) brought together psychometric theory, behaviorist psychology, and contrastive structural linguistics. For Lado, language tests ought to isolate and test the elements of a language – "distinct systems of pronunciation, stress, intonation, grammatical structure and vocabulary" – "that native speakers understand by the mere fact of being native speakers of the language" (p. 205).

Lado opposed established techniques such as reading aloud and dictation because of the uncertainty about exactly which aspects of language ability they were testing and on the grounds that presenting words in a context might give listeners clues as to their meaning that would allow them to guess a word without perceiving it accurately in the input. He also argued against the use of input texts taken from real-life settings on the grounds that this introduces "extraneous factors" such as technical knowledge, literary appreciation, or intelligence: "it is more economical and will result in more complete sampling to work from the language problems and then to seek situations in which particular problems can be tested" (p. 205).

Lado's approach implied the use of large numbers of very short input texts, especially constructed to target specific language points accompanied by "objective" multiple-choice questions. This discrete-point approach to testing fitted quite comfortably with contemporary audiolingual approaches to language teaching. Valette's (1967) practical handbook for teachers reflects the traditional purposes of the high school language program: "to enjoy the literature written in the target language, to appreciate the culture of the target country and especially to converse freely with its people" (p. 4). However, her recommendations on crafting scripts for use in a classroom test of listening comprehension reflect this discrete point approach to language: "the teacher should, a couple of days in advance, prepare a first draft of the script ... making sure that he has used all the structures and vocabulary used that week"

(Valette, 1967, p. 18). Although theories of language learning have moved on, the diagnostic appeal remains obvious: If the learners have failed to master one or more of the taught elements, this would be reflected in their test performance and they could be given remedial instruction.

In a highly influential paper written at around the same time as Lado's book, Carroll (1961) warned against overreliance on discrete-point testing. He argued for the addition of "integrative" language tests with "less attention paid to specific structure points or lexicon than to the total communicative effect of an utterance" (p. 37). Such tests (the example he gave involved spoken sentences to be matched to pictures) would, he suggested, better reflect the pressures of real-time communication and focus attention on how well learners could function in the target language.

The influence of both points of view can be seen in early developments in the assessment of English for academic purposes, which is often (and for obvious reasons) a focus for academics specializing in language testing. The Test of English as a Foreign Language (TOEFL), first administered in 1964, was introduced to assess the language skills of the growing numbers of international students studying in U.S. universities. From its launch, TOEFL, alongside more discrete tests of "structure and written expression" and vocabulary, included tests of reading comprehension (5 passages of 100–250 words from social science, fiction, and natural science texts, each with 4–5 questions) and listening (including recordings of 20 sentences with written response options, 15 dialogues with comprehension questions, and a 5-minute lecture with 15 questions) (Spolsky, 1995).

Harris (1969), one member in the TOEFL development team, dedicated two pages of his handbook to the selection of texts as reading passages. He specified four features to consider: *length*, *subject matter*, *style*, and *language*. Without distinguishing between intensive and extensive reading and the implications of different reading skills for text selection, Harris recommended the selection of passages of between 100 and 250 words, because these could support 6 or 7 comprehension questions to accompany each text for trialing, but they would allow for a wide sampling of types of material within the time available for a typical reading test. *Subject matter* addresses the work sample element. In a test of English for foreign applicants to American universities, texts "should reflect the various kinds of reading material assigned in basic university courses" (p. 60) and should not require cultural knowledge.

Harris advised avoiding passages that focus on a single proposition, recommending instead those that "(a) deal chronologically with a series of events, (b) compare or contrast two or more people, objects, or events, or (c) present an author's individualistic opinions on a familiar subject" (p. 61). He suggested that language could be used as a basis for grading texts; passages that included too many difficult words or were too complex should be simplified to take account of the level of the test takers.

A U.K. contemporary of TOEFL, the English Proficiency Testing Battery (EPTB), popularly known as the Davies test after its author, was developed for a similar purpose by the British Council. In this test, listening abilities were addressed through discrete-point tests of phonemic discrimination (deciding which, if any, of three words were the same: either heard as isolated words: *stipple – steeple – staple*, or in a brief context: *I like the old-fashioned* ports/ ports/parts *of England*) and intonation (recognizing attitudes in brief conversational exchanges). Alongside the testing of such language elements, the EPTB, like the TOEFL, also incorporated elements of a work sample approach. There was a listening comprehension component, which was based on a short lecture accompanied by multiple-choice questions based on summarizing statements.

Echoing the concerns voiced by Lado (1961), Davies (2009) pointed to the tensions that emerged between the authenticity of the lecture content, the requirements of efficient testing, and the theoretical rationale for the lecture-listening component. Extracts from genuine lectures did not seem to provide enough detail to support the intended 15–20 questions on the

274 Chapter 19 Adapting or Developing Source Materials

test and gave rise to concerns about differences in learners' levels of content knowledge. A compromise was arrived at by using a lecture that did not involve specialist knowledge: one given by a doctor about services available to students.

The reading texts were also chosen to reflect the kinds of material that students would encounter at university. Two texts were included: The first was a form of cloze text – a text with some words replaced by gaps – the first letter of each of the missing words being provided. The second was a lengthier passage, of around 1200 words, with additional words inserted at random. In the former (testing reading comprehension), test takers needed to insert the missing word; in the latter (testing reading speed), they needed to identify the intrusive words.

Published in 1975, Heaton, like Valette (1967), offered advice on testing both discrete elements such as phoneme discrimination or vocabulary knowledge and passage comprehension. In reading, Heaton distinguished between the kinds of text that can be used in testing the beginning stages of reading (matching of words and sentences) and higher levels (comprehension questions based on longer passages). He was critical of tests that were limited to brief extracts of a few sentences because these seemed to restrict the focus to intensive, word-by-word reading rather than involving skimming or scanning strategies.

In listening, Heaton was concerned with the distinctive features of spoken language, making the point that "impromptu speech is often easier to understand than carefully prepared (written) material when the latter is read aloud" (Heaton, 1975, p. 58). This is because of the more frequent occurrence of features like redundancy and restatements in the former and the greater information density of the latter. However, Heaton offered little advice on how to select reading texts beyond suggesting that these should be appropriate to the learners' ability, that text difficulty depends on the structural and lexical complexity of the language used, and that longer passages are often associated with greater propositional complexity and hence are better suited to higher-level learners.

The increasing availability of good-quality recording and playback equipment made the use of recordings for listening tests increasingly practical from the 1960s, and Heaton weighed up the advantages of employing recordings. On the one hand, a live (or videorecorded) presentation has the advantage that "it is helpful if the speaker can be seen by the listener ... a disembodied voice is much more difficult for the foreign learner to follow," while, on the other, recordings made by native speakers both "present perfect models of the spoken language, an important advantage in countries where native speakers are not available to administer the test" (p. 58) and make it possible to use authentic recordings of texts made for purposes other than testing. While the appropriateness of native speaker models has been increasingly questioned over the intervening years, authenticity was to emerge, as we shall see, as an increasingly important, if problematic, concern.

Influenced by the reaction during the 1970s against discrete-point approaches in applied linguistics more generally, Oller Jr. (1979) argued that language tests should be integrative, testing language elements in combination rather than attempting to separate them out. Oller favored dictation and cloze techniques as integrative task types engaging multiple elements of language at the same time, and so providing a good indication of general language proficiency. Oller was relatively unconcerned with issues of text selection, noting with regard to cloze tests that, as long as the source text is long enough to support around 50 deletions, the "procedure is probably appropriate to just about any text" and that "it has been demonstrated that for some purposes (e.g., testing ESL proficiency of university-level students) the level of difficulty of the task does not greatly affect the spread of scores that will be produced" (p. 364). He did, however, suggest that potentially disturbing or offensive material should be avoided and that esoteric or highly technical topics would not generally be suitable. His conclusion was that "material intended for fifth grade geography students" (p. 365) might work well as a basis for cloze tests aimed at these university-level students – presumably because this kind of material seemed widely accessible, yet plausibly academic. He took a similar line on dictation, suggesting that "dictation at an appropriate rate, of kinds of material that learners are expected to cope with, is a promising way of investigating how well learners can handle a variety of school-related discourse processing tasks" (p. 269).

Harris, Heaton, and Oller all recognized some virtue in the "realism" afforded by incorporating into tests the kinds of texts that learners might expect to encounter in the real world. Such texts would supplement questions constructed to target linguistic elements. Advocates of "communicative testing" such as Carroll (1980) went much further and wholeheartedly embraced a work sample approach. Carroll dismissed discrete-point testing as a "monotonous series of linguistic manipulations only distantly related to real communicative tasks" (p. 37). He took a lead from the growing interest in teaching English for specific purposes and was influenced by the functional orientation of the Council of Europe Threshold Level (van Ek, 1975). His point was to test not the knowledge of a language, whether as discrete elements or as an integrated whole, but the ability to use that language to carry out real-world tasks.

Carroll's approach to text selection was therefore based not on abstract linguistic analysis but on how learners would be expected to use the target language in relevant contexts. Authenticity was prioritized: Material for tests should be drawn directly from what Bachman and Palmer (2010) have subsequently termed the target language use (TLU) domain – the content classroom, the university, the workplace, and the public sphere – for use in tasks that would simulate real-world behaviors. Carroll suggested that "in a test of English for Life Sciences, a booklet may be prepared dealing with such topics as 'Antibiotic therapy,' 'Inheritance,' 'Lipids,' 'Lactation curves,' 'Nutrition,' 'Correlation of Ecological studies,' 'Weights and Measures' and appropriate 'Contents,' 'Bibliography' and 'Index'" (pp. 37–38). The texts would be chosen and prepared "by an inter-disciplinary team of language and subject specialists" (p. 38) guided by the analysis of learner needs.

Where Lado (1961) used the phrase "integrated skills" to refer to listening or reading (as distinct from discrete elements such as vocabulary or intonation), B.J. Carroll used the same phrase to refer to the integration of modalities involved in carrying out tasks: listening and speaking integrated in conducting a conversation or discussion; reading, listening, and writing along with graphics or other supporting visual material in preparing a simulated academic assignment.

By the early 1980s, the first communicative tests had begun to appear. Weir (1983) carried out an empirical analysis of the ways in which international students used English in pursuit of their studies and of the difficulties they encountered. The outcome of this needs analysis, the Test of English for Academic Purposes (TEAP), was a simulation of the cycle of assessment found in universities across academic disciplines. It involved responding to short answer questions based on a lengthy reading passage of around 1000 words taken from an academic textbook or journal; responding to questions on a recording of a 10-minute lecture extract; and, finally, integrating information from both the listening and the reading sections to respond to an essay prompt. B.J. Carroll was involved in the development of the English Language Testing System (ELTS, subsequently IELTS), which tested the use of reference material (in a component titled "Study Skills"), integrated reading and writing, and offered test takers a choice of modules linked to different disciplinary areas.

Enthusiasm for communicative testing was tempered by criticism from language-testing researchers. Echoing Carroll's (1961) complaint that Lado's use of contrastive linguistic analysis implied the need for a separate test for learners from each different language background, Alderson (1988) pointed out that the English for specific purposes orientation of communicative testing seemed to imply tests individually tailored to each learner to take account of their personal communication needs. Another key concern was the prioritization of content – the imperative that material be taken from the TLU domain – over theory – any account of the knowledge, skills, or abilities that language learners would require to process this material. Bachman (1990) showed that, without providing a coherent theory of an underlying language ability to replace Lado's (1961) contrastive structuralist model or Oller's (1979) pragmatic

Chapter 19 Adapting or Developing Source Materials

expectancy grammar, the appeal to "real-world" uses of language could not justify the assumption that test performance would predict performance on tasks beyond the test situation.

In short, the history of tests of second and foreign language reading and listening skills during the 20th century saw a movement away from translation and toward the use of comprehension questions. In earlier tests, input texts were composed or chosen to exemplify aspects of the linguistic system. The selection of sources took on greater importance in later tests, as they came to represent the types of material that language learners might expect to encounter outside the test, when undertaking specified social roles. The authenticity of source material emerged both as a central consideration and as a matter of debate. There were differences between those who gave priority to task accomplishment – comprehension of material representing real-life language use – and those who looked for evidence of underlying abilities.

What Characteristics Count in Text Selection?

The period following 1989 saw something of a compromise (or synthesis) between the cognitive and the contextual. In revisions made in 1989 and 1995, IELTS retreated from many of its more "communicative" features, including the testing of study skills, the integration of reading and writing, and the provision of alternative test modules for students in different disciplines (although test takers may still choose between "academic" and more vocationally oriented "general training" versions of the reading and writing papers). Moving in the opposite direction, the revision of TOEFL that led to the Internet-based test saw the incorporation of TLU analyses (Rosenfeld et al., 2001), introduced more extensive passages based on TLU sources for reading (700 words) and listening (3–5 minutes), and brought in integrated reading-into-writing or listening-into-writing tasks. The PTE Academic, a more recent entrant to this area of testing, also includes components integrating skills such as reading and writing or speaking (summarizing written texts) or listening and speaking (retelling a lecture extract).

Handbooks published after 1985 – such as Weir (1993), Alderson et al. (1995), Davidson and Lynch (2002), and Hughes (2003) – although broadly preferring the use of authentic texts and recordings drawn from the TLU domain, advised flexibility according to test purpose – discrete point tests have greater diagnostic and therefore educative potential – and pointed to the importance of test specifications in guiding text selection. Hughes (2003) advised teachers preparing tests to "keep specifications constantly in mind" (p. 142) and offered guidance on length, variety, and topic. His conclusion was that "successful choice of texts depends ultimately on experience, judgement and a certain amount of common sense" (p. 142). Alderson et al. (1995) offered similarly practical guidance: "for many tests, the item writer's next task is to find appropriate texts. In this case, 'appropriate' means not only texts that match the specifications, but also texts that look as if they will yield suitable items" (p. 43). Such texts can be difficult to find, and readers were advised to build up collections of promising material against future needs. Weir stressed the need to consider learner level and purpose:

> for lower-level general English students we need to look at the range of language forms candidates can be expected to handle. Does the text contain too many unknown lexical items? For higher-level ESP students we need to examine whether the lexical range is appropriate in terms of common core, technical and sub-technical vocabulary.
>
> (Weir, 1993, p. 67)

Grading text difficulty is, of course, a traditional educational concern dating back to Thorndike and beyond, but the debate over authenticity, together with developments in areas of applied linguistics such as discourse and genre analysis, raised new issues. Readability formulas like the Flesch Reading Ease index for English had already been used for many years to grade material for schoolchildren. These relied on word and sentence lengths to provide an indication of the difficulty of the vocabulary (longer words tend to be less common) and grammar (longer sentences tend to be more complex) of a text, and so they might be helpful in meeting Weir's (1993) suggestions on grading. However, they provided no real guidance on what types of text learners at different levels of ability might be able to process and what kinds of information they might be able to obtain.

Views of difficulty can be more fully explored by looking at how test developers have specified their tests at different levels of proficiency, for example, in the Cambridge suite of tests, the Common European Framework of Reference (Council of Europe, 2001), and in other frameworks used in national assessments of foreign language ability. One such characterization is contained in the American Council on the Teaching of Foreign Languages (ACTFL) Guidelines for Reading (Child, 1987; see Table 19.1). The ACTFL Guidelines divided reading proficiency into three areas – content, function, and accuracy – organized into two parallel hierarchies of difficulty level: one made up of text types and the other of reading skills. The evidential basis for these hierarchies has been questioned, and not all text types readily fit the categories presented, but attempts to characterize textual features more fully have continued.

As noted above, Bachman (1990) and Bachman and Palmer (2010) argued that it is not sufficient simply to take material from the TLU domain and use it in a test, as communicative testers had advocated, first because tests cannot provide sufficient space for all the material that might be encountered in the real world and, second, because listening to a lecture in

---

TABLE 19.1

Child's (1987) typology of text modes

Level 1: orientation mode	Texts in this mode serve to orient the reader to situations and events. Examples include street signs, arrival and departure notices, and greetings. These are often abbreviated, assume conventional knowledge on the part of the recipient, and may be heavily reliant on context. Problems in comprehension for learners are more likely to result from a lack of vocabulary and relevant knowledge than from syntax
Level 2: instructive mode	Texts in this mode involve extended discourse and straightforwardly convey facts and information (but not opinions) about situations and events. Examples of Level 2 texts given by Child include factual newspaper reports; assembly instructions; straightforward historical narratives; directions to and descriptions of geographical areas; and technical descriptions of a chemical compound
Level 3: evaluative mode	Points of view explain conduct, defend policy, etc. Examples include analytic and affective texts such as newspaper editorials disapproving or advocating some course of action; evaluative biographies; and personal correspondence attempting to repair a breach. Child makes the point that such texts, reflecting their social character, are often governed by more or less explicit formal conventions or received practices, which make them more accessible to those who are familiar with the conventions
Level 4: projective mode	This mode is "the natural realm of artistic creativity," as it involves individual responses, eschewing shared assumptions or conventional thinking, generating new approaches to a problem, or challenging received ideas. Reflecting the novelty of the writer's approach, texts may make use of abstract metaphors and symbolism and may be formally innovative. Child suggests as examples literary texts, philosophical discourse, and "think pieces" that advocate rethinking social, economic, or political policy or that put forward a novel approach to a technical question

a lecture theater will inevitably be a different kind of experience from listening to the same lecture as part of a test. Instead, test developers will need to determine how the test taker's language knowledge is involved in reading or listening in the TLU domain and attempt in their tests to engage that knowledge in similar ways (Bachman & Palmer, 2010).

To help language testers to achieve this, Bachman and Palmer (2010) introduced frameworks for describing the key characteristics of TLU tasks that should be simulated or replicated in the form of test tasks. Similarly, Alderson et al. (2006) provided a framework for describing key features of reading and listening input texts (Table 19.2) that can be used in locating them in relation to the Common European Framework of Reference (Council of Europe, 2001, 2009).

Recent work by Bejar et al. (2000) and by Weir (2005) – among others – went a step further in suggesting frameworks that bring together the contexts within which language tasks are undertaken and the different cognitive processes that are involved in carrying them out. Working from this socio-cognitive perspective, Khalifa and Weir (2009) considered how cognitive processes are reflected in the texts employed as input for the Cambridge ESOL tests of reading. Studies using questionnaires, verbal protocols, and eye-tracking tools have been used to explore how purpose and context shape the reading and listening process in tests and in TLU domains and how closely these processes resemble each other in the different contexts (see for example Green et al., 2010).

Current Issues and Future Trends

The degree of realism that can be achieved in the texts and recordings used in tests remains an intractable issue today. Buck (2001) called attention to the dilemma facing test writers. There is a balance to be struck between clear and detailed specification and textual authenticity. Found texts are unlikely to have the features that a test developer would like to see; but adapting texts in ways that are sympathetic both to the original writer's and the test developer's purposes is a very demanding task, even for the most experienced item writers. Where specifications set out in advance what reading or listening skills are to be tested but also call for the use of authentic input texts, practical compromises will need to be reached. The issue affects both reading and listening tests, but its impact is more obvious in listening, as any changes beyond minor edits will probably require a rerecording and so will substantially alter the nature of the material.

Increased awareness of the differences between spoken and written language means that readings of written source texts such as excerpts from novels are no longer very widely used in listening tests. On the other hand, many of the recordings that are used are based on scripts or outlines intended to approximate spoken language but prepared specifically for the test. These scripts may be modeled closely on source recordings of authentic speech (and so they claim a degree of authenticity), or they may be simply invented. Tests sometimes include recordings of scripted, semiscripted, or rehearsed speech (which may or may not be edited) made for purposes other than testing: news broadcasts, lectures, interviews, dramas, or public announcements. In other cases, unrehearsed, unedited recordings may be used. While these are certainly more authentic, they are more likely to involve uncontrolled variations in content, rate of speech, articulation, and accent. As shown in Table 19.2, features of listening tests such as the number of participants in conversations and the number of opportunities to listen further add to the potential for differences across forms of a test.

Authentic texts rarely feature all the characteristics that a test developer may wish to target in a format that will easily fit into testing templates, but substantially adapting texts may reduce their similarity to those found in the TLU domain, threatening the validity of the test. The growing availability of video resources, although it makes video-based tests increasingly practical, further limits the options for realistic adaptation.

Current Issues and Future Trends **279**

> **TABLE 19.2**

Frameworks for describing text characteristics

Bachman and Palmer (2010, pp. 66–67)

A. Format
    1. Channel (aural, visual, or both)
    2. Form (language, nonlanguage, or both)
    3. Language of input (native, target, or both)
    4. Length/time
    5. Vehicle (live, reproduced, or both)
    6. Degree of speededness
    7. Type (item, prompt, or input for interpretation)

B. Language of input
    1. Language characteristics
       a) Organizational characteristics (rhetorical or conversational)
          1) Grammatical
             a. Vocabulary
             b. Syntax
             c. Phonology/graphology
          2) Textual
             a. Cohesion
             b. Organization (rhetorical or conversational)
       b) Pragmatic characteristics
          3) Functional (ideational, manipulative, heuristic, or imaginative)
          4) Sociolinguistic (genre, dialect/variety, register, naturalness, cultural references, and figures of speech)
    2. Topical characteristics

Alderson et al. (2006), Council of Europe (2009)

Listening/Reading comprehension in ... (language) ...
    1. Target level in the curriculum:
    2. Item types
    3. Source
Interviews, news broadcasts, public announcements, etc.
    4. Length
Words for reading or duration for listening
    5. Authenticity
Genuine, adapted/simplified, or pedagogic
    6. Discourse type
Mainly argumentative, mainly descriptive, mainly expository, mainly instructive, mainly narrative, or mainly phatic
    7. Domain
Personal, public, occupational, or educational
    8. Topic
Personal identification; travel; shopping; house and home, environment, etc.
    9. Curriculum linkage
An optional category
    10. Number of speakers
    11. Pronunciation
Text speed: artificially slow, slow, normal, or fast; Accent: standard accent, slight regional accent, strong regional accent, or non-native accent; Clarity of articulation: artificially/clearly/normally/sometimes unclearly articulated
    12. Content
Only concrete content, mostly concrete content, fairly abstract content, or mainly abstract content

(Continued)

Chapter 19 Adapting or Developing Source Materials

> **TABLE 19.2**
>
> **(Continued)**
>
> 13. Grammar
> *Only simple structures. mostly simple structures. limited range of complex structures, or wide range of complex structures*
> 14. Vocabulary
> *Only frequent/mostly frequent/rather extended/extended vocabulary*
> 15. Number of listenings
> 16. Input text comprehensible at CEFR level
> *A1/ A2/ B1/ B2/ C1/ C2*
> 17. Items comprehensible at CEFR level
> *A1/ A2/ B1/ B2/ C1/ C2*

The challenges involved in using authentic recordings is well illustrated by the account given by Brindley et al. (1997) of the problems faced by developers of a test designed for migrants to Australia. Sometimes the recordings proved to be too long, but

> at other times they contained either too much or too little information or would have required extensive contextualization. Even some texts which were capable of generating a considerable number of items had to be edited when it was found, for example, that the items followed one another too closely and thus placed an overly demanding processing burden on candidates or that a text contained specific cultural references which would be difficult for some candidates to interpret.
>
> (Brindley et al., 1997, pp. 40–41)

Ultimately the recordings employed in the test were either entirely scripted or adapted from broadcast material and rerecorded using actors.

Buck (2001) dedicated a whole chapter (chapter 6) to the selection of recordings for tests of listening, noting the additional difficulties that this process involves by comparison with selecting and adapting reading texts. There can be no doubt that using scripted speech (including speech from broadcast sources) allows test developers to exert control over the recordings and to achieve greater consistency in test content – an important consideration when multiple forms must be produced. Scripted and controlled forms of speech may also be more suitable for beginners in language learning. On the other hand, Buck renewed the warning that scripted dialogue tends to be unrepresentative of spontaneous speech and that greater authenticity can be achieved when recordings are not crafted by the test developers. Buck suggested a range of strategies for obtaining more realistic spoken samples, while exercising some control over content. These strategies included semiscripted scenarios and directed interviews.

Khalifa and Weir (2009, p. 110) provided a list of the kinds of adaptation currently considered appropriate in Cambridge tests of reading:

- cutting to make the text an appropriate length;
- removing unsuitable content to make the text inoffensive;
- cutting or amending the text to avoid candidates being able to get the correct answer simply by word matching, rather than by understanding the text;
- glossing or removing cultural references if appropriate, especially where cultural assumptions might impede understanding;
- deleting confusing or redundant references to other parts of the source text; and
- glossing, amending, or removing parts of the text that require experience or detailed understanding of a specific topic.

Recent research by Salisbury (2005) for listening and by Green and Hawkey (2012) for reading has provided direct insights into how item writers approach text selection. Salisbury found that expert writers were more aware of the test specifications, were quickly able to recognize texts with potential as test material, and could add contextualizing elements to a script to make it accessible to listeners. Writers often started from ideas for questions and then modified the script to make it fit with them. For example, they might change words in the text to avoid giving direct clues to the correct answer, or they might add text to the script to introduce distraction and make answers less guessable. Green and Hawkey similarly found that questions of authenticity played relatively little part in item writers' editing processes. Writers focused instead on the relationship between the text and the tasks, including matters such as coherence and avoiding the repetition of key information. Both studies have illustrated the role that effective group moderation can play both in reviewing text selection and in editing processes.

One promising avenue has been the use of automated text analysis tools for text selection. Recent approaches to measuring readability using automated text analysis have incorporated a wider range of textual features. The lexile approach is an example of this (see http://www. lexile.com), and lexile measures have been linked to test scores on tests such as TOEFL. However, lexiles are based on L1 readers of English and so may not be the optimal metric for L2 readers. It is also problematic that the proprietary nature of the tool makes it difficult for users to see exactly how lexile values are arrived at. Green (2011) used computational measures of features listed by Alderson et al. (2006) and Khalifa and Weir (2009) to differentiate between texts used in educational materials targeting learners at different levels of proficiency and found that vocabulary range played a greater role in distinguishing between lower levels (up to level B2 of the Common European Framework of Reference), while syntax measures emerged as more salient at the higher levels. Sheehan et al. (2007) reported on a computer system that can be used to retrieve texts with characteristics that might make them suitable as reading input texts for a specific test: the Graduate Record Examinations (GRE). They reported that identifying texts in this way leads to dramatic improvement in the number of texts that item writers can locate to use on the test in a given time. In addition to aiding text selection, such tools can also help test developers evaluate how closely their texts reflect key texts from the TLU domain and the impact of editorial changes. Green and Hawkey (2012), for example, were able to trace how changes made by item writers impact on the nature of the texts presented to test takers.

The Internet has provided the item writer with a hitherto unimaginable wealth of potential input material in all modes from which to choose. However, for the present, there is no doubt that finding suitable sources for use in tests of comprehension remains a subtle and challenging activity. Increasing use of integrated multimedia resources is only adding to the complexity of the challenge, bringing a growing need for research into the impact on comprehension of different combinations of textual, graphic, and auditory input (Khabbazbashi et al., 2022; Suvorov & He, 2022).

This chapter has mainly been concerned with tests originating in the "Anglo-Saxon" countries and with the testing of English. However, recent years have seen increasing professionalism in the production of language tests globally and innovations are now coming from more diverse sources. One issue for testers of English and other international languages that might perhaps be more easily tackled outside the historic center is the shift away from the perception of English as the expression of Anglo-Saxon cultural heritage toward its use as *lingua franca* (Elder & Davies, 2006) or as an international basic skill (Graddol, 2006), used more in interactions between second language speakers than between second and first language speakers. In the future, which non-native accents should be included on a test of listening? Which locally current expressions should be allowed on a test of reading? To what extent might it be desirable and acceptable to incorporate multiple languages and translingual or

282 **Chapter 19** Adapting or Developing Source Materials

plurilingual competences (Chalhoub-Deville, 2019; Saville & Seed, 2021) into comprehension tests? Validity concerns may argue for the inclusion of the wide range of languages, varieties, and accents that users typically encounter, but in tests with an international candidature the imperative to avoid bias argues for the use of a limited range of standard native varieties, all similarly familiar to test-taker groups. The experience of test developers has also shown that learners themselves have often favored "Inner Circle" varieties over locally more prevalent varieties (Elder & Davies, 2006).

Discussion Questions

1. When preparing items to assess comprehension of spoken input, is it better to work from a transcript, or only to listen to the recording? Or to do both? What might be the advantages of each approach?

2. Much of the reading people do these days is done on digital devices, giving them ready access to dictionaries, translation tools, and other sources of support. To better reflect the realities of language use, should our reading assessments allow people to use these kinds of tool?

References

Alderson, J. C. (1988). Testing English for specific purposes: how specific can we get? In A. Hughes (Ed.), *Testing English for university study* (pp. 16–28). London, England: Modern English Publications/The British Council.

Alderson, C., Clapham, C., & Wall, D. (1995). *Language test construction and evaluation*. Cambridge, England: Cambridge University Press.

Alderson, J. C., Figueras, N., Kuijpers, H., Nold, G., Takala, S., & Tardieu, C. (2006). Analysing tests of reading and listening in relation to the CEFR: the experience of the Dutch CEFR construct project. *Language Assessment Quarterly, 3*(1), 3–30.

Bachman, L. F. (1990). *Fundamental considerations in language testing*. Oxford, England: Oxford University Press.

Bachman, L. F., & Palmer, A. S. (2010). *Language assessment in practice*. Oxford, England: Oxford University Press.

Barnwell, D. P. (1996). *A history of foreign language testing in the United States: From its beginnings to the present*. Tempe, AZ: Bilingual Press.

Bejar, I., Douglas, D., Jamieson, J., Nissan, S., & Turner, J. (2000). *TOEFL® 2000 listening framework: A working paper* (TOEFL report MS-19). Princeton, NJ: Educational Testing Service.

Brindley, G., Hood, S., McNaught, C., & Wigglesworth, G. (1997). Test design and delivery. In G. Wigglesworth & G. Brindley (Eds.), *Access: Issues in English language test design and delivery* (pp. 31–64). Sydney: NCELTR.

Buck, G. (2001). *Assessing listening*. Cambridge, England: Cambridge University Press.

Carroll, J. B. (1961). Fundamental considerations in testing for English language proficiency of foreign language students. In *Testing the English proficiency of foreign students* (pp. 30–40). Washington, DC: Center for Applied Linguistics.

Carroll, B. J. (1980). *Testing communicative performance*. Oxford, England: Pergamon.

Chalhoub-Deville, M. B. (2019). Multilingual testing constructs: theoretical foundations. *Language Assessment Quarterly, 16*(4–5), 472–480.

Child, J. R. (1987). Language proficiency levels and the typology of texts. In H. Byrnes & M. Canale (Eds.), *Defining and developing proficiency: Guidelines, implementations and concepts* (pp. 97–106). Lincolnwood, IL: National Textbook.

Council of Europe. (2001). *Common European framework of reference for languages: Learning, teaching, assessment*. Strasbourg, France: Language Policy Division.

Council of Europe. (2009). *Relating language examinations to the common European framework of reference for languages: Learning, teaching, assessment (CEFR). A manual*. Strasbourg, France: Language Policy Division.

Davidson, F., & Lynch, B. (2002). *Testcraft: A teacher's guide to writing and using language test specifications*. New Haven, CT: Yale University Press.

Davies, A. (2009). Assessing academic English: testing English proficiency 1950–1989. In *The IELTS solution. Studies in language testing* (Vol. *23*). Cambridge, England: Cambridge University Press/Cambridge ESOL.

van Ek, J. A. (1975). *The threshold level*. Strasbourg, France: Council of Europe.

Elder, C., & Davies, A. (2006). Assessing English as a lingua franca. *Annual Review of Applied Linguistics, 26*, 282–304.

Graddol, D. (2006). *English next*. London, England: British Council.

Green, A. (2011). *Language functions revisited: Theoretical and empirical bases for language construct definition across the ability range*. Cambridge, England: Cambridge University Press.

Green, A., & Hawkey, R. A. (2012). Re-fitting for a different purpose: a case study of item writer practices in adapting source texts for a test of academic reading. *Language Testing, 29*(1), 109–129.

Green, A., Ünaldi, A., & Weir, C. J. (2010). Empiricism versus connoisseurship: establishing the appropriacy of texts for testing reading for academic purposes. *Language Testing, 27*(3), 1–21.

Harris, D. (1969). *Testing English as a second language*. New York, NY: McGraw Hill.

Hawkey, R. A. (2004). The CELS: developing a modular approach to testing English language skills. In *Studies in language testing* (Vol. *16*). Cambridge, England: Cambridge University Press/Cambridge ESOL.

Heaton, B. (1975). *Writing English language tests*. London, England: Longman.

Hughes, A. (2003). *Testing for language teachers* (2nd ed.). Cambridge, England: Cambridge University Press.

Khabbazbashi, N., Chan, S., & Clark, T. (2022). Towards the new construct of academic English in the digital age. *ELT Journal, 2022*, ccac010. https://doi.org/10.1093/elt/ccac010.

Khalifa, H., & Weir, C. J. (2009). Examining reading: research and practice in assessing second language reading. In *Studies in language testing* (Vol. *29*). Cambridge, England: Cambridge University Press/Cambridge ESOL.

Lado, R. (1961). *Language testing*. London, England: Longmans.

Oller, J. W. Jr. (1979). *Language tests at school*. London, England: Longman.

Rosenfeld, M., Leung, S., & Oltman, P. K. (2001). *The reading, writing, speaking, and listening tasks important for academic success at the undergraduate and graduate levels* (TOEFL Report MS-21). Princeton, NJ: Educational Testing Service.

Salisbury, K. (2005). *The edge of expertise: Towards an understanding of listening test item writing as professional practice* (Unpublished doctoral dissertation). King's College London, England.

Saville, N., & Seed, G. (2021). Language assessment in the context of plurilingualism. In *The Routledge handbook of plurilingual language education* (pp. 360–376). Abingdon, England: Routledge.

Sheehan, K. M., Kostin, I., & Futagi, Y. (2007). *Supporting efficient, evidence-centered item development for the GRE verbal measure* (ETS research report RR-07-29). Princeton, NJ: Educational Testing Service.

Spolsky, B. (1995). *Measured words: The development of objective language testing*. Oxford, England: Oxford University Press.

Suvorov, R., & He, S. (2022). Visuals in the assessment and testing of second language listening: a methodological synthesis. *International Journal of Listening, 36*(2), 80–99.

Thorndike, E. L. (1918). Reading as reasoning: a study of mistakes in paragraph reading. *Journal of Educational Psychology, 8*, 323–332.

Valette, R. (1967). *Modern language tests: A handbook* (1st ed.). New York, NY: Harcourt Brace & World.

Weir, C. J. (1983). *Identifying the language needs of overseas students in tertiary education in the United Kingdom* (Unpublished doctoral dissertation). University of London, England.

Weir, C. J. (1993). *Understanding and developing language tests*. Hemel Hempstead, England: Prentice Hall.

Weir, C. (2005). *Language testing and validation: An evidence based approach*. Basingstoke, England: Palgrave Macmillan.

Weir, C. J., & Milanovic, M. (Eds.). (2003). Continuity and innovation: the history of the CPE 1913–2002. In *Studies in language testing* (Vol. *15*). Cambridge, England: Cambridge University Press.

Suggested Readings

Alderson, C. (2000). *Assessing reading*. Cambridge, England: Cambridge University Press.

Brindley, G. (1998). Assessing listening abilities. *Annual Review of Applied Linguistics, 18*, 171–191.

Field, J. (2019). *Rethinking the second language listening test*. Sheffield, England: Equinox.

Green, A. B. (2021). *Exploring language assessment and testing*. New York, NY: Routledge.

CHAPTER 20

Automated Writing Assessment and Feedback

Sara T. Cushing and Sha Liu

Introduction

In traditional writing assessments, raters evaluate a performance sample against a rating scale or set of criteria with the help of exemplar scripts that instantiate aspects of the scale with actual student performance. However, there is a growing trend among researchers and test developers toward experimenting with, and increasingly using operationally, automated scoring for writing. Reasons for this trend include the desire to move away from discrete items toward more performance items in large-scale tests, advances in natural language processing, and the ability of computers to analyze very large data sets, along with a growing need to test more and more students quickly and economically.

The most obvious potential advantages of automated scoring for large-scale assessment are the savings in terms of time and costs, given the labor-intensive nature of human scoring, and the reliability of automated scoring in producing the same score for a given essay. Many large-scale and institutional tests require double rating of some if not all performances for reliability, using a third rater if the first two disagree or diverge beyond an acceptable threshold. At a single institution with a test for only a few hundred students, scoring essays can require several raters working over multiple days; international tests, of course, are much larger scale, sometimes requiring many thousands of raters working in different locations and time zones around the world. An automated system that can accomplish this scoring in a matter of minutes represents a major saving of both time and money.

Some large-scale international tests have already incorporated automated scoring into their test systems. For example, the Test of English as a Foreign Language, Internet-Based Test (TOEFL iBT) uses a scoring engine developed by Educational Testing Service called *e-rater*® as one of two raters on two writing tasks: an independent (non-source-based and an integrated (source-based) writing task. Similarly, the Graduate Management Admission Test (GMAT) utilizes *Intellimetric* for assessing responses in its Analytical Writing Assessment section. The Pearson Test of English Academic (PTE Academic) relies entirely on automated scoring for both speaking and writing, as does the Duolingo English Test (DET). However, employing automated scoring for summative writing assessment is not without its critics. Major concerns arise from its perceived reliance on proxy indicators instead of true writing performance, and

The Concise Companion to Language Assessment, First Edition. Edited by Antony John Kunnan.
© 2025 John Wiley & Sons, Inc. Published 2025 by John Wiley & Sons, Inc.

potential negative influence on writing instruction. These reservations have been expressed in the position statement endorsed by the U.S.-based Conference on College Composition and Communication (2004) which states unequivocally: "We oppose the use of machine-scored writing in the assessment of writing."

For anyone involved in language testing, either at the classroom level or in developing or interpreting large-scale tests, it is important to understand the capabilities and limitations of automated writing assessment techniques. Such an understanding is crucial for making informed decisions about adopting this technology or accepting automatically generated scores. In this chapter, we chart the developmental trajectory of automated writing assessment, focusing on its two primary applications: automated essay scoring (AES), i.e., generating automated ratings, primarily for large-scale assessments, and automated writing evaluation (AWE), which provides various types of feedback to writers in formative assessment. We highlight recent trends and feature examples of systems currently in use. Further, we explore the utilization of automated writing assessment, emphasizing key considerations when implementing AES for summative assessments in large-scale testing scenarios. Concluding this chapter, we address the factors that influence the efficacy of AWE systems in classroom settings, drawing on comprehensive reviews of recent research. We also discuss implications for the successful implementation of automated writing assessment.

History and Current Trends

It may surprise some to learn that the history of automated writing assessment dates back to the 1960s. During this period, Page (1966) launched Project Essay Grade (PEG), an innovative initiative aimed at emulating human assessment techniques for written content. PEG's strategy was grounded in regression analysis, examining quantifiable linguistic elements such as average word and sentence lengths, and the frequency of prepositions and punctuation. Even with the technological limitations of its era, PEG's performance was found to be on par with trained human raters (Page, 2003; Shermis et al., 2013). Such achievements led Page (1966) to predict that automated scoring might soon be standard practice.

In the years that followed, a spectrum of automated scoring instruments emerged to address both academic and commercial demands. Advancements in natural language processing (NLP) enabled these tools to incorporate statistical, rule-based, or hybrid algorithms. Distinct from PEG's approach, these methods extract and analyze a wide variety of linguistic characteristics ranging from syntactic patterns to intricate semantic connotations (Burstein et al., 2013a). This depth of analysis enhanced the accuracy of essay evaluations. Consequently, these approaches solidified their position as dominant methods in automated scoring. A comprehensive discussion of these techniques will be presented in the subsequent section. Due to their primary function of assigning scores, such tools are commonly categorized as machine scoring, automated scoring, or, as introduced earlier, AES systems. We will use the more widely accepted term AES for consistency. Prominent among the AES systems are *e-rater*® from the Educational Testing Service, the *Intelligent Essay Assessor* from Pearson Education Inc., and *Intellimetric* by Vantage Learning.

To expand the educational applications of AES, developers integrated feedback mechanisms to address learners' needs for constructive feedback in the 2000s. Consequently, *e-rater*® evolved into *Criterion*, Intelligent Essay Assessor became *WriteToLearn*, and Intellimetric transformed into *MyAccess*. Beyond mere scoring, these advanced systems furnish immediate, formative feedback across various writing aspects – from basic mechanics and grammar to usage and style. These refinements signaled a transition from AES to automated writing evaluation (AWE), marking a more formative approach to writing assessment.

In the past decade, AWE has witnessed significant advancements, paralleling the rapid developments in natural language processing, machine learning, and the ascendancy of generative AI. Strobl et al. (2019) identified 44 AWE systems, a number that has undoubtedly increased since then. Within this expansion, Liu (2024) identifies three prominent trends in AWE:

- The integration of insights from second language acquisition (SLA) and second language (L2) writing research with the design of AWE represents a significant shift in recent years. Such close alignment helps ensure that these tools are more attuned to the specific needs of L2 learners (Ranalli, 2021). Products that exemplify this trend include the Automated Causal Discourse Evaluation Tool (Chukharev-Hudilainen & Saricaoglu, 2016), Research Writing Tutor (Cotos et al., 2020), Writing Pal (Roscoe & McNamara, 2013), and Write & Improve with Cambridge (Liu & Yu, 2022). It should be noted that Write & Improve with Cambridge is a product of a renowned test provider – Cambridge Assessment University & Press. In contrast, other systems primarily originate from research initiatives aimed at achieving pedagogical objectives, such as enhancing academic writing proficiency. Furthermore, Write & Improve with Cambridge mirrors the traditional design of AWE systems which are typically associated with AES systems and promise added value through automated feedback. The other three researcher-led AWE systems, however, predominantly concentrate on delivering feedback, sidelining automated score generation.
- A proliferation of context-sensitive AWE tools, particularly tailored for specific L2 learner demographics, has been observed (Shermis et al., 2013). This trend is most evident in tools crafted for Chinese EFL learners, epitomized by platforms like Pigai and iWrite. Pigai, in particular, has attracted extensive academic attention and is the most frequently studied system in AWE research in L2 contexts (Shadiev & Feng, 2023).
- The AWE horizon is expanding with the incorporation of AI-driven platforms, especially those developed using models such as OpenAI's GPT (Alharbi, 2023; Mizumoto & Eguchi, 2023). Tools emblematic of this shift include WordTune and GrammarlyGo – a more advanced AI rendition of Grammarly. Intriguingly, in response to concerns from Chinese educators about potential GPT misuse in student compositions, iWrite recently augmented its feedback tools with a GPT detector.

The development of automated scoring and feedback systems originated in the commercial sector rather than educational research, with little reference to current theories of learning or assessment (Xi, 2010). Those systems that were based in learning science and backed by a rigorous validation program, such as Criterion, tended to be proprietary and only available by subscription. However, a recent shift is evident. Writing educators and researchers are increasingly contributing to AWE development, making them more appropriate for use in pedagogical contexts. It is important to note that many contemporary AWE tools are freely accessible, while others, like Grammarly, PaperRater, and Write & Improve with Cambridge, offer premium features for an added fee.

Understanding the distinction between AES and AWE is crucial, given their unique objectives, intended applications, and validation methods. While AES is optimized for summative assessments in large-scale exams, aiming to streamline grading, reduce costs, and bolster scoring reliability, AWE is inherently tailored for formative assessment. It acts as a supporting tool to enrich writing instruction in classroom environments (Burstein et al., 2020; Shi & Aryadoust, 2023; Stevenson & Phakiti, 2019; Ware, 2011; Xi, 2010). In the following sections, we first discuss the fundamentals of AES systems and then turn to considerations for the use of AWE in classrooms.

Setting the Stage: When to Consider Automated Writing Assessment

Claims about the benefits of automated scoring and feedback are often made by purveyors of commercial systems but are frequently greeted with some skepticism by educators. To sort out the validity of these claims, it is useful to distinguish between high-stakes, typically large-scale assessments, and lower-stakes, classroom-based assessments. In high-stakes situations, what is typically desired is a single score that can be used in informing decisions such as admission, placement, or certification. A reliable AES system that generates scores similar to human ratings (which themselves are never completely reliable) may be useful, provided that there are sufficient checks within the system to ensure ongoing accuracy and reliability of scoring, along with evidence in addition to computer-generated scores on which to base important decisions about a student's proficiency such as placement or university admission. On the other hand, the case for AES is weakest as a tool for summative assessment in the classroom, where the classroom teacher is the most appropriate person to make the ultimate evaluation as to how much students have learned or achieved. Teachers are rightly concerned about the dangers of handing over critical decision-making to a computer that may be focusing on the wrong skill, and de-professionalizing teaching by using automated grading to make critical decisions about students' education. Conversely, classroom settings are the most relevant venue for AWE (i.e., automated feedback for formative assessment). Here, the important checks to be made are the degree to which feedback can be understood and used by students and how well teachers are trained in system use so that they can make use of its features appropriately.

AES for Summative Assessment

An informed decision about whether to use a commercially available automated scoring engine or to trust test scores that are generated automatically requires some knowledge of what these systems can and cannot do, how they work, and how the features used by AES systems relate to the features of language production that are valued by human raters in scoring. In this section of the chapter, we present some of these considerations.

Automated language analysis, as introduced previously, primarily employs two distinct approaches: statistical and rule-based methods. Statistical methods use very large language corpora to model patterns of language. Within statistical methods, there are two types: supervised and unsupervised modeling. Supervised modeling relates models to human ratings, while unsupervised models do not. For the purposes of this chapter, we are thus only considering supervised models, as they are most relevant to automated scoring. The process of supervised modeling, as described by Burstein et al. (2013), involves running a large number of randomly sampled scored responses to an essay topic (at least 250) through a computer program that extracts a variety of linguistic features from the essays and gives each feature or cluster of features a numerical value. These values are weighted through regression to arrive at a set of scores that most closely matches the human scores for the training essays. These weights are then converted to a formula, which is then used to generate scores for new essays on that topic. Such systems have been demonstrated to be as reliable as human raters on the prompts for which they have been trained (see, for example, Attali, 2007; Bridgeman, 2013; Bridgeman et al., 2012; Page, 2003).[1]

Rule-based methods of language analysis, as the name implies, involve creating rules to guide language pattern identification, such as specific syntactic structures. Both statistical

---

[1] It should be noted that not all AES systems use regression techniques; for example, Yannakoudakis et al. (2011) describe a system for scoring ESOL texts that is based on rank preference techniques rather than regression.

and rule-based methods are used to generate features for sophisticated AES systems such as e-rater (see Burstein et al., 2013).

While the scores generated by AES systems may be similar to human scores, it is not necessarily the case that those scores were derived in the same way – in other words, the features of an essay that can easily be counted are not always the same features that are valued by human raters. However, developers of AES systems should be able to describe to potential users how their system generates scores and how these scores correspond to descriptors on a rating scale used by human raters.

In the best case, features that are extracted from the essays can be associated with features of the rating scale that raters also focus on. As an illustration, we can look at the features of e-rater and compare them with the TOEFL Independent essay rating scale, for which e-rater served as one of the two raters (see also Enright & Quinlan, 2010 for a discussion of the relationship between e-rater scores and this scale). Note that in 2023, the Independent essay was replaced by a discussion task with a different rating scale and the e-rater engine is being continuously updated. This information is being presented here for illustrative purposes only. The highest score level (5) descriptor for the TOEFL Independent essay is as follows:

(5) An essay at this level largely accomplishes all of the following:

- effectively addresses the topic and task;
- is well organized and well developed, using clearly appropriate explanations, exemplifications, and/or details;
- displays unity, progression, and coherence; and
- displays consistent facility in the use of language, demonstrating syntactic variety, appropriate word choice, and idiomaticity, though it may have minor lexical or grammatical errors.

E-rater (v. 11, as reported in Ramineni et al., 2012), uses the following features in scoring TOEFL essays:

- Organization (number of discourse elements)
- Development (length of discourse elements)
- "Positive features" (including preposition usage and collocation density)
- Lexical complexity (average word length, sophistication of word choice)
- Errors in grammar, usage, mechanics, and style.

A cursory look at these two lists reveals both overlaps and gaps. Perhaps the most obvious overlap is the relationship between the last descriptor of the scale (a consistent facility in the use of language) and the e-rater features related to lexical complexity and errors, and the set of positive features that has recently been added to e-rater. While there is not 100% correspondence, it is clear that there is a strong relationship between the e-rater features and the rating scale in this area. In terms of gaps, as Enright and Quinlan (2010) acknowledge, there is little overlap between e-rater features and the descriptors "effectively addresses the topic and task" and "displays unity, progression, and coherence."

Finally, both lists include organization and development, though the way these notions are interpreted by raters and measured by e-rater is not identical. E-rater evaluates organization by automatically identifying the presence or absence of relevant discourse elements (e.g., introduction, thesis statements, main ideas, supporting details, and conclusion), and development by measuring the length of each discourse element. Human raters, by comparison, when rating organization and development, pay attention to such features as the logic and flow of an essay, whether it introduces the topic in an appropriate way, includes body paragraphs with sensible statements supporting the main ideas, and concludes the essay satisfactorily. These notions are expressed in the TOEFL rating scale as "clearly appropriate explanations, exemplifications, and/or details" and "unity, progression, and coherence." They may not be quantifiable, as they rely on the background knowledge and expectations that the

290 Chapter 20 Automated Writing Assessment and Feedback

rater brings to the reading, including other essays that he or she has read in the past, expectations about what a writer can accomplish in the time allowed, and world knowledge.

Furthermore, a skeptical reader might protest that the length of discourse elements is an invalid measure of development, given that length by itself is not a good measure of the quality of writing. However, it should be recognized that it is difficult to develop an essay well without expanding on main points and supporting them with relevant details, all of which have the effect of increasing the length of the different elements of the essay. As Deane and Raminatha (2014) note, "e-rater's organization and development features are affected by fluency (longer, more richly structured essays score well on these features). But someone who writes a longer essay with more structure and clear transitional elements hasn't necessarily written a better essay (though with typical populations, that's almost always true)."

In other words, while the features of the essay that e-rater can measure are not exactly the same as the features that humans value, these features can stand in as useful proxies for them in the majority of cases, if the goal is simply to provide a score that approximates a human score. We can see from this example that, at least in this case, there is a reasonable correspondence between the rating scale used by human raters and the algorithm used by e-rater, even though there are features of the scale that are not evaluated by e-rater. As Enright and Quinlan (2010) point out, e-rater looks at fewer aspects of writing than humans do, but does so more consistently than humans, who vary both in what they attend to and how they weight different features of writing when evaluating it.

Of course, in some cases, an AES system will not give the same score as a trained human rater. This is primarily because AES systems cannot "read" a text as a person does. That is, while AES systems can parse sentences and identify propositions within a text, they cannot relate those propositions or texts to world knowledge or evaluate the logic of an argument or the reasonableness of evidence. Thus, AES systems are not well suited to evaluate many features of writing that are valued by human raters such as authorial voice or strength of argument, which depend on shared knowledge and assumptions between reader and writer (although research is underway to close this gap; see, e.g., Burstein et al., 2013b; Chukharev-Hudilainen & Saricaoglu, 2016; Cotos et al., 2020). Similarly, an AES system cannot detect features of an essay that might be rewarded by a human rater, such as allusions to literature or cultural references, or the use of humor or irony. As an example, one version of an online demonstration of the criterion system included an essay marked for subject–verb agreement errors. This particular essay included the sentence "Monkey see, monkey do," which contained two subject–verb agreement errors, according to Criterion. From a strictly grammatical perspective, these are errors, but from a pragmatic perspective, it is a perfectly well-formed sentence, evoking the reader's (stereotyped) world knowledge about monkey behavior and the appropriate use of proverbs in writing, among other things. We have not yet reached a point in automated scoring where the computer can recognize pragmatically skillful uses of "incorrect" language like this.

Furthermore, computers cannot easily interpret the intended meaning of a writer when errors are made. ESL errors are often difficult to categorize (Polio, 1997), and AES systems are not always able to use context to distinguish among possible interpretations of sentences containing errors. Chodorow et al. (2010, p. 422) give the example "I fond car": does this involve a misspelling of "found" and a missing article (I found the car) or a missing copula, preposition, and plural marking (I am fond of cars)? In the context of an actual essay, a human rater would be able to deduce the most likely interpretation, but AESs are not yet at the point where they can reliably do so.

Another aspect of concern is that there are degrees of seriousness of errors, in terms of creating confusion for the reader or stigmatizing the writer. Some important work being done in error detection at ETS, for example, focuses on prepositions and articles; however, these errors are generally considered to be less important to address by teachers than errors such as word choice or verb tense (see Vann et al., 1984); we return to this issue later in the chapter.

To summarize, AES systems can be useful as a complement to human ratings. Double rating by human raters is the gold standard, but humans are not completely reliable and two different people may focus on different aspects of the writing, have slightly different interpretations of the rating scale descriptors, and may have other differences that result in different scores. An AES system will generate the same score for the same essay every time, even though it will use less information than a human rater to come up with that score. In the majority of cases, the agreement rate between two human raters will be approximately the same as between a human rater and the AES, with the cost and time saving of using AES substantial.

Because of the limitations of computer scoring vis-à-vis human scoring, it is important that there be checks in place to identify and deal with those essays that are anomalous in one way or another. For example, such checks would include an algorithm for identifying off-topic essays or essays that attempt to game the system. Such essays can be sent to a second human rater, and, it is generally agreed that the scores of human raters should always trump the scores of an AES system. Enright and Quinlan (2010), for example, describe the procedures in place that trigger a second human rater. First, if the difference between the first rater and e-rater is 1.5 points or greater, a second human rater is used, and the final score is the average of the three ratings. In the rare case that one of the ratings is 1.5 points away from the other two, the outlier is not included in the average. Second, if the human rater determines that the essay is off-topic, the essay is not scored by e-rater but rather by a second human rater. Finally, e-rater identifies anomalous essays for adjudication, including essays that are excessively long or short, or essays that contain an inordinate number of errors. In these cases, the essays are scored by two humans rather than by e-rater.

AWE and Classroom Use

AWE systems introduce a transformative approach to feedback, distinguishing it from traditional methods. Its immediacy can streamline the often time-consuming and laborious feedback-practice cycle. Learners can undertake several essay revisions without waiting for teacher feedback. Moreover, some AWE systems offer valuable resources such as portfolios, dictionaries, and sample essays. These tools empower students to track progress, revisit their submissions, and learn from the feedback. Ideally, this proactive engagement over time may help cultivate essential skills like independent revision and writing autonomy that are important for the growth of writing ability (see Fu et al., 2022; Li et al., 2015; Liao, 2016), freeing up teachers to provide feedback on higher-level concerns such as content, development of ideas, and organization. Another notable benefit of AWE is its anonymity, which can alleviate the anxiety and emotional challenges that learners often encounter with feedback from teachers or peers (see Alderson, 2005). This feature holds particular significance for L2 learners from Asian cultures, where the concept of "Mianzi" or maintaining one's dignity is deeply ingrained and influences how feedback is perceived (see Carless et al., 2006). By ensuring anonymity, AWE has the potential to create a conducive learning environment for these learners to address their weak points and make improvements without fear of public embarrassment.

Given the promising capabilities of AWE feedback, numerous studies have examined its classroom integration. As illustrated in Table 20.1, a total of 11 comprehensive reviews have distilled this extensive research, covering various periods. This compilation consists of six systematic reviews (see Fu et al., 2022; Hibert, 2019; Nunes et al., 2021; Shadiev & Feng, 2023; Stevenson, 2016; Stevenson & Phakiti, 2014) and five meta-analytical explorations (see Fleckenstein et al., 2023; Li, 2022; Mohsen, 2022; Ngo et al., 2022; Zhai & Ma, 2023).

Collectively, these reviews reported generally positive effects of AWE on student writing. They support the claim that AWE, especially when tailored to identify initial lower-level errors, complements traditional teacher or peer feedback, thereby enhancing students'

Chapter 20 Automated Writing Assessment and Feedback

TABLE 20.1

A synopsis of 11 studies reviewing previous AWE research

Study	Type	Scope	
		N	Period
Stevenson & Phakiti (2014)	Systematic review	33	1990–2011
Stevenson (2016)	Systematic review	29	1990–2013
Hibert (2019)	Systematic review	29	2007–2018
Fu et al. (2022)	Systematic review	48	Until 2021
Nunes et al. (2020)	Systematic review	8	2000–2020
Shadiev & Feng (2023)	Systematic review	82	2016–2022
Li (2022)	Meta-analysis	26	2000–2022
Mohen (2022)	Meta-analysis	14	Until 2020
Ngo et al. (2022)	Meta-analysis	44	1993–2021
Fleckenstein et al. (2023)	Meta-analysis	20	NA
Zhai & Ma (2023)	Meta-analysis	26	2010–2022

Note. N = The number of studies being reviewed

writing quality. While Stevenson and Phakiti's (2014) review, which examined the 1990–2011 period, identified limited supporting evidence for AWE's efficacy, more recent reviews have consistently found a more positive influence on writing performance across diverse educational tiers. This trend toward more favorable results in recent years may be attributed to advancements in AWE technology and, even more crucially, its thoughtful implementation, which takes into account a multitude of factors affecting a student's capacity to fully realize the benefits of AWE. In what follows, we briefly discuss these factors, aiming to outline strategies for optimizing the utility of AWE in classroom contexts. A comprehensive discussion of these elements exceeds this chapter's scope. For more in-depth discussions, readers are directed to the review studies mentioned in Table 20.1.

The Quality of Automated Feedback

The quality of automated feedback, encompassing the types of errors it addresses and the accuracy and actionability of its advice, is an important determinant of student engagement with AWE systems. Drawing a line between what teachers are most helpful for (giving feedback on content) and what computers do well (counting things), we might think that automated feedback on sentence-level grammar and word choice might be most useful, particularly for L2 students who want and appreciate error identification and correction. However, it is important to recognize some limitations of automated forms of error detection in currently available AWE systems. Two main issues have been raised in this regard.

First and foremost, many error types cannot be automatically tagged and detected. In fact, humans do not always agree on what an error is or how it should be categorized. Certain errors, such as preposition and article errors, are notoriously difficult to identify, and even experienced teachers do not always agree on whether a particular usage is an error. Since error identification is imprecise, developers need to decide whether it is more important to minimize false-positives (i.e., calling a correct usage an error) or false-negatives (i.e., not identifying actual errors). That is, an engine that identifies more errors will inevitably get some wrong, while an engine that identifies fewer errors but does so with more accuracy will inevitably miss some.

In designing AWE systems, developers often prioritize feedback accuracy over the breadth of error detection, as there's a prevailing concern that inaccurate feedback might misguide students into making unwarranted edits to their writing. As an illustration, Chodorow et al. (2010) report that the developers of Criterion have chosen to minimize false-positives in their feedback system; i.e., they wanted to be more confident of the errors that were identified, even though that means identifying fewer errors. As reported by Chodorow et al. (2010), Criterion can identify 25% of preposition errors with 80% accuracy, and 40% of article errors with 90% accuracy. A similar trend of prioritizing precision, even at the expense of detection breadth, is evident in other AWE systems like *Grammarly* (see John & Woll, 2020; Ranalli & Yamashita, 2022), *My Access* (Hoang & Kunnan, 2016), *Pigai* (Bai & Hu, 2017), *WriteToLearn* (Liu & Kunnan, 2016), and *Write & Improve* with Cambridge (Liu, 2024).

However, an emerging body of research (see Fu et al., 2022; Guo et al., 2023; Saricaoglu, 2019) has begun to challenge this prevailing approach, emphasizing its potential drawbacks, especially in L2 contexts. When an AWE system's detection rate is low, it inevitably overlooks a considerable number of errors. Such omissions can hinder students from recognizing and rectifying their mistakes. On the flip side, when students are given ample opportunities to engage with AWE feedback, particularly concerning their most significant errors, they stand a better chance of deriving meaningful benefits from such interactions (see Fu et al., 2022). For instance, in Liu's (2024) study of Chinese EFL students using *Write & Improve*, feedback on word choice errors, even when doubted for their accuracy, prompted students to recognize their frequent misuse of terms that appeared synonymous but had subtle differences in use (e.g., "however" versus "on the contrary"). This heightened students' awareness regarding the need to improve their accuracy in word choice. Students also voiced frustrations over the system overlooking certain errors (e.g., possessive case), which made self-correction daunting without automated guidance. Given these findings, AWE developers need to strike a delicate balance between ensuring feedback accuracy and offering comprehensive feedback. Students and teachers should also be cognizant of the fact that the majority of errors may be missed by such systems.

Further compounding this issue, the error types that are identified by AWE systems may not be those that are important for teachers and students to address. For instance, Dikli and Bleyle (2014) compared the errors in a set of essays marked by the teacher with those found by Criterion and found that Criterion only identified about 25% as many errors as the teacher did, with only about 60% accuracy. The categories of error that were most likely to be missed by Criterion included wrong or missing word, preposition errors, wrong form of word, and ill-formed verbs. Unfortunately, these are some of the error types that are of most concern to teachers. In a similar vein, Liu and Kunnan (2016) observed that *WriteToLearn* frequently failed to detect errors commonly made by Chinese EFL students, including mistakes related to prepositions, word choice, and verb forms. Adding to these concerns, Pigai, although specifically designed and widely adopted for Chinese EFL students, consistently missed key errors, such as those associated with articles, prepositions, subject–verb agreement, and verb forms (see Bai & Hu, 2017; Chen et al., 2022; Zhang & Hyland, 2018).

At this point in time, therefore, it seems that, while automated feedback systems can identify some errors, and thus provide some useful feedback to students, teachers should not rely solely on these systems for providing feedback on linguistic errors to students. This understanding sets the stage for our exploration of how contextual factors shape the efficacy of automated feedback within classroom settings.

The Contextual Attributes of AWE Implementation

The context in which AWE is employed plays a significant role in how students engage with automated feedback. How the teacher uses the system and integrates it into the classroom can make a large difference in how successful it is (see Chen et al., 2022; Chen & Cheng, 2008; Xu & Zhang, 2022; Zhang, 2020). For example, Chen and Cheng (2008) report on the experiences of three teachers using MyAccess in an EFL classroom. In the most successful classroom, the teacher had students use the program only in the early stages of drafting; once they received a minimum score from the system she would conference with students and give them her feedback. In the second class, the teacher used the system only for summative feedback and did not grade essays at all until her students complained, at which point she went back to grading essays by hand. In the third class, the teacher did not take time to learn the system and gave up on it altogether after a few weeks.

Such varied outcomes highlight the necessity for robust administrative backing and adequate teacher training. Given the multifaceted features of AWE platforms, the learning curve can be steep for some teachers. Ware (2011) asserts that these systems frequently allow a great deal of flexibility in how they are used and include features that teachers may not be aware of at first; in order for teachers to be able to buy into the system they need to be thoroughly familiar with the capabilities of the system and how these might work with their own teaching style. The importance of administrative support is also mentioned by Grimes and Warschauer (2010), who studied the use of MyAccess in three different middle school districts and attributed greater success in one district to "stronger top-down support ... primarily through systematic peer support and the inspired leadership of the district writing project director" (p. 24). Such support is particularly essential in L2 contexts, where teachers face immense workloads and often lack ample time to provide in-depth feedback on student writing (see Zhang, 2017, 2020). Furthermore, the institutional stance on the importance of revising for writing improvement significantly impacts the successful use of AWE (see Zhang & Hyland, 2018).

The Personal Characteristics of Students

It is important to recognize that the personal characteristics of the students who use AWE will have an impact on how successful the system is. Students' perception of AWE feedback can directly affect student engagement, motivation, and willingness to employ the feedback for writing improvement. This perception, often shaped by English language proficiency, varies. While learners with lower proficiency levels might appreciate AWE feedback for its capacity to pinpoint and rectify surface errors, those with higher proficiency might find it lacking, especially in terms of honing higher-order writing skills and addressing issues of content.

A considerable volume of research on multiple AWE systems underscores the influential role of English language proficiency in molding how learners perceive, comprehend, and modify their writing based on AWE feedback (e.g., Bai & Hu, 2017; Chapelle et al., 2015; Chen & Cheng, 2008; Grimes & Warschauer, 2010; Liao, 2016; Liu, 2024; Thi et al., 2022; Tian & Zhou, 2020; Xu & Zhang, 2022; Zhang, 2020; Zhang & Hyland, 2018). To illustrate, Grimes and Warschauer (2010) report that teachers had different opinions on which learner groups would benefit from the system. One teacher felt that lower-proficiency English language learners would not benefit as they were unable to write enough for their writing to be scored. Others noted that high-ability honors students were able to game the system to get higher scores, for example, by repeating words, and were not motivated to use the system to improve their writing.

However, findings on how English language proficiency impacts students are varied. Some research (see Chen & Cheng, 2008; Thi et al., 2022; Tian & Zhou, 2020) has found that advanced learners feel discouraged with AWE due to its limited focus on meaning and development of advanced writing abilities. In contrast, other studies (see Koltovskaia, 2020; Liao, 2016; Zhang & Hyland, 2018) advocate AWE for proficient learners, suggesting that lower proficiency students might struggle to understand the feedback. These studies indicate a potential pitfall for less advanced students: over-reliance on AWE might encourage mere acceptance of feedback without truly understanding it.

Based on the discussions in this section, we recommend a judicious application of AWE, leveraging its full technological potential and actively involving key stakeholders. AWE systems, ideally, should initially be employed to identify lower-level errors during the early stages of essay revision. This automated feedback can then be augmented and eventually followed by feedback from teachers or peers. Such an integrative approach has been proven effective in an expanding body of research (see Yao et al., 2021; Zhang & Hyland, 2018, 2022; Zhang & Xu, 2022). Additionally, within the AWE-mediated writing process, students should not merely be seen as passive feedback recipients. Instead, they should be central to the process, with efforts directed toward fostering sustained engagement. For such active involvement to occur, teachers must continually oversee students' AWE utilization, offering timely scaffolding as required. This guidance helps cultivate an environment promoting student–teacher and student–student collaboration, maximizing learning outcomes of using AWE. For instance, Shi et al. (2022) documented a strategy where teachers created "essay revision pairs," enabling students to collaboratively engage with automated feedback during revisions. This method was found to significantly enhance students' comprehension and application of the feedback, leading to improved academic writing.

We also wish to highlight the rapidly increasing prominence of GPT-powered AWE systems and the potential revolutionary changes they might introduce in classroom settings. Traditional AWE systems often faced criticism for their inability to genuinely "read" content and for lacking the personal interaction inherent in human feedback. These enduring concerns, however, might soon be mitigated by generative AI. A study of *Wordtune* by Rad et al. (2023) indicated that L2 learners relished the experience of "communicating" with the tool, seeking its tailored feedback. This dialogic interaction highlights a fundamental distinction between conventional and GPT-powered AWE tools. While the application of this cutting-edge technology remains in its early stages, any definitive conclusions regarding its effectiveness might be premature. Teachers and students should be conscious of both the potential advantages and challenges posed by its deployment (Barrot, 2023).

Conclusion

In this chapter we have provided an overview of AES and AWE systems as they relate to human scoring of writing. AES has progressed to the point where it is used operationally as a check on human scoring in at least one major large-scale international test that includes extended writing and without human scoring on other tests that use shorter writing tasks. AWE systems are being marketed to and widely used in educational institutions with the promise of reducing teacher workload and improving student outcomes in writing, with some successes noted. The technology of automated writing assessment will certainly continue to develop and become more pervasive in educational settings. We believe that whatever their views of AES and AWE systems, teachers, and administrators need to be informed of how such systems operate and what their strengths and limitations are so they can make intelligent choices about using them.

Discussion Questions

1. Reflecting on the varied purposes and stakes of different assessment scenarios, how can educators and test developers effectively leverage the capabilities of AES for summative, large-scale assessments and AWE for classroom settings?

2. As generative AI-powered AWE systems grow in prominence and potentially address some limitations of traditional AWE tools, how might they reshape the classroom dynamic between students, teachers, and technology?

296   **Chapter 20** Automated Writing Assessment and Feedback

References

Alderson, J. C. (2005). *Diagnostic foreign language proficiency: The interface between learning and assessment*. London: Continuum.

Alharbi, W. (2023). AI in the foreign language classroom: a pedagogical overview of automated writing assistance tools. *Education Research International, 23*, 4253331. https://doi.org/10.1155/2023/4253331.

Attali, Y. (2007). *Construct validity of e-rater® in scoring TOEFL® essays. Research Report-Educational Testing Service. Princeton RR, 7*.

Bai, L., & Hu, G. (2017). In the face of fallible AWE feedback: how do students respond? *Educational Psychology, 37*(1), 67–81.

Barrot, J. S. (2023). Using automated written corrective feedback in the writing classrooms: effects on L2 writing accuracy. *Computer Assisted Language Learning, 36*(4), 584–607. https://doi.org/10.1080/09588221.2021.1936071.

Bridgeman, B. (2013). 13 human ratings and automated essay evaluation. In M. D. Shermis & J. Burstein (Eds.), *Handbook of automated essay evaluation: Current applications and new directions* (pp. 221–232). Routledge.

Bridgeman, B., Trapani, C., & Attali, Y. (2012). Comparison of human and machine scoring of essays: differences by gender, ethnicity, and country. *Applied Measurement in Education, 25*(1), 27–40.

Burstein, J., Tetrault, J., & Madnini, N. (2013a). The E-rater® automated essay scoring system. In M. D. Shermis & J. Burstein (Eds.), *Handbook of automated essay evaluation: Current applications and new directions* (pp. 55–67). Routledge.

Burstein, J., Tetreault, J., Chodorow, M., Blanchard, D., & Andreyev, S. (2013b). Automated evaluation of discourse coherence quality in essay writing. In M. D. Shermis & J. Burstein (Eds.), *Handbook of automated essay evaluation: Current applications and new directions* (pp. 267–280). Routledge.

Burstein, J., Riordan, B., & McCaffrey, D. (2020). Expanding automated writing evaluation. In D. Yan, A. A. Rupp & P. Foltz (Eds.), *Handbook of automated scoring: Theory into practice* (pp. 329–346). Taylor and Francis Group/CRC Press.

Carless, D., Joughin, G., & Liu, N. (2006). *How assessment supports learning: Learning-oriented assessment in action*. Hong Kong: Hong Kong University Press.

Chapelle, C. A., Cotos, E., & Lee, J. (2015). Validity arguments for diagnostic assessment using automated writing evaluation. *Language Testing, 32*(3), 385–405. https://doi.org/10.1177/0265532214565386.

Chen, C. F. E., & Cheng, W. Y. E. (2008). Beyond the design of automated writing evaluation: pedagogical practices and perceived learning effectiveness in EFL writing classes. *Language Learning & Technology, 12*(2), 94–112.

Chen, Z., Chen, W., Jia, J., & Le, H. (2022). Exploring AWE-supported writing process: an activity theory perspective. *Language Learning & Technology, 26*(2), 129–148. https://hdl.handle.net/10125/73482.

Chodorow, M., Gamon, M., & Tetreault, J. (2010). The utility of article and preposition error correction systems for English language learners: feedback and assessment. *Language Testing, 27*(3), 419–436.

Chukharev-Hudilainen, E., & Saricaoglu, A. (2016). Causal discourse analyzer: improving automated feedback on academic ESL writing. *Computer Assisted Language Learning, 29*(3), 494–516. https://doi.org/10.1080/09588221.2014.991795.

Conference on College Composition and Communication (2004). *Position statement on teaching, learning, and assessing writing in digital environment.*

Cotos, E., Huffman, S., & Link, S. (2020). Understanding graduate writers' interaction with and impact of the research writing tutor during revision. *Journal of Writing Research, 12*(1), 187–232. https://doi.org/10.17239/jowr-2020.12.01.07.

Deane, P. & Raminatha, C. (2014). *Construct representation and the structure of an automated scoring engine: issues and uses*. Paper presented at AILA, August 2014.

Dikli, S., & Bleyle, S. (2014). Automated essay scoring feedback for second language writers: how does it compare to instructor feedback? *Assessing Writing, 22*, 1–17.

Enright, M. K., & Quinlan, T. (2010). Complementing human judgment of essays written by English language learners with e-rater® scoring. *Language Testing, 27*(3), 317–334.

References 297

Fleckenstein, J., Liebenow, L. W., & Meyer, J. (2023). Automated feedback and writing: a multi-level meta-analysis of effects on students' performance. *Frontiers in Artificial Intelligence, 6,* 1162454. https://doi.org/10.3389/frai.2023.1162454.

Fu, Q.-K., Zou, D., Xie, H., & Cheng, G. (2022). A review of AWE feedback: types, learning outcomes, and implications. *Computer Assisted Language Learning,* 1–43. https://doi.org/10.1080/09588221.2022.2033787.

Grimes, D., & Warschauer, M. (2010). Utility in a fallible tool: a multi-site case study of automated writing evaluation. *Journal of Technology, Learning, and Assessment, 8*(6). Retrieved from: https://files.eric.ed.gov/fulltext/EJ882522.pdf.

Guo, Q., Feng, R., & Hua, Y. (2023). *Automated written corrective feedback in research paper revision: The good, the bad, and the missing.* Taylor & Francis Group.

Hibert, A. I. (2019). Metacognitive processes and self-regulation in the use of automated writing evaluation programs. *Lecture Notes in Computer Science,* 655–658. https://doi.org/10.1007/978-3-030-29736-7_60.

Hoang, G. T., & Kunnan, A. J. (2016). Automated essay evaluation for English language learners: a case study of my access. *Language Assessment Quarterly, 13*(4), 359–376. https://doi.org/10.1080/15434303.2016.1230121.

John, P., & Woll, N. (2020). Using grammar checkers in an ESL context. *CALICO Journal, 37*(2), 193–196. https://doi.org/10.1558/cj.36523.

Koltovskaia, S. (2020). Student engagement with automated written corrective feedback (AWCF) provided by Grammarly: a multiple case study. *Assessing Writing, 44,* 1–12. https://doi.org/10.1016/j.asw.2020.100450.

Li, R. (2022). Still a fallible tool? Revisiting effects of automated writing evaluation from an activity theory perspective. *British Journal of Educational Technology, 54,* 773–789.

Li, J., Link, S., & Hegelheimer, V. (2015). Rethinking the role of automated writing evaluation (AWE) feedback in ESL writing instruction. *Journal of Second Language Writing, 27,* 1–18. https://doi.org/10.1016/j.jslw.2014.10.004.

Liao, H. (2016). Enhancing the grammatical accuracy of EFL writing by using an AWE-assisted process approach. *System, 62,* 77–92.

Liu, S. (2024). *Investigating the efficacy of automated writing evaluation as a diagnostic assessment tool in L2 writing instruction: A mixed-method study. (Unpublished doctoral dissertation).* University of Bristol.

Liu, S., & Kunnan, A. J. (2016). Investigating the application of automated writing evaluation to Chinese undergraduate English majors: a case study of WriteToLearn. *CALICO Journal, 33*(1), 71–91.

Liu, S., & Yu, G. (2022). L2 learners' engagement with automated feedback – an eye-tracking study. *Language Learning & Technology, 26*(2), 78–105. https://doi.org/10125/73480.

Mizumoto, A., & Eguchi, M. (2023). Exploring the potential of using an AI language model for automated essay scoring. *Research Methods in Applied Linguistics, 2,* 1–13.

Mohsen, M. A. (2022). Computer-mediated corrective feedback to improve L2 writing skills: a meta-analysis. *Journal of Educational Computing Research, 60*(5), 1253–1276. https://doi.org/10.1177/07356331211064066.

Ngo, T. T.-N., Chen, H. H.-J., & Lai, K. K.-W. (2022). The effectiveness of automated writing evaluation in Efl/ESL writing: a three-level meta-analysis. *Interactive Learning Environments,* 1–18. https://doi.org/10.1080/10494820.2022.2096642.

Nunes, A., Cordeiro, C., Limpo, T., & Castro, S. L. (2021). Effectiveness of automated writing evaluation systems in school settings: a systematic review of studies from 2000 to 2020. *Journal of Computer Assisted Learning, 38*(2), 599–620. https://doi.org/10.1111/jcal.12635.

Page, E. B. (1966). The imminence of grading essays by computer. *Phi Delta Kappan, 48*(1), 238–243.

Page, E. B. (2003). Project essay grade: PEG. In M. D. Shermis & J. Burstein (Eds.), *Automated essay scoring: A cross-disciplinary perspective* (pp. 43–54). Lawrence Erlbaum Associates Publishers.

Polio, C. G. (1997). Measures of linguistic accuracy in second language writing research. *Language learning, 47*(1), 101–143.

Rad, H. S., Alipour, R., & Jafarpour, A. (2023). Using artificial intelligence to foster students' writing feedback literacy, engagement, and outcome: a case of Wordtune application. *Interactive Learning Environments.* https://doi.org/10.1080/10494820.2023.2208170.

Ramineni, C., Trapani, C. S., Williamson, D. M., Davey, T., & Bridgeman, B. (2012). Evaluation of the e-rater® scoring engine for the TOEFL® independent and integrated prompts. *ETS Research Report Series, 2012*(1), 1–51. https://doi.org/10.1002/j.2333-8504.2012.tb02288.x.

Ranalli, J. (2021). L2 student engagement with automated feedback on writing: potential for learning and issues of trust. *Journal of Second Language Writing, 52*, 1–16. https://doi.org/10.1016/j.jslw.2021.100816.

Ranalli, J., & Yamashita, T. (2022). Automated written corrective feedback: error-correction performance and timing of delivery. *Language Learning & Technology, 26*(1), 1–25. http://hdl.handle.net/10125/73465.

Roscoe, R. D., & McNamara, D. S. (2013). Writing pal: feasibility of an intelligent writing strategy tutor in the high school classroom. *Journal of Educational Psychology, 105*(4), 1010–1025. https://doi.org/10.1037/a0032340.

Saricaoglu, A. (2019). The impact of automated feedback on L2 learners' written causal explanations. *ReCALL, 31*(2), 189–203. https://doi.org/10.1017/s095834401800006x.

Shadiev, R., & Feng, Y. (2023). Using automated corrective feedback tools in language learning: a review study. *Interactive Learning Environments*, 1–29. https://doi.org/10.1080/10494820.2022.2153145.

Shermis, M. D., Burstein, J., & Bursky, S. A. (2013). Introduction to automated essay evaluation. In M. D. Shermis & J. Burstein (Eds.), *Handbook of automated essay evaluation: Current applications and new directions* (pp. 1–15). Routledge.

Shi, H., & Aryadoust, V. (2023). A systematic review of automated writing evaluation systems. *Education and Information Technologies, 28*, 771–795. https://doi.org/10.1007/s10639-022-11200-7.

Shi, Z., Liu, F., Lai, C., & Jin, T. (2022). Enhancing the use of evidence in argumentative writing through collaborative processing of content-based automated writing evaluation feedback. *Language Learning & Technology, 26*(2), 106–128. https://doi.org/10.10125/73481.

Stevenson, M. (2016). A critical interpretative synthesis: the integration of automated writing evaluation into classroom writing instruction. *Computers and Composition, 42*, 1–16.

Stevenson, M., & Phakiti, A. (2014). The effects of computer-generated feedback on the quality of writing. *Assessing Writing, 19*, 51–65.

Stevenson, M., & Phakiti, A. (2019). Automated feedback and second language writing. In K. Hyland & F. Hyland (Eds.), *Feedback in second language writing: Contexts and issues* (pp. 125–142). Cambridge University Press.

Strobl, C., Ailhaud, E., Benetos, K., Devitt, A., Kruse, O., Proske, A., & Rapp, C. (2019). Digital support for academic writing: a review of technologies and pedagogies. *Computers & Education, 131*, 33–48. https://doi.org/10.1016/j.compedu.2018.12.005.

Thi, N. K., Nikolov, M., & Simon, K. (2022). Higher-proficiency students' engagement with and uptake of teacher and Grammarly feedback in an EFL writing course. *Innovation in Language Learning and Teaching, 17*(3), 690–705. https://doi.org/10.1080/17501229.2022.2122476.

Tian, L., & Zhou, Y. (2020). Learner engagement with automated feedback, peer feedback and teacher feedback in an online EFL writing context. *System, 91*, 102247. https://doi.org/10.1016/j.system.2020.102247.

Vann, R. J., Meyer, D. E., & Lorenz, F. O. (1984). Error gravity: a study of faculty opinion of ESL errors. *TESOL Quarterly, 18*(3), 427–440.

Ware, P. (2011). Computer-generated feedback on student writing. *TESOL Quarterly, 45*, 769–774.

Xi, X. (2010). Automated scoring and feedback systems: where are we and where are we heading? *Language Testing, 27*(3), 291–300.

Xu, J., & Zhang, S. (2022). Understanding AWE feedback and English writing of learners with different proficiency levels in an EFL classroom: a sociocultural perspective. *The Asia-Pacific Education Researcher, 31*(4), 357–367. https://doi.org/10.1007/s40299-021-00577-7.

Yannakoudakis, H., Briscoe, T., & Medlock, B. (2011, June). *A new dataset and method for automatically grading ESOL texts. In Proceedings of the 49th annual meeting of the association for computational linguistics: Human language technologies (Vol. 1, pp. 180–189). Association for Computational Linguistics.*

Yao, Y., Wang, W., & Yang, X. (2021). Perceptions of the inclusion of automatic writing evaluation in peer assessment on EFL writers' language mindsets and motivation: a short-term longitudinal study. *Assessing Writing, 50*, 1–14. https://doi.org/10.1016/j.asw.2021.100568.

Zhai, N., & Ma, X. (2023). The effectiveness of automated writing evaluation on writing quality: a meta-analysis. *Journal of Educational Computing Research, 61*(4), 875–900. https://doi.org/10.1177/07356331221127300.

Zhang, Z. (2017). Student engagement with computer-generated feedback: a case study. *ELT Journal, 71*(3), 317–328. https://doi.org/10.1093/elt/ccw089.

Zhang, Z. (2020). Engaging with automated writing evaluation (AWE) feedback on L2 writing: student perceptions and revisions. *Assessing Writing, 43*, 1–14. https://doi.org/10.1016/j.asw.2019.100439.

Zhang, Z., & Hyland, K. (2018). Student engagement with teacher and automated feedback on L2 writing. *Assessing Writing, 36*, 90–102.

Zhang, Z., & Hyland, K. (2022). Fostering student engagement with feedback: an integrated approach. *Assessing Writing, 51*, 100586. https://doi.org/10.1016/j.asw.2021.100586.

Zhang, Z., & Xu, L. (2022). Student engagement with automated feedback on academic writing: a study on Uyghur ethnic minority students in China. *Journal of Multilingual and Multicultural Development*. https://doi.org/10.1080/01434632.2022.2102175.

Suggested Readings

Barrot, J. S. (2023). Using ChatGPT for second language writing: pitfalls and potentials. *Assessing Writing, 57*, 1–6. https://doi.org/10.1016/j.asw.2023.100745.

Buckingham Shum, S., Lim, L., Boud, D., Bearman, M., & Dawson, P. (2023). A comparative analysis of the skilled use of automated feedback tools through the lens of teacher feedback literacy. *International Journal of Educational Technology in High Education, 20*, 1–42. https://doi.org/10.1186/s41239-023-00410-9.

Fu, Q.-K., Zou, D., Xie, H., & Cheng, G. (2022). A review of AWE feedback: types, learning outcomes, and implications. *Computer Assisted Language Learning*, 1–43. https://doi.org/10.1080/09588221.2022.2033787.

Mizumoto, A., & Eguchi, M. (2023). Exploring the potential of using an AI language model for automated essay scoring. *Research Methods in Applied Linguistics, 2*, 1–13.

Yan, D., Rupp, A. A., & Foltz, P. (Eds.). (2020). *Handbook of automated scoring: Theory into practice*. Taylor and Francis Group/CRC Press.

THEME 4

Assessment Contexts

CHAPTER 21

Classroom-Based Assessment Issues for Language Teacher Education

Constant Leung

Introduction

Assessment as an integral part of teacher education has received increasing attention in recent years. Although teachers have always been involved in assessment activities in their professional work, teacher education generally did not give assessment literacy – that is, the professional knowledge and repertoire regarding assessment – a great deal of curriculum prominence. Recent developments in education and assessment reforms have, however, pointed to the need for teachers to have a good grasp of assessment issues. Furthermore, the current trends toward increasing accountability in public services have been reflected in greater use of the assessment of student attainment as an index of effective pedagogy and cost-efficient educational provision. With few exceptions, practicing teachers are required to administer externally produced tests as well as to carry out teacher-led assessment. The more they understand the educational and technical issues involved, the better they are able to make principled decisions that would lead to beneficial uses of assessment, especially classroom-based assessment, in their professional practice. For these reasons, assessment literacy is now a very important aspect of teachers' professional repertoire (see Giraldo, 2022; Inbar-Lourie, 2008; Kremmel & Harding, 2020; Levi & Inbar-Lourie, 2020 for further discussion).

This chapter will focus on classroom-based assessment issues for teacher education with reference to teachers working in the broad field of English language teaching (ELT); the conceptual issues raised in this discussion are, however, relevant to language teacher education more generally. English language teachers work in a range of diverse contexts in different world locations. Some work in conventionally labeled foreign language contexts (e.g., universities and schools in parts of Africa, East Asia, and South America), some in places such as Hong Kong and Singapore, where English is regarded as a second language, and some in international schools (in all parts of the world) where English is used as the medium of instruction. In many educational jurisdictions in places such as Australia, England, and United States, where a significant number of students come from linguistically diverse backgrounds, English language teaching can take place as part of mainstream content lessons. The discussion will be oriented toward some of the key issues related to teacher-led

---

The Concise Companion to Language Assessment, First Edition. Edited by Antony John Kunnan.
© 2025 John Wiley & Sons, Inc. Published 2025 by John Wiley & Sons, Inc.

classroom-based assessment that are relevant to preservice and in-service additional/second-language teacher education. For reasons of scope, this chapter will not address issues related to peer and (student) self-assessment (but see cross-references at the end of this chapter). The term "assessment" is used inclusively in this discussion, to refer to all the types of evaluating, monitoring, and measuring of student learning and attainment that are carried out by teachers; the narrower terms "test" and "examination" will be used, where appropriate, to indicate the use of particular assessment instruments.

Some Key Issues

Classroom-based assessment has been the subject of curriculum developments in different parts of the world (e.g., DeLuca et al., 2016; Leung et al., 2021; Willis et al., 2013). At the same time, assessment is being increasingly recognized as an important part of the ELT teacher education curriculum. For instance, in the Cambridge ESOL (English for speakers of other languages) Delta syllabus (University of Cambridge Local Examinations Syndicate, 2022), assessment was in two of its three modules. Similarly, out of a 47-page statement, the TESOL/NCATE standards for initial teacher education programs (Teachers of English to Speakers of Other Languages, 2010) devoted some 12 pages to specifying the types and levels of knowledge in assessment for trainee teachers. In general teacher education, curriculum statements tend to cover issues such as formative and summative assessment purposes, specialist concepts such as validity and reliability, and professional considerations such as appropriate choice of externally produced assessment instruments and practicality. Classroom-based assessment tends to be subsumed within these topics, with the exception of the TESOL/NCATE curriculum statement (Teachers of English to Speakers of Other Languages, 2010), which provided a separate subsection on "Classroom-Based Assessment for ESL" within the "Assessment" domain. The inclusion of a separate subsection on classroom-based assessment signals a growing awareness that this is an important area of professional knowledge and practice. For reasons of scope, this discussion will focus on four major issues: purposes of assessment, validity, and reliability of assessment, perspectives on language and language learning, and the relationship between language and curriculum content. The overall aim is to help produce a teacher education agenda that would promote teachers' assessment literacy. The discussion will be broadly framed within a classroom-based assessment perspective.

Purposes and Uses of Assessment

Assessment has been conventionally seen as serving two main purposes: formative and summative. Assessment activities in themselves are essentially purpose-neutral; it is the way(s) in which we make use of the assessment process and outcome that would render them purpose-bound. For instance, the scores of a teacher-made vocabulary test administered at the end of a reading course could be used to indicate how much (or how many words) students have learned and retained. This would be a summative use of the test. At the same time, it is possible to use the results of the same test as a basis to work out what has and what has not been learned and why, and to develop alternative teaching strategies and/or curriculum content to try to improve future teaching and learning. This "assessment-to-teaching/learning" orientation would serve a formative purpose.

The term "assessment" in formal education generally signals particular moments within the curriculum when teaching, learning, and other related activities come to a halt, and students' performance is being checked and evaluated in specially designed activities. End-of-year school examinations and termly tests are examples of these set-piece activities. This conventional notion of assessment still holds for formal summative assessment.

However, in the past 25 years or so, the developments in formative assessment have added a process and learning orientation. This orientation to formative assessment is often discussed under the banner of assessment for learning. The influential Assessment Reform Group's (2002, p. 2) 10 principles of assessment for learning, for instance, include the following:

- *Assessment for learning should be part of effective planning of teaching and learning.* A teacher's planning should provide opportunities for both learner and teacher to obtain and use information about progress toward learning goals ... Planning should include strategies to ensure that learners understand the goals they are pursuing and the criteria that will be applied in assessing their work. How learners will receive feedback, how they will take part in assessing their learning, and how they will be helped to make further progress should also be planned.
- *Assessment for learning should focus on how students learn.* The process of learning has to be in the minds of both learner and teacher when assessment is planned and when the evidence is interpreted. Learners should become as aware of the "how" of their learning as they are of the "what."
- *Assessment for learning should be recognized as central to classroom practice.* Much of what teachers and learners do in classrooms can be described as assessment. That is, tasks and questions prompt learners to demonstrate their knowledge, understanding, and skills. What learners say and do is then observed and interpreted, and judgments are made about how learning can be improved. These assessment processes are an essential part of everyday classroom practice and involve both teachers and learners in reflection, dialogue, and decision-making.

Active open dialogic interaction between teachers and pupils seems to lie at the heart of this approach to formative assessment; from a teacher's point of view, this kind of assessment is embedded in everyday teacher–student interaction. The formativeness resides in the efforts made by the teacher to make use of the information given by the student as a basis of developing additional and/or alternative teaching strategies and of providing learning opportunities. When teachers engage students in learning activities and analyze their performance with a view to determining how much or how well the target content (in terms of language or other subject knowledge or both) has been learned, they are effectively conducting a diagnosis of what has been learned or achieved (as part of their formative assessment). The diagnosis can be used to form the basis of teachers' pedagogic guidance for further learning (also referred to as "feedback" designed to enhance student understanding and "feed forward" for further learning). Perhaps it is worth highlighting the point that diagnosing student learning can take place as a one-off teacher-centered event that takes place at planned moments, or it can be built into teaching activities on an ongoing basis, with students playing an active part through dialoguing with others and reflecting on their own work (see Fox & Hartwick, 2011; Harding et al., 2015; Read, 2008 for further discussion).

Rea-Dickins (2006) provided an empirical account of how language teachers, working in collaborative teaching situations with subject teachers, orient toward different purposes in planned assessment and informal "assessing while teaching" activities. She notes that both the summative and the formative orientations may be observed during the moments when teachers carry out the assessment of student performance in the classroom. In the classroom-based English as an additional language assessment framework designed for use by elementary and secondary school teachers in content lessons, Leung et al. (2021) made an explicit point that assessment outcomes can be used for formative and summative purposes. From the point of view of teacher education, particularly initial teacher education, an important point to emphasize is that formative and summative purposes are not tied to specific assessment

306 Chapter 21 Classroom-Based Assessment Issues for Language Teacher Education

activities – the marks of an end-of-term teacher-made test can be used for formative purposes, e.g., analyzing student performances to identify curriculum areas for development and/or change; likewise, teacher assessment of individual students' knowledge and understanding carried out during teaching can form part of a summative assessment of overall attainment over a course.

Validity and Reliability in Classroom-Based Assessment

Issues of validity are key to the consideration of quality in assessment. There is a considerable body of research literature devoted to these issues, particularly in relation to large-scale psychometrically oriented standardized assessment in the form of tests and examinations (e.g., Bachman & Palmer, 2010; McNamara & Roever, 2006; Messick, 1989; Ockey & Green, 2020; Stoynoff & Chappelle, 2005; also see Bachman & Damböck, 2018 for a discussion for teachers). Broadly speaking, validity refers to the extent to which an assessment can be justified in terms of a number of considerations such as whether an assessment taps into the knowledge and skills that it claims to be focusing on (this is generally referred to as construct validity); what interpretation and use is made of the assessment outcomes; and what consequences the assessment may have on the key stakeholders (e.g., the students). Traditionally reliability – accuracy and consistency in sampling of language abilities and reporting student performance – is seen as a key quality in any assessment (a separate consideration from validity). From the point of view of classroom-based assessment, reliability issues should be seen in conjunction with the focus of the assessment and its intended purpose(s) and use(s). There is a case for suggesting that, for classroom-based assessment, reliability, and validity work hand in hand, as the following discussion will indicate.

In planned and specially designed teacher-made summative assessment activities that attempt to establish what has been learned, for example, an end-of-term test, it would be important to be clear about what is meant to be assessed (i.e., what is the construct?), and how the chosen focus of assessment is being translated into the test itself. For instance, in developing a test on listening and speaking, the following questions could be asked:

- What counts as listening and speaking (in a specific curriculum context)? Listening to and giving a monologic talk (e.g., an account of an experiment)? Listening and responding to a recorded multiparty conversation? Listening to (and watching) a video-recorded conversation and responding to questions from the teacher? Listening to others while participating in a live discussion?
- What content should be included in listening tasks? Should the tasks be on topics covered in the course? Or should they be general topics appropriate for the age and for the stage of language development?

There is not a single, universal correct answer to any of the above questions; the important consideration is fitness for purpose in context. Language teachers in academic language programs at university, for instance, are likely to have different concerns and priorities from those of teachers who are in school content classes, teaching English collaboratively with content teachers. Test tasks should reflect the aim and content of the teaching program concerned. Furthermore, interpreting the value of the outcomes of such teacher-made tests should take account of intended use(s). If the purpose of the test is to sort students for a particular purpose, for instance, to identify students with relevant background knowledge to fill 10 spaces for a general language course at a particular level, then it would probably be sufficient to use test scores from a relevant programme to establish the students' attainment relative to one another in terms of general language proficiency. The 10 students with the top 10 highest scores would be allocated the 10 spaces.

However, if the intended use of a test is to find suitable candidates for a competition, say in oratory, then it would be necessary to identify those students who have the attributes that the competition is known to require. In other words, a stronger criterion-based consideration would need to be applied. One of the advantages of teacher-made tests over externally produced tests is that teachers, by using their local knowledge, are generally better placed to develop tasks that would tap into their students' achievements. On the other hand, the close relationship between teacher-influenced content and teacher-made tests may be a limiting factor in validity, because the teaching may only have covered the content partially or from a particular perspective.

When teachers carry out formative assessments as part of teaching in an informal way, validity issues become more complex. When a teacher asks probing questions in order to find out about students' knowledge, the live and contingent nature of this kind of "on the run" assessment may lead to an unexpected change or detour in topic. For instance, an elicitation question such as "What is the capital city of China?" might yield a variety of responses from students. While for summative assessment purposes, there is only one acceptable and correct answer to this question, formatively the answers provided by students are the entry point for further action. A correct answer may be the result of a lucky guess, an incorrect answer might be triggered by a momentary confusion over the different capitals at different historical periods, or the different Anglicized names being used, and so on. On receiving an answer, the teacher might ask a further question such as "why?" in order to elicit further information that might help establish the underlying reason(s). The point here is that the formative imperative cannot be served adequately just by having a well-defined construct in terms of desired knowledge and skills. To conduct effective formative assessment that is embedded within classroom interaction, the teacher should offer students opportunities to express the basis of their answers and should use this information to design alternative teaching strategies and learning activities where necessary. Thus, the validity considerations discussed earlier in relation to teacher-made tests or examinations would not be sufficient for classroom-embedded formative assessment, the validity of which depends, additionally, on improved learning outcomes. Colby-Kelly and Turner (2007) used the metaphor of "assessment bridge" to highlight this distinct relationship between assessment, teaching, and learning. Also, see Davison and Leung (2009) and Giraldo (2022).

The discussion so far has addressed some of the key concerns regarding assessment purposes and validity. There are, however, two other conceptually relevant issues that should be taken into account when developing teachers' professional repertoire in classroom-based assessment: view(s) on language and their relationship to language learning and assessment; and the relationship between content meaning and language.

Perspectives on Language and Language Learning

Teachers' beliefs and perceptions of what counts as language and language learning can bear on their assessment practices. Language learning can be understood in a variety of ways from different theoretical perspectives. For instance, a behaviorist view would suggest that learning is a form of response to external stimulus; a cognitive view of learning would foreground the importance of understanding and problem-solving by individual students; and a sociocultural perspective would emphasize the importance of the interaction between the individual learner and the social environment (including other people's actions in any given social situation). At the same time, language can be conceptualized at a number of levels and in a variety of ways. For instance, a grammar-oriented teacher may regard language as primarily consisting of a set of rules at the lexical (e.g., spelling and tense inflection) and syntactical

308 Chapter 21 Classroom-Based Assessment Issues for Language Teacher Education

levels (e.g., active or passive voice). A discourse-minded teacher, on the other hand, may see language as a set of resources for meaning making that can embody social values and power relationships. (For a further discussion on pedagogic perspectives, see James, 2006.)

At any one time, language teachers, like other subject specialists, tend to hold particular views on language and language learning, some of which may be espoused and some may be implicit (Leung, 2022; Rea-Dickins, 2008; Tsagari & Vogt, 2017). In various combinations, these epistemological views held by teachers can impact their pedagogic and assessment practices. For instance, *a grammar-oriented teacher* who sees learning in behaviorist terms would tend to favor the vocabulary and sentence-level work presented in discrete-point material for practice. *A discourse-oriented teacher*, aligned with a sociocultural view of learning, is likely to organize language learning tasks as group work in which the teacher would act as expert informant and the students would be encouraged to participate in discussions and to build on them in order to set their own objectives and tasks. In each of these cases, the teacher's epistemological position and the associated pedagogy would impact his/her assessment priorities. The grammarian would likely be focusing on the learning of discrete points of language (e.g., third-party verb inflection in the present tense); the socio-culturalist would be interested in assessing the language learning outcome, say, a piece of writing, against the backdrop of the students' current levels of proficiency and use of the available resources – such as a teacher's exposition of ideas, learning materials, and discussions with peers. So, both the process and the product would be part of the assessment.

The examples above are illustrative. In practice, teachers often hold a complex of views regarding language, language learning, and other education-related matters. In a study of assessment practice, for example, Leung (2012) reported that the participant teachers applied a range of criteria when marking English language learners' writing:

- *Skills*: using grammatical rules correctly
- *Process*: making use of recommended process in writing (e.g., drafting and revision)
- *Genre*: using appropriate text types and language expressions for particular audiences
- *Effort*: evidence of a student trying hard
- *Second/additional language*: being mindful of the limits to the amount of language learning possible at any one time, thus accepting some unclear language expressions.

From the point of view of teacher education, it is important that the relationship between these language-related views and assessment be made explicit. A degree of conscious understanding of this relationship would be important for any reflection on the merits and problems in one's own classroom-based assessment practices. Furthermore, such knowledge would also help teachers to analyze and understand the often-implicit language models and assumptions underlying externally produced tests and assessment frameworks. This would in turn enable them to make informed decisions as to how best to support their students' overall language learning and their preparation for assessment on the one hand, and how to avoid "teaching to the test" on the other (see Alderson & Wall, 1992; Cheng, 2005; Stiggins, 2001 for further discussion).

Relationship Between Curriculum Content and Language

The way language is construed has an impact on how the relationship between language and curriculum content is handled in assessment. It is noncontroversial to say that meaning is expressed through language. Furthermore, the communicative approach that has been predominant in English language teaching worldwide since the late 1970s has tried to focus on meaning in context. In turn, large-scale public language-testing systems such as International English Language Testing Systems (IELTS) have been designed to address language proficiency in specific contexts – the use of English in academic contexts, in this case. So, at the level of broad conceptualization, there is an acknowledgment of the links between language and curriculum content meaning. In practice, this means that academic English, for instance, is assessed through test items that represent some form of typified and decontextualized proficiency. The actual relationship between wording (what is actually said or written in real contexts) and meanings in particular subject areas has, however, remained underarticulated and underrepresented (see Staples et al., 2018 for an analysis of the lack of correspondence between subject-based language use and language test). For classroom-based language assessment, this state of affairs is unhelpful. Teachers, from their professional experience, know that it is possible to communicate the meaning of any curriculum content in a variety of formal and informal ways. Gibbons (1998, p. 101) offers an illustrative example:

Text 1 (working on the topic of magnetism, spoken by three 10-year-old students while doing an experiment using metal and nonmetal objects):

1. this ... no it doesn't go ... it doesn't move ...
2. try that ...
3. yes it does ... a bit ... that won't ...
4. won't work it's not metal ...
5. these are the best ... going really fast.

Text 2 (spoken by one student about the action, after the experiment):
we tried a pin ... a pencil sharpener ... some iron filings and a piece of plastic ... the magnet didn't attract the pin but it did attract the pencil sharpener and the iron filings ... it didn't attract the plastic.

Text 3 (written by the same student):
Our experiment was to find out what a magnet attracted. We discovered that a magnet attracts some kinds of metal. It attracted the iron filings, but not the pin. It also did not attract things that were not metal.

All three texts can be said to be about magnetism, but they differ in the lexical and grammatical resources being used. From the point of view of language assessment, the teacher would need to address questions such as: Is the assessment at hand concerned with interactional talk, spoken (monologic) reporting, or written formal reporting? Effective classroom-based assessment, for both formative and summative purposes, would require a clear and explicit sense of the language resources students are expected to use in curriculum-based tasks.

Concluding Remarks

Current developments in curriculum reform and innovation in different world locations call for increasing teacher expertise in formative and summative assessment. The discussion in this chapter suggests that additional or second-language teacher education should address some of the key concepts, such as validity and reliability, but should do so in ways that would sensitize teachers to the specific affordances and purposes of classroom-based assessment. Furthermore, given that classroom-based assessment is often carried out at close proximity to pedagogy and learning, teacher education should promote a higher level of awareness of the relationship between teachers' own beliefs and perspectives on matters such as "what is language?" and "how is language/how should language be taught/learned?" and their assessment practices. In both preservice and in-service phases, teacher education programs can help develop a higher level of expertise in this increasingly important area of teacher professionalism.

Discussion Questions

1. If you are developing a language teacher education program, would you give more prominence to formative or summative assessment, or pay equal attention to both? Give an account of your reasoning, taking into consideration of the specific educational program and environment involved.

2. How might language teachers' own (preferred) views of what counts as effective teaching and learning impact on the way/s in which they approach classroom-based formative assessment?

References

Alderson, C., & Wall, D. (1992). *Does washback exist? The educational and social impacts of language tests.* Languahe Testing Research Colloquium, Vancouver, Canada.

Assessment Reform Group. (2002). *Assessment for learning: 10 principles.* Retrieved July 25, 2011 from: http://www.assessment-reform-group.org/CIE3.PDF.

Bachman, L., & Damböck, B. (2018). *Language assessment for classroom teachers.* Oxford University Press.

Bachman, L., & Palmer, A. (2010). *Language assessment in practice: Developing language assessments and justifying their use in the real world.* Oxford University Press.

Cheng, L. (2005). *Changing language teaching through language testing: A washback study.* Cambridge University Press.

Colby-Kelly, C., & Turner, C. E. (2007). AFL research in the L2 classroom and evidence of usefulness: taking formative assessment to the next level. *The Canadian Modern Language Review/La Revue canadienne des langues vivantes, 64*(1), 9–37.

Davison, C., & Leung, C. (2009). Current issues in English language teacher-based assessment. *TESOL Quarterly, 43*(3), 393–415.

DeLuca, C., LaPointe-McEwan, D., & Luhanga, U. (2016). Teacher assessment literacy: a review of international standards and measures. *Educational Assessment, Evaluation and Accountability, 28*, 251–272.

Fox, J., & Hartwick, P. (2011). Taking a diagnostic turn: reinventing the portfolio in EAP classrooms. In D. Tsagari & I. Csépes (Eds.), *Classroom-based language assessment* (pp. 47–61). Peter Lang.

Gibbons, P. (1998). Classroom talk and the learning of new registers in a second language. *Language and Education, 12*(2), 99–118.

Giraldo, F. (2022). *Language assessment literacy and the development of pre-service foreign language teachers.* Universada de Caldas.

Harding, L., Alderson, C., & Brunfaut, T. (2015). Diagnostic assessment of reading and listening in a second or foreign language: elaborating on diagnostic principles. *Language Testing, 32*(3), 317–336.

Inbar-Lourie, O. (2008). Constructing a language assessment knowledge base: a focus on language assessment courses. *Language Testing, 25*(3), 385–402.

James, M. (2006). Assessment, teaching and theories of learning. In J. Gardner (Ed.), *Assessment and learning* (pp. 47–60). Sage.

Kremmel, B., & Harding, L. (2020). Towards a comprehensive, empirical model of language assessment literacy across stakeholder groups: developing the Language Assessment Literacy Survey. *Language Assessment Quarterly, 17*(1), 100–120.

Leung, C. (2012). Qualitative research in language assessment. In C. Chapelle (Ed.), *The Encyclopedia of applied linguistics.* Wiley. https://doi.org/10.1002/9781405198431.wbeal0979.

Leung, C. (2022). English as an additional language: a close-to-practice view of teacher professional knowledge and professionalism. *Language and Education, 36*(2), 170–187.

Leung, C., Evans, M., & Liu, Y.-C. (2021). English as an additional language assessment framework: filling a void in policy and provision in school education in England. *Language Assessment Quarterly, 18*(3), 296–315. https://doi.org/10.1080/15434303.2020.1869745.

Levi, T., & Inbar-Lourie, O. (2020). Assessment literacy or language assessment literacy: learning from the teachers. *Language Assessment Quarterly, 17*(2), 168–182.

McNamara, T., & Roever, C. (2006). *Language testing: The social dimension*. Blackwell.

Messick, S. (1989). Validity. In R. L. Linn (Ed.), *Educational measurement* (3rd ed., pp. 13–103). Macmillan.

Ockey, G. J., & Green, B. A. (Eds.). (2020). *Another generation of fundamental considerations in language assessment: A festschrift in honor of Lyle F. Bachman*. Springer.

Read, J. (2008). Identifying academic language needs through diagnostic assessment. *Journal of English for Academic Purposes, 7*(3), 180–190.

Rea-Dickins, P. (2006). Currents and eddies in the discourse of assessment: a learning- focused interpretation. *International Journal of Applied Linguistics, 16*(2), 164–189.

Rea-Dickins, P. (2008). Classroom-based language assessment. In E. Shohamy & N. H. Hornberger (Eds.), *Encyclopedia of language and education* (2nd ed.). Springer.

Staples, S., Biber, D., & Reppen, R. (2018). Using corpus-based register analysis to explore the authenticity of high-stakes language exams: a register comparison of TOEFL iBT and disciplinary writing tasks. *The Modern Language Journal, 102*(2), 310–332.

Stiggins, R. J. (2001). *Student-involved classroom assessment* (3rd ed.). Prentice Hall.

Stoynoff, S., & Chappelle, C. A. (Eds.). (2005). *ESOL tests and testing*. Alexandria, VA: Teachers of English to Speakers of Other Languages.

Teachers of English to Speakers of Other Languages. (2010). *TESOL/NCATE standards for the recognition of initial programmes in P-12 ESL teacher education*. TESOL.

Tsagari, D., & Vogt, K. (2017). Assessment literacy of foreign language teachers around Europe: research, challenges and future prospects. *Papers in Language Testing and Assessment, 6*(1), 41–63.

University of Cambridge Local Examinations Syndicate. (2022). *Delta syllabus specifications*. UCLES.

Willis, J., Adie, L., & Klenowski, V. (2013). Conceptualising teachers' assessment literacies in an era of curriculum and assessment reform. *Australian Educational Researcher, 40*(2), 241–256.

Suggested Readings

Assessment Reform Group. (2006). *The role of teachers in the assessment of learning*. Retrieved February 6, 2013 from: http://www.assessment-reform-group.org/ASF%20booklet%20English.pdf.

Black, P., Harrison, C., Lee, C., Marshall, B., & Wiliam, D. (2003). *Assessment for learning: Putting it into practice*. Open University Press.

Black, P., & Wiliam, D. (2003). The development of formative assessment. In B. Davies & J. West-Burnham (Eds.), *Handbook of educational leadership and management* (pp. 409–418). Pearson.

Black, P., & Wiliam, D. (2018). Classroom assessment and pedagogy. *Assessment in Education, 25*(3), 551–575.

Chapelle, C. A., Enright, M. K., & Jamieson, J. M. (2008). Test score interpretation and use. In C. A. Chapelle, M. K. Enright & J. M. Jamieson (Eds.), *Building a validity argument for the Test of English as a Foreign Language* (pp. 1–25). Routledge.

Davidson, F., & Lynch, B. K. (2002). *Testcraft: A teacher's guide to writing and using language test specifications*. Yale University Press.

Leung, C. (2004). Developing formative teacher assessment: knowledge, practice and change. *Language Assessment Quarterly, 1*(1), 19–41.

Leung, C. (2020). Learning-oriented assessment: more than the chalkface. In M. E. Poehner & O. Inbar-Lourie (Eds.), *Toward a reconceptualization of second language classroom assessment* (pp. 85–106). Springer Nature.

Leung, C. (2022). Curriculum-embedded EAL assessment. In H. Chalmers (Ed.), *The researchED guide to English as an Additional Language: An evidence-informed guide for teacher* (pp. 67–80). John Catt.

Mohan, B., Leung, C., & Slater, T. (2010). Assessing language and content: a functional perspective. In A. Paran & L. Sercu (Eds.), *Testing the untestable in language and education* (pp. 217–240). Multilingual Matters.

Tsagari, D., & Cheng, L. (2017). Wasback, impact and consequences revisited. In E. Shohamy & S. May (Eds.), *Language testing and assessment (part of Encyclopedia of language and education)* (pp. 359–372). Springer.

CHAPTER 22

Assessment of Young Language Learners

Mikyung Kim Wolf

Introduction

Around the world, the number of children who learn an additional, foreign, or second language (L2) alongside their mother tongue or first language (L1) is steadily increasing. This trend can be attributed not only to the benefits of early L2 learning (Jaskow & Ellis, 2019) but also to the increased mobility of individuals across international borders (Betalova, 2022). Children from immigrant, migrant, and refugee populations need to acquire L2 when their L1 is not the primary language of the society or the medium of instruction. To support effective instruction and facilitate children's L2 learning, the appropriate use of assessment is essential. Appropriate assessment practices involve both the careful design of assessments and their valid use, taking into consideration the unique characteristics of young L2 learners.

This chapter focuses on the characteristics of young learners and key considerations related to such characteristics in the development and implementation of language assessments for young L2 learners. While the term L2 is used to refer to a second, foreign, or additional language collectively throughout this chapter, the specific contexts of L2 learning and assessment will be described where appropriate. In addition, this chapter highlights recent research and practices in L2 assessments of young language learners (YLLs). Readers may refer to Bailey et al. (2014) in the first edition of the Companion to Language Assessment for earlier literature on the assessment of YLLs.

YLLs in this chapter are defined as children aged 5–13, which approximately corresponds to kindergarten through lower secondary or middle school grades. Certainly, there are younger children under the age of five who are learning an L2 before entering school. Yet, this chapter focuses on school-aged children, as L2 assessments are predominantly used in school settings for specific purposes (McKay, 2006). In the literature on the assessment of YLLs, school-aged children are often divided into two or three age/grade groups primarily due to their rapidly evolving developmental and instructional characteristics (Bailey et al., 2014; Hasselgreen, 2021). For example, the transition between elementary and middle school grades (i.e., Grade 5 or 6, depending on the schooling system) can serve as one grouping point for YLLs. YLLs in the elementary grades can also be further divided into lower (e.g., kindergarten to Grade 3) and upper elementary segments (e.g., Grades 4 and 5). In this chapter, key considerations for L2 assessment will be discussed for YLLs in general, unless age/grade-specific features need to be addressed.

The Concise Companion to Language Assessment, First Edition. Edited by Antony John Kunnan.
© 2025 John Wiley & Sons, Inc. Published 2025 by John Wiley & Sons, Inc.

312

This chapter is organized into four main sections. It begins with an overview of the developmental characteristics of YLLs, which are crucial to consider when developing and using L2 assessments. Next, it delves into the contextual and curricular characteristics that influence the potential L2 ability YLLs can achieve. The subsequent section presents various L2 assessment types for YLLs, along with key validation concerns. Finally, the chapter concludes by exploring future directions in research and practice for the continued improvement of L2 assessments for YLLs. Considering that the most prevalent L2 for school-aged children is English as an international lingua franca, this chapter is primarily drawn from research and practices in the contexts of English as an additional, foreign, or second language (EAL, EFL, or ESL).

Developmental Considerations in the Assessment of YLLs

In the assessment of YLLs, their developmental factors should be taken into careful consideration. The cognitive, social, and emotional characteristics of children constitute important developmental components in the assessment of YLLs, given their mutual relationships with L2 development. For instance, concerning cognitive aspects, research has shown that children's cognitive abilities have a substantial impact on their phonological processing skills and vocabulary acquisition (Kormos & Safar, 2009). Major learning theories (e.g., the sociocultural theory) and second language acquisition theories (e.g., the complex adaptive system/complexity theory, the input hypothesis theory) also underscore the role of social interaction in children's development and language acquisition (Bailey, 2017a). That is, children's L2 development is contingent upon their social interactions and contexts (this aspect is further described in the section of contextual considerations). With respect to children's emotions (or affective factors), research has also demonstrated that students' positive feelings and attitudes toward language learning are associated with their success in L2 learning (Ehrman et al., 2003). The following sections describe salient developmental aspects in relation to the L2 assessment for YLLs.

Cognitive Factors

Children's cognitive development is inextricably intertwined with their language development as well as with their performances on language assessments. Cognitive capacity includes a range of mental abilities (Barac et al., 2014) such as attention (the ability to focus on specific tasks for varying lengths of time), short-term and long-term memory (the ability to hold information for a short period or over an extended period), working memory (the ability to keep information in mind and manipulate it to perform tasks), visual–spatial processing (the ability to understand and analyze spatial relationships among objects), abstract reasoning (the ability to contemplate objects and concepts that are not in a physical or concrete state), metalinguistic awareness (the ability to understand the functions of language), executive functions (a suite of mental skills pertaining to cognitive flexibility, inhibitory control, and working memory), among others. These cognitive abilities evolve in conjunction with both the progress of brain development and the expansion of social experiences. Thus, YLLs' constantly growing cognitive capacity should be appropriately reflected in the assessment of L2 abilities.

Let us consider a few examples of YLLs' cognitive characteristics in the context of L2 assessment. Children's attention spans are relatively short compared to adults. Younger children (those below seven years old) typically have shorter attention spans, usually lasting around 10–15 minutes for a specific task. This factor is important when determining the

314 Chapter 22 Assessment of Young Language Learners

duration of both individual tasks and the overall assessment. Malloy (2015) suggests that, for younger children, a formal assessment should last no more than 30 minutes in a single sitting to prevent loss of concentration. To facilitate continued concentration, it is crucial to keep YLLs engaged in assessment tasks within their attention spans, and therefore devise assessment tasks in a way they are relevant and intriguing to the students.

Importantly, the complexity of assessment tasks should align with the children's stages of cognitive development (i.e., age-appropriate cognitive complexity). As children grow in their executive functions, tasks that demand working memory, flexible thinking, and self-regulation should be developmentally appropriate for YLLs. For instance, Blything et al. (2015) found that complex sentence structures, specifically those with temporal connectives, posed memory challenges, constraining the sentence comprehension of younger children (aged 4–7 in their study). Similarly, Pyykkönen and Järvikivi (2012) observed that children's difficulties in understanding complex sentences with temporal connectives persisted even up to the age of 12. This challenge was partly attributed to the memory demands imposed by the tasks. These studies suggest that the interplay between linguistic complexity and cognitive complexity is a critical element in designing assessment tasks for YLLs.

While much of the existing literature on children's cognitive development and its relation to language development primarily focuses on native language speakers, a burgeoning body of research is on the rise examining the effects of YLLs' cognitive abilities on L2 assessments (e.g., Brunfaut et al., 2021; Michel et al., 2019). This area of research is mainly concerned with cognitive validity to ensure that assessment tasks involve the mental processes that YLLs would typically utilize in authentic situations. For instance, Winke et al. (2018) conducted retrospective interviews with YLLs aged 7–9, who took English language assessments designed for young learners of English, in order to examine the students' test-taking processes and experiences. Additionally, the inclusion of native English-speaking students in the study allowed the researchers to identify potential construct-irrelevant variance that might stem from children's cognitive functioning, rather than the intended language ability. The researchers argued for the importance of examining both L2 and native language speakers when performing cognitive validation of L2 assessments for YLLs. Concerning a specific aspect of cognitive abilities, Michel et al. (2019) investigated the effects of YLLs' working memory on their performance in an L2 writing assessment. The YLL sample comprised sixth and seventh graders who began learning English in first grade in Hungary. Unexpectedly, the researchers found that working memory exerted only a marginal impact on the writing tasks of the assessment (email writing, opinion writing, and an integrated listening-and-writing task). They posited that this finding lent validity evidence, suggesting that the tasks of this particular assessment were appropriately crafted to fit within the cognitive capacity of the target YLLs. However, they observed differential effects of working memory on the task of editing, implying the need for further investigation into the interaction between task characteristics and YLLs' cognitive abilities.

Collectively, this body of research highlights the relationship between the cognitive load involved in L2 assessments and the cognitive developmental stages of YLLs. Related to this, Wolf and Butler (2017) offer practical recommendations for developing and administering L2 assessments for YLLs, particularly in the aspects of assessment length, the nature of assessment stimuli, clarity of task instructions, task content, and administration settings.

Affective Factors

Affective factors encompass a learner's emotions such as attitude, anxiety, motivation, self-esteem, and the like and have a profound influence on L2 learning. Bachman and Palmer (2010) assert that affective schemata play a crucial role in individuals' performance on language assessments. For YLLs, the sway of these affective elements can be more pronounced than for adult learners, because children's ability to control their emotions is not yet fully matured. Research shows that the relationship between affective factors and L2 assessment performance is complex, varying depending on individual learners' characteristics (e.g., age, L2 proficiency, familiarity with testing) and the specific nature of assessments and tasks (Mihaljević Djigunović, 2016).

Test anxiety emerges as one of the key concerns among affective factors in the assessment of YLLs. Previous literature has highlighted the significance of testing environments and familiarity with the test format to address this concern as they are intricately associated with YLLs' levels of test anxiety (Jang et al., 2017; McKay, 2006). In a recent study, Lee and Winke (2018) conducted an empirical investigation utilizing eye-movement tracking and drawing-based survey data to analyze the experiences of ESL students aged 8–10 in the United States. They discovered that the participants were distracted by the countdown timer embedded in a computerized speaking assessment, which heightened test-taking anxiety among the YLLs. The researchers noted that this distraction and test-taking anxiety were seemingly associated with the participants' relatively limited English proficiency. That is, the participating students lacked confidence in their L2 proficiency, leading to increased test anxiety. It is also noteworthy that the participants were unfamiliar with the format used in the specific assessment (i.e., the countdown timer), suggesting the importance of having YLLs take sample or practice tests beforehand. Such preparation can help alleviate students' test-taking anxiety by increasing familiarity with the testing format and tools. Likewise, a cognitive lab study by Wolf et al. (2020), which involved close observation of test-taking processes followed by retrospective interviews, found that younger children of L2 English (kindergarteners to first graders in US schools) were not accustomed to computer-based L2 assessments. The children in their study frequently sought confirmation from adults before advancing to the next screen during testing. This study was carried out in the context of developing a large-scale standardized assessment and helped test developers and relevant stakeholders make informed decisions about the appropriate administrator-to-student ratio for testing (i.e., one-on-one for kindergarteners and a 1:5 ratio for first to second graders).

Lately, the impact of YLLs' motivation on their performance on L2 assessments has also been empirically investigated (Kormos et al., 2020; Sok et al., 2021). While the role of motivation in L2 learning and acquisition is firmly established, research on YLLs' motivation within L2 assessment contexts has yielded mixed results. In a study involving Hungarian students learning English in Grades 6–8, Kormos et al. (2020) examined students' appraisal of the given assessment tasks prior to completing the tasks (i.e., an integrated listen–speak task and an integrated listen–write task). The students generally evaluated the listen–speak task as more challenging and expressed greater anxiety compared to the listen–write task. Notwithstanding, no significant differences were found in the students' performances on the two task types. The researchers pointed to the low stakes of the assessment, the appropriate level of cognitive demands in the tasks, and the participating students' generally high L2 competence as plausible reasons for the lack of motivational impact in the study results. On the other hand, Sok et al. (2021) found a differential impact of YLL's motivation on L2 listening and reading assessments. They examined a sample of sixth graders learning English in Korea and found a significant correlation between students' motivation ratings and performances on the listening assessment, but not on the reading assessment. The researchers speculate that students' performances were impacted by the interaction of motivation and cognitive demands in assessments. They conclude that the listening assessment posed greater cognitive demands than the reading assessment for their participants.

Clearly, research illustrates that the influence of YLLs' affective factors varies based on assessment characteristics such as the stakes involved, differing cognitive demands of task types, task instructions, and administration settings. Considering YLLs' emotional vulnerability, special attention must be given to assessment design and its potential to generate positive testing experiences for YLLs.

Contextual and Curricular Considerations in the Assessment of YLLs

Early theories of learning and language use such as sociocultural theory (Vygotsky, 1978) and systemic functional linguistics and more recent ones like complex dynamic systems theory (see Larsen-Freeman, 2019), underscore the importance of social interaction and contextual aspects in L2 development. Sociocultural theory, in particular, postulates how social interactions and cultural practices shape the process of learning in child development. Systemic functional linguistics theory, from a language development standpoint, views language through a social semiotic lens, stressing that language use is highly dependent on contexts. In a similar vein, complex dynamic systems theory emphasizes the dynamic nature of language use norms and their adaptability to situations. Considering these theories, it is important to recognize that YLLs have a narrower spectrum of social interactions and contexts compared to adults. They are in the midst of gaining more knowledge in the use of L2 appropriately for specific contexts (e.g., sociolinguistic and pragmatic knowledge). More importantly, YLLs' social interaction and L2 learning are predominantly influenced by their educational and instructional contexts. Therefore, factors such as the type of instruction, curriculum, and standards are important aspects to be considered in L2 assessment. They inform the specific assessment needs and help determine the expected L2 abilities for YLLs. The following subsections deal with YLLs' instructional contexts and their implications for L2 assessment, using the case of English as an L2.

L2 Learning Environments: Curriculum Standards and Instructional Programs in ESL and EFL Contexts

The distinctions between the contexts of English as a second language (ESL) and English as a foreign language (EFL) have been well documented in previous literature. This subsection elucidates different instructional foci and English language learning standards in ESL and EFL contexts, which implicates the expected L2 skills for YLLs.

In ESL contexts where the target language is the dominant language of the society, YLLs are immersed in English-medium environments both inside and outside of school. As a result, the main objective of ESL instruction for YLLs is to equip them with English proficiency needed to fully participate in society and to access academic content in school. To this end, ELP standards for school-aged L2 learners are often established at the national or state/provincial level. In the United States, federal law mandates that state education agencies develop or adopt ELP standards and ensure that schools provide instruction aligned with these standards for L2 learners of English. The recent law known as the Every Student Succeeds Act (ESSA, 2015) explicitly stipulates that states' ELP standards must also align with states' academic content standards such as English language arts, mathematics, and science standards. The premise herein is that the English language knowledge and skills delineated in ELP standards should correspond to the academic language demands implicated in the content-area standards (Council of Chief State School Officers, 2012). Consequently, ESL instruction and assessment in K-12 schools aims to aid L2 learners of English (or so-called English learners in US federal documents) in developing English proficiency to meet these academic standards in content areas. Thus, a greater emphasis has been placed on academic English proficiency starting from the early elementary grades (Bailey & Wilkinson, 2022).

Accordingly, the language abilities expected of YLLs in the US K-12 school context are highly academic and sophisticated. WIDA's (2020) English language development standards, adopted by over 35 states, provide examples of such expectations. One of the standards for

L2 learners in Grades 2–3 (ages 7–9) states, "Analyzing relevant information from one or two sources to develop claims in response to compelling questions" (p. 97). Within this grade band, learners are expected to acquire linguistic forms including a variety of cohesive devices to connect larger chunks of text, expanded noun groups with embedded clauses, simple and compound sentences, and a diverse range of words and phrases (p. 102). This example illustrates the rigorous expectations set for YLLs in US K-12 schools, suggesting a demanding academic language construct for the assessment of language ability.

In other English-speaking countries such as Australia, Canada, and the United Kingdom, various proficiency standards and frameworks have also been developed to guide the education of linguistically diverse students and support their academic learning (Papp, 2018). For instance, the Ministry of Education of British Columbia, in collaboration with educators, introduced the English Language Learning Standards for K-12 English language learners. These standards, much like those in the United States, aim to facilitate English language learners "in accessing the provincial curriculum and succeeding in academic achievement" (British Columbia Ministry of Education, 2017, p. 5). For example, the writing standards for Grades 1–3 include the following, "Produce a text that has a number of logically sequenced stages or series of events" and "Produce examples of a variety of genres (life cycles, flow charts, summaries, narratives, recounts, personal responses) to suit purpose" (p. 12). As seen in these examples, academic English language proficiency has been an important construct for school-aged YLLs in ESL contexts.

In EFL contexts, many countries place English as a compulsory subject starting in elementary grades. Since the predominant language in these societies is not English, YLLs' L2 use situations are mainly constrained to the English classroom (Hasselgreen & Caudwell, 2016), and the type and the quality of L2 input and interaction are largely driven by instructional materials and class activities. Hence, school curricula and instructional programs become vital in determining the L2 competencies that YLLs can attain. At the national level, EFL curriculum policies often prioritize communicative language abilities accompanied by an emphasis on cross-cultural understanding (Copland et al., 2013). For younger children, there is a marked focus on oral language proficiency. This is attributed not only to the curriculum emphasis on communicative ability but also to their L1 literacy, which is still under development (McKay, 2006).

Despite the advocacy for communicative language ability in national curriculum policies, research has pointed to considerable discrepancies in the implementation of such policies in EFL contexts. In many EFL countries, examinations were typically found to focus on forms including grammar and vocabulary (Copland et al., 2013). A review by Butler (2015) of EFL policies and research in East Asian countries also suggests a prevailing trend of form-based instruction in the region.

Additionally, insufficiency in teachers' English proficiency and pedagogical training tailored to young L2 learners has also been posed as a notable challenge in the literature (Butler, 2015; Copland et al., 2013; Hasselgreen, 2017). For example, Szpotowicz's (2012) study found that EFL teachers from elementary schools in Poland often struggled to integrate interactive oral language tasks into their classrooms. This limitation resulted in students' reliance on formulaic chunks or repetition of memorized chunks in a performance assessment. In a similar vein, Patekar (2021) examined writing tasks created by elementary English language teachers in Croatia. He found that tasks were not oriented for communicative language ability in general and that some tasks did not consider the unique characteristics of YLLs, such as the need for scaffolding. These studies underline the importance of teachers' skills and their role in YLLs' L2 development. Additionally, it is worth highlighting the relatively basic level of language skills outlined in the national English curriculum in Patekar's study. For Year 3 students, some writing expectations included "Copying very short texts that have been previously taught orally" and "Independent writing of guided shorter descriptions as part of familiar, previously orally practiced content" (Patekar, 2021, p. 462). Compared to the US and

Canadian standards exemplified earlier, the anticipated English language skills for YLLs in this context remain foundational. These examples indicate varying expectations for language skills among YLLs across different contexts, depending on the respective educational standards.

Coupled with the variability of teacher qualifications, EFL instructional programs have a great influence in shaping YLLs' L2 abilities. Inbar-Lourie and Shohamy (2009) categorized different EFL instructional programs in terms of the degrees to which language and content are integrated as the L2 instructional goals. On their language-content continuum, one extreme end is a program focusing on language awareness (i.e., learning language knowledge) and the other opposite end is an immersion program where both L1 and L2 develop simultaneously in the course of learning academic content. Closer to the immersion program side, the authors identified the Content and Language Integrated Learning (CLIL) program wherein the L2 is utilized within disciplinary areas. This content-based language learning approach has gained popularity in Europe and is now expanding to Asia and South America due to students' enriched exposure to L2 usage (Papp, 2018).

Research has also pointed to the socioeconomic factor that comes into play in YLLs' L2 development because of the affordances of attending various instructional programs (Butler, 2015; Chik & Besser, 2011). These varied programs represent a wide range of teaching and learning contexts to which YLLs can be exposed. Consequently, different L2 constructs and their associated assessments are being employed depending on the specific instructional settings (Inbar-Lourie & Shohamy, 2009; Nikolov & Timpe-Laughlin, 2021).

Common European Framework of References for YLLs

As reviewed above, in both ESL and EFL contexts, national or local standards, and curricula have been the major impetus that influences the ways in which YLLs learn English as an L2. In addition, the Common European Framework of References for Languages (CEFR) (Council of Europe, 2001, 2020) has been widely adopted as an international guideline in developing L2 curricula and assessments. The six levels from A1 to C2 and their descriptors in the CEFR have been instrumental as a common yardstick to compare the proficiency and progress of L2 learners. As the CEFR was initially developed for adult learners, not all descriptors were relevant or achievable for YLLs. As a result, efforts were made to distill the CEFR descriptors that YLLs can achieve (e.g., Hasselgreen & Caudwell, 2016) or to modify the descriptors to be suitable to YLLs (e.g., Papageorgiou & Baron, 2017). Although high-level descriptors tend to postulate abstract and technical language use along with the sociolinguistic competence, Hasselgreen (2021) explicates that some high-level descriptors are still applicable to YLLs (e.g., understanding the main points of standard speech in one of the B1 level descriptors). Papageorgiou and Baron (2017) took an approach of modifying the CEFR descriptors to report the CEFR levels based on the assessments specifically designed for YLLs (i.e., TOEFL Junior and TOEFL Primary tests). For instance, in the original B1 level descriptor, "Can understand straightforward factual information about common every day or job related topics . . ." (Council of Europe, 2020, p. 48), the phrase, "job related topics" was replaced with "school-related topics" for the TOEFL Primary tests.

In recognition of the increasing demand for CEFR application to YLLs, the Council of Europe produced *Collated Representative Samples of Descriptors of Language Competences Developed for Young Learners* for two age groups (7–10 and 11–15) in 2018. These compilations feature pertinent CEFR descriptors for YLLs and have been influential in defining the construct of L2 assessments for YLLs.

Types of L2 Assessments and Key Validation Issues for YLLs

The aforementioned diverse contexts necessitate a variety of assessment strategies. For YLLs, most assessment activities take place within the classroom, orchestrated by their teachers for both summative and formative purposes (Lewkowicz & Leung, 2021). These assessments are mainly intended to promote students' L2 development. In addition to teacher-made assessments, standardized English proficiency assessments have been increasingly utilized in recent years, due to the exponential increase in the number of YLLs learning English and the need to evaluate their English proficiency in comparison with national or international standards (Nikolov, 2016; Wolf & Butler, 2017). This section illustrates the features of classroom assessments and standardized assessments for YLLs, followed by key validation considerations in the assessment of YLLs.

Classroom-Based Assessments

Teachers often create their own classroom assessments to gauge students' learning outcomes in relation to curricula and standards. Traditionally, teachers in L2 classroom have been accustomed to collecting summative information through end-of-unit tests, school progress tests, and final examinations (Rixon, 2016). Over the past decade, there has been renewed attention to such classroom-based formative assessment due to increasing research interest in the assessment process involving both teachers and learners (Gan & Leung, 2020). In the formative assessment process, teachers elicit students' learning evidence on an ongoing basis and provide forward-looking feedback toward the specific learning goals that students are expected to achieve. The elicitation techniques used in classroom assessments can be wide-ranging, including questioning, discussions, observations, assignments, projects, and tests, to name a few. This collected evidence informs instructional adjustments tailored to students' needs. Students should also play an active role in formative assessment by responding to the feedback and engaging in self-assessment. Through the process, students' perspectives are taken into consideration, enhancing students' autonomy and self-directed learning.

Formative assessment can benefit YLLs not only in their L2 development but also in their cognitive and social–emotional development. As a good formative assessment practice, teachers must communicate learning goals and success criteria with students. Certainly, it is essential for teachers to explain these in a language that children can access. It is equally important to check children's understanding of the goals and expected criteria. On the same token, teachers' feedback should be specific and concrete so as for students to understand and enact on. While feedback should be positive given YLLs' emotional vulnerability, the overuse of rewarding feedback should be avoided. The feedback should center on the task performance, not on the learner (Hasselgreen, 2021) to help students use the feedback to plan the next steps toward the learning goals. Prior literature indicates that YLLs are in fact capable of understanding the learning goals, success criteria, and feedback while engaging in self-assessment (Butler et al., 2021).

In eliciting students' learning evidence, it is important to take YLLs' characteristics into consideration. If classroom interaction serves as an assessment event, students should be given ample opportunities, with appropriate probing, to speak and thereby demonstrate their knowledge and skills. Scaffolding is often necessary to adequately assess YLLs in L2 classroom. Scaffolding refers to the instructional support provided to learners, enabling them to complete tasks they would otherwise struggle with (Rogers & Rogers, 2004). It pertains to Vygotsky's (1978) concept of the zone of proximal development (ZPD), which is defined as the

Chapter 22 Assessment of Young Language Learners

"distance between the actual developmental level as determined by independent problem solving and the level of potential development as determined through problem solving under adult guidance or in collaboration with more capable peers" (p. 86). For YLLs who are in developmental stages across many facets, providing scaffolding is crucial for teachers to properly identify children's capacities including their ZPD. In doing so, teachers can better address the individual needs of YLLs.

Large-Scale Standardized Assessments

As mentioned above, standardized ELP assessments are increasingly used to assess YLLs in the United States. Among international standardized ELP assessments, Cambridge's Young Learner English tests, ETS's TOEFL Young Student Series tests, and Pearson's International Certificate Young Learners tests have been widely used around the world. These assessments are designed in alignment with the CEFR and confer certificates that include CEFR levels. The assessments are intended for relatively low- to medium-stakes use such as determining a student's proficiency level, monitoring progress, and guiding instruction on a macro scale. Standardized assessments typically undergo a thorough development process that includes multiple rounds of item review and large-scale pilot/ field testing. The technical qualities of the assessments allow for a high degree of confidence in measuring students' current level and tracking their progression based on the assessment scale. Owing to this nature of standardized assessments, schools often use the results as evidence to demonstrate the qualities of their programs and instruction to parents (Chik & Besser, 2011; Wolf et al., 2023). In Wolf et al.'s (2023) study, teachers and school administrators reported feeling pressured to prove the quality of their instruction to parents. They perceived these external standardized assessments as an "objective" measure for parents and themselves.

Standardized ELP assessments have also been used for accountability purposes at the national level. In the US K-12 school context, schools are federally mandated to ensure the adequate attainment and progress of English proficiency among English language learners. Therefore, YLLs starting in kindergarten are required to take a large-scale standardized ELP assessment that measures all four language skills of listening, reading, speaking, and writing. Standardized ELP assessments are also used to identify students who need ESL or bilingual program support and to determine whether students are ready to exit such language support programs. These uses entail relatively high-stakes decisions with the assessments acting as a gatekeeping function even for YLLs.

Key Validation Areas for YLLs

The various uses of L2 assessments in different formats described above warrant the collection of validity evidence to ensure their appropriate use for YLLs. The types of such validity evidence are intrinsically linked to the specific purposes and claims associated with the assessments. Yet, considering the unique characteristics of YLLs, certain areas of validation become more prominent. Specifically, as L2 assessments for YLLs are ultimately intended to promote students' L2 proficiency development, consequential and construct validity are the key areas where validation efforts should be focused.

Bachman and Palmer (2010) argue that the consequences resulting from the use of assessments are central to constructing a validity argument, since the assessment uses must be justified to stakeholders. For L2 assessments targeting YLLs, it is vital that assessments provide a positive experience, ensuring that YLLs remain motivated to learn and improve their L2 proficiency. Validating the intended consequences, impact, or washback of assessments requires multi-faceted investigations (Tsagari & Cheng, 2017). In the case of the classroom-based formative assessment discussed in the previous section, one aspect of consequential validity is the extent to which students evolve into self-directed learners. To investigate this consequence, one must consider the interplay among the quality of classroom-based assessment method, the roles of teachers, and the individual characteristics of students as part of validity investigations. The impacts that standardized assessments have on YLLs and their relevant stakeholders represent critical areas of validation, given their direct relevance to YLLs' academic paths and learning trajectories.

Examining construct validity, especially in distinguishing between construct-relevant and construct-irrelevant factors, is a critical area of validation given the developmental characteristics of YLLs. The previous section has portrayed the diverse instructional settings that lead to different L2 constructs for assessing YLLs (e.g., academic language versus basic language proficiency). As part of construct validity investigations, it is important to determine whether the cognitive demand, cultural background, and sociolinguistic knowledge embedded in the assessments are developmentally appropriate for YLLs. As reviewed earlier, there is a growing body of research that examines the appropriateness of the assessment construct and task types in light of YLLs' cognitive and affective factors (e.g., Kormos et al., 2020; Winke et al., 2018). This body of research not only offers validity evidence but also advances our understanding of best practices for L2 assessments for YLLs.

Future Directions in Research and Practice

Over the past two decades, considerable research and development effort has been focused on language assessment for YLLs. However, the constantly evolving contexts in which YLLs from tremendously diverse backgrounds are situated demand far more work to ensure adequate L2 assessments for them. This section outlines four critical areas for future research, which have the potential to advance the practice of language assessment for YLLs: (i) new domain analyses to define the construct of L2 assessments, (ii) corpus analysis to inform L2 progression models, (iii) the use of technology to foster learner-centered assessments, and (iv) professional support to empower teachers of YLLs.

Redefining the Target Language Use Domain for YLLs

In today's digital era, children encounter a plethora of information across various formats. The ways in which they learn an L2 have vastly diversified compared to times when access to digital devices and information is limited. As discussed in earlier sections, the anticipated language skills for YLLs differ depending on the context. For instance, one of the reading standards used in US K-12 schools delineates that by Grade 4, they should be able to "interpret information presented visually, orally, or quantitatively (e.g., in charts, graphs, diagrams, timelines, animations, or interactive elements on Web pages) . . ." (Common Core State Standards Initiative, 2010, p. 14). This expectation indicates an evolution in the traditional reading skill construct, suggesting it extends beyond just interpreting printed texts. The notion of multiliteracies (literacy that encompasses multimodal and multimedia formats) is becoming increasingly crucial for L2 learners. Consequently, there is an urgent need to empirically analyze the target language use domains for YLLs to refine the L2 construct and to improve assessment design accordingly. Such endeavors will not only allow for more accurate inferences about YLLs' language abilities but also make assessments more useful for pedagogical purposes.

Utilizing Corpus Analysis Research

While a range of language proficiency standards exists, featuring different levels of proficiency exists (e.g., CEFR, K-12 English language proficiency standards), they often lack empirical validation. Moreover, because these proficiency levels are typically described in broad and general terms, they offer limited guidance for fine-tuned teaching and learning strategies tailored to YLLs. As Bailey (2017b) notes, L2 progression models based on empirical data can be beneficial to educators, assessment specialists, and curriculum developers in devising more effective instruction and assessment. Numerous research projects and assessments focusing on YLLs have produced a wealth of data. This has facilitated the creation of L2 acquisition corpora from young multilingual learners, gathered in both natural and assessment settings (e.g., Dirdal et al., 2022). Analyzing the corpora of young L2 learners, especially when paired with background data, can illuminate the path toward establishing practical guidelines to develop L2 assessments with varying granularity (e.g., age/grade-specific lexical and syntactic complexities). Such assessments can be instrumental to support the L2 development of YLLs from diverse backgrounds.

Leveraging Technology for Learner-Centered L2 Assessment

As previously highlighted, the use of technology is becoming increasingly widespread in educational settings including the context of L2 assessment. In particular, technology opens the door to the design of more learner-centric and learning-oriented language assessments for YLLs. For example, scenario-based assessment design is gaining its prominence in the language testing field due to its advantages of simulating immersive contexts of language usage as well as providing learning opportunities for test takers simultaneously (Purpura, 2016). The seamless presentation of the scenarios in assessments would be challenging without the aid of technology. Kim et al. (2022) have also demonstrated how technology helps implement innovative task types, allowing YLLs to engage in L2 assessments in interactive ways. Furthermore, to better elicit YLLs' language knowledge and skills, research has been undertaken to weave scaffolding into standardized L2 assessments using technology (Choi et al., 2019; Wolf et al., 2016). This area of research has offered valuable insights into the potential benefits of integrating technology in L2 assessments for YLLs. Given the swift advancements in technology and artificial intelligence capabilities, it is imperative to further explore how these capabilities can be harnessed for the creation of effective and efficient L2 assessments, as well as to provide useful feedback for YLLs.

Enhancing Teacher Support and Language Assessment Literacy

Teachers undoubtedly hold the central role in guiding YLLs' L2 development and in utilizing their assessment results. Much research has consistently echoed the pressing need for professional support and training (Butler, 2019; Hasselgreen, 2017; Tsagari & Vogt, 2017; Wolf et al., 2023). YLLs constitute a tremendously heterogeneous group. However, it is common that teachers find themselves tasked with instructing mixed-level classes comprising students of varying L1 and L2 proficiencies, without receiving the requisite training. Teachers need to gain both pedagogical skills and keen knowledge about L2 learning and assessments, specific to YLLs. For instance, in classrooms with linguistic minority students, the strategic allowance for the use of students' L1 or translanguaging can be integrated into L2 instruction and assessment depending on the intended objectives. Consequently, researching ways to effectively deliver professional training and bolster teachers' language assessment literacy is of paramount importance for enhancing YLLs' learning outcomes and positive experiences.

While the areas addressed above are by no means exhaustive, investigations into these identified areas promise to provide much-needed support in advancing and innovating the field of language assessment for YLLs. Assessments grounded in a robust research foundation will in turn elevate the education for YLLs, aiding them in honing their L2 skills and realizing their full potential.

Discussion Questions

1. How can assessments be designed to foster a positive learning experience for young L2 learners?
2. What could be the potential benefits and challenges of utilizing technology in the assessment of young L2 learners?

References

Bachman, L. F., & Palmer, A. S. (2010). *Language assessment in practice*. Oxford University Press.

Bailey, A. L. (2017a). Theoretical and developmental issues to consider in the assessment of young learners' English language proficiency. In M. K. Wolf & Y. G. Butler (Eds.), *English language proficiency assessments for young learners* (pp. 25–40). Routledge.

Bailey, A. L. (2017b). Progressions of a new language: characterizing explanation development for assessment with young language learners. *Annual Review of Applied Linguistics*, *37*, 241–263.

Bailey, A. L., & Wilkinson, L. C. (2022). Linguistics and education article collection. Introduction: tracing themes in the evolution of the academic language construct. *Linguistics and Education*, *71*, 101063.

Bailey, A. L., Heritage, M., & Butler, F. A. (2014). Developmental considerations and curricular contexts in the assessment of young language learners. In A. J. Kunnan (Ed.), *The companion to language assessment* (pp. 423–439). John Wiley & Sons, Inc.

Barac, R., Bialystok, E., Castro, D. C., & Sanchez, M. (2014). The cognitive development of young dual language learners: a critical review. *Early Childhood Research Quarterly*, *29*, 699–714.

Betalova, J. (2022). *Top statistics on global migration and migrants*. Migration Policy Institute.

Blything, L. P., Davies, R., & Cain, K. (2015). Young children's comprehension of temporal relations in complex sentences: the influence of memory on performance. *Child Development*, *86*(6), 1922–1934.

British Columbia Ministry of Education. (2017). *English language learning (ELL) standards*.

Brunfaut, T., Kormos, J., Michel, M., & Ratajczak, M. (2021). Testing young foreign language learners' reading comprehension: exploring the effects of working memory, grade level, and reading task. *Language Testing*, *38*(3), 356–377.

Butler, Y. G. (2015). English language education among young learners in East Asia: a review of current research (2004–2014). *Language Teaching*, *48*, 303–342.

Butler, Y. G. (2019). Assessment of young English learners in instructional settings. In X. Gao (Ed.), *Second handbook of English language teaching* (pp. 477–496). Springer.

Butler, Y. G., Peng, X., & Lee, J. (2021). Young learners' voices: towards a learner-centered approach to understanding language assessment. *Language Testing*, *38*(3), 429–455. https://doi.org/10.1177/0265532221992274.

Chik, A., & Besser, S. (2011). International language test taking among young learners: a Hong Kong case study. *Language Assessment Quarterly*, *8*(1), 73–91.

Choi, I., Wolf, M. K., Pooler, E., Sova, L., & Faulkner-Bond, M. (2019). Investigating the benefits of scaffolding in assessments of young English learners: a case for scaffolded retell tasks. *Language Assessment Quarterly*, *16*(2), 161–179. https://doi.org/10.1080/15434303.2019.1619180.

Common Core State Standards Initiative. (2010). *Common core state standards for english language arts & literacy in history/social studies, science, and technical subjects*.

Copland, F., Garton, S., & Burns, A. (2013). Challenges in teaching English to young learners: global perspectives and local realities. *TESOL Quarterly*, *48*(4), 738–762.

324   Chapter 22 Assessment of Young Language Learners

Council of Chief State School Officers. (2012). *Framework for English language proficiency development standards corresponding to the common core state standards and the next generation science standards*.

Council of Europe. (2001). *Common European framework of reference for languages: Learning, teaching and assessment*. Cambridge University Press.

Council of Europe. (2020). *Common European Framework of reference for languages: Learning, teaching, assessment – companion volume*. Council of Europe Publishing.

Dirdal, H., Hasund, I. K., Drange, E. D., Vold, E. T., & Berg, E. M. (2022). Design and construction of tracking written learner language (TRAWL) corpus: a longitudinal and multilingual young learner corpus. *Nordic Journal of Language Teaching and Learning, 10*(2). https://doi.org/10.46364/njltl.v10i2.1005.

Ehrman, M. E., Leaver, B. L., & Oxford, R. L. (2003). A brief overview of individual differences in second language learning. *System, 31*, 313–330.

Every Student Succeeds Act (ESSA). (2015). *Public Law No. 114–354*.

Gan, Z., & Leung, C. (2020). Illustrating formative assessment in task-based language teaching. *ELT Journal, 74*(1), 10–19.

Hasselgreen, A. (2017). Assessing young learners. In G. Fulcher & F. Davidson (Eds.), *The Routledge handbook of language testing* (pp. 93–105). Routledge.

Hasselgreen, A. (2021). Assessing the language of children. *The European Journal of Applied Linguistics and TEFL, 10*(2), 61–77.

Hasselgreen, A., & Caudwell, G. (2016). Assessing the language of young learners. In *British Council Monographs 1*. Equinox.

Inbar-Lourie, O., & Shohamy, E. (2009). Assessing young language learners: what is the construct? In M. Nikolov (Ed.), *The age factor and early language learning* (pp. 83–96). Mouton de Gruyter.

Jang, E. E., Vincett, M., van der Boom, E., Lau, C., & Yang, Y. (2017). Considering young learners' characteristics in developing a diagnostic assessment intervention. In M. K. Wolf & Y. G. Butler (Eds.), *English language proficiency assessments for young learners* (pp. 193–213). Routledge.

Jaskow, R. J., & Ellis, M. (Eds.). (2019). *Early instructed second language acquisition: Pathway to competence*. Multilingual Matters.

Kim, A. A., Tywoniw, R. L., & Chapman, M. (2022). Technology-enhanced items in grades 1–12 English language proficiency assessments. *Language Assessment Quarterly, 19*(4), 343–367.

Kormos, J., & Safar, A. (2009). Phonological short-term memory, working memory and foreign language performance in intensive language learning. *Bilingualism: Language and Cognition, 11*(2), 261–271.

Kormos, J., Brunfaut, T., & Michel, M. (2020). Motivational factors in computer-administered integrated skills tasks: a study of young learners. *Language Assessment Quarterly, 17*(1), 43–59.

Larsen-Freeman, D. (2019). On language learner agency: a complex dynamic systems theory perspective. *The Modern Language Journal, 103*, 61–79.

Lee, S., & Winke, P. (2018). Young learners' response processes when taking computerized tasks for speaking assessment. *Language Testing, 35*(2), 239–269.

Lewkowicz, J., & Leung, C. (2021). Classroom-based assessment. *Language Teaching, 54*, 47–57.

Malloy, A. (2015). Seven essential considerations for assessing young learners. *Teaching Young Learners, 24*(1), 20–23.

McKay, P. (2006). *Assessing young language learners*. Cambridge University Press.

Michel, M., Kormos, J., Brunfaut, T., & Ratajczak, M. (2019). The role of working memory in young second language learners' written performances. *Journal of Second Language Writing, 45*, 31–45.

Mihaljević Djigunović, J. (2016). Individual learner differences and young learners' performance on L2 speaking tests. In M. Nikilov (Ed.), *Assessing young learners of English: Global and local perspectives* (pp. 243–262). Springer.

Nikolov, M. (2016). Trends, issues, and challenges in assessing young language learners. In M. Nikolov (Ed.), *Assessing young learners of English: Global and local perspectives* (pp. 1–18). Springer.

Nikolov, M., & Timpe-Laughlin, V. (2021). Assessing young learners' foreign language abilities. *Language Teaching, 54*, 1–37.

Papageorgiou, S., & Baron, P. (2017). Using the common European framework of reference to facilitate score interpretations for young learners' English language proficiency assessments. In M. K. Wolf & Y. G. Butler (Eds.), *English language proficiency assessments for young learners* (pp. 136–152). Routledge.

Papp, S. (2018). Assessment of young English language learners. In S. Garton & F. Copland (Eds.), *The Routledge handbook of teaching English to young learners* (pp. 389–408). Routledge.

Patekar, J. (2021). A look into the practice and challenges of assessing young EFL learners' writing in Croatia. *Language Testing, 38*(3), 456–479.

Purpura, J. (2016). Second and foreign language assessment. *The Modern Language Journal, 100*(Supplement 2016), 190–208.

Pyykkönen, P., & Järvikivi, J. (2012). Children and situation models of multiple events. *Developmental Psychology, 48*, 521–529.

Rixon, S. (2016). Do development in assessment represent the 'coming of age' of young learners English language teaching initiatives?: the international picture. In M. Nikolov (Ed.), *Assessing young learners of English: Global and local perspectives* (pp. 19–41). Springer.

Rodgers, E. M., & Rodgers, A. (2004). The role of scaffolding in teaching. In A. Rodgers & E. M. Rodgers (Eds.), *Scaffolding literacy instruction: Strategies for K-4 classrooms* (pp. 1–10). Heinemann.

Sok, S., Shin, H. W., & Do, J. (2021). Exploring which test-taker characteristics predict young L2 learners' performance on listening and reading comprehension tests. *Language Testing, 38*(3), 378–400.

Szpotowicz, M. (2012). Researching oral production skills of young learners. *Center for Educational Policy Studies (C.E.P.S) Journal, 2*(3), 141–166.

Tsagari, D., & Cheng, L. (2017). Washback, impact, and consequences revisited. In E. Shohamy, I. Or & S. May (Eds.), *Language testing and assessment, Encyclopedia of language and education* (pp. 2–12). Springer.

Tsagari, D., & Vogt, K. (2017). Assessment literacy of foreign language teachers around Europe: research, challenges, and future prospects. *Papers in Language Testing Assessment, 6*(1), 41–63.

Vygotsky, L. (1978). *Mind in society: The development of higher psychological processes*. Harvard University Press.

WIDA. (2020). *WIDA English language development standards framework* (2020th ed.). Wisconsin Center for Education Research.

Winke, P., Lee, S., Ahn, J. I., Choi, I., Cui, Y., & Yoon, H.-J. (2018). The cognitive validity of child English language tests: what young language learners and their native-speaking peers can reveal. *TESOL Quarterly, 52*(2), 274–303.

Wolf, M. K., & Butler, Y. G. (2017). An overview of English language proficiency assessments for young learners. In M. K. Wolf & Y. G. Butler (Eds.), *English language proficiency assessments for young learners* (pp. 3–21). Routledge. https://doi.org/10.4324/9781315674391-1.

Wolf, M. K., Guzman-Orth, D., Lopez, A., Castellano, K., Himelfarb, I., & Tsutagawa, F. (2016). Integrating scaffolding strategies into technology-enhanced assessments of English learners: task types and measurement models. *Educational Assessment, 21*(3), 151–175. https://doi.org/10.1080/10627197.2016.1202107.

Wolf, M. K., Guzman-Orth, D., Still, C., & Winter, P. (2020). Examining students' response processes in a computer-based English language proficiency assessment. In M. K. Wolf (Ed.), *Assessing English language proficiency in U.S. K-12 schools* (pp. 111–133). Routledge. https://doi.org/10.4324/9780429491689-7.

Wolf, M. K., Lopez, A. A., & Lee, J. (2023). An investigation of the use of standardized and local assessments for young EAL students. In G. Brooks, J. Clenton & S. Fraser (Eds.), *EAL research for the classroom: Practical and pedagogical implications* (pp. 164–184). Routledge. https://doi.org/10.4324/9781003274889-13.

Suggested Readings

Garton, S., & Copland, F. (Eds.). (2019). *The Routledge handbook of teaching English to young learners*. Routledge.

Oliver, R., & Azkarai, A. (2017). Review of child second language acquisition: examining theories and research. *Annual Review of Applied Linguistics, 37*, 62–76.

Papp, S., & Rixon, S. (2020). *Examining young learners: Research and practice in assessing the English of school-age learners*. Cambridge University Press.

CHAPTER 23

Monitoring Progress in the Classroom

Matthew E. Poehner and Rama Mathew

Introduction

In our chapter in *The Companion to Language Assessment* (2014), we noted that for at least the preceding 15 years there had been a growing interest in assessment practices that support language teaching and learning. Since then, this trend has shown no sign of slowing down. Indeed, professional meetings such as those organized by the International Language Testing Association (ILTA), the American Association of Applied Linguistics (AAAL), and the Asian Association for Language Assessment (AALA) continue to feature colloquia/main themes devoted to this topic, and a review of journals reveals regular publications referencing notions of assessment-for-learning, dynamic assessment, and learning-oriented assessment, among others. Debates in many countries over the deleterious effects of frequent large-scale, standardized testing have no doubt contributed to interest in other means of understanding learner abilities and progress. In addition, the growing popularity of models of learning that emphasize the social origins of abilities, together with the dominance of communicatively oriented language curricula, has further fostered an environment that more readily recognizes assessment as a natural feature of teaching and learning activities rather than a stand-alone endeavor that requires learners to perform under unique testing conditions.

This chapter proceeds from the perspective that assessment can best support teaching and learning when these two activities are aligned. Put another way, we argue that assessment may function not merely to measure learner achievement or mastery at the end of a learning cycle but also – and perhaps more importantly for many teachers and learners – to monitor learner progress, and in so doing it provides the necessary basis from which instructional decisions may be made. We are thus clearly more concerned in this chapter with assessments undertaken for *formative* rather than *summative* purposes. This is not to undermine the value of the latter for language education. Rather, it reflects a commitment to understanding learner abilities while they are in the process of developing and while feedback may be offered. After all, that is when classroom instruction can be attuned to support learners' continued development. It is in this regard that one may contrast summative assessment, or assessments of the products of learning at the completion of an instructional cycle or program, with formative assessment, where the express purpose is to know about the current state of learner development to determine the way forward (Broadfoot et al., 2002). The emphasis on

---

The Concise Companion to Language Assessment, First Edition. Edited by Antony John Kunnan.
© 2025 John Wiley & Sons, Inc. Published 2025 by John Wiley & Sons, Inc.

monitoring as well as guiding learner development is also brought out explicitly in recent research in dynamic assessment (see Poehner, this volume, Dynamic Assessment in the Classroom).

In what follows, we offer an overview of current conceptualizations of assessment that attempt to help teachers monitor and support learner development in an ongoing manner. We also discuss important innovations in how learner progress itself may be understood. We then turn to issues that must be overcome, at conceptual and systemic levels, for effective assessment practices to be implemented in the classroom.

Clarifying Terms

Before moving on, we wish to disambiguate certain terms that are sometimes used interchangeably but that in fact have particular meanings. Following Harris and McCann (1994), *assessment* refers to activities designed to provide information relevant to drawing inferences about learning processes as well as learner progress. Bell and Cowie (2001) specify that formative assessment denotes *processes* used by *teachers and students* to *recognize* and *respond* to *student learning* in normal, non-contrived classroom activities. It is worth noting that Bell and Cowie differentiated *planned* formative assessments, involving more formal tasks, and *interactive* formative assessments that may occur more spontaneously as a natural part of classroom activity. We include both in our discussion in the present chapter as, in our view, both kinds of formative assessment emphasize learning over measurement or accountability. In this regard, we also recognize that the term *learning-oriented assessment* (LOA) has been used by some (e.g., Carless, 2007; Leung, 2020) as a superordinate label encompassing any kind of assessment that focuses on learning. However, we note that LOA itself has a distinctive history in the L2 field (Turner & Purpura, 2016) and that what constitutes LOA as well as its relation to other forms of assessment continues to be a topic of discussion (see Saville, 2021). To avoid confusion, we employ the traditional term formative assessment (henceforth, FA) throughout this chapter. In our usage, FA requires comparing actual (present) and reference (future) levels of performance and using the resultant information to bridge the gap between these levels. In this way, successfully orchestrating assessments that are both informative of learner abilities and that support their continued development is critical to monitoring progress.

Previous Views or Conceptualization

The idea of monitoring progress in the classroom has emerged from developments in two somewhat distinct but overlapping areas: the development of educational evaluation models with particular reference to language evaluation, and the shift from curricula that are objectives-based to those that are communicatively oriented. Beretta (1992) traced developments in the history of language evaluation to major conceptual shifts beginning in the 1960s (e.g., Bloom, 1969; Scriven, 1967; Stufflebeam et al., 1971). While Bloom (1969) had proposed a formative role for evaluation which provided for giving feedback and correctives at each stage of the teaching–learning process, models of evaluation at the time were found to be sorely lacking in this respect. Researchers increasingly realized that no matter how well specified the objectives are at the beginning of an instructional program, restricting evaluation exclusively to learning outcomes does not account for unexpected outcomes and outcomes that are hard to define let alone capture through external tests. This gave rise to a host of new models that emphasized the need for descriptive data and value judgments that could improve programs. Scriven (1967) proposed a distinction between *formative* and *summative* assessments,

328 Chapter 23 Monitoring Progress in the Classroom

with the former tracking process and progress while the latter seeks to determine the outcomes of a program. Others offered practical recommendations for monitoring learner progress through the CIPP model (context, input, process, and product) and advocated a "process of delineating, obtaining, and providing useful information for judging decision alternatives" (Stufflebeam et al., 1971, p. 43) using systematic observation, interviews, diaries, and rating scales aside from product assessment.

During roughly the same period, the shift toward communicative language teaching ushered in a view of language teaching as involving the use of language for meaningful communication as a means of learner language development and not simply as an end goal. Communicative language teaching views the negotiating of meaning that occurs in ongoing interaction among teachers and learners to be the key element in second language development (see Brumfit & Johnson, 1979). This perspective implies that different learners could be learning different things from the same interactions. This state of affairs rendered assessment far more complex than it had been previously. Specifically, it was recognized that rather than understanding assessment in terms of learning outcomes derived in a linear relation from particular teacher input, it is necessary to examine these processes as they occur in the classroom over time.

Against this backdrop, evaluation during the 1980s shifted from an activity focused on testing learners at the end of a program to integrating an evaluation system into curriculum design in order to investigate processes of learner development and how instruction could best meet learner needs. The need for understanding and interpreting data about language learning from the classroom was recognized (see Lewkowicz & Moon, 1985). At around the same time, Stenhouse's (1975) proposal for *research-based teaching* began to gain attention. He argued:

> It is difficult to see how teaching can be improved or how curricular proposals can be evaluated without self-monitoring on the part of teachers. A research tradition which is accessible to teachers and which feeds teaching must be created if education must be significantly improved. (p. 165)

This confluence of shifts in educational evaluation and growing research into processes of second language acquisition, particularly in classroom settings, set the stage for the considerable research beginning in the 1990s and continuing today on FA vis-à-vis the pivotal role of teachers.

Black and Wiliam (1998) provided a watershed moment in educational assessment in their reframing of the summative-formative divide as *assessments of learning* and *assessments for learning (AfL)*. Among other important contributions of this work, Black and Wiliam convincingly argued for the importance of AfL in its own right, asserting that there is likely no other way of monitoring learner progress and working to support gains across age groups and school subjects. In the L2 field, Rea-Dickins and Gardner (2000) added that classroom FAs are often the basis for very high-stakes decisions, such as allocation of resources, identification of learners with special needs, and placement of learners in courses of study. Such rethinking of the relevance of FA also led to curriculum documents specifying its integration in educational systems (see, for example, Broadfoot et al., 2002; Curriculum Development Council, 2001).

Regardless of whether one recognizes FA as a high-stakes undertaking, it has also been argued that FA cannot, and should not, be judged according to the same criteria as formal testing as these represent fundamentally different activities, each with their own goals and underlying assumptions about learners (e.g., Leung & Mohan, 2004). However, it is also to be noted that FA, unlike SA, does not have a robust conceptual framework to guide its practice. That said, the dialogue surrounding how FA may be conceptualized has increased in recent years, and we comment on some of the major trends below.

Current Views

Although there is no standard procedure that can be recommended for monitoring progress in the classroom, the processes involved in FA highlight the need for full participation of both teachers and learners in an attempt to make it more responsive to individual learners, to promote learning and equity in education. It can be seen to consist broadly of a two-part activity (Black & Wiliam, 1998) that begins with the perception by the learner or teacher of a gap between the present state of learner ability and the intended goal. This may be achieved through self-assessment or self-monitoring as well as through both spontaneous and planned observation of individual students, pairs, or groups; it may entail asking questions, offering feedback, and maintaining records of how students progress from one activity or unit to another. This leads to the second part, in which action is taken by the teacher and learner to bridge the gap between their current level of performance and curricular goals. The tools for monitoring can virtually be all "teaching" tasks such as oral, listening, and reading tasks, portfolios, group projects, and teacher-made tests along with checklists, reflective journals/diaries, interviews, and online discussions. It is beyond the scope of this chapter to provide a detailed discussion of "how" monitoring can be carried out in the classroom, and we refer readers to a number of valuable resources (e.g., Bachman & Damböck, 2018; Brown, 1999; Cheng, 2013; De Florio, 2023).

The central role played by learners in FA has led some to identify effective FA practices with a broader, learner-centered classroom culture. From this perspective, learners and teachers must have a shared understanding of the goals of particular activities, must be involved in assessing work (their own as well as others') and should not be regarded as passive recipients of knowledge but should be empowered to guide their own learning (for discussion, see Mathew, 1998). Of course, in reality, successful implementation of FA practices is dependent upon both teacher and learner orientation to classroom activities. For instance, learners may be content to get by with minimal effort and they may avoid taking risks to solve difficult problems or fail to recognize helpful feedback (Black & Wiliam, 1998). Similarly, teachers may not be willing to give up their position of power, a characteristic of a teacher-dominated classroom, and allow students to take charge of their learning. However, there is evidence to show that with adequate orientation to learner-centered pedagogies, teachers can effectively participate in the assessment of their learners instead of relying on a one-off snapshot taken by an outsider (e.g., Davison, 2004; Hasselgren, 2000).

As regards teacher roles, their understanding of assessment and actual classroom practices can be visualized within the broad concept of teacher's language assessment literacy (LAL) which has seen a shift in the last two decades, from a technical activity to that of a complex social practice (O'Loughlin, 2013). School culture, of which teachers are a part, has come to be understood as existing within a larger education system that exerts a strong influence on classroom assessment practices. To understand and investigate the complex nature of LAL, Fulmer et al. (2015) recommend adopting a model connecting three levels: the *micro* (the immediate classroom processes), *meso* (factors external to but that have a direct influence on the classroom, and *macro* (educational policies at various levels and cultural and social norms). Scarino (2013) and Giraldo (2020), for example, advocate incorporating teacher interpretive frameworks that emanate from their teaching contexts, practices, beliefs, values, and attitudes, all of which shape their own LAL.

Finally, a crucial aspect of the teacher's role in FA is of course to provide feedback. De Florio (2023), based on the important characteristics of effective feedback (as opposed to unproductive feedback) discussed in Green (2021), makes a strong case for using different forms of feedback and exemplifies them in concrete contexts. The three-step model, suggested by Hattie and Timperley (2007) is crucial for ensuring an effective feedback culture and emphasizes that learners involved should find answers to the three questions: *feed up*

(What are my goals? Where do I stand?); *feed back* (How am I progressing?); and *feed forward* (Where to next?). Overall, feedback is most powerful when learners understand what it means and when it provides an adequate basis upon which learners can move forward. This model therefore reinforces independent learning and necessitates a fundamental shift from teacher-dominated approaches to ELT to those of learner-centered ones.

Before moving on, we wish to briefly comment on two approaches to framing how assessment may be used to monitor learner progress in the classroom and that have both received considerable attention in the L2 field: learning-oriented assessment (LOA) and dynamic assessment (DA). Other chapters in this volume address these topics in detail, and so we limit our remarks here to noting some of the trends that have emerged in recent years and how they pertain to monitoring learner progress. To begin, LOA does not refer to a specified assessment method, approach, or framework, but rather "it is the elicitation and appropriate use of the evidence for specified teaching and learning purposes that is at the heart of the LOA concept" (Saville, 2021, p. 17). Turner and Purpura (2016, p. 255) similarly express that in LOA the "premise is to begin with learning, that is, to prioritize learning when considering the interrelationships across instruction, assessment, and learning." From these statements, it appears that LOA offers first and foremost a way of thinking about assessment that contrasts with the uses to which large-scale, standardized tests are often put (i.e., decisions such as program completion, acceptance into a program, overall academic achievement, general language proficiency, etc.). In this regard, we are reminded of the formative-summative distinction as well as the differentiation between assessment-of-learning and assessment-for-learning that we discussed earlier.

Recent research has sought to identify assessment practices in various contexts that might be discussed as contrasting with standardized testing and as illustrative of LOA. For example, Amer (2021) reports efforts to introduce LOA into Egyptian schools. A particularly interesting finding concerns the perceptions of what constitutes LOA among various stakeholders. While Amer found a general shift toward assessments that align with teaching and learning goals through the adoption of projects and performance-based assessment practices, he further noted that these continued to be conceptualized in terms that reflect the broader assessment culture dominated by high-stakes standardized testing. Amer's (2021) findings are intriguing because they suggest that, absent a general LOA framework, teachers may resort to their knowledge of assessment, shaped by formal testing, to conceptualize what they do and to interpret outcomes. The tendency toward documenting local assessment practices that may be considered in terms of their emphasis on learning also orients Banerjee's (2021) review of research into classroom language assessment. Taking a broad view of LOA to encompass several related but distinct forms of assessment, including FA, AfL, and DA, Banerjee argues for the importance of qualitative research methods, including observations, narrative inquiry, and conversation and discourse analytic approaches in order to understand how teachers approach assessment and their reasoning from the information they obtain about learners. This, for Banerjee, may offer insights into what constitutes LOA in a given context.

Turning to DA, a key feature that sets it apart from other forms of assessment is its close adherence to a theoretically coherent account of human abilities and their development, namely, the Sociocultural Theory of mind that originated in the writings of Russian psychologist L.S. Vygotsky (1978). As such, DA proceeds from the perspective that the primary aim of education is not to impart factual knowledge but to guide learner development of new ways of understanding the world and ultimately acting. For Vygotsky (2012), making learner development the focus of educational activity requires that assessment identify both an individual's present, or actual, abilities and abilities that are emerging, or ripening, and that are most amenable to instructional intervention. While *actual abilities* may be determined through observation of *learner independent performance*, as occurs in most assessments, abilities that are *ripening* may be interpreted according to their engagement in *joint activity*, and in particular their responsiveness to mediation intended to support them as difficulties arise. As Poehner and Wang (2021) explain, the teacher or assessor who engages in DA (often referred to as a *mediator*) endeavors both to observe learner performance of assessment tasks and to interact with learners to obtain a robust developmental diagnosis. Thus, DA proceeds from the view that understanding learner development entails an element of intervention, or teaching, that usually manifests through providing prompts, reminders, leading questions, examples, models, and explanations to learners as part of the assessment. Particularly important for the topic of this chapter, learner progress in DA may be interpreted not only as improved independent performance of tasks but also through changes in the amount or quality of mediation they require.

Current Research

In this section, we wish to begin with the observation that in recent years traditional assumptions concerning who gets to do research have in fact been challenged, with teachers themselves taking a more central role in such work. Poehner and Inbar-Lourie (2020) have proposed a re-examination of the relationship between assessment researchers and classroom teachings, arguing for a new partnership framework that aims to simultaneously advance researcher understanding of classroom assessment and improve practices for teachers and learners. Situating this framework within a Marxian critical philosophy of science, the authors refer to it as praxis. They explain that praxis "reflects an epistemology that runs counter to the more conventional stance that research and theory building (including the elaboration of principles and models) might be pursued exclusively by researchers and then conveyed to teachers for them to apply it" (Poehner & Inbar-Lourie, 2020, p. 3). Instead "praxis regards theory as providing principles and concepts that *allow teachers to build their practice* in a reasoned, reflective manner ... [while] *practice serves as a testing ground for theory*, pointing to areas in need of revision and expansion" (ibid., emphasis added). In this way, praxis seeks to promote dialogue and cooperation between language assessment researchers and classroom teachers in lieu of either directing how teachers ought to conduct assessments or simply identifying their preferred assessment practices.

As one example of such researcher–teacher partnership, Baker and Germain (2020) followed a narrative inquiry approach to examining assessment practices in a nature-based immersion program that is part of a larger language revitalization effort focused on Mi'gmaq language and culture in Canada. The authors identify their positionality at the outset as, respectively, a language assessment researcher documenting assessment practices among Indigenous communities in Canada (Baker) and a veteran Mi'gmaq immersion educator with particular expertise at the kindergarten level (Germain). Recognizing the importance of creating a relationship of mutual respect and trust, the authors explain that Baker approached the partnership not to *teach* Germain but to *learn* with her (Baker & Germain, 2020, p. 111). Their joint project followed a narrative research approach in which regular open-ended interviews about Germain's language assessment practices with Indigenous learners were recounted and became the data that were thematical analyzed by both Baker and Germain. Particular exchanges with learners that were reported shed light on the ways in which Germain made use of one learner's responses to elaborate the language of another and how she integrated and built upon the comments, questions, feedback, and discoveries of learners in outdoor environments to gain insights into their current thinking and extend it. The authors argue that this process not only allowed for connections between Germain's practices and theoretical constructs associated with DA and LOA but also served to decolonize assessment research by enabling the voices of minoritized Indigenous populations to be heard.

332 Chapter 23 Monitoring Progress in the Classroom

While praxis emphasizes teacher–researcher partnerships, another, somewhat related body of research that has developed substantially in the last two decades is in practitioner or action research led by teachers themselves, sometimes supported by mentors who are also practitioners. Here teachers look critically at their own classroom teaching/assessment practices and also involve learners as researchers with a view to get a deeper understanding of the phenomena of interest (see, for example, Dikilitaş et al., 2015; Hanks, 2019; Pinter et al., 2016 among others). There have also been many teacher research reports emanating from projects in low- to middle-income countries that provide first-hand accounts of how they went about their investigation and what improvements it led to, not only for their students but also for their own professional development (see, for example, Teachers' Voices: Capturing the dynamics of change. English in Action, Bangladesh, 2017; Teachers as Change Agents: Classroom research in Sierra Leone secondary schools, 2021). What is important here is that teacher research offers a way for teachers to self-observe, self-analyze, and self-evaluate their work situated in their own cultural contexts, leading to reflectively acquired self-knowledge. It also shifts the focus from being implementers of "good" practices to one of taking responsibility for classroom decision-making.

Alongside praxis-oriented and teacher-led assessment research, more conventional approaches continue to be employed and yield valuable insights into assessment's relationship to teaching and learning, conflicts between assessment policies and practices, and the experiences of various stakeholders. In research on LAL of teachers for instance, teachers reported having little confidence in any of the assessment areas investigated, especially the more innovative methods of formative assessment such as using student portfolios, self- and peer-assessment (Tsagari & Vogt, 2017). Similarly, Hatipoğlu (2015) and Kömür (2018) noted that preservice teachers had difficulty in applying assessment knowledge to real classroom practices. A questionnaire-based study carried out by Kunnan et al. (2021) on LAL of teachers in Goa (India) revealed that teachers conformed quite rigidly to the School-Board's assessment requirements which in turn were mandated by the Indian government's "no detention" policy, and were constrained to "push" students to the next higher class regardless of their language level, Although teachers are a central stakeholder group in doing language assessments, also endorsed by Giraldo (2020) and Tsagari and Vogt (2017), teachers in Goa were mere implementers of a top-down policy that was seemingly learner-centered. However, the Goa study also sought to address the *why* and *how* of teachers' assessment practices qualitatively which portrayed distinctly how in spite of the diktats from the authorities, some teachers managed to carry out assessments that helped learning (see Mathew & Kunnan, 2021). The analysis of data from classroom observations and in-depth interviews of teachers gave rise to two almost distinct scenarios, one where *Assessment was tedious, a waste of teacher's and students' time,* and the other where *it helped learning* and identified some features that characterized these two scenarios (Mathew & Kunnan, 2021, p. 1381). A main feature that demarcated one from the other was the type of school that teachers worked in (i.e., private/semi-private as opposed to government ones). The former seemed to care for students and their learning more than the latter and supported teachers which in turn helped teachers to carry out learner-friendly assessments. The study also demonstrated that "... teachers' LAL is functional and effective to the extent the school culture including the parents it caters to and other macro aspects, such as the Board's policy of language proficiency and how it is operationally defined support it" (ibid., p. 1383). The dilemma one would need to address is whether a training program in language assessment should precede a systemic curricular reform or vice versa.

Challenges

Although the importance and value of FA have been endorsed by curriculum bodies and assessment experts alike, there are several conceptual and implementation issues that need to be addressed. One issue involves establishing effective FA practices in contexts traditionally dominated by a high-stakes testing culture. For SA and FA to coexist and each meet their intended purpose, it is important that FA not be subordinated to or fashioned after practices that are successful in meeting summative goals. As Harlen and James (1997) observe, it is widely and erroneously assumed that any assessment conducted by teachers in classroom contexts necessarily represents FA. Indeed, Cheng et al. (2004), following a three-year comparative survey of teacher assessment practices in Canada, Hong Kong, and China, observe that while teachers do see value in classroom assessment as an instructional tool, very often what they do in class is colored by the mandated external assessments as well as by their own beliefs about assessment. The authors report that teachers' work in the classroom valued discrete item formats targeting lower-order cognitive processes in a manner parallel to external, formal exams.

It is increasingly clear therefore that assessment exists within a broader educational culture that includes assumptions regarding teaching, learning, and assessing. Unless schools and secondary boards officially acknowledge the need to carry out continuous assessments that feed back into teaching, both students and teachers are not likely to attach importance to the activity, let alone engage in it. The performance or grade-oriented students and parents, used to high-stakes assessment that they (incorrectly) regard as scientific, fair, and objective, may not appreciate assessments focused on learning processes. Moreover, teachers may not be fully comfortable with the emphasis placed on engaging *with* learners in FA as co-participants. While this is crucial to helping learners eventually gain greater autonomy and more effectively participate in self- and peer assessment, teachers may feel that their expertise and authority is undermined. As one example, Mathew (2012) reports that in India classroom assessment is frequently a mirror image of what SA demand, with the result that FA is reduced to a series of "mini-SAs" done several times over.

Perhaps the single greatest challenge in recent years to not only assessment but to education more generally has been the COVID-19 global pandemic. This caused unprecedented disruptions to all areas of life. The sudden closure of universities and primary/secondary schools and the subsequent shift to online instruction created numerous difficulties and inequities, including access to the Internet and computers, as well as more self-directed learning which not all learners and teachers were prepared for. As regards online assessment, some challenges related to creating appropriate materials and inadequate electronic devices, especially in marginalized contexts have been responded to. While these events are extremely recent and time has not permitted a good deal of research into language assessment during the pandemic, as we enter a post-pandemic phase several questions are of concern: What new practices and ways of thinking may have already begun to emerge as teachers, researchers, and learners endeavored to respond to the unprecedented circumstances created by the pandemic? How well did these work, given their intended purpose? Perhaps most important, which of these practices might continue to be relevant and valuable?

Research has begun to explore such questions. For example, an International Language Testing Association webinar organized by Poehner and Inbar-Lourie in 2023 showcased three ongoing studies in different parts of the world in order to initiate discussion of these issues within the international research community. One of these studies, reported by Vogt and Tsagai (2023), examined perceptions among teachers and language assessment experts and revealed the need to generate new approaches to developing teacher LAL. Similarly, the 2022 Asian Association for Language Assessment conference saw several presentations focusing on how teachers and researchers investigated newer ways of handling hybrid approaches to classroom assessment.

With post-COVID issues looming large, an enduring challenge is that of teachers' and their students' unexamined beliefs about the merits of assessments that are informal and continuous. In India, Kunnan et al.'s (2021) and Mathew and Kunnan's (2021) studies of teachers' classroom assessment practices vis-a-vis their perspectives on their work revealed a case of near-illiteracy in language assessment. They had understood the notion of supporting learning

334 **Chapter 23** Monitoring Progress in the Classroom

as implementing a top-down policy that seemingly helped the learner by passing (promoting) them to the next higher grade level. Shepard (1995, p.43) suggests that "if teachers are being asked to make fundamental changes in what they teach and how they teach it, then they need sustained support to try out new practices, learn new theory, and make it their own." Furthermore, such radical change takes time. Even in countries where there is professional support for teachers to remain up to date on emerging teaching and assessment practices (e.g., Europe, New Zealand), deep-rooted tensions often remain between recommendations from professionals regarding "best practices" and policy decisions that create the contexts in which teachers must operate.

The matter of best practices is also far from straightforward. Teachers are faced with a number of choices when implementing a systematic program for monitoring learning, and ultimately their decisions must reflect what they know of their learners and the goals they and their learners set. Decisions must be made regarding tasks appropriate to meeting curricular goals, criteria for scoring or rating student work, whether work is to be conducted (and scored) on an individual basis or by groups, and the forms of assistance or scaffolding that are permitted. In addition, the research recommendations to which teachers might turn while making these decisions are not always consistent.

Another area that appears to be conspicuous by its absence is multilingual assessment in multilingual contexts. Even when we teach multilingual learners, classroom assessment in their (home) languages has remained a rarity. Gottlieb (2021) argues that if we could explore the rich repertoire – linguistic, academic, and cultural – teachers and students in a multilingual context bring to the classroom, a different view of learner abilities would likely emerge. In a country like India, although the policy actually encourages the use of learners' languages in classroom pedagogy including translanguaging, both classroom-based and summative tests have always been monolingual, with learners being penalized if they use a mix of languages (see Pallavi & Mathew, 2022 for research-based evidence).

Finally, the need for orientation in pre-service and in-service teacher workshops to the characteristics of FA and how it could be translated into classroom processes cannot be overemphasized. In traditional setups, one-off teacher orientations typically focus on modern teaching methodologies and techniques, if within a communicative language teaching framework, to a total exclusion of how teachers can and should monitor students' learning; follow-up workshops that could build progressively on how teachers mediate learning to guide them to an understanding of iterative cycles of teaching and assessment are frequently not included in professional development programs. Physical and infrastructural facilities are further constraints to implementing progressive practices since FA practices are, if at all, incorporated into old structures that have nurtured SA.

Future Directions

As the reader will appreciate from the preceding discussion, monitoring progress in the classroom is a complex process and needs to be understood both at macro (policy) and micro (classroom) levels. Since FA is embedded within the curriculum, all aspects of FA would need to focus on assessing – and, more important, supporting student progress – in relation to the curriculum. At the macro level, when introducing FAs, we need to be aware of the *what* and *how* of introducing this innovation: the more exam-orientated the culture, the lower the level of acceptance of FA among stakeholders, including administrators, principals, teachers, students, and parents, is likely to be, even if on the surface some of the features may appear to have been absorbed. Further, reforms would have to address all three components (i.e., teaching, learning, and assessment) simultaneously, as in the case of some Boards, for instance, the Hong Kong "learning to learn" curriculum reform that fosters students' whole-person development (https://www.edb.gov.hk/en/curriculum-development/renewal/index.html).

In contrast, piecemeal approaches tend to get distorted or diluted and are frequently met with resistance; in some cases, such initiatives finish by being abandoned altogether (see Mathew, 2012).

It seems that any model of FA, to be meaningful and comprehensive, would have to bring together, at a minimum, the following three domains: the teacher's agenda, the learner's level of development and capabilities, and the interaction between the two within the social world of the classroom and the school. While there is no one optimum model that will serve all FA purposes, a way forward might be to accept the plurality of different perspectives and work with them. Eventually researchers and, more important, teachers will have to be able to understand the underlying principles so that they can adapt and extend the models in real classroom contexts. Changes in classroom practice are central rather than marginal, and each teacher will have to make meaning of the model of FA in his or her own way and help in turn to enrich the model(s). In this regard, the innovations that emerged during the pandemic may continue to be employed by some teachers, and research into these practices may, on the one hand, help to systematize them into a coherent framework and, on the other hand, generate new conceptualizations of formative assessment itself. For this, s/he will need continuing support from both school personnel and researchers.

With this in mind, a key direction for future research lies in the development of teachers' understanding and use of classroom assessment skills. Teachers must learn to work within a collaborative framework and adopt assessment strategies involving group or interview and portfolio approaches, questioning, and observation techniques while being aware of the social and cultural influences on assessment and developing competencies to be able to interpret student learning. Teachers need time and space to develop a sense of ownership and to articulate and critique their own implicit constructs and interpretations. We need to provide opportunities in our initial and in-service teacher training programs for teachers to develop confidence and expertise in making and using judgments about and for learning. Such programs may be informed, in turn, by further research into the strategies teachers adopt to monitor progress, students' language learning processes, and the kind of fine-tuned support they need, especially low-achieving learners. This may also help to illuminate the kind of training teachers and students need for carrying out self- and peer-assessment.

Research-based, empirical accounts by teachers themselves of how they monitor students' progress in their classrooms and how they can problematize their pedagogical practices have seen a rise in the last decade. However, it is still the assessment "expert" or outsider who is investigating classroom processes, elevating assessment to a level of scholarly discourse although teachers are involved in research as participants. Since monitoring progress is *research-based teaching* (Stenhouse, 1975, p. 141) and is the business of the teacher, teachers documenting the processes they (and students) go through, and drawing insights from that, should form an urgent research agenda if the enterprise of FA is to come of age. Practitioner/action research seems to be an important way forward.

Discussion Questions

1. Assessment in this chapter is seen as a natural feature of teaching and learning activities that reveals not only learner achievement or mastery at the end of a learning cycle but that also helps to monitor learner progress and provide information relevant to instructional decision-making. What challenges might teachers and learners face when pursuing assessment for this purpose in their instructional context? Based on the ideas presented in this chapter, how might they respond to such challenges?

2. Research suggests that teachers often express a lack of confidence in their assessment knowledge, especially when they attempt to implement more innovative approaches to formative assessment. What might be some reasons for this? How can this issue be addressed by assessment researchers and practitioners?

References

Amer, W. (2021). Implementing learning-oriented assessment in Egyptian schools: a case study. In A. Gebril (Ed.), *Learning-oriented language assessment. Putting theory into practice* (pp. 123–139). Routledge.

Bachman, L., & Dambóck, B. (2018). *Language assessment for classroom teachers*. Oxford University Press.

Baker, B., & Germain, J. (2020). Narrative inquiry as praxis: examining formative assessment practices in a nature-based Indigenous language classroom. In M. E. Poehner & O. Inbar-Lourie (Eds.), *Toward a reconceptualization of second language classroom assessment: Praxis and researcher–teacher partnership* (pp. 107–127). Springer.

Banerjee, H. L. (2021). Approaches to researching learning-oriented assessment in second and foreign language classrooms. In A. Gebril (Ed.), *Learning-oriented language assessment. Putting theory into practice* (pp. 49–68). Routledge.

Bell, B., & Cowie, B. (2001). The characteristics of formative assessment in science education. *Science Education, 85*(5), 536–553.

Beretta, A. (1992). Evaluation of language education: an overview. In J. C. Alderson & A. Beretta (Eds.), *Evaluating second language education* (pp. 5–24). Cambridge University Press.

Black, P., & Wiliam, D. (1998). Assessment and classroom learning. *Assessment in Education: Principles, Policy & Practice, 5*(1), 7–74.

Bloom, B. S. (1969). Some theoretical issues relating to educational evaluation. In R. W. Tyler (Ed.), *Educational evaluation: New roles, new means. National Society for the Study of Education Yearbook*, (*Vol. 68* (Part 2), pp. 26–50). University of Chicago Press.

Broadfoot, P., Daugherty, R., Gardner, J., Harlen, W., James, M., & Stobart, G. (2002). *Assessment for learning: 10 principles. Research-based principles to guide classroom practice*. Assessment Research Group. Retrieved June 14, 2023 from https://www.researchgate.net/publication/271849158_Assessment_for_Learning_10_Principles_Research-based_principles_to_guide_classroom_practice_Assessment_for_Learning.

Brown, K. (1999). *Monitoring learner progress*. Australia: National Centre for English Language Teaching and Research.

Brumfit, C. J., & Johnson, K. (Eds.). (1979). *The communicative approach to language Teaching*. Oxford University Press.

Carless, D. (2007). Learning-oriented assessment: conceptual bases and practical implications. *Innovations in Education and Teaching International, 44*(1), 57–66.

Cheng, L. (2013). *Language classroom assessment*. TESOL International Association.

Cheng, L., Rogers, T., & Hu, H. (2004). ESL/EFL instructors' assessment practices: purposes, methods and procedures. *Language Testing, 21*(3), 360–389.

Curriculum Development Council. (2001). *Learning to learn: The way forward in curriculum development*. Hong Kong: The Printing Department.

Davison, C. (2004). The contradictory culture of teacher-based assessment: ESL teacher assessment practices in Australian and Hong Kong secondary schools. *Language Testing, 21*(3), 305–334.

De Florio, I. (2023). *From assessment to feedback: Applications in the second/foreign Language classroom*. Cambridge University Press.

Dikilitaş, K., Smith, R., & Trotman, W. (Eds.). (2015). *Teacher–researchers in action*. IATEFL Research Special Interest Group.

Fulmer, G. W., Lee, I. C. H., & Tan, K. H. K. (2015). Multi-level model of contextual factors and teachers' assessment practices: an integrative review of research. *Assessment in Education: Principles, Policy & Practice, 22*(4), 475–494. https://doi.org/10.1080/0969594X.2015.1017445.

Giraldo, F. (2020). A post-positivist and interpretive approach to researching teachers' language assessment literacy. *Profile: Issues in Teachers' Professional Development, 22*(1), 189–200. https://doi.org/10.15446/profile.v22n1.78188.

Gottlieb, M. (2021). *Classroom assessment in multiple languages: a handbook for teachers*. Corwin.

Green, A. (2021). *Exploring language assessment and testing: Language in action* (2nd ed.). Routledge.

Hanks, J. (2019). From research-as-practice to exploratory practice-as-research in language teaching and beyond. *Language Teaching, 52*(2), 143–187. https://doi.org/10.1017/S0261444819000016.

References 337

Harlen, W., & James, M. (1997). Assessment and learning: differences and relationships between formative and summative assessment. *Assessment in Education: Principles, Policy & Practice, 4*(3), 365–379.

Harris, M., & McCann, P. (1994). *Assessment.* Heinemann.

Hasselgren, A. (2000). The assessment of the English ability of young learners in Norwegian schools: an innovative approach. *Language Testing, 17*(2), 261–277.

Hatipoğlu, C. (2015). English language testing and evaluation (ELTE) training in Turkey: expectations and needs of pre-service English language teachers. *ELT Research Journal, 4*(2), 111–128.

Hattie, J., & Timperley, H. (2007). The power of feedback. *Review of Educational Research, 77,* 81–112.

Kömür, S. (2018). Preservice English teachers' assessment awareness: level of readiness for classroom practice. *Journal of Language Teaching and Learning, 8*(1), 109–121.

Kunnan, A. J., Mathew, R., & Zhang, E. (2021). Language assessment literacy among teachers in Goa: analyses of a survey questionnaire and teacher-made tests. *The Journal of Asia TEFL, 18*(3), 904–922. https://doi.org/10.18823/asiatefl.2021.18.3.10.904.

Leung, C. (2020). Learning-oriented assessment: more than the chalkface. In M. E. Poehner & O. Inbar-Lourie (Eds.), *Toward a reconceptualization of second language classroom assessment: Praxis and researcher-teacher partnership* (pp. 85–106). Springer.

Leung, C., & Mohan, B. (2004). Teacher formative assessment and talk in classroom contexts: assessment as discourse and assessment of discourse. *Language Testing, 21*(3), 335–359.

Lewkowicz, J. A., & Moon, J. (1985). Evaluation: a way of involving the learner. In C. Alderson (Ed.), *Evaluation. Lancaster practical papers in English language education* (Vol. 6, pp. 45–80). Pergamon Press.

Mathew, R. (1998). *Development of English language tests at the school level: a report of an ERIC project.* Delhi, India: National Council of Educational Research and Training.

Mathew, R. (2012). Understanding washback: a case study of a new exam in India. In C. Tribble (Ed.), *Managing change in English language teaching: Lessons from experience* (pp. 195–202). British Council.

Mathew, R., & Kunnan, A. J. (2021). Language assessment literacy among school–teachers in Goa: two teacher scenarios. *The Journal of Asia TEFL, 18*(4), 1370–1384. https://doi.org/10.18823/asiatefl.2021.18.4.17.1370.

O'Loughlin, K. (2013). Developing the assessment literacy of university proficiency test users. *Language Testing, 30*(3), 363–380. https://doi.org/10.1177/0265532213480336.

Pallavi & Mathew, R. (2022) *The paradox of multilingual education and multilingual assessment in India. Paper presented at the 8th annual international conference of the Asian Association for language assessment, held in Chennai, India, October, 2022.*

Pinter, A., Mathew, R. & Smith, R. (2016). *Children and teachers as co-researchers in Indian primary English classrooms. ELT Research Papers 16.03, British Council.*

Poehner, M. E., & Inbar-Lourie, O. (Eds.). (2020). *Toward a reconceptualization of second language classroom assessment: Praxis and researcher–teacher partnership.* Springer.

Poehner, M. E., & Wang, Z. (2021). Dynamic assessment and second language development. *Language Teaching, 54,* 472–490.

Rea-Dickins, P., & Gardner, S. (2000). Snares and silver bullets: disentangling the construct of formative assessment. *Language Testing, 17*(2), 215–243.

Teachers' voices: Capturing the dynamics of change. (2017). *English in Action.* Accessed April 5, 2024, from https://www.eiabd.com/publications/research-publications/tvc-book.html.

Teachers as change agents: Classroom research in Sierra Leone secondary schools. (2021). Accessed April 5, 2024, from https://mbsseknowledgeplatform.gov.sl/wp-content/uploads/2022/01/LWL_Teacher-Research-Book.pdf.

Saville, N. (2021). Learning-oriented assessment. Basic concepts and frameworks in using assessment to support language learning. In A. Gebril (Ed.), *Learning-oriented language assessment. Putting theory into practice* (pp. 13–33). Routledge.

Scarino, A. (2013). Language assessment literacy as self-awareness: understanding the role of interpretation in assessment and in teacher learning. *Language Testing, 30*(3), 309–327. https://doi.org/10.1177/0265532213480128.

Scriven, M. (1967). The methodology of evaluation. In R. Tyler, R. Gagne & M. Scriven (Eds.), *Perspectives on curriculum evaluation* (Vol. 1, pp. 39–83). Rand McNally.

338 Chapter 23 Monitoring Progress in the Classroom

Shepard, L. A. (1995). Using assessment to improve learning. *Educational Leadership, 52*(5), 38–43.

Stenhouse, L. (1975). *An introduction to curriculum research and development*. Heinemann.

Stufflebeam, D. L., Foley, W. J., Gephart, W. J., Guba, E. G., Hammon, R. L., Merriman, H. O., & Provus, M. M. (1971). *Educational evaluation and decision-making*. Peacock.

Tsagari, D., & Vogt, K. (2017). Assessment literacy of foreign language teachers around Europe: research, challenges, and future prospects. *Papers in Language Testing and Assessment, 6*(1), 41–63.

Turner, C., & Purpura, J. (2016). Learning-oriented assessment in second and foreign language classrooms. In D. Tsagari & J. Banerjee (Eds.), *Handbook of second language assessment* (pp. 255–272). De Gruyter.

Vogt, K. & Tsagai, D. (2023). *The impact of COVID-19 on language assessment in higher education. Paper presented as part of the International Language Testing Association webinar on Formative language assessment in the time of COVID-19: Lessons learned.*

Vygotsky, L. S. (1978). *Mind in society: The development of higher psychological processes*. Harvard University Press.

Vygotsky, L. S. (2012). *Thought and language*. MIT Press.

Suggested Readings

De Florio, I. (2023). *From assessment to feedback: Applications in the second/foreign language classroom*. Cambridge University Press.

Mathew, R., & Kunnan, A. J. (2021). Language assessment literacy among school-teachers in Goa: two teacher scenarios. *The Journal of Asia TEFL, 18*(4), 1370–1384. https://doi.org/10.18823/asiatefl.2021.18.4.17.1370.

Poehner, M. E., & Inbar-Lourie, O. (Eds.). (2020). *Toward a reconceptualization of second language classroom assessment: Praxis and researcher–teacher partnership*. Springer.

Saville, N. (2021). Learning-oriented assessment. Basic concepts and frameworks in using assessment to support language learning. In A. Gebril (Ed.), *Learning-oriented language assessment. Putting theory into practice* (pp. 13–33). Routledge.

CHAPTER 24

Diagnostic Assessment Feedback in the 21st-Century Technology-Rich Classroom

Eunice Eunhee Jang, Maryam Wagner, Liam Hannah, and Hyunah Kim

Introduction

Assessment feedback plays a critical role in personalizing students' learning by providing them with information about their learning progress and areas on which they need to focus their efforts (Hattie & Timperley, 2007). Classroom teachers can use feedback in their instruction adapting to students' learning profiles. Yet, students remain the primary agents who decide whether to confirm, reject, or restructure the information contained in feedback (Butler & Winne, 1995); therefore, the maximal effect of assessment feedback may depend on students' ability to metacognitively self-regulate their learning and act on the feedback.

Feedback, that is pedagogically diagnostic, requires precision so that it can pinpoint both strengths and weaknesses in students' knowledge base and skills (Alderson, 2005). Focusing on strengths enables the identification of the level a student has reached, and focusing on weaknesses or areas for improvement leads to remediation or further instruction. Diagnostic feedback should be generated through clear and consistent assessment processes to ensure accuracy and eliminate (or minimize) its potential biases and subjectivity.

Recent technological innovations have made a profound impact on how we teach, assess, and mediate students' learning. Yet, an existing body of research on feedback tends to focus on the type and delivery mode of feedback (Ferris, 2003; Ferris & Roberts, 2001; Hedgcock & Lefkowitz, 1996; Hyland & Hyland, 2006a; Lee, 2003; Lyster & Ranta, 1997). In this chapter, we examine the centrality of diagnostic assessment feedback to advancing students' learning in a technology-rich classroom environment. We begin by reconceptualizing the framework of assessment feedback in terms of six interrelated dimensions called Purpose, Agency, Latency, Mechanism, Environment, Reference (PALMER) and discuss various assessment approaches oriented toward the utilization of feedback.

The Concise Companion to Language Assessment, First Edition. Edited by Antony John Kunnan.
© 2025 John Wiley & Sons, Inc. Published 2025 by John Wiley & Sons, Inc.

340 Chapter 24 Diagnostic Assessment Feedback

PALMER Framework of Assessment Feedback

Learning is a complex process involving a myriad of intra- and interpersonal, social, and environmental factors. A feedback loop integrated into the learning process allows agents, such as teachers and students in the classroom, to co-achieve pedagogical goals. Assessment feedback is defined as actionable information generated based on task performance and used by learners for improvement (Hattie & Timperley, 2007). Brookhart (2008) characterized feedback in terms of its types, timing, frequency, volume, and delivery mechanism. Despite its potential pedagogical benefits, existing research on the effect of feedback on student learning is inconclusive, partly due to various compounding factors (Kluger & DeNisi, 1996). Furthermore, rapid advances in technologies are changing assessment practice and learning environments, which necessitate a reconceptualization of our understanding of assessment feedback. We consider a PALMER feedback framework comprising six interrelated dimensions to advance this reconceptualization as shown in Figure 24.1.

Purpose

Feedback may differ depending on the purpose of the assessment (Black & Wiliam, 1998). The purpose of the assessment can determine the content and focus of the feedback, the type of feedback delivery mechanism used, and the timing of the feedback. For example, if the purpose of the assessment is to measure students' proficiency in a specific skill or knowledge area, then feedback may be focused on identifying specific areas where students need to improve and providing guidance on how to improve in those areas (Shute, 2008). This type of feedback can support the formative purpose of assessment. In contrast, if feedback is mainly focused on the relative standing of students in their performance against their peers or a norm, it may be best suited to provide summative information about students' achievement or proficiency in a relative sense. When the purpose of the assessment is to provide diagnostic information about students' strengths and weaknesses, the feedback may be more specific and individualized. In addition, if the purpose of the assessment is to promote students' awareness of their own ability, feedback may be self-referenced or peer-referenced, meaning that students are provided with feedback based on their own performance or the performance of their peers. Feedback that is clearly aligned with a specific purpose of assessment has the potential to achieve the intended effects of the assessment.

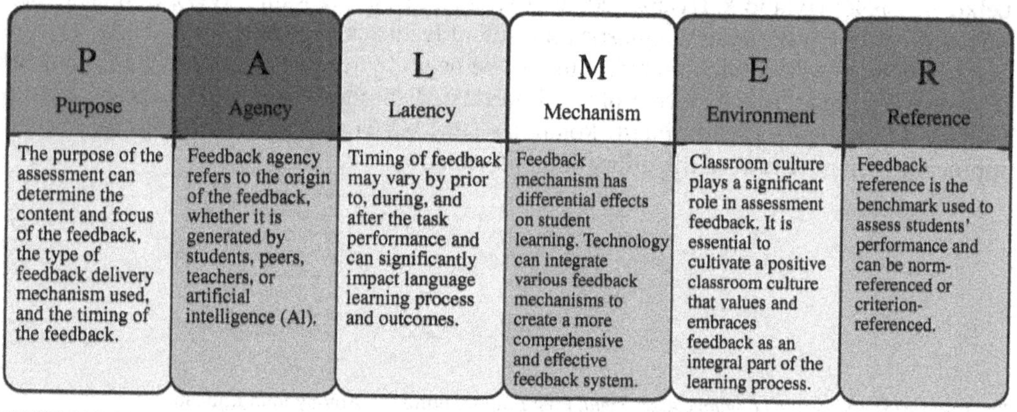

P Purpose	**A** Agency	**L** Latency	**M** Mechanism	**E** Environment	**R** Reference
The purpose of the assessment can determine the content and focus of the feedback, the type of feedback delivery mechanism used, and the timing of the feedback.	Feedback agency refers to the origin of the feedback, whether it is generated by students, peers, teachers, or artificial intelligence (AI).	Timing of feedback may vary by prior to, during, and after the task performance and can significantly impact language learning process and outcomes.	Feedback mechanism has differential effects on student learning. Technology can integrate various feedback mechanisms to create a more comprehensive and effective feedback system.	Classroom culture plays a significant role in assessment feedback. It is essential to cultivate a positive classroom culture that values and embraces feedback as an integral part of the learning process.	Feedback reference is the benchmark used to assess students' performance and can be norm-referenced or criterion-referenced.

FIGURE 24.1 PALMER dimensions of assessment feedback.

Agency

Feedback recipients are typically considered to be the primary agents of feedback. Likewise, in their seminal paper, Hattie and Timperley's (2007) discussion on feedback agency primarily focused on how recipients seek, receive, process, and utilize feedback to improve their performance. However, to gain a more comprehensive understanding of feedback agencies, it is equally imperative to consider it from the perspective of feedback providers, including students, peers, teachers, and artificial intelligence (AI). Therefore, feedback agency needs to be understood from both the receivers' and providers' perspectives.

Self-assessment encourages students to take ownership of their learning, promotes self-awareness, and helps students reflect on their strengths and weaknesses. When students engage in self-assessing their own learning ability and progress, they may improve their self-regulating ability and increase their motivation to learn. While it may not necessarily provide an accurate assessment of performance, students are more likely to accept other referenced feedback seriously when there is a significant discrepancy between their self-referenced feedback and externally referenced feedback (Jang et al., 2015). Peers' feedback may encourage collaboration and understanding of learners' performance from a different perspective. However, students may lack the necessary knowledge or skills to accurately assess their own or peers' performance and may be biased or overly critical, which may lead to a cognitive bias called the Dunning–Kruger effect (Kruger & Dunning, 1999).

Teachers can provide personalized, detailed, and nuanced feedback based on curricular goals, and the specific needs and goals of the student. This type of feedback can also consider learners' unique learning styles, backgrounds, and experiences. Teachers' feedback can be more effective in providing qualitative feedback that extends beyond identifying errors, but also providing explanations, examples, and suggestions for improvement. Teachers may deliver feedback verbally during instruction or through student–teacher conferences. Teachers' verbal feedback that encourages students' participation, drawing from a student's idea, is shown to be associated with effective teaching (Berliner, 1985; Richards, 1990). Teachers also spend a considerable amount of time providing written feedback. Teachers' feedback on students' writing can be distinguished in terms of whether an error is explicitly identified alongside its corrected form (direct or corrective feedback), or if errors are identified, but without the provision of the correct form (indirect or facilitative feedback) (Bitchener et al., 2005). Indirect forms of feedback may be further categorized according to whether the teacher uses a set of linguistic error codes. Teachers often use error codes to indicate linguistic errors in student writing, hoping that their comments help their students to pay attention to recurring error types and correct them on their own.

Latency

Research on the latency of feedback in language assessment suggests that the timing of feedback can significantly impact language-learning outcomes. Providing feedback while learners perform tasks, also known as real-time or concurrent feedback, has been found to be effective in language learning. Real-time feedback can help learners identify and correct errors as they occur, which can enhance their performance on the task (Lyster & Ranta, 1997). Further, real-time feedback can help learners improve their accuracy and fluency in speaking tasks. It has been demonstrated that learners who receive real-time feedback during a speaking task produce more accurate and fluent output than those who do not receive feedback (Sheen, 2004).

Delayed feedback may be less effective than immediate feedback in improving learners' performance on language tasks (Metcalfe et al., 2009). For example, feedback provided immediately after an assessment task was shown to be more effective in improving learners' writing performance than feedback provided after a longer delay. However, delayed corrective feedback that highlights errors and suggests a correction may be more effective than immediate corrective feedback in improving accuracy (Lyster & Ranta, 1997). Research further suggests that the impact of feedback latency may also depend on learner characteristics, such as their proficiency level and cognitive processing ability as well as the type of assessment task (Shute, 2008).

AI-based automated scoring and feedback systems have the potential to significantly reduce the latency of feedback. These automated systems can provide immediate feedback to learners after they complete language tasks. They can also provide feedback to teachers, allowing them to identify areas where learners may need additional support and adjust their teaching accordingly (Weigle, 2013).

Mechanism

The mechanism of feedback delivery is shown to have differential effects on student learning (Hattie & Timperley, 2007). Studies have shown that verbal and symbolic feedback (e.g., checkmarks) are more effective in promoting learning than tangible feedback (e.g., rewards and stickers) because they can direct students' attention to relevant cues in the learning materials (Barringer & Gholson, 1979). Further, tangible feedback presented solely to reward correct responses can rather hinder performance by distracting students from the learning targets.

The mechanism of feedback delivery can also be considered by reviewing the impact of written and verbal feedback. Written feedback can be an effective mechanism for delivering feedback in language assessment, particularly for writing tasks (Ferris, 2010), and may be more effective than verbal feedback in improving language learners' writing performance (Shintani et al., 2016). When the written feedback uses visual elements such as graphs or charts to illustrate performance, it can be effective in enhancing learner self-efficacy and promoting self-regulated learning (Zimmerman & Moylan, 2009). Verbal feedback can also positively impact students' intrapersonal variables by increasing their motivation and engagement. Learners who received verbal feedback during language tasks reported feeling more motivated and engaged than those who did not receive feedback (Lyster & Ranta, 1997).

AI can be capitalized to integrate various feedback mechanisms, such as written, verbal, and visual feedback to create a more comprehensive and effective feedback system (Attali & Burstein, 2006). Gamification techniques, such as badges, leaderboards, or points, can be used to generate feedback that engage young students and motivate them to learn (Dicheva et al., 2015). Furthermore, learner dashboards can be used to communicate feedback on students' progress over time, allowing them to self-regulate their learning trajectories.

Environment

Classroom culture plays a significant role in the impact of assessment feedback (Shepard, 2000). It is essential for teachers to cultivate a positive classroom culture that values and embraces feedback as an integral part of the learning process. This environment can be achieved by creating a safe and nonjudgmental learning space where students feel comfortable receiving feedback, emphasizing a growth mindset (Dweck, 2007) that views mistakes and challenges as opportunities for learning and development.

If classroom environments are highly competitive and performance-oriented, feedback from assessments may have a detrimental effect on student learning. Ames (1992) argued that students' learning is hindered when a classroom context is performance-oriented with excessive focus on grades and competitions. She further suggested that if feedback is provided with an opportunity for students to improve their skills, rather than with a numerical score only, then learners exert more effort and are concerned with self-improvement rather than "performing." Therefore, the learning environment influences how students receive and use feedback according to their individual goal orientations, and equally, the context may also shape the learners' orientations. As Hyland and Hyland (2006b) aptly stated, "we actively construct a context that relates feedback to specific *learners*" (p. 213, emphasis in text).

The interpretation and use of feedback by learners may also be influenced by their cultural influences and individual backgrounds (Hyland & Hyland, 2006a; Nelson & Carson, 2006; Sully de Luque & Sommer, 2000). Additionally, teachers' belief systems and cultural experiences can influence the delivery of feedback. Hyland and Hyland (2006a) noted:

> Ideologies help establish cohesion and coordinate understanding through mutual expectations but cultural variation in these assumptions can intrude into classrooms through the expectations that teachers and students have about instruction and the meanings they attach to the feedback they are given. (p. 11)

The delivery and use of feedback may be mediated by the shared and individual cultural experiences in a classroom; however, the extent to which culture plays a role in these exchanges is not easily understood. Sully de Luque and Sommer (2000) examined the relationship between feedback and four "cultural syndromes," which they identify as follows: specific holistic orientation, tolerance of ambiguity, individualism–collectivism, and status identity. These authors proposed these syndromes following a comprehensive search of the literature across multiple disciplines and identify characteristics that inform the interaction between the receiver and provider of feedback. Sully de Luque and Sommer subsequently proposed a feedback model incorporating these cultural facets across various feedback activities. For example, these authors proposed that in classrooms where there is a low tolerance for ambiguity, the feedback provided will be more structured and procedural than in a high tolerance context. At the same time, learners with low tolerance for ambiguity will seek feedback more frequently than students who are not similarly influenced. At the same time, Hyland and Hyland (2006a) cautioned against an overdependence on cultural factors as explanatory tools in the feedback loop. While aspects of students' cultural dimensions should be used to inform interactions and multiple perspectives, particularly in language-learning contexts where multiple cultures are represented, overused labels and stereotypes should be avoided.

In addition, external pressures can have a significant impact on the classroom culture and the way assessment feedback is perceived and valued (Hargreaves, 2020). If the society places a strong emphasis on high-stakes testing, it can create a culture of competition and anxiety whereby students and teachers may prioritize test scores over other aspects of learning. In such a culture, assessment feedback may be seen as less important than the results of standardized tests. Students may feel pressured to perform well on tests and may view feedback as a distraction from their preparation for exams. Teachers may also feel pressured to prioritize test preparation over other aspects of their curriculum, which can result in less time and attention being devoted to feedback. Similarly, if parents or other external stakeholders place a strong emphasis on grades and academic achievement, it can also create a culture of pressure and competition where feedback is viewed primarily to improving grades.

To mitigate the impact of external pressures on classroom culture, it is essential for educators to maintain a focus on the importance of feedback and to communicate its value to students and parents. Teachers can emphasize that learning should not focus solely on improving grades or test scores, but on developing skills and knowledge that will be useful in the future. Feedback should be recognized as an essential part of this learning process.

Reference

Feedback reference is the norm- or criterion-referenced standard or benchmark used to evaluate students' performance. In the classroom, standardized measures are often compared to a norm established based on the performance of a representative sample, typically expressed as percentiles or standard scores (Bachman & Palmer, 2010). Norm-referenced feedback can provide students with a general sense of their performance standing relative to others and using performance-level descriptors such as below, at, or above the average. However, these descriptors may provide limited information about the specific areas on which a student needs to work and can discourage learners and/or create an unhealthy sense of competition.

In contrast, criterion-referenced feedback can be more helpful for providing diagnostic feedback. It focuses on how well students meet a set of predetermined criteria or standards. Diagnostic feedback is designed to help learners identify and address their specific strengths and weaknesses, target their efforts on areas of improvement, and tailor instruction to meet their needs (Fulcher & Davidson, 2007).

Current Research on Diagnostic Assessment and Feedback

Cognitive(ly) Diagnostic Assessment

Research on cognitively diagnostic assessment feedback focuses on its potential to provide learners with descriptions of their cognitive strengths, weaknesses, and strategies – rather than focusing on the effects of different types or modes of feedback limited to their learning outcomes. The role of diagnostic feedback is not simply to provide learners with error corrections, but rather to address a cognitive gap or a proficiency level between a current level of performance and some desired level of performance or goal. Such feedback can motivate students to attain higher levels of effort.

Specificity, a measure of granularity, however, should not be confused with quantity. That is, the amount of feedback that is provided to a student is not equivalent to its specificity. For example, students' L2 writing development is positively impacted by the provision of judicious error feedback, not feedback that addresses all errors (Ferris, 2002, 2003; Goldstein, 2001). It is the specificity of feedback (or lack thereof) that is a primary distinguishing feature between the various types of feedback addressed in previous research and diagnostic feedback. To address a cognitive gap for diagnosis, the level of feedback specificity should be considered. Cognitively diagnostic feedback (Jang, 2005) requires cognitively engineered tasks so that they can elicit and collect the traces of learners' cognitive processes. Therefore, it is not only the content of the feedback that contributes to advancing students' learning; the tasks on which the feedback is based play an equally pivotal role.

Cognitive diagnostic assessment (CDA) whose primary goal is to provide cognitively diagnostic feedback has become a viable approach to providing detailed accounts of individual learners' cognitive profiles in reading (Jang et al., 2015; Li et al., 2016), listening (Min et al., 2022; Yi, 2017), and writing (e.g., Effatpanah et al., 2019; Xie, 2017). CDA begins by specifying a set of core skills, processes, or strategies guided by the relevant theory, followed by a careful design of tasks that elicit the skills. CDA bases its inferences on the classification of learners according to the probabilistic mastery level of each tested skill. The cognitive base comprises skills that learners use to process knowledge required for tasks. Using multidimensional latent class models, CDA estimates individual learners' mastery standing for each of the skills assessors specified a priori and provides detailed feedback for both learners and teachers.

Ideal implementation of CDA for language testing includes the design of diagnostic tasks specifically built with diagnostics in mind (Jang, 2005). Some research has implemented this approach by designing and implementing diagnostic assessments a priori based on multidimensional cognitive theories of language ability (Min et al., 2022; Toprak & Cakir, 2021). Nonetheless, demand for more detailed information from large-scale assessment programs has promoted the practice of retrofitting analyses to existing large-scale tests not designed to be diagnostic (Sessoms & Henson, 2018). In response to such limitations, efforts have been made to improve the diagnostic utility of retrofitted tests by using traditional cognitive diagnostic models (CDMs) to extract the diagnostic information from tests (e.g., Kim, 2015), as well as an integration of CDMs with standard setting (Min et al., 2022).

Despite its potential to provide detailed information beyond what a single test score can, skill profiling through CDMs has had limited applications to real-life testing programs due to various factors, including a lack of tests developed with CDM design principles and computationally intensive estimation methods, such as Markov chain Monte Carlo, over standard maximum likelihood estimation methods (von Davier & Lee, 2019). The complex nature of inter-skill relationships in most language constructs including reading comprehension ability has been a significant factor in determining appropriate CDM techniques (Jang, 2010; Lee & Sawaki, 2009; Ravand & Robitzsch, 2018). Another critical issue with CDM applications lies in the fact that its multidimensional discrete latent classification approach is at odds with high-stakes decision-making practices based on test scores derived from unidimensional scaling methods.

Research on feedback based on CDM has not been fully explored yet, as noted. Jang (2005, 2008) examined the effect of CDM-based diagnostic feedback on students' language learning in a university setting. While most students appreciated diagnostic feedback, students with low proficiency responded to their skill profiles with embarrassment and disappointment. Conversely, a high-proficiency student questioned what it meant to have all the skills mastered, indicating that his skill mastery profile confused him because there was no further direction for future action. Those who reported that the feedback was of little use were the students who had "flat" skill profiles (mastery of either none or all the skills), suggesting that the usefulness of feedback depends on whether it provides information about what future action needs to be taken.

Kim (2010) developed proficiency descriptor-based assessment checklists for L2 writing teachers and learners and constructed individual students' writing skill profiles using CDA. Her study demonstrated that teachers found the detailed, diagnostic writing information beneficial as it contributed to their understanding of the domains in which all students required help as well as those that necessitated further instruction for individual students. Her study also highlighted that some teachers believed that provision of excessive diagnostic information (e.g., identification of all grammatical errors) could be "demotivating" and create contexts of "disempowerment" for students. Additionally, teachers suggested that the diagnostic information should be offered incrementally for students at different proficiency levels because they perceived that motivated students would benefit more from the detailed feedback than more proficient students. Kim's investigation also focused on the impact of the diagnostic information on teachers' practice, not on students' use of feedback to improve their writing.

Dynamic Assessment

As noted, diagnostic assessment is distinguished from other general tests by its focus on assessing the gap between a student's existent (actual) ability and cognitive functions, and short- and long-term potential (future) development. Dynamic assessment is an interactive approach to determining students' potential learning ability by providing them with mediation to develop cognitive functions that are emergent in the zone of proximal development (Minick, 1987; Vygotsky, 1986). These emergent cognitive functions become internalized through interpersonal, collaborative interaction (Kozulin & Garb, 2004). This feature is the main characteristic of dynamic assessment (Lantolf & Poehner, 2004). Dynamic assessment typically involves pretesting of a student's current cognitive ability, a mediated intervention,

346 **Chapter 24** Diagnostic Assessment Feedback

which is indispensable for the student's future development, and post-testing of the student's actualization of emergent cognitive functions. Lantolf and Poehner (2004) pointed out that "assessing without mediation is problematic because it leaves out part of the picture – the future – and it is difficult to imagine an assessment context that is not interested in the future" (p. 251, emphasis in text).

In dynamic assessment, feedback can reduce the learner's cognitive load through facilitative feedback that scaffolds language tasks. Such mediated and immediate feedback is especially pivotal for low-ability learners faced with complex language-learning tasks. For example, teachers can mediate through scaffolding by questioning the learners to reorient their attention when they face difficulty, and by demonstrating how to accomplish the task.

Kletzien and Bednar (1990) demonstrated how the dynamic assessment procedure can be used to determine at-risk students' cognitive strategy use and attitude to reading instruction. A strategy analysis of a grade 10 student, Suzana, indicated her overreliance on background knowledge in understanding the text. As she became more frustrated with her lack of reading ability, which was lower than her grade level, she tended to avoid making an effort and attributed her difficulty to inability (i.e., she considered herself to be "really stupid" and "not good at this"). The teacher provided her with a subsequent mediated intervention by discussing both her strengths and limitations when interacting with the text. Identifying visualization as her strength, the teacher used a think-aloud procedure to model how the student could use the strategy with an expository paragraph. Suzana was asked to visualize her mental images while reading a new paragraph, and the teacher continued to provide oral feedback for clarification and reinforcement. A post-assessment indicated that the student could understand materials at a much higher level using visualization. This research demonstrates that orally mediated feedback from dynamic assessment can be valuable for at-risk readers and that it helps them gain a greater sense of control and confidence in learning.

While dynamic assessment can be easily integrated into instruction, it is not clear how an assessor or mediator determines a learner's current proficiency level. Mediation also requires a developmental theory that articulates how learners make progress. Research on the potential of dynamic assessment can offer insights into a learner's cognitive processes, as well as the role of mediation (e.g., graduated prompt and oral feedback) on a learner's developmental growth trajectory.

Technology-Enhanced Automated Feedback

Technology-enhanced feedback based on AI-powered automated scoring has emerged as a rapidly growing area of research. Significant progress has been made in natural language processing and automatic speech recognition, enabling advancements in this field. Parallel to the growing interest in the potential of automated feedback systems for computer-assisted language learning, research has focused on the potential benefits of automated feedback for both teachers and students in language classrooms. While some educators have expressed concerns for the replacement of teacher feedback with machine-generated feedback (e.g., Foltz, 2020), most researchers promote automated feedback to be supplementary to teacher (or other human) feedback (Gu et al., 2021; Kellogg et al., 2010). Automated feedback, ideally, should free teachers' time while augmenting their more tailored and holistic understanding of students' needs. Wilson and Czik (2016) conducted a study examining the effects of automated feedback in conjunction with teacher feedback, alongside a control group that only received teacher feedback as usual. The authors found when providing feedback alongside automated feedback, teachers saved about one-third of their time and focused more on higher-level writing skills and students demonstrated increases in writing persistence though there were no differences in final-draft writing quality.

One important consideration in automated feedback is its level of specificity. Many automated scoring and feedback systems evaluate each student's written or oral responses holistically (to predict human rater judgment) and present the student's position in relation to peer performance (Ke & Ng, 2019). Yet, there has more recently begun to be a push for feedback systems to provide more fine-grained feedback at the subskill level or even for specific linguistic features. Koskey and Shermis (2013) analogized holistic feedback to "a student receiving a marking of 'B' on a paper with a few general comments but no descriptive feedback" (p. 201). For example, Gu et al. (2021) reported that in the TOEFL preparation context, the vast majority of student and teacher participants found both the subscores for different criteria domains (e.g., delivery and language use) and the percentile ranks for speech features helpful. These aspects were included in a feedback report. In writing, the "6 + 1" trait model has been used as a framework for teaching six core (voice, ideas, conventions, organization, word choice, and sentence fluency) and one additional (presentation) writing traits (Culham, 2003). The 6 + 1 model is meant to focus teachers and students on the independent components that build toward high-quality writing overall, making use of a "chunking" model to simplify the learning process. The 6 + 1 model has been shown to produce significantly better writing when taught to fifth graders compared to those taught using traditional methods (Jarmer et al., 2000).

When feedback provided for users includes performance information about specific linguistic features, careful consideration is required to select meaningful features to be communicated (Xi et al., 2006). Although feature selection may vary to a certain extent across the assessment purpose and context, the feature selection criteria used for the feedback report of the TOEFL Practice Online test (Zechner & Loukina, 2020) offered useful insight:

> Selection criteria for the features included their empirical performance (e.g., correlations with human holistic scores), their interpretability by non-experts, their discriminatory properties across the range of speaking proficiency, and the extent to which they may inform subsequent language learning activities. (p. 377)

Following these criteria, the feedback report of the TOEFL Practice Online includes performance information for three fluency features (number of words without pause of fillers, number of long pauses, number of fillers, and number of repetitions), one pronunciation feature (native-live word pronunciation), and one vocabulary feature (vocabulary range) along with a brief description of each feature (Gu et al., 2021). It is also noteworthy that, because of those criteria, the set of features used for feedback may not be the same as the feature set used for the purpose of scoring (Zechner & Loukina, 2020). With regard to writing, Ke and Ng (2019) described categories of writing features used in automated essay evaluation, including length-based, lexical, embeddings, word category, prompt-relevant, readability, syntactic, argumentation, semantic, and discourse features.

Some automated feedback systems provide corrective feedback on student errors (e.g., Cucchiarini et al., 2009; de Vries et al., 2015; Franco et al., 2010; Guo et al., 2022; Koltovskaia, 2020; Lee et al., 2014) although its effectiveness is a contentious topic in the field. Many automated corrective feedback systems for written responses such as ones embedded in Microsoft and Grammarly have been commercialized and are widely in use in language classrooms (Guo et al., 2022; Koltovskaia, 2020). Less common, but significant research has also been conducted for spoken responses. Lee et al.'s (2014) gamified English-learning application focused on corrective feedback on grammar and vocabulary such as morphological, syntactic, and lexical errors. Another example is de Vries et al.'s (2015) experimental study, in which immediate corrective feedback on errors of word order in Dutch spoken responses was provided for adult Dutch learners. In this study, feedback was found to positively affect the learners in terms of learning behaviors (e.g., more attempts and self-corrections) and perceived effectiveness of the feedback system.

348 **Chapter 24** Diagnostic Assessment Feedback

Recent research has extended the boundaries of performance that can be evaluated by automated scoring and feedback systems. In the evaluation of written responses, some content-related writing traits have been modeled (Zhang, 2021) such as discourse coherence (Burstein et al., 2013; Hannah et al., 2023), the use of text evidence (Correnti et al., 2020; Mao et al., 2018; Rahimi et al., 2017), organization (Kumar & Boulanger, 2021; Rahimi et al., 2017), and quality of ideas (Kumar & Boulanger, 2021). Hannah et al. (2023), for example, created separate models for task fulfillment, organization and coherence, and vocabulary and expression trained on samples of grades 3–6 students' writing. Task fulfillment (also referred to as relevance to the prompt above) is related to the degree to which the essay fulfills the requirements of the prompt. Some of the features included in the task fulfillment feedback model were topic modeling features, keyword and synonyms features, and argumentation features. The organization and coherence feedback model evaluated the sentence flow and effective use of writing conventions, using features including discourse features, sentence similarity, and parts of speech tagging. Automated feedback based on this model supports students and teachers at the syntactic and discourse level. Vocabulary and expression scored the use of grade-level words and appropriate descriptors using word frequency features, readability features, and formality features. Future research in feedback on student writing is likely to continue to expand the list of specific writing traits that can be evaluated, especially with the growth of word embeddings (i.e., BERT and GloVe) that can represent more semantic meaning than the traditional writing features described above.

In contrast, research on content-related feedback on spoken responses is still in its nascency. Previous studies suggest significant challenges in applying the feature extraction processes and scoring algorithms used for automated writing scoring and feedback (Zechner & Loukina, 2020). Most importantly, scoring of and feedback on the content domain of spoken responses heavily rely on transcripts generated by automated speech recognition systems. However, the error rate of the state-of-the-art automated speech recognition systems for non-native speeches is still being reported as above 10% at best, and as high as 30% for spontaneous, less predictable speeches of non-native children despite recent breakthroughs brought about by deep learning techniques (Hannah et al., 2022; Ziman et al., 2018). Furthermore, as punctuation needs to be estimated, rather than given, in transcribing spoken responses, the incorrectly estimated or even ambiguous sentence boundaries present additional challenges in providing feedback on the content domain (Zechner & Loukina, 2020). Thus, future research is warranted to address these complex issues and enhance the feedback quality for spoken responses by expanding the coverage of feedback from delivery and language use to the content domain.

BalanceAI

BalanceAI (Jang et al., 2023) is an example of an automated feedback system that combines many of the ideas highlighted in this chapter. BalanceAI is an online assessment platform designed to provide holistic, diagnostic information to teachers, students, and parents. It is holistic in that it does not only evaluate language-related constructs but also assess five broad domains including learning orientation, reading, writing, speaking, and cognitive functioning. The focus on learning orientations derives from the concept of agency discussed earlier in this chapter in which one critical component of a student's response to feedback is their personal relationship to it. The learning orientations evaluated by BalanceAI include the so-called big four of self-efficacy (Bandura, 1999), goal orientation (Dweck, 1986), self-regulation (Zimmerman & Schunk, 2011), and grit, also known as perseverance (Duckworth et al., 2007), all of which are core to developing a robust profile of a student. The other four domains of BalanceAI combine traditional and innovative assessment techniques, including multiple-choice questions following a reading passage, and the use of machine learning models to score prosody from acoustic features of language. The system is also somewhat gamified to create a more enjoyable experience for students. Finally, a core principle of BalanceAI is scaffolding, which was discussed earlier in the context of dynamic assessment. Scaffolding is incorporated based on dynamic complexity theory (Larsen-Freeman, 2011; Wolf-Branigin, 2013) in which the goal is to promote students' intrinsic self-organizing agency. BalanceAI attempts to promote self-organization through iterative learning-oriented tasks that provide real-time feedback.

Challenges and Future Directions

In this chapter, based on the PALMER framework of assessment feedback, we examined how the six dimensions of assessment feedback, assessment purpose, agency, latency, mechanism, environment, and reference, influence the nature and effect of feedback. We further considered current research on diagnostic and dynamic assessment approaches designed to provide feedback for students and teachers in a technology-rich environment.

Despite the numerous benefits, research suggests that many teachers do not use information from assessment to its full potential, due to various factors (Bennett, 2011; Brookhart, 2013). These factors include a lack of time, a lack of training and professional development, a lack of resources, and a lack of support from school and district leaders (Brookhart, 2013; Heritage, 2010). One of the primary challenges teachers face is the lack of time to administer, score, and interpret formative assessments (Heritage, 2010). For example, it requires time to create and administer assessment activities, which can be a challenge for teachers who are already facing significant time constraints. Some formative assessment approaches require specialized tools or technologies, which may be beyond the budget or resources available for teachers. Teachers also struggle to interpret the data they collect through formative assessment and use that data to improve instruction.

Lastly, teachers may also face resistance or pushback from students or parents who are not familiar with formative assessment practices (Brookhart, 2013). Implementing formative assessment may require a shift in teaching practices or school culture, which can be difficult to achieve if teachers or administrators are resistant to change. Despite these challenges, many teachers continue to use formative assessment as a tool for providing feedback to students. By addressing these challenges proactively and finding ways to integrate formative assessment into their instructional practices, teachers can reap the benefits of this powerful tool.

Teachers can be supported in several ways to overcome the challenges in implementing formative assessment and maximizing the effect of feedback in their classrooms. As we discussed in this chapter, some of those challenges can be addressed by leveraging technology to automate some aspects of the formative assessment process. In recent years, technology has been increasingly used to facilitate assessment by automated data processing and scoring, allowing teachers to focus on interpreting the data and using feedback for instructional decisions. Technology can be used to provide teachers with real-time feedback on student learning, which is a critical aspect of effective formative assessment. Specifically, machine learning can also be leveraged to provide teachers with automated feedback on student learning based on their responses to formative assessments. Overall, there is limited research on how technology can enhance classroom formative assessment and its pedagogical impact on students' learning and motivation. We encourage further research in this emerging area to advance our understanding.

Discussion Questions

1. Generating and delivering feedback is an essential component of teachers' language assessment competence. How can PALMER be used to advance teachers' language assessment competence in 21st-century technology-rich classrooms?

2. Continual technological progress, such as generative AI, reshapes and expands language assessment practices. How do they enhance the nature and utilization of assessment feedback? What potential issues might arise from integrating advanced technological innovations into assessments?

350 Chapter 24 Diagnostic Assessment Feedback

References

Alderson, J. C. (2005). *Diagnosing foreign language proficiency: The interface between learning and assessment.* Continuum.

Ames, C. (1992). Classrooms: goals, structures, and student motivation. *Journal of Educational Psychology, 84,* 261–271. https://doi.org/10.1037/0022-0663.84.3.261.

Attali, Y., & Burstein, J. (2006). Automated essay scoring with e-rater® V.2. *The Journal of Technology, Learning and Assessment, 4*(3), 3. https://ejournals.bc.edu/index.php/jtla/article/view/1650.

Bachman, L. F., & Palmer, A. S. (2010). *Language assessment in practice: Developing language assessments and justifying their use in the real world.* Oxford University Press.

Bandura, A. (1999). Social cognitive theory of personality. In D. Cervone & Y. Shoda (Eds.), *The coherence of personality: Social-cognitive bases of consistency, variability, and organization* (pp. 185–241). Guilford Press.

Barringer, C., & Gholson, B. (1979). Effects of type and combination of feedback upon conceptual learning by children: implications for research in academic learning. *Review of Educational Research, 49*(3), 459–478. https://doi.org/10.3102/00346543049003459.

Bennett, R. E. (2011). Formative assessment: a critical review. *Assessment in Education: Principles, Policy & Practice, 18*(1), 5–25. https://doi.org/10.1080/0969594X.2010.513678.

Berliner, D. C. (1985). Effective classroom teaching: the necessary but not sufficient condition for developing exemplary schools. In G. R. Austin & H. Garber (Eds.), *Research on exemplary schools* (pp. 127–155). Academic Press. https://doi.org/10.1016/B978-0-12-068590-5.50013-9.

Bitchener, J., Young, S., & Cameron, D. (2005). The effect of different types of corrective feedback on ESL student writing. *Journal of Second Language Writing, 14,* 191–205. https://doi.org/10.1016/j.jslw.2005.08.001.

Black, P., & Wiliam, D. (1998). Assessment and classroom learning. *Assessment in Education: Principles, Policy & Practice, 5*(1), 7–74. https://doi.org/10.1080/0969595980050102.

Brookhart, S. M. (2008). *How to give effective feedback to your students.* ASCD.

Brookhart, S. M. (2013). *How to create and use rubrics for formative assessment and grading.* ASCD. https://doi.org/10.4135/9781452218649.n15.

Burstein, J., Tetreault, J., Chodorow, M., & Blanchard, D. (2013). Automated evaluation of discourse coherence quality in essay writing. In M. D. Shermis & J. Burstein (Eds.), *Handbook of automated essay evaluation* (pp. 289–302). Routledge. https://doi.org/10.4324/9780203122761.

Butler, D. L., & Winne, P. H. (1995). Feedback and self-regulated learning: a theoretical synthesis. *Review of Educational Research, 65*(3), 245–281. https://doi.org/10.3102/00346543065003245.

Correnti, R., Matsumura, L. C., Wang, E., Litman, D., Rahimi, Z., & Kisa, Z. (2020). Automated scoring of students' use of text evidence in writing. *Reading Research Quarterly, 55*(3), 493–520. https://doi.org/10.1002/rrq.281.

Cucchiarini, C., Neri, A., & Strik, H. (2009). Oral proficiency training in Dutch L2: the contribution of ASR-based corrective feedback. *Speech Communication, 51*(10), 853–863. https://doi.org/10.1016/j.specom.2009.03.003.

Culham, R. (2003). *6+1 traits of writing: The complete guide grades 3 and up.* Scholastic. https://www.scholastic.com/teachers/teaching-tools/articles/6-1-traits-of-writing--the-complete-guide--grades-3-and-up.html.

von Davier, M., & Lee, Y. S. (2019). Introduction: from latent classes to cognitive diagnostic models. In M. von Davier & Y. S. Lee (Eds.), *Handbook of diagnostic classification models, methodology of educational measurement and assessment* (pp. 1–17). Springer. https://doi.org/10.1007/978-3-030-05584-4_1.

Dicheva, D., Dichev, C., Agre, G., & Angelova, G. (2015). Gamification in education: A systematic mapping study. *Journal of Educational Technology & Society, 18*(3), 75–88.

Duckworth, A. L., Peterson, C., Matthews, M. D., & Kelly, D. R. (2007). Grit: perseverance and passion for long-term goals. *Journal of Personality and Social Psychology, 92*(6), 1087–1101. https://doi.org/10.1037/0022-3514.92.6.1087.

Dweck, C. S. (1986). Motivational processes affecting learning. *American Psychologist, 41,* 1040–1048. https://doi.org/10.1037/0003-066X.41.10.1040.

Dweck, C. S. (2007). Self-theories: the mindset of a champion. In P. T. Morris & S. Gordon (Eds.), *Sport and exercise psychology: International perspectives.* Fitness Information Technology.

References   351

Effatpanah, F., Baghaei, P., & Boori, A. A. (2019). Diagnosing EFL learners' writing ability: a diagnostic classification modeling analysis. *Language Testing in Asia*, 9, 1–23. https://doi.org/10.1186/s40468-019-0090-y.

Ferris, D. R. (2002). *Treatment of error in second language student writing*. University of Michigan Press.

Ferris, D. R. (2003). *Response to student writing: Implications for second language students*. Routledge.

Ferris, D. R. (2010). Second language writing research and written corrective feedback in SLA: intersections and practical applications. *Studies in Second Language Acquisition*, 32(2), 181–201. https://doi.org/10.1017/S0272263109990490.

Ferris, D., & Roberts, B. (2001). Error feedback in L2 writing classes: how explicit does it need to be? *Journal of Second Language Writing*, 10, 161–184. https://doi.org/10.1016/S1060-3743(01)00039-X.

Foltz, P. W. (2020). Practical considerations for using AI models in automated scoring of writing. In H. Jiao & R. W. Lissitz (Eds.), *Application of artificial intelligence to assessment* (pp. 101–113). Information Age Publishing, Inc.

Franco, H., Bratt, H., Rossier, R., Rao Gadde, V., Shriberg, E., Abrash, V., & Precoda, K. (2010). EduSpeak®: a speech recognition and pronunciation scoring toolkit for computer-aided language learning applications. *Language Testing*, 27(3), 401–418. https://doi.org/10.1177/0265532210364408.

Fulcher, G., & Davidson, F. (2007). *Language testing and assessment: An advanced resource book*. Routledge. https://doi.org/10.4324/9780203449066.

Goldstein, L. M. (2001). For Kyla: what does the research say about responding to student writers. In T. Silva & P. K. Matsuda (Eds.), *On second language writing* (pp. 73–89). Lawrence Erlbaum Associates.

Gu, L., Davis, L., Tao, J., & Zechner, K. (2021). Using spoken language technology for generating feedback to prepare for the TOEFL iBT® test: a user perception study. *Assessment in Education: Principles, Policy & Practice*, 28(1), 58–76. https://doi.org/10.1080/0969594X.2020.1735995.

Guo, Q., Feng, R., & Hua, Y. (2022). How effectively can EFL students use automated written corrective feedback (AWCF) in research writing? *Computer Assisted Language Learning*, 35(9), 2312–2331. https://doi.org/10.1080/09588221.2021.1879161.

Hannah, L., Jang, E. E., Shah, M., & Gupta, V. (2023). Validity arguments for automated essay scoring of young students' writing traits. *Language Assessment Quarterly*, 20(4–5), 399–420. https://doi.org/10.1080/15434303.2023.2288253.

Hannah, L., Kim, H., & Jang, E. E. (2022). Investigating the effects of task type and linguistic background on accuracy in automated speech recognition systems: Implications for use in language assessment of young learners. *Language Assessment Quarterly*, 19(3), 289–313. https://doi.org/10.1080/15434303.2022.2038172.

Hargreaves, A. (2020). Large-scale assessments and their effects: the case of mid-stakes tests in Ontario. *Journal of Educational Change*, 21, 393–420. https://doi.org/10.1007/s10833-020-09380-5.

Hattie, J., & Timperley, H. (2007). The power of feedback. *Review of Educational Research*, 77(1), 81–112. https://doi.org/10.3102/003465430298487.

Hedgcock, J., & Lefkowitz, N. (1996). Some input on input: two analyses of student response to expert feedback on L2 writing. *Modern Language Journal*, 80, 287–308. https://doi.org/10.1111/j.1540-4781.1996.tb01612.x.

Heritage, M. (2010). *Formative assessment and next-generation assessment systems: Are we losing an opportunity?* National Center for Research on Evaluation, Standards, and Student Testing.

Hyland, K., & Hyland, F. (2006a). Contexts and issues in feedback on L2 writing: an introduction. In K. Hyland & F. Hyland (Eds.), *Feedback in second language writing: Contexts and issues* (pp. 1–20). Cambridge University Press. https://doi.org/10.1017/CBO9781139524742.003.

Hyland, K., & Hyland, F. (2006b). Interpersonal aspects of response: constructing and interpreting teacher written feedback. In K. Hyland & F. Hyland (Eds.), *Feedback in second language writing: Contexts and issues* (pp. 206–224). Cambridge University Press. https://doi.org/10.1017/CBO9781139524742.

Jang, E. E. (2005). *A validity narrative: The effects of cognitive reading skills diagnosis on ESL adult learners' reading comprehension ability in the context of Next Generation TOEFL* [Unpublished doctoral dissertation]. University of Illinois at Urbana Champaign.

Jang, E. E. (2008). A framework for cognitive diagnostic assessment. In C. A. Chapelle, Y. R. Chung & J. Xu (Eds.), *Towards adaptive CALL: Natural language processing for diagnostic language assessment* (pp. 117–131). Iowa State University.

352 Chapter 24 Diagnostic Assessment Feedback

Jang, E. E. (2010). Demystifying a Q-matrix for making diagnostic inferences about L2 reading skills: the author responds. *Language Assessment Quarterly*, 7, 116–117. https://doi.org/10.1080/15434300903559225.

Jang, E. E., Dunlop, M., Park, G., & van der Boom, E. H. (2015). How do young students with different profiles of reading skill mastery, perceived ability, and goal orientation respond to holistic diagnostic feedback? *Language Testing*, 32(3), 359–383. https://doi.org/10.1177/0265532215570924.

Jang, E. E., Hunte, M., Barron, C., & Hannah, L. (2023). Exploring the role of self-regulation in young learners' writing assessment and intervention using BalanceAI automated diagnostic feedback. In K. Sadeghi & D. Douglas (Eds.), *Fundamental Considerations in Technology Mediated Language Assessment*. Routledge. https://doi.org/10.4324/9781003292395-4.

Jarmer, D., Kozol, M., Nelson, S., & Salsberry, T. (2000). Six-trait writing model improves scores at Jennie Wilson elementary. *Journal of School Improvement*, 1(2), 29–32. https://doi.org/10.5539/elt.v11n9p68.

Ke, Z., & Ng, V. (2019). *Automated essay scoring: a survey of the state of the art*. Proceedings of 28th international joint conference on artificial intelligence, pp. 6300–6308. https://doi.org/10.24963/ijcai.2019/879

Kellogg, R. T., Whiteford, A. P., & Quinlan, T. (2010). Does automated feedback help students learn to write? *Journal of Educational Computing Research*, 42(2), 173–196. https://doi.org/10.2190/EC.42.2.c.

Kim, A.-Y. (2015). Exploring ways to provide diagnostic feedback with an ESL placement test: Cognitive diagnostic assessment of L2 reading ability. *Language Testing*, 32(2), 227–258. https://doi.org/10.1177/0265532214558457.

Kim, Y. (2010). *An argument-based validity inquiry into the empirically-derived descriptor-based diagnostic (EDD) assessment in ESL academic writing* [Unpublished doctoral dissertation]. University of Toronto.

Kletzien, S., & Bednar, M. (1990). Dynamic assessment for at-risk readers. *Journal of Reading*, 33(7), 528–533.

Kluger, A. N., & DeNisi, A. (1996). The effects of feedback interventions on performance: a historical review, a meta-analysis, and a preliminary feedback intervention theory. *Psychological Bulletin*, 119(2), 254–284. https://doi.org/10.1037/0033-2909.119.2.254.

Koltovskaia, S. (2020). Student engagement with automated written corrective feedback (AWCF) provided by Grammarly: a multiple case study. *Assessing Writing*, 44, 100450. https://doi.org/10.1016/j.asw.2020.100450.

Koskey, K. L. K., & Shermis, M. D. (2013). Scaling and norming for automated essay scoring. In *Handbook of automated essay evaluation* (pp. 221–242). Routledge. https://doi.org/10.4324/9780203122761.

Kozulin, A., & Garb, E. (2004). Dynamic assessment of literacy: English as a third language. *European Journal of Psychology of Education*, 19(1), 65–77. https://doi.org/10.1007/BF03173237.

Kruger, J., & Dunning, D. (1999). Unskilled and unaware of it: how difficulties in recognizing one's own incompetence lead to inflated self-assessments. *Journal of Personality and Social Psychology*, 77, 1121–1134. https://doi.org/10.1037/0022-3514.77.6.1121.

Kumar, V. S., & Boulanger, D. (2021). Automated essay scoring and the deep learning black box: how are rubric scores determined? *International Journal of Artificial Intelligence in Education*, 31(3), 538–584. https://doi.org/10.1007/s40593-020-00211-5.

Lantolf, J. P., & Poehner, M. E. (2004). Dynamic assessment: bringing the past into the future. *Journal of Applied Linguistics*, 1, 49–74. https://doi.org/10.1558/japl.1.1.49.55872.

Larsen-Freeman, D. (2011). A complexity theory approach to second language development/acquisition. In D. Atkinson (Ed.), *Alternative approaches to second language acquisition* (pp. 60–84). Routledge. https://doi.org/10.4324/9780203830932-8.

Lee, I. (2003). L2 writing teachers' perspectives, practices and problems regarding error feedback. *Assessing Writing*, 8(3), 216–237. https://doi.org/10.1016/j.asw.2003.08.002.

Lee, K., Kweon, S., Lee, S., Noh, H., & Lee, G. G. (2014). POSTECH immersive English study (POMY): dialog-based language learning game. *IEICE Transactions on Information and Systems*, E97.D(7), 1830–1841. https://doi.org/10.1587/transinf.E97.D.1830.

Lee, Y.-W., & Sawaki, Y. (2009). Application of three cognitive diagnosis models to ESL reading and listening assessments. *Language Assessment Quarterly*, 6(3), 239–263. https://doi.org/10.1080/15434300903079562

Li, H., Hunter, C. V., & Lei, P. W. (2016). The selection of cognitive diagnostic models for a reading comprehension test. *Language Testing*, 33(3), 391–409. https://doi.org/10.1177/0265532215590848.

Lyster, R., & Ranta, L. (1997). Corrective feedback and learner uptake: negotiation of form in communicative classrooms. *Studies in Second Language Acquisition*, 19, 37–66. https://doi.org/10.1017/S0272263197001034.

Mao, L., Liu, O. L., Roohr, K., Belur, V., Mulholland, M., Lee, H.-S., & Pallant, A. (2018). Validation of automated scoring for a formative assessment that employs scientific argumentation. *Educational Assessment, 23*(2), 121–138. https://doi.org/10.1080/10627197.2018.1427570.

Metcalfe, J., Kornell, N., & Finn, B. (2009). Delayed versus immediate feedback in children's and adults' vocabulary learning. *Memory & Cognition, 37*(8), 1077–1087. https://doi.org/10.3758/MC.37.8.1077.

Min, S., Cai, H., & He, L. (2022). Application of bi-factor MIRT and higher-order CDM models to an in-house EFL listening test for diagnostic purposes. *Language Assessment Quarterly, 19*(2), 189–213. https://doi.org/10.1080/15434303.2021.1980571.

Minick, N. (1987). Implications of Vygotsky's theory for dynamic assessment. In C. Lidz (Ed.), *Dynamic assessment* (pp. 116–140). Guilford Press.

Nelson, G., & Carson, J. (2006). Cultural issues in peer response: revisiting 'culture'. In K. Hyland & F. Hyland (Eds.), *Feedback in second language writing: Contexts and issues* (pp. 42–59). Cambridge. https://doi.org/10.1017/CBO9781139524742.005.

Rahimi, Z., Litman, D., Correnti, R., Wang, E., & Matsumura, L. C. (2017). Assessing students' use of evidence and organization in response-to-text writing: using natural language processing for rubric-based automated scoring. *International Journal of Artificial Intelligence in Education, 27*(4), 694–728. https://doi.org/10.1007/s40593-017-0143-2.

Ravand, H., & Robitzsch, A. (2018). Cognitive diagnostic model of best choice: a study of reading comprehension. *Educational Psychology, 38*(10), 1255–1277. https://doi.org/10.1080/01443410.2018.1489524.

Richards, J. C. (1990). The dilemma of teacher education in second language teaching. In J. C. Richards & D. Nunan (Eds.), *Second language teacher education* (pp. 3–15). Cambridge University Press.

Sessoms, J., & Henson, R. A. (2018). Applications of diagnostic classification models: a literature review and critical commentary. *Measurement: Interdisciplinary Research and Perspectives, 16*(1), 1–17. https://doi.org/10.1080/15366367.2018.1435104.

Sheen, Y. (2004). Corrective feedback and learner uptake in communicative classrooms across instructional settings. *Language Teaching Research, 8*(3), 263–300. https://doi.org/10.1191/1362168804lr146oa.

Shepard, L. A. (2000). The role of assessment in a learning culture. *Educational Researcher, 29*(7), 4–14. https://doi.org/10.3102/0013189X029007004.

Shintani, N., Aubrey, S., & Donnellan, M. (2016). The effects of pre-task and post-task metalinguistic explanations on accuracy in second language writing. *TESOL Quarterly, 50*(4), 945–955. https://doi.org/10.1002/tesq.323.

Shute, V. J. (2008). Focus on formative feedback. *Review of Educational Research, 78*(1), 153–189. https://doi.org/10.3102/0034654307313795.

Sully de Luque, M. F., & Sommer, S. M. (2000). The impact of culture on feedback-seeking behavior: an integrated model and propositions. *Academy of Management Review, 25*, 829–849. https://doi.org/10.2307/259209.

Toprak, T. E., & Cakir, A. (2021). Examining the L2 reading comprehension ability of adult ELLs: developing a diagnostic test within the cognitive diagnostic assessment framework. *Language Testing, 38*(1), 106–131. https://doi.org/10.1177/0265532220941470.

de Vries, B. P., Cucchiarini, C., Bodnar, S., Strik, H., & van Hout, R. (2015). Spoken grammar practice and feedback in an ASR-based CALL system. *Computer Assisted Language Learning, 28*(6), 550–576. https://doi.org/10.1080/09588221.2014.889713.

Vygotsky, L. (1986). *Thought and language*. MIT Press.

Weigle, S. C. (2013). English as a second language writing and automated essay evaluation. In *Handbook of automated essay evaluation* (pp. 58–76). Routledge. https://doi.org/10.4324/9780203122761.

Wilson, J., & Czik, A. (2016). Automated essay evaluation software in English language arts classrooms: effects on teacher feedback, student motivation, and writing quality. *Computers & Education, 100*, 94–109. https://doi.org/10.1016/j.compedu.2016.05.004.

Wolf-Branigin, M. (2013). *Using complexity theory for research and program evaluation*. Oxford University Press.

Xi, X., Zechner, K., & Bejar, I. (2006). *Extracting meaningful speech features to support diagnostic feedback: An ECD approach to automated scoring*. San Francisco, CA, USA: Annual Meeting of National Council on Measurement in Education.

Xie, Q. (2017). Diagnosing university students' academic writing in English: is cognitive diagnostic modelling the way forward? *Educational Psychology, 37*(1), 26–47. https://doi.org/10.1080/01443410.2016.1202900.

354 **Chapter 24** Diagnostic Assessment Feedback

Yi, Y. S. (2017). Probing the relative importance of different attributes in L2 reading and listening comprehension items: an application of cognitive diagnostic models. *Language Testing, 34*(3), 337–355. https://doi.org/10.1177/0265532216646141.

Zechner, K., & Loukina, A. (2020). Automated scoring of extended spontaneous speech. In D. Yan, A. A. Rupp & P. W. Foltz (Eds.), *Handbook of automated scoring* (pp. 365–382). Chapman and Hall/CRC. https://doi.org/10.1201/9781351264808-20.

Zhang, S. (2021). Review of automated writing evaluation systems. *Journal of China Computer-Assisted Language Learning, 1*(1), 170–176. https://doi.org/10.1515/jccall-2021-2007.

Ziman, K., Heusser, A. C., Fitzpatrick, P. C., Field, C. E., & Manning, J. R. (2018). Is automatic speech-to-text transcription ready for use in psychological experiments? *Behavior Research Methods, 50*(6), 2597–2605. https://doi.org/10.3758/s13428-018-1037-4.

Zimmerman, B. J., & Moylan, A. R. (2009). Self-regulation: where metacognition and motivation intersect. In D. J. Hacker, J. Dunlosky & A. C. Graesser (Eds.), *Handbook of metacognition in education* (pp. 299–315). Routledge/Taylor & Francis Group.

Zimmerman, B. J., & Schunk, D. H. (Eds.). (2011). *Handbook of self-regulation of learning and performance*. Routledge/Taylor & Francis Group.

Suggested Readings

Gu, L., Davis, L., Tao, J., & Zechner, K. (2021). Using spoken language technology for generating feedback to prepare for the TOEFL iBT® test: a user perception study. *Assessment in Education: Principles, Policy & Practice, 28*(1), 58–76. https://doi.org/10.1080/0969594X.2020.1735995.

Hattie, J., & Timperley, H. (2007). The power of feedback. *Review of Educational Research, 77*(1), 81–112. https://doi.org/10.3102/003465430298487.

Jang, E. E., & Sinclair, J. (2021). Diagnostic assessment in language classrooms. In G. Fulcher & L. Harding (Eds.), *The Routledge handbook of language testing* (pp. 187–205). Routledge.

Lee, Y. W. (2015). Diagnosing diagnostic language assessment. *Language Testing, 32*(3), 299–316. https://doi.org/10.1177/0265532214565387.

CHAPTER 25

Evolution and Future Trends in Tests of English for University Admissions

Xiaoming Xi, Brent Bridgeman, and Cathy Wendler

Introduction

For more than a century, applicants to universities have been tested to gauge their level of subject matter knowledge, reasoning ability, and level of proficiency in specific areas considered important by the university. Admissions tests are used to determine whether applicants have the requisite level of certain knowledge, skills, and abilities deemed necessary for success at the institution.

In this chapter, we first present a brief historical overview of the origins and development of tests of English for academic purposes (EAP) used for admissions. This overview is followed by a discussion of current trends in EAP tests in defining and operationalizing test constructs, test delivery methods, scoring methods and technologies, and score reporting and interpretation. In this discussion, emphasis is placed on validation research associated with EAP tests for admissions. Finally, we conclude with a discussion of research and development issues and future trends.

The History and Growth of EAP Tests in Higher Education Admissions

Measuring the language proficiency of applicants to postsecondary institutions is now a well-established practice. One of the earliest admissions tests for speakers of other languages, the Cambridge English Proficiency Exam, was introduced in 1913 by the University of Cambridge. However, given the relatively small number of international students, few other institutions screened non-native English speakers at that time.

In the early days of the United States, admissions tests were unique to the institutions that created them. Due to disparities across tests at different institutions, the College Entrance Examination Board was formed in 1900 to establish more uniform standards for admission to American institutions. The development and use of standard admissions tests continued to expand during the 20th century, focusing on applicants' knowledge in specific subjects and on

---

The Concise Companion to Language Assessment, First Edition. Edited by Antony John Kunnan.
© 2025 John Wiley & Sons, Inc. Published 2025 by John Wiley & Sons, Inc.

356 Chapter 25 Evolution and Future Trends in Tests of English

verbal and quantitative reasoning skills. The SAT® and its derivatives were administered beginning in 1926, the American College Test (ACT®) in 1959, and the Graduate Record Examinations (GRE®) in 1949. The 20th century also saw continued growth in student diversity in higher education, with more and more international students seeking admissions.

In 1961, the National Council on the Testing of English as a Foreign Language, comprising of representatives from 30 governmental and private organizations, was formed to address the issue of English proficiency for non-native speakers of English applying to U.S. institutions. Ultimately, the Council recommended creating an English proficiency examination. In 1964, the first large-scale test measuring the English proficiency of non-native English speakers, the Test of English as a Foreign Language (TOEFL®), was introduced.

Since the late 1970s, with gradually increasing numbers of graduate students seeking university education in English-speaking contexts, the landscape of EAP testing at the tertiary level has changed significantly. The TOEFL test has gone through major revisions to respond to test-user demands and continuing developments in theories and practices of language learning, teaching, and testing. Until 1979, the TOEFL test included reading, listening, and structure and written expression. With the emergence of communicative language teaching (CLT) in the 1980s, the Test of Spoken English (TSE) was introduced into the TOEFL suite in 1979 and the Test of Written English (TWE) added to the TOEFL test in 1986. The computer-based TOEFL was created in 1998 and included reading, listening, and writing sections. In 2005, a completely redesigned TOEFL Internet-based test (iBT™) debuted. The TOEFL iBT tasks assess reading, writing, listening, and speaking in more authentic communication contexts that require the ability to use multiple language skills in an integrated fashion.

Institutions in other English-speaking countries also called for English proficiency tests for non-native students. In the mid-1960s, the English Proficiency Test Battery (EPTB) was introduced for screening applicants to institutions in the United Kingdom. In 1980, the EPTB was replaced by the English Language Testing Service (ELTS), and in 1989 the ELTS was replaced by the International English Language Testing System (IELTS). Changes to the content, format, and delivery mode were introduced to IELTS during its growth spurts between 1995 and 2005. In 1995, the three field-specific reading and writing modules were replaced by one academic reading module and one academic writing module (Charge & Taylor, 1997; Clapham, 1996). The revised IELTS Speaking Test was introduced in 2001, and a computer-based IELTS test for reading, listening, and writing was piloted in 2005 at several test centers and is now offered worldwide along with the paper-based version.

A more recent addition is the Pearson Test of English (PTE) Academic introduced in 2010, a computer-based test (CBT) that assesses reading, listening, speaking, and writing that is scored using automated scoring engines exclusively.

Two newer entrants to the admissions space include the Duolingo English Test (DET) introduced in 2016, and a recent player, the PSI Skills for English tests. The DET was introduced as a remote-proctored test consisting of machine-generated discrete items only that were not representative of the language skills essential in the academic domain (see Wagner & Kunnan, 2015). It experienced rapid growth during the COVID pandemic due to unavailability of other well-known admissions tests, which has provided impetus for its test revisions in the last few years to include more item types relevant to the measurement of some productive language skills scored by the machine. The PSI Skills for English is a suite of English proficiency tests used for work, study, travel, and residency purposes created through a partnership between the Scottish Qualifications Authority (SQA) and PSI. The tests are designed as multilevel tests corresponding to CEFR levels. The tests at B2 and above include all four skills, at A1, A2 listening and speaking only, and at B1, options for examinees to take a four-skill or a two-skill test.

Some locally developed English tests are also accepted for college admissions both locally and internationally. An example is the Hong Kong Diploma of Secondary Education (HKDSE)

English Language Test, which is locally developed and administered in Hong Kong but is accepted by a few hundred academic institutions around the world. It includes four sections, reading, writing, listening and integrated skills, and speaking, and is the only admissions test that uses a group discussion format to assess speaking. The integrated skills tasks integrate reading, listening, and writing skills, where examinees are expected to produce short to extended writing outputs. The topics across the four papers cover a range of subdomains such as school, general training, and social–interpersonal contexts. Another unique design feature is the incorporation of School-based Assessment (SBA) administered by schools with guidance and score moderation from the test developer for all school candidates into the final score with a weight of 15%, which takes the form of a group interaction and an individual presentation.

Current Trends of EAP Testing in Higher Education Admissions

This section discusses current trends associated with EAP tests for higher education admissions. It focuses on approaches to operationalizing test constructs, test delivery mode, scoring methods and technologies, and score reporting and interpretation.

Test Constructs and Approaches to Operationalization

The definition of constructs for academic English proficiency tests should draw on an analysis of the target language use domain of English-medium institutions. Based on analyses of the English language knowledge, skills, and abilities required for success in academic studies and typically encountered instructional tasks and materials (see Bridgeman & Carlson, 1984; Hale et al., 1996; Rosenfeld et al., 2001), the TOEFL iBT captures three subdomains of English language use: *general academic, navigational,* and *social/interpersonal,* with emphasis on general academic use contexts (see Xi et al., 2021). The reading and writing sections primarily use materials on general academic course content, and argumentative texts are used as stimulus materials, whereas the listening and speaking sections include general academic course, university environment navigational, and everyday familiar topics. The IELTS Academic Module includes academic reading, academic writing, general listening, and general speaking. The materials used in academic reading are for a nonspecialist audience and written in narrative, descriptive, or argumentative styles. Academic writing focuses on general academic materials. General listening uses materials on everyday social situations and general educational and training contexts. General speaking elicits conversations, brief presentations, and discussions about everyday familiar topics. Overall, the IELTS Academic Module puts less emphasis on using academic content materials. The PTE Academic uses reading and listening materials for both academic work and extracurricular activities on a university campus (e.g., dealing with university administration). For the PSI Skills for English, the tests for CEFR levels B1 and higher include more tasks that are relevant to the academic domain while the lower levels use more social interpersonal contexts. Most of the DET tasks target the social language use domain, rather than the academic domain. The HSDSE English Language test uses tasks that are mostly on school, social, and general academic contexts.

It is now common practice for communicative language tests to assess all four modalities, but a growing trend is the use of integrated tasks that require the use of multiple skills to complete test tasks successfully. The extensive use of tasks that integrate language skills in the writing and speaking sections is a key feature of the TOEFL iBT test. Separate reading and listening sections that primarily use selected response items provide distinct measures of reading and listening abilities. This test design approach reflects the integrated nature of

358 Chapter 25 Evolution and Future Trends in Tests of English

language use while yielding relatively distinct measures of reading, listening, speaking, and writing. The PTE Academic has also adopted this practice of using some integrated tasks that require summarization of written or spoken texts. The PSI Skills for English speaking tests integrate listening and speaking skills. The HKDSE English Language exam has a Listening and Integrated Skills section that normally includes three tasks requiring examinees to listen to and/or read and produce written outputs. However, IELTS reading and writing have moved away from this practice in order not to confuse the measurement of abilities associated with different modalities, removing the thematic link between reading and writing tasks (see University of Cambridge ESOL Examinations, 2012). DET does not use any integrated tasks.

Test Delivery and Administration Mode

Most EAP tests for admissions are offered in a computer-based mode with some supporting parallel paper- and computer-based administrations. The TOEFL CBT introduced in 1998 was the first large-scale computer-based EAP test. The TOEFL iBT, an Internet-based test, was introduced in 2005. IELTS has followed a similar path: It started as a paper-based test under the name of ELTS in 1980 and launched a CBT for its reading, listening, and writing sections in 2005 (see Maycock & Green, 2005), with its paper-based test remaining as the dominant delivery mode. The PTE Academic and DET, as the newer additions, were launched as a CBT in 2010 and 2016, respectively. The PSI Skills for English tests are offered as a CBT test as well. The HKDSE English Language test has remained paper-based since its introduction in 2012, although pilot studies have been conducted on the use of video conferencing technology for administering the group discussion speaking test (Smart et al., 2024).

A noteworthy development in the administration model is at-home administration utilizing remote proctoring technologies. DET uses human proctors to review recordings of at-home test sessions post hoc, and TOEFL, PTE Academic, and PSI Skills for English tests use artificial intelligence (AI) technology and live online proctors to monitor the test-taking process of at-home examinees.

Scoring Technologies

The use of automated technologies in scoring constructed response tasks has been a major trend in EAP testing for admissions in recent years. For example, TOEFL iBT uses automated scoring engines as the second rater to score writing and as the sole rater for the independent speaking tasks and the second rater for the integrated tasks. PTE Academic and DET, on the other hand, are fully automated, using natural language processing (NLP) and speech technologies to score writing and speaking. PSI Skills for English tests and the HKDSE English Language test use human raters solely to score writing and speaking.

Score Reporting and Interpretation

Although large-scale EAP admissions testing is moving toward the use of integrated tasks that engage multiple modalities of language, current score-reporting practices conform to the traditional partition of reading, listening, speaking, and writing. Essentially, TOEFL iBT, IELTS, and PTE Academic report scores on each modality in addition to a total score. For TOEFL iBT, this practice has been motivated by theoretical expectations that reading, listening, writing, and speaking skills are distinct and supported by empirical research that shows the scores on the four modalities still emerge as separate factors, although loading on an overall language ability factor (see Sawaki et al., 2009). IELTS reports a band-level score for each modality and an overall band level (1–9). The PTE Academic test also reports scores on a

10–90-point scale for enabling skills including, for example, grammar, oral fluency, pronunciation, spelling, vocabulary, and written discourse (Pearson Education, 2010b). DET reports a total score of 10–160 with 5 points increment and sub-scores of literacy, comprehension, conversation, and production on the same scale, with overlapping skills among them. The PSI Skills for English tests adopt an interesting reporting approach, providing pass/fail distinctions for CEFR C1, C2, and A1 and A2 tests, and finer-grained distinctions of pass/pass with merit/fail for CEFR B1 and B2 level tests (https://skillsforenglish.com/test/). The HKDSE English Language test is reported on a 5-level scale for both the total and section scores, with a very small proportion at 5* and 5** levels.

Using performance descriptors is another characteristic. The TOEFL iBT score reports for examinees, for example, include performance feedback on each modality, which provides descriptions of language competencies for typical students at three to four levels. The levels and associated performance descriptors were derived using scale anchoring research for reading and listening (see Gomez et al., 2007), and through summarizing the typical characteristics of samples at different score levels for writing and speaking. The IELTS test provides band-level scores (0–9) with half-point bands and a brief performance descriptor for each whole-score band. The PTE Academic score report does not provide detailed performance descriptors. DET provides very brief descriptors for the total scores. The PSI Skills for English tests include multilevel tests corresponding to various CEFR levels, using adapted CEFR level descriptors as the performance descriptors. The HKDSE English Language test provides descriptors in reading, listening and integrated skills, speaking, and writing, respectively, corresponding to the standards for the five levels (https://www.hkeaa.edu.hk/en/hkdse/hkdse_subj.html?A1&1&2_4).

Another major trend in score interpretation is linking test scores to the Common European Framework of Reference for Languages (CEFR). The intention is to provide a common set of benchmarks for test users to select the appropriate cut scores on each test. Almost all EAP test providers have published information on how their test score levels correspond roughly to CEFR levels, as well as methodologies and results of their CEFR linking studies (e.g., Lim et al., 2012; Pearson Education, 2010a), and the PSI Skill for English tests are designed to be pegged to the CEFR levels.

Current Research

This chapter focuses on the validation of the fundamental claim made by EAP tests used for admissions that the test scores are relevant and useful for making admissions decisions.

One of the clearest links between theory and practice is the argument-based approach to validation developed by Kane (2006). Following Kane's approach and Chapelle's (2008) extension of Kane's work, we use validity inferences to organize exemplary research studies related to tests for admissions purposes.

Domain Description

The domain description is based on the warrant that test tasks represent relevant knowledge, skills, and abilities in the target domain of academic discourse in an English-medium university. Support for this warrant should show the link between the critical language tasks and skills in the target use domain and the test tasks. In the late 1970s and 1980s, linguists emphasized the importance of communicative competence, and not merely knowledge of grammar rules, for success in the classroom (e.g., Munby, 1978), and this insight heavily influenced the development of the first IELTS test. The development of the IELTS as a four-skill test was influenced by the work of Munby as well as by EAP teachers, language testers, applied linguists, and score users (see Milanovic & Saville, 1996).

360 Chapter 25 Evolution and Future Trends in Tests of English

The communicative competence movement also influenced the development of the TOEFL in the late 1970s and 1980s with the addition of productive speaking and writing skills in the form of the TSE and TWE. In 2005, the TOEFL iBT was introduced as a four-skill test that makes extensive use of integrated tasks. The design of the new test was heavily influenced by needs analyses that identified the academic language tasks and skills deemed important for academic success in all four skill areas in tertiary classrooms (see Rosenfeld et al., 2001), and the work that was specifically targeted at identifying the types of writing tasks that were assigned in academic degree programs (see Bridgeman & Carlson, 1984; Hale et al., 1996).

Evaluation

The evaluation inference requires a link between the targeted abilities and the actual observed scores on the test. As noted by Chapelle et al. (2008), three assumptions about scoring, task administration conditions, and statistical properties need to be supported: (i) Rubrics for scoring responses are linked to the constructs of interest; (ii) task administration conditions elicit evidence of targeted language abilities; and (iii) the statistical characteristics of items, measures, and test forms support the intended decisions.

The kind of work needed to validate rubric development and rater training is illustrated by Bridges and Shaw (2004), who describe a revision project for the IELTS writing test. Based on the research, definitions were provided for five scoring criteria of writing, with descriptions for each criterion provided for each band level.

TOEFL iBT writing and speaking scoring rubrics were developed from research that examined the dimensions that raters attended to when scoring responses to prototype writing and speaking tasks (see Brown et al., 2005; Cumming et al., 2001, 2002). In addition, the task characteristics and scoring rubrics of writing and speaking tasks were modified based on the characteristics of the responses from the prototype studies and on raters' actual experience working with the preliminary scoring rubric (see Pearlman, 2008).

The PTE speaking and writing tasks are scored exclusively by machine. In order to accomplish this, rubrics had to first be developed for human scoring so that the human scores could be used to train the machine. The reliability of these human scores was demonstrated and the comparability of the human and machine scores established (see de Jong & Zheng, 2011). However, limited information has been provided on the automated features used and how they are combined to generate the automated scores for individual tasks in the test. It is therefore difficult to make fair evaluations of the extent to which automated scoring models capture targeted language abilities.

Evidence for the evaluation inference should also demonstrate the psychometric quality of the scores, including evidence that test tasks are at an appropriate difficulty level for the population and have the ability to meaningfully discriminate among different levels of examinee proficiency. Such data are critical during initial development and implementation (e.g., Chapelle et al., 2008; Clapham, 1996; Pearson Education, 2011). Because examinee populations and their test preparation strategies can change over time, the psychometric characteristics of test items must be continuously monitored, as initial positive results do not guarantee the maintenance of quality over time.

The HKDSE English Language test targets students with a wide range of ability levels. To ensure that statistical characteristics of test items and forms support the intended admissions decisions, two sections, Reading and Listening & Integrated Skills, allow examinees to select an easier or more difficult part in addition to a compulsory part and examinees can choose based on the advice of their teachers if they prefer (see Smart et al., 2014). This design feature allows the paper-based exam to better match examinees' levels with appropriate test difficulty levels, leading to reduced measurement errors for high- and low-level examinees and providing support for the evaluation inference. However, based on qualitative research, Tsang and Isaacs (2021) speculated that students' self-assessment of their levels with advice from their teachers may not be accurate and result in wrong choices for the test difficulty level. This could potentially yield increased measurement errors for these students and needs to be further investigated.

Another study investigated the group discussion task of the SBA of the HKDSE English Language test with extended (4–5 hours) versus limited planning time (10 minutes) (see Lam, 2019). Discourse analysis of candidates' speech suggested that extended planning may make the task less discriminating than limited planning, thus impacting the strength of the evaluation inference.

Generalization

Evidence is needed to support the warrant that scores on test tasks are good estimates of scores that would be received with comparable tasks, test forms, and rating conditions. There must be a sufficient number of tasks that are reliably scored so that parallel forms can be created and their comparability demonstrated.

Reliability is a deceptively complex concept, and it is easy to make inappropriate comparisons across tests that report "reliability" estimates, especially for constructed response tasks. Reliability estimates reported for constructed response tasks include inter-rater reliability (see University of Cambridge ESOL Examinations, 2006), Cronbach's alpha (see Pearson Education, 2011), test–retest reliability (Zhang, 2008), and reliability based on the generalizability theory that accounts for multiple sources of error such as errors associated with rater judgments and task variability (see Educational Testing Service, 2011; Lee & Kantor, 2005; Shaw, 2004; Taylor & Jones, 2001). When comparing reliability estimates, we should distinguish the different types discussed above, and in the case of reliability estimates based on G theory, we should look closely at the sources of measurement error modeled. For example, since the PTE Academic test is exclusively machine scored, the reliability of constructed response tasks concerns task variability only and is typically reported as Cronbach's alpha.

In general, these EAP tests report very high total score reliability in the range of 0.94–0.97 (see Educational Testing Service, 2011; Pearson Education, 2011; University of Cambridge ESOL Examinations, 2011).

Explanation

Evidence is needed to show that scores may be attributed to the target construct of academic language proficiency. This evidence may come in the form of test-taking processes and strategies or the factor structure of the test. Factor analyses of the TOEFL iBT indicate the presence of a strong general proficiency factor, with group factors for the four skills (see Sawaki et al., 2009). Investigations of the processes and strategies involved in responding to TOEFL iBT reading and speaking test tasks have revealed that they are meaningful and consistent with the test designers' expectations (Cohen & Upton, 2006; Swain et al., 2009). Through think-aloud and questionnaire responses, Bridges (2010) provided evidence that the cognitive processes used by examinees in responding to IELTS writing prompts reflect the kinds of processes important for academic writing. Using screen capture and stimulated recall techniques, Chan (2011) demonstrated that the written summarization and essay tasks in the PTE Academic test engage different cognitive processes, as expected in real-world academic writing tasks.

Extrapolation

Evidence is needed to support the warrant that the knowledge, skills, and abilities (KSAs) measured by the test are related to KSAs and language performance in the university context. Non-test data might include self-assessments, instructor judgments, or other relevant

362 Chapter 25 Evolution and Future Trends in Tests of English

indicators of language performance in an academic setting, or discourse produced in real-world academic contexts. Sawaki and Nissan (2009) provided evidence that TOEFL iBT listening scores were related to performance on listening tests created by subject matter experts using video-based academic lectures covering introductory topics in a few subjects. Weigle (2011) reported moderate relationships between TOEFL iBT writing scores and measures of writing proficiency in an academic context including instructor ratings of students' general writing proficiency and ratings of students' writing samples from a non-test environment. Bridgeman et al. (2012) found strong relationships between the scores assigned by TOEFL iBT speaking section raters and undergraduate students' comprehension and ratings of TOEFL iBT examinees' speech samples.

Weir et al. (2009) examined the academic reading activities and problems of first-year students at a British university in relation to the construct measured by IELTS reading and reported encouraging results that the reading problems experienced by the students differed significantly across IELTS band levels, with fewer problems reported by students scoring at higher levels. Breeze and Miller (2008) examined students' IELTS listening scores and final grades in the courses taught in English and found small positive correlations between them.

Additionally, discourse analyses of examinees' speech or written outputs in relation to discourse produced in authentic academic language use tasks have provided insights into the strength of the extrapolation inference. Ducasse and Brown (2009) investigated the validity of IELTS speaking, comparing interview interaction and university classroom interaction, and found that both types of interactions require students to produce information and opinions in response to questions, although classroom interaction involves a wider range of interactional and interaction management functions, which may not be evident in IELTS interviews. A few studies on the speaking section of the HKDSE English Language test found that the produced group discussion discourse shares some characteristics with authentic interaction, although some deviations are also found. These include the more scripted nature of the test discourse given its high-stakes nature (see Lam, 2015), longer examinee turns than real-life discussion discourse, and less display of convergent interaction expected in authentic discourse such as contradictions and disagreements (see Smart, 2017).

Utilization

The ultimate evidence needed for the validity argument is that the scores are actually relevant and useful for making appropriate admissions decisions. Evidence supporting this link includes predictive validity research that investigates the extent to which test scores predict academic success, and standard-setting research that helps users to understand score meaning and set admissions standards.

Academic success has typically been defined in terms of grades of international students, although grades can be impacted by a host of factors beyond English language proficiency, such as subject-area knowledge and expertise and motivation. Evidence of the ability of IELTS to predict academic success comes from a number of small-scale studies (e.g., Feast, 2002; Kerstjens & Nery, 2000; Lloyd-Jones et al., 2007). A study of a few thousand undergraduate and graduate international students from 10 U.S. universities indicated that at both undergraduate and graduate levels, students with higher TOEFL iBT scores tended to be more successful in their studies (reflected in higher GPAs) than students with lower scores. At the graduate level, TOEFL iBT scores tended to predict academic performance over and beyond GRE scores (see Cho & Bridgeman, 2012).

The TOEFL program has provided score users with descriptive information to help them to interpret test scores (see Educational Testing Service, 2004), a standard-setting manual that provides guidance on how to set cut scores for admissions purposes (see Educational Testing Service, 2005), and empirical research on setting standards on the TOEFL iBT speaking section for the initial screening of international teaching assistants (see Xi, 2007). A few case studies have been conducted to establish the appropriate IELTS cut scores for individual programs at different universities (see Golder et al., 2009; Singh & Sawyer, 2011).

The evidence cited here gives but a few examples that illustrate the six-step validity argument for the use of EAP tests in university admissions, and many more relevant studies exist. But even if we cited all existing studies, additional evidence would be warranted as tests and the academic environment continue to evolve.

Critical Research and Development Issues and Future Directions

In previous sections, we discussed current trends in EAP testing for university admissions and exemplary, wide-ranging research that pertains to various inferences supporting test score interpretations and uses. As the domain of academic language use evolves, especially in terms of the growing attention to the use of English as a lingua franca and technology-mediated language communication, the need arises to refine the constructs. AI technology has advanced beyond our imagination, with the emergence of generative AI in recent years, which have far-reaching implications for the language assessment field, such as how language constructs are conceptualized and operationalized and how the whole assessment process is conducted. Since the early 2000s, automated scoring technologies have seen increased applications in large-scale EAP tests for university admissions. This fast growth rate calls for scrutiny of each application of automated scoring to ensure appropriate and responsible use. Furthermore, the use of AI technology to enable automated test development or facilitate test development and to support at-home administrations of high-stakes admissions has been on the rise in the last few years, raising some critical issues for the field to debate on regarding the effects on examinee performances and test item quality and validity. In addition, a potential paradigm shift from EAP admissions tests capturing a snapshot of examinees' ability at a given time to prediction of future capacity to develop academic skills may be anticipated.

Need for Refining the Constructs of Academic English Proficiency

English language tests used for admissions purposes are expected to reflect the communication demands in English-medium university environments. One impetus for refining the construct is continual changes in the academic language use domain. Two notable developments in the domain may prompt us to refine the constructs: increasing diversification of the academic language use domain and the changing nature of communication at colleges and universities.

English as a Lingua Franca

English-medium academic environments for higher education have become increasingly diverse. This diversification manifests itself in a rapid significant growth in the number of programs that primarily use English for content instruction in countries where English is not a dominant language (see Coleman, 2006). This suggests that students are being increasingly exposed to both standard and nonstandard varieties of English in their interactions in classrooms and on campus.

These standard and nonstandard English varieties come with variations in the phonological and prosodic properties of spoken discourse, in the syntactic, lexical, and discourse characteristics of both spoken and written discourse, and in culture and pragmatics. The extent to which these variations should be represented in the constructs of English as a second or

364 Chapter 25 Evolution and Future Trends in Tests of English

foreign language remains controversial. Debates are continuing about whether and which educated speakers of standard varieties of English should set the norms for English teaching and testing (see Davies et al., 2003). Although English language teachers have started to embrace the notion of ELF (see Seidlhofer, 2004), language testers have adopted a more cautious approach to defining the role of English varieties in constructs. Taylor (2006) argues that the purpose and intended uses of a test drive the decision to include English varieties in tests. Elder and Davies (2006) contend that if language varieties are part of the target language use domain, including them in language tests will likely enhance score meaning and interpretation and bring about a positive impact on teaching (see Elder & Davies, 2006). Xi and Mollaun (2011) make a similar argument that design decisions regarding linguistic standards and norms to be used in tests need to be based on the intended use of the test and the context in which the learners will be expected to use English for communication.

The research on ELF may have different implications for test content and scoring criteria for university admissions tests. In terms of test content, for the assessment of listening, the most common practice is to include standard varieties of English. As for the inclusion of non-native accents, although an argument can be made that they are a prominent part of the language use domain, the multiplicity of nonstandard English varieties presents challenges in conceptualizing and operationalizing constructs that include them. The sampling of non-native accents and its implications for test validity and fairness need to be carefully considered (e.g., What non-native accents to include? What degrees of an accent should be targeted? Would non-native speakers of English be held to higher standards than their peers who are native speakers of English?). As for the assessment of speaking, some characteristics of ELF have been incorporated into the scoring rubrics of EAP admissions tests, where the emphasis is on the impact of accents on the overall intelligibility and comprehensibility rather than on degree of "nativeness." The writing rubrics still adopt standard English norms by educated speakers who speak standard varieties of English. A key aspect of real-life communicative competence that remains outside the scope of EAP admissions testing is culture and pragmatics associated with different English varieties. Therefore, although the conceptualization may have changed as our understanding of the target language use domain evolves, the practice is lagging because of some operational challenges.

Technology-mediated Communication

The growing use of computers and multimedia technologies in communication has implications for how we define the constructs for EAP admissions tests. Do we define the constructs based on the belief that technology is considered a nonessential component of the construct (e.g., testing writing using handwritten essays), or even as a potential source of construct irrelevance? Or do we define certain computer literacy skills (e.g., reading on the computer screen and keyboarding skills) as an integral part of the constructs, to reflect computer-mediated reading and writing literacy required for the target language use domain? Or do we even go one step further and define the constructs as communication skills that are fully integrated with computer literacy and digital information literary skills, such as using the full set of assistive tools such as dictionary, thesaurus, spelling and grammar checker, and even generative AI tools to accomplish a communication task and the ability to use digital technologies to find needed information and evaluate, organize, and synthesize it to fulfill a task? How far do we go, and where do we draw the line in delineating the constructs?

Currently large-scale EAP tests for admissions are taking a very careful approach to specifying the role of computer technologies in the construct definition, given the large variation in computer and digital information literacy skills among global examinees. None of the EAP tests for admissions has gone a step further to allow examinees access to assistive tools while taking the tests, although progressive ideas about assistive technologies being part of the language constructs have emerged (see Voss et al., 2023).

A notable development is the use of video conferencing technology in conducting interactive speaking tests such as oral interviews or group discussions. For example, IELTS has offered the speaking test via a video call (https://www.ielts.org/for-test-takers/ielts-online/faqs). Pilot research has been conducted on the HKDSE English Language test to compare face-to-face and zoom-based group discussions. Drawing on the conclusion that virtual group discussion is largely comparable to that conducted face to face (see Smart et al., 2024), it was recommended that the HKDSE English Speaking be conducted in a virtual format, complementing the face-to-face format of the SBA, which contributes to the final HKDSE English Speaking score. The descriptors regarding interactional competence for the HKDSE English Language Examination would need to be revised accordingly to reflect the nature of virtual interactions. One can argue that given the increasing prevalence of technology use in academic settings, virtual communication has become an important part of authentic language use and thus the comparability with face-to-face interactions may become irrelevant to our conceptualization and inquiry of test validity unless a speaking test is conducted in both face-to-face and virtual formats.

In a similar vein, with the increasingly prevalent use of technology around the globe, arguing for or against a construct definition encompassing technology-mediated English communicative abilities may become irrelevant eventually. However, regardless of our approach to construct definition, research that investigates how computer literacy skills interact with foundational language skills to impact the overall communication needs to continue.

Future Trends of Using Technology in the Entire Assessment Process

Growing Use of AI Technology in Simulating Real-World Tasks

The use of computers in delivering EAP university admissions tests has afforded new opportunities for the development of innovative tasks, such as integrated tasks that involve the use of written, spoken, and visual materials as stimulus materials. However, the potential of using AI technologies such as text- and voice-based chatbots in simulating real-world interactive writing and speaking tasks is yet to be fully utilized to help expand the construct representation. Voice-based chatbot, or spoken dialogue system, has been used to enable automated interactive speaking assessment (see Ockey et al., 2023) and has the potential to be enhanced and scaled for large-scale speaking tests. With the emergence of generative AI, it may indeed be possible for the use of interactive writing tasks or more open-ended conversations with a computer agent on complex topics such as discussing the pros and cons of an idea to become a reality for large-scale tests.

Opportunities and Challenges Offered by Automated Scoring Technologies

Automated scoring technologies offer many benefits, including improving the efficiency and reliability of scoring. However, limitations of current state-of-the-art technology still put constraints on the kinds of test tasks that can be included, thus compromising the construct coverage and representation of tests that rely solely on automated scoring technologies. The use of automated scoring solely would also increase the probability of examinees gaming the system to gain higher scores that are not warranted, because the state-of-the-art automated scoring systems still rely on surface features for assessing some higher-order skills such as content, coherence, quality of argument, etc., and cannot access them the same way human raters do. Although the use of automated scoring as the single rater for high-stakes EAP tests for admissions would have generated quite a lot of controversy and debates 10 years ago, in the last few years, especially during the pandemic, test users have become more receptive to the use of automated scoring as the sole rater and less concerned about the potential negative consequences. They have shifted their focus to how the acceptance of more tests can help them broaden their candidate pools to increase international student enrollment. We, as a field though, bear this important responsibility of educating the users and advocating for more critical evaluation and acceptance of automated EAP tests for admissions to ensure truly equal opportunities for all examinees and a positive impact on teaching and learning.

Use of AI Technology for Item Development

In recent years, AI technologies have increasingly been used in developing test items for large-scale standardized English tests, notably generative AI technologies that can create long, complex texts and other types of stimulus materials such as images. DET is the first EAP test for admissions that uses generative AI technology for creating some of the test items reviewed by test developers. While generative AI can facilitate the generation of stimulus materials such as reading passages and scripts for listening and the creation of item types such as multiple-choice, true or false, cloze, short answer, etc., some known vulnerabilities have been documented such as inaccuracies and bias in the generated materials. It is also known to have limited capacity in creating items that measure diverse skills, especially higher-order skills. Therefore, it is critical to adopt a model where humans are closely in the loop (Bolender et al., 2023).

Use of AI Technology for Remote-Proctored Tests

Traditionally, high-stakes language tests for university admissions have been conducted in certified test centers with very rigorous proctoring procedures. However, the COVID pandemic has accelerated users' acceptance of remote-proctoring technology for high-stakes admissions tests, which has been used for very low-stakes classroom assessments. Duolingo, the TOEFL iBT Home Edition, the IELTS Indicator, and the PTE Academic Home Edition have all been accepted by many academic programs, and for some programs, the at-home versions may be here to stay. Currently, two major technological vulnerabilities have been identified regarding remote proctoring technology: The first one is that the web camera used in most remote-proctored tests does not capture a 360-degree view of the room during the test-taking process even though the online human proctor does a sweep of the room initially. Even with a second camera from a smartphone capturing the side of the examinee and the screen, the two cameras still do not cover a 360-degree view. The second is the use of remote access software that takes control of the examinee's computer device so that the test is actually done by a proxy. In addition to technological vulnerabilities that may lead to security issues and untrustworthy scores, remote-proctored test administrations introduce other issues that challenge the fairness and justice of tests, such as accommodations for students with disabilities, comparability of scores obtained through test center and at-home administrations, and potential alteration of the cognitive processes in test taking due to examinees' intention to comply with remote proctoring guidelines involving eye gaze. Isbell and Kremmel provide a comprehensive analysis of the fairness and justice issues introduced by remote proctoring using Kunnan's framework of test justice (Isbell & Kremmel, 2023). However, as remoted proctoring technology and practices mature, it is conceivable that remote test administrations may become dominant in the future and gradually eliminate the role of physical test centers.

Prediction of Future Capacity to Develop Academic Skills in an Immersion Environment

Current academic English tests for admissions provide a snapshot of examinees' English skills at the time of test taking and have an exclusive focus on a static view of language ability. However, prior exposure to English language training and use and language learning aptitude of learners may have a differential impact on their language skill development once they can benefit from access to an English immersion environment and exposure to English language instruction in both language and/or content classes. English language tests that can provide information about learners' future capacity to develop academic skills given variations in their prior exposure and instruction could be better utilized for admissions decisions, especially for those who have obtained provisional admissions provided that their English language skills can advance to a satisfactory level within a defined period.

Conclusion

In this chapter, we have presented an overview of the history and current landscape of EAP admissions testing for higher education, focusing on current trends and critical issues to resolve. The field of EAP admissions testing has attracted the most significant research and development efforts in language testing. Therefore, it is critical that research efforts be maintained and increased to continue to set the benchmark for the development and validation of language tests around the world.

The unexpected COVID pandemic has caused major disruptions to the field, leading to the rise of unconventional English tests for admissions that would otherwise have a very low probability of gaining wide acceptance because of undifferentiated acceptance of English language tests by universities around the world (Xi & Norris, 2021). The priority for test users was shifted to increasing their international student enrollment to get their schools through financial difficulty, and fundamental issues of test validity, fairness, and impact were largely pushed aside in selecting English tests to accept. The normalcy regained post-pandemic will hopefully prompt users to be more critical and demanding of admissions test providers so that they continue to revise their tests to help facilitate examinees' eventual success in higher education academic settings and to help promote a positive impact on teaching and learning.

Discussion Questions

1. How do you think technology-mediated communication in the real world would impact our construct definition of language ability?

2. What would the next generation of language tests for admissions purposes look like 20 years from now?

References

Bolender, B., Foster, C., & Vispoel, S. (2023). The criticality of implementing principled design when using AI technologies in test development. *Language Assessment Quarterly.*, *20*(4–5), 512–519.

Breeze, R., & Miller, P. (2008). Predictive validity of the IELTS listening test as an indicator of student coping ability in Spain. In L. Taylor (Ed.), *IELTS research reports* (Vol. *12*, pp. 201–234). Cambridge University Press and Assessment.

368   **Chapter 25** Evolution and Future Trends in Tests of English

Bridgeman, B., & Carlson, S. B. (1984). Survey of academic writing tasks. *Written Communication, 1*(2), 247–280.

Bridgeman, B., Powers, D., Stone, E., & Mollaun, P. (2012). TOEFL iBT speaking test scores as indicators of oral communicative language proficiency. *Language Testing, 29*(1), 91–108.

Bridges, G. (2010). Demonstrating cognitive validity of IELTS academic writing task 1. *Cambridge ESOL: Research Notes, 42,* 24–33.

Bridges, G., & Shaw, S. D. (2004). IELTS writing: revising assessment criteria and scales (phase 4). *Cambridge ESOL: Research Notes, 18,* 8–12. Retrieved January 14, 2013 from http://www.cambridgeesol.org/rs_notes/rs_nts18.pdf.

Brown, A., Iwashita, N., & McNamara, T. (2005). *An examination of rater orientations and examinee performance on English-for-academic-purposes speaking tasks (TOEFL® Monograph No. MS-29).* Princeton, NJ: ETS.

Chan, S. H. C. (2011). *Demonstrating cognitive validity and face validity of PTE academic writing items summarize written text and write essay (PTE Academic Research Note).*

Chapelle, C. A. (2008). The TOEFL validity argument. In C. A. Chapelle, M. K. Enright & J. M. Jamieson (Eds.), *Building a validity argument for the Test of English as a Foreign Language* (pp. 319–352). Routledge.

Chapelle, C. A., Enright, M. K., Jamieson, J. M., & (Eds.). (2008). *Building a validity argument for the Test of English as a Foreign Language.* Routledge.

Charge, N., & Taylor, L. (1997). Recent developments in IELTS. *English Language Testing Journal, 51*(4), 374–380.

Cho, Y., & Bridgeman, B. (2012). Relationship of TOEFL IBT™ scores to academic performance: some evidence from American universities. *Language Testing, 29*(3), 421–442.

Clapham, C. (1996). *The development of IELTS: A study of the effect of background knowledge on reading comprehension.* Cambridge University Press.

Cohen, A., & Upton, T. (2006). *Strategies in responding to the new TOEFL reading tasks (TOEFL Monograph No. MS-33).* ETS.

Coleman, J. A. (2006). English-medium teaching in European higher education. *Language Teaching, 39,* 1–14.

Cumming, A., Kantor, R., & Powers, D. (2001). *Scoring TOEFL essays and TOEFL 2000 prototype writing tasks: An investigation into raters' decision making and development of a pre- liminary analytic framework (ETS RR-01-04; TOEFL-MS-22).* ETS.

Cumming, A., Kantor, R., & Powers, D. E. (2002). Decision making while rating ESL/EFL writing tasks: a descriptive framework. *Modern Language Journal, 86,* 67–96.

Davies, A., Hamp-lyons, L., & Kemp, C. (2003). Whose norms? International proficiency test in English. *World Englishes, 22*(4), 571–584.

Ducasse, A. M., & Brown, A. (2009). The role of interactive communication in IELTS speaking and its relationship to candidates' preparedness for study or training contexts. In L. Taylor (Ed.), *IELTS research reports* (Vol. 12, pp. 125–150). Cambridge University Press and Assessment.

Educational Testing Service. (2004). *English language competency descriptors.* Author.

Educational Testing Service. (2005). *Standard setting materials for the Internet-based TOEFL test* [Compact disk]. Author.

Educational Testing Service. (2011). *Reliability and comparability of TOEFL iBT scores. TOEFL iBT® research insight series,* 3. Author.

Elder, C., & Davies, A. (2006). Assessing English as a lingua franca. *Annual Review of Applied Linguistics, 25,* 282–301.

Feast, V. (2002). The impact of IELTS scores on performance at university. *International Education Journal, 3*(4), 70–85.

Golder, K., Reeder, K., & Fleming, S. (2009). Determination of appropriate IELTS band score for admission into a program at a Canadian post-secondary polytechnic institution. In J. Osborne (Ed.), *IELTS research reports* (Vol. 10, pp. 1–25). Cambridge University Press and Assessment.

Gomez, G. P., Noah, A., Schedl, M., Wright, C., & Yolkut, A. (2007). Proficiency descriptors based on a scale-anchoring study of the new TOEFL iBT reading test. *Language Testing, 24*(3), 417–444.

Hale, G. A., Taylor, C., Bridgeman, B., Carson, J., Kroll, B., & Kantor, R. (1996). *A study of writing tasks assigned in academic degree programs (TOEFL Report No. 54; ETS RR-95-44).* ETS.

Isbell, D. R., & Kremmel, B. (2023). Remote proctoring in language testing: implications for fairness, justice, and validity. *Language Assessment Quarterly, 20*(4/5), 469–487. https://doi.org/10.1080/15434303.2023.2288251.

de Jong, J. H. A. L., & Zheng, Y. (2011). *Applying EALTA guidelines: A practical case study on Pearson Test of English Academic*. Retrieved January 14, 2013 from http://www.pearsonpte.com/research/Documents/EALTAguidelinesPTEAcademic.pdf.

Kane, M. T. (2006). Validation. In R. L. Brennan (Ed.), *Educational measurement* (4th ed., pp. 17–64). ACE/Praeger.

Kerstjens, M., & Nery, C. (2000). Predictive validity in the IELTS test. In R. Tulloh (Ed.), *IELTS research reports* (Vol. *3*, pp. 85–108). Cambridge University Press and Assessment.

Lam, D. M. K. (2015). Contriving authentic interaction: task implementation and engagement in school-based speaking assessment in Hong Kong. In G. Yu & Y. Jin (Eds.), *Assessing Chinese learners of English: Language constructs, consequences and conundrums* (pp. 38–60). Palgrave Macmillan.

Lam, D. M. K. (2019). Interactional competence with and without extended planning time in a group oral assessment. *Language Assessment Quarterly, 16*(1), 1–20. https://doi.org/10.1080/15434303.2019.1602627.

Lee, Y.-W., & Kantor, R. (2005). *Dependability of new ESL writing test scores: Evaluating proto- type tasks and alternative rating schemes (ETS RR-05-14)*. ETS.

Lim, G., Geranpayeh, A., Khalifa, H., & Buckendahl, C. (2012). Standard setting to an international framework: implications for theory and practice. *Internal Journal of Testing, 13*(1), 32–49.

Lloyd-Jones, G., Neame, C., & Medaney, S. (2007). A multiple case study of the relationship between the indicators of students' English language competence on entry and students' academic progress at an international postgraduate university. In L. Taylor (Ed.), *IELTS research reports* (Vol. *11*, pp. 1–54). Cambridge University Press and Assessment.

Maycock, L., & Green, T. (2005). The effects on performance of computer familiarity and attitudes towards CB IELTS. *Research Notes, 20*, 3–8.

Milanovic, M., & Saville, N. (1996). *Considering the impact of Cambridge EFL examinations (Internal Report)*. Cambridge ESOL.

Munby, J. (1978). *Communicative syllabus design: A sociolinguistic model for defining the content of purpose-specific language programmes*. Cambridge University Press.

Ockey, G., Chukharev-Hudilainen, E., & Hirch, R. R. (2023). Assessing international competence: ICE versus a human partner. *Language Assessment Quarterly, 20*(4/5), 377–398. https://doi.org/10.1080/15434303.2023.2237486.

Pearlman, M. (2008). Finalizing the test blueprint. In C. A. Chapelle, M. K. Enright & J. M. Jamieson (Eds.), *Building a validity argument for the Test of English as a Foreign Language* (pp. 227–258). Routledge.

Pearson Education. (2010a). *Aligning PTE academic test scores to the Common European Framework of Reference for Languages* (Pearson Research Note). Retrieved June 6, 2012 from http://pearsonpte.com/research/Documents/Aligning_PTEA_Scores_CEF.pdf

Pearson Education. (2010b). *The official guide to Pearson Test of English Academic*. Author.

Pearson Education. (2011). *Validity and reliability in PTE Academic (Pearson Research Summary)*. Retrieved June 2, 2012 from http://pearsonpte.com/research/Documents/Validity_and_Reliability_in_PTEA_4Aug10_v2.pdf

Rosenfeld, M., Leung, S., & Oltman, P. K. (2001). *The reading, writing, speaking, and listening tasks important for academic success at the undergraduate and graduate levels (ETS RM-01-03; TOEFL-MS-21)*. ETS.

Sawaki, Y., & Nissan, S. (2009). *Criterion-related validity of the TOEFL® iBT listening section (ETS RR-09-02; TOEFL iBT Report No. iBT-08)*. ETS.

Sawaki, Y., Stricker, L. J., & Oranje, A. H. (2009). Factor structure of the TOEFL Internet-based test. *Language Testing, 26*(1), 5–30.

Seidlhofer, B. (2004). Research perspectives on teaching English as a lingua franca. *Annual Review of Applied Linguistics, 24*, 209–239.

Shaw, S. D. (2004). IELTS writing: revising assessment criteria and scales (phase 3). *Research Notes, 16*, 3–7.

Singh, M., & Sawyer, W. (2011). Learning to play the "classroom tennis" well: IELTS and international students in teacher education. In L. Taylor (Ed.), *IELTS research reports* (Vol. *11*, pp. 1–54). Cambridge University Press and Assessment.

Smart, C. (2017). Linear unit discourse analysis: the case of peer group interaction in the HKDSE public examination. *The Asian Journal of Applied Linguistics, 4*(2), 148–160.

370 Chapter 25 Evolution and Future Trends in Tests of English

Smart, C., Drave, N., & Shiu, J. (2014). Implementing innovation: a graded approach to English language testing in Hong Kong. In *English Language Education and Assessment: Recent Developments in Hong Kong and the Chinese Mainland* (pp. 257–273). Springer.

Smart, C., Shiu, J., Drysdale, M., & Chan, A. (2024). Exploring the use of an Internet-delivered speaking test in a Kong Kong secondary school public examination. *China Examinations, 382*(2), 47–55.

Swain, M., Huang, L., Barkaoui, K., Brooks, L., & Lapkin, S. (2009). *The speaking section of the TOEFL iBT™ (SSTiBT): Test-takers' reported strategic behaviors (TOEFL iBT™ Report No. iBT-10)*. ETS.

Taylor, L. (2006). The changing landscape of English: implications for language assessment. *ELT Journal, 60*(1), 51–60.

Taylor, L., & Jones, N. (2001). Revising the IELTS speaking test. *Research Notes, 4*, 9–11.

Tsang, C. L., & Isaacs, T. (2021). Hong Kong secondary students' perspectives on selecting test difficulty level and learner washback: effects of a graded approach to assessment. *Language Testing, 39*(2), 212–238.

University of Cambridge ESOL Examinations. (2006). IELTS test performance data 2004. *Research Notes, 23*, 13–15. Retrieved June 6, 2012 from http://www.cambridgesol.org/rs_notes/rs_nts23.pdf.

University of Cambridge ESOL Examinations. (2011). *Analysis of test data*. Retrieved June 6, 2012 from http://www. ielts.org/researchers/analysis_of_test_data.aspx

University of Cambridge ESOL Examinations. (2012). *History of IELTS*. Retrieved June 6, 2012, from http://www.ielts. org/researchers/history_of_ielts.aspx

Wagner, E., & Kunnan, A. J. (2015). The Duolingo English Test. *Language Assessment Quarterly, 12*(3), 320–331. https://doi.org/10.1080/15434303.2015.1061530.

Weigle, S. C. (2011). *Validation of automated scores of TOEFL iBT® tasks against nontest indicators of writing ability* (TOEFL iBT Report No. iBT-15). ETS.

Weir, C., Hawkey, R., Green, A., Unaldi, A., & Devi, S. (2009). The relationship between the academic reading construct as measured by IELTS and the reading experiences of students in their first year of study at a British university. In L. Taylor (Ed.), *IELTS research reports* (Vol. 9, pp. 97–156). Cambridge University Press and Assessment.

Voss, E., Cushing, S. T., Ockey, G. J., & Yan, X. (2023). The use of assistive technologies including generative AI by test takers in language assessment: A debate of theory and practice. *Language Assessment Quarterly, 20*(4/5), 520–532.

Xi, X. (2007). Validating TOEFL® iBT speaking and setting score requirements for ITA screening. *Language Assessment Quarterly, 4*(4), 318–351.

Xi, X., & Mollaun, P. (2011). Using raters from India to score a large-scale speaking test. *Language Learning, 61*(4), 1222–1255.

Xi, X., & Norris, J. (Eds.). (2021). Assessing academic English for higher education admissions. In *Language assessment at ETS: Innovation and validation*. Routledge.

Xi, X., Norris, J., Ockey, G., Fulcher, G., & Purpura, J. (2021). Assessing academic speaking. In X. Xi & J. Norris (Eds.), *Assessing academic English. Innovations in language learning and assessment at ETS*. Routledge.

Zhang, Y. (2008). *Repeater analyses for TOEFL iBT (ETS Research Report RM-08-05)*. ETS.

Suggested Readings

Chalhoub-Deville, M., & Turner, C. (2000). What to look for in ESL admission tests: Cambridge certificate exams, IELTS, and TOEFL. *System, 28*, 523–539.

Cumming, A. (2007). New directions in testing English language proficiency for university entrance. In J. Cummins & C. Davison (Eds.), *International handbook of English language teaching* (pp. 473–485). Springer.

Xi, X., & Norris, J. (Eds.). (2021). Assessing academic English for higher education admissions. In *Language assessment at ETS: Innovation and validation*. Routledge.

CHAPTER 26

Assessing Health and Other Professionals

Lynda Taylor and John Pill

Introduction

Language assessment for professional purposes (LAPP) can be located within the broader, well-established concept of language for specific purposes (LSP), which incorporates the notion of language for academic purposes as well as language in workplace contexts. Knoch and Macqueen (2020) define LAPP as "any assessment process, carried out by and for invested parties, which is used to determine a person's ability to understand and/or use the language of a professionally-oriented domain to a specified or necessary level" (p. 3).

The decade since the publication of the first version of this chapter (Taylor & Pill, 2014) saw continued growth in the global movement of professionals in multiple work domains, including the health professions. Knoch and Macqueen (2020) attribute this to rapid globalization, transnational migration flows in response to economic or security pressures, massive technologization, and the continuing spread of English as a means of communication internationally. Issues involved in assessing the language and communication skills of healthcare workers are complex, touching upon testing policy and practice, as well as concerns of a moral and ethical nature.

Our 2014 chapter focused on the assessment of health professionals, principally doctors, seeking to practice in predominantly English language contexts. This was because of the prevalence of migration of doctors, as a clearly defined group, to English-speaking, more economically developed regions (i.e., the United Kingdom, North America, and Australasia), leading to established and well-documented language assessment policy and practice in those contexts. Furthermore, the approaches adopted by national medical registration boards at that time were somewhat diverse, requiring a comprehensive explanation and discussion. In the decade after 2014, significant changes in policy and practice took place in the three specific regions originally surveyed.

In this updated chapter, we explore changing patterns and new developments in the language assessment of doctors since 2014 to discern emerging trends. Though the focus of this chapter remains firmly on doctors, many of the principles and practices adopted for medical registration apply similarly to other health professionals, such as nurses, physiotherapists, dentists, and even veterinarians. The issues and challenges involved in assessing the language skills of doctors and other health professionals are comparable in many professional domains. As constraints of space make it impossible to address all professional contexts, we shall once again use the case of

---

The Concise Companion to Language Assessment, First Edition. Edited by Antony John Kunnan.
© 2025 John Wiley & Sons, Inc. Published 2025 by John Wiley & Sons, Inc.

internationally trained doctors wishing to cross borders to register and practice as a means of exploring more generally the needs and priorities in other professions and domains, e.g., the aviation/manufacturing industry, call centers, and international law/accountancy.

We begin with an update on current approaches for certifying internationally trained medical graduates (IMGs)[1] in the same three regional contexts. We describe some of the theory and research to have emerged in the field of LAPP over recent years, using the Occupational English Test (OET) as a case study that illustrates how a language test intended for a specific purpose can evolve in terms of its design, operationalization, and implementation based on theory and research, as well as through market take-up in response to policy changes. A section on challenges and issues highlights various questions and considerations confronting anyone working in the area of LSP and LAPP, drawing on useful conceptual frameworks for thinking and action on the part of assessment providers. The final section reflects on key themes to emerge over the past 10 years and speculates on what lies ahead for the field, including directions for future research.

Approaches to Language Assessment of Health Professionals

The 2014 version of this chapter discussed patterns of language assessment at that time for doctors in the United Kingdom, Australia, and the United States. Differing assessment policies and procedures were described, together with a discussion of their history to contextualize developments over time; to avoid repetition, we refer readers to that chapter for details of the specific policy and practice for IMGs in those jurisdictions and cultural contexts. Significant changes took place over the next decade, partly in light of developments in language assessment theory and research, but also for sociopolitical and economic reasons, including the impact of the COVID-19 pandemic and consequences of the United Kingdom's exit from the European Union in 2020. Regulatory bodies found themselves having to review and revise arrangements for licensing and registering internationally trained health professionals to practice and work in the destination country. In this section, we provide a brief update on current approaches to illustrate how policy and practice have changed. It is important to note that the situation in each context remains fluid and continues to evolve in an environment of rapid change. Readers are advised to consult the websites of individual regulatory bodies to check on the latest policy and practice.

Doctors in the United Kingdom

The General Medical Council (GMC) registers all doctors wishing to practice medicine in the United Kingdom, and different regulations may apply based on an applicant's nationality and country of training. In addition to holding acceptable primary medical and postgraduate qualifications, international doctors who graduated outside the United Kingdom, the European Economic Area, or Switzerland are usually required to demonstrate that they can communicate effectively in English, in the interests of patient safety.

---

[1]The term *international medical graduate* and its abbreviation IMG are still in common use to describe doctors trained in one country and seeking registration in another. The population it describes varies from context to context, as IMGs are not a homogeneous group. Similar terms exist in other professions, e.g., *internationally educated nurse*. Once professionals have obtained registration in a jurisdiction, their status is no different from any other practitioner; nevertheless, these terms may continue to be applied, often to indicate problematic cases where a difference or deficit (e.g., in language, professional knowledge, or cultural competence) is perceived.

The International English Language Testing System (IELTS), a general-purpose language test, continues to be used by the GMC. To meet the requirements, candidates need an overall score of band 7.5 (increased from 7.0 in 2014) on IELTS Academic, with a minimum band of 7.0 in each component area (speaking, reading, writing, and listening) at a single (the most recent) test sitting. In 2018, the GMC approved an additional English language proficiency (ELP) test, the specific-purpose OET, as appropriate evidence of language competence. This decision was informed by a GMC-commissioned study (Taylor & Chan, 2015) investigating the increasing range of international ELP tests available in the marketplace. International applicants for GMC registration take the Medicine version of OET, 1 of 12 test variants covering a range of health professions. Candidates require a grade B in each OET component (speaking, reading, writing, and listening), with the four grades obtained at the same test sitting.

Having demonstrated satisfactory ELP, IMGs provide evidence of their current level of medical knowledge and skill by passing the GMC Professional and Linguistic Assessments Board (PLAB). The two-part assessment is delivered in English. Part 1 is a written test with multiple-choice questions testing medical knowledge and skills. Part 2 is a practical objective structured clinical examination (OSCE) involving short scenarios designed to test clinical skills, including the ability to communicate effectively with patients, relatives, and other healthcare workers.

Doctors in Australia

Originally designed in Australia (McNamara, 1996), the specific-purpose OET was used there from the 1990s to evaluate the language competence of medical and other health professionals seeking registration. IMGs with medical qualifications awarded outside Australia or New Zealand must provide evidence of eligibility to undertake one of three assessment pathways set by the Medical Board of Australia (MBA): competent authority, standard, or specialist. The assessment process evaluates their medical knowledge and clinical skills and also includes a registration standard for English language skills.

A revised English language skills registration standard was announced by the Australian Health Practitioner Regulation Agency (AHPRA) in July 2015. It provided for four international ELP tests to be accepted by the MBA: the OET; IELTS Academic; the Test of English as a Foreign Language internet-based test (TOEFL iBT); and the Pearson Test of English Academic (PTE Academic). Information on score requirements for each test is available from the AHPRA website. For OET, for example, a minimum score of grade B in each component (reading, writing, listening, and speaking) is required on either the paper- or computer-based format, and scores can be achieved at up to two test sittings in a six-month period if no score in any component is below grade C. The MBA also accepts successful completion of two profession-specific tests: the New Zealand Registration Examination (NZREX) and the U.K. PLAB, both of which have an OSCE format (see above for details of the PLAB). The Australian Medical Council (AMC) assesses the professional knowledge and skills of IMGs on the standard pathway using a format similar to the PLAB in the United Kingdom.

Doctors in the United States

In the United States, the Educational Commission for Foreign Medical Graduates (ECFMG) provides certification for IMGs to confirm their readiness to enter residency and fellowship programs. All applicants must satisfy a medical science examination requirement, a clinical skills requirement, and a communication skills requirement. In addition, each State Medical Board requires doctors to pass examinations for licensure.

In 2014, IMGs were required to pass three separate steps of the United States Medical Licensing Examination (USMLE) and this requirement was universal, applying equally to newly trained U.S. doctors. It was necessary to pass all four tests – Step 1, Step 2 (with two parts, including a Clinical Skills [CS] component with a communication element), and Step 3 – and there was no additional requirement for an ELP test.

In 2020, the Step 2 CS component of the USMLE was suspended due to the COVID-19 pandemic and was subsequently discontinued in 2021 (Mladenovic et al., 2023). In its place, the ECFMG recognized the Medicine variant of OET to assess the ELP of applicants pursuing one of the six new pathways leading to ECFMG certification. The OET grades required of IMGs were set at a minimum score of 350 (grade B) for each of the 4 OET components at one test sitting. (In April 2022, the writing requirement was reduced to a minimum score of 300.) All pathway applicants, regardless of native language, language of instruction at medical school, or citizenship, must satisfy this ELP/communication skills requirement in addition to meeting the certification requirements of their specific pathway.

Reasons given for the ECFMG choosing OET are that it is designed for health professionals, and it offers a test variant specifically for physicians (i.e., OET Medicine). The ECFMG regards the OET as assessing the healthcare-specific ELP of physicians, with emphasis on the language needed to communicate effectively in a clinical setting with peers and patients, including the ability to show empathy and to break down complex medical terminology and procedures into simpler language.

Summary

Over a period of 10 years, approaches to assessing the ELP of doctors changed in the three contexts. In the United Kingdom, a specific-purpose test (OET) was approved alongside the existing general-purpose test (IELTS), and both are now used as measures of ELP. However, the language tests still serve as initial screening followed by a separate professional competence test that includes an assessment of specific work-related communication skills (i.e., the OSCE-format PLAB). In Australia, the range of approved ELP tests broadened to include three general-purpose tests – IELTS Academic, TOEFL iBT, and PTE Academic – alongside the specific-purpose OET. Some flexibility is shown in how test scores are obtained (e.g., from more than one test setting and using paper- or computer-based formats). In the United States, the original USMLE Step 2 CS test, formerly taken by IMGs and U.S.-trained doctors alike, was abandoned in favor of the separate and specific-purpose OET, taken by IMGs only.

Several interesting trends are discernible. First, there was a noticeable shift toward increased use of a specific-purpose test of language proficiency for health professionals (i.e., the acceptance of OET in all three contexts), perhaps suggesting that, when available, this is an attractive option for professional registration bodies. Second, the move to approve and accept a wider range of high-stakes ELP tests on offer in the international marketplace (at least for the U.K. and Australian regulators) may be for reasons of cost and accessibility for test takers. This raises questions about the perceived and actual equivalence of cut-scores across different tests; the required scores for tests accepted in the Australian context illustrate this well. Third, the issue of whether an LSP test is a sufficient measure of professional (clinical) communication skills appears unresolved: In the United States, the OET (a specific-purpose language test) now replaces the previous OSCE-format test (Step 2 CS), while in the United Kingdom and Australia the same test is used alongside OSCE-format tests – the GMC PLAB and AMC clinical examination, respectively – indicating different views on the intended purpose of the OET and the assessment required of the same pool of IMGs.

Theory and Research

The domain of healthcare provision, particularly relating to medicine and nursing, is one of the more fully researched contexts of professional life from a language testing perspective. For example, a useful body of research in LSP testing has continued to grow around both IELTS and the OET as used in the United Kingdom and Australia. However, this focus does not imply that other areas are being neglected. Assessment of aviation English, for example, is also an area of substantial research interest at present (see Friginal et al., 2020; Kim, 2018).

In an IELTS-sponsored study, Sedgwick et al. (2016) investigated the language needs of international nurses in the United Kingdom, while Séguis and Lim (2020) focused on investigating the writing that nurses do. A study for the Nursing and Midwifery Council (NMC; Lim, 2022) summarized recommendations for standards to use for nurses in the United Kingdom, and the NMC cut-score for the OET writing component was lowered as a result. Two major research projects relating to the OET were funded by the Australian Research Council. They resulted in special issues of the journals *Language Testing* (Elder, 2016), focusing on the challenge of seeking authenticity, and *Assessing Writing* (Knoch et al., 2020b), presenting LSP tests as tools to manage risk and mediate the views of domain insiders and applied linguists. In these projects, researchers considered questions fundamental to theory-building for LSP testing as well as practical implications for a particular test (OET) in which their findings are operationalized. The first project considered how the conventional, language-focused criteria used in the speaking component of the OET might be extended to include the assessment of features of test-taker performance more attuned to qualities in interaction between practitioners and patients that are found to be valued by healthcare professionals (e.g., patient-centeredness and effective information-gathering). The second project reviewed the types of writing done by healthcare professionals and how examples were appraised in the domain, before considering how features of appraisal could be integrated into the OET writing assessment criteria. We focus in turn on four (overlapping) themes to structure the presentation of recent developments relating to the OET: assessment criteria, test tasks, examiners, and standard setting.

The concept of *indigenous assessment criteria*, first introduced by Jacoby and McNamara (1999), featured strongly in the two projects. The goal to understand what matters in the domain and to represent this in the assessment scheme for the test is based on the belief that test performance assessed from this perspective serves as an effective predictor of performance in the domain. The challenge of accessing the criteria used by domain insiders is considerable (Elder & McNamara, 2016): They are often taken for granted and go unstated; they can be observed only fleetingly as part of long-term, diffuse professional mentoring practices (e.g., hospital ward rounds) and so remain inaccessible to study. To overcome this, in the speaking project, health professional educators watched recordings of trainee performance and discussed the feedback they would give the novices to help them develop their skills in interacting with patients (Pill, 2016); in the writing project, health professionals reviewed patients' hospital records, commenting on their adequacy (Knoch et al., 2020a).

Insights from this type of investigation can then inform the production of appropriate *test tasks*. As the scope of the criteria for assessment is expanded or changed to be more relevant to the domain, test developers need to ensure that task prompts elicit spoken or written performances to which these criteria can be applied. The construct for the receptive skills has also changed, and, over recent years, the OET reading and listening components have been updated to include a wider range of task types and represent more fully content from each of the 12 healthcare domains the test serves. Further revisions have been made for practical reasons, for example, to permit automated marking.

376 Chapter 26 Assessing Health and Other Professionals

As assessment criteria expand to focus on features of performance more closely related to professional skills, the capacity of *examiners* to apply them to test performances effectively must also be considered. For example, OET examiners involved in the research projects had backgrounds in language teaching and were therefore "outsiders" to the healthcare domain. Nevertheless, the new criteria required them to act to some extent as proxies for the insiders whose priorities the criteria represented, recognizing features of performance relevant to each criterion and observing salient differences in their quality. In the speaking test criteria, a distinction was sought between professional communication skills (work done through language) and clinical skills, which were excluded from the scope of the OET; a pilot study investigated how well existing examiners could apply the revised criteria (O'Hagan et al., 2016). An article on the writing project (Knoch et al., 2020c) considers the tensions for examiners created by a realignment of assessment priorities, tensions that remain despite the examiners' application of the new criteria being statistically satisfactory.

A further way to engage the perspective of insiders and apply their indigenous criteria is to involve them in setting cut-scores for the test, that is, establishing the quality of performance sufficient for entry into the professional domain. *Standard-setting* methods have developed in recent years, and it is now more common for representatives of the professional bodies who use language tests such as the OET to be actively involved in this task. Standard-setting exercises were carried out as part of the research projects mentioned above (e.g., Davidson, 2022), and a speaking test panel was also convened that included representatives of allied health professions who use the OET (Séguis & McElwee, 2019).

In an earlier initiative for the General Medical Council, when IELTS was the sole ELP test accepted for doctors registering in the United Kingdom, Berry and O'Sullivan (2016) carried out standard-setting panels to review appropriate cut-scores for IELTS. Most interestingly, as well as involving practitioners and employers, some panels were constituted of members of the public and patients, a vital constituency to engage given their insider status as users of the healthcare system and on the receiving end of the communication skills being assessed.

The standard-setting studies and other commissioned research also demonstrate how language testing researchers and practitioners can collaborate with professional registration bodies, leading to greater mutual understanding between key stakeholders and positive outcomes for those involved (e.g., Chan & Taylor, 2020).

Challenges and Issues

The three "problematic" aspects of LSP tests identified by Douglas (2001, p. 45) – *authenticity, specificity,* and *inseparability* – remain a helpful way of discussing challenges and issues in LSP assessment. In addition, this updated chapter draws on a recent framework proposed by Knoch and Macqueen (2020) that conceptualizes LAPPs as tools for risk management: risks to test takers, to fellow professionals, to clients and consumers, and to society more generally.

Authenticity

Simulating tasks and content from the workplace in a test provides a context in which test takers can feel "at home" with the routine and topics of their profession. When a test seeks to reflect the workplace, the preparation materials and courses that invariably develop alongside it are also likely to reflect that content; this may create a positive washback that goes beyond the test to help set appropriate expectations among test takers for their future roles as well. However, tensions arise because a test cannot fully replicate the workplace, and what constitutes an authentic response can be contested (Harding et al., 2023). This challenge was discussed in detail in the previous section. Tensions persist between the practicalities of test administration (delivery, marking, and maintaining similar difficulty across test versions) and the authenticity of a test (tasks, content, and assessment criteria). For example, while test users request that a range of writing skills should be assessed, practitioners may complain that they rarely write extended text at work, instead using templates set up on a computer. A mismatch may also arise between linguistically oriented assessment criteria and the authentic performance criteria of the workplace. (See articles in Knoch et al., 2020b, for evidence of both issues.) Nevertheless, the OET-related research presented in the previous section demonstrates the viability and value of extending the scope of assessment criteria to reflect better what matters to health professional "insiders," thereby making "weak" performance tests – dealing only with linguistic features of performance – "stronger," to use McNamara's definition (McNamara, 1996, p. 197), i.e., more focused on task achievement in the domain.

Specificity

The section above on approaches to language assessment of health professionals reveals continuing variation in the three contexts reviewed but also significant changes in the take-up of general- and specific-purpose testing tools for assessing language proficiency. Interestingly, the trend over the past decade, perhaps compelled further by the recent COVID-19 pandemic, appears to be toward accreditation boards embracing a broader range of internationally available ELP tests, particularly the specific-purpose OET with its multiple healthcare-related variants, e.g., for medicine, nursing, and dentistry. The sufficiency of primarily general-purpose language tests for use in a specialized context such as medicine remains contested (for IELTS, see Read, 2022).

The issue of specificity should perhaps be viewed as one of degree. Domain description and needs analysis in the development of LSP tests help test designers understand the demands of the workplace and the tasks and content that participants (insiders) engage with. A test representing these aspects is likely to be viewed as more suitable for the domain than a general-purpose test is. Specific-purpose test takers can be confused by task prompts or topics that appear irrelevant to their working context (Pym, 2017), and even LSP test content is open to criticism that it is not sufficiently pertinent to the needs of particular test takers. Introducing greater variety into test tasks and their content, as noted in the previous section on research, can help reduce any sense of lack of relevance for test takers.

Another view of specificity concerns how local or national characteristics are reflected in a test. Health professionals moving to work in Australia, for instance, might be criticized for not understanding aspects of informal language or so-called "slang" in common use, and this might be suggested as an area for assessment in a language test. However, including such content would disadvantage health professionals who have not had the chance to visit and become familiar with the country. This type of culturally specific knowledge, also including brand names for medication or procedures for providing a "sick note," for example, is perhaps best acquired in situ; nevertheless, it remains a matter of degree. Localizing a test to suit a particular regional context may seem attractive and offer certain benefits, but it also risks limiting its international reach and relevance beyond certain borders, thus making it potentially less viable and useful in a global sense.

Inseparability

If language knowledge can be reliably separated out from other domain-related knowledge, then using a general, decontextualized measure of language proficiency makes sense, since the test scores can justifiably be used to predict performance, even in a highly specialized context. However, if this is not the case, there are significant test development implications in terms of content sampling, task design, assessment criteria, and score interpretation. Collaboration between language specialists and content specialists (also known as subject matter experts) is required at every stage of test development, along with input from test users such as accreditation bodies. Evidence of this is found in the research section above, where studies have involved domain insiders (healthcare practitioners and patients) and test stakeholders (regulatory bodies) in the ongoing development of an LSP test (OET) and in standard-setting procedures to determine or review passing standards. The importance of including the views of nonlanguage specialists in the assessment of performance for specific and general domains is considered by Elder et al. (2017), who argue that a test's validity may be greatly limited if it operationalizes only a language-focused construct.

Current assessment practice for doctors registering in three jurisdictions, as described above, illustrates the continuing challenge of how to deal with language, communication, and professional skills. Although it remains impossible to discern a single model that the three contexts are moving toward, it is interesting that the different approaches presented appear to share a view that communication skills can be fundamentally linked with professional skills, to a greater or lesser degree. All three jurisdictions now accept the specific-purpose OET for the certification of medical and some other health professionals. The United Kingdom also uses PLAB, while Australia recognizes PLAB and NZREX – two tests that integrate communication and professional skills in an OSCE format. This view may be due to the underlying understanding in the health professions that good communication skills are essential, as health care evolves both socially and technologically. The concept of patient-centered care continues to be valued highly in Western healthcare practice.

Managing Public Risk

A significant contribution since 2014 is the work of Knoch and Macqueen (2020) in their volume *Assessing English for professional purposes*. The authors begin by introducing the sociological concept of risk to conceptualize LAPPs as tools for risk management on the part of different stakeholder groups within the context of rapid socio-technological development. They propose a socially oriented theory of *construct* for LAPP, starting with the dimensions of an assessment construct and then suggesting how these relate to the micro and macro contexts of an assessment, for example, in terms of language varieties and professional registers. They advocate a broadened approach to the *needs analysis* stage of test development that samples from the gamut of linguistic repertoires that inhabit professional workplaces. They describe the complex process of reconciling the findings of a needs analysis and developing a *test blueprint and test specifications*, including the elicitation and development of scoring criteria based on indigenous criteria (i.e., criteria valued by domain insiders). Finally, Knoch and Macqueen model an argument-based approach for validating LAPP use in a given context and discuss the sometimes-confused distinction between language assessments and language-associated policies. Their work seeks to extend the remit of the field and to theorize about its various tools: for understanding constructs, for conducting needs analyses, for developing assessment instruments, for validation, and for evaluating policy. It also suggests some important directions for future research together with a broader agenda for the field of LAPP.

Practical Considerations and Policy Constraints

In addition to the challenges and issues discussed above, matters of practicality and issues of policy and fairness must be addressed. It is important to acknowledge that decisions by health professional registration bodies to create, adopt, or recognize tests are shaped not only by considerations of test content, quality, and relevance but also by pragmatic issues, including the availability of test centers and online test versions; convenience and frequency of test administrations; cost to test takers and other stakeholders; test security, integrity, and turn-around of results; transparency of the scoring system; and documentary support for stakeholders (e.g., online score validation services). Language testing researchers and practitioners would do well to seek to understand the perspectives of LAPP stakeholders, such as representatives of regulatory bodies, employers, and test takers themselves. Macqueen et al.'s (2021) research presents stakeholders' views on test impact and their trust in tests.

Furthermore, the political dimension must not be underestimated: Workforce flows are managed by governments, and language tests and test providers inevitably become involved in legislation and public policy. Changes in the political, legal, or economic environment trigger policy changes, and political priorities may override language testing sensibilities. Test users demand and expect a single, clear "answer," something language testers rarely want to provide. For their part, registration bodies face the complex task of balancing the management of public policy and risk while seeking to facilitate fair access and professional development opportunities for individual health professionals.

Future Directions

In addition to the challenges and issues discussed above, other factors are likely to focus the attention of language test developers and users in the future.

One impact of the COVID-19 pandemic in 2020 was a major shift to online, video-, and telephone-based interaction in business, industry, and education, as well as health-related contexts. Much assessment practice has also moved online as test providers pivoted to a new digital environment with computer-based testing becoming increasingly the norm for both general- and specific-purpose tests. Developments in digital communication will continue to shape approaches to the design and delivery of LAPP, e.g., the creation of new, "born digital" assessments (cf. Duolingo English Test), or multimodal assessments that combine language skills. Applied linguistics and language assessment research will need to keep pace with changing communication demands in an interconnected, digitally mediated world in order to implement appropriate domain and delivery changes.

A second factor, related to technology, concerns the growing presence of tools using artificial intelligence (AI) and the potential these may have to shape LAPP approaches and the workplace environment more broadly. Automated scoring for writing and speaking performances has been used in some language tests for several years. The impact of this on LSP testing is limited so far, perhaps because the specialist nature of the performance, i.e., the inseparability of language and professional content, makes its assessment a particularly challenging endeavor. It would be a backward step to impose the application of automated scoring prematurely and so reverse recent advances made, for example, in the broadening of the scope of assessment criteria for an LSP domain to include profession-specific features. Nevertheless, technology is constantly improving, and the situation will change. Currently, the scope for wider social change due to AI and a timeline for this change are difficult to predict. In time, instant automated interpretation between languages may remove the need for language proficiency tests, while robot carers may take over human workers' roles in many healthcare contexts.

Third, from an ethical perspective, the increasing dependence of healthcare systems in more economically developed countries on health professionals trained elsewhere risks depleting the resources and systems of the countries providing this valued "commodity." Many of the latter countries have a great need for health professionals' skills among their own populations but are unable to compete in a global marketplace (see, e.g., Grimley &

380 Chapter 26 Assessing Health and Other Professionals

Horrox, 2023). A further moral and ethical challenge is to avoid setting migrants on "pathways to nowhere" (Breakey et al., 2019, p. 11), where they cannot maintain their professional status in the new country (perhaps because they are unable to obtain the necessary language certification) and their professional skills consequently become unavailable. The language testing community needs to reflect on its role in this complex situation through a lens of professional ethics and social justice (Kunnan, 2018).

Though much was achieved in the decade following our 2014 publication, the interrelationship of language proficiency, communicative competence, and clinical communication skills undoubtedly merits further study. The goals we suggested then are still pertinent. All health professionals, regardless of language or cultural background, can be trained to communicate more effectively. When language is considered a fundamental tool in doing the work of health and other professionals, such training should focus more explicitly on improving practitioners' understanding of how particular linguistic choices and strategies can facilitate efficient communication. Current research on interactional competence and its assessment may make a valuable contribution in this regard (e.g., Roever & Dai, 2021).

Language tests used in professional and workplace contexts are still viewed essentially as hurdle requirements to establish that performance of "non-native" speakers meets a minimum standard. A more constructive role for assessment is the ongoing improvement of the language and communication skills of *all* practitioners for the specialist contexts in which they work. These contexts could include those where more than one language is used as a matter of routine and where English, for example, is a lingua franca. In addition, the growing role and contribution of multilingualism and translanguaging within professional and workplace contexts merit greater attention. Training and assessment must be developed in and for the workplace to meet the actual needs of practitioners; they must also be developed in parallel, as complementary aspects of professional development and support. Moreover, the role of language in accomplishing effective communication should be acknowledged further in national professional standards and regulatory documents. Representing language as the essential tool for effective communication in this way would help generate a new and progressive agenda for research on language assessment for health and other professionals.

Discussion Questions

1. Consider the similarities/differences in the language (assessment) needs of:
    a. related professions (e.g., doctors, nurses, physiotherapists, and radiographers)
    b. different professional fields (e.g., health care, aviation, engineering, and tourism)
    c. different geographical/political/social contexts (e.g., economically more/less developed countries).
2. What are the likely reasons for the differences you note, and what implications do such differences have for the design and implementation of language assessments?

References

Berry, V., & O'Sullivan, B. (2016). Language standards for medical practice in the UK: issues of fairness and quality for all. In J. Banerjee & D. Tsagari (Eds.), *Contemporary second language assessment* (pp. 225–241). Bloomsbury.

Breakey, H., Ransome, W., & Sampford, C. (2019). The ethical significance of migrating health professionals' legitimate expectations: Canadian and Australian pathways to nowhere? In V. Harris (Ed.), *Ethics in a crowded world: Globalisation, human movement and professional ethics* (pp. 11–31). Emerald Publishing. https://doi.org/10.1108/S1529-209620190000022003.

References 381

Chan, S., & Taylor, L. (2020). Comparing writing proficiency assessments used in professional medical registration: a methodology to inform policy and practice. *Assessing Writing, 46*, 100493. https://doi.org/10.1016/j.asw.2020.100493.

Davidson, S. (2022). The domain expert perspective: a qualitative study into the views expressed in a standard-setting exercise on a language for specific purposes (LSP) test for health professionals. *Language Testing, 39*(1), 117–141. https://doi.org/10.1177/02655322211010737.

Douglas, D. (2001). Three problems in testing language for specific purposes: authenticity, specificity and inseparability. In C. Elder, A. Brown, E. Grove, K. Hill, N. Iwashita, T. Lumley, T. McNamara & K. O'Loughlin (Eds.), *Experimenting with uncertainty: Essays in honour of Alan Davies* (pp. 45–52). Cambridge University Press.

Elder, C. (Ed.). (2016). Authenticity in LSP testing (special issue). *Language Testing, 33*(2).

Elder, C., & McNamara, T. (2016). The hunt for "indigenous criteria" in assessing communication in the physiotherapy workplace. *Language Testing, 33*(2), 153–174. https://doi.org/10.1177/0265532215607398.

Elder, C., McNamara, T., Kim, H., Pill, J., & Sato, T. (2017). Interrogating the construct of communicative competence in language assessment contexts: what the non-language specialist can tell us. *Language & Communication, 57*, 14–21. https://doi.org/10.1016/j.langcom.2016.12.005.

Friginal, E., Mathews, E., & Roberts, J. (2020). *English in global aviation: Context, research and pedagogy*. Bloomsbury Academic.

Grimley, N., & Horrox, C. (2023, June 6). *Ghana patients in danger as nurses head for NHS in UK – medics. BBC News.* https://www.bbc.co.uk/news/world-africa-65808660

Harding, L., Macqueen, S., & Pill, J. (2023). Assessing communicative competence. In M. Solon & M. Kanwit (Eds.), *Communicative competence in a second language: Theory, method, and applications* (pp. 187–207). Routledge. https://doi.org/10.4324/9781003160779-14.

Jacoby, S., & McNamara, T. (1999). Locating competence. *English for Specific Purposes, 18*(3), 213–241. https://doi.org/10.1016/S0889-4906(97)00053-7.

Kim, H. (2018). What constitutes professional communication in aviation: is language proficiency enough for testing purposes? *Language Testing, 35*(3), 403–426. https://doi.org/10.1177/0265532218758127.

Knoch, U., & Macqueen, S. (2020). *Assessing English for professional purposes*. Routledge.

Knoch, U., Elder, C., Woodward-Kron, R., Manias, E., Flynn, E., McNamara, T., Huisman, A., & Zhang, B. Y. (2020a). Capturing domain expert perspectives in devising a rating scale for a health specific writing test: how close can we get? *Assessing Writing, 46*, 100489. https://doi.org/10.1016/j.asw.2020.100489.

Knoch, U., Macqueen, S., & Elder, C. (Eds.). (2020b). Assessing writing for workplace purposes (special issue). *Assessing Writing, 46*.

Knoch, U., Zhang, B. Y., Elder, C., Flynn, E., Huisman, A., Woodward-Kron, R., Manias, E., & McNamara, T. (2020c). "I will go to my grave fighting for grammar": exploring the ability of language-trained raters to implement a professionally-relevant rating scale for writing. *Assessing Writing, 46*, 100488. https://doi.org/10.1016/j.asw.2020.100488.

Kunnan, A. J. (2018). *Evaluating language assessments*. Routledge.

Lim, G. S. (2022). *English language standards for internationally educated nurses seeking to work in the United Kingdom: Recommendations for standard setting exercises*. Cambridge Boxhill Language Assessment. https://www.nmc.org.uk/globalassets/sitedocuments/english-language-consultation/oet-standards-report/

Macqueen, S., Pill, J., & Knoch, U. (2021). Trust the test: score-user perspectives on the roles of language tests in professional registration and skilled migration. *Papers in Language Testing and Assessment, 10*(1), 49–69. https://doi.org/10.58379/MAKH4553.

McNamara, T. F. (1996). *Measuring second language performance*. Longman.

Mladenovic, J., van Zanten, M., & Pinsky, W. W. (2023). Evolution of Educational Commission for Foreign Medical Graduates certification in the absence of the USMLE Step 2 clinical skills examination. *Academic Medicine, 98*(4), 444–447. https://doi.org/10.1097/ACM.0000000000005051.

O'Hagan, S., Pill, J., & Zhang, Y. (2016). Extending the scope of speaking assessment criteria in a specific-purpose language test: operationalizing a health professional perspective. *Language Testing, 33*(2), 195–216. https://doi.org/10.1177/0265532215607920.

382   Chapter 26   Assessing Health and Other Professionals

Pill, J. (2016). Drawing on indigenous criteria for more authentic assessment in a specific-purpose language test: health professionals interacting with patients. *Language Testing, 33*(2), 175–193. https://doi.org/10.1177/0265532215607400.

Pym, H. (2017, August 22). *Do I have to understand jam-making to be a nurse? BBC News.* https://www.bbc.co.uk/news/health-41010021

Read, J. (2022). Test review: the International English Language Testing System (IELTS). *Language Testing, 39*(4), 679–694. https://doi.org/10.1177/02655322221086211.

Roever, C., & Dai, D. W. (2021). Reconceptualising interactional competence for language testing. In M. R. Salaberry & A. R. Burch (Eds.), *Assessing speaking in context* (pp. 23–49). Multilingual Matters. https://doi.org/10.21832/9781788923828-003.

Sedgwick, C., Garner, M., & Vicente-Macia, I. (2016). *Investigating the language needs of international nurses: insiders' perspectives. IELTS Research Reports Online Series*, 2016/2. https://www.ielts.org/for-researchers/research-reports/online-series-2016-2

Séguis, B., & Lim, G. S. (2020). The writing that nurses do: investigating changes to standards over time. *Assessing Writing, 46*, 100491. https://doi.org/10.1016/j.asw.2020.100491.

Séguis, B., & McElwee, S. (2019). Assessing clinical communication on the Occupational English Test. In S. Papageorgiou & K. M. Bailey (Eds.), *Global perspectives on language assessment: Research, theory, and practice* (pp. 63–79). Routledge.

Taylor, L. & Chan, S. (2015). *IELTS equivalence research project (GM133) – final report.* General Medical Council. www.gmc-uk.org/-/media/documents/GMC_Final_Report___Main_report__extended____Final___13May2015.pdf_63506590.pdf

Taylor, L., & Pill, J. (2014). Assessing health professionals. In A. J. Kunnan (Ed.), *Companion to language assessment* (Vol. 1, pp. 497–512). Wiley-Blackwell. https://doi.org/10.1002/9781118411360.wbcla137.

Suggested Readings

Douglas, D. (2000). *Assessing languages for specific purposes.* Cambridge University Press.

Knoch, U., & Macqueen, S. (2020). *Assessing English for professional purposes.* Routledge.

Kunnan, A. J. (2018). *Evaluating language assessments.* Routledge.

CHAPTER 27

Acoustic and Temporal Analysis for Assessing Speaking

Okim Kang and Lucy Pickering

Introduction

Oral assessment in language learning has received increasing attention among second-language (L2) acquisition researchers. This growing interest is likely a product of the increased interpretability of test scores and potential validity of the scores when linked to real-world criteria (Bonk & Ockey, 2003; Kang & Ginther, 2017). However, assessing speaking skills can be more challenging than assessing other skills because of the possible subjective nature of listener comprehension, the complexity of rater reliability, and the validity of the performance itself. Of these challenges, the potential variability in rater judgments has been of particular concern for language assessment, as sources of measurement error (e.g., Bachman et al., 1995; Kang et al., 2019).

A variety of human rater biases are attested to in the perceptions of speaking proficiency, and the speaking assessment may have a limited basis in the linguistic characteristics of the speaker's oral production. Although sophisticated statistical techniques derived from Rasch scaling or G-theory can in principle equate practiced ratings that may display different degrees of rigor or leniency among raters (Lumley & McNamara, 1995), a technology-based measurement strategy that compensates for the need for rater judgments in oral proficiency is much to be desired (Kang et al., 2010). In fact, certain acoustical and temporal features of non-native speaker's (NNS) pronunciation – measurable by means of instrumentation rather than by listener impressions – can now provide supplementary parameters for "degree of accentedness."

Thanks to advances in speech science, we can readily identify acoustic and temporal features of pronunciation that affect listeners' comprehensibility. That is, computer-assisted instruments can conveniently examine some elements of the physical facts of human utterances. In this chapter, the primary focus lies in a discussion of instrumental measures with regard to speaking assessment in general and addresses both temporal (voice time and duration) and acoustic (e.g., fundamental frequency, amplitude, or spectral behavior for intonation in particular) parameters used for various operational constructs of NNS speech evaluation. For this purpose, the constructs of listeners' judgments such as intelligibility, comprehensibility, and accentedness are construed in one broad sense of listeners' evaluation

---

The Concise Companion to Language Assessment, First Edition. Edited by Antony John Kunnan.
© 2025 John Wiley & Sons, Inc. Published 2025 by John Wiley & Sons, Inc.

384 Chapter 27 Acoustic and Temporal Analysis for Assessing Speaking

of NNS speech, even though they are addressed separately in the literature (Derwing & Munro, 2005).[1] This broad approach also includes listeners' ratings of NNSs' oral proficiency and fluency. This chapter also addresses the difference between automated scoring systems and systems such as those discussed thus far that rely on both instrumental and auditory analyses.

One caveat to note initially is that the instrumental analysis can be indeed dependent upon perceptual subjectivity itself to some extent, although it is known to objectively describe and evaluate speech data. (See the section, "Challenges for objective measures of the speech signal in oral assessment" later in this entry.) Thus, this entry posits that the instrumental analysis alone should not be the sole basis for objective interpretation of candidates' scores in speaking assessment, but instead a useful methodology to identify information about a candidate's speech that would contribute to scoring decision-making or to assessment rubric development.

Background of Acoustic and Temporal Measures

Perceptual ratings in oral assessment such as measurement of the percentage of correctly identified words or rating scales using 5-, 7-, or 9-point scales may suffer from measurement errors due to their dependency on raters' backgrounds, subjectivity, and other social issues (Kang & Rubin, 2009). In the social contexts, up to a quarter of the variance in listener judgment is attributed to factors such as listeners' expectations, attitudes, and stereotypes as opposed to the nature of the speech itself (Derwing et al., 2014). An alternative approach to supplement this human rater variability is the application of instrumental analysis that can objectively evaluate candidates' speech. Since computers began to become available to speech researchers in the 1960s, speech analysis research has evolved substantially. For example, computer-assisted speech analysis (e.g., use of a KayPentax Computerized Speech Laboratory known as CSL or freeware such as PRAAT: http://www.praat.org/) is becoming more commonplace in the assessment of speech patterns (e.g., Kang et al., 2020; Pickering, 2004).

The instrumental analysis can examine the production of NNS at both segmental and suprasegmental levels. While the segmental analysis often focuses on the "accuracy" of NNS' consonant and vowel formation, the suprasegmental analysis takes account of the role that differences in speaking rates, intonation patterns, and other prosodic features may play in listeners' comprehension. This methodology often incorporates discourse analysis to supplement the instrumental analysis, wherein an analyst identifies a pragmatic context in which a particular intonational contour would be expected (Pickering, 2001). Following the discourse analysis, computer-based analysis is used to confirm (or disconfirm) that the expected contour does indeed appear at that site in the speech stream. This is especially one of the big methodological differences between computer-programmed automated scoring systems, which are described in the following paragraph, and auditory-instrumental-combined analysis. Studies have suggested that features (e.g., pitch range) identified via the combined acoustic analysis explain a large portion of variance in listeners' judgments of NNS speech (e.g., Kang et al., 2010).

Finally, and more recently, instrumentally identified measures are used to help understand the process of automated scoring. This is the latest development in language assessment and testing due to advances in speech recognition and processing technologies (see, for example, the 2010 special issue of *Language Testing*). Currently, tests are in some use in the ESL field: for example, Versant, also known as PhonePass produced by Ordinate Corporation,

---

[1] Unlike intelligibility that refers to the extent to which a listener understands an utterance, comprehensibility pertains to the degree of difficulty the listener reports in attempting to understand an utterance, and accentedness represents the extent to which an L2 learner's speech is perceived to differ from native speaker norms (Derwing & Munro, 2005).

Speech Rater developed by Educational Testing Services alongside their internet-based (iBT) TOEFL test, the Aptis English Test by the British Council, or the Duolingo English Test. For instance, sub-scores of Versant tests for reading fluency and repeat fluency are measures of suprasegmental features (timing, pause, or rhythm). However, as Chapelle and Chung (2010) note, the mechanisms that underlie these tests remain largely opaque and unknown to most professionals in L2 assessment, not least because these are commercial not academic ventures. That is, the algorithms or the features that are assessed are mostly proprietary, and not available for public examination or academic research. In addition, adopting these automated speech scoring systems still faces various challenges in terms of establishing validity for test score use and decisions made on the basis of automated test scores, or accurately evaluating communicative functions (Kang et al., 2021a). The lack of adequacy in testing the communicative competence of candidates is an ongoing concern for those who seek a valid means to automatically test and score learner speech.

Acoustic and Temporal Parameters Measured in Assessing Speaking

Various aspects of NNS pronunciation can be considered in listeners' assessments of speaker proficiency. Studies have investigated the impact of acoustic and temporal features on listeners' judgments of NNSs' oral performance (e.g., Kang et al., 2010) or the correlations between objective measures of speech rates and listeners' rating scores (e.g., Cucchiarini et al., 2002; Hsieh et al., 2019). In the early 1980s and 1990s, acoustic studies largely compared NNSs' speech production with the patterns of native speakers' (NSs) speech. Gradually, however, they began to use acoustic and temporal parameters as indicators of listeners' perceptions.

Segmental acoustic parameters include features of accent such as consonants, the voice onset time (VOT), or vowel formants. VOT refers to the duration of the period of time between the release of a stop consonant and the beginning of voicing. An easy way to visualize VOT is by reference to the waveform of a sound. Figure 27.1 shows a waveform of the word "tie" in English spoken by the first author, an advanced Korean speaker of English. The left vertical line indicates the moment of release of the stop consonant /t/ pronounced as [tʰaɪ]. The VOT is about 0.08 ms from the spike indicating the release of the stop consonant to the start of the oscillating line indicating the vibration of the vocal folds in the vowel of [aɪ]. An example of the VOT study using NNSs' speech is Flege and Eefting's (1987) research, which compared

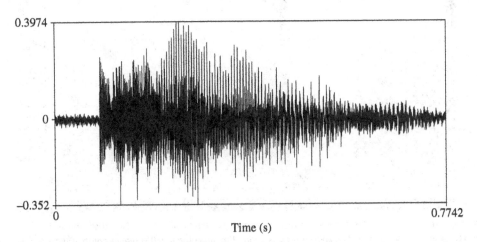

FIGURE 27.1 The waveform of the word "tie."

VOT differences of English stop consonants (e.g., /p/, /t/, and /k/) produced by NSs and Spanish L2 speakers. Spanish speakers of English produced shorter VOTs in English initial voiceless stops than did NSs.

In acoustic phonetics, vowels are classified according to particular values called formants, which are a concentration of acoustic energy, i.e., a group of overtones corresponding to a resonating frequency of the air in the vocal track (Ladefoged, 2001). (Examples of the formants are shown as dark voice bars in Figure 27.2.) Accordingly, English vowels are characterized by three formants (F1, F2, and F3) that are used to describe vowel structures. For example, in Wilson et al.'s (2009) study analyzing the speech of low-intermediate Japanese speakers, when a consonant /s/ occurs before a high front vowel /i/, it becomes palatalized as in /ʃ/ (i.e., "sea" and "sit" are pronounced as "she" and "shit"). As for the vowel formants, Japanese speakers' F1 value of the low back vowel as in /ɑ/ is considerably lower than that of NSs. (In Figure 27.2, examples of the F1 formant are illustrated as the lowest voice bars.) Overall, using speech analysis programs we can identify the characteristics of individual phonemes, the location of formants, or the presence of voicing.

Numerous studies have investigated the relationships between temporal measures and listeners' judgments of NNS speech (e.g., Kang, 2010; Kang & Johnson, 2018; Préfontaine et al., 2015; Saito et al., 2022; Suzuki & Komos, 2019). After Munro and Derwing's (2001) finding, a common belief is that there is a curvilinear relationship between speaking rates and listeners' judgments of L2 comprehensibility and accent. This curvilinear relationship has been recently confirmed by Kang and her colleagues' research (Kang et al., 2022). NNS utterances should be somewhat slower than the typical rate for an NS utterance but faster than what L2 learners often produce. Parameters of speaking rates are measured via syllables per second, articulation rate (mean number of syllables per second excluding pauses), phonation–time ratio (percentage of time producing audible speech), and mean length of run (an average number of syllables between pauses). Some or all of these temporal variables often strongly predict L2 performance judgments.

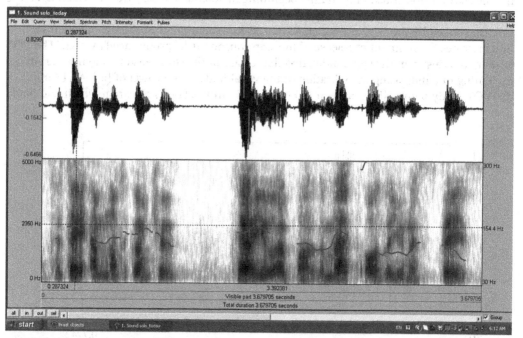

FIGURE 27.2 An example of a spectrogram showing the waveform (the upper) and the fundamental frequency (the lower, wavy lines). The speech used is *Today I'm not going to tell you about map of the United States* by an advanced Chinese speaker.

Pauses are an especially important element in regard to speaking rate, and relationships between pausing and speaking assessment have been also widely investigated. Pauses are measured by variables such as the number, the length, and the location of silent and filled (e.g., "eh" or "um") pauses. Thus far, pause studies (e.g., Anderson-Hsieh & Venkatagiri, 1994; Kormos & Denes, 2004) have demonstrated that low-proficiency speakers tend to pause frequently and inappropriately, and their pause durations are longer, whereas higher proficiency learners speak faster with less pausing and fewer unfilled pauses. Methodologically speaking, there has been an ongoing debate among researchers about the cut-off point of pause length. That is, the cut-off point of silent pauses can vary, i.e., 0.1 second (Anderson-Hsieh & Venkatagiri, 1994), 0.2 second (Zeches & Yorkston, 1995), or 0.25 (Towell et al., 1996). Terminology-wise, the terms "pauses" and "silences" are often used synonymously in automated scoring systems (e.g., Zechner et al., 2009). They use disfluency as a substitute for the term, "filled pause." What is also important is the location of pauses. A recent study (Moran & Kang, 2021) showed that there were big differences in highly intelligible speakers between inner circle (North American and British) speakers and other outer and expanding circle varieties.

Speaking rate and pause measures are often preferred by automatic speech recognition (ASR) systems as objectively measurable parameters that show a high correlation with L2 fluency judgments (Cucchiarini et al., 2002; Saito et al., 2022). De Jong and Wempe (2007) provide an example of the relationship between machine-based and human-based coding of temporal measures. In this study, PRAAT was used to automatically calculate the number of syllables in the utterance based on intensity (the amount of acoustic energy) and pitch peaks. The correlation between the human and automatic speech rate calculations was 0.71 (see more detail in De Jong & Wempe, 2007). Ginther et al. (2010) also report robust correlations between temporal variables and other rated measures of oral proficiency; however, these measures alone did not distinguish adjacent levels in the same way that human raters were able to. The authors add that automated rating systems are thus only able to measure a "narrow sense of fluency" (p. 394).

Prosodic features such as stress and intonation patterns also have a crucial role to play in L2 speaking assessment. First, stress features have been emphasized as nonstandard word stress has been shown to undermine intelligibility (Field, 2005). Misplacement of stress in disyllabic words has detrimental effects in speech processing (Cutler & Clifton, 1984). Stress patterns can be obscured in NNS speech production. Low-proficiency NNSs often misuse primary stress, placing equal stress on every content word in the unit (Wennerstrom, 2000). In terms of fluency and oral proficiency judgments, advanced L2 learners used stressed words more appropriately than low-intermediate students (Kang, 2010; Kang et al., 2021a). Acoustic parameters used for these analyses are numbers of stressed words per minute and proportion of stressed words to the overall number of words, or the duration of stressed and unstressed syllables.

Non-native intonation patterns, particularly tone choices, have been studied in native listeners' perception of L2 English learners' speech (e.g., Kang et al., 2021a, b; Kang & Johnson, 2018). The intonation characteristics of many East Asian speakers may cause U.S. listeners to lose concentration or to misunderstand the speaker's intent (Pickering, 2001). In particular, the choice of a rising, falling, or level pitch on the focused word of a tone unit can affect both perceived information structure and social cues in L2 discourse. A tone unit is a basic unit of intonation known also as tone group, which is a means of breaking up stretches of spoken discourse (Brazil, 1997). Another intonation feature that affects NSs' comprehension of NNSs' speech is pitch range variation. Low proficient/NNSs tend to show a compressed pitch range and a lack of variety in pitch-level choices (Wennerstrom, 2000). This contracted pitch range particularly affects NNSs' ability to indicate the beginning or the end of their discourse. Not surprisingly, this narrow pitch range factor exerts a significant negative effect on proficiency and comprehensibility ratings (Kang et al., 2010).

388   Chapter 27 Acoustic and Temporal Analysis for Assessing Speaking

The intonation-related variables investigated as part of acoustic measures have included tone choices (high-rising, high-level, high-falling, mid-rising, mid-level, mid-falling, low-rising, low-level, and low-falling), pitch prominent syllables, pitch non-prominent syllables, and other spoken discourse-related measures (Kang et al., 2021a). (See the later section of this entry subtitled "Applications of acoustic analysis and sample analyses" for a fuller discussion of prominence.) In a study that distinguished these variables, Kang et al. (2010) reported that mid-rising and high-rising tone choices and pitch range variables were the strongest predictors for NNSs' oral proficiency and comprehensibility ratings.

These physical features listed above along with suggestions from the literature (e.g., Cucchiarini et al., 2002; Kang & Johnson, 2018; Saito et al., 2022) are used as bases for automated scoring systems. Indeed, the knowledge of acoustic and temporal properties of sound can be helpful for understanding how speech recognition works. Acoustic models exclusively trained on non-native speech can extract these temporal and acoustic features that are scaled and transformed into fluency and pronunciation scores in the system (Bernstein et al., 2010). For example, the TOEFL Practice Online (TPO) has a set of 11 features for use in the scoring model, whose focus is mainly on fluency, with pronunciation, vocabulary diversity, and grammatical accuracy added to the mix (Zechner et al., 2009). Among the 11 selected features, 8 of them deal with fluency aspects (e.g., articulation rate or duration of silence per word) with 1 pronunciation, and 2 other language use features. One of the rationales for choosing these features is high correlations between these features and human rating scores as they are known to represent the overall quality of speech ($r = 0.55$).

In a similar vein of research, Evanini and Wang (2013) used automated proficiency scoring with English oral responses given by non-native speaking middle school students. The computer calculated 10 linguistic measures with suprasegmental (mostly fluency features) and other linguistic skills (e.g., reading accuracy). The results showed Pearson's correlation ranged from 0.62 to 0.70 between human and computer ratings. Similarly, Black et al.'s (2015) study reported the best predictors of the "degree of nativeness" involving pauses in speech, speaking rate, rhythm, and stress, along with the segmental feature of goodness of phone pronunciation. Kang and Johnson (2018) examined 35 suprasegmental features in predicting oral proficiency scores and demonstrated the Pearson's correlation of 0.72 between the computer and human proficiency levels. More recently, research has explored issues related to the intonation aspect and its interpretation in the pragmatic context (Kang et al., 2021b), but this area of topic is still yet to be applied into these automated systems.

Applications of Acoustic Analysis and Sample Analyses

In the following section of the entry, some sample analyses of spoken discourse assessment are presented by using a combination of auditory and instrumental measures (Kang, 2010; Kang et al., 2010). In other words, they combine the subjective auditory perceptions of a human analyst with the objective instrumental measurements of the speech signal. As noted above, although temporal measures can be fairly successfully scored automatically, crucial prosodic features such as intonation and stress are less easily scored. This is particularly the case when dealing with discourse as opposed to more constrained language samples. Combinations of auditory and instrumental analysis of acoustic features tend to use hardware and software programs such as a CSL or PRAAT for pitch-related measures. As for sole temporal measures, sound editing programs such as *Audacity* or *Soundforge* can be employed.

Speech samples are recorded in digital .wav format and transcribed orthographically and prosodically (see Excerpt 27.1). As acoustic parameters are gradient in nature, a range of baseline native speaker realizations of the features is also measured. As described in Ladefoged's

(2001) book, *A Course in Phonetics*, sound consists of small variations in air pressure that occur rapidly one after another. Actions of the speakers' vocal organs cause these variations, which move through the air somewhat like the ripples on a pond. When they reach the ear of a listener, they cause the eardrum to vibrate, which creates sound waves. These waveforms of speech sounds can be readily observed on a computer program such as a CSL or PRAAT.

For analysis, three acoustic indicators are generated: (i) spectrograms; (ii) frequency or pitch of fundamental formant (F_0); and (iii) intensity (volume of vocalization). Spectrograms are a "graphic representation of sounds in terms of their component frequencies, in which time is shown on the horizontal axis, frequency on the vertical axis, and the intensity of each frequency at each moment in time by the darkness of the mark" (Ladefoged, 2001, p. 276). Frequency is a technical term for an acoustic property of a sound. It refers to the number of complete cycles of variation in air pressure occurring in a second. The unit of this frequency measurement is the Hertz, known as Hz. Figure 27.2 shows a spectrogram of an advanced Chinese speaker's speech *Today I'm not going to tell you about map of the United States* using the PRAAT. The upper part of the figure shows the waveform. The fundamental frequency (pitch) is illustrated in the lower part with wavy lines. Time is shown on the horizontal axis, and frequency (from 0 to 5000 Hz on the left and from 30 to 300 Hz on the right) on the vertical axis.

From the three indicators listed above, plotted against the transcripts of the speech samples, the variables of interest are derived. Figure 27.3 taken from Kang et al. (2010) exemplifies a picture of the pitch analysis matched with a script via the PRAAT freeware program, using the same Chinese speaker's speech in Figure 27.2. Note that the pitch of a sound depends on the rate of vibration of the vocal folds. A high-pitch sound involves a higher frequency of vibration than a low-pitch sound. Different sounds mean that there are differences in pitch, loudness, and quality. Especially the higher pitch and louder volume (the darkness of the waveform) are represented as prominence (a peak of intonation) syllables.

In Figure 27.3, words such as "toDAy, GOing, TEll, mAp, UNIted, StATes" appear to have received the prominence; therefore, they have been transcribed prosodically in capitalized letters. Note that in the final decision of these prominent syllables, the auditory judgments

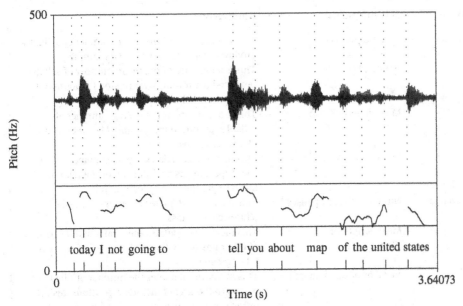

FIGURE 27.3 An example of the transcription shown for pitch ranges in PRAAT (as in Kang, 2010, p. 306). (*Note:* Due to the contraction of the spectrogram itself for the limited space, the pitch contour and phonological segments may not appear to be exactly paralleled.)

390 Chapter 27 Acoustic and Temporal Analysis for Assessing Speaking

need to be combined with this instrumental analysis. In order to measure the proportion of prominent words, for example, we can calculate the proportion of these prominent words to the total number of words. For the pitch range measure, we look at the midpoint of the vowel in the prominent syllable and read F_0 values and calculate the range of the sample by subtracting the minimum F_0 from the maximum F_0 across the speech sample. In Figure 27.2, the dotted lines point at the word "toDAy" of which F_0 value is 154.4 Hz shown at the end of the right side. More examples of variable measures particularly for suprasegmental features are presented in Table 27.1.

Excerpt 27.1 shows the prosodic transcription of the same speech sample.

Combining measures used in a variety of studies, Kang et al. (2010, 2021a) completed a detailed analysis of the speech signal comprising rate, pause, stress, and pitch measures as shown in Table 27.1.

EXCERPT 27.1

(0.10) //todAY I'm not GOing to // (0.47) // TELL you about the MAP of the UNITED STATES/ (0.22)
     154.4 147.2   142.   145.5   124.48   111.3

(The numbers in parentheses =the length of pauses produced; // = dividing run or tone unit; capitalized letters=prominent syllables; the numbers below the stressed syllables = the F_0 reading of the vowel measured in Hz at the midpoint of the vowel).

TABLE 27.1

Selected suprasegmental measures

Measures	Sub-measures	Descriptions
Rate measures	Syllable per second	This is a measure of the mean number of syllables produced per second for the 60 s sample
	Articulation rate	This is a measure of the mean number of syllables produced per minute over the total amount of time talking and excluding pause time
	Mean length of run	This is a measure of the average number of syllables produced in utterances between pauses of 0.1 s and above
	Phonation time ratio	This measure calculates the percentage of time spent speaking as a proportion of the total time taken to produce the speech sample
Pause measures	Number of silent pauses	This measure calculates the number of silent pauses per 60 s task
	Mean length of silent pauses	This measure calculates the total length of pauses of 0.1 or greater by the total number of pauses of 0.1 or greater
	Number of filled pauses	This measure calculates the number of filled pauses (but does not include repetitions, restarts, or repairs) per 60 s task
	Mean length of filled pauses	This measure calculates the average of length of filled pauses occurring per 60 s task

Measures	Sub-measures	Descriptions
Stress measures	Number of prominent syllables per run (pace)	This measure calculates the average number of prominent syllables per run
	Proportion of prominent words (space)	This measure calculates the proportion of prominent words to the total number of words
	Prominence characteristics	This measure calculates the proportion of tone units (a run may have more than one unit) that do not contain a nuclear syllable (or final termination)
Pitch measures	Overall pitch range	This measure calculates the pitch range of the sample based on the point of F_0 minima and maxima appearing on prominent syllables per task
	Tone choice	This is the second measure of discourse-appropriate across-utterance pitch. Each complete unit is counted as comprising either a high, mid, or low termination accompanied by a rising (R), falling (P), or level (O) tone
	Average pitch difference between prominent and non-prominent syllables[a]	This is calculated by measuring the F_0 of five prominent and five non-prominent syllables and calculating the average F_0 value for each category
	Average pitch difference between new and given items	This is calculated by measuring the F_0 of the same lexical item presented initially as new information and thus appearing in following instances as given information. Where possible, five lexical items were used to calculate the average F_0 for each category

[a] Prominent syllables are divided into two categories based on where they appear in the tone unit. The first prominent syllable is called the *onset*, and the last is called the *tonic* syllable. It is the pitch level and pitch movement on these syllables that form the basis for the assessment of their communicative value within three systems (high, mid, and low). These systems realized on these two syllables (the onset and the tonic syllable) are *key*, realized on the onset syllable, and *termination*, realized on the tonic syllable (Brazil, 1986).

Challenges for Objective Measures of the Speech Signal in Oral Assessment

It is clear following decades of research that the nature of spoken language proficiency is complex. The studies reviewed here suggest that non-native temporal and intonation patterns account, at least in part, for native listeners' assessment of L2 English learners' speech. In fact, Kang et al. (2010) found that suprasegmental features alone accounted for approximately 50% of the variance in L2 speakers' proficiency ratings. Machine-based acoustic analysis suggests an additional resource to supplement human ratings in the field of language assessment. However, this objective technique still has challenges to overcome.

Acoustic analyses are indeed subject to perceptual limitations. As Crystal (2008) argues, it is important not to become too reliant on acoustic analyses because they rely on accurate calibration of measuring devices and are often open to multiple interpretations:

> Sometimes, indeed, acoustic and auditory analyses of a sound conflict – for example, in intonation studies, one may hear a speech melody as rising, whereas the acoustic facts show the fundamental frequency of the sound to be steady. In such cases, it is for phoneticians to decide which evidence

392 **Chapter 27** Acoustic and Temporal Analysis for Assessing Speaking

they will pay more attention to; there has been a longstanding debate concerning the respective merits of physical (i.e., acoustic) as opposed to psychological (i.e., auditory) solution to such problems, and how apparent conflicts of this kind can be resolved.

(Crystal, 2008, p. 7)

Possible ways to overcome such limitations include (i) using a combination of auditory and instrumental analysis and (ii) checking inter-/intra-analyst reliability to ensure the consistency of the analysis. According to Kang et al. (2010) and Kang et al. (2020) in suprasegmental analyses, the internal consistency reliability between two phonetic analysts was relatively lower in stress and pitch analyses (0.86 or lower), but higher in temporal measures (0.95 or higher). Discrepancies between the two analysts took place either in determining the start and end of each pause or in identifying prominent syllables. Therefore, a calibrating procedure having two analysts reach consensus may be required to ensure the reliability of the analysis. What people consider "objective" still relies on the "subjective" nature of listener perception.

Another caveat involves gender difference in acoustic analysis. Due to a gender confounding factor (i.e., male speakers having lower pitch voice than female speakers in general) especially in intonation measures, some studies tend to use a single gender (e.g., Kang et al. (2010) investigate only male speakers). It is becoming increasingly common to make gender adjustments for pitch before starting any analysis with different gender. That is, prior to any kind of pitch comparison between male and female voices, the pitch is transformed into semitones (Couper-Kuhlen, 1996).

Differences in spoken genre can result in additional variance to the accuracy of acoustic analysis. Scholars have used various speech stimuli for their analysis: NNS's oral presentation speech for different proficiency levels (Hincks, 2005); international teaching assistants' in-class lectures (Kang, 2010; Pickering, 2001); iBT TOEFL responses to speaking tasks (Kang et al., 2010); read versus spontaneous speech (Cucchiarini et al., 2002). Depending on the types of speech samples used for analysis, speech patterns may appear differently, assuming that test-taker performance varies in response to various tasks (Crowther et al., 2015).

When considering the practicality or applicability of an acoustic approach that combines auditory and instrumental analysis, one must take into account the labor-intensiveness involved. For a 1-minute NNS speech sample, it takes at least 30–45 minutes to identify runs and the location or length of pauses (silent and filled). It takes approximately another 45 minutes to perform the prosodic analysis (i.e., measure fundamental frequency [F_0] for prominent syllables and analyze tone choice).

Acknowledging this labor intensity, automatic speech assessment tools have received growing attention (Franco et al., 2010; Kang et al., 2021a). However, the ASR still faces numerous problems in terms of its accuracy of the measures and feedback (Kang et al., 2021a; Neri et al., 2008). Speech recognition systems, at least up until now, seem to offer more accuracy for NS speech than for NNS speech (Ehsani & Knodt, 1998; Xu, 2021). With accented NNSs' speech, the accuracy of the speech program significantly dropped (95% with NS speech in Ehsani & Knodt, 1998, but 70% in Derwing et al., 2000). In addition, as the speech recognition systems tend to measure prosody of speech without reference to linguistic organization, the precision problem especially arises with suprasegmental errors (Kang & Johnson, 2018). For instance, when it comes to tone choice analysis, there is great difficulty in identifying a tone unit especially with the speech of a low-proficiency speaker. Following Brazil's (1997) protocol, a tone unit contains one or two prominent syllables, which may coincide with syntactic and pause boundaries. However, low-proficient NNSs frequently use primary stress on every word in a message unit, regardless of its function or semantic importance (Wennerstrom, 2000). Their pauses often appear randomly and irregularly. As a result, recognizing tone unit boundaries is not a clear-cut procedure in much NNS speech.

Future Directions

To the degree that conformity to native speaker comprehensibility constitutes a criterion for oral proficiency, acoustic and temporal parameters measured via instrumentation can help interpret candidates' scores in assessing speaking skills. The knowledge of these instrumentally analyzed properties can be also used for the rubric development or rater training in oral proficiency testing. Currently, descriptors of rubrics used in high-stakes testing are still relatively general in terms of describing the pronunciation features, in particular. For example, part of descriptors for a delivery dimension in the TOEFL iBT speaking rubric for Score 4 (the highest score of the holistic rating) has a statement as follows: "... *It may include minor lapses or minor difficulties with pronunciation or intonation ....*" Raters can be still confused with the term of "difficulties with intonation," as it can be still ambivalent when it comes to their decision-making. Acoustically identified prosodic features such as pitch range or level (flat)-tones can be used as the objects of sensitization in rater training and in developing the assessment criteria those raters will employ.

In addition, the physical properties of the acoustic and temporal measures can build bases for speech recognition and processing techniques, which has increasingly drawn attention of language testers as they can help develop automated scoring and feedback systems. Despite some existing drawbacks as listed in the previous section, this objective analysis approach or the combined method with a human rating may also be of use to the automatic assessment of speech production. As topics on the improvement of ASR effectiveness for NNS speech continue to be of interest to L2 researchers (Zechner & Evanini, 2019), the improvement of this ASR approach to speech assessment is certainly necessary.

Nowadays, acoustic research has been relatively widely applied to the field of assessment of oral performance (e.g., Versant by Pearson or the Duolingo English Test, or TOEFL speaking e-Rater at the Educational Testing Service). In fact, human raters are considered to be more able to decipher meaning from utterances in response to test questions (Godwin-Jones, 2009). Xi (2010) notes that automatic feedback systems may only "be acceptable in low-stakes practice environments with instructor support" (p. 298). For example, as seen from the set of features used for the TOEFL Practice Online (Zechner et al., 2009), the focus of the automatic scoring model is mainly on fluency (temporal features) with some segmental acoustic aspects. Moreover, the ASR models still fall short in that they do not examine the aspects of communicative ability on the part of the candidates. This lack of adequacy in testing the communicative or interactional competence of test takers is of ongoing concern for those who seek a valid means to automatically test and score candidates' speech (Chapelle & Chung, 2010). Therefore, incorporating more of the acoustic suprasegmental features such as intonation (e.g., tone choices or pitch ranges) in the automated scoring models as seen in Kang and Johnson (2018) or Kang et al. (2021a) can reconcile the issue of communicative competence to some extent, as tones are associated with particular communicative values (e.g., proclaiming with falling tones and referring with rising tones) (Brazil, 1997). Thus, proactive collaborative projects among researchers in language assessment and linguistic analysis are much more needed to better develop assessment criteria and to improve assessment training.

Whereas studies have traditionally tended to examine segmental and suprasegmentals separately, future research may investigate a constellation of acoustic features conjointly for both segmentals and suprasegmentals. This will help to answer the question to what extent non-prosodic features of speech contribute to ratings of oral performance, compared to suprasegmentals. In addition, these pronunciation aspects of speech identified through acoustic analysis must be interpreted in conjunction with other linguistic features. That is, further research is necessary regarding whether grammatical and lexical performance variables contribute additional variance to oral assessment ratings, and the degree to which those other linguistic elements can compensate for dysfunctional features of pronunciation.

394   Chapter 27 Acoustic and Temporal Analysis for Assessing Speaking

The main discussion of this entry has focused on issues in large-scale assessment. Yet, advances made on instrumental analysis and ASR can be possibly (although somewhat limitedly at the moment) used in the classroom-based assessment of speech in the future. De Jong and Wempe (2007) provide good evidence of practical application by describing a method to automatically measure speech rate without the need of a transcription using PRAAT. The program can quickly identify silence in speech and ultimately provide information on speech rate for learners. The Higgins et al. (2011) study has advanced the technique and built into speech recognizers a component that is able to identify speech rate. A possible scenario is that free-downloadable programs such as the PRAAT can be used for formative assessments in which teachers can informally evaluate students' oral fluency development without labor-intensive scoring procedures (e.g., Hirschi et al., 2023; Kang et al., 2022). How this instrumental analysis can be used in classroom-based speaking assessment is an important topic for future research.

A qualitative approach to acoustic measures may be much in need for future language assessment. Speech evaluation often falls back on quantitative methods such as using a large speech corpus data to explore the impact of certain acoustic features on listeners' judgments. On the other hand, in-depth interviews or discussions with NNSs (e.g., why they paused at certain locations or why they emphasized certain words) can provide insights into understanding the relationship between NNSs' speech production and the listeners' evaluation. This approach will not only help clarify the acoustically identified features of accented speech but will also increase the validity and reliability of the measures.

Overall, the future direction of acoustic studies involves expanding the scope of interpretation of the parameters analyzed for assessing speaking. The features measured instrumentally (i.e., particularly acoustic properties such as tone choices) should be interpreted in a more contextualized sense, recognizing the social nature of oral performance through the discourse and interaction analysis. Moreover, a sociolinguistic approach may help us find out whether or not the test taker is disadvantaged by his or her interlocutors' particular speech patterns. For example, if an interlocutor does not use rising tones appropriately or frequently, the other interlocutor may feel offended or less supported (Pickering, 2001, 2018). Overuse of falling tones by NNSs can give NS listeners an impression of arrogance. Much research needs to be done in this area and to expand the capacity of acoustic research itself. Finally, this entry has not touched on an important topic of sociopolitical issues regarding NNSs' accent such as identity and motivation as it is not a main concern of the arguments. Another area of future research should lie in the relationship between the speech properties and physiological traits.

Discussion Questions

1. Some people can say "instrumental measures or analyses can be subjective"? What does this mean? What can we do to reduce this subjectivity?

2. How can we address the Global Englishes-related issues in the automated scoring systems?

References

Anderson-Hsieh, J., & Venkatagiri, H. (1994). Syllable duration and pausing in the speech of intermediate and high proficiency Chinese ESL speakers. *TESOL Quarterly, 28*, 807–812. https://doi.org/10.2307/3587566.

Bachman, L. F., Lynch, B. K., & Mason, M. (1995). Investigating variability in tasks and rater judgments in a performance test of foreign language speaking. *Language Testing, 12*, 238–247. https://doi.org/10.1177/026553229501200206.

Bernstein, J., van Moere, A., & Cheng, J. (2010). Validating automated speaking tests. *Language Testing, 27*(3), 355–377. https://doi.org/10.1177/0265532210364404.

Black, M. P., Bone, D., Skordilis, Z. I., Gupta, R., Xia, W., Papadopoulos, P., & Narayanan, S. S. (2015). *Automated evaluation of non-native English pronunciation quality: combining knowledge- and data-driven features at multiple time scales. Proceedings of Interspeech. Dresden, Germany: 16th annual conference of the International Speech Communication Association* (pp. 493–497). Retrieved from http://toc.proceedings.com/29080webtoc.pdf

Bonk, W. J., & Ockey, G. J. (2003). A many-facet Rasch analysis of the second language group oral discussion task. *Language Testing, 20*(1), 89–110. https://doi.org/10.1191/0265532203lt245oa.

Brazil, D. (1997). *The communicative value of intonation in English.* Cambridge University Press.

Chapelle, C. A., & Chung, Y.-R. (2010). The promise of NLP and speech processing technologies in language assessment. *Language Testing, 27,* 301–315. https://doi.org/10.1177/0265532210364405.

Couper-Kuhlen, E. (1996). The prosody of repetition: on quoting and mimicry. In E. Couper-Kuhlen & M. Selting (Eds.), *Prosody in conversation: Interactional studies* (pp. 366–405). Cambridge: Cambridge University Press. https://doi.org/10.1017/CBO9780511597862.

Crowther, D., Trofimovich, P., Isaacs, T., & Saito, K. (2015). Does a speaking task affect second language comprehensibility? *The Modern Language Journal, 99*(1), 80–95. https://www.jstor.org/stable/43651879.

Crystal, D. (2008). *A dictionary of linguistics and phonetics.* Oxford: Blackwell. https://doi.org/10.1002/9781444302776.

Cucchiarini, C., Strik, H., & Boves, L. (2002). Quantitative assessment of second language learners' fluency: comparisons between read and spontaneous speech. *Journal of the Acoustical Society of America, 111*(6), 2862–2873. https://doi.org/10.1121/1.1471894.

Cutler, A., & Clifton, C. F. (1984). The use of prosodic information in word recognition. In H. Bouma & D. G. Bouwhuis (Eds.), *Attention and performance x: Control of language processes* (pp. 183–196). Hillsdale, NJ: Lawrence Erlbaum. https://hdl.handle.net/11858/00-001M-0000-0013-36DA-5.

De Jong, N. H., & Wempe, T. (2007). Automatic measurement of speech rate in spoken Dutch. *ACLC Working Papers, 2,* 51–60. Retrieved from https://pure.uva.nl/ws/files/4414196/53194_dejong_automaticfluency_toweb.pdf.

Derwing, T., & Munro, M. (2005). Second language accent and pronunciation teaching: a research-based approach. *TESOL Quarterly, 39,* 379–397. https://doi.org/10.2307/3588486.

Derwing, T., Munro, M., & Carbonaro, M. (2000). Does popular speech recognition software work with ESL speech? *TESOL Quarterly, 34*(3), 592–603. https://doi.org/10.2307/3587748.

Derwing, T., Frazer, H., Kang, O., & Thompson, R. (2014). Accent and ethics: issues that merit attention. In A. Mahboob & L. Barratt (Eds.), *English in a multilingual context: Language variation and education* (pp. 63–80). Dordrecht: Springer. https://doi.org/10.1007/978-94-017-8869-4_5.

Ehsani, F., & Knodt, E. (1998). Speech technology in computer-aided language learning: strengths and limitations of a new CALL paradigm. *Language Learning and Technology, 2*(1), 54–73. http://hdl.handle.net/10125/25032.

Evanini, K., & Wang, X. (2013). *Automated speech scoring for non-native middle school students with multiple task types. Proceedings of Interspeech. 14th annual conference of the international speech communication association* (pp. 2435–2439). Lyon, France. Retrieved from http://evanini.com/papers/evaniniWang2013toefljr.pdf

Field, J. (2005). Intelligibility and the listener: the role of lexical stress. *TESOL Quarterly, 39,* 399–423. https://doi.org/10.2307/3588487.

Flege, J. E., & Eefting, W. (1987). Cross-language switching in stop consonant perception and production by Dutch speakers of English. *Speech Communication, 6,* 185–202. https://doi.org/10.1016/0167-6393(87)90025-2.

Franco, H., Bratt, H., Rossier, R., Gadde, V. R., Shriberg, E., Abrash, V., & Precoda, K. (2010). EduSpeak: a speech recognition and pronunciation scoring toolkit for computer-aided language learning applications. *Language Testing, 27,* 401–418. https://doi.org/10.1177/0265532210364408.

Ginther, A., Dimova, S., & Yang, R. (2010). Conceptual and empirical relationships between temporal measures of fluency and oral English proficiency with implications for automated scoring. *Language Testing, 27,* 379–399. https://doi.org/10.1177/0265532210364407.

Godwin-Jones, R. (2009). Emerging technologies: speech tools and technologies. *Language Learning and Technology, 13*(3), 4–11. https://www.learntechlib.org/p/74404/.

Higgins, D., Xi, X., Zechner, K., & Williamson, D. (2011). A three-stage approach to the automated scoring of spontaneous spoken responses. *Computer Speech and Language, 25*(2), 282–306. https://doi.org/10.1016/j.csl.2010.06.001.

Hincks, R. (2005). Measures and perceptions of liveliness in student oral presentation speech: a proposal for an automatic feedback mechanism. *System, 33*, 575–591. https://doi.org/10.1016/j.system.2005.04.002.

Hirschi, K., Kang, O., Hansen, J., & Looney, S. D. (2023). *Fluency benchmarks and impacts of practice with instantaneous assessment on International Teaching Assistants' speech rate and pause units.* In R. I. Thomson, T. M. Derwing, J. Levis, & K. Hiebert (Eds.), *Proceedings of the 13th pronunciation in second language learning and teaching conference,* held June 2022 at Brock University, St. Catharines, ON. https://doi.org/10.31274/psllt.15711.

Hsieh, C.-N., Zechner, K., & Xi, X. (2019). Features measuring fluency and pronunciation. In K. Zechner & K. Evanini (Eds.), *Automated speaking assessment: Using language technologies to score spontaneous speech.* New York and London: Routledge. https://doi.org/10.4324/9781315165103-7.

Kang, O. (2010). Relative salience of suprasegmental features on judgments of L2 comprehensibility and accentedness. *System, 38*, 301–315. https://doi.org/10.1016/j.system.2010.01.005.

Kang, O., & Ginther, A. (Eds.). (2017). *Assessment in second language pronunciation.* New York: Routledge. https://doi.org/10.22158/selt.v6n2p155.

Kang, O., & Johnson, D. (2018). Contribution of suprasegmental to English speaking proficiency: human rater and automated scoring system. *Language Assessment Quarterly, 15*(2), 150–168. https://doi.org/10.1080/15434303.2018.1451531.

Kang, O., & Rubin, D. (2009). Reverse linguistic stereotyping: measuring the effect of listener expectations on speech evaluation. *Journal of Language and Social Psychology, 28*, 441–456. https://doi.org/10.1177/0261927X09341950.

Kang, O., Rubin, D., & Pickering, L. (2010). Suprasegmental measures of accentedness and judgments of English language learner proficiency in oral English. *Modern Language Journal, 94*, 554–566. https://doi.org/10.1111/j.1540-4781.2010.01091.x.

Kang, O., Rubin, D., & Kermad, A. (2019). Effect of training and rater differences on oral proficiency assessment. *Language Testing, 36*(4), 481–504. https://doi.org/10.1177/0265532219849522.

Kang, O., Thomson, R., & Moran, M. (2020). Which features of accent affect understanding? Exploring the intelligibility threshold of diverse accent varieties. *Applied Linguistics, 41*(4), 453–480. https://doi.org/10.1093/applin/amy053.

Kang, O., Johnson, D., & Kermad, A. (2021a). *Second language prosody and computer modeling.* New York: Routledge. https://doi.org/10.4324/9781003022695.

Kang, O., Kermad, A., & Taguchi, N. (2021b). The interplay of proficiency and study abroad experience on the prosody of L2 speech acts. *Journal of Second Language Pronunciation.* https://doi.org/10.1075/jslp.20024.kan.

Kang, O., Hirschi, K., Hansen, J., & Looney, S. (2022). *Characterization and normalization of second language speech intelligibility through lexical stress, speech rate, rhythm, and pauses.* TN: Acoustic Society of America. https://doi.org/10.1121/10.0016224.

Kormos, J., & Denes, M. (2004). Exploring measures and perceptions of fluency in the speech of second language learners. *System, 32*, 145–164. https://doi.org/10.1016/j.system.2004.01.001.

Ladefoged, P. (2001). *A course in phonetics.* Harcourt College Publishers. https://doi.org/10.1017/S0025100302220150.

Lumley, T., & McNamara, T. F. (1995). Rater characteristics and rater bias: implications for training. *Language Testing, 12*, 54–71. https://doi.org/10.1177/026553229501200104.

Moran, M., & Kang, O. (2021). *The effect of pause location on listening comprehension. 2021 AAAL virtual conference.*

Munro, M. J., & Derwing, T. M. (2001). Modeling perceptions of the accentedness and comprehensibility of L2 speech: the role of speaking rate. *Studies of Second Language Acquisition, 23*, 451–468. https://doi.org/10.1017/S0958344008000724.

Neri, A., Cucchiarini, C., & Strik, H. (2008). The effectiveness of computer-based speech corrective feedback for improving segmental quality in L2 Dutch. *ReCALL, 20*(2), 225–243.

Pickering, L. (2001). The role of tone choice in improving ITA communication in the classroom. *TESOL Quarterly, 35*(2), 233–255. https://doi.org/10.2307/3587647.

Pickering, L. (2004). The structure and function of intonational paragraphs in native and nonnative speaker instructional discourse. *English for Specific Purposes, 23*(1), 19–43. https://doi.org/10.1016/S0889-4906(03)00020-6.

Pickering, L. (2018). *Discourse intonation: A discourse-pragmatic approach to teaching the pronunciation of English.* University of Michigan Press. https://doi.org/10.3998/mpub.6731.

Préfontaine, Y., Kormos, J., & Johnson, D. E. (2015). How do utterance measures predict raters' perceptions of fluency in French as a second language? *Language Testing, 33*(1), 53–73. https://doi.org/10.1177/0265532215579530.

Saito, K., Macmillan, K., Kachlicka, M., Kunihara, T., & Minematsu, N. (2022). Automated assessment of second language comprehensibility: review, training, validation, and generalization studies. *Studies in Second Language Acquisition*, 1–30. https://doi.org/10.1017/S0272263122000080.

Suzuki & Komos. (2019). Automated assessment of second language comprehensibility: review, training, validation, and generalization studies. *SSLA*, 1–25. https://doi.org/10.1017/S0272263119000421.

Towell, R., Hawkins, R., & Bazergui, N. (1996). The development of fluency in advanced learners of French. *Applied Linguistics, 17*, 84–119. https://doi.org/10.1093/applin/17.1.84.

Wennerstrom, A. (2000). The role of intonation in second language fluency. In H. Riggenbach (Ed.), *Perspectives on fluency* (pp. 102–127). University of Michigan Press.

Wilson, I., Fujinuma, J., Horiguchi, N., & Yamauchi, K. (2009). *Acoustic analysis of the English pronunciation of Japanese high school teachers and university students. Meeting of the Acoustical Society of America, San Antonio, TX, Oct 30, 2009*. https://doi.org/10.1121/1.3249531

Xi, X. (2010). Automated scoring and feedback systems: where are we and where are we heading. *Language Testing, 27*, 291–300. https://doi.org/10.1177/0265532210364643.

Xu, J. (2021). *Understanding automated assessment of speaking*. Cambridge University Press, ELT. Retrieved from https://www.youtube.com/watch?v=Jh7gqNhJv8s&t=738s.

Zeches, J. T., & Yorkston, K. M. (1995). Pause structure in narratives of neurologically impaired and control subjects. *Clinical Aphasiology, 23*, 155–164.

Zechner, K., & Evanini, K. (2019). *Automated speaking assessment: Using language technologies to score spontaneous speech*. Routledge. https://doi.org/10.4324/9781315165103.

Zechner, K., Higgins, D., Xi, X., & Williamson, D. M. (2009). Automatic scoring of non-native spontaneous speech in tests of spoken English. *Speech Communication, 51*, 883–895. https://doi.org/10.1016/j.specom.2009.04.009.

Online Resources

KayPENTAX Computerized Speech Lab (CSL). http://www.kayelemetrics.com/

Test of English as a Foreign Language (TOEFL) IBT® Scoring Guides – ETS. http://www.ets.org/Media/Tests/TOEFL/pdf/Speaking_Rubrics.pdf

Speech Technology and Research Laboratory. http://www.speech.sri.com/

PRAAT: Doing Phonology by Computer. http://www.fon.hum.uva.nl/praat/

PRAAT Language Lab. http://www.tc.umn.edu/~parke120/praatwebfiles/

Suggested Readings

Suzuki & Komos. (2019). Automated assessment of second language comprehensibility: review, training, validation, and generalization studies. *SSLA*, 1–25. https://doi.org/10.1017/S0272263119000421.

Wennerstrom, A. (2001). *The music of everyday speech: Prosody and discourse analysis*. Oxford: Oxford University Press. https://doi.org/10.1017/S0047404503244055.

Yu, D., & Deng, L. (2016). *Automatic speech recognition: A deep learning approach*. London: Springer. https://doi.org/10.1007/978-1-4471-5779-3.

Zechner, K., & Evanini, K. (2019). *Automated speaking assessment: Using language technologies to score spontaneous speech*. New York and London: Routledge. https://doi.org/10.4324/9781315165103.

THEME 5

Assessment for Immigration and Citizenship

CHAPTER 28

Language Testing for Residence and Citizenship in Europe: Justifications, Consequences, and Debates

Cecilie Hamnes Carlsen

Introduction

Over the past 20 years, an increasing number of European countries have made residence and citizenship and even entrance to the country for family reunification, dependent on a migrant's ability to learn the official language and pass formal language tests. To meet these requirements is disproportionately challenging for adult migrants and refugees with low levels of prior schooling and limited or no alphabetic print literacy (see Gujord, 2023; Jensen et al., 2021; Kurvers et al., 2015; Vanbuel et al., in progress). The use of language tests to regulate migrants' residence and democratic rights is fundamentally different from the traditional use of language tests for admission to the labor market or to higher education: While it is logical that migrants need a certain level of proficiency in the language(s) of the receiving country to manage the different language tasks they face in their work or studies, it is less obvious that the interpretation and use of language test scores for migrants' entry, residence, and citizenship is valid and ethical from a test professional point of view (Carlsen & Rocca, 2021). Scholars have also questioned the legitimacy of this use of tests from a social justice and social consequences perspective (see Kunnan, 2012, 2017; McNamara & Roever, 2006; Shohamy, 2001, 2007a; Van Avermaet & Pulinx, 2013).

The increasing use of language tests as gatekeepers to residence and citizenship rights marks a restrictive shift in immigration and integration policy in Europe, referred to as the "civic turn" in the citizenship literature (see Fernández, 2019; Goodman, 2012, 2018; Joppke, 2013; Mouritsen et al., 2019). This development has been likened to a re-assertion of 19th century nationalist ideology of "one country, one language" in which multilingualism and multiculturalism are considered a threat to social cohesion and national security (see Anderson, 1983; Blackledge, 2009; Khan & McNamara, 2017)[1] and has prompted political and social scientists

---

[1]The language and KoS requirements are added to other requirements, such as economic demands of self-sustenance, non-criminality, and increased number of years of residence.

The Concise Companion to Language Assessment, First Edition. Edited by Antony John Kunnan.
© 2025 John Wiley & Sons, Inc. Published 2025 by John Wiley & Sons, Inc.

Chapter 28 Language Testing for Residence and Citizenship in Europe

to describe immigration policies in Europe since the start of the millennium as the "return of assimilation" (see Brubaker, 2001; Joppke & Morawska, 2003; Michalowski, 2011).

This chapter focuses on the political *justifications* behind the use of language tests as a requirement for residence and citizenship. Central questions addressed in this chapter are to what degree language requirements contribute to social justice and equal rights for migrants, or whether it is more likely that they result in discrimination and exclusion. These questions are addressed through a summary of research on the *consequences* of such requirements on those subject to them. Particular attention is paid to migrant groups for whom the requirements represent real barriers, as advocated by Strik et al. (2010, p. 132). The requirement policy has sparked a scholarly debate across different scientific disciplines, not least in the field of language testing and assessment. A third aim of this chapter is to refer to the key points of the *debate*. In this chapter, I adopt a critical language testing perspective, building on a Messickian definition of validity that highlights the underlying values as well as the social consequences of tests on test takers and on society, in keeping with the influential writings of critical language testers such as Elana Shohamy, Tim McNamara, Piet Van Avermaet, and others. As a background, a brief presentation of language requirements in the migration context in Europe will be given.

European Requirement Policy from 2002 to 2022

In a 2002 survey of language requirements for residence and citizenship, the Association of Language Testers in Europe (ALTE) found that only four out of fourteen European countries surveyed (29%) had formal language requirements for citizenship (Van Avermaet & Pulinx, 2013, p. 4). Sixteen years later, a similar survey conducted on behalf of ALTE and the Council of Europe (CoE) found that 33 out of 41 CoE member states surveyed (80%) reported such requirements (see Rocca et al., 2020). A similar trend was found for residence and entry to the country. In addition, many countries require aspiring residents or citizens to pass a knowledge of society (KoS) test, which, almost without exception, is available only in the official language and accordingly functions as a *de facto* additional language test (see Khan & McNamara, 2017, p. 454; Rocca et al., 2020). Since most European countries link their language requirements to the proficiency scales of the *Common European Framework of Reference for Languages* (CEFR) describing language proficiency from A1 (lowest) to C2 (highest) (Council of Europe, 2001, 2020), it is possible to compare the relative severity of language requirements across contexts, across countries, and over time. In their cross-country comparison, Rocca et al. (2020) found that requirements are generally less strict for pre-entry and temporary residence than for permanent residence and citizenship, that the number of countries setting requirements has increased, and also that the proficiency levels required have been raised over the past 15 years.

As is clear from Table 28.1, the apparent *convergence* regarding the presence of language requirements for citizenship in Europe reflects a considerable degree of *divergence* regarding the proficiency levels required for similar contexts: In 2018, 7 countries had no language or KoS requirements for citizenship, 10 countries had requirements but either not linked to the CEFR or not specified, 2 countries had differentiated requirements, while 7 countries had an A2 requirement, 8 countries a B1 requirement, and 4 countries a B2 requirement in all four skills. In 2022, the ALTE LAMI project group (Language Assessment for Migration and Integration) gathered updated information on policy changes between 2018 and 2022, finding that permanent residence language requirements had become stricter in 3 out of the 15[2] countries covered (Austria, the Netherlands,

---

[2] Austria, Belgium (Flemish speaking), Denmark, Finland, France, Germany, Greece, Ireland, Italy, the Netherlands, Norway, Slovenia, Spain, Sweden, and the United Kingdom.

European Requirement Policy from 2002 to 2022   **403**

TABLE 28.1

Language requirements for citizenship, 2018 CoE/ALTE survey (Rocca et al., 2020), updated by the IMPECT project and ALTE LAMI group (Language Assessment for Migration and Integration) in 2022[a]

Country	Listening	Reading	Speaking	Writing	Data update 2022
Andorra, Bulgaria, Ireland, Monaco, San Marino, Serbia, and Sweden	No formal language requirements for citizenship				Sweden has proposed to introduce language requirements
Romania	A1	A1	A1	A1	
Norway			A2		B1 (speaking)
Luxembourg	B1		A2		
Switzerland	B1	A2	B1	A2	
Belgium (Fl.)	A2	A2	A2	A2	No change
Belgium (Fr.)	A2	A2	A2	A2	
Netherlands	A2	A2	A2	A2	No change
Portugal	A2	A2	A2	A2	
Russian Federation[b]	A2	A2	A2	A2	
Slovenia	A2	A2	A2	A2	No change
Spain	A2	A2	A2	A2	No change
Czech Republic	B1	B1	B1	B1	
Finland	B1	B1	B1	B1	No change
France	B1	B1	B1	B1	No change
Germany	B1	B1	B1	B1	No change
Iceland	B1	B1	B1	B1	
Italy	B1	B1	B1	B1	No change
Poland	B1	B1	B1	B1	
UK	B1	B1	B1	B1	No change
Greece	B2	B2	B2	B2	B1
Austria	B2	B2	B2	B2	No change
Denmark	B2	B2	B2	B2	No change
Moldova	B2	B2	B2	B2	
Albania, Armenia, Croatia, Hungary, Latvia, Lithuania, Malta, North Macedonia, Slovak Republic, and Turkey	Unspecified (requirements not linked to the CEFR)				

[a] The 2022 update also reveals some changes regarding requirements for permanent residence: In Austria and in the Netherlands, the CEFR level required for permanent residence was increased from level A2 to level B1 in all four skills. Slovenia replaced no requirement with an A2 requirement in all four skills.

[b] The Russian Federation was excluded from the Council of Europe in an extraordinary meeting in the Committee of Ministers on March 16, 2023 due to the invasion of Ukraine.

Source: Adapted from Rocca and Carlsen (2022).

and Slovenia) and citizenship language requirements had become stricter in one country (Norway) and less strict in another (Greece). In addition, in one of the few countries without language or KoS requirements for permanent residence and citizenship in 2018 (Sweden), such requirements have been proposed by the government and are very likely to be introduced in the near future. These findings mirror Van Avermaet and Gysen's (2009) observation that an apparent universal process of introducing and tightening the conditions for integration and citizenship through formal language requirements in Europe obscures considerable differences in the relative strictness of these policies across countries. I will return to possible interpretations of this paradox later.

Citizenship and Language: A Symbolic Link

Citizenship is normally defined as membership of a political community, and a person holding citizenship enjoys the rights and assumes the duties of this membership (see Joppke, 2013). Citizenship grants specific legal rights, which in most European states mean the right to vote at national elections, the right to be elected to the national assembly, freedom of movement, protection against deportation, full protection and support by the receiving state, facilitation of citizenship for family members, and, in the case of EU states, the right to freely settle and work in other countries within the European Union (see Gathmann & Garbers, 2022, p. 2). Successful application for citizenship (referred to as naturalization) gives migrants the same formal status and the same rights and duties as native-born citizens. But in addition to legal rights, holding a European-country passport signals where you come from and is filled with symbolic power linked to national identity and (assumed) feeling of belonging (see Brubaker, 2001; Goodman, 2012, p. 670). Even though permanent residence confers many of the same rights, citizenship is the ultimate formal sign of a person's membership of a state, "the most important privilege a host country can bestow on its immigrant population" (Gathmann & Garbers, 2022, p. 1).

To understand the link between citizenship and language requirements, it is necessary to recognize that in addition to its functional role, language has an important symbolic role (see Evans, 2018). Language is not only a means of communication but also a means through which we signal who we are and who we want to be (see McNamara, 2019). Language is a marker of group belonging as well as of group distancing, hence a sign through which we define "us" and "them" (see Anderson, 1983; Carlsen & Rocca, 2021; Slade & Möllering, 2010). In the context of migration, the ability to speak the official language(s) has become a symbol of national belonging (see Blackledge, 2009; Extra et al., 2009) where the national language is "viewed in ideological terms as part of a national identity embedded with notions that language is an indicator of loyalty, patriotism, belonging, inclusion, and membership" (Shohamy, 2006, p. 174). Similarly, a lack of mastery of the national language could be interpreted as a sign of non-belonging or even as a sign of unwillingness to integrate (Van Avermaet & Gysen, 2009, p. 119).

Political Justifications

When language and knowledge tests are introduced as an obligatory part of migration and integration policies, they are typically framed by politicians as an incentive for migrants to acquire the skills needed for successful integration (see Löwenheim & Gazit, 2009, p. 161). In a comparative study of policies, practices, and consequences of language requirements in nine European states[3] (INTEC project), Strik et al. (2010) found that in every country where migrants were required to to pass a language or KoS test to achieve residence or citizenship status, the stated aim was to foster migrants' integration into the new society (pp. 64–65). Han et al. (2010) also found that language and citizenship tests are portrayed by governments as a way of motivating migrants to develop the competences believed necessary for social integration (p. 63). This point is also made by Khan and McNamara (2017) who asserted that discourses of integration play a key role in justifying the use of language and KoS requirements for citizenship (p. 452). Van Avermaet and Pulinx (2013) summarized the arguments

---

[3] Austria, Belgium, Denmark, France, Germany, Hungary, Latvia, the Netherlands, and the United Kingdom.

dominating the political justifications for language requirements for residence and citizenship in Europe as follows:

The use of a singular language by all members of society is a prerequisite for achieving social cohesion, since

a. the goal of social cohesion can only be guaranteed by acquiring the standard variety of the national language;
b. language proficiency is a condition for social participation and must therefore be acquired beforehand;
c. language proficiency is seen as a marker for knowledge of the culture and social norms and values; and
d. unwillingness or refusal to learn and use the dominant language is regarded as a sign of disloyalty and defective integration and a threat to social cohesion.

(Van Avermaet & Pulinx, 2013, p. 7)

Importantly, Van Avermaet and Pulinx pointed out that these arguments continue to be used by policymakers even though they are repeatedly refuted by research. This has led scholars in different scientific fields to question whether the *stated* political aims are indeed the *real* aims and to discuss hidden agendas behind the policy of requirements (see Shohamy, 2006). As Strik et al. (2010) argued, it is more than likely that behind the stated aims of fostering integration and motivation for learning, there are other latent aims and concerns, such as the desire to reduce the number of migrants coming into the country, to limit access to residence and citizenship to "well integrated" migrants, or to assure the majority population that the government is dealing with migration and integration issues in an effective manner (p. 65).

Consequences

Despite the proliferation of language tests for residence and citizenship in Europe, the use of such tests typically lacks an empirical underpinning (see Bonotti & Willoughby, 2022, p. 452). Indeed, only 8 of the 33 European countries that have such requirements for citizenship report that the requirement policy is based on research (see Rocca et al., 2020). In addition, relatively little is known about the consequences of these requirements on those subject to them (see Böcker & Strik, 2011; Goodman & Wright, 2015; Neureiter, 2019), and only a few validity studies have investigated their impact (see McNamara & Roever, 2006, p. 35; Pochon-Berger & Lenz, 2014). In particular, more research is needed into how these requirements affect vulnerable migrant groups who are less likely to meet the requirements and, therefore, at greater risk of being excluded from entry, permanent residence, or citizenship when this status is made dependent upon passing formal tests as advocated by Strik et al. (2010), Frost and McNamara (2018), Khan and McNamara (2017), and Pochon-Berger and Lenz (2014). The following section summarizes research findings on the impact of language (and KoS) requirements on migrants in Europe, taking as a starting point the three political justifications presented above.

Firstly, governments typically justify language requirements for residence and citizenship by claiming that *migrants need the language proficiency required* to cope with the linguistic tasks they encounter as residents or citizens. However, as Böcker and Strik (2011) and Khan and McNamara (2017) argued, if the requirements were really reflecting communicative needs, one would expect the levels required for identical contexts to be broadly the same across countries. No such convergence exists for language requirements for citizenship or residence. On the contrary, as Figure 28.1 clearly demonstrates, there is a striking lack of agreement as to what level of language proficiency is considered necessary and sufficient for the same context. For citizenship, for example, the requirements range from no requirements or only a very basic level, A1, up to an academic level, B2.

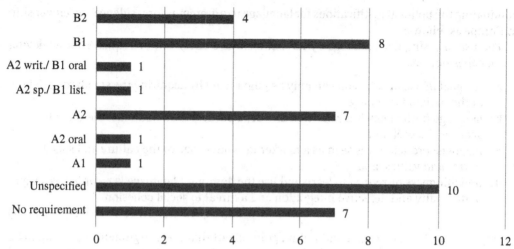

FIGURE 28.1 Numbers of European countries setting different CEFR levels for citizenship (Rocca et al., 2020, p. 32).

The second political justification is that requirements are *necessary in order to motivate migrants to learn the language(s)* of the host country. As Bonotti and Willoughby (2022) showed, however, there is little empirical underpinning for the assumption that lack of motivation is a valid explanation as to why (some) migrants fail to learn the majority language(s). On the contrary, research on language and integration from different countries has repeatedly shown that migrants are generally highly motivated to learn the language of the new society (p. 455). In their interviews with migrants from nine European countries, Strik et al. also noted that migrants are highly motivated to participate in language education (see Strik et al., 2010, p. 115), a finding mirrored by Hyltenstam et al. (2012) who in a review of SLA research found no support for the claim that adult migrants lack motivation to learn the language of the host country. Similarly, the IMPECT project investigating the consequences of language and KoS requirements for residence and citizenship on low-literate adult migrants (LESLLA[4] learners) found that the majority of LESLLA learners' teachers (58% of $n = 1078$) in 20 European countries agree or strongly agree that LESLLA learners are highly motivated to learn the language(s) of the host country. Only 21% of the teachers disagree with this statement. Etzioni (2007) too argues that migrants' lack of motivation is a politically constructed truth, stating that in the United Kingdom "[...] immigrants are very keen to learn English, yet there is a great shortage of English classes for adults and there are long waiting lines where they do exist" (p. 357). In summary, the political discourse that migrants lack motivation for language learning is not only empirically false but also potentially harmful because it places the responsibility for an eventual lack of language learning success on the migrants and refugees alone ignoring the responsibility of the receiving country in providing migrants with opportunities to learn.

A third policy argument is that these *requirements* are *beneficial for migrants' integration* into the host country and therefore in migrants' best interest. This argument too lacks empirical support. Indeed, the most striking outcome of research into the consequences of language (and KoS) requirements for entry, residence, or citizenship is a dramatic decrease in the numbers of individuals who apply for, or successfully achieve, family reunification, permanent residence, and citizenship (see Löwenheim & Gazit, 2009, p. 160; Pochon-Berger & Lenz, 2014, p. 19; Strik et al., 2010). A clear drop in the number of new citizens after the introduction or tightening of requirements was found in almost all European countries where this has been surveyed

---

[4]LESLLA stands for Literacy Education and Second Language Learning for Adults (https://www.leslla.org/).

statistically. Strik et al. (2010) found that the number of applications and/or naturalizations declined in Austria, Denmark, Latvia, and the Netherlands (Strik et al., 2010). In Denmark, the number of naturalizations dropped from just above 9000 to just above 2000 after the introduction of language requirements in 2002 (see Carlsen, 2014). In the Netherlands, the introduction of the requirements led to a decrease by two-thirds (see van Oers, 2013), while in Norway the number halved after the introduction of requirements in 2017 (see Carlsen & Hamidi, 2023). These findings confirm the assertion of citizenship researchers that naturalization has become a function not only of migrants' desire or need for obtaining citizenship but also of their ability to overcome the formal barriers, such as passing language tests (see Goodman, 2014; Howard, 2009; Jensen et al., 2021, p. 1047). It is highly relevant to consider this effect on the numbers of naturalizations in relation to Gathmann and Garbers' (2022) study in which they found evidence that citizenship status in itself works as a driver for integration as it seems "to speed up the convergence between natives and immigrants and helps immigrants improve their position in the host country" (p. 34). If citizenship status does indeed function as a driver for integration and inclusion, measures that primarily contribute to limiting migrants' access to citizenship and accordingly reduce the number of new citizens would lead to exclusion, rather than to inclusion. (It probably goes without saying that knowing the language of the host country and having knowledge about the society is beneficial for integration, but as Carens (2010) argued, encouraging migrants to acquire language or civic knowledge is very different from requiring that they pass tests to prove their competence and punishing those who fail (p. 19).)

The most important factors influencing migrants' likelihood to meet formal requirements include level of prior schooling and alphabetic print literacy, age, and typological distance between the L1 and the L2 (see Brinch et al., 2020; Gujord, 2023). Lack of prior schooling and low levels of print literacy affect both the rate and outcome of the L2-learning process (see Gujord, 2023; Kurvers et al., 2015) as well as language test scores (Carlsen & Hamidi, 2023; Vanbuel et al., in progress). Consequently, linking residence and citizenship rights to language learning and test-taking abilities is likely to be more onerous for migrant groups already defined as vulnerable, including those from the Global South, women, low-literate learners, and refugees (see Bonotti & Willoughby, 2022, p. 454; Jensen et al., 2021; van Oers, 2013).[5]

Scholarly Debates

The introduction of language and KoS tests as requirements for settlement and citizenship has been a topic of controversy and debate not only within the language testing community. Social and political scientists, political and moral philosophers, and migration researchers, as well as sociolinguists and SLA researchers, have been discussing this practice for several decades. To present these debates in their completeness is outside the aim and scope of this chapter. The overview presented here will therefore refer primarily to issues of most relevance to language testers, commencing with a discussion of different ideological conceptions of what citizenship is and what role it assumes in relation to integration. This is followed by a review of debates around possible underlying political motivation for this particular use of language tests. Finally, I will refer to debates and critiques from within the professional community of language testing and assessment and discuss the question of whether language tests for residence and citizenship can be justified from a test-professional perspective. And, results from a recently conducted survey among language testers about social justice and responsibility for justice related to test use (see Carlsen, in progress).

---

[5]The consequences of language and KoS tests for residence and citizenship on LESLLA learners are the topic of the ongoing research project IMPECT (Bugge et al., 2023; Carlsen et al. in progress; Mouti & Rocca, 2023).

Citizenship: Tool or Reward?

Political scientists have suggested that the apparent divergences in the relative severity of requirements observed between countries can best be explained by referring to their differing conceptions of what citizenship is and what role it is assumed to play in the integration process. Jurado (2008) and Gathmann and Garbers (2022) suggested that a rough line can be drawn between policies that portray citizenship as a *crown* for a successfully completed integration process on the one hand and policies that portray it as a *catalyst* for integration on the other (Jurado, 2008, p. 5). Michalowski (2011) linked this dichotomy to an assimilationist versus a liberal societal model, in which the first views citizenship as a reward to be granted to individuals who have proven their loyalty to the state, while in the second instance rights and responsibilities that come with citizenship are themselves considered a factor in encouraging further integration. Brochmann and Seland (2010) and Fernández (2019) convincingly explained the different requirement policies in the three Scandinavian countries, Sweden, Denmark, and Norway, through reference to whether citizenship is considered a reward for successful integration in society (Denmark, and, after 2015–2016, also Norway) or as an encouragement to further integration (Sweden) (Brochmann & Seland, 2010; Fernández, 2019, p. 15). van Oers (2013) too explained differences between European countries' requirement policies by reference to whether states consider citizenship as a right or as something migrants should demonstrate that they have deserved (see van Oers, 2013). Van Avermaet and Pulinx referred to this as moral citizenship (Van Avermaet & Pulinx, 2013), Schinkel (2010) as the virtualization of citizenship (Schinkel, 2010) conceptualized by Burke with reference to "the good citizen" (Burke et al., 2018).

The Real Aims?

As demonstrated above, there is little research supporting the claim that formal language requirements are beneficial for migrants' integration. Moreover, as Joppke argued, if requirements were indeed introduced for the benefit of migrants, one would expect political parties typically associated with a concern for equality, human rights, and non-discrimination to be the most eager in introducing such requirements. This is clearly not the case (see Carlsen & Bugge, 2021; Etzioni, 2007; Goodman, 2014; Joppke, 2013; Kostakopoulou, 2010). Finally, as Böcker and Strik (2011) argued, since there is little practical reason why some countries should have higher language requirements than others for the same context, like citizenship, "these differences throw doubt on the argument that immigrants need the knowledge they are required to demonstrate in order to successfully integrate" (p. 182). Nonetheless, governments continue to introduce and tighten language requirements in the migration context. Why is this?

There is general agreement in the literature that behind the stated aims of integration and beneficence for migrants, the real aim of linking entry, residence, and citizenship to scores on language and civic tests is to reduce the number of (certain) migrants entering, settling permanently, or becoming citizens (see Blackledge, 2009; Byrne, 2017; Etzioni, 2007; Han et al., 2010; Joppke & Morawska, 2003; Khan, 2021; Khan & McNamara, 2017; Shohamy, 2007a; van Oers, 2013). Scholars point to the 9/11 terror attack in the United States and other hostile events followed by the increase of refugees to Europe in 2015/16 after the Syrian war, as likely drivers for this turn toward stricter border controls. This is reflected not only in an increase in physical border fences (EU/Schengen, 2023) but also by the growing presence of invisible gatekeepers such as language and KoS tests. Khan and McNamara (2017, p. 464) argued that the changes witnessed over the past 20 years cannot be fully understood without reference to the anti-immigration sentiment and advances of the far-right movement in several European countries in recent years; this point is also made by Byrne (2017, p. 334), Burke et al. (2018), Brubaker (2001), and Joppke and Morawska (2003).

Can This Use of Tests Be Justified by Test Theory?

Messick's definition of validity, outlined in a series of papers in the 1980s and 1990s (Messick, 1989, 1998), introduced to the language testing community by Bachman (1990), further elaborated and interpreted by McNamara (2006), and embraced by critical language testers such as Shohamy (2007b, pp. 144–145), while also criticized and expanded over the past 30 years, remains central in the field of language testing and assessment (see Chalhoub-Deville and O'Sullivan (2020) for a comprehensive overview). Without devaluing other important theoretical or methodological innovations related to validity, it is impossible to ignore Messick when addressing questions of test use and consequences. Messick's contribution has been fundamental for our field in broadening the scope of validity and validation studies to encompass not only the empirical or evidential aspect of validity, e.g., whether the test score reflects the test construct as completely and at the same time as purely as possible, but also the underlying values of test constructs, the interpretation of test scores, and the consequences of test use for test takers (see Table 28.2).

Central to the concept of validity, even in its narrowest sense, is the relationship between the underlying construct of the test and test score interpretation. In Europe, most standardized language tests developed by professional language test providers set out to measure the construct of functional language proficiency or communicative competence as described by Canale and Swain (1980) and later referred to as communicative language ability (CLA) by Bachman (1990) and Bachman and Palmer (1996), further specified in the CEFR (CoE, 2001, 2020). The *ALTE Principles of Good Practice*, which 33 European test organizations subscribe to, emphasize CLA as the central construct for ALTE members (ALTE, 2020, p. 17). Even within a narrow conceptualization of validity, it is difficult to demonstrate that the interpretation and use of language test scores as gatekeepers to family reunion, permanent residence, and citizenship are valid. As demonstrated, there is little, if any, evidence to support the claim that scores from language tests set as requirements in the migration context are interpreted and used as representing CLA at a given level. If this were the case, as argued above, one would expect similar proficiency levels of CLA to be required for the same context across countries. Rather than reflecting the construct of CLA, Khan and McNamara (2017, p. 454) argued that the interpretation and use of language test scores reflect the political "heat" of the debate concerning immigration in different countries and, as McNamara (2009, p. 161) argued, "[...] the construct of language proficiency in the context of tests for immigration and citizenship is best understood in terms of ideology, not functional language proficiency." It is the symbolic, not the communicative, function of language that is central when language tests are used for residence and citizenship purposes, pointing to a mismatch between the underlying theoretical construct and the interpretation and use of test scores. Moreover, as the Council of Europe has repeatedly stressed, the CEFR was developed in line with the CoE's human rights values and aims to support the development of the learners' plurilingual and intercultural competences, clearly stating that "[i]t has never been the intention that

---

TABLE 28.2

Facets of validity

	Test interpretation	Test use
Evidential basis	Construct validity	Construct validity + Relevance/utility
Consequential basis	Value implications	Social consequences

Source: Messick (1989, p. 20) / Scientific Research Publishing.

410   **Chapter 28** Language Testing for Residence and Citizenship in Europe

the CEFR should be used to justify a gate-keeping function of assessment instruments" (CEFR CV, 2020, p. 11). Given its original purpose, it is paradoxical that the CEFR is being used as a tool to justify monolingual policies based on the requirement of given national languages (see Bruzos et al., 2018, p. 423).

Another central aspect of Messick's validity concept is the consequential basis including underlying values and social consequences of tests addressing questions like: Is the use of language tests for residence and citizenship purposes valid from a social consequence point of view? Can the use be justified ethically? Asking these questions is at the core of a responsible and ethical professional conduct, as described in the ILTA Code of Ethics, the ALTE Code of Practice, and the EALTA Guidelines for Good Practice. A valid test should bring about beneficial, non-harmful consequences for test takers (Bachman & Palmer, 2010). As the research referred to above clearly demonstrates, using language tests as gatekeepers to residence, citizenship, or family reunification is hardly beneficial, especially for the most vulnerable migrants, such as refugees with little prior schooling as failing the tests may have negative consequences for migrants' possibilities not only for study or work but also for a secure future for themselves and their families. The use of language tests to control migration and integration could also potentially come into conflict with migrants' basic human rights (see Carrera & Vankova, 2019). In certain instances, there may be implications for the right to respect for family and private life, a fundamental right under the European Convention on Human Rights (Article 8).

Language Testers' Opinions

The language testing research community has been vigorously opposed to the use of language tests as policy tools for gatekeeping purposes (as Bonotti & Willoughby, 2022, p. 452 contend). It is true that many professionals in our field have questioned the legitimacy and also expressed their clear opposition to this use of language tests (see Bruzos et al., 2018; Carlsen & Rocca, 2021, 2022; Kunnan, 2021; McNamara, 2005, 2009; McNamara & Roever, 2006; Shohamy, 2001, 2007a,b, 2009; Van Avermaet & Gysen, 2009; Van Avermaet & Pulinx, 2013). But how representative are these vigorously opposing voices of the wider language testing community? With the purpose of shedding some light on this question, Carlsen (in progress) conducted an online survey among language testers through the member lists of ALTE, EALTA, and ILTA in March 2023. A total of 284 individual test professionals responded to the questionnaire, two-thirds of whom were from Europe. 39% of the respondents report to work as test developers, 23% work as language test researchers, and 22% as leaders of a team of language test developers. It is noted that 40% of the respondents work for a higher education or research institution and 37% work on assignment of the government, while 19% work for a commercial company. A large majority of 83% report that they are familiar with the language requirements for residence and citizenship in their countries. According to the respondents, the language tests they develop are used for access to higher education (54%), for employment purposes (39%), as a requirement for citizenship (32%), permanent residence (29%), or entrance to the country for family reunification (10%). The respondents were asked to state their agreement on a 5-point Likert scale (strongly agree – agree – not relevant/I don't know – disagree – strongly disagree) with statements related to social justice, test misuse, and language testers' perceived ethical responsibility. Table 28.3 summarizes the main findings.[6]

The results show quite clearly that most professional language testers are concerned about social consequences and social justice issues in relation to the use of their tests.

---

[6]When the total percentage does not add up to 100%, it is because "Not relevant/I don't know" and "missing" are not included in this overview. For more detailed analyses, see Carlsen (in progress).

TABLE 28.3

Results from a survey among language testers, 2023 (*N* = 284)

Language testers' agreement with the following statements	Agree/Strongly agree (%)	Disagree/Strongly disagree (%)
I consider the use of language tests for residency and citizenship purposes one of the biggest challenges for our field today	60	16
The consequences of tests on test candidates are a source of great concern to me	84	6
Test developers have a responsibility to investigate how their tests are used and the consequences tests have on test takers	82	7
Test developers have a responsibility to do what they can to prevent uninformed or deliberate misuse of their tests	81	3
As a test developer, my job is to make good tests, not to worry about how they are used by others	18	58
Test score users (policymakers, employers, etc.) are the only ones responsible for how tests are used	15	66
International organizations like ALTE, EALTA, and ILTA should help prepare language testers for advocacy and dialog with test users (policymakers, employers, etc.)	79	4

The majority (60%) see the use of language tests for residence and citizenship as challenging for the field, and they clearly see it as their professional responsibility both to investigate test use and consequences (82%) and to try to prevent test misuse (81%). Only a small minority (15%/16%) consider questions of test use to be outside of their professional responsibility. The large agreement (79%) with the last statement about test organizations' role in preparing testers for advocacy and dialog with test users can be interpreted as a confirmation of McNamara's (2006) supposition that language testers are generally not well prepared for policy interaction (p. 37). The results of the survey suggest that this is a role language testers are ready to take on, but also that many testers feel they need more training in how to do so. Communication between language testers and policymakers about the use of language tests in the migration context is important in order to (try to) prevent test misuse.

Conclusion and Way Forward

As I have demonstrated in this chapter, there is little research supporting the policy claim that language testing for entrance, residence, and citizenship is beneficial for migrant integration. On the contrary, the introduction of requirements leads to a dramatic drop in the numbers of migrants obtaining family reunification, permanent residence, and citizenship. Since some studies find that citizenship is a driver for integration, if integration were indeed the real political agenda, politicians should make it easier, not harder, to become a citizen. Moreover, at an emotional level, the requirements are often judged as useless, stressful, and discouraging for migrants (see Böcker & Strik, 2011; Strik et al., 2010; Carlsen et al., under review) and discriminate against the most vulnerable groups of migrants (Carlsen & Hamidi, 2023; Vanbuel et al., in progress). Several scholars have pointed to the fact that the political discourse of integration and beneficence disguises a reality of gatekeeping and exclusion. Whether gatekeeping is the real political intention is less important from a human rights and nondiscrimination point of view, I would argue: What matters are the consequences. The use of language tests as gate-keepers in migration policy has been criticized both outside and within the language testing community for decades, and as the recently conducted survey among language testers reveals, test developers are generally seriously concerned about the problems posed by this use (or misuse) of language tests. Professional language testers consider it part of their professional responsibility to try to counteract this trend. At the same time, European governments are tightening the requirements as we write. So, what can we do?

In a recent paper, Carlsen and Rocca (2022) argued that individual language testers can take action at different levels in order to prevent or counteract test misuse. Some language testers work for the government and may have frequent dialog with policymakers, but less opportunities to oppose their government politics publicly, while others work in academia, further away from the decision-making processes, but in a freer position to speak out against political misuse of language tests publicly. As the testers responding to the survey clearly state, there is a need for more focus on advocacy in our field, and international organizations such as ALTE, EALTA, and ILTA can play an important role in preparing test professionals to act as advocates and to dialog with policymakers. Professional networks as well as individual test developers are invaluable if we are going to achieve the aim of preventing deliberate or uninformed misuse of our tests. Taking a clear stance against discrimination, as EALTA does in its online mission statement, is an important aspect, as is the work of ALTE to include a stronger focus on detecting and preventing test misuse through the inclusion of a new minimum standard on preventing test misuse within the ALTE audit system (Taylor, 2023). Also, the stronger focus on matters of justice, equity, diversity and inclusion, often referred to as JEDI, in international language tester organizations, like ILTA, is another important step. In Europe, the Council of Europe continues to work to promote human rights, equity, and protection of migrants in its 46 member states and represents another clear voice against discrimination and racism in Europe.

I would like to end this chapter by echoing what Shohamy and other critical language testers have argued for a long time already that language tests are powerful tools that can give people opportunities they would otherwise not have, but equally can be political tools of exclusion, discrimination, and marginalization (Shohamy, 2001). Given the symbolic power of language, it would be naïve to ignore the role of language and language tests in structural racism (see Carlsen & Hamidi, 2023; Khan, 2021). We also need to note Blackledge's argument that racism and discrimination exist in spite of linguistic proficiency (Blackledge, 2006, p. 39). As a community of professionals with specialist insight into what our tests measure, and what they do not measure, what represent valid interpretations and use of test scores, which candidate groups would fail if the bar is raised, etc., I would argue that few scholars are better equipped than language testers to speak out against a use of language tests that is not valid from a professional point of view and highly questionable from an ethical and social justice perspective.

Discussion Questions

1. How can language tests be used as a driver for integration in the migration context?
2. How can you, in your current position, work to prevent the (intended or unintended) misuse of language tests?

References

ALTE. (2020). *ALTE principles of good practice 2020*. ALTE Online Publication.

Anderson, B. (1983). *Imagined communities: Reflections on the origin and spread of nationalism* (1st ed.). Verso books.

Bachman, L. F. (1990). *Fundamental considerations in language testing*. Oxford University Press.

Bachman, L. F., & Palmer, A. (1996). *Language testing in practice: Designing and developing useful language tests*. Oxford University Press.

Bachman, L. F., & Palmer, A. (2010). *Language assessment in practice*. Oxford University Press.

Blackledge, A. (2006). The magical frontier between the dominant and the dominated: sociolinguistics and social justice in a multilingual world. *Journal of Multilingual and Multicultural Development, 27*(1), 22–41.

Blackledge, A. (2009). *"As a Country We Do Expect"*: the further extension of language testing regimes in the United Kingdom. *Language Assessment Quarterly, 6*(1), 6–16.

Böcker, A., & Strik, T. (2011). Language and knowledge tests for permanent residence rights: help or hindrance for integration? *European Journal of Migration and Law, 13*(2), 157–184.

Bonotti, M., & Willoughby, L. (2022). Citizenship, language tests, and political participation. *Nations and Nationalism, 28*(2), 449–464.

Brinch, K., Olseth, T., von Mehren, L., Salomonsen, L. I. A., Cej, A., Winsnes, K., Rossow, A. O., & Birkeland, P. (2020). *Utredning av hvilke personlige forutsetninger som kan være avgjørende for at en person ikke klarer å bestå prøve i norsk muntlig på nivå B1 ("Investigation of personal characteristics that could be decisive for whether a person would be able to pass a test of Norwegian at level B1")*. Kompetanse Norge.

Brochmann, G., & Seland, I. (2010). Citizenship policies and ideas of nationhood in Scandinavia. *Citizenship Studies, 14*(4), 429–443.

Brubaker, R. (2001). The return of assimilation? Changing perspectives on immigration and its sequels in France, Germany, and the United States. *Ethnic and Racial Studies, 24*(4), 531–548.

Bruzos, A., Erdocia, I., & Khan, K. (2018). The path to naturalization in Spain: old ideologies, new language testing regimes and the problem of test use. *Language Policy, 17*(4), 419–441.

Bugge, E., Nordanger, M. & Karim, S. (2023). *Migration tests and low-literate migrants: Preliminary outcomes from the IMPECT project. [Conference presentation]. ALTEs 8th international conference, April 26–28, Madrid.*

Burke, R., Thapliyal, N., & Baker, S. (2018). The weaponisation of language: English proficiency, citizenship and the politics of belonging in Australia. *Journal of Critical Thoughts and Praxis, 7*(1), 84–102.

Byrne, B. (2017). Testing times: the place of the citizenship test in the UK immigration regime and new citizens' responses to it. *Sociology, 51*(2), 323–338.

Canale, M., & Swain, M. (1980). Theoretical bases of commuicative approaches to second language teaching and testing. *Applied Linguistics, 1*(1), 1–47.

Carens, J. (2010). The most liberal citizenship test is none at all. In R. Bauböck & C. Joppke (Eds.), *How liberal are citizenship tests?* (pp. 19–20). EUDO Citizenship.

Carlsen, C. H. (2014). Språkkrav og statsborgerskap – Et testetisk dilemma. (Language requirements and citizenship – a test ethical dilemma). In E. Brunstad, A.-K. Helland Gujord & E. Bugge (Eds.), *Rom for språk. Nye innsikter i språkleg mangfald. («Room for languages. New insights in linguistic diversity»)* (pp. 99–115). Novus.

Carlsen, C., Rocca, L., Shohamy, E., & Kurvers, J. (under review). "They are right to worry"– the emotional impact of language requirements for permanent residence and citizenship on LESLLA learners.

Carlsen, C. H., & Bugge, E. (2021). Språkkrav for statsborgerskap og hvordan de begrunnes ("Language requirements for citizenship and how they are justified"). In *Andrespråkslæring hos voksne. Vitenskapelige innsikter og didaktiske refleksjoner. ("Second language learning in adults. Scientific insights and didactical reflections")* (pp. 191–215). Cappelen Damm Akademisk.

Carlsen, C. H., & Hamidi, H. (2023). Språklig rasialisering – Språk og språkkravs rolle i strukturell rasisme ("Linguistic racialization – The role of language and language requirements in structural racism"). In E. Bugge & C. H. Carlsen (Eds.), *Norsk som andrespråk – Voksne innvandrere som utvikler skriftkyndighet på et andrespråk.*

("*Norwegian as a second language – Adult migrants who develop literacy in a second language*") (pp. 74–96). Cappelen Damm Akademisk.

Carlsen, C. H., & Rocca, L. (2021). Language test misuse. *Language Assessment Quarterly, 18*(5), 477–491.

Carlsen, C. H., & Rocca, L. (2022). Language test activism. *Language Policy, 21*(4), 597–616.

Carlsen, C. H. (in progress). *Language testers' opinions on social justice aspects and testers' responsibility for justice.*

Carlsen, C. H., Rocca, L., & van Oers, R. (in progress). *Language and knowledge of society requirements in the migration context – a cross national study of language policy effects on low-literate adult migrants.*

Carrera, S., & Vankova, Z. (2019). *Human rights aspects of immigrant and refugee integration policies. A comparative assessment in selected Council of Europe member states. (Council of Europe Issue Paper). Council of Europe.*

Chalhoub-Deville, M., & O'Sullivan, B. (2020). *Validity: Theoretical development and integrated arguments* (Illustrated ed.). Equinox Publishing Ltd.

Council of Europe. (2001). *Common European framework of reference for languages: Learning, teaching, assessment.* Council of Europe Publishing.

Council of Europe. (2020). *Common European framework of reference for languages: Learning, teaching, assessment; companion volume.* Council of Europe Publishing.

Etzioni, A. (2007). Citizenship tests: a comparative, communitarian perspective. *The Political Quarterly, 78*(3), 353–363.

EU/Schengen. (2023). *EU countries are building fences all around their borders with third countries & this is how they look. Schengenvisa News.* https://www.schengenvisainfo.com/news/eu-countries-are-building-fences-all-around-their-borders-with-third-countries-this-is-how-they-look/

Evans, D. (Ed.). (2018). *Language, identity and symbolic culture.* Bloomsbury Academic.

Extra, G., Spotti, M., & Van Avermaet, P. (Eds.). (2009). *Language testing, migration, and citizenship: Cross-national perspectives on integration regimes.* Continuum.

Fernández, C. (2019). The unbearable lightness of being Swedish? On the ideological thinness of a liberal citizenship regime. *Ethnicities, 19*(4), 674–692.

Frost, K., & McNamara, T. (2018). Language tests, language policy, and citizenship. In J. W. Tollefson & M. Pérez-Milans (Eds.), *The Oxford handbook of language policy and planning* (pp. 280–298). Oxford University Press.

Gathmann, C., & Garbers, J. (2022). Citizenship and integration. *IZA Institute of Labor Economics Discussion Paper Series, 15786,* 1–38.

Goodman, S. W. (2012). Fortifying citizenship policy strategies for civic integration in Western Europe. *World Politics, 64*(4), 659–698.

Goodman, S. W. (2014). *Immigration and membership politics in Western Europe.* Cambridge University Press.

Goodman, S. W. (2018). The civic integration turn. In A. Weinar, S. Bonjour & L. Zhyznomirska (Eds.), *The Routledge handbook of the politics of migration in Europe* (1st ed., pp. 167–178). Routledge.

Goodman, S. W., & Wright, M. (2015). Does mandatory integration matter? Effects of civic requirements on immigrant socio-economic and political outcomes. *Journal of Ethnic and Migration Studies, 41*(12), 1885–1908.

Gujord, A.-K. H. (2023). Who succeeds and who fails? Exploring the role of background variables in explaining the outcomes of L2 language tests. *Language Testing, 40*(2), 227–248.

Han, C., Starkey, H., & Green, A. (2010). The politics of ESOL (English for speakers of other languages): implications for citizenship and social justice. *International Journal of Lifelong Education, 29*(1), 63–76.

Howard, M. M. (2009). *The politics of citizenship in Europe.* Cambridge University Press.

Hyltenstam, K., Axelsson, M., & Lindberg, I. (Eds.). (2012). *Flerspråkighet: En forskningsöversikt.* («*Multilingualism: An overview of research*»). Vetenskapsrådet.

Jensen, K. K., Mouritsen, P., Bech, E. C., & Olsen, T. V. (2021). Roadblocks to citizenship: selection effects of restrictive naturalisation rules. *Journal of Ethnic and Migration Studies, 47*(5), 1047–1065.

Joppke, C. (2013). *Citizenship and immigration.* John Wiley & Sons.

Joppke, C., & Morawska, E. T. (2003). *Toward assimilation and citizenship: Immigrants in liberal nation-states.* Palgrave Macmillan.

References   **415**

Jurado, E. (2008). *Citizenship – Tool or reward? The role of citizenship policy in the process of integration. Policy Network Paper.*

Khan, K. (2021). Raciolinguistic border-making and the elasticity of assessment and believeability in the UK citizenship process. *Ethnicities, 21*(2), 333–351.

Khan, K., & McNamara, T. (2017). Citizenship, immigration laws, and language. In S. Canagarajah (Ed.), *The Routledge handbook of migration and language* (pp. 451–467). Routledge.

Kostakopoulou, D. (2010). What liberalism is committed to and why current citizenship policies fail this test. In R. Bauböck & C. Joppke (Eds.), *How liberal are citizenship tests?* (pp. 15–18). European University Institute.

Kunnan, A. J. (2012). Language assessment for immigration and citizenship. In G. Fulcher & F. Davidson (Eds.), *The Routledge handbook of language testing* (pp. 162–177). Routledge.

Kunnan, A. J. (2017). *Evaluating language assessments.* Taylor & Francis.

Kunnan, A. J. (2021). Revisiting language assessment for immigration and citizenship. In G. Fulcher, & L. Harding (Eds.), *The Routledge handbook of Language Testing.* (pp. 96–116). Routledge.

Kurvers, J., van de Craats, I., & van Hout, R. (2015). Footprints for the future: cognition, literacy and second language learning by adults. In I. van de Craats, J. Kurvers & R. van Hout (Eds.), *Adult literacy, second language, and cognition* (pp. 7–32). Nijmegen, CLS.

Löwenheim, O., & Gazit, O. (2009). Power and examination: a critique of citizenship tests. *Security Dialogue, 40*(2), 145–167.

McNamara, T. (2005). 21st century shibboleth: language test, identity, and intergroup conflict. *Language Policy, 4,* 351–370.

McNamara, T. (2006). Validity in language testing: the challenge of Sam Messick's legacy. *Language Assessment Quarterly, 3*(1), 31–51.

McNamara, T. (2009). Language tests and social policy: a commentary. In G. Hogan-Brun, C. Mar-Molinero & P. Stevenson (Eds.), *Discourses on language and integration. Critical perspectives on language testing regimes in Europe* (pp. 153–163). John Benjamins Pub. Co.

McNamara, T. (2019). *Language and subjectivity.* Cambridge University Press.

McNamara, T., & Roever, C. (2006). *Language testing: The social dimension.* Blackwell Pub.

Messick, S. (1989). Validity. In *Educational measurement* (pp. 13–104). American Council on Education and Macmillan.

Messick, S. (1998). Test validity: a matter of consequence. *Social Indicators Research, 45,* 35–44.

Michalowski, I. (2011). Required to assimilate? The content of citizenship tests in five countries. *Citizenship Studies, 15*(6–7), 749–768.

Mouritsen, P., Kriegbaum Jensen, K., & Larin, S. J. (2019). Introduction: theorizing the civic turn in European integration policies. *Ethnicities, 19*(4), 595–613.

Mouti, A., & Rocca, L. (2023). Linguistic integration of adult migrants in Greece and Italy: Language requirements and learning opportunities in L2 Greek and L2 Italian. *Social Sciences, 12*(12), 1–12.

Neureiter, M. (2019). Evaluating the effects of immigrant integration policies in Western Europe using a difference-in-differences approach. *Journal of Ethnic and Migration Studies, 45*(15), 2779.

van Oers, R. (2013). *Deserving citizenship: Citizenship tests in Germany, the Netherlands and the United Kingdom.* Brill Nijhoff.

Pochon-Berger, E., & Lenz, P. (2014). *Language requirements and language testing for immigration and integration purposes.* Institute of Multilingualism, University of Freiburg.

Rocca, L., Carlsen, C. H., & Deygers, B. (2020). *Linguistic integration of adult migrants: Requirements and learning opportunities.* Council of Europe.

Rocca, L., & Carlsen, C. H. (2022). *Association of Language Testers in Europe (ALTE), Language Assessment for Migration and Integration (LAMI) meeting, November 10, 2022, Presentation,* Prague.

Schinkel, W. (2010). The virtualization of citizenship. *Critical Sociology, 36*(2), 265–283.

Shohamy, E. (2001). *The power of tests. A critical perspective on the uses of language tests.* Longman.

Shohamy, E. (2006). *Language policy: Hidden agendas and new approaches.* Routledge.

Shohamy, E. (2007a). Language tests as language policy tools. *Assessment in Education: Principles, Policy & Practice,* *14*(1), 117–130.

Shohamy, E. (2007b). Tests as power tools: looking back, looking forward. In J. Fox, M. Wesche, D. Bayliss, L. Cheng, C. Turner & C. Doe (Eds.), *Language testing reconsidered* (pp. 141–152). Ottawa University Press.

Shohamy, E. (2009). Language tests for immigrants: why language? Why tests? Why citizenship? In G. Hogan-Brun, C. Mar-Molinero & P. Stevenson (Eds.), *Discourses on language and integration: Critical perspectives on language testing regimes in Europe* (pp. 45–60). John Benjamins Pub. Co.

Slade, C., & Möllering, M. (2010). *From migrant to citizen: Testing language, testing culture.* Palgrave Macmillan.

Strik, T., Böcker, A., Luiten, M., & Oers, R. V. (2010). *Synthesis report integration and naturalisation tests: The new way to European citizenship (No. 04; Nijmegen Migration Law Working Papers Series p. 135). Radboud University.*

Taylor, C. (2023, April). *Developing a new ALTE Minimum Standard for test use and misuse [Conference presentation]. ALTE 8th international conference, Madrid.*

Van Avermaet, P., & Gysen, S. (2009). One nation, two policies: language requirements for citizenship and integration in Belgium. In G. Extra, M. S. Potti & P. van Avermaet (Eds.), *Language testing, migration and citizenship* (pp. 107–124). Continuum.

Van Avermaet, P., & Pulinx, R. (2013). Language testing for immigration to Europe. In A. J. Kunnan (Ed.), *The companion to language assessment* (pp. 376–389). John Wiley & Sons, Inc.

Vanbuel, M., Bugge, E., & Carlsen, C. H. (in progress). *Test taker background variables and outcomes of language and KoS tests for citizenship in Norway.*

Suggested Readings

Extra, G., Spotti, M., & Van Avermaet, P. (Eds.). (2009). *Language testing, migration, and citizenship: Cross-national perspectives on integration regimes.* Continuum.

McNamara, T., & Roever, C. (2006). *Language testing: The social dimension.* Blackwell.

Strik, T., Böcker, A., Luiten, M., & Oers, R. V. (2010). *Synthesis report integration and naturalisation tests: The new way to European citizenship (No. 04; Nijmegen Migration Law Working Papers Series, p. 135). Radboud University.*

CHAPTER 29

Language Assessment for Immigration in Australia: Test-Policy-Discourse Entanglements and Their Ethical Implications

Kellie Frost

Introduction

Language testing for immigration and citizenship is by now a widespread phenomenon. In Australia, like in the United States, the United Kingdom, Canada, and a growing number of European countries, many migrants now face language test requirements as part of their migration efforts, often at more than one point in their trajectories. However, in contrast to Europe, where it has become increasingly common for language test requirements to be imposed upon family migrants from non-European Union countries to restrict access to entry, permanent residency, and citizenship (see Rocca et al., 2020), in Australia, only those categorized as skilled migrants need to fulfill English language test requirements. For skilled migrants in Australia, these requirements are part of various temporary visa processes as well as selection for permanent residency, while those entering through other streams in the migration program – namely family and humanitarian migrants – are not required to take an English language test at any point in their trajectories.[1] Permanent residency provides a pathway to citizenship across all streams of the migration program in Australia, and there is no explicit language test requirement in the process for gaining citizenship.[2]

That said, for more than two decades, skilled migrants have accounted for around two-thirds of Australia's annual permanent visa allocation (Department of Home Affairs, n.d.),

---

[1] To those familiar with Australia's notoriously inhumane border "protection" measures against those seeking humanitarian visas, this can hardly be viewed as an inclusive policy stance.

[2] Citizenship is available to all permanent residents of Australia as long as they are deemed to be of good character, but the process of becoming a citizen does involve a knowledge of society test, which is in English. Various measures are now in place to enable high pass rates – test preparation booklets are offered in various languages, migrants who cannot read in English can choose to listen instead to test questions, and the test can be taken multiple times at no cost. Nonetheless, it remains controversial, not least because humanitarian migrants are more likely to need repeated attempts than migrants in other categories.

The Concise Companion to Language Assessment, First Edition. Edited by Antony John Kunnan.
© 2025 John Wiley & Sons, Inc. Published 2025 by John Wiley & Sons, Inc.

which makes this English test-regulated trajectory the primary pathway to citizenship in the country (Australian Bureau of Statistics, 2023). In addition, for the last decade, many migrants in the skilled category have been required to achieve highly restrictive English test scores in order to transition from temporary to permanent status, a significant proportion of whom are graduates of Australian universities, already living and working in the country on temporary visas (for which they also had to satisfy an English test requirement) (see Frost, 2021).

This proliferation of language testing for immigration and citizenship represents an increasing preference for selective migration, especially skilled migration, over family migration and reunification. This has been occurring over the past decade or more, not only in more wealthy Western countries, including Australia, but in an increasing number of non-Organisation for Economic Co-operation and Development countries (see Boucher, 2020; Koslowski, 2018; Rocca et al., 2020). Many argue that a parallel shift has occurred in conceptualizations of citizenship, away from social citizenship toward what Ellermann (2020) terms "human capital citizenship," whereby the focus is now on the immediate market value of individual migrants rather than on intergenerational social contributions traditionally associated with permanent migration (see Bassel et al., 2021; Boucher, 2020; Burke et al., 2018). As Ellerman explains, migrants with high-level educational qualifications and other abstracted "desirable" attributes, including dominant language proficiency, are increasingly privileged in immigration policies because these profiles correlate with high earnings (high individual market value), which, in turn, are viewed unproblematically as a measure of productivity. Thus, workers with high earnings are credited with being the primary drivers of productivity and growth in national economies, and the contributions of lower and unskilled workers in meeting labor market needs, as well as contributions in the form of unpaid labor to national and global economies, are rendered invisible.

In this chapter, I focus on the role and effects of English testing within Australia's selective skilled migration policy, which, as mentioned, encompasses the main pathway to citizenship in the country. As I have argued elsewhere (see Frost, 2019, 2021), language testing effects cannot be readily disambiguated from the effects of other policy processes in this and other similar policy contexts and thus cannot be readily identified nor evaluated within existing validation and fairness frameworks. This represents a significant and ongoing challenge to the field of language testing, hindering our capacity to contribute substantively to important debates about the appropriateness of testing practices in these high-stakes, value-laden policy domains. As a result, I argue for a reframing of language testing as a social practice, embedded and entangled not only within policy aims and intentions (Knoch & Macqueen, 2020) but also within wider discursive webs that render problems of language and of policy visible and amenable to particular kinds of solutions.

Building on earlier conceptualizations of the disciplinary power of language tests (see Frost & McNamara, 2018; McNamara, 2012; Shohamy, 2001, 2006), I situate testing for immigration in Australia within globally circulating discourses of uncertainty, which position resilience in the face of unrelenting uncertainties as the inherent "project" of contemporary governance, of the self, and of societies (see Joseph, 2013; Rose & Lentzos, 2017). As Rose and Lentzos (2017) set out:

> We have come to think of ourselves and our societies as vulnerable in so many ways: vulnerable ecosystems, vulnerable infrastructure, vulnerable food supplies, vulnerability to climate change, vulnerability to economic shocks and turbulence, vulnerability to terrorism, or just vulnerability to the challenges of a rapidly changing world in which our children have to live. And, it seems, resilience is the best response. (p. 39)

Within this policy-discursive context, I argue, language tests serve to produce racialized and gendered notions of human capital (see Peters, 2016) and to reinforce ideologies of human agency as a class-neutral set of enterprising, responsive, and adaptive capacities that rise within and extend beyond individuals, to enable resilience. A logic linking English and human capital to a national program of resilience in Australia (as elsewhere) provides a veil of legitimacy to the use of language tests for immigration and citizenship purposes, resonating with a problem–solution nexus that is increasingly pervasive across all aspects of life. To conclude this chapter, I discuss the implications of this expanded view of the role of language tests as policy instruments, in terms of the ethical dilemmas it poses and also the potential it offers for creating the conditions for more inclusive and relevant language teaching and testing programs.

The Dynamics of the Australian Immigration Policy Space

Changes to Australia's immigration policy over the past decade and a half have included a progressive tightening of English test requirements for skilled migration, and by extension citizenship, as set out further below (also see Frost & McNamara, 2018 for an overview). This trend in Australia has been consistent with and in some cases a driver for immigration and citizenship policy trends elsewhere, with countries including the United Kingdom (e.g., Khan, 2019), the United States (e.g., Kunnan, 2018; Schissel, 2019), and numerous others across Europe (see Rocca et al., 2020), as noted above, either introducing or tightening national language testing criteria within these domains.

In Australia, the aims of the skilled migration stream of policy are focused on enhancing the labor force in order to promote the nation's economic growth and prosperity, by addressing the challenges of an aging population and skill shortages in Australia, as well as pressures associated with increasing global competition, rapid technological change, and the changing nature of work (Department of Home Affairs, n.d.). Consistent with a human capital orientation to immigration and citizenship, mentioned at the outset, the program places a heavy emphasis on the income-earning potential of migrants, in terms of their employability, and their potential to contribute to the growth of the economy as a whole, via the high-level skills they possess, as well as through their spending and tax contributions. Particularly over the last decade and a half, selection processes have been configured to enable longer term strategic labor force planning, while prioritizing flexibility to meet short-term economic and labor force needs.

The role of skilled migration in longer term labor market planning, managed by the Department of Home Affairs, is undertaken via a mechanism known as the points test. The points test is essentially a list of weighted criteria, including core criteria related to age range, number of years of employment experience, level of tertiary education, and English language proficiency (see Table 29.1).

As shown in Table 29.1, all core criteria, including English proficiency, are subdivided into discreet descriptors and assigned a numerical value, and migrants must accumulate a total of at least 65 points[3] across different categories to meet the eligibility requirements for a permanent skilled visa. These criteria comprise the human capital possessed by a migrant, with their aggregate points total serving as an indicator of their potential value in the labor market and of the associated benefit they offer to the Australian economy. Skilled visa applicants who meet the 65-point eligibility requirement are subsequently invited to submit an expression of interest (EOI) for a permanent visa. EOIs are categorized by skill area, and applicants within a skill area are ranked based on their points total. Visas are allocated from the highest-ranking applicant downward, until a visa allocation quota, as set by the government

---

[3] 2023 eligibility requirements (https://immi.homeaffairs.gov.au/visas/getting-a-visa/visa-listing/skilled-independent-189/points-tested#Eligibility).

TABLE 29.1

Summary of core points test criteria[a]

Age	
At least 18 but less than 25 years	25
At least 25 but less than 33 years	30
At least 33 but less than 40 years	25
At least 40 but less than 45 years	15
English	
Competent English (IELTS 6 or equivalent[b])	0
Proficient English (IELTS 7 or equivalent)	10
Superior English (IELTS 8 or equivalent)	20
Skilled employment experience[c]	
Overseas skilled employment (outside Australia)	
Less than 3 years	0
At least 3 but less than 5 years	5
At least 5 but less than 8 years	10
At least 8 years	15
Australian skilled employment (in Australia)	
Less than 1 year	0
At least 1 but less than 3 years	5
At least 3 but less than 5 years	10
At least 5 but less than 8 years	15
At least 8 years	20
Education	
Doctorate	20
At least a bachelor's degree	15
Diploma or trade qualification	10

[a] Information summarized from Home Affairs website: https://immi. homeaffairs.gov.au/visas/getting-a-visa/visa-listing/skilled-independent-189/ points-table (accessed April 29, 2023).

[b] IELTS 6 represents the minimum English requirement and is a prerequisite to applying for a skilled migrant visa. Scores from PTE Academic, TOEFL-iBT, and Cambridge C1 Advanced are also accepted for skilled migration purposes.

[c] The maximum number of points that can be claimed for skilled employment experience is 20 across the two subcategories of overseas and Australian employment.

based on labor market estimates, is reached. For an individual migrant, what this means is that a total of more than 65 points may be needed, if the number of eligible applicants exceeds the supply of permanent visas. However, this will depend on the number and profile of other applicants and cannot be specified in advance, thereby introducing a source of inherent uncertainty for would-be permanent migrants. This uncertainty creates an impetus for applicants to attempt to maximize their points for English, since points in other categories such as age cannot be altered, and others, such as educational level and often employment status (see further below), cannot be easily altered in the short term.

The aim of the points test is to select the "best and the brightest" skilled workers – those who will be most rapidly integrated into the labor market at a level commensurate with their qualifications and thereby able to quickly generate value in the Australian economy. To this end, existing core selection criteria in the points test were originally derived from longitudinal studies of migrant survey data, in which different migrant characteristics, including their ability to speak English, were correlated with labor market integration outcomes over time. These criteria were then refined based on a study into the efficacy of selection criteria in meeting the aims of the skilled migration program, conducted by Birrell et al. (2006). The most highly valued criteria for selection purposes (as manifest in the number of points they generate) became those that were associated with rapid labor market integration, that is, where migrants gained employment at a level commensurate with their skills soon after being granted a permanent visa.

However, as noted previously by Frost and McNamara (2018), the level of English associated with rapid labor market integration was derived from migrants' self-reports of English proficiency on a qualitative scale (i.e., from a response of *I speak English "very well"*), and this was then translated, solely on the basis of intuition, into a recommendation by Birrell et al. (2006) to include IELTS 7 in the points test, in addition to the minimum requirement of IELTS 6. This occurred in 2007, and in 2011, IELTS 8 was also added to the points test, as part of a tightening of selection processes to address an excess of demand for permanent visas in certain skill areas, as was the introduction of a more restrictive visa quota system, mentioned above. These changes have meant that achieving the higher English score of IELTS 8 has become the primary means for migrants to gain an edge over other applicants in an increasingly competitive system (see Frost, 2021).

While the approach built into the skilled migration program is intended to promote the selection of the most highly skilled and competitive migrants from an international pool of mobile workers, the reality, as mentioned earlier, is that a significant proportion (typically more than half) of permanent skilled visa applicants each year are migrants who have completed degrees at Australian universities, and who have already been living and working in Australia for a number of years on temporary visas (Department of Home Affairs, n.d.). In this context, the gatekeeping function of shifting and contingent English requirements in regulating access to permanent visas has been widely criticized, with many suggesting that English testing is functioning to promote a permanent supply of temporary workers, faced with ongoing precariousness and uncertainty, and especially vulnerable to unscrupulous employers (see Dickie, 2016; Lising, 2017; Piller & Lising, 2014; Robertson & Runganaikaloo, 2014).

Before turning to a discussion of these and other implications of the situated nature of English testing, in policy and in its wider discursive context, the next section addresses limitations in the way tests are currently conceptualized in language testing frameworks, using the example of the arbitrariness of score meanings inherent to the points test and surrounding selection processes in Australia. Following this, the role of tests will be reconceptualized in terms of a policy logic as situated within wider discourses of resilience, as a means of a new basis for ethical inquiry, including future research agendas.

Undoing the Logic of Testing: Policy-Induced "Validity Chaos"

The embeddedness of a range of English test scores within a suite of other core selection criteria, as is the case in the points test system, as outlined above, renders it impossible to define score meanings in relation to any language demands a migrant might face in employment in Australia.[4] English test scores instead interact with other categories of individual attributes in the points test to serve the general purpose of selecting migrants with the desired aggregate of human capital value. For example, it is possible for two migrants with exactly the same

---

[4]This term was coined by Fulcher and Davidson (2009, p. 125) to refer to the impossibility of evaluating validity in situations in which the intended test purpose, from the perspective of language testers, fails to align with the policy purposes tests are used to serve.

422   **Chapter 29** Language Assessment for Immigration in Australia

educational and employment profile, but who differ in age by as little as one year, to require different English test scores to meet the minimum points test total for skilled migration (see Frost, 2021). In addition, the points test pass mark has been changed by the government at least three times since 2010, from 65 to 60 and back to 65 again, in response to labor market indicators and other pressures. This means that the English test score required by a single migrant shifts randomly, in line with changes the government makes to the points test total (for reasons unrelated to language). From a language testing perspective, as pointed out in Frost (2019), this embeddedness is associated with an inherent arbitrariness, caused by the contingent and shifting nature of the score requirement any particular migrant will face as part of the overall selection process.

The role of individual employers in the selection of skilled migrants, derived from the role of employment experience in Australia in the points test, also functions to further confound the English requirements a migrant may face as part of gaining permanent status in Australia. Migrants from non-English-speaking countries, for example, face significant challenges in accessing skilled work opportunities in Australia, despite ongoing skill shortages. Studies have consistently shown that these challenges are not necessarily attributable to English proficiency per se, but rather to a range of complex and often implicit obstacles. These include employer perceptions that certain groups of migrants from non-English-speaking backgrounds are more likely than others to lack the "soft skills" needed to engender trust and relationship building with clients and colleagues (e.g., Almeida & Fernando, 2017; Gribble, 2014; Parry & Jackling, 2015) and are less likely to "fit in" with existing workplace norms and values (see Almeida & Fernando, 2017; Blackmore & Rahimi, 2019).

In addition, it is not uncommon for individual employers to impose their own language policies as part of recruitment processes, either explicitly or implicitly. Parry and Jackling (2015), for example, found that large, international accounting firms in Australia specify English proficiency scores of IELTS 8 as a prerequisite to graduate recruitment. The authors explain that this occurs because recruitment is undertaken well in advance of job commencement dates, with English test requirements functioning partly to mitigate against a risk of recruited graduates being unable to gain a permanent resident visa to remain in the country to take up their positions. Others have noted that job advertisements in some skill areas, such as information technology, include the need for a permanent visa as part of the core selection criterion, thereby excluding migrants on temporary visas seeking to gain the employment experience required to transition to permanent status (see Arkoudis et al., 2009; Gribble, 2014). The latter requirement for a permanent visa as a condition of eligibility for employment embodies an implicit English requirement, since, as shown above, English test scores are necessary for gaining such a visa. Moreover, migrants blocked from employment are under pressure to gain the highest number of points possible for English (by achieving IELTS 8) to enhance their likelihood of visa success, since they cannot gain points for skilled employment experience in Australia.

With English test scores and employment experience in Australia both operating as key criteria in the allocation of permanent visas, additional barriers are therefore produced through interactions between these kinds of employer practices and other skilled migration policy practices, potentially creating a perpetual cycle of exclusion. As noted, if migrants are unable to access skilled employment experience in Australia, they will likely need instead to strive to achieve higher than the minimum English test score to meet or exceed the minimum points test requirement for a visa. If they are unable to achieve the higher score, they may be forced to remain on temporary visas, which, as also shown above, acts as further a barrier to skilled employment.

Consequently, restrictive English test requirements have been found to lead to prolonged periods of repeat test taking for international graduates (see Frost, 2017; Knoch et al., 2020) and have also been widely associated with limited access to job opportunities,

Language Testing as Embedded and Entangled in a Policy-Discourse Space **423**

underemployment, and various forms of social exclusion (e.g., Arkoudis et al., 2009; Berg, 2011; Dickie, 2016; Hamid et al., 2019; McNamara & Ryan, 2011; Piller, 2016). Moreover, it has been found that migrants on temporary visas who do manage to gain employment in their skill area in some cases feel compelled to leave their jobs to be able to dedicate more time to English test preparation (Frost, 2017; Robertson, 2016). Such actions on the part of migrants likely lead to de-skilling, which hinders rather than facilitates future employment success; a perverse effect, given that the fundamental aim of skilled migrant selection processes is to promote labor market integration.

As demonstrated above, English testing plays an ambiguous, but clearly consequential role across different and intersecting layers of policy enactment involved in migrant trajectories to permanent status in Australia. The complex and dynamic roles of testing in this policy context conflict with the fundamental logic of testing underlying existing validation frameworks (e.g., Bachman & Palmer, 2010; Chapelle et al., 2010; Kane, 2006; Xi, 2008), which, as discussed elsewhere (Frost, 2019), is premised on the idea that score meanings can be specified in relation to a real-world domain of language use. This conflict is not specific to the Australian context, with many noting that language test criteria used in other immigration policy contexts, in Europe and elsewhere, appear to serve a primarily ideological purpose, rather than a legitimate measurement function (e.g., Shohamy, 2009; Van Avermaet, 2009).

Thus, the issue of arbitrariness in test score meanings and uses in policy contexts is likely the norm rather than the exception, thereby highlighting an inherent limitation in current conceptualizations of tests and their roles. Interrogation of the nuance and complexity of test purposes and effects in immigration policy contexts arguably requires different research approaches and methods to those typically engaged in the field. In order to proceed toward a deeper engagement with the societal consequences of testing practices in immigration and other policy spaces, it is necessary to move beyond the logic of testing, and toward this end, I suggest a reconceptualization of tests as situated within a policy and a discursive context, as set out in the following section.

Language Testing as Embedded and Entangled in a Policy-Discourse Space

As we have seen, within Australia's skilled migration selection processes, different English scores, rather than representing different levels of English ability in relation to any actual work-relevant communication demands, are instead transformed into a value of English as a human capital attribute. The human capital value of an English test score is expressed via a number of points in the points test, thereby placing English proficiency on the same measurement scale as other aspects of human capital (age, education, and employment experience). This enables the production of an overall measure of a migrant's potential value to the Australian economy (expressed as an aggregate of points). English test scores of IELTS 8 are valued more highly than English test scores of IELTS 7, as indicated by their relative numerical point value (20 compared to 10), not because they correspond to an actual ability to communicate in the context of a particular job or even skill area as such, but simply because higher scores amount to "more" English, which translates to more potential human capital value.

As outlined earlier in this chapter, the points test aim of selecting migrants according to their aggregate human capital value represents part of a broader policy aim focused on utilizing migration to promote economic growth and prosperity, through the production of a skilled workforce capable of meeting the pressures of competitive global markets and rapidly changing conditions related to technological disruptions. The aim is to generate a labor force with a capacity to not only deal with but also capitalize on a rapidly evolving global landscape.

424 **Chapter 29** Language Assessment for Immigration in Australia

The changing nature of work, one of the preoccupations underlying Australia's skilled migration program agenda, is a problem space echoed by industry leaders and global companies operating in the Australian context, with numerous calls for a shift in tertiary and vocational educational agendas to better generate flexible, adaptable workers of the future, well-suited to what has been termed the "fourth industrial revolution." This fourth industrial revolution involves rapid technological development, enabling an increasing number of routine and predictable cognitive functions to be fulfilled by machines. These changes are creating shifts in the capital value of workers, privileging attributes that are thought to be uniquely human, particularly communication and other so-called soft skills, such as empathy, creativity, and cultural sensitivity (e.g., Gray, 2016; McGowan, 2019).

A focus on the value of flexibility and adaptability of workers, and the soft skills that underpin these capacities, can be related to employer recruitment practices in the context of skilled migration in Australia, in which, as discussed earlier, vaguely articulated notions of cultural assimilability are embedded within job selection criteria. As noted, notions of "fitting in" can rest on implicit employer bias and potentially hegemonic norms and values, functioning to legitimize the exclusion of migrants from non-English-speaking backgrounds, who are assumed to lack the "soft skills" that "fitting in" entails. Soft skills, which include communication and other traits associated with effective workplace interactions, can thus be thought of as relating to but extending well beyond any given level of English proficiency and cannot be separated from implicit norms and biases that give value to certain communication practices over others. While the role of English tests in enacting the exclusion of migrants is ambiguous across different aspects of policy and practice in the skilled migration space, as discussed throughout, these tests are nonetheless clearly implicated, thereby raising ethical questions concerning the assumptions upon which measurement practices are based, including assumptions about humans, language, and communication, as discussed in the next section, further below.

The various ways in which language testing functions as part of policy enactments, summarized above, suggest that test purpose would be better characterized as an entanglement of measurement-ideology, posited here to be in contrast to a traditional view of tests as serving separate measurement and/or ideological purposes; English, human capital, and associated soft skills are simultaneously constituted as "things" of economic and social value through measurement processes, broadly construed, which comprise language testing embedded in point-based selection, and recruitment practices embedded in this testing-policy space. These diverse measurement processes, effectively processes of evaluation and selection, are themselves derived from and contingent on culturally and temporally situated ways of seeing and knowing the world, which constitute widely circulating discourses of resilience (see Joseph, 2013; Rose & Lentzos, 2017). Such discourses have enabled new forms of neoliberal governance to emerge, which are legitimized around an underlying problem of uncertainty and which call for solutions that align with what has been termed *a logic of resilience*, as set out below.

Neoliberal forms of governance derive from a particular set of assumptions about the world, which emphasize the complexity and unpredictability of interrelated economic, political, and social forces, now operating on a global scale and defying "rational and linear models of calculation and intervention" (Rose & Lentzos, 2017, p. 34). Joseph (2013) argues that a shared commitment to an ontology that "assumes a world that is increasingly complex but also contingent" (p. 39) has rendered possible new forms of governance, in a Foucauldian sense, in which the focus is on the responsibility of individuals to self-govern in ways that are consistent with rationalities of competitive practice, which include not only risk mitigation but also appropriate risk-taking behaviors. According to Rose and Lentzos (2017), idealizations of individual responsibility are entwined with an increasingly pervasive logic of resilience, which functions to produce new connections between individuals, communities, and societies at large and which enables new forms of management of these relations, on the part of policymakers and governments. They explain the logic of resilience, as it manifests in neoliberal forms of governance, as follows:

> Absolute security is impossible. We will experience adversity, although we cannot accurately predict when, how, and in what form. Preparedness, planning, precaution, pre-emption, pre-clusion, and prevention – all these are necessary endeavours, but they can never be completely successful: the anticipation work of experts and authorities fails to predict many of the danger-ous events that actually occur; ... painstakingly organised systems of communication and direction break down in the face of disasters and crisis. Hence such anticipatory activities are insufficient. How shall we respond? Shall our defenses crumble, shall our systems collapse, shall our populations panic, shall each of us be paralyzed with dread ...? Or can we resist ..., bounce back ..., recover ..., adapt ..., ... emerge even stronger, fitter, more resourceful – in other words, be resilient?
>
> (Rose & Lentzos, 2017, p. 36)

The project of governance is thus the production of conditions to enable resilience, which entails responsible, agentive behavior on the part of individuals, communities, and institu-tions, including government, as well as flexibility, adaptability, and an associated capacity to exploit changing circumstances and conditions. This represents a shift away from conceptual-izations of governance as a form of disciplinary power enacted directly on the body to produce submissive, "docile" subjects (see Foucault, 1977), as set out in earlier work in language test-ing by Shohamy (2001) and McNamara (2012), and represents instead a shift toward governance at a distance, whereby the role of the state is to manage and organize the conditions that enable subjects the freedom to act in ways which align with the rationalities of the neoliberal self (see Foucault, 2008).

This notion of governance at a distance, and its underlying logic of resilience as a solution to the problem of uncertainty that pervades contemporary life, has arguably become a tenet of governance in the Australian skilled migration space, where policy interventions, particu-larly those enacted over the past decade and a half, have focused on encouraging migrants to make themselves as attractive as possible in terms of their human capital profile, through the tightening of selection criteria, including English test score criteria (Department of Home Affairs, n.d.). By gaining a higher English score, a migrant effectively mitigates against the contingencies of the selection process and of the labor market, including diverse employer recruitment practices and potentially implicit job selection criteria. The policy-embedded encouragement for migrants to enhance their human capital attributes, particularly English, thereby produces a means of generating resilience, at both the individual level, by promoting a migrant's agility and capacity to align with newly emerging labor market opportunities, and at the societal level, through the role skilled migrants play in the production of a labor force capable of dealing with rapid technological change and the changing nature of work, as artic-ulated in the policy aims, described earlier.

To summarize then, language testing for immigration purposes, in this particular testing-policy-discursive context, operates as a part of a technology of governance at a distance, thereby playing a role in producing policy objectivity and legitimacy, made possible by assumptions about fairness in measurement, while simultaneously producing the active, enterprising individuals who, as subjects of human capital, constitute the resilience needed for enhancing the competitiveness and prosperity of society in the face of global challenges. Migrants, and indeed citizens, are tasked with enhancing their own employability, opera-tionalized via the point system as a mix of attributes, skills, and experiences, or human capital. English proficiency test scores in this space constitute one aspect of an expression of an idealized migrant-worker identity, while simultaneously functioning to guide migrants' own self-related and employment-related aspirations, in terms of attributes they should attempt to acquire to be successful, not only in the visa program but also in work and in life. This expanded view of testing as an embedded, entangled practice, as shown in the section below, further implies an expanded view of ethics, to encompass its wider implications.

An Expanded View of the Ethical Implications of Testing

The ideology of English as human capital, as it manifests in this and many other policy spaces in Australia and elsewhere in the world, has been associated with a global commodification of English (e.g., Heller, 2010; Kubota & Takeda, 2020; Urciuoli, 2008, 2020). Such an ideology reflects particular assumptions about the nature of English, which have been widely critiqued in the literature. These include conceptualizations of English as a fixed, bounded object (see Canagarajah, 2018) and communication as a predictable set of discreet language-in-use skills (see Urciuoli, 2008, 2020), which migrants who are willing to make the necessary investment will succeed in acquiring (see Cameron, 2005; Kubota & Takeda, 2020). While it has been acknowledged that such conceptualizations are inconsistent with the nature of contemporary workplace communicative practices (e.g., Canagarajah, 2017, 2018; Piller & Lising, 2014), they remain fundamental to large-scale standardized test design.

The positioning of English in such terms can be seen as an effect emerging from particular constructions of the self as responsible, self-regulating, agentive, and entrepreneurial, which are characteristic of discourses of neoliberalism (see Joseph, 2013; Miller, 2016; Rose & Lentzos, 2017). Within this discursive context, behaviors directed at enhancing English skills are associated with not only individual success but also the prosperity and ongoing strength of industry, and of nations (see Lo Bianco, 2021). Not surprisingly, the focus on individual responsibility underlying neoliberal expressions of self has been widely criticized in the applied linguistics literature, mainly in terms of the effacement of structural inequalities and the invisibility of power hierarchies such a focus perpetuates (e.g., Block et al., 2012; Flores, 2013; Kubota, 2014; Miller, 2016). However, as Miller (2016) has pointed out, similar ideologies underlie the promotion of individual agency as a means of enhancing language learning success across much of the work in applied linguistics, which, she suggests, similarly risks effacing the complex interactions between different social, cultural, and economic factors implicated in learning outcomes.

The ethical questions surrounding contemporary discourses of responsibilities and assumptions about English and communication, summarized above, speak to wider questions of the appropriateness of large-scale, standardized tests, especially English tests, which appear to be increasingly at odds with workplace settings in Australia and in other English-dominant countries of migration, where English would arguably be more appropriately situated as a lingua franca. Drawing on studies of linguistically and culturally diverse workplaces in such contexts, Canagarajah (2017, 2018), for example, has pointed out that communicative practices in professional settings are highly situated, with nonverbal semiotic resources frequently privileged over verbal resources, as procedural knowledge and technical expertise, rather than shared language norms and values, increasingly represent the common ground from which mutual understandings emerge. These communicative practices, as he notes, undermine notions of individual languages with distinct and closed structures, which underlie both ideologies of English as human capital as well as the measurement constructs of standardized language tests. Moreover, they raise complex questions about how the language proficiency needed by skilled migrant workers might be conceptualized, given that effective communication is a mutual, not individual, achievement.

Nonetheless, standardized English proficiency tests hold much appeal to policymakers. As Knoch and Macqueen (2020) point out, these tests offer governments a means of reducing "the complexity of language-education-culture-ethnicity to a linear scale" (p. 165), thereby enabling some sort of principled decision-making in the face of numerous contingencies. Language testing practices provide a means for governments to quantify a migrant's potential for integration into the labor market, albeit with very little, if any, precision, enabling an otherwise abstract notion, since it relates to a future time and is not tied to any actual employment position, to be rendered concrete and measurable for policy decision-making purposes; migrants with complex and diverse backgrounds and experiences are thereby constituted as comparable and sortable bundles of human capital, the complexities and diversities of situated professional communicative practices are neutralized, and some form of procedural fairness in selection processes, while imperfect, is enabled.

The role of testing in supporting the intentions of migrants, on the other hand, remains ambiguous at best. As already discussed, the embedded nature of English score requirements within points-based selection processes creates an impetus for migrants to strive for the highest possible number of points for English, those associated with IELTS 8. A growing body of research suggests such aspirations come at a significant cost to migrants, in terms of both time and money, not to mention impacts on their emotional, psychological, and physical health of prolonged precariousness (see Arkoudis et al., 2009; Frost, 2017; Gribble, 2014; Robertson, 2016). Moreover, as already mentioned, migrants can feel compelled to prioritize test preparation over skilled employment, to the extent that they leave jobs in their skill area, as findings by Frost (2017) and Robertson (2016) suggested. As also variously mentioned throughout this chapter, a range of evidence suggests that English test score criteria, through interactions with employment processes as much as other policy mechanisms, create rather than remove barriers to migrant employment, as employers work to mitigate against risks to productivity as they envisage them, in terms of perceived soft skill deficiencies and/or the impermanence of workers.

Given Australia's reliance on skilled migrants, such effects are counterproductive, to say the least. It seems that government aims would be better served by de-emphasizing high levels of standard language proficiency, which function to exclude workers who possess in-demand skills and qualifications, while simultaneously offering no evidence that migrants who succeed in gaining high English scores will possess the communication skills valued by employers. Although it is likely that employer values are imbued with hidden cultural biases, migrant and industry "resilience" would nonetheless be better served by a focus in both language teaching and assessment on the localized and multifaceted communicative practices that are relevant to migrant experiences of social and work integration. There is thus an urgent need for a research agenda focused not only on migrant and employer understandings of valued communication and other soft skills across diverse contexts of social and working life, but especially on the actual practices through which abstract, value-laden notions of such skills become manifest. Such an agenda demands interdisciplinarity and a sense of ethical responsibility that extends across all the areas, layers, and levels of policy in which tests are implicated in consequences, including those that fall outside testing expertise. While this implies, to some extent, a need for language testers to better align test constructs with the lived experiences of migrants, evidence thus far suggests that the communicative practices involved in such experiences are unlikely to be readily deconstructed into the discreet, observable, relatively fixed parts, required to enable reliable, standardized measurement. The question then becomes one of how to best assess the kinds of language-related capacities migrants need in order to meet the expectations of employers and, more importantly, to enable the fulfillment of their own life goals, including employment goals. Whatever new form this might entail, it is unlikely to resemble large-scale, standardized testing practices.

Conclusion

With the aim of moving beyond the conundrums created by the use of tests as immigration and citizenship policy instruments, I argue in this chapter for a view of testing that includes not only surrounding policy conditions, as has been suggested by Knoch and Macqueen (2020), but also the wider discourses underlying contemporary forms of governance, which enable immigration and other policy problems to be rendered sensible and open to being addressed in certain ways (see Foucault, 1977, 2008; Joseph, 2013; Rose & Lentzos, 2017). I suggest that adopting this wider lens enables a move beyond the need to specify test and/or policy intentions and consequences in unambiguous terms and instead foregrounds the tensions and complexities of testing as a situated practice, within policy and within its wider discursive context. A view of testing as an embedded social practice further creates space for a renewed, more reflexive, critical language testing, encompassing not only an interrogation of the ideologies and intentions behind policy uses of tests but also the role of language testing expertise in producing idealized language users, workers, and migrants, together with the inclusions and exclusions these entail.

Discussion Questions

1. As Roever and Kasper (2018) have argued, none of speaking sections of the existing major international English language tests include a meaningful measure of interactional ability, despite that fact that research has demonstrated that the construct is, at least to some extent, measurable. Given the emphasis on soft skills in conceptualizations of employability in Australia and elsewhere, to what extent would an expansion of speaking test constructs to include interactional ability support or hinder the needs of migrants, employers, and other policy stakeholders in the Australian skilled migration policy space?

2. What kinds of ethical dilemmas might such an expanded construct raise?

References

Almeida, S., & Fernando, M. (2017). Making the cut: occupation-specific factors influencing employers in their recruitment and selection of immigrant professionals in the information technology and accounting occupations in regional Australia. *The International Journal of Human Resource Management, 28*(6), 880–912.

Arkoudis, S., Hawthorne, L., O'Loughlin, K., Leach, D., & Bexley, E. (2009). *The impact of English language proficiency and workplace readiness on the employment outcomes of tertiary international students.* Canberra: The Department of Employment, Education and Workplace Relations.

Australian Bureau of Statistics. (2023). *Permanent migrants in Australia: Characteristics of permanent migrants who arrived in Australia between 1 January 2000 and 10 August 2021.* Retrieved 30 May, 2023 from: https://www.abs.gov.au/statistics/people/people-and-communities/permanent-migrants-australia/2021.

Bachman, L., & Palmer, A. (2010). *Language assessment in practice: Developing language assessments and justifying their use in the real world.* Oxford University Press.

Bassel, L., Montforte, P., Bartram, D., & Khan, K. (2021). Naturalization policies, citizenship regimes, and the regulation of belonging in anxious societies. *Ethnicities, 21*(2), 259–270. https://doi.org/10.1177/1468796820963959.

Berg, L. (2011). Mate speak English, you're in Australia now – English language requirements in skilled migration. *Alternative Law Journal, 36*(2), 110–115. https://doi.org/10.1177/1037969X1103600208.

Birrell, B., Hawthorne, L., & Richardson, S. (2006). *Evaluation of the general skilled migration categories report.* Canberra: Commonwealth of Australia.

Blackmore, J., & Rahimi, M. (2019). How "best fit" excludes international graduates from employment in Australia: a Bourdeusian perspective. *Journal of Education and Work, 32*(5), 436–448.

Block, D., Gray, J., & Holborrow, M. (2012). *Neoliberalism and applied linguistics*. Routledge.

Boucher, A. (2020). How 'skill' definition affects the diversity of skilled immigration policies. *Journal of Ethnic and Migration Studies, 46*(12), 2533–2550. https://doi.org/10.1080/1369183X.2018.1561063.

Burke, R., Thapliyal, N., & Baker, S. (2018). The weaponization of language: English proficiency, citizenship and the politics of belonging in Australia. *Journal of Critical Thought and Praxis, 7*(1), 84–102. https://doi.org/10.31274/jctp-180810-107.

Cameron, D. (2005). Communication and commodification: Global economic change in sociolinguistic perspective. In G. Erreygers & G. Jacobs (Eds.), *Language, communication and the economy* (pp. 9–23). John Benjamins Publishing. https://doi.org/https://doi.org/10.1075/dapsac.16.04cam

Canagarajah, S. (2017). *Translingual practices and neoliberal policies: Attitudes and strategies of African skilled migrants in anglophone workplaces*. Springer. https://doi.org/10.1007/978-3-319-41243-6.

Canagarajah, S. (2018). Translingual practice as spatial repertoires: expanding the paradigm beyond structuralist orientations. *Applied Linguistics, 39*(1), 1–25. https://doi.org/10.1093/applin/amx041.

Chapelle, C., Enright, M., & Jamieson, J. (2010). Does an argument-based approach to validity make a difference? *Educational Measurement: Issues and Practice, 29*, 3–13. https://doi.org/10.1111/j.1745-3992.2009.00165.x.

Department of Home Affairs. (n.d.). *Visa statistics*. Retrieved September 15, 2021 from https://www.homeaffairs.gov.au/research-and-statistics/statistics/visa-statistics/live.

Dickie, M. (2016). Introduction. In M. Dickie, D. Gozdecka & S. Reich (Eds.), *Unintended consequences: The impact of migration law and policy* (pp. 1–8). ANU Press.

Ellermann, A. (2020). Human–capital citizenship and the changing logic of immigrant admissions. *Journal of Ethnic and Migration Studies, 46*(12), 2515–2532. https://doi.org/10.1080/1369183X.2018.1561062.

Flores, N. (2013). The unexamined relationship between neoliberalism and plurilingualism: a cautionary tale. *TESOL Quarterly, 47*(3), 500–520.

Foucault, M. (1977). *Discipline and punish: The birth of the prison*. Translated by A. Sheridan. Allen Lane.

Foucault, M. (2008). *The birth of biopolitics* (Vol. 2008). Palgrave.

Frost, K. (2017). *Test impact as dynamic process: Individual experiences of the English test requirements for permanent skilled migration in Australia. Unpublished Doctoral Dissertation, University of Melbourne*.

Frost, K. (2019). Language testing in immigration policy: transitioning from fairness to social justice. In C. Roever & G. Wigglesworth (Eds.), *Social perspectives on language testing: Papers in honour of Tim McNamara* (pp. 43–54). Peter Lang.

Frost, K. (2021). Negotiating the boundaries of responsibility: rethinking test takers and the ethics of testing. *Papers in Language Testing and Assessment, 10*(1), 70–83. https://doi.org/10.58379/YKQJ4733.

Frost, K., & McNamara, T. (2018). Language tests, language policy, and citizenship. In J. W. Tollefson & M. Pérez-Milans (Eds.), *The Oxford handbook of language policy and planning* (pp. 280–298). Oxford University Press. https://doi.org/10.1093/oxfordhb/9780190458898.013.14.

Fulcher, G., & Davidson, F. (2009). Test architecture, test retrofit. *Language Testing, 26*(1), 123–144. https://doi.org/10.1177/0265532208097339.

Gray, A. (2016). *The 10 skills you need to thrive in the fourth industrial revolution. World Economic Forum*. Retrieved from: https://www.weforum.org/agenda/2016/01/the-10-skills-you-need-to-thrive-in-the-fourth-industrial-revolution.

Gribble, C. (2014). *Employment, work placements & work integrated learning of international students in Australia* (p. 2). International Education Association of Australia, Research Digest.

Hamid, O., Hoang, N., & Kirkpatrick, A. (2019). Language tests, linguistic gatekeeping and global mobility. *Current Issues in Language Planning, 20*(3), 226–244.

Heller, M. (2010). The commodification of language. *Annual Review of Anthropology, 39*(1), 101–114. https://doi.org/10.1146/annurev.anthro.012809.104951.

Joseph, J. (2013). Resilience as embedded neoliberalism: a governmentality approach. *Resilience, 1*(1), 38–52.

Kane, M. (2006). Validation. In R. L. Linn (Ed.), *Educational measurement* (4th ed., pp. 17–64). MacMillan.

Khan, K. (2019). *Becoming a citizen: Linguistic trials and negotiations*. Bloomsbury.

Knoch, U., & Macqueen, S. (2020). *Assessing English for professional purposes*. Routledge. https://doi.org/10.4324/9780429340383.

430   Chapter 29 Language Assessment for Immigration in Australia

Knoch, U., Huisman, A., Elder, C., Kong, X., & McKenna, A. (2020). Drawing on repeat test takers to study test preparation practices and their links to score gains. *Language Testing*, *37*(4), 550–572. https://doi.org/10.1177/0265532220927407.

Koslowski, R. (2018). Shifts in selective migration policy models. In M. Czaika (Ed.), *High-skilled migration: Drivers and policy*. Oxford University Press. https://doi.org/10.1093/oso/9780198815273.003.0006.

Kubota, R. (2014). The multi/plural turn, postcolonial theory, and neoliberal multiculturalism. *Applied Linguistics*, *33*, 1–22.

Kubota, R., & Takeda, Y. (2020). Language-in-education policies in Japan versus transnational workers' voices: two faces of neoliberal communication competence. *TESOL Quarterly*, *55*(2), 458–485. https://doi.org/10.1002/tesq.613.

Kunnan, A. (2018). *Evaluating language assessments*. Routledge. https://doi.org/10.4324/9780203803554.

Lising, L. (2017). Language in skilled migration. In S. Canagarajah (Ed.), *The Routledge handbook of migration and language* (pp. 296–311). Taylor and Francis. https://doi.org/10.4324/9781315754512-17.

Lo Bianco, J. (2021). The discourse of the edge: marginal advantage, positioning and linguistic entrepreneurship. *Multilingua*, *40*(2), 261–275. https://doi.org/10.1515/multi-2020-0188.

McGowan, H. (2019). *What if the future of work starts with high school? Forbes*. Retrieved from: https://www.forbes.com/sites/heathermcgowan/2019/04/03/what-if-the-future-of-work-starts-with-high-school/?sh=1e231a5b5964.

McNamara, T. (2012). Language assessments as shibboleths: a poststructuralist perspective. *Applied Linguistics*, *33*(5), 564–581.

McNamara, T., & Ryan, K. (2011). Fairness versus justice in language testing: the place of English literacy in the Australian citizenship test. *Language Assessment Quarterly*, *2*, 161–178.

Miller, E. (2016). The ideology of learner agency and the neoliberal self. *International Journal of Applied Linguistics*, *26*(3), 348–365. https://doi.org/10.1111/ijal.12129.

Parry, N., & Jackling, B. (2015). How do professional financial services firms understand their skill needs and organise their recruitment practices? *Accounting Education*, *24*(6), 514–538.

Peters, M. (2016). Education, neoliberalism, and human capital: homo economicus as "Entrepreneur of Himself". In S. Springer, K. Birch & J. MacLeavy (Eds.), *The handbook of neoliberalism* (pp. 297–307). Routledge.

Piller, I. (2016). *Linguistic diversity and social justice: An introduction to applied sociolinguistics*. Oxford University Press.

Piller, I., & Lising, L. (2014). Language, employment, and settlement: temporary meat workers in Australia. *Multilingua*, *33*, 35–59.

Robertson, S. (2016). Intertwined mobilities of education, tourism and labour: the consequences of 417 and 485 visas in Australia. In M. Dickie, D. Gozdecka & S. Reich (Eds.), *Unintended consequences: The impact of migration law and policy* (pp. 53–80). Canberra: ANU Press.

Robertson, S., & Runganaikaloo, A. (2014). Lives in limbo: migration experiences in Australia's education-migration nexus. *Ethnicities*, *14*(2), 208–226.

Rocca, L., Carlsen, C., & Deygers, B. (2020). Linguistic integration of adult migrants: requirements and learning opportunities. In *Report on the 2018 Council of Europe and ALTE survey on language and knowledge of society policies for migrants*. Council of Europe.

Roever, C., & Kasper, G. (2018). Speaking in turns and sequences: interactional competence as a target construct in testing speaking. *Language Testing*, *35*(3), 331–355.

Rose, N., & Lentzos, F. (2017). Making us resilient: responsible citizens for uncertain times. In S. Trnka & C. Trundle (Eds.), *Competing responsibilities: The ethics and politics of contemporary life* (pp. 27–48). Duke University Press.

Schissel, J. L. (2019). *Social consequences of testing for language-minoritized bilinguals in the United States*. Multilingual Matters. https://doi.org/10.21832/9781788922715.

Shohamy, E. (2001). *The power of tests: A critical perspective of the uses of language tests*. Longman.

Shohamy, E. (2006). *Language policy: Hidden agendas and new approaches*. London and New York: Routledge. https://doi.org/10.4324/9780203387962.

Shohamy, E. (2009). Language tests for immigrants: why language? Why tests? Why citizenship? In G. Hogan-Brun, C. Mar-Molinero & P. Stevenson (Eds.), *Discourses on language and integration* (pp. 45–60). Amsterdam and Philadelphia: John Benjamins. https://doi.org/10.1075/dapsac.33.07sho.

Urciuoli, B. (2008). Skills and selves in the new workplace. *American Ethnologist, 35*, 211–228.

Urciuoli, B. (2020). Leadership communication "skills" and undergraduate neoliberal subjectivity. In L. Martin Rojo & D. Percio (Eds.), *Language and neoliberal governmentality* (pp. 91–109). Routledge.

Van Avermaet, P. (2009). Fortress Europe? Language policy regimes for immigration and citizenship. In G. Hogan-Brun, C. Mar-Molinero & P. Stevenson (Eds.), *Discourses on language and integration* (pp. 15–44). John Benjamins Publishing.

Xi, X. (2008). Methods of test validation. In E. Shohamy & N. H. Hornberger (Eds.), *Encyclopedia of language and education, Volume 7: Language testing and assessment* (2nd ed., pp. 177–196). Springer.

Suggested Readings

Dickie, M., Gozdecka, D., & Reich, S. (Eds.). (2016). *Unintended consequences: The impact of migration law and policy* (pp. 1–8). Canberra: ANU Press.

Macqueen, S., & Ryan, K. (2019). Test mandate discourse: debating the role of language tests in citizenship. In C. Roever & G. Wigglesworth (Eds.), *Social perspectives on language testing: Papers in honour of Tim McNamara* (pp. 55–71). Peter Lang.

CHAPTER 30

U.S. Immigration, Citizenship, and the Naturalization Test: Policies and practices

Antony John Kunnan

Introduction

It is often stated that the United States is a land of immigrants as it attracts the largest number of immigrants in the world. Even today, most people in the country can trace part of their ancestry to an immigrant – either decades or even centuries ago, except for those who are descendants of Native Americans and enslaved Africans.

In the (almost) last 250 years in the United States, the concept of naturalization and citizenship in terms of ideology, legislation, and court rulings has swung like a pendulum, sometimes favoring inclusion and tolerance of immigrants and citizenship, sometimes exclusion, racism, and self-righteousness. The first of these attitudes was encapsulated in the words of Emma Lazarus on the pedestal of the Statue of Liberty on an island overlooking New York City: "Give me your tired, your poor, your huddled masses yearning to breathe free" (cited by Kennedy, 1964, p. 45). The other attitude was (and has been) on display when resistance was (and is) seen toward new immigrants; for example, in the riots against Italians, the branding of Irish as criminals, anti-Semitism that targeted Jewish people, the racist denials of citizenship to Chinese residents, the shameful internment of Japanese American citizens, and the ban of immigrants based on Muslim religion, among many other crimes and indignations.

Despite these conflicting ideologies and practices, the volume of immigrants and naturalized persons has been steady and totally unprecedented. Based on historical data from the Department of Homeland Security over the 202-year period (1820–2021), a total of 87,437,532 (about 87.4 million) persons obtained lawful permanent residents (LPRs) to live in the United States. Of these LPRs, between 1907 and 2022, 33,677,000 (about 33.7 million) became naturalized citizens. To put this in a global perspective, no country in the world has had such high immigration volumes in the past or even now. Currently, according to the Migration Policy Institute tabulations of U.S. Department of Homeland Security, Office of Immigration Statistics, as of January 1, 2022, there were 12.9 million LPRs living in the United States and of these 9.2 million LPRs are eligible to naturalize. Table 30.1 provides yearly information of LPRs for the last 10 years.

This chapter reviews how U.S. immigration and citizenship policy vacillated between permitting and restricting immigration and citizenship, a discussion of naturalization rates and the beginnings and current language assessment practice, an evaluation of the U.S. naturalization test, and a brief consideration of what is meant by immigrant language attainment and integration.

The Concise Companion to Language Assessment, First Edition. Edited by Antony John Kunnan.
© 2025 John Wiley & Sons, Inc. Published 2025 by John Wiley & Sons, Inc.

432

TABLE **30.1**	
Persons who obtained lawful permanent residents status by fiscal year	
Year	Number of LPRs
2012	1,031,631
2013	990,553
2014	1,016,518
2015	1,051,031
2016	1,183,505
2017	1,127,167
2018	1,096,611
2019	1,031,765
2020	707,362
2021	740,002

Source: Adapted from https://www.migrationpolicy.org/programs/data-hub/charts/annual-number-of-us-legal-permanent-residents.

Permitting and Restricting Citizenship

After the American revolutionaries gave up their allegiance to the British monarch in 1776, the idea of citizenship emerged "grounded in contract, consent, and volition ... [but] not everyone in the native-born population was deemed a citizen or granted the rights of one. Native Americans and free Black people were classified as 'aliens' or mere 'inhabitants'" (Parker, 2015, p. 80). George Washington, the first president of the United States (1789–1797), emphatically declared in 1783 that "the bosom of America was open to receive not only the opulent and respectable stranger, but the oppressed and persecuted of all nations and religions." He was obviously oblivious of the fact that Native Americans and Blacks were living in the country.

The first federal regulation that followed was the Naturalization Act of 1790, which stated that

> any alien, who was a free white person and who had resided within the limits and under the jurisdiction of the United States for the term of two years may be admitted to become a citizen on application to any common law court of record, in any one of the States where he had resided for the term of one year at least, and making proof to the satisfaction of such court that he is a person of good character, and taking the oath or affirmation prescribed by law to support the Constitution of the United States.
>
> *U.S. Statutes at Large, Vol. 1, 1st Congress/2nd Session/Chapter 3.*

Although Washington's statement came a few years before the Naturalization Act of 1790, once again, the founders were untroubled by the presence of non-white persons as citizenship was restricted to "free white persons." This original white supremacist law was used to exclude free white women, Black people, and Native Americans, in contrast to the much-quoted line from the Declaration of Independence: "We hold these truths to be self-evident, that all men are created equal."

Several new acts were passed and repealed regarding citizenship over the centuries, particularly regarding non-white immigrants. In 1795, Congress repealed the 1790 Act, raised the

434 Chapter 30 U.S. Immigration, Citizenship, and the Naturalization Test

residence requirement for citizenship to five years, and required a declaration of intention to seek citizenship at least three years before naturalization. In 1798, the residency requirement for citizenship was raised to 14 years; in 1802, it was repealed. During the American antebellum period (1812–1861), there was westward expansion, mass migration, and extremely piecemeal and limited rights for non-white people.

In 1855, Congress passed a law that provided alien women (i.e., women not born in the United States) to become naturalized citizens upon marriage to a husband who was a U.S. citizen. While free white men and white women were granted citizenship rights, Black people, Native Americans, Mexicans, and Asians were still considered alien, foreign, or inhabitants but not citizens. Two years later, in 1857, the U.S. Supreme Court infamously ruled in the *Dred Scott v. Sandford* case that the Constitution was not meant to include citizenship for Black people, whether they were slaves or free. Thus, the rights and privileges that the Constitution conferred upon American citizens could not apply to them.

In 1868, with the passing of the 13th Amendment to the U.S. Constitution, slavery was abolished, but Black people were recognized as citizens only in the 14th Amendment. The 14th Amendment granted citizenship to all persons "born or naturalized in the United States," including formerly enslaved people, and provided all citizens with "equal protection under the laws." Yet a little more than a decade after expounding the 14th Amendment's guarantees of equal protection, due process, and consent, Congress reverted to a more restrictive immigration policy. Responding to a national xenophobic clamor for the exclusion of Chinese immigration, Congress passed the Chinese Exclusion Act of 1882. This Act included the suspension of immigration of Chinese laborers (merchants, teachers, students, and tourists were exempt) to the United States for 10 years and prohibition of Chinese immigrants becoming citizens through the naturalization process. In the next few years, vigilantes drove out Chinese residents mainly from California, Oregon, and Washington through harassment, intimidation, arson, bombing, assault, and murder (see Lew-Williams, 2018, for details).

In 1898, a landmark ruling that stands until today was issued: The U.S. Supreme Court ruled in *United States v. Wong Kim Ark* that any child born in the United States, regardless of race or parents' citizenship status, is an American citizen. Based on this ruling, these individuals do not need to go through the naturalization process.

Finally, in 1924, what seemed like an afterthought considering how long this took, Congress enacted the Indian Citizenship Act that granted citizenship to all Native Americans born in the United States after decades of caricaturing them as savages needing to be civilized. Imagine the situation of Native Americans whose lands were occupied by colonizers and then being disenfranchised in their own country. But the Immigration Act of 1924 also brought new restrictions on immigration through a numerical limit of 155,000 per year. According to Lee (2019), the quota for Western Europeans was 87% and for Eastern and Southern Europe, 11%, hardening the lines between whites and non-whites.

In the West, during the economic stresses of the 1930s, Mexican and Mexican Americans bore the brunt of mass deportation and repatriation. According to Lee (2019), "families that included naturalized U.S. citizens and U.S.-born citizens faced just as much pressure to repatriate as noncitizens families" (p. 176). "[B]y the end of the Great Depression, the U.S. had turned into a 'deportation nation' that made no distinction between foreign born and the undocumented ... and lawful resident and naturalized citizens, and American born citizens of Mexican descent" (p. 180).

In February 1942, three months after the Japanese military attacked Pearl Harbor in Hawai'i in December 1941, President Roosevelt signed Executive Order 6066, authorizing the Secretary of War to prescribe certain areas as military zones. This cleared the way for the incarceration of Japanese Americans, German Americans, and Italian Americans in U.S. concentration camps. But far more Americans of Japanese descent were forcefully interned than Americans of European descent, both in total and as a share of relative population. About 120,000 Japanese

Americans were interned in ten relocation centers in California, Arizona, etc. In December 1944, in *Korematsu v. United States*, a divided U.S. Supreme Court in a 6-3 decision upheld the constitutionality of internment camps during World War II as a "military necessity" not based on race. In 1983, a federal judge in San Francisco overturned Korematsu's conviction in the same San Francisco courthouse where he was convicted almost 40 years earlier.

Alongside these actions, the United States also welcomed Jewish immigrants from the 1880s onward, and from the 1960s to 1980s, it received immigrants from South Korea, Vietnamese refugees, the Mariel boatlift refugees from Cuba, and Central American immigrants. In addition, the U.S. government granted amnesty to all immigrants who had overstayed in 1986 and offered legal permanent residency to all Chinese residents in the United States after the post-Tiananmen Square protests in 1989. In most recent times, after disastrous interventions by the United States, in Afghanistan and Iraq, refugees from these countries have been admitted. Thus, the pendulum swings have continued.

These immigration policies and practices have repercussions regarding who and how many come to the United States as immigrants and subsequently become U.S. citizens. That is why it is critical that a study of the United States naturalization process considers past and present immigration policies. Appendix 30.A lists the various policy measures taken by the government and courts from the 18th century to the early 21st century.

Naturalization Trends

Applications, Approvals, and Denials

Table 30.2 shows the numbers of applications and naturalizations approved and denied for the last eight years (2015–2022). The numbers of applicants have remained high (from 700,000 to 800,000 each year), and the numbers of approved naturalizations are going up overall except for a dip in 2020. However, the actual numbers and percentage of denials are also up with a record of 14.29% in 2022. It would be useful to know if either of the tests caused the denials to rise.

Table 30.3 presents the numbers of approved naturalizations for the year 2022 by country of birth of the applicants, states they are residing in, and the class of admission. The top three countries of birth of the approved naturalized citizens were Mexico, India, and the

---

> TABLE **30.2**

Naturalizations approved and denied

Year	Applications filed	Persons naturalized	Applications denied	Denied %
2015	783,062	730,259	75,810	9.68
2016	972,151	753,060	86,033	8.85
2017	986,851	707,265	83,176	8.43
2018	837,168	761,901	92,631	6.00
2019	830,560	843,593	97,789	11.77
2020	967,755	628,254	80,609	8.32
2021	789,119	813,861	85,170	10.79
2022	781,075	969,380	111,637	14.29

In all DHS reports, "years" refer to U.S. fiscal years, which run from October 01 to September 30.
Source: Adapted from https://www.dhs.gov/immigration-statistics/naturalizations.

436 Chapter 30 U.S. Immigration, Citizenship, and the Naturalization Test

TABLE **30.3**

Approved naturalizations for FY 2022 by top 10 countries of origin, top 10 states of residence, and class of admission

Country of birth	Numbers	State of residence	Numbers	Class of admission	Numbers	%
Mexico	128,300	California	184,700	Spouses	248,300	25.7
India	65,800	Texas	108,300	Parents	58,400	6.0
Philippines	53,300	Florida	106,000	Children	44,500	4.6
Cuba	46,700	New York	102,300	Family pref.	197,500	20.5
Dominican Republic	34,400	New Jersey	53,700	Refugees	103,100	10.6
China	32,700	Illinois	32,800	Asylees	34,000	3.5
Vietnam	23,200	Washington	32,100	Employment pref.	128,000	13.2
Jamaica	22,800	Georgia	28,400	Diversity	48,400	5.0
El Salvador	21,300	Virginia	27,600	Unknown	68,900	7.1
Colombia	18,000	Pennsylvania	27,000	Other	36,000	3.7
All others	521,000	All others	264,500			
Total	967,500	Total	967,500	Total	967,500	100.0

Notes: Due to rounding, the totals may not sum.
Source: Adapted from USCIS, ELIS. Data accessed December 2022. https://www.dhs.gov/immigration-statistics/naturalizations.

Philippines, and the top four states they resided in were California, Texas, Florida, and New York. It is important to note here that applicants from the top 10 countries listed in Table 30.3 are most likely to use a first language that is not English.

Despite these uniformly high numbers of approved naturalizations (800,000 or more a year in the last eight years), there is a high denial rate too. Close to 100,000 applicants are denied naturalization for many reasons (the English test, the civics test, other factors such as the lawful permanent residency and moral character requirement, and filing fees – currently $640 filing and $85 biometrics fees per applicant).

In summary, the tables presented above show that a high number of legal permanent residents want to become naturalized U.S. citizens every year. The approved naturalizations from the top 10 countries show that these citizens are not likely to use English as a first language. However, the percentage of denials is going up in actual numbers and as a percentage of applicants. It will be necessary to probe the reasons for this increase.

Language Tests

The Literacy Test

In 1906, the Bureau of Immigration and Naturalization was established, and standardized naturalization procedures were introduced. The Bureau changed the process from an informal approach conducted by county judges in each state. Soon, naturalization examiners, instead of judges, began asking the civics questions orally, with examiners choosing their own questions.

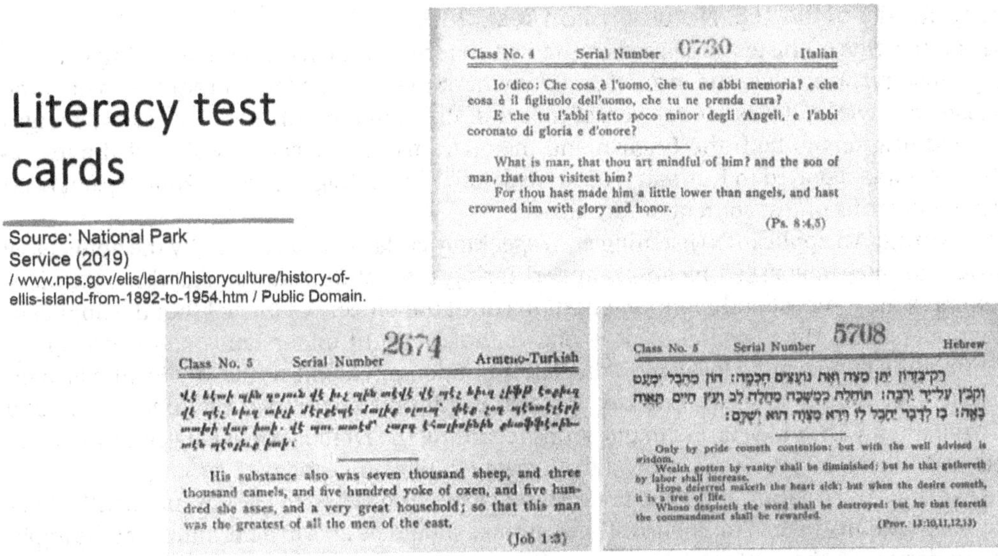

Literacy test cards

Source: National Park Service (2019) / www.nps.gov/elis/learn/historyculture/history-of-ellis-island-from-1892-to-1954.htm / Public Domain.

FIGURE 30.1 Literacy test cards in Italian, Armenio-Turkish, and Hebrew. *Source:* History of Ellis Island from 1892 to 1954 National Park Service (2019) / www.nps.gov/elis/learn/historyculture/history-of-ellis-island-from-1892-to-1954.htm / Public Domain.

Language criteria were added for the first time in the 1893 Act, when Congress added *the ability to read and write* (but not specifically in English), and in the 1906 Act, Congress required applicants *to sign their petitions in their own handwriting and speak English*. In 1896, Congress passed the Literacy Test Bill, promoted by the Immigration Restriction League, who wanted to have a barrier in place to restrict immigrants from the "inferior" races of Europe (immigrants from Eastern and Southern Europe). The test was expected to assess the ability of applicants for immigration to read at least 40 words in any language as a requirement for admission to the United States, but this bill was vetoed by President Cleveland.

In 1917, as wartime hysteria fed American xenophobia, Congress passed the Literacy Test Bill again, overriding President Wilson's veto this time. This instrument of racial exclusion became the first literacy requirement that required potential immigrants over 16 years of age to read at least 30 words and not more than 80 words in ordinary use in any language. Thus, from 1917 onward, the test resulted in effectively restricting immigrants from Eastern and Southern Europe, Irish Catholics, and Asians. Figure 30.1 shows literacy test cards in Italian, Armenio-Turkish, and Hebrew. In the most prominent card, Italian immigrants had to read to the immigration officer what was printed on the card. Similar cards were prepared for many languages.

The U.S. Naturalization Test

In 1952, The Immigration and Nationality Act of 1952 (1952) enshrined both the English language and the history and government requirements for citizenship (see Appendix 30.B). The Act itself was controversial in many aspects: It was too conservative to some and more restrictive to others. The Act was vetoed by President Truman. His veto was overridden by a vote of 278 to 113 in the House and 57 to 26 in the Senate. del Valle (2003) noted, "in passing the English literacy provision, Congressmen clearly linked the inability to speak or understand English to political suspicion" (p. 93). The U.S. government enforced the requirements for naturalization in diverse ways over time.

438 Chapter 30 U.S. Immigration, Citizenship, and the Naturalization Test

Components of the U.S. Naturalization Test, 2018

The components of the test are based on the INA in terms of the requirements of English language, history, principles, and form of government of the United States. From 1986, when the English and civics test was used as part of the naturalization process, there have been changes and modifications to both the English and the civics parts. A recent revision of the test in 2007–2008 was reported in Kunnan (2009a) in detail. The redesigned test in 2018 has not been changed in terms of test content or format.

Speaking: An applicant's (listening and) speaking skills are determined by the applicant's answers to questions asked by an examiner during the naturalization eligibility interview. Examiners must repeat and rephrase questions until the officer is satisfied that the applicant fully understands the question or does not. If the applicant understands and can respond meaningfully to questions relevant to the determination of eligibility, the applicant has demonstrated the ability to speak English. The test is administered by an examiner orally and individually, and it could start with questions regarding the N-400 form and everyday matters (such as "Where do you live?" "How did you come to this office today?" etc.).

Reading: An applicant must read one sentence out of three sentences to sufficiently demonstrate the ability to read in English. The examiner should be able to determine that the applicant understands the sentence's meaning. Once the applicant reads one of three sentences correctly, the examiner will stop administering the reading test. Applicants will not be failed because of their accent when speaking English. The examiner will score the reading as follows:

Writing: An applicant must write one sentence (on a piece of paper) out of three sentences to sufficiently demonstrate the ability to write in English in a manner that would be understandable to the examiner. An applicant must not abbreviate any dictated word in the written sentence. Once the applicant writes one of three sentences correctly, the examiner will stop administering the writing test. An applicant will not fail because of spelling, capitalization, or punctuation errors unless the errors would prevent understanding the meaning of the sentence. The examiner will score the writing as follows:

Civics: Applicants will be asked at least 10 questions based on the 100 questions on U.S. history and civics list on the USCIS website. Questions are about American government and history that are under the following sections: *American government* (principles of American democracy, the system of government, rights, and responsibilities); *American history* (colonial period and independence, the 1800s, recent American history, and other historical information); *Symbols and holidays* (symbols and holidays).

Several problems regarding the test were identified: (i) Examiners used different sentences for reading and writing; (ii) examiners used different content for listening and speaking; some used history and civics test questions (although these questions could be answered in the applicant's first language); some used daily life, current events, sports, etc.; (iii) the level of difficulty varied as sentences for the writing test differed in topic, length, and complexity; some words were more difficult in terms of spelling (allegiance, president, and television); and (iv) the history and government questions encouraged memorization of discrete facts with little understanding of the material; some were memory-type questions.

Test redesign, 2023

Due to these problems and a general rethink by the USCIS, President Biden issued an Executive Order (No. 14012 on February 2, 2021)[1] (see Appendix 30.B for the full text). Its main purpose was "Restoring Faith in Our Legal Immigration Systems and Strengthening Integration and Inclusion Efforts for New Americans." It called for "eliminating barriers in,

---

[1] https://www.whitehouse.gov/briefing-room/presidential-actions/2021/02/02/executive-order-restoring-faith-in-our-legal-immigration-systems-and-strengthening-integration-and-inclusion-efforts-for-new-americans/.

and otherwise improving, the existing naturalization process, with particular emphasis on the civics and English language tests. Create a consistent, fair, and transparent process to ensure that applicants have the information they need to study and prepare for all parts of the naturalization test" (Executive Order 14012, p. 1).

The naturalization test redesign would include a new speaking test and a new proposed civics test. The parts of the naturalization test that would not change are the reading test and the writing test. The test would be standardized, and the speaking test would be separated from general talk about the application. The test would also be aligned to the National Reporting System (NRS) with an ESL Level 3 – High Beginner. Applicants would be given three attempts to complete at least one sufficiently for a pass. For the civics test, instead of open-ended questions, a multiple-choice format would be introduced. The other aspects of the test would remain the same: The passing score would be 6 correct out of 10 questions.

Previous redesigns have resulted in minimal change to the test. Thus, we may not expect much change except for the inclusion of the picture-description task.

Pass Percentage Rates

Table 30.4 presents the pass percentage rates for the year 2021: The first percentage (89.5%) denotes the pass rate of applicants who took the initial exam only and includes applicants who were exempt from one of more portions of the naturalization test. The second percentage (96.1%) denotes the pass rate of applicants who took the initial and re-exam and includes applicants who were exempt from one of more portions of the naturalization test. The English skills breakdown (speaking, understanding, writing, and reading) shows a 95% pass rate. The last column (civics test pass %) shows the pass percentages for applicants who are exempt from the English test based on their age and years of residency. Surprisingly, those applicants who are 65 and above and have 20 years of residency and above have the highest pass percentage (93.1%).

TABLE 30.4

Median years spent as LPRs by applicants' country of origin, FY 2022

Applicants' country of origin	Median years spent as LPRs
Mexico	12.5
Canada	11.1
United Kingdom and El Salvador	10.3
Dominic Republic	9.8
Haiti	9.1
South Korea	9.0
Jamaica	8.0
Colombia	7.7
Philippines	7.5
China	7.2
Cuba	6.8
Vietnam, India, and Brazil	6.4
Pakistan	6.1
Afghanistan, Iran, Venezuela, Bangladesh, Nigeria, and Iraq	6.0

Notes: Due to rounding, the totals may not sum.
Source: Adapted from USCIS, ELIS. Data accessed December 2022. https://www.dhs.gov/immigration-statistics/naturalizations.

Overall Evaluation: Is the Test Beneficial or a Barrier?

Kunnan (2021) discussed an overall evaluation of the USNT; he argued that an unambiguous way to examine whether the USNT is beneficial to the applicants for citizenship and the community is to use a framework that accounts for principles of fairness of the assessment and justice of the assessment institution (see Kunnan, 2018 for a detailed explication of these two principles). Briefly, the fairness principle is composed of the five sub-principles: (i) opportunity to learn, (ii) meaningfulness, (iii) absence of bias, (iv) access and accommodations, and (v) consequences; the justice principle is composed of two sub-principles: (i) reasoning or justifying the assessment and (ii) advancing justice.

Using Fairness and Justice Principles

A detailed examination using these principles listed above is available in Kunnan (2021). Additional descriptions of the bases and processes of the U.S. naturalization are also available in Kunnan (2008, 2009a,b, 2013, 2018) including its ideological bases, cumbersome processes, the tests and its revisions, and consequences to applicants. Here is a summary of the detailed examination.

Fairness 1: Opportunity to learn
Question: Do applicants have an opportunity to learn for the test? The evidence in support of the question is as follows:

USCIS websites: Several USCIS websites provide guidance that is meant to be useful for the English test. Vocabulary practice for the reading and writing tests and topics for the speaking test covered on Form N-400, application for naturalization, and the interview are offered. For the civics test, topics such as American history and government and integrated civics with 100 civics questions and answers are available in many languages.

Community college courses: Applicants can attend community college courses to prepare for the for English and civics tests. In California, noncredit courses titled English and civics (meant for residents planning to go through the naturalization process) are available for free at community colleges or at advocacy or community centers.

Pass Rates: As we have seen in Table 30.5, the pass rate is above 89.5% for the first attempt and 96.1% for the re-exam. However, given that there are about 800,000 applicants a year, the pass rate still leaves 88,000 failing in their first attempt at the test.

All this opportunity is based on the expectation that applicants would have the resources to have access to their websites or be able to take a community college course. In summary, given the circumstances, it could be concluded that the opportunity to learn and opportunity for success is high (in English and Spanish) but more needs to be done for applicants from other languages.

Fairness 2: Meaningfulness
Question: Do applicants find the test meaningful? The evidence in support of the question is as follows:

Constructs: The constructs of the English test (through the skills of speaking, reading, and writing) clearly underrepresent basic abilities in language proficiency. The tasks asked of the applicants are clearly considerably basic (following directions as in the listening and speaking tasks), and reading and writing can be considered as basic. If we map the tasks on the Common European Framework, we could place the test at an A1 for listening and speaking and A2 for reading and writing.

Overall Evaluation: Is the Test Beneficial or a Barrier?

TABLE 30.5

Pass percentage rates, FY 2021

	Initial pass %	Initial pass + Re-exam %	Civic test pass %
Overall test (English + Civics)	89.5	96.1	
Overall English	93.0		
Speaking	94.0		
Understanding/Listening	93.0		
Writing	95.0		
Reading	98.0		
Overall civics test			93.8
English test exempt applicants			
Age 50 with 20 years of residency			90.0
Age 55 with 15 years of residency			87.9
Age 65 with 20 years of residency			93.1

Source: Adapted from USCIS, ELIS. Data accessed December 2022. https://www.dhs.gov/immigration-statistics/naturalizations.

The history and civics test, on the other hand, requires both memory of information (with 100 questions) as well as ability to read the questions and multiple-choice options.

Consistency: Concern with the lack of consistency in the difficulty level of the questions was one of the reasons why the test was redesigned (see Kunnan, 2009a). In the English test, sentences are created by using the vocabulary practice for reading and writing. However, it is not clear whether applicants will get sentences for reading and writing that are of equal level of difficulty. Similarly, in terms of the history and civics test, the questions are selected carefully in terms of content.

Besides, there are no questions on pivotal moments in American history that applicants may be familiar with, such as the treatment of Native Americans, the great migration of African Americans from the Jim Crow South to the North and West starting in 1915, the Great Depression of the 1930s, the 1945 atomic bombings of Hiroshima and Nagasaki, the House Un-American Activities Committee, the assassination of John F. Kennedy and Martin Luther King, protests of the Vietnam War, Cesar Chavez and the farm movement, the Chinese Exclusion Act, the Japanese internment, the Mariel boatlift, the Vietnamese refugee crisis, etc. Thus, in summary, it could be concluded that the test is not meaningful to the test takers.

Fairness 3: Absence of bias

Question: Is the test absent of bias? The evidence in support of the question is as follows:

Item difficulty: As noted earlier, it is not clear that the applicants are administered items with the same level of difficulty on either the English test or the history and civics test. Thus, test bias cannot be ruled out as it is hard to know as no interview data is made available on whether there is adequate consistency across examiners in the country.

Item topics and content: The topics and content of the reading and writing sentences as well as the history and civics test items may also be biased. There is no information concerning whether the administrative procedures for both item difficulty and item topics and content are balanced. Thus, again, *bias cannot be ruled out* as there is no information regarding pass rates for applicants with low income and/or applicants from countries that do not share similar government structure with the United States. Thus, in summary, it must be concluded that it is possible there is bias in the administration.

442 Chapter 30 U.S. Immigration, Citizenship, and the Naturalization Test

Fairness 4: Access and accommodations

Question: Does the test offer enough access and adequate accommodations to applicants? The evidence in support of the question is as follows:

Costs: The cost of filing an application is high (currently, it is $640 for filing the application and $85 biometrics fees per applicant; the reduced rate of $320 is available if your documented annual household income is greater than 150% and not more than 200% of the Federal Poverty Guidelines).

Considerations: Due consideration exceptions are available for taking the English test for the following groups: applicants who are 50, 55, and 65 years old.

Accommodations: Accommodations are available for those with medical disabilities. However, there is no mention of American Sign Language for applicants who need this service.

In summary, while considerations and accommodations available make the test accessible to most applicants, *the filing fees are extremely high*. There is no doubt that the fee is a barrier to citizenship applications for many low- and moderate-income applicants. The lack of American Sign Language is another barrier.

Fairness 5: Consequences

Question: Is the test bringing about beneficial consequences to the applicant and their community? The evidence in support of the question is as follows:

Naturalizations and denials: Applications filed for naturalizations and persons naturalized from 1907 to now show more than 37 million applied and 33 million received citizenship. Tables 30.2–30.4 present current figures for applications, approvals, and denials. The pass rates indicate that the test is not difficult to pass for most applicants, but the high number of denials dampens the encouragement from the pass rate. Further, there is no evidence that the successful applicants will go on to improve their English language ability and knowledge of American government and civics because of the USNT.

Justice 1: Reasoning or justification

Question: Does the institution administering the test provide adequate reasoning for the test? The evidence in support of the question is as follows:

Civic nationalism: There is no recent reasoning or justification for the tests that were developed based on the 1952 Act. Thus, the study concluded that the U.S. naturalization process did not help toward the goal of more civic nationalism.

Reluctance to file applications: As attractive as U.S. citizenship may seem to many, there are legal permanent residents who do not apply for citizenship until many years after they are eligible. Persons naturalizing in 2019 spent a median of eight years in LPR status before becoming U.S. citizens. The median years spent as an LPR varies by the applicants' country of origin. The countries with the largest number of new citizens in FY 2022 and their median years spent as LPRs are shown in Table 30.5. Out of these countries, applicants from Mexico spent the longest time (12.5 years) as LPRs before applying for citizenship, while applicants from Afghanistan, Iran, Venezuela, Bangladesh, Nigeria, and Iraq spent the shortest time before they applied for citizenship (with six years).

In addition, while LPRs in New York have the highest naturalization rates (about 50%), LPRs from the southern border states (Arizona, New Mexico, and Texas) have the lowest rates of naturalization (about 30% of eligible LPRs).

There are many reasons why applicants delay applying for citizenship such as proximity to the United States (the southern border states, for example), filing fee costs, low perceived benefits, and renunciation of loyalty and legal ties with previous nationality (except in the case of dual citizenship). On the other hand, reasons for why applicants may apply as soon as they are eligible include securing a U.S. passport, and unemployment, low earning capacity, poverty, violence, or persecution in the home country.

Justice 2: Advancing justice

Question: Does the institution administering the test advance justice related to the test? The evidence in support of the question is as follows:

Remedies: According to the regulations, an applicant who passes the tests is informed by the examiner in person that they have been successful. In the event the applicant fails any portion of the English test and/or civics test during their first examination, the applicant will be re-scheduled to appear for a second opportunity to take the test(s) within 90 days. If the applicant fails any portion of the test a second time, the examiner will deny the application. This means the applicant will have to start all over again with the filing of application, pay fees, and so on.

Legal challenges: A legal challenge is another way of checking the process and government's policies. But the naturalization process itself cannot be challenged in court as there is no appeal process and pass and fail rates are not available for public review.

In summary, in addition to the analysis presented above, many well-known noted scholars have commented on the U.S. naturalization test in terms of its meaning and its overall purpose. An early commentator was Pickus (2005) who raised a fundamental issue: "Questions (in the tests) deal with rights and freedoms but none speaks of its obligations ... civic knowledge does not make one a good citizen—native-born Americans do not have to take any such test" (p. 25A). Etzioni (2007) concluded the "test hinders those who do not speak English and favours immigrants from English-speaking countries and persons who can afford extensive English education prior to their arrival, or once they are in the U.S." (p. 355). Later, in a provocative book, Pickus (2005) presented an account of nationalism in which he argued that instead of focusing on the wild swings of political discourse and actions of immigration and citizenship, there should be "a renewed civic nationalism that melds principles and people-hood" (p. 1). Similar analyses of tests of immigration and citizenship in Europe have argued that such tests only hinder and do not promote immigration and citizenship (see Carlsen & Rocca, 2021, 2022).

Language Attainment and Integration

It is asserted that one of the most critical factors in immigration integration (and assimilation) is the language attainment of the receiving country's national or most used language. In the United States, the expectation is that immigrants will be able to function well and be integrated into society if their English language proficiency is high enough for employment and general living.

Language Attainment

English is not the first language of most immigrants; many arrive from countries where English is the main language or the medium of instruction in school or college study. These immigrants are from Australia, Canada, Jamaica, and the United Kingdom but also from countries where English is an official language such as India, Nigeria, and the Philippines. Most others learn English through formal instruction in school or informally at their place of work or in the community. Success through these programs depends on numerous factors related to immigrants. Here are the most salient personal, educational, cognitive, employability, and availability of support systems:

A. *Personal variables*: (i) Age and gender at the time of immigration (a range of primary school level children to adults who are seniors), (ii) marital status and partner (single, married to a non-L1 English partner, or married to an L1 English-speaking partner), (iii) length of residence in the United States, (iv) future plans for residence (in the United States or elsewhere), and (v) the individual need and motivation.

B. *Educational variables*: (i) General education level at the time of immigration (a range of no education or low literacy to college graduate) and (ii) home country English language instruction or exposure (a range of no English to L1 English).

C. *Cognitive and linguistic variables*: (i) Age, (ii) motivation, (iii) language exposure and environment, (iv) language aptitude and memory, (v) L1 and L1 learning success, (vi) attention and awareness to language features, (vii) personality, and (viii) beliefs and attitude toward language learning.

D. *Employability variables*: (i) Employability at the time of immigration (range of no skills to less skilled to highly skilled) and (ii) means in terms of time and leisure to pursue English language study and watch English-language TV or other programs.

E. *Availability variables*: (i) Federal, state, or local government instructional programs in English language and civics (a range of website information to full-fledged courses in English and civics), (ii) community activities that promote English language learning and social activities (playing mah-jongg, pickleball, or tennis, cooking and dancing classes, driving lessons, watching films, filing tax returns, etc.), and (iii) the role of the immigrant community they belong to (from a range of only L1 to bilingual L1-English).

Obviously, success in language learning depends on these variables coming together in an optimal manner and for a sustained period, especially for limited English proficiency students. Hakuta et al. (2000) examined limited English proficiency students in two California districts and concluded that "oral proficiency takes three to five years to develop, and academic English proficiency can take four to seven years" (p. 1).

With reference to immigrants in the United States, Freeman and Tendler (2012) reported survey results of *lack of attainment* of English at "less than very well" by immigration and L1 status although no information in this study is available regarding what is meant by "less than very well." Could it be literate, functional in high school, employment or workspace, or college? Table 30.6 provides this information although the results are from 15 years ago. The nationwide rates show that noncitizens (62.2%) report a much higher rate of "less than very

---

TABLE 30.6

Attainment of English language as "less than very well" as % of population in 10 states

State	Total	Native/L1 English	Foreign-born not naturalized	Naturalized citizen	Noncitizen
Arizona	12.1	3.1	59.2	37.0	68.9
California	19.9	4.0	58.8	46.0	68.9
Colorado	7.5	1.9	54.8	32.4	65.2
Florida	11.7	2.4	49.1	37.1	59.3
Illinois	9.8	1.9	55.5	42.7	65.8
Nevada	13.0	2.2	55.0	37.5	65.5
New Jersey	11.7	2.5	46.3	35.6	57.1
New Mexico	10.2	4.6	58.6	40.2	66.6
New York	13.2	3.3	46.8	37.8	56.5
Texas	14.5	4.7	62.2	44.2	70.4
Nationwide	**8.6**	**1.9**	**52.3**	**38.9**	**62.2**

Source: US Census Bureau; American Community Survey, 2006–08 (cited in Freeman & Tendler, 2012).

Language Attainment and Integration   **445**

well" English language proficiency than foreign-born not naturalized (52.3%) and naturalized citizens (38.9%). The state-wise results show that the southern border states (New Mexico, Texas, and Arizona) have high rates of "less than very well" English language proficiency.

Integration

As immigration integration (and assimilation) seems to be an implicit goal in the United States through the naturalization process, it is critical to identify the facilitators or barriers immigrants and new citizens face in terms of the various dimensions of integration: legal, political, geographical, socioeconomic, sociocultural, family, education, and health. The U.S. National Academies of Sciences, Engineering and Medicine (2015) defined the term:

> Integration is the term the panel uses to describe the changes that both immigrants – and their descendants – and the society they have joined – undergo in response to migration ... (it) is a process by which members of immigrant groups and host societies come to resemble one another (Brown & Bean, 2006) ... Integration is a two-fold process: it happens both because immigrants experience change once they arrive and because native-born Americans change in response to immigration ... The process of integration takes time, and the panel considers the process in two ways: first for the first generation, by examining what happens in the time since arrival; for the second and third generations – the children and grandchildren of immigrants – by comparisons across generations. (p. 19)

But many authors have doubts over the governmental or institutional sense of integration. Castles et al. (2002) pointed out that "the broadness of the integration process makes it hard to define in any precise way. Integration of newcomers to a society takes place at every level and in every sector of society. It involves a wide range of social players: public officials, political decision-makers, employers, trace union officials, fellow-workers, service providers, neighbors, and so on. The immigrants...themselves play a crucial role in the integration process (p. 113). However, the concept of integration remains an implicit policy goal of governments; in the case of the United States, their implicit policy goal is buried in the U.S. naturalization process.

The key questions that could be asked if we were to adopt the notion of immigrant integration would be: how would successful integration be measured? What would be the *indicators or markers* of successful integration? What would be the *blockers or hurdles* for successful integration? Harder et al. (2018) proposed a multidimensional measure of immigrant integration capturing six dimensions: psychological, economic, political, social, linguistic, and navigational. They claimed that their framework can measure be used across countries, over time, and across different immigrant groups and can be administered through short questionnaires. Ager and Strang (2008) too offered a conceptual framework defining core domains of integration. These include the *Foundation* (rights and citizenship), *Facilitators* (language and cultural knowledge and safety and stability), *Social connection* (social bridges, social bonds, and social links), and *Markers and means* (employment, housing, education, and health).

Keeping theseframeworks in mind, questions that are salient in immigrant integration are raised here. First, if all of the domains mentioned above are taken into consideration, immigrants who might be able to reach full integration would only be the educated, English-speaking, reasonably well-employed, middle- and upper-class persons who have sufficient time and disposable income to participate in activities that would facilitate integration.

Second, is it reasonable to expect *all* new citizens, young and older, (after the naturalization process) to be ready to integrate into many integration-promoting institutions? Would it not be the case that integration would also depend on premigration engagement of

446 Chapter 30 U.S. Immigration, Citizenship, and the Naturalization Test

immigrants to political, social, cultural, or civic matters in the country of origin? In other words, would engagement in the home country prepare immigrants for integration more easily? But would it also be possible that some immigrants who have never been engaged in their home country might be ready to be engaged in the United States (because of perceived easiness to engage)? Third, should the goal of integration hinge on *success in the English and civics test* alone? In other words, would preparation for the test and taking the test bring about integration?

Would other civic and social activities contribute as well? Also, would integration be found in small incremental activities (for example, participation in political, cultural, social, or religious) that new citizens might participate in rather than a big integration event (such as stand for a political seat in a local or regional election)?

Fourth, would some immigrants who have come from countries that are more autocratic find it difficult to engage as they might have had unpleasant experiences in the past? And, relatedly, immigrants who have come from countries that are more democratic find it easier to engage as they may have had pleasant experiences in the past. Fifth, would it be the case that the immigrants who want to become citizens may not want to integrate and adapt the political, cultural, and civic ways? Is it possible that the goal of some immigrants is not to want to engage in full integration and adaptation and only benefit from other aspects of becoming a citizen (such as receiving a U.S. passport? Not all citizens are active participants in political, cultural, or civic activities. Sixth, is it possible for some immigrants integration may only take place over a few generations? Second- or third-generation immigrants might find success in integration than first-generation immigrants. Finally, could it be the case that immigrant integration can take place only if the host government and society are providing resources to help integrate immigrants into host communities? As mentioned in the extract above, integration is a twofold process.

Conclusion

In summary, immigration and citizenship policies as they stand do not favor non-English-speaking applicants and low-income applicants for citizenship. The naturalization process is not painless to applicants as the whole endeavor is expensive, untransparent, unnecessarily long, and fraught with anxiety. The xenophobia of the past (and, in the present, in some political quarters) is reflected in some of the recent manufactured obstacles (such as excessive bureaucratic measures, meaningless tests, high application costs, and delayed processing). But it is also the case that despite all these daunting obstacles, large numbers of LPRs apply for citizenship each year (close to 800,000) because they believe in the aspiration of American democracy: a nation bound not by race or religion but by the shared values of freedom, liberty, and equality, and for the practical benefits, which include permanent residence, employment, and opportunity to participate politically and have a voice in how the city, state, and nation are governed. And immigrant integration in terms of attainment of high English language proficiency and other dimensions will depend on many factors combining well for success.

A way forward then would be to rethink the naturalization process for the new transnational immigrants of the 21st century. This new conceptualization would have to include ways to cancel the xenophobia of the past in all branches of federal and state governments, legislatures, and the judiciary; to embrace multilingualism and multiculturalism; and to welcome and support LPRs to apply to become citizens with lower fees, smoother bureaucratic measures, and more support systems. This rethink requires the review and reflection of American political and moral theory and of thinking by immigrants by the citizenry of the country as contributors to society.

Discussion Questions

1. How do ESL/Citizenship classes prepare immigrants to be successful at the U.S. naturalization test in your city?

2. Does the U.S. naturalization test deter non-English-speaking and less resourced immigrants from becoming citizens in your region?

Appendix A: Key Dates Related to Citizenship, 18th to Early 21st Century

1776: Declaration of Independence protests England's limiting naturalization of foreigners in the colonies.

1789: U.S. Constitution, under Article I, states that Congress is "to establish an uniform Rule of Naturalization," eventually giving the federal government the sole authority over immigration.

1789: Bill of Rights outlines basic rights under the new government.

1790: Naturalization Act of 1790 provides the first rules to be followed by the United States in granting national citizenship to "free white people."

1848: Treaty of Guadalupe Hidalgo extends citizenship to all inhabitants living in the territory annexed to the United States following the Mexican War.

1865: 13th Amendment abolishes slavery, although it did not grant formerly enslaved persons the full rights of citizenship.

1868: 14th Amendment grants that all persons born or naturalized in the United States are citizens and are guaranteed "equal protection of the laws."

1870: Naturalization Act of 1870 extends naturalization rights to former African slaves not born in the United States; Asian immigrants remain excluded from citizenship.

1882: Chinese Exclusion Act of 1882 is the first U.S. law to ban immigration based on race or nationality; it would be repealed in 1943.

1898: U.S. Supreme Court rules in *United States v. Wong Kim Ark* that any child born in the United States, regardless of race or parents' citizenship status, is an American citizen.

1917: Jones–Shafroth Act grants U.S. citizenship to residents of Puerto Rico.

1921: First quota law is passed limiting the annual number of immigrants based on country of origin.

1924: Indian Citizenship Act extends U.S. citizenship to all Native Americans.

1940: Alien Registration Act requires all noncitizen adults to register with the government and empowers the president to deport foreigners suspected of espionage or being a security risk.

1952: Immigration and Nationality Act eliminates race as a bar to immigration or citizenship.

1965: Hart-Celler Act abolishes the national origins quota system, replacing it with a preference system that focuses on immigrants' skills and family relationships with citizens or U.S. residents.

1986: Immigration Reform and Control Act of 1986 grants amnesty to millions of individuals living in the United States who entered the country before January 1, 1982.

2001: USA Patriot Act amends the Immigration and Nationality Act to broaden the scope of aliens ineligible for admission or deportation to include terrorist activities.

2005: REAL ID Act created national standards for state-issued ID cards.

2008: Secured communities allowed for data sharing between states and localities and federal government to identify and deport immigrants with criminal convictions.

448 Chapter 30 U.S. Immigration, Citizenship, and the Naturalization Test

2012: The Department of Homeland Security (DHS) announced that it would not deport certain undocumented youth who came to the United States as children; these individuals may be granted a type of temporary permission to stay in the United States called "deferred action." The Obama administration called this program Deferred Action for Childhood Arrivals, or DACA.

Source: https://americanhistory.si.edu/democracy-exhibition/creating-citizens/defining-citizenship.

Appendix B: Requirements as to Understanding the English Language, History, Principles, and Form of Government of the United States

a. No person except as otherwise provided in this subchapter shall hereafter be naturalized as a citizen of the United States upon his own application who cannot demonstrate
   1. An understanding of the English language, including an ability to read, write, and speak words in the English language: provided that the requirements of this paragraph relating to the ability to read and write shall be met if the applicant can read or write simple words and phrases to the end that a reasonable test of his literacy shall be made and that no extraordinary or unreasonable condition shall be imposed upon the applicant.
   2. A knowledge and understanding of the fundamentals of the history, and of the principles and form of government, of the United States.

Exemptions
b.
   1. The requirements of section (a) shall not apply to any person who is unable because of physical or developmental disability or mental impairment to comply therewith.
   2. The requirements of section (a) shall not apply to any person who, in the date of the filling of the person's application for naturalization as provided in section 334, either
      a. is over 50 years of age and has been living in the United States for periods of totaling at least 20 years subsequent to a lawful admission for permanent residence or
      b. is over 55 years of age and has been living in the United States for periods of totaling at least 15 years subsequent to a lawful admission for permanent residence.
   3. The Attorney General, pursuant to regulations, shall provide for special consideration, as determined by the AG, concerning the requirement of subsection (a) (2).

Exceptions
The U.S. naturalization test does not apply to the following two groups:

1. Children born in the United States, including the 50 States and the District of Columbia and, in most cases, U.S. territories such as Puerto Rico, Guam, the Northern Maraina Islands, and the United States. Virgin Islands as well as current States that were territories at the time of the birth of some individuals now living (for example,

Alaska and Hawaii) are considered U.S. citizens at birth (unless born to foreign diplomatic staff), regardless of the citizenship or nationality of the parents (the *jus solis* principle, the "right of soil").

2. Children born outside the United States to at least one parent who is a U.S. citizen are granted U.S. citizenship (the *jus sanguinis* principle, the "right of blood").

Source: Immigration and Nationality Act, Sec 312 [8 U.S.C. 1423].

References

Ager, A., & Strang, A. (2008). Understanding integration: a conceptual framework. *Journal of refugee studies*, *21*(2), 116–191.

Brown, S. & Bean, F., (2006). Assimilation Models, Old and New: Explaining a Long-Term Process, *Migration Information Source*. United States of America. Retrieved from https://policycommons.net/artifacts/1356344/assimilation-models-old-and-new/1968503/ on 28 May 2024. CID: 20.500.12592/tbhs3r.

Carlsen, C. (2024). Language testing for residency and citizenship in Europe. Justification, consequences and debate. In A. J. Kunnan (Ed.), *The concise companion to language assessment* (pp. 401–416). John Wiley & Sons, Inc.

Carlsen, C. H., & Rocca, L. (2021). Language test misuse. *Language Assessment Quarterly*, *18*(5), 477–491.

Carlsen, C. H., & Rocca, L. (2022). Language test activism. *Language Policy*, *21*(4), 597–616.

Etzioni, A. (2007). Citizenship tests: a comparative, communitarian perspective. *Political Quarterly*, *78*, 353–363. https://doi.org/10.1111/j.1467-923X.2007.00864.x.

Freeman, G., & Tendler, S. (2012). United States of America. In C. Joppke & F. Seidle (Eds.), *Immigrant integration in federal countries* (pp. 192–220). McGill-Queen's University Press.

Frost, K. (2024). Language assessment for immigration in Australia: test-policy-discourse entanglements and their ethical implications. In A. J. Kunnan (Ed.), *The concise companion to language assessment* (pp. 417–431). John Wiley & Sons, Inc.

Hakuta, K., Butler, Y., & Win, D. (2000). *How long does it take English learners to attain proficiency? The University of California Linguistic Minority Research Institute. Project 2000-1.*

Harder, N., Figueroa, L., Gillum, R., Hangartner, D., Laitin, D., & Hainmueller, J. (2018). Multidimensional measure of immigrant integration. *PNAS*, *115*(45), 11483–11488.

Kennedy, J. F. (1964). *A nation of immigrants*. Harper.

Kunnan, A. J. (2008). Towards a model of test evaluation: using the test fairness and wider context frameworks. In L. Taylor & C. Weir (Eds.), *Multilingualism and assessment: Achieving transparency, assuring quality, sustaining diversity* (Papers from the ALTE conference, Berlin, pp. 229–251). Cambridge University Press.

Kunnan, A. J. (2009a). Politics and legislation in immigration and citizenship testing: the U.S. case. *Annual Review of Applied Linguistics*, *29*, 37–48. https://doi.org/10.1017/S0267190509090047.

Kunnan, A. J. (2009b). The U.S. naturalization test. *Language Assessment Quarterly*, *6*, 89–97. https://doi.org/10.1080/15434300802606630.

Kunnan, A. J. (2013). Language assessment for immigration and citizenship. In G. Fulcher & F. Davidson (Eds.), *The handbook of language testing* (pp. 152–166). Routledge.

Kunnan, A. J. (2018). *Evaluating language assessments*. New York, NY: Routledge.

Kunnan, A. J. (2021). Revisiting language assessment for citizenship: the case of U.S. citizenship and the naturalization test. In G. Fulcher & L. Harding (Eds.), *The handbook of language testing* (2nd ed., pp. 96–115). Routledge.

Lee, E. (2019). *America for Americans: A history of xenophobia in the United States*. Basic Books.

Lew-Williams, B. (2018). *The Chinese must go*. Harvard University Press.

National Academies of Sciences, Engineering and Medicine. (2015). *The integration of immigrants into American Society*. The National Academies Press.

National Park Service (2019). *History of Ellis Island from 1892 to 1954*. www.nps.gov/elis/learn/historyculture/history-of-ellis-island-from-1892-to-1954.htm.

450 **Chapter 30** U.S. Immigration, Citizenship, and the Naturalization Test

Parker, K. (2015). *Making foreigners*. Cambridge University Press.

Pickus, N. (2005). *True faith and allegiance: Immigration and American civic nationalism*. Princeton University Press.

The Immigration and Nationality Act of 1952. (1952). *Pub. L. No. 82-414, Stat. 163, Title 8 of the U.S. Code, Chapter 12. USCIS, Department of Homeland Services*.

U.S. Department of Homeland Security, Office of Immigration Statistics. *Yearbook of Immigration Statistics (various years)*. Available at www.dhs.gov/files/statistics/publications/yearbook.shtm.

del Valle, S. (2003). *Language rights and the law*. Multilingual Matters.

Suggested Readings

Canagarajah, S. (Ed.). (2017). *The Routledge handbook of migration and language*. Routledge.

Cisneros, J. D. (Ed.). (2013). *The border crossed U.S.* University of Alabama Press.

Loring, A., & Ramanathan, V. (Eds.). (2016). *Language, immigration, and naturalization*. Multilingual Matters.

National Academies of Sciences, Engineering and Medicine. (2015). *The integration of immigrants into American society*. The National Academies Press.

Ngai, M. (2004). *Impossible subjects*. Princeton University Press.

Court Cases

Korematsu v. United States, 323 U.S. 214 (1944). https://supreme.justia.com/cases/federal/us/323/214/

United States v. Wong Kim Ark, 169 U.S. 649 (1898). https://www.loc.gov/item/usrep169649/.

THEME 6

Qualitative Research Methods

CHAPTER 31

Introspective Methods
Miyuki Sasaki and Yuhang Hu

Introduction

In this chapter, we follow Gass and Mackey (2017, p. 1), who define an introspective method as "a means of eliciting data about the thought processes that take place while a learner is doing a task or an activity" on the basis of the two assumptions: that "it is possible to tap into and document a learner's internal processes in much the same way as one can observe external real-world events," and that "humans have access at some level to their internal thought processes and can verbalize those processes." Introspective methods provide internal processing data that cannot be obtained from simple observation or quantitative measures such as test scores. This chapter focuses on three introspective methods that have been frequently used in applied linguistics: think-aloud reports, retrospection without memory aids, and stimulated recalls. When carefully used, all three are known to maximize the merits and minimize the demerits of introspective methods (see Green, 1998).

Below we briefly describe how and why introspection became a legitimate research method, first in the field of second language acquisition (SLA) and later in language assessment (LA). We define and explain the three methods and report on how they have been used in both fields. We discuss the possible advantages and disadvantages of all three methods when applied to SLA and LA research. Finally, we present three representative studies to demonstrate how introspective data have been collected and analyzed in past LA research. In critically evaluating these three studies, we review both the positive and negative features researchers should consider when planning to use these methods. We conclude with possible directions for future studies.

History of Introspective Methods

Introspective Methods in the Humanities

In the 1950s, mainly in reaction to the limited focus of behaviorism, as researchers in various fields (e.g., psychology, linguistics) began to pay more attention to human cognitive mechanisms and to experiment with people's thinking processes, behaviorism began to wane. This "cognitive revolution" created the need for introspective methods as tools for eliciting data. This time, however, researchers were much more systematic about data collection processes to ensure that the collected data would be both valid and reliable from a (then) dominant

The Concise Companion to Language Assessment, First Edition. Edited by Antony John Kunnan.
© 2025 John Wiley & Sons, Inc. Published 2025 by John Wiley & Sons, Inc.

positivist epistemology that valued empirically-based "objective truth" (for a definition, see, for example, Denzin & Lincoln, 2000). Among various introspective methods, those used for collecting verbal report data became especially popular from the 1980s onward and have now become "major sources of data on subjects' cognitive processes in specific tasks" (Ericsson & Simon, 1993, p. xi) in the fields of psychology and education.

Introspective Methods in SLA

Around the beginning of the 1980s, SLA researchers began to pay more attention to the *process* of second language (L2) development. This was a reaction against the prevalent investigations of the *product* of SLA through methods such as error analysis (or the classifications of learner errors, e.g., Richards, 1974) or morpheme studies, including studies of the acquisition order of particular grammatical morphemes (e.g., Dulay & Burt, 1973). Because "reconstructing unobservable phenomena from performance data will always entail situations where the ambiguity between product and process cannot be solved" (Færch & Kasper, 1987, p. 9), researchers sought methods that more directly probed learners' thinking processes. In the event, they found that introspective methods, which began to gain legitimacy in the social sciences around the same time, served this purpose. As SLA research methods became more rigorous, introspective methods were increasingly used in studies of learner strategies (e.g., Cohen & Upton, 2007), language processing (e.g., Smith et al., 2020), problem-solving (e.g., López-Serrano et al., 2020), and classroom research (e.g., Mackay, 2006). Furthermore, some researchers (e.g., Suzuki & Storch, 2020) began to approach L2 learners' introspection from a sociocultural perspective, claiming that the approach could be used not only as data to be investigated but also as a set of tools for facilitating learning by mediating and sharpening learners' thinking processes.

Introspective Methods in Language Assessment

Compared to SLA, the field of LA has been slower to adopt introspective methods, probably because of its inclination toward quantification. It was not until the notion of test validity was redefined in the early 1990s as "an inductive summary of both the existing evidence for and the potential consequences of score interpretation and use" (Messick, 1989, p. 13) that introspective methods began to be used in LA research. Though revolutionary, Messick's theory was too abstract to make the "positioning constructs ... the basis for test score interpretation" (Chapelle, 2021, p. 11). To make this step more amenable to research, Kane (2001, 2006) devised the "argument-based approach," which requires "the tester to specify claims expressing the meaning of the score and the inferences required to make such claims" (Chapelle, 2021, p. 11). In LA, this approach was further developed by Bachman and Palmer (2010) and has led to numerous studies of accountability and fairness in the use of specific tests toward all relevant stakeholders, particularly in North America. In Europe and the United Kingdom, many researchers owe the theoretical framework for their validation studies to Weir's (2005) socio-cognitive approach. This approach was also influenced by Messick (1989) and Kane (2001, 2006) and may be seen as similar to the argument-based approach in that it provides researchers with stages, thanks to which studies become more feasible. Since test validation has long been a pressing issue in every era of LA (see Aryadoust, 2023), the advent of these two approaches has allowed validation studies to include introspective data, which ideally should include stakeholders' thinking processes at every stage of the test. Furthermore, research on the application of test results to learning also flourishes (e.g., Şahan & Razı, 2020), with introspective data from stakeholders often used in this endeavor.

Definitions and Characteristics of Introspective Methods

The three methods discussed in this chapter differ in terms of time variation and the existence of memory aids (i.e., prompts). Due to space limitations, we mainly focus here on spoken, not written reports (cf. Bryfonski, 2023). Moreover, we distinguish between *think*-aloud and *talk*-aloud as methods with the latter referring to "the case where a subject utters thoughts that are already encoded in verbal form from the case where the subject records verbally and utters thoughts that may have been held in memory in some other form (e.g., visually)" (Ericsson & Simon, 1993, p. 222). In this chapter, we only deal with the former (i.e., think-aloud).

Think-Aloud Reporting

In think-aloud reporting, participants are asked to concurrently verbalize what they are thinking about. Ericsson and Simon (1993) explain how this type of verbalization comes closest to what is actually paid attention to, especially when a participant's verbal report is not mediated by specific instructions such as "Request for Explanations, Motions, etc." (p. 17). Compared to retrospective methods, this method is less likely to allow participants to produce accounts affected by knowledge stored in long-term memory and may therefore fail to truly reflect what they were thinking at the time. In a think-aloud procedure, participants are asked to simply verbalize their thought processes.

To this end, the researcher usually trains participants to be familiar with the "say everything that comes to your mind" process by using a task that is similar to the task participants are asked to think aloud. This makes data collection more reliable. However, despite this training, some participants may not verbalize their concurrent thinking processes accurately, especially when the task is cognitively demanding or the language participants are required to use is not their strongest (typically their L1). In such cases, researchers should encourage participants to keep talking while taking care not to force participants to produce additional explanations or justifications beyond their thinking processes.

These problems are related to potentially the most serious disadvantage of the think-aloud method, namely reactivity. Although Ericsson and Simon (1993) claimed that the method does not significantly influence participants' thinking process (except by making task completion longer), a number of studies have reported either a negative impact (e.g., Goo, 2010) or a positive one (e.g., Sanz et al., 2009). Furthermore, few studies have examined the effects of think-aloud on L2 learners with weak L2 proficiency because talking while performing a task in the L2 places too heavy a burden on the learners' cognition (e.g., Sasaki, 2000; but see also Sachs & Polio, 2007). Consequently, previous studies claiming little effect of think-aloud on accuracy may have been biased toward L1 speakers or L2 speakers with high proficiency.

Retrospective Methods Without Memory Aids

Retrospective methods ask participants to recall their thinking processes after the task is completed and to verbalize as much of the process as possible. Retrospective methods are used in both SLA and LA studies when applying think-aloud methods is too difficult for participants or when the task in question (e.g., making a speech) does not permit the use of such methods. Retrospective methods are also advantageous compared to think-aloud methods in that they usually require no specific training. However, despite such merits, content recalled through retrospective methods may not be as accurate as that elicited through think-aloud protocols, and the data collected through such methods may include information not directly relevant to

456 Chapter 31 Introspective Methods

what was thought about during task completion (for example, "post hoc rationalization," see Blackwell et al., 1985, p. 400).

To mitigate such demerits, researchers often use various aids to stimulate participant recall. Nevertheless, this can be operationally difficult, even impossible. For example, researchers may ask participants to recall what they were thinking about while listening to a recorded text in the L2 because collecting concurrent protocols from them is not possible during listening activities. In such cases, the time lag between participants' working on the task and their verbalization of it should be minimized so that they can recall their thinking processes while their memory is still fresh (e.g., Gass & Mackey, 2017; Green, 1998). For example, researchers might insert a pause after participants listen to a coherent chunk of text and immediately ask what they were thinking about while listening to it. However, providing participants with some form of memory aid (e.g., the videotaped performance) during each reporting session may be logistically impossible or simply unsettling.

Retrospective Methods with Memory Aids (Stimulated Recall)

Except in cases where providing memory aids is either impossible or unsettling, researchers using retrospective methods should use memory aids to stimulate participants' recall processes. Using "some tangible (perhaps visual or aural) reminder of the event" (Gass & Mackey, 2017, p. 14) should encourage participants to produce reports that will be closer to what was thought about during task completion. Examples include the videotaped performance of a participant's task completion and the audiotaped performance of an L2 teacher's activities over one entire lesson. Such aids are especially helpful when short or frequent interventions designed to elicit participants' recall are impossible (e.g., in classroom observations) because being part of the retrospective method family, this method may elicit false information or extra explanations or justifications being retrieved from long-term memory compared to concurrent think-aloud data gathering.

The advantages and disadvantages of these three methods along with possible steps for mitigating these disadvantages are summarized in Table 31.1. In addition, these methods may be combined to mitigate the disadvantages of each one.

Studies Using Introspective Methods Published in *Language Testing* and *Language Assessment Quarterly*

We present how the three introspective methods reviewed above have been used in the LA field. Because investigating every paper published in the LA field is beyond the scope of this chapter, we selected *Language Testing* (*LT*) and *Language Assessment Quarterly* (*LAQ*) as representative cases due to their long history and prestige, and we present general trends over the past 10 years by classifying all studies using the three above methods published between 2013 and 2022. Of the 341 published articles (*LT*: 189; *LAQ*: 152) excluding editorials, introductions to special issues, and book reviews, 34 (10%) employed one or two of the three methods discussed here (Tables 31.2 and 31.3). (A full list of all 34 articles is presented in Appendix 31.A.)

In Sasaki (2014), the author classified all studies using the three introspective methods published in *LT* between 1991 and 2010. However, we did not investigate *LAQ* because it was not founded until 2004. Compared to the trends we observed in *LT*, Tables 31.2 and 31.3 show that: (i) more studies (17 out of 34, or 50%) used more stimulated recall compared to think-aloud between 2013 and 2022, with only 40% using stimulated recall and 50% using think-aloud between 1991 and 2010 (these percentages add up more than 100% because some studies use more than one method); (ii) an increasing number of studies collected qualitative data (e.g., interviews) in addition to introspective data to supplement the qualitative analysis

TABLE 31.1

Advantages and disadvantages of three methods

	Advantages	Disadvantages	Ways of mitigating disadvantages
Think aloud	Considered to most faithfully reflect the participants' thinking processes	May influence participants' thinking processes (reactivity problems). May not be conducted in the L2 if weak	Provide appropriate training and appropriate instructions before and during participant reporting
Retrospective without memory aids	Can be applied when collecting concurrent reporting is not possible or providing participants with memory aids is impractical or impossible. Requires no special training	Resulting data may not faithfully reflect the content of actual thinking processes	Minimize time lag between task and reporting
Stimulated recall	Can be applied when collecting verbal reports is not possible but when providing participants with memory aids is possible. Requires no special training. Memory aids help participants produce more accurate reports of past thinking processes	Resulting data may not faithfully reflect the content of actual thinking processes	Minimize time lag between task and reporting. Use memory aids that most help participants

(29 out of 34 studies, or 85%) between 2013 and 2022, and thanks to technological advances such as eye-tracking, these data are becoming increasingly sophisticated in both type and content or are supported by interdisciplinary methods such as thematic analysis; however (iii) since some authors gave no details of the introspective method they used, we could not determine whether they truly used the methods they claimed to have used, which is why, regrettably, Table 31.3 contains two question marks; (iv) overall, the use of the three introspective methods became even more popular between 2013 and 2022 compared to the period 1991–2010, when they were used by only 6% of all articles in *LT*.

Representative Recent Studies Using the Three Methods

Three Studies and Evaluation Criteria

Below we report on studies by Wei and Llosa (2015), a representative study using think-aloud, and Lee and Winke (2018), a representative study using stimulated recall. For a sample study using an introspective method, we chose Crosson et al. (2019). The three studies were chosen from those listed in Tables 31.2 or 31.3 so as to satisfy as many of the following criteria as possible: (i) published in either *LT* or *LAQ*; (ii) used new technologies (e.g., eye-tracking) as research tools; (iii) used multiple data sources; and (iv) used LA for novel purpose (e.g., pedagogy).

Studies published in *Language Testing* between 2013 and 2022 employing the three introspective methods

Study	Year published	Participants	Targeted tasks	What was investigated	Method employed	Language of reports	Other data analyzed
Winke et al.	2013	107 raters	Rating 82 TOEFL iBT™ speech samples	Impact of accent familiarity on rater bias	Stimulated recall	Not reported	Questionnaire; Speech sample ratings
Bax	2013	71 Malaysian undergraduates with various L1s	IELTS reading passage scores; 11 reading items	Investigation of test takers' cognitive processing while completing onscreen IELTS reading test items	Stimulated recall	Not reported	Eye-tracking data
Zhao	2013	Six qualified and experienced raters who were PhD candidates at a US university	Rating voice strength in 400 TOEFL iBT writing samples	Development and validation of analytic rubric measuring voice strength in L2 argumentative writing	Think aloud	L1/L2	Voice strength ratings; Interviews
Li and Suen	2013	Six East-Asian and four Romance-language ESL learners	MELAB reading test	Examination of native language group differences in subskills of reading	Think aloud; Retrospective	L2	Expert ratings
Chapelle et al.	2015	130 students enrolled in ESL writing courses	Completing tasks in Criterion, an online Automated Writing Evaluation (AWE) program	Validation of diagnostic assessment using AWE	Think-aloud	L2	Likert-scale questions; Semi-structured interviews; Observation
Lam	2018	Student from co-educational public secondary schools in Hong Kong	Group interaction task	Investigation of nature of contingent responses in assessed group interactions	Stimulated recall	Not reported	Video-recorded candidate discourse; Mock assessment
Lee and Winke	2018	28 children	Computerized sample TOEFL® Primary™ speaking tasks	Investigation of young learners' response processes when taking computerized tasks for speaking assessment	Stimulated recall	L1	Questionnaire; Speaking test; Draw-a-picture task; Computer skills assessment; Eye-tracking data

					Think aloud	Not reported	None
Şahan and Razı	2020	33 raters	Rating 50 EFL essays	Impact of quality of essays and rater's scoring experience on variability in EFL essay scores	Think aloud	Not reported	None
May et al.	2020	Six trained B2 examiners	Evaluating interactional features of 12 paired interaction performances	Development of tools for learning-oriented assessment of interaction competence	Stimulated recall	Not reported	Focus group interviews
Rukthong and Brunfaut	2020	72 Thai-L1, English-L2 students from four UK universities	Listening-to-summarize tasks	Investigation of listening construct underlying integrated tasks with oral input and effect on summary accuracy	Stimulated recall	L1	Questionnaires; Notes; Oral and written summaries
Batty	2021	12 Japanese-L1, English L2 students	Video-mediated listening tests	Investigation of attention to visual cues in L2 listening tests	Stimulated recall	L1	Eye-tracking data
Lukácsi	2021	14 writing examiners	Proposed checklist for assessing EFL writing	Development of level-specific checklist for assessing EFL writing	Stimulated recall; Think-aloud	Not reported	Interviews; Items scores
Davidson	2022	18 health professionals in Australia	Rating the writing sub-test of the Occupational English Test (OET)	Views expressed in standard setting exercise on Language for Specific Purposes (LSP) test for health professionals	Think-aloud	L1/L2	None
Tsang and Isaacs	2022	162 Hong Kong secondary students	Washback on students' learning questionnaire	Investigation of washback effect of HKDSE-English on Hong Kong secondary students	Think-aloud	Not reported	Focus group interviews; Questionnaire

Note. Retrospective = retrospective method without memory aids; Stimulated recall = retrospective method with memory aids.

TABLE 31.3

Studies published in *Language Assessment Quarterly* between 2013 and 2022 employing the three introspective methods

Study	Year published	Participants	Targeted tasks	What was investigated	Method employed	Language of reports	Other data analyzed
Isaacs and Thomson	2013	38 L2 English speakers; 40 L1 Canadian English raters	Rating L2 speech samples on six tasks	Effects of rating scale length and rater experience on listeners' judgments of L2 speech	Retrospective[a]	L1	Rating scores; Interviews
Weigle et al.	2013	Five ESL learners	Reading-into-writing task involving responding to short-answer questions	Reading processes in academic test	Think-aloud; Retrospective	L2	Semi-instructed interviews
Li and He	2015	Nine qualified raters of Chinese College English Test Band (CET-6)	Rating CET-6 essays	Comparing essay-rating processes between holistic and analytic rating scales of CET-6	Think-aloud	L1	Semi-instructed interviews; Questionnaire
Wei and Llosa	2015	Three US and three Indian raters	Rating 60 Indian test takers' speech responses to TOEFL™ speaking tasks	Impact of raters' language background on rating test takers' speaking ability	Think-aloud	L1/L2	Rating scores; Interviews
Nakatsuhara et al.	2017	32 IELTS test takers; Four certified IELTS examiners; Three researchers as observers	Rating IELTS speaking test produced by 32 test takers	Use of video-conferencing technology in assessing spoken language	Stimulated recall	Not reported	Rating scores; Examiners' written notes; Examiners' feedback questionnaire; Observers' field notes
Wang	2017	EFL teacher from China; 25 first-year English-major undergraduates	Classroom assessment practices	Assessment of oral English at a university in China	Stimulated recall	Not reported	Class observation and recording; Interviews; Students' journals; Questionnaire

Winke and Lim	2017	63 English language learners	IELTS listening tests	Effects of test preparation on L2 listening test performance	Stimulated recall	Not reported	Questionnaire
Javidanmehr and Anani Sarab	2019	4000 test takers (10 for think-aloud)	Reading comprehension questions	Examination of reading comprehension attributes underlying high-stake test to evaluate capability of Cognitive Diagnostic Assessment (CDA) model	Think-aloud	Not reported	Test scores
Crosson et al.	2019	124 L1 English middle school students	Evaluation of Academic Vocabulary test	Development of vocabulary test to assess students' depth of knowledge of academic words	Retrospective	L1	Test scores
Schissel et al.	2019	44 pre-service English teachers in Mexico	Reading comprehension assessment	Classroom-based assessment in linguistically diverse communities	Stimulated recall (?)[b]	L2	Questionnaire
Baker and Hope	2019	14 university instructors or professors	Translanguaging listening task	Development of trans languaged French/English listening task of a revised test for professors in bilingual Canadian university	Stimulated recall	Not reported L1 assumed (?)	Survey
Lam	2019	Four female student-candidates	Group interaction task	Impact of extended planning time on interactional competence in group oral assessment	Stimulated recall	Not reported	Test scores; video-recording of assessed group interactions; Mock assessments

(Continued)

TABLE **31.3**

(Continued)

Study	Year published	Participants	Targeted tasks	What was investigated	Method employed	Language of reports	Other data analyzed
Xie	2020	338 students (20 for think-aloud or retrospective interview)	Proposed test items	Development and validation of item bank to diagnose linguistic problems in English academic writing of university students in Hong Kong	Think aloud; Retrospective	Not reported	Item scores
Yeom and Jun	2020	84 Korean middle school EFL learners	Paper and a computer-based reading comprehension test	Young Korean EFL learners' reading and test taking strategies in paper and computer-based reading comprehension tests	Stimulated recall	L1	Test scores; Questionnaire
Burton	2020	58 trained IELTS examiners as raters	Rating eight speech samples using speech production rating scales with five items for authenticity and four items for proficiency	Raters' views of authenticity in speaking performance tests	Stimulated recall	L1	Rating scores; Questionnaire
Kim	2015	Nine MA students or recent graduates of TESOL and Applied Linguistics programs; 18 ESL learners	Speaking placement test	Investigation of rater behavior on L2 speaking assessment	Think-aloud (?)	Not reported	Rating score; Questionnaire

Nakatsuhara et al.	2021	Six IELTS examiners; 36 test-takers	Two retired versions of IELTS speaking test	Comparison of IELTS examiners' scores when assessing spoken performances under live and two non-live testing conditions using audio and video recordings	Stimulated recall	Not reported	Test scores; Examiners' written commentaries
Frost et al.	2021	38 international students in Australia	Integrated speaking test performances	Investigation of strategies used by test takers at different levels of proficiency	Stimulated recall	L1/L2	Test scores
Liu and Read	2021	Ten participants providing expert judgments; Ten undergraduates	Two sets of reading test tasks	Comparison between language expert judgments on the content of two sets of reading test tasks and ten university students' verbal reports on solving those tasks	Think-aloud; Retrospective	Not reported	Expert judgments
Altherr Flores	2021	14 ESL learners enrolled in classes for refu-gee students	Two experimental assessments aiming to examine how participants made meaning via varied, intentionally selected, visual and multimodal design and composi-tion choices	Meaning-making processes in language and literacy assessments	Think-aloud	L1	Test scores; Semi-structured interviews

[a] Retrospective = retrospective method without memory aids; Stimulated recall = retrospective method with memory aids.

[b] (?) = The method claimed to have been used in the paper could not be verified in the absence of specific explanation about how it may have been implemented.

464 Chapter 31 Introspective Methods

By describing and evaluating the details of the methodologies used in these studies, we show how studies such as these have been conducted in the LA field over the past 10 years. To provide theoretical support for our evaluation, we drew on Green's (1998, p. 15) list of 13 "distinct phases in gathering and analyzing verbal reports regardless of the task or domain" because it is one of the most comprehensive and practical guides available for conducting studies using introspective methods. Though we do not refer below to all 13 phases for each study, the full list is as follows: (1) Task identification; (2) Task analysis; (3) Selecting an appropriate procedure; (4) Selecting subjects; (5) Training subjects (for concurrent methods only); (6) Collecting verbal reports; (7) Collecting supplementary data (optional); (8) Transcribing verbal reports; (9) Developing a coding scheme; (10) Segmenting protocols; (11) Encoding protocols; (12) Calculating encoder reliability; and (13) Analyzing the data.

Wei and Llosa (2015): Using Think-Aloud

Wei and Llosa's study is a good example of a mixed-methods approach that employed a convergent parallel design (Creswell & Clark, 2011, p. 69), with quantitative and qualitative results interpreted in an equal and complementary manner, leading to more compelling conclusions than when only quantitative or qualitative data are available. The purpose of this study was to examine whether raters' linguistic background affects their evaluation processes and scores on speaking tests. Three American and three Indian raters rated 60 responses (45-60 seconds each) to TOEFL iBT™ speaking tasks (both independent and integrated). They scored 60 responses spoken by Indian test-takers (quantitative data) and provided think-aloud accounts for four samples from the same sample pools as those probed for the above scores. Participants' rating processes were analyzed through think-aloud protocols (TAPs) while they rated each response (Green's Phase 2). The authors' choice of TAPs for exploring their thinking processes while rating was appropriate because this is one of the few options for obtaining such data (Green's Phrase 1). The selected group of six participants (Green's Phase 4) was large enough since the authors carefully chose each one in order to have sufficient within-group variation in terms of familiarity with Indian accents as well as being multilingual users of English (for the American raters), teaching experience, and "identity as an 'Indian English speaker'" (p. 288).

Though the TAP method employed here (Green's Phase 3) did not consist of the usual verbalization of thoughts, it was appropriate as a method for collecting introspection data for rating purposes, and it compensated for the shortcomings of standard TAPs. First, raters listened to one speech sample, scored it, and then listened to the same speech sample again (Green's Phase 6). They were asked to comment not only on the response they were hearing but also on their own judgment. One of the authors sat beside the rater so that raters could answer any questions about the rating. The only drawback of this approach is that it is time-consuming: five hours per rater in total (according to the paper) including score collection, and thus the fatigue factor that may have affected the data. Otherwise, based on the data used as an example, none of the language stagnation occasionally seen in TAPs was apparent. This may be partly due to the fact that the raters' most proficient language (i.e., English) was that required by the TAP approach and also that all raters were teachers who were supposed to be skilled communicators. Furthermore, the authors had all raters trained for TAP (Green's Phase 5) and ensured that all received a one-hour score norming session. Additionally, the TAP data were supplemented by a 30-minute interview (Green's Phase 7). The only flaw is that the coding reliability of these two datasets was not reported (Green's Phase 11).

The value of Wei and Llosa's (2015) study is in how raters with different backgrounds could reach similarly fair and reliable scores through different processes (e.g., Indian raters were better at understanding Indian English than American raters) even though this does not always lead to higher or lower scores, which are influenced by the raters' various backgrounds), as revealed by means of a robust quantitative analysis (Multifaceted Rasch

Analysis) and validly conducted qualitative analyses. In this sense, this study demonstrated the essence of the mixed-methods approach and is thus an important pioneering study of its kind (Green's Phase 13).

Lee and Winke (2018): Using Stimulated Recall

Lee and Winke examined how English L2 learners aged 8–10 would answer L2 English-speaking test items designed for them and what scores they would receive (Green's Phase 2). The authors' selection of 20 L2 English speakers (the targeted group) and 8 L1 English speakers (the baseline group) was appropriate (Green's Phase 4) in that these 2 groups came from similar age groups and may realistically have taken the test. Though small, the two groups' sample sizes were appropriate in that they produced descriptive results for comparison purposes, and the target group's size was not so large that its size would make collecting various types of introspective data (Green's Phase 6) excessively labor-intensive and time-consuming. All participants completed seven sample tasks taken from an online TOEFL® Primary™ speaking test. The tasks were noninteractive, as in "describing pictures" (p. 249), and took 10–20 seconds. Like Wei and Llosa (2015), Lee and Winke (2018) chose a convergent parallel design (Creswell & Clark, 2011, p. 69), where quantitative and qualitative data are collected simultaneously and their results are interpreted in a complementary manner (Green's Phase 13). Lee and Winke's quantitative data consisted of means of three to five points according to task types (e.g., scored by trained raters based on the TOEFL® Primary™ holistic rubric assessing language use, content, and delivery). Additionally, the authors used a fluency measure based on silent pauses and speed fluency (for details, see de Jong et al., 2015).

The authors' selection of methods for exploring participants' introspective test-taking processes were tailored to 8–10 years old test takers, who may have found it difficult to put their thoughts into words. Thus, the qualitative data combined number, type, mode, and whether concurrent or retrospective and verbal or nonverbal. For concurrent data, various types of eye-tracking data (different locations on the screen, length, and frequency of eye fixation, etc.) were used. Immediately upon test completion, to explore test takers' attitudes toward the test, they were asked to draw pictures of one, several, or all speaking tasks, a process considered equivalent to retrospective data without memory aids. However, as insufficient information was provided about these data, we inferred the above information from the three examples provided in figure 6 of the study (i.e., Lee and Winke, 2018). As regards stimulated recall data, the focus of this section, more explanation was provided. Test takers were interviewed after drawing their picture while looking at "the same material they had seen on screen" (p. 259). Because the authors used this picture as a memory aid while the participants were talking, we refer to these data as "stimulated recall data" (Green's Phase 1). Together with this somewhat unusual data collection procedure, the participants' age, and the novelty of the test, using multiple data sources to explore participants' test taking processes to ascertain test validity was justifiable (Green's Phase 7).

Turning to the analysis phase of the study, probably due to the small sample size, quantitative test scores were presented only descriptively in order to interpret the qualitative results (Table 31.2). In contrast, the stimulated recall data were analyzed in greater detail. Following the test, participants "provided their thoughts ... on the test through one-on-one interviews" (p. 250). The authors then transcribed all interview response data (Green's Phase 8). Furthermore, drawing on Winke et al. (2015), they classified these data "according to the children's overall view (positive or negative)" and labeled those codes ... in relation to: (i) task (1–7); (ii) test features delineated by Area of Interest (AoI) on the screen; and (iii) test mode (recording or not-recording) (p. 252) (Green's Phase 8). However, readers are not told how this coding system worked in the analysis because the authors used very few examples to support their argument except in the last paragraph (p. 252) dealing with participants' drawings, which were also classified as positive, negative,

466 **Chapter 31** Introspective Methods

or neutral and in order to support one of the findings of the eye-tracking (e.g., "nervousness" and "embarrassment," p. 258). Overall, the authors devoted ample space (seven paragraphs and four Excerpts, pp. 254–258) to their eye-tracking results compared to introspection (drawing and stimulated recall) (three paragraphs, pp. 258–261). However, this is not surprising since eye-tracking was then a groundbreaking tool for exploring subjects' introspection. As the authors write, "eye-tracking can tap into lower-level unconscious processing in a non-intrusive way" (p. 246). However, they conceded that other methods also proved valid, and these could have been assigned more weight for the sake of method triangulation.

Crosson et al. (2019): Using Retrospective Methods Without Memory Aids

Crosson et al. (2019) aimed to develop a vocabulary assessment tool (the Evaluation of Academic Vocabulary – EAV) in order to measure students' depth of knowledge of academic words, a learning process sensitive to time. Participants were adolescent native English-speaking learners. While the authors also employed a mixed-methods research design, unlike Wei and Llosa (2015), they collected quantitative and qualitative data non-simultaneously. Their quantitative analysis was grounded in classic psychometric assessment methods and aimed to evaluate the validity and technical quality of the assessment tool, while the qualitative data complemented the quantitative data in explaining and interpreting the quantitative results.

In Study 1 (quantitative analysis), the authors conducted an academic vocabulary intervention study for 105 native English-speaking middle school students in the United States using *Robust Academic Vocabulary Encounters (RAVE)*. The intervention was conducted over a 20-week period and taught 99 general academic words to students in 11 instructional units. In Study 2 (qualitative analysis), the authors adopted a retrospective interview protocol without memory aids to further assess the validity of the assessment tool. Although they referred to their method as consisting of "cognitive interviews," the definition they provided matched that of retrospective methods without memory aids. We therefore decided to refer to retrospective methods here.

Crosson et al. interviewed a subsample of students ($n = 8$) regarding their decision-making processes over nine target academic words while completing the EAV. Their choice of the retrospective method was deemed appropriate because think-aloud methods interrupt students' thinking processes as they complete the task (Green's Phase 3). To mitigate the limitations of retrospective methods, the researchers devised a set of interview questions to guide students' thought processes. One potential flaw of this design is that the students they interviewed did not participate in the intervention study (Study 1). According to the authors (p. 207), they were selected because "their teacher was willing to permit the research team to administer EAV and interviews" (Green's Phase 4). Ideally, Crosson et al. would have interviewed a subsample of Study 1 participants. However, all researchers understand the challenge of recruiting research participants. On the positive side, the eight students were selected based on their academic performance (two high-, four mid-, and two low-achieving students), which allowed the authors to collect interview data from different proficiency levels. After completing the EAV task, the research team interviewed the selected students for about 25–30 minutes in a quiet place in their school (Green's Phase 6). They selected nine target words on which to interview the students based on pretest results from Study 1 and representing a wide range of lexical knowledge without instruction. The researchers then collaboratively transcribed and analyzed the interview data (Green's Phases 8 and 13). Although it is recommended to have multiple coders involved in coding decisions and to report intercoder agreement, the authors did not do so (Green's Phase 12).

However, Crosson et al.'s study contributed to the field with a new instrument for assessing in-depth knowledge of academic vocabulary among L1 English native speakers. To analyze their quantitative data, they adopted different statistical methods, including Bayesian network methods, an advanced statistical method designed to compensate for students' guessing behavior in their study. To conclude, the Crosson et al. study is a good example of using a mixed-methods approach and advanced statistical methods in test development and validation.

Additional Recommendations for Researchers

Based on our review of three representative studies, we add the following recommendations to Green's (1998) list for conducting studies using introspection processes. The studies in parentheses show the source of each recommendation.

1. Choose the think-aloud method if your targeted task allows its use, you can allow participants to use their L1 when necessary, and the task is not so cognitively demanding that it may and distract participants' thinking-aloud processes (Wei & Llosa, 2015).
2. If you choose retrospective methods, devise the procedure so that what participants recall is as authentic and accurate as possible (e.g., make the time lag between task and retrospective session as short as possible) (Crosson et al., 2019).
3. Although it may be preferable to start with theoretically well-informed baseline categories when coding the data, do not hesitate to add more categories or to revise existing ones if the data require it (Lee & Winke, 2018).
4. Report how transcribing was conducted and how the data were segmented for analysis.
5. Employ another coder and report intercoder reliability (Crosson et al., 2019; Wei & Llosa, 2015).
6. Describe how you analyzed the data in as much detail as possible (Lee & Winke, 2018).

Conclusion and Future Directions for Introspective Methods

Overall, in the field of LA, there has long been an "argument" (Chapelle et al., 2003, p. 411) over how well test scores are interpreted and used in each situation. Consequently, investigating participants' test-taking processes through introspection has become increasingly important to this debate. Among the methods used for eliciting test takers' introspection, the three methods described above are most frequently used to obtain as close and accurate access as possible to participants' thinking processes. This focus on learners' thinking in situ has also been advocated as part of the long-standing sociocultural orientation in the field of SLA (e.g., *Modern Language Journal*, 2007). Given this almost serendipitous synchronization of attention toward learners' internal processes, we present several possible directions for future introspective research in the LA field.

First, the number of studies using introspective data to supplement quantitative data analysis, as in Lee and Winke's (2018) study, will continue to grow. Such mixed-methods studies have been recommended ever since the above-mentioned consensus on test validation emerged as a result of seminal work by researchers such as Messick (1989). These studies will become even more desirable if qualitative data analysis is as carefully and rigorously conducted as in their quantitative counterparts so that they complement the findings as equal contributors rather than merely as supplements. Thus, how convincingly qualitative data such as participants' test-taking processes can be analyzed for the benefit of readers in the LA field with predominantly positivist orientations remains a key issue in the future.

468   Chapter 31 Introspective Methods

Second, if we believe that test validation should consider the impact of test scores, we should reflect on how LA research results can be used to help test takers' subsequent learning. In this sense, Wei and Llosa's (2015) findings are valuable in that Indian raters found it easier to comprehend Indian varieties of English than did American raters, who had less exposure to Indian varieties. As Wei and Llosa (2015) discussed, their findings led to the argument whereby "large-scale standardized assessment programs may consider hiring both Inner and Outer Circle English speakers as raters" (p. 299). Now that the status of English as a lingua franca is firmly established (Pennycook, 2017), the relationship between the concept of comprehensibility and the background of those who evaluate it is being debated outside the field of LA (e.g., Trofimovich & Isaacs, 2012). Today, becoming more comprehensible rather than more native-like is recommended as a realistic goal for L2 learners (Derwing & Munro, 2015). In these increasingly multilingual and highly globalized times, rigorous studies such as Wei and Llosa's are needed if LA researchers are to bridge the gap between assessment and education.

Finally, we should consider the educational impact of verbal reporting itself. If it is true that "ideas are crystallized and sharpened and inconsistencies become more obvious" (Swain, 2006, p. 100) while participants are taking a test and thinking aloud simultaneously, that impact may be negative in that this introspective method interferes with accurate descriptions of cognition, or positive in that the talking itself can facilitate participants' learning. In fact, the three participants with higher L2 proficiency in Plakans (2009) "felt that talking while writing helped them. It moved their thinking along and assisted in their proofreading" (p. 567). Future studies could adopt a negative "method-effect" stance and investigate the reactivity of using introspective methods on the investigation of test-taking processes. Alternatively, they could take the approach employed by researchers from a sociocultural perspective such as those who believe in "dynamic assessment" (e.g., Poehner, 2008) and promote a combination of "assessment and instruction as a development-oriented activity" (p. 1). Findings from studies based on the latter view can also contribute to knowledge accumulation in the field by adding a wealth of studies with non-positivist perspectives.

Discussion Questions

1. Thinking about a research project you are currently working on or a research topic you are interested in, how can you incorporate introspective methods in your study?

2. Identify an empirical study in language testing that uses at least one of the introspective methods reviewed in this chapter. What is the author's justification for choosing the method(s)? Did you have any validity concerns? How would you improve this/these method(s), if needed and if possible?

Appendix A: Sources Listed in Tables 31.2 and 31.3

Language Testing

Batty, A. O. (2021). An eye-tracking study of attention to visual cues in L2 listening tests. *Language Testing*, *38*(4), 511–535. https://doi.org/10.1177/0265532220951504.

Bax, S. (2013). The cognitive processing of candidates during reading tests: evidence from eye-tracking. *Language Testing*, *30*(4), 441–465. https://doi.org/10.1177/0265532212473244.

Chapelle, C. A., Cotos, E., & Lee, J. (2015). Validity arguments for diagnostic assessment using automated writing evaluation. *Language Testing*, *32*(3), 385–405. https://doi.org/10.1177/0265532214565386.

Davidson, S. (2022). The domain expert perspective: a qualitative study into the views expressed in a standard-setting exercise on a language for specific purposes (LSP) test for health professionals. *Language Testing*, 39(1), 117–141. https://doi.org/10.1177/02655322211010737.

Lam, D. M. K. (2018). What counts as "responding"? Contingency on previous speaker contribution as a feature of interactional competence. *Language Testing*, 35(3), 377–401. https://doi.org/10.1177/0265532218758126.

Lee, S., & Winke, P. (2018). Young learners' response processes when taking computerized tasks for speaking assessment. *Language Testing*, 35(2), 239–269. https://doi.org/10.1177/0265532217704009.

Li, H., & Suen, H. K. (2013). Detecting native language group differences at the subskills level of reading: a differential skill functioning approach. *Language Testing*, 30(2), 273–298. https://doi.org/10.1177/0265532212459031.

Lukácsi, Z. (2021). Developing a level-specific checklist for assessing EFL writing. *Language Testing*, 38(1), 86–105. https://doi.org/10.1177/0265532220916703.

May, L., Nakatsuhara, F., Lam, D., & Galaczi, E. (2020). Developing tools for learning oriented assessment of interactional competence: bridging theory and practice. *Language Testing*, 37(2), 165–188. https://doi.org/10.1177/0265532219879044.

Rukthong, A., & Brunfaut, T. (2020). Is anybody listening? The nature of second language listening in integrated listening-to-summarize tasks. *Language Testing*, 37(1), 31–53. https://doi.org/10.1177/0265532219871470.

Şahan, Ö., & Razı, S. (2020). Do experience and text quality matter for raters' decision-making behaviors? *Language Testing*, 37(3), 311–332. https://doi.org/10.1177/0265532219900228.

Tsang, C. L., & Isaacs, T. (2022). Hong Kong secondary students' perspectives on selecting test difficulty level and learner washback: effects of a graded approach to assessment. *Language Testing*, 39(2), 212–238. https://doi.org/10.1177/02655322211050600.

Winke, P., Gass, S., & Myford, C. (2013). Raters' L2 background as a potential source of bias in rating oral performance. *Language Testing*, 30(2), 231–252. https://doi.org/10.1177/0265532212456968.

Zhao, C. G. (2013). Measuring authorial voice strength in L2 argumentative writing: the development and validation of an analytic rubric. *Language Testing*, 30(2), 201–230. https://doi.org/10.1177/0265532212456965.

Language Assessment Quarterly

Altherr Flores, J. A. (2021). The interplay of text and image on the meaning-making processes of adult L2 learners with emerging literacy: implications for test design and evaluation frameworks. *Language Assessment Quarterly*, 18(5), 508–529. https://doi.org/10.1080/15434303.2021.1984491.

Baker, B., & Hope, A. (2019). Incorporating translanguaging in language assessment: the case of a test for university professors. *Language Assessment Quarterly*, 16(4–5), 408–425. https://doi.org/10.1080/15434303.2019.1671392.

Burton, J. D. (2020). "How scripted is this going to be?" Raters' views of authenticity in speaking performance tests. *Language Assessment Quarterly*, 17(3), 244–261. https://doi.org/10.1080/15434303.2020.1754829.

Crosson, A. C., McKeown, M. G., & Ward, A. K. (2019). An innovative approach to assessing depth of knowledge of academic words. *Language Assessment Quarterly*, 16(2), 196–216. https://doi.org/10.1080/15434303.2019.1612899.

Frost, K., Wigglesworth, G., & Clothier, J. (2021). Relationships between comprehension, strategic behaviors, and content-related aspects of test performances in integrated speaking tasks. *Language Assessment Quarterly*, 18(2), 133–153. https://doi.org/10.1080/15434303.2020.1835918.

Isaacs, T., & Thomson, R. I. (2013). Rater experience, rating scale length, and judgments of L2 pronunciation: revisiting research conventions. *Language Assessment Quarterly*, 10(2), 135–159. https://doi.org/10.1080/15434303.2013.769545.

Javidanmehr, Z., & Anani Sarab, M. R. (2019). Retrofitting non-diagnostic reading comprehension assessment: application of the G-DINA model to a high stakes reading comprehension test. *Language Assessment Quarterly*, 16(3), 294–311. https://doi.org/10.1080/15434303.2019.1654479.

Kim, H. J. (2015). A qualitative analysis of rater behavior on an L2 speaking assessment. *Language Assessment Quarterly*, 12(3), 239–261. https://doi.org/10.1080/15434303.2015.1049353.

Lam, D. M. K. (2019). Interactional competence with and without extended planning time in a group oral assessment. *Language Assessment Quarterly*, 16(1), 1–20. https://doi.org/10.1080/15434303.2019.1602627.

470 **Chapter 31** Introspective Methods

Li, H., & He, L. (2015). A comparison of EFL raters' essay-rating processes across two types of rating scales. *Language Assessment Quarterly*, *12*(2), 178–212. https://doi.org/10.1080/15434303.2015.1011738.

Liu, X., & Read, J. (2021). Investigating the skills involved in reading test tasks through expert judgment and verbal protocol analysis: convergence and divergence between the two methods. *Language Assessment Quarterly*, *18*(4), 357–381. https://doi.org/10.1080/15434303.2021.1881964.

Nakatsuhara, F., Inoue, C., Berry, V., & Galaczi, E. (2017). Exploring the use of video-conferencing technology in the assessment of spoken language: a mixed-methods study. *Language Assessment Quarterly*, *14*(1), 1–18. https://doi.org/10.1080/15434303.2016.1263637.

Nakatsuhara, F., Inoue, C., & Taylor, L. (2021). Comparing rating modes: analyzing live, audio, and video ratings of IELTS speaking test performances. *Language Assessment Quarterly*, *18*(2), 83–106. https://doi.org/10.1080/15434303.2020.1799222.

Schissel, J. L., López-Gopar, M., Leung, C., Morales, J., & Davis, J. R. (2019). Classroom-based assessments in linguistically diverse communities: a case for collaborative research methodologies. *Language Assessment Quarterly*, *16*(4–5), 393–407. https://doi.org/10.1080/15434303.2019.1678041.

Wang, X. (2017). A Chinese EFL teacher's classroom assessment practices. *Language Assessment Quarterly*, *14*(4), 312–327. https://doi.org/10.1080/15434303.2017.1393819.

Wei, J., & Llosa, L. (2015). Investigating differences between American and Indian raters in assessing TOEFL iBT speaking tasks. *Language Assessment Quarterly*, *12*(3), 283–304. https://doi.org/10.1080/15434303.2015.1037446.

Weigle, S. C., Yang, W., & Montee, M. (2013). Exploring reading processes in an academic reading test using short-answer questions. *Language Assessment Quarterly*, *10*(1), 28–48. https://doi.org/10.1080/15434303.2012.750660.

Winke, P., & Lim, H. (2017). The effects of test preparation on second language listening test performance. *Language Assessment Quarterly*, *14*(4), 380–397. https://doi.org/10.1080/15434303.2017.1399396.

Xie, Q. (2020). Diagnosing linguistic problems in English academic writing of university students: an item bank approach. *Language Assessment Quarterly*, *17*(2), 183–203. https://doi.org/10.1080/15434303.2019.1691214.

Yeom, S., & Jun, H. (2020). Young Korean EFL learners' reading and test-taking strategies in paper and computer-based reading comprehension tests. *Language Assessment Quarterly*, *17*(3), 282–299. https://doi.org/10.1080/15434303.2020.1731753.

References

Aryadoust, V. (2023). The vexing problem of validity and the future of second language assessment. *Language Testing*, *40*(1), 8–14. https://doi.org/10.1177/02655322221125204.

Bachman, L., & Palmer, A. (2010). *Language assessment in practice*. Oxford University Press.

Blackwell, R. T., Galassi, J. P., Galassi, M. D., & Watson, T. E. (1985). Are cognitive assessment methods equal? A comparison of think aloud and thought listing. *Cognitive Therapy and Research*, *9*(4), 399–413. https://doi.org/10.1007/BF01173089.

Bryfonski, L. (2023). Collecting and analyzing L2 introspective data. In A. Mackey & S. Gass (Eds.), *Research methods in second language learning: Current approaches* (pp. 120–142). Wiley-Blackwell.

Chapelle, C. A. (2021). *Argument-based validation in testing and assessment*. Sage.

Chapelle, C. A., Jamieson, J., & Hegelheimer, V. (2003). Validation of a web-based ESL test. *Language Testing*, *20*(4), 409–439. https://doi.org/10.1191/0265532203lt266oa.

Cohen, A. D., & Upton, T. A. (2007). "I want to go back to the text": response strategies on the reading subtest of the new TOEFL. *Language Testing*, *24*(2), 209–250. https://doi.org/10.1177/0265532207076364.

Creswell, J. W., & Clark, V. L. P. (2011). *Designing and conducting mixed methods research* (2nd ed.). Sage.

Crosson, A. C., McKeown, M. G., & Ward, A. K. (2019). An innovative approach to assessing depth of knowledge of academic words. *Language Assessment Quarterly*, *16*(2), 196–216. https://doi.org/10.1080/15434303.2019.1612899.

de Jong, N. H., Groenhout, R., Schoonen, R., & Hulstijn, J. H. (2015). Second language fluency: speaking style or proficiency? Correcting measures of second language fluency for first language behavior. *Applied Psycholinguistics*, *36*(2), 223–243. https://doi.org/10.1017/S0142716413000210.

References · **471**

Denzin, N. K., & Lincoln, Y. S. (Eds.). (2000). *Handbook of qualitative research*. Sage.

Derwing, T. M., & Munro, M. J. (2015). *Pronunciation fundamentals: Evidence-based perspectives for L2 teaching and research*. John Benjamins.

Dulay, H., & Burt, M. (1973). Should we teach children syntax? *Language Learning, 23*(2), 245–258. https://doi.org/10.1111/j.1467-1770.1973.tb00659.x.

Ericsson, K. A., & Simon, H. A. (1993). *Protocol analysis* (revised ed.). MIT Press.

Færch, C., & Kasper, G. (Eds.). (1987). *Introspection in second language research*. Multilingual Matters.

Gass, S. M., & Mackey, A. (2017). *Stimulated recall methodology in second language research* (2nd ed.). Routledge.

Goo, J. (2010). Working memory and reactivity. *Language Learning, 60*(4), 712–752. https://doi.org/10.1111/j.1467-9922.2010.00573.x.

Green, A. (1998). *Verbal protocol analysis in language testing research: A handbook*. Cambridge University Press.

Kane, M. T. (2001). Current concerns in validity theory. *Journal of Educational Measurement, 38*, 319–342. https://doi.org/10.1111/j.1745-3984.2001.tb01130.x.

Kane, M. T. (2006). Validation. In R. Brennan (Ed.), *Educational measurement* (4th ed., pp. 17–64). Praeger.

Lee, S., & Winke, P. (2018). Young learners' response processes when taking computerized tasks for speaking assessment. *Language Testing, 35*(2), 239–269. https://doi.org/10.1177/0265532217704009.

López-Serrano, S., Roca de Larios, J., & Manchón, R. M. (2020). Processing output during individual L2 writing tasks: an exploration of depth of processing and the effects of proficiency. In R. M. Manchón (Ed.), *Writing and language learning: Advancing the research agenda* (pp. 230–253). John Benjamins.

Mackay, S. L. (2006). *Researching second language classrooms*. Erlbaum.

Messick, S. (1989). Validity. In R. L. Linn (Ed.), *Educational measurement* (3rd ed., pp. 13–103). Macmillan.

Modern Language Journal. (2007). *91(S1). Special Issue on Second Language Acquisition*.

Pennycook, A. (2017). *The cultural politics of English as an international language*. Taylor & Francis.

Plakans, L. (2009). Discourse synthesis in integrated second language writing assessment. *Language Testing, 26*(4), 561–587. https://doi.org/10.1177/0265532209340192.

Poehner, M. E. (2008). *Dynamic assessment: A Vygotskian approach to understanding and promoting L2 development*. Springer.

Richards, J. C. (1974). *Error analysis: Perspectives on second language acquisition*. Longman.

Sachs, R., & Polio, C. (2007). Learners' uses of two types of written feedback on a L2 writing revision task. *Studies in Second Language Acquisition, 29*(1), 67–100. https://doi.org/10.1017/S0272263107070039.

Şahan, O., & Razı, S. (2020). Do experience and text quality matter for raters' decision-making behaviors? *Language Testing, 37*(3), 311–332. https://doi.org/10.1177/0265532219900228.

Sanz, C., Lin, H., Lado, B., Bowden, H. W., & Stafford, C. A. (2009). Concurrent verbalizations, pedagogical conditions, and reactivity: two CALL studies. *Language Learning, 59*(1), 33–71. https://doi.org/10.1111/j.1467-9922.2009.00500.x.

Sasaki, M. (2000). Toward an empirical model of EFL writing processes: an exploratory study. *Journal of Second Language Writing, 9*(3), 259–291. https://doi.org/10.1016/S1060-3743(00)00028-X.

Sasaki, M. (2014). Introspective methods. In A. J. Kunnan (Ed.), *The companion to language assessment, Vol. 3: Evaluation, methodology, and interdisciplinary themes* (pp. 1340–1357). Wiley-Blackwell.

Smith, P., Kim, D., Vorobel, O., & King, J. (2020). Verbal reports in the reading processes of language learners: a methodological review. *Review of Education, 8*(1), 37–114. https://doi.org/10.1002/rev3.3170.

Suzuki, W., & Storch, N. (Eds.). (2020). *Languaging in language learning and teaching; A collection of empirical studies*. John Benjamins.

Swain, M. (2006). Verbal protocols: what does it mean for research to use speaking as a data collection tool? In M. Chalhoub-Deville, C. A. Chapelle & P. Duff (Eds.), *Inference and generalizability in applied linguistics: Multiple perspectives* (pp. 97–113). John Benjamins.

Trofimovich, P., & Isaacs, T. (2012). Disentangling accent from comprehensibility. *Bilingualism: Language and Cognition, 15*, 905–916. https://doi.org/10.1017/S1366728912000168.

Wei, J., & Llosa, L. (2015). Investigating differences between American and Indian raters in assessing TOEFL iBT speaking tasks. *Language Assessment Quarterly, 12*(3), 283–304. https://doi.org/10.1080/15434303.2015.1037446.

472 **Chapter 31** Introspective Methods

Weir, C. (2005). *Language testing and validation: An evidence-based approach.* Palgrave MacMillan.

Winke, P., Lee, S., Ahn, I., Choi, I., Cui, Y., & Yoon, H.-J. (2015). *A validation study of the reading section of the Young Learners Tests of English (YLTE).* Working Paper. Cambridge–Michigan Language Assessment (CaMLA).

Suggested Readings

Bryfonski, L. (2023). Collecting and analyzing L2 introspective data. In A. Mackey & S. Gass (Eds.), *Research methods in second language learning: Current approaches* (pp. 120–142). Wiley-Blackwell.

Mackey, A., & Gass, S. (2022). *Second language research: Methodology and research* (3rd ed.). Routledge.

McKinley, J., & Rose, H. (Eds.). (2021). *The Routledge handbook of research methods in applied linguistics.* Routledge.

Phakiti, A., De Costa, P., Plonsky, L., & Starfield, S. (Eds.). (2018). *The Palgrave handbook of applied linguistics research methodology.* Palgrave.

CHAPTER 32

Test-Taking Strategies

Yuyang Cai

Introduction

Test takers consciously engage in complex cognitive and affective processes in language testing situations. These processes are called test-taking strategies in the language testing literature. These mental activities are thus, in contrast, to automatic processes that have been internalized into the higher-order construct of language competence.

Test-taking strategies have therefore been recognized as an important research theme in language testing since they can facilitate the understanding of test-takers' mental processes and test score interpretation. First, the core objective of language tests is to measure the ability that language users must rely on to accomplish communication tasks in various contexts (Bachman & Palmer, 2010; Messick, 1989). To achieve this goal, the design of language test tasks should be oriented to measure test-takers' competencies in linguistics, pragmatics, and cognitive and metacognitive processing (Bachman & Palmer, 2010).

Research in test-taking strategies may help to understand the extent a test can successfully activate such construct-relevant test-taking strategies, such as language use strategies (see Cohen, 2011) or strategic competence (see Bachman & Palmer, 1996; Cai & Kunnan, 2020) and test-management strategies (see Cohen, 2014; Cohen et al., 2023). Findings on the function of test-management strategies may also help test-takers develop useful strategies to ensure more efficient deployment of cognitive resources during the test-taking process. Another value of conducting test-taking strategies research is to reveal how undesired strategies (i.e., test wiseness strategies) are activated among the test takers (see Chen et al., 2020; Xu & Wu, 2011). Such information can help language testers identify task features that may lead to unwanted construct-irrelevant activities, for example, blind guessing.

Although explicit attention to test-taking strategies has a history of over three decades, research on this issue is still in its childhood stage. This can be reflected by the inconsistent conceptualization of test-taking strategies (e.g., Cohen, 2014). To promote a better understanding of test-taking strategies in second/foreign language (L2) contexts, this chapter covers studies after Cohen's (2014) overview. This review first revisits the construct of test-taking strategies. Next, empirical studies on test-taking strategies are covered, with emphasis on the prevalence of different types of test-taking strategies, the variation of test-taking strategy use across L2 skills (or media of communication as preferred by some language

The Concise Companion to Language Assessment, First Edition. Edited by Antony John Kunnan.
© 2025 John Wiley & Sons, Inc. Published 2025 by John Wiley & Sons, Inc.

Revisiting the Construct of Test-Taking Strategies

Cohen (2011) defines test-taking strategies as "the processes that the test takers made use of in order to produce acceptable answers to questions and tasks, as well as the perceptions that they have about these questions and tasks before, during, and after responding to them" (p. 305). The literature offers different ways of categorizing test-taking strategies. Based on response time, test-taking strategies can be divided into before-test strategies (e.g., reading instructions carefully), while-test strategies (e.g., answering questions in sequential order), and after-test strategies (e.g., revising answers) (see Wenden, 1991). Based on the question type, test-taking strategies can include essay writing strategies, multiple-choice strategies, and closed question strategies (see Amer, 2007). In addition, depending on the media of communication (or language skills as conventionally called), test-taking strategies can be classified as reading test-taking strategies, writing test-taking strategies, speaking strategies, listening strategies (see Amer, 2007), and test-taking strategies in integrated tasks (see Cumming, 2024) that combines multiple language skills such as reading and writing (Golparvar & Khafi, 2021; Plakans & Gebril, 2012) or reading/listening and speaking (Huang et al., 2018).

Cohen (2011) provided the most-cited classification by language testing researchers based on the functions of test-taking strategies: language learner strategies, test management strategies, and test wiseness strategies. Language learner strategies refer to "Thoughts and actions, consciously chosen and operationalized by language learners, to assist them in carrying out a multiplicity of tasks from the very onset of learning to the most advanced levels of target-language performance." (Cohen, 2011, p. 7). Cohen (2011) further distinguished language learner strategies as language learning strategies (strategies to identify, manage, and memorize learning materials) and language use strategies (e.g., cognitive processes such as retrieving, rehearsing, coping, and communication strategies when working on language tasks). The latter partly corresponds to the construct of strategic competence in language testing research or cognitive and metacognitive strategy use during language testing situations (Bachman & Palmer, 2010; Cai, 2020; Phakiti, 2008; Purpura, 1998). There is a subtle difference between them: while language use strategies emphasize the frequency of strategy use (Cohen, 2011; Oxford & Amerstorfer, 2018), strategic competence relates more to test-takers' competence in using these strategies efficiently (Bachman & Palmer, 1996; Cai, 2020; Phakiti, 2008).

The second category of test-management strategies is strategy use bound to test questions and tasks that test-takers call upon to control their test responses to answer the questions correctly. Examples of test-management strategies include going back and forth between a passage and a given question to obtain more information, managing response time to ensure sufficient attention to items with the highest point, studying multiple options systematically to justify the best choice, taking notes, translating some words/sentences, guessing from other sentences, and using clues in other questions (see Wu & Stone, 2016). As these strategies enable test takers to use their linguistic knowledge more efficiently, they are considered construct-relevant.

The third category, test-wiseness strategies, or test-deviousness strategies as Cohen et al. (2023) preferred, refer to strategies test-takers use to craft a correct answer without activating construct-relevant linguistic knowledge or cognitive processes. Examples of test-wiseness strategies include selecting an option containing a word matching the same word in the text without knowing what the word means, guessing blindly, selecting an option with an important word, or choosing the least wrong answer.

Note that among the most-cited categories of test-taking strategies, Cohen and colleagues (Cohen, 2014; Cohen et al., 2023) dropped learner-use strategies from the list of test-taking strategies. They argued that these strategies are not test-related (Cohen, 2014) but did not offer intensive analyses to justify this exclusion. However, this argument contradicts scholars investigating strategy use in test situations (Bachman & Palmer, 2010; Cai, 2020; Phakiti, 2008). After all, it is unavoidable that test takers must activate cognitive and metacognitive strategies during the process of test response. This broad view of test-taking strategies is widely applied in other empirical studies in test-taking strategies (see Bumbálková, 2021). Given this concern, we stick to this broad taxonomy of test-taking strategies (Cohen, 2006, 2011) when reviewing relevant literature conducted after Cohen's (2014) review. At the same time, the review aligns with Cohen's (2014) call for more attention to test management and test-wiseness strategies.

Research on Test-Taking Strategies

Prevalence of Different Types of Test-Taking Strategies

Since Cohen's (2014) call for exclusive attention to test management and test-wiseness strategies, responses to his call have accumulated. Table 32.1 provides an overview of these studies. A few scholars followed Cohen's call and focused on test-management and test-wiseness strategies (Estaji & Banitalebi, 2023; Suvorov, 2018; Winke & Lim, 2017). For instance, Suvorov (2018) investigated test-management and test-wiseness strategies used during a computer-delivered test consisting of listening, reading, and grammar. Drawing on data obtained from eye-tracking and a survey questionnaire, the researcher revealed a large variety of test-management strategies that test takers applied and placed them into three subcategories: strategies related to item elements (i.e., question-first versus prompt-first), strategies used for interaction with the text prompt, and strategies used for interaction with the question/options and answer selection. Besides, they identified a cluster of test-wiseness strategies, such as random guessing, using background knowledge to select the answer, or selecting an option based on clues from other items. A similar focus also emerged in studies such as Winke and Lim (2017) and Estaji and Banitalebi (2023). For instance, Estaji and Banitalebi (2023) observed the change in the use of test management and test-wiseness strategies by Iranian IELTS repeaters. They found increased use in test management and a decreased use in test-wiseness strategies.

Another strand of studies continues to cover language use strategies, test management, and test-wiseness strategies simultaneously. Wu and Stone (2016) derived a working taxonomy of reading-specific test-taking strategies. They formulated a measure of test-taking strategies consisting of three subscales: comprehending meaning, test management, and test-wiseness. The comprehending meaning subscale contained three items measuring cognitive reading strategies (e.g., "understanding the main ideas"). The test-management subscale had four items measuring ability-relevant actions dealing with question answering (e.g., "guessing from other sentences"). The third dimension contained three items measuring test-wiseness strategies (e.g., "guessing blindly"). The results of exploratory factor analysis confirmed the three-factor structure (of the three subscales). A further comparison of the prevalence of strategy use indicated that test-takers applied language use strategies (i.e., comprehending meaning) more frequently than they did with test-management and test-wiseness strategies.

Other studies go to the extreme of only focusing on language use strategies. Acknowledging the importance of test management and test-wiseness strategies, Huang (2016) referred to the construct of strategic competence in language testing literature (Bachman & Palmer, 2010; Purpura, 1999) and argued that to accomplish a speaking test task, test takers must master the competence to efficiently use different learner strategies (e.g., cognitive, communicative, and

476 Chapter 32 Test-Taking Strategies

> **TABLE 32.1**

Features of test-taking strategies (TTS) in different studies

Author	Year	Journal/Book	Strategies	Participants	Study level	Targeted test
Phakiti	2008	*Language Assessment Quarterly*	1. Language learner strategies	561 Thai students	University	Midterm and final reading tests
Xie	2015	*Assessing Writing*	1. Test-wiseness strategies (i.e., impression management strategies)	886 Chinese learners with low English proficiency	University	Essay test from College English Test Band 4 (CET4)
Wu & Stone	2016	*Journal of Psychoeducational Assessment*	1. Language learner strategies (comprehending meaning) 2. Test-management strategies 3. Test-wiseness strategies	189 participants from Canada with different English proficiency levels	Adults	Canadian English Language Proficiency Index Program-General (CELPIP-General) reading pilot test
Huang	2016	*Perceptual and Motor Skills*	1. Language learner strategies (cognitive strategy, communication strategy, affective strategy)	215 Taiwanese English learners	University	Test of English for International Communication Speaking Test (TOEIC-S)

Skills	Test language	Instruments	Names of questionnaire	Findings	TTS and language performance
Reading	English as foreign language (EFL)	Test; Questionnaire	State and trait cognitive and metacognitive strategy use questionnaires	1. Strategic competence directly influenced trait metacognitive strategy use (MSU), which in turn regulated trait cognitive strategy use and state MSU 2. State MSU in turn directly influenced state CSU	/
Writing	English as second language (ESL)	Questionnaire	Test-taking strategy questionnaire about test-taker perceptions (Xie, 2013; Xie & Andrews, 2013)	1. Strategies to manage rater management impressions included a risk-taking approach and a defensive approach 2. Test-takers with higher values to the defensive approach achieved significantly higher scores than test-takers with lower values 3. Defensive writers writing longer essays and committing fewer linguistic errors, while risk-takers used slightly more sophisticated words and sentences but also committed more errors	/
Reading	English as second language (ESL)	Reading pilot test; Questionnaire	Cognitive test-taking strategies survey (Cohen & Upton, 2006, 2007)	1. Test takers used more language learner strategies (i.e., comprehending meaning), less in test-management skills, and least in test-wiseness 2. Task characteristics (e.g., difficulty) influenced test takers' different types of test-taking strategies, which, in turn, led to differences in predicting task performance 3. Test management showed a small negative association with test performance 4. Test-wiseness led to poorer performance 5. Higher language learner strategies (comprehending meaning) led to higher test performance	1. Students who used language learner strategies (comprehending meaning strategies) more frequently had higher L2 reading test scores
Speaking	English as foreign language (EFL)	Test; Questionnaire	Strategy Inventory for English Speaking Tests (SIEST)	1. Participants used communication strategy use and cognitive strategy use of language learner strategies positively and significantly influenced speaking performance 2. Affective strategies were not significantly related to test performance	1. The use of language learner strategies (communication strategy use and cognitive strategy use) had a significantly positive association with speaking performance while affective strategy did not

(Continued)

TABLE 32.1

(Continued)

Author	Year	Journal/Book	Strategies	Participants	Study level	Targeted test
Assiri	2016	*Studies in English Language Teaching*	1. Test-management strategies; 2. Test-wiseness strategies	/	University	TOEFL-iBT reading section
Guo et al.	2016	*Reading and Writing*	1. Test management strategies (previewing response choices, item response accuracy, and response time)	95 undergraduate students	University	Reading material adopted from SAT practice questions
Winke & Lim	2017	*Language Assessment Quarterly*	1. Test-wiseness strategies	76 English-language learners	University	IELTS listening test
Stenlund et al.	2017	*Assessment in Education: Principles, Policy & Practice*	1. Structural organization 2. Time-management 3. Test-wiseness strategies	1129 individuals who completed the SweSAT for the first time	High school	Swedish scholastic aptitude test (SweSAT)

Skills	Test language	Instruments	Names of questionnaire	Findings	TTS and language performance
Reading	/	Test; Questionnaire; Verbal report	/	1. The integration of three procedures of verbal reporting, namely stimulated recall, self-observation, and retrospective interview, in computer-assisted research can tremendously help capitalize on their strengths and control their weaknesses	/
Reading	English as first and second language	Test; Eye tracking	/	1. Test management strategy of previewing was associated with a significantly lower probability of answering an item correctly but not with significantly longer response time 2. The relations of test management strategy of previewing to response accuracy and response time were moderated by English proficiency levels 3. Test management strategy of previewing does not facilitate performance on a sentence comprehension task, but instead interferes with the comprehension process, particularly for individuals with relatively high language proficiency	1. Participants with higher proficiency performed better without previewing, but there was no difference for lower-intermediate learners of English
Listening	English as first and second language	Experiment; Questionnaire	Test-taking strategy questionnaire (Cohen & Upton, 2007)	1. No group differences in post-test scores attributable to the type of instruction 2. Explicit, implicit, or none instructional types had no measurable, differential effects on test-wiseness strategies 3. Test taker' pretest score is significantly related to whether or not a test taker would obtain a large gain pre-testing to post-testing	1. The pre-test score is significantly associated with test performance improvement
Verbal/ Reading	Swedish as first language	Test; Questionnaire	/	1. In terms of structural organization, high achievers reported using successful strategies to a higher extent. Extreme low achievers reported to a higher extent that they answered the items in the order they were displayed in the test booklet compared to extreme high achievers 2. Females reported using test-wiseness strategies (i.e., random guessing) to a higher extent than males	1. High achievers skipped items they did not know the answer to a higher extent compared to low achievers 2. Among learners with time-management strategies, there are statistically significant differences between low and high achievers in one of the four strategies

(Continued)

480 Chapter 32 Test-Taking Strategies

TABLE 32.1

(Continued)

Author	Year	Journal/Book	Strategies	Participants	Study level	Targeted test
Suvorov	2018	*Cambridge Michigan Language Assessment (CaMLA) Working Papers*	1. Test-management strategies (e.g., item elements, text prompt, question and answer selecting) 2. Test-wiseness strategies (random guessing, selecting the answer based on background knowledge or on clues form other items)	15 non-native speakers of English	University	Michigan English Test (MET)
Waiprakhon & Jaturapitakkul	2018	*PASAA: Journal of Language Teaching and Learning in Thailand*	1. Language learner strategies 2. Test-management 3. Test-wiseness strategies	5 Thai Engineers and Technologists	University	Reading section of the Test of English for Thai Engineers and Technologists (TETET)
Lin et al.	2019	*Studies in Educational Evaluation*	1. Language learner strategies	552 test takers who were learning Chinese as a second language (L2) in universities in mainland China	University	A Chinese reading test (the reading subtest of HSK Level 5
Cai & Kunnan	2020	*Language Testing*	1. Language learner strategies (strategy use ability)	1491 nursing students	University	A Grammar Knowledge Test (GKT) The Nursing English Reading Test (NERT)

Skills	Test language	Instruments	Names of questionnaire	Findings	TTS and language performance
				3. Low achievers to a higher extent reported that it was more important to ensure accuracy in their answers than certifying time to answer all items 4. Test-taking behavior might bring additional variance to test scores, whether or not this is irrelevant variance is discussed	3. In terms of test-wiseness strategies, there are statistically significant differences between high and low achievers
Listening, reading, and grammar	English as foreign language (EFL)	Eye-tracking Verbal report Test Background questionnaire	/	1. Participants used a wide variety of test-management and test-wiseness strategies 2. Most test-taking strategies were used across all item types, some of the strategies appeared to be applicable only to a specific item type 3. Some test-management strategies were used to interact with text prompts when completing reading set items 4. Test-wiseness strategies imposed construct-irrelevant variance and affect scores for computer-delivered items adapted from the MET	1. Test-wiseness strategies had construct-irrelevant variance and influenced EFL test scores
Reading	English as second language	Test Stimulated recall interview	/	1. Test-management strategies were the most frequently used strategy type across all sub-sections of the TETET reading section 2. Test-wiseness strategies were the least frequently used strategy type 3. There was concordance between the types of strategies used and the item types in the sub-sections	/
Reading	Chinese as L2	Test; Questionnaire	The strategy use questionnaire (Purpura, 1999; Oxford, 2011)	1. Only cognitive strategy use directly influenced Chinese reading test performance while both metacognitive and affective strategy use did so in an indirect way 2. Affective strategy use had direct effects on both metacognitive and cognitive strategy use 3. Metacognitive strategy use exerted a strong and direct effect on cognitive strategy use	1. Among language learner strategies, only cognitive strategy use directly influenced Chinese reading test performance 2. Both metacognitive and affective strategy use affect performance in an indirect way
Reading	English as second language	Test; Questionnaire	Strategy Use Ability Scale	1. The effect of strategy use ability on nursing English reading performance fluctuated in a down-up-down pattern with the increase of students' language knowledge	1. The Island Ridge Curve pattern

(Continued)

TABLE 32.1

(Continued)

Author	Year	Journal/Book	Strategies	Participants	Study level	Targeted test
Leddo et al.	2020	*International Journal of Advanced Educational Research*	1. Language learner strategies	29 students from USA	High school	SAT
Aryadoust	2020	*Computer Assisted Language Learning*	1. Test-management strategies	28 Singaporean students	Secondary	A computerized while-listening performance (WLP) test
Yeom & Jun	2020	*Language Assessment Quarterly*	1. Language learner strategies (reading strategies) 2. Test-management strategies 3. Test-wiseness strategies	84 Korean students	Middle school	TOEFL Junior reading comprehension test (a shortened version)
Singh et al.	2021	*Studies in English Language and Education*	1. Language learner strategies (cognitive, metacognitive, compensating, social, affective, compensation, and memory strategies) 2. Test-wiseness strategies (compensation)	44 ESL learners with weak language proficiency in Malaysia	University	Malaysian University English Test (MUET)
Low & Aryadoust	2021	*International Journal of Listening*	1. Language learner strategies (meta-cognitive strategies: planning, monitoring, and evaluating)	66 participants in Singapore	University	An academic listening test designed for the study

Skills	Test language	Instruments	Names of questionnaire	Findings	TTS and language performance
Writing	English as first language	Experiment	/	1. Students using the metacognitive writing strategies scored higher than those using standard test taking strategies 2. Metacognitive writing strategies can lead to higher Writing and Language scores on the SAT and further research can indicate whether this applies to other standardized tests as well	/
Listening	English as first language	Test; Eye-tracking	/	1. Listeners tended to quickly skim the test items, distractors, and answers during pre-listening in hearing 1 and pre-listening in hearing 2 2. During while-listening in hearing 1 and while-listening in hearing 2, significantly more attention was paid to the written stems, distractors, and options 3. The increment in attention to the written stems, distractors, and options was greater for the matching items and interactions between item format and item reading were also detected 4. A mixed answer changing pattern (i.e., incorrect-to-correct and correct-to-incorrect), although the dominant pattern for both item formats (67%) was wrong-to-correct	/
Reading	English as a foreign language	Test; Questionnaire	Reading and test-taking strategies (Cohen & Upton, 2006)	1. There were marginal statistical differences in strategy use between the paper-based and computer-based modes 2. Learners with different levels of English reading proficiency had significant differences in strategy use	1. More use of test-taking strategies does not always lead to higher L2 achievement
Reading	English as second language (ESL)	Think-aloud; In-depth focus group interviews	/	1. Participants employed various strategies: cognitive strategies (repetition and translation), metacognitive strategies (the content of the passage to real life, self-questioning and using prior knowledge), and compensation strategies (guessing) 2. Understanding and reading the passage allowed learners to draw conclusions better in answering the multiple-choice questions 3. Learners used a compensation strategy whereby they tried guessing the answers on a number of occasions	/
Listening	English as first and second language	Eye-Tracking; Self-Report Questionnaires	Self-reported test-taking strategies	1. Results suggest that gaze measures (visit duration and fixation frequency) predicted participants' final test performance, while self-reports had moderate predicting power	1. Self-report moderated the relation between language learner strategies and test performance

(Continued)

484 Chapter 32 Test-Taking Strategies

TABLE 32.1

(Continued)

Author	Year	Journal/Book	Strategies	Participants	Study level	Targeted test
Kim	2021	*Assessing Writing*	1. Test-wiseness strategies	4 Korean students in South Korea	/	TOEFL iBT Writing test
Joseph et al.	2021	*Quarterly Journal of Experimental Psychology*	1. Test management strategies (inference making, comprehension monitoring)	64 children	Age 8–13 years old	1. Test of Word Reading Efficiency (TOWRE) 2. York Assessment of Reading for Comprehension (YARC)
Estaji & Banitalebi	2023	*International Journal of Testing*	1. Test management strategies 2. Test-wiseness strategies	178 Iranian IELTS repeaters	University	IELTS
Kwon & Yu	2023	*System*	1. Language learner strategies (cognitive and metacognitive strategies)	116 students in South Korea	High school	Listening materials from College Scholastic Ability Test (CSAT)
Zawoyski et al.	2023	*School Psychology*	1. Test management strategies (the passage-first (PF) and questions-first (QF) strategies)	84 participants in the southeastern United States	Elementary	Gates Mac Ginitie Reading Tests (GMRT)

The author would like to acknowledge Xiuyue Xu and Keke Xing for their assistance in building Table 32.1.

Skills	Test language	Instruments	Names of questionnaire	Findings	TTS and language performance
Writing	English as second language (ESL)	In-depth interviews	/	1. All interviewees reported that the coaching of test-wiseness strategies had improved their TOEFL iBT writing scores and perceived direct test preparation efficiency	/
Reading	English as first language	Experiments; Eye movements	/	1. Children appear to prioritize efficiency over completeness when reading, generating inferences spontaneously only when they are necessary for establishing a coherent representation of the text	/
Listening, speaking, writing, and reading	English as foreign language (EFL)	Mixed method: closed-ended questionnaire and open-ended questionnaire	Test-Taking Strategy Questionnaire	1. An increased use of test management strategies and a decreased use in test-wiseness strategies were found during three test occasions 2. The use of test-management strategies positively influenced test scores 3. The use of test-wiseness strategies negatively affect test scores	1. The relation of test scores to test-management and test-wiseness strategies is linear
Listening	English as second language (ESL)	Test; Questionnaire	Cognitive and metacognitive strategy use questionnaire (Phakiti, 2016)	1. There was no significant difference in the use of language learner strategies (i.e., cognitive and metacognitive strategies) between audio test and video conditions, but the video group outperformed the audio-only group in terms of test scores achieved 2. Specific language learner strategies such as "planning" and "comprehending and retrieval" had significant positive effects on the overall test score, while the "monitoring and evaluation" factor exerted a significant negative effect on listening performance	1. Different language learner strategy has different effects on test performance
Reading	English as first or foreign language	Eye movements	/	1. The PF condition was superior to the QF condition for elementary readers in terms of efficiency in reading and responding to questions 2. The PF strategy supports a more comprehensive understanding of the text 3. Within the PF condition, students required less time to obtain the same accuracy outcomes they attained when reading in the QF condition	/

486 Chapter 32 Test-Taking Strategies

affective). They adopted a three-dimensional scale called the Strategy Inventory for English Speaking Tests (SIEST) and administered the questionnaire to 215 Taiwanese English learners after they took the Test of English for International Communication Speaking Test (TOEIC-S). The results of exploratory factor analysis supported eight factors falling into three higher-order factors: cognitive strategy use (i.e., rehearing, attending, processing inductively, and organizing), communication strategy use (i.e., simplifying, structuring, and elaborating), and affective strategy use (i.e., self-encouraging, self-calming, self-comforting, and self-talk). Cohen and colleagues (Cohen et al., 2023) challenged this three-factor structure, which expanded the construct of test-taking strategies to include language use strategies (especially the affective aspects). The critique by Cohen et al. (2023) was rational in that the social and affective elements have rarely been formally conceptualized as elements of language ability (Bachman & Palmer, 2010). Regardless, the re-consideration of the cognitive elements as test-taking strategies can find support from more recent proposals of language ability (Bennett et al., 2016; Cai & Cheung, 2021) and empirical studies investigating test-taking strategies for the sake of test validation (Lin et al., 2019; Phakiti, 2008).

Variation of Test-Taking Strategy Use Across Media of Communication, Test Formats, and L2 Proficiency

During the past decade, many studies have been conducted to examine test-taking strategies across different media of communication. The majority has found that all three types of strategies are commonly used by test takers across different media of communication. These widely used strategies include language use strategies such as *cognitive strategies* (e.g., memorizing, retrieving, comprehending) and *metacognitive strategies* (e.g., planning before responding, monitoring during responding and evaluating after selecting the question options) in reading tests (see Cai & Kunnan, 2020; Singh et al., 2021; Wu & Stone, 2016), cognitive, affective, and communication strategies used in speaking tests (Huang, 2016), cognitive listening strategies in listening tests (see Kwon & Yu, 2023; Low & Aryadoust, 2021; Winke & Lim, 2017), and *metacognitive writing strategies* in writing tests (Leddo et al., 2020). Regarding test-management strategies, studies during the past decade have shown that there is a list of commonly used strategies across different media of communication. These strategies include strategies related to item elements (i.e., question-first versus prompt-first), strategies used for interaction with the text prompt, and strategies used for interaction with the question/options and answer selection. Besides, test-wiseness strategies such as random guessing are commonly used in tests of reading (see Assiri & Alodhahi, 2018), listening, and grammar (see Suvorov, 2018).

Another important finding of existing studies is that some test-taking strategies are skill-specific or sensitive to different test formats. Suvorov (2018) found that some test-management strategies are task-specific (e.g., skimming through the text prompt only applied to Reading tasks). Research also suggested that test-taking strategies may vary across different testing formats. For example, in some listening testing conditions, test takers are allowed to preview test questions before playing the recording, whereas in other situations, this previewing might not be allowed (see Low & Aryadoust, 2021). The different formats of listening tests inevitably incur different applications of test-taking strategies (see Aryadoust, 2020; Low & Aryadoust, 2021). For instance, in a small-scale study involving five undergraduate students, Waiprakhon and Jaturapitakkul (2018) found that students' test-taking strategies varied across different test sections. Specifically, students reported more use of test-management strategies for the Internet-Reading Section. In contrast, they reported more use of cognitive strategies for the Technical Manuals section.

The third research theme regards the variation of test-taking strategy use across different L2 proficiency levels. An important finding is that low- and high-achievers differed in their use of test-taking strategies. Through a literature review, Assiri and Alodhahi (2018) concluded that test takers with high L2 proficiency use more test-taking strategies and more intensively than their peers with low L2 proficiency. Specifically, high-achievers combine a high level of language use strategies (e.g., textual information comprehension) with superior test-management strategies (e.g., confirming the selected answers, evaluating potential options, consulting background knowledge to enhance their understanding of the item content), skipping items they cannot answer, and eliminating based on clues in the text (Stenlund et al., 2017). In contrast, low-achievers stick rigidly to test-wiseness strategies (Suvorov, 2018), such as blind guessing (Assiri, 2016; Stenlund et al., 2017), looking at the questions before reading the passage, rereading the whole passage or part of it to compensate their comprehension deficiency, jumping between items or subtests, sticking to the original item sequence, and caring accuracy more than allocating time appropriately to all items (see Stenlund et al., 2017).

Yeom and Jun (2020) further compared the different use of test-taking strategies across low-, medium-, and high-L2 reading proficiency groups and discovered more complex patterns of test-taking strategy use. They found that high-achievers read the passage more carefully and used more metalinguistic knowledge than those with lower proficiency. The medium-proficiency group used a variety of strategies, such as rereading the passage and questions, translating into their first language (L1), and using elimination more frequently than the high- and low-proficiency groups. The lower L2-proficiency group, however, was more ready than the other two groups to use blind guessing, select options based on background knowledge without much relating to the textual information, look for clues in other items to answer the questions, and choose the option carrying a same word from the passage. This finding suggested a possible nonlinear relationship between the frequency of test-taking strategy use and L2 reading proficiency.

Effects of Test-Taking Strategies and L2 Test Performance

As reviewed earlier, higher-achievers do not necessarily use more test-taking strategies than medium- or low-achievers. This suggests that more use of test-taking strategies does not always lead to higher L2 achievement. For this reason, scholars have started to look into the actual effects of test-taking strategies on L2 achievement. Despite some inconsistency, existing evidence in general suggests a significant relationship between test-taking strategies and L2 test performance.

A few studies examined the relationship between *language use strategies* and L2 test performance. Huang (2016) discovered that cognitive strategies (i.e., rehearsing, attending, processing inductively, and organizing) and communication strategies (simplifying, structuring, and elaborating) were positively related to speaking test performance. This positive association was also observed in Wu and Stone (2016). They found that students who used comprehending meaning strategies more frequently also had higher reading L2 test scores. In another large-scale study on the English for Specific Purposes reading test, Cai and Kunnan (2020) revealed that test-takers' perceptions of the efficiency of using cognitive and metacognitive strategy use are in general positively related to the test scores of the Medical English Test Systems Reading Subtest. Besides, they found that this effect fluctuates up and down with increase in English proficiency, a pattern which they called the Island Ridge Curve (IRC). See Figure 32.1 for an illustration of this fluctuation of strategy use effect on language performance.

Other researchers focused on the relationship between test-wiseness strategies and L2 test performance. Xie (2015) examined the impact of impression management strategies, one type of test-wiseness strategies, on essay writing performance. The study compared two aspects of impression management strategies: the risk-taking approach (e.g., using advanced vocabulary) and the defensive approach (e.g., avoiding unfamiliar grammar/words). Results of

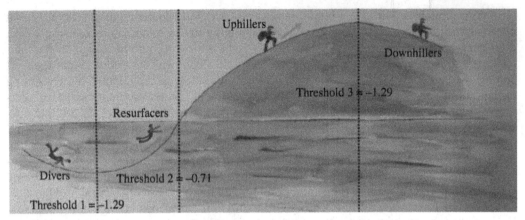

FIGURE 32.1 A metaphoric illustration of the island ridge curve (IRC). *Source:* Cai and Kunnan (2020), p. 296 / SAGE Publications.

multiple regression analysis showed that test takers who applied the defensive approach obtained significantly higher writing scores. Drawing on the results of textual analyses, she found that highly defensive test takers used simpler words, wrote shorter sentences, and made fewer mechanical mistakes, thereby achieving higher test scores. In contrast, risk-takers used more sophisticated words and were easily penalized due to more lexical and grammatical errors. Despite the positive effect of the defensive approach, the author caveated its possible harm to the development of English writing ability.

Kim (2021) also examined the relationship between test-wiseness strategies and L2 writing test performance. The researcher interviewed four TOEFL iBT candidates recruited from a Cram school in South Korea regarding their perceptions of the usefulness of coaching test-wiseness strategies (i.e., familiarizing with the test formats, memorizing the templates, and intensive exercising). All interviewees reported that the coaching had helped them enhance their TOEFL iBT writing scores. According to one interviewee, the drill they received during the coaching enabled them to respond to the test prompts in an energy-saving way which has been known to inflate writing test scores (Xie, 2015).

The positive relationship between test-wiseness strategies and L2 test performance was confirmed by Suvorov (2018). The researcher identified 7 specific test-wiseness strategies among 15 participants: random guessing, eliminating, selecting the option with a word irrelevant to the prompt, using clues from other items, using background knowledge, and using clues from the speakers' tone of voice. Ultimately, he found that test-wiseness strategies significantly inflated the test scores.

However, mixed results also emerged. For instance, Huang (2016) found that affective strategies were non-significantly related to test-takers' TOEIC speaking test scores. Wu and Stone (2016) found that more use of test-wiseness strategies (i.e., "choosing the least wrong answer," "selecting an option that has an important word," and "guessing blindly") was related to lower reading test scores. One possible reason for this inconsistency is the difference in the media of communication used in different studies (i.e., productive versus receptive). Coaching test-wiseness strategies for productive skills more or less enables students to activate their use of linguistic knowledge (e.g., memorizing some useful cohesive devices), whereas coaching for receptive skills does not necessarily work.

Likewise, studies on test-management strategies and their relation to L2 test performance also provide mixed results. Wu and Stone (2016) found that more use of test-management strategies (i.e., taking notes, translating, guessing based on textual clues, and using clues in other questions) negatively predicted L2 reading test scores. A possible reason for the negative relation might be that these specific test-wiseness strategies were related to lower-level local information processing but not on test-management per se.

Guo et al. (2016) examined the effect of previewing test questions before reading the passages, one specific strategy for test management among Chinese English learners and native-English speakers. They revealed that previewing was negatively associated with response accuracy but not response time. They also zoomed into the previewing–reading relationship across three English proficiency groups: lower intermediate, upper intermediate, and advanced. The results revealed a significant moderation of English proficiency on the previewing-reading relation. Specifically, previewing was negatively associated with the response accuracy of the upper-intermediate and advanced proficiency groups but nonsignificantly associated with that of the lower-intermediate group. Meanwhile, previewing cost additional response time for the two higher-proficiency groups but not for the lower-intermediate proficiency group. The results suggested that previewing is negatively associated with response accuracy and costs additional response time, though the effect only occurs with the higher-proficiency group.

Other studies conducted in non-L2 settings may also shed new light on our understanding of test-management strategies in L2 testing situations. Joseph et al. (2021) compared the effect of question location (before and after the passage) on children's local inference (information in working memory) and global inference (comprehension of textual information) and their task-response time. They found that previewing had no effect on global inference but a detrimental effect on local inference. They also observed that reading the questions first costs more response time. The researchers argued that reading the questions first may burden working memory, eventually leading to deteriorated task performance. This finding of the decreased performance accuracy is consistent with what Guo et al. (2016) found in L2 settings with students performing sentence-completion tasks. However, the finding regarding the increased response time due to previewing contradicts what was revealed by Guo et al. (2016). A possible reason is that the reading tasks used by Joseph et al. (2021) required more working memory than the sentence-completion tasks used in Guo et al. (2016).

Zawoyski et al. (2023) compared the passage-first strategies and question-first strategies of 84 elementary school students performing 2 English reading comprehension tasks. They found nonsignificant differences in the test scores derived from the two strategies. In line with Joseph et al. (2021), they found that the passage-first strategies enabled students to spend less time achieving the same accuracy.

Challenges for Researchers

The double-fold purpose of test-taking strategies research is to understand and distinguish construct-relevant and construct-irrelevant processes that test-takers activate during their test-taking process and to help language testers develop tasks to assess language ability. Research during the past decade has enriched the list of test-taking strategies, revealed the prevalence of these different types of test-taking strategies, and uncovered their actual function in raising or reducing test scores, but challenges remain.

The first challenge relates to the construct of test-taking strategies. Despite Cohen et al.'s (2023) reasonable call for the focus on test-management and test-wiseness strategies, general language use strategies such as cognitive and metacognitive strategies (or affective strategies) still remain on the menu of test-taking strategies researchers. To researchers of such an inclusive view, learner strategies such as cognitive, metacognitive, and motivation regulation strategies involved during language learning are also inevitably involved during the test-taking process (see Huang, 2016). This disagreement makes the construct of test-taking strategies an open issue.

490   Chapter 32 Test-Taking Strategies

Another challenge relates to the continuous enrichment of the list of test-taking strategies. Although the number of test-taking studies has increased significantly during the past decade, this number is still relatively small. Reported test-taking strategies, especially test-management and test-wiseness strategies, are still limited to those proposed more than one decade ago. In addition, most of these strategies are observed for close-ended multiple-choice questions and relatively fewer are for open-ended question types, especially for integrated tasks. Besides, several strategies have been derived from small-scale narrative studies and categorized according to researchers' intuition. The subjective categorization of these strategy categories (e.g., guessing from clues as test-wiseness strategies) leaves its validity to be tested by further researchers.

The third challenge lies in distinguishing between construct-relevant and -irrelevant strategies. There has been a widely accepted criterion for determining whether a strategy is construct-relevant or not, that is, whether a strategy can enable or avoid the use of language ability. However, the actual activation of test-taking strategies is quite complex. Often, a mental process may involve a mixture of construct-relevant and construct-irrelevant strategies. For instance, guessing is generally considered construct-irrelevant. However, if test takers make a logical guess drawing on their comprehension of the testing materials, it is hard to tell if this guessing is purely construct-irrelevant.

A final challenge deals with the link between test-taking strategies and test-task design. A major goal of test developers is to design test tasks that can minimize the score variances due to test-takers' activation of construct-irrelevant mental processes. However, it is unrealistic to expect that there is a perfect test task design (e.g., task prompts for a writing test) that can sufficiently prevent test takers from taking shortcuts by rote-learning some templates to avoid the profound activation of linguistic resources.

Future Directions: Ensuring Validity and Accounting for Heterogeneity

Fine-Tuning Measures of Test-Taking Strategies

Measurements of test-taking strategies during the past decades have moved from the prevalence of verbal reports of test-takers' thinking processes and self-revelation (e.g., concurrent or stimulated recall) (Yeom & Jun, 2020) to the use of large-scale surveys that ask test takers to report the frequency of their behaviors (Wu & Stone, 2016) and to the use of eye-tracking technique (Suvorov, 2018). One limitation of these measurement approaches deals with the directness of strategy measurement. Although verbal reports can be used as a reliable measure of strategy use frequency or occurrence (i.e., whether a specific strategy is used), this measurement cannot tell how these strategies are used and whether these activated strategies can enhance test-takers' L2 test performance. Future studies may extend their measurements to test-takers' perceived efficiency of using specific test-taking strategies (e.g., Cai & Kunnan, 2020).

Besides, in quite a few studies, the measurement quality of the self-reported measures did not go through psychometric evaluation (e.g., Suvorov, 2018). Future studies using surveys to measure test-taking strategies must ensure psychometric quality before further exploring other more in-depth issues.

Furthermore, the past decade has seen a fast development in technology. As existing studies have shown (Suvorov, 2018; Zawoyski et al., 2023), eye-tracking techniques can be used to obtain more direct and accurate measurements of test-taking strategies through eye movement data. Other advanced techniques such as Electroencephalography (EEG), Functional Near-Infrared Spectroscopy (fNIRS), and Functional magnetic resonance imaging (fMRI) can also be appropriate instruments for obtaining test-taking strategies data.

Future Directions: Ensuring Validity and Accounting for Heterogeneity **491**

Accounting for the Heterogeneity of Test-Taking Strategies

Test-taking strategies research aims to identify strategies that can raise or decrease L2 test scores. However, a review of the literature has shown that the effect of the same test-taking strategy may vary with different characteristics of test-takers (e.g., demographic, psychological, cognitive, physiological, etc.), tests (e.g., different tests, media of communication, test methods, or test modes), and contexts (e.g., on-site test taking or test preparation situations). Future studies on test-taking strategies need to account for these variables that may lead to the heterogeneous effects of test-taking strategies.

One direction would be to compare the relative importance of different test-taking strategies to test performance and scores. It would be helpful to compare whether one type of test-taking strategy (i.e., on-site use of cognitive and metacognitive strategies, test management strategies, or test-wiseness strategies) plays a relatively more important role in predicting test performance than others. Second, in situations where a specific type of test-taking strategy is not directly related to test performance, it would be helpful to find out whether these strategies still contribute to test performance by improving other types of test-taking strategies that directly benefit test performance. For instance, some metacognitive strategy factors are occasionally reported to produce nonsignificant direct effects on test performance; meanwhile, they are found to indirectly affect test performance through cognitive strategies (e.g., Cai, 2020; Purpura, 1999).

A third direction is to examine the moderated effects of test-taking strategies on test performance. It would be helpful to compare the variation of different types of test-taking strategies across different media of communication (i.e., independent writing tasks and integrated writing tasks), the importance of one type of test-taking strategies conditioned on other types of test-taking strategies (e.g., test-wiseness strategies or test-management strategies conditioned on metacognitive strategies), background knowledge, or language proficiency. Among these moderators, language proficiency is especially recommended, given its importance recognized in existing studies that cover all three types of test-taking strategies, such as language use strategies (see Cai & Kunnan, 2020; Purpura, 1999), test-management strategies (see Assiri, 2016), and test-wiseness strategies (see Assiri, 2016; Yeom & Jun, 2020).

To examine the moderation, researchers may divide test takers into different L2 proficiency groups based on some predefined cut-off scores (e.g., top 30% and bottom 30% of the total sample; −1 and +1 standard deviations; or −1.29, −0.71, 1.29 as recommended in Cai and Kunnan, 2020) and compare the relationship between test-taking strategies and L2 test performance across different proficiency groups. Alternatively, future researchers may apply the person-centered approach to group participants using latent class analysis and then compare the effects of test-taking strategies across different latent groups (e.g., Cai & Lei, 2019). More sophisticatedly, researchers may include a measure of L2 proficiency and conduct a Multilayered Moderation Analysis (MLMA), which allows for a continuous projection of the fluctuation of test-taking strategies on L2 test performance (see Cai & Kunnan, 2019, 2020). For a philosophical interpretation of the fluctuation phenomenon, interested readers may refer to the series of studies with the label of Island Ridge Curve (Cai, 2024; Cai & Chen, 2022; Cai & Yang, 2022; Wang et al., 2021).

More recently, Cai (2023) encapsulates the abovementioned strategies for heterogeneity testing and proposes the competition-mediation-moderation (CMM) approach. According to the CMM, researchers can examine three types of effects independently or simultaneously: the relative importance of different test-taking strategies to L2 test performance (i.e., competition), the mediation of one type of test-taking strategies on the effect of another type of test-taking strategies, and the moderation of one type of test-taking strategies on the effect of another type of test-taking strategies on L2 test performance. Results derived from this CMM approach can allow the researchers to reveal more subtle information regarding the

492   **Chapter 32** Test-Taking Strategies

interaction mechanism long-posited in the Communicative Language Ability (Bachman & Palmer, 1996, 2010).

The final direction is to link test-taking strategies to other individual characteristics that may significantly affect L2 test performance. The list includes age, gender, critical thinking, self-efficacy (e.g., Esfahani, 2022), self-concept, test anxiety, motivation, design thinking, and systems thinking (Cabrera et al., 2021), to name but a few. By including these variables, researchers can explore whether any of these variables mediate the effects of specific test-taking strategies. Alternatively, they may explore whether test-taking strategies can mediate the relationships between these individual factors and L2 test performance. Moreover, researchers can explore whether these variables can reduce or amplify the relationship between interested test-taking strategies and test performance. Wherever necessary, such exploration can be conducted by applying the CMM approach.

Discussion Questions

1. Are there different patterns of test-taking strategies? Do different patterns of test-taking strategies make a difference to the language test scores?

2. What factors (e.g., personality, motivation, emotion, cognition, language proficiency, school climate, culture) determine test-takers' choice of test-taking strategies? Do these factors make a difference to the *de facto* effect of test-taking strategies on the test scores?

References

Amer, A. (2007). *EFL/ESL test-wiseness and test-taking strategies (ED497399)*. https://files.eric.ed.gov/fulltext/ED497399.pdf

Aryadoust, V. (2020). Dynamics of item reading and answer changing in two hearings in a computerized while-listening performance test: an eye-tracking study. *Computer Assisted Language Learning, 33*(5–6), 510–537. https://doi.org/10.1080/09588221.2019.1574267.

Assiri, M. S. (2016). Integration of stimulated recall, self-observation, and retrospective interview in the collection of strategy data in computer-assisted language testing. *Integration, 4*(1), 104–122. https://core.ac.uk/download/pdf/268085089.pdf.

Assiri, M., & Alodhahi, E. (2018). Test-taking strategies on reading comprehension tests: a review of major research themes. *Studies in English Language Teaching, 6*(3), 207–227. https://doi.org/10.22158/selt.v6n3p207.

Bachman, L. F., & Palmer, A. S. (1996). *Language testing in practice: Designing and developing useful language tests.* Oxford University Press.

Bachman, L. F., & Palmer, A. S. (2010). *Language assessment in practice: Developing language assessments and justifying their use in the real world.* Oxford University Press.

Bennett, R. E., Deane, P. D., & van Rijn, P. W. (2016). From cognitive-domain theory to assessment practice. *Educational Psychologist, 51*(1), 82–107. https://doi.org/10.1080/00461520.2016.1141683.

Bumbálková, E. (2021). Test-taking strategies in second language receptive skills tests: a literature review. *International Journal of Instruction, 14*(2), 647–664. https://doi.org/10.29333/iji.2021.14236a.

Cabrera, L., Sokolow, J., & Cabrera, D. (2021). Developing and validating a measurement of systems thinking: the systems thinking and metacognitive inventory (STMI). In D. Cabrera, L. Cabrera & G. Midgley (Eds.), *Routledge handbook of systems thinking* (pp. 1–42). Routledge.

Cai, Y. (2020). *Examining the interaction among components of English for Specific Purposes ability in reading: The Triple-Decker Model.* Peter Lang.

Cai, Y. (2023). Accounting for interaction in language test validation: applying the competition-mediation-moderation (CMM) approach to enhance the transparency of test score interpretation. *Language Testing and Assessment, 2,* 48–64. https://sns.wanfangdata.com.cn/perio/yuycsypj.

References 493

Cai, Y. (2024). Metacognitive strategy use in L2 learning fluctuates from both ends towards the middle: longitudinal evidence for the Island Ridge Curve. *System*. https://doi.org/10.1016/j.system.2024.103324.

Cai, Y., & Chen, H. (2022). The fluctuating effect of thinking on language performance: new evidence for the Island Ridge Curve. *Language Assessment Quarterly, 19*(5), 465–479. https://doi.org/10.1080/15434303.2022.2080553.

Cai, Y., & Cheung, H.-T. (2021). A dynamic language ability system framework for diagnosing EMI students' readiness of English language ability. In L. I.-W. Su, H. Cheung & J. R. W. Wu (Eds.), *Rethinking EMI: Rethinking EMI multidisciplinary perspectives from Chinese speaking regions* (pp. 141–160). Taylor & Francis. https://doi.org/10.4324/9780429352362.

Cai, Y., & Kunnan, A. J. (2019). Detecting the language thresholds of the effect of background knowledge on a Language for Specific Purposes reading performance: a case of the island ridge curve. *Journal of English for Academic Purposes, 42*, 100795. https://doi.org/10.1016/j.jeap.2019.100795.

Cai, Y., & Kunnan, A. J. (2020). Mapping the fluctuating effect of strategy use ability on English reading performance for nursing students: a multi-layered moderation analysis approach. *Language Testing, 37*(2), 280–304. https://doi.org/10.1177/0265532219893384.

Cai, Y., & Lei, C. (2019). Profiling the efficiency of strategy use across different levels of L2 readers. *Educational Studies*. https://doi.org/10.1080/03055698.2019.1655712.

Cai, Y., & Yang, Y. (2022). The fluid relation between reading strategies and mathematics learning: a perspective of the Island Ridge Curve. *Learning and Individual Differences, 98*, 102180. https://doi.org/10.1016/j.lindif.2022.102180.

Chen, M. Y., Wu, A. D., & Liu, Y. (2020). Linking test-taking process to performance through mixed-effects regression models: a response process-based validation study. *Journal of Psychoeducational Assessment, 38*(3), 389–401. https://doi.org/10.1177/0734282919861269.

Cohen, A. D. (2006). The coming of age of research on test-taking strategies. *Language Assessment Quarterly, 3*(4), 307–331. https://doi.org/10.1080/15434300701333129.

Cohen, A. D. (2011). *Strategies in learning and using a second language*. Pearson.

Cohen, A. D. (2014). Using test-wiseness strategy research in task development. In A. J. Kunnan (Ed.), *The companion to language assessment* (pp. 1–13). Wiley.

Cohen, A. D., Rahmati, T., & Sadeghi, K. (2023). Test-taking strategies in technology-assisted language assessment. In *Fundamental considerations in technology mediated language assessment* (pp. 235–254). Routledge.

Cohen, A. D., & Upton, T. A. (2006). *Strategies in responding to the new TOEFL reading tasks (TOEFL Monograph Series No. MS-33) (0898-2236)*.

Cohen, A. D., & Upton, T. A. (2007). I want to go back to the text: response strategies on the reading subtest of the new TOEFL(R). *Language Testing, 24*(2), 209–250. https://doi.org/10.1177/0265532207076364.

Cumming, A. (2024). Assessing integrated skills. In A. J. Kunnan (Ed.), *The concise companion to language assessment* (pp. 42–54). John Wiley & Sons, Inc.

Esfahani, F. R. (2022). Predictive power of test-taking strategies, critical thinking, and self-efficacy in accounting for female Iranian Ph.D. students' language proficiency: the case of EPT. *International Journal of Foreign Language Teaching and Research, 10*(41), 151–163. https://jfl.iaun.iau.ir/article_689396_10ef39d31d16ec8290afc08680e3f8df.pdf.

Estaji, M., & Banitalebi, Z. (2023). A study of test-taking strategies of Iranian IELTS repeaters: any change in the strategy use? *International Journal of Testing*, 1–26. https://doi.org/10.1080/15305058.2023.2195662.

Golparvar, S. E., & Khafi, A. (2021). The role of L2 writing self-efficacy in integrated writing strategy use and performance. *Assessing Writing, 47*, 100504. https://doi.org/10.1016/j.asw.2020.100504.

Guo, Q., Kim, Y.-S. G., Yang, L., & Liu, L. (2016). Does previewing answer choice options improve performance on reading tests? *Reading and Writing, 29*, 745–760. https://doi.org/10.1007/s11145-016-9626-z.

Huang, H.-T. D. (2016). Test-taking strategies in L2 assessment: the test of English for international communication speaking test. *Perceptual and Motor Skills, 123*(1), 64–90. https://doi.org/10.1177/0031512516660699.

Huang, H.-T. D., Hung, S.-T. A., & Plakans, L. (2018). Topical knowledge in L2 speaking assessment: comparing independent and integrated speaking test tasks. *Language Testing, 35*(1), 27–49. https://doi.org/10.1177/0265532216677106.

Joseph, H., Wonnacott, E., & Nation, K. (2021). Online inference making and comprehension monitoring in children during reading: evidence from eye movements. *Quarterly Journal of Experimental Psychology, 74*(7), 1202–1224. https://doi.org/10.1177/1747021821999.

494   Chapter 32 Test-Taking Strategies

Kim, S. (2021). Prepping for the TOEFL iBT Writing test, Gangnam style. *Assessing Writing, 49*, 100544. https://doi.org/10.1016/j.asw.2021.100544.

Kwon, S. K., & Yu, G. (2023). Investigating differences in test-takers' use of cognitive and metacognitive strategies in audio-only and video-based listening comprehension test. *System, 114*. https://doi.org/10.1016/j.system.2023.103017.

Leddo, J., Sengar, A., Liang, I., & Chilumula, R. (2020). Improving SAT writing and language scores by using metacognitive strategies. *International Journal of Advanced Educational Research, 5*(1), 24–26. https://www.researchgate.net/publication/338968856_Improving_sat_writing_and_language_scores_by_using_metacognitive_strategies.

Lin, L., Lam, J. W.-I., & Tse, S. K. (2019). Test takers' strategy use and L2 Chinese reading test performance in mainland China: a structural equation approach. *Studies in Educational Evaluation, 60*, 189–198. https://doi.org/10.1016/j.stueduc.2019.01.002.

Low, A. R. L., & Aryadoust, V. (2021). Investigating test-taking strategies in listening assessment: a comparative study of eye-tracking and self-report questionnaires. *International Journal of Listening, 1-20*. https://doi.org/10.1080/10904018.2021.1883433.

Messick, S. (1989). Validity. In R. L. Linn (Ed.), *Educational measurement* (3rd ed., pp. 13–103). Macmillan.

Oxford, R. (2011). *Teaching and researching language learning strategies.* Routledge.

Oxford, R., & Amerstorfer, C. M. (2018). *Language learning strategies and individual learner characteristics: Situating strategy use in diverse contexts.* Bloomsbury Publishing.

Phakiti, A. (2008). Strategic competence as a fourth-order factor model: a structural equation modeling approach. *Language Assessment Quarterly, 5*(1), 20–42. https://doi.org/10.1080/15434300701533596.

Phakiti, A. (2016). Test takers' performance appraisals, appraisal calibration, and cognitive and metacognitive strategy use. *Language Assessment Quarterly, 13*(2), 75–108. https://doi.org/10.1080/15434303.2016.1154555.

Plakans, L., & Gebril, A. (2012). A close investigation into source use in integrated second language writing tasks. *Assessing Writing, 17*(1), 18–34. https://doi.org/10.1016/j.asw.2011.09.002.

Purpura, J. E. (1998). Investigating the effects of strategy use and second language test performance with high- and low-ability test takers: a structural equation modelling approach. *Language Testing, 15*(3), 333–379. https://doi.org/10.1177/026553229801500303.

Purpura, J. E. (1999). *Learner strategy use and performance on language tests: A structural equation modeling approach.* Cambridge University Press.

Singh, C. K. S., Ong, E. T., Singh, T. S. M., Maniam, M., & Mohtar, T. M. T. (2021). Exploring ESL learners' reading test taking strategies. *Studies in English, Language and Education, 8*(1), 227–242. https://doi.org/10.24815/siele.v8i1.18130.

Stenlund, T., Eklöf, H., & Lyrén, P.-E. (2017). Group differences in test-taking behaviour: an example from a high-stakes testing program. *Assessment in Education: Principles, Policy & Practice, 24*(1), 4–20. https://doi.org/10.1080/0969594X.2016.1142935.

Suvorov, R. (2018). Investigating test-taking strategies during the completion of computer delivered items from Michigan English Test (MET): evidence from eye tracking and cued retrospective reporting. *Cambridge Michigan Language Assessment (CaMLA) Working Papers, 2*, 1–20.

Waiprakhon, T., & Jaturapitakkul, N. (2018). Test-taking strategies used in the reading section of the test of English for Thai engineers and technologists: a computer-based ESP test. *PASAA: Journal of Language Teaching and Learning in Thailand, 55*, 149–177. https://eric.ed.gov/?id=EJ1191741.

Wang, C., Cai, Y., Zhao, M., & You, X. (2021). Disentangling the relation between motivation regulation strategy and writing performance: a perspective of the Island Ridge Curve. *Foreign Languages World (Chinese), 204*(3), 46–54. https://www.cnki.com.cn/Article/CJFDTotal-WYJY202103007.htm.

Wenden, A. (1991). *Learner strategies for learner autonomy.* Prentice Hall.

Winke, P., & Lim, H. (2017). The effects of test preparation on second-language listening test performance. *Language Assessment Quarterly, 14*(4), 380–397. https://doi.org/10.1080/15434303.2017.1399396.

Wu, A. D., & Stone, J. E. (2016). Validation through understanding test-taking strategies: an illustration with the CELPIP-General reading pilot test using structural equation modeling. *Journal of Psychoeducational Assessment, 34*(4), 362–379. https://doi.org/10.1177/0734282915608575.

Xie, Q. (2013). Does test preparation work? Implications for score validity. *Language Assessment Quarterly (SSCI, A), 10*(2), 196–218. https://doi.org/10.1080/15434303.2012.721423.

Xie, Q. (2015). "I must impress the raters!" An investigation of Chinese test-takers' strategies to manage rater impressions. *Assessing Writing*, 25, 22–37. https://doi.org/10.1016/j.asw.2015.05.001.

Xie, Q., & Andrews, S. (2013). Do test design and uses influence test preparation: testing a model of washback with StructuralEquation Modeling. *Language Testing*, 30(1), 49–70. https://doi.org/10.1177/0265532212442634.

Xu, Y., & Wu, Z. (2011). A review of the research on test-taking strategies in the past 50 years. *Foreign Language Learning Theory and Practice*, 21(4), 43–51. http://www.teachlanguage.ecnu.edu.cn/EN/abstract/abstract8356.shtml.

Yeom, S., & Jun, H. (2020). Young Korean EFL learners' reading and test-taking strategies in a paper and a computer-based reading comprehension tests. *Language Assessment Quarterly*, 17(3), 282–299. https://doi.org/10.1080/15434303.2020.1731753.

Zawoyski, A. M., Ardoin, S. P., & Binder, K. S. (2023 January). The impact of test-taking strategies on eye movements of elementary students during reading comprehension assessment. *School Psychology*, 38(1), 59–66. https://doi.org/10.1037/spq0000526.

Suggested Readings

Cohen, A. D. (2021). Test-taking strategies and task design. In A. D. Cohen (Ed.), *The Routledge handbook of language testing* (2nd ed., pp. 372–396). Routledge. https://doi.org/10.4324/9781003220756-29.

Jensen, J. L., McDaniel, M. A., Woodard, S. M., & Kummer, T. A. (2014). Teaching to the test. . . or testing to teach: exams requiring higher order thinking skills encourage greater conceptual understanding. *Educational Psychology Review*, 26, 307–329. https://doi.org/10.1007/s10648-013-9248-9.

Kane, M. (2013). Validating the interpretations and uses of test scores. *Journal of Educational Measurement*, 50(1), 1–73. https://doi.org/10.1111/jedm.12000.

Lee, J.-Y. (2019). Teaching test-taking strategies to EFL student readers with different language proficiencies: an empirical reassessment. *ESP Today*, 7(2), 165–181. https://doi.org/10.18485/esptoday.2019.7.2.3.

CHAPTER 33

Consequences, Impact, and Washback

Liying Cheng

Introduction

The prevalence of large-scale high-stakes testing and its impact on its stakeholders have been well documented in education. There are a set of relationships, intended and unintended, between testing, teaching, and learning that need to be considered. The phenomenon of testing consequences is not new; it has existed ever since the birth of modern testing. The core issue of this phenomenon resides in the use (or misuse) of test scores and the values and stakes attached to a test within society and within the teaching and learning context where a particular test exists. Given the range and extent of testing consequences reported worldwide, it is critical that testing practices yield valid data about student achievement and performance.

The term "consequences" is used as a general concept in educational assessment. It is therefore used in this chapter to discuss testing consequences in general. The terms "impact" and "washback" – both now commonly used in applied linguistics – are, however, used here as specific research concepts. Washback (also "backwash" in early literature) is a term used specifically in applied linguistics since the well-known and well-cited publication of "Does Washback Exist?" (see Alderson & Wall, 1993). Bachman and Palmer (1996) defined testing consequences as "test impact" – the effect that testing has on individuals (teachers and students), educational systems, and the society at large. They treat "impact" as one of the six qualities of test usefulness – reliability, construct validity, authenticity, interactiveness, impact, and practicality. McNamara (2000), however, used two terms to distinguish between two levels of this phenomenon: "impact" – the effects of tests on macro-levels of education and society, and "washback" – the effects of language tests on micro-levels of language teaching and learning inside the classroom. In this sense, the difference between impact and washback resides in the scope of the effects of testing – which gives us a view of test consequences falling between the narrower one of washback and the all-encompassing one of impact (see Hamp-Lyons, 1997). These two specific terms are discussed in this chapter as individual researchers use them. In addition, "testing" (or "tests") is used consistently in this chapter, where it bears a meaning similar to that of "examination," as cited by individual researchers. To note, the testing and examination practices referred to here are of a large-scale high-stakes nature. Consequences, impact, and washback of classroom-based teacher-led formative assessments are not discussed in this chapter as such issues require quite a different consideration (see Brookhart, 2004). It is possible that the consequences of

The Concise Companion to Language Assessment, First Edition. Edited by Antony John Kunnan.
© 2025 John Wiley & Sons, Inc. Published 2025 by John Wiley & Sons, Inc.

large-scale high-stakes testing could be lessened if more quality classroom-based teacher-led formative assessments were conducted in combination with large-scale high-stakes testing – a combination of assessment *for* learning and assessment *of* learning (see the section "Future Directions").

Considering the nature of testing consequences, Messick (1996, p. 243) regarded washback as "only one form of testing consequence that needs to be weighted in evaluating validity, and testing consequences are only one aspect of construct validity needing to be addressed." Messick also pointed out that the consequences of tests are likely to be a function of factors both within the test itself and within the setting of the test. He recommended the examination of the two threats to construct validity – construct under-representation and construct-irrelevant variance – in order to enhance the quality of the test and thus promote positive washback. Bailey (1996, p. 268), however, argued that any test, whether good or bad (in terms of validity), can have either negative or positive washback, depending on whether "it impedes or promotes the accomplishment of educational goals held by learners and/or program personnel." She focused on the specificity of this phenomenon, which could induce a differential impact on test stakeholders within a range of teaching and learning contexts – a view increasingly shared by many language testers (e.g., Cheng, 2008). In a sense, positive or negative washback is likely defined by test stakeholders, possibly differentially, as they see how a test serves its purposes and uses from their own points of view. More recently, Bachman (2005) proposed a validity framework with a set of principles and procedures for linking test scores and score-based inferences to test use and the consequences of test use – an area in which he argues for more research to be conducted.

In addition, testing consequences have increasingly been discussed from the point of view of critical language testing (Shohamy, 2001), which focuses on ethics and fairness in language testing (see Hamp-Lyons, 1997; Kunnan, 2004). Shohamy (2001) pointed out the political uses and abuses of language tests and calls for examining the hidden agendas of the testing industry and of high-stakes tests. Kunnan (2004) discussed the role of tests as instruments of social policy and control, drawing on research in ethics to link test validity and test consequences to create a test fairness framework. Hamp-Lyons (1997) argued for an encompassing ethics framework to examine the consequences of testing on language learning at the classroom and the educational, social, and political levels. The study of testing context is highlighted from this point of view.

The above literature has examined testing consequences either by using a theoretical framework focusing on test validity or by using a philosophical framework illustrating the social concerns of language testing. In order to provide a context for the discussion of the phenomenon of testing consequences, I will address below research literature derived from both the fields of educational assessment and applied linguistics, where language testing and assessment are situated. Further, in order to understand the relationship between testing, teaching, and learning within a society and a teaching and learning context, it is important to review the previous and current views of testing consequences, as well as the empirical research conducted in understanding this educational phenomenon. Due to the relatively short history of empirical research on impact and washback in applied linguistics, I will discuss the views and research published prior to and during the 1990s as *previous* and those in the 2000s as *current* views and research. The timing of this division is arbitrary, yet significant to the field of applied linguistics because the research in the 1990s had just started to explore the existence and nature of the phenomenon and its potential relationship with teaching and learning. The research in the 2000s has provided increasing empirical evidence about the nature and scope of the phenomenon from a range of teaching and learning contexts around the world. After that, I will present the current conceptualization of testing consequences, pose the challenges for conducting empirical research, and point out future research directions in the end.

Previous Views and Research

Testing consequences have been an issue of long-standing concern in education. The earliest literature can be traced back to Latham (1877), who referred to an examination system as an "encroaching power" and pointed out "how it influences the prevalent view of life and work among young men, and how it affects parents, teachers, the writers of educational books, and the notion of the public about education" in the United Kingdom (p. 2). Indeed, the use of examinations for selection purposes in education and employment has existed for a very long time. In many parts of the world, examinations were valued by society as ways to encourage the development of talent, to upgrade the performance of schools and colleges, and to counter to some degree nepotism, favoritism, and even outright corruption in the allocation of scarce opportunities, such as in the case of the imperial examinations in China (Eckstein & Noah, 1992). If the initial spread of examinations can be traced to the above, the very same reasons appear to be as powerful today as ever. Linn (2000) classified the use of tests and assessments as key elements in relation to five waves of educational reform over the past 50 years in the United States: their tracking and selecting role in the 1950s; their program accountability role in the 1960s; minimum competency testing in the 1970s; school and district accountability in the 1980s; and the standards-based accountability systems in the 1990s. Clearly, tests and assessments have played a crucial and critical role in education and society. Testing consequences are influenced by the ideological, social, and political milieu surrounding particular educational systems.

In spite of its long and well-established place in educational history, the use of tests has been constantly subject to criticism. Nevertheless, tests continue to occupy a leading place in the educational policies and practices of most countries around the world. Aware of the power of tests, policymakers in many parts of the world continue to use them to manipulate the local educational systems, to control curricula, and to impose (or promote) new textbooks and new teaching methods. Testing is "the darling of the policymakers" (Madaus, 1985, p. 5), and it would not be too much of an exaggeration to say that testing has become the engine for implementing educational policy despite the fact that tests have been the focus of controversy for as long as they have existed. One reason for their longevity in the face of such criticism is that tests are viewed as the primary tools through which changes in the educational system can be introduced without other educational components, such as teacher education and curricula, having to change – a naive and simplistic view of the power of testing practices. Shohamy et al. (1996, p. 299) pointed out the strong authority of external testing in a study conducted in Israel:

> the power and authority of tests enable policy-makers to use them as effective tools for controlling educational systems and prescribing the behavior of those who are affected by their results – administrators, teachers and students. School-wide exams are used by principals and administrators to enforce learning, while in classrooms, tests and quizzes are used by teachers to impose discipline and to motivate learning.

It is because of the potential and actual misuse of tests that washback has become a well-known concept in applied linguistics (now appearing in education literature). It is an increasingly prominent phenomenon in education, as what is assessed becomes what is valued and taught. Since the early 1990s, we have seen an increasing number of washback research studies conducted. There seem to be at least two major approaches of empirical studies to this phenomenon: an approach that relates to traditional, multiple choice, large-scale high-stakes tests, which are perceived to have had mainly negative influences on the quality of teaching and learning; and one where a specific test or examination has been introduced, modified, or improved upon in order for it to exert a positive influence on teaching and learning, e.g., communicative language teaching (see Wall & Alderson's, 1993 study in Sri Lanka). Studies in earlier applied linguistics literature in the 1990s fell mostly into this latter category. In this approach, researchers investigated how and what happened when a new or revised test was used to bring about changes in teaching and learning (see Cheng et al., 2004 – a collection of studies conducted in all major parts of the world). Further, most of these studies were conducted within the context of teaching English as a foreign language.

The work of Alderson and Wall (1993) and Wall and Alderson (1993) marked a significant development in shaping the constructs of washback studies for the field of language testing in this period. Alderson and Wall (1993) explored the potentially positive and negative relationships between testing, teaching, and learning. They questioned whether washback could be a property of test validity, as suggested by Messick (1989). They subsequently proposed 15 hypotheses regarding the potential influences of language testing on various aspects of language teaching and learning and posed the intriguing question: "Does washback exist?" Of the 15 hypotheses, half are about teaching and half on aspects of learning.

Prior to their major work, only a few empirical studies on washback had been published. Li's (1990) work is the first piece well known to the field of language testing for its delineation of how powerful a test can be in China. Morrow (1986, p. 6) adopted the concept of "washback validity" to describe the quality of the relationship between testing, teaching, and learning. He claims that "in essence an examination of washback validity would take testing researchers into the classroom in order to observe the effect of their tests in action." Accordingly, most of the earlier washback research had responded to the call by focusing on the classroom – most specifically on teachers, their teaching practices, their materials, and their methodology.

In 1996, a collection of the six most cited washback works was published in a special issue of *Language Testing*, volume 3, issue 3, edited by Alderson and Wall. Messick linked washback with validity, as mentioned above. Bailey, employing a model of washback, explored the nature of the phenomenon, the mechanism by which it worked, and how it could be investigated. The next three empirical studies were conducted by Alderson and Hamp-Lyons, who investigated how washback likely changed what teachers taught and how they taught; by Shohamy and colleagues on the differential stakes of testing; and by Watanabe on the teacher factor in washback research. The last paper, by Wall, explored why tests do not always have the effect we desire or fear they would have. Indeed, most of the studies conducted in the 1990s investigated the perceptions and practices of teachers (e.g., Alderson & Hamp-Lyons, 1996; Shohamy et al., 1996; Watanabe, 1996). However, much remains unknown about the washback effects of tests on learners and their learning processes. Of the 15 washback hypotheses proposed by Alderson and Wall (1993), eight are related to learners but very few of them were empirically examined in the 1990s. Meanwhile, empirical studies of testing consequences on parents and employers are almost nonexistent. These areas are, however, seen to be researched increasingly in the 2000s.

Current Views and Research

The 2000s witnessed an increasing number of research studies on the phenomenon of testing consequences. Major works included

- Cheng et al. (2004);
- another special issue on "investigating washback in language testing and assessment" in *Assessment in Education*, volume 14, issue 1, 2007, edited by Pauline Rea-Dickins and Catriona Scott; and
- a number of large-scale empirical studies published in the *Studies in Language Testing* (SILT) series (e.g., Cheng, 2005; Green, 2007; Hawkey, 2006; Wall, 2005).

500 Chapter 33 Consequences, Impact, and Washback

In addition, roughly more than 20 doctoral dissertations and 10 journal articles have been completed and published in applied linguistics journals including *Language Testing* and *Language Assessment Quarterly*. All these studies continued to investigate the influence of testing on various aspects of teaching, and increasingly on various aspects of learning. These studies also expanded our understanding of test impact on other testing stakeholders like parents (Cheng et al., 2011), employers (Pan, 2010), and publishers (Hawkey, 2006). In addition, more studies investigated the issue of test use using a validity framework (Abdul Kadir, 2008; Cheng et al., 2007; Wang, 2010; Xie, 2011).

The Cheng et al. (2004) review was the first systematic attempt to capture the essence of the washback phenomenon and has, through its collection of washback studies from around the world, responded to the question "what does washback look like?" (p. ix) – a step further from the question "does washback exist?" posed by Alderson and Wall (1993).

Four major sources of evidence have been produced over this period of time, predominantly in response to the question of what washback looks like in teaching and learning. First of all, we have empirical evidence that testing influences teaching. Language tests are seen to have a more direct washback effect on teaching content than on teaching methodology. For example, Alderson and Hamp-Lyons's (1996) washback study in the context of Test of English as a Foreign Language (TOEFL) preparation courses found that the TOEFL affected both *what* and *how* teachers taught; but the effect was not the same in degree or kind from teacher to teacher, and the simple difference between different types of courses – e.g., TOEFL versus non-TOEFL courses – did not explain why teachers taught the way they did. Over the years, a number of studies continued to investigate the influence of testing on teachers (including teaching assistants: see Saif, 2006), on teaching practices (see the works of Burrows, Ferman, Hayes, & Read, and Qi in Cheng et al., 2004),[1] and on textbooks (see Hawkey, 2006; Tsagari, 2007). Although the studies of textbooks are not encompassed by Alderson and Wall's 15 hypotheses, these studies indirectly investigated the *rate* and *sequence* as well as the *degree* and *depth* of teaching and learning (Alderson & Wall, 1993). However, these studies have not yet produced sufficient and direct evidence about the relationship between testing, teaching, and learning. Watanabe (1996, also in Cheng et al., 2004) was the first to point out that teacher factors, including personal beliefs, past education, and academic background, seemed to be more important in determining the teaching methodology a teacher employs. It is the teacher (who s/he is and what s/he brings as a teacher), rather than the testing, that decides how s/he teaches. In addition, washback studies have investigated other teacher- and teaching-related factors such as teacher ability, teacher understanding of the test and of the approach the test was based on, classroom conditions, lack of resources, and management practices within the school (see Tan, 2009; Wang, 2009, 2011; Yu, 2010). Among other teaching factors also studied are: the status of the subject being tested in the curriculum, feedback mechanisms between the testing agency and the school, and the time elapsed since the introduction of the test (see Tan, 2009; Yu, 2010); teacher style, commitment, and willingness to innovate (Cheng, 2005); teacher background (Watanabe in Cheng et al., 2004); the general social and political context (see Wall, 2005; Wang, 2009); and the role of publishers in material design and teacher training (see Cheng, 2005; Hawkey, 2006; Wall, 2005).

Second, compared with washback studies on teaching and teachers, the studies on learning and learners are still limited. Wall (2000) pointed out that, while it would be useful to continue to study the effects of tests on teaching, it is extremely important to investigate the effects on student learning, as students receive the most direct impact of testing. This reminds us that, if we wish to establish the relationship between testing, teaching, and learning, it is not sufficient only to study, indirectly along with other instructional variables, teaching and

---

[1]Individual studies in Cheng et al. (2004) are not cited in the reference list due to the limited number of references allowed in this companion.

the instructional context where learning is studied. So far we have seen a number of research studies conducted on the relationship between testing, learners, and their learning (see Andrews et al., 2002; Qi, 2007), students' attitudes toward testing (Cheng, 2005), and test preparation behaviors (Stoneman, 2006). For instance, in a recent investigation of stakeholder perceptions of test impact on learners in the primary school context in the United Kingdom, Scott (2007) found that the degree of test impact varied in different grades. The higher the grades, the more intensive the testing effects felt among the students. In another recent study, Qi (2007) examined students' perceptions of writing in comparison with those of the test constructors embodied in the writing task of the national matriculation English test in China. A mismatch was identified in relation to perceptions concerning writing. The test constructors' intention, as reflected in the input of the writing tasks, was that students would be encouraged to learn to write for communicative purposes. However, students were found to focus only on those aspects of writing that they believed would help achieve better scores, while neglecting the development of the ability to write communicatively in real-life situations. Andrews et al. (2002) studied a major examination change intended to bring about a positive washback on teaching and learning. They found that the introduction of the Use of English oral examination as a requirement for university admission in Hong Kong appeared to lead to general improvements in students' spoken performance; however, some students' inappropriate use of transitional words and discourse markers seemed to indicate a rote-learning of exam-targeted strategies and formulaic phrases rather than meaningful internalization. What needs further research in that context is the reason why students think that memorization can help them cope with a speaking exam. Though not discussed in the above two studies, these findings seem to suggest that students may not always fully understand the construct of a test. This may happen especially in the public exam context, where test-related information may not be directly accessible to students. In addition, students' perceptions of tests are likely to be shaped by the school context, for example, by students' teachers and peers. Therefore, it is important to examine not only what students understand about a test, but also how they obtain such knowledge.

In recent years, more attention has been paid to test the impact on students' learning practices and test preparation activities. Ferman (in Cheng et al., 2004), in a study investigating the washback of an oral examination on teaching and learning in Israel, found that intensive learning for the test is prevalent among students and that low-ability students tend to learn for the test more intensively than their high ability peers (see also Cheng et al., 2011), believing that cramming can help them achieve a better score. Also, not surprisingly, more students with low language ability than those with high language ability turn to private tutors for help. Such findings have resonance in Gosa's (2004) study within the Romanian context, which reported that students feel a strong need to practice exam tasks intensively and actually do so in their personal learning environment. Stoneman's (2006) study in Hong Kong provided further evidence that students faced with a high-stakes exam tended to choose activities mainly intended for test orientation or test-specific coaching. A contribution of her study to our knowledge about washback on learners is that students' past learning and test-taking experiences have a major influence on their choice of types of test preparation activities. Green (2007) emphasized that it is important for us to know how students understand test demands and whether/how that understanding is related to the test preparation practices they undertake. These studies discussed above suggest that washback on learners does not seem to be any simpler than it is on teachers. Tests used as an agent to promote desirable changes in learners and their learning may not necessarily be efficient tools for change and may not have the desired consequences predicted. The unpredictability of test washback on learners may be due to our lack of understanding about learners' beliefs and expectations in a testing situation (Stoneman, 2006). We need more direct research evidence, for example, student behavioral and test performance data, to demonstrate the relationship between testing and learning.

502 **Chapter 33** Consequences, Impact, and Washback

Third, another area that lacks empirical research is washback on parents (also on other stakeholders). The limited research in the literature shows that very often parents see the evaluative and normative values in the test results more than anything else (see James, 2000; Scott, 2007). According to Scott (2007), most parents have very little understanding of what tests usually entail and what the test information they receive actually means. James (2000) argued that the function of tests in reporting to parents about their children's learning progress remains unfulfilled. Contrary to what teachers believe, parents have been found to have an interest in knowing more about assessments and to feel responsible for helping their children prepare for exams. A recent study by Cheng et al. (2011) linked parent and student questionnaire responses toward an assessment change and found that parents' views were directly associated with the views of their children and with their children's perceptions of what they did in schools.

Lastly, since Shohamy et al. (1996) first pointed out that the degree of impact of a test is often influenced by several other contextual factors – the status of the subject matter tested, the nature of the test (low- or high-stakes), and the uses to which the test scores are put – a number of studies investigated the impact of test use (see Abdul Kadir, 2008; Cheng et al., 2007; Wang, 2010; Xie, 2011). These studies adopted the framework that testing consequences are part of test validity, and they responded to the call launched by Bachman (2005) when he proposed a framework with a set of principles and procedures for linking test scores and score-based inferences to test use and to the consequences of test use. For example, Cheng et al. (2007) conducted a multiphased mixed-method study investigating the impact of a large-scale literacy test on second language students in the province of Ontario in Canada. These second-language students come to the Ontario secondary school system from other countries and learn their school subjects in English as their additional language. Employing large data sets of student literacy test performance, the study has shown that testing constructs – represented by test formats, text types, skills, and strategies of reading, as well as by different writing tasks – impacted second language students differently and significantly in comparison with first language students (those who were born and grew up in Canada). The study also showed the direction of test impact and the specific areas of performance gaps of second language students. In addition, these students' after-school reading and writing activities predicated their reading and writing performance differently. Apart from linking learners' variables with their test performance, the researchers also used cognitive verbal protocols to listen to student accounts of their test-taking processes (Fox & Cheng, 2007). The findings can be used to inform test validity and to ensure that testing practices yield valid interpretations and uses of test data on the basis of student achievement and performance. This multiphased study investigated a wider range of cognitive and sociocultural variables in relation to test impact on students and on their literacy test performance. The study has investigated far more issues than the 15 washback hypotheses proposed by Alderson and Wall (1993) and has explored the relationship between testing, teaching, and learning by attempting to link test validity, test use, and the consequences of test use.

Current Conceptualization

Empirically, as mentioned above, researchers have studied washback of existing tests and have also explored the use of testing in bringing about new changes in language teaching and learning. The latter approach takes into account the value and stakes of testing in a particular social, teaching, and learning context. The consequences of testing have been closely associated with test validity (consequential validity) and, specifically, with the consequences of test use. Theoretically, the concept of consequential validity has been well argued for in Messick (1989, 1996); see also Cronbach, 1989; Kane, 2002). Messick's (1989) validity framework remains the most influential current theory of validity in language testing and assessment

(McNamara & Roever, 2006). This framework details two interconnected facets of the unitary validity concept. One facet is the source of the justification of testing, which is based on the appraisal of either evidence or consequence. The other facet is the function of the test score, which is either interpretation or use. Drawing on Messick's facets of the validity matrix (Messick, 1989),[2] Haladyna and Downing (2004) echoed the importance of collecting evidence that contributes to construct under-representation and construct-irrelevant variance in test performance. *Construct under-representation* involves error in test performance that is attributed directly to the measurement of the specific test construct, whereas *construct-irrelevant variance* involves factors that are disconnected from the test construct but influence test performance. For example, when a test designed for English for academic purposes and for university admission is used for job or professional certification purposes, construct under-representation could occur. When a test taker is too anxious due to social (e.g., family pressure), educational (e.g., entrance to university pending the score), and economic reasons (e.g., costly test registration fee), construct-irrelevant variance would likely contribute greatly to test performance. Construct-irrelevant variance also occurs when cultural and linguistic bias could potentially disadvantage certain subgroups of students (see Fox & Cheng, 2007). However, as pointed out by Loevinger (1957) more than 50 years ago, every test under-represents its constructs to some degree and contains sources of construct-irrelevant variance. What is needed in empirical research is the evidence on what specific constructs are under-represented and on what the sources of irrelevant variance are from multiple stakeholder perspectives.

Contemporary validation practices rely on multiple frameworks to establish evidence to justify score interpretation and test use. While some of these frameworks focus on establishing internal validity through an examination of psychometric processes within testing programs (Bachman, 2005), others maintain a broader scope, considering contextual factors and social consequences on test validity (see McNamara & Roever, 2006). Across these frameworks, there is a growing emphasis on collecting valid evidence from multiple stakeholders and by using multiple methods. For example, Moss et al. (2006) have suggested a hermeneutic methodology to access teachers' perspectives toward large-scale and classroom assessment practices. Kane (2002) used an argument-based model to systematically collect valid evidence at various assessment stages. Focusing on the assessment of language ability, Bachman (2005) has expanded upon this argument-based approach and has proposed the assessment use argument (AUA) framework, which links test scores to interpretations about language ability, and also explicitly links these interpretations to test use.

Challenges

Researchers have not yet been able to establish methodological frameworks for *how* to link test validation with test use in language testing and assessment. Further, the majority of previous studies on consequential validity have been conducted from the perspectives of test designers (Bachman, 2000), which focus on test validation and on the cognitive dimension of testing (see McNamara & Roever, 2006). Studies have rarely included the social dimension of language testing, despite the fact that washback is likely to be a function of factors both within the test itself and within the setting where the test is situated (see Messick, 1996). In fact, even fewer studies have considered both the cognitive dimension of language testing (e.g., the interaction of motivation and test anxiety with test takers' test performance) and its social dimension (e.g., potential test uses/misuses within a context) (see Cheng, 2008). These two

---

[2]Messick (1989) presented a 2 × 2 matrix, termed the *facets of validity matrix*. The matrix classified four aspects of validity, including evidential and consequential bases of test interpretation and test use. The latter portion is referred to as "consequential validity" in the literature.

504 **Chapter 33** Consequences, Impact, and Washback

dimensions can result in construct under-representation and in construct-irrelevant variance. So the challenges facing researchers as to how to empirically examine the link between test validation and test use remain.

Given the range and the extent of testing consequences, it is critical that testing practices yield valid data about student achievement and performance. Research in language assessment has demonstrated strong evidence of test validation from the perspective of test developers, albeit with foci exclusively on intended test uses and consequences. However, validity evidence from the perspectives of test takers is still limited in language assessment. Even fewer studies have included the perspectives of parents, employers, and other stakeholders. For example, the impact of public media on a testing context – the impact of how schools are ranked by newspapers – has rarely been studied. Further, only a few language assessment researchers have attempted to draw a link between test validation and test use. Bachman (2005, p. 7) observed that "the extensive research on validity and validation has tended to ignore test use, on the one hand, while discussions of test use and consequences have tended to ignore validity, on the other." The application of contemporary validity theory in educational assessment contexts (e.g., classroom assessment, large-scale achievement assessment, and dynamic assessment) has established grounds for the inclusion of consequences and uses within validation studies (see Kane, 2002, 2006; Messick, 1989, 1996). Specifically, there is an increasing recognition that constructs underrepresentation and construct-irrelevant variance, together with their attending factors – social consequences, test-taking experiences, and multiple test uses – contribute toward test validation (see Haladyna & Downing, 2004). Thus it is critical that the link between test validity and consequences of test use be established from multiple stakeholder perspectives within language assessment. Only then can we better justify the use of test scores in pedagogical practices. Moss et al. (2006) argued that validation studies must include multiple stakeholder perspectives in order to expose sources of evidence that would otherwise stand to invalidate test inferences and uses. If increased, and therefore more informative, measures of validity are desired, an under-representation of test takers' perspectives in language assessment contexts is clearly problematic. Validation evidence from test takers should include, for instance, an analysis of "how test-takers interpret test constructs and the interaction between these interpretations, test design, and accounts of classroom practice" (Fox & Cheng, 2007, p. 9). The same argument should apply to research on other testing stakeholders. The challenge remains as to how to delineate evidence that was collected from multiple stakeholders and by using multiple methods so as to justify the use of test scores. Criteria for such delineation could be epistemology, paradigms, methods, and funding, just to mention a few.

Future Directions

The phenomenon of testing consequences has existed for a long time and will remain for many years to come. Although empirical research on impact and washback is relatively recent in the field of applied linguistics, it is likely that such effects have occurred for an equally long time. It is also likely that these testing, teaching, and learning relationships are to become closer, more complex, and more contextual in the future, for example, with the increasing research on classroom assessment (see the two special issues, in *Language Testing* in 2004 and *Language Assessment Quarterly* in 2007). How can teaching and learning be understood in the current test-oriented pedagogical and assessment culture? And how can learner-centered and constructive learning take place in a test-oriented culture? What is the relationship between large-scale high-stakes testing and classroom-based teacher-led formative assessment? Research evidence in this area, though still limited to the field of applied linguistics, points out that classroom assessment (or assessment outcomes that are used formatively), when used appropriately, can better inform teachers for their curriculum planning and instruction and can better support student learning (see Andrade & Cizek, 2010). If this is true, such assessment practices should be able to minimize the negative consequences of our assessment practices. Teachers could be more willing to adopt quality formative assessment practices than simply to accept and mirror large-scale testing, which in many cases serves purposes beyond classroom practice. It is therefore essential that the members of the educational community (including all testing stakeholders) work together to understand and evaluate the consequences of testing on all of the interconnected aspects of teaching and learning within different education systems around the world. As pointed out earlier, the impact and washback of classroom-based assessments will likely be different from those of assessments derived from large-scale high-stakes testing, yet they may be equally complex, if not more so.

Researchers who are interested in conducting research in this area will first need to make deliberate attempt to understand the test they plan to investigate, e.g., by working with the test developers and in the context where the test exists. Their studies need to go beyond the micro-level of the classroom (washback) to the macro-level of society (impact), to analyze the social factors that lead to assessment practices in the first place and to explain why some forms of assessment practice (such as large-scale testing) are valued more than others. Their studies also need to link the use/misuse of test scores with what happens at the micro- and macro-levels of the context. Future research directions, based as they should be on contemporary validation practices, should employ multiple theoretical and conceptual frameworks to establish evidence to justify test score interpretation and test use. This means that empirical studies need to be conducted not only to establish internal validity through an examination of psychometric processes within a testing program (see Bachman, 2005), but also to consider contextual factors and social consequences of test validity (see McNamara & Roever, 2006). Only by doing so can we link test scores to interpretations about language ability within the teaching and learning context, and also explicitly link these interpretations to test use. Further, researchers will need to collect valid evidence from multiple stakeholders, and also by using multiple methods – including mixed methods explanatory, exploratory, and concurrent design. Methodologically, researchers must collect sufficient data; they must also attempt to link them from multiple stakeholder perspectives and by using multiple and/or mixed methods. Only then can we confidently make the claim that the testing consequences we find at the micro- and macro-levels are exclusively the results of a testing program, and confidently say what these consequences are.

Discussion Questions

1. What are the relationships among assessment (testing), teaching, and learning within your instructional context? What are the most important values held within your society (region and country) among assessment (testing), teaching, and learning three?

2. What are the key factors and who are key players in your instruction and societal context?

References

Abdul Kadir, K. (2008). *Framing a validity argument for test use and impact: The Malaysian public service experience (Unpublished doctoral dissertation)*. Urbana-Champaign: University of Illinois.

Alderson, J. C., & Hamp-Lyons, L. (1996). TOEFL preparation courses: a case study. *Language Testing, 13*, 280–297.

Alderson, J. C., & Wall, D. (1993). Does washback exist? *Applied Linguistics, 14*, 115–129.

Andrade, H., & Cizek, G. (Eds.). (2010). *Handbook of formative assessment*. New York, NY: Routledge.

Andrews, S. J., Fullilove, J., & Wong, Y. (2002). Targeting washback: a case study. *System, 30*, 207–233.

506 **Chapter 33** Consequences, Impact, and Washback

Bachman, L. F. (2000). Modern language testing at the turn of the century: assuring that what we count counts. *Language Testing, 17,* 1–42.

Bachman, L. F. (2005). Building and supporting a case for test use. *Language Assessment Quarterly, 2,* 1–34.

Bachman, L. F., & Palmer, A. S. (1996). *Language testing in practice.* Oxford, England: Oxford University Press.

Bailey, K. (1996). Working for washback: a review of the washback concept in language testing. *Language Testing, 13,* 257–279.

Brookhart, S. M. (2004). Classroom assessment: tensions and intersections in theory and practice. *Teachers College Record, 106*(3), 429–458.

Cheng, L. (2005). Changing language teaching through language testing: a washback study. In *Studies in language testing* (Vol. 21). Cambridge, England: Cambridge University Press.

Cheng, L. (2008). Washback, impact and consequences. In E. Shohamy & N. H. Hornberger (Eds.), *Encyclopedia of language and education. Vol. 7: Language testing and assessment* (2nd ed., pp. 349–364). New York, NY: Springer Science + Business Media LLC.

Cheng, L., Watanabe, Y., & Curtis, A. (Eds.). (2004). *Washback in language testing: Research contexts and methods.* Mahwah, NJ: Lawrence Erlbaum Associates.

Cheng, L., Klinger, D., & Zheng, Y. (2007). The challenges of the Ontario Secondary School Literacy Test for second language students. *Language Testing, 24*(2), 185–208.

Cheng, L., Andrews, S., & Yu, Y. (2011). Impact and consequences of school-based assessment in Hong Kong: views from students and their parents. *Language Testing, 28*(2), 221–250.

Cronbach, L. J. (1989). Construct validity after thirty years. In R. L. Linn (Ed.), *Intelligence: Measurement, theory, and public policy* (pp. 147–171). Urbana, IL: University of Illinois Press.

Eckstein, M. A., & Noah, H. J. (Eds.). (1992). *Examinations: Comparative and international studies.* Oxford, England: Pergamon Press.

Fox, J., & Cheng, L. (2007). Did we take the same test? Differing accounts of the Ontario Secondary School Literacy Test by first and second language test-takers. *Assessment in Education: Principles, Policy and Practice, 14*(1), 9–26.

Gosa, C. M. C. (2004). *Investigating washback: A case study using student diaries (Unpublished doctoral dissertation).* Lancaster University, England.

Green, A. B. (2007). *IELTS washback in context: Preparation for academic writing in higher education.* In *Studies in language testing* (Vol. 25). Cambridge, England: Cambridge University Press/Cambridge ESOL.

Haladyna, T. M., & Downing, S. M. (2004). Construct-irrelevant variance in high-stakes testing. *Educational Measurement: Issues and Practice, 23,* 17–27.

Hamp-Lyons, L. (1997). Washback, impact and validity: ethical concerns. *Language Testing, 14,* 295–303.

Hawkey, R. A. H. (2006). *Impact theory and practice: Studies of the IELTS test and Progetto Lingue 2000. Studies in language testing* (Vol. 24). Cambridge, England: Cambridge University Press/Cambridge ESOL.

James, M. (2000). Measured lives: the rise of assessment as the engine of change in English schools. *Curriculum Journal, 11*(3), 343–364.

Kane, M. (2002). Validating high-stakes testing programs. *Educational Measurement: Issues and Practices, 21*(1), 31–41.

Kane, M. T. (2006). Validation. In R. L. Brennan (Ed.), *Educational measurement* (4th ed., pp. 17–64). Westport, CT: American Council on Education.

Kunnan, A. J. (2004). Test fairness. In M. Milanovic, C. Weir & S. Bolton (Eds.), *European language testing in a global context: Selected papers from the ALTE conference in Barcelona* (pp. 27–48). Cambridge, England: Cambridge University Press.

Latham, H. (1877). *On the action of examinations considered as a means of selection.* Cambridge, England: Deighton, Bell and Company.

Li, X. J. (1990). How powerful can a language test be? The MET in China. *Journal of Multilingual and Multicultural Development, 11,* 393–404.

Linn, R. L. (2000). Assessments and accountability. *Educational Researcher, 29*(2), 4–16.

Loevinger, J. (1957). Objective tests as instruments of psychological theory. *Psychological Reports, 3,* 635–694.

References **507**

Madaus, G. F. (1985). Public policy and the testing profession: you've never had it so good? *Educational Measurement: Issues and Practice*, *4*(4), 5–11.

McNamara, T. (2000). *Language testing*. Oxford, England: Oxford University Press.

McNamara, T., & Roever, C. (2006). *Language testing: The social dimension*. Oxford, England: Blackwell Publishing.

Messick, S. (1989). Validity. In R. L. Linn (Ed.), *Educational measurement* (3rd ed., pp. 13–103). New York, NY: Macmillan.

Messick, S. (1996). Validity and washback in language testing. *Language Testing*, *13*, 243–256.

Morrow, K. (1986). The evaluation of tests of communicative performance. In M. Portal (Ed.), *Innovations in language testing: Proceedings of the IUS/NFER conference* (pp. 1–13). London, England: NFER/Nelson.

Moss, P. A., Girard, B. J., & Haniford, L. C. (2006). Validity in educational assessment. *Review of Research in Education*, *30*, 109–162.

Pan, Y. (2010). *Consequences of test use: Educational and societal effects of English certification exit requirements in Taiwan (Unpublished doctoral dissertation). Australia: University of Melbourne.*

Qi, L. (2007). Is testing an efficient agent for pedagogical change? Examining the intended washback of the writing task in a high-stakes English test in China. *Assessment in Education*, *14*(1), 51–74.

Saif, S. (2006). Aiming for positive washback: a case study of international teaching assistants. *Language Testing*, *23*(1), 1–34.

Scott, C. (2007). Stakeholder perceptions of test impact. *Assessment in Education*, *14*(1), 27–49.

Shohamy, E. (2001). *The power of tests: A critical perspective on the uses of language tests*. Essex, England: Longman.

Shohamy, E., Donitsa-Schmidt, S., & Ferman, I. (1996). Test impact revisited: washback effect over time. *Language Testing*, *13*, 298–317.

Stoneman, B. W. H. (2006). *The impact of an exit English test on Hong Kong undergraduates: A study investigating the effects of test status on students' test preparation behaviors (Unpublished doctoral dissertation). Hong Kong, China: Hong Kong Polytechnic University.*

Tan, M. H. (2009). *Changing the language of instruction for mathematics and science in Malaysia: The PPSMI policy and the washback effect of bilingual high-stakes secondary school exit exams (Unpublished doctoral dissertation). Montreal, Canada: University of McGill.*

Tsagari, D. (2007). *Investigating the washback effect of a high-stakes EFL exam in the Greek context: Participants' perceptions, material design and classroom applications (Unpublished doctoral dissertation). Lancashire, England: Lancaster University.*

Wall, D. (2000). The impact of high-stakes testing on teaching and learning: can this be predicted or controlled? *System*, *28*, 499–509.

Wall, D. (2005). The impact of high-stakes examinations on classroom teaching: a case study using insights from testing and innovation theory. In *Studies in language testing* (Vol. 22). Cambridge, England: Cambridge University Press.

Wall, D., & Alderson, J. C. (1993). Examining washback: the Sri Lankan impact study. *Language Testing*, *10*(1), 41–69.

Wang, W. (2009). *Teachers' beliefs and practices in the implementation of a new English curriculum in China: Case studies of four secondary school teachers (Unpublished doctoral dissertation). Hong Kong, China: University of Hong Kong.*

Wang, H. (2010). *Investigating the justifiability of an additional test use: An application of assessment use argument to an English as a foreign language test (Unpublished doctoral dissertation). Los Angeles: University of California.*

Wang, J. (2011). *A study of role of the "teacher factor" in washback (Unpublished doctoral dissertation). Montreal, Canada: University of McGill.*

Watanabe, Y. (1996). Does grammar translation come from the entrance examination? Preliminary findings from classroom-based research. *Language Testing*, *13*(3), 318–333.

Xie, Q. (2011). Is test taker perception of assessment related to construct validity? *International Journal of Testing*, *11*(4), 324–348.

Yu, Y. (2010). *The washback effects of school-based assessment on teaching and learning: A case study (Unpublished doctoral dissertation). Hong Kong, China: University of Hong Kong.*

Suggested Readings

Brunfaut, T. (2014). A lifetime of language testing: an interview with J. Charles Alderson. *Language Assessment Quarterly, 11*, 103–119. https://doi.org/10.1080/15434303.2013.869818.

Chapelle, C. A. (2020). An introduction to language testing's first virtual special issue: investigating consequences of language test use. *Language Testing, 37*, 638–645. https://doi.org/10.1177/0265532220928533.

Cheng, L., & Sultana, N. (2021). Washback: looking backward and forward. In G. Fulcher & L. Harding (Eds.), *Routledge handbook of language testing*. Routledge. https://doi.org/10.4324/9781003220756-12.

Cheng, L., Sun, Y., & Ma, J. (2015). Review of washback research literature within Kane's argument-based validation framework. *Language Teaching, 48*(4), 436–470.

CHAPTER 34

Language Testing in the Dock

Glenn Fulcher

Introduction

Language testing becomes embroiled in litigation whenever an individual from an identifiable subgroup of the test-taking population feels that they have been unfairly treated (Childs, 1990; Fulcher & Bamford, 1996). This normally means they believe that their score does not reflect their true ability. This state of affairs arises when a decision taken on the basis of a test score (and associated documentation) may deny them access to education, employment, or some other economically desirable opportunity. In technical terms, they believe they are a false negative: Their observed score was below the pass mark or cut score for an intended decision-making purpose, but their true score is higher.

This chapter investigates the relationship between language testing and the law. This begins with a consideration of the role of high-stakes testing as a social tool designed for allocating resources, and the values underlying current practices. When decisions are made about the future of individuals using tests, the question asked is whether these are "fair" or "just." Test takers may question the outcome of the test and litigation may follow. A range of situations are considered in which fairness or justice may be questioned and litigation has occurred or is likely to take place. Illustrative cases are discussed in order to explore emerging themes. These cases are drawn almost exclusively from the United States, with a smaller number from Europe, because these are the regions in which testing and assessment have been explicitly related to issues of discrimination, either in primary legislation or through precedent. Searches in legal databases such as Westlaw and Lexis Library reveal very little legal activity around testing and assessment in other countries, with the single exception of the prosecution for fraud of test takers or officials in cases of cheating.

The research reported in this chapter and the synthesis of key legal issues as they relate to testing and assessment are key resource for institutions and individuals involved in assessment development, test use and administration, and score reporting.

High-Stakes Decisions

High-stakes testing is an enterprise explicitly designed to classify or select individuals for decision-making purposes. For Plato (1987, p. 190), testing was used to ensure that members of the Republic could "devote their full energy to the one particular job for which they are naturally suited." This meant using tests and assessments to maintain social castes and ensure

---

The Concise Companion to Language Assessment, First Edition. Edited by Antony John Kunnan.
© 2025 John Wiley & Sons, Inc. Published 2025 by John Wiley & Sons, Inc.

510 Chapter 34 Language Testing in the Dock

that only the most able guardians became rulers. In ancient China, testing was the tool of choice to reduce the power of the aristocracy over the state, while maintaining traditional values in what knowledge was taught to the administrative classes (Miyazaki, 1981). These two examples illustrate the union of merit, social standing, and income, mediated by testing and assessment, that is foundational for the cultures of both East (Zeng, 1999) and West (Roach, 1971).

As a powerful social tool that allocates resources to individuals and brings opportunities in life, testing is also a value-laden enterprise. Our choices in how to use tests reveal our political and philosophical preferences (Fulcher, 2009), clearly exemplified by the haste with which the German Nazi party seized control of the examination system upon coming to power in 1933 (Cecil, 1971). This is clearly an extreme case, but it serves to demonstrate most vividly how testing and assessment, perhaps more than any other social tool, are both governed by, and revealing of, our beliefs and values.

E. M. Forster is reputed to have said:

> As long as learning is connected with earning, as long as certain jobs can only be reached through exams, so long must we take this examination system seriously. If another ladder to employment was contrived, much so-called education would disappear, and no one would be a penny the stupider.

The meritocratic view of the world that links effort to material success, and back to motivation to learn, is taken for granted today. It also provides the backdrop to notions of fairness and how perceived unfairness may be challenged.

Values and Fairness

What we value in our testing and assessment practices, and therefore how decisions are made, is intimately related to society's current sense of what is "fair." This is inherent when decisions are made that favor some – the successful – and disadvantage others – the unsuccessful. What we ask is "Is the decision fair?"

This raises the question of what "fairness" is, to which there are many different answers on offer. Messick (1988, p. 2) says:

> In general, fairness implies impartiality, and the question arises as to how fairness is manifested in educational and psychological measurement. In particular, the impartiality entailed in test fairness is achieved through comparable construct validity across individuals, groups, and settings. That is, score levels should have the same meaning and consequences in different population groups and environmental contexts. This does not imply that fair test use yields equal group outcomes, however, because fair tests may validly document unequal outcomes resulting from, among other things, unequal opportunities to learn as well as differential experiences in learning and development.

While "fairness" is notoriously difficult to define for the purposes of assessment (Camilli, 2006; Kunnan, 2000, 2004; Xi, 2010), its use in daily life is not (Walters, 2012, p. 469). In line with Messick, it is taken to mean "just and honest," "impartial," "unprejudiced," and "free from discrimination." For legal purposes, this is the heart of the matter. The law asks the question: "Does the process of assessment lead to discrimination against a subgroup of the test-taking population?" Much of the interface between assessment and the law is therefore concerned with discrimination. However, as Walters (2012, p. 470) points out, "What most language testing views of fairness have in common is a desire to avoid the effects of any construct-irrelevant factors on the entire testing process, from the test-design stage through post-administration decision making."

Discrimination and Bias **511**

This is the second principle that informs legal practice. Messick (1989, p. 34) describes construct irrelevance in terms of assessment contexts where "the test contains excess reliable variance that is irrelevant to the interpreted construct." This means that the scores of some individuals or groups may be artificially low because of what Carroll (1961/1965, p. 319) called "extraneous variables." Such variables may range from the conditions under which a test is administered, to test content that requires particular background knowledge, or sensitive content that is likely to cause offence or distress. The test is therefore seen as parallel to a controlled experiment for the findings to be meaningfully interpreted (Fulcher, 2010, pp. 254–260).

It is here that legal issues and litigation intersect with assessment theory and practice. If testing and assessment are used for classification and selection, the outcome of which is to distribute scarce resources and opportunities, it is inevitable that the fairness of the system will be questioned primarily by those who are classified unfavorably or are not selected. The law becomes interested in testing and assessment whenever it is asserted that practices are biased, prejudiced, or discriminatory.

Messick (1989, pp. 86–87) discusses the question as part of his conception of validity under the heading of the consequential basis of test use, which he explicates in terms of distributive justice (Rawls, 1971). Claims of injustice or unfairness may be targeted at:

- the rules by which the distribution is made;
- the implementation of the rules;
- the decision-making procedures; and
- the values underpinning the rules or procedures.

Examples of such claims will be investigated within a legal classification of the grounds for litigation, beginning with the most important, which is discrimination and bias. The vast majority of legal cases associated with testing and assessment fall into this category.

Discrimination and Bias

Discrimination is defined as denying equitable treatment, rights, benefits, or access to social goods, on the basis of a protected characteristic. This has two parts: what may not be denied, and those to whom it may not be denied. Most countries legislate to cover both parts. With regard to the first, the most relevant categories to language assessment are employment and education, although in Europe this is now impacting upon marriage and rights of residence (see the discussion below of *Chapti, Ali, & Bibi v. The Secretary of State for the Home Department*, 2011). With regard to the second, a protected characteristic is an identifiable attribute showing an individual to be a member of a particular group, which may not be used as a basis for decision-making. Under the 2010 Equality and Diversity Act in the United Kingdom, for example, protected characteristics included: age, disability, gender, gender reassignment, marriage or civil partnership, pregnancy and maternity, race, religion or belief, and sexual orientation. With these two aspects of discrimination clarified, it is possible to proceed to consider what would count as bias in language testing.

Cole and Moss (1989, p. 205) define bias in the following way:

> An inference is biased when it is not equally valid for different groups. Bias is present when a test score has meanings or implications for a relevant, definable subgroup of test takers that are different from the meanings or implications for the remainder of the test takers. Thus, *bias is differential validity of a given interpretation of a test score for any definable, relevant subgroup of test takers.* (Italics in original)

From a legal perspective, bias is an unequal outcome on a test for a subgroup of the test-taking population that is identified by a protected characteristic, *because of construct-irrelevant*

512 Chapter 34 Language Testing in the Dock

(*extraneous*) *factors*, and affects access to education or employment, or restricts civil rights. The following sections discuss the two protected characteristics that have attracted legal attention in the field of testing and assessment.

Ethnicity

The earliest legal cases were brought in the United States after the passage of the Civil Rights Act of 1964, of which Title VII abolished discriminatory employment practices, and the Fourteenth Amendment (see Phillips & Camara, 2006, for a detailed discussion of Title VII). *Hobson v. Hansen* (1967, 1969) set the trend, claiming that state tests systematically and unfairly placed Black children in remedial educational provision (Reschly et al., 1988a, pp. 16–17). In all subsequent cases in which the defendants were unable to show that bias was not the cause of observed differences between groups, the petitioners would win, as in the landmark case of *Larry P. v. Riles* (1984). As a result of this case, the use of IQ tests was banned in the United States due to the larger number of Black students classified as mentally retarded (MacMillan & Barlow, 1991; Prasse & Reschly, 1986; Reschly et al., 1988a, b, c). In *Larry P. v. Riles,* the court ruled that no attempt had been made to validate the use of the test (and hence comparable score meaning) for ethnic minorities, and that test content was culturally biased against them.

Perhaps the most important case in the United States was *Golden Rule Insurance Company v. Washburn/Mathias* in 1984. In 1975, the State of Illinois introduced an insurance agent licensing test that had been developed by the Educational Testing Service (ETS). The plaintiffs argued and eventually proved that the pass rates of White and Black test takers were of the order of 83% and 59%, respectively. This was ruled discriminatory, and as a result, testing agencies in the United States were obliged to report test statistics broken down by race and to conduct some form of differential item functioning for individual test items by ethnic group. Most importantly, it became a requirement to define the domain from which test content was derived and select questions written to domain specifications on the basis of (i) achieving predetermined minimum facility values for all test takers, and Black and White test takers separately and (ii) achieving a predetermined maximum difference in facility values for Black and White test takers (Shapiro et al., 1989).

However, as indicated in the above quotation from Messick, a difference in scores between test takers classified by protected characteristics is a necessary, but not sufficient, condition for the identification of bias. The observed (statistically significant) difference must be traced to a source of construct-irrelevant variance for bias to be proved. This principle was established in two important cases. In *Wards Cove Packing Co. v. Antonio* (1989), it was alleged that the salmon packing company had discriminatory appointments processes because low-paid cannery jobs were mostly filled with non-Whites, whereas more highly paid noncannery jobs were filled with Whites. The statistically significant difference, however, was held to be irrelevant, because the most appropriate space of events for an analysis of the probability of this distribution was not the employees of the packing company, but the population from which the workforce was drawn. That is, if the distribution of qualifications and abilities in the population was represented in the workforce, the unequal distribution would not be evidence of bias in the selection processes. It may very well tell the authorities something about the social and educational opportunities available to the different ethnic groups, but not about assessment bias.

Furthermore, the only way to achieve equality in this case would be to introduce ethnic quotas, and this would lead to having unqualified individuals in noncannery jobs. It was established that for the plaintiffs to be successful they would have to show that "specific practices by the state or the testing company caused the discrimination and had a specific impact on minorities" (Hood & Parker, 1991, p. 604). The second case is that of *Debra P. v. Turlington* (1981), in which it was argued that the State of Florida's Student Assessment Test (SSAT II), a test of functional literacy, discriminated against Blacks. The evidence was that fewer Blacks

Discrimination and Bias **513**

than Whites passed, and they were not therefore awarded a High School Diploma. The State of Florida undertook a survey of all schools to discover what teachers had done to prepare pupils for the test, and of students to find out if they thought they had been properly prepared. The court ruled that there was no evidence of bias in the test and that all pupils had been given appropriate opportunities to prepare. Thus, any attempt to produce equal pass rates would constitute a threat to the value of the High School Diploma. In this case, the variance associated with differential outcomes was deemed to be construct relevant.

These important cases have established the principle that equality of opportunity at the moment of testing is of primary concern, rather than equal outcomes. The legal issues arising from these cases may be summarized under the following three categories, annotated with reference to other relevant litigation.

The predictive aspect of validity

Wards Cove Packing Co. v. Antonio was also concerned with the relation between the method of assessment and the outcomes. However, it placed the burden of proof on the plaintiff. This was a change from the principle laid down in *Griggs v. Duke Power Co.* in 1971, that the burden of proof lay with the employer. Duke Power Co. had introduced the requirements of a High School Diploma and IQ testing for entrance to higher paid jobs, thus discriminating against Blacks in the population who had had an inferior education. A study showed that White employees who had been employed prior to the new requirements performed just as well as employees appointed after the introduction. It was concluded that the Diploma and the tests were not related to job performance and were therefore likely to discriminate against ethnic minority applicants. The court ruled that, if differential impact could be demonstrated, the burden of proof lay with the employer to justify the use of assessments as a "business necessity" (Crow, 2004). The Civil Rights Act of 1991 reinstated the Griggs principles, thus establishing "disparate impact" as grounds for litigation. This has not been used as much as a direct impact as grounds for litigation in succeeding years (Shoben, 2003), but it has established the principle that any assessment used for employment decisions must be shown to be directly relevant to, and predictive of, workplace performance.

The content aspect of validity

Wards Cove, Griggs, and other cases already mentioned illustrate the necessity for tests that are used for employment decisions to demonstrate content that is directly related to the domain of interest. In the Golden Rule case, plaintiffs claimed that the test allegedly contained many questions subject to different interpretations and different answers by individuals experienced and competent as insurance agents and brokers. Additionally, the exam allegedly tested levels of cognition of subject matter substantially and rationally unrelated to a determination of an applicant's competency as an insurance agent or broker. The plaintiffs alleged that the test was given without any job validation to determine whether in fact it appropriately measured competency to engage in the business of an insurance agent or broker and was not fairly designed to measure an applicant's competency. Instead, the test served as a method of artificially limiting and controlling the number of individuals entering the business of insurance agents or brokers without regard for competency (Shapiro et al., 1989, p. 244).

This aspect of the interface between language testing and the law is relevant to debates around the relevance of general language tests for domain-specific decisions, and the use of tests for specific purposes for which they were not designed (see test retrofit, below).

Test preparation

The Debra P. case has particular relevance to test preparation. First, the ruling established the principle that, if a new test is to be introduced or significant modifications are to be made to a test, the test developer must leave a reasonable period of time between publishing information on the changes and their introduction to allow teachers and learners time to adjust.

514 Chapter 34 Language Testing in the Dock

The principle should be that the changes themselves should not become a source of construct-irrelevant variance. Second, what is tested should be adequately reflected in educational materials and texts, thus providing equality of learning opportunity for all.

Disability

The second major area of concern to the law is the provision of equal opportunities for any test taker with a physical or learning disability. This is often enshrined in primary legislation. In the United States, this is the Americans with Disability Act, and in the United Kingdom the Disability and Equality Act. Legislation requires test providers to offer accommodations to any individual whose score on a test may be negatively affected by a disability unrelated to the construct of interest (Abedi, 2012). The most frequently granted accommodation is extended time, but may also include

a. someone to read the instructions or text in the test;
b. amanuensis for those unable to write or type responses;
c. Sign Language interpreter for spoken information;
d. audio recordings of written texts;
e. braille;
f. large print versions;
g. selectable font type and size (in computer-based tests); and
h. selectable colors (in computer-based tests).

The issue of construct-irrelevant variance is equally pertinent to disability. First, if a disability is construct relevant there is a case for denying an accommodation. If the test is one of listening, for example, it is arguably the case that Sign Language should not be offered as an alternative for the deaf as the construct definition is changed. Second, any accommodation offered to a test taker with a disability should not also significantly increase the scores of a test taker who does not suffer from that disability. Under this scenario, the accommodation itself impacts upon the construct. This particularly affects increased time, which may lead to all test takers improving their scores (Lovett, 2010). Accommodations are not always effective (Abedi, 2012), and so care should be taken in their use. Changes in the construct can result in score interpretations that are not equally valid across groups, thus introducing rather than eradicating discrimination.

However, the provision of accommodations has not been the focus of legal attention. Rather, it is the practice of "flagging." This is the procedure of noting on a score report the fact that a test taker has taken the test under a nonstandard condition, such as an accommodation, when there is no validation evidence to suggest that the construct has not been altered. The double negative is important here: If a nondisabled test taker may have benefited from the accommodation, the score obtained by the disabled test taker *may not* be completely comparable with that obtained by a non-disabled test taker without the accommodation. The score is therefore "flagged" for the score user, who is thereby warned of a potential problem with interpretation.

Flagging first came before the U.S. courts in the case of *Doe v. The National Board of Medical Examiners* in 1999, but it was *Breimhorst v. Educational Testing Service* (ETS) in 2000 that led to widespread changes in testing practice. Mark Breimhorst took the Scholastic Aptitude Test (SAT) with the accommodation of a trackball and additional test-taking time, with the purpose of applying to business school. His scorecard was flagged with the accommodations. Under the Americans with Disabilities Act, the first argument of the plaintiff was that flagging was an act of discrimination as it identifies and stigmatizes the test taker as disabled. Further, the act of flagging is contrary to the reason for providing the accommodation in the first place: to remove any effect of the disability from the score. In other words, the act of flagging by ETS suggests they suspect that their accommodations compromise the validity of their own test scores. Finally, the plaintiff argued that the policy of flagging intimidated the disabled into not requesting accommodations due to the knowledge that their disability would be disclosed through the flag. The court ruled that flagging violated the Americans with Disability Act.

Following this ruling the College Board, which owns the SAT, established the "Blue Ribbon Panel" of experts to make recommendations on flagging. In their review, Gregg et al. (2002) found that there was not sufficient validation evidence to suggest that scores from standard and accommodated administrations were comparable, but nevertheless recommended the abolition of flagging:

> Many students are reluctant to request extended time on the SAT I because the presence of the flag forces them to reveal a disability. Since the overwhelming majority of students who request extended time demonstrate learning disabilities, the presence of a flag denotes a special personal characteristic of the examinee – a learning disability. The detrimental effect of such a designation is further supported by findings that students with learning disabilities with flagged scores are under admitted to colleges. Thus, flagging appears to single out and treat the group with learning disabilities unequally, to diminish fair chances for college admission, and to discourage the use of a mandated ADA accommodation. The Majority concluded that there are situations when it is necessary to treat people differently in order to treat them equally, and that this is one of them.
>
> (Gregg et al., 2002, p. 10)

The recommendation was implemented in 2003, bringing flagging to an end. However, Leong (2005) reports on the unintended consequences of the abolition of flagging: the increased incentive for those without disabilities to seek a diagnosis as learning disabled in order to gain additional testing time. Applications for psychological assessment have risen significantly since 2003, primarily among those with the ability to pay, in the knowledge that the additional testing time will never be revealed. Leong expresses the concern that this provides additional advantages to those with socioeconomic backgrounds to manipulate the system. She suggests that the only solution to the problem is to make all tests non-speeded so that a time accommodation is not required, but suspects that the resource implications will deter test providers for the foreseeable future. In the meantime, testing agencies are tightening up on the kind of evidence for disability that they will accept before allowing accommodations.

Test Design and Retrofit

This section identifies two design issues that have arisen in some court cases: the use of inappropriate samples, and the use of tests for purposes different from those envisioned at the time of test design. This is likely to become an area of further concern and legal challenge in the future as testing agencies come to rely on standard-setting techniques as a defense for a change in test purpose without paying attention to the need for test retrofit.

Selection of Samples for Pretesting and Standard Setting

The law becomes interested in test design processes when a test or assessment is used to make high-stakes decisions about a population that was not intended, and not adequately represented in a sample used for preoperational testing (prototyping and piloting). In the case of *Larry P v. Riles* (1984), for example, the tests in question had been pretested on an all-White population, but subsequently used to make decisions about ethnic minority children.

This problem is exacerbated in standard-setting studies where the purpose of the test is being changed. The clearest example is in the use of academic English tests to make high-stakes judgments about the communicative abilities of health professionals. Failure to reach

516   Chapter 34 Language Testing in the Dock

cut scores on these tests can result in nurses being refused professional status (Castledine, 2000), or medical doctors being required to spend long periods of time studying a language not directly related to the medical domain (Cacanus, 2002). Such stories reach the popular press, as well as the courts. Some examination boards have resorted to standard-setting practices in order to legitimize the new test use. O'Neil et al. (2007, p. 295) explicitly state that standard setting is used to establish a "legally defensible passing standard on the test."

Standard setting is primarily a policy judgment informed by perceptual data, as frequently acknowledged by practitioners in the field:

> a passing standard is a function of informed professional judgment that relies on the panelists' content expertise and their experience with the abilities of the target examinee population. There are no passing standards that are empirically correct. A passing score reflects the values of those professionals who participate in its definition and adoption, and dif.ferent professionals may hold different sets of values.

> (O'Neil et al., 2007, p. 299)

Content experts were asked to make judgments about whether minimally competent health practitioners would answer a test item correctly. The average responses with the error estimates were used to arrive at cut scores. As part of the process, the panelists were shown item statistics from operational test data to help them modify their judgments. These data were drawn from the IELTS population at large (O'Neil et al., 2007, p. 304). They did not reflect the performance of medical personnel on the test, nor was there any group difference information regarding successful and nonsuccessful practitioners on the target criterion.

This use of standard setting would not provide the test users with a "legally defensible passing standard" were it to be challenged in the courts because of the very different samples, but the problem is much deeper than this.

"Repurposing" and Retrofit

The use of a test for a new (unintended) population, as in the case described above, is sometimes referred to as "repurposing" the test (Wendler & Powers, 2009). The content aspect of validity becomes critical in order to ensure that it is directly relevant to the domain of inference (Shapiro et al., 1989, pp. 223–224, 244) in order to avoid bias, as shown in the Griggs, Wards Cove, and Golden Rule cases.

As we saw in the previous section, the data that support a standard-setting judgment when attempting to repurpose a test are usually the perceptions of individual experts (language testing and content) of the likely outcome of a response to a given item by minimally competent practitioners. In the case of health professionals the IELTS has no content that is relevant to the specific needs of this population as outlined in table 3 of the paper (O'Neil et al., 2007, p. 303). For example, there are no reading tasks that measure the ability to understand medication lists or diagnostic reports. Expert judges are therefore being asked to decide how well a minimally competent nurse could perform on generic first-year university academic tasks, and an inference is being made from that judgment to how well they would perform medical communication tasks in a hospital or surgery.

This assumption would not stand up in court. It has recently been argued that any use of a test for a new population and decision context should be subject to retrofit procedures (Fulcher & Davidson, 2009; Fulcher, 2013). The minimum requirement of retrofit practice is that a new validation argument is constructed to support the use of the scores for the new intended use (AERA, 1999, pp. 17–18, Standards 1.1 and 1.4). However, it is much more likely that significant changes are required to test specifications and content in order to make that argument plausible.

Misclassification

The legal system has recognized that test scores do not provide certainty. Even if there is sufficient validation evidence for the use of a score for an intended purpose, there are always sources of unreliable variance. The legal system, at least, has heard the message of "inescapable error" (Spolsky, 1997, p. 246).

While test takers may be misclassified, there is also a notion of reasonable and unreasonable measurement/classification error. If the reliability of a test is known and published, it is unlikely that a challenge to a score would succeed if it fell within known error ranges and the rationale for establishing cut scores for specific decisions had been articulated in terms of the effects of false positives or false negatives on both individuals and the wider public. However, if it can be demonstrated that sources of error have not been identified and adequately dealt with, legal challenges are likely to succeed. The main areas for legal concern include taking appropriate measures to establish defensible cut scores (as discussed above), producing rating scales/scoring procedures that are not ambiguous or difficult to use, and training human raters to make consistent and construct-relevant decisions (Kleinman & Faley, 1985).

Any such claim must be related to an instance of disadvantage. One such case was reported in the Pakistan Times (2009): Dr. Jaffrey took an IELTS test in 2008 in order to apply for an Australian work visa. The score was below that required under Australian immigration law and Dr. Jaffrey appealed. Cambridge Assessment had the test rescored and the band was raised as a result, but not before the date for issuing the visa had passed (*Dr. Syed Jaffer Abbas Jafri v. The British Council and Others*, 2009). This case was unfortunately not heard; court records suggest that the lawyers and plaintiff did not appear at the required hearings and the case was dismissed. Similar misclassification concerns have been aired by judges in Australia (Lane, 2011) in cases where there was prima facie evidence that IELTS scores may have been unreliable, particularly where the plaintiffs had acquired degrees from English-medium universities. However, in all such cases to date, judges have ruled that internationally recognized tests are at least more likely to be reliable than other measures of proficiency.

Although no successful cases have been brought under the heading of misclassification because of unreasonable measurement error, this may be because language-testing experts have not been called as expert witnesses. This is an area in which future litigation may be successful unless test providers conduct and place into the public domain classification reliability data and risk estimates.

Immigration

A closely related area is that of immigration. The use of language tests to restrict immigration is rapidly growing around the world (Kunnan, 2012) and has proved to be highly controversial, not least because it is difficult to clearly identify key ethical principles upon which stakeholders can agree (Bishop, 2004). However, from a legal perspective, the key issue is likely to revolve around discrimination. The most important case to date is that of *Chapti, Ali, and Bibi v. The Secretary of State for the Home Department* (2011) in the United Kingdom. In 2010, new legislation was passed that required spouses of U.K. citizens to demonstrate a working knowledge of English before they were allowed to remain in the United Kingdom. In this case, it was claimed that the use of language tests for this policy purpose was an infringement of Articles 8 and 12 of the European Convention on Human Rights, which protect the right to marry and live together. It was further claimed that the law was discriminatory because it would have a differential impact on spouses from poor educational backgrounds, and countries where access to English learning opportunities are limited.

The key aspects of the defense were that Article 8 does "not oblige a state to respect the choice by married couples of the country of their matrimonial residence" (*Chapti, Ali, and*

518 **Chapter 34** Language Testing in the Dock

Bibi v. The Secretary of State for the Home Department, 2011, section 5), and as the plaintiffs had not lived with their spouses in the United Kingdom at the time of marriage the requirement that they pass a language test did not interfere with their married life. Evidence considered in favor of the defense included reports on the need to speak English for social integration, the cost of translation services for non-English speakers in public services, and research into employment rates among non-English-speaking immigrants. The central argument therefore was that there are good social reasons for using language tests to deny residence, and no violation of human rights had occurred. The entire case deserves close reading by applied linguists and language testers for the nuanced approach to the use of language in policy aims. However, the judge, Mr. Justice Beatson, commented in relation to discrimination:

> I first deal with direct discrimination. I have concluded (at [82]–[84]) that the aim of requiring a minimum level of English from those seeking entry as spouses of British citizens and other persons settled in the United Kingdom is a legitimate aim. Those who can speak English will have no difficulty in meeting it. Non-English speakers are not in a relevantly similar position to English speakers and it is rational to exempt those who do speak English to the required standard from the test. A lack of English is not an immutable characteristic like race or gender. A distinction based on it should not be regarded in the same way as they are; that is, accorded a "specially protected status", "special vigilance and a vigorous reaction", and require "very weighty reasons" in order to be justified.

(Ibid., p. 128)

> I turn to indirect discrimination. For the reasons in [140], I have not determined whether the new rule constitutes indirect discrimination on the ground of gender. In relation to the other categories, I have concluded that, while the rule has a disparate impact on some, that disparate impact arises from personal circumstances such as financial means, education or knowledge of English, and does not amount to discrimination contrary to Article 14.

(Ibid., p. 139)

These observations led to the ruling that the purpose served by the language tests was legitimately in the public interest and did not represent direct discrimination because it was not targeting a protected characteristic. Although there was evidence of indirect discrimination, this does not contravene human rights; it merely reflects the fact that those from disadvantaged backgrounds find it harder to obtain a share of the limited resources available. In legal terms, it may be of great social concern, but using a language test to limit their rights of residence is neither direct nor indirect discrimination.

There is evidence that this use of language testing spreads rapidly in times of economic turmoil and is therefore a topic that will dominate the pages of journals and newspapers for many years to come. The reasoning in this landmark case should be carefully studied and re-evaluated in light of new research and practices.

The Unusual Case of False Positives

There have been no legal cases to date regarding a test taker receiving a score higher than they should have done as a result of unreasonable error. In other words, they should have received a score below some cut score for decision making, but nevertheless "passed." It is not hard to see why this is the case given the previous discussion: There is no possible basis for a claim of discrimination.

Passing due to Error or Misuse

However, testing agencies and other professional bodies should not discount the possibility that litigation may happen at some point. The example of using IELTS to certify nurses and doctors to practice in the United Kingdom is apposite. The call for testing health professionals from the European Union working in the British National Health Service was a direct result of the death of a patient at the hands of a German doctor who did not have the language skills necessary to practice in the United Kingdom. New legislation establishes systematic language testing with decisions to be taken by "responsible officers" (BBC, 2012). The General Medical Council (GMC) has been given responsibility for the new system, and a tender to establish appropriate cut scores on the IELTS issued.

It is almost inevitable that a health professional who has achieved the cut score will at some point in the future be responsible for an error that will lead to medical tragedy. The family or a patient support agency may bring a case against the health professional, the GMC, or one of the responsible officers, on the grounds that the health professional was not able to communicate with the patient, understand medical records, or write out prescriptions or notes. Content and cut score issues will immediately be the evidential focus of the litigation, in addition to the reliability of classification. However, the challenge will be that the individual was a false positive, and should not have passed the test. Similar scenarios can be imagined for other high-stakes decision contexts, such as pilots and air traffic controllers. False-positives, in these cases, may clearly not be in the public interest.

Language testers and test providers should be very wary of the possibility of litigation related to false positives. A failure to take into account potential consequences could lead to those who conduct the standard-setting studies to be held personally responsible, and the test provider could face penalties for failure to advise what a test should not be used for.

Cheating

Cheating is an attempt to create false positives by an act of dishonesty on the part of a test taker, individuals employed by a testing agency, or their representatives. It is usually dealt with under fraud legislation. Cheating usually takes place in high-stakes contexts where the fear of being prosecuted is outweighed by the desire for economic or social benefits to be accrued by achieving a test score that appears unobtainable (Fulcher, 2011a).

Cheating takes many forms, such as the use of electronic devices to receive answers from outside the test venue, smuggling crib sheets into the test venue, and transmitting questions over time zones. Most recently the provision of "ghost writers," test-taker substitutes, has grown into a substantial business activity. On the provision side, there have been a number of cases of teachers changing student answers after the test, and providing copies of test papers prior to the test. The range of activities that attract prosecution is discussed and illustrated in Fulcher (2011b).

Test providers and those responsible for test delivery attempt to reduce the number of false positives created in this way by developing test security procedures that guarantee test confidentiality and ensure test-taker identity and score integrity throughout the assessment process. While there are numerous prosecutions of test takers and individuals who abuse the system each year, there have been no cases in which a test provider has been prosecuted for poor security systems. However, as language test use grows as a component of immigration policy, border agencies increasingly produce lists of tests that providers claim are "secure." This has pushed providers to invest in new security measures, such as biometric identification. It is therefore at least possible that lapses in security that allow false-positives may attract prosecution in the future.

Standards and Codes

Most of the issues raised in this chapter are covered to varying degrees by the standards and codes that have evolved to guide testing and assessment practice. Individual testing agencies produce standards for use within their own institutions, and internationally recognized standards are produced by organizations such as the International Language Testing Association (ILTA). However, it is the *Standards for Educational and Psychological Testing* (AERA, 1999) and its predecessors that are frequently cited in court. In many cases, including those involving flagging such as *Doe v. The National Board of Medical Examiners* (1999), the interpretation of the *Standards* has been a critical element in legal argument. It behoves testing and assessment producers to pay close attention to the *Standards* and to develop research agendas that address the key questions upon, which they are most likely to be at risk from litigation.

Conclusions

The law is relevant to language testing and educational assessment primarily when test use and interpretation give rise to the possibility of discrimination in decision-making. Whenever discrimination is suspected, specific aspects of current practice and test data become evidence in legal proceedings that challenge the fairness of outcomes. Litigation is usually motivated by the potential loss associated with unjustifiably low scores. In the future, there is additional potential for litigation to be associated with damage to the public good through misclassification.

Basic procedures to avoid bias and discrimination are built into routine testing and assessment practice, including content sensitivity and bias reviews during test development, and evaluation of differential item functioning in operational testing. New practices such as those associated with test retrofit (Fulcher, 2013; Fulcher & Davidson, 2009) will add to the language-testing tool kit.

When institutionalized, these will inevitably provide some defense against a charge of discrimination. However, it is unclear whether test providers, individual language-testing researchers, or nominated "responsible officers" have considered the breadth of potential sources and reasons for litigation in the field. With issues of fairness and accountability permeating every aspect of our societies, and the growing use of language testing in such a wide range of policy contexts, the escalation of litigation is inevitable. The research and synthesis of legal issues presented in this chapter, and an awareness of the relevant standards and codes, should inform a risk-aware approach to professional practice.

Discussion Questions

1. Imagine there is a testing institution that discriminates test takers based on race, gender, first language, marital status, or disability in your country, what are the grounds available to you for taking the testing institution to court?

2. Imagine a test that is designed for a particular purpose (such as for university admission) is used for another purpose (such as for healthcare employment). Decisions based on test taker scores result in some test takers feeling they were given an inappropriate test and thus discriminated against. Could this be grounds for litigation in your country?

References

Abedi, J. (2012). Validity issues in designing accommodations for English language learners. In G. Fulcher & F. Davidson (Eds.), *The Routledge handbook of language testing* (pp. 48–63). London, England: Routledge.

AERA. (1999). *Standards for educational and psychological testing*. Washington, DC: American Educational Research Association.

BBC. (2012). *Consultation over language tests for foreign doctors. Retrieved December 5, 2012, from* http://www.bbc.co.uk/news/uk-17746069.

Bishop, S. (2004). Thinking about professional ethics. *Language Assessment Quarterly, 1*(2–3), 109–122.

Cacanus, Z. (2002 July 1). *Starting all over again: refugees who have fled their country to stay alive face another tough test to continue a career.* London Evening Standard.

Camilli, G. (2006). Test fairness. In R. Brennan (Ed.), *Educational measurement* (4th ed., pp. 221–256). Westport, CT: American Council on Education/Praeger.

Carroll, J. B. (1961/1965). Fundamental considerations in testing for English language proficiency of foreign students. In H. B. Allen & R. N. Campbell (Eds.), *Teaching English as a second language: A book of readings* (pp. 313–330). New York, NY: McGraw-Hill.

Castledine, G. (2000). Nurses who seek to regain their professional status. *British Journal of Nursing, 9*(13), 821.

Cecil, R. (1971). *Education and elitism in Nazi Germany. ICR monograph series, 5.* London, England: Institute for Cultural Research.

Childs, R. A. (1990). *Legal issues in testing. Retrieved December 5, 2012 from* http://www.eric.ed.gov/PDFS/ED320964.pdf.

Cole, N., & Moss, P. (1989). Bias in test use. In R. L. Linn (Ed.), *Educational measurement* (3rd ed., pp. 201–219). New York, NY: Macmillan/American Council on Education.

Crow, A. (2004). May I speak? Issues raised by employer's English-only policies. *Journal of Corporation Law, 30*(3), 593–608.

Fulcher, G. (2009). Test use and political philosophy. *Annual Review of Applied Linguistics, 29*, 3–20.

Fulcher, G. (2010). *Practical language testing.* London, England: Hodder Education.

Fulcher, G. (2011a). *Cheating gives lie to our dependence on language testing. Retrieved December 5, 2012 from* http://www.guardian.co.uk/education/2011/oct/11/why-more-language-test-cheating?INTCMP=SRCH.

Fulcher, G. (2011b). *Cheating on language tests. Retrieved December 5, 2012 from* http://languagetesting.info/features/examination/cheating.php.

Fulcher, G. (2013). Test design and retrofit. In C. A. Chapelle (Ed.), *The encyclopedia of applied linguistics* (pp. 5809–5817). Malden, MA: Wiley-Blackwell.

Fulcher, G., & Bamford, R. (1996). I didn't get the grade I need. Where's my solicitor? *System, 24*(4), 437–448.

Fulcher, G., & Davidson, F. (2009). Test architecture, test retrofit. *Language Testing, 26*(1), 123–144.

Gregg, N., Mather, N., Shaywitz, S., & Sireci, S. (2002). *The flagging test scores of individuals with disabilities who are granted the accommodation of extended time: A report of the majority opinion of the Blue Ribbon Panel on flagging.* Washington, DC: The College Board.

Hood, S., & Parker, L. (1991). Minorities, teacher testing, and recent U.S. Supreme Court holdings: a regressive step. *Teachers College Record, 92*(4), 603–618.

Kleinman, L., & Faley, R. H. (1985). The implications of professional and legal guidelines for court decisions involving criterion-related validity: a review and analysis. *Personnel Psychology, 38*(4), 803–833.

Kunnan, A. J. (2000). Fairness and justice for all. In A. J. Kunnan (Ed.), *Fairness and validation in language assessment: Selected papers from the 19th Language Testing Research Colloquium, Orlando, Florida (Studies in language testing, 9)* (pp. 1–14). Cambridge, England: Cambridge University Press.

Kunnan, A. J. (2004). Test fairness. In M. Milanovic & C. Weir (Eds.), *European language testing in a global context: Proceedings of the ALTE Barcelona conference* (pp. 27–48). Cambridge, England: Cambridge University Press.

522   **Chapter 34** Language Testing in the Dock

Kunnan, A. J. (2012). Language assessment for immigration and citizenship. In G. Fulcher & F. Davidson (Eds.), *The Routledge handbook of language testing* (pp. 162–177). London, England: Routledge.

Lane, B. (2011). *Judges air concerns about English tests in visa cases. Retrieved December 5, 2012 from* http://www.theaustralian.com.au/higher-education/judges-air-concerns-about-english-tests-in-visa-cases/story-e6frgcjx-1226093298468.

Leong, N. (2005). Beyond Breimhorst: appropriate accommodation of students with learning disabilities on the SAT. *Stanford Law Review, 57*, 2135–2155.

Lovett, B. J. (2010). Extended time testing accommodations for students with disabilities: answers to five fundamental questions. *Review of Educational Research, 80*(4), 611–638.

MacMillan, D. L., & Barlow, I. H. (1991). Impact of Larry P. on educational programs and assessment practices in California. *Diagnostique, 17*(1), 57–69.

Messick, S. (1988). *Consequences of test interpretation and use: The fusion of validity and values in psychological assessment (ETS research report, 48). Princeton, NJ: Educational Testing Service. Retrieved December 5, 2012 from* http://www.ets.org/Media/Research/pdf/RR-98-48.pdf.

Messick, S. (1989). Validity. In R. L. Linn (Ed.), *Educational measurement* (3rd ed., pp. 13–103). New York, NY: Macmillan/American Council on Education.

Miyazaki, I. (1981). *China's examination hell: The civil service examinations of Imperial China*. New Haven, CT: Yale University Press.

O'Neil, T. R., Buckendahl, C. W., Plake, B. S., & Taylor, L. (2007). Recommending a nursing specific passing standard for the IELTS examination. *Language Assessment Quarterly, 4*(4), 295–317.

Pakistan Times (2009). *October 14. Citizen sues British Council/IELTS.*

Phillips, S. E., & Camara, W. J. (2006). Legal and ethical issues. In R. Brennan (Ed.), *Educational measurement* (4th ed., pp. 733–755). Westport, CT: American Council on Education/Praeger.

Plato. (1987). *The Republic (Desmond Lee, Trans., 2nd rev. ed.). London, England: Penguin Classics.*

Prasse, D. P., & Reschly, D. J. (1986). Larry P.: a case of segregation, testing, or program efficacy? *Exceptional Children, 52*(4), 333–346.

Rawls, J. A. (1971). *A theory of justice*. Cambridge, England: Cambridge University Press.

Reschly, D. J., Kicklighter, R., & McKee, P. (1988a). Recent placement litigation, Part I: regular education grouping: comparison of Marshall (1984, 1985) and Hobson (1967, 1969). *School Psychology Review, 17*(1), 9–21.

Reschly, D. J., Kicklighter, R., & McKee, P. (1988b). Recent placement litigation, Part II: minority EMR overrepresentation: comparison of Larry P. (1979, 1984, 1986) with Marshall (1984, 1985) and S-1 (1986). *School Psychology Review, 17*(1), 22–38.

Reschly, D. J., Kicklighter, R., & McKee, P. (1988c). Recent placement litigation, Part III: analysis of differences in Larry P., Marshall and S-1 and implications for future practices. *School Psychology Review, 17*(1), 39–50.

Roach, J. (1971). *Public examinations in England 1850–1900*. Cambridge, England: Cambridge University Press.

Shapiro, M. M., Slutsky, M. H., & Watt, R. F. (1989). Minimizing unnecessary differences in occupational testing. *Valparaiso University Law Review, 23*(3), 213–265.

Shoben, E. W. (2003). Disparate impact theory in employment discrimination: what's Griggs still good for? What not? *Brandeis Law Journal, 42*(3), 597–622.

Spolsky, B. (1997). The ethics of gatekeeping tests: what have we learned in a hundred years? *Language Testing, 14*(3), 242–247.

Walters, S. (2012). Fairness. In G. Fulcher & F. Davidson (Eds.), *The Routledge handbook of language testing* (pp. 469–478). London, England: Routledge.

Wendler, C., & Powers, D. (2009). *What does it mean to repurpose a test? Retrieved December 5, 2012 from* http://www.ets.org/Media/Research/pdf/RD_Connections9.pdf.

Xi, X. (2010). How do we go about investigating test fairness? *Language Testing, 27*(2), 147–170.

Zeng, K. (1999). *Dragon Gate: Competitive examinations and their consequences*. London, England: Cassell.

Case References

Breimhorst v. Educational Testing Service, *C-99-3387 WHO (N.D. Cal, March 27,* 2000).

Chapti, Ali, & Bibi v. The Secretary of State for the Home Department. (2011). Case in the High Court of Justice, Queen's Bench Division. Case No. [2011] EWHC 3370 (Admin).

Debra P. v. Turlington, *644 F.2d 397 (5th Cir.* 1981).

Doe v. The National Board of Medical Examiners (1999 *WL 997141 (E.D.Pa.)).*

Dr. Syed Jaffer Abbas Jafri v. The British Council and Others. Suit 1430/2009 (S.B.), Principal Seat Karachi (2009).

Golden Rule Insurance Company v. Washburn/Mathias, 419-76 Illinois Cir. Ct. (7th Ind. Cir. Ct. 1984).

Griggs v. Duke Power Co., *401 U.S. 424, 431-32* (1971).

Hobson v. Hansen, *269 F. Supp. 401 (D.D.C. 1967* 1969).

Larry P. v. Riles, *United States Court of Appeals, 793 F.2d 969 (9th Cir. 1984). Wards Cove Packing Co. v. Antonio, 490 US 642* (1989).

Suggested Readings

Bersoff, D. N. (1981). Testing and the law. *American Psychologist, 36*(10), 1047–1056.

Outtz, J. L. (2010). *Adverse impact: Implications for organizational staffing and high stakes selection.* London, England: Routledge.

Popham, W. J. (2012). *Assessment bias: How to banish it.* Boston, MA: Pearson. Retrieved December 5, 2012 from http://www.ati.pearson.com/downloads/chapters/Popham_Bias_BK04.pdf.

Sireci, S. G. (2005). Unlabeling the disabled: a perspective on flagging scores from accommodated test administrations. *Educational Researcher, 34*(1), 3–12.

THEME 7

Quantitative Research Methods

CHAPTER 35

Historical Overview of Classical Theory: Reliability

James Dean Brown

Introduction

When we measure anything, we need that measurement to be consistent. Let's say I go to the post office and hand the clerk a package. She weighs it and says it is one pound, but that I forgot the return address. I write the return address on the package, and she weighs it again saying that it is one and a half pounds. Should I think, *wow, that ink was heavy*? Or should I question the consistency of the scale she is using? This is exactly the sort of problem that this chapter addresses: How consistent are our measurements? However, here I am concerned not with the relatively trivial issue of consistency in weighing packages, but rather with the consistency, or reliability, of the important measurements that language-teaching professionals make in determining students' scores on tests. These measurements are important because they lead to decisions about college admissions, the level of placement in a language program, passing or failing a course, the grade a student will get in a course, and so forth. Clearly, we need these decisions to be reliable because they affect students' lives in important ways that can cost students time, money, opportunities, and so forth.

The purpose of this chapter is to define and discuss classical theory reliability approaches to test score consistency, with the ultimate goal of helping readers decide whether classical theory reliability is appropriate for their particular tests and score interpretations, and if so which classical theory reliability strategy they should use. While several formulas will be presented to illustrate conceptual issues, space precludes me from explaining in detail how to compute each and every reliability estimate that I cover. However, I will present conceptually important equations with example calculations and some explanation; I will also reference language-testing sources that readers can refer to for further explanations of how to compute the relevant statistics. All classical theory equations will appear in Roman letters and will be the simplest available version of each equation. While this chapter will assume minimal knowledge of descriptive statistics like the mean, the standard deviation, and test variance (i.e., the standard deviation squared), all other statistics will be defined as the discussion develops. To review basic descriptive statistics, see Bachman (2004, pp. 41–77) or Brown (2005, pp. 89–138).

The Concise Companion to Language Assessment, First Edition. Edited by Antony John Kunnan.
© 2025 John Wiley & Sons, Inc. Published 2025 by John Wiley & Sons, Inc.

528 Chapter 35 Historical Overview of Classical Theory: Reliability

Reliability and Norm-Referenced Testing

Norm-referenced tests (NRTs) focus on spreading examinees out along a continuum of scores so that educators can make grouping decisions about the examinees. Examples include language proficiency testing used to help in making admissions decisions (admit versus deny), and language placement tests used to determine the level that students should enter their language studies (e.g., beginning, intermediate, or advanced). Much program-level norm-referenced testing was developed and is conducted using *classical theory* (CT) statistics and methods of estimating reliability. Since CT formed the basis of psychometrics during much of the first half of the 20th century and is alive and well today (as argued in Brown, 2012), all language-teaching professionals interested in testing should understand these basics.

Within CT, reliability can be defined simply as the consistency of a set of test scores. CT reliability has typically been conceptualized, examined, and estimated in terms of psychological *constructs*. In language testing, we are usually interested in *language constructs* like overall English language proficiency, academic English ability, and so forth. As a result, within CT, we are often trying to measure differences among individuals in a particular construct. Test scores are then considered reliable if they are shown to be measured consistently.

It is important to note that, where reliability focuses on the consistency of the scores on a test, validity focuses on the degree to which the interpretations and uses of the scores on the test are appropriately related to the construct that the test designer purports to be measuring. Thus reliability and validity are different but related concepts. In a sense, reliability is a precondition for validity; that is, the scores on a test must first be reasonably consistent (and therefore systematic) before they can be shown to be systematically measuring what they are purported to measure.

It is also important to note that all of the concepts discussed in this chapter can, and often should, be applied to subtest scores as well as total test scores. Too often test developers look at the reliability of all of the items on a test without considering the reliabilities of the subtests for listening, reading, grammar, and so forth separately. For example, the Test of English as a Foreign Language Internet-based test (TOEFL iBT) score reliability was reported to be 0.87, 0.87, 0.86, 0.80, and 0.95 for the reading, listening, speaking, and writing subtests' scores and total scores, respectively (see table 1 on p. 7 at https://origin-www.ets.org/s/toefl/pdf/toefl_ibt_research_s1v3.pdf). Clearly, subtest and total test reliability estimates provide different but useful information, so it may be foolish to ignore either.

Some CT Background

Histories of CT usually begin with Pearson's groundbreaking (Pearson, 1896) demonstration that the best value for a correlation coefficient for two sets of numbers can be determined by dividing their covariance (i.e., the degree to which the two sets vary together) by the product of their two standard deviations (i.e., measures of how much each of the two sets of numbers is dispersed). A consensus was developing among scientists at that time that measurements were not perfect, that is, measurements contained error. CT developed out of these notions. A number of other striking moments occurred in the history of CT. Spearman (1904) used reliability estimates to correct for attenuation (i.e., for lack of reliability) for the first time. Brown (1910) and Spearman (1910) described how to calculate reliability from a single set of test items using what is commonly called the split-half reliability adjusted with the Spearman–Brown prophecy formula. Spearman (1913) systematized the basic principles of what we now call CT. Kuder and Richardson (1937) critiqued the existing reliability methods (i.e., split half and test–retest) and derived the now-famous KR-20 and KR-21 formulas. Guttman (1945) demonstrated that reliability estimates from a single administration of a test can be considered *lower bounds* estimates (i.e., underestimates) of the correlation between the examinees' observed scores and true scores, which means that any error in estimating the reliability should occur on the conservative side, that is, the estimates should be lower than or equal to the actual state of affairs. Cronbach (1951) first presented the famous alpha (α) reliability statistic and showed that under certain conditions (discussed below) α is equivalent to KR-20. Amusingly, Cronbach (in Cronbach & Shavelson, 2004) points out that:

> So many articles tried to offer sets of assumptions that would lead to the [same] result that there was a joke that "deriving K-R20 in new ways is the second favorite indoor sport of psychometricians." Those articles served no function once the general applicability of alpha was recognized. (p. 397)

All of these CT developments are explained at length in Lord and Novick (1968), and the development and nature of CT reliability are also described in depth in Stanley (1971), Feldt and Brennan (1989), and Haertel (2006).

The Basis of CT Reliability Theory

CT score reliability distinguishes between *observed scores*, which are the examinees' actual scores on a given test, and *errors*, which are random effects due to factors that are not being measured. The variation in observed scores, or the differences among examinees, is called *observed score variance*, and the variation in errors among examinees is called *error variance*. Such error variance is considered random because it comes from nonsystematic sources that are extraneous to testing purposes. Brown (2005, pp. 171–175) lists a number of error sources that may not be accounted for in the environment (e.g., noise, lack of space, high or low temperatures, and lack of lighting), administration procedures (e.g., faulty equipment, unclear directions, and differences in timing), scoring procedures (mathematical errors in calculating scores, or rater subjectivity and biases), test items (e.g., low item quality, item types unfamiliar to some examinees, and lax test security), or examinees (e.g., poor health, fatigue, and lack of motivation).

True scores are the theoretical results that would be obtained if there were no errors in measurement. *True score variance* is the variation among examinees that would occur if there were no errors in measurement. A *true score* can be conceptualized as follows: "Roughly speaking, the person's *true score* is the average score he or she would obtain on a great number of independent applications of the measuring instrument" (Cronbach & Shavelson, 2004, p. 395). If a set of observed scores is completely random, the *true score variance* will theoretically be 0% and *error variance* will be 100%. However, since any test is designed to measure some construct, it is much more likely that at least some portion of the observed score variance will be attributable to true abilities in that construct. Hence, some portion of the variation in observed scores is likely to be true score variance and some proportion error variance. Conceptually, those relationships are often represented as follows:

$$\text{Observed score variance} = \text{True score variance} + \text{Error variance}$$

The CT framework for reliability is based on the observation that the proportion of observed score variance attributable to true score variance is the *proportion of reliable variance* and the rest is error variance. For example, if the reliability of the scores on a test is reported to be 0.95, this means that the proportion of reliable variance was 0.95 (or 95%), and the rest, 0.05 (or 5%), is error.

Within this CT framework, two types of approaches are traditionally used to examine reliability statistically: proportions-of-reliability approaches and error-estimation approaches. The remainder of this chapter will be divided into two sections explaining those two approaches (for more information on CT reliability in language testing, see Bachman, 2004, pp. 153–191; Brown, 2005, pp. 169–198).

530 **Chapter 35** Historical Overview of Classical Theory: Reliability

Proportions-of-Reliability Approaches

Most often, the reliability of a set of scores is reported as a proportion on a scale of 0.00–1.00, indicating that the scores are not consistent at all (0.00, or 0%) or completely consistent (1.00, or 100%), or somewhere in between. For instance, say the reliability for a set of scores is 0.85. That means that the scores are 85% reliable (and by extension 15% unreliable). But is 0.85 good enough? Shrout (1998, p. 308) suggested some rule-of-thumb standards for interpreting reliability estimates:

0.00 to 0.10	virtually none
0.11 to 0.40	slight
0.41 to 0.60	fair
0.61 to 0.80	moderate
0.81 to 1.00	substantial

I personally interpret reliability estimates more conservatively, something like:

0.00 to 0.30	virtually none
0.31 to 0.50	slight
0.51 to 0.70	fair
0.71 to 0.89	moderate
0.90 to 1.00	substantial

Since such interpretations depend heavily on additional information like the type of test, test length, testing conditions, and so forth, language professionals will have to decide for themselves how to take all of the relevant factors into consideration in interpreting particular reliability estimates.

Four proportions-of-reliability strategies are commonly used for estimating CT reliability: test–retest, equivalent forms, internal consistency, and rater.

Test–Retest Reliability

Test–retest reliability addresses the consistency of a set of test scores over time. The tester begins by administering the items to the same group of examinees twice with testing sessions far enough apart so examinees won't remember the test items, and yet close enough together so they are not likely to have learned anything substantial related to the items. A *Pearson product–moment correlation coefficient* is then calculated between the two sets of scores (henceforth referred to simply as *correlation coefficient*; for more on this concept and instructions for calculating it by hand, see Bachman, 2004, pp. 78–109; or with a spreadsheet program, see Brown, 2005, pp. 139–162). This correlation coefficient provides a test–retest reliability estimate, which represents the proportion of reliable (or true score) variance over time for the scores. This approach is conceptually fairly easy to understand, but it has the drawback that the examinees must take the same test twice.

Equivalent-Forms Reliability

Traditionally, *equivalent-forms reliability* addresses the stability of test items across forms. It requires developing two equivalent tests and administering them to a single group of examinees. Next a correlation coefficient is calculated for the two sets of resulting scores.

Proportions-of-Reliability Approaches **531**

This coefficient provides an equivalent-forms reliability estimate that indicates the proportion of reliable (or true score) variance on either form of the test. This approach is conceptually fairly easy to understand. However, it has the drawbacks of requiring that the examinees take two very similar tests and that the two forms are equivalent.

Internal-Consistency Reliability

In order to overcome the drawbacks of test–retest and equivalent-forms reliabilities, test designers most often use *internal-consistency reliability*, which has the distinct advantages of being based on only one test form and only one test administration. Internal-consistency reliability estimates come in many forms, but the most common are splithalf, Kuder–Richardson formulas 20 and 21, and Cronbach's alpha reliabilities.

Split-half reliability is conceptually the simplest internal-consistency strategy. It is similar to the equivalent-forms strategy except that the equivalent forms in this case are created by separating a single test into two equal parts, usually by scoring the odd-numbered and even-numbered items separately for each examinee. The tester then calculates a correlation coefficient between the odd-numbered and even-numbered scores and that provides an estimate of the reliability for either the odd-numbered scores or the even-numbered scores. However, since testers are normally interested in the full-test reliability (i.e., the scores for all items combined) and since a longer test is typically more reliable than a short one, an adjustment must be made to the half-test correlation using the *Spearman–Brown prophecy formula* (Brown, 1910; Spearman, 1910) in order to estimate the full-test reliability. That formula is

$$r_{xx'} = \frac{2r}{1+r}$$

where $r_{xx'}$ = full-test reliability and r = half-test reliability. For example, consider a 30-item test that has a half-test (15-item) reliability of 0.80. The full-test (30-item) reliability would be

$$r_{xx'} = \frac{2r}{1+r} = \frac{2.80}{1+0.80} = \frac{1.60}{1.80} = 0.8888 \approx 0.89$$

A more general version of the Spearman–Brown prophecy formula can be used for estimating the reliability of a test that is increased in length by any number of times (e.g., 3 times, 4 times, 2.5 times, etc.):

$$r_{xx'} = \frac{nr}{(n-1)r+1}$$

where the symbols are the same except for n = number of times length is increased. For instance, for the same example, let's say that we want to make it a 45-item test and would like to estimate the reliability that we are likely to get if all other factors except length are held constant. In this case, 45 is three times ($n = 3$) as long as the half-test reliability of 15, so the adjustment would be:

$$r_{xx'} = \frac{nr}{(n-1)r+1} = \frac{3.60}{(3-1)0.60+1} = \frac{2.40}{(2)0.80+1} = \frac{2.40}{1.60+1} = \frac{2.40}{2.60} = 0.9231 \approx 0.92$$

For more on calculating split half reliability, see Bachman (2004, pp. 161–162), Bachman and Kunnan (2005, p. 86), or Brown (2005, pp. 176–179, 190–192).

532 Chapter 35 Historical Overview of Classical Theory: Reliability

Rulon (1939) offered an alternative formula for calculating split-half reliability that is slightly easier to calculate because it avoids the Spearman–Brown adjustment:

$$r_{xx'\text{Rulon}} = 2\left(1 - \frac{S_{\text{odd}}^2 + S_{\text{even}}^2}{S_{\text{total}}^2}\right)$$

where $r_{xx'\text{Rulon}}$ = Rulon's split-half reliability for the full test; S_{odd} = standard deviation for the odd-numbered items; S_{even} = standard deviation for the even-numbered items; and S_{total} = standard deviation for the total test scores. Like the regular split-half estimate, Rulon's method has the drawback that it requires scoring the test three times: once each for the odd, even, and total scores. Rulon's method also assumes that the two halves have equal covariances. For example, say the test above turned out to have $S_{\text{odd}} = 3.92$, $S_{\text{even}} = 4.15$, and $S_{\text{total}} = 7.11$. Then:

$$r_{xx'\text{Rulon}} = 2\left(1 - \frac{S_{\text{odd}}^2 + S_{\text{even}}^2}{S_{\text{total}}^2}\right) = 2\left(1 - \frac{3.92^2 + 4.15^2}{7.11^2}\right) = 2\left(1 - \frac{15.37 + 17.22}{50.55}\right)$$

$$= 2\left(1 - \frac{32.59}{50.55}\right) = 2(1 - 0.6447) = 0.7106 \approx 0.71$$

For more on calculating split half reliability this way, see Bachman (2004, p. 162) and Bachman and Kunnan (2005, pp. 84–85), where it is called the Guttman split half in both cases; or Brown (2005, p. 174), where it was labeled *Cronbach α* because Cronbach (1970, p. 161) called it α_2, which "is really just the first α_k formula, with $k = 2$," and because it was easier to calculate than the original alpha equation.[1]

Kuder–Richardson formulas 20 and 21 (KR-20 and KR-21, respectively) are widely taught and used in language testing (for the original derivation, see Kuder & Richardson, 1937). KR-21 is the easiest of the two to calculate because it only requires knowing the number of items (k), as well as the mean (M) and the standard deviation (S) for the total test scores. It can be expressed as follows:

$$KR-21 = \frac{k}{k-1}\left(1 - \frac{M(k-M)}{kS^2}\right)$$

Consider a test where $k = 50$, $M = 24.91$, and $S = 8.12$. The KR-21 reliability in this case would be:

$$KR-21 = \frac{k}{k-1}\left(1 - \frac{M(k-M)}{kS^2}\right) = \frac{50}{50-1}\left(1 - \frac{24.91(50-24.91)}{50(8.12^2)}\right)$$

$$= 1.0204\left(1 - \frac{24.91(25.09)}{50(65.93)}\right) = 1.0204\left(1 - \frac{624.99}{3296.5}\right)$$

$$= 1.0204(1 - 0.1896) = 1.0204(0.8104) = 0.8269 \approx 0.83$$

---

[1]Note that there is some confusion in the labeling of these formulas in both Bachman (2004) and Brown (2005), which is not to say that either is wrong, but rather that the literature (especially when using secondary sources) is sometimes very confusing. For example, for the equation labeled $r_{xx'\text{Rulon}}$ in this chapter, Rulon (1939) is the earliest primary source I was able to locate, but he attributed it to Flanagan, and Guttman (1945) published an algebraically equivalent formula. So is it Rulon, or Flanagan, or Guttman? I chose Rulon because he published my earliest primary source. The bottom line is that the labels and equations used in this chapter have been checked against primary sources and are my current best shot at getting all of this right.

Proportions-of-Reliability Approaches **533**

KR-20 is somewhat more difficult to calculate because it involves item-level computations, but it does provide a more accurate (sometimes much more accurate) estimate of reliability than KR-21. KR-20 is often given as follows:

$$KR-20 = \frac{k}{k-1}\left(1 - \frac{\Sigma p(1-p)}{S^2}\right)$$

where k = number of items; Σ = sum, or add up; p = proportion answering each item correctly; and S^2 = total score variance. The hard part is calculating $\Sigma p(1 - p)$, which is done as follows: the item facility (p) must be calculated for each item, then subtracted from 1.00; then the result of $(1 - p)$ is multiplied times p for each item. For example, if $p = 0.40$, $(1 - p) = 0.60$ and $0.40 \times 0.60 = 0.2400$. That needs to be done for each item on the test. Then to get $\Sigma p(1 - p)$, the individual item results must be added up. With that sum in hand, the tester is ready for the final steps in calculating KR-20. For example, for a test with 50 items (k), where $\Sigma p(1 - p) = 8.99$, and $S = 7.94$, KR-20 would be:

$$KR-20 = \frac{k}{k-1}\left(1 - \frac{\Sigma p(1-p)}{S^2}\right) = \frac{50}{50-1}\left(1 - \frac{8.99}{7.94^2}\right) = 1.0204\left(1 - \frac{8.99}{63.0436}\right)$$
$$= 1.0204(1 - 0.1426) = 0.8748 \approx 0.87$$

Both KR-20 and KR-21 have the limitation that they can only be applied to items that are dichotomously scored (i.e., right or wrong). KR-21 additionally assumes that items are of equal difficulty, which is sometimes far from true in language testing. For example, the item difficulties in cloze tests often vary wildly from 0.00 to 1.00 (i.e., everyone answering incorrectly to everyone answering correctly, respectively); such violations of the assumption can cause serious underestimates of reliability when using KR-21 as compared to other strategies (Brown, 2005, p. 181). For more on calculating KR-20 and KR-21, see Bachman (2004, pp. 163–164), or for a spreadsheet approach, see Brown (2005, pp. 179–185, 193–195).

Cronbach's alpha (α) is the most commonly reported internal-consistency estimate in language testing and research, probably because it is flexible (i.e., it can be applied to items that are scored right or wrong, but also to items that are not dichotomously scored, e.g., weighted items, Likert scales, etc.). Other reasons for the apparent pre-eminence of Cronbach's alpha (or simply "alpha") in CT are described by Cronbach (in Cronbach & Shavelson, 2004, p. 396):

> One of the bits of new knowledge I was able to offer in my 1951 article was a proof that coefficient alpha gave a result identical with the average coefficient that would be obtained if every possible split of a test were made and a coefficient calculated for every split. Moreover, my formula was identical to K-R 20 when it was applied to items scored one and zero. This, then, made alpha seem preeminent among internal consistency techniques.

Thus, alpha is equivalent to KR-20 when applied to dichotomously scored items but is also more flexible. The original Cronbach (1951) alpha equation was

$$\alpha = \frac{k}{k-1}\left(1 - \frac{\Sigma S_i^2}{S_t^2}\right)$$

where k = number of items; Σ = sum or add up; S_i^2 = item variances (item standard deviation squared); and S_t^2 = total score variance (test score standard deviation squared).

534   Chapter 35 Historical Overview of Classical Theory: Reliability

If the same dichotomously scored item data were used to calculate α that was used above to calculate KR-20, $\Sigma p(1 - p)$ would equal $\Sigma S_i^2 = 8.99$ and S would equal $S_t = 7.94$, and of course, there would still be 50 items, so the result would be exactly the same for KR-20 and α, as follows:

$$\alpha = \frac{k}{k-1}\left(1-\frac{\Sigma S_i^2}{S_t^2}\right)=\frac{50}{50-1}\left(1-\frac{8.99}{7.94^2}\right)=1.0204\left(1-\frac{8.99}{63.0436}\right)$$
$$=1.0204\left(1-0.1426\right)=0.8748 \approx 0.87$$

However, calculating ΣS^2 would mean calculating the standard deviation and then squaring it for each and every item, then adding them up. For dichotomously scored items (coded 1 for correct and 0 for incorrect), the result would be the same as for $\Sigma p(1 - p)$. However, if the data were for items with weighted scoring, say 2 for factually and grammatically correct, 1 for factually correct, and 0 for completely incorrect, only ΣS_i^2 could be calculated, and therefore only α is applicable if the items are not dichotomously scored. Note that calculating either ΣS_i^2 or $\Sigma p(1 - p)$ by hand takes inordinate amounts of time (see Brown, 2005, pp. 181–185), but it can be done quickly in a spreadsheet program (as explained in Brown, 2005, pp. 193–195). In addition, for those who have it available, the SPSS statistical program can be used to calculate α and several of the other reliability estimates discussed here (as shown in Bachman & Kunnan, 2005, pp. 83–84). Additional information about alpha is available in Bachman (2004, pp. 163, 170). Note also that, because α can handle weighted scores, it can also be used for ratings, as explained below.

Rater Reliability

Rater reliability is a common concern in language testing because situations are common where raters are asked to make judgments about the language performances of examinees (e.g., examinees' productive speaking and writing skills as in essay writing, oral interviews, role plays, task performance, etc.). Within CT, such reliability estimates typically take the form of inter-rater, intra-rater, or alpha reliability estimates.

Inter-rater reliability is calculated by lining up the scores produced by two raters for a single group of examinees and calculating a correlation coefficient between those two sets of scores. The resulting coefficient provides an estimate of the inter-rater reliability of the ratings of either rater. If the scores are to be added up or averaged and then serve as the basis for decision-making, the tester may wish to use the first Spearman–Brown prophecy formula described above to estimate the two-rater reliability (or use the more general formula to estimate reliability for other multiples like three or four raters). Inter-rater reliability coefficients provide estimates of the reliability of judgments between raters. For instance, let's say that the correlation between the ratings assigned to a set of compositions by Randy and Jeanne produces a correlation coefficient of 0.63. That would indicate that either Randy's ratings or Jeanne's ratings are 63% reliable (and 37% unreliable). If that is not a satisfactory level of reliability in a given situation, they might consider adding their ratings together (or averaging them) for each student, in which case the Spearman–Brown prophecy formula could be used to estimate the reliability for both raters combined as follows:

$$r_{xx'} = \frac{2r}{1+r}=\frac{2\times.63}{1+0.63}=\frac{1.26}{1.63}=0.7730 \approx 0.77$$

If they were thinking about the possibility of bringing in more raters, they could also estimate what the reliability would be for three raters, four raters, and so forth, based on their

Proportions-of-Reliability Approaches **535**

current data, by using the more complex Spearman–Brown prophecy formula discussed earlier in the chapter.

Intra-rater reliability is calculated in a similar manner. However, the two sets of scores are produced by the same rater for a single group of examinees on two separate occasions, followed by calculating a correlation coefficient for the two sets of scores. That coefficient provides an estimate of the intra-rater reliability of the ratings on either of the two occasions. However, if the two sets of ratings are to be added up or averaged and then serve as the basis for decision-making, again, the tester may wish to use the Spearman–Brown prophecy formula described above to estimate the reliability for the two ratings taken together. Intra-rater reliability coefficients provide estimates of the reliability of a rater's judgments over time. For instance, let's say that Randy must also rate a set of interviews that he taped with students, but he cannot coerce Jeanne into doing the ratings too. So he rates the interviews on two occasions one week apart. He can then calculate the correlation coefficient between his two sets of interview ratings to determine the single-occasion reliability. Let's say that turns out to be 0.73. If that level of reliability does not seem satisfactory to Randy, he might consider adding his ratings from the two occasions together (or averaging them) for each student. Again, the Spearman–Brown prophecy formula could be used to estimate the reliability of the scores combined from both rating occasions as follows:

$$r_{xx'} = \frac{2r}{1+r} = \frac{2 \times .73}{1+0.73} = \frac{1.46}{1.73} = 0.8439 \approx 0.84$$

Randy could also estimate what the reliability would be for three occasions, four occasions, and so forth, based on his current data, by using the more complex Spearman–Brown prophecy formula discussed earlier in the chapter.

Using *alpha for ratings* is another possibility. If the scores assigned by each rater are viewed as items, then the standard deviations for each rater's scores can be squared and added up as follows:

$$\Sigma_r^2 = S_{r1}^2 + S_{r2}^2 + S_{r3}^2 + S_{r4}^2$$

Since ΣS_r^2 is the same conceptually as ΣS_i^2,

$$\alpha = \frac{k}{k-1}\left(1 - \frac{\Sigma S_i^2}{S_t^2}\right) = \frac{k}{k-1}\left(1 - \frac{\Sigma S_r^2}{S_t^2}\right)$$

For example, consider a situation in which four raters (so $k = 4$) on a 6-point holistic rating scale for a possible total of 24 points assigned scores to 30 compositions, where the standard deviation for the total scores (S_t^2) was 3.96 for the four raters' scores combined, where the standard deviations for the four sets of ratings separately were 1.11, 1.06, 1.23, and 1.01, respectively, and where the squared values of those standard deviations were 1.2321, 1.1236, 1.5129, and 1.0201, respectively, and their sum (ΣS_r^2) was 4.8887. In that case:

$$\alpha = \frac{k}{k-1}\left(1 - \frac{\Sigma S_i^2}{S_t^2}\right) = \frac{k}{k-1}\left(1 - \frac{\Sigma S_r^2}{S_t^2}\right) = \frac{4}{4-1}\left(1 - \frac{4.887}{3.96^2}\right) = 1.33\left(1 - \frac{4.88}{15.6816}\right)$$
$$= 1.33(1 - 0.3116) = 0.9516 \approx 0.92$$

Clearly, Cronbach's α is very flexible, since it is applicable not only to dichotomously scored tests (as are the KR-20 and -21 internal-consistency estimates), but also to tests with weighted

536   Chapter 35 Historical Overview of Classical Theory: Reliability

scoring schemes, and to ratings. This flexibility also means that α is applicable to questionnaire data like Likert scales. All in all, α is a very useful tool for language testers and researchers. Unfortunately, it is more difficult to calculate by hand than some of the other reliability estimates, but with minimal skills in a spreadsheet program like Excel, the calculations are relatively easy, and for those who know how to use the SPSS statistical program, α is very easy to calculate (see Bachman & Kunnan, 2005, pp. 83–84). For more on rater reliability, see Bachman (2004, pp. 169–170) or Brown (2005, pp. 185–188).

Error-Estimation Approaches

Reliability estimates help testers examine the proportion of consistent variance on a test. However, another, more practical and perhaps more useful, way to examine the consistency of a set of scores is to estimate the amount of error in test score points by calculating the *standard error of measurement* (SEM):

$$SEM = S\sqrt{1 - r_{xx'}}$$

where S = the standard deviation of the scores on a test and $r_{xx'}$ = the reliability estimate for those scores. Consider a test that has $S = 6.34$ and $r_{xx'} = 0.87$. The SEM would be:

$$SEM = S\sqrt{1 - r_{xx'}} = 6.34\sqrt{1 - 0.87} = 6.34\sqrt{0.13} = 6.34(0.3606) = 2.2862 \approx 2.29$$

The resulting SEM of 2.29 can be used to further estimate *confidence intervals* (CIs) that indicate how many score points of variation can be expected with 68%, 95%, or 98% probability (based on percentages under the normal distribution) around any given point (e.g., a cut point). Let's say that the SEM for that test with the SEM of 2.29 points had a cut point for passing the test of 55. The tester will know that the score for any examinee falling within one SEM plus or minus (55 + 2.29 = 57.29; 55 − 2.29 = 52.71; or a band from 52.71 to 57.29) is likely to fluctuate within that band 68% of the time by chance alone if the test were administered repeatedly. Similarly, any examinee falling within two SEMs plus or minus (2 × 2.29 = 4.58; 55 + 4.58 = 59.58; 55 − 4.58 = 50.42; or a band from 50.42 to 59.58) is likely to fluctuate within that band 95% of the time by chance alone, and an examinee falling within three SEMs plus or minus (3 × 2.29 = 6.87; 55 + 6.87 = 61.87; 55 − 6.87 = 48.13; or a band from 48.13 to 61.87) is likely to fluctuate within that band 98% of the time. Practically speaking, testers may want to at least consider gathering additional information about any examinees who have scores within the band of plus or minus one SEM of any cut point in order to increase the reliability of the decision-making. Whether the tester decides to choose a 68%, 95%, or 98% CI is a judgment call.

For example, let's consider a placement test that has scores ranging from 20 to 80 and a cut point of 60 between the intermediate and advanced level English as a second language (ESL) courses. The test designer dutifully calculates the SEM and finds that it is 4.33. He then informs the decision makers that they should gather additional information (e.g., additional test scores, a writing sample, an interview, etc.) for any examinee falling within the 68% confidence interval between 55.67 and 64.33 (i.e., 60 − 4.33 = 55.67; 60 + 4.33 = 64.33) to make reasonably sure the placement decisions for these particular examinees are consistent and accurate.

For additional information on SEM, see Bachman (2004, pp. 171–174) or Brown (2005, pp. 188–190, 193–195).

Conclusions

Table 35.1 summarizes the material in this chapter, but with an eye to helping readers determine which reliability statistic(s) they might want to use in a given testing situation. That said, it is important to first recognize that this chapter, and therefore the table, only cover the reliability of NRTs as analyzed within CT. However, NRTs are common and CT statistics are relatively easy to understand and calculate. For readers who prefer ease of understanding and calculation and who want to analyze the reliability of NRTs from a CT perspective, this chapter and table are perfect. If, however, ease of understanding and calculation are not crucial and readers are interested in (i) analyzing NRTs from a more sophisticated point of view where sources of measurement error can be studied and accounted for, (ii) investigating the dependability of their criterion-referenced test scores, or (iii) studying the dependability of the decisions they are making at certain cut points, then, other more complex methods of analysis are available that will better serve their purposes. So the first decision in selecting the form of reliability analysis is to decide whether to use this chapter or the other more complex methods.

For those readers who have decided on this chapter, the next step is to look at column one of Table 35.1 and decide on the form of the estimate, that is, whether they are interested in the proportion of reliability of their test or in an estimate of the amount of error in test score points. If the goal is to find out the proportion of reliability, then the reader must decide which strategy to use: test–retest, equivalent forms, internal consistency, or rater reliability. Then, for example, if readers choose the internal consistency reliability strategy, the next step is to examine the specific statistics available and read through the pros and cons of each. From all of that, readers should be able to decide what the most appropriate statistic would be for their purposes. Referring back to the associated section of the chapter will provide the appropriate equation(s), show how to do the actual calculations, and supply additional references on the specific statistic so the reader can easily find further information if needed.

For example, let's say a group of teachers is interested in using a reliability statistic that is relatively easy to understand and calculate for a set of NRT placement test scores, and that they are interested in both the proportion-of-reliability and the error-estimation forms. After reading through the specific statistics column as well as the pros and cons, they decided to use the internal-consistency type that is easiest (i.e., requires only one administration of one test and is relatively easy to calculate); the table indicates that KR-21 would be appropriate but warns in the last column that the items must be dichotomously scored and be of about equal difficulty. These teachers also decide to use the SEM and CIs, and then refer back to the appropriate sections of the chapter and are able to calculate both KR-21 and the SEM and use the SEM by interpreting it in terms of CIs for their placement test. It turns out that KR-21 = 0.92 and the SEM = 4.18. These results tell them that their scores are substantially reliable and, because they only need the 68% CI, they realize that they should gather additional information about any students within a range of plus or minus one SEM of 4.18 points of any cut point. Thus these teachers are able to make more reliable and professional decisions.

Alternatively, the table can be used to quickly learn about any of the specific reliability statistics by searching it out in column three and reading the material to the left and right of it in the same row. For instance, say the reader wants to remember what KR-20 is. Reading to the left, it is clearly a proportion-of-reliability statistic that estimates the internal consistency of a set of scores. Reading to the right, KR-20 can be used for a single test administered once, is accurate, is appropriate only for dichotomously scored items, and is relatively difficult to calculate.

TABLE **35.1**

Selecting the appropriate reliability strategy

Form of estimate	Reliability strategy	Specific statistic	Pros	Cons
Proportion-of-reliability	Test–retest	Correlation coefficient for scores from test administered twice	Conceptually clear	Must administer the same test twice to same examinees
	Equivalent-forms	Correlation for scores on two equivalent forms administered	Conceptually clear	Typically done by developing two equivalent tests and administering both to same examinees
	Internal-consistency	Split half $r_{xx'}$	One administration and one test; Conceptually easy	Must score separate halves and total; Spearman–Brown needed for full-test reliability
		Rulon's split half $r_{xx'Rulon}$	One administration and one test; Fewer steps than plain split-half	Must score separate halves and total; Assumes equal covariances
		Kuder–Richardson formula 21 (KR-21)	One administration and one test; Relatively easy to calculate	Only for dichotomous items; may seriously underestimate if equal item difficulty assumption not met
		Kuder–Richardson formula 20 (KR-20) Cronbach's alpha (α)	One administration and one test; Accurate One administration and one test; Accurate and flexible (complex scoring possible)	Only for dichotomous items; Relatively difficult to calculate Relatively difficult to calculate
	Rater	Inter-rater reliability is correlation between scores produced by two raters	Conceptually clear because similar to equivalent-forms reliability	Must use Spearman–Brown for two (or more) rater reliability
		Intra-rater reliability is correlation of scores produced by same rater twice	Conceptually clear because similar to test–retest reliability	Must use Spearman–Brown for two (or more) occasion reliability
		Alpha α for ratings	One administration and one test; Accurate and flexible (complex scoring possible)	Relatively difficult to calculate
Error-estimation	Standard error and confidence intervals	Calculate SEM and use	Conceptually clearer than the proportion of reliability	A step beyond reliability; subject to same cons as reliability estimate used
		CIs at 68%, 95%, or 98% in decision making		

Factors Affecting the Reliability of NRTs

For readers who would like to maximize the possibility of reliability in their test scores, it is worth considering factors that might affect reliability. Both Bachman (2004, pp. 190, 204–205) and Brown (2005, pp. 171–175, 222) discuss factors that affect the reliability of NRTs. Here, I will combine, reorganize, and liberally adapt from those observations. To begin with, in planning, developing, revising, implementing, and interpreting the test items, sources of error should be minimized in the environment, administration procedures, scoring procedures, test items, and examinees. In addition, the possibility of high reliability will be maximized for any set of test scores by making sure the test is as long as is reasonable (without sacrificing the quality of the items), is well written and designed, and is as homogeneous in what it tests as makes sense in the situation. In addition, reliability will be maximized if items are selected for the test that have been shown to discriminate (between the high- and low-achieving students), if the distribution of total scores is normal, and if the examinees to whom the items are administered range in ability as widely as makes sense in the particular testing situation.

Again, I remind readers that score reliability and validity are different concepts. Reliability is concerned with the consistency of scores on a test, while validity is focused on the degree to which the interpretations and score uses are appropriately related to the construct that the test designer purports to be measuring. In addition, reliability is a reasonable precondition for validity, that is, the scores on a test must logically be consistent before they can be shown to be consistently measuring what they are purported to measure.

Future Directions

I have shown in this chapter how research and practice in CT reliability for NRTs have developed and changed over time and how they stand today in language testing. Such developments will no doubt continue. In my view, the language-testing community would benefit from further developing some or all of the following topics:

1. What are the effects on reliability for test scores that are made up of testlets (collections of items considered together as units or clusters, e.g., the items associated with a particular reading passage, those associated with a specific listening test lecture, etc.)?
2. The importance of using the SEM and CI in interpreting and using reliable information. As Cronbach (in Cronbach & Shavelson, 2004, p. 413) put it:
    "I am convinced that the standard error of measurement is the most important single piece of information to report regarding an instrument, and not a coefficient.
    The standard error, which is a report on the uncertainty associated with each score, is easily understood not only by professional test interpreters but also by educators and other persons unschooled in statistical theory, and also to lay persons to whom scores are reported."
3. The benefits of examining *conditional errors* in language testing. One of the great benefits often touted for item response theory (IRT) is that, unlike the CT SEM, which is the same at all score levels, IRT can supply estimates of measurement error for each score level. This state of affairs is true for the CT SEM because generally only *unconditional errors* (i.e., errors that are assumed to be the same for all examinees) have been considered, but if *conditional errors* (i.e., errors that vary depending on examinees' true scores) are considered, language testers will indeed be able to estimate errors at each score level within a CT framework (see Haertel, 2006, pp. 82–84, 98–99; Qualls-Payne, 1992). Clearly, research examining applications of errors conditioned on true scores would be useful in language testing.

540 Chapter 35 Historical Overview of Classical Theory: Reliability

Discussion Questions

1. Why is reliability important in CT?
2. How is reliability a precondition for validity in CT?

References

Bachman, L. F. (2004). *Statistical analyses for language assessment*. Cambridge University Press.

Bachman, L. F., & Kunnan, A. J. (2005). *Statistical analyses for language assessment workbook and CD ROM*. Cambridge University Press.

Brown, W. (1910). Some experimental results in the correlation of mental abilities. *British Journal of Psychology, 3*, 296–322.

Brown, J. D. (2005). *Testing in language programs: A comprehensive guide to English language assessment*. McGraw-Hill.

Brown, J. D. (2012). Classical test theory. In G. Fulcher & F. Davidson (Eds.), *Routledge handbook of language testing* (pp. 303–315). Routledge.

Cronbach, L. J. (1951). Coefficient alpha and the internal structure of tests. *Psychometrika, 16*(3), 297–334.

Cronbach, L. J. (1970). *Essentials of psychological testing* (3rd ed.). Harper & Row.

Cronbach, L. J., & Shavelson, R. J. (2004). My current thoughts on coefficient alpha and successor procedures. *Educational and Psychological Measurement, 64*, 391–418.

Feldt, L. S., & Brennan, R. L. (1989). Reliability. In R. L. Linn (Ed.), *Educational measurement* (3rd ed., pp. 105–146). American Council on Education/Collier Macmillan.

Guttman, L. A. (1945). A basis for analyzing test–retest reliability. *Psychometrika, 10*, 255–282.

Haertel, E. H. (2006). Reliability. In R. L. Linn (Ed.), *Educational measurement* (4th ed., pp. 65–110). American Council on Education/Praeger.

Kuder, G. F., & Richardson, M. W. (1937). The theory of estimation of test reliability. *Psychometrika, 2*, 151–160.

Lord, F. M., & Novick, M. R. (1968). *Statistical theories of mental test scores*. Addison-Wesley.

Pearson, K. (1896). Mathematical contributions to the theory of evolution: on a form of spurious correlation which may arise when indices are used in the measurement of organs. *Proceedings of the Royal Society of London, 60*, 489–498.

Qualls-Payne, A. L. (1992). A comparison of score level estimates of the standard error of measurement. *Journal of Educational Measurement, 29*, 213–225.

Rulon, P. J. (1939). A simplified procedure for determining the reliability of a test by split halves. *Harvard Educational Review, 9*, 99–103.

Shrout, P. E. (1998). Measurement reliability and agreement in psychiatry. *Statistical Methods in Medical Research, 7*, 201–317.

Spearman, C. (1904). The proof and measurement of association between two things. *American Journal of Psychology, 15*, 72–101.

Spearman, C. (1910). Correlation calculated from faulty data. *British Journal of Psychology, 3*, 271–295.

Spearman, C. (1913). Correlations of sums or differences. *British Journal of Psychology, 5*, 417–476.

Stanley, J. C. (1971). Reliability. In R. L. Thorndike (Ed.), *Educational measurement* (2nd ed., pp. 359–442). American Council on Education.

Suggested Readings

Cronbach, L. J. (1947). Test "reliability": its meaning and determination. *Psychometrika, 12*(1), 1–16.

Novick, M. R. (1966). The axioms and principal results of classical test theory. *Journal of Mathematical Psychology, 3*, 1–8.

Traub, R. E. (2005). Classical test theory in historical perspective. *Educational Measurement: Issues and Practice, 16*(4), 8–14.

CHAPTER 36

Classical Test Theory – Reliability

Yasuyo Sawaki

Introduction

Classical test theory (CTT) is a measurement theory that developed over the last century and has been used widely ever since, as a framework for examining the precision of measurements obtained from various types of tests. While other complex measurement theories have been developed more recently, knowledge of CTT remains fundamental to their understanding. Quite often, a CTT analysis of assessment data provides us with valuable information as to whether examinee performance data for a target ability of interest, obtained from a given test, are of high enough quality for further score interpretation. Accordingly, CTT data analyses play important roles in constructing and validating tests as well as in interpreting and using test scores in practice. While CTT is a broad framework that deals with test reliability, validity, and test construction (Allen & Yen, 1979), this chapter focuses specifically on how test reliability is conceptualized in CTT.

Key CTT Concepts

Fundamental CTT Equations

Suppose that you are a non-native speaker of English just starting a degree program at a university in an English-speaking country. Suppose, further, that you need to take a placement test for the university's ESL (English as a second language) program the day after you arrive on campus. In such a situation, you might not perform as well as usual: fatigue from the long trip may mean that you cannot concentrate on the test. If the score you have earned is unexpectedly low, you might conclude that this is not because of your English ability but because you happened to take the test on a bad day. As can be seen from this example, a test score reflects not only the ability we purport to assess but also other factors that might affect test performance, such as fatigue. The greater the contribution of factors other than the target ability (in this case, English language ability is of interest), the more difficult it is to interpret a given candidate's test score as a measure of his/her ability (in this case, English

---

The Concise Companion to Language Assessment, First Edition. Edited by Antony John Kunnan.
© 2025 John Wiley & Sons, Inc. Published 2025 by John Wiley & Sons, Inc.

541

542 **Chapter 36** Classical Test Theory – Reliability

language ability). This is because the effects of such "extraneous" factors make the candidate's score discrepant from the score that would reflect his/her "true" English language ability.

The example above illustrates the relationship among three key CTT concepts: observed score, true score, and measurement error. The observed score is the score we actually obtain when we test a candidate. The true score is the score reflecting a given candidate's true ability. Note that the true score is a hypothetical entity, because we can never observe one's true language ability. Measurement error is the difference between the observed score and the true score, reflecting the effects of various factors other than the target ability. In CTT, the relationship between the observed score (X), the true score (T), and the measurement error (E) is expressed in equation 36.1:

$$X = T + E \tag{36.1}$$

Equation 36.1 communicates some fundamental ideas of CTT. First, a score that we actually observe is a linear combination of a true score and a measurement error. That is, the smaller the measurement error, the closer the observed score is to the true score. Any measurement that we obtain in real life includes some degree of measurement error. Thus E in equation 36.1 is never equal to zero in practice.

Equation 36.1 is extended to explain the variability of test scores across examinees as well. A measure of score variability often used in assessment research is variance, which is the average of squared differences between individual test scores and the mean score across all examinees being analyzed. When we administer a test, we often expect that candidates will differ from one another in terms of the ability being tested. However, parallel to what we have seen in equation 36.1, the score variance that we observe reflects not only candidate ability differences but also various sources of measurement error. Accordingly, CTT defines the observed score variance (σ_x^2) as a linear combination of score variance due to true ability differences (true score variance; σ_t^2) and score variance due to measurement error (error variance; σ_e^2):

$$\sigma_x^2 = \sigma_t^2 + \sigma_e^2 \tag{36.2}$$

Equations 36.1 and 36.2 serve as the basis for various CTT concepts that evaluate the consistency of measurement described in this chapter. Before moving on, however, a discussion of two important assumptions of CTT is in order. First, the CTT true score is defined as the theoretically expected score, which is the average score across all scores one would obtain when measurements of a person were taken an infinite number of times under the same measurement conditions. An important assumption here is that each testing is independent, in other words, a candidate's performance on one testing occasion does not affect his/her performance on another. As shown above, the concept of the true score in CTT is mathematical. Thus, the definition is not directly associated with how one conceptually defines the ability of interest, although this point is often confused (Willse, 2010).

Secondly, measurement error is treated as random in CTT. That is, error in CTT is conceptualized as the random variation of an examinee's score from his/her true score unrelated to his/her ability. A random error is temporary in nature. In the ESL placement test example above, the score you obtain the day after you arrive on campus might be lower than usual because you happen to be extremely tired and lack focus during the test session. Alternatively, you might score better on the same test if you happen to take the test when you are in a good physical and mental condition.

It is worth noting that the concept of CTT measurement error above does not make a distinction between random (unsystematic) sources of measurement error that affect individuals differently and systematic sources of error that affect multiple individuals systematically. Bachman (2004) distinguishes two general types of systematic sources of measurement error: those associated with the personal characteristics of candidates; and others, associated with the test method. An example of a systematic source of error concerning personal characteristics is knowledge about the topic of a text used in a reading comprehension test. Candidates who are familiar with the topic – a specific physics theory, for instance – may score systematically better than others on a reading task about this theory. Sources of measurement error pertaining to the test method include those related to the test design, how the test is administered, and how candidate responses are scored. An example is the severity of raters who score candidates' responses in performance assessments. Scores assigned to essays by a harsh rater may be systematically lower than those assigned by a lenient rater. Language assessments often involve these systematic sources of error. Thus, the lack of distinction between unsystematic and systematic sources of error is often considered a limitation of CTT, as discussed in more detail later.

Definition of CTT Reliability

The fundamental equations of CTT above extend to defining the notion of reliability of measurement. Reliability refers to the consistency of measurement across different test occasions, different test forms, and different raters, among other things. The notion of reliability is closely related to how we interpret test scores. Two major types of score interpretation often distinguished in the literature are norm-referenced testing (NRT) and criterion-referenced testing (CRT). A primary goal of NRT is to rank-order candidates for decision-making (e.g., admission, placement, hiring), where decisions about candidates are made on the basis of how well they perform in relation to others. Selecting the top three candidates on the basis of their English-speaking test scores as trainees of court interpreters, no matter how high or how low they score, is an example of an NRT situation. In contrast, in a CRT setting, candidate decisions are based on whether their performance levels satisfy a predetermined criterion of performance. In such a situation, only those candidates whose speech samples have earned the rating of "fully functional English speaker" would be selected as trainees of court interpreters, for instance, regardless of how many candidates pass the exam.

The distinction between the types of test score interpretation above is critical in a consideration of reliability, because reliability of measurement is defined differently in NRT and in CRT. In NRT, reliability means how consistently candidates are rank-ordered no matter when they take the test, what forms are used to test them, and who judges their performance. This definition is distinct from the notion of reliability in CRT, in which reliability concerns how consistently candidates are classified into different performance levels of interest, again, no matter when they take the test, what forms are used to test them, and who judges their performance. Various CTT-based reliability coefficients discussed below are more closely associated with NRT, while CRT reliability coefficients have been developed outside of CTT. Thus CRT reliability coefficients are not discussed further in this chapter. (See Bachman, 2004, Brown & Hudson, 2002, for more details about CRT.)

Equation 36.2 serves as the basis of the mathematical definition of CTT reliability. In CTT, reliability, denoted as $r_{xx'}$, is defined as the proportion of observed score variance that is explained by true score variance. Equation 36.3 provides the formal definition of reliability, which is denoted as $r_{xx'}$:

$$r_{xx'} = \sigma_t^2 / \sigma_x^2 \tag{36.3}$$

Following equation 36.2, equation 36.3 can be rewritten as equation 36.4:

$$r_{xx'} = \sigma_t^2 / \left(\sigma_t^2 + \sigma_e^2 \right) \tag{36.4}$$

544 Chapter 36 Classical Test Theory – Reliability

Given that reliability is a measure of proportion, it ranges from 0.0 to 1.0. Reliability takes its maximum value when the true score variance equals the observed score variance – a situation that is virtually impossible in practice, where the target ability is measured without measurement error. In contrast, reliability approaches 0 as the error variance increases. In language assessment, we normally expect our measurements to tell us about candidate ability differences. Thus, our goal is to maximize the reliability of our tests.

It should be noted that the definition of reliability above is only a theoretical one, because the true score variance (σ_t^2) is unknown, and thus reliability cannot be obtained directly from equation 36.3 or 36.4. For this reason, we need an operational definition of reliability, so that reliability can be estimated. CTT reliability is defined operationally as a correlation between observed scores on at least two sets of parallel measures. In CTT, two measures are considered parallel to each other when they satisfy the following four criteria: (i) the measures must be based on the same test specification, so that they are equivalent in content and the ability being measured; (ii) they must have the same mean and variance; (iii) their correlations to a third measure must be the same; and (iv) individual sets of scores must be independent of one another – that is, an examinee's performance on one test does not affect his/her performance on another.

Types of CTT Reliability Coefficients

There are various ways in which CTT reliability estimates are obtained operationally. Table 36.1 provides selected CTT reliability coefficients in three broad categories, according to the type of information they offer about measurement consistency. All coefficients in Table 36.1 except KR-20 and KR-21 are applicable to both dichotomous data (examinee responses to test items scored for two categories such as correct and incorrect) and polytomous data (examinee responses to test items scored for more than two categories, such as fully correct, partially correct, and incorrect), while KR-20 and KR-21 are for dichotomous data only. There are some other important differences within and across the three categories as well, including how measurement error (the error variance, σ_e^2, in equation 36.4) is conceptualized, how strictly the four criteria for parallel measures above should be satisfied, and what statistics are used for calculation. In the circumstances, it is important for researchers and practitioners to carefully choose a coefficient that provides information about measurement consistency that is appropriate for their specific purposes.

As will be noted later, computer programs can be used to obtain the coefficients in Table 36.1. However, the basic formulas for the calculation of these coefficients will be introduced through discussions of conceptual issues of consideration below, in order to help the reader to better understand the meaning behind the statistics. For more details about the indices in Table 36.1, see volumes such as Brown and Hudson (2002), Bachman (2004), and Brown (2005). Moreover, note that the list of CTT reliability coefficients in Table 36.1 is by no means exhaustive. Interested readers should refer to Haertel (2006) for information about a wider variety of CTT reliability coefficients. A given coefficient can also be calculated in various ways. For example, Cronbach's alpha in Table 36.1 can be obtained by using other procedures, such as Hoyt's ANOVA (Hoyt, 1941) and generalizability theory (Brennan, 2001; Shavelson & Webb, 1991).

Category A in Table 36.1 includes two reliability coefficients, a test–retest reliability coefficient and a parallel forms reliability coefficient. These two coefficients are similar in that they both provide information about the consistency of candidate performance across two test sessions. While both require examinees to be tested twice, the nature of the measurement error that these coefficients address is not the same. The test–retest reliability coefficient highlights the degree to which the information obtained from a given test is stable across time (testing occasions) when the test content is held constant. Thus, the same test is given twice

Definition of CTT Reliability 545

TABLE 36.1

CTT reliability coefficients for norm-referenced tests

Reliability coefficient	Definition	Features
A. Reliability coefficients based on data obtained from two test sessions		
1. Test–retest	Correlation between two administrations of the same test given to the same examinees	• *Advantage*: The coefficients are transparent, closely reflecting the operational definition of CTT reliability
2. Parallel forms	Correlation between two parallel forms given to the same examines	• *Limitation*: Both require testing examinees twice
B. Internal consistency reliability coefficients		
3. Split half (Spearman–Brown)	Based on the correlation between halves of a single test (e.g., random split, odd–even, first/second)	• *Advantage*: Only a single test administration is required
4. Split half (Guttman)	Based on variances of halves of a single test (e.g., random split, odd–even, first/second)	• *Limitations*: Split-half methods are relatively less stable; all coefficients under this category ignore performance differences across occasions and may overestimate reliability
5. Cronbach's α	Based on variances of individual items treated as parallel measures	• Reliability is underestimated when the parallel measure assumption is not met for the Spearman–Brown split-half reliability coefficient and when the essential tau-equivalence assumption is not met for the other four coefficients listed under this category
6. KR-20	A special case of Cronbach's α (for dichotomous data only)	
7. KR-21	A short-cut estimate of KR-20 (for dichotomous data only)	
C. Rater consistency reliability coefficients		
8. Intra-rater reliability	Correlation between scores assigned to a set of examinees by the same rater	• *Advantage*: The coefficients are transparent because they closely reflect the operational definition of CTT reliability
9. Inter-rater reliability	• *Only two raters*: Correlation between scores assigned to a set of examinees by the rater pair • *More than two raters*: Cronbach's α where each rater is treated as an "item"	• *Limitation*: Multiple sources of error that often affect the reliability of performance assessments cannot be modeled simultaneously

to each candidate, and a correlation coefficient between the two sets of the test's total score is obtained as the reliability coefficient. In contrast, the parallel forms reliability coefficient focuses on the equivalence of information about candidate performance obtained across different test forms. Accordingly, two different test forms, designed to be parallel to each other, are administered to the same candidates. One can then obtain either a correlation coefficient between the two or a Cronbach's alpha coefficient, as discussed below, as a parallel forms reliability coefficient. (See Bachman, 2004, p. 168, for further details.)

Carefully planned test administration is essential for obtaining test–retest reliability and parallel forms reliability coefficients that provide meaningful information about the consistency

546 **Chapter 36** Classical Test Theory – Reliability

of measurement. A primary issue of consideration, for three reasons, is to allow a long enough interval between the two test sessions when obtaining data required for calculating these coefficients. First, too short an interval (e.g., administering both measures on the same day by making the test session twice as long) would introduce another, unwanted source of measurement error: candidate fatigue. Second, a reliability coefficient based on data collected at once is likely to overestimate the consistency of measurement, because the coefficient would not reflect the variability of candidate performance across separate testing occasions. Third, allowing a sufficiently long interval between the two sessions is important in order to control for a practice effect (Suzuki & Koizumi, 2021). That is, candidates may remember what was on the test from the first session when the same form is administered for a second time to obtain the test–retest reliability coefficient. This also applies when obtaining a parallel forms reliability coefficient. There is a possibility that candidates will score systematically higher on the second form than on the first, simply because they become accustomed to the test format and procedure. One way to address this issue is to have a random selection of half the candidates start with one form, and to have the other half start with the other form (Bachman, 2004). When data are obtained by taking account of important administration issues such as those above, test–retest and parallel forms reliability coefficients provide useful information about measurement consistency.

Haertel (2006) notes that the parallel forms reliability coefficient is often considered an ideal reliability coefficient if the data used for the calculation are obtained properly. This is because the coefficient shows the extent to which a combination of two important sources of measurement error – testing occasions and test forms – affects measurement consistency.

However, obtaining the data required for the calculation of this coefficient is not easy, because it requires two test sessions. This is one reason why reliability coefficients that can be calculated on the basis of data from one test session are used widely. Five commonly used reliability coefficients of this type, called "internal consistency reliability coefficients," are listed under Category B in Table 36.1. These coefficients indicate the extent to which information obtained about a candidate ability is consistent across different parts of a single test. When scored candidate response data related to individual test items are available, these indices can be obtained by splitting the test into multiple parts, in different ways.

The first two coefficients in Category B are two types of split-half reliability coefficients based on test halves. The Spearman–Brown split-half reliability coefficient can be calculated by plugging a correlation coefficient between the total scores on the halves ($r_{hh'}$) into equation 36.5:

$$r_{xx'} = \frac{2r_{hh'}}{1+r_{hh'}} \tag{36.5}$$

However, this coefficient assumes that the two halves are strictly parallel measures, which is difficult in practice. Accordingly, reliability coefficients based on a weaker assumption, called "essential tau-equivalence," have been proposed. When test halves are essentially tau-equivalent, they have the same true score variance but possibly different measurement error variances. The observed mean scores of the halves may also be different. Guttman (1945) and Rulon (1939) proposed equivalent formulas for a split-half reliability on the basis of the essential tau-equivalence assumption. The version proposed by Guttman, which was based on the variances of the halves (designated as s_{h1}^2 and s_{h2}^2) and on that of the total score (designated as s_x^2), is presented in equation 36.6. This formula is often implemented in statistical packages as the Guttman split-half reliability coefficient:

$$r_{xx'} = 2\left(1 - \frac{s_{h1}^2 + s_{h2}^2}{s_x^2}\right) \tag{36.6}$$

When calculating split-half reliability coefficients, it is extremely important to obtain halves that can reasonably be treated as comparable to each other. Let us take a vocabulary test comprising items that require identification of the definitions of individual words. If the items are ordered according to difficulty (e.g., on the basis of vocabulary frequency measures), splitting the test into odd- and even-numbered items is a reasonable approach. Alternatively, if the items are positioned in the test with no specific order in mind, one might decide to randomly split the items into halves. Unlike in the example above, however, language assessments often include items that share the same stimulus text (e.g., listening comprehension items based on the same lecture; gap-filling items based on the same reading passage). Because candidate performance on items that share the same stimulus text is related across questions, assigning these items to different halves of the test contributes to inflation of the reliability estimate. It is therefore recommended that such items are kept together when calculating split-half reliability coefficients.

The remaining three coefficients under Category B in Table 36.1 – Cronbach's alpha, KR-20, and KR-21 – treat individual items, instead of halves of the test, as measures that are essentially tau-equivalent to one another and offer information about the degree to which consistent information about candidate ability is obtained across items within a single test. The formula for the Cronbach's alpha coefficient is shown in equation 36.7, where k is the number of items in the test, s_i^2 is the item variance, and s_x^2 is the variance of the entire test:

$$r_{xx'} = \frac{k}{k-1}\left(1 - \frac{\sum s_i^2}{s_x^2}\right) \tag{36.7}$$

KR-20 and KR-21 are versions of Cronbach's alpha applicable to dichotomous data only. The advantage of these coefficients is the simplicity of the calculation. KR-20 can be obtained when the number of items in the test, the variance of the test, and the proportion of candidates answering individual items correctly are known. KR-21, a shortcut of KR-20, requires only the number of items in the test, as well as the variance and the mean of the total test score.

Cronbach's alpha is the most widely used index of test reliability. As already noted, it is practical because data from only one test session are required for its calculation. Another advantage is its stability. While the split-half reliability coefficients yield different reliability estimates depending on how test halves are obtained, Cronbach's alpha is equivalent to the mean across Guttman split-half reliability estimates on the basis of all possible ways in which halves of the test are obtained (Haertel, 2006). Thus Cronbach's alpha offers more stable reliability estimates than the split-half reliability coefficients.

While these advantages make Cronbach's alpha attractive, caution should be exercised concerning its interpretation and application. First, given that Cronbach's alpha treats individual items as essentially tau-equivalent measures, using this coefficient is appropriate only when individual items are comparable in test design, the ability being assessed, and statistical functioning. When different parts of a test are not essentially tau-equivalent to one another, the coefficient underestimates reliability. For example, a language test often comprises parts designed to assess different aspects of language ability (e.g., grammar, vocabulary, and reading). Examinee performance on this test may not be consistent across the different parts. Likewise, it is not appropriate to use Cronbach's alpha for obtaining reliability estimates for speed tests. This is because it is likely that at least some of the candidates do not perform well on items toward the end of the test due to lack of time. This instability of candidate performance across items leads to an underestimation of reliability. Thus, when a test is speeded, it is more appropriate to use either a test–retest or a parallel forms reliability coefficient. Finally, it is often said that Cronbach's alpha is a conservative estimate of reliability, offering a lower-bound estimate of internal consistency reliability. As noted by Haertel (2006), however, internal consistency reliability estimates, including Cronbach's alpha, ignore

548   **Chapter 36** Classical Test Theory – Reliability

candidate performance consistency across time. In this sense, Cronbach's alpha can overestimate reliability as well.

While the reliability coefficients discussed so far are often applied to tests in traditional formats comprising a fairly large number of items, some approaches to obtaining CTT reliability estimates for candidate responses scored by human raters have also been discussed in the literature. Human raters are often used to evaluate speech and writing samples in language performance assessments (e.g., oral interview tests and writing tests requiring candidates to write essays). This introduces human judgment into the scoring process, yielding another source of measurement error: consistency of ratings assigned by raters. (See McNamara, 1996, for a detailed discussion on the role of human rater scoring in measurements obtained in language performance assessments.) Even after careful training and monitoring of the raters, the ratings they provide fluctuate for various reasons. Previous research has shown that rater training may help raters to apply scoring rubrics consistently but that such training may not necessarily eliminate systematic differences among them, such as harshness or leniency (e.g., Weigle, 1998).

In NRT approaches to estimating rater reliability for performance assessments, two aspects of the reliability of ratings provided by human raters are widely recognized. One is called intra-rater reliability, which is the extent to which a given rater assigns ratings to a set of candidates' responses consistently across rating occasions. The other is called inter-rater reliability, which is the extent to which ratings assigned to a given set of candidates' responses are consistent across raters. Category C in Table 36.1 offers some approaches to calculating inter- and intra-rater reliability coefficients within the CTT framework. For calculation of an intra-rater reliability coefficient, one can have a given rater score the same set of candidate responses twice. What has been said above on the careful planning of the test administration when obtaining the test–retest and parallel forms reliability coefficients also applies here. It is thus important to secure a sufficient interval between the two rating sessions in order to control for fatigue in the rater and to present candidate responses to the rater in a different order across the two rating sessions in order to minimize practice effects. A correlation between the two sets of scores obtained from the two rating occasions can then be calculated as an intra-rater reliability coefficient for the specific rater. Meanwhile, a few approaches are possible when examining inter-rater reliability. If there are only two raters involved in scoring examinee responses, a correlation coefficient can be calculated between two sets of scores obtained from the pair of raters on the same set of candidate responses. By contrast, when there are more than two raters, Bachman (2004) recommends calculating Cronbach's alpha by treating ratings obtained from different raters as different "items" (See equation 36.7).

The CTT approaches to rater reliability investigation discussed above provide useful information about how consistently raters assign scores to examinee responses. However, a few words of caution are in order for the appropriate interpretation of the rater reliability information. First, a correlation coefficient tells us how consistently a set of candidate responses are rank-ordered by the same rater across different occasions, or by different raters. Accordingly, as long as the rank ordering of the candidates is the same across the two sets of scores, a perfect correlation ($r_{xx'} = 1.0$) can be obtained between two sets of scores under certain conditions, even when the scores assigned to a given candidate response are not the same. Thus it is recommended that correlation-based inter- and intra-rater reliability coefficients are examined, along with rater agreement information. (See Xi, 2007, for a sample of a study reporting rater agreement information.) Second, the inter- and intra-rater reliability coefficients focus on one source of error at a time, despite the fact that other sources of error, including task difficulty and rater background such as native language and professional training and experience (e.g., Brown, 1995; Johnson & Lim, 2009), are often thought to affect the reliability of language performance assessments as well. This issue will be revisited in the "Challenges" section.

Spearman–Brown Prophecy Formula

Another important notion developed within CTT is a formula called "the Spearman–Brown prophecy formula," which is often used to estimate how score reliability changes by adding/reducing the number of items in a test. The assumption here is that the items to be added to lengthen a test, as well as those that are already in the test, parallel one another. This formula is also useful in order for us to understand how score reliability is related to test length. The Spearman–Brown prophecy formula is presented as equation 36.8, in which $r_{xx'}$ refers to the reliability estimate of the shortened or lengthened test, N refers to the factor by which the original test is lengthened, and $r_{yy'}$ refers to the reliability estimate of the original test:

$$r_{xx'} = \frac{Nr_{yy'}}{1+(N-1)r_{yy'}} \tag{36.8}$$

It should be clear from equation 36.8 that the longer the test, the higher the test reliability becomes. For example, imagine that you have constructed a 30-item grammar test with an internal consistency reliability estimate of 0.75. You may wonder to what extent the reliability of your test may improve if the length is doubled. The reliability of a test containing 60 items, which is twice as long as the original (hence $N = 2$), can be estimated by plugging the appropriate numbers into equation 36.8:

$$r_{xx'} = \frac{Nr_{yy'}}{1+(N-1)r_{yy'}} = \frac{(2)(0.75)}{1+(2-1)(0.75)} = \frac{1.5}{1.75} = 0.86 \tag{36.9}$$

As this example illustrates, the Spearman–Brown prophecy formula is useful for test construction and revision. The formula can be used, for instance, to estimate the number of items required to secure a certain level of reliability in a test based on pilot test data. In such a case, the reliability estimate of the pilot test and the desired level of reliability of the actual test can be plugged into the formula as $r_{yy'}$ and $r_{xx'}$, respectively. The equation can then be solved for N to calculate the number of additional items required.

Standard Error of Measurement

While reliability estimates provide us with information about the consistency of measurements obtained from a test as a whole, they do not tell us how one might go about interpreting individual test scores. Standard error of measurement (SEM) is a measure developed to do just that. SEM refers to the standard deviation of error scores (a square root of the error variance) under repeated independent testing with the same test or parallel tests, assuming that the error is the same across all candidates (Allen & Yen, 1979). Equation 36.10 shows the formula for calculating SEM:

$$SEM = S_x \sqrt{1-r_{xx'}} \tag{36.10}$$

S_x in equation 36.10 is the standard deviation of the observed scores, and $r_{xx'}$ is the reliability estimate. Equation 36.10 tells us two things. First, the larger the standard deviation of a test, the larger its SEM. Thus, a test that spreads candidates widely across a given scale would yield a relatively large SEM. Second, as $r_{xx'}$ becomes larger, the SEM becomes smaller. One would normally want an SEM to be small, and a test with high reliability helps us minimize it.

550 **Chapter 36** Classical Test Theory – Reliability

SEM is often used to construct a confidence interval around an observed score of interest in order to estimate the true score with which it is associated. The confidence interval can be set by using the statistical notion of a normal curve and a z score, a standardized score that tells us the location of a specific score in the score distribution. When scores on a given test are distributed normally, 95% of the scores fall between the z scores of -1.96 and $+1.96$ under the normal curve. This concept allows us to estimate where a given person's true score falls. Suppose, for example, that a student earns a score of 50 on a test. If S_x for the test is 10 and $r_{xx'}$ is .90, then the SEM for this test can be obtained as in equation 36.11:

$$\text{SEM} = 10\sqrt{1-0.90} = (10)(0.37) = 3.7 \tag{36.11}$$

The 95% confidence interval for the score of 50 can be obtained by using equation 36.12, in which the observed score is denoted as X and the absolute value of the z score associated with the 95% confidence level as $|z_{0.95}|$:

$$\text{CI}(0.95) = X \pm \text{SEM}|z_{0.95}| = 50 \pm (3.7)(1.96) \tag{36.12}$$

Equation 36.12 shows that the lower bound of the 95% confidence interval is 43.8 and its upper bound is 56.2. This suggests that we are 95% confident that the true score of a person who has scored 50 on the test lies somewhere between 43.8 and 56.2. The 95% confidence interval is often used when accurate estimates of true scores are required. Similar confidence intervals can be constructed for other desired levels of confidence by referring to a z-score table available in basic statistics references to look up the z scores associated with the specific confidence levels of interest.

Disattenuated Correlations

In language assessment research, correlation coefficients are often obtained to examine interrelationships among different parts of the same test and between a test and other external measures. As discussed above, however, all measurements we obtain from a test are affected by measurement error. The same applies to an observed correlation coefficient calculated from two sets of observed scores. In other words, an observed correlation coefficient may not present an accurate picture of the relationship between two variables because measurement error masks the true relationship between them. For this reason, the observed correlation is often corrected for the reliability of the variables for further interpretation. The resulting correlation coefficient is called "the disattenuated correlation" or "the true score correlation," which is an estimate of the correlation between two variables measured with perfect reliability, that is, with no measurement error. Equation 36.13 shows the formula for calculating the disattenuated correlation coefficient (r_{TaTb}), in which the observed correlation coefficient between variables A and B is denoted as r_{ab} and the reliability estimates of these two variables as $r_{aa'}$ and $r_{bb'}$, respectively:

$$r_{TaTb} = \frac{r_{ab}}{\sqrt{r_{aa'}r_{bb'}}} \tag{36.13}$$

Computer Programs

Although there are few computer programs dedicated to CTT data analysis, widely available statistical packages such as R, SAS, and SPSS implement the internal consistency reliability coefficients listed in Table 36.1. Moreover, all basic statistics introduced in this chapter (mean, variance, standard deviation, and correlation) can be obtained from these programs. They can be used for hand calculation of SEMs (equation 36.10), disattenuated correlations (equation 36.13), and estimated reliability with different test lengths, on the basis of the Spearman–Brown prophecy formula (equation 36.8).

Current Practice

In the field of language assessment, the different types of CTT-based information about the quality of measurements obtained from the language tests discussed above are reported routinely. First, reporting test reliability is, in all circumstances, the responsibility of any test developer, and doing so is of paramount importance for maintaining good testing practice. To this end, guidelines for reporting reliability in a form that is suitable for a specific test purpose and context are provided in professional standards such as the *Standards for educational and psychological testing* (American Educational Research Association et al., 2014) and the International Language Testing Association's (2020) *ILTA guidelines for practice in English*. While high reliability is usually preferred, expected reliability depends on various issues such as the purpose, stakes, length, and design of a given test. Accordingly, there is no "one size fits all" criterion for how high test reliability should be. Nunnally (1978) offers a useful rule of thumb for suggested levels of test reliability for different purposes, ranging from 0.70 to 0.95 (pp. 245–246). In order to ensure a desired level of test reliability, the quality of individual test items should be scrutinized carefully by conducting pilot tests and item analyses concerning, for instance, item difficulty and discrimination (how well an item distinguishes high-ability candidates from low-ability candidates). Revising test items according to the results of such analyses should in turn contribute to improving the overall test reliability. (See Chapter 50, Statistics for Test Revisions, for further details.)

Second, the SEM discussed earlier in this chapter should be reported along with information about test reliability, because it facilitates the interpretation of individual test scores. One context in particular where the availability of SEM is critical is setting standards for making decisions about candidates on the basis of their test scores. Suppose, for instance, that the example cited in the SEM section above is a high-stakes test used for admitting candidates to a university. If the institution wishes to accept candidates whose true score is 55 or above, the institution may as well consider accepting a candidate who earns a score of 50 in the example. This is because, as shown in the example above, the 95% confidence interval for the observed score of 50 ranges from 43.8 to 56.2, which includes 55. By following this procedure to construct confidence intervals for different scores, the institution can adjust the cut score.

Finally, disattenuated correlation coefficients play an important role in test validation studies that employ correlational analyses of test data. Some previous studies that have reported disattenuated correlation coefficients include an investigation of the comparability of test scores between paper-based and computer-based administrations, by Choi et al. (2003), and a validation study of the TOEIC® test for South American learners of English by Sinharay et al. (2009).

Challenges

While CTT has wide applications in measurement, it has some notable limitations that have been discussed elsewhere in the literature. A first limitation is the underestimation of reliability through recourse to frequently used coefficients such as Cronbach's alpha. However, recent research suggests ways to adjust the value of alpha when the assumption of essential tau-equivalence is violated. For example, an approach based on structural equation modeling

552 Chapter 36 Classical Test Theory – Reliability

(e.g., Raykov, 1997; Raykov & Shrout, 2002) is applicable when different parts of the test are congeneric, a situation where the true score variances of the test parts are not the same, thereby violating the essential tau-equivalence assumption.

A second limitation is that, essentially, CTT treats only one type of measurement error at a time (e.g., Bachman, 2004; Shavelson & Webb, 1991). As we saw in Table 36.1, different CTT reliability indices feature different aspects of measurement consistency, such as the stability of information obtained across occasions (test–retest reliability and intra-rater reliability), across forms (parallel forms reliability), across different items on a single test (internal consistency reliability), and across raters (inter-rater reliability). Another closely related issue is that CTT does not distinguish between different types of error. As shown in Haertel's (2006) statement about the parallel forms reliability coefficient mentioned above, it is possible to calculate a reliability coefficient reflecting more than one type of measurement error with careful collection of data. The limitation is, however, that the resulting CTT reliability estimate tells us only about the combined effect of the different sources of error; it does not give us fine-grained information about how individual sources of error and their interactions contribute to measurement error.

Together with the fact that CTT does not distinguish unsystematic or systematic errors, the lack of fine-grained information about the effects of multiple sources of error on test score variability is a cause of concern. This is because, as already noted, multiple sources of systematic error and their interactions (e.g., rater severity, rater background, task difficulty) are often thought to affect the reliability of language assessments. Understanding the way in which different sources of error affect measurement consistency is essential for controlling the test design appropriately enough to maximize test reliability. A final concern about CTT, often pointed out by various researchers, is that CTT assumes SEM to be equal across all score levels, which is not the case. It is well-known that measurement error tends to be larger at the higher and lower ends of a score distribution. However, CTT provides only a single, average SEM across all score levels.

Recent advances in measurement models have made it possible to address some of the limitations of CTT listed above. For instance, generalizability theory (G theory) and a special type of item response theory (IRT) called "many-facet Rasch measurement" are often employed in language assessment research to examine multiple sources of measurement error simultaneously. Both frameworks offer separate estimates of SEMs for different score levels. These measurement models have additional advantages as well. For instance, G theory allows score reliability investigation for both NRT and CRT. Meanwhile, IRT approaches allow the estimation of score reliability to be unaffected by the sample taking the test. This is considered advantageous, because CTT reliability calculation depends on the test performance of the specific sample on which the calculation of the statistics is based. For further details about G theory and many-facet Rasch measurement, see the chapters on these topics in this volume, as well as introductory texts such as Shavelson and Webb (1991), McNamara (1996), Eckes (2015), and Sawaki and Xi (2019).

Future Directions

Currently multiple frameworks for test validation are widely used in the field (e.g., Bachman & Palmer, 2010; Chapelle et al., 2008; Kane, 2006, 2013; Weir, 2005). Despite variations in specific ways in which test validity is theorized across them, an important commonality is the treatment of test reliability as a fundamental quality of language tests on which the soundness of test score interpretation and use hinges. CTT often serves as a flexible framework for analyzing test reliability, offering a range of statistical information that enables the investigator to assess how a given test is functioning and how it should be revised to enhance the quality of measurement obtained from it. Even when a modern test theory such as generalizability theory and IRT is applicable to analyzing a given language test, CTT is quite often the only available option for a preliminary investigation, particularly when one needs to work with a small sample. While test validity theories may change across time, it is expected that CTT reliability analysis discussed in this chapter will continue to play critical roles in investigating measurement quality toward justifying an intended test score interpretation and use.

Discussion Questions

1. Suppose that you will develop a test of academic English for university admissions. This test comprises a vocabulary section (40 stand-alone multiple-choice items), a reading section (30 multiple-choice items based on six reading passages), and a writing section (1 essay). Each student essay is scored by two raters. There are 1000 applicants taking the test, and the top-scoring 100 would be admitted. How would you go about examining the reliability of this test? Which reliability coefficients presented in Table 36.1 would you use? Why?

2. This chapter presented an example of how a confidence interval constructed based on an SEM could be used to determine a cut score for a language test. Now consider a placement test where students are divided into three levels on the basis of the test score. Describe how confidence intervals could be constructed based on the SEM to inform the decision.

References

Allen, J., & Yen, W. M. (1979). *Introduction to measurement theory*. Brooks/Cole Pub. Co.

American Educational Research Association, American Psychological Association, & National Council on Measurement in Education (2014). *Standards for educational and psychological testing*. American Educational Research Association.

Bachman, L. F. (2004). *Statistical analyses for language assessment*. Cambridge University Press.

Bachman, L. F., & Palmer, A. (2010). *Language assessment in practice*. Oxford University Press.

Brennan, R. L. (2001). *Generalizability theory*. Springer-Verlag.

Brown, A. (1995). The effect of rater variables in the development of an occupation-specific language performance test. *Language Testing, 12*, 1–15. https://doi.org/10.1177/026553229501200101.

Brown, J. D. (2005). *Testing in language programs*. McGraw-Hill.

Brown, J. D., & Hudson, T. (2002). *Criterion-related language testing*. Cambridge University Press.

Chapelle, C. A., Enright, M. K., & Jamieson, J. M. (2008). *Building a validity argument for the Test of English as a Foreign Language*. Routledge.

Choi, I.-C., Kim, K. S., & Boo, J. (2003). Comparability of a paper-based language test and a computer-based language test. *Language Testing, 20*(3), 295–320. https://doi.org/10.1191/0265532203lt258oa.

Eckes, T. (2015). *Introduction to many-facet Rasch measurement: Analyzing and evaluating rater-mediated assessments* (2nd rev. and updated ed.). Peter Lang.

Guttman, L. A. (1945). A basis for analyzing test–retest reliability. *Psychometrika, 10*(4), 255–282.

Haertel, E. H. (2006). Reliability. In R. L. Brennan (Ed.), *Educational measurement* (4th ed., pp. 65–110). American Council on Education and Praeger Publishers.

Hoyt, C. (1941). Test reliability estimated by analysis of variance. *Psychometrika, 6*(3), 153–160. https://doi.org/10.1007/BF02289270.

International Language Testing Association. (2020). *International Language Testing Association guidelines for practice in English*. Retrieved April 21, 2023, from https://www.iltaonline.com/page/ILTAGuidelinesforPractice.

Johnson, J. S., & Lim, G. S. (2009). The influence of rater language background on writing performance assessment. *Language Testing, 26*(4), 485–505. https://doi.org/10.1177/0265532209340186.

554   Chapter 36 Classical Test Theory – Reliability

Kane, M. (2006). Validation. In R. Brennan (Ed.), *Educational measurement* (4th ed., pp. 17–64). American Council on Measurement in Education and Praeger Publishers.

Kane, M. T. (2013). Validating the interpretations and uses of test scores. *Journal of Educational Measurement, 50*(1), 1–73. https://doi.org/10.1111/jedm.12000.

McNamara, T. (1996). *Measuring second language performance*. Longman.

Nunnally, J. C. (1978). *Psychometric theory* (2nd ed.). New York, NY: McGraw-Hill.

Raykov, T. (1997). Scale reliability, Cronbach's alpha, and violations of essential tau-equivalence with fixed congeneric components. *Multivariate Behavioral Research, 32*(4), 329–353. https://doi.org/10.1207/s15327906mbr3204_2.

Raykov, T., & Shrout, P. E. (2002). Reliability of scales with general structure: point and interval estimation using a structural equation modeling approach. *Structural Equation Modeling, 9*(2), 195–212. https://doi.org/10.1207/S15328007SEM0902_3.

Rulon, P. J. (1939). A simplified procedure for determining the reliability of a test by split-halves. *Harvard Educational Review, 9*, 99–103.

Sawaki, Y., & Xi, X. (2019). Univariate generalizability theory in language assessment. In V. Aryadoust & M. Raquel (Eds.), *Quantitative data analysis for language assessment. Vol. I: Fundamental techniques* (pp. 30–53). Routledge.

Shavelson, R. J., & Webb, N. M. (1991). *Generalizability theory: A primer*. Sage.

Sinharay, S., Powers, D. E., Feng, Y., Saldivia, L., Giunta, A., Simpson, A., & Weng, V. (2009). Appropriateness of the TOEIC Bridge test for students in three countries of South America. *Language Testing, 26*(4), 589–619. https://doi.org/10.1177/0265532209340195.

Suzuki, Y., & Koizumi, R. (2021). Using equivalent test forms in SLA pretest-posttest design research. In P. Winke & T. Brunfaut (Eds.), *The Routledge handbook of second language acquisition and language testing* (pp. 457–467). Routledge.

Weigle, S.-C. (1998). Using FACETS to model rater training effects. *Language Testing, 15*, 263–287. https://doi.org/10.1177/026553229801500205.

Weir, C. (2005). *Language testing and validation: An evidence-based approach*. Palgrave.

Willse, J. T. (2010). Classical test theory. In N. Salkind (Ed.), *Encyclopedia of research design* (pp. 149–153). Sage.

Xi, X. (2007). Evaluating analytic scoring for the TOEFL Academic Speaking Test (TAST) for operational use. *Language Testing, 24*(2), 251–286. https://doi.org/10.1177/0265532207076365.

Suggested Readings

Carr, N. T. (2011). *Designing and analyzing language tests*. Oxford.

Lord, F. M., & Novick, M. R. (1968). *Statistical theories of mental test scores*. Addison-Wesley.

Traub, R. E. (1997). Classical test theory in historical perspective. *Educational Measurement: Issues and Practice, 16*(4), 8–14. https://doi.org/10.1111/j.1745-3992.1997.tb00603.x.

CHAPTER 37

Norm-Referenced and Criterion-Referenced Score Interpretations in Language Assessment

Ikkyu Choi

Introduction

A test score is rarely useful on its own. What makes a test score useful is our interpretation, which takes the form of an answer to the following question: What does the score of X on this test mean? Despite the simplicity of the question, it is not easy to come up with an accurate answer. This difficulty is inherent to the construct of interest because target constructs of language tests are abstract concepts that cannot be observed directly. Another source of difficulty comes from a wide range of potential interpretations of a test score. Even measurements of physical traits with a small amount of measurement error (e.g., height) can have different interpretations across different personal views, use cases, and contexts. It is thus not surprising that a language test score, a number without any associated physical trait and with a large amount of measurement error, can be interpreted differently. The abstract construct and the large potential variability in interpretation highlight the importance of proper score interpretation.

To facilitate the discussion about score interpretation, educational measurement researchers have devised two distinct classes of interpretations. The deciding factor has to do with comparison: what should a test score be compared against? One class of interpretations focuses on the relative comparison of a test score to those of other test takers. Specifically, a test taker's score is compared to the distribution of scores from others who are deemed relevant and comparable. Because this comparison involves summary statistics of the relevant score distribution, which are called *norms*, this class of interpretations is called norm-referenced (NR). The other class anchors interpretations to a set of external criteria, such as standards and minimum requirements, and is thus called criterion-referenced (CR). Glaser (1963) is credited as the first use of the terminology "criterion-referenced testing" (Geisinger, 2022) in the educational measurement literature, and the differences between NR and CR were highlighted

The Concise Companion to Language Assessment, First Edition. Edited by Antony John Kunnan.
© 2025 John Wiley & Sons, Inc. Published 2025 by John Wiley & Sons, Inc.

556 Chapter 37 Norm- and Criterion-Referenced Score Interpretations

by many researchers (Millman, 1974). Since then, the NR–CR distinction has been used in the literature for multiple decades to understand, discuss, and study score interpretation.

This chapter introduces the NR–CR distinction in the context of language assessment. The goal of this chapter is to help readers understand the distinction, apply it to real-world tests, and consider challenges relevant to the distinction. The remainder of this chapter is organized as follows. First, we present the concepts of NR- and CR-interpretations in detail. We then review a few real-world language tests as examples. The examples are followed by a discussion about relevant challenges, some of which apply to both NR- and CR-interpretations while others are specific to one class of interpretations. Lastly, we conclude the chapter with remarks on promising lines of future research.

Norm-Referenced and Criterion-Referenced Interpretations

The NR–CR distinction has to do with the interpretation of scores (American Educational Research Association et al., 2014; Hudson, 2014). A language test can (and often does) yield scores that are designed to be interpreted in multiple ways, even across the NR–CR distinction. It can thus be misleading to consider the distinction as inherent to a test. In the remainder of this chapter, we sometimes omit the term *interpretation* after NR or CR for simplicity, because there is no ambiguity in their reference. They always refer to an interpretation.

Whether an intended interpretation is justified is an empirical question at the core of validation: the developer of a test should make an explicit claim about each intended interpretation and provide backing as part of its validity argument (e.g., Bachman & Palmer, 2010; Kane, 2013). Such backing is often derived from item and test development processes as well as evidence gathered from research efforts. In this section, we discuss NR and CR score interpretations in detail, with a particular emphasis on their impact on item and test development and research.

Norm-Referenced Interpretations

Commonly used norms

A norm is a summary statistic of a test score distribution from the relevant population group. Summary statistics that frequently form the basis of NR interpretations include the mean, standard deviation, and percentiles of a score distribution. The mean of a distribution is a measure of where its center is located, and the corresponding standard deviation indicates the amount of variability around the mean. Figure 37.1 gives three examples of score distributions with different mean and standard deviation values. With the mean and standard deviation of a score distribution, any given score can be interpreted in terms of how many standard deviations it is away from the mean in which direction. For example, consider a score distribution with mean 50 and standard deviation 10 (in the top panel of Figure 37.1). The score of, say, 75 is 2.5 standard deviations higher than the mean, whereas the score of 30 is 2 standard deviations below the mean.

Percentiles convey information about the location of a score with a different focus: they show exactly how many percentage of test takers in the reference distribution received higher or lower scores than a given score. More precisely, a pth percentile, $0 \leq p \leq 100$, is the score point that is higher than the scores of $p\%$ of the reference distribution. For example, if a score is at the 27th percentile, it means that the score is higher than those of 27% of the reference population (equivalently, lower than those of 73%). The 50th percentile value is called the median of a distribution and is another common measure of the central location (in addition to the mean).

Norm-Referenced and Criterion-Referenced Interpretations 557

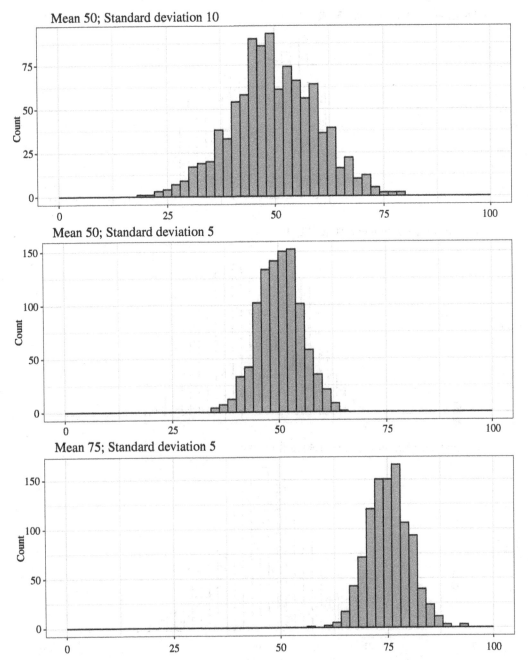

FIGURE 37.1 Example score distributions with different means and standard deviations.

There is a long history of using a normal distribution to describe the reference score distribution (see, e.g., Briggs, 2022). Distributions can have the same mean and the same standard deviation and yet have very different shapes. For example, Figure 37.2 shows three different distributions, all with the same mean of 50 and the same standard deviation of 10. A normal distribution, on the other hand, is completely determined by its mean and standard deviation: there exists only a single normal distribution with a given mean and a given standard deviation. To put it another way, the mean and standard deviation of a distribution tell us where its

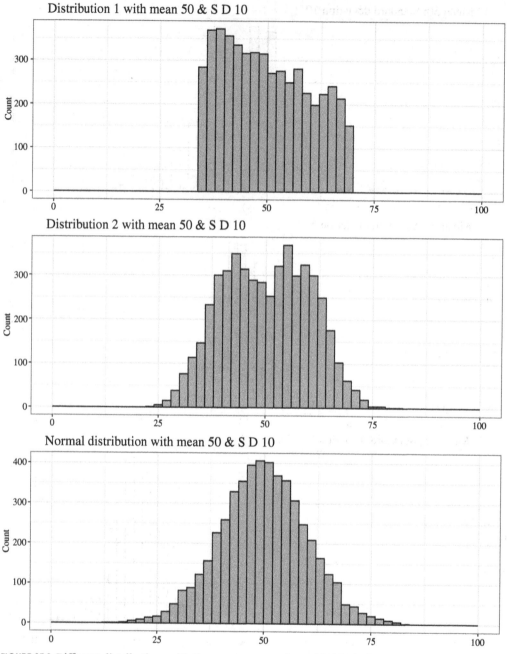

FIGURE 37.2 Different distributions with the same mean and standard deviation.

central location is and how variable individual scores are around that location, whereas a normal distribution (with the same specified mean and standard deviation) tells us exactly how probable every single score is. This use of a normal distribution thus amounts to a strong assumption on the shape of the reference distribution. The bottom panel of Figure 37.2 shows the normal distribution with mean 50 and standard deviation 10.

The additional assumption of a normally distributed reference score distribution provides more information in interpreting a given score relative to the mean and standard deviation.

Specifically, by utilizing the cumulative distribution function[1] of a normal distribution, one can make the relative location interpretation similar to that from a percentile. Suppose the score of 75 in the distribution with mean 50 and standard deviation 10. If this distribution follows the normal distribution (with the same mean and standard deviation), the score of 75 is higher than 99% of those in the reference population. This additional information comes at the cost of the additional normality assumption; if the empirical score distribution is far from the assumed normal distribution, the additional information would not be accurate and may even be detrimental to score interpretation.

Considerations for items

The most important quality to support NR interpretations is a large standard deviation in the reference score distribution. To understand why, let us consider a scenario in which everyone's score is highly concentrated around the mean, say 50, with a very small standard deviation, say 1. This hypothetical scenario (with the additional normality assumption) is depicted in the top panel of Figure 37.3. Here, a small score difference can lead to substantially different interpretations. For example, the score of 50 corresponds to the 50th percentile, but a single score point increase puts the resulting score (of 51) to the 84th percentile. That is, with a single score point difference, a test taker would go from being in the middle of the pack to belonging to the top 20%. It is not desirable to have such a large swing in interpretation based on a small score difference, because even a small amount of measurement error can substantially distort score interpretation. Let us now consider a much more desirable scenario with the same mean but 10 times larger standard deviation, which is depicted in the bottom panel of Figure 37.3. The scores of 50 and 51 in this scenario correspond to the 50th and 54th percentiles, which would lead to largely the same interpretations. These contrasting examples show why large variability in the reference score distribution is desirable.

Tests whose scores are to be interpreted against norms are thus designed to maximize score variability in the reference population. The maximization task is carried out by assembling a test form consisting of items at the desirable level of difficulty and discrimination. Specifically, the desirable items in this context are those that are not too difficult or easy (i.e., mid-level difficulty), with much more correct responses coming from high-proficiency test takers than from low-proficiency ones (i.e., high discrimination). These preferences make an intuitive sense. If all test takers respond to an item correctly (i.e., an extremely easy item) or incorrectly (i.e., an extremely difficult item), everyone's score on that item would be the same, and that item would not contribute at all to the variability of the reference score distribution. Moreover, if most correct responses on an item come from low-proficiency test takers and most incorrect responses from high-proficiency test takers, then the score on that item sends the opposite signal to the proficiency level measured by the test. The difficulty and discrimination of an item are also related. Specifically, if an item is too difficult or too easy, it is in general difficult to achieve high discrimination power because the score on that item does not vary in the first place. Moreover, a small amount of

---

[1]The cumulative distribution function of a random variable X evaluated at a given realized value of x represents the probability of $X \leq x$. The cumulative distribution function of the normal distribution, often denoted by $\phi(\cdot)$, with mean μ and standard deviation σ is defined as follows:

$$\phi(x) = \frac{1}{\sqrt{2\pi\sigma^2}} \int_{-\infty}^{x} \exp\left(-\frac{(t-\mu)^2}{2\sigma^2}\right) dt.$$

This function is implemented in virtually all modern software platforms with computing capabilities. For example, in Microsoft Excel, the cumulative distribution function value for the score of 75 with mean 50 and standard deviation 10 can be obtained by =NORM.DIST(x = 75, mean = 50, standard_dev = 10, cumulative = 1).

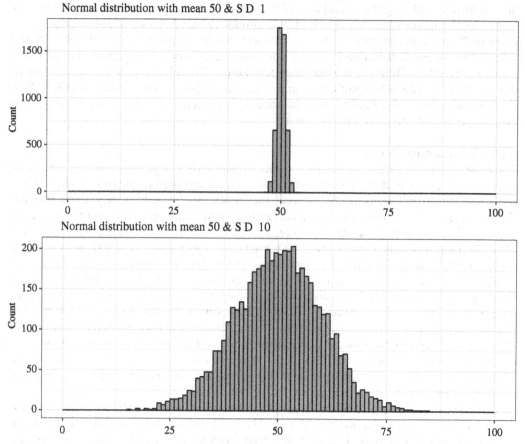

FIGURE 37.3 Normal distributions with the same mean but different standard deviations.

measurement error, such as random guesses by low-proficiency test takers or occasional slips by high-proficiency ones, can make the discrimination unstable for items with such extreme difficulty levels.

The standard process of obtaining item difficulty and discrimination involves collecting response data from a representative group of test takers. The data collection can take place as part of ongoing test administrations (e.g., in the form of pretest items) or separate pilot administrations. Item difficulty and discrimination values can then be estimated from the collected responses under the classical test theory (CTT) or item response theory (IRT) models. The CTT and IRT models differ in their operational definitions of difficulty and discrimination, but there are mature estimation routines for either model. The estimated item difficulty and discrimination values are reviewed at the individual item level as well as the aggregated test level to ensure all items contribute toward score variability.

Considerations for tests

The quality of a test score is determined not only by the quality of individual items but also by the quantity and coverage of items in the test form. In general, it is desirable to include as many items as possible, because the number of items in a test is closely related to the amount of measurement error associated with its scores. A large amount of measurement error makes it difficult to trust any given score, which in turn makes it difficult to interpret its location relative to the norms. All else being equal, the more items a test has, the more reliable its scores are, and the less measurement error. Each individual item can be considered as a measurement contributing information about a test taker's relative location in terms of the target construct.

As the number of items increases, the amount of information increases as well (assuming well-constructed items), which leads to higher reliability and smaller measurement error.

Another important test-level consideration is to ensure that scores across administrations are equally comparable to the norms and to one another. If all test takers respond to the same set of items across all administrations, the resulting scores would be comparable by design (assuming no meaningful differences across administration conditions). However, not every test can be administered that way because of logistical challenges (e.g., time zone differences; test center and proctor availability) and potential concerns about item exposure and security breaches. A popular alternative is to develop multiple test forms that consist of different sets of items (potentially with a subset of overlapping items) yet are as comparable as possible in content coverage and item characteristics at the test form level. Remaining differences across test forms can be adjusted via a psychometric procedure called equating (for a detailed discussion about this topic, see, e.g., Kolen & Brennan, 2014) to further ensure score comparability.

Criterion-Referenced Interpretations

Classification and categories

CR interpretations are designed such that they are anchored to standards and/or classifications (i.e., criteria) that are external to the test. Scores are thus interpreted in reference to the external criterion of interest in an absolute manner. For example, the score of X on a test indicates that the test taker has met Standard Y or belongs to Class Z. From an idealized perspective, relative interpretations in comparison with other test takers' scores may not be relevant at all. For example, let us consider a driver's license test designed to classify applicants into two groups: those who have enough knowledge and skills to be allowed driving on public roads and those who do not. An applicant would receive a score that is associated with one of the two groups, and how well he or she did within each group or across all applicants would be of little, if any, practical importance. The external criterion of interest can be as simple as two ordered groups (as shown in the driver's license test example) or more involved with multiple groups without an inherent order (e.g., classification of soldiers into different training foci).

Hudson (2014) noted varying degrees of specificity and relevance of CR interpretations in relation to the external criterion of interest. On one end of the spectrum, its reference can be as broad and inclusive as any interpretation that is not NR. On the other hand, a CR interpretation can be made based on a principled and specific reference to a target domain that is well-defined (Popham, 1978). The usefulness of a CR interpretation is closely related to the degree of its specificity and relevance.

A related consideration is the amount of effort needed to map a score to the external criterion of interest in a specific and relevant manner. Few external criteria render themselves naturally and inherently to a test score scale. For example, what does it mean to have enough knowledge and skills to be allowed driving on public roads when the observable outcome on which to make that distinction comes in on the scale of, say, 0–30 on a paper-and-pencil driving test? To address questions along this line, test developers and researchers need to make deliberate efforts to map a test score to a specific classification within the target domain and to make a case for (or against) the resulting mapping with evidence. The classification relies on preset scores that divide a given test score scale into the desired number of categories. Such scores are called cut scores, and the process of determining where on the test score scale the cut scores should be positioned is called (performance) standard setting.

In the context of language assessment, meaningful categories (e.g., different target language proficiency levels) are rarely inherent in the domain but often constructed based on research and practice of language learning and acquisition. This leads to the need for

562 Chapter 37 Norm- and Criterion-Referenced Score Interpretations

describing each category in detail in terms of what language learners in that category can do with the target language. When categories are defined in terms of target language proficiency, resulting descriptions are often called proficiency-level descriptors. The central role of the classification and the category description for CR interpretations is often represented explicitly in score reports, as will be shown in the third section.

Considerations for items and tests

The primary source of the mapping between a category in the target domain and a test score is item and test design and development. Specifically, items are written, reviewed, and evaluated to ensure that they provide discrimination and cover important content in the target domain. The discrimination in this context applies to categories and differs in meaning from that in the NR context which the primary concern is the relative standing of an individual test taker in comparison to others. To make this distinction more explicit, let us consider a hypothetical item for a driver's license test about which color of traffic lights indicate cars should stop. It may be safe to assume that the key, the red light, is a common knowledge, and that this item would be very easy, with almost every test taker responding correctly. This item would thus have almost zero discrimination in the NR context. However, in the CR context, this item may still be considered important because not knowing what the red light means can be strong evidence against allowing a person to drive on a public road. Items for CR interpretation should also cover the range of knowledge, skills, and abilities relevant to the classification. The lack of coverage presents a severe challenge for CR interpretations in that it amounts to classification based on missing information.

The focus on category classification and content coverage presents concrete guidelines for the evaluation of individual items and tests to support CR interpretations. The primary concern in writing individual items has to do with content: individual items should reflect content characterizing different categories within the target domain. A test then should consist of multiple such items that can, as a whole, provide sufficient content coverage of the target domain. The number of items included in a test also plays an important role in determining the reliability of the classification made based on the resulting scores.

There have been multiple proposals to quantify the reliability of classification for CR interpretations. Feldt and Brennan (1989) considered these proposals as part of two broad approaches. The first approach is to modify the reliability coefficient such that the modified index can take into account the (aggregated) distance between test takers' scores and cut scores (e.g., Brennan & Kane, 1977a, b; Livingston, 1972). The second approach is to quantify the consistency of classification across multiple (hypothetical) administrations. Livingston and Lewis (1995) proposed a generally applicable method under this approach to estimate classification accuracy and consistency around a set of cut scores for tests consisting of items with different scoring weights.

Standard setting

Let us consider again the hypothetical paper-and-pencil driver's license test that results in a score on the 0–30 scale. Suppose further that the meaningful categories include pass (possesses enough knowledge to be allowed to drive on public roads) and fail (does not possess such knowledge), and the classification is made at the score of 15: anyone who scored 15 or higher belong to the pass category, and the others in the fail category. The cut score in this case is 15. How does one know whether the dividing point between pass and fail should be 15, as opposed to, say, 17 or 11? The process of answering this question is standard setting.

Meaningful categories in a target language use domain (Bachman & Palmer, 1996) are general and conceptual. For example, whether a language learner can convey complex ideas in the target language is a general concept that is not specific to any given test. Even task-specific categories (e.g., can order a set of food and drinks in the target language) are general in the sense that they are not tied to any given test. On the other hand, cut scores are specific to a test and concrete. Standard setting is thus a process of mapping generic, conceptual categories into a set of concrete scores on a specific scale. In this sense, standard setting operationalizes conceptual categories (Kane, 1994). Like any operationalization process, standard setting involves judgment (Shepard, 1979). Consequently, the standard procedure for standard setting is to gather expert judgments of test content and/or test-taker performance and synthesize them to decide on a set of cut scores.

There is an extensive literature on standard-setting methods. In one recent count (Kaftandjieva, 2010), there are more than 60 different published standard-setting methods. A proper discussion of these methods goes beyond the scope of this chapter and is available elsewhere (e.g., Cizek, 2012; Hambleton & Pitoniak, 2006). For the purpose of this chapter, we can consider these methods as representing different options to elicit and aggregate expert judgments in an effective and systematic manner. Many researchers have compared the results from different standard-setting methods and observed varying sets of cut scores depending on which method was used, and the findings are summarized by Zieky (2012) as: "That different methods of setting cut scores will give different results is probably one of the most widely replicated findings in the research on setting cut scores" (p. 26). It is thus reasonable to consider a specific set of cut scores as those constructed by a specific expert panel of experts following a specific method, rather than some kind of underlying "truth" discovered by mechanically following an objective protocol.

The variability across standard-setting methods highlights the need for thorough and transparent documentation of standard-setting procedures, as explicitly mentioned in Standard 5.21 in the current edition of Standards for Educational and Psychological Testing (American Educational Research Association et al., 2014). A typical report from a standard-setting study includes details about the expert panel, the information the panel was given, specific procedures for panel discussions, and methodologies used to determine cut scores based on panel discussions. Each of these details helps stakeholders understand the process that led to the specific set of cut scores and test developer's justification for it.

Why the Distinction?

The NR–CR distinction described in this section represents an idealized view. Real-world score interpretations may not fall neatly or exclusively into one of the two categories. It is thus advisable to consider the distinction as a model: a simplified and idealized depiction of a phenomenon of interest that helps us comprehend its complexity. The NR–CR distinction "model" is wrong like any others (Box, 1976) but has proven its usefulness over the past several decades in the literature. Particularly useful is the model's conceptual clarity in presenting intended score interpretation as a central feature that accounts for different characteristics observed across tests and its rich vocabulary to describe such characteristics. With this in mind, we now apply the NR–CR distinction to understand real-world examples.

Real-World Examples

We now consider real-world language tests as case studies to apply and contextualize our understanding of the NR–CR distinction. The examples are selected to represent a variety of target test takers and intended use cases among tests that include published information and guidelines for score interpretation.

564 Chapter 37 Norm- and Criterion-Referenced Score Interpretations

The TOEIC® Listening and Reading Test

The first example comes from the TOEIC Listening and Reading test. According to its website,[2] the test assesses one's "English-language listening and reading skills for the workplace" using items that "simulate real-life situations that are relevant to the global workplace." It consists of two sections, Listening and Reading, and each section includes 100 items. The score on each section is reported on a scale ranging from 5 to 495. The sum of the two section scores, which ranges from 10 to 990, is also reported as the total score.

Many pieces of information are provided in the test program's annual report on score distributions of various test taker groups (Educational Testing Service, 2022b). An example of such information is given in Table 37.1. Specifically, the table gives the mean and standard deviation of two section scores on the TOEIC Listening and Reading test across five geographical regions. The regions differ in terms of the mean and standard deviation. Thus, one could gauge their relative standing amongst test takers within a particular region (and a particular year) based on their score and the regional norms. This in no way implies that a score of, say, 320, has a different CR interpretation for a test taker in Asia or Europe but highlights how information about norms can be used to facilitate comparisons within a referenced group.

Another set of norms is given in Table 37.2. Specifically, the table presents the means and standard deviations of the section and total scores across job types. For example, a total score of 660 would be right around the mean score for Professional Specialists. The same total score would be positioned at about a half standard deviation higher than the mean score for Technicians.

The availability of these norms does not mean that the TOEIC Listening and Reading test is a NR "test." The official website includes a link to another document that provides descriptions of strengths and weaknesses at different score ranges for each section (Educational Testing Service, 2018a). These descriptors indicate what a typical test taker with a given TOEIC Listening score range can do using English (under the "Strengths" column) as well as what they may find difficult to do (under the "Weaknesses" column). This type of information thus facilitates CR interpretations of the TOEIC Listening and Reading scores.

> **TABLE 37.1**
>
> **The means and standard deviations of the TOEIC Listening and Reading test scores across five regions**
>
> | | Listening | | Reading | |
> |---|---|---|---|---|
> | | Mean | SD | Mean | SD |
> | Africa | 355 | 104 | 302 | 108 |
> | Asia | 331 | 97 | 269 | 106 |
> | Europe | 372 | 98 | 330 | 110 |
> | North America | 327 | 128 | 275 | 130 |
> | South Amrica | 350 | 110 | 312 | 117 |
>
> **Source:** Adapted from figure 1 in Educational Testing Service (2022b).

---

[2] https://www.ets.org/toeic/test-takers/scores.html.

TABLE 37.2

The means and standard deviations of the TOEIC Listening and Reading test scores across four types of jobs

	Listening		Reading		Total	
	Mean	SD	Mean	SD	Mean	SD
Professional Specialist	350	89	306	99	656	181
Management	346	101	301	110	647	204
Services	347	98	287	107	633	196
Technician	309	100	255	104	564	196

Source: Adapted from figure 1 in Educational Testing Service (2022b).

ACTFL Assessment of Performance Toward Proficiency in Languages

The ACTFL Assessment of Performance toward Proficiency in Languages (AAPPL) measures the proficiency and performance of US language learners in Grades 3–12. The test focuses on the following three modes of communication: Interpersonal Listening & Speaking (ILS), Presentational Writing (PW), and Interpretive Reading (IR) and Listening (IL). A separate score is reported for each mode, except for the interpretive mode for which IR and IL scores are provided separately. The total number of scores is thus four.

Each of the four scores is reported on 10-point scale that is divided into three proficiency ranges, which are Novice, Intermediate, and Advanced Low according to ACTFL Proficiency Guidelines (ACTFL, 2012). A single test form covers a subset of the scale. Specifically, Forms A1, A2, and E cover the first eight score points (N-1 through I-4), and Forms B1 and B2 do not cover the first three score points. This information is summarized in Table 37.3.

TABLE 37.3

AAPPL score and form information

ACTFL proficiency guidelines	ACTFL performance scale	AAPPL performance score	Form	
Advanced low	Advanced	A-1		B
Intermediate high	Intermediate	I-5		
Intermediate mid		I-4	A & E	
Intermediate mid		I-3		
Intermediate mid		I-2		
Intermediate low		I-1		
Novice high	Novice	N-4		
Novice mid		N-3		
Novice mid		N-2		
Novice low		N-1		

Source: Reproduced from ACTFL (2023).

The AAPPL score points represent different categories of test taker performances rather than numeric information. The categories are aligned to ACTFL Proficiency Guidelines, which provide descriptions of what language learners in each category can do with the target language. In this sense, the AAPPL scores facilitate CR interpretations. The support for CR interpretations is further demonstrated in the score report. A sample score report is available on the AAPPL website.[3] It shows the score on the ILS mode and provides descriptions of the scores as well as strategies for improving proficiency and performance. The score descriptions indicate what this test taker can do in the target language without any mention of norms or other test takers. AAPPL scores are intended for CR interpretations, and the score report makes it clear.

Challenges

The usefulness of the NR–CR distinction "model" lies in its capacity to account for major differences across tests. The model also has limitations and challenges. Knowledge of such limitations and challenges is useful because it helps us identify the consequences of using the model as well as aspects of the model that can be improved. In this section, we discuss such limitations and challenges.

Challenges for NR–CR Distinction Model

A major challenge for the NR–CR distinction model is a strong practical preference toward multiple uses and interpretations of test scores. Preparing for and taking a test is often an expensive and time-consuming process that requires financial, emotional, and intellectual investment from test takers and stakeholders. It is understandable that they want as much information as possible from a test score report. They may expect (and even demand) a test score intended to be interpreted against norms to also have a criterion-related interpretation, and vice versa. The NR–CR distinction model, on the other hand, is rooted in the binary distinction between NR and CR interpretations and thus may underestimate the importance of the fundamental desire for more information.

The predilection toward multiple score interpretations presents a related challenge for test developers and researchers: how to communicate intended score interpretations with stakeholders? Justifying an intended score interpretation and use often requires multiple research studies and thorough documentation to build up a necessary validity argument. It can be difficult to communicate the resulting validity argument in an accurate yet succinct manner. Multiple intended interpretations across the NR–CR divide could make the development and communication of validity arguments even more demanding and involved.

NR-Specific Challenges

There are also challenges specific to NR interpretations. The most fundamental challenge in this context has to do with the definition of relevant population groups. Because the norms are summary statistics of a population, they are specific to how the population is defined. NR score interpretations are in turn specific to the population definition and would in general

---

[3] https://www.actfl.org/assessments/k-12-assessments/aappl/aappl-scores-reporting.

change across different definitions. A related challenge is the agency in, and the responsibility of, the population definition; that is, who should have a say in defining population groups for score interpretations. Traditionally, population groups have often been defined at an aggregated level (e.g., grade level) by policy-makers and test developers. However, recent advancements in socio-culturally responsible assessments (Bennett, 2023) and quantitative critical race theory (e.g., Castillo & Gillborn, 2022) have raised questions about whether such practices can be justified and presented alternative approaches that emphasize the role of test-taker experiences and choices.

CR-Specific Challenges

The central challenge specific to CR interpretations involves the mapping between test scores and external criteria. The mapping relies on the standard setting process, which has multiple sources of variability including the sampling of test takers, items, and experts, as well as their interactions. Researchers have reported empirical evidence suggesting that their combined effects can be large (e.g., Clauser et al., 2014). The uncertainty associated with the outcome of a standard-setting process can be estimated as suggested by Clauser et al., but it is rare to see such estimates reported in practice. It is thus often difficult to evaluate a mapping process and the resulting output. Moreover, the lack of information about this uncertainty leads to other related questions: How much uncertainty is there in the output mapping from a well-designed mapping process, and how much difference is there between the outputs from a well-designed and those from a not so well-designed one? Answers to these questions would help stakeholders interpret test scores and test developers allocate resources under contexts in which CR interpretations are desired.

Conclusion and Future Steps

In this chapter, we introduced the distinction between NR- and CR-interpretations of test scores, applied it to real-world examples, and discussed its usefulness and challenges, in the context of language assessment. The distinction centers around how scores can and should be interpreted, which in turn affects upstream decisions about how tests are designed and developed to support a given score interpretation. We framed the distinction as a model, whose usefulness comes from its capacity to account for differences in test design and development processes with the simple, binary NR–CR distinction.

Its long history in the educational measurement field notwithstanding, the NR–CR distinction is still evolving with learning and assessment research and practice. The previous edition of this volume included two chapters on this topic, one for NR interpretations (Bae, 2014) and the another for CR interpretations (Hudson, 2014). The unified treatment in this chapter framed the distinction as a model and discussed its usefulness and challenges. Contemporary topics in the relevant fields will lead to new questions to which the distinction will be exposed and applied. Our understanding and view toward the usefulness and limitations of the NR–CR distinction will evolve.

Discussion Questions

1. What are common classroom assessment practices to facilitate NR- and CR-interpretations?
2. Consider a score report that you liked the most as a test taker. Which information in that report made you like it? What research activities are needed to support and justify that information?

568 Chapter 37 Norm- and Criterion-Referenced Score Interpretations

References

ACTFL. (2012). *ACTFL proficiency guidelines 2012*. https://www.actfl.org/uploads/files/general/ACTFLProficiency Guidelines2012.pdf.

ACTFL. (2023, August 12). *AAPPL scores & reporting*. https://www.actfl.org/assessments/k-12-assessments/aappl/aappl-scores-reporting.

American Educational Research Association, American Psychological Association, & National Council on Measurement in Education (Eds.). (2014). *Standards for educational and psychological testing*. American Educational Research Association.

Bachman, L. F., & Palmer, A. S. (1996). *Language testing in practice: Designing and developing useful language tests*. Oxford University Press.

Bachman, L. F., & Palmer, A. S. (2010). *Language assessment in practice* (2nd ed.). Oxford University Press.

Bae, J. (2014). Norm-referenced approach to language assessment. In A. J. Kunnan (Ed.), *The companion to language assessment* (Vol. 2, pp. 542–560). John Wiley & Sons.

Bennett, R. E. (2023). *Toward a theory of socioculturally responsive assessment*. Educational Assessment: Advanced online publication.

Box, G. E. P. (1976). Science and statistics. *Journal of the American Statistical Association, 71*, 791–799.

Brennan, R. L., & Kane, M. T. (1977a). An index of dependability for mastery tests. *Journal of Educational Measurement, 14*, 277–289.

Brennan, R. L., & Kane, M. T. (1977b). Signal/noise ratios for domain-referenced tests. *Psychometrika, 42*, 609–625.

Briggs, D. C. (2022). A history of scaling and its relationship to measurement. In B. E. Clauser & M. B. Bunch (Eds.), *The history of educational measurement: Key advancements in theory, policy, and practice* (pp. 263–291). Routledge.

Castillo, W., & Gillborn, D. (2022). *How to "QuantCrit": Practices and questions for education data researchers and users (EdWorkingPaper: 22-546)*. Retrieved from Annenberg Institute at Brown University: https://doi.org/10.26300/v5kh-dd65.

Cizek, G. J. (Ed.). (2012). *Setting performance standards: Foundations, methods, and innovations* (2nd ed.). Routledge.

Clauser, J. C., Margolis, M. J., & Clauser, B. E. (2014). An examination of the replicability of Angoff standard setting results within a generalizability theory framework. *Journal of Educational Measurement, 51*, 127–140.

Educational Testing Service. (2018a). *TOEIC® Listening and Reading score descriptors*. https://www.ets.org/pdfs/toeic/toeic-listening-reading-score-descriptors.pdf.

Educational Testing Service. (2022b). *TOEIC® Listening and Reading 2022 report on test takers worldwide*. https://www.ets.org/pdfs/toeic/toeic-listening-reading-report-test-takers-worldwide.pdf.

Feldt, L. S., & Brennan, R. L. (1989). Reliability. In R. L. Linn (Ed.), *Educational measurement* (3rd ed., pp. 105–146). American Council on Education and Macmillan.

Geisinger, K. F. (2022). The history of norm- and criterion-referenced testing. In B. E. Clauser & M. B. Bunch (Eds.), *The history of educational measurement: Key advancements in theory, policy, and practice* (pp. 42–64). Routledge.

Glaser, R. (1963). Instructional technology and the measurement of learning outcomes: some questions. *American Psychologist, 18*, 519–521.

Hambleton, R. K., & Pitoniak, M. J. (2006). Setting performance standards. In R. L. Brennan (Ed.), *Educational measurement* (4th ed., pp. 433–470). Praeger.

Hudson, T. (2014). Criterion-referenced approach to language assessment. In A. J. Kunnan (Ed.), *The companion to language assessment* (Vol. 2, pp. 561–577). John Wiley & Sons.

Kaftandjieva, F. (2010). *Methods for setting cut scores in criterion-referenced achievement tests: A comparative analysis of six recent methods with an application to tests of reading in EFL*. CITO.

Kane, M. T. (1994). Validating the performance standards associated with passing scores. *Review of Educational Research, 64*, 425–461.

Kane, M. T. (2013). Validating the interpretations and uses of test scores. *Journal of Educational Measurement, 50*, 1–73.

Kolen, M. J., & Brennan, R. L. (2014). *Test equating, scaling, and linking: Methods and practices* (3rd ed.). Springer.

Livingston, S. A. (1972). Criterion-referenced applications of classical test theory. *Journal of Educational Measurement, 9*, 13–26.

Livingston, S. A., & Lewis, C. (1995). Estimating the consistency and accuracy of classifications based on test scores. *Journal of Educational Measurement, 32*, 179–197.

Millman, J. (1974). Criterion-referenced testing. In W. J. Popham (Ed.), *Evaluation in education: Current applications* (pp. 309–397). McCutchan.

Popham, W. J. (Ed.). (1978). *Criterion-referenced measurement*. Prentice-Hall Inc.

Shepard, L. (1979). Standard setting issues and methods. *Applied Psychological Measurement, 4*, 447–467.

Zieky, M. J. (2012). So much has changed: an historical overview of setting cut scores. In G. J. Cizek (Ed.), *Setting performance standards: Foundations, methods, and innovations* (2nd ed., pp. 15–32). Routledge.

Suggested Readings

Geisinger, K. F. (2022). The history of norm- and criterion-referenced testing. In B. E. Clauser & M. B. Bunch (Eds.), *The history of educational measurement: Key advancements in theory, policy, and practice* (pp. 42–64). Routledge.

Kane, M. T. (1994). Validating the performance standards associated with passing scores. *Review of Educational Research, 64*, 425–461.

CHAPTER 38

Practical Uses of EFA and SEM for Language Assessment Researchers

Gary J. Ockey

Introduction

Exploratory factor analysis (EFA) and structural equation modeling (SEM) are techniques commonly used in the field of language assessment. Both are multivariate statistical techniques, which have their basis in correlational analysis. EFA is a data-driven approach which is generally used as an investigative technique to identify relationships among variables. This usually means determining the smallest number of factors which can reasonably account for the correlations among the scores on test or survey items for language assessment researchers. For instance, EFA might help determine that a 30-item multiple-choice test aimed at assessing reading comprehension largely measures only three subconstructs of reading. Each of the 30 items mostly measures one of the three constructs. For instance, it might be determined that 7 items measure reading for general understanding, 12 for finding details, and 6 for making inferences. Test users could use this information to better interpret the meaning of test scores, and test developers could use it to help them revise the test to better align their targeted construct of reading with what the test actually measures.

SEM is an a priori theory approach that is most often used to determine the extent to which an already established theory, generally based on previous research, about relationships among variables is supported by observed data. The aim of an analysis is to test a hypothesized set of relationships, often among scores on items. For instance, if a researcher believes that reading comprehension is composed of the three sub-constructs of reading for general understanding, finding details, and making inferences, a confirmatory factor analysis (CFA), which is a particular type of SEM analysis, could be used to test this hypothesis.

EFA uses correlational statistics, and SEM uses correlational statistics as well as multiple regression analysis. Readers who are not familiar with correlation and regression are encouraged to explore these topics before embarking on this chapter. An appropriate source is Larson-Hall's (2016) *A guide to doing statistics in second language research using SPSS and R*.

The following definitions are helpful for understanding some of the concepts introduced in this chapter. Observed variables, or measured variables, are the actual scores on a particular test or survey, such as the scores on a multiple-choice listening test or responses to a Likert scale self-evaluation. *Latent variables*, or *factors*, are unobservable *constructs*, *traits*, or *abilities*,

---

The Concise Companion to Language Assessment, First Edition. Edited by Antony John Kunnan.
© 2025 John Wiley & Sons, Inc. Published 2025 by John Wiley & Sons, Inc.

570

like second language speaking ability that we cannot observe directly. The term *factor* is most often used when the concept is defined mathematically, but all five of these terms refer to the same concept and are used synonymously throughout this chapter. A model is a set of mathematical relationships among variables. In SEM, a researcher tests a hypothesized mathematical model believed to best explain the relationships among the variables of interest.

This chapter is divided into two major sections, the first introduces EFA and the second SEM, with a focus on CFA. Theoretical explanations are accompanied by a practical example from real data.

Exploratory Factor Analysis

EFA is most often used to determine how many factors or constructs underlie a set of test scores and to what extent these factors are related to each other. For language assessment researchers, EFA is generally used to help identify theoretical constructs, which are measured by an assessment instrument, such as the ability to comprehend a written passage or sub-constructs, like the ability to comprehend details or global ideas in a written passage.

EFA analyzes the pattern of correlations among many observed variables in order to determine which of them measure similar constructs. The process converts a set of observed variables into a set of unobservable factors. The factors are interpreted by using the factor loadings, usually the correlations between the observed variables and the unobservable factors. Observed variables are said to *load on* a factor when they correlate with it. After factors have been identified, a content analysis of the set items that load on each factor can be conducted to help determine the abilities or other features that are measured by the set of items.

An EFA generally follows five steps. First, the data are screened and prepared for analysis; second, factors are extracted; third, the number of factors to retain for the solution is determined; fourth, a rotation method is selected and employed; and fifth, the solution is interpreted. To demonstrate this five-step process, data from a study, which aimed to identify the factors measured by an academic abilities self-assessment questionnaire, is used. The researchers were particularly interested in determining the ways and extent to which language ability might be manifested as a construct measured by the instrument. Three hundred test takers completed the assessment. The test takers responded to 20 five-point Likert scale items, 5 = strongly agree, 4 = agree, 3 = neither agree nor disagree, 2 = disagree, and 1 = strongly disagree. The item correlations are presented in Table 38.1.

As can be seen, all correlations are positive, and the sizes of the correlations are diverse, ranging from a high of 0.86 to a low of 0.09. From looking at the matrix of correlations, it is clear that these variables measure related concepts (because all variables correlate with each other), but with so many correlations, it is difficult to determine much more about the relationships among the items. EFA can be used to make the patterns in large correlation matrices, such as this one, more salient.

Data Screening

The first step in an EFA is data screening. EFA relies on the following assumptions: independence of observations, linearity of relationships among all pairs of variables, the absence of multicollinearity and singularity, and potentially multivariate normality. Insufficient sample sizes and outliers can also lead to meaningless analyses. The assumption of independence holds that scores of the individuals in the experiment are independent. A violation of this assumption would be test takers working together or cheating from each other. Collecting one's own data and paying careful attention to the behaviors of the test takers can

TABLE **38.1**

Data matrix for example dataset of self-assessed academic abilities

Item	1	2	3	4	5	6	7	8	9	10	11	12	13	14	15	16	17	18	19	20
1	1.00																			
2	0.46	1.00																		
3	0.49	0.34	1.00																	
4	0.34	0.60	0.45	1.00																
5	0.43	0.22	0.36	0.18	1.00															
6	0.66	0.53	0.42	0.39	0.37	1.00														
7	0.37	0.63	0.33	0.59	0.14	0.41	1.00													
8	0.29	0.23	0.52	0.35	0.61	0.33	0.21	1.00												
9	0.33	0.46	0.41	0.69	0.12	0.31	0.56	0.26	1.00											
10	0.51	0.34	0.48	0.35	0.49	0.54	0.34	0.44	0.30	1.00										
11	0.49	0.29	0.31	0.24	0.62	0.49	0.22	0.55	0.17	0.49	1.00									
12	0.26	0.16	0.50	0.31	0.53	0.28	0.15	0.84	0.27	0.35	0.48	1.00								
13	0.35	0.51	0.49	0.61	0.15	0.33	0.52	0.20	0.71	0.34	0.14	0.21	1.00							
14	0.47	0.37	0.70	0.48	0.41	0.39	0.31	0.48	0.44	0.44	0.35	0.47	0.49	1.00						
15	0.34	0.26	0.52	0.39	0.53	0.37	0.24	0.79	0.27	0.40	0.56	0.81	0.23	0.53	1.00					
16	0.43	0.39	0.71	0.47	0.37	0.45	0.36	0.58	0.42	0.40	0.37	0.50	0.47	0.69	0.59	1.00				
17	0.30	0.48	0.39	0.69	0.09	0.33	0.58	0.26	0.75	0.32	0.19	0.27	0.64	0.41	0.33	0.51	1.00			
18	0.51	0.38	0.49	0.33	0.45	0.55	0.40	0.35	0.34	0.60	0.44	0.34	0.36	0.46	0.43	0.48	0.37	1.00		
19	0.34	0.27	0.55	0.33	0.58	0.34	0.16	0.80	0.30	0.39	0.55	0.82	0.28	0.50	0.86	0.57	0.29	0.39	1.00	
20	0.45	0.40	0.72	0.50	0.37	0.50	0.39	0.52	0.47	0.46	0.33	0.48	0.50	0.69	0.56	0.83	0.49	0.51	0.56	1.00

Exploratory Factor Analysis   **573**

help ensure that this assumption is met. Linearity assumes that the observed variables are related in a straight-line relationship, which can be assessed by inspecting bivariate scatter plots. Data transformations (Keppel & Wickens, 2004) can be used as a remedy for non-linear relationships between pairs of variables. The assumption of the absence of singularity and multicollinearity is that the variables are not too highly correlated. Only in extreme cases is this usually a problem for a factor analysis. Measures of tolerance or variance inflation factor can be used to check this assumption. Tolerance values of less than 0.10 or VIF values greater than 10.00 indicate serious levels of multicollinearity (Kline, 2016) and suggest that an FA analysis may not produce meaningful results. When multicollinearity is present, one or more of the highly correlated variables may be combined with each other or excluded from the analysis. Satisfying the assumption of multivariate normality is only necessary when statistical inference is used to determine the number of factors – which is not common in language assessment research. This assumption is discussed in the SEM section.

While there are no agreed upon guidelines for what is a sufficient sample size for an EFA, researchers have provided some suggestions. Kline (1994) argued that a sample size of 100 is quite reliable but 50 may be tolerable when researchers accept that the findings may not be highly reliable. More recently, de Winter et al. (2009) agree indicating that sample sizes of 50 or even smaller may produce acceptably reliable results, depending on the context. Importantly, when assumptions are clearly met, and there are no outliers, fewer cases will be needed for accurate estimates.

It is crucial that procedures for collecting and screening data are reported. Procedures for determining the extent to which assumptions are tenable should be described, and if for example, outliers are excluded or data transformations are conducted, a description of these data manipulations accompanied by a rationale for the changes should be reported. Particular attention should be paid to outliers since they can have a considerable effect on an EFA. Based on the guidelines above, all variables in the self-assessment of academic ability dataset satisfied the assumptions, and no outliers were detected. As a result, no data manipulations were used for the analysis.

Factor Extraction

Factor extraction is a procedure that mathematically determines the type of model and the number of factors in a dataset (Tabachnick & Fidell, 2019). Various procedures for factor extraction are available, including principal components (PCA), principal factors, maximum likelihood (ML), and weighted or unweighted least squares factoring. Because of somewhat differing mathematical procedures, some researchers consider PCA separate from EFA, while others consider it a type of EFA (Blunch, 2013). In this paper, it will be considered a type of EFA. PCA is commonly encountered in the language assessment literature and is a relatively simple model compared to (other) EFA extraction methods. For factor extraction using PCA, the total variance among the observed variables is partitioned so that a linear combination of them that accounts for the most possible variance is identified. The value placed on this linear combination is referred to as the first eigenvalue. The process continues so that a second linear combination, one that is uncorrelated with the first, is found that accounts for the most possible remaining variance. This linear combination is the second eigenvalue. This process continues until all of the variance has been accounted for (Pituch & Stevens, 2016). This process will produce the same number of eigenvalues as there are test items, decreasing in size from the first to the last (20th for the questionnaire data). ML factor extraction is also commonly used by language assessment researchers. In this approach, factor loadings are calculated by maximizing the probability of sampling the correlation matrix from a population (Tabachnick & Fidell, 2019).

A PCA, using EQS 6.1, was used to extract the eigenvalues from the self-assessment of academic ability data. The magnitudes of the eigenvalues were as follows: 9.27, 2.77, 1.59, 1.09, 0.68, 0.58, 0.51, 0.44, 0.42, 0.38, 0.36, 0.33, 0.28, 0.27, 0.23, 0.22, 0.20, 0.16, 0.12, and 0.10. It is quite clear that most of the variance in scores can be quite accurately represented with fewer than 20 items since a number of the eigenvalues are very small – close to zero. This means that many of the items are measuring highly similar factors – not 20 distinct ones.

Determining the Number of Factors in a Solution

Multiple methods for determining the number of factors in a solution are available, and it is recommended that a combination of them be used. The default in most computer programs is set to the Kaiser rule, which is to retain factors that have eigenvalues greater than one. The logic for the Kaiser rule is that a factor should account for at least as much unique variance as one item. Unfortunately, this easy-to-follow rule is not always an effective indicator of the number of factors, especially when there are many items, as is the case with most language tests. Parallel analysis (Horn, 1965) is a technique for identifying the number of factors, which takes into account sample size and number of items. The number of factors in a parallel analysis is determined based on a comparison of the sizes of the eigenvalues in the dataset to the sizes of eigenvalues in a randomly generated dataset.

A third indicator of the number of factors for a set of scores is a scree plot, which is a visual representation of the size of the eigenvalues. When the decrease in size from one eigenvalue to the next smallest becomes insubstantial relative to the decrease in size from the next largest, it is determined that this is the point at which no more factors should be included in the solution. Figure 38.1 presents the scree plot of the self-assessment of academic ability data.

The scree plot presents eigenvalues as dots on the line. The horizontal axis shows the number of eigenvalues or components, beginning with one on the left and progressing to 20 on the right (because the test has 20 items). The vertical axis shows the size of the eigenvalue, starting with zero at the bottom. An eigenvalue of one is highlighted to remind users of Kaiser's rule.

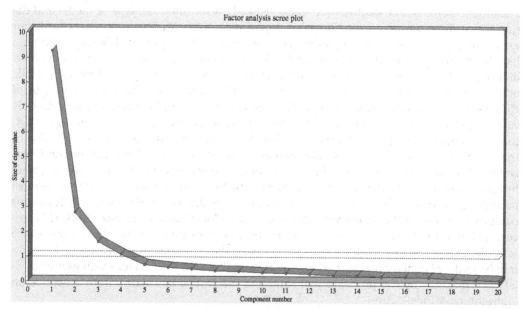

FIGURE 38.1 Scree plot of self-assessment of academic ability data.

The first eigenvalue in the analysis can be seen at the dot where the line begins in the top left corner. The eigenvalue for this first factor is above nine, suggesting that much of the variance in scores can be accounted for by one underlying trait or factor. The second eigenvalue, which can be seen at the second dot on the line, is near three, and the third, which is at the third dot on the line is at about 1.5. The 20th eigenvalue is near zero at the far right hand of the scree plot. As can be seen, there is a sharp drop from the first to the second and the second to the third eigenvalues. Between the third and fourth and between the fourth and fifth, there is much less decrease in size. After the fifth, the line is almost horizontal.

Interpreting scree plots can be difficult because the researcher has to determine at what point the decrease in variance accounted for by a factor, that is, the difference in magnitudes of eigenvalues, is no longer large enough to justify including the factor in the solution. In the scree plot shown in Figure 38.1, it is clear that there are at least three factors present in the data because the drop is quite sharp from the first to the second and the second to the third points on the line. It is also quite clear that after the fifth point on the line, there is almost no decrease. However, determining whether there are three, four, or five factors requires some judgment on the part of the researcher.

Although EFA is largely a quantitative approach, researchers should also consider content and theory when determining the number of factors in a dataset. This will be discussed further in the section on *Interpreting factor loadings*. Based on Kaiser's rule, the scree plot, a parallel analysis, content, and theory, a four-factor solution was selected.

Selecting a Rotation Method

After factors have been extracted, a rotation method is used to improve the interpretability of the solution. Rotation maximizes or minimizes different statistics to emphasize interpretative patterns. Various rotation methods can be used, some of which simplify the factors, some the variables, and others both the factors and variables. For example, varimax rotation aims to simplify factors by maximizing variance for each of the within-factor loadings across variables, and quartimax simplifies variables by maximizing the variance of the loadings for a variable across factors (Tabachnick & Fidell, 2019). The most important distinction for language testers is whether or not the rotation method employs an uncorrelated, also referred to as orthogonal, technique, or a correlated, also referred to as an oblique, technique. Orthogonal approaches assume that the factors are not correlated while oblique approaches assume that they are. In the social sciences, factors are most often correlated (Bentler, 2008), and it is therefore usually more defensible for language assessment researchers to use oblique techniques. Orthogonal approaches include Varimax, Quartimax, and Equamax and oblique approaches include Oblimin and Promax. The results from the computer program EQS 6.1 based on the selection of four factors and using an Oblimin rotation for the self-assessment of academic ability data are presented in Table 38.2. In Table 38.2, items which load highly (>0.55) on each factor have been bolded. For instance, items 3, 14, 16, and 20 correlate highly with, or more technically, load on factor one.

Interpreting Factor Loadings

The relative magnitudes of the factor loadings drive an analysis. Specific guidance for determining the magnitude of a factor loading to use as a cutoff is somewhat unclear. Some researchers suggest that values above 0.30 indicate a legitimate factor loading while others recommend conducting statistical tests that take sample size into account (Pituch & Stevens, 2016). It generally requires very large sample sizes for loadings as low as 0.30 to be considered large enough. Thus, 0.30 should be used as a cutoff only when sample sizes

576 Chapter 38 Practical Uses of EFA and SEM for Language Assessment Researchers

TABLE 38.2

Four-factor solution for self-assessment of academic ability data

	Factor 1	Factor 2	Factor 3	Factor 4
Item 1	0.21	0.07	**0.68**	−0.06
Item 2	−0.10	**0.64**	0.32	−0.02
Item 3	**0.71**	0.02	0.15	0.11
Item 4	0.03	**0.79**	−0.05	0.14
Item 5	−0.02	−0.14	0.41	**0.57**
Item 6	0.11	0.16	**0.68**	−0.01
Item 7	−0.13	**0.76**	0.19	−0.03
Item 8	0.09	0.04	−0.03	**0.84**
Item 9	0.08	**0.80**	−0.12	0.05
Item 10	0.16	0.05	**0.58**	0.12
Item 11	−0.20	0.02	0.48	**0.55**
Item 12	0.09	0.04	−0.13	**0.86**
Item 13	0.28	**0.66**	−0.01	−0.10
Item 14	**0.66**	0.06	0.14	0.12
Item 15	0.12	0.08	−0.02	**0.80**
Item 16	**0.65**	0.10	0.08	0.19
Item 17	0.09	**0.80**	−0.10	0.06
Item 18	0.25	0.08	**0.56**	0.05
Item 19	0.14	0.05	−0.04	**0.81**
Item 20	**0.68**	0.12	0.13	0.12

are large. When loadings are much higher than 0.30, and sample sizes are fairly large as in the self-assessment of academic abilities dataset, judgments based on relative magnitudes of factor loadings generally provide an appropriate interpretation.

Items that load highly on one factor only measure one construct, that is, they are unidimensional. Items that load on more than one factor, such as item 11, which substantially loads on factors three (0.48) and four (0.55), are multidimensional, that is, they measure aspects of two or more factors. When many items have split loadings, like item 11, it can suggest that the solution should have a different number of factors. For instance, instead of four factors, maybe there are actually five for this dataset. For the most part, however, this factor structure provides a clear solution. All of the items loaded at 0.55 or above on one factor, and only two items, 5 (0.41), and 11 (0.48), loaded above 0.35 on a second factor.

After identifying the items that load on each factor, a content analysis of the items should be conducted to determine what the items for each factor have in common. This makes it possible to identify the constructs that underlie the test items. For the self-assessment of academic ability data, items that loaded on factor one were about enjoying school, items that loaded on factor two were about enjoying and doing well in language, items that loaded on factor three were about feeling confident to do well in school, and items that loaded on factor four were about enjoying and doing well in math. The self-assessment instrument could therefore be shown to measure these four constructs. In this case, the content analysis of the four-factor model led to a reasonable outcome. When content analysis does not align with the quantitative findings, it may be appropriate to reanalyze the data with a different number of factors. A solution where the number of factors is supported by both content/theory and the quantitative analysis is most defensible.

Origins and Applications in Language Testing

The logic underlying EFA might have originated with 5th-century Greek philosophers, who believed that what is observable can only be explained by what cannot be observed. However, Spearman (1907), who worked on finding intelligence factors in the early 20th century, is usually given credit for founding factor analysis (Mulaik, 1987).

A common use of EFA in language assessment has been to assess the factor structure of a test or dimensionality of a dataset (e.g., Green & Weir, 2004; Ockey, 2007). EFA has also been used to reduce the number of variables to investigate in research studies (e.g., Saito et al., 2019) and to determine the number of factors in cognitive strategy use when taking an examination (Song & Cheng, 2006).

Structural Equation Modeling

SEM is a set of statistical techniques that can be used to show and verify the relationships among a set of variables. More specifically, SEM combines multiple regression, factor analysis, and path analysis techniques to model the relationships among measured and latent variables. CFA is a commonly encountered type of SEM in the language assessment literature. Various computer software programs and notational schemes are used by SEM researchers. This chapter is based on the Bentler and Weeks (1980) model, and the example analyses are conducted using this model in the EQS program.

Model diagrams are often used to help researchers picture relationships among the variables in an SEM analysis, and they often appear in published studies as visual representations of the models under investigation. These diagrams represent the hypothesized relationships in a covariance matrix. Arrows between variables indicate that the variables are expected to be meaningfully related. The absence of arrows between variables indicates that the magnitude of the relationships, that is, the covariances among these variables, are not expected to be large enough to be meaningful. A model diagram that shows a hypothesized relationship between compliance, shyness, and second language oral ability is presented in Figure 38.2.

The 11 rectangles represent observed variables, usually test or survey items in language assessment research, and the ovals, labeled, shyness, compliance, and oral ability, indicate factors, latent variables, or constructs. When one variable is hypothesized to predict another, a single-headed arrow pointing toward the predicted variable is used. For example, in Figure 38.2, the latent variable of shyness is hypothesized to predict three observed variables: avoid crowds, keep quiet, and loner. Double-headed arrows indicate that the variables are expected to correlate with each other, but the direction of the relationship is not assumed. An example in Figure 38.2 is the relationship between compliance and shyness. Error is labeled as either E for error or D for disturbance. Errors are used when a latent variable predicts an observed variable, for instance, E (error) 11 for compliance predicting agreeable. Disturbance (D) is used when a latent variable predicts another latent variable, for example, the $D1$ for shyness and compliance predicting oral ability.

In SEM, a distinction is generally made between the part of the model that relates the measured variables to the latent variables, referred to as the measurement model, and the relationships among the latent variables, referred to as the structural model. In the model in Figure 38.2, there are three measurement models. One relates the latent variable of shyness to three observed variables: avoid crowds, keep quiet, and loner. Another measurement model relates the latent variable of compliance to three observed variables: agreeable, follower, and rarely argue. The third measurement model is the relationship of the latent variable of oral ability to the observed variables of strategies, vocabulary, grammar, fluency, and pronunciation.

578 Chapter 38 Practical Uses of EFA and SEM for Language Assessment Researchers

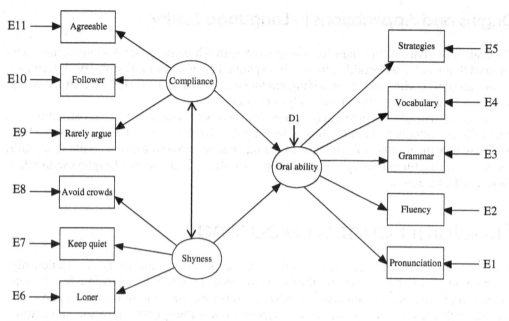

FIGURE 38.2 Example SEM model diagram which relates compliance, shyness, and second language oral ability.

There is one structural model in Figure 38.2 that relates the latent variables of shyness, compliance, and oral ability.

Researchers present the steps in an SEM analysis in slightly different ways. The seven-step approach that follows is recommended for language testers using a strictly confirmatory approach: (i) a model is proposed; (ii) the proposed model is shown to be identified; (iii) suitable data for the model is collected and screened; (iv) the model parameters are estimated; (v) the fit of the model to the data is assessed; (vi) parameters are interpreted; and (vii) competing models are evaluated.

Despite the fact that SEM is a confirmatory technique, researchers may not always base their final analysis on their originally proposed model. This generally happens when the proposed model does not fit the observed data to an acceptable extent. Procedures for identifying parameters that are missing from a model are available when model fit is not acceptable. One of these procedures is the Lagrange Multiplier (LM) test. The LM test identifies parameters that have been excluded from the model, which if included will have the largest effect on increasing model fit. The LM test's counterpart is the Wald test. It is used to identify parameters that have been hypothesized as meaningful in the proposed model but are not found to be substantial in the observed data. When the originally proposed model is respecified because it does not fit the data, it is crucial that the researcher provides a relevant theory to support changes in the model as well as indicate that the analysis is no longer strictly confirmatory. The results should be considered exploratory since an a priori model driven by theory and relevant research is no longer the object of investigation (Ockey & Choi, 2015).

In language assessment research, CFA is frequently used to confirm the underlying constructs of an assessment instrument. To determine the extent to which the four underlying constructs found in the self-assessment of academic abilities assessment instrument could be confirmed, data from a different group of 560 test takers, who completed the same self-assessment, were analyzed using SEM techniques. The procedures follow the seven steps introduced above.

Proposal of Hypothesized Model

Because SEM is an a priori method, models should be hypothesized prior to the analysis. The proposed model for the self-assessment of academic abilities example is presented in Figure 38.3 and is based on previous research (the EFA conducted in the first section of this chapter).

Based on the results of the EFA described in the first half of this chapter, the items were hypothesized to load as follows: items 3, 14, 16, and 20 on factor 1, items 2, 4, 7, 9, 13, and 17 on factor 2, items 1, 6, 10, and 18 on factor 3, and items 5, 8, 11, 12, 15, and 19 on factor 4.

Identification of Proposed Model

To perform an SEM analysis, it must be possible to identify a unique set of estimates for each of the parameters in the hypothesized model. All SEM models must satisfy two requirements to be identified. First, the number of unique elements in the variance–covariance matrix, or data points, must be equal to or greater than the number of parameters to be estimated. Data points are based on number of observed variables multiplied by the number of observed variables plus one, all divided by 2 [$p(p+1)/2$, where p = number of observed variables]. Parameters to be estimated are based on the number of variances, covariances, and regression coefficients that are estimated in the model. The number of parameters to be estimated is then subtracted from the number of data points in the dataset to give model degrees of freedom. When this number is zero or greater, the first condition for identification is satisfied. Second, all latent variables must be set to a particular scale (Kline, 2016). This means that each factor variance or one of the regression paths from a factor variance to an observed variable must be fixed to a specified value – which is usually 1.0. It is best to fix the path to the most reliably measured variable. In addition, for unidimensional CFA models with two or more factors, each factor must predict at least two observed variables. When the model has only one factor, three or more observed variables are required.

The self-assessment of academic abilities example satisfies both conditions for model identification. As can be seen in Figure 38.3, there are 20 observed variables (based on the number of rectangles). Replacing p with 20 in the formula $p(p+1)/2$, gives 20(21)/2 = 210 unique elements for the observed variance–covariance matrix. The number of parameters to be estimated is equal to 46. These 46 parameters are indicated by asterisks in Figure 38.3. There are 24 variances based on the 20 error rectangles and 4 factor ovals. There are 16 regression coefficients, or factor loadings, based on 16 of the 20 one-headed arrows from factors to observed variables with asterisks; the four regression coefficients with 1.0 rather than an asterisk have to be fixed – one for each factor, to satisfy the second condition of identification. Finally, there are six covariances based on the six two-headed arrows. Subtracting 46 from 210 results in 164 model degrees of freedom, which is greater than zero and therefore satisfies the first requirement. To satisfy the second requirement of model identification, one regression path for each of the factors was fixed as can be seen by the 1.0 on four of the paths in the model, and all of the paths from error variances to the observed variables that were fixed to 1.0. Moreover, each of the four factors predicts more than two observed variables (four for factors 1 and 3 and six for 2 and 4).

Collection and Screening of Data

After the data are collected, they must be screened to determine the extent to which they are appropriate for an SEM analysis. Like EFA, SEM techniques generally rely on the independence of observations, linear relationships between variables (although nonlinear relationships

580 Chapter 38 Practical Uses of EFA and SEM for Language Assessment Researchers

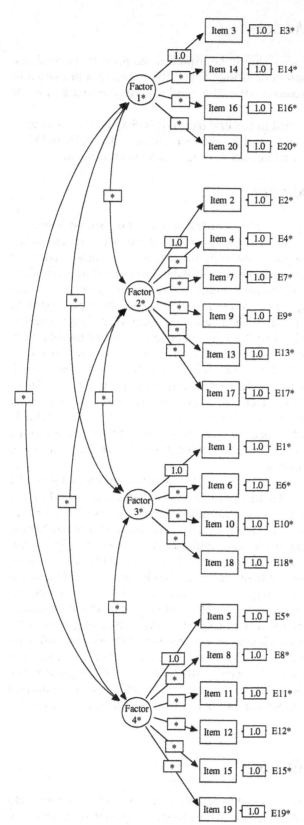

FIGURE 38.3 Proposed model for the self-assessment of academic abilities example.

Structural Equation Modeling **581**

between variables can be modeled with advanced techniques), and the absence of multicollinearity and singularity. Outliers can also negatively affect an SEM analysis. See data screening in the EFA section for a discussion on diagnosing and remedying violations of these assumptions. Because of the use of test statistics, an additional assumption of an SEM analysis, for most estimation procedures, is that the dataset is multivariate normal (Ullman, 2001). The first step for assessing multivariate normality is to assess the univariate normality of each variable in the analysis. Variables with skewness absolute values above 3.0 or kurtosis absolute values greater than 10.0 "suggest a problem" (Kline, 2016). Transformations are commonly used to normalize a variable (Keppel & Wickens, 2004). Univariate normality of all the variables in an analysis, however, does not insure multivariate normality of a dataset, and therefore multivariate normality tests, such as Mardia's coefficient of multivariate kurtosis, should be satisfied.

Because the assumption of multivariate normality in a dataset is commonly violated, procedures for working with such datasets have been developed. One approach is to remove cases that have a large effect on multivariate normality. This approach is usually not favorably viewed in language assessment research, however, because of the difficulty of collecting data and the questions associated with the ways in which dropping scores can affect the generalizability of the results. A more common approach for working with data that are not multivariate normal in the language assessment field is to use a corrected normal theory method, which is discussed in the Assessment of Model Fit section.

Appropriate sample size in an SEM analysis depends on various factors, including complexity of the model and the degree of precision that the researcher expects. More complex models and higher degrees of precision require larger sample sizes. Analyses that include reliably measured variables require smaller samples than ones that include unreliable measures. Even with quite simple models, however, SEM analyses require rather large datasets. Kunnan (1998) stated that sample sizes of less than 150 are unlikely to provide stable estimates. Techniques that require smaller samples, however, continue to be developed as researchers develop SEM techniques appropriate for more contexts.

Estimation of Proposed Model Parameters

The purpose of an estimation procedure is to identify the best possible approximations for each of the parameters (e.g., factor variances, factor loadings, error variances, disturbance variances) in the hypothesized model. These estimates aim to minimize the difference between the observed and hypothesized covariance matrices. The process is iterative. It begins with an initial set of estimates and then evaluates other similar estimates in an attempt to get closer to the optimal solution. The process ends when the solution that best fits the data is found. The most commonly encountered estimation procedure in language assessment research and in most other fields of study is ML. ML estimation is based on probabilities and patterns in the data (Bentler, 2008).

To estimate the self-assessment of academic abilities proposed four-factor model, ML estimation as implemented in the computer program EQS 6.1 with robust standard errors, corrected test statistics, and scaled fit indices (Satorra & Bentler, 1988) was used. The estimates for this solution can be seen on the diagram in Figure 38.4, which is discussed in the Interpretation of Parameter Estimates section.

Assessment of Model Fit

Model fit indicates the degree to which the observed data can plausibly be explained by the proposed model. The data must fit the model to an acceptable extent if the proposed model is to be accepted. For normal theory data, the chi-square statistic along with various fit indices

582 Chapter 38 Practical Uses of EFA and SEM for Language Assessment Researchers

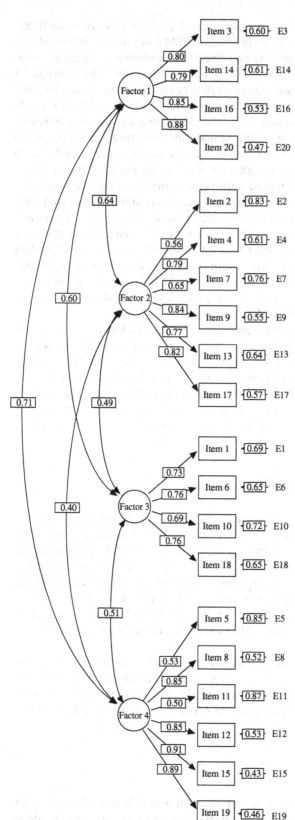

FIGURE 38.4 Standardized estimates for the self-assessment of academic abilities example.

are used. The chi-square statistic tests the hypothesis that the difference between the estimated population covariance matrix based on the model and the sample covariance matrix based on the actual data is not significantly different. The logic is that if there is not a significant difference between the proposed model data and the data, the model fits the data. It is important, however, to point out that this logic is not a guarantee of model fit. Chi-square statistics are almost always used to assess model fit; however, because they are sample size dependent, the null hypothesis can be rejected when the proposed model data and actual data are only slightly different in large datasets (Kline, 2016). Thus, fit indices that take into account sample size, among other factors, should accompany chi-square statistics.

There are many fit indices and each focuses on a particular aspect of model fit. For this reason, multiple fit indices should be reported. Ockey and Choi (2015) recommend that language assessment researchers report the chi-square statistic, the Comparative Fit Index (CFI), the Root Mean Square Error of Approximation (RMSEA) index, and the Standardized Root Mean Square Residual (SRMR) because they address different aspects of model fit and are commonly found in language assessment research.

CFI assesses fit compared to other models. Fit is seen as a continuum ranging from 0 to 1, in which zero indicates that the model is not at all accounting for the covariances among the variables, and one indicates that the model accounts for all of the covariances perfectly. RMSEA compares the lack of fit in a model to a completely saturated model, that is, a model in which all variables are correlated. A value of zero indicates a perfect fit. SRMR is based on a standardized average of the differences between the actual and hypothesized covariances. These differences, or residuals, would be zero if the actual data and the modeled data were identical. While acceptable fit values depend on the context of the study, Kline (2016) suggests that a CFI of greater than or equal to 0.95, RMSEA of 0.08 or lower, and SRMR of 0.10 or lower indicate acceptable fit. These values should be considered together when judging model fit, and all should be reasonable to justify a model.

Scaled fit indices developed to function when the assumption of multivariate normality is violated are often encountered in the language assessment literature. When data violate the assumption of multivariate normality, ML parameter estimates are fairly accurate, but standard error estimates are usually lower than they should be. As a result, parameter estimates are accurate, but true factor structures can be rejected when standard fit indices are used on non-normal data. To remedy this problem, a corrected normal theory method (Bentler, 2008) can be used. In this procedure, ML procedures along with Satorra and Bentler (1988) robust standard errors, corrected test statistics, and scaled fit indices which are adjusted for the degree of observed kurtosis, can be used. These scaled fit indices can be interpreted using the same cut-off values as normal theory fit indices.

For the self-assessment of academic abilities data, the proposed model and the observed data fit approximately. The chi-square value was 610 on 164 degrees of freedom $p < 0.05$; CFI = 0.91; RMSEA = 0.07; and SRMR = 0.07. Based on the criteria discussed above, the chi-square value indicates poor fit, CFI slightly unacceptable, and RMSEA and SRMR acceptable. Taken as a whole, along with the fact that the model is based on previous research and relevant theory, the indicators suggest that the proposed model may acceptably fit the data.

Interpretation of Parameter Estimates

SEM analyses lend themselves to a great deal of information of which only a small fraction is discussed here. Parameter estimates, standard errors of these estimates, and test statistics that assess the significance of these estimates are provided. Both unstandardized and standardized estimates are important in SEM output. While unstandardized estimates are generally difficult to interpret, they are crucial because standard errors and complementary test statistics do

584 Chapter 38 Practical Uses of EFA and SEM for Language Assessment Researchers

not accompany standardized estimates. However, because standardized estimates are more easily interpreted, they are the basis of most interpretations.

In addition to model fit, most language assessment SEM research emphasizes the interpretation of factor loadings, error estimates, factor correlations, and relationships between observed and latent variables. Factor loadings, indicated by arrows pointing from a factor to an observed variable provide estimates of the change of the observed variable based on a 1-unit change in the factor (holding other variables constant). High factor loadings indicate that the observed variables are good indicators of the factors. The magnitudes of the correlations between factors provide evidence of the extent to which factors are distinct constructs. Low correlations indicate that the factors are largely separate constructs. Factors that correlate above 0.85 are generally viewed as too similar to be distinct (Brown, 2015). However, higher or lower cut-offs may be defensible depending on the research questions and the context of the study. Direct effects between two variables (latent or observed) can also be interpreted in SEM. High path coefficients from one variable to another indicate that the factor to which the arrow is pointing is strongly predicted by the other factor. Measurement error is also modeled and accounted for in an SEM analysis. Two types of error are indicated by error terms associated with the measurement of the effect of a latent variable on an observed variable. The first is random error due to score unreliability, and the second is systematic error, which is not due to the factors. Relationships between factors in a model are purified estimates. That is, measurement error, due to the imperfect reliability of an assessment instrument, is not included in the error term associated with the relationship between two latent variables (Ockey, 2011).

The self-assessment of academic abilities data provides an example of parameter interpretation for a CFA model. The standardized estimates are presented in Figure 38.4.

All relationships in the model were significant. The large factor loadings from the latent variable, like from factor 1, to the observed variables, such as item 3 (0.80), suggest that the observed variables are good indicators of the latent traits. A couple of the loadings on factor 4 (for items 5 and 11) and one on factor 2 (for item 2) are medium-sized loadings (0.53, 0.50, and 0.56, respectively), but overall, the loadings suggest that the observed variables provide good measures of the factors that they were hypothesized to assess. The correlations between factors, indicated by the coefficients with the two-headed arrows, such as between factors 1 and 2 – correlation is 0.64, are all significant but well below the cut-off point of 0.85, suggesting that the four sub-constructs of self-perceived academic ability are related but distinct enough to be viewed as separate constructs. The paths from errors to observed variables suggest a fair amount of measurement error in the assessment instrument and/or procedures (a high of 0.87 for item 11). This is a common finding in studies that use self-assessment data obtained from Likert-scale items and underscores the value of using SEM techniques, which attempt to remove measurement error, when comparing constructs measured by such item types (Ockey, 2011).

Evaluation of Competing Models

A final step in an SEM analysis is to provide evidence that other plausible models have been investigated to determine if they fit the data better or equally well as the proposed model. In fact, one approach to SEM analysis, referred to as model comparison, is to compare competing models to see which best fits the observed data. Turner's (1989) study, one of the first SEM studies to appear in the language testing literature, provided a detailed example of how competing theoretical models can be compared to determine which is most plausible for a given dataset. Given that the self-assessment of academic abilities data was used only as an example here, other possible competing models will not be investigated.

Origins and Applications in Language Testing

Sewell Wright is generally credited as the father of SEM because he was the first to propose path analysis techniques in the 1920s. It was in the 1970s when Jöreskog presented LISREL software, which incorporates factor analysis, simultaneous equation models, and path analysis into a general covariance structure model that SEM exploded as a field.

Uses of SEM in language assessment have been to confirm a test's structure or the abilities measured by a test (e.g., Gholam et al., 2021; Gu et al., 2015), assess the effect of test methods on test performance (e.g., Llosa, 2007; Sawaki, 2007), assess the equivalency of models for different populations (e.g., Llosa, 2005; Shin, 2005), and understand the effects of test taker characteristics, test tasks, or types of language on a construct or test performance (e.g., Ockey, 2011; Romhild et al., 2011).

Challenges and Future Directions

EFA and SEM research have been disparaged on different fronts. EFA has been criticized because it is a technique that can be used given almost any dataset. As a result, it is commonly used when not much else can be done. SEM, on the other hand, has been criticized because researchers can inappropriately use the LM test to add parameters to a model that will make it fit a dataset. Theory to justify the model modifications can be crafted ex post facto to justify the changes. When such an approach is used, results can be based on idiosyncrasies in the data that are unique to the data collection procedures and/or test-taker population, leading to models that are not at all indications of real-world language assessment phenomena.

To limit the misuse and resulting criticisms of EFA and SEM, an important challenge for the language assessment community is to ensure that appropriate procedures are followed and reported. Accurate and detailed reporting is crucial because the degree to which the data satisfy necessary assumptions, decisions such as how many factors to retain, the rotation method used in an EFA, and the extent to which an SEM analysis is strictly confirmatory, are crucial to the claims that can be made from findings.

EFA and SEM are techniques that can be used to increase knowledge about language assessment. By following the best practice guidelines laid out in this chapter and by Kunnan (1998), In'nami and Koizumi (2011), and Ockey and Choi (2015), many of the criticisms of the uses of these techniques can be avoided. Future research employing these techniques will undoubtedly continue to become more stringent and sophisticated, and as a result, more enlightening.

Discussion Questions

1. How can EFA and CFA help language assessment developers or researchers evaluate the effectiveness of language assessments?

2. A language assessment researcher wants to determine how well an assessment measures the constructs it was designed to assess. Should the researcher use EFA or CFA? Why?

References

Bentler, P. M. (2008). *EQS program manual*. Encino, CA: Multivariate Software Inc.

Bentler, P. M., & Weeks, D. G. (1980). Linear structural equation with latent variables. *Psychometrika, 45*, 289–308.

Blunch, N. (2013). *Introduction to structural equation modeling using IBM SPSS statistics and Amos* (2nd ed.). Sage.

Gholam, H. K., MacIntyre, P. D., & Hariri, J. (2021). A closer look at grit and language mindset as predictors of foreign language achievement. *Studies in Second Language Acquisition, 43*, 379–402.

Green, A., & Weir, C. (2004). Can placement tests inform instructional decisions? *Language Testing, 21*(4), 467–494.

Gu, L., Turkan, S., & Gomez, P. G. (2015). *Examining the internal structure of the test of English-for-teaching (TEFT™). Educational Testing Service, Research Report: ETS RR-15-16.*

Horn, J. L. (1965). A rationale and test for the number of factors in factor analysis. *Psychometrica, 30*(2), 179–185.

In'nami, Y., & Koizumi, R. (2011). Structural equation modeling in language testing and learning research: a review. *Language Assessment Quarterly, 8*(3), 250–276.

Keppel, G., & Wickens, T. (2004). *Design and analysis: A researcher's handbook.* Pearson-Prentice Hall.

Larson-Hall, J. (2016). *A guide to doing statistics in second language research using SPSS and R.* Routledge.

Llosa, L. (2005). *Building and supporting a validity argument for a standards-based classroom assessment of English proficiency (Unpublished PhD dissertation). Los Angeles: University of California.*

Llosa, L. (2007). Validating a standards-based classroom assessment of English proficiency: a multitrait-multimethod approach. *Language Testing, 24*, 489–515.

Mulaik, S. (1987). A brief history of the philosophical foundations of exploratory factor analysis. *Multivariate Behavioral Research, 22*, 267–305.

Ockey, G. J. (2007). Investigating the validity of math word problems for English language learners with DIF. *Language Assessment Quarterly, 4*(2), 149–164.

Ockey, G. J. (2011). Assertiveness and self-consciousness as explanatory variables of L2 oral ability: a latent variable approach. *Language Learning, 61*(3), 968–989.

Ockey, G. J., & Choi, I. (2015). Structural equation modeling reporting practices for language assessment. *Language Assessment Quarterly, 12*(3), 305–319.

Romhild, A., Kenyon, D., & MacGregor, D. (2011). Exploring domain-general and domain-specific linguistic knowledge in the assessment of academic English language proficiency. *Language Assessment Quarterly, 8*(3), 213–228.

Saito, K., Tran, M., Suzukida, Y., Sun, H., Magne, V., & Ilkan, M. (2019). How do second language listeners perceive the comprehensibility of foreign-accented speech? Roles of first language profiles, second language proficiency, age, experience, familiarity, and metacognition. *Studies in Second Language Acquisition, 41*, 1133–1149.

Satorra, A., & Bentler, P. M. (1988). Scaling correction for chi-square statistics in covariance structure analysis. *Proceedings of the American Statistical Association*, 308–313.

Sawaki, Y. (2007). Construct validation of analytic rating scales in a speaking assessment: reporting a score profile and a composite. *Language Testing, 24*, 355–390.

Shin, S. (2005). Did they take the same test? Examinee language proficiency and the structure of language tests. *Language Testing, 22*, 31–57.

Song, X., & Cheng, L. (2006). Language learner strategy use and test performance of Chinese learners of English. *Language Assessment Quarterly, 3*(3), 243–266.

Tabachnick, B., & Fidell, L. (2019). *Using multivariate statistics* (7th ed.). Pearson.

Turner, C. (1989). The underlying factor structure of L2 close test performance in Francophone, university-level students: causal modelling as an approach to construct validation. *Language Testing, 6*, 172–197.

de Winter, J., Dodou, D., & Wieringa, P. (2009). Exploratory factor analysis with small sample sizes. *Multivariate Behavioural Research, 44*(2), 147–181.

Suggested Readings

Brown, T. A. (2015). *Confirmatory factor analysis for applied research.* New York: Guilford.

In'nami, Y., & Koizumi, R. (2011). Structural equation modeling in language testing and learning research: a review. *Language Assessment Quarterly, 8*(3), 250–276.

Kline, P. (1994). *An easy guide to factor analysis.* New York: Routledge.

Kline, R. (2016). *Principles and practice of structural equation modeling* (4th ed.). The Guilford Press.

Kunnan, A. J. (1998). An introduction to structural equation modeling for language assessment research. *Language Testing, 15*(3), 295–332.

Pituch, K. A., & Stevens, J. P. (2016). *Applied multivariate statistics for the social sciences: Analysis with SAS and IBM's SPSS* (6th ed., Chapter 11 ed.). Lawrence Erlbaum Associates.

Spearman, C. (1907). Demonstration of formulae for true measurement of correlation. *American Journal of Psychology, 18*, 161–169.

Ullman, J. (2001). Structural equation modeling. In B. Tabachnick & L. Fidell (Eds.), *Using multivariate statistics* (4th ed., pp. 653–771). Boston: Allyn and Bacon.

CHAPTER 39

Item Response Theory in Language Assessment

Shangchao Min and Lianzhen He

Introduction

Item Response Theory (IRT) is an extension of classical true score theory (CTT). It utilizes mathematical models that involve parameters such as item discrimination, difficulty, and guessing to describe the likelihood of a person's response to a test item based on his or her ability level. In contrast to CTT, which analyzes aggregated test scores, IRT provides insights into the unique properties of individual test items. A major drawback of CTT is its failure to differentiate between the characteristics of the test and the abilities of the test takers. IRT overcomes this limitation through its property of item parameter invariance and ability parameter invariance (see Baker & Kim, 2017). This implies that the estimated parameters of an item and the estimated abilities of test takers remain consistent regardless of the specific group of test takers or items being administered. These advantages have contributed to the widespread adoption of IRT in educational measurement research (van der Linden, 2016) and practice (see Meijer & Tendeiro, 2018) in recent decades.

IRT has its roots in Binet and Simon's (1905) publication in French (see van der Linden, 2016). However, it was not until Lord and Novick's (1968) findings that the field of educational measurement began to recognize the benefits of IRT. The initial connection between IRT and the Rasch model led to the latter being referred to as "the one-parameter logistic model," representing the simplest form of IRT models developed by Lord and Novick. Nevertheless, there was an ongoing debate between the founders of IRT and Rasch measurement, such as Ben Wright and Fred Lord, regarding whether the Rasch model was indeed an IRT model. A recent study on Rasch measurement revealed that publications related to the Rasch model have become a distinct area of research separate from the IRT literature (see Aryadoust et al., 2019). Thus, this chapter differentiates between IRT and Rasch measurement, only focusing on IRT models in language assessment, with Rasch measurement such as many-facet Rasch modeling (MFMR) excluded (see Aryadoust et al. (2021) for a detailed overview of how Rasch models have been applied in language assessment).

Depending on the dimensionality of the construct being measured, different IRT models can be used, including unidimensional and multidimensional IRT models. In language assessment, both unidimensional and multidimensional IRT models have been employed to investigate a diverse range of topics, such as design of computerized adaptive language tests (CALT; see Huang et al., 2022), differential item functioning (DIF; Ockey, 2007; Pae, 2012),

---

The Concise Companion to Language Assessment, First Edition. Edited by Antony John Kunnan.
© 2025 John Wiley & Sons, Inc. Published 2025 by John Wiley & Sons, Inc.

588

and scaling, equating, and scoring (see Warnby et al., 2023). A recent systematic review on IRT (see Min & Aryadoust, 2021) showed that researchers in the field of language assessment have shifted over time from employing unidimensional IRT models by asserting the existence of essential unidimensionality to adopting more sophisticated multidimensional IRT models that can handle the presence of multidimensionality in language tests.

In this chapter, we will begin by providing a brief overview of how the dimensionality of language ability is conceptualized and operationalized in language assessment and then move on to an introduction of unidimensional and multidimensional IRT models. Following that, we will delve into the issues and considerations in applying IRT and provide an overview of key research areas where IRT has been applied in language assessment. Finally, we will conclude by highlighting current research trends and suggesting potential avenues for further investigation.

Dimensionality of Language Ability

Despite controversies surrounding the nature of language ability in early research, it is now widely accepted that language ability is a multidimensional system comprising many components (see Bachman & Palmer, 2010; Purpura, 2016). The discussion of language ability can be traced back to Chomsky's competence versus performance dichotomy where competence is narrowly defined as grammatical knowledge. Such a narrow conceptualization was later extended by Hymes from a sociolinguistic perspective and further developed by Canale and Swain (1980) in their communicative competence framework to include not only grammatical competence but also sociolinguistic competence (i.e., sociocultural rules), discourse competence (i.e., cohesion and coherence), and strategic competence (i.e., compensatory communication strategies). Since the publication of Canale and Swain's (1980) seminal paper, several researchers have adopted communicative competence in designing models of language assessment for classrooms and large-scale assessment (e.g., Bachman, 1990; Bachman & Palmer, 1996; Chapelle, 1998). Among them, the communicative language ability (CLA) model has exerted the greatest impact on the development and score interpretation of language tests (see Harding, 2014). The CLA model provided the most comprehensive conceptualization of language ability based on three components: language competence, strategic competence, and psychophysiological mechanisms. It provided a more detailed account of strategic competence than that in Canale and Swain (1980) and highlighted the interaction of language competence and strategic competence with the attributes of language use context. This conceptualization, however, does not recognize the separation of the four language skills of listening, reading, speaking, and writing. It has been criticized for being too complex for operationalization in designing language tests or, by contrast, for not being rich enough to reflect communication in real life (see Elder et al., 2017). There is also little empirical evidence supporting the psychometric validity of CAL. The question that arises, then, is how language tests can be designed to measure the intractable multidimensionality of language ability without inducing construct underrepresentation (see Klem et al., 2015).

Two approaches to addressing this question have emerged from the literature: *the hierarchical approach* and *the multidimensional IRT approach*. A general approach to conceptualizing language ability assumes a hierarchical structure for language (see Klem et al., 2015). The majority of existing language test batteries comprise listening, reading, speaking, and writing subtests to measure language abilities in different linguistic domains (e.g., International English Language Testing System [IELTS]). Even for tests that include integrated tasks, such as the Test of English as a Foreign Language Internet Based Test (TOEFL iBT), a four-skill language model was supported (see Sawaki et al., 2009). Thus, unidimensional IRT models are typically used to score each individual domain (i.e., listening, reading, speaking, and

590 Chapter 39 Item Response Theory in Language Assessment

writing) and the subtest scores of each domain are reported to test takers as indicators of their linguistic abilities in distinct domains. Additionally, the subtest scores are combined into a composite score, indicating the presence of a unitary language ability factor that accounts for performance in all domains (e.g., IELTS, TOEFL). Language ability in this approach is thus broken down into two layers: (i) an overarching general language ability and (ii) low-level constructs of listening, reading, speaking, and writing abilities.

An alternative to modeling the multidimensionality of language constructs is to use multidimensional IRT models such as the bifactor multidimensional IRT model (see Gibbons & Hedeker, 1992) and the two-tier full-information IRT model (see Cai, 2010). Compared with the hierarchical approach, the multidimensional IRT approach would provide rich and less ambiguous psychometric information, including reliable composite and subtest scores (see Chen & Zhang, 2018). Several studies have used multidimensional IRT models to capture multidimensionality in language tests (e.g., Cai & Kunnan, 2018, 2019). Cai and Kunnan (2018) conducted a bifactor multidimensional IRT analysis of an English for Specific Purposes (ESP) assessment and concluded that content knowledge is inseparable from ESP reading ability. The findings lend support to Douglas's (2000) interactionist approach to ESP language ability, where the contextual feature is specified as part of the construct. In the context of English for general purposes assessment, Longabach and Peyton (2018) demonstrated the utility of the multidimensional IRT model in drawing upon information across subtest scores to improve score reliability. They called into question the current practice of simply adding subtest scores to form composite scores, stating that "the view of language proficiency as the additive function of unrelated domains lacks theoretical support" (p. 299).

In sum, language ability is typically viewed as multidimensional, but debate prevails on what comprises its constituents and the possible interactions among them. Stemming from the theoretical disputes regarding the components of language ability are the practical issues of how to measure the multidimensionality of language ability in language tests.

Item Response Theory (IRT) models

Unidimensional and multidimensional IRT models are two distinct approaches utilized in psychometrics and educational measurement to analyze test data. The choice between these two types of models depends on the nature of the test and the specific measurement goals.

Unidimensional IRT models

Unidimensional IRT models are statistical models that assume the underlying construct being measured can be adequately represented by a single latent ability or trait. Depending on the number of response categories in an item, two main types of unidimensional IRT models are used, namely dichotomous and polytomous IRT models. Dichotomous IRT models are applied when an item has only two response options, such as a multiple-choice question with correct or incorrect answers. Several examples of dichotomous IRT models include the one-parameter logistic model (1PLM), two-parameter logistic model (2PLM), and three-parameter logistic model (3PLM) (see Birnbaum, 1968). The 1PLM involves calibrating items using only the item difficulty parameter, whereas the 2PLM utilizes two item parameters – the item discrimination parameter and item difficulty parameter. Similarly, the 3PLM employs three item parameters – the item discrimination parameter, item difficulty parameter, and pseudo-guessing parameter.

On the other hand, polytomous IRT models are used for items with more than two response categories, like a Likert scale. Polytomous IRT models can be categorized into difference models and divide-by-total models, depending on how the response process is modeled.

The graded response model (GRM) is an example of a difference model (see Samejima, 1969), while the partial credit model (PCM) (Masters, 1982) and the generalized partial credit model (GPCM) (Muraki, 1992) are commonly used divide-by-total models.

Multidimensional IRT models

Multidimensional IRT (MIRT) models are statistical models that are designed to handle the presence of multiple dimensions or latent traits or factors that contribute to test performance. These models acknowledge that language ability, for example, may involve distinct sub-skills or domains such as listening, reading, speaking, and writing. Depending on whether latent dimensions are considered (in)dependent and (non)compensatory, the multidimensional IRT models can be classified into compensatory multidimensional IRT models and non-compensatory multidimensional IRT models. Multidimensional IRT models allow for trade-off between the dimensions, stipulating that good performance in one dimension can compensate for bad performance in another, while non-compensatory multidimensional IRT models assume that performance in each dimension is independent and cannot compensate for performance in other dimensions. The commonly used multidimensional IRT models include multidimensional generalizations of the unidimensional IRT models (Reckase, 2009), testlet response theory model (TRT; see Wainer et al., 2007), bifactor multidimensional IRT model (see Gibbons & Hedeker, 1992), mixture IRT model (see Mislevy & Verhelst, 1990), hierarchical two-tier IRT model (see Cai, 2010), and explanatory IRT model (see De Boeck & Wilson, 2004).

Issues and Considerations in IRT

Several issues need to be considered when applying IRT, including its basic assumptions, the required sample size, and the evaluation of model-data fit.

Assumptions

Two fundamental assumptions must be satisfied for the application of IRT models. The first assumption, known as unidimensionality, applies to unidimensional IRT models, which states that all the items in the test measure predominantly a single latent ability or trait. Various techniques have been suggested to assess the unidimensionality of tests, including reliability statistics, component analysis, exploratory factor analysis (EFA), confirmatory factor analysis (CFA), IRT fit statistics, DETECT, and the DIMTEST procedure (see Guo & Choi, 2023; Min & Aryadoust, 2021). However, reliability statistics and eigenvalues derived from component analysis and EFA have faced increasing criticism for providing limited and indirect information regarding the suitability of applying unidimensional IRT models (2019). Reise et al. (2014) critically reviewed evaluation methods for dimensionality and argued that a "comparison modeling" approach, involving the comparison of parameter estimates derived from unidimensional IRT models with those from multidimensional models, offers a more promising and direct method to assess the potential distortion caused by fitting unidimensional IRT models to datasets that are typically multidimensional to some extent. Nevertheless, there is no specific recommendation provided regarding the exact value that constitutes a meaningful difference. The choice of which model to utilize depends on substantive and practical factors.

The second assumption in IRT is known as local independence (LI). In both unidimensional and multidimensional IRT models, LI must be satisfied. LI entails local item independence and local person independence. The former is more frequently covered in language testing, which states that the likelihood of responding to an item is statistically unrelated to the likelihood of responding to any other items in the test, given the test takers' ability

592   **Chapter 39** Item Response Theory in Language Assessment

(see Embretson & Reise, 2000). Another way to understand LI is as a lack of correlation among the items, once the influence of the measurement construct (θ) has been removed from the item scores. In the context of a unidimensional test, the LI assumption is equivalent to the assumption of unidimensionality. Therefore, methods used to assess unidimensionality can also indirectly evaluate LI at a test level. Various tests have been developed to evaluate the LI assumption at the level of item pairs. These include the Q_3 statistic, the χ^2 statistic, the G_2 statistic, Cramer's V statistic, and modification indices of structural equation modeling (see Min & Aryadoust, 2021).

The unidimensionality and LI assumptions are not easy to satisfy in language tests, due to the multidimensional nature of language ability as well as the prevalent uses of testlets (i.e., a group of items pertaining to one passage) in language tests. Empirical research shows that when the unidimensionality and LI assumptions are violated, the application of unidimensional IRT models leads to biased item parameter estimates and person ability estimates (e.g., Min & He, 2014) and to overstated test information and measurement precision (e.g., Zhang, 2010).

Sample Size

A key question frequently asked in IRT application concerns the required minimum sample size for accurate and stable parameter estimation. This question does not admit to a unique answer: it depends on the specific IRT models being used. The one-parameter logistic model (1PLM) typically yields reliable estimates with sample sizes as small as 150–200 test takers (Lord, 1980). The two-parameter logistic model (2PLM) and three-parameter logistic model (3PLM) generally require larger sample sizes for estimating discrimination and/or guessing parameters. For 2PLM, if the items have moderate difficulty and the abilities follow a normal distribution, effective estimation of item parameters can be achieved with samples of 500 (Woods & Thissen, 2006) or even fewer, such as 250 test takers for 30 items (Sahin & Anil, 2017). In the case of 3PLM, at least 1000 test takers are needed for reliable parameter calibration, although for easier or less-discriminating items, the guessing parameter may need to be fixed rather than estimated (see Woods, 2008).

In the case of polytomous IRT models, the accurate estimation of category thresholds or step difficulty parameters depends on the number of test takers per category (see DeMars, 2010). Samples as small as 250 have been reported as adequate for three-category items using the PCM (see Choi et al., 1997), an extension of the Rasch model. For the GRM (see Samejima, 1969) or GPCM (see Muraki, 1992), which are polytomous extensions of the 2PLM, a minimum of 500 test takers is needed for reliable calibration (see DeMars, 2010).

When dealing with multidimensional IRT models, it is generally agreed that a sample size of 1000 or more cases is required to obtain stable results due to the additional parameters involved (Millsap et al., 2014). However, recent research indicates that a sample size of 500 is sufficient for stable item parameter estimation in the bifactor multidimensional IRT model (see Reise et al., 2014) and the multidimensional extension of GRM (see Jiang et al., 2016). It is important to note that these recommendations signify the minimal sample sizes necessary and should be considered as approximate guidelines. Their applicability may vary across different contexts. The choice of sample size depends on the specific data analysis purpose, real-life applications, and financial or operational considerations.

Model Fit

In addition to sample size, the selection of an appropriate IRT model is a critical issue in IRT application. Simply using an IRT model randomly chosen by researchers does not guarantee the success of specific IRT applications. Instead, researchers should initially identify a set of potentially suitable IRT models and then determine the best-fitting model by assessing how well it aligns with the test data of interest. However, it should be noted that, in real-world scenarios, it is rare for a model to perfectly match the data.

The most common method for evaluating model-data fit is through statistical tests of model fit. However, caution is warranted as these tests are sensitive to the sample size of the test takers. This means that even slight deviations between the empirical data and the model under consideration may lead to the conclusion that the model does not fit the data if the sample size is sufficiently large. To compare the goodness of fit among different models, several metrics might be used, such as the deviance ($-2\log$-likelihood), Akaike information criterion (AIC), and Bayesian information criterion (BIC) (see Rijmen, 2010). Generally, the preferred model is the one with the lowest values on these three indices. This indicates that the model achieves the best balance between fitting the data (as indicated by the deviance) and model complexity (as indicated by AIC and BIC values). If one model is nested within another model, the significance of the difference in deviance can be tested using a chi-square difference test with degrees of freedom equal to the difference in the number of parameters. The outcome of this test can help inform the decision of whether one model should be rejected in favor of another.

Apart from assessing the overall fit of the model to the data, it is important to evaluate item-level fit and person fit. Item-level fit can be examined using the $S-\chi^2$ item-fit statistic developed by Orlando and Thissen (2000, 2003), where a significant p-value indicates items that do not fit well. For person fit, likelihood-based (L-B) indices, such as the l_z index proposed by Drasgow et al. (1985), are commonly used. The l_z index can be computed for both unidimensional and multidimensional IRT models. A small l_z value, such as below -2 or -3, is typically considered a threshold for identifying individuals with potentially problematic response patterns indicating misfit (see Paek & Cole, 2020). Items that demonstrate a satisfactory fit to a specific IRT model are assumed to effectively measure the construct as specified by the model (see Chan, 2015). Conversely, items that exhibit poor fit may be measuring a different dimension that is not captured by the specified model. It should be noted, however, item-level fit and person fit are rarely reported in IRT research in language assessment in general, except in many-facet Rasch measurement (MFRM) research typically seen in performance assessments.

Application of IRT in Language Assessment

IRT has been utilized in language assessment to explore a broad spectrum of research areas, such as the development of CALT, DIF detection, and scaling, equating, and scoring.

Computer Adaptive Language Testing

IRT is the psychometric foundation that makes CALT implementation feasible. CALT operates by administering test items that closely match the estimated ability of each individual test taker, moving away from the traditional use of the same set of items for everyone. An important property of IRT is that the item parameter estimates obtained from IRT can stay stable and be generalized to different administrations. Thus, CALT developers can estimate and compare different test takers' abilities on the same scale though they are administered different sets of items (see van der Linden, 2016).

CALT has become an efficient and popular alternative to fixed-item testing, whether in paper-and-pencil or computer-based formats. It drastically reduces testing time and enhances efficiency in estimating abilities while increasing measurement precision, when compared to traditional paper-and-pencil or computer-based formats (see Mizumoto et al., 2019). Aside

594 Chapter 39 Item Response Theory in Language Assessment

from this primary advantage, CALT offers several additional benefits that make it highly applicable in educational settings. These advantages include preventing test taker boredom and frustration, providing immediate feedback and self-pacing options, offering new task types, and providing flexibility in test scheduling (see He & Min, 2017). Nevertheless, CALT presents specific challenges for test developers, notably the need for a large sample for IRT calibration and a large pool of test items (see Hambleton et al., 1991). As a result, many assessments have shifted from item-level adaptive formats to multistage adaptive testing, as seen in the Graduate Record Examination (GRE; see Robin et al., 2014) and the National Assessment of Educational Progress (NAEP; see Yamamoto et al., 2019). Instead of employing adaptation at the individual item level, multistage adaptive testing uses a prebuilt module of items, offering several advantages like better item exposure control, well-balanced content representation, item review, and reduced demand on the size of the item pool (see Pohl, 2013). Nonetheless, MST comes with its own set of challenges. These include the complexities of pre-constructing test modules, which might add complications to test assembly, and having a limited number of adaptive points, which could potentially influence measurement precision.

Both unidimensional and multidimensional IRT models are used in CALT, depending on how multidimensionality is conceptualized and operationalized in language assessment. Earliest CALT research primarily relied on Rasch modeling (e.g., Young et al., 1996), partly due to limited sample size in pilot testing, and partly for the sake of easier implementation in CALT function. Applications of IRT in later CALT are gradually extended to 2PLM (see He, 2004), and even 3PLM (see Laurier, 1999). Yet, it should be noted that, no matter whether it is Rasch model, or 2PLM or 3PLM that is used, the LI assumption is difficult to satisfy and easy to violate, as most large-scale assessments are composed of testlets that include a set of items using a common passage as a stimulus.

When the LI assumption cannot be satisfied, using conventional dichotomous IRT models leads to inflated estimates of item discrimination parameters, test information, and measurement precision (see Min & He, 2014). Therefore, to circumvent this problem, some later CALT applications either choose to group items within a testlet together, and then apply polytomous IRT models by treating them as a single polytomous item (see He & Min, 2017), or resort to multidimensional IRT models to directly capture the multidimensionality present in language assessments (see Frey & Seitz, 2011). It should be noted, however, that the polytomous IRT model approach tends to result in lower reliability coefficients because of the loss of information that could have been obtained from the exact item response pattern within each testlet (see Alpizar et al., 2023). It is encouraging to see that studies adopting multidimensional IRT models in developing CALTs have started to appear in language assessment (see Huang et al., 2022).

That said, a plethora of recent CALT studies still adopt dichotomous 2PLM (see Kaya et al., 2022) and the easy-to-understand Rasch model for item calibration (see MacGregor et al., 2022), probably due to the computational simplicity and ease to communicate with stakeholders.

Differential Item Functioning

IRT has also been employed to investigate DIF. DIF occurs when individuals with the same ability but belonging to different groups have different probabilities of answering an item correctly (see Min & He, 2020). DIF indicates that the group membership variable may favor one group of test takers while putting another group at a disadvantage, posing a significant threat to test fairness. To detect DIF, researchers in educational measurement have proposed various statistical approaches, generally classified into two categories based on their theoretical frameworks. One category is grounded in CTT, where observed scores are used to approximate underlying ability. The other category is based on IRT, where estimated latent variable scores are used as the matching criterion (see Min & He, 2020). Previous researchers have suggested that the IRT-based approach is more powerful than other methods in detecting DIF (see Thissen et al., 1993).

The most commonly used IRT-based method for detecting DIF is the likelihood ratio test for parametric IRT models (IRT-LRT; Thissen et al., 1993). This approach assumes that if the item parameters obtained from the IRT model vary for the same ability level between different groups, then the item is exhibiting DIF. More specifically, it compares a compact model, which constrains parameters for the studied item to be equal across groups, and an augmented model, which allows these parameters to vary between groups. Then a likelihood ratio test is conducted to determine if the augmented model provides a significantly better fit to the data than the compact model. If the augmented model significantly improves data fit, it suggests that the studied item exhibits DIF.

The IRT-LRT can detect both uniform DIF (related to the difficulty parameter) and non-uniform DIF (related to the discrimination parameter). Uniform DIF occurs when one group of test takers consistently outperforms the other group across the ability spectrum (i.e., a main effect of group), while non-uniform DIF occurs when one group is advantaged in one part of the ability spectrum and disadvantaged in another (i.e., an interaction of group by ability). However, it is important to note that the test of uniform DIF is contingent on the absence of non-uniform DIF because meaningful assessment of DIF on the difficulty parameter relies on the item not exhibiting DIF on the discrimination parameter (see Woods, 2008). A drawback of this approach is that it tends to flag even a small amount of DIF as significant due to its high statistical power. In addition, there is no consensus yet on what effect size measures to use, despite the clear importance of including such information (see Chalmers, 2023).

IRT-LRT has been extensively used in language assessment research to explore DIF across distinct groups, such as gender (see Min & He, 2020), age (see Geranpayeh & Kunnan, 2007), language background (see Ockey, 2007), and academic background (see Pae, 2004). The IRT models used in these studies are primarily unidimensional IRT models, but more and more multidimensional IRT models are used in DIF studies in language assessment in recent years, including mixture IRT models (see Nijlen & Janssen, 2011), multidimensional multi-level mixture models (Finch & Finch, 2013), and bifactor multidimensional IRT models (see Fukuhara & Kamata, 2011). Almost all researchers adopting multidimensional IRT models advocate their use by stating that the multidimensional models provide more complete information regarding the nature of DIF and produce better estimates of DIF magnitude and DIF detection rates.

Scaling, Equating, and Scoring

Another extensively utilized area of IRT in the field of language assessment involves scaling, equating, and scoring. Both scaling and equating serve as linking processes, aiming to connect scores obtained from various test versions, yet they differ in their approach. Scaling represents a more relaxed method of linking, commonly employed to connect scores from different tests that measure similar but not necessarily identical constructs (Holland & Dorans, 2006). On the other hand, equating is the most demanding and strongest form of linking, typically used to connect scores from tests that measure the same construct and share the same test specifications for each alternative form (see Radwan et al., 2013).

One of the most widely used scaling and equating procedures in language assessment research is unidimensional IRT scaling/equating (see Kim et al., 2020). Exemplification of such procedures on language test data can be found in Warnby et al. (2023). However, the assumptions of the unidimensional IRT models are not usually met by language test data, in that case, the accuracy of the equating relationships derived from the unidimensional IRT framework may be compromised. To address this issue, an alternative approach gaining popularity involves scaling and equating methods based on the multidimensional IRT framework. Recent years have seen the emergence of two types of multidimensional IRT equating procedures in language assessment research: (i) simple-structure multidimensional IRT models, as demonstrated in studies by Kim et al. (2020) and (ii) bifactor multidimensional IRT models, studied by Lee et al. (2020). Kim et al. (2020) demonstrated that, in cases where the data was multidimensional, simple-structure multidimensional IRT models generally produced more accurate equating results compared to traditional unidimensional IRT equating. Likewise, Lee et al. (2020) found that the simple-structure and bifactor multidimensional IRT models yielded similar results, whereas the unidimensional IRT model, as compared to the two multidimensional IRT models, consistently produced lower estimates of reliability and classification consistency/accuracy indices.

Similar findings have been reported in previous research on IRT scoring. For example, Longabach and Peyton (2018) investigated various approaches for assigning subscores to the four domains of an English test. The methods explored included CTT, unidimensional IRT, augmented IRT, and multidimensional IRT. The results indicated that multidimensional IRT models demonstrated the highest level of reliability among the tested methods. Cai and Kunnan (2018, 2019) conducted a bifactor multidimensional IRT analysis to compute the test scores of an ESP assessment to enhance the meaningfulness of subtest and composite scores. Min et al. (2022) reported that although the ACCESS reading test could be well fit by the unidimensional 2PL model, the bifactor multidimensional IRT model would be preferred to model the general and content-specific factors simultaneously to account for how Grade 1 students and those with low proficiency across all grade clusters responded to the reading items.

Conclusions and Some Areas for Future Exploration

In a nutshell, multidimensional IRT models hold promise for accommodating local item independence in CALT, producing accurate estimates of DIF magnitude, and providing appropriate scoring of test takers on both the overall trait and specific domain traits. They can help capture the complexities of language performance in language assessment and contribute to theoretical models that account for the multifaceted nature of language ability. Despite their potential, multidimensional IRT models have not been widely implemented in practical settings for several reasons. These include challenges in interpreting item parameters within multidimensional IRT models, limited accessibility of these techniques for a wide range of language assessment researchers, and, most significantly, the increased complexity involved in effectively communicating scores to users (see Choi & Papageorgiou, 2019).

That said, low-dimensional multidimensional IRT models hold great potential for widespread use due to their theoretical simplicity and computational ease. For instance, bifactor multidimensional IRT models, one of the most widely used low-dimensional multidimensional IRT models in language assessment, offer an appealing approach not only for scoring the overall trait and specific domain traits but also serve as a potential alternative to cognitive diagnostic models (CDM) to provide diagnostic information on the specific domain traits (see Min et al., 2022). Recent research even suggests that the multidimensional IRT models provide a more robust approach to quantifying growth in longitudinal settings than CDMs (see Huang & Bolt, 2023). Cognitive diagnostic assessment (CDA) is based on the notion that language skills encompass multiple dimensions, which is congruent with the underlying philosophy of multidimensional IRT models. Expanding CDA research to include latent trait models, such as bifactor multidimensional IRT models, may help address the theoretical challenges related to the dimensionality paradox arising from the simultaneous application of unidimensional IRT and CDA models in current CDA research.

In this line of inquiry, the combination of CALT and CDA shows great potential in overcoming the difficulty of providing valid psychometric evidence for reporting detailed diagnostic information with a limited number of items. Despite a few attempts in educational measurement, CDA–CALT is seldom researched or operationalized in language assessment. Given the growing need for efficient and informative feedback from different parties involved, including students, parents, and teachers, work along this line is urgently needed.

Likewise, the utilization of multidimensional explanatory IRT analysis and Bayesian approaches to IRT modeling has been inadequately explored in previous research on language assessment. Multidimensional explanatory IRT analysis is a relatively new but emerging approach that encourages critical examination of the response process (see Revicki & Reise, 2014). Bayesian approaches incorporate prior information when modeling students' item responses. A promising direction for future research would involve employing multidimensional explanatory IRT analysis to capture the influence of various individual manifest and latent variables, such as age, cognitive style, and socioeconomic status, on item responses. Additionally, utilizing Bayesian IRT models would enable the incorporation of other pertinent information about the assessment, beyond the available data, to enhance the analysis.

To sum up, the recent advancements in the creation of advanced IRT models, along with the availability of free R packages like the *mirt* package (see Chalmers, 2012) for fitting these models, present a promising outlook for substantial improvements in IRT-based applications within language assessment. However, it is essential to note that these sophisticated techniques should not distract language assessment researchers and practitioners from addressing the fundamental concerns related to validating the interpretations and use of scores obtained from language assessment.

Discussion Questions

1. Can you provide examples of real-world language assessments that have benefited from the implementation of IRT? What are the specific improvements that can be observed?

2. Can you discuss the impact of multidimensionality on the application of IRT in language assessment? How can multidimensional IRT models address this issue?

References

Alpizar, D., Li, T., & Norris, J. M. (2023). Psychometric approaches to analyzing C-tests. *Language Testing, 40*(1), 107–132. https://doi.org/10.1177/02655322211062138.

Aryadoust, V., Tan, H., & Ng, L. (2019). A scientometric review of Rasch measurement: the rise and progress of a specialty. *Frontiers in Psychology, 10*, 2197. https://doi.org/10.3389/fpsyg.2019.02197.

Aryadoust, V., Ng, L. Y., & Sayama, H. (2021). A comprehensive review of Rasch measurement in language assessment: recommendations and guidelines for research. *Language Testing, 38*(1), 6–40. https://doi.org/10.1177/0265532220927487.

Bachman, L. (1990). *Fundamental considerations in language testing.* Oxford University Press.

Bachman, L., & Palmer, A. (1996). *Language testing in practice.* Oxford University Press.

Bachman, L., & Palmer, A. (2010). *Language assessment in practice.* Oxford University Press.

Baker, F. B., & Kim, S. H. (2017). *The basics of item response theory using R.* Springer.

Binet, A., & Simon, T. (1905). Méthodes nouvelles pour le diagnostic du niveau intellectuel des anormaux. *L'Année Psychologique, 11*, 191–244. https://doi.org/10.3406/psy.1904.3675.

Birnbaum, A. (1968). Some latent traits and their use in inferring an examinee's ability. In F. M. Lord & M. R. Novick (Eds.), *Statistical theories of mental test scores* (pp. 19–20). Reading, MA: Addison-Wesley.

Cai, L. (2010). A two-tier full-information item factor analysis model with applications. *Psychometrika*, *75*(4), 581–612. https://doi.org/10.1007/s11336-010-9178-0.

Cai, Y., & Kunnan, A. J. (2018). Examining the inseparability of content knowledge from LSP reading ability: an approach combining bifactor-multidimensional item response theory and structural equation modeling. *Language Assessment Quarterly*, *15*(2), 109–129. https://doi.org/10.1080/15434303.2018.1451532.

Cai, Y., & Kunnan, J. A. (2019). Detecting the language thresholds of the effect of background knowledge on a language for specific purposes reading performance: a case of the island ridge curve. *Journal of English for Academic Purposes*, *42*, 1–12. https://doi.org/10.1016/j.jeap.2019.100795.

Canale, M., & Swain, M. (1980). Theoretical bases of communicative approaches to second language teaching and testing. *Applied Linguistics*, *1*, 1–47. https://doi.org/10.1093/applin/1.1.1.

Chalmers, R. P. (2012). *mirt*: a multidimensional item response theory package for the R environment. *Journal of Statistical Software*, *48*(6), 1–29. https://doi.org/10.18637/jss.v048.i06.

Chalmers, R. P. (2023). A unified comparison of IRT-based effect sizes for DIF investigations. *Journal of Educational Measurement*, *60*(2), 318–350. https://doi.org/10.1111/jedm.12347.

Chan, M. C. E. (2015). Young learners: an examination of the psychometric properties of the early literacy knowledge and skills instrument. *Journal of Psychoeducational Assessment*, *33*(7), 607–621. https://doi.org/10.1177/0734282915569436.

Chapelle, C. (1998). Construct definition and validity inquiry in SLA research. In L. Bachman & A. Cohen (Eds.), *Interfaces between second language acquisition and language testing research* (pp. 32–70). Cambridge University Press.

Chen, F. F., & Zhang, Z. (2018). Bifactor models in psychometric test development. In P. Irwing, T. Booth & D. J. Hughes (Eds.), *The Wiley handbook of psychometric testing: A multidisciplinary reference on survey, scale and test development* (1st ed., pp. 413–443). Wiley Blackwell.

Choi, I., & Papageorgiou, S. (2019). Evaluating subscore uses across multiple levels: a case of reading and listening subscores for young EFL learners. *Language Testing*, *37*(2), 1–26. https://doi.org/10.1177/0265532219879654.

Choi, S. W., Cook, K. F., & Dodd, B. G. (1997). Parameter recovery for the partial credit model using MULTILOG. *Journal of Outcome Measurement*, *1*(2), 114–142. https://doi.org/10.1111/j.1745-3984.1990.tb00738.x.

De Boeck, P., & Wilson, M. (Eds.). (2004). *Explanatory item response models*. Springer.

DeMars, C. E. (2010). *Item response theory*. Oxford University Press.

Douglas, D. (2000). *Assessing languages for specific purposes*. Cambridge: Cambridge University Press.

Drasgow, F., Levine, M. V., & Williams, E. A. (1985). Appropriateness measurement with polychotomous item response models and standardized indices. *British Journal of Mathematical and Statistical Psychology*, *38*(1), 67–86. https://doi.org/10.1111/j.2044-8317.1985.tb00817.x.

Elder, C., McNamara, T., Kim, H., Pill, J., & Sato, T. (2017). Interrogating the construct of communicative competence in language assessment contexts: what the non-language specialist can tell us. *Language & Communication*, *57*, 14–21. https://doi.org/10.1016/j.langcom.2016.12.005.

Embretson, S. E., & Reise, S. P. (2000). *Item response theory for psychologists*. Lawrence Erlbaum Associates.

Finch, W. H., & Finch, M. E. H. (2013). Investigation of specific learning disability and testing accommodations based differential item functioning using a multilevel multidimensional mixture item response theory model. *Educational and Psychological Measurement*, *73*(6), 973–993. https://doi.org/10.1177/0013164413494776.

Frey, A., & Seitz, N. (2011). Hypothetical use of multidimensional adaptive testing for the assessment of student achievement in the programme for international student assessment. *Educational and Psychological Measurement*, *71*(3), 503–522. https://doi.org/10.1177/0013164410381521.

Fukuhara, H., & Kamata, A. (2011). A bifactor multidimensional item response theory model for differential item functioning analysis on testlet-based items. *Applied Psychological Measurement*, *35*(8), 604–622. https://doi.org/10.1177/0146621611428447.

Geranpayeh, A., & Kunnan, A. J. (2007). Differential item functioning in terms of age in the certificate in advanced English examination. *Language Assessment Quarterly*, *4*(2), 190–222. https://doi.org/10.1080/15434300701375758.

Gibbons, R. D., & Hedeker, D. R. (1992). Full-information bi-factor analysis. *Psychometrika*, *57*(3), 423–436. https://doi.org/10.1007/bf02295430.

References **599**

Guo, W., & Choi, Y.-J. (2023). Assessing dimensionality of IRT models using traditional and revised parallel analyses. *Educational and Psychological Measurement, 83*(3), 609–629. https://doi.org/10.1177/00131644221111838.

Hambleton, R. K., Swaminathan, H., & Rogers, H. J. (1991). *Fundamentals of item response theory*. Sage.

Harding, L. (2014). Communicative language testing: current issues and future research. *Language Assessment Quarterly, 11*(2), 186–197. https://doi.org/10.1080/15434303.2014.895829.

He, L. (2004). *Computerized cognitive adaptive testing*. Zhejiang University Press.

He, L., & Min, S. (2017). Development and validation of a computer adaptive EFL test. *Language Assessment Quarterly, 14*(2), 160–176. https://doi.org/10.1080/15434303.2016.1162793.

Holland, P. W., & Dorans, N. J. (2006). Linking and equating. In R. L. Brennan (Ed.), *Educational measurement* (4th ed., pp. 155–186). Praeger.

Huang, Q., & Bolt, D. M. (2023). Relative robustness of CDMs and (M)IRT in measuring growth in latent skills. *Educational and Psychological Measurement, 83*(4), 808–830. https://doi.org/10.1177/00131644221117194.

Huang, H.-T., Hung, S.-T., Chao, H.-Y., Chen, J.-H., Lin, T.-P., & Shih, C.-L. (2022). Developing and validating a computerized adaptive testing system for measuring the English proficiency of Taiwanese EFL university students. *Language Assessment Quarterly, 19*(2), 162–188. https://doi.org/10.1080/15434303.2021.1984490.

Jiang, S., Wang, C., & Weiss, D. (2016). Sample size requirements for estimation of item parameters in the multidimensional graded response model. *Frontiers in Psychology, 7*, 109. https://doi.org/10.3389/fpsyg.2016.00109.

Kaya, E., O'Grady, S., & Kalender, İ. (2022). IRT-based classification analysis of an English language reading proficiency subtest. *Language Testing, 39*(4), 541–566. https://doi.org/10.1177/02655322211068847.

Kim, S. Y., Lee, W. C., & Kolen, M. J. (2020). Simple-structure multidimensional item response theory equating for multidimensional tests. *Educational and Psychological Measurement, 80*(1), 91–125. https://doi.org/10.1177/0013164419854208.

Klem, M., Gustafsson, J.-E., & Hagtvet, B. (2015). The dimensionality of language ability in four-year-olds: construct validation of a language screening tool. *Scandinavian Journal of Educational Research, 59*(2), 195–213. https://doi.org/10.1080/00313831.2014.904416.

Laurier, M. (1999). The development of an adaptive test for placement in French. In M. Chalhoub-Deville (Ed.), *Issues in computer-adaptive testing of reading comprehension* (pp. 122–135). Cambridge University Press.

Lee, W., Kim, S. Y., Choi, J., & Kang, Y. (2020). IRT approaches to modeling scores on mixed-format tests. *Journal of Educational Measurement, 57*(2), 230–254. https://doi.org/10.1111/jedm.12248.

van der Linden, W. J. (2016). Introduction. In W. J. van der Linden (Ed.), *Handbook of item response theory, volume one: Models* (pp. 1–10). Taylor & Francis Group.

Longabach, T., & Peyton, V. (2018). A comparison of reliability and precision of subscore reporting methods for a state English language proficiency assessment. *Language Testing, 35*(2), 297–317. https://doi.org/10.1177/0265532217689949.

Lord, F. M. (1980). *Applications of item response theory to practical testing problems*. Lawrence Erlbaum Associates Inc.

Lord, F. M., & Novick, M. R. (1968). *Statistical theories of mental test scores*. Reading, MA: Addison-Wesley.

MacGregor, D., Yen, S., & Yu, X. (2022). Using multistage testing to enhance measurement of an English language proficiency test. *Language Assessment Quarterly, 19*(1), 54–75. https://doi.org/10.1080/15434303.2021.1988953.

Masters, G. N. (1982). A Rasch model for partial credit scoring. *Psychometrika, 47*(2), 149–174. https://doi.org/10.1007/bf02296272.

Meijer, R. R., & Tendeiro, J. N. (2018). Unidimensional item response theory. In P. Irwing, T. Booth & D. J. Hughes (Eds.), *The Wiley handbook of psychometric testing: A multidisciplinary reference on survey, scale and test development* (Vol. 1, pp. 413–443). Wiley Blackwell.

Millsap, R. E., Gunn, H., Everson, H. T., & Zautra, A. (2014). Using item response theory to evaluate measurement invariance in health-related measures. In S. P. Reise & D. A. Revicki (Eds.), *Handbook of item response theory modeling: Applications to typical performance assessment* (pp. 364–385). Routledge.

Min, S., & Aryadoust, V. (2021). A systematic review of item response theory in language assessment: implications for the dimensionality of language ability. *Studies in Educational Evaluation, 68*, 100963. https://doi.org/10.1016/j.stueduc.2020.100963.

Min, S., & He, L. (2014). Applying unidimensional and multidimensional item response theory models in testlet-based reading assessment. *Language Testing, 31*(4), 453–477. https://doi.org/10.1177/0265532214527277.

Min, S., & He, L. (2020). Test fairness: examining differential functioning of the reading comprehension section of the GSEEE in China. *Studies in Educational Evaluation, 64*, 100811. https://doi.org/10.1016/j.stueduc.2019.100811.

Min, S., Bishop, K., & Cook, H. G. (2022). Reading is a multidimensional construct at child-L2-English-literacy onset, but comprises fewer dimensions over time: evidence from multidimensional IRT analysis. *Language Testing, 39*(2), 265–288. https://doi.org/10.1177/02655322211045296.

Mislevy, R. J., & Verhelst, N. (1990). Modeling item responses when different subjects employ different solution strategies. *Psychometrika, 55*(2), 195–215. https://doi.org/10.1007/bf02295283.

Mizumoto, A., Sasao, Y., & Webb, S. A. (2019). Developing and evaluating a computerized adaptive testing version of the word part levels test. *Language Testing, 36*(1), 101–123. https://doi.org/10.1177/0265532217725776.

Muraki, E. (1992). A generalized partial credit model: application of an EM algorithm. *Applied Psychological Measurement, 16*, 159–176. https://doi.org/10.1002/j.23338504.1992.tb01436.x.

Nijlen, V. D., & Janssen, R. (2011). Measuring mastery across grades: an application to spelling ability. *Applied Measurement in Education, 24*(4), 367–387. https://doi.org/10.1080/08957347.2011.607064.

Ockey, G. J. (2007). Investigating the validity of math word problems for English language learners with DIF. *Language Assessment Quarterly, 4*(2), 149–164. https://doi.org/10.1080/15434300701375717.

Orlando, M., & Thissen, D. (2000). Likelihood-based item fit indices for dichotomous item response theory models. *Applied Psychological Measurement, 24*(1), 50–64. https://doi.org/10.1177/01466216000241003.

Orlando, M., & Thissen, D. (2003). Further investigation of the performance of S-X2: an item fit index for use with dichotomous item response theory models. *Applied Psychological Measurement, 27*(4), 289–298. https://doi.org/10.1177/0146621603027004004.

Pae, T. (2004). DIF for examinees with different academic backgrounds. *Language Testing, 21*(1), 53–73. https://doi.org/10.1191/0265532204lt274oa.

Pae, T. (2012). Causes of gender DIF on an EFL language test: a multiple-data analysis over nine years. *Language Testing, 29*(4), 533–554. https://doi.org/10.1177/0265532211434027.

Paek, I., & Cole, K. (2020). *Using R for item response theory model applications*. Routledge Taylor & Francis Group.

Pohl, S. (2013). Longitudinal multistage testing. *Journal of Educational Measurement, 50*(4), 447–468. https://doi.org/10.1111/jedm.12028.

Purpura, J. (2016). Second foreign language assessment. *The Modern Language Journal, 100*(S1), 190–208. https://doi.org/10.1111/modl.12308.

Radwan, N., Reckase, M. D., & Rogers, W. T. (2013). Linking cut-scores given changes in the decision-making process, administration time, and proportions of item types between successive administrations of a test for a large-scale assessment program. *Educational and Psychological Measurement, 73*(1), 125–142. https://doi.org/10.1177/0013164412448652.

Reckase, M. D. (2009). *Multidimensional item response theory*. Springer Verlag.

Reise, S. P., Cook, K. F., & Moore, T. M. (2014). Evaluating the impact of multidimensionality on unidimensional item response theory model parameters. In S. P. Reise & D. A. Revicki (Eds.), *Handbook of item response theory modeling: applications to typical performance assessment* (pp. 13–40). New York: Routledge.

Revicki, D. A., & Reise, S. P. (2014). Summary: new IRT problems and future directions. In S. P. Reise & D. A. Revicki (Eds.), *Handbook of item response theory modeling: Applications to typical performance assessment* (pp. 457–461). Routledge.

Rijmen, F. (2010). Formal relations and an empirical comparison among the bi-factor, the testlet, and a second-order multidimensional IRT model. *Journal of Educational Measurement, 47*(3), 361–372. https://doi.org/10.1111/j.1745-3984.2010.00118.x.

Robin, F., Steffen, M., & Liang, L. (2014). The multistage test implementation of the GRE revised general test. In D. Yan, A. A. von Davier & C. Lewis (Eds.), *Computerized multistage testing: Theory and applications* (pp. 325–341). CRC Press.

Sahin, A., & Anil, D. (2017). The effects of test length and sample size on item parameters in item response theory. *Educational Sciences: Theory and Practice, 17*(1), 321–335. https://doi.org/10.12738/estp.2017.1.0270.

Samejima, F. (1969). Estimation of latent ability using a response pattern of graded responses. *Psychometrika, 34*, 1–97. https://doi.org/10.1007/bf03372160.

Sawaki, Y., Stricker, L. J., & Oranje, A. H. (2009). Factor structure of the TOEFL Internet-based test. *Language Testing, 26*(1), 5–30. https://doi.org/10.1177/0265532208097335.

Thissen, D., Steinberg, L., & Wainer, H. (1993). Detection of differential item functioning using the parameters of item response models. In P. W. Holland & H. Wainer (Eds.), *Differential item functioning* (pp. 35–66). Lawrence Erlbaum.

Wainer, H., Bradlow, E. T., & Wang, X. (2007). *Testlet response theory and its applications.* Cambridge University Press.

Warnby, M., Malmström, H., & Hansen, K. Y. (2023). Linking scores from two written receptive English academic vocabulary tests – the VLT-Ac and the AVT. *Language Testing, 40*(3), 548–575. https://doi.org/10.1177/02655322221145643.

Woods, C. M. (2008). Ramsay-curve item response theory for the 3PL item response model. *Applied Psychological Measurement, 32*(6), 447–465. https://doi.org/10.1177/0146621607308014.

Woods, C. M., & Thissen, D. (2006). Item response theory with estimation of the latent population distribution using spline-based densities. *Psychometrika, 71*(2), 281–301. https://doi.org/10.1007/s11336-004-1175-8.

Yamamoto, K., Shin, H. J., & Khorramdel, L. (2019). *Introduction of multistage adaptive testing design in PISA 2018 (OECD Education Working Paper No. 209).* OECD Publishing. https://doi.org/10.1787/b9435d4b-en.

Young, R., Shermis, M. D., Brutten, S. R., & Perkins, K. (1996). From conventional to computer-adaptive testing of ESL reading comprehension. *System, 24*, 23–40. https://doi.org/10.1016/0346-251X(95)00051-K.

Zhang, B. (2010). Assessing the accuracy and consistency of language proficiency classification under competing measurement models. *Language Testing, 27*(1), 119–140. https://doi.org/10.1177/0265532209347363.

Suggested Readings

Paek, I., & Cole, K. (2020). *Using R for item response theory model applications.* Routledge.

Reckase, M. D. (2009). *Multidimensional item response theory.* Springer Verlag.

van der Linden, W. J. (2016). *Handbook of item response theory: Models* (Vol. 1). Taylor & Francis.

CHAPTER 40

Many-Facet Rasch Analysis for Evaluating Second Language Tests

Khaled Barkaoui

Introduction

Identifying and measuring the factors that contribute to variability in assessment results is central to evaluating tests. This chapter focuses on the use of Rasch models, specifically the many-facet Rasch model (MFRM), for evaluating second language (L2) tests.

Rasch models are a family of probabilistic measurement models that use sophisticated mathematical procedures to calibrate parameters in the assessment setting (e.g., test-taker ability, item difficulty) independently of each other (Bond et al., 2021; Eckes, 2023; McNamara et al., 2019). According to the basic Rasch model, as proposed by Rasch (1960), the probability of a correct response to a dichotomously scored test item (e.g., true/false) is a function of the difference between test-taker ability and item difficulty. Estimates of test-taker ability and item difficulty are computed and placed on a common frame of reference, called the logit scale. As McNamara (1996) explained, a logit scale is a true interval scale to express the relationship between item difficulty and test-taker ability; logits being log-odd transformations of observed scores across all test takers and items. When the ability of a test taker matches exactly the difficulty of an item, the model predicts success for the test taker half of the time (50%). For test takers with ability higher than the difficulty of a given item, the model predicts that they will answer the item correctly more than 50% of the time.

Various models have been developed from the basic, dichotomous Rasch model, including the rating scale model (RSM) (Andrich, 1978), the partial-credit model (PCM) (Masters, 1982), and the MFRM (Linacre, 2023). The RSM extends the dichotomous Rasch model to polytomously scored items (i.e., items scored on a rating scale). An item with k possible score categories needs $k - 1$ *step difficulty* parameters, or *thresholds*, to separate the score categories. The PCM is an extension of the RSM that addresses this issue by allowing the number of score categories and their threshold estimates to vary across items in the same test (Bond et al., 2021). The PCM also allows the examination of responses that could be given partial credit (e.g., incorrect, partially correct, and correct).

The Concise Companion to Language Assessment, First Edition. Edited by Antony John Kunnan.
© 2025 John Wiley & Sons, Inc. Published 2025 by John Wiley & Sons, Inc.

The MFRM

The MFRM (e.g., Linacre, 2023) is an extension of the PCM to assessment settings in which factors, called *facets*, other than test-taker ability and item difficulty can systematically influence test scores and, thus, need to be identified and measured (Bond et al., 2021). Examples of facets that can influence test scores include task type, rater, rating criteria, and rating occasion. The MFRM allows test developers to estimate the impact of each facet on the measurement process by estimating its difficulty (e.g., severity of each rater) and then including that difficulty estimate in computing the probability of any test taker responding to any item for any score category threshold for any rater (Bond et al., 2021).

The MFRM thus enables researchers to model various facets in the assessment setting, estimate their effects on test scores, and place them on the same logit scale for comparison. Each facet is calibrated from the raw, potentially ordinal, ratings, when a rating scale is used, and all facets are placed on a single common linear scale called a *variable* or *facets map*. For example, in a writing test that involves responding to multiple tasks and then rating test takers' responses on multiple rating criteria by multiple raters, there are four facets: test taker, task, rater, and rating criterion. The MFRM sees each rating as a function of the interaction (and computes measures) of test-taker ability, task difficulty, criterion difficulty, and rater severity/leniency (Bond et al., 2021; McNamara, 1996; McNamara et al., 2019).

The computer program FACETS (Linacre, 2023) operationalizes MFRM. FACETS uses the ratings that raters assign (observed scores) to provide parameter estimates for each facet (i.e., rater severity, task difficulty, and test-taker ability) as well as information about the reliability of each of these estimates, in the form of standard error (SE), and the validity of the measure in the form of fit statistics for each element in each modeled facet. Each facet is calibrated from the relevant observed ratings, and, depending on the purpose of the analyses, all facets except one, usually the test taker, are set at zero (Lunz et al., 1996). When the rating scale includes several rating criteria (e.g., analytic scale), FACETS allows the estimation of rating criteria difficulty as well.

FACETS also permits rating scale diagnosis and bias analysis. Scale diagnosis aims to assess the quality of the rating scale by examining how *scale steps* (or score levels) are functioning to create an interpretable measure and whether *scale-step thresholds* indicate a hierarchical pattern to the rating scale (Bond et al., 2021). Bias analysis is similar to differential item functioning (*DIF*) analysis in that it aims to identify any systematic sub-patterns of behavior occurring from an interaction of a particular rater (or any other facet) with a particular aspect of the rating situation (e.g., rating criteria, task, test taker) and to estimate the effects of these interactions on test scores (Kondo-Brown, 2002; Lumley & McNamara, 1995). The different analyses of FACETS thus permit us to move beyond raw scores to understand the effects of the conditions of assessment on test scores (Bond et al., 2021; McNamara et al., 2019).

The MFRM provides a powerful framework and tool for evaluating L2 assessment tools and procedures. It can help L2 test developers address several important questions concerning the assumptions underlying the interpretive argument of L2 tests, such as the following:

1. What are the effects of the assessment setting and conditions (e.g., rater, task, and rating occasion) on test scores? (e.g., Eckes, 2005; Ockey, 2022; Weigle, 1999)
2. Are there any biased interactions between facets in the assessment setting? (e.g., Kondo-Brown, 2002)
3. How do we account and compensate for the effects of facets in the assessment setting when interpreting and using assessment results? (e.g., Kozaki, 2004)

In the following section, the MFRM, as operationalized by FACETS, is applied to scores from an L2 writing test to illustrate the kind of questions that the MFRM can address and the

604   **Chapter 40** Many-Facet Rasch Analysis for Evaluating Second Language Tests

types of insights it can provide about the quality of L2 assessments. Readers interested in the technical aspects of the MFRM and how to implement it should consult the references listed at the end of this chapter.

MFRM Analysis: An Illustration

Data for this analysis consist of the scores of 161 test takers on the writing section of an L2 test to place internationally trained pharmacists in courses to improve their English language proficiency. The writing section includes three writing tasks. Task 1 consists of reading a medical alert in English and then writing a message to a colleague that summarizes the key points of the alert (i.e., a reading-based task). Task 2 consists of listening to and summarizing a four-minute lecture on a pharmacy-related topic (i.e., a listening-based task). Tasks 1 and 2 are rated analytically in terms of content, vocabulary, grammar, appropriacy, and effectiveness. Task 3 consists of writing an essay on one of three independent topics (i.e., an independent task). For the purposes of this analysis, these three topics are treated as three different tasks (Tasks 3–5). Tasks 3–5 are rated analytically in terms of organization, coherence, vocabulary, grammar, and effectiveness. Each rating criterion is rated on a 5-point scale (0–4). One rater rated all the writing samples ($n = 470$ samples), while a second rater rated the writing samples ($n = 149$ samples) of a random sample of 50 test takers. The dataset consisted of 3094 scores.

The scores were analyzed using the RSM as operationalized by FACETS (Linacre, 2023) to estimate test-taker writing ability, task and criterion difficulty, rater severity and self-consistency, scale-step difficulty, and any biased interactions between facets. A four-facet Rasch model was employed for analyzing the scores: test taker ($n = 161$), task ($n = 5$), rater ($n = 2$), and rating criterion ($n = 7$). Formally, the Rasch model for score analysis is as follows (Bond et al., 2021; Linacre, 2023; McNamara, 1996):

$$\log\left(P_{nmijk}\, P_{nmijk-1}\right) = B_n - D_m - E_i - C_j - F_k,$$

where P_{nmijk} = probability of test taker n achieving on task m, for criterion i, by rater j, a score k; $P_{nmijk-1}$ = probability of test taker n achieving on task m, for criterion i, by rater j, a score immediately below k ($k - 1$); $\log(P_{nmijk}/P_{nmijk-1})$ = log odds of achieving a score k, given the task, criterion, and rater, versus the probability of being rated $k - 1$; B_n = ability (B) of test taker n, the test-taker facet, $n = 1$–161; D_m = difficulty (D) of task m, the task facet, $m = 1$–5; E_i = difficulty (E) of criterion i, the criterion facet, $i = 1$–7; C_j = severity (C) of rater j, the rater facet, $j = 1$–2; F_k = score category threshold (F) defined as the point where the probability of achieving a score of k and $k - 1$ is equal.

FACETS provides various statistics for each facet, including parameter estimates and SE for each element of each facet, strata index, reliability of separation, fixed X^2, various rater agreement statistics, and infit and outfit mean square (IMS and OMS) statistics.[1] For each element of each facet, FACETS provides a measure of that parameter on a logit scale together with an SE that indicates the uncertainty of (i.e., error associated with) the parameter estimate.

Strata indicates the number of levels within a given facet (e.g., number of levels of rater severity and number of levels of task difficulty), while the *reliability of separation* indicates the degree to which the analysis reliably distinguishes between different strata within a given facet. It also provides information concerning the replicability of the placement of elements within each facet relative to each other (see below). *Fixed (all same) X^2* tests the null hypothesis that all the elements of the facet are equal. If fixed X^2 is significant at p, this indicates

---

[1] Issues of data screening and assumptions are discussed below.

MFRM Analysis: An Illustration **605**

that the elements are not equal (e.g., raters are not equal in severity). While FACETS provides strata and reliability indices and fixed X^2 for each facet, the interpretation of these indices differs depending on the facet under consideration, as will be discussed below.

FACETS reports infit and outfit mean-squares (*IMS* and *OMS*) statistics for each element in each facet. IMS statistics show the degree of variability in individual elements of a facet (e.g., rater and task) relative to the amount of variability in the entire set (of raters, tasks, etc.). Ideally, if the observed data conform to the model, the infit statistic is expected to have a value of 1.0. The closer the fit statistics are to this ideal, the better the assessment. As will be discussed below, there is no general agreement about what is considered acceptable fit since the range of acceptable IMS (and OMS) indices depends on a variety of factors (Bond et al., 2021). For illustrative purposes, the upper and lower control limits for IMS in this analysis are set at 0.5 and 1.5, respectively. Elements with $IMS \leq 0.5$ indicate overfit; elements with $IMS \geq 1.5$ indicate misfit, while elements with $0.5 < IMS < 1.5$ indicate acceptable fit. OMS has the same form as IMS, but is more sensitive to outliers (Linacre, 2023). The acceptable range for identifying misfitting OMS is the same as for IMS. Elements (e.g., raters and tasks) with IMS and OMS statistics outside the acceptable range are reviewed for inconsistency (misfit) or over consistency (overfit) in score patterns.[2]

Test-Taker Ability

The MFRM can help L2 test developers address several questions about their tests in relation to the test-taker facet, such as whether the test discriminates among test takers in terms of the ability being measured; how replicable the placement of test takers relative to each other is across other tests that measure the same construct; and whether the abilities of test takers are measured "properly" by the test (as indicated by fit statistics).

A summary of FACETS results for the test-taker facet is reported in Table 40.1. It shows that test takers' ability estimates ranged between −4.07 and 4.20 logits, with a mean of −0.15 (SD = 1.64). The negative mean (*M*) suggests that the test was slightly difficult for this group

TABLE 40.1

Summary of test-taker facet statistics

Test-taker ability estimates ($N = 161$)	
M (Model SE)	−0.15 (0.35)
SD (Model SE)	1.64 (0.08)
Min	−4.07
Max	4.20
Infit	
M	0.98
SD	0.66
Separation statistics	
Strata	6.23
Reliability of separation	0.95
Fixed X^2 statistic (df)	2838.9 (160), $p < 0.001$

SD refers to the spread of scores between test takers. SE refers to the spread of estimates for a test taker.

---

[2] In this chapter, only IMS statistics are discussed to keep the discussion brief and because OMS statistics are often interpreted in the same way as IMS (but see Bond et al., 2021; McNamara, 1996) and the IMS and OMS statistics for the current dataset were almost identical for all facets.

606 Chapter 40 Many-Facet Rasch Analysis for Evaluating Second Language Tests

of test takers. The mean SE is 0.35; SE indicates the uncertainty or precision of the estimates of test-taker ability and depends on the amount of information about the element in a facet (McNamara, 1996). Generally, the more scores assigned to each test taker, the lower the SE. In this case, a large number of scores (3 tasks × 5 criteria = 15 scores) were assigned to each test taker. Consequently, the SE is quite low as compared to what we typically encounter in most test settings. The X^2, which tests the hypothesis that all test takers are equal in terms of the ability being measured, is statistically significant at $p < 0.001$.

The strata and reliability indices for the difference in test-taker ability are high (6.23 and 0.95, respectively). The high strata index indicates that the variance among test takers is substantially larger than the error of estimates and that the test separates the 161 test takers into approximately 6 statistically distinct levels in terms of the ability being measured. The high-reliability statistic indicates that the same ordering of test takers would be more likely to obtain if test takers were to take another test measuring the same ability, thus increasing our confidence in the consistency of score-based inferences.

In addition to ability estimates, FACETS reports fit statistics for each test taker, providing useful information about the validity of the assessment (Bond et al., 2021). Table 40.1 shows that the mean fit (0.98) is close to the expected value of 1.0. Table 40.2 classifies test takers according to the magnitude of their IMS statistics. Acceptable fit indicates a pattern of ratings that closely approximates the predicted Rasch-model rating pattern based on the test-taker ability estimate. Overfit indicates that ratings for a test taker are closer to expected ratings than the model predicts they should be. In contrast, model misfit indicates that test takers' scores do not agree with each other; the scores they obtained on different items and from different raters are more different than expected. In this case, misfit indicates that the observed ratings are farther from what the model expects given the test-taker ability. This may be due to inter-rater disagreement on the quality of that test taker's performance. Both misfit and overfit suggest that the test-taker ability is not being measured appropriately by the test, but misfit is usually considered to be a more serious problem than overfit (see Bond et al., 2021; McNamara, 1996).

Table 40.2 shows that about two-thirds of the test takers (68%) had fit statistics within the acceptable range. There is a larger proportion of test takers with overfit than with misfit. Overfit may occur if test takers are assigned the same scores regardless of differences in their proficiency levels. Overfit also indicates a halo effect; test takers are assigned similar scores on the different rating criteria. Misfit indicates noisiness or unusual rating patterns and can occur when the dataset includes few observations per test taker. Concerning analytic scales, Bonk and Ockey (2003) noted that because Rasch models treat rating criteria as "items," these models tend to flag departures from expected patterns of behavior as misfitting, even when they are not. For example, if a test taker is assigned different scores on different rating criteria, as some test takers may perform differently on different aspects of writing, Rasch models may consider the pattern of ratings unexpected and flag the test taker as misfitting. For this reason, Bonk and Ockey (2003) noted that test-taker misfit may not be a major problem with rating data and does not disqualify such data from inclusion in Rasch models.

TABLE **40.2**

Frequencies (%) of test-taker IMS statistics

Range of Infit MS	Frequency (%)
Overfit: fit < 0.50	28 (17%)
Acceptable: 0.50 < fit < 1.50	109 (68%)
Misfit: fit > 1.50	24 (15%)

Rater Severity and Self-Consistency

A major contribution of the MFRM is that it allows test developers and users to detect and measure various types of rater effects, biases, and errors such as severity/leniency, halo, restriction of range, central tendency, and order effects (Eckes, 2015, 2023). Detecting and measuring such effects and errors is an important step in evaluating and improving L2 tests. For example, if it is found that several raters exhibit a halo effect, whereby similar scores are assigned to the same student on different criteria regardless of actual differences in the student's mastery of the various criteria, test developers may choose to revise and clarify the rating criteria, provide raters with feedback and additional training, or do both (see Myford & Wolfe, 2004a, b).

Some of the questions that the MFRM can help address in relation to the rater facet are whether raters differ in the severity/leniency with which they rate test takers' performances; whether raters can effectively distinguish among test takers in terms of their levels of performance; whether raters can effectively differentiate between rating criteria; how self-consistent raters are; and whether ratings show evidence of a restriction in range or halo effects (adapted from Myford & Wolfe, 2004a, b).

Table 40.3 summarizes FACETS results for the rater facet. It shows that the difference in severity between the two raters is very small (0.06 logits). The low reliability and strata indices and the nonsignificant X^2 statistic in Table 40.3 indicate that the raters were similar in severity. Note that reliability in this context refers not to the traditional index of inter-rater agreement, but to the ability of the analysis to reliably separate raters into different levels of severity. As a result, a reliability index of zero is desirable, as it indicates that raters are interchangeable (McNamara, 1996; Weigle, 1999). A low strata value and a nonsignificant fixed X^2 are desirable outcomes too as they indicate that the assumption of equivalence among raters is held (Weigle, 1998).

FACETS reports the observed and expected percentages of exact rater agreement too. If the observed agreement rate is too low in comparison with the expected agreement rate, a model for predicting agreement is problematic. By contrast, when the observed agreement rate is higher than the expected rate, there is a possibility that raters do not perform ratings independently (Linacre, 2023). Table 40.3 shows that the percentage of observed exact agreement between raters is 59% of the total possible opportunities for agreement ($n = 745$), which is higher than the expected level of agreement (41%).

FACETS also reports rater fit statistics, which indicate the degree to which a rater is internally self-consistent across test takers, criteria, and tasks, and whether raters are able to implement the rating scale to make distinctions among test takers' performances (Bond et al., 2021; Weigle, 1998). As Table 40.3 shows, both raters have fit statistics close to the

TABLE **40.3**

Rater measurement report

	Measure	Model SE	Infit MS
Rater 1	−0.03	0.03	0.95
Rater 2	0.03	0.05	1.15
$M\ (n = 2)$	0.00	0.04	1.05
SD	0.04	0.02	0.15

Strata 0.42 reliability (not inter-rater) 0.00.

Fixed (all same) X^2: 1.0 df: 1 significance (probability): 0.32.

Inter-rater agreement opportunities: 745 exact agreements: 438 = 58.8% Expected: 301.8 = 40.5%.

608 Chapter 40 Many-Facet Rasch Analysis for Evaluating Second Language Tests

expected value of 1.0, suggesting that they used the rating scale consistently and maintained their personal level of severity across test takers, tasks, and criteria (i.e., intra-rater agreement). Misfit indicates inconsistency in applying the rating scale across tasks and test takers, while overfit indicates that the rater is unusually consistent or overly cautious in using the upper and lower levels of the rating scale (i.e., a central tendency) (Eckes, 2015, 2023; Myford & Wolfe, 2004a, b). Rater misfit is a more serious threat to validity than rater overfit or test-taker misfit because it indicates that a rater's ratings deviate from the norm and its effect on all other facet measure estimates can be strong. Rasch models cannot adjust scores for rater misfit, as is the case with rater severity, because scores need to be consistent for the model to apply a reasonable adjustment (see Bonk & Ockey, 2003, p. 101; Myford & Wolfe, 2004a, b).[3]

Task Difficulty

Some of the questions that the MFRM can help L2 test developers address in relation to the task facet are how difficult each task is; whether tasks (e.g., tasks that are assumed to be equivalent) differ significantly in terms of their difficulty; whether there are tasks that are redundant and can be deleted; and whether all tasks contribute to the measurement of the same underlying construct, and so scores on those tasks can be combined into a composite score or not.

As Table 40.4 shows, the five tasks, ordered from least to most difficult, differed significantly in terms of their difficulty, as indicated by the high reliability and strata indices and the significant X^2 statistic. The analysis reliably separated the tasks into seven levels of difficulty. Task 5 was the easiest and Task 1 the most difficult. Note that Tasks 3–5, which are assumed to be equivalent and hence test takers can choose which topic to respond to, are not equal in terms of difficulty; Task 5 was the easiest followed by Task 4 and then Task 3. Note also that tasks based on reading and listening (Tasks 1 and 2) were generally more difficult than the independent tasks. The task reliability index indicates the replicability of task placements in terms of difficulty if these same tasks were given to another sample with comparable ability levels (Bond et al., 2021). For example, Task 3 will be more difficult than Task 5 with another sample of test takers.

TABLE **40.4**

Task measurement report

	Measure	Model SE	Infit MS
Task 5	−0.44	0.08	0.72
Task 4	−0.28	0.07	1.77
Task 2	0.10	0.04	0.99
Task 3	0.12	0.10	0.78
Task 1	0.50	0.04	0.80
$M\ (n = 5)$	0.00	0.07	1.01
SD	0.37	0.02	0.44

Strata 7.18 reliability 0.96.
Fixed (all same) X^2: 156.0 df: four significance (probability): 0.00.

---

[3] The results presented here are not typical, and so readers should not expect similar results. For example, unlike in this example, most studies report high reliability of separation for the rater facet and significant fixed X^2 tests.

Table 40.4 reports fit statistics for each task. While the mean IMS is close to 1.0, the fit for individual tasks varies between 0.72 and 1.77. Task 4 exhibits misfit, which suggests that the task is poorly written or that it is perfectly good in itself but does not form part of a set of tasks that together define a single measurement trait (McNamara, 1996). In the first instance, misfitting tasks need to be revised or deleted from the test. In the second scenario, scores on the tasks should be reported separately. Overfit, by contrast, indicates that the task is redundant; that is, the pattern of response to the task is too predictable from the overall pattern of responses to other tasks (see McNamara, 1996). The task can therefore be revised or removed. None of the tasks in Table 40.4 shows overfit.

Criterion Difficulty

Concerning rating criteria, the MFRM can help L2 test developers address questions such as how difficult the rating criteria are; whether the rating criteria differ significantly in terms of their difficulty; whether raters are able to effectively distinguish among the rating criteria; whether there are rating criteria that are redundant and can be deleted; and whether all criteria contribute to the measurement of the same underlying construct, and so scores on different criteria can be combined into a composite score or not.

Table 40.5 reports FACETS analysis results for the rating criteria, with criteria ordered from least to most difficult. It shows that it was hardest for test takers to obtain high ratings on Effectiveness, with a difficulty of 0.35 logits, and easiest to get high ratings on Organization, with a difficulty of −0.22 logits. The strata and reliability indices indicate that the analysis reliably (0.80) distinguishes between about three distinct levels of difficulty among the rating criteria. These results indicate that the test takers performed significantly differently in the various aspects of writing, or the raters perceived these rating criteria differently, or both. The fit statistics of the seven rating criteria are within the acceptable range of 0.5 to 1.5. Organization exhibited a larger degree of misfit than did the other criteria. Misfit indicates that a criterion does not form part of the same dimension as defined by the other criteria in the rating scale and is therefore measuring a different construct or trait (i.e., evidence of psychometric multidimensionality; see below). This suggests that "it would not be appropriate to sum or average scores across the different [criteria]" (McNamara, 1996, p. 275). If there is no misfit, then this indicates that the criteria work together, that ratings on one criterion correspond

TABLE 40.5			
Rating criteria measurement report			
	Measure	**Model SE**	**Infit MS**
Organization	−0.22	0.10	1.49
Appropriateness	−0.04	0.07	0.93
Coherence	−0.03	0.10	1.19
Vocabulary	−0.03	0.06	0.97
Content	−0.02	0.07	1.00
Grammar	−0.01	0.06	0.94
Effectiveness	0.35	0.06	0.92
M ($n = 7$)	0.00	0.07	1.06
SD	0.17	0.02	0.21

Strata 2.96 reliability 0.80.
Fixed (all same) X^2: 39.1 df: six significance (probability): 0.00.

610 Chapter 40 Many-Facet Rasch Analysis for Evaluating Second Language Tests

well to ratings on other criteria, and that a single summary measure (e.g., average or total score) can appropriately capture the essence of test-taker performance across the different criteria of the rating scale. Overfit, on the other hand, indicates that a criterion is redundant (i.e., is measuring the same ability as other criteria); it significantly affected the scores assigned to the essays on the other criteria (i.e., halo effect) (McNamara, 1996) or both.

Rating Scale Functioning

Scale functioning analysis assesses the quality of the rating scale by addressing such questions as follows: whether the rating scale functions well in estimating the construct being measured; whether raters use all parts of the rating scale; whether raters use the rating scale consistently, so the scale is associated with a progression of test-taker ability; whether raters employ the scale in the same way or interpret and use it differently; and whether there is evidence of a restriction of range or a central tendency (Bond et al., 2021; Bonk & Ockey, 2003, p. 102). Answers to these questions can help L2 test developers identify problems in the rating scale and rating process and address them by, for example, further clarifying and differentiating the rating criteria and score levels; increasing or reducing the number of criteria and score levels on the rating scale (Myford & Wolfe, 2004a, b); or doing both.

Table 40.6 reports the results of FACETS scale analysis for the current dataset. Column 1 shows the scale levels from 0 to 4. Columns 2 and 3 report the frequency and percentage of times a given score is assigned across all raters and writing samples. Bond et al. (2021) suggest that, as a rule of thumb, each scale level should be assigned to at least 10 essays to allow scale diagnostics. Column 4 reports the (observed) average test-taker ability measure associated with each score level. This is computed by averaging the test-taker ability measures (in logits) for all test takers in the sample who were assigned that score. These measures are expected to increase monotonically[4] in size as the variable being measured increases, indicating that, on average, those with higher ability will be assigned higher scores (Bond et al., 2021; Linacre, 2023). Scale levels that violate the monotonicity pattern are flagged. Table 40.6 shows that the rating scale functioned as expected in that a higher score is always associated with a higher average measure. Column 5 reports the expected measure for each scale level, that is, the test-taker ability measure that the measurement model would predict for that scale level if the data were to fit the model.

TABLE **40.6**

Scale statistics

| | Observed counts | | Average measure | Expected measure | Outfit MS | Step calibration | |
Score level	Freq.	%				Measure	SE
0	260	8	−2.45	−2.42	1.0		
1	772	25	−1.27	−1.23	0.9	−2.90	0.08
2	1047	34	−0.06	−0.15	1.0	−0.99	0.05
3	854	28	0.90	0.98	1.1	0.61	0.05
4	161	5	2.38	2.29	0.9	3.29	0.09

---

[4]That is, as the value of one increases, the value of the other increases as well.

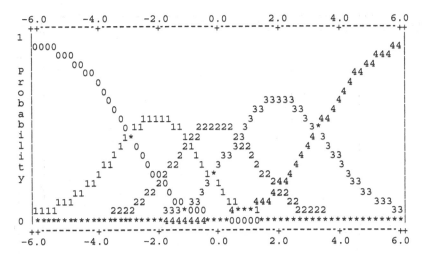

FIGURE 40.1 Scale category probability curves.

Column 6 reports the OMS index for each scale level. The expected value of this index is 1.0, indicating that the observed and expected test-taker ability measures are equal. The larger the difference between the observed and expected measures, the larger the OMS index will be. An OMS index greater than 2.0 suggests that a rating in that level for one or more test takers' essays may not be contributing to meaningful measurement of the variable (Linacre, 2023). Note that, because OMS indices are sensitive to outlying ratings, scores at the ends of the scale are more likely to exhibit high OMS indices than are scores in the middle. The OMS indices in Table 40.6 are around 1.0. The last two columns in Table 40.6 report step or threshold calibrations, which are the difficulties estimated for choosing one response category over another (e.g., how difficult it is to endorse 4 over 3) (Bond et al., 2021; Linacre, 2023).

MFRM software also provides *scale category probability curves* when an RSM is used. Figure 40.1 displays the scale category probability curves for the current dataset. The probability curves enable one to see the structure of the rating scale and, particularly, whether raters are using all the score categories on the scale. The horizontal axis represents the test-taker ability scale (in logits); the vertical axis represents probability (from 0 to 1). There is a probability curve for each of the scale levels (0 to 4). As Davidson (1991) explained, when examining such a graph, the chief concern is whether there is a separate peak for each score category probability curve or not, and whether the curves appear as an evenly spaced series of hills. A score category curve without a separate peak that rises above the peaks for adjacent category curves is problematic as it indicates that the category is never the most probable rating on any point along overall test-taker ability. Davidson (1991) suggested three ways to address this problem: rewriting the level descriptors to clarify what the level is intended to measure; removing that step from the scale if it is not needed; or providing rater training to explain the meaning of the underused step. The probability curves for the rating scale in Figure 40.1 show that each level is the most probable across some section of the ability being measured, indicating that the scale functions well.

Facets Variable Map

MFRM software provides a visual display of the relationships between facets in the form of a *facets variable map*. An example of such a map appears as Figure 40.2. The map displays visually, from left to right, the relative abilities of the test takers, the relative severity of the raters, and the relative difficulties of the tasks, the rating criteria, and the scale steps. The information

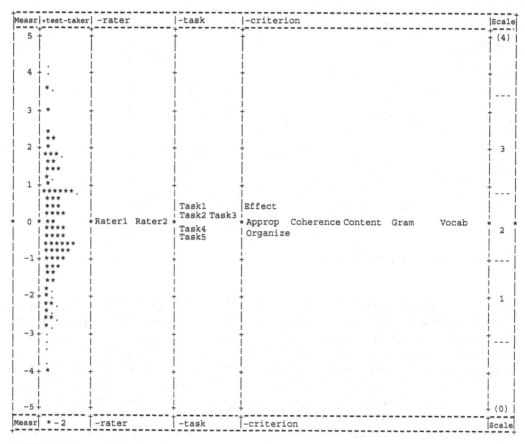

FIGURE 40.2 Facets variable map.

in columns 2–5 in Figure 40.2 is given in terms of the scale in column 1, which can be seen as a "scale of the chances of success of candidates and the degree of challenge presented by particular raters and particular [tasks, rating criteria and scale levels]" (McNamara, 1996, p. 134). Column 1, then, acts as a "ruler" against which each of the four facets, as well as scale step difficulty, is measured in "logit" units (McNamara, 1996). A positive sign (above 0 on the "ruler" in column 1) indicates that a test taker is more able, a task or criterion is more difficult, and a rater is more severe. A negative sign (below 0) indicates the opposite. Test takers' locations are plotted so that any test taker has a 50% probability of succeeding with a task located at the same point on the logit scale.

Bias Analysis

Bias analysis in the MFRM investigates whether a particular aspect of the assessment setting elicits a consistently biased pattern of scores. As McNamara (1996) explained, bias analysis consists in comparing expected and observed values in a set of data (i.e., *residuals*). After estimating overall rater severity (across all tasks), task and criterion difficulty (across all raters), and test-taker ability (across all tasks, criteria, and raters), the MFRM estimates the most likely score for each test taker with a given rater on a specific task "if the rater were rating that [task and criterion] in the way he or she rated the other [tasks and criteria]" (p. 142). These individual scores are totaled across all test takers to produce a total *expected* score from each rater on each task, which is then compared to the *observed* total score for all the test takers. If the observed score for a given task is higher than the expected score, then the task seems to have elicited more lenient behavior than usual from the raters. The difference, which is measured on the logit scale, reveals "precisely how much less of a challenge was presented by this [task] with this rater than might have been expected" and indicates how this impacts "the chances of success for candidates under those conditions" (p. 142). Fit statistics summarize the extent to which the differences between expected and observed values are within a normal range (for each rater, task, and test taker). In MFRM, sub-patterns of bias are identified in relation to pairs of facets such as rater by test taker, rater by rating criterion, rater by task, test taker by task, and so forth.

Bias analyses can help address important questions about the quality of L2 tests, such as whether there is evidence of bias in the test; whether rater severity varies across test takers, rating criteria, tasks, time, or a combination of these; whether raters exercise differential severity depending on test taker's race, ethnicity, age, or gender; and whether some tasks, rating criteria, or both are more prone to rater bias than others.

For the current dataset, the following possible interactions between facets were examined: rater by test taker, rater by task, rater by criterion, test taker by task, test taker by criterion, and task by criterion. Few significantly biased interactions were identified. To illustrate how bias analysis results are interpreted, the following paragraph focuses on the significantly biased rater-by-criterion interactions (see Table 40.7).

FACETS identified two significantly biased rater-by-criterion interactions (out of 14 possible interactions), both involving rater 2. Table 40.7 reports five types of information: the elements of the facets under investigation and their measures in logits; the observed and expected total raw scores for each combination of elements (e.g., rater 2 and grammar); the average difference between observed and expected raw scores; an estimate of the discrepancy between observed and expected values in logits and their SE; and z scores and IMS for each combination of elements of facets. z scores assess whether a discrepancy is due to chance. Ideally all the z scores should be equal to zero. z-values larger than $+2$ or less than -2 indicate significantly biased interactions. For example, Table 40.7 shows that rater 2 was significantly more severe when rating grammar ($z > +2$) but significantly more lenient when rating appropriateness ($z < -2$) than is normal for this rater. Fit MS tells us how consistent this pattern of bias is across all the test takers involved on these criteria with this rater. McNamara (1996) and Kondo-Brown (2002) recommended that only biased interactions with z-values equal to or higher than the absolute value of 2 and with IMS values within the range of two SDs around the mean of infit are considered. Significant biased interactions point to the need for more training for the raters on the criteria they interact with.

TABLE **40.7**								
Significantly biased rater-by-criterion interactions								
Criterion (Measure)	Rater (Measure)	Observed score	Expected score	Obs-exp. average	Bias (Logit)	Model SE	z	Infit MS
Appropriateness (−0.04)	2 (0.03)	221	204.6	16	−0.34	0.14	−2.33	1.0
Grammar (−0.01)	2 (0.03)	291	316.8	−17	0.35	0.12	3.02	1.1
M ($n = 14$)		433.7	433.7	0.00	0.00	0.12	0.00	1.1
SD		284.0	282.8	0.07	0.15	0.05	1.27	0.3

Fixed (all = 0) X^2: 21.0 df: 14 significance (probability): 0.10.

Issues and Considerations in the MFRM

This section discusses four main issues and considerations in the MFRM: sample size, model fit, dimensionality, and the interpretation of fit statistics.

Sample Size

As with other statistical models, users often want to know what "minimum sample size" is required to conduct MFRM analyses. However, to my knowledge, sample size is not discussed in the MFRM literature, although it is obvious that for the analysis to run, each facet (e.g., rater, task, and test taker) must include at least two elements. M. Linacre (personal communication, June 22, 2012) explained that sample size is usually controlled by operational and financial considerations. But he added that "a reasonable FACETS analysis would contain 30 test-takers, 10 raters, and 3 tasks, although researchers have used much smaller datasets" (for more recent discussions of sample size in MFRM, see Eckes, 2023; McNamara et al., 2019; Ockey, 2022).

One practical advantage of the MFRM is that it is robust in the presence of missing data. This means that "sufficiently accurate estimates" of facets can be computed with substantially incomplete designs (Bond et al., 2021). The only design requirement for the MFRM is that there is "enough linkage between all elements of all facets that all parameters can be estimated within one frame of reference without indeterminacy" (Linacre, 1994, p. 138; see Bond et al., 2021; Linacre, 2023; McNamara et al., 2019). This can be achieved by, for example, having all raters rate the same small subset of performances in addition to those performances they have to rate as part of their normal workload in a scoring session (see McNamara et al., 2019 for advice on how to ensure appropriate linkage). However, it is important to keep in mind that as the sample size decreases (e.g., because of missing data), parameter estimates become less precise and stable, SEs of the parameter estimates become larger, and statistical power of the fit statistics becomes weaker (M. Linacre, personal communication, June 22, 2012). Future studies could examine empirically the effects of different sample sizes and missing data on parameter estimates and other indices in the MFRM.

Model-Data Fit

Model fit relates to the number of item parameters to be estimated. The Rasch model is sometimes referred to as a one-parameter IRT model as it estimates only item difficulty. Other IRT models include other parameters such as item discrimination (two-parameter models) and guessing (three-parameter models). Although this is an important issue in dichotomously scored items, as McNamara (1996) pointed out, model fit is not a resolvable concern in performance assessment because currently only the Rasch models can operationally deal with judge-mediated scores. However, an issue often raised in relation to model fit is whether the measurement model should fit the data or the data should fit the measurement model. Rasch proponents insist that the data should fit the measurement model if valid measurement is the goal. As Bond et al. (2021) have argued:

> The Rasch model provides a mathematical framework against which test developers can compare their data. The model is based on the idea that useful measurement involves examination of only one human attribute at a time (unidimensionality) on a hierarchical "more than/less than" line of inquiry. This line of inquiry is a theoretical idealization against which we can compare patterns of responses that do not coincide with this ideal. Person and item performance deviations from that line (fit) can be assessed, alerting the investigator to reconsider item wording and score interpretations from these data. (p. 41)

Issues and Considerations in the MFRM   **615**

In the Rasch model, the criterion for success is not that the model fits the data, but that the data fit the model. However, because the Rasch model is probabilistic or stochastic, the data do not have to fit the model perfectly for the analysis to be successful (Bond et al., 2021). Misfitting data can be tolerated and may be revised or removed if it is found that, for example, the ratings of a rater are inconsistent. To diagnose the quality of overall data-model fit, one examines the overall fit of each facet and its elements through fit statistics and the responses that are unexpected given the assumptions of the model.[5]

Fit statistics provide information about how well the data for each element in each facet in the analysis "fit" or match the expectations of the measurement model that was used (McNamara, 1996). These statistics also allow test developers to determine to what extent the observed measures are drifting away from the expected measures (Bond et al., 2021). Fit is evaluated as the difference between the observed and predicted or expected score patterns. As noted above, the model expects that as ability increases, the chances of success on each item increase. If this relationship between ability (or difficulty) and performance breaks down, the fit statistic indicates the extent to which the relationship has been lost. Generally, the expected mean square value of the fit for each facet is 1.0 for the data to conform to the Rasch model. Mean square fit values very different from 1.0 indicate an unanticipated problem, mostly with the quality of the item or its interaction with a specific context. As Masters (1998) noted, item misfit can be an indication that performance on the test is multidimensional and cannot be summarized in a single score. As reported above, the overall fit of each of the facets in the dataset (test taker, task, rater, and rating criterion) was around 1.

Overall data-model fit can also be investigated through examining the responses that are unexpected given the assumptions of the Rasch measurement model. These unexpected responses result in large (absolute standardized) residuals, that is, differences between expected and observed scores. According to Linacre (2023), satisfactory model fit is indicated when about 5% or less of (absolute) standardized residuals are equal to or greater than 2, and about 1% or less of (absolute) standardized residuals are equal to or greater than 3.[6] A standardized residual with absolute value greater than 2 indicates a rating that is two SDs away from the expected value of zero (Linacre, 2023). One could examine the residuals and unexpected response patterns for a given element in a given facet (e.g., a rater) to find out why it showed misfit. For the current dataset, model-data fit was found to be satisfactory. About 3% ($n = 100$) of the 3094 valid responses were associated with (absolute) standardized residuals equal to or greater than 2, and 0.3% ($n = 10$) were associated with (absolute) standardized residuals equal to or greater than 3. If these expectations are not met, elements in facets that exhibit high misfit (e.g., rater and task) could be excluded from the analysis.

Psychometric Dimensionality

Rasch analysis rests on an assumption of unidimensionality, that is, the measurement of a latent trait along a single linear scale at a time (Bond et al., 2021; Eckes, 2005; McNamara, 1996). As Eckes (2005) explained, the main question in judge-mediated scores is "whether ratings on one criterion follow a pattern that is markedly different from ratings on the others, indicating that [test-takers'] scores relate to different dimensions, or whether the ratings on one

---

[5] In traditional statistics (e.g., analysis of variance [ANOVA]), assumptions about data characteristics (e.g., distribution) are checked before conducting the statistical test. In the MFRM, data screening is done during data analysis using the various indicators discussed in this section.

[6] Strictly speaking, according to the statistical theory of the normal distribution (to which standardized residuals are modeled to conform), about 5% of the standardized residuals should fall outside the absolute value of 1.96, and about 1% should fall outside the absolute value of 2.58 (M. Linacre, personal communication, September 22, 2007).

616 **Chapter 40** Many-Facet Rasch Analysis for Evaluating Second Language Tests

criterion correspond well to ratings on the other criteria, indicating unidimensionality of the data" (p. 211).

Many authors have voiced concern about the Rasch models' assumption of unidimensionality and its appropriateness when dealing with performance scores. As McNamara (1996) explained, the major concern is that while performance on language tasks (e.g., writing) is complex or multidimensional because it involves drawing on various abilities and skills (e.g., planning, editing, grammar, and content), measurement models assume that the test is unidimensional, measuring one trait. As a result, Rasch models have been branded as being simplistic (or reductionistic) and lacking in validity, as they reduce multidimensional performance to a single score.

In response to this critique, McNamara (1996) emphasized the need to distinguish between *psychometric* (i.e., measurement) and *psychological* (i.e., language ability) unidimensionality. Performance on any language task is necessarily *psychologically* multidimensional, as models of language ability suggest. The psychometric model, however, deals with the question of whether it makes sense *in measurement terms* to use a single score to summarize test-taker performance on different items or on one task that involves a variety of skills (i.e., psychologically multidimensional) (cf. Henning, 1992). As Bejar (1983) explained,

> Unidimensionality does not imply that performance on items is due to a single psychological process. In fact, a variety of psychological processes are involved in responding to a set of test items. However, as long as they are involved in unison – that is, performance on each item is affected by the same process and in the same form – unidimensionality will hold. (p. 31)

Traditionally, unidimensionality is evaluated by submitting test scores to factor analysis; if all items load on a single factor, then unidimensionality can be assumed to be present. An alternative approach is to examine fit statistics. Specifically, all facets must have infit and outfit statistics within the acceptable range for the unidimensionality assumption to be met (Eckes, 2005; Linacre, 2023). As McNamara (1996) noted, the Rasch model does not assume or take for granted measurement unidimensionality. Rather, it "*hypothesizes* a single *measurement* dimension of ability and difficulty. Its analysis of test data represents *a test of this hypothesis* in relation to the data [through fit statistics]" (p. 275, emphasis added). Table 40.5 shows that the IMS values for the seven rating criteria were within the quality control limits of 0.50 and 1.50, providing evidence of psychometric unidimensionality in the current dataset.

Interpreting Fit Statistics

Another issue concerns the interpretation of fit statistics in Rasch models. While fit statistics as discussed above are central to the MFRM, there are no hard-and-fast rules for determining the "acceptable ranges" for fit statistics or for how to interpret them (Bond et al., 2021; Weigle, 1998). Some researchers recommend using the lower and upper limits of 0.7 and 1.3, respectively (e.g., McNamara, 199), while others recommend using a wider range of 0.5–1.5 (e.g., Linacre, 1994). Still others (e.g., Kondo-Brown, 2002) used a range of two SDs around the mean of the fit statistics for each facet as a criterion for misfit. If an element in a facet has a fit statistic higher or lower than that range, then there is misfit (high unpredictability) or overfit (lack of independence), respectively.

Bond et al. (2021) and Myford and Wolfe (2004a), on the other hand, argued that different fit ranges are appropriate for different assessment contexts and purposes. Other factors such as the type of test or rating scale, type of observation, examination design, expectations for rater agreement, or a combination of these can also affect the acceptable range and interpretation of fit statistics. In addition, interpreting the meaning of fit mean square indices is context-bound and thus not an easy, straightforward process. Myford and Wolfe (2004a), for example, argued that if the results from the analyses are to inform high-stakes decision-making, then more stringent upper and lower control fit limits might be set. By contrast, if the results are to be used for making low-stakes decisions, more relaxed fit limits might be set.

Concluding Remarks

The MFRM has proven a valuable tool for investigating the effects of different facets in the L2 assessment context and interactions among them on L2 assessment results. However, one has to be aware of the concerns discussed above when using and interpreting findings from this approach to score analysis. While the MFRM can make significant contributions to L2 test development and evaluation, combining it with other types of data and data collection and analyses strategies, such as interviews, discourse analysis, and observation, can help L2 test developers better interpret and use MFRM results, gain significant insights into the quality and impact of their L2 assessments, and improve these assessments and their interpretive arguments.

Discussion Questions

1. For an L2 assessment of your choice, what are the main facets (and their elements) involved in the assessment? What are some possible sources of biased interactions in the assessment?
2. MFRM provides a powerful tool to identify instances of biased interactions or misfit among different facets in the assessment setting, but it cannot explain how or why these patterns occur. What are some of the possible data collection and analysis strategies to identify why and how misfit and biased patterns occur among raters, test takers, tasks, and rating criteria?

References

Andrich, D. (1978). Rating formulation for ordered response categories. *Psychometrika*, *43*(4), 561–573.

Bejar, I. I. (1983). *Achievement testing: Recent advances*. Sage.

Bond, T. G., Yan, Z., & Heene, M. (2021). *Applying the Rasch model: Fundamental measurement in the human sciences* (4th ed.). Routledge.

Bonk, W. J., & Ockey, G. J. (2003). A many-facet Rasch analysis of the second language group oral discussion task. *Language Testing*, *20*, 89–110.

Davidson, F. (1991). Statistical support for training in ESL composition rating. In L. Hamp-Lyons (Ed.), *Assessing second language writing in academic contexts* (pp. 155–164). Ablex.

Eckes, T. (2005). Examining rater effects in TestDaF writing and speaking performance assessments: a many-facet Rasch analysis. *Language Assessment Quarterly*, *2*, 197–221.

Eckes, T. (2015). *Introduction to many-facet Rasch measurement: Analyzing and evaluating rater-mediated assessments* (2nd rev. and updated ed.). Peter Lang.

Eckes, T. (2023). *Many-facet Rasch measurement*. Peter Lang.

Henning, G. (1992). Dimensionality and construct validity of language tests. *Language Testing*, *9*, 1–11.

Kondo-Brown, K. (2002). A FACETS analysis of rater bias in measuring Japanese second language writing performance. *Language Testing*, *19*, 3–31.

Kozaki, Y. (2004). Using GENOVA and FACETS to set multiple standards on performance assessment for certification in medical translation from Japanese into English. *Language Testing*, *21*, 1–27.

Linacre, J. M. (1994). Constructing measurement with a many-facet Rasch model. In M. Wilson (Ed.), *Objective measurement: Theory into practice* (Vol. *2*, pp. 129–144). Ablex.

Linacre, J. M. (2023). *A user's guide to FACETS Rasch-model computer programs: Program manual 3.86.0.* http://www.winsteps.com/manuals.htm.

Lumley, T., & McNamara, T. F. (1995). Rater characteristics and rater bias: implications for training. *Language Testing, 12,* 54–71.

Lunz, E. M., Stahl, J. A., & Wright, B. D. (1996). The invariance of judge severity calibration. In G. Engelhard & M. Wilson (Eds.), *Objective measurement: Theory into practice* (Vol. *3,* pp. 99–112). Ablex.

Masters, G. N. (1982). A Rasch model for partial credit scoring. *Psychometrika, 47*(2), 149–174.

Masters, G. N. (1998, November). *Item misfit and item selection [Rasch model list service discussion].* Retrieved March 14, 2013 from http://www.Rasch.org.

McNamara, T. (1996). *Measuring second language performance.* Longman.

McNamara, T., Knoch, T., & Fan, J. (2019). *Fairness, justice, and language assessment.* Oxford University Press.

Myford, C. M., & Wolfe, E. W. (2004a). Detecting and measuring rater effects using many-facet Rasch measurement: Part I. In E. V. Jr. Smith & R. M. Smith (Eds.), *Introduction to Rasch measurement: Theory, models and applications* (pp. 460–517). JAM Press.

Myford, C. M., & Wolfe, E. W. (2004b). Detecting and measuring rater effects using many-facet Rasch measurement: Part II. In E. V. Jr. Smith & R. M. Smith (Eds.), *Introduction to Rasch measurement: Theory, models and applications* (pp. 518–574). JAM Press.

Ockey, G. (2022). Item response theory and many-facet Rasch measurement. In G. Fulcher & L. Harding (Eds.), *The Routledge handbook of language testing* (pp. 462–476). Routledge.

Rasch, G. (1960). *Probabilistic models for some intelligence and attainment tests.* Danmarks Paedagogiske Institut.

Weigle, S. C. (1998). Using FACETS to model rater training effects. *Language Testing, 15,* 263–287.

Weigle, S. C. (1999). Investigating rater/prompt interactions in writing assessment: quantitative and qualitative approaches. *Assessing Writing, 6,* 145–178.

Suggested Readings

Bond, T. G., Yan, Z., & Heene, M. (2021). *Applying the Rasch model: Fundamental measurement in the human sciences* (4th ed.). Routledge.

Eckes, T. (2023). *Many-facet Rasch measurement.* Peter Lang.

McNamara, T. (1996). *Measuring second language performance.* Longman.

McNamara, T., Knoch, T., & Fan, J. (2019). *Fairness, justice, and language assessment.* Oxford University Press.

CHAPTER 41

Psychometric Considerations for a Computerized Adaptive Language Test

Steven W. Nydick, J.R. Lockwood, and Mancy Liao

Introduction

This chapter explains the psychometrics of computerized adaptive testing for those interested in applying it to a language test. We will discuss the history of adaptive testing, how adaptive testing works, the limitations of adaptive tests, and alternative methods of test administration. Finally, we will discuss a few examples of adaptive testing in language testing as well as technological developments that promise to change the way that language can be assessed within an adaptive testing context.

Traditional high-stakes language tests typically involve test takers answering a fixed set of items at a testing center, with many of the responses being assessed by human graders. However, recent advancements in language technology and artificial intelligence (AI) have paved the way for more efficient, accurate, and accessible testing methods. Remote, computer-based, automated assessments that capitalize on these technological advancements, such as computerized adaptive or multistage tests, may reduce testing time and costs without sacrificing psychometric quality.

Computerized adaptive testing was created to maintain high measurement precision with decreased testing time (e.g., Weiss, 1982). Computerized adaptive tests (CATs) often contain a large set of administrable items (i.e., items or other measurement opportunities), only a small proportion of which are administered to any individual test taker. The items are chosen sequentially based on an estimate of the test taker's proficiency computed from the responses to previous items. This method can reduce how often test takers are presented items that are either too difficult or too easy for them, thus reducing "wasted" measurement opportunities, relative to nonadaptive tests. CATs are often variable in length and depend on how well the chosen items match a test taker's skill level to determine when the test should end.

Because of the adaptive nature of CATs, it is often challenging to control item exposure or constrain test properties to reflect required specifications. Alternative computer-based delivery methods, such as multistage (e.g., Yan et al., 2014) and linear-on-the-fly tests (e.g., Becker & Bergstrom, 2013), control test properties by reducing adaptivity.

Adaptive tests require automated scoring, as the results need to be available immediately to inform the selection of the next item. By nature, and tradition, language tests often include

The Concise Companion to Language Assessment, First Edition. Edited by Antony John Kunnan.
© 2025 John Wiley & Sons, Inc. Published 2025 by John Wiley & Sons, Inc.

620 Chapter 41 Psychometrics of Computerized Adaptive Testing

complex, open-ended items that demonstrate speaking and writing fluency, which can be difficult to score. Human graders using rubrics traditionally have assessed responses to these types of items. However, modern language processing technology allows for automated scoring of these items, either by analyzing parts of the response that predict human ratings or using large language models (LLMs) to mimic human reasoning (see Chapelle & Chung, 2010, for a review). As language models improve, they will more closely resemble the decision-making process of human raters. However, before discussing how technological advancements might transform and better personalize adaptive testing, we should consider why adaptive testing exists and what problems it first attempted to solve.

History of Computer-Adaptive Testing

Computerized adaptive testing arose from Binet's intelligence test of the early 1900s (Weiss, 1982). To administer the Stanford-Binet intelligence test, an examiner would choose the starting point of the test based on information about an examinee, typically using a vocabulary scale (e.g., Becker, 2003). Subsequent items would be administered only if they were "appropriate for that examinee" (Becker, 2003, p. 3). One issue with early psychometric theory was that the definition of classical statistics (such as a true score, standard error, and reliability and validity coefficients) was defined using a fixed-form tested on an explicit population (Traub, 2005). Early adaptive tests were able to administer slightly different tests to examinees by making assumptions about responses to the items that examinees did not see (e.g., unadministered items that were harder than a test taker's mental age would be assumed to be answered incorrectly).

To address some of the issues with classical theory, Thurstone examined the proportion of correct responses to the Binet scale based on a function of examinee age. As described in Bock (2005), "a child's mental age is judged, not from the number of items successfully completed, but by the highest age-graded items the child can complete successfully" (p. 21). The Thurstone scaling procedure better allowed the examiner to draw conclusions about examinee age from responses to the observed items. Yet even this method was based on classical statistics with populations defined by external attributes, namely an examinee's age. By determining how respondents of different ages typically respond to items on a test, one can estimate an examinee's "mental" age by how they respond to the same items.

Rather than a fixed attribute of a population that results in response tendencies, modern test theory based on item response theory (IRT) posits one or more hypothetical variables that affect responses to test items. These hypothetical variable(s) are typically referred to as "ability" or "proficiency" (e.g., Bock, 2005, p. 21) and are latent (i.e., unobserved). Modern test theory was based on advancements in statistical and psychometric theory (see Bock, 2005, for more details).

Modern test theory provides the theoretical underpinning of most adaptive testing methods. By positing a model-defined ability that influences responses to test items, the thing we care about as test users (performance on a test) is detached from the specific items any examinee takes. We can then estimate this "ability" given any set of items, as long as we make some assumptions about the relationship between the relevant items. Using a model-defined ability that is not dependent on testing cohort or specific test items allows us to target the items to the test taker.

Fred Lord developed many of the procedures still used in adaptive testing (see Lord, 1980, for more details), and David Weiss sought to disseminate and popularize the methods in associations, conferences, and journals (Weiss, 1982). However, adaptive testing was not feasible until the development of powerful computers that could quickly implement the required statistical estimation algorithms (e.g., van der Linden & Glas, 2010). Once more powerful computers became available, several high-profile tests, such as the Armed Services Vocational Aptitude Battery (ASVAB), the National Council of State Boards of Nursing (NCLEX), and the Graduate Record Examination (GRE) switched to an adaptive testing format (van der Linden & Glas, 2010, p. vi).[1]

Although adaptive testing better targets items to the estimated test-taker ability, few language tests use CAT delivery methods. Part of the reason for the limited application of CAT to language tests is IRT's historical emphasis on scoring multiple-choice or multi-select item types and language testing's purported requirement of complex simulations (Meunier, 2013). Traditionally, migrating language tests to a CAT format requires translating items to multiple-choice or multi-select format. This modification is justified from research indicating that multiple-choice items can measure higher-order reasoning (Scully, 2017). However, as described by Scully (2017), "[multiple choice] items measuring complex cognitive processes are simply rarely constructed" (p. 10). Alternatively, one can apply more complicated measurement models based on natural language processing (NLP) to quantify examinee ability from responses to complex item types. Modern language proficiency tests are able to capitalize on advancements in quantitative psychometrics to obtain better information from these responses (Langenfeld et al., 2022).

Theory of Computer-Adaptive Testing

The adaptivity of a CAT is primarily determined by immediate decisions of the next items to administer (item selection rules) and when to end a test (stopping rules). All other decisions commonly associated with adaptive tests, such as the administrable items, item response models, person and item fit, and differential item functioning (DIF), also apply to linear fixed-form (LFF) assessments (although they are also described in depth in van der Linden & Glas, 2010, with respect to adaptive tests).

In this section, we summarize the core elements required to implement adaptive tests. These include specifying item response theory (IRT) models that quantify how item and person attributes interact to determine response quality, defining the set of items eligible for administration (the "item pools"), specifying the algorithm that determines which items are administered to each test taker, and deciding when to stop the assessment. All of the methods will be described with respect to adaptivity at the item level, which we refer to as a "fully adaptive test."

Item Response Models

Item response theory describes how responses to a set of test items depend on the interaction between items and person attributes (see Bock, 2005; Embretson & Reise, 2013, for more information about typical IRT models). For example, in a simple case where item responses are either correct or incorrect, an IRT model specifies how item attributes influence the probability that a test taker of a given ability will answer the item correctly.[2] Test developers use item response functions (IRFs) to model how response tendencies depend on both item and person attributes. Figure 41.1 displays the IRF for six simple items modeled with a 2-parameter logistic (2PL) model. Logistic functions are typically used as IRT models due to useful

---

[1] The GRE switched from an adaptive test to a multistage test in 2011 due to security issues. It is currently still adaptive at the section and not at the individual item level.

[2] We adopt the "random sampling" perspective of probability in this context, in which the probability of a correct response to a given item for people of a given ability refers to the fraction of hypothetical test takers in a given population, of the given ability, who would correctly answer the item (Holland 1990).

Chapter 41 Psychometrics of Computerized Adaptive Testing

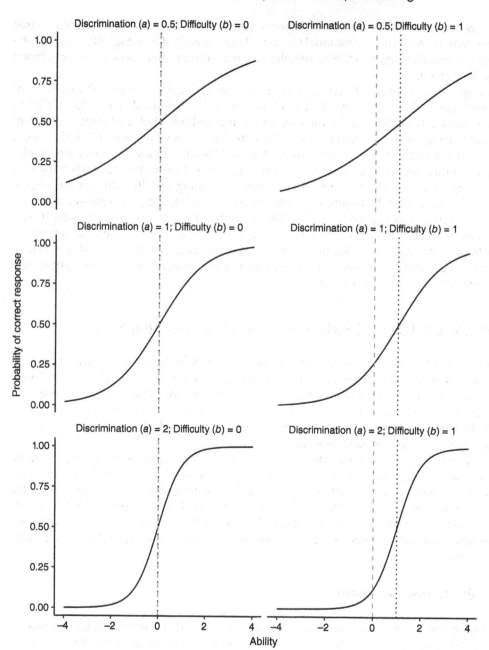

FIGURE 41.1 Item response function for example 2PL items with different discrimination parameters.

statistical properties. The 2PL model has two parameters: discrimination (usually referred to as a) and difficulty (usually referred to as b). In Figure 41.1, the y-axis indicates the model-predicted probability of a correct response given ability (on the x-axis).[3] For a 2PL model, difficulty refers to the ability such that 50% of test takers with this ability will answer the item

---

[3] Neither item parameters nor ability have absolute meaning and only depend on their relative relationship. Test developers typically pick a scale for the model by, for example, assuming that ability comes from a distribution with a mean of 0 and a standard deviation of 1.

correctly. The dotted vertical line in Figure 41.1 corresponds to the difficulty of each item and intersects with a probability of 0.5 on the y-axis. Alternatively, discrimination refers to the difference in probabilities comparing ability slightly above and below the item difficulty. As discrimination increases, as it does down the rows of Figure 41.1, this difference also increases. In practice, for 2PL items, difficulty indicates the ability for which the item provides the most information, and (squared) discrimination corresponds to the amount of information.

Additional parameters can be added to the 2PL model to account for guessing and/or slipping effects (see Yen et al., 2012, for more information). Moreover, alternative item response models exist with differences in (i) response formats, for example, polytomous models (Nering, 2010), continuous response models (Mellenbergh, 1994), or paired-comparison models (Brown & Maydeu-Olivares, 2011); (ii) assumptions in the relationship between person ability and item responses, for example, nonparametric models (Meijer et al., 1990); and (iii) auxiliary variables, for example, response time models (Thissen, 1983).

Item Pools

In adaptive tests, items are selected from item pools. Because different test takers are likely to see a different subset of items from any item pool, practitioners need to ensure that the meaning of scores remains the same regardless of administered items. Wise and Kingsbury (2000) described several considerations when developing item pools for adaptive tests, including item pool size, scale dimensionality, and scale consistency. In general, item pools should be large enough with items of a reasonable range of difficulty. This statement is purposely vague as it depends on the purpose of the test, security considerations, ease of writing and testing items, the size of the test-taker population, the method of item selection, the length of the test, etc. (see Veldkamp & van der Linden, 2009, for more information in how to design, specify, and build appropriate item pools). For instance, a computerized language test designed to determine only whether a test taker performs at least to B2 on the Common European Framework of Reference for Languages (CEFR; Europarat, 2020) required many items on the border between B1 and B2 and fewer items elsewhere (e.g., Thompson, 2009). However, a test designed to assess ability across the range of CEFR levels would require a much wider distribution of item difficulties.

The size of an item pool also depends on the purpose of the test. For a low-stakes, relatively short, formative language assessment with all multiple-choice items, a sufficiently large item bank might contain 500 items. However, a high-stakes language test used for admissions decisions with a larger test-taker population may require tens of thousands of items. A large item pool ensures that test takers of all ability levels have enough targeted items to make high-stakes decisions. Moreover, large item pools discourage malicious actors from stealing items in the pool and selling those items to test takers (Wise & Kingsbury, 2000).

Item Selection Algorithms

Designing an adaptive test requires determining how items should be selected. As described by Sulak and Kelecioglu (2019), the optimal method of item selection depends on the required decision. Assuming that the goal is to minimize the error in the estimate of ability (i.e., estimate ability with the smallest standard error in the fewest number of items), one would typically choose subsequent items that result in maximum information at the current ability estimate (e.g., Chang, 2015; Weiss, 1982). Information is inversely related to the variability of the estimate, so choosing an item to maximize information should result in a more precise estimate.

Choosing the next item to maximize information at the current ability estimate seems reasonable. However, ability is poorly estimated early in a test. Moreover, this method would

624 Chapter 41 Psychometrics of Computerized Adaptive Testing

overexpose items with the highest a-parameters, as those items yield the largest maximum information. One could instead choose items with lower values for discrimination early in the test (a-stratified item selection Chang & Ying, 1999; Leung et al., 2002), as those items result in high information across a wider range of ability. Alternatively, items could be chosen to have the best aggregate information across a range weighted on how much is currently known about a test taker's ability (likelihood-weighted or posterior-weighted information; van der Linden & Pashley, 2009, pp. 15–16). Additionally, test takers sometimes answer the first few items incorrectly due to nerves rather than anything inherent about their ability. Using non-targeted methods for the first few items on an adaptive test can prevent poor responses to the first few items from severely affecting an examinee's final score (e.g., Rulison & Loken, 2009, p. 99).

Even after limiting item exposures early in an adaptive test, some items might still be exposed more than others, risking the security of the item bank. Test developers might want to add additional randomness to the item selection algorithm by choosing 1 of the top 5 or 10 items that optimize the selection criterion or by randomly deciding whether an item should be administered based on how often it has been administered relative to the maximum desired exposure rate (the Randomesque method and the Sympson–Hetter method, respectively, Revuelta & Ponsoda, 1998). Revuelta and Ponsoda (1998) list several other methods of exposure control, all based on probabilistically reducing the administration of the most exposed items.

Unfortunately, the statistically optimal item cannot always be administered next. Most tests have some content requirements or item-administration requirements. Language tests typically require some measure of speaking, writing, reading, and listening. Initially, these constraints were implemented as heuristics (e.g., Stocking & Swanson, 1993). However, van der Linden proposed a more sophisticated (and computationally intensive) method (van der Linden & Veldkamp, 2004). Rather than selecting items one-by-one, the CAT algorithm can build the best remaining test after each item (e.g., one that yields the lowest expected error in the ability estimate given the items already administered and matching the required constraints). The first item from this "shadow test" is then administered, and the remaining items are updated based on the test-taker response.

Adaptive tests are often attractive due to their efficiency. Efficiency can be thought of both in terms of number of items required and time required. By taking the test on a computer, test administrators have information about the time required to respond to any given item. Test developers can use response time information to ensure that the total testing time is less than a particular amount, either by using time as a constraint in a shadow test or by adding a penalty for items that are expected to take too long (e.g., Veldkamp, 2016). Rather than administering the item with maximum information, one could administer the item that has maximum information per minute. Tests can thus be short, if not in number of items than in total required seat time.

Stopping Rules

CAT stopping rules indicate when enough items have been administered to end a test for variable-length CATs. Any test requires a summative judgment, either an estimate of examinee ability on one or more scales or some classification or pass/fail decision. CAT developers want to balance the accuracy of a decision against the efficiency of the test: Will more items lead to a drastically different decision given additional exposures and testing time? Adaptive tests typically fall into two groups: precision-based tests, in which ability is estimated, and classification-based tests, in which a classification decision is made.[4]

---

[4]The distinction between precision-based and classification-based tests is roughly analogous to that between norm-referenced and criterion-referenced tests.

Stopping rules for precision-based adaptive tests are typically based on the estimated error in the ability estimate or the change in estimated ability between subsequent items (Babcock & Weiss, 2012). We do not necessarily want to end a test if the estimate of ability is optimal, but rather if the estimate of ability is good enough or there are not enough remaining items to drastically improve the estimate (e.g., Choi et al., 2011).

Unlike precision-based tests, the goal of classification adaptive tests is to make a decision that is sufficiently accurate. Most of the stopping rules for classification tests are based on statistical procedures that quantify how likely the decision is to be incorrect after any given item (Thompson, 2011). Once the likelihood that the decision is wrong is sufficiently low or we do not have enough remaining items to change the decision (e.g., Finkelman, 2008), the test is ended.

Imagine two different English language proficiency tests, one trying to rank test takers on English knowledge and one trying to determine whether test takers are at B2 level in reading on the CEFR. In the first case, all test takers would need similar numbers of items to adequately differentiate their abilities. In the second case, expert English speakers should require many fewer items to make a decision than those test takers on the cusp between B1 and B2 levels.

Adaptive tests might also require additional constraints, such as minimum/maximum number of test items, time limitations, content requirements, and item-type requirements. See van der Linden and Jiang (2020) for one possible approach to include a variety of stopping rules in a single algorithm and Braecken and Papp (2020) for more details about adaptive tests when measuring multiple traits.

Example CAT Tracelines

Item selection algorithms are typically paired with stopping rules. That is, stopping rules indicate how we quantify evidence, and item selection algorithms choose items that yield as much of that type of evidence as possible. For example, information-based item selection algorithms are typically implemented with precision-based adaptive tests due to information relating to the precision of a common method of estimating ability, so that selecting items by maximizing information typically leads to shorter tests than other item selection methods.

Figures 41.2 and 41.3 depict example adaptive tests for three generated simulees (simulated test takers) with ability of -1, 0, and 1 on an ability scale with a mean of 0 and a standard deviation of 1. Note also that the Greek symbol theta (θ) is typically used in IRT to represent person ability. The tracelines displayed in Figure 41.2 show example adaptive tests that are precision-based, in that they end when the estimated standard error is below a particular amount. To result in a maximally efficient test, items are selected using maximum information at each ability estimate. The vertical dotted lines represent confidence intervals around ability estimates at each step in the test. The confidence interval after the last item is approximately the same width for each test taker, but the test taker with ability at 0 has a shorter test than the other two test takers. The shorter test for simulee 2 results from more targeted items available for this simulee.

Figure 41.3 shows adaptive tests for the same three simulees for an example classification CAT with a cut-score of 0. Unlike the CAT processes displayed in Figure 41.2, these tests are much longer for test takers with ability close to the cut-point. In a classification CAT, test-taker ability is not measured to the same degree of precision: The test ends for simulee 2 after more items with a shorter confidence interval width for ability than simulees 1 and 3. However, the final decision (classification into categories) is estimated with similar degrees of precision for all three candidates.[5]

---

[5]For simulees 1 and 3, the final decision is correct based on simulated ability. For simulee 2, the final decision cannot be correct, as the cut-score matches that candidate's actual ability. This scenario is only for illustrative purposes and is unlikely to play out in practice.

626 Chapter 41 Psychometrics of Computerized Adaptive Testing

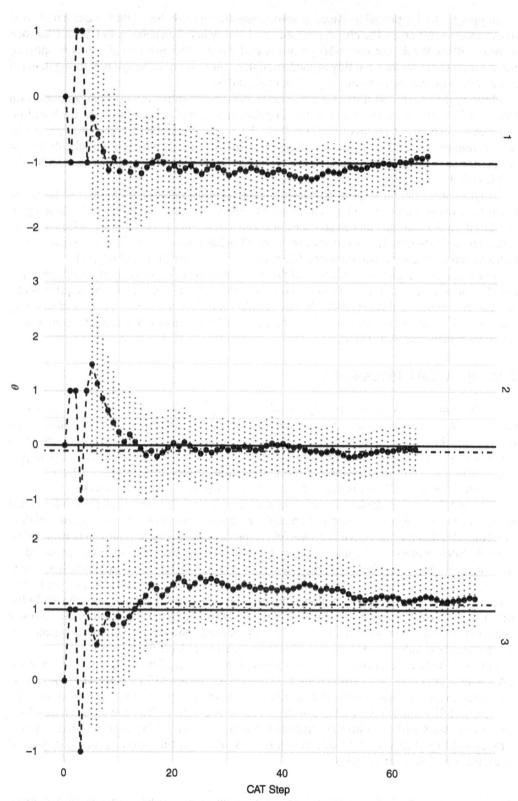

FIGURE 41.2 Ability estimates and confidence intervals after each item for a variable-length adaptive test from a bank of 500 items. *Note:* The panels depict example adaptive tests with true ability of −1, 0, and 1, respectively. The solid horizontal line is the ability used to simulate responses. The dashed and dotted line is the estimate of ability after administering all of the items in the bank.

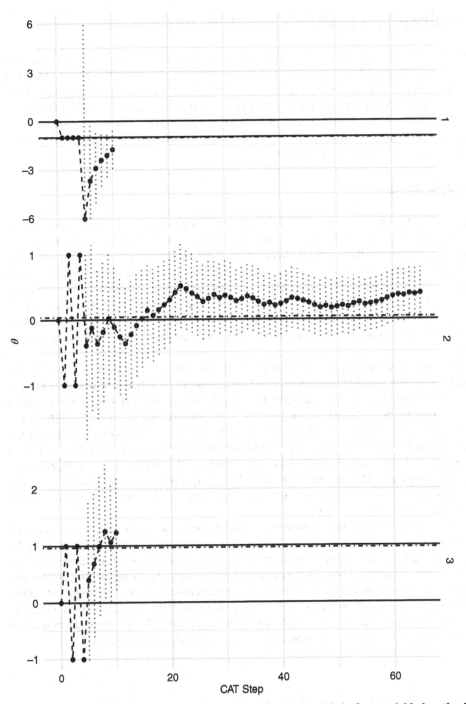

FIGURE 41.3 Ability estimates and confidence intervals after each item for a variable-length adaptive test from a bank of 500 items. *Notes:* The panels depict example adaptive tests with true ability of −1, 0, and 1, respectively. The thicker solid horizontal line is the ability used to simulate responses. The thinner solid horizontal line (at $\theta = 0$) corresponds to the cut-point separating categories. The dashed and dotted line is the estimate of ability after administering all of the items in the bank.

Alternatives to Fully Adaptive Tests

As described by Rulison and Loken (2009), the efficient targeting of an adaptive test to person ability results in a trade-off between efficiency and redundancy. We gain efficiency in terms of seat time and number of items at the expense of additional, redundant items that can better account for the performance of real test takers who respond less consistently than those in a computer simulation. Some less-than-adaptive tests sacrifice some degree of efficiency for additional test developer control and test-taker redundancy. The following subsections describe alternatives to purely adaptive tests.

Multistage Tests

A common alternative item administration design to fully adaptive or linear assessments is multistage tests (MSTs; Yan et al., 2014). Many high-volume, high-stakes standardized tests, such as the GRE and the Certified Public Accountant (CPA) examination, are administered as MSTs (Yang & Reckase, 2020). Rather than administering items one-by-one, as in a fully adaptive CAT, MSTs administer items together in modules and route test takers between these modules based on their scores to previous modules (e.g., Sari & Raborn, 2018). As described by Rotou et al. (2007), MSTs are "a special case of CAT that allows for item review, reduces the number of items exposed, [and] makes the implementation of quality assurance more feasible" (p. 1).

Some differences between MSTs and fully adaptive CATs are shown in Figure 41.4. An MST design contains a number of stages as well as a number of levels within a given stage. Figure 41.4 displays an MST 1-3-3 design. In a 1-3-3 design, all test takers start with a medium-difficulty module. Based on their performance on the first module, they are either routed to an easy, moderate, or hard module. Finally, based on their performance on the second module as well as the level of the second module, they are again either routed to an easy, moderate, or hard module. Ability is then estimated from performance to all items across all of the modules. The design depicted in Figure 41.4 is somewhat simplistic, in that typically, multiple modules exist at each level for each stage, and examinees are assigned a random module based on their target level.

Unlike in fully adaptive tests, MSTs can allow test takers to review responses to all items within a module because routing does not take place until after the module is completed (Mead, 2006). Moreover, fully adaptive tests assume that all items in an item pool are administrable to any test taker (with some restrictions for content coverage and invalid item pairs). MSTs provide stronger mechanisms for test developers to review item sets for content coverage, module length, and other complex or difficult-to-define constraints prior to test administration. Test developers willing to sacrifice some control of test content for efficiency can also generate MSTs during administration of the test, although they would not be subject to review (see Zheng & Chang, 2015).

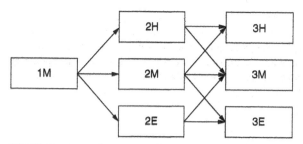

FIGURE 41.4 Example stages and routing for a 1-3-3 MST design.

For MSTs, practitioners need to determine the number of stages, number of modules within a stage, number of items within a module, how modules are assembled and verified, how test takers navigate between modules, etc. (e.g., Luo & Kim, 2018). Many of these decisions are analogous to those required to implement a fully adaptive test, as MSTs are a specific type of CAT. MacGregor et al. (2022) described the benefits of using MST for balancing content constraints, adaptivity, and additional targeting/review of test items within the context of language assessment as well as how language assessment developers would design an MST based on an existing linear test.

Linear Fixed-Form Methods

Linear fixed forms can also be automatically generated to reduce item overlap and account for content constraints. For instance, linear-on-the-fly testing (LOFT) uses binary programming, similar to that used in shadow testing (van der Linden & Veldkamp, 2004), to construct individual forms that match constraints and have minimal overlap of items across other forms (Becker & Bergstrom, 2013, p. 1). Like MSTs, these forms can be constructed ahead of time and reviewed by experts for content and statistical requirements (Pallet Assembly; Becker & Bergstrom, 2013).

Becker and Bergstrom (2013) compared different test construction and delivery methods on different attributes. They claimed that linear form methods sacrifice measurement efficiency for better pool utilization and test developer control, especially given small item pools and over-exposure risk. As described by Becker and Bergstrom (2013), these attributes might be preferable when developing classification tests rather than precision-based tests given how practitioners typically implement computerized classification tests.

CAT in Language Testing (CALT)

Due to perceived limitations of technology and item formats for capturing higher-order language thinking, few computerized adaptive language tests (CALTs) existed until recently. Most adaptive language tests as of 2013 were either based on cloze tests or multiple-choice tests and not language simulations (Meunier, 2013). For example, Nogami and Hayashi (2010) described a version of the TOEFL modified to work as a CALT on the entire test by replacing simulations with standard multiple-choice questions, and Curi and Silva (2019) detailed the transition of a Brazilian university's multiple-choice English proficiency test from paper-and-pencil to CAT administration.

With more advanced computer power, NLP theory, as well as accessibility concerns, test developers are starting to rethink how language tests should be constructed. Several modern language tests, such as the Test of English as a Foreign Language (TOEFL) Essentials, the Kaplan International Tools for English Test, Linguaskill, the Duolingo English Test (DET), Webscape, Test of Chinese as a Foreign Language (TOCFL), and the Goethe-Test PRO for German language proficiency are at least partially adaptive. In some modern language tests, innovative question types can also be adaptively administered. For example, the CAT section of the Duolingo English Test contains an assortment of question types, including those with more complex scoring methods beyond simply correct/incorrect, such as text highlighting and speech processing (Cardwell et al., 2023). In the Kaplan English Test, the writing and speaking tasks are selected adaptively based on the ability estimates derived from the preceding listening, reading, and grammar sections (Kaplan, 2022). Finally, the TOEFL Essentials is a multi-stage language test (MSLT), with the second stage containing free-response writing and speaking questions (Papageorgiou et al., 2021).

Future Directions in CALT

Researchers continue to develop new models to faithfully represent how people express and learn language. Several advancements are occurring inside and outside of psychometrics that impact how language is assessed. For instance, psychometricians are currently exploring an area called "Computational Psychometrics." According to past president of the National Council on Measurement in Education (NCME) Derek Briggs, computational psychometrics "sits behind the scenes to facilitate an adaptive and often gamified experience in which the student is placed in a position to seek out assessment opportunities, rather than have them be imposed by someone else" (Briggs, 2022, p. 405). Traditional adaptive tests personalize which items to present, whereas current developments from machine learning, NLP, and computing power promise to personalize the entire testing experience. Currently, computational psychometrics is in its infancy, mostly adaptive predictive models from machine learning to improve extant algorithms. However, other areas of psychology are exploring gamified assessment for rapidly assessing employee suitability for jobs (e.g., Georgiou et al., 2019). Standard psychometric assessments can be gamified by adding story, fantasy, or additional interactive elements (e.g., Landers & Sanchez, 2022). Gamified assessments tend to be more difficult to assess psychometrically as they can induce multidimensionality and local item dependencies (Landers & Sanchez, 2022, p. 6). However, as models improve and computational power increases, a variety of personalized data points can be used to construct candidate profiles and allow consumers of test results to make more comprehensive decisions. These methods could even be used in language assessment by having test takers communicate with different avatars to solve tasks.

More immediately impactful for language assessment is the development of LLMs and other advanced AI models. Examples of LLMs include the Bidirectional Encoder Representations from Transformers (BERT) introduced by Google and the Generative Pre-trained Transformer (GPT) models introduced by OpenAI. LLMs can replicate patterns in human decisions and text generation. GPT, for example, predicts future text from past text given a model with billions of parameters and trained on billions of tokens. These models are able to synthesize patterns and consistency in human text and reproduce them when generating new text. GPT is already being used to quickly generate content for language assessments, and BERT is being used to predict item parameters given question properties to reduce the need for large training samples (e.g., Langenfeld et al., 2022; McCarthy et al., 2021). By using LLM for item generation and model estimation, test developers are able to efficiently maintain a large item bank size by extracting more information from the intersection between item content and item responses.

As described above, many of the text processing algorithms for these assessments use either human raters or standard text scoring features, such as distance, fluency, word counts, and readability metrics. Future assessments will integrate LLMs into a personalized process to "enable an effective natural communication and interaction between users and the system" (Kasneci et al., 2023, p. 6). Imagine an adaptive test where test takers talk to a simulated professor generated via a LLM, where information from that interaction is used to determine subsequent reading passages or audio processing tasks, and where corresponding algorithms based on LLMs are able to determine how much information that interactive provides and how likely it is for the test taker to succeed communicating in the tested language. There are certainly many challenges with implementing LLMs for fair and equitable assessments, including data privacy, training bias, and setting content guardrails (see Kasneci et al., 2023, pp. 6–9 for a list of examples). However, CAT has always benefited from technological advancement. As described at the beginning of this chapter, CATs were conceived prior to the technology being available for their implementation. LLMs and AI tools promise to provide additional measurement opportunities that test developers can harness to create more precise and efficient algorithms.

Discussion Questions

1. Why is it important to consider both psychometric and non-psychometric aspects when developing and maintaining computerized adaptive language tests?
2. How might technological advancements change the way that CALTs are developed and maintained?

References

Babcock, B., & Weiss, D. (2012). Termination criteria in computerized adaptive tests: do variable-length CATs provide efficient and effective measurement? *Journal of Computerized Adaptive Testing*, 1–18. https://doi.org/10.7333/1212-0101001.

Becker, K. A. (2003). *History of the Stanford-Binet intelligence scales: Content and psychometrics (Stanford-Binet Intelligence Scales, Fifth Edition Assessment Services Bulletin No. 1)*. Itasca, IL.

Becker, K. A., & Bergstrom, B. A. (2013). Test administration models [Publisher: University of Massachusetts Amherst]. *Practical Assessment, Research, and Evaluation, 18*, 1–7. https://doi.org/10.7275/PNTR-YZ21.

Bock, R. D. (2005). A brief history of item response theory. *Educational Measurement: Issues and Practice, 16*(4), 21–33. https://doi.org/10.1111/j.1745-3992.1997.tb00605.x.

Briggs, D. C. (2022). NCME presidential address 2022: turning the page to the next chapter of educational measurement. *Journal of Educational Measurement, 59*(4), 398–417. https://doi.org/10.1111/jedm.12350.

Braecken, J., & Paap, M. C. S. (2020). Making fixed-precision between-item multidimensional computerized adaptive tests even shorter by reducing the asymmetry between selection and stopping rules. *Applied Psychological Measurement, 44*(7), 531–547. https://doi.org/10.1177/0146621620932666.

Brown, A., & Maydeu-Olivares, A. (2011). Item response modeling of forced-choice questionnaires. *Educational and Psychological Measurement, 71*(3), 460–502. https://doi.org/10.1177/0013164410375112.

Cardwell, R., Naismith, B., LaFlair, G. T., & Nydick, S. W. (2023). Duolingo English Test: Technical Manual (Duolingo Research Report). Duolingo. https://duolingo-papers.s3.amazonaws.com/other/technical_manual.pdf.

Chang, H.-H. (2015). Psychometrics behind computerized adaptive testing. *Psychometrika, 80*(1), 1–20. https://doi.org/10.1007/s11336-014-9401-5.

Chang, H.-H., & Ying, Z. (1999). A-stratified multistage computerized adaptive testing. *Applied Psychological Measurement, 23*(3), 211–222. https://doi.org/10.1177/01466219922031338.

Chapelle, C. A., & Chung, Y.-R. (2010). The promise of NLP and speech processing technologies in language assessment. *Language Testing, 27*(3), 301–315. https://doi.org/10.1177/0265532210364405.

Choi, S. W., Grady, M. W., & Dodd, B. G. (2011). A new stopping rule for computerized adaptive testing. *Educational and Psychological Measurement, 71*(1), 37–53. https://doi.org/10.1177/0013164410387338.

Curi, M., & Silva, V. (2019). Academic english proficiency assessment using a computerized adaptive test. *Tendencias em Matematica Aplicada e Computacional, 20*(2), 381. https://doi.org/10.5540/tema.2019.020.02.381.

Embretson, S. E., & Reise, S. P. (2013). *Item response theory*. Psychology Press. https://doi.org/10.4324/9781410605269.

Europarat (Ed.). (2020). *Common European framework of reference for languages: Learning, teaching, assessment; companion volume*. Council of Europe Publishing.

Finkelman, M. (2008). On using stochastic curtailment to shorten the SPRT in sequential mastery testing. *Journal of Educational and Behavioral Statistics, 33*(4), 442–463. https://doi.org/10.3102/1076998607308573.

Georgiou, K., Gouras, A., & Nikolaou, I. (2019). Gamification in employee selection: the development of a gamified assessment. *International Journal of Selection and Assessment, 27*(2), 91–103. https://doi.org/10.1111/ijsa.12240.

Holland, P. W. (1990). On the sampling theory foundations of item response theory models. *Psychometrika, 55*(4), 577–601. https://doi.org/10.1007/BF02294609.

Kaplan. (2022, March). Kaplan International Tools for English Adaptive Assessment Development and Validation (English Technical Report No. 2.2). Kaplan. Retrieved May 10, 2023, from https://www.kaplanenglishtest.com/documents/Kaplan International Tools for English White Paper.pdf.

632 **Chapter 41** Psychometrics of Computerized Adaptive Testing

Landers, R. N., & Sanchez, D. R. (2022). Game-based, gamified, and gamefully designed assessments for employee selection: definitions, distinctions, design, and validation. *International Journal of Selection and Assessment, 30*(1), 1–13. https://doi.org/10.1111/ijsa.12376.

Kasneci, E., Sessler, K., Küchemann, S., Bannert, M., Dementieva, D., Fischer, F., Gasser, U., Groh, G., Günnemann, S., Hüllermeier, E., Krusche, S., Kutyniok, G., Michaeli, T., Nerdel, C., Pfeffer, J., Poquet, O., Sailer, M., Schmidt, A., Seidel, T., et al. (2023). ChatGPT for good? On opportunities and challenges of large language models for education. *Learning and Individual Differences, 103*, 102274. https://doi.org/10.1016/j.lindif.2023.102274.

Langenfeld, T., Burstein, J., & von Davier, A. A. (2022). Digital-first learning and assessment systems for the 21st century. *Frontiers in Education, 7*, 857604. https://doi.org/10.3389/feduc.2022.857604.

Leung, C.-K., Chang, H.-H., & Hau, K.-T. (2002). Item selection in computerized adaptive testing: improving the a-stratified design with the Sympson–Hetter algorithm. *Applied Psychological Measurement, 26*(4), 376–392. https://doi.org/10.1177/014662102237795.

van der Linden, W. J., & Glas, C. A. (Eds.). (2010). *Elements of adaptive testing.* Springer. https://doi.org/10.1007/978-0-387-85461-8.

van der Linden, W. J., & Jiang, B. (2020). A shadow-test approach to adaptive item calibration. *Psychometrika, 85*(2), 301–321. https://doi.org/10.1007/s11336-020-09703-8.

van der Linden, W. J., & Pashley, P. J. (2009). Item selection and ability estimation in adaptive testing. In W. J. van der Linden & C. A. Glas (Eds.), *Elements of adaptive testing* (pp. 3–30). Springer. https://doi.org/10.1007/978-0-387-85461-8_1.

van der Linden, W. J., & Veldkamp, B. P. (2004). Constraining item exposure in computerized adaptive testing with shadow tests. *Journal of Educational and Behavioral Statistics, 29*(3), 273–291. https://doi.org/10.3102/10769986029003273.

Lord, F. M. (1980). *Applications of item response theory to practical testing problems.* Erlbaum Associates.

Luo, X., & Kim, D. (2018). A top-down approach to designing the computerized adaptive multistage test: top-down multistage. *Journal of Educational Measurement, 55*(2), 243–263. https://doi.org/10.1111/jedm.12174.

MacGregor, D., Yen, S. J., & Yu, X. (2022). Using multistage testing to enhance measurement of an English language proficiency test. *Language Assessment Quarterly, 19*(1), 54–75. https://doi.org/10.1080/15434303.2021.1988953.

McCarthy, A. D., Yancey, K. P., LaFlair, G. T., Egbert, J., Liao, M., & Settles, B. (2021). Jump-starting item parameters for adaptive language tests. *Proceedings of the 2021 Conference on Empirical Methods in Natural Language Processing*, 883–899. https://doi.org/10.18653/v1/2021.emnlp-main.67.

Mead, A. D. (2006). An introduction to multistage testing. *Applied Measurement in Education, 19*(3), 185–187. https://doi.org/10.1207/s15324818ame1903_1.

Meijer, R. R., Sijtsma, K., & Smid, N. G. (1990). Theoretical and empirical comparison of the Mokken and the Rasch approach to IRT. *Applied Psychological Measurement, 14*(3), 283–298. https://doi.org/10.1177/014662169001400306.

Mellenbergh, G. J. (1994). A unidimensional latent trait model for continuous item responses. *Multivariate Behavioral Research, 29*(3), 223–236. https://doi.org/10.1207/s15327906mbr2903_2.

Meunier, L. E. (2013). Computer adaptive language tests (CALT) offer a great potential for functional testing. Yet, why don't they? *CALICO Journal, 11*(4), 23–39. https://doi.org/10.1558/cj.v11i4.23-39.

Nering, M. L. (Ed.). (2010). *Handbook of polytomous item response theory models.* Routledge.

Nogami, Y., & Hayashi, N. (2010). A Japanese adaptive test of English as a foreign language: Developmental and operational aspects. In W. J. van der Linden & C. A. W. Glas (Eds.), *Elements of Adaptive Testing* (pp. 191–211). Springer.

Papageorgiou, S., Davis, L., Norris, J. M., Gomez, P. G., Manna, V. F., & Monfils, L. (2021). Design framework for the TOEFL essentials test 2021 (Research Memorandum RM-21-03).

Revuelta, J., & Ponsoda, V. (1998). A comparison of item exposure control methods in computerized adaptive testing. *Journal of Educational Measurement, 35*(4), 311–327. https://doi.org/10.1111/j.1745-3984.1998.tb00541.x.

Rotou, O., Patsula, L., Steffen, M., & Rizavi, S. (2007). Comparison of multistage tests with computerized adaptive and paper-and-pencil tests. *ETS Research Report Series, 2007*(1), 1–27. https://doi.org/10.1002/j.2333-8504.2007.tb02046.x.

Rulison, K. L., & Loken, E. (2009). I've fallen and I can't get up: can high-ability students recover from early mistakes in CAT? *Applied Psychological Measurement, 33*(2), 83–101. https://doi.org/10.1177/0146621608324023.

Sari, H. I., & Raborn, A. (2018). What information works best?: A comparison of routing methods. *Applied Psychological Measurement, 42*(6), 499–515. https://doi.org/10.1177/0146621617752990.

Scully, D. (2017). Constructing multiple-choice items to measure higher-order thinking [Publisher: University of Massachusetts Amherst]. *Practical Assessment, Research, and Evaluation, 22*, 1–13. https://doi.org/10.7275/SWGT-RJ52.

Stocking, M. L., & Swanson, L. (1993). A method for severely constrained item selection in adaptive testing. *Applied Psychological Measurement, 17*(3), 277–292. https://doi.org/10.1177/014662169301700308.

Sulak, S., & Kelecioglu, H. (2019). Investigation of item selection methods according to test termination rules in CAT applications. *Egitimde ve Psikolojide Olcme ve Degerlendirme Dergisi*, 315–326. https://doi.org/10.21031/epod.530528.

Thissen, D. (1983). Timed testing: an approach using item response theory. In D. J. Weiss (Ed.), *New horizons in testing* (pp. 179–203). Elsevier. https://doi.org/10.1016/B978-0-12-742780-5.50019-6.

Thompson, N. A. (2009). Item selection in computerized classification testing. *Educational and Psychological Measurement, 69*(5), 778–793. https://doi.org/10.1177/0013164408324460.

Thompson, N. A. (2011). Termination criteria for computerized classification testing [Publisher: University of Massachusetts Amherst]. *Practical Assessment, Research, and Evaluation, 16*, 1–7. https://doi.org/10.7275/WQ8M-ZK25.

Traub, R. E. (2005). Classical test theory in historical perspective. *Educational Measurement: Issues and Practice, 16*(4), 8–14. https://doi.org/10.1111/j.1745-3992.1997.tb00603.x.

Veldkamp, B. P. (2016). On the issue of item selection in computerized adaptive testing with response times: item selection in CAT with response times. *Journal of Educational Measurement, 53*(2), 212–228. https://doi.org/10.1111/jedm.12110.

Veldkamp, B. P., & van der Linden, W. J. (2009). Designing item pools for adaptive testing. In W. J. van der Linden & C. A. Glas (Eds.), *Elements of adaptive testing* (pp. 231–245). New York: Springer. https://doi.org/10.1007/978-0-387-85461-8_12.

Weiss, D. J. (1982). Improving measurement quality and efficiency with adaptive testing. *Applied Psychological Measurement, 6*(4), 473–492. https://doi.org/10.1177/014662168200600408.

Wise, S. L., & Kingsbury, G. G. (2000). Practical issues in developing and maintaining a computerized adaptive testing program. *Psicologica, 21*(1), 135–155. Retrieved April 21, 2023, from https://www.redalyc.org/pdf/169/16921108.pdf.

Yan, D., Davier, A. A. v., & Lewis, C. (Eds.). (2014). *Computerized multistage testing: Theory and applications*. CRC Press Taylor & Francis Group.

Yang, L., & Reckase, M. D. (2020). The optimal item pool design in multistage computerized adaptive tests with the p-optimality method. *Educational and Psychological Measurement, 80*(5), 955–974. https://doi.org/10.1177/0013164419901292.

Yen, Y.-C., Ho, R.-G., Laio, W.-W., Chen, L.-J., & Kuo, C.-C. (2012). An empirical evaluation of the slip correction in the four parameter logistic models with computerized adaptive testing. *Applied Psychological Measurement, 36*(2), 75–87. https://doi.org/10.1177/0146621611432862.

Zheng, Y., & Chang, H.-H. (2015). On-the-fly assembled multistage adaptive testing. *Applied Psychological Measurement, 39*(2), 104–118. https://doi.org/10.1177/0146621614544519.

Suggested Readings

Bock, R. D. (2005). A brief history of item response theory. *Educational Measurement: Issues and Practice, 16*(4), 21–33.

van der Linden, W. J., & Glas, C. A. (Eds.). (2000). *Computerized adaptive testing: Theory and practice*. Springer.

Wainer, H., Dorans, N. J., Flaugher, R., Green, B. F., & Mislevy, R. J. (2000). *Computerized adaptive testing: A primer*. Routledge.

THEME 8

The Role of Technology

The Role of
Technology

CHAPTER 42

Computer-Assisted Language Testing

Ruslan Suvorov, Yasin Karatay, and Volker Hegelheimer

Introduction

Computer-assisted language testing (CALT) is an area within the field of language testing and assessment that studies the use of technology for designing, delivering, scoring, and evaluating test takers' performance in a second language. CALT encompasses various applications of technology for test design, delivery, scoring, and test security. Chapelle (2010) distinguishes three main motives for using technology in language testing: efficiency, equivalence, and innovation. Efficiency can be achieved through computer-adaptive testing and analysis-based assessment that utilizes automated writing evaluation (AWE) or automated speech evaluation (ASE) systems. Equivalence refers to research on making computerized tests equivalent to paper and pencil tests that were traditionally considered to be "the gold standard" in language testing. Innovation – where technology can create a true transformation of language testing – is revealed in the reconceptualization of the L2 ability construct in CALT as "the ability to select and deploy appropriate language through the technologies that are appropriate for a situation" (Chapelle & Douglas, 2006, p. 107). In addition, innovation can be exemplified in the applications of artificial intelligence (AI), for instance, to automatically generate prompts and items for computerized language tests.

We begin this chapter with an overview of CALT followed by a discussion of some key attributes and values used for describing computer-assisted language tests. Next, we introduce several major computer-assisted language tests followed by a brief summary of key research areas in CALT. In our last section, we conclude with a discussion of current issues and future directions for using technology in language testing.

Overview of Computer-Assisted Language Testing

Computer-assisted language testing can be defined as a type of language testing that uses technology for test design, delivery, administration, scoring, and/or evaluation. It can be viewed as part of computer-assisted language assessment (CALA), which is a broader umbrella term used to refer to different applications of technology in a variety of language assessment contexts, including alternative types of assessment such as electronic portfolios and self-assessment systems (Winke & Isbell, 2017, p. 2). To highlight the increasingly sophisticated

The Concise Companion to Language Assessment, First Edition. Edited by Antony John Kunnan.
© 2025 John Wiley & Sons, Inc. Published 2025 by John Wiley & Sons, Inc.

638 **Chapter 42** Computer-Assisted Language Testing

role of not only computers but also digital technology in all of its permutations, many researchers in recent years have started to adopt the word "technology" instead of "computer," leading to an array of new terms such as technology-infused language assessment (Winke & Isbell, 2017), technology-assisted language assessment (Sadeghi, 2023), technology-enhanced language assessment (Li, 2023), and technology-mediated language assessment (Sadeghi & Douglas, 2023). Other related terms that can be found in the literature include web-based language testing (Carr, 2023), computer-adaptive language testing (Chalhoub-Deville & Deville, 1999), computer-based language testing (Douglas & Hegelheimer, 2007), computer-based language assessment (Jamieson, 2005), computer-mediated language assessment (Malabonga & Kenyon, 1999), and mobile-assisted language assessment (Chen & Lin, 2023). This diversity in nomenclature reflects the complexity of this topic and the varied approaches that have been adopted to leveraging technology for language testing purposes.

The COVID-19 pandemic precipitated "normalization" of CALT (Sadeghi & Douglas, 2023). As the global health crisis unfurled and national lockdowns were put in place to slow the spread of the coronavirus, everyone from individual language teachers to major test development companies had to quickly adapt to the new reality and rethink how to continue testing remotely. High-stakes language tests originally designed for remote delivery, such as Duolingo English Test (DET), witnessed a huge surge in popularity and demand, while many other language testing companies rushed to develop and launch online versions of their tests that could be taken at home. As a result of this seismic shift, once-unthinkable high-stakes at-home language proficiency tests became the only option available to test takers during the pandemic (Isbell & Kremmel, 2020).

The use of technology in language testing offers a number of important benefits. One of such benefits is increased efficiency of the testing process (Chapelle & Voss, 2017). Unlike paper-based language tests, computer-delivered language tests can be quickly administered to large numbers of test takers. Responses to both selected-response and constructed-response items on such tests can be automatically scored and relayed to the test takers, administrators, and other stakeholders (Van Moere & Downey, 2016). Technology also offers greater accessibility to language tests: An online test that can be taken anywhere and at any time can reduce logistical barriers for test takers who – for various reasons – might not be able to travel to a testing center, resulting in a more equitable assessment landscape (Zhang & Isaacs, 2023). Another benefit is enhanced authenticity of language assessment instruments that can be achieved, for instance, through the integration of multimedia in listening stimuli (Suvorov, 2019) or the use of video-conferencing tools for assessing speaking (Nakatsuhara et al., 2021). Finally, technology allows for creating more personalized assessments by leveraging computer adaptivity (Mizumoto et al., 2019). In a computer-adaptive test, test takers' responses to the previous items predetermine the difficulty level of the subsequent items, which are selected by the algorithm to create a more tailored test-taking experience. Such adaptivity can arguably provide a more precise measurement of an individual test taker's language abilities, while also reducing the amount of time necessary to complete the test.

Attributes and Values

In this section, we discuss several key attributes and associated values that can be used to describe computer-assisted language tests (see Table 42.1).

Technology Purpose

Technology can be used in CALT for several important purposes, including test design, test delivery, test scoring, and test security. When used for *test design* purposes, technology enables

Attributes and Values **639**

TABLE **42.1**		
Attributes and associated values of computer-assisted language tests		
#	Attributes	Values
1	Technology purpose	Test design, test delivery, test scoring, and test security
2	Test progression	Linear, adaptive, and semi-adaptive
3	Media format	Text-based, audio-based, video-based, and multimedia-based
4	Scoring method	Human, automated, and hybrid
5	Delivery mode	Remote and onsite
6	Delivery medium	Computer-delivered and mobile-delivered
7	Content generation	Human-based generation and automatic generation

the integration of multimedia elements in stimuli and test items to create more authentic language input that simulates real-life language use (e.g., video-based mini-lectures in academic listening tests; see Ockey & Wagner, 2018). In addition, technology can be leveraged to design innovative item types and formats, such as drag-and-drop items or simulated conversations with avatars, that are not possible in paper-based tests (Parshall et al., 2000). Technology can also be used for *test delivery* purposes, enabling online tests such as remote at-home high-stakes tests that can be taken anytime and anywhere, in either synchronous or asynchronous configurations (Ockey, 2021). Another important application of technology in CALT is *test scoring*. With recent advancements in machine learning (ML) and AI, technology can now be harnessed to automatically score both selected and constructed responses of test takers (Van Moere & Downey, 2016). Finally, technology plays a crucial role in ensuring *test security* through various methods, such as test takers' authentication, remote proctoring, monitoring of the test-taking process to detect any anomalies, forensic analysis of the responses to identify potential cheating, and protection of the test content and test takers' data.

Test Progression

Computer-assisted language tests can be linear, adaptive, or semi-adaptive (Davey et al., 2015; Ockey, 2009). Linear tests administer the same number of test items in the same order to all test takers. In some linear tests, test takers can go back to the previous questions and review their responses or preview the upcoming questions, whereas in other linear tests such unrestricted browsing is not permitted. In a computer-adaptive test, each item is selected by the computer based on the test taker's performance on the previous item or a set of items. If a test taker answers an item correctly, they will be presented with a more difficult item. However, in case of an incorrect response, the test taker will be provided with easier items. By dynamically adjusting the difficulty level of the test based on the accuracy of the test taker's responses, a computer-adaptive test requires ostensibly fewer items and less time to assess the language proficiency level of individual test takers.

Due to limitations of earlier computer-adaptive tests – including high cost, increased exposure of test items, issues with algorithms for item selection, and difficulties with satisfying strict item response theory (IRT) assumptions – semi-adaptive tests have been proposed and used as an alternative. Compared to adaptive tests in which adaptivity occurs at the item level (i.e., the difficulty level of the next item is determined by the test taker's performance on the current item), semi-adaptive tests are adaptive at the level of a group of items called testlets (Winke & Fei, 2008) or at the level of the whole test where test takers are given a version of the test that corresponds to their proficiency level as determined by a pretest (Ockey, 2009).

640 Chapter 42 Computer-Assisted Language Testing

It should be noted, however, that the term "semi-adaptive" is not universally accepted: While some researchers distinguish semi-adaptive tests from purely adaptive tests (Ockey, 2009; Winke, 2006), others consider such tests to be just a variant of an adaptive test (Davey et al., 2015).

Media Format

One of the key affordances offered by technology is different media formats that can be integrated into the design of language tests. In particular, tests can use a single medium (e.g., an audio-only listening test or a text-based reading test) or multimedia (e.g., a listening test with a video or a reading test with text and images). In recent years, the use of multimedia, such as images, videos, animation, and graphics, has gained much attention among researchers studying L2 listening tests (e.g., Lesnov, 2017; Suvorov, 2019; Wagner, 2007), partly because multimedia is believed to have the potential for enhancing the authenticity of language assessment tasks (Ockey & Wagner, 2018). Douglas and Hegelheimer (2007), however, warn that this issue is not as straightforward as it might first seem because the implementation of multimedia in computer-assisted language tests can alter the constructs measured, which, in turn, can have implications for the validity of test interpretation and use.

Scoring Method

Three general approaches to scoring can be found in CALT: human scoring, automated scoring, and hybrid scoring. Traditionally, the scoring of extended written and oral responses has been done by human raters using rubrics, checklists, or other types of evaluation criteria. Technological innovations in the second half of the 20th century gave rise to automated scoring methods, such as exact answer matching, automated essay scoring (AES), automated writing evaluation (AWE), and automated speech scoring (Van Moere & Downey, 2016; Xi, 2010). Exact answer matching entails matching test takers' responses with the correct preset responses (for instance, responses to multiple-choice or matching questions). This type of scoring is typically used for the evaluation of receptive skills (i.e., reading and listening) and, occasionally, productive skills (e.g., writing) in the form of one-word or even short-phrase answers provided that the test has a pre-piloted list of acceptable answers, including the ones with common spelling errors. While both AES and AWE systems leverage various natural language processing (NLP) and ML techniques, the primary concern of AES is to score test takers' writing, whereas AWE aims at providing different types of feedback for language learning purposes (Van Moere & Downey, 2016). Harnessing the power of automatic speech recognition (ASR), automated speech scoring is used to recognize, process, and score test takers' oral responses (Xi, 2010). Finally, some computer-based language tests utilize hybrid scoring.

Delivery Mode and Medium

Computer-assisted language tests can be delivered onsite (e.g., in a physical classroom or a test center) or remotely (e.g., at home). The COVID-19 pandemic has precipitated many changes to how language tests are delivered. Specifically, it forced both language teachers and test developers to quickly adapt to the new reality where the delivery of onsite assessments was not an option, thereby giving rise to remote at-home tests (Ockey, 2021). Such remote at-home assessments can be delivered either synchronously (i.e., when test takers and proctors or test administrators are connected online simultaneously during the test) or asynchronously (i.e., when direct human supervision or proctoring in real time is not required and test takers have an option to complete the test on their own).

Two main mediums are available for the delivery of language tests: computers, such as desktops and laptops, and mobile devices, such as smartphones and tablets. While computer-based delivery of language tests remains the most dominant method, mobile technologies have been playing an increasingly important role in language learning and assessment practices. García Laborda et al. (2014), for instance, report on two research projects that examined the feasibility of utilizing mobile phones to deliver a language test for the Spanish College Entrance Examination. Some of the high-stakes tests such as Versant English Test can also be taken on a mobile device. Despite calls from some researchers to expand the use of mobile technology for delivering both classroom-based and high-stakes assessments (Isbell & Kremmel, 2020), mobile-delivered language tests still remain a rarity.

Content Generation

The content of computer-assisted language tests, which comprises stimuli and test items, can be created by humans or generated automatically. Various approaches to automatic item generation (AIG) – also referred to as automatic question generation (AQG, see Kurdi et al., 2020) – have been utilized for a number of years, with varying degrees of success (Gierl & Haladyna, 2013). However, recent advances in AI, ML, and computational language modeling have opened new possibilities for test developers to automate the process of item development and significantly expand the number of available items. In addition to item generation, language modeling techniques have also been applied for generating test content such as reading passages. Undoubtedly, the ongoing proliferation of AI-driven tools will further transform and improve the existing approaches to generating content for CALT.

Major Computer-Assisted Language Tests and Their Applications

Rapid technological advances and the ensuing quick expansion of CALT have resulted in a variety of commercial computer-assisted language tests. Over the past few decades, numerous CALT projects have been initiated by academic institutions and test development companies. As a representative sample of computer-delivered language tests has already been reviewed in previous publications (e.g., Chalhoub-Deville, 2010; Stoynoff & Chapelle, 2005), this section focuses only on the most recent and innovative developments in CALT that go beyond a simple adaptation of paper-and-pencil tests for computer delivery. All the tests listed in Table 42.2 are divided into three main groups: academic and general English proficiency tests, English proficiency in a professional/workplace-context tests, and non-English language proficiency tests.

Key Research Areas

In this section, we provide a brief overview of three main research areas in CALT: test validation, development of computer-based language tests (i.e., computer-adaptive tests, spoken dialog system-mediated assessments, and digital-first language assessments), and research on automated assessment.

Validation Research

In language testing, one of the primary goals of researchers is to determine the suitability of tests for their intended purposes. Validation research utilizes both quantitative and qualitative

Chapter 42 Computer-Assisted Language Testing

> **TABLE 42.2**
>
> **Summary of major computer-based language tests**

Primary purpose	Test
Academic and General English Proficiency	ACTFL Test of English Proficiency (TEP)
	Aptis (British Council)
	Cambridge English Qualifications
	Duolingo English Test (DET)
	International English Language Testing System (IELTS) Online
	Linguaskill General (Cambridge English)
	Michigan English Test (MET)
	Pearson Test of English (PTE) Academic
	Test of English Language Learning (TELL™)
	The Canadian Academic English Language (CAEL)
	Test of English as a Foreign Language Internet-based Test (TOEFL iBT)
English Proficiency in a Professional/Workplace Context	Basic English Skills Test Plus (BEST Plus™)
	Test of English for International Communication (TOEIC)
	Versant English Test
	Linguaskill Business (Cambridge English)
Non-English Language Proficiency	Versant Tests for Other Spoken Languages

approaches that are tailored to the test, its objectives, and the target audience. The research design and interpretation can vary depending on the test developer, the researcher, and other factors (Chapelle & Voss, 2021). Numerous validation research methods have been proposed in language testing, with more recent methodologies centering on construct validation and argument-based validity. Aryadoust (2022) underlines the constraints of two approaches in language assessment, drawing attention to the difficulties and uncertainties in appraising evidence and establishing test validity. In particular, he advocates for a shift toward more authentic assessment methods, embracing AI and interdisciplinary approaches, such as computational linguistics and cognitive neuroscience, to develop more precise language usage profiles.

These ideas gain importance in light of three major changes in language assessment, suggested by Chapelle and Voss (2021). Firstly, the expanding roles of language assessments in various contexts such as learning, education, workplace, and government call for context-sensitive research approaches to investigate test validity. Secondly, advancements in test methods using technology for development, delivery, and scoring necessitate a reevaluation of language constructs assessed by the tests. For instance, scores based on tasks that require test takers to converse with an interactive computer program might differ from those eliciting speaking in a monologic or face-to-face format. Thirdly, the surge in the number and variety of test takers aligns with new technologies, demographics, mobility, economic systems, and political trends.

A range of studies have attempted to address some of these challenges by examining the construct validity of computer-based tests, exploring their limitations, and suggesting interdisciplinary approaches to develop more accurate language use profiles. For example, Park (2018) employed virtual environments to enhance construct interpretations of aviation English assessment outcomes, while Isaacs et al. (2023) investigated the predictive validity of DET test scores in relation to university students' academic achievement. Meanwhile, Gokturk and Chukharev-Hudilainen (2023) and Karatay (2022) analyzed the cognitive processes involved in spoken dialog system (SDS)-delivered tasks, focusing on strategic competence in L2 oral communication.

Development of Computer-Based Language Tests

Computer adaptive testing (CAT)

An important line of research in CALT focuses on reporting the development of CAT. Despite the large number of existing commercial tests with an adaptive component (e.g., DET and Pearson), individual researchers and institutions pursue the development of "homemade" language tests to match their specific needs. In a study by Huang et al. (2022), for example, researchers developed a computerized adaptive English proficiency testing (E-CAT) system specifically tailored for assessing Taiwanese EFL university students' L2 reading and listening skills. The E-CAT system was carefully constructed through a six-stage process, which included determining the test's purpose, defining the construct, creating test items, designing administration processes, conducting field testing, and finalizing the system. The test incorporated CAT and IRT to offer a localized, free-of-charge English proficiency assessment. Upon logging into the E-CAT system, the test taker is assigned an initial proficiency level. The system then presents an item from the item bank tailored to the test taker's response to the previous item, continually adjusting and estimating the individual's proficiency. This process is repeated until a predetermined stopping rule is met, culminating in a final score report for the test taker. Another example of a customized CAT is presented in He and Min (2017) who designed it as a high-stakes graduation requirement for non-English majors at a major Chinese university. The study outlines the procedures employed to develop a CAT that evaluates test takers' listening and reading proficiency in English using dichotomous and polytomous IRT models, while also addressing validity concerns.

Spoken-dialog system (SDS)-mediated assessment

Spoken-dialog system (SDS)-mediated assessment leverages computer-generated scenarios to evaluate language proficiency in contextually relevant situations. Test takers engage with tasks that simulate real-life interactions, such as negotiating, problem-solving, or making requests, providing a more authentic assessment of their language abilities. These autonomous systems, known as chatbots, dialog systems, robots, or conversational agents, enable learners to participate in meaningful dialogs, thereby enhancing their proficiency in the target language (Bibauw et al., 2019). Utilizing AI, conversational agents can comprehend spoken phrases and generate appropriate verbal responses. The process consists of four stages: transcribing speech to text through ASR, determining the meaning or intent of the utterance using natural language understanding, generating a response with natural language generation, and converting the response to speech via text-to-speech technology.

Building on this foundation, Karatay (2023) developed an SDS-mediated Tourism English test tailored for classroom-based assessment. In this test, students assumed the role of a receptionist, while the computer played the part of a hotel guest lodging a complaint about a problem in their room. The study's findings revealed that the test effectively elicited ratable speech samples from test takers and engaged them with test tasks that are relevant to their future profession. In a similar study, Gokturk and Chukharev-Hudilainen (2023) discovered that strategic competence played a key role in determining test takers' performance when engaged in computer-assisted scenario-based tasks.

Digital-first language assessment

As technology advances rapidly, digital-first language assessment systems (LASs) have emerged to harness the benefits of improved accessibility, interactivity, and real-time feedback. These cutting-edge assessment methods are designed to provide broader access and tailored

644 Chapter 42 Computer-Assisted Language Testing

adaptation, promoting fairness in educational opportunities. By merging automated tools with sophisticated measurement techniques, a seamless technological infrastructure is created.

The progress in AI and NLP in recent years has enabled the growth of digital-first LASs. These advancements support various processes, including the creation of automated test items and automatic scoring of constructed responses. An example of such an innovative, digital-first, computer-adaptive English language proficiency assessment is the DET. Contrary to conventional assessments, the DET incorporates "human-in-the-loop AI" throughout the process, which covers the automatic generation of test items and scoring of test takers' responses (Settles et al., 2020). Human participation is still present in test proctoring processes, review of automatically generated test items, and supervision of automated scoring.

Another example of a digital-first assessment is the Versant test, which was created specifically to use technology to optimize the evaluation process. It integrates CAT, AI, NLP, and speech recognition to automatically and accurately analyze and score spoken and written responses. The entire Versant test is administered online thanks to its digital-first design, which makes it convenient for both test takers and administrators. Additionally, the Versant test's automated nature allows for quick scoring and reporting, which significantly cuts down on the time it takes for test takers to receive their results.

Research on Automated Assessment

Significant research efforts have been made in the area of automated assessment of productive skills. Automated evaluation has been in use for more than two decades in various capacities. Specifically, in the context of language testing, tools such as e-rater have been operational for scoring writing tasks on high-stakes tests such as TOEFL and GMAT since 1999. Research on automated writing evaluation has led to the development of operational systems used in high-stakes, large-volume tests, such as the Intelligent Essay Assessor (Pearson), e-rater (ETS), and IntelliMetric® (Vantage Learning). These tools are adept at analyzing lexical measures, syntax, and discourse structure of essays.

In addition, researchers have also made efforts to develop automated writing evaluation systems, which, while promising, have not been commercially deployed on a large scale. The Intelligent Academic Discourse Evaluator (IADE) is one such example of a web-based AWE program that harnesses NLP techniques to provide feedback at the level of rhetorical functions in research writing (Cotos, 2011). IADE later became the prototype of a more complex AWE system called Research Writing Tutor (RWT) developed at Iowa State University.

Although AWE systems are used extensively in many educational institutions, these systems are not universally accepted. Proponents of AWE suggest that such systems are generally in close agreement with human raters and are thus more time- and cost-effective. They may also foster learner autonomy, promote the process writing approach that involves writing multiple drafts, and lead to individualized assessment. Critics, however, claim that the use of such systems encourages students to focus on surface features such as grammar and vocabulary rather than meaning. In addition, automated assessment of essays diminishes the role of instructors and impels students to adjust their writing to the evaluation criteria of these systems (Cotos, 2011).

Unlike automated writing assessment, automated speech scoring involves an additional layer of complexity in that the test takers' oral output must first be recognized before it can be evaluated (Van Moere & Downey, 2016). While technologies for automated speech processing have improved significantly due to recent advances in ML algorithms (Evanini & Zechner, 2020), any variations in ASR accuracy can pose a serious threat to the validity of the scores generated by ASE systems (Hannah et al., 2022). Research suggests that the quality of automated speech scoring partly depends on the types of speaking tasks, with ASE systems performing more accurately on constrained tasks such as elicited imitation compared to the tasks that elicit more spontaneous L2 speech (Evanini & Zechner, 2020). Consequently, how a construct of L2 speaking is defined in a test has a direct impact on the performance of the ASE system. According to Litman et al. (2018), two contrasting approaches to construct definition can be found in tests that use ASR-based technology for automated speech scoring. In a psycholinguistic approach (adopted by Pearson for its speaking tests), the construct of L2 speaking is defined as the ability to perform restricted speaking tasks viewed as building blocks of more complex oral performance. Meanwhile, a communicative approach to construct definition (adopted by ETS for the speaking section of TOEFL iBT) views L2 speaking as the ability to engage in interaction. As a result, the L2 speaking construct measured by Pearson's tests can be scored by ASR-based technology quite accurately, whereas the speaking construct measured by TOEFL iBT poses additional challenges for automated scoring.

Current Issues and Future Directions

There are several important issues related to the use of technology in language testing: test security issues, ethical issues, and construct-related issues. Test security issues include theft of test content (i.e., prompts, items, and/or answers), identity fraud (impersonation), cheating and plagiarism during the test, and unauthorized access to test takers' data (Clark et al., 2023). While a widespread adoption of remote and at-home language assessments during the COVID-19 pandemic heightened security concerns, a number of solutions for remote proctoring have been proposed to address and mitigate such concerns.

Technology integration in language tests also poses ethical issues, including equity, fairness, and social justice (Chapman et al., 2023). Such issues may arise when technology use favors a particular group of test takers (for example, based on their L1 background, socioeconomic status, or educational background), while introducing biases against other groups (e.g., test takers who do not possess adequate computer literacy skills). Ethical concerns may also arise when test takers' performance is tracked and recorded using privacy-invasive technology (e.g., eye tracking or facial recognition) and when their data are not properly secured and stored or used for purposes other than language testing.

Another set of important issues in CALT are related to the constructs measured by computerized language tests. Sadeghi and Douglas (2023), for example, caution that the addition of a computer (or any other digital device) as a medium for test delivery may have an impact on test takers' performance, thereby affecting the validity of the interpretations that can be made on the basis of their test scores. Any such impact would inevitably have theoretical and practical implications for the construct measured by the test and test fairness, especially if using a computer as a delivery mode introduces construct-irrelevant variance (Lynch, 2022).

There is no doubt that the efforts to address these issues will continue as advances in ML models, AI, and data analytics will provide test developers and researchers with new tools and methods. One possible direction is to leverage technology for tracking, recording, and measuring test takers' response processes. Response processes that include both cognitive processes and physical processes (e.g., navigating the test content and changing the answer) can be captured using eye tracking, pupillometry, keystroke logging, brain imaging techniques such as electroencephalography (EEG) or functional near-infrared spectroscopy (fNIRS), and other similar methodologies. Another interesting proposition is to exploit gesture recognition technology for assessing pragmatics (Van Moere & Downey, 2016). Technological advancements will also allow for creating innovative item types and increasing the authenticity of existing assessment tasks, for instance, by using a chatbot to engage a test taker in a simulated job interview. While it remains to be seen whether Gruba's (2019) prediction that "[l]anguage testing, as we know it, will cease to exist within a generation" (p. 229) due to

646   **Chapter 42** Computer-Assisted Language Testing

advances in data analytics will come true, more sophisticated ML techniques, AI, and the Big Data will undoubtedly contribute to the evolution of language assessment practices and research.

Discussion Questions

1. How might modern digital innovation affect CALT?
2. How might modern digital innovation in CALT impact language teaching and washback?

References

Aryadoust, V. (2022). The known and unknown about the nature and assessment of L2 listening. *International Journal of Listening, 36*(2), 69–79. https://doi.org/10.1080/10904018.2022.2042951.

Bibauw, S., François, T., & Desmet, P. (2019). Discussing with a computer to practice a foreign language: research synthesis and conceptual framework of dialogue-based CALL. *Computer Assisted Language Learning, 32*(8), 827–877. https://doi.org/10.1080/09588221.2018.1535508.

Carr, N. T. (2023). Web-based testing and automated scoring: construct conceptualization and improving reliability. In K. Sadeghi & D. Douglas (Eds.), *Fundamental considerations in technology mediated language assessment* (pp. 1–16). Routledge. https://doi.org/10.4324/9781003292395-11.

Chalhoub-Deville, M. (2010). Technology in standardized language assessments. In R. Kaplan (Ed.), *The Oxford handbook of applied linguistics* (2nd ed., pp. 511–526). Oxford University Press. https://doi.org/10.1093/oxfordhb/9780195384253.013.0035.

Chalhoub-Deville, M., & Deville, C. (1999). Computer adaptive testing in second language contexts. *Annual Review of Applied Linguistics, 19*, 273–299. https://doi.org/10.1017/S0267190599190147.

Chapelle, C. A. (2010). *Technology in language testing [video].* http://languagetesting.info/video/main.html.

Chapelle, C. A., & Douglas, D. (2006). *Assessing language through computer technology.* Cambridge University Press. https://doi.org/10.1017/CBO9780511733116.

Chapelle, C., & Voss, E. (2017). Utilizing technology in language assessment. In E. Shohamy, I. Or & S. May (Eds.), *Language testing and assessment. Encyclopedia of language and education.* Springer. https://doi.org/10.1007/978-3-319-02261-1_10.

Chapelle, C. A., & Voss, E. (Eds.). (2021). *Validity argument in language testing: Case studies of validation research.* Cambridge University Press. https://doi.org/10.1017/9781108669849.

Chapman, M., Kemp, J. A., Kim, A. A., MacGregor, D., & MacMillan, F. (2023). Testing young multilingual learners remotely: prioritizing equity, fairness, and social justice. In K. Sadeghi & D. Douglas (Eds.), *Fundamental considerations in technology mediated language assessment.* Routledge.

Chen, M. Y., & Lin, Y. M. (2023). Mobile-assisted language assessment for adult EFL learners: recommendations from a systematic review. In S. W. Chong & H. Reinders (Eds.), *Innovation in learning-oriented language assessment* (pp. 237–256). Palgrave Macmillan. https://doi.org/10.1007/978-3-031-18950-0_14.

Clark, T., Holland, M., & Spiby, R. (2023). Seeking empirical evidence to support online test validation: building on the IELTS indicator assessment model. In K. Sadeghi (Ed.), *Technology-assisted language assessment in diverse contexts: Lessons from the transition to online testing during COVID-19* (pp. 16–33). Routledge.

Cotos, E. (2011). Potential of automated writing evaluation feedback. *CALICO Journal, 28*(2), 420–459. http://www.jstor.org/stable/calicojournal.28.2.420.

Davey, T., Pitoniak, M. J., & Slater, S. C. (2015). Designing computerized adaptive tests. In S. Lane, M. R. Raymond & T. M. Haladyna (Eds.), *Handbook of test development* (2nd ed., pp. 467–484). Routledge. https://doi.org/10.4324/9780203102961.

Douglas, D., & Hegelheimer, V. (2007). Assessing language using computer technology. *Annual Review of Applied Linguistics, 27*, 115–132. https://doi.org/10.1017/CBO9780511733116.

Evanini, K., & Zechner, K. (2020). Overview of automated speech scoring. In K. Zechner & K. Evanini (Eds.), *Automated speaking assessment: Using language technologies to score spontaneous speech* (pp. 3–20). Routledge. https://doi.org/10.4324/9781315165103-1.

García Laborda, J. G., Magal-Royo, T. M., Litzler, M. F., Giménez, L. J., & L. G. (2014). Mobile phones for Spain's university entrance examination language test. *Educational Technology & Society, 17*(2), 17–30. https://www.jstor.org/stable/10.2307/jeductechsoci.17.2.17.

Gierl, M. J., & Haladyna, T. M. (2013). *Automatic item generation: Theory and practice.* Routledge. https://doi.org/10.4324/9780203803912.

Gokturk, N., & Chukharev-Hudilainen, E. (2023). Strategy use in a spoken dialog system-delivered paired discussion task: a stimulated recall study. *Language Testing, 40*(3), 630–657. https://doi.org/10.1177/02655322231152620.

Gruba, P. (2019). The challenge of theory: social media and language assessment. In C. Roever & G. Wigglesworth (Eds.), *Social perspectives on language testing: Papers in honor of Tim McNamara* (pp. 229–242). Peter Lang.

Hannah, L., Kim, H., & Jang, E. E. (2022). Investigating the effects of task type and linguistic background on accuracy in automated speech recognition systems: implications for use in language assessment of young learners. *Language Assessment Quarterly, 19*(3), 289–313. https://doi.org/10.1080/15434303.2022.2038172.

He, L., & Min, S. (2017). Development and validation of a computer adaptive EFL test. *Language Assessment Quarterly, 14*(2), 160–176. https://doi.org/10.1080/15434303.2016.1162793.

Huang, H. T. D., Hung, S. T. A., Chao, H. Y., Chen, J. H., Lin, T. P., & Shih, C. L. (2022). Developing and validating a computerized adaptive testing system for measuring the English proficiency of Taiwanese EFL university students. *Language Assessment Quarterly, 19*(2), 162–188. https://doi.org/10.1080/15434303.2021.1984490.

Isaacs, T., Hu, R., Trenkic, D., & Varga, J. (2023). Examining the predictive validity of the Duolingo English Test: evidence from a major UK university. *Language Testing, 40*(3), 748–770. https://doi.org/10.1177/02655322231158550.

Isbell, D. R., & Kremmel, B. (2020). Test review: current options in at-home language proficiency tests for making high-stakes decisions. *Language Testing, 37*(4), 600–619. https://doi.org/10.1177/0265532220943483.

Jamieson, J. (2005). Trends in computer-based second language assessment. *Annual Review of Applied Linguistics, 25*, 228–242. https://doi.org/10.1017/S0267190505000127.

Karatay, Y. (2022). *Development and validation of spoken dialog system-based oral communication tasks in an ESP context (Publication No. 2725255274) [Doctoral dissertation, Iowa State University].* ProQuest Dissertations and Theses Global. https://www.proquest.com/dissertations-theses/development-validation-spoken-dialog-system-based/docview/2725255274/se-2.

Karatay, Y. (2023). Using spoken dialog systems to assess L2 learners' oral skills in a local language testing context. In X. Yan, S. Dimova & A. Ginther (Eds.), *Local language testing: Practice across contexts* (pp. 231–252). Springer. https://doi.org/10.1007/978-3-031-33541-9_12.

Kurdi, G., Leo, J., Parsia, B., Sattler, U., & Al-Emari, S. (2020). A systematic review of automatic question generation for educational purposes. *International Journal of Artificial Intelligence in Education, 30*, 121–204. https://doi.org/10.1007/s40593-019-00186-y.

Lesnov, R. O. (2017). Using videos in ESL listening achievement tests: effects on difficulty. *Eurasian Journal of Applied Linguistics, 3*(1), 67–91. https://doi.org/10.32601/ejal.461034.

Li, L. (2023). Developing language teacher cognition about technology-enhanced assessment: A case of student teachers in a TESOL programme. In S. W. Chong & H. Reinders (Eds.), *Innovation in learning-oriented language assessment* (pp. 277–294). Springer.

Litman, D., Strik, H., & Lim, G. S. (2018). Speech technologies and the assessment of second language speaking: approaches, challenges, and opportunities. *Language Assessment Quarterly, 15*(3), 294–309. https://doi.org/10.1080/15434303.2018.1472265.

Lynch, S. (2022). Adapting paper-based tests for computer administration: lessons learned from 30 years of mode effects studies in education. *Practical Assessment, Research, and Evaluation, 27*(22), 1–16. https://scholarworks.umass.edu/pare/vol27/iss1/22/.

Malabonga, V. A., & Kenyon, D. M. (1999). Multimedia computer technology and performance-based language testing: a demonstration of the Computerized Oral Proficiency Instrument (COPI). In M. B. Olsen (Ed.), *Association for Computational Linguistics/International Association of Language Learning Technologies Symposium proceedings. Computer mediated language assessment and evaluation in natural language processing* (pp. 16–23). Association for Computational Linguistics.

648 **Chapter 42** Computer-Assisted Language Testing

Mizumoto, A., Sasao, Y., & Webb, S. A. (2019). Developing and evaluating a computerized adaptive testing version of the Word Part Levels Test. *Language Testing, 36*(1), 101–123. https://doi.org/10.1177/0265532217725776.

Nakatsuhara, F., Inoue, C., Berry, V., & Galaczi, E. (2021). Video-conferencing speaking tests: do they measure the same construct as face-to-face tests? *Assessment in Education: Principles, Policy & Practice, 28*(4), 369–388. https://doi.org/10.1080/0969594X.2021.1951163.

Ockey, G. J. (2009). Developments and challenges in the use of computer-based testing for assessing second language ability. *The Modern Language Journal, 93*, 836–847. https://doi.org/10.1111/j.1540-4781.2009.00976.x.

Ockey, G. J. (2021). An overview of COVID-19's impact on English language university admissions and placement tests. *Language Assessment Quarterly, 18*(1), 1–5. https://doi.org/10.1080/15434303.2020.1866576.

Ockey, G. J., & Wagner, E. (2018). *Assessing L2 listening: Moving towards authenticity.* John Benjamins. https://doi.org/10.1075/lllt.50.

Park, M. (2018). Innovative assessment of aviation English in a virtual world: windows into cognitive and metacognitive strategies. *ReCALL, 30*(2), 196–213. https://doi.org/10.1017/S0958344017000362.

Parshall, C. G., Davey, T., & Pashley, P. J. (2000). Innovative item types for computerized testing. In W. J. Van der Linden & C. A. W. Glas (Eds.), *Computerized adaptive testing: Theory and practice* (pp. 129–148). Kluwer.

Sadeghi, K. (Ed.). (2023). *Technology-assisted language assessment in diverse contexts: Lessons from the transition to online testing during COVID-19.* Taylor & Francis. https://doi.org/10.4324/9781003221463.

Sadeghi, K., & Douglas, D. (2023). Technology mediated language assessment: key considerations. In K. Sadeghi & D. Douglas (Eds.), *Fundamental considerations in technology mediated language assessment* (pp. 1–14). Routledge.

Settles, B., LaFlair, G. T., & Hagiwara, M. (2020). Machine learning-driven language assessment. *Transactions of the Association for Computational Linguistics, 8*, 247–263. https://doi.org/10.1162/tacl_a_00310.

Stoynoff, S., & Chapelle, C. (2005). *ESOL tests and testing.* TESOL.

Suvorov, R. (2019). Multimedia in the teaching and assessment of listening. In M. A. Peters & R. Heraud (Eds.), *Encyclopedia of educational innovation* (pp. 1–6). Springer. https://doi.org/10.1007/978-981-13-2262-4_87-1.

Van Moere, A., & Downey, R. (2016). Technology and artificial intelligence in language assessment. In D. Tsagari & J. Banerjee (Eds.), *Handbook of second language assessment* (pp. 341–358). De Gruyter Mouton. https://doi.org/10.1515/9781614513827-023.

Wagner, E. (2007). Are they watching? Test-taker viewing behavior during an L2 video listening test. *Language Learning & Technology, 11*(1), 67–86. http://hdl.handle.net/10125/44089.

Winke, P. (2006). Online assessment of foreign language proficiency: meeting development, design, and delivery challenges. In S. Howell & M. Hricko (Eds.), *Online assessment and measurement: Case studies from teacher education, K-12 and corporate* (pp. 82–97). Information Science Publishing. https://doi.org/10.4018/978-1-59140-497-2.ch006.

Winke, P., & Fei, F. (2008). Computer-assisted language assessment. In N. Van Deusen-Scholl & N. H. Hornberger (Eds.), *Encyclopedia of language and education* (Vol. 4, pp. 353–364). Springer.

Winke, P. M., & Isbell, D. R. (2017). Computer-assisted language assessment. In S. L. Thorne & S. May (Eds.), *Language, education and technology* (pp. 313–325). Springer. https://doi.org/10.1007/978-3-319-02237-6_25.

Xi, X. (2010). Automated scoring and feedback systems: where are we and where are we heading? *Language Testing, 27*(3), 291–300. https://doi.org/10.1177/0265532210364643.

Zhang, S., & Isaacs, T. (2023). Can interactions happen across the screens? The use of videoconferencing technology in assessing second language pragmatic competence. In K. Sadeghi (Ed.), *Technology-assisted language assessment in diverse contexts: Lessons from the transition to online testing during COVID-19* (pp. 196–211). Routledge.

Suggested Readings

Sadeghi, K. (Ed.). (2023). *Technology-assisted language assessment in diverse contexts: Lessons from the transition to online testing during COVID-19.* Taylor & Francis. https://doi.org/10.4324/9781003221463.

Sadeghi, K., & Douglas, D. (Eds.). (2023). *Fundamental considerations in technology mediated language assessment.* Routledge. https://doi.org/10.4324/9781003292395.

CHAPTER 43

Computer-Adaptive Language Testing: Focus on Language Issues

Ramsey Cardwell, Ben Naismith, and Micheline Chalhoub-Deville

Introduction

Computer-adaptive testing is a method of assessment administered via a computer that adapts to a test taker's ability in real time by selecting items of appropriate difficulty based on responses to preceding items (see Chalhoub-Deville & Deville, 1999). This tailored approach is what sets computer-adaptive tests (CATs) apart from conventional tests, wherein a group of examinees receive the same items (i.e., fixed-form tests). In CAT administration, an approximate estimate of ability is first obtained via one or more initial items of predetermined difficulty. A subsequent item is then selected corresponding to the test taker's estimated ability level. The process of estimating a test taker's ability and selecting items accordingly is repeated until a sufficiently accurate ability estimate is achieved, at which point the test ends (see Sawaki, 2021).

In this chapter, we focus on a specific subset of CATs: computer-adaptive testing in *language* assessment (a.k.a., computer-adaptive language tests [CALTs]).[1] Due to the complex, multidimensional nature of language proficiency, developing CATs suitable for this purpose presents additional challenges and considerations for test developers (e.g., construct coverage and automated scoring of production). We begin with key components and then discuss specific CALT advantages and challenges. This chapter primarily focuses on item-level adaptive tests and general issues relevant to all types of adaptive testing.

Essential Components

We provide a brief summary of five essential CAT components and characteristics. As CALTs are a type of CAT, all CALTs share these same attributes. The components or characteristics listed below are presented primarily from the perspective of item-level CATs (in which each

---

[1] Throughout this chapter, we use "CALT" when referring specifically to CATs of language proficiency constructs and "CAT" when referring more generally to all CATs. Some statements made about CALTs are also applicable to CATs.

The Concise Companion to Language Assessment, First Edition. Edited by Antony John Kunnan.
© 2025 John Wiley & Sons, Inc. Published 2025 by John Wiley & Sons, Inc.

649

650 Chapter 43 Computer-Adaptive Language Testing: Focus on Language Issues

item is administered separately and adaptively), but they also apply to varying degrees in multistage testing (MST), in which adaptivity is at the level of groups of items.

1. *Method for estimating test-taker ability*: Prior to test administration, the true value of a test taker's ability is unknown. For CALTs, this ability is overall language proficiency or proficiency in specific language systems or skills. The CAT algorithm generates proximate ability estimates based on the responses to the given items, updating this estimate after each item is administered. Ability estimation methods include maximum likelihood (MLE), maximum a posteriori (MAP, a.k.a. Bayes modal estimate [BME]), and expected a posteriori (EAP).

2. *Starting point*: Approaches to selecting the initial item include using items with average difficulty or near an important cut point (e.g., the threshold between pass and fail; Stevenson & Gross, 1991), test-taker self-assessment, presenting multiple items of differing difficulty and basing the first adaptive item on the collective responses, or considering demographic data and/or previous test scores. For example, in terms of CALTs, DIALANG uses a combination of a self-assessment and results from a yes/no vocab test to determine the starting point for the main test.

3. *Termination criterion*: Setting the criteria for an exit (or termination) point in a CAT (i.e., stopping rules) is important as it impacts test length, test takers' scores, and desirable item bank size. Stopping rules generally fall into two categories: fixed-length and variable-length (see He & Min, 2017). Variable-length stopping rules, typically based on the precision of the ability estimate, can be supplemented with constraints on testing time and/or the number of items. CALTs tend to be essentially fixed-length, with narrow total testing time ranges (e.g., WebCAPE), presumably in part for reasons of standardization and perceived fairness. MSTs such as TOEFL Essentials are by definition fixed-length.

4. *Item selection algorithm*: Item selection algorithms determine which items to administer based on the test taker's responses. Optimal item selection depends on the intended decision, with strategies including maximizing information (e.g., maximized Fisher information), choosing items with lower discrimination earlier in the test (e.g., a-stratified selection), or weighting information based on current knowledge of test-taker ability (e.g., weighted likelihood information criterion). An item selection algorithm that focuses on efficiently maximizing the precision of estimating an examinee's ability may sacrifice content coverage and representativeness.

5. *Item bank (pool) characteristics*: The item bank for a CAT consists of all items available for administration and their corresponding metadata such as content tags and IRT item parameters. Depending on factors such as the ability range of the test-taker population and frequency of test sessions, an adaptive testing program can require a larger item bank compared to fixed-form tests. Since predetermined content coverage is typically desired for all test-taker proficiency levels, as more item-type attributes and properties are added, the required item pool size increases. High-stakes CALTs typically have item banks of thousands of items to cover the four traditional skills (see Starr-Egger, 2001).

Advantages of CALTs

CALTs offer a range of benefits that set them apart from traditional, nonadaptive language testing methods; these benefits motivate their continued development and use despite some unique challenges and resource requirements. As a subset of computer-based tests (CBTs), CALTs offer the same advantages of nonadaptive CBTs plus additional advantages due to their adaptive nature. For example, like nonadaptive CBTs, CALTs allow for more innovative item types that are not possible on paper-based tests (PBTs) and nearly instantaneous scoring of test-taker responses, among other advantages (see Chalhoub-Deville & Deville, 1999 for a more detailed list of CBT advantages). This section discusses specifically salient advantages of CALTs, including administration efficiency, classification consistency, measurement precision, and test security.

Administration Efficiency

One of the primary motivations for the development of CALTs in the late 1900s was administration efficiency. CALTs generally require less testing time because they select a subset of items from an item bank, quickly homing in on the test taker's proficiency level. As a result, they often require fewer items to achieve an accurate measurement compared to traditional fixed-form tests. This advantage applies to test takers with varying proficiency levels, as long as the item bank contains enough items at the appropriate difficulty levels.

In addition to the efficiency of the actual testing session, CALTs can also be more efficient in terms of cost and logistics. Traditional large-scale, high-stakes tests are administered in person simultaneously to large groups of examinees, requiring resources for transporting exam materials and scoring test-taker responses (for PBTs), or providing computers with sufficient technical specifications and secure IT infrastructure (for computer-based tests). Adaptive testing's efficiency was therefore desirable for cost reduction, as shorter test durations meant fewer resources, such as proctoring time and test center operation costs, were needed per test taker.

Measurement Precision

CALTs offer the advantage of measurement precision due to their adaptive nature. Unlike fixed-form tests that include items from a wide range of difficulty levels (see Chalhoub-Deville & Deville, 1999), CALTs maximize test information at each test taker's ability level, leading to relatively high and uniform measurement precision across all ability levels adequately covered by the item bank. As a result, CALTs can reliably classify test takers into multiple proficiency levels, such as those of the Common European Framework of Reference (CEFR; Council of Europe, 2001), using a single test. In contrast, a comparable PBT program could require multiple distinct test levels or much longer testing time to adequately cover the same proficiency range.

CALTs also enable the reduction of construct-irrelevant variance due to practice effects and item preknowledge. It is possible to record the items administered to each test taker in order to prevent repeat test takers from receiving the same item on multiple test attempts. By maximizing measurement precision, CALTs produce more accurate and reliable classifications, such as pass/fail or proficiency levels. Furthermore, it is possible to design the item selection algorithm specifically to select items that maximize classification accuracy based on the test taker's mid-test ability estimate and location of the nearest cut score. In this way, CALTs can be optimized for classification accuracy even when there are multiple outcome categories.

The Test of Chinese as a Foreign Language[2] (TOCFL), a high-stakes Mandarin proficiency exam developed and primarily administered in Taiwan, is an example of a test that transitioned from PBT to CAT. As a PBT test, TOCFL offered four separate levels, corresponding to CEFR levels pre-A1, A1/A2, B1/B2, and C1/C2; it was the test taker's responsibility to choose the appropriate level when registering for the test. Conversely, the adaptive version of the TOCFL assesses all proficiency levels with a single undifferentiated test.

---

[2] https://tocfl.edu.tw/

Test Security

The adaptive nature of CALTs also confers several security advantages. Since each test taker receives a unique set of items based on their performance, when CALTs are administered in exam centers, test takers have minimal chance of successfully cheating off a neighbor's test. CALTs also minimize the benefit of item preknowledge (i.e., access to items before encountering them on the test), given that test takers cannot predict with any great certainty which items will appear on the test. However, both of these security advantages are proportional to the size of the item bank.

In recent years, the confluence of CALTs' efficiency and security features with the proliferation of ever more powerful personal computers have made it feasible to administer high-stakes tests remotely (i.e., the test taker is at home or another private location and takes the test on a personal computer). The Duolingo English Test[3] (DET) was a relatively early example of a remote high-stakes CALT. The COVID-19 pandemic created an urgent need for such tests due to the closure of physical test centers. Even after the pandemic subsided and physical test centers reopened, remote testing options have persisted.

Challenges in CALTs

CALTs offer several key advantages, but like all assessment approaches, they also present challenges that vary by context. Advances in CAT research and technology have provided partial solutions to previously significant challenges, such as item bank development, automated scoring, exam administration, parameter calibration, and test comparability (see Chalhoub-Deville & Deville, 1999). However, there remain considerable practical and theoretical obstacles for CALT developers. Some concerns, such as those related to technology and psychometric theory, may lessen with continued research, but issues surrounding construct coverage and validity are likely to persist as barriers to widespread CALT adoption. Generally speaking, CALT challenges reflect the need to balance efficiency and resource constraints on the one hand with construct coverage and item complexity on the other, as exemplified by the trade-offs between machine-generated and human-directed test development. In this section, we discuss some common challenges posed by CALTs, what progress has been made in recent years, and what barriers remain.

Construct Coverage

A fundamental challenge of CALT is ensuring a more comprehensive coverage of the construct being measured, meaning that the test items must sufficiently represent the language skills and abilities for the intended score interpretation and use to be valid. Language proficiency is inherently multidimensional, encompassing various competencies such as grammatical, textual, and sociolinguistic (see Bachman & Palmer, 1996). While consensus is lacking in terms of how these variables interact at different proficiency levels and in different modalities, the field is in general agreement based on research and practice that the L2 construct is multidimensional. To assess these diverse aspects, mainstream L2 assessment typically employs a variety of task types, often emphasizing authentic skill use and demonstrable communicative competence.

In contrast, the IRT models commonly used in adaptive testing assume a unidimensional trait, although test-taker ability on distinct subconstructs can be estimated separately.

---

[3] https://englishtest.duolingo.com

To check this assumption, dimensionality analyses can be performed, such as factor analysis and DIMTEST (see Nandakumar & Stout, 1993). However, numerous scholars have expressed concerns about the unidimensionality assumption of IRT models in CALTs. A comprehensive discussion of dimensionality and IRT models can be found in Min and Aryadoust's review (2021). The fact that all major high-stakes language tests provide an overall score can be seen as a response to demands by test score users and policymakers, who tend to conceptualize and operationalize language proficiency as quasi-unidimensional. As a result of this inherent tension, developing tasks that align with and satisfy both paradigms presents a significant challenge (see Sawaki, 2021), and CALTs have faced criticism about their lack of capability to assess productive skills and other open-ended task types (see He & Min, 2017).

One way to increase authenticity and construct coverage is through complex item types comprising multiple subitems (e.g., a multi-turn dialog) and sets of distinct items that share a common stimulus (e.g., multiple-choice questions about a passage). Also known as testlets, these subsets of tests are developed as a unit and share a common context and thus must be administered together. However, given that the subitems naturally vary in difficulty, testlets dilute the efficiency of CALTs and complicate item selection. They also increase chances of violating IRT's *local item independence* assumption, which may result in a number of psychometric issues including inaccurate estimates of item parameters, reduced measurement precision, and an overestimation of test takers' proficiency levels.

Consequently, future CALT development must continue to focus on striking a balance between authentic language assessment and satisfying psychometric requirements. Achieving this balance will require ongoing research and development, particularly in the areas of automated scoring and parameter estimation for open-ended productive skills tasks.

Item Bank Development and Maintenance

Developing and maintaining CALTs requires ongoing investment in research and development, which can be costly. A large item bank is a crucial aspect of CALT development, as the success of the adaptive testing model depends on having a large pool of test items from which to draw. What constitutes a sufficiently large item bank depends on many factors, such as the stakes and purpose of the test and the size of the test-taker population; a high-stakes CALT with many test takers might need tens of thousands of items in the item bank. Moreover, items need to be continually added to the pool to compensate for item exposure and leakage, which pose threats to test security and score use validity. Controlling for item exposure (i.e., limiting the number of times or rate at which an item can be administered) can force the item selection algorithm to administer suboptimal items, leading to slightly longer CATs and further increasing the required size of the item bank. The large item bank requirement has been a factor in some testing programs moving away from item-level adaptivity (e.g., TOEFL and GRE).

Developing large sets of items was historically resource-intensive, requiring expert item writers, piloting items on large samples, and digital storage and data transfer infrastructure (see Nogami & Hayashi, 2010). Costs have decreased with advances in item-writing software, improved digital storage, and more robust internet infrastructure. Automated item generation (AIG) can reduce item development costs by leveraging item templates or large language models (LLMs) such as GPT-3 to create content orders of magnitude faster (e.g., Attali et al., 2022), though in such cases it is critical to carefully put in place human-directed quality control measures. Ongoing challenges in CALT development are thus the trustworthiness of AI-based item generation to accurately represent authentic language use and balancing human resources with machine capabilities.

654 Chapter 43 Computer-Adaptive Language Testing: Focus on Language Issues

Test-Taker Computer Literacy

Computer literacy used to be a concern for developing CBTs, but widespread computer usage has increased test takers' familiarity. For example, in 2019 an estimated 50% of households worldwide owned a computer, a proportion that has continually increased in recent years (International Telecommunication Union, 2019). In the L2 assessment field, ETS researched computer experience and test performance in the 1990s for the computer-based TOEFL. A survey of 90,000 TOEFL test takers revealed 16% low, 34% moderate, and 50% high computer familiarity (see Kirsch et al., 1998). To address this issue, a pretest tutorial and TOEFL Sampler CD-ROM were developed (see Jamieson et al., 1998). A study with 1100 test takers found no significant score differences between computer-familiar and computer-unfamiliar groups after the tutorial (see Taylor et al., 1998). With increasingly widespread computer access, basic computer literacy is generally assumed for most test takers, except in specific populations like the very young or those with potentially limited computer access such as refugees.

CALT developers must now focus on test takers' perceptions of the specific user interface of the test platform (e.g., Langenfeld et al., 2022) as well as their understanding of adaptive testing. Ortner and Caspers (2011) investigated the relationship between test-taker anxiety and performance on CATs versus fixed-form tests. Interestingly, negative effects of CAT administration were only present in the condition when test takers did not receive any prior information about how CATs work. During the test itself, uncertainty may be alleviated by providing feedback to the test taker, for example, by praising, reminding, warning, or giving feedback in the form of correct answers. Such messages have been found to be effective, though some test takers can potentially find messaging of this nature to be distracting (see Vispoel, 1993). Online practice tests and test-specific tutorials are generally provided to help test takers get accustomed to the platform and adaptive testing in advance of their test session.

Despite the ever-increasing availability of computers, some concerns about technological literacy remain relevant. Keyboarding skills, varying among individuals, can introduce construct-irrelevant variance in test scores involving timed extended writing items (see Barkaoui, 2014). Nowadays, students frequently use smartphones or tablets to compose digital texts, possibly limiting their experience with physical keyboards required in high-stakes CBTs. Barkaoui (2014) identified a small yet significant impact of keyboarding skills on TOEFL writing task scores. Additionally, with the rise of remote testing options, remote test takers are now responsible for ensuring the suitability of their personal hardware as well as internet connection and have less access to technical support than they would in a physical test center, introducing a new aspect of technology literacy to high-stakes standardized testing.

Score Comparability

Bennett (2000) proposed three CBT adoption phases, with the first focusing on computerizing paper-based item types for efficiency. During this early CBT and CAT development period, score comparability between PBT and CBT was a major concern, in part due to concerns about test-taker unfamiliarity with computers and CBTs. An early review on the topic by Bunderson et al. (1989) found a small effect favoring PBTs, while Mead and Drasgow's (1993) meta-analysis observed no mode effect for well-constructed CBT/CAT power tests, but a substantial effect for speeded tests. Sawaki (2001) highlighted that score comparability depends on assessed abilities and that computerization can impact test aspects like completion time, test-taker affect, and score meaning. However, as computer-based language tests are now more familiar to learners, concerns over PBT–CBT score comparability have lessened.

Score comparability is a concern when decisions are based on scores from different modes, such as PBT and CBT during transitions or concurrent offerings. However, with the rise of CBT-only tests (e.g., PTE and DET), PBT–CBT comparability is becoming less relevant.

Still, some high-stakes tests offer both versions. The TOEFL iBT Paper Edition is offered in select countries "for test takers who prefer to test on paper" (ETS, 2023), and the scores are claimed to be interchangeable with the CBT version. Similarly, the IELTS is also offered concurrently on paper and computer, but Read (2022) noted a lack of published comparability studies since the early 2000s when the test was delivered on a different platform.

"Comparability study" has typically implied PBT–CBT comparisons. But of increasing importance are comparisons of different CBT versions and administration conditions. Test programs like TOCFL have transitioned from nonadaptive CBT to CALT, while the GRE has moved from item-level CAT to MST. Precipitated by the COVID-19 pandemic, remote/at-home versions of center-based tests such as TOEFL iBT Home Edition, IELTS Online, and PTE Academic Online have emerged. Comparability with the center-based versions seems to be assumed on the basis of identical test structure and content, but currently, no published research exists on the impact of different test administrations. This is a crucial area of study, as Bachman and Palmer (2010) have noted: the influence of test environment on performance and scores.

Automated Scoring of Writing and Speaking

In addition to resource and consistency considerations, automated real-time scoring of writing and speaking is a prerequisite for a (computer-based) test of language proficiency to be fully adaptive while covering all language modalities. However, automated scoring of open-ended production responses is a significant challenge in CALT development. While advances have been made in the accuracy of automated scoring systems, human raters are still often considered the gold standard of assessing certain more subjective aspects of language, such as creativity in the case of writing, or appropriacy of content in the case of speaking (see Wang & Evanini, 2020). Furthermore, automated scoring systems are still dependent on human raters, as human-rated datasets are required for the development and evaluation of scoring models.

Advances in automated writing evaluation (AWE) have understandably outpaced those of speaking, since speech scoring requires additional steps of speech recognition, speech segmentation, and processing of audio signals. AWE has thus been used to score high-stakes tests for some time; both the GRE and TOEFL use the *e-rater* automated scoring system to score open-ended writing responses, albeit in conjunction with a human rater. The PTE Academic and the DET are two prominent examples of high-stakes tests employing fully automated scoring of both writing and speaking items.

In all of these examples, subconstructs of speaking and writing are typically based on rubrics used by human raters and findings from the research community (see Zechner & Evanini, 2020). Terminology for these subconstructs varies, though they typically cover aspects of speaking/writing related to content (task achievement, relevance, etc.), discourse (clarity, cohesion, etc.), lexis (lexical diversity, lexical sophistication, etc.), grammar (grammatical complexity, grammatical accuracy, etc.), fluency (speed, chunking, etc.), and pronunciation (intonation, intelligibility, etc.). Automated (often complex) features then operationalize these different aspects, for example, the mean length of clauses as one measure of grammatical complexity, or the cosine similarity between the prompt's embedding and the response's embedding to measure relevance. Weights are given to each feature to calculate overall scores, though feature weights used on operational tests are typically not made publicly available.

Unfortunately, to our knowledge, no operational high-stakes language test has yet implemented real-time scoring of open-ended responses such that they contribute to the adaptive item selection process. Additionally, judging the difficulty of open-ended tasks is inherently challenging. As in many other areas of educational technology, recent advances in AI have also opened possibilities for using LLMs to assess language constructs historically difficult for automated scoring systems to capture, for example, discourse coherence in writing (Naismith et al., 2023).

CALTs and Test Contexts

CATs have evolved significantly since their early beginnings in the 1970s, when the development of the Computerized Adaptive Testing System marked a major milestone in the field. From the 2000s onward, the popularity of CATs continued to grow, driven by technological advancements, such as the proliferation of internet access, as well as increased societal demand for assessments to support data-driven decision-making.[4] Turning to CALTs specifically, the field of second language (L2) assessment began to adopt computer-adaptive elements in the 1980s (see Chalhoub-Deville & Deville, 1999). A significant development was Brigham Young University's introduction of its first CALT in 1986, a Spanish placement test known as S-CAPE, a predecessor of WebCAPE (see Larson, 1989). Subsequently, in the 1990s, several commercial CALTs were launched, including the Business Language Testing Service (BULATS), the Test of English as a Foreign Language computer-based test (TOEFL CBT), and the Versant suite of tests[5] (see Pearson, 2019). The first conference on CALT, "Issues in Computer-Adaptive Testing on L2 Reading Proficiency," was held in March 1996, based on which an edited volume was published (see Chalhoub-Deville, 1999).

Throughout the 21st century, several trends have shaped the development and usage of modern CALTs. In terms of the languages assessed via CALTs, English[6] is currently the most common, reflecting the large market – and therefore resources – for English proficiency testing. Such CALTs often produce an overall determination of language proficiency (e.g., EF SET and Oxford Test of English). In addition, there have been numerous English CALTs targeting specific language skills and systems, especially vocabulary (e.g., Aviad-Levitzky et al., 2019), receptive skills (e.g., ACTFL, 2023), and productive skills (e.g., Malabonga & Kenyon, 1999). The majority of CALTs have been developed to assess adults, although some exist for young learners (e.g., Oxford University Press, 2023).

CALTs also exist for assessing a wide range of languages besides English, including French (e.g., Laurier, 1999), German (e.g., Goethe-Institut., 2023), Hausa (e.g., Dunkel, 1999), Japanese (e.g., Imai et al., 2009), Mandarin (e.g., Taiwan Mandarin Educational Resources Center, 2020), and Spanish (e.g., OSU, 2023). In addition, some CALTs offer a range of language options, for example, Avant (45 languages; Avant, 2023), DIALANG (currently 15 languages; Chapelle, 2006), and WebCAPE (7 languages), typically for low- or medium-stakes purposes.

CALTs can be used for tests of different stakes: high (e.g., admissions), medium (e.g., placement), and low (e.g., formative; Bachman & Damböck, 2018), reflecting both the magnitude of impact from and reversibility of the decision(s) made based on test results (Bachman & Palmer, 2010). A test's stakes have important implications for the test's design and operations due to differences in requirements for test security, content coverage, and measurement precision.

High stakes bring high incentives to cheat, so high-stakes CALTs generally require larger item banks to compensate for item leakage and to control item exposure. A large item bank, facilitated by automatic item generation, is a key component in the security framework of such tests (LaFlair et al., 2022). In medium- and low-stakes contexts, technological advances have allowed CALTs to become accessible via mobile devices.[7] Although mobile CALTs are currently not generally considered to be sufficiently secure for high-stakes purposes, they are

---

[4] For a list of many operational CAT programs around the world, see the International Association of Computerized Adaptive Testing (IACAT) resources page: http://iacat.org/resources.
[5] https://www.pearson.com/languages/hr-professionals/versant.html
[6] https://www.efset.org/
[7] In this chapter, we consider adaptive tests on mobile/handheld devices to be included under the overarching CAT category.

used in other contexts. The English First Standard English Test (EF SET) is one such CALT, offering a free placement/advancement/certification test that can be taken in 50 minutes on a smartphone or tablet.

For medium-stakes tests such as placement tests, covering all language skills and modalities (i.e., receptive and productive and oral and written) is less crucial than in high-stakes contexts, and it is therefore common to see medium- and low-stakes CALTs that only assess receptive skills through selected-response items. An example is the WebCAPE tests, which are commonly used for source placement in foreign language programs at North American postsecondary institutions. WebCAPE is currently available in multiple languages (e.g., Spanish, French, German, and Chinese) and assesses reading, grammar, and listening through selected-response items.

The often more lenient requirements for medium- and low-stakes tests with respect to test security, construct coverage, and standardization – coupled with the availability of easy-to-use software and online platforms for adaptive testing – make CALT development less onerous for medium- and low-stakes use cases. These factors potentially explain why examples of CALTs used for placement purposes have been particularly numerous.

Conclusions

Technological and measurement advancements have facilitated the creation of CATs and CALTs. With the development of sophisticated IRT measurement technology and software, test developers have been able to maximize test information at each test taker's ability level, achieving high measurement precision across ability levels, provided these ability levels are adequately covered by the item bank. CALTs have seen progress in the assessment of a variety of languages and age groups for different purposes. However, there remains an ongoing debate on whether CALTs sacrifice construct representation to improve measurement efficiency. Technological progress, including the implementation of robust security algorithms in CATs and CALTs, has facilitated the adoption of at-home, high-stakes testing. This trend has notably improved accessibility for test takers in challenging environments or with disabilities. These developments align with the increasing societal focus on issues related to access, equity, and fairness.

CALTs increasingly incorporate complex texts and integrated task types that better represent the target language use domain and enhance test takers' engagement and overall experience. There is a disconnect, however, between the unidimensional assumption of the construct in IRT and how the broader field of applied linguistics views this construct, which is often multidimensional. Balancing the demand for a single, monolingual score to meet the needs of traditional test score users, such as admissions officers and policymakers, with the prevalent understanding that language use is multifaceted and often multilingual, poses another challenge. The automated scoring of productive skills, particularly speaking, remains a concern with CALTs. Future research and development in CALTs should focus on bridging the gap between the requirements of test user groups and the insights from applied linguistics.

Discussion Questions

1. What are some of the challenges specific to developing and administering computer-adaptive language tests?

2. In which contexts do you think the advantages of computer-adaptive language tests outweigh the disadvantages?

References

ACTFL. (2023). *L&RCAT: Computer adaptive listening & reading test.* https://www.actfl.org/assessments/postsecondary-assessments/l-rcat.

Attali, Y., Runge, A., LaFlair, G. T., Yancey, K., Goodwin, S., Park, Y., & von Davier, A. (2022). The interactive reading task: Transformer-based automatic item generation. *Frontiers in Artificial Intelligence, 5,* https://doi.org/10.3389/frai.2022.903077.

Avant. (2023). *Avant: Language assessment and professional learning solutions.* Avant Assessment. https://avantassessment.com/.

Aviad-Levitzky, T., Laufer, B., & Goldstein, Z. (2019). The new computer adaptive test of size and strength (CATSS): Development and validation. *Language Assessment Quarterly, 16*(3), 345–368. https://doi.org/10.1080/15434303.2019.1649409.

Bachman, L. F., & Damböck, B. (2018). *Language assessment for classroom teachers.* Oxford University Press.

Bachman, L. F., & Palmer, A. S. (1996). *Language testing in practice: Designing and developing useful language tests* (Vol. 1). Oxford University Press.

Bachman, L. F., & Palmer, A. S. (2010). *Language assessment in practice: Developing language assessments and justifying their use in the real world.* Oxford University Press.

Barkaoui, K. (2014). Examining the impact of L2 proficiency and keyboarding skills on scores on TOEFL-iBT writing tasks. *Language Testing, 31*(2), 241–259. https://doi.org/10.1177/0265532213509810.

Bennett, R. E. (2000). *Reinventing assessment: Speculations on the future of large-scale educational testing.* ETS.

Bunderson, C. V., Inouye, D. K., & Olson, J. B. (1989). The four generations of computerized educational measurement. In R. L. Linn (Ed.), *Educational measurement* (pp. 367–407). American Council on Education.

Chalhoub-Deville, M. (Ed.). (1999). *Issues in computer-adaptive testing of reading proficiency.* Cambridge University Press.

Chalhoub-Deville, M., & Deville, C. (1999). Computer adaptive testing in second language contexts. *Annual Review of Applied Linguistics, 19,* 273–299. https://doi.org/10.1017/S0267190599190147.

Chapelle, C. A. (2006). DIALANG: A diagnostic language test in 14 European languages. *Language Testing, 23*(4), 544–550. https://doi.org/10.1191/0265532206lt341xx.

Council of Europe. (2001). *Common European framework of reference for languages: Learning, teaching, assessment.* Press Syndicate of the University of Cambridge.

Dunkel, P. A. (1999). Research and development of a computer-adaptive test of listening comprehension in the less-commonly taught language Hausa. In M. Chalhoub-Deville (Ed.), *Issues in computer-adaptive testing of reading proficiency* (pp. 91–121). University of Cambridge Local Examinations Syndicate.

ETS. (2023). *April 1 TOEFL Paper Edition.* ETS India. https://www.etsindia.org/toefl-paper-edition/.

Goethe-Institut. (2023). *Goethe-Test PRO.* Swiss Exams. https://goethe-pruefungen.swiss-exams.ch/exams-and-certifications/goethe/exams/levels/young-people/goethe-test-pro.

He, L., & Min, S. (2017). Development and validation of a computer adaptive EFL test. *Language Assessment Quarterly, 14*(2), 160–176. https://doi.org/10.1080/15434303.2016.1162793.

Imai, S., Ito, S., Nakamura, Y., Kikuchi, K., Akagi, Y., Nakasono, H., Honda, A., & Hiramura, T. (2009). Features of J-CAT (Japanese computerized adaptive test). In D. J. Weiss (Ed.), *Proceedings of the 2009 GMAC conference on computerized adaptive testing* (pp. 1–8). Graduate Management Admission Council.

International Telecommunication Union. (2019). *November 5. New ITU data reveal growing Internet uptake but a widening digital gender divide [Press release].* https://www.itu.int/en/mediacentre/Pages/2019-PR19.aspx.

Jamieson, J., Taylor, C., Kirsch, I., & Eignor, D. (1998). Design and evaluation of a computer-based TOEFL tutorial. *System, 26*(4), 485–513. https://doi.org/10.1016/S0346-251X(98)00034-7

Kirsch, I., Jamieson, J., Taylor, C., & Eignor, D. (1998). *Computer familiarity among TOEFL examinees. TOEFL Research Report No. 59.* Educational Testing Service.

LaFlair, G. T., Langenfeld, T., Baig, B., Horie, A. K., Attali, Y., & von Davier, A. A. (2022). Digital-first assessments: A security framework. Journal of Computer Assisted Learning, 38(4), 1077–1086. https://doi.org/10.1111/jcal.12665

References 659

Langenfeld, T., Burstein, J., & von Davier, A. A. (2022). Digital-first learning and assessment systems for the 21st century. *Frontiers in Education, 7*, 857604. https://doi.org/10.3389/feduc.2022.857604.

Larson, J. W. (1989). S-CAPE: A Spanish computerized adaptive placement exam. In *In W. F. Smith (Ed.) Modern technology in foreign language education: Applications and projects* (pp. 277–289). National Textbook Co.

Laurier, M. (1999). The development of an adaptive test for placement in French. In M. Chalhoub-Deville (Ed.), *Issues in computer-adaptive testing of reading proficiency* (pp. 122–135). University of Cambridge Local Examinations Syndicate.

Malabonga, V. A., & Kenyon, D. M. (1999). *Multimedia computer technology and performance-based language testing: A demonstration of the Computerized Oral Proficiency Instrument (COPI).* In *Proceedings of a Symposium on Computer Mediated Language Assessment and Evaluation in Natural Language Processing.* Association for Computational Linguistics. https://aclanthology.org/W99-0404

Mead, A. D., & Drasgow, F. (1993). Equivalence of computerized and paper-and-pencil cognitive ability tests: A meta-analysis. *Psychological Bulletin, 114*, 449–458. https://doi.org/10.1037/0033-2909.114.3.449.

Min, S., & Aryadoust, V. (2021). A systematic review of item response theory in language assessment: Implications for the dimensionality of language ability. *Studies in Educational Evaluation, 68*, 100963. https://doi.org/10.1016/j.stueduc.2020.100963.

Naismith, B., Mulcaire, P., & Burstein, J. (2023). Automated evaluation of written discourse coherence using GPT-4. In E. Kochma et al. (Eds.), *Proceedings of the 18th Workshop on Innovative Use of NLP for Building Educational Applications (BEA 2023)* (pp. 394–403). Association for Computational Linguistics. https://doi.org/10.18653/v1/2023.bea-1.32.

Nandakumar, R., & Stout, W. (1993). Refinements of Stout's procedure for assessing latent trait unidimensionality. *Journal of Educational Statistics, 18*(1), 41–68. https://doi.org/10.2307/1165182.

Nogami, Y., & Hayashi, N. (2010). A Japanese adaptive test of English as a foreign language: Developmental and operational aspects. In W. J. van der Linden & C. A. W. Glas (Eds.), *Elements of adaptive testing* (pp. 191–211). Springer New York. https://doi.org/10.1007/978-0-387-85461-8_10.

Ortner, T. M., & Caspers, J. (2011). Consequences of test anxiety on adaptive versus fixed item testing. *European Journal of Psychological Assessment, 27*(3), 157–163. https://doi.org/10.1027/1015-5759/a000062.

OSU. (2023). *Language placement testing.* https://cllc.osu.edu/undergraduate/testing.

Oxford University Press. (2023). *Oxford placement test for young learners.* https://elt.oup.com/feature/global/young-learners-placement/.

Pearson. (2019). *VersantTM English test: Test description and validation summary.* https://www.pearson.com/content/dam/one-dot-com/one-dot-com/english/SupportingDocs/Versant/ValidationSummary/Versant-English-Test-Description-Validation-Report.pdf.

Read, J. (2022). Test review: The International English Language Testing System (IELTS). *Language Testing, 39*(4), 679–694. https://doi.org/10.1177/02655322221086211.

Sawaki, Y. (2001). Comparability of conventional and computerized tests of reading in a second language. *Language Learning and Technology, 5*, 38–59. https://doi.org/10125/25127.

Sawaki, Y. (2021). Computer-based testing. In G. Fulcher & L. Harding (Eds.), *The Routledge handbook of language testing* (2nd ed., pp. 530–544). Routledge. https://doi.org/10.4324/9781003220756.

Starr-Egger, F. (2001). German computer adaptive language tests – Better late than never. *German as a Foreign Language, 3*, 12–30.

Stevenson, J. W., & Gross, S. (1991). Use of computerized adaptive testing model for ESOL/bilingual entry/exit decision making. In P. A. Dunkel (Ed.), *Computer-assisted language learning and testing: Research issues and practice* (pp. 237–257). Newbury House.

Taiwan Mandarin Educational Resources Center. (2020). *The Test of Chinese as a Foreign Language.* TOCFL. https://lmit.edu.tw/lc/tocfl.

Taylor C., Jamieson, J., Eignor, D., & Kirsch, I. (1998). *The relationship between computer familiarity and performance on computer-based TOEFL test tasks. TOEFL Research Report No. 61.* Educational Testing Service.

Vispoel, W. P. (1993). Computerized adaptive and fixed-item versions of the ITED vocabulary subtest. *Educational and Psychological Measurement, 53*(3), 779–788. https://doi.org/10.1177/0013164493053003022.

Wang, X., & Evanini, K. (2020). Features measuring content and discourse coherence. In K. Zechner & K. Evanini (Eds.), *Automated speaking assessment: Using language technologies to score spontaneous speech* (pp. 138–156). Routledge.

Zechner, K., & Evanini, K. (Eds.). (2020). *Automated speaking assessment: Using language technologies to score spontaneous speech*. Routledge.

Suggested Readings

Chalhoub-Deville, M., & Deville, C. (1999). Computer adaptive testing in second language contexts. *Annual Review of Applied Linguistics, 19*, 273–299. https://doi.org/10.1017/S0267190599190147.

He, L., & Min, S. (2017). Development and validation of a computer adaptive EFL test. *Language Assessment Quarterly, 14*(2), 160–176. https://doi.org/10.1080/15434303.2016.1162793.

Min, S., & Aryadoust, V. (2021). A systematic review of item response theory in language assessment: implications for the dimensionality of language ability. *Studies in Educational Evaluation, 68*, 100963. https://doi.org/10.1016/j.stueduc.2020.100963.

CHAPTER 44

Automated Writing Evaluation

Jill Burstein and Yigal Attali

Introduction

Automated writing evaluation (AWE) is a field of research, as well as a technology used to evaluate the quality of written text in educational settings (such as, assessment and instruction). AWE is a cross-disciplinary field. For instance, it draws expertise from computational linguistics to identify methods for automatically extracting linguistic information, from educational measurement to examine performance and validity, and from writing studies to inform the relevant constructs that need to be measured. While this chapter provides an overview of AWE for assessment and instruction, it also provides a discussion about how natural language processing (NLP) methods have been used for AWE to automatically identify linguistic characteristics in text-based writing samples (e.g., automated grammatical error detection) to evaluate writing quality for assessment and instruction (Shermis & Burstein, 2002, 2013; Shermis & Wilson, 2024; Yan et al., 2020). For illustration, the chapter discusses AWE use cases for high-stakes writing assessment, writing instruction applications, and broader academic writing research. The chapter also provides a discussion about the impact of generative AI (GenAI) such as OpenAI's ChatGPT (OpenAI, 2023; Radford et al., 2019).

Page (1966) first discussed an automated essay scoring capability, Project Essay Grade (PEG), as a solution to relieve English teachers from the burden of grading writing assignments. Page's early method relied heavily on a word count measure (i.e., the fourth root of essay word count). While word count is not substantively aligned with well-accepted writing construct features (such as grammatical accuracy, vocabulary choice, and organization), it has been shown in AWE research to be strongly correlated with writing quality for *expository essay writing tasks* (such as standardized writing assessment tasks (Chodorow & Burstein, 2004).

Page's early efforts were visionary. His work was a catalyst for later, more sophisticated, construct-rich AWE systems for large-scale writing assessments that revolutionized the testing industry. Approximately 30 years after Page's PEG system, Educational Testing Service's (ETS) e-rater scoring engine was the first to score constructed-response writing responses on a high-stakes assessment – the Graduate Management Admissions Test (GMAT). Later, e-rater was used for scoring the writing assessment responses on the Test of English as a Foreign Language (TOEFL) and the Graduate Record Exam (GRE; Attali & Burstein, 2006). Millions of test-taker responses are now scored by AWE systems for high-stakes assessments—including English language proficiency tests, such as the Duolingo English Test (DET; Settles et al., 2020), ETS's TOEFL (Attali & Burstein, 2006), the Pearson Test of English (PTE; Foltz et al., 1998), and state assessments in the US (Lottridge, in press).

While AWE began as a scoring technology, the education community soon realized its greater potential to provide diagnostic feedback to learners above and beyond grammar error

The Concise Companion to Language Assessment, First Edition. Edited by Antony John Kunnan.
© 2025 John Wiley & Sons, Inc. Published 2025 by John Wiley & Sons, Inc.

662 **Chapter 44** Automated Writing Evaluation

detection/correction and word usage feedback provided by commercial applications, such as Grammarly.[1] Examples of earlier AWE feedback systems designed to assist developing writers include ETS's *Criterion* online essay evaluation system[2] (Burstein et al., 2003), Writing Mentor (Burstein et al., 2018), Saavas' revision assistant,[3] Vantage Learning's MyAccess,[4] and MI Write[5] (Palermo & Thomson, 2018). More recently, Grammarly has become a widely-used writing feedback application adopted by institutional stakeholders in K-12 and higher education settings (Alikaniotis & Raheja, 2019).

The remainder of the chapter provides an overview of current NLP methods used in automated scoring and feedback systems and offers examples for illustration. For more detailed information, refer to research publications written about individual systems (e.g., Shermis & Wilson, 2024; Shermis & Burstein, 2002, 2013). The chapter also discusses how AWE capabilities have been used for writing analytics research to examine relationships between writing features as captured by AWE and broader academic outcomes.

Automated Writing Evaluation Use Cases

AWE systems have been commonly used for *scoring* and *feedback*. The impact of AWE systems is seen in the large-scale, operational scoring of high-stakes writing assessments (such as the TOEFL and the DET), and U.S. state writing assessments that provide information about K-12 students' academic writing performance. Detailed descriptions are available for major systems, including ETS's e-rater, Intelligent Essay Assessor, Vantage's IntelliMetric, Measurement Inc.'s PEG (see Shermis & Burstein, 2003, 2013), and Cambium's automated essay scoring system (Lottridge, in press). In the context of instruction, applications provide corrective or stylistic feedback (such as grammar error detection and organization suggestions, respectively). These systems are primarily designed for developing student writers in the U.S. K-12 education. The writing feedback space is quite large and dynamic. Some applications have been available for a number of years, such as ETS's *Criterion* online essay evaluation system (Burstein et al., 2004), Vantage's MyAccess,[6] Measurement Inc.'s MI Write (Palermo & Thomson, 2018), and Writing Pal[7] (Roscoe & McNamara, 2013).

AWE Scoring and Feedback

Natural language processing is the computational analysis of language applied to written text. While the scope of this chapter is writing evaluation, it is important to note that NLP methods can be applied to a spoken response once it has been converted to text through automated speech recognition. This section provides a brief overview of NLP methods commonly used to build AWE systems used in real-world, operational contexts (such as high-stakes writing assessments). AWE methods discussed represent state-of-the-art NLP methods at the time this chapter was written. Yaneva and von Davier (2023) include discussions of advances in NLP across different assessment contexts. A broader and more in-depth discussion of NLP may be found in Jurafsky and Martin (2023)[8] – a well-recognized, online, open-access book.

---

[1] See https://www.grammarly.com/.
[2] See https://www.ets.org/criterion.html.
[3] See https://www.turnitin.com/products/revision-assistant.
[4] See https://about.myaccess.com/#toggle-writing-stats.
[5] See https://www.measurementinc.com/miwrite.
[6] See https://about.myaccess.com/#toggle-interactive-writing-tools.
[7] See http://www.adaptiveliteracy.com/writing-pal.
[8] See https://web.stanford.edu/~jurafsky/slp3/.

Currently, AWE feedback applications largely use rule-based and statistical NLP. In rule-based NLP applications, human experts (such as computer scientists or computational linguists) write code that implements linguistic rules (such as part-of-speech sequences) and lexical resources (e.g., word lists composed of transition words). These rules and lexical resources tend to be highly accurate at identifying linguistic structures and words, respectively. However, they have lower coverage, meaning that they will not cover the breadth of linguistic structures and vocabulary possible in writing. For example, if a dictionary of transition words is created, it is likely to cover only a subset of examples that writers use to make transitions across sentences and paragraphs. An example of statistical NLP is latent semantic analysis (LSA; Landauer et al., 1998). This is an unsupervised method and does not use labeled data, unlike supervised machine learning methods that require human labeling. Instead, LSA requires thousands of documents to model document similarity. LSA uses information from the documents to show relationships between terms. For instance, it will show that documents containing the term "doctor" are more likely to also contain the term "nurse." This method is used in automated essay scoring to identify essays that appear similar in terms of their level of quality (i.e., score; Foltz et al., 1998). Large language models (LLMs) are also statistically based, built by modeling word sequences from terabytes of data. For instance, GPT-3 is built using 45 terabytes of text data.[9] These GenAI models are designed to predict language sequences (e.g., what is the next word likely to be in a text). This is why they work well for automated text generation. With regard to AWE, these models can also be used for grammatical error correction (Alikaniotis & Raheja, 2019).

Operational AWE systems (i.e., real-life learning and assessment systems) score learner or test-taker writing proficiency or provide feedback in instructional contexts. For both scoring and feedback, AWE systems use NLP methods to identify and extract linguistic characteristics (i.e., *features*) relevant to writing subconstructs. Typically, these features reflect human scoring rubric criteria, which has been the gold standard for evaluating learner and test-taker writing. The scoring rubric criteria illustrate what is important to measure in learner and test-taker writing (such as essays on high-stakes writing assessments). Subconstructs may include, but are not limited to, grammatical accuracy (Leacock et al., 2010); use of mechanics (e.g., punctuation and spelling); appropriateness of vocabulary choice (Attali & Burstein, 2006); organization and development (Burstein et al., 2003); discourse coherence (Somasundaran et al., 2014); use of sources (Beigman Klebanov et al., 2014); topic coherence and relevance (Burstein et al., 2018; Foltz et al., 1998, 1999); and process data (e.g., keystroke logs; Sinharay et al., 2019).

The most common use of automated scoring is for summative writing assessment (Attali & Burstein, 2006; Settles et al., 2020; Shermis & Burstein, 2002, 2013; Shermis & Wilson, 2024) and writing instruction support (Burstein et al., 2004; Woods et al., 2017). To generate scores, statistical models are built using learner or test-taker writing response data that is representative of a population (such as from L2 English learners for English language proficiency tests). The sample is commonly referred to as *training data* and is typically scored by human raters using human-created rubric criteria. These rubric criteria are often *holistic*, meaning that the rater provides a score based on the overall quality of the writing considering features, such as grammatical accuracy, vocabulary choice, coherence, organization, and topic relevance. This is in contrast to a specific *trait* scoring where raters assign scores based on a specific trait (such as grammatical accuracy). Ideally, the training dataset should represent the target population (such as a sample across different L1 subgroups) and include a distribution of responses across the score range.

AWE scoring models can be built to perform holistic or trait scoring. To train the model, the relevant features are extracted from the training data. For example, let's say that for an essay from a high-stakes writing assessment that the testing organization defines writing quality based on grammatical and spelling accuracy, appropriateness of vocabulary choice, discourse

---

[9] Note that 1 terabyte equals 1000 gigabytes.

664   Chapter 44 Automated Writing Evaluation

coherence quality, and topical relevance. To perform the feature extraction, NLP methods are used to identify grammatical and spelling errors (Alikaniotis & Raheja, 2019; Leacock et al., 2010), sophistication of vocabulary choice (Attali & Burstein, 2006), discourse coherence (Burstein et al., 2013; Graesser et al., 2004), and topic relevance (Foltz et al., 1998). The features are converted to values that can be used for model building. For instance, the number of grammatical errors may be converted to a normalized error count (such as a log value), the measure of vocabulary choice might be converted into a value based on word frequency, the discourse coherence feature may be a normalized value of the transition terms, and the topic relevance may be a value based on a statistical model, such as latent semantic analysis, which serves as a proxy for topic relevance (Foltz et al., 1998).

A common method for building statistical AWE scoring models is linear regression. Using this example, each writing sample (essay) in the training data is converted into a vector (row) of values that represents each of the relevant features listed above. The vectors of numerical feature values are used as input to the linear regression. The regression model outputs weights for each of the features. The model is evaluated to determine how well it can predict new, unseen data. A common metric for determining model fit is the R-squared (R^2) value that explains how well the model features explain the variance in the data. In addition, a test dataset is created that contains a data sample similar in composition to the training data. The statistical scoring model is evaluated on the test set to see how well the model generalizes to the new, unseen test data. Model performance is typically evaluated by comparing human rater scores assigned to the test set and examining agreement between human raters and the system scores. Common metrics used to evaluate agreement are the percentage of exact and adjacent agreement, Pearson correlations, and quadratic weighted kappa (Bridgeman, 2013).

In contrast to AWE for summative high-stakes writing assessment, a number of AWE feedback applications have been designed for classroom use and support *formative* assessment for developing writers – most commonly in U.S. K-12 and early higher education settings. Early applications of AWE feedback appeared in Writer's Workbench (Cherry, 1982), and in word processing packages, such as early versions of Microsoft Word's grammar error detection feedback from the early 1990s. The growth of AWE writing instructional applications seemed to follow advances in AWE for automated scoring and its use in large-scale, high-stakes assessments.

Classroom writing instruction systems have leveraged advances in NLP methods to generate qualitative, diagnostic feedback. Similar to scoring, the feedback was informed by subconstructs relevant to writing quality, including grammatical accuracy, vocabulary choice, coherence, organization, and topic relevance. Grammarly is an AWE-driven application that delivers explicit writing feedback in educational settings; the application uses NLP to generate feedback related to grammatical accuracy, word choice, and citation use. As mentioned earlier, examples of well-known AWE-driven writing feedback applications designed specifically for classroom use include ETS's *Criterion®*, Measurement Inc.'s *MI Write*, and Vantage Learning's *MyAccess*. These applications aim to support best practices in the teaching of writing. They provide immediate feedback to support learners in the full writing process: planning, drafting, and revising based on feedback. These applications use AWE to provide scores (*holistic* and *trait* scores) for learner drafts and final submissions; in addition, they provide specific feedback, similar to an instructor "marking up" a paper. The most common feedback across the different applications is identification of errors in grammar, spelling, and writing mechanics (e.g., capitalization and punctuation). Other types of AWE-based qualitative feedback provided by these applications include explicit system comments related to aspects of organization (e.g., thesis statement identification), and appropriate vocabulary choice (e.g., "their" versus "there"). More varied and advanced AWE feedback can be seen in research feedback systems in addition to standard grammar error and word usage features. For example, *Writing Mentor* (Burstein et al., 2018) includes feedback related to topic development, text coherence, and argumentation, and *ArgRewrite* (Litman et al., 2022) provides feedback about the nature of writing revisions (i.e., surface or content-based revision).

Automated Writing Evaluation Use Cases **665**

In contrast to system performance for summative scoring uses of AWE, feedback research methods and metrics are much more varied. Much of the system usage happens in the class-room context, and it is difficult to access school-based data at the same scale as summative assessment data, which test providers have access to. However, there is a significant body of research that examines AWE feedback efficacy (Cassidy et al., 2016; Foltz & Rosenstein, 2017; Wilson & Czik, 2016), and specifically for L2 English learners (e.g., Dikli & Bleyle, 2014; Li et al., 2015; Ranalli, 2018, 2021; Stevenson & Phakiti, 2014).

Writing Analytics Research

Writing analytics research emerged as a new opportunity to use fine-grained AWE features to examine relationships between writing skill and broader outcomes (e.g., Allen et al., 2016; Arthurs, 2018; Burstein et al., 2017; McCaffrey et al., 2023). This section provides an overview of a few writing analytics studies.

Allen et al. (2016) investigated how linguistic properties in students' writing could be used to model individual differences in postsecondary students' vocabulary knowledge and reading comprehension skills. For argumentative essays in response to a standardized test prompt, AWE features were computed using an automated text analysis tool that computes linguistic and rhetorical text indices. Allen et al. (2016) tested the relationship between AWE feature scores and Gates-MacGinitie Vocabulary and Reading Comprehension tests for the students. They found that a subset of AWE features accounted for vocabulary and the reading compre-hension scores. The study has implications for how linguistic features in student writing can provide information about broader skill sets.

Burstein et al. (2017) conducted an exploratory, secondary data analysis with students enrolled at U.S. 4-year institutions to examine relationships between student writing charac-teristics and grade-point average (GPA). Students completed a standardized essay writing assessment, and AWE features were extracted from students' writing responses. Regression analyses suggested that AWE features, such as grammatical accuracy, sophisticated word usage, use of argumentative vocabulary, and topic development were found to be predictors of GPA. Burstein et al. (2017) also found relationships between AWE features in students' writing samples and success predictors, including test scores from standardized reading, math, and science assessments (i.e., SAT and ACT).

Arthurs (2018) conducted a writing analytics study using a dataset containing 15,000 argu-mentative and personal writing samples from Stanford University undergraduate students from humanities, social science, and STEM disciplines. The writing was produced across students' four years of college. AWE features were extracted from the student writing representing topic-based features, stance-based features associated with argument framing, and sentence complexity features. Based on the features examined, findings suggested that students' writing developed primarily in their first two years and developed differently in the different disciplines.

McCaffrey et al. (2023) studied relationships between AWE features in student writing and college retention. AWE features were extracted from a standardized essay writing assessment and coursework writing data for students enrolled in U.S. universities. Findings from this exploratory writing analytics study had implications for using AWE for retention analytics to identify students at risk of dropping out. Using a Cox proportional hazards regression (Cox & Oakes, 1984), the study findings suggested that AWE vocabulary features were associated with students' risk of dropping out. Specifically, increased use of more sophisticated vocabulary on the standardized writing assessment was associated with a lower risk of dropout. Further, increased use of vocabulary associated with personal reflection (such as, singular first-person pronoun "I") in either coursework or the standardized writing assessment was associated with a higher risk of dropout.

Validity and Reliability

The validity of test scores can be defined as the degree to which evidence and theory support the interpretation of the scores (American Educational Research Association et al., 2014). With AWE, the validation process is established with the meaning of individual features and relating features to writing skills. A key aspect in determining the meaning of a feature is its interpretability. This refers to the logical connection between the feature and the linguistic characteristic it represents. Some features, such as grammar or fluency, are easily understood. Others, while representing a relevant construct, such as discourse coherence, are based on numerous signals and have only a predictive relationship to human scores. Establishing the meaning of a feature can be informed by linguistic and cognitive research in various areas, such as second language development (see Wolf-Quintero et al., 1998) or readability (see Shee-han et al., 2010). By drawing from these sources, AWE can develop theories on writing quality and how feature variations influence essay quality.

Establishing the meaning of features can also benefit from empirical analyses of their relation with human scores and with other features. In particular, through factor analysis methods, the patterns of correlations between features could provide additional support for their interpretation as measures of particular dimensions of writing quality (Attali, 2007, 2012). For example, in the context of the e-rater system, Attali (2012) found empirical support for four factors: word choice, grammatical conventions within a sentence, development and organization, and content. Such results strengthen the validity argument of AWE by further clarifying what individual features measure and how related features can be interpreted as measures of writing constructs.

The consistency of measurement of individual features also influences feature validity because consistency determines how well we can generalize from one measurement opportunity to another. The empirical evidence for generalizing over repeated measurement procedures is the focus of reliability studies (Haertel, 2006). Attali and Burstein (2006) report *test–retest* reliability of individual features, and the relation between feature values computed from multiple essays written by the same students. With features that are computed within individual sentences, it is possible to estimate *internal consistency* reliability by computing the relation between feature values in odd versus even sentences.

As discussed earlier in this chapter, individual feature scores are normally aggregated into AWE scores, usually as a weighted average of feature scores. The weights represent the relative importance of the different features, and surely different weighting schemes will result in AWE scores that have different meanings. An advantage of AWE over human scoring is that it is possible to adopt different approaches for aggregating features (Bennett & Bejar, 1998), thereby controlling (to some degree) what Embretson (1983) calls "construct representation," meaning scores based on internal evidence, and "nomothetic span," meaning scores based on relationships with external variables.

The most common weighting scheme for AWE has been based on optimizing the relation of the AWE score with human scores of the same essays. Clearly, the rationale for human prediction weighting is to imitate human scores with the assumption that human scores are the gold standard. However, alternative feature weighting schemes have been suggested. One such scheme is based on the premise of maximizing reliability and internal consistency of the AWE scores (see Attali, 2015).

Many studies (as early as Page, 1966) have compared AWE scores with human scores (for a review, see Attali, 2013). The relationship between two human ratings of the same response is often as high as that of AWE scores with human scores. However, the test–retest reliability (i.e., correlations across two responses) of human scores is considerably lower than AWE scores. With respect to other subscores of the same general ability test (such as reading, speaking, and listening for TOEFL and verbal scores for GRE), AWE scores show similar correlations as human scores. Note, however, that AWE scores can be manipulated by changing the weights of features. Attali (2015) found that reliability-based feature weights give rise to comparable or even superior reliability and validity coefficients, even though they do not optimize the relation with any external scores.

Future Directions

AWE evolved in parallel with advances in NLP. The first automated essay scoring system, reported in Page (1966), was driven by a normalized word count measure. Advances in NLP supported a wider range of AWE features, which afforded greater construct coverage (Attali & Burstein, 2006; Burstein et al., 1998; Foltz et al., 1998; Shermis & Burstein, 2003, 2013). AWE's widespread use for large-scale, high-stakes assessments and classroom writing instruction was possible due to advances in computing infrastructure that allowed fast and efficient processing of vast amounts of data and web-based applications that supported broad access to classroom applications. AWE use cases also expanded beyond scoring and feedback to writing analytics, offering new research opportunities to examine relationships between writing and broader outcomes. Insights from writing analytics research could inform best practices for learning and assessment.

In 2022, GenAI models disrupted education with the ChatGPT application that was available to anyone with a computer. Applications that leveraged GenAI models became a game changer in writing instruction. Given text "seeds," these models could generate text that looks similar to human writing. Students could use ChatGPT to complete tasks associated with the writing process, from generating outlines and ideas to essay writing. This set off alarms in terms of the greater potential of plagiarism and bad-faith writing responses (Cahill et al., 2018; Higgins et al., 2006). Widespread availability of ChatGPT sparked novel research, such as examining how to computationally distinguish between human and writing produced from GenAI models (Tian, 2023). While technology misuse is a reality, there is a flip side with regard to the use of GenAI for AWE. Specifically, it can be leveraged as support in writing instruction. For instance, writing instruction activities can use this technology to help learners with idea generation. Further, the technology can be leveraged to generate automated scaffolding (such as feedback) for interactive writing assessment tasks, especially in the context of practice.

As a result of the emergence of GenAI, stakeholder communities are developing new research agendas for digital learning and assessment. New research questions should examine the impact of GenAI on AWE as it pertains to assessment, writing feedback, and writing analytics. With regard to assessment, research questions should address cheating behaviors. For example, do we need AWE methods that help us distinguish between human or machine-generated text in learning and assessment contexts? In high-stakes digital assessment, GenAI models are already being used to generate writing items on the DET (Attali et al., 2022). The benefit is the ability to efficiently produce large item banks that mitigate item exposure and cheating behaviors; might this limit test takers' ability to memorize leaked assessment questions that they are likely to encounter on the actual test, and encourage them to improve their writing skills? Further, as item banks grow, will GenAI models produce writing prompts on a wider range of topics, and if so, how might this impact AWE scoring performance? With regard to AWE for scoring, studies are already examining accuracy of GenAI models for automated essay scoring (Mizumoto & Eguchi, 2023). Advances in AI, and GenAI in particular, impact AWE. As with early AWE, education stakeholders across many fields will need to ensure that new applications to AWE are responsibly applied.

Discussion Questions

1. What novel automated writing evaluation research in language assessment might we see as a result of generative AI?

2. What should the language assessment community be thinking about with regard to responsible use of AI, especially for automated writing evaluation on high-stakes language assessment?

668 Chapter 44 Automated Writing Evaluation

References

Alikaniotis, D., & Raheja, V. (2019). The unreasonable effectiveness of transformer language models in grammatical error correction. In *Proceedings of the Fourteenth Workshop on Innovative Use of NLP for Building Educational Applications* (pp. 127–133). Florence, Italy: Association for Computational Linguistics.

Allen, L., Dascalu, M., McNamara, D. S., Crossley, S., & Trausan-Matu, S. (2016). Modeling individual differences among writers using Reader Bench. In *EDULEARN16 Proceedings* (pp. 5269–5279). IATED. https://doi.org/10.21125/edulearn.2016.2241.

American Educational Research Association, American Psychological Association, & National Council on Measurement in Education (Eds.). (2014). *Standards for educational and psychological testing.* American Educational Research Association.

Arthurs, N. (2018). Structural features of undergraduate writing: a computational approach. *Journal of Writing Analytics, 2,* 138–175. https://doi.org/10.37514/JWA-J.2018.2.1.06.

Attali, Y. (2007). *Construct validity of e-rater in scoring TOEFL essays.* Educational Testing Service. https://doi.org/10.1002/j.2333-8504.2007.tb02063.x.

Attali, Y. (2012). *April 14–16. Factor structure of the e-rater automated essay scoring system. [Paper presentation] National Council of Measurement in Education: 2012 annual meeting, Vancouver, BC, Canada.*

Attali, Y. (2013). Validity and reliability of automated essay scoring. In M. D. Shermis & J. Burstein (Eds.), *Handbook of automated essay evaluation* (pp. 181–198). Routledge.

Attali, Y. (2015). Reliability-based feature weighting for automated essay scoring. *Applied Psychological Measurement, 39*(4), 303–313. https://doi.org/10.1177/0146621614561630.

Attali, Y., & Burstein, J. (2006). Automated essay scoring with e-rater® V. 2. *The Journal of Technology, Learning, and Assessment, 4*(3).

Attali, Y., Runge, A., LaFlair, G. T., Yancey, K., Goodwin, S., Park, Y., & von Davier, A. A. (2022). The interactive reading task: transformer-based automatic item generation. *Frontiers in Artificial Intelligence, 5.* https://doi.org/10.3389/frai.2022.903077.

Beigman Klebanov, B., Madnani, N., Burstein, J., & Somasundaran, S. (2014). Content importance models for scoring writing from sources. In *Proceedings of the 52nd annual meeting of the association for computational linguistics: Vol 2. Short papers* (pp. 247–252). Association for Computational Linguistics. https://doi.org/10.3115/v1/P14-2041.

Bennett, R. E., & Bejar, I. I. (1998). Validity and automated scoring: it's not only the scoring. *Educational Measurement: Issues and Practice, 17*(4), 9–16. https://doi.org/10.1111/j.1745-3992.1998.tb00631.x.

Bridgeman, B. (2013). Human ratings and automated essay evaluation. In M. D. Shermis & J. Burstein (Eds.), *Handbook of automated essay evaluation* (pp. 243–254). Routledge. https://doi.org/10.4324/9780203122761.

Burstein, J., Kukich, K., Wolff, S., Lu, C., Chodorow, M., Braden-Harder, L., & Harris, M. D. (1998). Automated scoring using a hybrid feature identification technique. In *36th annual meeting of the Association for Computational Linguistics and 17th international conference on computational linguistics: Vol. 1* (pp. 206–210). Association for Computational Linguistics. https://doi.org/10.3115/980845.980879.

Burstein, J., Marcu, D., & Knight, K. (2003). Finding the WRITE stuff: automatic identification of discourse structure in student essays. *IEEE Intelligent Systems, 18*(1), 32–39. https://doi.org/10.1109/MIS.2003.1179191.

Burstein, J., Chodorow, M., & Leacock, C. (2004). Automated essay evaluation: the Criterion online writing service. *AI Magazine, 25*(3), 27–36. https://doi.org/10.1609/aimag.v25i3.1774.

Burstein, J., Tetreault, J., Chodorow, M., Blanchard, D., & Andreyev, S. (2013). Automated evaluation of discourse coherence quality in essay writing. In M. D. Shermis & J. Burstein (Eds.), *Handbook of automated essay evaluation: Current applications and new directions* (pp. 267–280). Routledge. https://doi.org/10.4324/9780203122761.

Burstein, J., McCaffrey, D., Beigman Klebanov, B., & Ling, G. (2017). Exploring Relationships between Writing and Broader Outcomes with Automated Writing Evaluation. In *Proceeding of the 12th Workshop on Innovative Use of NLP for Building Educational Applications (BEA), EMNLP 2017, Copenhagen, Denmark.*

Burstein, J., Elliot, N., Beigman Klebanov, B., Madnani, N., Napolitano, D., Schwartz, M., Houghton, P., & Molloy, H. (2018). Writing mentor: writing progress using self-regulated writing support. In *Journal of writing analytics: Vol. 2. Methodological and conceptual developments* (pp. 285–313). WAC Clearinghouse. https://doi.org/10.37514/JWA-J.2018.2.1.12.

References   **669**

Cahill, A., Chodorow, M., & Flor, M. (2018). Developing an e-rater advisory to detect Babel-generated essays. *Journal of Writing Analytics, 2*, 203–224. https://doi.org/10.37514/JWA-J.2018.2.1.08.

Cassidy, L., Yee, K., Schmidt, R., Vasquez, S., Means, B., & Krumm, A. (2016). *Classroom trials: A study of instruction with writing software.* SRI Education. https://www.sri.com/wp-content/uploads/2021/12/classroom-trials_jan_29_2016_1.pdf.

Cherry, L. (1982). Writing tools. *IEEE Transactions on Communications, 30*(1), 100–105. https://doi.org/10.1109/TCOM.1982.1095396.

Chodorow, M., & Burstein, J. (2004). Beyond essay length: Evaluating e-rater®'s performance on TOEFL® essays. *ETS Research Report Series, 2004*(1), i–38.

Cox, D. R., & Oakes, D. (1984). *Analysis of survival data.* Chapman & Hall; CRC Press.

Dikli, S., & Bleyle, S. (2014). Automated essay scoring feedback for second language writers: how does it compare to instructor feedback? *Assessing Writing, 22*, 1–17. https://doi.org/10.1016/j.asw.2014.03.006.

Embretson, S. E. (1983). Construct validity: construct representation versus nomothetic span. *Psychological Bulletin, 93*, 179–197. https://doi.org/10.1037/0033-2909.93.1.179.

Foltz, P. W., Kintsch, W., & Landauer, T. K. (1998). The measurement of textual coherence with latent semantic analysis. *Discourse Processes, 25*(2–3), 285–307. https://doi.org/10.1080/01638539809545029.

Foltz, P. W., Laham, D., & Landauer, T. K. (1999). The intelligent essay assessor: applications to educational technology. *Interactive Multimedia Electronic Journal of Computer-Enhanced Learning, 1*(2). http://imej.wfu.edu/articles/1999/2/04/index.asp.

Foltz, P. W., & Rosenstein, M. (2017). Data mining large-scale formative writing. In C. Lang, G. Siemens, A. Wise, & D. Gašević (Eds.), *Handbook of learning analytics* (pp. 199–210). *Society for Learning Analytics Research.* https://doi.org/10.18608/hla17.

Graesser, A. C., McNamara, D. S., Louwerse, M., & Cai, Z. (2004). Coh-Metrix: Analysis of text on cohesion and language. *Behavior Research Methods, Instruments, & Computers, 36*, 193–202. https://doi.org/10.3758/BF03195564.

Haertel, E. H. (2006). Reliability. In R. L. Brennan (Ed.), *Educational measurement* (4th ed., pp. 65–110). American Council on Education; Praeger.

Higgins, D., Burstein, J., & Attali, Y. (2006). Identifying off-topic student essays without topic-specific training data. *Natural Language Engineering, 12*(2), 145–159. https://doi.org/10.1017/S1351324906004189.

Landauer, T. K., Foltz, P. W., & Laham, D. (1998). An introduction to latent semantic analysis. *Discourse Processes, 25*(2–3), 259–284. https://doi.org/10.1080/01638539809545028.

Leacock, C., Chodorow, M., Gamon, M., & Tetreault, J. (2010). *Synthesis lectures on human language technologies: Vol. 7. Automated grammatical error detection for language learners* (2nd ed.). Morgan & Claypool Publishers.

Li, J., Link, S., & Hegelheimer, V. (2015). Rethinking the role of automated writing evaluation (AWE) feedback in ESL writing instruction. *Journal of Second Language Writing, 27*, 1–18. https://doi.org/10.1016/j.jslw.2014.10.004.

Litman, D., Afrin, T., Kashefi, O., Olshefski, C., Godley, A., & Hwa, R. (2022). An automated writing evaluation system for supporting self-monitored revising. In M. M. Rodrigo, N. Matsuda, A. I. Cristea & V. Dimitrova (Eds.), *Lecture notes in computer science: Vol. 13355. Artificial intelligence in education. AIED 2022* (pp. 581–587). Springer International Publishing. https://doi.org/10.1007/978-3-031-11644-5_52.

Lottridge, S. (in press). Applications of transformer neural networks in processing examinee text. In H. Jiao & R. Lissitz (Eds.), *Machine learning, natural language processing, and psychometrics: A volume in the MARCES book series.* University of Maryland Press.

McCaffrey, D., Burstein, J., et al. (2023). Making sense of college students' writing achievement and retention with automated writing evaluation. In V. Yaneva & M. von Davier (Eds.), *Advancing natural language processing in educational assessment. NCME educational measurement and assessment book series.* Taylor & Francis.

Mizumoto, A., & Eguchi, M. (2023). Exploring the potential of using an AI language model for automated essay scoring. *Research Methods in Applied Linguistics, 2*(2). https://doi.org/10.1016/j.rmal.2023.100050.

OpenAI (2023). *GPT-4 technical report.* https://arxiv.org/pdf/2303.08774.

Page, E. B. (1966). The imminence of . . . grading essays by computer. *The Phi Delta Kappan, 47*(5), 238–243.

Palermo, C., & Thomson, M. M. (2018). Teacher implementation of self-regulated strategy development with an automated writing evaluation system: effects on the argumentative writing performance of middle school students. *Contemporary Educational Psychology, 54*, 255–270. https://doi.org/10.1016/j.cedpsych.2018.07.002.

670   Chapter 44 Automated Writing Evaluation

Radford, A., Wu, J., Child, R., Luan, D., Amodei, D., & Sutskever, I. (2019). *February 14. Language models are unsupervised multitask learners. OpenAI.* https://insightcivic.s3.us-east-1.amazonaws.com/language-models.pdf.

Ranalli, J. (2018). Automated written corrective feedback: how well can students make use of it? *Computer Assisted Language Learning, 31*(2), 653–674. https://doi.org/10.1080/09588221.2018.1428994.

Ranalli, J. (2021). L2 student engagement with automated feedback on writing: potential for learning and issues of trust. *Journal of Second Language Writing, 52.* https://doi.org/10.1016/j.jslw.2021.100816.

Roscoe, R. D., & McNamara, D. S. (2013, September 9). Writing Pal: feasibility of an intelligent writing strategy tutor in the high school classroom. *Journal of Educational Psychology, 105*(4), 1010–1025. https://doi.org/10.1037/a0032340.

Settles, B., LaFlair, G. T., & Hagiwara, M. (2020). Machine learning–driven language assessment. *Transactions of the Association for computational Linguistics, 8*, 247–263.

Sheehan, K. M., Kostin, I., Futagi, Y., & Flor, M. (2010). Generating automated text complexity classifications that are aligned with targeted text complexity standards. *ETS Research Report Series, 2010*(2). https://doi.org/10.1002/j.2333-8504.2010.tb02235.x.

Shermis, M. D., & Burstein, J. C. (2002). *Automated essay scoring: A cross-disciplinary perspective. Routledge.* https://doi.org/10.4324/9781410606860.

Shermis, M. D., & Burstein, J. C. (2003). *Automated essay scoring: a cross-disciplinary perspective.* Routledge.

Shermis, M. D., & Burstein, J. (2013). *Handbook of automated essay evaluation: Current applications and new directions.* Routledge. https://doi.org/10.4324/9780203122761.

Shermis, M. D., & Wilson, J. (2024). *Routledge international handbook of automated writing evaluation.* Routledge.

Sinharay, S., Zhang, M., & Deane, P. (2019). Prediction of essay scores from writing process and product features using data mining methods. *Applied Measurement in Education, 32*(2), 116–137.

Somasundaran, S., Burstein, J., & Chodorow, M. (2014). Lexical chaining for measuring discourse coherence quality in test-taker essays. In J. Tsujii & J. Hajic (Eds.), *Proceedings of COLING 2014, the 25th international conference on computational linguistics: Technical papers* (pp. 950–961). Dublin City University; Association for Computational Linguistics. https://aclanthology.org/C14-1090.

Stevenson, M., & Phakiti, A. (2014). The effects of computer-generated feedback on the quality of writing. *Assessing Writing, 19*, 51–65. https://doi.org/10.1016/j.asw.2013.11.007.

Tian, E. (2023). *Identifying GPT: First principles for generative AI detection [Undergraduate senior thesis, Princeton University] Dataspace.* http://arks.princeton.edu/ark:/88435/dsp0100000330z.

Wilson, J., & Czik, A. (2016). Automated essay evaluation software in English Language Arts classrooms: effects on teacher feedback, student motivation, and writing quality. *Computers & Education, 100*, 94–109. https://doi.org/10.1016/j.compedu.2016.05.004.

Wolf-Quintero, K., Inagaki, S., & Kim, H. Y. (1998). *Second language development in writing: Measures of fluency, accuracy, and complexity.* University of Hawaii Press.

Woods, B., Adamson, D., Miel, S., & Mayfield, E. (2017 August). Formative essay feedback using predictive scoring models. In *Proceedings of the 23rd ACM SIGKDD international conference on knowledge discovery and data mining* (pp. 2071–2080). Association for Computing Machinery. https://doi.org/10.1145/3097983.3098160.

Yan, D., Rupp, A. A., Foltz, P. W., & . (2020). *Handbook of automated scoring: Theory into practice.* Chapman and Hall; CRC Press. https://doi.org/10.1201/9781351264808.

Yaneva, V., & von Davier, M. (2023). *Advancing natural language processing in educational assessment* (p. 261). Taylor & Francis.

Suggested Readings

Attali, Y., & Burstein, J. (2006). Automated essay scoring with e-rater® V. 2. *The Journal of Technology, Learning, and Assessment, 4*(3).

Shermis, M., & Wilson, J. (2024). *Routledge international handbook of automated writing evaluation.* Routledge.

Yan, D., Rupp, A. A., Foltz, P. W., & . (2020). *Handbook of automated scoring: Theory into practice.* Chapman and Hall; CRC Press. https://doi.org/10.1201/9781351264808.

CHAPTER 45

Detecting Plagiarism and Cheating

Ardeshir Geranpayeh

Introduction

Professional vigilance about threats to the accuracy and dependability of test information is a key aspect of data quality control. Against this background, cheating may directly put into question the validity of a test (see Geranpayeh, 2014). Any single examination score obtained by fraudulent means is not valid; it cannot be interpreted as a fair reflection of the candidate's abilities. Results obtained through cheating have a negative impact on the validity of scores obtained by other candidates. Plagiarism and cheating have been serious problems in schools and colleges alike for a long time. The 2011 cheating scandal in Atlanta, the biggest in U.S. history, which involved 178 teachers and principals, showed how Atlanta public school officials cheated to raise student scores on high-stakes standardized tests. Many teachers confessed that they erased students' answers and corrected tests. This widespread scandal testified that cheating was no longer seen as an old-fashioned battle between teachers and students. When the stakes are high, teachers are also willing to cheat. More recently the availability of free artificial intelligence (AI) software such as ChatGPT raised concerns among many universities around the world to ban the use of ChatGPT on university networks. The eight UK Russell Group Universities reported one million visits to ChatGPT from their Wi-Fi network during the winter exam session in 2022/23.

In this chapter, the concept of cheating and plagiarism is reviewed in the context of educational measurement and its implication for language assessment. Plagiarism is treated here as a special act of cheating that only relates to coursework assessments and that may not be directly related to standardized language assessment. The discussion first briefly reviews the concept of plagiarism, its definition, manifestation, and techniques associated with the detection of plagiarism for essay-type coursework. This chapter then reviews the cheating concept and its manifestations and focuses extensively on various psychometric techniques for the detection of various forms of cheating in high-stakes standardized language assessments. The practical and political dimensions of cheating are discussed, and recommendations are made to help test developers prevent cheating.

The Concise Companion to Language Assessment, First Edition. Edited by Antony John Kunnan.
© 2025 John Wiley & Sons, Inc. Published 2025 by John Wiley & Sons, Inc.

672   Chapter 45 Detecting Plagiarism and Cheating

Prevention of Cheating in Assessment

According to Cizek (1999), any action that violates the rules for administering a test is considered cheating. Cheating can take a wide variety of forms and may involve any of the stakeholders in the testing process, including candidates, their teachers, and those responsible for administering the test. Cheats may be motivated by material rewards such as access to life chances, by personal needs such as competitiveness or a lack of self-confidence, or, in the case of school examinations, by the publication of league tables, as was the case in the Atlanta scandal. Whatever the cause, teachers, examination boards, and their agents clearly have a responsibility to discourage cheating on their tests and to minimize it wherever possible. There are many explicit statements in the *Standards for Educational and Psychological Testing* (American Educational Research Association et al., 1999) for the prevention of cheating. For example, Standard 11.7 requires that test publishers "protect the security of their tests." There is a whole section on test security in the fourth edition of Educational Measurement (Brennan, 2006). The importance of test security is reiterated in Standard 10.18 of the 2014 *Standards for Educational and Psychological Testing* (American Educational Research Association et al., 2014).

Plagiarism

Definition

Plagiarism is a special act of cheating associated with essay writing. According to Webster's *Third New International Dictionary*, "to plagiarize" means "to steal and pass off as one's own [the ideas or words of another] or use without crediting the source." It goes on to say that it is "to commit literary theft." The problem with plagiarism is twofold. It involves stealing someone else's work and then lying about it. Although plagiarism is a serious offense in academic contexts, its nebulous boundary with copying (legitimate) is not always clear-cut. There are guidelines about what counts as plagiarism. According to www.plagiarism.org, the following are considered acts of plagiarism:

- turning in someone else's work as your own;
- copying words or ideas from someone else without giving credit;
- failing to put a quotation in quotation marks;
- giving incorrect information about the source of a quotation;
- changing words but copying the sentence structure of a source without giving credit; and
- copying so many words or ideas from a source that it makes up the majority of your work, whether you give credit or not.

Educational researchers have repeatedly found academic dishonesty to be disturbingly common, and more common than is generally believed by educators. It is not uncommon to hear from students that they frequently plagiarize papers or defy honesty codes in other ways. Cizek (1999, p. 3), reviewing a large body of survey and experimental research, states that "nearly every research report on cheating ... has concluded that cheating is rampant." Cizek reports that about 40% of sixth graders copy and that about 60% of undergraduates do so at some point during their college careers. Cheating can significantly compromise the assessment process (see Cizek, 1999; Frary, 1993). These percentages have significantly increased with easier accessibility of online resources, which has led to even higher widespread electronic cheating within higher and further education institutions. With the widespread availability of Generative AI (ChatGPT and the like) in recent years, the detection of plagiarism has become a challenging task for any system to handle, let alone individual faculty members.

Detection software

The increase in online cheating brings about the need for the availability of online detection solutions. Many colleges and higher education institutions in the last decade started to use commercial online-detecting software tools to check the originality of an essay. There were numerous online detection software tools available before the pandemic in 2020, which checked essays submitted by students against a huge quantity of electronic media. Turnitin (turnitin.com), Dupli Checker (duplichecker.com), iThenticate (ithenticate.com), WriteCheck (writecheck.com), and AntiPlagiarism.net (antiplagiarism.net) were but a few examples of such online cheating detection solutions. Online verbatim copied manuscripts could have been identified by such tools. Some academic institutions that were interested in the use of a dual antiplagiarism tool that could detect and deter students from plagiarism had taken further steps to investigate not only the reliability of such detection techniques but also their user-friendliness for staff and students alike. For example, Humes et al. (2003) conducted a survey of antiplagiarism software at the Claremont McKenna College. One of the interesting findings from their research was that, after one semester's deployment of antiplagiarism software, it appeared that faculty could detect student plagiarism with higher accuracy and that students felt comfortable with both the detection program and learning the rules of academic honesty. More recently, Abdelhamid et al. (2022) carried out a wide survey on anti-plagiarism software in three different languages: English, French, and Arabic. They noticed that plagiarism detection software has evolved significantly in recent years.

AI plagiarism

With the widespread availability of Generative AI (ChatGPT) since December 2022, most traditional detection online software tools have become inadequate to deal with the new challenge of AI-generated plagiarism.

ChatGPT is based on the Generative Pre-trained Transformer (GPT) architecture and has been trained on a large dataset of internet text. ChatGPT is designed to generate human-like text and can be fine-tuned for a variety of NLP tasks, such as language translation, summarization, and question answering. ChatGPT can generate text that is grammatically correct and semantically meaningful, which makes it very difficult to detect by current online cheating detection tools. There have been some attempts to develop software to detect AI-generated essays (GPTZero – https://gptzero.me/) but they are still in trial/proof of concept phases and are not very promising to detect AI-generated texts. GPTZero scores text on its perplexity and burstiness. It looks at how complicated a text is and how randomly it is written. There is a plethora of software developed in recent years to address online plagiarism including using AI. Here is a list of software claiming to detect online plagiarism: *Quetext, Dupli Checker, Grammarly, Paper Rater, ProWritingAid, Copyscape, WhiteSmoke, Copyleaks Plagiarism Checker, Plagiarism Detector, Noplag, Plagscan from Ouriginal, Turnitin, iThenticate,* and *Texta.ai.*

Cheating in High-Stakes Language Assessment

All high-stakes language tests are expected to provide a snapshot of candidates' language proficiency at the time of testing. The results from language tests are often used to make decisions about a candidate's preparedness to cope with the target language of communication. The candidate's performance on a language test could be reported as simply passing or failing or scored against a system of ordered descriptors of performance such as the Common European Framework of Reference for Languages (CEFR). With the increasing importance of candidate test performance in contexts such as immigration, access to higher education, or job opportunities, the stakes associated with the use of test results will increase. This is particularly true of international standardized language proficiency tests such as IELTS,

674 Chapter 45 Detecting Plagiarism and Cheating

TOEFL iBT, PTE Academic, and Duolingo English Test. The consequences of results of such tests become quite weighty; such tests are called high stakes. Once a test is used for high-stakes decision-making, candidates will try harder to succeed in the test, even if it means by means of cheating. One can argue that cheating is an inevitable consequence and a by-product of high-stakes testing.

Definition

Cheating can take various shapes and forms. As mentioned earlier, Cizek (1999) defines cheating as any action that violates the rules for administering a test. Cizek (2001, p. 5) furthermore defines cheating as any behavior that gives an examinee an unfair advantage over other examinees, or any action on the part of an examinee or test administrator that decreases the accuracy of the intended inferences arising from the examinee's test score or performance.

This definition is quite broad and includes a range of test administration violations by either candidates or the people involved in the testing process. Caveon, a test security company, categorized cheaters in 10 different classes: the Impersonator, the Smuggler, the Storyteller, the Chain Gang, the Time Traveler, the Collaborators, Robin Hood, the Hacker, the Ticket Scalper, and the Insider and the Fence.

The *impersonator*, also known as proxy test taker, is the person who takes the test on behalf of someone else. The *smuggler* is someone who brings into the test setting materials or devices intended to provide an advantage over honest examinees. The *storyteller* is the individual who memorizes test items only to "retell" them later to others. The *chain gang* is the group that memorizes and sells items, typically through the Internet. The *time traveler* is the person who shares test materials that are used in multiple time zones. The *collaborators* are candidates who work together as a team to share responses to the test or steal the test material. The *Robin Hood* category refers to test takers who are not involved, but whose teachers or other authorities are involved in changing student responses with or without the students' knowledge. The Atlanta scandal falls under this category. The *hacker* is the person who infiltrates computer systems to change candidate results. The *ticket scalper* sits an exam's beta test for the sole purpose of obtaining a free voucher that they will then sell to others for a profit, interrupting the pretesting development of a test. The *insider* steals the question and the fence sells the results. People in the latter category are most difficult to identify, as they work for the testing organization and know how to avoid being recognized. We now need to add the AI-assisted cheating to that list.

Cheating detection indices

There are many ways, statistical or otherwise, to detect any number of cheating behaviors that may occur in a language test, but this chapter focuses only on cheating detection techniques that are based on candidates' item response analysis. Cizek and Wollack (2017) have a comprehensive review of various cheating detection techniques.

Most instances of cheating take place through copying responses or collusion of some kind. The collusion phenomenon has been known for many decades, and numerous statistical indices have been developed to detect collusion or cheating in examinations since 1927. The very first collusion detection methods were developed by Bird (1927, 1929), Crawford (1930), Dickenson (1945), Anikeef (1954), and Saupe (1960). Due to the complexity of computing and the unavailability of statistical software at that time, the detection power of such indices could not be thoroughly investigated. Angoff (1974) developed eight statistical indices by a variety of variables to detect cheaters using the same method as Saupe (1960). He found that the variables involving counts of right and wrong answers were more successful in detecting copying cases. Since then, many other indices have been developed by Frary et al. (1977), Schumacher (1980), Cody (1985), Hanson et al. (1987), Roberts (1987), Belleza and Belleza (1989), Harpp et al. (1996), Holland (1996), Wollack (1997), Kadane (1999), Ercole et al. (2002), Sotaridona and Meijer (2002), van der Linden and Sotaridona (2004, 2006), Sotaridona et al. (2006), Belov and Armstrong (2010), and van der Linden and Jeon (2012).

Prevention of Cheating in Assessment **675**

Statistical methods for collusion detection can be divided into two groups based on their theoretical foundation: classical test theory (CTT) and item response theory (IRT). Many existing techniques are modeled using CTT. They are designed to compare the response-pattern similarity between examinees with an expected amount of similarity. CTT item statistics are dependent on the trait levels of all examinees. The response pattern of each examinee is usually compared with the response patterns of everyone in the group who took the test including those who were not within physical copying distance. Thus, biased estimates of the expected number of matches between pairs of examinees are obtained.

The alternative method for detecting collusion is the use of IRT. There are different IRT models that can be used to detect cheating, depending on the test format/method. For example, for a multiple-choice option test, a nominal response model is used. Under IRT, the probability of an examinee answering an item correctly given an estimate of his or her ability is independent of the other examinees taking the test. IRT detection models take into account the item parameter of the test: difficulty level of the items and discrimination indices of the alternatives or choices of the test. They are also designed to compare patterns of responses for an examinee with those of other examinees of a similar ability level. Despite various advantages of IRT detection approaches to CTT, the cheating literature only mentions two IRT-based indices: the ω index of Wollack (1997) and the index proposed by van der Linden and Sotaridona (2006).

The CTT detection techniques are discussed first. The following indices are just a few examples of numerous available detection methods in the CTT literature.

The Bird Index: The earliest method documented in the literature was proposed by Bird (1927, 1929). For pairs of examinees, Bird suggested three approaches based on the inspection of observed distributions of the number of identical wrong responses.

The Dickenson Index: Dickenson (1945) derived a theoretical ratio of identical errors that he called probable percentage of errors.

The Regression Index: Saupe (1960) proposed a technique based on linear regression analysis to identify the suspected examinees. Saupe incorporated both correct and incorrect identical responses and derived two detection indices applicable to the number of right and wrong similarities in the responses.

The Angoff Index: Angoff (1974) proposed eight similar cheating detection methods of which he found three (A, B, and H) to be promising. The procedure was expressed as follows. Let candidate I answer R_i questions correctly in an exam, candidate J answer R_j questions correctly, and R_{ij} be the number of correct answers shared by the two candidates. R_{ij} is not a good measure of similarity because the number of similar answers increases with examinee knowledge. To examine R_{ij} in relation to R_i and R_j, one needs to assess the unusualness of R_{ij} by calculating the residual of R_{ij} after regression on $\sqrt{(R_i \cdot R_j)}$ and $R_i \cdot R_j$. Residuals are distributed normally and expressed as probabilities. Alternatively, Index B could be computed in a similar way as defined above for Index A by calculating the residual of Q_{ij} after regression on $\sqrt{(W_i \cdot W_j)}$ and $W_i \cdot W_j$. Index H was based on identical incorrect responses in the longest string of items and number of items answered incorrectly. Pairs with positive standardized residuals beyond a certain critical value could be treated as suspicious. The regression expressions for indices A, B, and H are as follows:

$$R_{ij} = \sqrt{\left(R_i - R_j\right)} + R_i \cdot R_j$$

$$Q_{ij} = \sqrt{\left(W_i - W_j\right)} + W_i \cdot W_j + \varepsilon$$

$$K_{ij} = \sqrt{Si} + S_i + \varepsilon$$

676   Chapter 45 Detecting Plagiarism and Cheating

where Q_{ij} = the number of items answered incorrectly in the same way by both i and j; $W_i \cdot W_j$ = the number of items answered incorrectly by i times the number of items answered incorrectly by j; S_i = the number of items answered incorrectly by either i or j + the number of items omitted by the examinee whose number of items answered incorrectly is smaller; and K_{ij} = identically marked incorrect and omitted responses in the longest string of items.

The Score Difference Index: Roberts (1987) applied a score difference method where alternate test forms, with different answer keys, were administered in the same room without the direct knowledge of the examinees. The procedure involved (i) scoring each answer document using the key appropriate to the examinee's form, (ii) scoring the answer document using the alternative, inappropriate keys, and (iii) finding the difference between the scores obtained from the appropriate and inappropriate keys. A large difference, especially upward, was taken as evidence of cheating.

The NBME Index: In NBME, two statistical methods were used to flag suspected pairs of examinees. The method suggested by Schumacher (1980) was a detection method based on the chi-square and required knowledge of seating locations of suspected examinees to evaluate the likelihood of independence of identical and nonidentical responses. Another requirement was that examinees be seated close to each other for one part of an examination and apart for another.

The Error Similarity Analysis Index: Belleza and Belleza (1989) suggested an error similarity analysis based on binomial probabilities. This computed the probability that a pair of examinees should have a certain number of identically incorrect responses to test items. If the probability was low enough for any pair of examinees, that pair was flagged as potentially engaging in collusion.

The K-Index: The K-index is a statistic that can be used to assess the degree of unusual agreement between incorrect answers on the multiple-choice test of two examinees: one referred to as the source (s) and the other as the copier (c). The copier is suspected of copying answers from the source. The K-index only takes the incorrect answers of the examinees into account.

Scrutiny!: Scrutiny! has received very little attention in the measurement literature. Scrutiny! is similar to the K-index in that it uses information from only the incorrect answers. Scrutiny! detects answer copying by implementing a modification of the error similarity analysis (ESA) first proposed by Belleza and Belleza (1989). Scrutiny! uses a normal approximation to the binomial (corrected for continuity), which compares the number of answer matches on incorrectly answered items with the number expected by chance, given the number of items answered incorrectly (though not necessarily identically) by both c and s.

The S-Index: Sotaridona and Meijer (2002) proposed two new indices called S_1 and S_2 to describe the probability of the suspect having at least the same incorrect answers as other examinees in the same subgroup, based on an assumed Poisson probability distribution. Examinees were also divided into R subgroups based on the number of incorrect answers, in such a way that examinees in each subgroup have the same number of wrong answers.

The Shifted Binomial Index: van der Linden and Sotaridona (2004) proposed a similar index related to the S-index, based on shifted binomial distribution. The test is based on the idea that examinees' answers to test items might be the result of three possible processes: (i) knowing, (ii) guessing, and (iii) copying, but that examinees who do not have access to the answers of other examinees can arrive at their answers only through the first two processes. This assumption leads to a distribution for the number of matched incorrect alternatives between the examinee suspected of copying and the examinee believed to be the source that belongs to a family of "shifted binomials."

The Kappa Index: A statistical test for answer copying on multiple choice tests based on Cohen's kappa was developed by Sotaridona et al. (2006). The test was free of any assumptions on the response processes of the examinees suspected of copying and having served as the source, except for the usual assumption that these processes are probabilistic.

The most common CTT cheating detection index used is the Angoff index. The index logic is very simple, although the significance of the outcome is statistically very strong. It is also very easy to implement in any testing program without the need to write complex syntax codes or use a specialized statistical package. Despite the popularity and simplicity of CTT cheating detection, it is limited in what it can detect. All CTT indices are based on the number of correct/incorrect responses and ignore any other information available in a test. Hence, they suffer from power test and are subject to type I and type II errors. In recent years, there has been a shift toward using IRT cheating detection indices that control type I and type II errors while adding power to the detection methods. There are two well-developed IRT cheating detection methods: the ω statistics and the Sotaridona and van der Linden index.

The ω statistics: Wollack (1997) proposed the ω copying index that is formulated in the context of the nominal response model (NRM) developed by Bock (1972).

The van der Linden and Sotaridona Index: van der Linden and Sotaridona (2006) have provided a comprehensive IRT-based framework for modeling collusion between examinees. The assumption of the procedure is that the probabilities with which a test taker who has not copied any answers chooses a response alternative follow a known response model.

In addition to the above two IRT models, there has recently been an interest in item preknowledge detection investigation (see Belov, 2020; Belov & Toton, 2022; Belov & Wollack, 2021; Gorney & Wollack, 2022a, 2022b).

Application of Cheating Indices in Language Testing

Testing organizations rarely discuss what method they use for detection of cheating in their examinations. It is assumed that some of the indices listed above are used in the detection of cheating in language tests. Geranpayeh and Khalid (2012) reported on a comprehensive study where they applied the *K-index*, *Scrutiny!*, ω, and the *van der Linden/Sotaridona index* to investigate the type I error rate and power of the cheating indices using real test data over a number of sessions of an English language proficiency test. Using simulations, they studied different impacts of varying test length, sample sizes, and proportion of answer copying in the study. They demonstrated that all the aforementioned indices were powerful enough to detect collusion in the test with relative consistency. However, the *van der Linden/Sotaridona index* (IRT-based) was found to be the most powerful index that could identify copying even in small sample sizes and mixed-format item types.

Geranpayeh (2009, 2011) also reported several cheating detection methods for high-stakes language assessments. Those methods looked for:

- unusually high scores on one measure in relation to others;
- identical/similar pattern of responses: copying or collusion; and
- grouping candidates' responses on some meaningful external criterion, such as seating plan, class membership, school, and so on.

678 **Chapter 45** Detecting Plagiarism and Cheating

Conclusion

In conclusion, cheating detection is a critical issue in education, as cheating undermines the integrity of the educational system and can lead to unfair advantages for some students. Various methods of cheating detection have been developed, including traditional methods, as well as newer technologies that are being used to combat cheating. Despite these efforts, cheating remains a persistent problem in education, and it is important for educators, parents, and students to work together to create an environment where academic integrity is valued and upheld. Notwithstanding the various methods that are being used to detect cheating, it remains a persistent problem in education. Cheating is often motivated by a desire for better grades or to get ahead in the competition. However, it is important to remember that cheating is a violation of academic integrity and can have serious consequences, including expulsion or a tarnished academic record.

Future Directions

Geranpayeh (2014) argues that cheating is an inevitable consequence and a by-product of high-stakes testing; as the stakes of a test increases, so does the level of cheating. The first two decades of the 21st century has seen a significant increase in innovative approaches to cheating. The new fraudulent activities tended to happen mostly by means of technology, using imposters and engaging local schools. New gadgets such as cell phones, pen scanners, calculators, memory devices, tiny button cameras, and advanced micro earphones, to name but a few, have facilitated cheating and have introduced serious challenges to combating this widespread phenomenon. In response to these ingenious cheating methods, examination boards have taken various actions, including prohibiting the use of electronic devices in test centers, implementing surveillance through CCTV cameras, and introducing stringent identification procedures like passport checks and biometrics, all of which must be completed before candidates gain access to examination halls. Nevertheless, it's important to note that none of these measures can effectively tackle the emerging issue of security threats driven by AI.

Since AI threats to assessment security are very recent, they aren't many well-established methods to investigate them. Lack of published literature does not mean there are no threats to test security in modern time. LaFlair et al. (2022) describe a comprehensive framework for test security in a digital-first assessment. They list a number of ways that AI-generated new exams can be exposed to test security breaches and how they can be addressed. There are also more recent studies where detection techniques are used by means of machine learning techniques (see Pan et al., 2022; Zhou & Jiao, 2022a, 2022b.)

The growing popularity of LLMs for language assessment underscores the significance of secure language evaluation in our progressively digitalized world. Traditional cheating detection methods, initially tailored for paper-based tests, have become inadequate for identifying irregular or malicious conduct among test takers in this digital age. As we enter the third decade of the 21st century, the prevalence of AI-driven plagiarism and cheating has reached alarming levels. It is imperative for examination boards to swiftly adopt AI-based remote proctoring techniques to combat the rising threats posed by Generative AI in cheating, and concurrently utilize AI to enhance the security of their assessments.

Discussion Questions

1. What strategies should the assessment industry employ to address test security in the digital era?
2. Explore how language assessments can shift their focus on test security toward content evaluation methods.

References

Abdelhamid, M., Batat, S. and Azouaou, F. (2022). *A survey of plagiarism detection systems: Case of use with English, French and Arabic languages.* https://arxiv.org/pdf/2201.03423.pdf.

American Educational Research Association, American Psychological Association, & National Council on Measurement in Education (1999). *Standards for educational and psychological testing.* American Educational Research Association.

American Educational Research Association, American Psychological Association, & National Council on Measurement in Education. (2014). *Standards for educational and psychological testing.* American Educational Research Association, The American Psychological Association, & the National Council on Measurement in Education.

Angoff, W. H. (1974). The development of statistical indices for detecting cheaters. *Journal of the American Statistical Association, 69,* 44–49.

Anikeef, A. M. (1954). Index of collaboration for test administrators. *Journal of Applied Psychology, 38,* 174–177.

Belleza, F. S., & Belleza, S. F. (1989). Detection of cheating on multiple-choice tests by using error-similarity analysis. *Teaching of Psychology, 16,* 151–155.

Belov, D. I. (2020). Monte Carlo detection of examinees with item preknowledge. *Behaviormetrika, 48*(1), 23–50. https://doi.org/10.1007/s41237-020-00110-y.

Belov, D. I., & Armstrong, R. D. (2010). Automatic detection of answer copying via Kullback–Leibler divergence and k-index. *Applied Psychological Measurement, 34,* 379–392.

Belov, D., & Toton, S. L. (2022). Detecting examinees with item preknowledge on real data. *Applied Psychological Measurement, 46,* 273–287. https://doi.org/10.1177/01466216221084202.

Belov, D., & Wollack, J. A. (2021). Graph theory approach to detect examinees involved in test collusion. *Applied Psychological Measurement, 45,* 253–267. https://doi.org/10.1177/01466216211013902.

Bird, C. (1927). The detection of cheating in objective examinations. *School and Society, 25,* 261–262.

Bird, C. (1929). An improved method of detection cheating in objective examinations. *Journal of Educational Research, 19*(5), 341–348.

Bock, R. D. (1972). Estimating item parameters and latent ability when responses are scored in two or more nominal categories. *Psychometrika, 46,* 443–459.

Brennan, R. L. (Ed.). (2006). *Educational Measurement* (4th ed.). American Council on Education and Praeger Publishers.

Cizek, G. J. (1999). *Cheating on tests: How to do it, detect it, and prevent it.* Erlbaum.

Cizek, G. J. (2001 April). *An overview of issues concerning cheating on large-scale tests. Paper presented at the annual meeting of the National Council on Measurement in Education, Seattle, WA.*

Cizek, G. J., & Wollack, J. A. (Eds.). (2017). *Handbook of quantitative methods for detecting cheating on tests.* Routledge.

Cody, R. P. (1985). Statistical analysis of examinations to detect cheating. *Journal of Medical Education, 60,* 136–137.

Crawford, C. C. (1930). Dishonesty in objective tests. *School Review, 38*(10), 776–781.

Dickenson, H. F. (1945). Identical errors and deception. *Journal of Educational Research, 38,* 534–542.

Ercole, A., Whittlestone, K. D., Melvin, D. G., & Rashbass, F. (2002). Collusion detection in multiple choice examinations. *Medical Education, 36,* 166–172.

Frary, R. B. (1993). Statistical detection of multiple-choice answer copying: review and commentary. *Applied Measurement in Education, 6,* 153–165.

Frary, R. B., Tideman, T. N., & Watts, T. M. (1977). Indices of cheating on multiple-choice tests. *Journal of Educational Statistics, 6,* 152–165.

Geranpayeh, A. (2009 February). *Security trends in large scale testing in education. Paper presented at the Association of Test Publishers, Palm Springs, CA.*

Geranpayeh, A. (2011 November). *Detecting cheating in language assessment. Paper presented at the Language Testing Forum, Warwick, England.*

Geranpayeh, A. (2014). A look at unintentional cheating in the testing industry: professional credentialing. *NCME Newsletter, 22*(1), 5–7.

Geranpayeh, A., & Khalid, M. N. (2012 April). *Robustness of cheating indices in language assessment. Paper presented at the National Council on Measurement in Education, Vancouver, Canada.*

680 Chapter 45 Detecting Plagiarism and Cheating

Gorney, K. N., & Wollack, J. A. (2022a). Generating models for item preknowledge. *Journal of Educational Measurement, 59*, 22–42. https://doi.org/10.1111/jedm.12309.

Gorney, K. N., & Wollack, J. A. (2022b). Two new models for item preknowledge. *Applied Psychological Measurement, 46*, 447–461. https://doi.org/10.1177/014662162211081.

Hanson, B. A., Harris, D. J., & Brennan, R. L. (1987). *A comparison of several statistical methods for examining allegations of copying (ACT research report series, Vol. 87*(15)). American College Testing.

Harpp, D. N., Hogan, J. J., & Jennings, J. S. (1996). Crime in the classroom: part II, an update. *Journal of Chemical Education, 73*, 349–351.

Holland, P. W. (1996). *Assessing unusual agreement between the incorrect answers of two examinees using the K-index: Statistical theory and empirical support (Research Report RR-94-4). Princeton, NJ: Educational Testing Service.*

Humes, C., Stiffler, J., & Malsed, M. (2003). *Examining anti-plagiarism software: Choosing the right tool.* http://net.educause.edu/ir/library/pdf/EDU03168.pdf.

Kadane, J. B. (1999). An allegation of examination copying. *Chance, 12*, 32–36.

LaFlair, T., Langenfeld, T., Baig, B., Horie, A. K., Attali, Y., & von Davier, A. A. (2022). Digital-first assessments: a security framework. *Journal of Computer Assisted Learning*, 1–10. https://doi.org/10.1111/jcal.12665.

van der Linden, W. J., & Jeon, M. (2012). Modeling answer changes on test items. *Journal of Educational and Behavioral Statistics, 37*(1), 180–199.

van der Linden, W. J., & Sotaridona, L. S. (2004). A statistical test for detecting answer copying on multiple-choice tests. *Journal of Educational Measurement, 41*, 361–378.

van der Linden, W. J., & Sotaridona, L. S. (2006). Detecting answer copying when the regular response process follows a known response model. *Journal of Educational and Behavioral Statistics, 31*, 283–304.

Pan, Y., Sinharay, S., Livne, O., & Wollack, J. A. (2022). A machine learning approach for detecting item compromise and preknowledge in computerized adaptive testing. *Journal of Psychological Test and Assessment Modeling, 64*(4), 385–424.

Roberts, D. M. (1987). Limitations of the score-difference method in detecting cheating in recognition test situations. *Journal of Educational Measurement, 24*, 77–81.

Saupe, J. L. (1960). An empirical model for the corroboration of suspected cheating on multiple-choice tests. *Educational and Psychological Measurement, 20*, 475–489.

Schumacher C. F. (1980 April). *A method for detection of confirmation of collaborative behaviour. Paper presented at the annual meeting of the American Educational Research Association, Boston, MA.*

Sotaridona, L. S., & Meijer, R. R. (2002). Statistical properties of the K-index for detecting answer copying. *Journal of Educational Measurement, 39*, 115–132.

Sotaridona, L. S., van der Linden, W. J., & Meijer, R. R. (2006). Detecting answer copying using the kappa statistic. *Applied Psychological Measurement, 30*, 412–431.

Wollack, J. A. (1997). A nominal response model approach to detect answer copying. *Applied Psychological Measurement, 21*, 307–320.

Zhou, T., & Jiao, H. (2022a). Data augmentation in machine learning for cheating detection in large-scale assessment: an illustration with the blending ensemble learning algorithm. *Psychological Test and Assessment Modeling, 64*(4), 425–444.

Zhou, T., & Jiao, H. (2022b). Exploration of the stacking ensemble machine learning algorithm for cheating detection in large-scale assessment. *Educational and Psychological Measurement*. https://doi.org/10.1177/00131644221117193.

Suggested Readings

Cizek, G. J., & Wollack, J. A. (Eds.). (2017). *Handbook of quantitative methods for detecting cheating on tests.* Routledge.

LaFlair, T., Langenfeld, T., Baig, B., Horie, A. K., Attali, Y., & von Davier, A. A. (2022). Digital-first assessments: a security framework. *Journal of Computer Assisted Learning*, 1–10. https://doi.org/10.1111/jcal.12665.

INDEX

A

academic language, 44, 306, 316–317, 321, 360–363. *See also English for academic purposes*

ACCESS for ELLs, 161

accommodation, 33, 36, 80–81, 90, 147, 248–251, 366, 440, 442, 514–515
  dictionaries, 291
  effectiveness, 5, 27, 61, 121, 159, 173, 176, 182, 191, 201, 236, 260, 295, 347, 393, 585, 604, 609
  linguistic complexity, 246, 314
  relevance, 10, 13, 46, 55, 57, 60, 163, 193, 199–200, 246, 256, 321, 328, 348, 377, 379, 407, 409, 513, 561, 655, 663–664
  translation, 62–63, 148, 162–163, 205, 208, 271–272, 276, 482–483, 518, 673

accountability, 3, 7–8, 19, 25, 28, 30, 77, 165, 303, 320, 327, 454, 498, 520

achievement, 5, 11, 13–14, 16–17, 29, 64, 96, 155, 159, 193, 212, 246, 286, 307, 317, 326, 330, 335, 340, 343, 377, 426, 482–483, 487, 496, 502, 504, 642, 655
  growth assessment, 29, 85, 115–116, 121, 160, 245, 291, 342, 346, 348, 355–356, 363, 371, 418–419, 423, 596, 644, 664

achievement tests, 5, 96, 159

acoustic analysis, 384, 388, 391–393

ACTFL, 61, 187, 195, 220, 231, 277, 565–566, 642, 656. *See also ACTFL Proficiency Guidelines; American Council on the Teaching of Foreign Languages*

ACTFL Proficiency Guidelines, 231, 565–566. *See also ACTFL*

admission test, 285
  in the Netherlands, 403, 407

AERA. *See American Educational Research Association*

AI plagiarism, 673

ALTE. *See Association of Language Testers in Europe*

ALTE Code of Practice, 410

American Association of Applied Linguistics (AAAL), 326

American Council on the Teaching of Foreign Languages, 5, 61, 277. *See also ACTFL*

American Educational Research Association, 69, 77, 91, 120, 122, 551, 556, 563, 666, 672

American Psychological Association, 69, 80

American Sign Language, 442
  analysis of variance, 103, 615
  assessment types, 313
  and confidence, 346, 626–627
  and feedback, 57, 60, 117, 159, 170, 173, 176, 184, 201, 259–260, 264, 319, 342, 344–345, 347–348, 392–393, 662–663, 667

analysis of variance (ANOVA), 103, 544

Angoff index, 675, 677

ANOVA. *See analysis of variance (ANOVA)*

APA. *See American Psychological Association*

aptitude, 5, 80, 223, 367, 444, 478–479, 514, 621
  diagnosis, 25, 27–28, 33, 56, 59, 61, 63, 165, 305, 331, 344, 515, 603
  in second language acquisition, 140, 227

aptitude test
  applications, 56, 63, 112–117, 119–120, 143, 159, 172–173, 175, 212, 256, 286–287, 345, 363, 388, 407, 435, 442, 486, 515, 529, 539, 551, 577, 585, 592, 594, 597, 637, 641, 661–662, 664, 667
  innovations, 140, 157–158, 170, 175, 217, 281, 327, 335, 339, 349, 409, 640
  language aptitude, 444
  student placement, 165
  test format, 148, 208, 315, 546, 675

The Concise Companion to Language Assessment, First Edition. Edited by Antony John Kunnan.
© 2025 John Wiley & Sons, Inc. Published 2025 by John Wiley & Sons, Inc.

682 Index

argument-based approach, 70, 75, 144, 454
Armed Services Vocational Aptitude Battery
  (ASVAB), 621
Artificial Intelligence, 63, 112–116, 118,
  120, 122, 149, 171, 213, 227, 237, 322,
  341, 358, 379, 619, 637, 671
ASE. *See automated speech evaluation*
  (ASE); computer-assisted
  language testing
assessing accent, 134–135, 150, 216–217,
  221, 224, 226–227, 247, 278–279,
  281, 364, 385–386, 394, 438, 458, 464.
  See also assessing pronunciation;
  intelligibility; pronunciation accuracy;
  pronunciation assessment
  accent reduction, 216
  foreign accent, 133–134, 155, 216, 245–246,
    248–249, 276–277, 364
assessing linguistics resources
  complexity, 29, 34, 59–60, 163, 168,
    171, 184, 193, 198–201, 210, 246, 266,
    274, 281, 289, 313–314, 322, 349,
    383, 423–424, 427–428, 438, 563,
    581, 593–594, 596, 638, 644, 652,
    655, 665, 674
  grammatical knowledge, 185, 188–190,
    192, 194, 196–197, 589
  propositional meaning, 181–182, 192–194,
    197, 201
  semantic meaning, 183, 187, 191–192,
    196–198, 200–201, 348
  SFL proficiency, 25, 31, 34, 181–182,
    184–186, 189, 199–201
  topical knowledge, 23, 184–186, 188, 193,
    199, 255, 257, 263–264, 266
assessing listening, 129–130, 132, 134,
  136, 138, 140
  construct irrelevant variance, 131, 135
  interactive speaking and listening,
    132–133, 139–140
  item type, 45, 136, 157, 159, 225, 238, 259,
    279, 356, 366, 480–481, 529, 584, 621,
    639, 645, 650, 653–654, 677
  linguistics features, 133
  nonverbal component, 135, 139
  response format, 130, 136, 162,
    164, 208, 623
  test impact and washback, 139
  unplanned spoken discourse, 131,
    133–134, 139–140

assessing pragmatics, 645
assessing pronunciation, 216, 218, 220, 222,
  224, 226–227. *See also foreign accent*
  accentedness, 219–220, 222–223,
    226, 383–384
  auditory, 223–224, 281, 384, 388–389,
    391–392
  instrumental, 223–224, 318, 322, 383–384,
    388–389, 392, 394
  intelligibility principle, 219
  learnability, 221
  musical ability, 223
  nativeness principle, 219
  native speaker, 135, 188, 191, 209,
    213, 216, 219, 224–227, 232, 235,
    246–249, 272, 274, 364, 383–385, 388,
    393, 466, 541
  rater characteristics, 217, 223
  segmental items, 218
  teachability, 221
  word stress items, 218
assessing reading, 154, 156, 158, 160, 162,
  164–165, 570
  assessment for reading, 155
  content knowledge, 34, 62, 161, 274, 590
  diagnostic assessment, 26, 30, 75, 77, 160,
    164, 170, 259, 339–340, 342, 344–348,
    461, 468, 596
  L2 reading assessment, 158–161, 164
  objective testing, 155, 169
  oral reading fluency, 160
  reading ability, 49, 132, 154–158, 160–161,
    163–165, 174, 183, 263, 346, 590
  standardized reading assessment, 154,
    156–158, 164
assessing speaking, 43, 143–144, 146–150,
  238, 383–394, 638
  automatic speech recognition
    (ASR), 387, 640
  integrated argument, 144
  Levelt's model, 143–144
  objective measures, 384–385, 391
  sample analysis, 388
  scoring system, 116–118, 143–144, 148–150,
    173, 201, 224, 365, 379, 384–385, 387–388,
    394, 655, 662, 667
  temporal analysis, 383–384, 386, 388,
    390, 392, 394
  test system, 144–145, 147, 158, 285, 421, 487
  voice onset time (VOT), 385

Index **683**

assessing vocabulary, 205–206, 208,
210–212
breadth-depth distinction, 208
breadth of knowledge, 207
depth of knowledge, 206–207, 461, 466
L2 vocabulary, 209
productive knowledge, 206, 208
receptive knowledge, 206
Timed Yes/No (TYN), 212
vocabulary size, 207–213
word association, 207, 213
assessing writing, 168, 170, 172, 174, 176,
375, 476–477, 484–485
academic literacy, 169, 175
AI and technology in writing, 168, 172
alternative approaches, 172, 567
writing construct, 661, 666
assessment design, 28, 80, 170, 172, 174–176,
256, 263, 315, 321–322. *See also test
development*
assessment development, 9, 19, 82, 120, 154,
156, 161, 243, 509
task templates, 9, 15
writing prompt, 16–19, 361, 667
assessment for learning, 24, 29, 160, 165,
172, 260, 305, 497
Assessment in Education, 499
assessment justification, 3, 7–8, 19
assessment performance, 6–7, 19, 90, 315
assessment principles, 27–28
Assessment Reform Group, 29, 305
assessment use argument (AUA) approach,
8–10, 15, 19, 71, 503
Association of Language Testers in
Europe, 402
ASVAB, 621
asylum (seekers)
language situation, 121, 134
AUA. *See assessment use argument
(AUA) approach*
authenticity, 43, 46, 70–71, 117–118, 162,
170, 172, 273–276, 278–281, 375–377,
462, 496, 638, 640, 645, 653
automated essay scoring (AES), 114,
172, 286, 640
automated feedback, 173, 176, 225, 287–288,
292–293, 295, 346–349
automated speech evaluation (ASE), 637
automated speech recognition (ASR), 114
automated text analysis, 281, 665

automated writing assessment. *See also
automated writing evaluation (AWE)*
personal characteristics of students, 294
Project Essay Grade (PEG), 173,
286, 661
automated writing evaluation (AWE), 116,
172, 286, 637, 640, 655, 661. *See also
automated writing assessment*
automatic item generation (AIG), 116, 641
aviation English, 375, 642

B

backing, 8, 10–13, 19, 294, 556
beneficial consequences, 3, 6–7, 75, 442
bias analysis, 105–107, 603, 612–613
bias review, 520
bird index, 675
Boston Public School system, 5
British National Corpus (BNC), 210
Business Language Testing Service
(BULATS), 656

C

CAE, 157
CAEL. *See Canadian Academic English*
CALL. *See computer-assisted
language testing*
Cambridge Certificate of Proficiency in
English, 270
Cambridge English Proficiency Exam, 355
Canadian Academic English, 642
Canadian Language Benchmarks,
145, 186
case study, 37, 61, 170, 363, 372, 505, 563
CET, 162–163, 460
ChatGPT, 115–116, 119, 148, 150, 661,
667, 671–673
cheaters, 674
Chinese Imperial Civil Service
Examination, 3
citizenship. *See residence and citizenship*
CLA. *See communicative language ability*
Claims, 8–10, 15, 19, 23–24, 26–27, 37,
44–45, 68–72, 75–76, 122, 145–146, 149,
156, 182, 216, 222, 250, 264, 288, 306,
317, 320, 454, 499, 511, 585
classical test theory, 97, 541–542, 544,
546, 548, 550, 552, 560, 675. *See also
criterion-referenced testing (CRT)*
classical true score theory (CTT), 588

684 Index

classroom assessment, 32, 34, 64, 132, 143, 154, 159, 170–171, 212, 235–236, 319, 329, 331, 333–335, 366, 460, 503–504, 567
  teacher assessment, 30, 34, 306, 333
  teacher-student interaction, 305
classroom-based assessment, 26, 303–304, 306–309, 643
  curriculum content, 28, 304, 308–309
  L2 learning environment, 316
CLIL. *See content and language integrated learning*
COCA. *See Corpus of Contemporary American English*
Code of Ethics, 8, 82, 410
codes, 80, 341, 465, 520, 672, 677
code switching, 117, 248–249
cognition and assessment
  information processing, 32, 114, 175, 489
  internalization, 64, 149, 501
  strategic competence, 175, 185–186, 257–258, 473–477, 589, 643
Cognitive Based Assessment of, for, and as Learning (CBAL), 256
coherence, 46, 116, 184, 187, 197, 199–201, 256, 281, 289, 348, 365, 589, 604, 609, 612, 655, 663–664, 666
cohesion, 11, 13–14, 16–17, 46, 162, 189, 191, 199–200, 279, 343, 401, 405, 589, 655
College Entrance Examination, 5, 355, 641
College Entrance Examination Board, 5, 355
Common European Framework of Reference for Languages (CEFR), 45, 226, 245, 359, 402, 673
  communicative competence, 121, 156, 185, 217–218, 225–226, 251, 255, 257–258, 265, 359–360, 364, 380, 385, 393, 409, 589, 652. *See also communicative language ability*
communicative competence, 121, 156, 185, 217–218, 225–226, 251, 255, 257–258, 265, 359–360, 364, 380, 385, 393, 409, 589, 652
communicative competence movement, 360
communicative language ability, 129, 134, 185, 206, 218, 225, 233, 317, 409, 589. *See also communicative competence*

communicative language teaching, 156, 328, 334, 356, 499
compensation for misclassification, 88
comprehensibility, 219–223, 225–227, 246, 364, 383–384, 386–388, 393, 468
comprehensibility ratings, 221–223, 227, 387–388. *See also intelligibility*
computer-adaptive language testing, 638, 649–650, 652, 654, 656
  administration efficiency, 651
  construct coverage, 237, 257, 365, 649, 652–653, 657, 667
  measurement precision, 592–594, 619, 651, 653, 656–657
  score comparability, 561, 654
  test security, 120, 379, 519, 529, 637–639, 645, 651, 653, 656–657, 672, 674, 678
computer-assisted language testing, 637–638, 640, 642, 644
computer technology, 159, 173, 175, 212, 233, 364
conceptual assessment framework (CAF), 263
confidence intervals, 100–101, 536, 538, 550–551, 625–627
Confucianism, 4
constructed response tasks, 358, 361
construct-irrelevant variance, 645, 651, 654
  and bias, 107, 366, 511, 513, 520, 603
construct validity, 46, 69–72, 130–131, 140, 159, 174–175, 306, 320–321, 409, 496–497, 510, 642
content and language integrated learning, 318
content representativeness, 189
conversation analysis (CA), 36, 231
corpus, 75, 210, 221, 248, 321–322, 394
Corpus of Contemporary American English, 210
correlation coefficients, 550–551
correlations, 69, 97–99, 162, 218, 224, 347, 362, 385, 387–388, 544, 550–551, 570–571, 584, 664, 666–667
criterion-referenced, 543, 555–562, 564, 566. *See also criterion-referenced testing (CRT)*
criterion-referenced testing (CRT), 96–99, 104, 543, 552, 555. *See also classical test theory; criterion-referenced; generalizability (G) theory*

Index **685**

critical research, 363
Cronbach's alpha, 99, 233, 361, 531, 533,
  538, 544–545, 547–548, 551
CRT. *See criterion-referenced testing (CRT)*
CTT. *See classical test theory (CTT)*

D

data transformations, 573
deep learning, 113–116, 348
defective tasks, 88
delivery platforms, 260
DELNA. *See Diagnostic English Language
  Needs Assessment (DELNA)*
dependability, 238, 537, 671
descriptive statistics, 99, 101, 527
descriptors, 31, 108, 148–150, 183–184, 195,
  220, 222–223, 226–227, 246–247, 289,
  291, 318, 344, 348, 359, 365, 393, 419,
  562, 564, 611, 673
detection indices, 674–675, 677
developmental experiments, 56
diagnostic assessment feedback, 339–340,
  342, 344, 346, 348
  agency, 4–6, 76, 80–82, 88, 91, 196–197, 235,
    316, 339–341, 348–349, 373, 418, 426,
    500, 512, 515, 519–520, 567
  BalanceAI, 348–349
  cognitive diagnostic assessment (CDA),
    344, 461, 596
  cognitive diagnostic models (CDMs), 345
  environment, 22, 56, 63, 113, 165, 175,
    189, 218, 236, 246, 256, 258, 279,
    287, 291, 295, 307, 315–316, 326, 331,
    339–340, 342, 349, 357, 362–363, 367,
    372, 379, 393, 444, 501, 529, 539, 642,
    655, 657, 678
  latency, 339–342, 349
  mechanism, 10, 85–86, 91, 144, 286,
    339–340, 342, 349, 385, 419, 427, 453,
    499–500, 589, 628
Diagnostic English Language Needs
  Assessment, 45
diagnostic feedback, 75, 90, 339, 344–345,
  661, 664
  teacher knowledge, 62
DIALANG, 650, 656
Dickenson index, 675
dictation, 91, 137–138, 212, 271–272,
  274–275
DIF. *See differential item functioning
  (DIF)*

differential item functioning (DIF),
  232, 603, 621
disability, 80–81, 90, 147, 366, 442, 511,
  514–515, 520, 657
disattenuated correlation, 550–551
discourse analysis, 361–362, 384
discourse completion tests (DCTs), 231
discrimination index, 96–97, 675
Duolingo English Test, 119–120, 134, 158,
  213, 224, 285, 356, 379, 385, 393, 629,
  638, 642, 674
dynamic assessment (DA), 330

E

EALTA, 410–412
Educational Testing Service, 5, 44, 80,
  97, 172, 184, 220, 227, 247, 260,
  285–286, 361–362, 385, 393, 512, 514,
  564–565, 661
EFA. *See exploratory factor analysis (EFA)*
ELF. *See English as a Lingua
  Franca (ELF)*
ELP. *See English language
  proficiency (ELP)*
ELTS. *See English Language Testing
  Service (ELTS)*
English as a foreign language, 5, 44, 77, 97,
  133, 186, 205, 238, 245, 248, 273, 285,
  316, 356, 373, 499–500, 528, 589, 629,
  642, 656, 661
English as a Lingua Franca (ELF),
  221, 227, 245–246, 248, 250–251,
  363, 468
English as a Lingua Franca in Academic
  Settings (ELFA), 248
English, assessment
  Australia, 91, 232, 236, 246, 250, 280, 303,
    317, 372–375, 377–378, 417–424, 426–428,
    443, 459, 463, 517
  Bangladesh, 332, 439, 442
  Canada, 44, 250, 317, 331, 333, 417, 439,
    443, 476–477, 502
  China, 63, 81, 85, 235, 307, 333, 436, 439,
    460, 480–481, 498–499, 501, 510
  Europe, 4, 43, 49, 63, 80, 98, 146, 150, 184,
    226–227, 234, 246–247, 271, 275, 277–279,
    318, 334, 401–406, 408–410, 412, 417,
    419, 423, 434, 437, 443, 454, 509,
    511, 564, 651
  Hong Kong, 31, 247, 303, 333–334, 356–357,
    458–459, 462, 501

686 Index

English, assessment (*cont'd*)
  India, 81, 85, 332–334, 435–436, 439, 443
  Japan, 3, 76, 85, 210, 218, 232
  Korea, 3, 85, 315, 435, 439, 484–485, 488
  Malaysia, 37, 85, 482–483
  Mexico, 200, 435–436, 439, 442, 444–445, 461
  New Zealand, 45, 135, 209, 236, 250, 334, 373
  Singapore, 85, 303, 482–483
  USA, 482–483
  Vietnam, 436, 439, 441
English for academic purposes, 49, 221, 273, 275, 355, 503. *See also academic language*
English language proficiency (ELP), 294, 317, 322, 362, 373, 419, 428, 443, 445–446, 528, 604, 625, 641–642, 644, 663, 677
English Language Teaching (ELT), 246, 303
English language testing, 5, 44, 47, 133, 157, 245, 250, 275, 308, 356, 373, 589, 642
English Language Testing Service (ELTS), 356
English proficiency Testing Battery (EPTB), 273
English, varieties
  phonological, 133, 139, 143, 156, 189–190, 192, 194, 196–197, 199–200, 223, 226, 248, 313, 363, 389
e-rater, 116, 290–291, 644, 655
error similarity analysis index, 676
error variance, 529, 542, 544, 546, 549, 579, 581
estimating test-taker ability, 650
ethical implications, 417, 426–427
ethics, 6–8, 75, 80, 82–84, 120, 122, 380, 410, 426, 497
  fairness and justice argument, 7
ethnicity, 84, 427–428, 512, 613
explanation, 16, 59, 71, 75, 93, 97, 157, 159, 171, 219, 289, 331, 341, 361, 371, 406, 455–456, 463, 465, 527, 571
exploratory factor analysis (EFA), 475, 486, 570–571, 573, 575, 591
extrapolation, 71–72, 171, 233–236, 361–362
eye-tracking, 457–459, 465–466, 468

F
fairness and accountability, 3, 7, 520
fairness and justice, 7, 75, 80–84, 86–88, 90–91, 366, 440
field testing, 320, 643
first language, 48, 129, 155, 185, 217, 245, 248, 266, 271, 281, 312, 436, 438, 443, 478–479, 482–485, 487, 502, 520, 641, 643
first language assessment, 641, 643
flow, 248, 289, 317, 348, 371, 379
foreign accent, 216
foreign language, 5, 22–23, 43–44, 49, 61, 64, 77, 97, 133–134, 155, 165, 181, 186, 205, 232, 238, 245, 248–249, 257, 265, 270–273, 276–277, 285, 303, 316, 356, 364, 373, 394, 473, 482–485, 499–500, 528, 589, 629, 642, 656–657, 661
functional knowledge, 195–196

G
generalizability, 10, 13, 15, 46, 98, 104, 183, 226, 236, 361, 544, 552, 581. *See also generalizability (G) theory*
generalizability (G) theory, 98–99, 108, 183, 236, 361, 544, 552. *See also criterion-referenced testing (CRT); true score*
generalization, 71, 75, 93–95, 97, 108, 117, 171, 187, 361, 591
general principles, 86–87, 91
General Service List of English Words (GSL), 205
genetic method, 56
GENOVA, 99, 103–105, 108. *See also mGENOVA; urGENOVA*
Graduate Record Examination (GRE), 621
grammar assessment, 188, 206
grammatical ability, 71, 77, 102, 115, 163, 233
G theory. *See generalizability (G) theory*
Guidelines for Practice, 8, 551

H
health professionals, 236, 371–375, 377–380, 459, 515–516, 519
historical overview, 3, 5, 355, 527–528, 530, 532, 534, 536
Hong Kong Diploma of Secondary Education (HKDSE), 356

human rating, 117, 146, 149, 173, 224, 288, 291, 388, 391, 393, 620, 666. *See also human scoring*

human scoring, 172, 176, 225, 285, 291, 295, 360, 640, 663, 666. *See also human rating*

I

IELTS. *See International English Language Testing System (IELTS)*

ILTA, 326, 410–412, 520, 551

immersion, 318, 331, 367

immersion environment, 367

immigration policy space, 419

implicational knowledge, 196–198
  in assessment security, 119
  in Australia, 91, 236, 373–374, 377, 417–424, 426, 428, 459, 463, 517
  in the classroom, 55–56, 58, 60, 62, 64, 170, 205, 208, 288, 305, 326–330, 332–334, 340, 343, 359, 394, 665
  in grammar, 289, 664
  in language testing, 68–70, 72–73, 76–77, 218, 227, 247, 273, 286, 367, 421, 425, 456, 458, 468, 473–475, 497, 499, 502–504, 511, 528–529, 532–534, 539, 577, 585, 591, 597, 619, 629, 637–638, 641–642, 645, 677
  in sign language assessment, 118–119
  in speaking assessment, 117, 146, 384
  in writing assessment, 116, 120, 168, 170–173, 176

indigenous assessment, 375

Instrument for Research Into Second Language Learning and Teaching (IRIS), 108

integrated skills, 42, 44–49, 132, 257, 275, 357–360
  diagnostic value, 45–46
  discourse features, 46–47, 172, 347–348
  integrated skills assessment, 44–49, 132
  raters' perceptions, 46

integrated skills tasks, 45–48, 357

intelligibility, 199, 219–222, 224–227, 236, 246, 248–249, 364, 383–384, 387, 655. *See also comprehensibility ratings; foreign accent*

intended consequences, 7–9, 11–12, 19, 144–145, 321

interactional competence (IC), 230, 238

interactionist, 44, 49, 57–58, 170, 186, 590

International Civil Aviation Organization (ICAO), 250

International English Language Testing System (IELTS), 5, 47, 49, 51, 133–135, 152–155, 157–158, 162–163, 166–167, 179, 220, 224, 237, 240, 245, 247, 250–251, 275–276, 283, 308, 356–370, 373–377, 382, 420–423, 427, 458, 460–463, 470, 475, 478–479, 484–485, 493, 506, 516–517, 519, 522, 589–590, 642, 646, 655, 659, 673

International Language Testing Association, 8, 80, 326, 333, 520, 551

International Language Testing Association (ILTA), 326, 520

interventionist, 57

introspective data, 453–454, 456, 465, 467

introspective methods, 453–458, 460, 464, 466–468
  item analysis, 96, 98–99, 101–102, 209, 551
  memory aids, 453, 455–457, 459, 463, 465–466
  retrospective methods, 455–456, 466–467
  stimulated recall, 361, 453, 456–457, 459, 463, 465–466, 490
  think-aloud, 453, 455–464, 466–467

item and task development
  basic principles, 528
  item bank, 462, 623–624, 630, 643, 650–653, 656–657, 667. *See also pool*
  item difficulty, 96, 441, 533, 538, 551, 560, 590, 602–603, 614, 623
  Item Response Theory (IRT), 539, 552, 560, 588, 590, 620–621, 639, 675
  item selection, 188–189, 621, 623–625, 639, 650–651, 653, 655
  multidimensional IRT models, 588–597
  sample size, 94–95, 103, 465, 571, 573–576, 581, 583, 591–594, 614, 677

item bank, 623, 624, 630, 643, 650–653, 656, 657, 667

K

Kaiser rule, 574

Kappa index, 677

Kuder–Richardson formulas, 531–532

688 Index

L

language acquisition, 28, 129, 135, 140, 227, 287, 313, 328, 453. *See also language learning*

language assessment for professional purposes (LAPP), 371

inseparability, 376–377, 379

policy constraints, 378

practical considerations, 378

specificity, 74, 344, 347, 376–377, 497, 561

language assessment literacy (LAL), 322, 329

language for specific purposes (LSP), 186, 235, 371

language knowledge, 67, 181, 185–186, 188, 193, 197, 201, 216, 246, 256–257, 278, 316, 318, 322, 357, 377, 480–481

language learning, 28, 32, 46, 64, 108, 118, 121, 129, 132, 147, 164, 201, 221, 227, 238, 270–271, 273, 280, 304, 307–308, 313, 316–318, 328, 335, 341, 345–347, 356, 367, 383, 406–407, 426, 444, 474, 482–483, 489, 497, 561, 640–642. *See also language acquisition; second language acquisition*

language learning, 28, 32, 46, 64, 108, 118, 121, 129, 132, 147, 164, 201, 221, 227, 238, 270–271, 273, 280, 304, 307–308, 313, 316–318, 328, 335, 341, 345–347, 356, 367, 383, 406–407, 426, 444, 474, 482–483, 489, 497, 561, 640–642. *See also language acquisition; second language acquisition*

language performance, 6, 59, 76, 145, 264, 361–362, 474, 487, 534, 548, 596

large language models (LLMs), 116, 148, 150, 620, 653, 663

large-scale assessment, 32, 34

learner-centered, 25

learner independent performance, 330

learning-oriented language assessment, 22, 24, 26, 28, 30–36

affective dimension, 30, 35–36, 260–261, 263–264

contextual dimension, 30–31, 34–35, 259, 261

foreign language assessment, 23

instructional dimension, 30, 35–36, 259–260, 264

limitations, 61, 70, 119, 148, 154, 158, 266, 286, 291–292, 295, 345–346, 365, 391–392, 421, 455, 466, 545, 551–552, 566–567, 619, 625, 629, 639, 642

moderators, 28, 32, 34–35, 256, 266, 491

naturalistic conversation, 26

performance indicators, 25, 34

proficiency dimension, 30, 34–35, 259

second language assessment, 251, 380

technological dimension, 30, 35–36, 260

linguistic features, 112, 115, 117, 183–184, 245, 288, 347, 377, 393, 665

linguistic resources, 32, 34, 181–186, 188–193, 195–196, 198–201, 234–235, 490

literacy, 29–30, 34–37, 45, 120–122, 155, 158, 164, 169, 175–176, 256–258, 260, 262, 303–304, 317, 321–322, 329, 359, 364–365, 401, 406–407, 436–437, 444, 463, 502, 512, 645, 654

LOLA. *See learning-oriented language assessment*

L2 speech, 115–117, 217, 219, 222, 224, 226, 460, 645

M

machine learning (ML), 113, 639

machine-scored, 286

for listening, 5, 130, 135, 140, 148, 212, 270, 272, 274, 276, 278–281, 366, 438, 440, 528

meaningful communication, 32–33, 181–182, 184, 186, 188, 190, 192, 196, 198, 200–201

for reading, 130, 155, 157, 162–164, 256, 276–277, 279, 281, 356, 359, 385, 438, 440–441

for writing, 5, 46–47, 49, 75, 116, 168, 170, 285, 294, 342, 359, 379, 662

measurement error, 103, 360–361, 383–384, 517, 537, 539, 542–544, 546, 548, 550, 552, 555, 559–561, 584

mediation, 27, 55–64, 331, 345–346, 491

mGENOVA, 99

migration, 371, 402–405, 407–412, 417–426, 428, 432, 434, 441, 445

race, 84, 434–435, 437, 446, 511–512, 518, 520, 567, 613

misclassification, 88, 517, 520

miscommunication, 186, 248, 250

model fit, 107, 578, 581, 583–584, 592–593, 614–615, 664

multiple-choice questions, 119, 653

N

naturalization test, 432, 434, 436–440, 442–444, 446

  approvals, 435, 442

  denials, 432, 435–436, 442

  literacy test, 436–437, 502

  U.S. Naturalization Test, 432, 437–438, 443

natural language processing (NLP), 112, 171, 286, 358, 621, 640, 661

NBME index, 676

needs analysis, 45, 275, 360, 377–378

neoliberalism, 426

norm-referenced, 543, 555–562, 564, 566

O

observed score variance, 529, 542–544

Occupational English Test (OET), 235, 372

Oral Proficiency Interview (OPI), 5, 61

organization, 6, 14, 55, 57, 60, 82, 89, 134–135, 158, 161–162, 164, 168, 199–200, 211, 233–235, 247, 250, 260, 279, 289–291, 347–349, 356, 392, 409, 411–412, 478–479, 520, 604, 609, 661–664, 666, 674, 677

organizational knowledge, 185

Oxford Online Placement Test, 188

P

Pearson Test of English (PTE), 220, 271, 356, 642

peer assessment, 29–30, 333

plagiarism, 48, 120, 645, 667, 671–674, 676, 678

pool, 77, 175, 209, 366, 374, 421, 464, 594, 621, 623, 628–629, 650, 653. *See also item bank*

pragmatic knowledge, 183, 185, 187–188, 195–197, 230, 233, 316

  interactional meanings, 197, 199

  literary/religious meanings, 198

  psychological meanings, 183, 197–198

  rhetorical meanings, 197–198

  situational meanings, 197–198

  sociocultural/intercultural meanings, 197–198

  sociolinguistic meanings, 183, 185, 197–198

preparation, 43, 48, 62, 72, 247, 308, 315, 343, 347, 360, 376, 417, 423, 427, 446, 461, 484–485, 491, 500–501, 505, 513

pretesting, 82, 88, 345, 515, 674

prevention, 425, 672–673, 675

pricing, 90

pronunciation accuracy, 219, 225. *See also foreign accent*

pronunciation assessment, 216–219, 221, 224–227. *See also foreign accent*

public reasoning, 85–87, 90–91

punishment, 81, 85

Q

quality of the assessment, 89, 466

R

rater bias, 171, 223, 225, 458, 613

rater consistency, 97–98, 107, 545. *See also rater reliability*

rater reliability, 97, 171, 232, 234, 361, 383, 534–538, 548, 552. *See also rater consistency*

reading skills, 132, 256, 273, 277, 564

real-world examples, 563, 565, 567

Regents Examinations, 5

  High School Regents Examinations, 5

regression index, 675

relationships between testing, teaching, and learning, 499

reliability coefficients, 534–535, 543–548, 550, 553, 562, 594

reliability indices, 104, 552, 605–606, 609

reliability of measurement, 543, 546

reliability strategies, 530

reliability theory, 529

reporting test reliability, 551

residence and citizenship, 401–412

  aims, 8, 31–32, 36, 47, 59, 62, 316, 331, 405, 408–409, 418–419, 421, 425, 427, 491, 518, 575, 603, 640

  debate, 401–402, 407, 409

  justification, 3, 7–8, 19, 44, 67, 76–77, 82–84, 86, 90, 129, 132, 135, 213, 401–402, 404–406, 442, 455–456, 468, 503, 563

  symbolic link, 404

retrofit, 513, 515–517, 520

revitalization, 331

690 Index

rotation method, 571, 575, 585
Royal Society of Arts Examinations Board, 4

S
sandwich format, 58
Scalable Multimodal Sign Language
 Technology for Sign Language
 Learning and Assessment
 (SMILE), 118
scenario-based language assessment (SBLA)
 activate background knowledge, 256
 consolidate knowledge, 256, 263
 convey knowledge, 256, 263
 elicitation, 23–24, 30, 32, 34–36, 259,
 263–264, 307, 319, 330, 378
 Nutrition Ambassador, 257, 261–263
 understand the text, 132, 256
Scholastic Aptitude Tests (SATs), 5
 SAT Achievement Tests, 5
 SAT II, 5
scope, 62, 74–75, 80, 95, 97, 237, 256, 259,
 265, 292, 304, 329, 364, 375–377,
 379, 394, 407, 409, 456, 496–497,
 503, 563, 662
score difference index, 676
score interpretation, 70–71, 75, 86–87, 173,
 220, 359, 363, 378, 409, 454, 473, 503,
 505, 514, 527, 541, 543, 552, 555–556,
 559, 563, 566–567, 589, 614, 652
score reliability, 361, 528–529, 539,
 549, 552, 590
scoring criteria, 235, 360, 364, 378. *See also
 true score*
scrutiny!, 676–677
second language acquisition, 28, 135,
 140, 227, 287, 313, 328, 453. *See also
 language learning*
second or foreign language (SFL), 22, 181
shifted binomial index, 676
simultaneous, 183, 585, 596
skills assessment, 44–49, 132, 155
social-interactional dimension, 30, 35–36
socio-cognitive dimension, 30, 35–36
software, 93–94, 96, 98–100, 102, 104, 108,
 121, 223, 260, 366, 388, 559, 577, 585,
 611, 653, 657, 671, 673–674
sources of measurement error, 361, 383,
 537, 542–543, 546, 552
speaking assessment, 46, 115–118, 143,
 146, 183, 223, 315, 365, 383–384,
 387, 394, 462

Spearman–Brown prophecy formula, 528,
 531, 534–535, 549, 551
speech analysis, 223, 225, 384, 386
speech recognition, 114, 118, 121, 221,
 224–225, 238, 346, 348, 384, 387–388,
 392–393, 640, 644, 655, 662
spoken-dialog system (SDS)-mediated
 assessment, 643
standard error of measurement, 99,
 536, 539, 549
Standardized Root Mean Square Residual
 (SRMR), 583
Standardized test, 5, 23, 25, 64, 132–133,
 158, 164, 168, 330, 343, 426, 482–483,
 628, 665, 671
 entrance examination, 4–5, 355, 641
 Testing for university and college
 admissions, 5
Statistical analysis, 93, 108
 Comparative Fit Index (CFI), 583
 confirmatory factor analysis, 570, 591
 criterion difficulty, 603–604, 609, 612
 data screening, 571, 581, 604, 615
 distractor analysis, 96–97
 D study, 103–104
 EduG, 99
 facets variable map, 611–612
 factor extraction, 573
 G theory, 98–99, 108, 183, 361, 552. *See also
 generalizability*
 interpreting fit statistics, 616
 ITEMAN, 98–99
 item discrimination, 96–98, 102, 588,
 590, 594, 614
 item selection algorithms, 623, 625, 650
 kurtosis, 95, 98, 101, 581, 583
 Lagrange multiplier (LM), 578
 maximum likelihood (ML), 573
 mGENOVA, 99. *See also GENOVA*
 principal components (PCA), 573
 Rasch measurement, 98–99, 234, 552, 588,
 593, 597, 615
 rater severity, 98, 105, 107, 552, 603–604,
 607–608, 612–613
 rating scale functioning, 610
 rating scale model (RSM), 602
 rating scales, 93–94, 97–98, 103, 107,
 149, 171, 219–220, 222, 225–226, 328,
 384, 460, 517
 Root Mean Square Error of
 Approximation (RMSEA), 583

SAS, 25, 98–99, 333, 550
score distribution, 94, 96, 101, 550, 552, 555–559, 564
self-consistency, 604
skewness, 94–95, 98, 101, 581
SPSS, 98–99, 101, 534, 536, 550, 570, 585
standard deviation, 94, 98, 101, 491, 527–528, 532–536, 549, 551, 556–560, 564–565, 622, 625
stopping rules, 621, 624–625, 650
task difficulty, 98, 105, 548, 552, 603–604, 608
test revision, 93–98, 100, 102, 104, 108, 356, 551
urGENOVA, 99. *See also GENOVA*
structural equation modeling (SEM), 182, 570
summative assessment, 23, 31, 37, 286–289, 304, 306–307, 309, 326–327, 665
syntax, 101, 103, 108, 118, 181, 185, 195–196, 277, 279, 281, 644, 677

T
target language use (TLU), 10, 130, 139, 160, 171, 275
teacher-led, 303
termination criterion, 650
test administration, 148, 217, 258, 366, 377, 379, 531, 545, 548, 560, 619, 628, 650, 655, 674
test bias, 441
test design, 27–28, 33, 35, 42, 60, 145, 163, 261, 270–271, 357, 426, 504, 515, 517, 543, 547, 552, 562, 567, 637–639
test development, 36, 49, 99, 113, 139, 143–145, 150, 186, 211, 232–233, 237, 261, 363, 367, 378, 467, 520, 556, 638, 641, 652. *See also assessment design*
Test of Academic English (TAE), 257
Test of English as a Foreign Language (TOEFL), 5, 44–45, 47–54, 71, 97, 108–111, 120, 133–136, 141, 154–155, 157–158, 162, 166–167, 170, 172, 174, 177–179, 186, 205, 220, 224, 227, 237, 239, 245, 247, 251, 273, 276, 281–283, 285, 289, 296, 298, 311, 318, 320, 347, 351, 354, 356–362, 366, 368–370, 373–374, 385, 388, 392–393, 397, 420, 458, 465, 470–471, 478–479, 482–485, 488, 493, 500, 505, 528, 554, 589–590,

601, 629, 642, 644–645, 650, 653–656, 658–659, 661–662, 667–668, 674
Test of English for Academic Purposes (TEAP), 275
Test of English for International Communication (TOEIC), 54, 100, 109, 220, 227, 245, 247, 249–250, 476–477, 486, 488, 551, 554, 564–565, 568, 642
Test of Spoken English (TSE), 356
Test of Written English (TWE), 356
test-retest reliability, 361, 530, 538, 544–546, 552
tests of English for university admission, 49, 355
administration mode, 358
score reporting, 355, 357–358, 509
test delivery, 82, 143, 355, 357–358, 519, 638–639, 645
Test-taking strategies, 491
heterogeneity, 490–491
language use strategies, 473–475, 486–487, 489, 491
test formats, 43, 162, 205, 207–208, 213, 474, 486, 488, 502
test management strategies, 474, 491
test wiseness strategies, 473–474
TOEFL. *See* Test of English as a Foreign Language (TOEFL)
transcendental institutionalism, 84
true score, 509, 529–531, 539, 542–544, 546, 550–552, 588, 620. *See also generalizability (G) theory; scoring criteria*

U
unidimensionality, 210, 589, 591–592, 614–616, 653
University of Cambridge Local Examinations Syndicate, 4, 304
urGENOVA, 99
using technology in language testing, 637
utilitarianism, 83
utilization, 71, 75, 93, 118, 120, 171, 259, 286, 295, 339, 349, 362, 597, 629

V
validation of language assessment, 68, 70, 72, 74, 76
argument-based, 70, 75, 121, 144, 454, 642
evidence gathering, 68–70, 72, 74
usefulness, 28, 67–68, 70–72, 74, 170, 173, 176, 205, 212, 246, 345, 488, 496, 561, 563, 566–567

692 Index

validity, 67–72, 74–77
van der Linden and Sotaridona index, 677
vocabulary assessment, 205, 208,
212–213, 466
Vocabulary Levels Test (VLT), 208
Vygotskian Sociocultural Theory (SCT), 55

W
washback effects, 499
writing assessment. *See assessing writing*

Y
young language learners (YLLs), 312

affective factors, 260, 313–315, 321
cognitive factors, 171, 313
contextual considerations, 313
corpus analysis, 321–322
curricular considerations, 316–317
target language use, 10, 15, 130–131, 139,
160, 171, 257–258, 271, 275, 321, 357,
364, 562, 657
teacher support, 322

Z
zone of proximal development
(ZPD), 56, 319